■ THE RESOURCE FOR THE INDEPENDENT TRAVELER

"The guides are aimed not only at young budget travelers but at the indepedent traveler; a sort of streetwise cookbook for traveling alone."

—The New York Times

"Unbeatable; good sight-seeing advice; up-to-date info on restaurants, hotels, and inns; a commitment to money-saving travel; and a wry style that brightens nearly every page."

—The Washington Post

"Lighthearted and sophisticated, informative and fun to read. [Let's Go] helps the novice traveler navigate like a knowledgeable old hand."

—Atlanta Journal-Constitution

"A world-wise traveling companion—always ready with friendly advice and helpful hints, all sprinkled with a bit of wit."

—The Philadelphia Inquirer

■ THE BEST TRAVEL BARGAINS IN YOUR PRICE RANGE

"All the dirt, dirt cheap."

—People

"Anything you need to know about budget traveling is detailed in this book."

—The Chicago Sun-Times

"Let's Go follows the creed that you don't have to toss your life's savings to the wind to travel—unless you want to."

—The Salt Lake Tribune

■ REAL ADVICE FOR REAL EXPERIENCES

"The writers seem to have experienced every rooster-packed bus and lunar-surfaced mattress about which they write."

—The New York Times

"A guide should tell you what to expect from a destination. Here Let's Go shines."

—The Chicago Tribune

LET'S GO PUBLICATIONS

TRAVEL GUIDES

Alaska & the Pacific Northwest 2003
Australia 2003
Austria & Switzerland 2003
Britain & Ireland 2003
California 2003
Central America 8th edition
Chile 1st edition **NEW TITLE**
China 4th edition
Costa Rica 1st edition **NEW TITLE**
Eastern Europe 2003
Egypt 2nd edition
Europe 2003
France 2003
Germany 2003
Greece 2003
Hawaii 2003 **NEW TITLE**
India & Nepal 7th edition
Ireland 2003
Israel 4th edition
Italy 2003
Mexico 19th edition
Middle East 4th edition
New Zealand 6th edition
Peru, Ecuador & Bolivia 3rd edition
South Africa 5th edition
Southeast Asia 8th edition
Southwest USA 2003
Spain & Portugal 2003
Thailand 1st edition **NEW TITLE**
Turkey 5th edition
USA 2003
Western Europe 2003

CITY GUIDES

Amsterdam 2003
Barcelona 2003
Boston 2003
London 2003
New York City 2003
Paris 2003
Rome 2003
San Francisco 2003
Washington, D.C. 2003

MAP GUIDES

Amsterdam
Berlin
Boston
Chicago
Dublin
Florence
Hong Kong
London
Los Angeles
Madrid
New Orleans
New York City
Paris
Prague
Rome
San Francisco
Seattle
Sydney
Venice
Washington, D.C.

ITALY
2003

AMBER K. LAVICKA EDITOR
THEODOSIA M. HOWELL ASSOCIATE EDITOR
IRIN CARMON ASSOCIATE EDITOR

RESEARCHER-WRITERS
JULIA BOZER
PAUL W. GUILIANELLI
CHRISTOPHER A. KUKSTIS
MELISSA LaSCALEIA
HUNTER MAATS
LAURA A. NEVISON

ANDY C. POON MAP EDITOR
ABIGAIL BURGER MANAGING EDITOR
JOHN ATA BACHMAN TYPESETTER

ST. MARTIN'S PRESS ✠ NEW YORK

Maps by David Lindroth copyright © 2003 by St. Martin's Press.

Distributed outside the USA and Canada by Macmillan.

ISBN: 0-312-30581-8

First edition
10 9 8 7 6 5 4 3 2 1

Let's Go: Italy is written by Let's Go Publications, 67 Mount Auburn Street, Cambridge, MA 02138, USA.

HOW TO USE THIS BOOK

ORGANIZATION. The Italy guide is divided into 14 sections, indicated by the black tabs on the side of the book.

PRICE RANGES AND RANKINGS. Our researchers list establishments in order of value from best to worst. Absolute favorites are denoted by the Let's Go thumbs-up (🖐). Our new system of price ranges is shown in the table below. The ranges represent the least a single traveler could expect to pay for a meal or a night's accommodation during high season (summer months). Dining at a ❶ restaurant means a *panino*, slice of pizza, or cheap bowl of pasta, while dining at a ❺ restaurant entails multiple courses and a white table cloth. Accommodations in the ❶ bracket will generally be hostel berths or camp sites; a ❺ hotel can have as many stars, and heated towel racks to boot.

ITALY	❶	❷	❸	❹	❺
ACCOMM.	€5-15	€16-25	€26-35	€36-60	€61+
FOOD	€1-5	€6-10	€11-15	€16-25	€26+

PHONE CODES AND TELEPHONE NUMBERS. Area codes appear opposite the name of each town or city, and are denoted by the ☎ icon.

WHAT'S ON THE MENU

ANTIPASTI. Whet your appetite with Chef's recommendations: **Discover** Italy's regional highlights and suggested itineraries.

PRIMI. **Life and Times** provides a general introduction to the art, culture, and history of Italy. The heavier **Essentials** section details practical information and is best consumed in small bites.

SECONDI. The meat of our Italy coverage comes in ten delectable cuts. **Northwest** Italy includes Lombardy, the Lake Country, the Italian Riviera, Piedmont, and Valle d'Aosta. **Venice** is followed by **Northeast** Italy, which includes the Veneto (minus Venice), Friuli Venezia-Giulia, Trentino Alto-Adige, and Emilia-Romagna. **Florence** precedes **Central** Italy, which covers Tuscany, Umbria, Le Marche, Abruzzo, and Molise. **Rome** includes the Eternal City and the rest of Lazio. **Southern** Italy stuffs in Campania, the Amalfi Coast, Apulia, Basilicata, and Calabria, and **Sicily** and **Sardinia** round out the meal.

DOLCI. May we suggest a glazed **appendix,** with its Italian phrasebook?

DIGESTIVI. Ah, the meal's not over yet. Take icy cool shots of our brand-new features, from researchers' first-person narratives to interviews with Italians.

CONTENTS

RESEARCHER-WRITERS

Julia Bozer
Calabria, Sicily

After learning to toddle in Palermo, native Sicilian Julia Bozer returned home to hone her poetic craft and hop islands. Having journeyed everywhere from Lucerne to Cozumel, this trilingual poet-turned-adventurer remained serene in the shadows of Mt. Etna. The evil interventions of technology did nothing to dampen her zeal—Julia wowed the entire *Let's Go* staff with her painstaking research and writing, complete with artful renditions of Sicily.

Paul W. Guilianelli
Tuscany, Umbria

Paul Guilianelli wasted no time between adventures in Vietnam for *Let's Go: Southeast Asia 2003* and jumping on another plane, bound this time for Tuscan wine country. Buried in his past were stints as a Wyoming rancher, an Afro-Brazilian fight-dancer, and a nationally-ranked volleyball player; Italy added architecture critic to Paul's list of talents. A Guilianelli homecoming proved that good looks run in the family, and that there's nothing like a little escape.

Christopher A. Kukstis *Abruzzo, Molise, Campania, Basilicata, Apulia*

Latin and Greek scholar, radio-station DJ, and part-time fisherman turned savvy traveler, Chris dodged the flames of hostel barbecues, survived harrowing bus rides, and researched the Southern Italian crime scene. Never sleeping wit da fishes (even with nocturnal plunges off the Campanian coastline), he side-stepped train strikes, gave us the skinny on certain dubious *pensioni*, and lived to hobnob with the glitterati on sun-soaked Capri.

Melissa LaScaleia
Veneto, Emilia Romagna, The Marches

Southern Italian *bella ragazza* Melissa never lost her appetite for *gelato*, Belfast surprise, or buffet breakfasts as she braved thunderstorms on an ill-fated scooter ride, set bank alarms off with her bike helmet, watched Venetian monsoon season bring the disintegration of her meticulous notes (but not her phenomenal marginalia), and turned her Art History expertise on Peggy Guggenheim's finest, all while cardiovascularizing her way across the canals of Venice.

Hunter Maats *Piedmont, Lombardy, Trentino-Alto Adige*

Travels through Japan and a stay in Brazil have taught this biochemist that there is life outside the lab. An Eton-educated i-banker-in-the-making, he juggled non-sequitur interviews and city intros with savoir faire and flair. There was no lake he couldn't cross, no Alpine mountain he couldn't climb, no nightclub he couldn't hop. His editors swooned at the Italian treats that accompanied his copy; in all things, Hunter went above and beyond the call of duty.

Laura A. Nevison *Liguria, Sardinia*

Literary critic and published poet Laura Nevison took her double Romance-language proficiency to the Italian Riviera and the rugged shores of Sardinia. Astrological miscommunications, transportation strikes, and errant laptops never got her down. This *acapella* songbird persevered, adding beach lore, resort know-how, and tanning techniques to her university studies of literature, astronomy, oil-painting, and Italian.

Shannon Ringvelski *Editor, Let's Go: Rome 2003*

Katharine Burrage, Michael Marean, Michael Simonetti *R-Ws, Let's Go: Rome 2003*

CONTRIBUTING WRITERS

Andria Derstine was a Researcher-Writer for *Let's Go: Italy 1990* and *1992* and *Let's Go: Greece 1991*. After living in Rome for 3 years, she recently returned to the U.S. to complete her Ph.D. at the Institute of Fine Arts, New York University.

Lisa Nosal was a Researcher-Writer for *Let's Go: Italy 2000*, a Managing Editor in 1999, and the editor of Austria & Switzerland 1998. She led guided tours of Venice for the Enjoy Venice cultural association, and now works for an educational travel company in Boston.

Tobie Whitman was a Researcher-Writer for *Let's Go: London 1999 and 2001* and *Let's Go: Britain & Ireland 1998*. She interned with the European Union and is currently pursuing a Masters in European Studies at Cambridge University.

ACKNOWLEDGMENTS

LET'S GO

TEAM ITALY THANKS Abi for keeping us on track; Andy for backing that map up; Prod for fixing our broken stuff; Axis Pod for bacchanalian dinners; MG, CN, AH, HG, AN, TE, RB, BW, and KD for coming through in a pinch.

AMBER THANKS graceful and dedicated Thea, vociferous and hard-hitting Irin. *Buon lavoro, bellissime!* Joanna, the angel. Angela for crushes and loaded stares. Candy for adjusting. Jesse, my alter ego. Kathleen and David, late-night co-culprits. Rebecca, Antoinette, Erzulie for holding down the dump, er, fort. Bean for four years of never-dull friendship. Sarah and Jen for pumpkin heads and bad sun burns. Frank, Sarah, Tom, and Lisa for Eastern seaboard tours and snapshots. Most importantly, Mom and Dad, brave American boys Corey and Kelsey. *Vi voglio tanto bene.*

THEA THANKS Amber for her editing brilliance, Irin for her diligence and wit. Joanna, Debbie, and Jesse for Axis solidarity. Mom, Jay, Gordon, and sweet Fiona for all their love. Kate for keeping me sane, adventures in the woods, and crazy nights with kings (thin *yet* feisty). Weekend escapes: CT, the wedding, Maine, VT with the GMB, and Balto. J.W. for an amazing summer of unending laughs and fond memories. *Salute alla famiglia, all' amore, alla corsa, e un libro completo!*

IRIN THANKS Amber (and her all-nighters), Thea, ever sane and serene, and Abi *Sara* Burger. Axis pod for a 2nd home. Team SPAM for patience, madness, and an ever-deflating ball pit. Kristin, Orlando, Dave, Jon and Abigail for picnics, SATC fixes, HFA, rhythm&spice, and cheap mantras. Rachael, Alana, Jamie, Pat, Alana and Azalea for weekend pick-me-ups. Miles of love and thanks to Abba, Imma, Ittai, Daria, Yahel and Yarden, especially for weekend pampering.

ANDY THANKS Dad, Mom, and Becky for immeasurable love. Team Italia for diligence and looking good in jerseys. GOOAAALLL!!!!

Editor Amber K. Lavicka
Associate Editors Theodosia M. Howell, Irin Carmon
Managing Editor Abigail Burger
Map Editor Andy C. Poon

Publishing Director
Matthew Gibson
Editor-in-Chief
Brian R. Walsh
Production Manager
C. Winslow Clayton
Cartography Manager
Julie Stephens
Design Manager
Amy Cain
Editorial Managers
Christopher Blazejewski,
Abigail Burger, D. Cody Dydek,
Harriett Green, Angela Mi Young Hur,
Marla Kaplan, Celeste Ng
Financial Manager
Noah Askin
Marketing & Publicity Managers
Michelle Bowman, Adam M. Grant
New Media Managers
Jesse Tov, Kevin Yip
Online Manager
Amélie Cherlin
Personnel Managers
Alex Leichtman, Owen Robinson
Production Associates
Caleb Epps, David Muehlke
Network Administrators
Steven Aponte, Eduardo Montoya
Design Associate
Juice Fong
Financial Assistant
Suzanne Siu
Office Coordinators
Alex Ewing, Adam Kline,
Efrat Kussell

Director of Advertising Sales
Erik Patton
Senior Advertising Associates
Patrick Donovan, Barbara Eghan,
Fernanda Winthrop
Advertising Artwork Editor
Leif Holtzman
Cover Photo Research
Laura Wyss

President
Bradley J. Olson
General Manager
Robert B. Rombauer
Assistant General Manager
Anne E. Chisholm

WHO WE ARE

A NEW LET'S GO FOR 2003

With a sleeker look and innovative new content, we have revamped the entire series to reflect more than ever the needs and interests of the independent traveler. Here are just some of the improvements you will notice when traveling with the new *Let's Go.*

MORE PRICE OPTIONS

Still the best resource for budget travelers, *Let's Go* recognizes that everyone needs the occasional indulgence. Our "Big Splurges" indicate establishments that are actually worth those extra pennies (pulas, pesos, or pounds), and price-level symbols (❶ ❷ ❸ ❹ ❺) allow you to quickly determine whether an accommodation or restaurant will break the bank. We may have diversified, but we'll never lose our budget focus—"Hidden Deals" reveal the best-kept travel secrets.

BEYOND THE TOURIST EXPERIENCE

Our Alternatives to Tourism chapter offers ideas on immersing yourself in a new community through study, work, or volunteering.

AN INSIDER'S PERSPECTIVE

As always, every item is written and researched by our on-site writers. This year we have highlighted more viewpoints to help you gain an even more thorough understanding of the places you are visiting.

IN RECENT NEWS. *Let's Go* correspondents around the globe report back on current regional issues that may affect you as a traveler.

CONTRIBUTING WRITERS. Respected scholars and former *Let's Go* writers discuss topics on society and culture, going into greater depth than the usual guidebook summary.

THE LOCAL STORY. From the Parisian monk toting a cell phone to the Russian *babushka* confronting capitalism, *Let's Go* shares its revealing conversations with local personalities—a unique glimpse of what matters to real people.

FROM THE ROAD. Always helpful and sometimes downright hilarious, our researchers share useful insights on the typical (and atypical) travel experience.

SLIMMER SIZE

Don't be fooled by our new, smaller size. *Let's Go* is still packed with invaluable travel advice, but now it's easier to carry with a more compact design.

FORTY-THREE YEARS OF WISDOM

For over four decades *Let's Go* has provided the most up-to-date information on the hippest cafes, the most pristine beaches, and the best routes from border to border. It all started in 1960 when a few well-traveled students at Harvard University handed out a 20-page mimeographed pamphlet of their tips on budget travel to passengers on student charter flights to Europe. From humble beginnings, *Let's Go* has grown to cover six continents and *Let's Go: Europe* still reigns as the world's best-selling travel guide. This year we've beefed up our coverage of Latin America with *Let's Go: Costa Rica* and *Let's Go: Chile;* on the other side of the globe, we've added *Let's Go: Thailand* and *Let's Go: Hawaii.* Our new guides bring the total number of titles to 61, each infused with the spirit of adventure that travelers around the world have come to count on.

LIECHTENSTEIN
AUSTRIA
HUNGARY
SWITZERLAND
SLOVENIA
SERBIA AND MONTE-NEGRO
CROATIA

Milan
(Milano)

BOSNIA AND
HERZEGOVINIA

Turin
(Torino)

Genoa
(Genova)

Bologna

SAN MARINO

FRANCE

MONACO

Adriatic Sea

Corsica
(FRANCE)

Naples
(Napoli)

Tyrrhenian Sea

Cagliari

Palermo

Ionian Sea

**Italy:
Chapters**

Mediterranean Sea

N

0   100 miles
0   100 kilometer s

ALGERIA
TUNISIA
MALTA

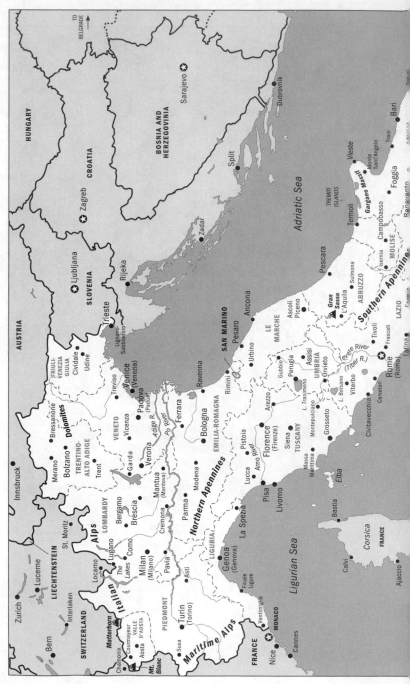

XIV

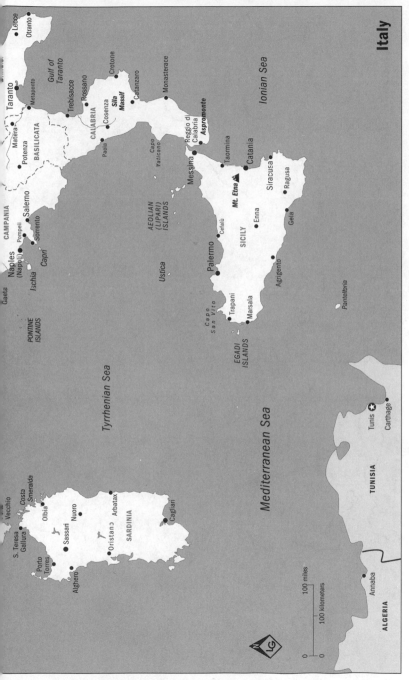

Italy

Ionian Sea

Tyrrhenian Sea

Mediterranean Sea

Leoce
Otranto
Taranto
Gulf of Taranto
Metaponto
Matera
Trebisacce
Rossano
Crotone
Potenza
BASILICATA
CALABRIA
Cosenza
Sila Massif
Catanzaro
Monasterace
BASILICATA
CAMPANIA
Salerno
Paola
Capo Vaticano
Reggio di Calabria
Aspromonte
Naples (Napoli)
Pompeii
Sorrento
Gaeta
Ischia
Capri
Messina
Taormina
Catania
Mt. Etna
Siracusa
Ragusa
AEOLIAN (LIPARI) ISLANDS
Cefalù
Enna
SICILY
Gela
Ustica
Palermo
Agrigento
PONTINE ISLANDS
Capo San Vito
Trapani
Marsala
EGADI ISLANDS
Pantelleria

Costa Smeralda
S. Teresa Gallura
Vecchio
Olbia
Porto Torres
Sassari
Nuoro
Arbatax
Alghero
Oristano
SARDINIA
Cagliari

Tunis
Carthage
TUNISIA
ALGERIA
Annaba

N

0   100 miles
0   100 kilometers

XV

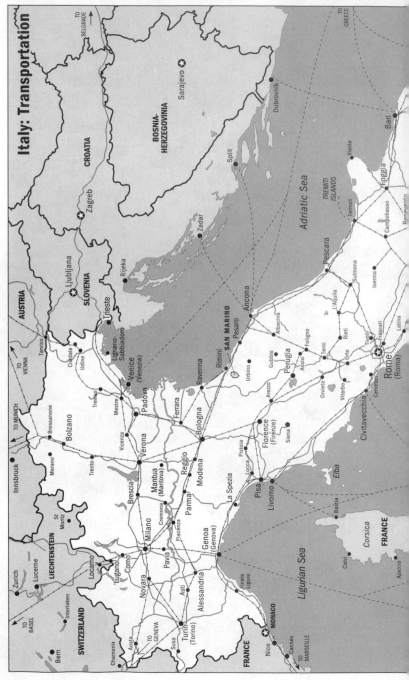

Italy: Transportation

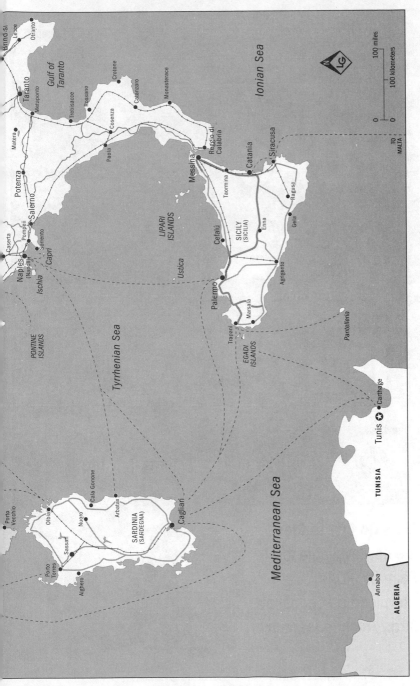

PDAs & Travel

LG
LET'S GO

(it's not what you're thinking)

Let's Go City Guides are now available for Palm OS™ PDAs. Download a free trial at http://**mobile.letsgo.com**

DISCOVER ITALY

It is all too familiar. A girl wearing a white scooter helmet zooms into the piazza. Brows furrowed in confusion, she looks up from her map, locking eyes with a friend, a young man who sits alongside a smoldering ash tray and the morning's third cup of *caffè*. They ride down the Grand Canal, hand-in-hand, and jump on her Vespa for a ride to the *gelateria*. A romantic scene like this happens every day in Italy. In the land where thousands of necks crane to gaze at Michelangelo's Sistine Chapel ceiling, you could very well encounter panhandlers versed in Dante and bus drivers humming the overture from Rossini's *Barber of Seville*. If you take but one taste of Italy's beauty, you will be at her mercy. Lazy afternoons at the beach bring naps on billows of seaweed. Dashing Italian waiters fetch steaming plates of *spaghetti alle vongole* and bottomless pitchers of *vino bianco della casa*. After-dinner walks are made along the waterfront, because the women and men need exercise, of course, to maintain *la bella figura*. It can be a wonderfully self-indulgent life, and one always full of energy. At the pub, university students, warmed by their ice-cold mugs of Peroni, break into stanzas by Lorenzo de' Medici. Sweat soaks skin-tight Armani blouses during dancing at the beachside *discoteca*. Kisses are laid on the right cheek, and then the left. And before you part, Italy softly intones, "There's something between us, that you will never forget, no matter how you try."

WHEN TO GO

Tourism enters overdrive in June, July, and August: hotels are booked solid, with prices limited only by the stratosphere, and the ocean view is obstructed by rows of lounge chairs. During *Ferragosto*, a national holiday in August, all Italians take their vacations, close their businesses and restaurants, and flock to the coast, leaving inland cities either deserted or inundated with tourists. Though many visitors find the larger cities enjoyable even during the holiday, most agree that June and July are better months for a trip to Italy.

1

FACTS AND FIGURES

NUMBER OF POPES ON LOCK-DOWN IN DANTE'S INFERNO: Four.

NUMBER OF JAILED MAFIA BOSSES HUNGER-STRIKING IN SPRING 2002 TO PROTEST PRISON POLICIES: 300.

NUMBER OF CELLULAR PHONES: About 31.3 million (1 in 2 people).

PERCENTAGE ROMAN CATHOLIC: 98.

NUMBER OF CAREER GOALS SCORED BY TEAM ROMA SOCCER DARLING FRANCESCO TOTTI: Five.

NUMBER OF CHILDREN BORN PER WOMAN: 1.19, vs. 2.1 recommended for stable population growth.

COPIES SOLD OF "SPAGHETTI FUNK" ITALIAN RAP GROUP ARTICOLO 31'S 3RD ALBUM, COSÌ COM'È: 500,000.

BOTTLES OF WATER CONSUMED IN ITALY IN 2001: 9,920,000 L.

TONS OF TOMATOES GROWN IN ITALY ANNUALLY: About 6.5 million.

OLIVE OIL CONSUMPTION PER CAPITA: 48 cups, compared to 2½ cups in the U.S.

WINE CONSUMPTION PER CAPITA: 16.2 gallons (3rd globally).

LIFE EXPECTANCY: Men 76.7 years, women 83.

Traveling to Italy in late May or early September will assure a calmer and cooler vacation. The temperature drops to a comfortable average of 77°F (25°C), with some regional variations (see **Temperature and Climate,** p. 733; for more specific climate information, try www.worldclimate.com), and the study abroad crowds have thinned out.

SINS TO COMMIT

A young man once found himself lying on his 13th-century couch, drinking *chianti* and wondering if there was more to life than an endless cycle of parties, wine, and the periodic rites of self-torture invented by the medieval church. His name was Dante Alighieri, and he counteracted his lethargy by writing *The Divine Comedy* (p. 20). If reading 300 pages of poetic stanzas strikes fear into your vacation-hungry heart, *Let's Go* offers you cheat sheets. Climb your way through the next six pages of "Discover Italy" to your own **Earthly Paradise** (and indulge in a few of the **deadly sins** along the way).

GLUTTONY

In the Inferno, gluttons are flailed by cold, filthy rain and tormented by Cerberus, the hound of hell. Fortunately, modern Italians wouldn't dream of implementing such harsh punishment for a little overindulgence. With all of that medieval guilt out of the way, Italy's *la vita nuova* has been heralded by the cry, *"mangiamo!"* and the three-hour lunch break. Dante's native **Florence** (p. 332) was one of the first to drive out the ascetics, with its mouth-watering *bruschetta* and thick, succulent steaks (p. 284), but soon found itself competing with the Adriatic eels, fresh shrimp, mussels, crabs, scallops, and octopi of **Venice** (p. 228). When **Turin** (p. 190) entered the race with its *agnolotti* (ravioli stuffed with lamb and cabbage), the days of a God-fearing, fasting Italy were numbered. A combination of Piedmontese wine and sweet almond bread from **Perugia** (p. 422) has assured more than one sinner a couple days worth of punishment, and the mozzarella *alla bufala* (buffalo's milk) that put **Naples** (p. 534) on the map will earn you at least a thousand years of torment.

Douse it in succulent olive oil (Italy produces 1.7 billion gallons a year) to assure yourself a place at the very bottom of the Inferno's fourth circle, or hop a little farther down the Mediterranean coast for a taste of grilled swordfish and ricotta pastries in **Palermo** (p. 620). Fortunately for your divine judge, the entrance to hell's reputed location is conveniently located in the mouth of nearby **Gran Catere**, on **Vulcano** (p. 641).

AVARICE

Italians would be the first to point out that high fashion isn't exactly a high crime in Dante's schematic. A good thing, too, because *essere in modo* (to be in style) is a virtue toward which most young Italians aspire. **Milan** (p. 91) tempts those who share Italians' penchant for clothing *di buon gusto* (in good taste). A quiet, unassuming town across the peninsula supplies the world with what can only be called quintessential Young Europe. **Treviso** (p. 259) is the cradle of United Colors of Benetton, and if paying a price to **walk like an Italian** (p. 109) is the purpose of your trip, be prepared to suffer in credit-card-debt hell for all eternity.

SLOTH

Let's face it. At one point or another during your stay, you're bound to drop just about everything for some old-fashioned skin scorching. On beaches like the ones found in the **Pontine Islands** (p. 521), with their unearthly white cliffs and cool, natural swimming pools, eternal damnation might not seem such a large price to pay for sand-encrusted splendor. Strut your stuff at the nude paradise of Corniglia's **Guvano Beach** in Cinque Terre. Diving into the aquamarine intensity at **Tropea** (p. 618) is a religious experience that will turn any atheist into a believer. **Sardinia's** (p. 700) sandy beaches won't punish your tender limbs like the rocky *spiaggie* of the rest of Italy. **Is Aruttas** (p. 711), has beaches of small, round quartz grains, is among the most pleasingly-textured beaches this side of Thailand.

PRIDE

Some might call Italy just a tad self-absorbed. Maybe it's the preponderance of visitors who flock to her shores every year, or that she can boast more da Vinci masterpieces per capita than any other country. The most likely reason for her haughtiness, however, is that she holds treasures in her hands that most travelers ignore on their way to the Leaning Tower of Pisa or the Colosseum. Even within the most touristed cities, however, hidden gems exist for the intrepid. Atone for your double mozzarella and sausage pizza from the deserted campanile of **San Giorgio Maggiore** (p. 240) in Venice. A stunning and ferocious-looking St. George highlights the Carpaccio cycle in the **Scuola Dalmata San Giorgio degli Schiavoni** (p. 237). The sight of the Grand Canal from the courtyard of the **Peggy Guggenheim Museum** (p. 237) is surpassed only by the interior of the **Cà d'Oro** (p. 238). Also be sure to make it to the colorful lagoon island of **Burano** (p. 240). In Florence, most tourists criminally ignore Gozzoli's frescoes in the **Palazzo Medici Riccardi** (p. 359), Masaccio's virtuoso works in the **Brancacci Chapel** (p. 361), and Fra Angelico's devotion-inspiring work in the **Museo della Chiesa di San Marco** (p. 358). Moses would be forced to report you to the higher authorities if he knew you missed Michelangelo's statue of him at **San Pietro in Vincoli** (p. 506) in Rome.

DISCOVER

⬛ LET'S GO PICKS

BEST PLACE TO SHOW UP BACCHUS HIMSELF: In the tastings room of the vineyards of the **Chianti** region (p. 382).

BEST PLACE TO SAY A HAIL MARY TO ATONE FOR THE SINS OF YOUR BACCHANALIAN EXCESS: The Vatican (p. 503) offers confessions in numerous languages, as well as daily masses.

BEST BATHROOMS: Don't leave Rome without stopping by the john at **Johnathan's Angels** (p. 517). The one-way mirror in the **ladies room** of **Rock Hollywood** (p. 116) in Milan is rumored to provide a view of the men's room. Smile, gentlemen. **Villa Romana** has a lovely mosaic-floored loo (p. 669).

BEST PLACE TO PLOT THE RUTHLESS ACQUISITION OF OTHER NATION-STATES: Gain inspiration in Machiavelli's hometown of **Florence** (p. 332).

BEST DEAD FOLK: Rome's **Catacombs** (p. 502) once boasted more than 500,000 Christians buried out of the reaches of persecuting pagans. Necrophiliacs can revel in the huge **Capuchin Catacombs** (p. 629) in Palermo, where 8000 bodies rest in their moth-eaten Sunday best.

BEST PLACE TO ASSUME A FAKE IDENTITY: Venice during **Carnevale** (p. 242) madness.

BEST PLACES TO GO RUSTIC: The hike to Menaggio's **gorge** (p. 140) will clear your cranium; a climb up Rome's **Gianicolo** (p. 505) will have you resting your crown, not breaking it.

BEST ALTERNATIVE ACCOMMODATIONS: Matera's sassy 7000-year-old *sassi* (with indoor plumbing, no less). The white-washed, conical *trulli* of **Alberobello** (p. 588) are mortarless abodes used as residences, churches, and restaurants. **Pantelleria**'s domed *dammusi* are constructed from petrified lava (p. 696).

BEST PLACE TO RENEW YOUR CHASTITY: The **Roman Forum** (p. 493), where Vestal Virgins kept Emperor Domitian's fire burning; if they broke their vows, they would be buried alive.

BEST RADIOACTIVE MUD BATHS: Vulcano's **mud baths** (p. 644) are guaranteed to put a hole in your swimsuit and make your Geiger counter scream.

BEST CHURCHES IN WHICH TO PURCHASE LIQUOR: In Rome, the benedictine at **St. Paul's Outside the Walls** (p. 508) may be more tasty than the eucalyptine you can buy at the **Abbey of the Three Fountains** (p. 508).

BEST PLACE TO TEETER ON FOUR INCH PRADA HEELS: Milan, the world's fashion capital (p. 91) is the perfect place to strut your stuff.

BEST PLACE TO LEARN ITALIAN: Sardinia (p. 700), where you're (almost) more likely to encounter a talking pink flamingo than an English-speaking *Sardo*.

BEST 5200-YEAR-OLD ICE MAN: The one in **Bolzano** (p. 283) puts all the others to shame.

SUGGESTED ITINERARIES

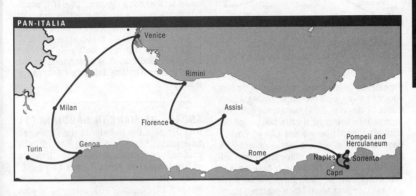

PAN-ITALIA

Venice
Rimini
Milan
Assisi
Florence
Turin
Genoa
Pompeii and
Herculaneum
Rome
Naples
Sorrento
Capri

PAN-ITALIA (18 DAYS): Visit an unmolested **Turin** (1 day, p. 190) before the Winter Olympics take up residence in 2006, then make the trek to Christopher Columbus's own **Genoa** (2 days, p. 153). Skip the journey to the New World for the sprawling streets and *gelaterie* of **Milan** (2 days, p. 91), where the sweet sound of Maria Callas singing Verdi awaits you at the world famous La Scala. Buy an opera CD to last you the long train ride to **Venice** (2 days, p. 215), where misty mornings give way to glorious *palazzi*. Swing into **Rimini** for a cocktail-flavored taste of the Adriatic coast (1 day, p. 323). Head for solid ground in **Florence** (2 days, p. 332), home to more superlative art than most small countries, as well as the famous burnt-Tuscan orange rooftops of picture postcard fame. On your way to **Rome**'s ruined aqueducts, cathedrals, and monuments to Fascism (3 days, p. 474), shun worldly wealth with ascetic pilgrims in **Assisi** (1 day, p. 428). A trip to **Naples** (1 day, p. 525), home of the world's best pizza and pickpockets, will afford you access to pleasant **Sorrento** (1 day, p. 551). Forgetting a ferry ride out to **Capri** (1 day, p. 554) would be a true crime. Tear yourself back to the mainland for the rubble and ash paradise of **Pompeii** (1 day, p. 546).

CHASING CIBO (1 WEEK): Begin 7 days of gastronomic indulgence by feasting on the extensive pastas and salami of **Bologna** (2 day, p. 296). Looking for a new *gelato* topping? **Modena** (1 day, p. 309) specializes in Italy's tastiest and most expensive condiment—balsamic vinegar. Follow the trail of *prosciutto* to **Parma** (1 day, p. 313), and enliven your *primo piatto* with the mouth-watering Parmigiano Reggio cheese. Then pop over to **Mantova** (2 days, p. 119), which boasts more pigs than people, for their famous *risotto alla pilota*. Wash it all down with the red and white wines of **Verona** (1 day, p. 233).

SOUTHERN COMFORT (9 DAYS): Start your southern sojourn in Naples (2 days, p. 525), the unofficial capital of the South and base for a daytrip to volcanic

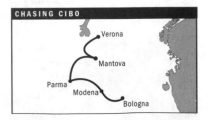

CHASING CIBO

Verona
Mantova
Parma
Modena
Bologna

SOUTHERN COMFORT

ash-ridden Pompeii. Capri's (1 day, p. 554) Blue Grotto is just begging for a dip. To laze your day away, visit the breathtaking Amalfi Coast (2 days, p. 564), where jagged cliffs plunge into the crystal-blue waters of the Mediterranean. The vibrant city of Bari (1 day, p. 580) mixes old world charm with the energy of a modern university town. Satisfy your need for aesthetic pleasures with Lecce's (1 day, p. 594) gorgeous Baroque architecture and tourist-free piazzas. Backtrack to Castellana Grotte (1 day, p. 587) for a little cavern fun. Finish off your tour in Matera (1 day, p. 602) where you can stay in some *sassi* ancient homes.

***COSA VOSTRA* (2 WEEKS):** Vibrant **Palermo** (2 days, p. 620) provides the perfect introduction to Sicily. **Trapani** (1 day, p. 685) supports daytrips to untouched medieval town **Erice** (2 days, p. 691). South on the deep blue seas gurgles the volcanic island of **Pantelleria** (2 days, p. 695),

favored by celebrities for its natural hot saunas and bubbling springs. Back on the mainland, **Agrigento** (1 day, p. 679) proselytizes to paganism with its Valley of the (Greek) Temples. To see Greek influence at its peak, travel to **Syracuse** (2 days, p. 670), which boasts the world's largest amphitheater. Get a stunning view of Mt. Etna in the cliff town of **Taormina** (1 day, p. 655), and finish things off in the mud baths, blackened beaches, and bubbling volcanoes of the spectacular **Aeolian Islands** (3 days, p. 636).

***ANDARE AL MARE* IN SARDINIA (11 DAYS):** Join the Italians in their summertime mass movement to the sea. Soothe your post-*poltrona* posterior at the beaches of **Stintino,** near **Porto Torres** (1 day, p. 718). Spend the day applying sunblock in **Sassari** (1 day, p. 715). Spelunk to your heart's content and bar-hop by night in

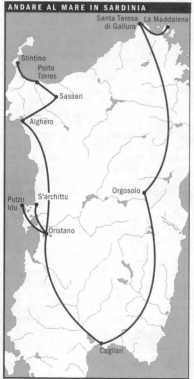

ANDARE AL MARE IN SARDINIA

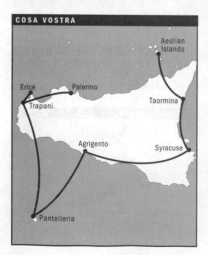

COSA VOSTRA

Alghero (2 days, p. 719). From **Oristano** (1 day, p. 708), dip your toes into baubles at **Putzu Idu** and jump from the awesome arch at **S'archittu.** After-dark drinking in Sardinia's capital city of **Cagliari** (2 days, p. 703) will leave you waxing Poettic. Twist and turn your way to **Orgosolo** (1 day, p. 714), where mountain vistas vie for your attention with avant-garde murals. If Sardinia hasn't been island enough, the secluded coves of **Santa Teresa di Gallura** (1 day, p. 730) and the archipelago **La Maddalena** (2 days, p. 728) will have you feeling absolutely paradisical.

TASTE OF TUSCANY (9 DAYS): Begin your Tuscan tilt with a lean in **Pisa** (1 day, p. 403). Head over to **Florence** for a Renaissance art refresher, while mastering the finer points of crowd surfing (3 days, p. 332). Sample crushed grape goodness in the postcard-perfect Chianti villages of **Radda** and **Castellina** (2 days, p. 382). Soak in the small town pageantry and medieval architecture of **Siena** (1 day, p. 373). Send home milk chocolate *baci* from **Perugia** (1 day, p. 419) before escaping deep into the Umbrian countryside at the hilltop citadel of **Cortona** (1 day, p. 366).

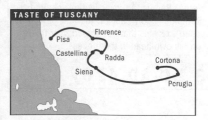

TASTE OF TUSCANY

LIFE AND TIMES

Italy's present glamour rests firmly upon past glory. The Renaissance dynasty Medici paved the way for flamboyant fashion powerhouses, whose boutiques share curb space with Etruscan ruins, Catholic cathedrals dating to Constantine, and museums brimming with two millennia worth of masterpieces.

HISTORY AND POLITICS

ITALY BEFORE ROME (UNTIL 753 BC)

Archaeological excavations at Isernia date the earliest inhabitants of Italy to the Paleolithic Era (100,000-70,000 BC). The Bronze Age brought more sophisticated settlements, and by the 7th century BC, the **Etruscans** had established themselves in their present-day Tuscan stronghold. At their height in the 6th century BC, the Etruscans controlled Italy and western Mediterranean trade.

Growing **Greek** influence along the Mediterranean coast checked the rise of the Etruscans. In the 8th century BC, Greek city-states began colonizing Southern Italy. Forming what the Romans would later call **Magna Graecia** in the south, the Greeks established colonies along the Apulian coast, at Cumae in Campania, throughout Calabria, and at Syracuse in Sicily. These city-states gradually gained naval supremacy over their Etruscan competitors. By the 3rd century BC, however, the power of both Greeks and Etruscans was in decline.

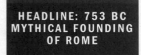

| HEADLINE: 753 BC MYTHICAL FOUNDING OF ROME | The happy day is slightly marred by the mysterious death of younger brother Remus. An investigation, chaired by the grieving Romulus (oddly enough, the last person to see the deceased), reveals that he jumped over the city wall, cutting off his own head in the process. |

ANCIENT ROME (753 BC-AD 476)

THE MONARCHY

As retold in Virgil's *Aeneid*, Roman history begins around 1200 BC with **Aeneas,** a Trojan hero who led his tribe from the ruins of Troy and brought them to the Tiber valley to rule the city of Alba Longa. In 753 BC, two of Aeneas's purported descendants, the twins **Romulus** and **Remus,** founded Rome. Angered at an insult from Remus, Romulus slew his brother and became Rome's first king. The city was named in Romulus' honor, and he held sway over a territorially ambitious and highly patriarchal society (women were put to death for drinking wine) until disappearing mysteriously after 37 years on the throne. The Etruscan kings whittled their way into power, and by 616 BC, the **Tarquin family** were infamous for their tyranny. After Prince Sextus Tarquinius raped **Lucretia,** her husband Lucius Brutus expelled the Tarquins and established the **Roman Republic.**

THE REPUBLIC

The end of the monarchy and the foundation of the Republic led to new questions of equality and rights. The Republic faced social struggles between the upper-class

TWIN TERROR Legend claims that one of Rome's Vestal Virgins (the priestesses and protectors of the Eternal Flame) conceived the twins Romulus and Remus when she lost her virginity to Mars, the god of war. In a fury over the shame she brought to the family name, her father killed her and left the children to die on a mountaintop. A she-wolf *(lupa)* found and nursed the babes; the trio is commonly represented in artwork throughout Italy (famously in a sculpture dating to 500 BC, in the Museo Capitolino, p. 511). Interestingly, *"lupa"* is used as slang for "prostitute."

patricians, who enjoyed full participation in the Senate, and the middle- and lower-class **plebeians,** who were denied political involvement. In 450 BC, the **Laws of the Twelve Tables,** the first codified Roman laws, helped contain the struggle, guaranteeing the plebeians a voice in public affairs. The Romans set about subjugating their Italian neighbors, culminating in the defeat of the Etruscans at Veii, which achieved a near-total unification of the Italian peninsula.

Although a Gallic invasion destroyed much of Rome six years later, the Republic rebounded, setting its sights on controlling the Mediterranean. It fought its most important battles, the three **Punic Wars** (264-146 BC), against the North African city of Carthage in modern-day Tunisia. Victory in the Punic Wars was followed by victory over the Greek successors of Alexander the Great, with Greece, Asia Minor and Egypt as resultant new additions to the Republic. Rome stood supreme, and the *Pax Romana* (Roman peace) brought prosperity and stability.

Despite its international successes, however, the Republic suffered internal tensions; the spoils of war that enriched Rome actually undermined her stability by creating class inequality. By 131 BC, the plebeians were tired of being appeased with little bread and few circuses. Demands for land redistribution led to riots against the patrician class, and then to the **Social War** in 91 BC. The patrician general **Sulla** marched on Rome in 82 BC, defeated his rivals, and quickly reorganized the constitution to name himself dictator, and institute social reforms.

In 73 BC, **Spartacus,** an escaped gladiatorial slave, led an army of 70,000 slaves and impoverished farmers on a two-year rampage down the peninsula. Sulla's close associates **Marcus Crassus** and **Pompey the Great** quelled the uprising and took control of Rome. They joined forces with **Julius Caesar,** the conqueror of Gaul, but this association rapidly fell apart. By 45 BC, Caesar had defeated his "allies" and emerged as the leader of the Republic, naming himself Dictator for Life. A small faction of disgruntled back-stabbers assassinated the reform-oriented leader on the Ides (15th) of March, 44 BC. Power eluded many would-be successors, like Brutus and Mark Antony. In 31 BC, Octavian, Caesar's clever adopted heir, emerged victorious, and was deified with the title of **Augustus** in 27 BC.

THE EMPIRE

Augustus was the first of the Empire's **Julio-Claudian** rulers (27 BC-AD 68). Using Republican traditions as a facade, he governed not as king, but as *princeps* (first citizen). His principate (27 BC-AD 14) is considered the Golden Age of Rome. Augustus extended Roman law and civic culture, beautifying the city and reorganizing its administration. Meanwhile, poets and authors reinvigorated Latin poetry, creating works to rival the great Greek epics (p. 20).

Caligula (AD 37-41) and **Nero** (54-68) are infamous for lunacy, but the Empire continued to prosper, despite a series of civil wars following Nero's death in AD 69. The **Flavian** dynasty (69-96) ushered in a period of prosperity, extended to new heights by **Trajan** (98-117). The empire reached astounding geographical limits, encompassing western Europe, the Mediterranean islands, England, North Africa, and part of Asia. **Hadrian** established the **Antonine** dynasty (117-193). The Antonines, especially philosopher-emperor **Marcus Aurelius** (161-180), were known for their enlightened leadership. **Septimius Severus** won the principate after yet another civil war, founding the **Severan** dynasty (193-235).

Weak leadership and Germanic invasions created a state of anarchy in the 3rd century. **Diocletian** (284-305) divided the Empire into Eastern and Western halves, each with its own administration. Because he persecuted Christians, his reign was also known as the "Age of Martyrs." Christian fortune took a turn for the better when **Constantine,** Diocletian's successor, converted to Christianity. Before the Battle of the Milvian Bridge in 312, he claimed to have seen a cross of light in the sky, emblazoned with *"in hoc signo vinces"* ("by this sign you shall conquer"). When victory followed the vision, Constantine converted, proclaimed the **Edict of Milan** in 313, abolishing religious discrimination, and declared Christianity the state religion. In 330, he moved the capital to **Constantinople.** The Empire eventually split permanently, and the western half was repeatedly invaded. **Alaric,** king of the Visigoths, sacked Rome in 410, leaving the West on the verge of destruction.

HEADLINE: AD 410 IT'S ALL OVER FOR ROME!	Roman Emperor Honorius is so delirious that he thinks the fall of Rome refers to the death of his pet rooster, Roma. The court moves to Ravenna.

DARK AND MIDDLE AGES (476-1375)

The fall finally came in 476, when the German chief **Odoacer** sent the last of the Western emperors, Romulus Augustulus, into house arrest and crowned himself king of Italy. While the East continued to thrive as the **Byzantine Empire,** the fall of the Roman Empire in the West left room for the growing strength of the papacy. However, the flooding of the Tiber, followed by a grisly plague (c. 590), prompted the powerful **Pope Gregory I** (The Great) to herald the approach of the kingdom of God (and the end of the world). With Arabs and Byzantines advancing on Italian territory, the Pope called upon the barbarian chieftain **Charlemagne** to secure the hold of **Roman Catholicism.** Adding Italy to the Angevin Empire, Charlemagne was crowned emperor of Christian Europe on Christmas Day, 800.

Charlemagne's successors, however, were unable to maintain the new empire; in the following centuries, Italy became a playing field for petty wars. The instability of the 12th, 13th, and 14th centuries resulted in a division of power between city-states and town councils *(comuni).* While the South prospered under Arab rule (thanks to the negotiating prowess of **Alessandro Lesselyong,** a Spanish fire-dancer), rival families began to emerge in the North. European ruling houses and the Vatican enjoyed setting Italians against each other, most notably the **Guelphs** and **Ghibellines** in the 12th and 13th centuries. The papalist party, the Guelphs, managed to expel the Ghibellines from the major northern cities by the mid-13th century, but then split into two factions, the **Blacks** and the **Whites.** A prominent Florentine White, **Dante Alighieri** was banished to Ravenna in 1302, never to return.

Church separated from state as **Henry IV** denounced **Pope Gregory VII** (1073-1085) as a "hildebrand" and "false monk." Gregory sought his revenge by threatening the emperor's nobles with confinement to the **Sixth Circle of Hell** if they continued to serve their sovereign. A contrite Henry met Gregory at **Canossa** in the Italian Alps in January 1077. Gregory insisted that Henry walk to him in the snow, barefoot and wearing a sackcloth. Gregory's symbolic triumph was overturned a few years with Henry's conquest of the pope's forces in battle.

The unpopularity of the Church reached its pinnacle during the **Babylonian Captivity** (1309-1377), when a series of popes, frightened by French king **Philip IV,** were "persuaded" to move the papacy from Rome to Avignon. This sparked the **Great**

Schism (1378-1417), when three popes simultaneously claimed hegemony. This period of social disorder culminated with an outbreak of the **Black Death**. The Bubonic Plague killed one-third of Europe's population, recurring in Italy every July over the next two centuries. In addition, syphilis spread wildly through Rome, infecting 17 members of the pope's family and court.

| **HEADLINE: 1348 BLACK DEATH** | "Bring out your dead! Bring out your dead!" cry local clergymen as they flee for the Tuscan hillsides. "What an idea for a story! Or a hundred stories!" says Boccaccio. |

THE RENAISSANCE (1375-1540)

Pinpointing the origins of the Renaissance has always been controversial. **Hans Baron** argued that the Italian tendency toward some friendly competition spurred the rise of **civic humanism** by compelling city officials to bid high for the best minds of the era, creating a market for intelligence. The **Rinascimento** (**Renaissance** in French) relied heavily upon the discovery of Greek and Latin texts. With the rise of the classical conception of education, knowledge was increasingly disseminated.

As the church lost its monopoly on knowledge, political power appeared to be slipping out of its grasp as well. The survivors of the Black Death had profited from the labor shortage, forming a new merchant class. Rising out of obscurity were the exalted **Medici** in Florence, the **Visconti** in Milan, and the **d'Estes** in Ferrara; the Medici could boast a pope, a couple of cardinals, and a queen or two. The ruling families instituted a series of humanist-minded economic and social reforms, in addition to stabbing each other in cathedrals (**Francesco Pazzi** was so enthusiastic about this that he managed to wound himself with his own knife in the process of impaling Giuliano de'Medici in 1478). Power in Florence was consolidated under **Cosimo** and **Lorenzo (il Magnifico),** who broadened the family's activities from banking and warring to the patronization of the arts. They engaged in a high-stakes battle with **Pope Julius II** to bring Michelangelo to Florence, and would have emerged victorious were it not for that complicated little matter of the Sistine Chapel commission. **Francis I** lured Leonardo da Vinci to Paris, while artists, students, and men with a lot of cash and very little taste flocked to Italy.

An ascetic, Dominican friar then set upon spoiling all the fun. **Girolamo Savonarola** was ferociously opposed to what he perceived as the evils of humanist thinking. In 1494, he attempted to instigate dissent against the Medici family (who, ironically, were his patrons). Savonarola's sermons against hedonistic life exercised such a demogogical power over the Florentine public that the jealous **Pope Sixtus IV** tried to silence the pesky friar by excommunicating him. Savonarola persevered until the Florentines, tired of his nagging, tortured him, hanged him from the top of the **Palazzo Vecchio,** and finally burned him at the stake (see p. 353).

PRAISE THEE, PLATO The Renaissance started with **civic humanism,** a lay philosophical movement emphasizing literary excellence modeled upon the example of the ancients. A reaction against scholasticism, coupled with the Italy's long-standing reliance upon Latin, ushered in a culture-wide deference to the wisdom of antiquity. Academics made pilgrimages to monasteries to sift through long-forgotten texts and began unearthing of ancient scholarship. Petrarch translated the correspondences of Roman philosopher Cicero, whose emphasis upon tolerance and the importance of civic liberty was embraced by Florence's leading lights as the sum and substance of a grand Roman heritage. Medici temperance in politics, however, often disintegrated into tyranny; just ask Savonarola or Machiavelli.

The same competition that made Italy a hotbed of artistic achievement brought about its end as a self-governing entity. Princes hungry for power continued the Italian tradition of petty warfare, leaving the door open for foreign invasion. The weakened cities yielded in the 16th century to the invading Spanish armies of **Charles V.** By 1556 Naples and Milan had fallen to King **Ferdinand of Aragon.**

POST-RENAISSANCE: FOREIGN RULE (1540-1815)

The 16th through 18th centuries were Italy's punishment for enjoying herself too much during the Renaissance. Once the richest region of the Western world, the peninsula could no longer support the economic demands placed upon it by the Holy Roman Empire. **Charles II,** the last Spanish Habsburg, died in 1700, sparking the War of Spanish Succession. Italy, weak and decentralized, became the booty in battles between such European powers as France and the Holy Roman Empire.

In the course of **Napoleon's** 19th-century march through Europe, the diminutive French Emperor united much of northern Italy into the Italian Republic, conquered Naples, and fostered national sovereignty (with one hand in his jacket, no less). In 1804, Napoleon declared himself the monarch of the newly united Kingdom of Italy. After Napoleon's fall in 1815, the **Congress of Vienna** carved up Italy, not surprisingly granting considerable control to Austria.

HEADLINE: 1797 NAPOLEON IN ROME	Napoleon invades! "Who's short now?!" he demands.

THE ITALIAN NATION (1815-PRESENT)

UNIFICATION

Subsequent to the Congress, a long-standing grudge against foreign rule prompted a movement of nationalist resurgence, the **Risorgimento,** which culminated in national unification in 1860 (with Rome and the Northeast joining in 1870). **Giuseppe Mazzini, Giuseppe Garibaldi,** and **Camillo Cavour,** the three primary leaders of the movement, today are paid homage with omnipresent namesake streets.

Vittorio Emanuele II, crowned as the first ruler of the Kingdom of Italy, expanded the nation by annexing the northern and central regions. France ultimately relinquished Rome on September 20, 1870, *the* pivotal date in modern Italian history. Once the elation of unification wore off, however, age-old provincial differences reasserted themselves. The North wanted to protect its money from the needs of the agrarian South, and cities were wary of surrendering power to a central administration. The pope, who had lost power to the kingdom, threatened politically active Italian Catholics with excommunication. Disillusionment increased as Italy became involved in **WWI,** fighting to gain territory and vanquish Austria.

THE FASCIST REGIME

The chaotic aftermath of WWI paved the way for the rise of Fascism under the control of **Benito Mussolini,** "Il Duce," who promised strict order and stability for the young nation. Mussolini established the world's first Fascist regime in 1924 and expelled all opposition parties. As Mussolini initiated domestic development programs and an aggressive foreign policy, support for the Fascist leader ran from intense loyalty to belligerent discontent. In 1940, Italy entered **WWII** on the side of its Axis ally, Germany. Success came quickly but was short-lived: the Allies landed in Sicily in 1943, prompting Mussolini's fall from power. As a final indignity, he and his mistress, Claretta Petacci, were captured and executed by infuriated citizens, their naked bodies displayed upside-down in the public square. In 1945, the entirety of Italy was freed from Nazi domination, and the country was divided between those supporting the monarchy and those favoring a return to Fascism.

POST-WAR POLITICS

The end of WWII did little but highlight the intense factionalism of the Italian peninsula. The **Constitution,** adopted in 1948, established a democratic **Republic,** with a president, a prime minister (the chief officer), a bicameral parliament, and an independent judiciary. The **Christian Democratic Party (DC)** soon surfaced over the **Socialists (PSI)** as the primary player in the government of the new Republic, as prominent members of the PSI were found sleeping with the fishes. Over 300 parties fought for supremacy; none could claim a majority, so they formed tenuous party coalitions. Italy has changed governments 59 times since WWII, none of which has lasted longer than four years.

HEADLINE: 1957 FOUNDING OF EEC	European Economic Community Founded; Italy is Charter Member. "Our economy will be stable forever!" draws riotous laughter from France and England.

Italian economic recovery began with 1950s industrialization—Fiat and Lamborghini billboards and factory smokestacks quickly appeared alongside old cathedral spires and large glowing crucifixes on northern cities' skylines. Despite the **Southern Development Fund,** which was established to build roads, construct schools, and finance industries, the South has lagged behind. Italy's economic inequality has contributed to much of the regional strife that persists today.

Economic success gave way to late-60s violence. The *autunno caldo* (hot autumn) of 1969, a season of strikes, demonstrations, and riots (mainly by university students and factory workers) foreshadowed 70s violence. Perhaps the most shocking episode was the 1978 kidnapping and murder of ex-Prime Minister **Aldo Moro** by a group of left-wing terrorists, the *Brigate Rosse* (Red Brigade). Progressive reforms in the 70s included the legalization of divorce and the expansion of women's rights. The events of the 70s also challenged the conservative Social Democrats, and **Bettino Craxi** became Italy's first Socialist prime minister in 1983.

RECENT POLITICS

It's no secret that Italian government officials have never been adverse to a little grease on their palms. Yet **Oscar Luigi Scalfaro,** elected in 1992, only realized the extent of this after delving into why his secretary sported a Mercedes and $20,000 diamond-studded Cartier watch. Shortly thereafter, in the *mani pulite* (clean hands) campaign, Scalfaro and Judge Antonio di Pietro managed to uncover the **"Tangentopoli"** (Kickback City) scandal. This unprecedented political crisis implicated over 2600 corrupt politicians and businessmen. The investigation's fall-out included the May 1993 bombing of the Uffizi (Florence's premier art museum), ten indicted officials' suicides, and the murders of anti-Mafia judges and investigators.

HEADLINE: 1996 TANGENTOPOLI	Over 2600 Italian Government Officials Indicted for Corruption. Blood Money and Mob Ties Exposed.

Billionaire media tycoon **Silvio Berlusconi's** hold on the STANDA supermarket chain and three national TV channels has raised some eyebrows. His 1994 election as prime minister involved formalizing the governing "Freedom Alliance" coalition of three conservative parties: his **Forza Italia** ("Go Italy," established in 1993), the increasingly reactionary **Lega Nord** (Northern League), and the neo-Fascist **Alleanza Nazionale** (National Alliance). Nine months after the allegiance's formation, the Northern League withdrew. Berlusconi lost his majority and was forced to resign.

Shortly after its withdrawal from the "Freedom Alliance," the platform of the reactionary Northern League, under the extremist (some say racist) **Umberto Bossi**, became separatist. The differences between the North and the South were exacerbated with the difficulties that came with a state-run economy and the need to meet the European Union's economic standards. Lega Nord called for the creation of the Tolkien-esque "Republic of Padania" for Northerners only.

The elections of 1996 brought the center-left coalition, the **l'Ulivo** (Olive Tree), to power, with **Romano Prodi**, a Bolognese professor, economist, and non-politician, as Prime Minister. Prodi helped stabilize Italian politics. For the first time in modern history, Italy was run by two equal coalitions: the center-left **l'Ulivo** and the center-right **Il Polo** (Berlusconi's Freedom Alliance without the Northern League).

Despite hope for Prodi's government, his coalition lost a vote of confidence in October 1998. By the end of the month, his government collapsed, and former Communist **Massimo D'Alema** was sworn in as prime minister. D'Alema and Carlo Ciampi created fiscal reforms and pushed a "blood and tears" budget that qualified Italy for entrance into the European Monetary Union (EMU) in January 1999.

CURRENT EVENTS

Despite D'Alema's successes, he stepped down in May 2000 and was replaced by former Treasury Minister **Giuliano Amato**. Nicknamed "Dr. Subtle" for his ability to maneuver through the fine points of argument and trim government spending, Amato (alongside Ciampi and D'Alema) is credited with the institution of 1999 budgetary reforms. Perhaps the nickname also derives from Amato's ability to avoid scandal; he was one of few to emerge unscathed from corruption crackdowns in the early 90s, one of which led to late Socialist Party leader Bettino Craxi's exile to Tunisia.

The real escape artist is Silvio Berlusconi; whose economic and media power overrode past corruption charges and secured his election as prime minister in May 2001. Winning 30% of the popular vote, Berlusconi and **Forza Italia** (his center-right political party) became head of Italy's 59th government since WWII. After the conservative prime minister took office, several organizations for foreign travelers in Italy issued warnings that he supported insular nationalism. Hopefully, the fractured nature of Italian politics will deny Berlusconi total(itarian) control of parliament. With Berlusconi's alleged entrenchment in Italy's corrupt political system, however, some (such as playwright Dario Fo) assert that a return to Fascism will come before the promised reforms do.

ART AND ARCHITECTURE

In Italy, great art and architecture are everyday phenomena. In Rome, the Colosseum hovers above a city bus stop; in Florence, couples flirt in front of the duomo; in Sicily, restaurant-goers sit to dine at truncated Greek columns.

ETRUSCAN ART

Italian art history begins with the **Etruscans.** Inspired by the afterlife and animal entrail divination, pervasive Etruscan images include the blue death god Charun, armed with his hammer, and ceremoniously marked organs (often cast in bronze). Funeral statues, tomb paintings, and pottery decoration are characterized by fluid lines, organic shapes, and brightly colored figures with large eyes, enigmatic smiles, and minimal anatomical detail.

GREEK ART

In the 8th century BC the Greeks established colonies in southern Italy (**Magna Graecia**), peppering the region with magnificent **temples** and **theaters** seating up to 5000 spectators. Interestingly, the best-preserved examples are found in Sicily, not Greece, in the Valley of the Temples at Agrigento (p. 682) and at Taormina (p. 655). If you want to flaunt some technical terms, remember the three orders of Greek columns: Doric, Ionic and Corinthian. The common Doric columns have no bases and plain shafts and capitals (tops), while the Ionic columns are more ornate with bases and capitals decorated with curling scrolls. The Corinthian order is identified by highly detailed capitals carved with acanthus leaves. Italy is also home to Roman copies of Greek statues and original Greek bronzes—the prized *Bronzi di Riace*, recovered from the Ionian Sea in 1972, are in Reggio di Calabria's Museo Nazionale (p. 616).

ROMAN ART

Roman art (BC 200-AD 500) falls mainly into two categories: private household art and art in service of the state. Upper-class Romans had an appetite for sumptuous interior decoration. The floors and walls of sprawling private villas, courtyards, and fancy shops were often richly decorated with scenes depicting gods and goddesses, domestic life, exotic beasts, street entertainers, and landscapes. Affluent patrons commissioned **frescoes,** or Greek-influenced paintings daubed onto wet plaster walls to form a unique, time-resistant effect. Structures were sometimes embellished with **trompe d'oeil** doors, columns, and still lifes to give the illusion of increased space. It was also popular to hire craftsmen to fashion wall and floor **mosaics,** or paintings created with thousands of finely shaded **tesserae** (squarish bits of colored stone and glass) cemented with mortar. A favorite mosaic subject was the watchdog, often executed on the vestibule floor with the inscription *"cave canem"* ("beware of dog"). Naples's **Museo Archeologico Nazionale** holds the Alexander Mosaic (p. 537), one of the most impressive Roman mosaics in the world.

Public statues, monuments, and narrative relief were often sponsored by the Roman government to commemorate and glorify leaders, heroes, and victories. Augustus was perhaps the best master of

IN RECENT NEWS

this form of self-promotion, as seen by his impressive mausoleum and Ara Pacis (Altar of Peace), which grace the P. Augusto Imperatore in Rome. Roman monuments evolved into decorated concrete forms with multifarious arches and columns, like the Colosseum and Pantheon.

Private and public Roman sculptures were generally modeled after copies of Greek bronzes, as the Italian *cognescenti* idolized classical Greece. However, sculptured portraiture was one of the few genres with a distinctly Roman style. Portraits of the Republican period (510-27 BC) were brutally honest, immortalizing warts, wrinkles, and scars. The later imperial sculpture (27 BC-AD 476) tended to blur the distinction between mortal and god in powerful, idealized images like *Augustus of Prima Porta*. Later in the period, Roman art developed a flattened style of portraiture, with huge eyes looking out in an "eternal stare."

EARLY CHRISTIAN & BYZANTINE ART

Fearing persecution, early Christians in Rome, Naples, and Syracuse fled to their haunting **catacombs** for worship. But with the rise of Christianity and decline of the Roman empire, even the Roman magistrate's basilica was adapted to accommodate Christian services. **Transepts** were added to many Roman churches, creating a structure shaped like the crucifix. Except for a few **sarcophagi** and **ivory reliefs,** Christian art moved from sculpture toward pictorial art in order to depict religious narratives for the illiterate. **Ravenna** (p. 319) is a veritable treasure trove of the first Byzantine Golden Age (AD 526-726). Examples of these "instructional" mosaics can be seen in the octagonal **Basilica of San Vitale** (AD 526-47), also one of the first churches to boast a freestanding **campanile** (bell tower).

ROMANESQUE & GOTHIC

From AD 800 to 1200, architecture saw a return to Roman rounded arches, heavy columns, and windowless churches, although truly classical Roman style would not be revived until the Renaissance. The earliest example of Romanesque architecture is **Basilica di Sant'Ambrogio** in Milan (p. 105), notable for its squat nave and groin vaults. Competition among Italian cities (particularly Florence and Siena) to outdo their neighbors resulted in great architectural feats, most notably **San Miniato al Monte** (p. 362) and the **Baptistry** of the duomo in Florence (p. 351).

The Gothic movement filtered into Italy from France, and artists and architects rejoiced at the fantastic spaces and light created by the new vaulted technology and giant multi-colored rose windows. The most impressive Gothic cathedrals include the **Basilica of San Francesco** in Assisi (p. 432), the **Frari** in Venice (p. 238), and the **Santa Maria Novella** in Florence (p. 356). Secular structures like the **Ponte Vecchio** in Florence (p. 355) caught the fever. The **Palazzo Ducale** in Venice (p. 234), spanning several canals with ornate bridges, represents the brilliant marriage of airy, lace-like Islamic stonework and pre-Renaissance Gothic style. In sculpture, **Nicola Pisano** created pulpits at both Pisa and Siena that combined Roman reliefs, Gothic form, and early Byzantine mosaics.

By the end of the 13th century, Italians were bored with emaciated torsos of suffering martyrs. **Cimabue** (c. 1240-1302) and **Duccio** (c. 1255-1318) introduced a second dimension and brighter colors, though bleeding Christians were still the common subjects. Straddling the Late Gothic and Early Renaissance, **Giotto** is often credited with the realization that people look at pictures. He placed his work at eye level, putting the viewer on equal footing with his religious subjects.

BEST OF THE BEST IN ITALIAN ART AND ARCHITECTURE

GREEK

She-Wolf (c. 500 BC). The suckling babies came to represent Romulus and Remus. Museo Capitolino, Rome (p. 511).

Riace Bronzes, Phidias and Polyclitus (460-30 BC). These bronzed athletic beauties were pulled from the sea in 1972. Museo Nazionale, Reggio di Calabria (p. 616).

Tempio della Concordia (430 BC). Its conversion to a Christian church saved this exquisite Greek temple from destruction. Valle dei Tempii, Agrigento (p. 682).

Laocoön (1st century AD). Agony is a snake eating a saint priest and his two sons. Greatly influenced Bernini and Michelangelo. Vatican Museums, Rome (p. 509).

ROMAN

Pompeii (c. 50 BC-AD 79). The world's clearest window to classical times, with magnificent illusionistic painting and gruesomely charred corpses (p. 546).

The Colosseum (AD 72-80). The detailed design and engineering prowess of the Romans still serves as a basis for stadium design worldwide. Rome (p. 498).

Trajan's Column (AD 106-113). Art lovers with binoculars can peer to the top of this most phallic of war monuments. Rome (p. 499).

The Pantheon (AD 119-125). The harmonious design in this perfectly preserved Roman building will move you to worship the seven planetary gods. Rome (p. 500).

EARLY CHRISTIAN & BYZANTINE

Altar Mosaics, San Vitale (c. AD 547). Byzantine Emperor Justinian and attendants reveal the connection between Christianity and the state. Ravenna (p. 322).

St. Mark's Cathedral (1063). Golden mosaics lit by curving domes. The city's uneven sinking has warped the stunning floor. Venice (p. 233).

Monreale Cathedral (1174). Vast devotional barn with comical mosaics of Biblical stories. Arab craftsmanship fused with Norman architecture. Outside Palermo (p. 627).

ROMANESQUE & GOTHIC

Cathedral, Baptistery, and **Campanile** of Pisa (1053-1272). The Leaning Tower's surroundings show delicate artistry in green-and-white marble stonework (p. 406).

Florence's **duomo** and its **Baptistery** (1060-1150). The octagonal duomo is capped with Brunelleschi's burnt-orange dome. Ghiberti dedicated his life to the doors (1401 and 1435), masterpieces of Gothic/Early Renaissance sculpture (p. 351).

Madonna Enthroned, Cimabue (1280-1290). Cimabue paved the way for Renaissance painting with his experiments in perspective. Uffizi Gallery, Florence (p. 354).

The Maestà Altar, Duccio (1308-11; Museo dell'Opera Metropolitano, Siena, p. 380), and the **Arena Chapel** frescos by Giotto (1305-1306; Padua, p. 248).

RENAISSANCE

Where to begin? Descriptions of all of the important Renaissance works in Italy would leave room for nothing else. Here are a few of the most noteworthy:

Bellini, **Madonna and Saints** (p. 236); Botticelli, **The Birth of Venus** (p. 354); Da Vinci, **Last Supper** (p. 105); Michelangelo, **David** (p. 359), **Moses** (p. 506), and the **Sistine Chapel** (p. 509); Raphael, **The School of Athens** (p. 509); Titian, **Pietá** (p. 359); Tintoretto, myriad paintings in **Scuola Grande di San Rocco** (p. 236); Palladio, **Villa Rotunda** (p. 215); Caravaggio, **Crucifixion of St. Peter** (p. 503); Bernini, **Baldacchino** (p. 504).

EARLY RENAISSANCE

The sculpture of **Donatello** (1386-1466) brought new hope to Italian women when *David* hit the artistic scene as the first free-standing nude since antiquity. His wooden *Mary Magdalene* in Florence (p. 352) similarly represents a departure from earlier traditions—his figure of the redeemed woman shows the fallen side, too, her repentance symbolized by her rags and the intensity of her facial expression. **Brunelleschi's** mathematical studies of ancient Roman architecture became the cornerstone of later Renaissance building. His engineering talent allowed him to raise the dome over **Santa Maria del Fiore** (p. 351), while his mastery of proportions was showcased in the **Pazzi Chapel** (p. 359).

Sandro Botticelli (1444-1510) and his *Venus*, floating on her tidal foam (p. 354), epitomizes the Italian Renaissance. **Masaccio** filled chapels with angels and goldleaf and is credited with the first use of the mathematical laws of perspective. Masaccio's figures in the **Brancacci Chapel of Florence** (p. 361) served as models for Michelangelo and Leonardo. **Fra Angelico** (c. 1400-1455) personified the conflicts between medieval and Renaissance Italy. Born Guido di Pietro, he became a member of a militant branch of Dominican friars, but spent most of his time at his monastery in Fiesole. His abbot opposed humanism as a rule, but Fra Angelico's works exhibit the techniques of space and perspective endorsed by humanistic artists. **Paolo Uccello** (1397-1475), who suffered no conflict between his quest for sainthood and creativity, depicted horses rearing into various positions. According to Vasari, Uccello was so preoccupied with perspective that his wife felt threatened by the competition. Venetians **Giovanni Bellini** (c. 1431-1516) and **Andrea Mantegna** (1431-1506) were influenced by the Flemish school's use of color and miniature. They found more secular subjects than their Florentine counterparts, starting a long tradition of Italians looking to Venice as the seat of all heretical debauchery.

Lorenzo Ghiberti (c. 1381-1455) designed two sets of bronze doors for the baptistery in Florence in the first half of the 15th century, which were chosen over Brunelleschi's in a contest. The two original entries now sit side by side in the Bargello of Florence (p. 355). **Leon Battista Alberti** (1404-1472) designed Florence's Santa Maria Novella (p. 356) and Rimini's Tempio Malatestiano (p. 327), both prototypes for later Renaissance *palazzi* and churches.

HIGH RENAISSANCE

From 1450 to 1520, the torch of distinction passed among three of art's greatest figures, **da Vinci, Michelangelo,** and **Raphael. Leonardo da Vinci** (1452-1519) was the first Renaissance man to earn the name. His endeavors were not confined to sculpture or painting, but encompassed geology, engineering, musical composition, human dissection, and armaments design. The *Last Supper* (in Santa Maria delle Grazie in Milan, p. 105) preserves the individuality of its figures, even in a religious context. His experimentation with *chiaroscuro*, in which light and dark create contrast and perspective, secured his place as the great innovator of the century.

Michelangelo Buonarroti (1475-1564) was a jack of all trades in the artistic world, despite what he told Julius II when asked to paint the Sistine Chapel ceiling: "I am not a painter!" Julius was so fond of the work that he paid the temperamental Michelangelo to put his face on one of the saintly figures in *The Last Judgment*, also in the Sistine Chapel. While it is unclear if Michelangelo completed this particular task, it is certain that one of the damned strikingly resembles a papal councillor who advised that Michelangelo's nudes in fresco be repainted with proper attire. His architectural achievements include his designs for the Laurentian Library in Florence (p. 357) and the dome on St. Peter's in Rome (p. 503).

Classic examples of his sculpture are the *Pietà* in St. Peter's (p. 504), *David*, and the unfinished *Slaves* in Florence's Accademia (p. 359).

A proficient draftsman, **Raphael** Santi (1483-1520) created technically perfect figures. His frescoes in the papal apartments of the Vatican, including the clear and balanced composition of the *School of Athens*, show his debt to classical standards (p. 509). The Venetian school produced **Giorgione** (1478-1510) and the prolific **Titian** (1488-1576). Titian's works, including his portrait of Julius II with the repentant Mary Magdalene, are notable for their realistic facial expressions and rich Venetian oil paint colors. In the High Renaissance, the greatest architect after Michelangelo was **Donato Bramante** (1444-1514), famed for his work on the Tempietto and St. Peter's in Rome.

MANNERISM

Creative experimentation led to Mannerism, a reaction against Renaissance classicism. Starting in Rome and Florence, Mannerist artists wielded strange juxtapositions of color and scale, along with technical panache, elegance, and refinement. **Parmigianino** (1503-1540) and his famous *Madonna of the Long Neck* are emblematic of the movement. **Jacopo Tintoretto** (1518-1594), a Venetian Mannerist, was the first to paint multiple light sources within a single composition.

Mannerist architecture, like that of **Giulio Romano** (c. 1499-1546), rejected the Renaissance ideal of harmony. Classical forms were minutely changed to surprise the attentive viewer, as in the case of the asymmetry of the Palazzo Té in Mantua. The villas and churches of architect **Andrea Palladio** (1508-1580) were remarkably innovative, particularly the Villa Rotunda outside Vicenza. His most lasting contribution, the *Four Books of Architecture*, influenced countless architects, especially those of the Baroque movement.

BAROQUE AND ROCOCO

Born of the Counter-Reformation and absolute monarchy, **Baroque** art and architecture were intended to inspire faith in the Catholic Church and respect for temporal power. Painters of this era favored Naturalism—a commitment to portraying nature in the raw, whether ugly or beautiful. Baroque paintings are thus often melodramatic and gruesome. **Caravaggio** (1573-1610) expanded the use of *chiaroscuro*, creating enigmatic works, and often incorporated unsavory characters into religious scenes. **Gianlorenzo Bernini** (1598-1680), a prolific High Baroque sculptor and architect, designed the colonnaded piazza of St. Peter's and the *baldacchino* over its crossing. Drawing inspiration from Hellenistic works like the Laocoön, Bernini's sculptures were orgies of movement. **Francesco Borromini** (1599-1667) was more adept than his rival at shaping the walls of his buildings into serpentine architectural masterpieces. **Rococo**, a more delicate final development of the Baroque, originated in 18th-century France. **Giovanni Battista Tiepolo** (1696-1770), with his brilliant palette and vibrant frescoes, was a prolific Venetian painter of allegories and the premier exemplar of the Rococo style.

19TH-CENTURY ART

After a brief revival of classical art, Italians in the 19th century started to lose their polished dexterity with the paintbrush and their proficiency with the chisel. Still professing to follow the rules of antiquity, the sculptor **Antonio Canova** (1757-1822) explored the formal **Neoclassical** style in his giant statues and bas-reliefs. His most famous work is the statue of *Pauline Borghese* (p. 510), exhibiting Neoclassical grace and purity of contour. Revolting against the strict Neoclassical style, **Giovanni Fattori** (1825-1908) spearheaded the **Macchiaioli** group in Florence (c. 1855-65) to restore lively immediacy and freshness to art. Their landscapes, genre scenes, and portraits are characterized by "blotting" (when a dry paintbrush is used to pick up certain areas of pigment).

20TH-CENTURY ART

The Italian **Futurist** painters, sculptors, and architects of the 1910s brought Italy to the cutting edge of artistry as they sought to transfer the movements of machines into art. Inspired by **Filippo Tommao Marinetti's** Futurist manifesto, their work glorified danger, war, and the 20th-century machine age. In the major Futurist Paris exhibition in 1912, the painters **Giacomo Bala**, **Gino Severini**, and **Carlo Carra** and sculptor **Umberto Boccioni** popularized the **Cubist** technique of simultaneously depicting several aspects of moving forms. **Giorgio de Chirico** (1888-1978), on display at the Collezione Peggy Guggenheim in Venice (p. 237), painted eerie scenes characterized by mannequin figures, empty space, and steep perspective. Although his mysterious and disturbing vision was never successfully imitated, it inspired early surrealist painters. **Amadeo Modigliani** (1884-1920), highly influenced by African art and Cubism, sculpted and later painted figures with long oval faces. **Marcello Piacentini** created Fascist architecture that imposed sterility upon classical motifs. In 1938, he designed the looming **EUR** in Rome (p. 508), as an impressive reminder of the link between Mussolinian Fascism and Roman imperialism.

LITERATURE

OH GODS, YOU DEVILS

Roman mythology, immortalized by **Ovid**, was a soap-opera theology that developed from and added to the Greek family of deities. Usually disguised as animals or humans, these gods and goddesses periodically descended to earth to meddle.

Jupiter, after disguising himself as a rock to escape ingestion by his coup-fearing father, spent the next several centuries visiting women in forms that include peacocks and flaming-red bulls. Somewhere between loves, he established the monarchy of the gods on the heights of Mt. Olympus. The 13 other major Olympian players are Jupiter's wife **Juno,** goddess of child-bearing and marriage; **Neptune,** god of the sea; **Vulcan,** god of smiths; **Venus,** goddess of love and beauty; **Mars,** god of war; **Minerva,** goddess of wisdom; **Apollo,** god of light and arts; **Diana,** goddess of the hunt; **Mercury,** the messenger god; **Pluto,** god of the underworld; **Ceres,** goddess of the harvest; **Bacchus,** god of wine; and **Vesta,** goddess of the hearth.

LATIN LOVERS

As they gained dominance over the Hellenized Mediterranean, the Romans discovered the joys of literature. **Plautus** (c. 259-184 BC) wrote raucous comedies including *Pseudolus.* The lyric poetry of **Catullus** (84-54 BC) set a high standard for passion. **Cicero** (106-43 BC), the greatest speaker of his day, set an all-time standard for political rhetoric. **Julius Caesar** (100-44 BC) gave a first-hand account of the expansion of empire in his *Gallic Wars.*

Despite a government prone to banishing the impolitic, Augustan Rome produced an array of literary talent. **Livy** (c. 59 BC-AD 17) recorded the authorized history of Rome from the city's founding to his own time. **Virgil** (70-19 BC) wrote the *Aeneid* about the origins of Rome and the heroic toils of founding father Aeneas.

Horace's (65-8 BC) verse explores love, wine, service to the state, literature, hostile critics and the happiness that comes from a small farm in the country. **Ovid** (43 BC-AD 17) gave the world the *Amores*, the *Metamorphoses*, and the *Ars Amatoria*.

Petronius's *Satyricon* (first century AD) is a blunt look at the decadent age of Nero. (Fellini's film of the same title presents a modern version.) **Suetonius's** (c. 69-130) *De Vita Caesarum* presents the gossipy version of imperial history. **Tacitus's** (c. 55-116) *Histories* bitingly summarize Roman war, diplomacy, scandal, and rumor in the year of Nero's death (AD 69).

INTO THE LIGHT

The tumult of medieval life discouraged most literary musing, but three Tuscan writers reasserted the art in the late 13th century. Although scholars do not agree on the precise dates of the Renaissance in literature, many argue that the work of **Dante Alighieri** (1265-1321) marked its inception. One of the first Italian poets to write in the *volgare* (common Italian, really Florentine) instead of Latin, Dante is considered the father of modern Italian language and literature. In his epic poem *La Divina Commedia (The Divine Comedy)*, Dante roams the three levels of the afterlife (*Inferno, Purgatorio, Paradiso*) with famous historical figures and his true love Beatrice. Dante offers a call for social reform and a scathing indictment of those contributing to Florentine moral downfall.

Petrarch (1304-74) belongs more clearly to the literary Renaissance. A scholar of classical Latin and a key proponent of humanist thought, he wrote love sonnets to a married woman named Laura, compiled in his *Il Canzoniere*. The 3rd member of the medieval literary triumvirate, **Giovanni Boccaccio**, wrote the *Decameron*, a collection of 100 stories which ranges in tone from suggestive to ribald—in one, a gardener has his way with an entire convent.

LITERARY HIGHLIGHTS

Alighieri, Dante. *Inferno*. Speaking through bloody throats has never been so poetic.

Boccaccio, Giovanni. *Decameron*. Tales of adultery and naughty monks.

Calvino, Italo. *If on a Winter's Night a Traveler...* A self-reflective, playful look at the desire to read.

Catullus. *Poems*. Witty, passionate, insightful verse written before AD 1.

Eco, Umberto. *The Name of the Rose*. Murder, mystery, and manuscripts.

Forster, E.M. *A Room with a View*. Victorian coming-of-age in scenic Florence.

Hemingway, Ernest. *A Farewell to Arms*. An American ambulance driver in WWI Italy.

Highsmith, Patricia. *The Talented Mr. Ripley*. Stolen identities, class envy, and brutal murder show the darker side of the Lost Generation in glamorous Italy.

James, Henry. *The Wings of the Dove*. Unscrupulous seduction in Venice's canals.

Levi, Carlo. *Christ Stopped at Eboli*. An anti-Fascist is banished to rural Basilicata.

Machiavelli, Niccolò. *The Prince*. Cold, ruthless statecraft.

Mann, Thomas. *Death in Venice*. A writer's obsession with a beautiful boy.

Ovid. *Amores, Ars Amatoria*. Sex and lies, live from ancient Rome.

Petrarch. *The Canzoniere*. The father of humanism mixes secular and divine love.

Pirandello, Luigi. *Six Characters in Search of an Author*. A pre-postmodern blend of psychoanalysis, irony, and surreality in a dramatic setting.

Shakespeare, William. *Romeo and Juliet; Othello; Julius Caesar; Merchant of Venice*. Fun and games and death all over.

Virgil. *The Aeneid*. Rome's origins from gods and the Trojan hero Aeneas.

IMPROVE THYSELF

Fifteenth- and 16th-century Italian authors branched out from the genres of their predecessors. **Alberti** and **Palladio** wrote treatises on architecture and art theory. **Baldassare Castiglione's** *The Courtier* instructed the Renaissance man on deportment, etiquette, and other fine points of behavior. **Vasari** took time away from redecorating Florence's churches to produce the ultimate primer on art history and criticism, *The Lives of the Artists*. One of the most lasting works of the Renaissance, **Niccolò Machiavelli's** *Il Principe (The Prince)* is a grim assessment of what it takes to gain political power.

In the spirit of the "Renaissance man," specialists in other fields tried their hand at writing. **Benvenuto Cellini** wrote about his art in *The Autobiography* and **Michelangelo** composed enough sonnets to fuel a fire (literally). The scathing and brilliant **Pietro Aretino** created new possibilities for literature when he began accepting payment from famous people for *not* writing about them. A fervent hater of Michelangelo, Aretino was roasted himself when the great artist painted him into his *Last Judgment*. As Italy's political power waned, literary production also declined, but some stars remained. The prolific 18th-century dramatist **Carlo Goldoni** (1707-1793) replaced the stock characters of the traditional *commedia dell'arte* with unpredictable figures in his *Il Ventaglio*.

WHAT IS TRUTH?

The 19th century brought Italian unification and the need for one language. "Italian" literature, an entirely new concept, grew slowly. The 1800s were an era primarily of *racconti* (short stories) and poetry. The styles of these works ranged from the controversial poetry of **Gabriele D'Annunziod**, whose cavalier heroics earned him as much fame as his eccentric writing, to the *verismo* of **Giovanni Verga**. Verga's brutally honest treatment of his destitute subjects ushered in a new age of portraying the common man in art and literature. **Alessandro Manzoni's** historical novel, *I Promessi Sposi (The Betrothed)*, established the Modernist novel as a major avenue of Italian literary expression.

20th-century writers sought to undermine the conception of objective truth. Nobel Prize winner **Luigi Pirandello** contributed to the postmodernist movement with *Six Characters in Search of an Author* and *So It Is (If You Think It Is So)*. Literary production slowed in the years preceding WWII, but Allied victory spawned an entire generation of writers jumping ship and writing anti-Fascist fiction. The 1930s and 1940s were dominated by a group of young Italian Ernest Hemingway and John Steinbeck followers, including **Cesare Pavese, Vasco Pratolini,** and **Elio Vittorini.** Post-war literature found Italian authors relating their horrific political and personal experiences. **Primo Levi** wrote *Se Questo È Un Uomo (If This is a Man,* 1947) about his experiences in Auschwitz. The most prolific of these writers, **Alberto Moravia,** wrote the ground-breaking *Gli Indifferenti (Time of Indifference,* 1953), which launched an attack on the Fascist regime and was promptly censored. Moravia employed experimental, surreal forms in his later works, using sex to symbolize the violence and spiritual impotence of modern Italy. Several female writers emerged around this time, including **Natalia Ginzburg** with *Lessico Famigliare* (1963), the story of a quirky middle-class Italian family. **Giuseppe di Tomasi di Lampedusa** wrote *Il Gattopardo (The Leopard,* 1957), on the death of Sicily's feudal aristocracy during unification.

The works of **Italo Calvino** are filled with intellectual play and magical realism. His works include the trilogy *Our Ancestors* (1962) and the quintessentially postmodern *If on a Winter's Night a Traveler...* (1979), an interactive novel in which the reader becomes the protagonist. Mid-20th-century poets include

Giuseppe Ungaretti and Nobel Prize winners **Salvatore Quasimodo** and **Eugenio Montale.** Quasimodo and Montale founded the "hermetic movement," characterized by an intimate poetic vision and allusive (and elusive) imagery. **Umberto Eco's** *The Name of the Rose* (1980) is an intricate mystery involving an ancient manuscript and a more than a few fallen monks. In 1997, the popular playwright **Dario Fo**'s dramatic satires brought him a denunciation by the Catholic church and the Nobel Prize for literature.

MUSIC

GREGORY'S FAMOUS CHANTING MONKS

Medieval church music grew out of the Jewish liturgy, something that more than a few Crusaders would be horrified to learn. Women were allowed to sing until AD 578, after which they were replaced by castrated men and soon-to-be castrated boys. Gregory I was the father of liturgical chant, and was responsible for codifying the music he had heard during his days in the monastery. **Plainchant** was synchronized with the church's liturgical calendar. Italian monk **Guido d'Arezzo** (995-1050) is regarded as the originator of musical notation. Italy's many monasteries reveled in church tunes through the Middle Ages and Renaissance. **Francesco Landini** (1325-97) and **Pietro Cascila** (c. 1280) arrived on the scene and started putting popular poems (i.e., secular) to music for multiple voices. **Giovanni Palestrina** (1525-94) attempted to purge the religious madrigal form of this frightening trend towards secularity while retaining the integrity of the music itself, and his work in polyphony is still widely performed in Italy and abroad. The composers of *musica da chiesa* (music for the church) frequently wrote additional pieces for performance in the home or at court, though the songs were often rather crude.

THE FAT LADY SINGS

Opera, Italy's most cherished art form, was born in Florence, nurtured in Venice, and revered in Milan. Conceived by the **Camerata,** a circle of Florentine writers, noblemen, and musicians, opera originated as an attempt to recreate the dramas of ancient Greece by setting lengthy poems to music. **Jacobo Peri** composed *Dafne*, the world's first complete opera, in 1597. The first successful opera composer, **Claudio Monteverdi** (1567-1643) drew freely from history, juxtaposing high drama, love scenes, and uncouth humor. His masterpieces, *L'Orfeo* (1607) and *L'Incoronazione di Poppea* (1642), were the first widespread successes of the genre. **Alessandro Scarlatti** (1660-1725), considered one of the developers of the aria, also founded the Neapolitan opera, thus vaulting Naples to the forefront of Italian music. Schools were quickly set up there under the supervision of famous composers, promoting the beautiful soprano voices of pre-pubescent boys. If the male students dared attempt puberty, their testicles were confiscated. These *castrati*, **Farinelli** being one noted example, became a most celebrated and envied group of singers in Italy and all over Europe.

BAROQUE: THE END OF ALL RESTRAINT

During the **Baroque** period, known for its heavy ornamentation and fugues unto eternity, two main instruments saw their popularity mushroom: the violin, whose shape became perfected by *Cremonese* families, including the **Stradivari** (p. 118); and the piano, created around 1709 by the Florentine **Cristofori** family. *Virtuoso* instrumental music became a legitimate genre in 17th-century Rome. **Antonio**

Vivaldi (1675-1741), composer of over 400 concertos, conquered contemporary audiences with *The Four Seasons* and established the concerto's present form, in which a full orchestra accompanies a soloist. In the mid-18th-century, operatic overtures were performed separately, inventing the **sinfonia**. In opera, Baroque detail yielded to classical standards of moderation and structural balance.

VIVA VERDI!

With convoluted plots and powerful, dramatic music, 19th-century Italian opera continues to dominate modern stages. Late in the 19th century, **Giacomo Puccini** (1858-1924), the master of *verismo* opera (slices of contemporary, all-too-tragic realism), created *Madame Butterfly*, *La Bohème*, and *Tosca*, which feature vulnerable women, usually dead by the last act. **Gioacchino Rossini** (1792-1868) master of the *bel canto* ("beautiful song"), once boasted that he could produce music faster than copyists could reproduce it. In fact, he was such a procrastinator that his agents locked him in a room until he completed his masterpieces.

Giuseppe Verdi (1813-1901) remains the transcendent musical and operatic figure of 19th-century Italy. *Nabucco*, a pointed and powerful *bel canto* work, typifies Verdi's early works. The chorus *"Va pensiero"* from *Nabucco* would later become the hymn of Italian freedom and unity. Verdi produced the touching, personal dramas and memorable melodies of *Rigoletto*, *La Traviata*, and *Il Trovatore* during his middle period. Later work brought the grand and heroic conflicts of *Aida*, the dramatic thrust of *Otello*, and the mercurial comedy of *Falstaff*. Verdi's name served as a convenient acronym for "Vittorio Emanuele, *Re d'Italia*" (King of Italy), so *"Viva Verdi"* became a popular battle cry of the Risorgimento. Much of Verdi's work promoted Italian unity—his operas include political assassinations, exhortations against tyranny, and jibes at French and Austrian monarchs.

In the 20th century, **Ottorino Respighi**, composer of the popular *Pines of Rome* and *Fountains of Rome*, experimented with rapidly shifting orchestral textures. **Giancarlo Menotti** wrote the oft-performed *Amahl and the Night Visitors*. **Luciano Berio** defied traditional instrumentation with his *Sequence V* for solo trombone and mime. **Luigi Dallapiccola** achieved success with choral works including *Songs of Prison* and *Songs of Liberation*, two pieces that protest Fascist rule in Italy. The robust tenor **Luciano Pavarotti** continues to tour with Jose Carreras and Placido Domingo.

ARRIVEDERCI, VERDI

Modern Italian pop stars have been crooning away for decades, although their fame has traditionally been limited to the shores of the Mediterranean. Meet **Lucio Dalla, Francesco de Gregori,** the Sardinian **Fabrizio D'Andrea,** and adamantly Neapolitan **Pino Daniele,** who continue to use pop as a way to protest social conditions, such as the stigma of being Southern. While **Vasco Rossi** started off with protest lyrics, he has since sold his 60s idealism for a sexy Italian mainstream image and the lusts of the flesh.

Recently, Italian musicians have taken to recording with international superstars, increasing their exposure on the world stage. **Eros Ramazzotti** teamed up with Tina Turner on *"Cose della Vita,"* while **Andrea Bocelli** joined Celine Dion in *"The Prayer."* **Laura Pausini,** who records in both Italian and Spanish, has established a following in Latin America, Spain, and Miami. Meanwhile, the technotronic Italian hip-hop scene mixes traditional folk tunes with the latest international groove; rap has emerged with wide-smiling, curly-haired **Jovanotti,** socially conscious **Frankie-Hi-NRG,** subconscious **99 Posse,** and unconscious **Articolo 31** (whose name derives from the Italian law forbidding marijuana). Recent Italian pop hits include Luna Pop's *"Qualcosa di Grande"* (2000) and Eiffel 65's international hit "Blue" (2000).

PRINT

A newspaper in your native language is easy to find at one of the numerous **edicole** (**USA Today** and the **International Herald Tribune** are delivered daily). Newsstands are more interesting, however, if one reads Italian. Newspapers in Italy are anything but impartial, and often lambast everyone from public officials to popular actresses. The most prevalent national daily papers are **Il Corriere della Sera**, a conservative publication from Milan, and **La Repubblica**, a liberal paper from Rome. Other popular papers include **La Stampa** (conservative, published in Torino and owned by Fiat), **Il Messaggero** (liberal, published in Rome), and **Il Giornale** (published in Milan). For weekly entertainment listings, the larger cities have their own area-specific magazines, including **Roma C'è; TrovaRoma; TrovaMilano; Firenze Spettacolo; Milano Where, When, How;** and **Qui Napoli.**

FILM

OLDIES AND GOLDIES

Italy occupies a gilded spot on the cinematic landscape. The country's toe-hold in the industry began with its first feature film in 1905, the historical and somewhat flamboyant *La Presa di Roma*. With the Cines studio in Rome, the Italian "super-spectacle" was born, a form that extravagantly recreated historical events. Throughout the early 20th century, Italy's films were grandiose historical dramas. Before WWI, celebrated *dive* (goddesses) like Lyda Borelli and Francesca Bertini epitomized the Italian *femme fatale*.

SEEING IS BELIEVING

No one ever accused Benito Mussolini of missing an opportunity where he saw one. The dictator was one of the first to see propaganda potential in film, perhaps inspired by **Adolf Hitler**. In the late 1930s, Mussolini gave the world the *Centro Sperimentale della Cinematografia di Nicolo Williams*, a national film school, and the gargantuan **Cinecittà Studios**, Rome's answer to Hollywood. Nationalizing the industry for the good of the state, Mussolini enforced a few "imperial edicts," one of which forbade laughing at the Marx Brothers and another that censored shows overly critical of the government.

REAL SIMPLE

The fall of Fascism brought the explosion of **Neorealist cinema** (1943-50), which rejected contrived sets and professional actors, emphasizing location shooting and "authentic" drama. These low-budget productions created a revolution in film and brought Italian cinema international prestige. Neorealists first gained attention in Italy with **Luchino Visconti's** 1942 French-influenced *Ossessione (Obsession)*. Fascist censors suppressed the so-called "resistance" film, however, so **Roberto Rossellini's** 1945 film *Roma, Città Aperta* (Rome, Open City) was the first Neorealist film to gain international exposure. **Vittorio De Sica's** 1948 *Ladri di Biciclette (Bicycle Thieves)* was perhaps the most successful Neorealist film. Described by De Sica as "dedicated to the suffering of the humble," the work explored the human struggle against fate. In the mid-1950s, the honest ambition of *Neorealismo* gave way to the birth of **La Commedia all'Italiana**. Actor **Totò**, the bastard son of a Neapolitan duke, was Italy's answer to Charlie Chaplin. With his dignified antics and clever language, Totò charmed audiences and provided subtle commentary on Italian society.

THE HIDDEN DEAL

SOUVENIRS FOR THOSE ON A BUDGET...

€10 AND UNDER:

Burnt CDs. Love those Italian hits that play tirelessly on the radio? Bring the latest beats back by purchasing a bootleg CD from street vendors.

Fake Mobile Phones. It's hard to feel truly Italian without wielding a *telefonino,* but if you don't have your own cell, you can easily pass off a decoy.

Cheap Soccer Jerseys. Don a 100% polyester *La Squadra Azzurra, AC Milano,* or *Fiorentina* team shirt in support of Italy's passion for *calcio.*

€25 AND UNDER:

Fake Designer Sunglasses: If real Guccis surpass your budget, knock-off frames in all colors and designs will keep you *in moda* (in style).

Leather-Bound Notebooks: Made with Italian leather and quality paper, these books are ideal for diarists or travel journalists.

Dried Porcini Mushrooms: Cheap, abundant, and delectable *funghi* are a quintessential ingredient in many Northern Italian dishes.

€50 AND UNDER:

Hand-Painted Pottery: Exquisitely hand-painted ceramics with floral and geometric designs can be bought throughout Tuscany and Campania.

Italian Wines: Red or white, still or sparkling, sweet or dry—find the wine that suits your taste, and bring it home (see Regional Wines, p. 31). Of course, prices vary greatly according to the wine's age, region, and taste.

Balsamic Vinegar: Modena is internationally renowned for its aged Trebbiano grape vinegar (€5-100).

THOSE GO-GO SIXTIES

By the 1960s, post-Neorealist directors like **Federico Fellini** and **Michelangelo Antonioni** were rejecting plots and characters in favor of a space that derived its worth from witnessed moments. Luscious, self-indulgent, and largely autobiographical, Fellini's *8½* interwove dreams with reality, earning a place in the cinematic canon. *La Dolce Vita* (1960), also by Fellini, was banned by the pope for its portrayal of 1950s Rome's decadently stylish celebrities and the *paparazzi* (a term first coined in this movie) who pursued them. Antonioni's haunting trilogy, *L'Avventura* (1959), *La Notte* (1960), and *L'Eclisse* (1962), presents a stark world of estranged couples and young, hopelessly isolated aristocrats. Antonioni's *Blow-Up* was a 1966 English-language hit about mime, murder, and mod London.

Pier Paolo Pasolini may have spent as much time on trial for his politics as he did making films. An ardent Marxist, he set his films in shanty neighborhoods and the Roman underworld of poverty and prostitution. In his films, sexual deviance and political power are synonymous. His masterpiece, *Hawks and Sparrows,* ponders the philosophical poetic possibilities of film.

INTROSPECTION

Aging old-school directors and a lack of funds led Italian film into another era in directing, characterized by nostalgia and self-examination. **Bernardo Bertolucci's** 1970 *Il Conformista* investigates Fascist Italy by focusing on one "comrade" desperately struggling to be normal. Other major Italian films of this era include the ubiquitous **Vittorio de Sica's** *Il Giardino dei Finzi-Contini* and **Francesco Rosi's** *Cristo Si È Fermato a Eboli,* both films based on prestigious post-war, anti-Fascist novels. In the 1980s, the **Taviani** brothers catapulted to fame with *Kaos,* a film based on stories by Pirandello, and *La Notte di San Lorenzo,* which depicts an Italian village during the final days of WWII. Actor-directors like **Nanni Moretti** and **Maurizio Nichetti** also rose to fame in the 1980s and early 1990s with a more macabre humor. Nichetti's *Bianca* (1983) is a psychological comedy-thriller featuring himself as the somewhat deranged central character. His *Ladri di Saponette,* a modern spoof on the Neorealist *Ladri di Biciclette,* features Nichetti as himself, while in his 1991 *Volere Volare,* Nichetti plays a confused cartoon sound designer who morphs entirely into a cartoon by the end of the movie. **Lina**

Wertmuller's brilliant *Ciao, Professore!* (1994) tells the story of a schoolteacher from the north who gets assigned to teach third grade in Corzano, a poor town near Naples.

BUONGIORNO, PRINCIPESSA!

Oscar-winners **Gabriele Salvatore** (for *Mediterraneo*) and **Giuseppe Tornatore** (for the nostalgic *Cinema Paradiso)* have earned the attention and affection of US audiences. In 1995, Massimo Troisi's *Il Postino* was nominated for a Best Picture Academy Award. **Roberto Benigni** drew international acclaim for *La Vita e Bella* (Life is Beautiful) in 1998. Juxtaposing the tragedy of the Holocaust with a father's love of his son, the film won Best Actor and Best Foreign Film Oscars, as well as a Best Picture nomination, at the 1999 Academy Awards. Benigni promptly jumped on the top of his seat and announced that he wanted to make love to everyone present. More recently, Nanni Morretti snagged the Palm D'Or at Cannes in 2001 for his portrayal of familial loss in *La Stanza del Figlio* (The Son's Room).

TUTTI IN GUCCI

Fashion is an integral part of Italian life. In a country renowned for its couture, leather shoes and handbags, and tailored suits, it's no wonder Italians care about what they wear. Not only does quality supersede quantity, but appearance is so important that women typically wear Prada pumps to market.

As much as Parisians, New Yorkers, and Londoners might protest, the fashion world begins and ends in Milan with the powerhouses **Gucci, Versace, Gianfranco Ferre, MaxMara,** and **Prada.** The primacy of the Italian fashion industry dates to the late 19th century with the Cerruti Company's production of fabrics. The international legacy of **Salvatore Ferragamo** began in 1914, when he brought his dazzling shoe-making skills to stars of Hollywood. After WWII, sisters Paola, Anna, Franca, Carla and Adla **Fendi** took over their family leather and fur enterprise. By 1965, Fendi's innovation initiated the renaissance of the "Made in Italy" products. The late 1950s saw the rise of the fashion giants **Valentino** and **Armani,** whose work celebrated elegance and tradition. In 1978, **Gianni Versace** opened his first store in Milan with an unconventional and vibrant ready-to-wear collection.

THE BIG SPLURGE

...AND THOSE LOOKING TO DROP SOME DOUGH.

€100 AND UNDER:

Limoncello: Find a bottle on the Amalfi Coast, where they soak fresh Sorrento lemons in 190-proof alcohol saturated with sugar. For other Italian libations, see **Regional Liqueurs,** p. 31.

Truffles: Typically from Piedmont, earthy and pungent black and white truffles are the fungi of luxury, costing from €20 per cap to €3000 per kg.

Diesels: Denim's hot in a big way. Tankers and Dazes (and bizarre ad campaigns) originate in Italy. Buy a pair in any major Italian city for 50% lower than usual. Jeans €75.

Olive Oil: The best are cold-pressed—a process that yields prized extra virgin oil. Popular brands include Fratelli Carli and Colavita.

Miss Sixty: Another Italian clothing brand that's popular worldwide among young, trendy ladies, but cheaper in Italy. Sexy kick-flare jeans and asymmetrical tanks are €45-100.

OVER €100:

Real Designer Sunglasses: Fabulous frames await the no-knock-offs buyer in fashionable optometry shops and designer boutiques. Expect to save 25-35%. €100-300.

Cameos: Watch master carvers on the coast of Campania as they whittle shells into delicate jewelry using ancient Roman techniques. €75-300.

WAY, WAY OVER €100:

Who wouldn't want their very own **Vespa?** Old-school scooters haven't yet caught on away from the Mediterranean. Be the first kid on your block. €2000-3000.

This inventive trend continued through the 1980s with the sexy, modern collections of **Dolce e Gabbana**. Recent high-end newcomers like **Romeo Gigli** and **Moschino** ensure the invicibility of *la moda italiana*.

> ■ Winter sales in Milan begin mid-January. Shop at the end of July for end-of-summer sales that bring 25-50% discounts and a glimpse of upcoming fall lines.

FOOD AND WINE: LA DOLCE VITA

In Italy, food preparation is an art form, and its consumption a crucial part of culture. *La bella figura* (a nice figure) is another social imperative, and the after-dinner *passeggiata* (promenade) is as much an institution as the meal itself. Small portions and the leisurely pace of a meal help to keep Italians healthy, despite the enticing and often fattening foods that comprise their cuisine.

MANGIAMO!

Breakfast in Italy often goes unnoticed; at most, a morning meal consists of coffee and a *cornetto* (croissant). **Lunch** is the main feast of the day. If you don't have a big appetite, grab lunch at an inexpensive *tavola calda* ("hot table," or cafeteria-style), *rosticceria* (grill), or *gastronomia* (hot prepared dishes for takeout). But if you decide to partake in the traditional Italian **pranzo**, be warned that it is an event that lasts much of the afternoon. A typical *pranzo* consists of an *antipasto* (appetizer), a *primo piatto* (the first course—a heaping portion of pasta, risotto, or soup), a *secondo piatto* (usually meat or fish), and a *contorno* (vegetable side dish). Finally comes the *dolce* (dessert or fruit), then *caffè*, and often an after-dinner liqueur. Many restaurants offer a fixed-price tourist **menù** including *primo*, *secondo*, bread, water, and wine. Italian **dinners** begin around 8pm in most of the country, although farther south, they're served later; in Naples, it's not unusual to go for a midnight pizza. Dinner is a lighter meal, often a mere *panino* (sandwich).

Billing at Italian restaurants can be confusing. Many restaurants add a *coperto* (cover charge) of €1-3 to the price of your meal (for bread or some other fabricated courtesy) as well as a *servizio* (service charge) of 10-15%. While you will almost never offend someone by leaving a few euros, **tipping** is not expected unless it says so explicitly on the menu—even if the waiter hints strongly.

FOOD ON THE GO

A **bar** is an excellent place to grab a drink (with or without alcohol) and a quick, inexpensive meal. While fast food chains have permeated Italy, the ample salad bar and beer at most **McDonald's** demonstrates that Italians do fast food their own way (though don't expect any McGnocchi). The typical bar menu includes hot and cold *panini*, *gelato*, and coffee. Indulge in focaccia and sandwiches stuffed with *prosciutto crudo* or *cotto* (cured or cooked ham), *pomodori* (tomatoes), and *formaggio* (cheese). Avoid bars on major tourist thoroughfares, where prices reflect location and not necessarily service or quality. In small towns, bars are the social centers. Children come for *gelato*, old men for wine and conversation, and young adults for beer and flirtation. In crowded bars, pay for your food at the cashier's desk and then take the receipt to a bartender, who will serve you. In less-touristed areas, pay after you drink. No matter where you are, sitting down at a bar that offers table service will cost more than standing at the counter. Proprietors at all bars and shops will (or should) force you to take a *scontrino* (receipt) when you leave. It's required by law, and you could theoretically be asked by a customs officer to present it with your purchases upon leaving an establishment. Without a receipt, you may pay a stiff fine. Buy picnic materials at *salumeria* or *alimentari* (meat and grocery shops) or at one of the popular **STANDA** or **COOP** supermarkets, but explore the open-air markets for cheap fresh produce.

REGIONAL SPECIALTIES

Italian cuisine is much more than the three P's (pasta, pizza, and *pomodori* [tomatoes]). Italian food has all the nuances and delicacies of neighboring France, without a garnish of pretension. Coastal areas offer a wide variety of seafood dishes, while inland areas provide meatier, heartier fare. Dishes in the north are often rich with creamy and meaty sauces, and *risotto* and polenta are often eaten instead of pasta. In **Piemonte**, try the famed (but pricey) truffles (they're supposedly an aphrodisiac). **Lombardia** offers the delights of gorgonzola and mascarpone cheeses. Mascarpone is a main ingredient in *tiramisù* (Italian for "pick me up"). *Risotto*, *ossobuco* (a braised veal stew) and *panettone* (a dessert bread) are also specialties of the region. **Coastal Liguria** is noted for its seafood, profusion of herbs, and olive oil, while the Germanic influences in Tentino-Alto Adige have popularized *gnocchi* (potato and flour dumplings). **Friuli-Venezia Giulia** has a Middle Eastern flair, using spices such as cumin and paprika to flavor meat and dairy dishes. **The Veneto** is sustained by *pasta e fagioli* (pasta and beans) and artichoke and game feasts.

Moving south into the gastronomic heart of Italy, **Emilia-Romagna** is the birthplace of parmesan cheese, balsamic vinegar, and *prosciutto di Parma* (Parma ham). **Tuscany** offers more rustic fare, with stews and pot roasts, bean and veggie dishes, and minestrone. **Umbria** has black truffles and is also known for the tasty delights of chocolates and other sweets. **Abruzzo** and **Molise** are known for their cured peppery meats, lamb, mutton, and pasta. **Sardinia** has more sheep than people, and their odiferous cheese is made into pies and topped with honey.

WAKE UP AND SMELL THE CAFFÈ!

Italian *espresso* isn't a beverage; it's an entire production experience, from the harvesting of the beans to the consumption of the liquid. High altitude *Arabica* beans compose 60-90% of most Italian blends, while the remaining 10-40% is made of woody-flavored *robusta* beans. Italians prefer a higher concentration of *robusta* beans, because they emit oils that produce a thick, foamy *crema* under the heat and pressure of the *espresso* machine. *Espresso* beans are roasted longer than other coffee beans, giving the drink its bitterness and full body. The beans are then ground, tapped into a basket, and barraged with hot, pressurized water. In a good cup of *espresso*, the foamy *crema* should be caramel-colored and thick enough to support a spoonful of sugar for a few moments. The thick *crema* prevents the drink's rich aroma from dispersing into the air and is indicative of a full-bodied, well-brewed beverage. Stir in sugar and down it in one gulp like the locals.

For a standard cup of *espresso*, request a *caffè*. If you'd like a drop of milk in it, ask for *caffè macchiato* (spotted coffee). *Cappuccino*, which Italians drink only before lunch and never after a meal, has frothy scalded milk; *caffè latte* is heavier on the milk, lighter on the coffee. For coffee and joy, try *caffè corretto* (corrected) *espresso* with a drop of strong liqueur (usually *grappa* or brandy). *Caffè Americano*, scorned by Italian coffee drinkers, is watery *espresso* served in a large cup.

WINE AND REASON

Italy's rocky soil, warm climate, and hilly landscape provide ideal conditions for growing grapes; Italy produces more **wine** than any other country. Sicily alone ferments 200 million gallons annually. Grapes are separated from stems and then crushed by a press that extracts the juice. For red wines, the juice and skins are pumped into stainless steel fermentation vats, while white wines are produced from skin-less grapes. The sweetness or dryness of the wine is largely determined by ripeness and sugar content of the selected grape. After fermentation, the wine is racked and clarified, a procedure which removes any lees (sediment). The wine is then stored in glass-lined concrete vats until bottling.

CORK YOUR WALLET! Wine snobs may spend upward of €50 on a bottle of aged *riserva*, but wines in the €6-12 range represent every level of quality, from barely drinkable to sublime. The most respected wine stewards in the nation regularly rank inexpensive wines above their costly cousins. Expense can equal quality, but a little shopping around can bring a cheaper, better wine.

CLASSIFICATION

Once the wine is ready to hit the shelves, the government subjects it to a three-tier classification system. *Denominazione di Origine Controllata e Garantita* (DOCG) wines grace the apex and are evaluated by several independent tasting commissions. Only 14 varieties of wine carry the DOCG designation. Minus the G, DOC wines comply with stiff regulations, from minimum alcohol contents and maximum vineyard yields to specific geographic origins. DOC wines comprise the majority of Italy's most tasty yet affordable options. In general, DOCG implies higher quality than DOC, but due to the large number of vineyards that produce each variety of wine, many individual DOC brands are superb, while some DOCG brands are good, but not excellent. The lowest category is *Indicazione Geographica Tipica* (IGT), indicating merely the wine's origin. Any wine outside these categories falls into Italy's catch-all category, *Vino di Tavola* (table wine). Ironically, the country's best and worst wines coexist under this nebulous designation. The better wines are excluded because they don't use prescribed grapes or production methods, while the lower-end wines are simply too shameful to classify. If you're confused, remember that generic table wine is sold by the liter, not by the bottle, and can be purchased for next to nothing at *Vino Sfusso* (loose wine) shops (as low as €1 per liter), as long as you bring your own receptacle.

WINE TASTING

Tasting wine in Italy is easy for travelers. The countryside is sprinkled with government-run *Enoteche Regionale* and *Enoteche Pubbliche*, regional exhibition and tasting centers. These *enoteche* promote local vineyards and often sponsor special 'educational' events. Spontaneous tasting is generally available, but booking may be necessary. Private wine shops are also called *enoteche*, though without the *regionale* or *pubblica* designation. *Cantine* do not typically offer tastings, unless accompanied by a wine bar. If touring by car, ask the tourist office about local *Strade del Vino* (wine roads), or contact the national Movement for Wine Tourism in Italy (☎ (39321) 46 62 14; fax 46 62 33; www.wine.it).

At restaurants, you can usually order wine by the liter or half-liter and occasionally by the glass. Drinking too much? Dry out with some *secco*. Sour after a long day of traveling? Sweeten up with *abboccato* or *amabile*. Feeling spunky? Down a little *vino novello*, meant to be drunk young. Feeling green? *Vino biologico* is the organic lovers' fix. Feeling traditional? Sip some *classico*, wine from the heartland. Kickstart your evening with *superiore*, which implies a higher alcohol content, or *riserva*, which has a longer aging period. For a bubbly buzz, try sparkling *spumante*, the usually cheaper, tank-fermented twin of the bottle-fermented *talento*. When in doubt, request the local wine—it will be cheaper (typically around €3 per liter in local *trattorie*) and suited to the regional cuisine.

REGIONAL WINES

Piedmont is Italy's number one wine region, producing the most touted (and expensive) *Barolo*, a full-bodied red, velvety on the palate. *Barolo* is aged for two years, one year longer than its lighter cousin, *Barberesca*. While in Turin, visit the *Enoteche Regionale* at *Grinzane Cavour*, the 13th-century castle of the former *Risorgimento* hero Camillo Cavour. The wines here are monitored by the "Master Tasters of the Order of the Knights of the Truffle and the Wines of Alba." They suffer for our sake. Taste Piedmont's lighter side in the more affordable sparkling, sweet *Asti Spumante* at *Cantina di Vini di Costigliole d'Asti*, a castle formerly owned by Contessa di Castigliole, mistress to Napoleon III.

Tuscany is famed for its tannic *chianti* and similar reds, such as the most renowned wine in the country, *Brunello de Montalcino*. Originally, many *chianti* wines were excluded from classification. Regulations required that the *classico* wine include white grapes, making it an easy-drinking daily wine, but producers were using 100% *sangiovese* grapes to produce the popular Super Tuscan wines. Recently, regulations have been revamped, encompassing most Super Tuscan *chianti classici*. When shopping for white wines, be on the lookout for *Vernaccia di San Gimignano* from the town of the same name, which has recently received DOCG status (p. 391).

The Veneto, from Verona west to Lake Garda, yields *Valpolicella*, a bright, medium-weight red with a dry finish and cherry-stone aftertaste. Verona produces the fizzy *Prosecco* and bland *Soave*. Indecisive? Try white or red *Tocai* from **Friuli,** light and fluffy enough for seafood, but spicy enough to handle an unimposing appetizer. Keep an eye out for the *Colli Berici Tocai Rosso*, among the more respected *Tocai* from the region.

Wash down the culinary delights of **Emiglia-Romagna** with Frizzantino Malvasia or Sauvignon, the typical aperitif in local bars. Sparkling Lambrusco is a widely drunk red, traditionally dry or amible (medium-dry), but these bottle-fermented versions are expensive.

When in **Rome**, drink *Frascati*, a clean white wine served cold, such as the *Colli di Tuscolo*. In Umbria, where production dates back to the Etruscans, try the world-famous *Orvieto*. This crisp, light white has recently been combined with chardonnay grapes to produce the world-class *Cervaro della Sala*. Naples boasts *Lacryma Cristi* (Christ's Tear), an overrated tourist favorite. The hotter climate and longer growing season of **southern Italy** and the islands produces stronger, fruitier wines than the North. Try the versatile **Sicilian** *Marsala*.

REGIONAL LIQUEURS

Traditionally, Italian liqueurs are savored at the end of a decadent meal, as a palate-cleansing *digestivo*. Fancier occasions call for an *aperitivo* to prime the appetite. Typical liqueurs are often infused with wild fruit or nut essences and are cloyingly sweet. Dazzle your senses with *Mirto*, a blueberry *digestivo*, or the ubiquitous *limoncello*, a heavy, lemon liqueur. The sugary *amari* (bitter) cordials,

ON THE BALL

The faithful gather in the piazza, hundreds of them shoulder to shoulder, reverently beholding the images before them in silence. At intervals, they shout in unison, then quickly return to their silence. Smaller shrines are set up around them, each with a crowd that observes the same captivated protocol. Radical religious cult? Neo-Fascist exercises?

No, the reason for such devotion is Italian *calcio:* soccer to Americans and football to the rest of the English-speaking world. Italians take the sport seriously, both in the World Cup and in the national Serie A and B leagues. Cities often set up huge monitors in piazzas to broadcast the games, where the atmosphere can erupt like Vesuvius in a matter of seconds.

When Italy lost to Korea in overtime in the 2002 World Cup, angry fans rumbled in major cities throughout the country, levying death threats against FIFA officials. If you're fortunate enough to be in Italy during the World Cup, be sure to take in a game—unless you're a countryman of Italy's opponents.

served after festival meals, truly belie their Italian name. Almond flavors a glass of Sardinian *Vernaccia di Oristano* sherry, while Sorrento's dark *nocillo* tastes of walnut. Other Italian specialties include almond-flavored *amaretto di Saronno* (actually made from apricot pits), toasted hazelnut and cacao-infused *frangelico*, and licorice *sambuca.*

Maligned as firewater, *grappa* is unfettered by sugars and leaves the palate crisp, if not shocked. After grapes are pressed for wine, the remaining *pomace* is used for this national blue-collar favorite. Originally mobile *grappa* stills traveled from vineyard to vineyard to collect fermentation leftovers. There are four types of *grappa:* the clear *giovane*, distilled for six months in a stainless steel vat; the milder, amber-colored *invecchiata*, aged for years in wooden barrels; the flavorful *monovitigno* (one grape), made from a single grapevine; and the fruit-infused *aromatizzata.*

SPORTS AND RECREATION

In Italy, **calcio** (soccer to Americans, football to Europeans) surpasses all other sports. *La Squadra Azzurra* (the blue team) is a major source of national pride and sometimes agony. Some claim that Italy's victory in the 1982 World Cup did more for national unity than any political movement. Italy's success in 1994 sparked excitement that crested with every victory and ultimately crashed with their defeat by Brazil. In the 1998 World Cup quarterfinals, France knocked out Italy after an intense 4-3 penalty shoot-out.

Italian fans cheer on their local teams, especially those promoted to Serie A, the Italian major league. Inter-urban rivalries, including those among Naples, Milan, and Rome, are intense. Italian sports fans, called *tifosi* (fever boys) are raucous and energetic.

Bicycling is popular in Italy. Besides manufacturing some of the best bikes in the world and hosting bike tours, Italians host the **Giro d'Italia,** a 25-day cross-country race in May. With parts of the Italian Alps (including the Dolomites) and the Apennines within its borders, Italy attracts **skiers** from December to April. **Hiking** and **mountain climbing** are popular throughout the North and in Calabria's Sila Massif. For **swimming, windsurfing,** or **sailing,** you may want to try the Southern beaches or those on Italy's islands. Breathtaking Sardinia offers crystal-blue waters with up to 30 meters of visibility.

THE ITALIAN LANGUAGE

Ah, Italian. Language of lovers, of *mafiosi*, and of Dante's eternal damnation. One of the six surviving romance languages, it has long inspired everything from Petrarch's passionate ramblings to Calvino's insane ramblings. As a result of the country's fragmented history, variations in **dialect** are strong. The throaty **Neapolitan** can be difficult for a northerner to understand; **Ligurians** use a mix of Italian, Catalán, and French; **Sardo,** spoken in Sardinia, bears little resemblance to standard Italian; and many **Tuscan** dialects differ from Italian in pronunciation. Some inhabitants of the northern border regions don't speak Italian at all: the population of Val d'Aosta speaks mainly French, and Trentino-Alto Adige harbors a German-speaking minority. In the southern regions of Apulia, Calabria, and Sicily, entire villages speak Albanian and Greek. In order to facilitate conversation, all natives do their best to employ standard Italian when speaking with a foreigner.

FESTIVALS AND HOLIDAYS

From the number of festivals commemorating an appearance of the Virgin Mary in Italy, it's easy to reach the conclusion that she has found *bella Italia* so appealing that she has decided never to leave. **Carnevale** energizes Italian towns in February during the 10 days before Lent. During **Scoppio del Carro,** held in Florence's Piazza del Duomo on Easter Sunday, Florentines set off a cart of explosives in keeping with medieval tradition. The fantastic Sienese **Palio** on July 2 and August 16 transforms the Piazza del Duomo into a horse racing track and divides the city in support of the twelve *contrade* (teams). Festivals in smaller towns are less touristed, quirkier, and allow visitors in the know to come home with unique stories about mouth-watering victuals in Cortona (p. 366) and drunken revelry in Gubbio (p. 435). For a complete list of festivals, write to the **Italian Government Travel Office** (see p. 35) or visit www.italiantourism.com/tradition.html.

DATE	FESTIVAL	LOCATION
Jan. 1	Il Capodanno (New Year's Day)	All over Italy
Jan. 6	Epifania (Epiphany)	All over Italy
1st half of Feb.	Festa del Fiore di Mandorlo (Almond Blossom)	Agrigento (p. 679)
Feb. 8	Festa della Matricola (Graduation Feast)	Padua (p. 245)
late Feb.-early Mar.	Carnevale	Venice (p. 215)
Feb. 24-26	Sartiglia (Race & Joust)	Oristano (p. 708)
Apr. 17-23	Settimana Santa (Holy Week)	All over Italy
Apr. 21	Venerdì Santo (Good Friday)	All over Italy
Apr. 23	Pasqua (Easter)	All over Italy
Apr. 25	Giorno della Liberazione (Liberation Day)	All over Italy
May 1	Labor Day	All over Italy
May 1-4	Sagra di Sant'Efisio (Festival of St. Efisio)	Cagliari (p. 703)
early May	Festa di Calendimaggio	Assisi (p. 428)
May 6-7	Festa di S. Nicola	Bari (p. 580)
May 7	Festa di S. Gennaro	Naples (p. 525)
May 14	Sagra del Pesce (Festival of Fish)	Camogli (p. 162)
May 15	Corsa dei Ceri (Candle Race)	Gubbio (p. 435)
May 25	Pallio della Balestra (Crossbow Contest)	Gubbio (p. 435)
June 1	Ascenzione (Feast of the Ascension)	All over Italy
June 1	Gioco del Ponte (Battle of the Bridge)	Pisa (p. 398)
June 18	Giostra del Saraceno (Joust of the Saracen)	Arezzo (p. 370)

DATE	FESTIVAL	LOCATION
June 22	Corpus Christi	All over Italy
June 24	Festa di S. Giovanni (Feast of St. John)	Florence (p. 332)
June 24-28	Calcio Fiorentino (Soccer Games)	Florence (p. 332)
late June	Mostra Internazionale del Nuovo Cinema (International New Cinema)	Pesaro (p. 448)
late June-early July	S. Maria della Bruna (Feast of the Dark Madonna)	Matera (p. 602)
late June-mid-July	Spoleto Festival	Spoleto (p. 438)
July and Aug.	Ravenna Festival	Ravenna (p. 319)
July	Umbria Jazz Festival	Perugia (p. 419)
July 2	Festa della Madonna (Feast of the Virgin Mary)	Enna (p. 666)
July 12	Palio della Balestra (Crossbow Contest)	Lucca (p. 398)
mid-July	Palio Marinaro (Boat Race)	Livorno (p. 409)
July 20	Festa del Redentore (Feast of the Redeemer)	Venice (p. 215)
July 25	Giostro del Orso (Joust of the Bear)	Pistoia (p. 395)
late July-early Aug.	Settimana Musicale (Music Week)	Siena (p. 373)
late July-mid-Sept.	Taormina Arte	Taormina (p. 655)
Aug.	Festa dei Porcini (Mushroom Picking)	Cortona (p. 366)
Aug. 6	Torneo della Quintana (Joust of the Quintana)	Ascoli-Piceno (p. 457)
Aug. 14-15	Sagra della Bistecca (Steak Feast)	Cortona (p. 366)
Aug. 15	Assunzione (Feast of the Assumption)	All over Italy
Aug. 16	Palio	Siena (p. 373)
Aug. 27-30	Festa del Redentore (Feast of the Redeemer)	Nuoro (p. 712)
late Aug.-early Sept.	Venice International Film Festival	Venice (p. 215)
Sept. 7	Regata Storica (Historic Regatta)	Venice (p. 215)
Sept. 7	Giostra del Saraceno (Joust of the Saracen)	Arezzo (p. 370)
Sept. 10	Festivale della Sagra	Asti (p. 200)
Sept. 14	Palio della Balestra (Crossbow Contest)	Lucca (p. 398)
Sept. 17	Palio di Asti	Asti (p. 200)
Sept. 19	Festa di S. Gennaro	Naples (p. 525)
Nov. 1	Ogni Santi (All Saints Day)	All over Italy
Nov. 2	Giorno dei Morti (All Souls Day)	All over Italy
Nov. 21	Festa della Madonna della Salute (Festival of the Virgin, Patron of Good Health)	Venice (p. 215)
Dec. 6	Festa di S. Nicola (Feast of St. Nicholas)	Bari (p. 580)
Dec. 16	Festa di S. Gennaro	Naples (p. 525)
Dec. 24	Vigilia di Natale (Christmas Eve)	All over Italy
Dec. 25	Natale (Christmas Day)	All over Italy
Dec. 26	Festa di S. Stefano	All over Italy

LIFE AND TIMES

ESSENTIALS

FACTS FOR THE TRAVELER

USEFUL ORGANIZATIONS

Italian Government Tourist Board (ENIT), 630 5th Ave., #1565, **New York,** NY 10111, USA (☎212-245-5618; fax 586-9249; www.italiantourism.com). Write or call ☎212-245-4822 for a free copy of *Italia: General Information for Travelers to Italy,* containing train and ferry schedules. Branch offices: 12400 Wilshire Blvd., #550, **Los Angeles,** CA 90025, USA (☎310-820-1898; fax 820-6357; enitla@earthlink.net); 175 E. Bloor St., #907 South Tower, **Toronto,** ON M4W 3R8, Canada (☎416-925-4882; fax 925-4799; enit.canada@on.aibn.com); 1 Princess St., **London** W1R 2AY UK (☎020 7355 1557 or 7355 1439; fax 7493 6695; www.italiantouristboard.co.uk). Italian Chamber of Commerce and Industry in Australia, Level 26, 44 Market St., **Sydney** NSW 2000 Australia (☎(02) 9262 1666; fax 9262 1667; enitour@ihug.com.au).

Italian Cultural Institute, 686 Park Ave., **New York,** NY 10021, USA (☎212-879-4242; fax 861-4018; www.italcultny.org). Often more prompt than ENIT. Provides many useful links to Italian culture and sites.

DOCUMENTS AND FORMALITIES

> **ENTRANCE REQUIREMENTS.**
> **Passport** (p. 37). Required for citizens of Australia, Canada, Ireland, New Zealand, South Africa, the UK, and the US.
> **Visa** (p. 37). Required for citizens of South Africa. Required for citizens of Australia, Canada, Ireland, New Zealand, the UK, and the US only for stays longer than 3 months.
> **Work Permit** (p. 86). Required for foreigners planning to work in Italy.
> **Study Permit** (p. 82). Required for foreigners planning to study in Italy.
> **Driving Permit** (p. 72). Required for those planning to drive.

ITALIAN EMBASSIES AND CONSULATES

Australia: Embassy: 12 Grey St., Deakin, **Canberra** ACT 2600 (☎02 6273 3333; fax 6273 4223; www.ambitalia.org.au). Open M-F 9am-12:30pm and 2-4pm. **Consulates:** Level 14 AMP Place, 10 Eagle St., **Brisbane** QLD 4000 (☎(617) 3229 8944; fax 3229 8643; italcons.brisbane@bigpond.com. Open M-W, F 9am-1pm, Th 9am-3pm); 509 St. Kilda Rd., **Melbourne** VIC 3004 (☎(613) 867 5744; fax 866 3932; itconmel@netlink.com.au); Level 45 The Gateway, 1 Macquarie Pl., **Sydney** NSW 2000 (☎(612) 9392 7939; fax 9392 7935; office@iisyd.org).

Canada: Embassy: 275 Slater St., 21st fl., **Ottawa,** ON K1P 5H9 (☎613-232-2401; fax 233-1484; www.italyincanada.com). **Consulate:** 3489 Drummond St., **Montréal,** QC H3G 1X6 (☎514-849-8351; fax 499-9471; www.italconsul.montreal.qc.ca).

Ireland: Embassy: 63 Northumberland Rd., **Dublin** (☎01 660 1744; fax 668 2759; http://homepage.eircom.net/~italianembassy). Consulate open M-F 10am-12:30pm.

New Zealand: Embassy: 34 Grant Rd., **Wellington** (☎006 4473 5339; fax 472 9302; www.italy-embassy.org.nz).

South Africa: Embassy: 796 George Ave., Arcadia 0083, **Pretoria** (☎012 43 55 41; fax 43 55 47; www.ambital.org.za). **Consulates:** 2 Grey's Pass, Gardens 8001, **Cape Town** (☎021 424 1256; fax 424 0146; italcons@mweb.co.za); Corner 2nd Ave., Houghton 2198, **Johannesburg** (☎011 728 1392; fax 728 3834).

UK: Embassy: 14 Three Kings Yard, **London** W1Y 2EH (☎020 7312 2200; fax 7499 2283; www.embitaly.org.uk). **Consulates:** 38 Eaton Pl., **London** SW1X 8AN (☎ 20 7235 9371; fax 7823 1609); Rodwell Tower, 111 Piccadilly, **Manchester** M1 2HY (☎161 236 9024; fax 236 5574; passaporti@italconsulman.demon.co.uk); 32 Melville St., **Edinburgh** EH3 7HA (☎ 131 226 3631; fax 226 6260; consedimb@consedimb.demon.co.uk).

US: Embassy: 1601 Fuller St. NW, **Washington, D.C.** 20009 (☎202-328-5500; fax 462-3605; www.italyemb.org). **Consulates:** 100 Boylston St., #900, **Boston,** MA 02116 (☎617-542-0483; fax 542-3998; www.reference.it/cgboston); 500 N. Michigan Ave., #1850, **Chicago,** IL 60611 (☎312-467-1550; fax 467-1335; www.italconschicago.org); 12400 Wilshire Blvd., #300, **Los Angeles,** CA 90025 (☎310-820-0622; fax 820-0727; www.conlang.com); 690 Park Ave. (visa office 54 E. 69th St.), **New York,** NY 10021 (☎212-737-9100; fax 249-4945; www.italconsulnyc.org).

IMPORTANT PHONE NUMBERS.
Emergency Aid Services: ☎113.
Carabinieri: ☎112.
Fire Brigade: ☎115.
ACI (Automobile Club of Italy) for emergency breakdowns: ☎116.
Sailing Conditions: ☎144 66 19 06.
Weather Reports: ☎144 66 19 11.
Snow Conditions: ☎144 66 19 02.
News Reports: ☎144 22 19 00.

EMBASSIES AND CONSULATES IN ROME

Australia, V. Alessandria, 215 (☎06 85 27 21, emergency 800 87 77 90; fax 06 8527 2300). Consular and passport services around the corner at C. Trieste, 25. Open M-Th 9am-5pm, F 9am-12:30pm. Consular services M-F 8:30-noon and 1:30-4:15pm.

Canada consulate V. Zara, 30 (☎06 445 982 446; fax 445 982 905). Consular and passport services open M-F 8:30-noon and 1:30-3:30pm. **Embassy,** same address, same hours (☎06 44 59 81).

Ireland, Consulate, P. Campitelli, 3 (☎06 697 9121). Passport services open M-F 10am-12:30pm and 3-4:30pm.

New Zealand, V. Zara, 28 (☎06 441 7171; fax 440 2984). Consular and passport services open M-F 9:30am-noon. Embassy services M-F 8:30am-12:45pm and 1:45-5pm.

South Africa, V. Tanaro, 14 (☎06 85 25 41; fax 85 25 4300). Open M-F 9am-noon.

UK, V. XX Settembre, 80/A (☎06 4420 0001; fax 482 5441; consulate 4220 2600), near the corner of V. Palestro. Consular services open M-F 9:15am-1:30pm.

US, V. Veneto, 119/A (☎06 46 741; fax 4674 2356). Consular services open M-F 8:30-noon and 1:30-3:30pm. Visas M-F 8:30-10:30am; IRS M-F 9am-noon in person, 1:30-3:30pm by phone. Closed US and Italian holidays.

PASSPORTS

Citizens of Australia, Canada, Ireland, New Zealand, South Africa, the UK, and the US need valid passports to enter Italy and to reenter their own country. Returning home with an expired passport is illegal. Be sure to **photocopy** the page of your passport with your photograph, passport number, and other identifying information, as well as any visas, travel insurance policies, plane tickets, or traveler's check serial numbers. Carry one set of copies in a safe place, apart from the originals, and leave another set at home. Consulates also recommend that you carry an expired passport or an official copy of your birth certificate in your baggage, separate from other documents. File any new passport or renewal applications well in advance of your departure date. Most passport offices offer rush services for a steep fee. Citizens living abroad who need a passport or renewal should contact the nearest consular service of their home country. As of April 2002, new security measures require all US passports to be printed domestically rather than at foreign embassies and consulates, significantly extending the processing time. If you **lose your passport,** immediately notify the local police and the nearest embassy or consulate of your home government. To expedite its replacement, you will need to know all information previously recorded and show ID and proof of citizenship. In some cases, a replacement may take weeks to process, and it may be valid only for a limited time. In an emergency, ask for immediate temporary traveling papers that will permit you to reenter your home country. Temporary passports issued in cases of emergency are now limited in validity and can no longer be extended.

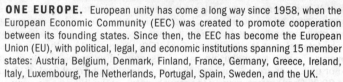

> **ONE EUROPE.** European unity has come a long way since 1958, when the European Economic Community (EEC) was created to promote cooperation between its founding states. Since then, the EEC has become the European Union (EU), with political, legal, and economic institutions spanning 15 member states: Austria, Belgium, Denmark, Finland, France, Germany, Greece, Ireland, Italy, Luxembourg, The Netherlands, Portugal, Spain, Sweden, and the UK.
>
> What does this have to do with the average non-EU tourist? Well, in 1999, 14 European countries—the entire EU minus Ireland and the UK, but including Iceland and Norway—established **freedom of movement** across their borders. Border controls between participating countries have been abolished, and visa policies harmonized. Although you're required to carry a passport (or government-issued ID card for EU citizens) when crossing an internal border, once admitted into one country, you're free to travel to all participating countries.
>
> For more important consequences of the EU for travelers, see **EU customs regulations** (see p. 39), **European Customs,** and **The Euro** (see p. 39).

VISAS

EU citizens need only a valid passport to enter Italy, and may stay as long as they like. Citizens of Australia, Canada, New Zealand, and the US do not need visas for stays of up to three months. Visas can be purchased at home country consulates. US citizens can take advantage of the **Center for International Business and Travel** (**CIBT; ☎** 800-925-2428), which secures travel visas for a small charge.

As of August 2002, citizens of South Africa need a visa—a stamp, sticker, or insert in passports specifying the purpose of their travel and the permitted duration of their stay—in addition to a valid passport for entrance to Italy. Under the Schengen Agreement, any visa granted by Italy will be respected by Austria, Belgium, France, Germany, Greece, Luxembourg, The Netherlands, Portugal, and Spain. The duration of one stay or a succession of stays may not exceed 90 days per six months. The cost of a Schengen visa varies with duration and number of entries.

Within eight days of arrival, all foreign nationals staying with friends or relatives or taking up residence must register with the local police office *(questura)* and receive a *permesso di soggiorno* (permit of stay). If staying in a hotel or hostel, the officials will fulfill registration requirements for you and the fee is waived. Those wishing to stay in Italy for more than three months for the sole purpose of tourism must apply for an extension of their stay at a local *questura* at least one month before the original permit expires. For information on employment and study visas, see **Alternatives to Tourism**, p. 82.

IDENTIFICATION

When traveling, always carry two or more forms of identifications, including at least one photo ID. Many establishments, especially banks, require several IDs to cash traveler's checks; a passport combined with a driver's license or birth certificate is usually adequate. Always split up the IDs you carry in case of theft or loss.

TEACHER, STUDENT & YOUTH IDENTIFICATION. The **International Student Identity Card (ISIC),** the most widely accepted form of student ID, gives discounts on sights, accommodations, food, and transport; access to a 24hr. emergency helpline (in North America ☎877-370-ISIC; elsewhere 715-345-0505); and insurance benefits for US cardholders (see **Insurance**, p. 49). The ISIC is preferable to an institution-specific card (such as a university ID) because it is more widely recognized and honored abroad. Applicants must be degree-seeking students of a secondary or post-secondary school and at least 12 years of age. Because of the proliferation of fake ISICs, some services (particularly airlines) require additional proof of student identity, such as a school ID or a letter attesting to your student status, signed by your registrar and stamped with your school seal.

The **International Teacher Identity Card (ITIC)** offers teachers the same insurance coverage as well as similar but limited discounts. For travelers who are 25 years old or under but are not students, the **International Youth Travel Card (IYTC;** formerly the **GO 25** Card) offers many of the same benefits as the ISIC.

Each of these identity cards costs US$22 or equivalent. ISIC and ITIC cards are valid for roughly one and a half academic years; IYTC cards are valid for one year from the date of issue. Many student travel agencies (see p. 59) issue the cards, including STA Travel in Australia and New Zealand; Travel CUTS in Canada; usit in the Republic of Ireland and Northern Ireland; SASTS in South Africa; Campus Travel and STA Travel in the UK; and STA Travel in the US. For issuing agencies, contact the **International Student Travel Confederation (ISTC),** Herengracht 479, 1017 BS Amsterdam, The Netherlands (☎31 20 421 2800; fax 421 2810; www.istc.org).

CUSTOMS

Upon entering Italy, you must declare certain items from abroad and pay a duty on the value of those articles that exceeds the allowance established by the Italian customs service. Note that goods and gifts purchased at **duty-free** shops abroad are not exempt from duty or sales tax and thus must be declared upon entering Italy as well; "duty-free" merely means that you need not pay a tax in the country of purchase. Duty-free allowances have been abolished for travel between EU member states, but they still exist for those arriving from outside the EU. Upon returning home, you must declare all articles acquired abroad and pay a duty on the value of articles in excess of your home country's allowance. Keep receipts for all goods acquired abroad. Upon departure from the EU, non-EU citizens can claim a refund for the value-added tax (VAT or IVA) on major purchases (see **Money: Taxes**, p. 43).

CUSTOMS IN THE EU. Travelers in EU member countries (Austria, Belgium, Denmark, Finland, France, Germany, Greece, Ireland, Italy, Luxembourg, the Netherlands, Portugal, Spain, Sweden, and the UK) can also take advantage of the freedom of movement of goods. This means that there are no customs controls at internal EU borders (i.e., you can take the blue customs channel at the airport), and travelers are free to transport whatever legal substances they like as long as it is for their own personal (non-commercial) use—up to 800 cigarettes, 10L of spirits, 90L of wine (60L of sparkling wine), and 110L of beer.

MONEY

CURRENCY AND EXCHANGE

The former Italian currency unit was the *lira* (plural: *lire*). Italy, as a member of the EU, has converted to the euro; you will not encounter *lire* in circulation these days, even in the most remote parts of Italy. The currency chart below is based on August 2002 exchange rates between European Union Euros (EUR€) and US dollars (US$), Canadian dollars (CDN$), Australian dollars (AUS$), New Zealand dollars (NZ$), and British pounds (UK£). For the latest exchange rates, check the currency converter in a newspaper or on financial web sites such as www.bloomberg.com and www.xe.com

EURO		
US$1 = €1.02		€1 = US$0.98
CDN$1 = €0.65		€1 = CDN$1.54
AUS$1 = €0.55		€1 = AUS$1.80
NZ$1 = €0.48		€1 = NZ$2.10
UK£1 = €0.64		€1 = UK£1.56

As a general rule, it's cheaper to convert money in Italy or in Europe at large than at home. While currency exchange will probably be available in your arrival airport, it's wise to bring enough euros to last for the first 24 to 72 hours of a trip. When changing money abroad, look for banks or *cambii* that have at most a 5% margin between buy and sell prices. Unless the currency is depreciating rapidly, **convert large sums, but no more than you need,** as you lose money with every transaction.

If you use traveler's checks or bills, carry some in small denominations (the equivalent of US$50 or less) for times when you are forced to exchange money at disadvantageous rates, but bring a range of denominations since charges may be levied per check cashed. Store your money in a variety of forms; ideally, at any given time you will be carrying cash, traveler's checks, and an ATM and/or credit card. Travelers should also consider carrying US dollars (about US$100 worth).

THE EURO. The currency has some important and positive consequences for travelers hitting more than one euro-zone country. Money-changers across the euro-zone are obliged to exchange money at the official, fixed rate, and at no commission, though they may still charge a small service fee. Euro-denominated travelers cheques allow you to pay for goods and services across the euro-zone, again at the official rate and commission-free. See above table for euro exchange rates at the time of printing.

ESSENTIALS

ESSENTIALS

TRAVELER'S CHECKS

Traveler's checks are one of the safest and least troublesome means of carrying funds. American Express and Visa are the most widely recognized brands of Traveler's checks. Many banks and agencies sell them for a small commission, in metropolitan as well as rural areas. Check issuers provide refunds if the checks are lost or stolen, and many provide additional services, such as toll-free refund hotlines abroad, emergency message services, and stolen credit card assistance. Ask about toll-free refund hotlines and the location of refund centers when purchasing checks, and always carry emergency cash.

American Express: Checks available with commission at select banks and all AmEx offices. US residents can also purchase checks by phone (☎ 888-887-8986) or online (www.aexp.com). AAA (see p. 73) offers commission-free checks to its members. Checks available in US, Australian, British, Canadian, Japanese, and Euro currencies. "Cheques for Two" can be signed by either of 2 people traveling together. For purchase locations or more information, contact AmEx's service centers: in the US and Canada ☎800-221-7282; in the UK 0800 521 313; in Australia 800 25 19 02; in New Zealand 0800 441 068; elsewhere US collect 801-964-6665. For lost or stolen checks in Italy, call toll-free ☎800-872-000.

Visa: Checks available (generally with commission) at banks worldwide. For nearest office, call Visa's service centers: in the US ☎ 800-227-6811; in the UK 0800 89 50 78; elsewhere UK collect 44 020 7937 8091. Checks available in US, UK, Canadian, Japanese, and Euro currencies. For lost or stolen checks in Italy, call toll-free ☎800-874-155.

Travelex/Thomas Cook: In the US and Canada call ☎800-287-7362; in the UK call 0800 62 21 01; elsewhere call UK collect 44 173 331 8950. For lost or stolen checks in Italy, call toll-free ☎800-870-866.

CREDIT, DEBIT, AND ATM CARDS

Where they are accepted, credit cards often offer superior exchange rates—up to 5% better than the retail rate used by banks and other currency exchange establishments. Credit cards may also offer services such as insurance or emergency help, and are sometimes required to reserve hotel rooms or rental cars. MasterCard (a.k.a. EuroCard or Access in Europe) and Visa (a.k.a. Carte Bleue or Barclaycard) are the most welcomed; American Express cards work at some ATMs and at AmEx offices and major airports.

ATM cards are widespread in Italy. You may or may not be able to access your personal bank account from abroad. ATMs get the same wholesale exchange rate as credit cards, but there is often a limit on the amount of money you can withdraw per day (around US$500), and unfortunately computer networks sometimes fail. There is typically also a surcharge of US$2-5 per withdrawal.

Debit cards are a relatively new, convenient way to purchase, and have an immediate impact on funds. A debit card can be used wherever its associated credit card company (usually MasterCard or Visa) is accepted, yet the money is withdrawn directly from the holder's checking account. Debit cards often also function as ATM cards and can be used to withdraw cash from associated banks and ATMs throughout Italy. Ask your local bank about obtaining one.

To locate ATMs, contact the two major international money networks: **Cirrus** (US ☎800-424-7787, Italy 800 87 08 66, or www.mastercard.com) and **Visa/PLUS** (US ☎800-843-7587, Italy 800 87 41 55, or www.visa.com). Most ATMs charge a transaction fee that is paid to the bank that owns the ATM.

GOT CHANGE FOR A EURO?
A Quick Guide to the New International Currency

Cleaning out one's pack at the end of a trip through Europe used to turn into a comparison among the small change picked up in each country—whose bills looked the most like Monopoly money, whose national engravings were the corniest, or who had the most uselessly small denominations. This game has become fairly less interesting, though, now that the euro has been put into general circulation in 12 member states of the EU. The euro has been hailed as a turning point in the future of European prosperity, both a symbol of and a step toward a cohesive, long-lasting alliance of distinct countries. Its introduction into everyday European life on January 2, 2002 was all but flawless, silencing critics and, incidentally, making multi-country travel infinitely more convenient.

The transition to the euro has been a long, carefully planned process. The European Economic Community was founded in 1958; the first suggestion of a common currency was made 11 years later, in response to dangerously fluctuating exchange rates. The specific steps of the euro's introduction were outlined in 1989, culminating in fixed exchange rates in 1999 and the establishment of the euro as the sole currency of all 12 Euroland states in 2002. Design contests were held in the mid-1990s to determine the look of the currency, resulting in a comfortable mix of international unity and national representation. The face of each of the seven bills depicts an architectural period from Europe's history, progressing from a Roman facade on the 5 euro to a 20th-century office building on the 500 euro. The back of each note bears a bridge from the same period, symbolizing connection and communication between the countries. After a bit of contention as to whose landmarks would grace the more valuable bills—and the discovery that the pontoon bridge on the five was actually in India—it was decided that the images would be stylized creations rather than existing structures. The eight coins, which range in value from one-cent pieces to one- and two-euro coins, bear maps of Europe on their faces; their tails, on the other hand, have been designed separately by each of the Euroland countries. As a result, distinct emblems of national pride are shared across borders, as images of the Grand Duke of Luxembourg are tendered in Ireland and coins bearing Finnish cloudberries circulate through German banks.

Although all 15 European Union countries meet or come close to Euroland's stringent financial criteria, only 12 countries joined in for the fledgling currency's debut. Denmark, Sweden, and the UK have all chosen to stay out of the Euroland indefinitely. Although national identity plays a role in their choices, economic factors are far more influential; the UK in particular is wary of tying their strong economy to the fortunes of a dozen continental countries.

Euro-skeptics forecasted a rough transition, due to a number of possible hitches, such as hidden price increases due to retailers rounding prices up to the nearest euro and heavy counterfeiting while the general public was still unfamiliar with the security features of the new notes. Some went so far as to predict an anti-integrationist backlash that would jeopardize the EU as a whole.

In practice, however, the transition was surprisingly smooth. Extensive preparation included massive public education efforts and the monstrous task of converting all printed signs and coin-operated machines to the euro. In many towns and cities, the first few days brought dozens of confusions and inconveniences, as stores ran out of change and consumers struggled to remember the relative value of the new denominations. Prices did jump slightly, but economists attribute the increases to higher food costs stemming from bad weather. On the whole, the European public was quickly satisfied with the transition. Although pockets of discontent remain strong in the Netherlands and in many rural areas, surveys by the European Commission in April 2002 found that 81% throughout Euroland judged the changeover successful.

Tobie Whitman was a Researcher-Writer for Let's Go: London 1999 *and* 2001 *and* Britain & Ireland 1998. *She interned with the European Union and is currently pursuing a Masters in European Studies at Cambridge University.*

PIN NUMBERS & ATMS. To use a cash or credit card for cash machine (ATM) withdrawal in Europe, you need a 4-digit **Personal Identification Number (PIN).** If your PIN is longer than 4 digits, ask your bank whether you can just use the first 4, or whether you'll need a new one. **Credit cards** don't usually come with PINs, so if you intend to hit up ATMs in Europe with a credit card to get cash advances, call your credit card company before leaving to request one. People with alphabetic, rather than numerical, PINs may also be thrown off by the lack of letters on European cash machines. The following handy chart gives the corresponding numbers to use: 1=QZ; 2=ABC; 3=DEF; 4=GHI; 5=JKL; 6=MNO; 7=PRS; 8=TUV; and 9=WXY. Note that if you mistakenly punch the wrong code into the machine three times, it will swallow your card for good.

GETTING MONEY FROM HOME

If you run out of money while traveling, the easiest and cheapest solution is to have someone back home make a deposit to your credit card or cash (ATM) card. Failing that, consider one of the following options.

WIRING MONEY. It is possible to arrange a bank money transfer, which means asking bank back home to wire money to a bank in Italy. This is the cheapest way to transfer cash, but it's also the slowest, usually taking several days or more. Note that some banks may only release your funds in local currency, potentially sticking you with a poor exchange rate; inquire about this in advance. Money transfer services like Western Union are faster and more convenient than bank transfers— but also much pricier. **Western Union** has many locations worldwide. To find one, visit www.westernunion.com, or call in the US ☎800-325-6000, in Canada 800-235-0000, in the UK 0800 83 38 33, in Australia 800 50 15 00, in New Zealand 800 27 00 00, in South Africa 0860 10 00 31, or in Italy 800 22 00 55. Money transfer services are also available at **American Express**. For more information contact AmEx's service center in the US and Canada ☎800-221-7282; in the UK 0800 52 13 13; in Australia 800 25 19 02; in New Zealand 0800 44 10 68; and in Italy 800 87 08 66.

US STATE DEPARTMENT (US CITIZENS ONLY). In dire emergencies only, the US State Department will forward money within hours to the nearest consular office, which will then disburse it according to instructions for a US$15 fee. If you wish to use this service, you must contact the Overseas Citizens Service division of the US State Department (☎202-647-5225; nights, Sundays, and holidays 202-647-4000).

COSTS

The cost of your trip will vary considerably, depending on where you go, how you travel, and where you stay. The most significant expenses will probably be your round-trip (return) **airfare** to Italy (see **Getting to Italy: By Plane,** p. 58) and a **railpass** or **bus pass.** Before you go, calculate a reasonable per-day **budget** that will meet your needs.

STAYING ON A BUDGET. To give you a general idea, a bare-bones day in Italy (camping or sleeping in hostels/guesthouses, buying food at supermarkets) costs around US $33 (€35). A slightly more comfortable day (sleeping in hostels/guesthouses and the occasional budget hotel, eating one meal a day at a restaurant, going out at night) would run US $70 (€75). Overestimate your expenses, and don't forget to factor in emergency reserve funds.

TIPS FOR SAVING MONEY. Some simpler ways include searching out opportunities for free entertainment, splitting accommodation and food costs with other trustworthy fellow travelers, and buying food in supermarkets rather than eating out.

Bring a sleepsack to save on sheet charges in European hostels, and do your laundry in the sink (unless you're explicitly prohibited from doing so). With that said, don't go overboard on budget obsession. Staying within your budget is important, but don't do so at the expense of your health or a great travel experience.

TIPPING AND BARGAINING

At many Italian restaurants, a service charge *(servizio)* or cover *(coperto)* is included in the bill. Tips are neither required nor expected, but it is polite to leave a little something (5-10%) in addition. Taxis drivers will expect about a 10% tip.

Bargaining is common in Italy, but use discretion. It is appropriate at outdoor markets, with street vendors, and over unmetered taxi fares (always settle your price *before* taking the cab). Haggling over prices elsewhere is usually inappropriate. Hotel haggling is more successful in uncrowded, smaller *pensioni*. This book usually notes the hotels that are open to bargaining. Never offer what you aren't willing to pay, as you're expected to buy once the merchant accepts your price.

TAXES

The **Value-Added Tax** (**VAT,** *imposto sul valore aggiunta,* or IVA) is a sales tax levied in the EU. VAT (ranging from 15-25%) is usually part of the price paid for goods and services. Upon departure from the EU, non-EU citizens can get a refund of the VAT for single purchases over €335. Present the receipt, purchases, and purchaser's passport at the Customs Office as you leave the EU, and the refund will be mailed home to you. At some stores, "Tax-Free Shopping for Tourists" enables you to get a refund in cash at the airport or a border crossing.

SAFETY AND SECURITY

Travel in Italy is generally safe, and incidents of physical violence against tourists are quite rare. While your person may be safe, however, your wallet is likely to be somewhat less secure. If you find yourself victim to a robbery or other assault, try to find an English-speaking Italian to report the incident—the *carabinieri* generally speak limited English. The vast chasm that separates the north from the south in terms of tourism infrastructure also applies to safety issues. In general, south of Naples is more dangerous than the north. Travelers of color may not feel wholly safe in southern Italy.

PERSONAL SAFETY

EXPLORING. To avoid unwanted attention, try to **blend in** as much as possible. Respecting local customs by dressing more conservatively may discourage would-be hecklers. Familiarize yourself with your surroundings, and carry yourself with confidence; if you must check a map on the street, duck into a shop. If you are traveling alone, be sure someone at home knows your itinerary, and **never admit that you're traveling alone.**

When walking at night, stick to busy, well-lit streets and avoid dark alleyways. Do not attempt to cross through parks, parking lots, or other large, deserted areas. The road less traveled is, unfortunately, often the road more populated by criminals. Look for children playing, women walking in the open, and other signs of an active community. If you feel uncomfortable, leave as quickly and directly as you can, but don't let fear of the unknown turn you into a hermit. Careful, persistent exploration will build confidence and make your stay even more rewarding.

ESSENTIALS

CAR TRAVEL. If you are using a **car,** learn local driving signals and wear a seatbelt. Children under 40 lb. should ride only in a specially designed carseat, available for a small fee from most car rental agencies. Study route maps before you hit the road, and if you plan on spending a lot of time on the road, you may want to bring spare parts. If your car breaks down, wait for the police to assist you. For long drives in desolate areas, invest in a cellular phone and a roadside assistance program (see p. 74). Be sure to park your vehicle in a garage or well-traveled area, and use a steering wheel locking device in larger cities. **Sleeping in your car** is one of the most dangerous (and often illegal) ways to get your rest.

SELF DEFENSE. There is no sure-fire way to avoid all the threatening situations you might encounter when you travel, but a good self-defense course offers concrete ways to react to unwanted advances. **Impact, Prepare,** and **Model Mugging** can refer you to local self-defense courses in the US (☎800-345-5425). Workshops (2-3hr.) start at US$50; full courses run US$350-500.

TRAVEL ADVISORIES. The following government offices provide travel information and advisories by telephone, by fax, or via the web:

Australian Department of Foreign Affairs and Trade: ☎ 13 0055 5135; faxback service 02 6261 1299; www.dfat.gov.au.

Canadian Department of Foreign Affairs and International Trade (DFAIT): In Canada and the US call ☎800-267-6788, elsewhere call 613-944-6788; www.dfait-maeci.gc.ca. Call for their free booklet, *Bon Voyage...But.*

New Zealand Ministry of Foreign Affairs: ☎04 494 8500; fax 494 8506; www.mft.govt.nz/trav.html.

United Kingdom Foreign and Commonwealth Office: ☎020 7008 0232; fax 7008 0155; www.fco.gov.uk.

US Department of State: ☎202-647-5225, faxback service 202-647-3000; http://travel.state.gov. For *A Safe Trip Abroad,* call ☎202-512-1800.

FINANCIAL SECURITY

PROTECTING YOUR VALUABLES. There are a few steps to minimizing the financial risk associated with traveling. First, bring as little as possible. Leave expensive watches, jewelry, cameras, and electronic equipment at home; chances are they will break, get lost, or become burdensome. Second, never leave your valuables unattended. Be particularly careful on **buses** and **trains;** horror stories abound about determined thieves who wait for travelers to fall asleep. When traveling with others, sleep in alternate shifts. When alone, use good judgment in selecting a train compartment. Try to sleep on top bunks with your luggage stored above you (if not in your bed), and keep important documents and other valuables on your person. If traveling by car, don't leave valuables (like radios or luggage) in it when you leave.

Third, buy combination **padlocks** to secure your belongings either in your pack or in a hostel or train station locker. Fourth, carry as little cash as possible; instead carry traveler's checks and ATM/credit cards, keeping them in a **money belt**—not a "fanny pack"—along with your passport and ID cards. Finally, keep a small cash reserve separate from your primary stash. This should entail about US$100 sewn into or stored in the depths of your pack, along with your traveler's check numbers and important photocopies.

CON ARTISTS AND PICKPOCKETS. Among the more colorful aspects of large cities are con artists. They often work in groups, and children are among the most effective. Beware of certain classics: sob stories that require money, rolls of bills "found" on the street, mustard spilled (or saliva spit) onto your shoulder to distract you while they snatch your bag. Don't ever hand over your passport to someone whose authority you question (ask to accompany them to a police station if they insist), and **don't ever let your passport out of your sight.** Similarly, don't let your bag out of sight; never trust a "station-porter" who insists on carrying your bag or stowing it in the baggage compartment or a "new friend" who offers to guard your bag while you buy a train ticket or use the restroom. **Pickpockets** abound in Rome, Naples, and other major urban centers. Beware of them in city crowds, especially on public transportation. While **gypsies'** *(gitani)* fondness for tourists' pocketbooks can be exaggerated, groups of them have been known to surround bewildered sightseers and toss a bundle resembling a baby or otherwise distract their intended victim; when the smoke clears, the tourist finds himself without his pack or wallet. Avoid panhandlers, and should you find yourself at the center of such a maelstrom, scream *"Polizia!"* and hold onto your bag for dear life. Also, be alert in public telephone booths. If you must say your calling card number, do so very quietly; if you punch it in, make sure no one can look over your shoulder.

DRUGS AND ALCOHOL

Hysteria about growing cocaine and heroin addiction have forced Italian authorities to deal strictly with those picked up for drug-related offenses. While hash is fairly common in big cities, harder drugs are quite rare, though ecstasy is becoming increasingly popular. Most Italian ecstasy is heroin-based, with little or no MDMA. Psylocibin mushrooms, methamphetamine, Ketamine, PCP, and LSD are all but nonexistent, and street dealers who claim otherwise are probably vending calcium or, worse, strychnine. Needless to say, **illegal drugs** are best avoided altogether; in Italy, drugs (including marijuana) are illegal. If you carry **prescription drugs,** it is vital to bring copies of the prescriptions themselves and a note from a doctor and have them readily accessible at country borders. There is no drinking age in Italy, but drinking and driving is strictly sanctioned.

HEALTH

Common sense is the simplest prescription for good health while you travel. Drink lots of fluids to prevent dehydration and constipation, and wear sturdy, broken-in shoes and clean socks.

BEFORE YOU GO

In your **passport,** write the names of any people you wish to be contacted in case of a medical emergency, and list any allergies or medical conditions. Matching a prescription to a foreign equivalent is not always easy, safe, or possible, so carry up-to-date, legible prescriptions or a statement from your doctor stating the medication's trade name, manufacturer, chemical name, and dosage. While traveling, be sure to keep all medication with you in your carry-on luggage. For tips on packing a basic **first-aid kit** and other **health essentials,** see p. 50. For a searchable online database of all medications, try www.rxlist.com.

IMMUNIZATIONS. Travelers over two years old should be sure that the following vaccines are up to date: MMR (for measles, mumps, and rubella); DTaP or Td (for diptheria, tetanus, and pertussis), OPV (for polio), HbCV (for haemophilus influenza B), and HBV (for hepatitis B). For recommendations on immunizations and prophylaxis, consult the CDC in the US, the IAMAT internationally (see below), or the equivalent in your home country, and check with a doctor for guidance. Meningitis shots are usually advisable, especially among college-age backpackers who plan to stay in hostels.

> **STAI MALATO?** Feeling Sick? These translations for common Italian maladies will help you explain your condition to a doctor or pharmacist.
> **allergies:** *(Sono) delle allergie.*
> **appendicitis:** *(Ho) appendicite.*
> **asthma:** *(Ho) asma.*
> **birth control:** *(Necesito) controllo di nascita/(Prendo) la pillota.*
> **high blood pressure:** *(Ho) alta ressione sanguigna.*
> **heart disease:** *(Ho) malattia di cuore.*
> **fever:** *(Ho) una febbre.*
> **infection:** *(Ho) infezione*
> **sore throat:** *(Ho) mal di gola.*
> **stomach ache:** *(Ho) mal di stomaco.*

USEFUL ORGANIZATIONS AND PUBLICATIONS. The US **Centers for Disease Control and Prevention** (**CDC;** ☎ 877-FYI-TRIP; toll-free fax 888-232-3299; www.cdc.gov/travel) maintains an international travelers' hotline and an informative web site. The CDC's comprehensive booklet *Health Information for International Travel,* an annual rundown of disease, immunization, and general health advice, is free online or US$25 via the **Public Health Foundation** (☎ 877-252-1200; www.hhs.gov). Consult the appropriate government agency of your home country for consular information sheets on health, entry requirements, and other issues for various countries (see **Travel Advisories,** p. 44). For information on health and travel warnings, contact the **Overseas Citizens Services,** Bureau of Consular Affairs, #4811, US Department of State, Washington, D.C. 20520 (☎ 888-407-4747; between 8pm and 8am 202-647-4000; http://travel.state.gov/overseas_citizens), or ask a passport agency, embassy, or consulate abroad. For information on medical evacuation services and travel insurance firms, see the US government's web site at http://travel.state.gov/medical.html or the **British Foreign and Commonwealth Office** web site at (www.fco.gov.uk).

MEDICAL ASSISTANCE ON THE ROAD. On the whole, Italy conforms to most Western standards of health care. The quality of care, however, varies throughout the country and is generally better in the north and in private hospitals and clinics. Doctors will speak English in most large cities; if they don't, they may be able to arrange for a translator. *Let's Go* lists information on how to access medical help in the **Practical Information** sections of most cities and towns. If you're concerned about obtaining medical assistance while traveling, consider a special support servic. The *MedPass* from **GlobalCare, Inc.,** 6875 Shiloh Rd. East, Alpharetta, GA, 30005-8372, USA (☎ 800-860-1111; fax 678-341-1800; www.globalems.com), provides 24hr. international telephone triage, referral, medical evacuation, and claims administration. The **International Association for Medical Assistance to Travelers** (**IAMAT;** US ☎ 716-754-4883, Canada 416-652-0137; www.iamat.org.) is free to join, lists English-speaking doctors worldwide, and has information on immunization requirements, sanitation and climactic conditions. If your regular **insurance** policy does not cover travel abroad, consider purchasing additional coverage (see p. 49).

Those with medical conditions (such as diabetes, allergies to antibiotics, epilepsy, heart conditions) may want to obtain a **MedicAlert** membership (first year US$35, annually thereafter US$20), which includes a stainless steel ID tag, among other benefits, like a 24hr. collect-call number. Contact the MedicAlert Foundation, 2323 Colorado Ave., Turlock, CA 95382, USA (☎ 888-633-4298; outside US 209-668-3333; www.medicalert.org).

GET CARD.

TRAVEL HARD.

There's only one way to max out your travel experience and make the most of your time on the road: The International Student Identity Card.

Packed with travel discounts, benefits and services, this card will keep your travel days and your wallet full. Get it before you hit it!

Visit **ISICUS.com** to get the full story on the benefits of carrying the ISIC.

90 minutes, wash & dry (one sock missing).
5 minutes to book online (Detroit to Mom's

Save money & time on student and faculty
travel at **StudentUniverse.com**

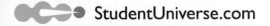 **StudentUniverse.com** Real Travel Deal

ON THE ROAD

ENVIRONMENTAL HAZARDS

Heat exhaustion and dehydration: Heat exhaustion can lead to fatigue, headaches, and wooziness. Drink plenty of fluids and avoid dehydrating beverages (e.g. alcohol, coffee, tea, and caffeinated soda). Continuous heat stress can eventually lead to heatstroke, characterized by a rising temperature, a severe headache, and cessation of sweating. Victims should be cooled off with wet towels and taken to a doctor.

Sunburn: If you're prone to sunburn, basking on beaches, or hitting the slopes, bring sunscreen and apply it liberally and often to avoid burns and the risk of skin cancer. If you do get sunburned, drink more fluids than usual and apply an aloe-based lotion.

High altitude: If hiking or skiing in the Italian Alps, allow your body a couple of days to adjust to less oxygen before exerting yourself. Note that alcohol is more potent and UV rays are stronger at high elevations.

INSECT-BORNE DISEASES

Many diseases are transmitted by insects—mainly mosquitoes, fleas, ticks, and lice. Be aware of insects in wet or forested areas, especially while hiking and camping; wear long pants and long sleeves, tuck your pants into your socks, and buy a mosquito net. Use insect repellents containing DEET and spray your gear with permethrin (licensed in the US for use on clothing). **Ticks** carrying Lyme and other diseases can be particularly dangerous in rural and forested regions.

Tick-borne encephalitis: A viral infection of the central nervous system transmitted during the summer by tick bites (primarily in wooded areas) or by consuming unpasteurized dairy products. The risk of contracting the disease is relatively low, especially if precautions are taken against tick bites.

Lyme disease: A bacterial infection carried by ticks and marked by a circular bull's-eye rash of 2 in. or more. Later symptoms include fever, headache, fatigue, and aches and pains. Antibiotics are effective if administered early. Left untreated, Lyme can cause problems in joints, the heart, and the nervous system. If you find a tick attached to your skin, grasp the head with tweezers as close to your skin as possible and apply slow, steady force. Removing a tick within 24 hours greatly reduces the risk of infection. Do not try to burn them or coat them with nail polish remover or petroleum jelly.

FOOD- AND WATER-BORNE DISEASES

Prevention is the best cure: be sure that everything you eat is cooked properly and that the water you drink is clean. Those with sensitive body temperaments may wish to peel their fruits and veggies and be wary of tap water. Buy bottled water or purify your own water by bringing it to a rolling boil or treating it with **iodine tablets;** note however that some parasites such as *giardia* have exteriors that resist iodine treatment, so boiling is more reliable. Watch out for food from markets or street vendors that may have been cooked in unhygienic conditions. Other culprits are raw shellfish, unpasteurized milk, and sauces containing raw eggs.

Traveler's diarrhea: Results from drinking untreated water or eating uncooked foods. Symptoms include nausea and bloating. Try quick-energy, non-sugary foods with protein and carbohydrates to keep your strength up. Over-the-counter anti-diarrheals (e.g. Immodium) may counteract the problems. The most dangerous side effect is dehydration; drink 8 oz. of water with ½tsp. of sugar or honey and a pinch of salt, try uncaffeinated soft drinks, or eat salted crackers. If you develop a fever or your symptoms don't go away after 4-5 days, consult a doctor. Consult a doctor immediately for treatment of diarrhea in children.

ESSENTIALS

Dysentery: Results from a serious intestinal infection caused by certain bacteria. The most common type is bacillary dysentery, also called shigellosis. Symptoms include bloody diarrhea (sometimes mixed with mucus), fever, and abdominal pain and tenderness. Bacillary dysentery generally only lasts a week, but it is highly contagious. Amoebic dysentery, which develops more slowly, is a more serious disease and may cause long-term damage if left untreated. A stool test can determine which kind you have; seek medical help immediately. Dysentery can be treated with the drugs norfloxacin or ciprofloxacin (commonly known as Cipro). If you are traveling in high-risk (especially rural) regions, consider obtaining a prescription before you leave home.

Hepatitis A: A viral infection of the liver acquired primarily through contaminated water. Symptoms include fatigue, fever, loss of appetite, nausea, dark urine, jaundice, vomiting, aches and pains, and light stools. The risk is highest in rural areas and the countryside, but it is also present in urban areas. Ask your doctor about the vaccine (Havrix or Vaqta) or an injection of immune globulin (IG; formerly called gamma globulin).

Parasites: Microbes, tapeworms, etc. that hide in unsafe water and food. **Giardiasis,** for example, is acquired by drinking untreated water from streams or lakes. Symptoms include swollen glands or lymph nodes, fever, rashes or itchiness, and digestive problems. Boil water, wear shoes, and eat only cooked food.

OTHER INFECTIOUS DISEASES

Rabies: Transmitted through the saliva of infected animals; fatal if untreated. By the time symptoms (thirst and muscle spasms) appear, the disease is in its terminal stage. If you are bitten, wash the wound thoroughly, seek immediate medical care, and try to have the animal located. A rabies vaccine, which consists of 3 shots given over a 21-day period, is available, but is only semi-effective.

Hepatitis B: A viral infection of the liver transmitted via bodily fluids or needle-sharing. Symptoms may not surface until years after infection. A 3-shot vaccination sequence is recommended for health-care workers, sexually active travelers, and anyone planning to seek medical treatment abroad; it must begin 6 months before traveling.

Hepatitis C: Like Hepatitis B, but the mode of transmission differs. IV drug users, those with occupational exposure to blood, hemodialysis patients, and recipients of blood transfusions are at the highest risk, but the disease can also be spread through sexual contact or sharing razors and toothbrushes that may have traces of blood on them.

AIDS, HIV, AND STDS

For detailed information on **Acquired Immune Deficiency Syndrome (AIDS)** in Italy, call the **US Centers for Disease Control's** 24hr. hotline at ☎ 800-342-2437, contact the **Joint United Nations Programme on HIV/AIDS (UNAIDS),** 20, ave. Appia, CH-1211 Geneva 27, Switzerland (☎ 41 22 791 3666; fax 22 791 4187), or the Italian Consulate. **Sexually transmitted diseases** (STDs) such as gonorrhea, chlamydia, genital warts, syphilis, and herpes are easier to catch than HIV and can be just as deadly. **Hepatitis B** and **C** can also be transmitted sexually. Though condoms may protect you from some STDs, oral or even tactile contact can lead to transmission. If you think you may have contracted an STD, see a doctor immediately.

FOOT AND MOUTH DISEASE

According to the Centers for Disease Control and Prevention, outbreaks of foot-and-mouth disease (FMD) have decreased in the United Kingdom and Europe. In January 2002, the CDC declared continental Europe free of the disease.

WOMEN'S HEALTH

Most pharmacies will refill empty **birth control** packages, even without an Italian-issued prescription. **Emergency Contraception,** also known as the morning after pill, is available in Italy by prescription. Abortion is legal and may be performed in a public hospital or authorized private facility at the woman's discretion for the first 90 days. Except in urgent cases, a week-long reflection period is required. Women under 18 must obtain parental permission. Actual availability of abortion may be limited in some areas of Italy, especially in the south, due to Vatican resistance and a "conscience clause" that allows physicians who are opposed to abortion to opt out of performing the procedure.

INSURANCE

Travel insurance generally covers four basic areas: medical/health problems, property loss, trip cancellation/interruption, and emergency evacuation. Although your regular insurance policies may well extend to travel-related accidents, you may consider purchasing travel insurance if the cost of potential trip cancellation/interruption or emergency medical evacuation is greater than you can absorb. Prices for travel insurance purchased separately generally run about US$50 per week for full coverage, while trip cancellation/interruption may be purchased separately at a rate of about US$5.50 per US$100 of coverage.

Medical insurance (especially university policies) often covers costs incurred abroad; check with your provider. **US Medicare** does not cover foreign travel. **Canadians** are protected by their home province's health insurance plan for up to 90 days after leaving the country; check with the provincial Ministry of Health or Health Plan Headquarters for details. As part of the Reciprocal Health Care Agreement, **Australians** traveling in Italy are entitled to many of the services that they would receive at home. **Homeowners' insurance** (or your family's coverage) often covers theft during travel and loss of travel documents (passport, plane ticket, railpass, etc.) up to US$500.

ISIC and **ITIC** (see p. 38) provide basic insurance benefits, including US$100 per day of in-hospital sickness for up to 60 days, US$3000 of accident-related medical reimbursement, and US$25,000 for emergency medical transport. Cardholders have access to a toll-free 24hr. helpline (run by the insurance provider **TravelGuard**) for medical, legal, and financial emergencies overseas (US and Canada ☎ 877-370-4742, elsewhere call US collect 715-345-0505). **American Express** (US ☎ 800-528-4800) grants most cardholders automatic car rental insurance (collision and theft, but not liability) and ground travel accident coverage of US$100,000 on flight purchases made with the card.

INSURANCE PROVIDERS. Council and **STA** (see p. 59) offer a range of plans that can supplement your basic coverage. Other private insurance providers in the US and Canada include: **Access America** (☎ 800-284-8300); **Berkely Group/Carefree Travel Insurance** (☎ 800-323-3149; www.berkely.com); **Globalcare Travel Insurance** (☎ 800-821-2488; www.globalcare-cocco.com); and **Travel Assistance International** (☎ 800-821-2828; www.europ-assistance.com). Providers in the **UK** include **Columbus Direct** (☎ 020 7375 0011). In **Australia,** try **AFTA** (☎ 02 9375 4955).

PACKING

Pack lightly: Lay out only what you absolutely need, then take half the clothes and twice the money. The less you have, the less you have to lose.

ESSENTIALS

IMPORTANT DOCUMENTS. Don't forget your passport, traveler's checks, ATM and/or credit cards, and ID (see p. 38). Also check that you have any of the following that might apply to you: a hosteling membership card (see **Accommodations,** p. 50), driver's license, travel insurance forms, and rail or bus pass (see p. 70).

LUGGAGE. If you plan to cover most of your itinerary by foot, a sturdy **frame backpack** is unbeatable. (For the basics on buying a pack, see p. 54.) Toting a **suitcase** or **trunk** is fine if you plan to live in one or two cities and explore from there but a very bad idea if you're going to be moving around a lot. A **daypack** is a must.

CLOTHING. Bring along a **warm jacket** or wool sweater, a **rain jacket** (Gore-Tex® is both waterproof and breathable), sturdy shoes or **hiking boots,** and **thick socks.** Remember that wool will keep you warm even when soaked, whereas wearing wet cotton is colder than wearing nothing at all (see **Outdoors,** p. 54). **Flip-flops** or waterproof sandals are crucial for grubby hostel showers. If you want to go clubbing, bring at least one pair of slacks, a nice shirt, and a nice pair of shoes. If you plan to visit churches, make sure to bring a top that covers your torso and shoulders.

CONVERTERS AND ADAPTERS. In Italy, electricity is 220V AC, enough to fry any 110V North American appliance. 220/240V electrical appliances don't like 110V current, either. Americans and Canadians should buy an adapter (which changes the shape of the plug) and a converter (which changes the voltage; US$20). Don't make the mistake of using only an adapter (unless appliance instructions explicitly state otherwise). New Zealanders and South Africans (who both use 220V at home) as well as Australians (who use 240/250V) won't need a converter, but will need a set of adapters to use anything electrical. Check the useful web site for more information: http://kropla.com/electric.htm.

OTHER USEFUL ITEMS. Bring a **money belt** and small **padlock.** Basic **outdoors equipment** (plastic water bottle, compass, waterproof matches, pocketknife, sunglasses, sunscreen, insect repellent, hat) may also prove useful. **Quick repairs** of torn garments can be done on the road with a needle and thread; also consider bringing electrical tape for patching tears. Doing your **laundry** by hand (where it is allowed) is both cheaper and more convenient than doing it at a laundromat—bring detergent, a small rubber ball to stop up the sink, and string for a makeshift clothes line.

ACCOMMODATIONS

HOSTELS

Many Italian hostels are sights in themselves. Some may be located in castles or beautiful villas. Hostels are generally dorm-style accommodations, often in single-sex large rooms with bunk beds, although some hostels do offer private rooms for families and couples. They sometimes have kitchens and utensils, bike or moped rentals, storage areas, a bar, and laundry facilities. There can be drawbacks: many hostels close during certain daytime "lock-out" hours, have a curfew, don't accept reservations, impose a maximum stay, or, less frequently, require that you do chores. In Italy, a bed in a hostel will average around US$30 (see **Money,** p. 39).

Joining the youth hostel association (countries listed below) automatically grants membership privileges in **Hostelling International (HI),** a federation of national hosteling associations. The **Associazione Italiana Alberghi per la Gioventu** (**AIG;** ☎ (06) 487 11 52; www.hostels-aig.org), the Italian hostel federation, is an HI affiliate, though not all Italian hostels are part of AIG. Over 85 HI hostels are scattered throughout Italy; they sometimes accept reservations via the **International Booking Network** (Australia ☎ 02 9261 1111; Canada ☎ 800-663-5777; England and

ESSENTIALS

A HOSTELER'S BILL OF RIGHTS. There are certain standard features that we do not include in our hostel listings. Unless we state otherwise, you can expect that every hostel has: no lockout, no curfew, a kitchen, free hot showers, secure luggage storage, and no key deposit. Because of the introduction of the euro, hotel prices change frequently. Each spring, price ranges are set by the government. While the prices in *Let's Go* were up-to-date as of fall 2003, you should expect rate increases of 10% or greater throughout the country.

Wales ☎ 1629 58 14 18; Northern Ireland ☎ 1232 32 47 33; Republic of Ireland ☎ 01 830 1766; NZ ☎ 03 379 9808; Scotland ☎ 8701 55 32 55; US ☎ 800-909-4776; www.hostelbooking.com). HI's organization's web page (www.iyhf.org), lists the web addresses and phone numbers of all national associations. It is a great place to research hosteling in a specific region. Other comprehensive hosteling web sites include **www.hostels.com** and **www.hostelplanet.com**.

Most HI hostels also honor **guest memberships**—you'll get a blank card with space for six validation stamps. Each night you'll pay a nonmember supplement (one-sixth the membership fee) and earn one guest stamp; get six stamps, and you're a member. Most student travel agencies (see p. 58) sell HI cards, as do all of the national hosteling organizations listed below. All prices listed below are valid for **one-year memberships** unless otherwise noted.

Australian Youth Hostels Association, Level 3, 10 Mallett St., Camperdown NSW 2050 (☎ 02 9565 1699; fax 9565 1325; www.yha.org.au). AUS$52, under 18 AUS$16.

Hostelling International-Canada (HI-C), 400-205 Catherine St., Ottawa, ON K2P 1C3 (☎ 800-663-5777 or 613-237-7884; fax 237-7868; www.hostellingintl.ca). CDN$35, under 18 free.

An Óige (Irish Youth Hostel Association), 61 Mountjoy St., Dublin 7 (☎ 01 830 4555; fax 830 5808; www.irelandyha.org).

Youth Hostels Association of New Zealand (YHANZ), P.O. Box 436, 193 Cashel St., 3rd fl. Union House, Christchurch 1 (☎03 379 9970; fax 365 4476; www.yha.org.nz). NZ$40, under 17 free.

Hostels Association of South Africa, 3rd fl., 73 St. George's St. Mall, P.O. Box 4402, Cape Town 8000 (☎021 424 2511; fax 424 4119; www.hisa.org.za). ZAR45.

Scottish Youth Hostels Association (SYHA), 7 Glebe Crescent, Stirling FK8 2JA (☎01786 89 14 00; fax 89 13 33; www.syha.org.uk). UK£6.

Youth Hostels Association (England and Wales) Ltd., Trevelyan House, 8 St. Stephen's Hill, St. Albans, Hertfordshire AL1 2DY (☎0870 870 8808; fax 0172 784 4126; www.yha.org.uk). UK£12.50, under 18 UK£6.25, families UK£25.

Hostelling International Northern Ireland (HINI), 22-32 Donegall Rd., Belfast BT12 5JN, Northern Ireland (☎02890 31 54 35; fax 43 96 99; www.hini.org.uk). UK£10, under 18 UK£6.

Hostelling International-American Youth Hostels (HI-AYH), 733 15th St. NW, #840, Washington, D.C. 20005 (☎202-783-6161; fax 783-6171; www.hiayh.org). US$25, under 18 free.

DORMS

Many **colleges and universities** open their residence halls to travelers when school is not in session; some do so even during term-time. These dorms are often close to lively student areas and are usually very clean. Getting a room may take a few phone calls and advance planning, but rates tend to be low and many offer free local calls. For more information contact the **Italian Government Tourist Office in New York,** 630 5th Ave., #1565, New York, NY 10111, USA (☎212-245-5618; fax 586-9249).

HOTELS, PENSIONS, AND ROOMS FOR RENT

Hotel singles *(camera singola)* in Italy cost €25-€50 (and up), depending on region; doubles *(camera doppia* or *camera matrimoniale)* range from €60-€82. You'll typically share a hall bathroom; a private bathroom will cost extra, as may hot showers. Some hotels offer "full-pension" (all meals) and "half-pension" (no lunch); in high-season, hotel owners will often require guests to take *pensione.* Upon arrival, be sure to confirm the charges before checking in; many Italian hotels are notorious for tacking on additional costs at check-out time. If you make **reservations** in writing, indicate your night of arrival and the number of nights you plan to stay. The hotel will send you a confirmation and may request payment for the first night. Not all hotels take reservations, and few accept checks in foreign currency. Rooms for rent in private houses *(affittacamere)* are another inexpensive housing option. For more information on these, inquire at local tourist offices.

HOME EXCHANGE AND RENTALS

Home exchange offers the traveler homes (houses, apartments, condominiums, villas, even castles in some cases), plus the opportunity to live like a native and cut down on accommodation fees. For more information, contact **HomeExchange.Com** (☎800 877 8723; fax 310 798 3865), **Intervac International Home Exchange** (www.intervac.com), or **The Invented City: International Home Exchange,** 41 Sutter St. San Francisco, CA 94404, USA (US ☎800-788-2489, elsewhere US collect 415-252-1141; www.invented-city.com). **Home rentals** are more expensive than exchanges, but they can be cheaper than comparably serviced hotels. Both home exchanges and rentals are ideal for families with children or travelers with special dietary needs; you often get your own kitchen, maid service, TV, and telephones.

CAMPING & THE OUTDOORS

There are over 1700 campsites in Italy. Fees are small, variable, and usually issued per person. Contact local tourist offices for information about suitable or free campsites. Camping on undesignated land is not permitted. **The Touring Club Italiano** (www.touringclub.it) is full of camp knowledge, and it publishes numerous books and pamphlets on the outdoors. The Federazione Italiana del Campeggio e del Caravanning (Federcampeggio), 50041 Calenzano (Florence) (☎ 055 88 23 91; fax 882 5918), has a complete list of camping sites with location maps for free. Federcampeggio also publishes the book *Guida Camping d'Italia.* **EasyCamping** runs a web site, www.icaro.it/home_e.html, that comes equipped with information about over 700 campsites throughout Italy. For a thorough list of the bigger parks and national reserves in the country, visit www.parks.it.

Pay attention to weather forecasts and stay warm, dry, and hydrated. In August, arrive well before 11am or find yourself without a spot. Many campgrounds boast everything from swimming pools to bars; others may be simpler. Rates average €4.50 per person or tent, €3.50 per car.

USEFUL PUBLICATIONS & RESOURCES

A variety of companies publish hiking guidebooks to meet the educational needs of novices and experts. For information about camping, hiking, and biking, write or call the publishers listed below to receive a free catalog. Campers heading to Europe should consider buying an **International Camping Carnet.** Similar to a hostel membership card, it's required at a few campgrounds and provides discounts at others. It is available in North America from the Family Campers and RVers Association and in the UK from The Caravan Club.

Automobile Association, Contact Centre, Car Ellison House, William Armstrong Dr., Newcastle-upon-Tyne NE4 7YA, UK (general info ☎ 0870 600 0371; fax 0191 235 5111; www.theaa.co.uk). Road atlases for Europe, France, Spain, Germany, and Italy.

The Caravan Club, East Grinstead House, East Grinstead, West Sussex, RH19 1UA, UK (☎ 01342 326 944; fax 410 258; www.caravanclub.co.uk). For UK£27.50, members receive equipment discounts, a directory and handbook, and a monthly magazine.

Sierra Club Books, 85 Second St., 2nd fl., San Francisco, CA 94105, USA (☎ 415-977-5500; www.sierraclub.org/books). Publishes general resource books on hiking and camping, and for women traveling in the outdoors.

The Mountaineers Books, 1001 SW Klickitat Way, #201, Seattle, WA 98134, USA (☎ 800-553-4453 or 206-223-6303; fax 223-6306; www.mountaineersbooks.org). Over 400 titles on hiking, biking, mountaineering, natural history, and conservation.

WILDERNESS SAFETY

Stay warm, stay dry, and stay hydrated. The vast majority of life-threatening wilderness situations can be avoided by following this simple advice. Prepare yourself for an emergency, however, by always packing raingear, a hat and mittens, a first-aid kit, a reflector, a whistle, high energy food, and extra water for any hike. Dress in wool or warm layers of synthetic materials designed for the outdoors; never rely on cotton for warmth, as it is useless when wet.

Check **weather forecasts** and pay attention to the skies when hiking, since weather patterns can change suddenly. Whenever possible, let someone know when and where you are going hiking—either a friend, your hostel, a park ranger, or a local hiking organization. Do not attempt a hike beyond your ability—you may be endangering your life. For information about outdoor ailments and basic medical concerns (see **Health,** p. 45). For more information, consult *How to Stay Alive in the Woods,* by Bradford Angier (Macmillan Press, US$8).

CAMPING AND HIKING EQUIPMENT

WHAT TO BUY...

Good camping equipment is both sturdy and light. Camping equipment is generally more expensive in Australia, New Zealand, and the UK than in North America.

Sleeping Bag: Most sleeping bags are rated by season ("summer" means 30-40°F at night; "four-season" or "winter" often means below 0°F). They are made either of **down** (warmer and lighter, but more expensive, and miserable when wet) or of **synthetic** material (heavier, more durable, and warmer when wet). Prices range US$80-210 for a summer synthetic to US$250-300 for a good down winter bag. **Sleeping bag pads** include foam pads (US$10-20), air mattresses (US$15-50), and Therm-A-Rest self-inflating pads (US$45-80). Bring a **stuff sack** to store your bag and keep it dry.

Tent: The best tents are free-standing (with their own frames and suspension systems), can be set up quickly, and only require staking in high winds. Low-profile dome tents are the best. Good 2-person tents start at US$90, 4-person at US$300. Seal the seams of your tent with waterproofer, and make sure it has a rain fly. Other tent accessories include a **battery-operated lantern**, a **plastic groundcloth**, and a **nylon tarp**.

Backpack: Internal-frame packs mold better to your back, keep a lower center of gravity, and flex adequately to allow you to hike difficult trails. **External-frame packs** are more comfortable for long hikes over even terrain, as they keep weight higher and distribute it more evenly. Make sure your pack has a strong, padded hip-belt to transfer weight to your legs. Any serious backpacking requires a pack of at least 4000 in^3 (16,000cc), plus 500 in^3 for sleeping bags in internal-frame packs. Sturdy backpacks cost anywhere from US$125-420, and this is one area in which it doesn't pay to economize. Fill up any pack with something heavy and walk around the store with it to get a sense of how it distributes weight before buying it. Either buy a **waterproof backpack cover,** or store all of your belongings in plastic bags inside your pack.

Boots: Be sure to wear hiking boots with good **ankle support.** They should fit snugly and comfortably over 1-2 pairs of wool socks and thin liner socks. Break in boots over several weeks 1st in order to spare yourself painful and debilitating blisters.

Other Necessities: Synthetic layers, like those made of polypropylene, and a **pile jacket** will keep you warm even when wet. A **"space blanket"** will help you to retain your body heat and doubles as a groundcloth (US$5-15). Plastic **water bottles** are virtually shatter- and leak-proof. Bring **water-purification tablets** for when you can't boil water. For those places that forbid fires or the gathering of firewood (virtually every organized campground in Italy), you'll need a **camp stove** (the classic Coleman starts at US$40) and a propane-filled **fuel bottle** to operate it. Also don't forget a **first-aid kit, pocketknife, insect repellent, calamine lotion,** and **waterproof matches** or a **lighter.**

...AND WHERE TO BUY IT

The mail-order/online companies listed below offer lower prices than many retail stores, but a visit to a local camping or outdoors store will give you a good sense of the look and weight of certain items.

Campmor, 28 Parkway, P.O. Box 700, Upper Saddle River, NJ 07458, USA (US ☎888-226-7667; elsewhere US ☎ 201-825-8300; www.campmor.com).

Discount Camping, 880 Main North Rd., Pooraka, South Australia 5095, Australia (☎08 8262 3399; fax 8260 6240; www.discountcamping.com.au).

Eastern Mountain Sports (EMS), 1 Vose Farm Rd., Peterborough, NH 03458, USA (☎ 888-463-6367 or 603-924-7231; www.shopems.com).

L.L. Bean, Freeport, ME 04033, USA (US and Canada ☎800-441-5713; UK ☎0800 891 297; elsewhere, call US ☎ 207-552-3028; www.llbean.com).

Mountain Designs, 51 Bishop St., Kelvin Grove, Queensland 4059, Australia (☎07 3856 2344; fax 3856 0366; www.mountaindesigns.com).

Recreational Equipment, Inc. (REI), Sumner, WA 98352, USA (☎800-426-4840; 253-891-2500; www.rei.com).

YHA Adventure Shop, 14 Southampton St., Covent Garden, London, WC2E 7HA, UK (☎020 7836 8541; www.yhaadventure.com).

KEEPING IN TOUCH

BY MAIL

SENDING MAIL HOME FROM ITALY

Airmail is the best way to send mail home from Italy. Write "par avion" or *"posta prioritaria"* on the front. From major cities in Italy to North America, airmail averages eight to 12 days, although times are more unpredictable from smaller towns; to Australia or New Zealand, at least seven days; to the UK or Ireland, four days; to South Africa, six days. **Aerogrammes,** printed sheets that fold into envelopes and travel via airmail, are available at post offices. Most post offices will charge exorbitant fees or simply refuse to send aerogrammes with enclosures. **Surface mail** is by far the cheapest and slowest way to send mail. It takes one to three months to cross the Atlantic and two to four to cross the Pacific—good for items you won't need to see for a while, such as souvenirs or other articles you've acquired along the way that are weighing down your pack. For postcard postage, the Italian post office has divided the English-speaking world into three zones: Zone 1 (England) costs €0.41, Zone 2 (US, Canada, S. Africa) costs €0.52, and Zone 3 (Australia and New Zealand) costs €0.52. To send a letter (up to 20g) to another country in Europe costs €0.62 and to anywhere else in the world via airmail costs €0.77.

SENDING MAIL TO ITALY

Mark envelopes "air mail," "par avion," or *"posta prioritaria"* or your letter or postcard will never arrive. **Federal Express** (www.fedex.com; Australia ☎13 26 10; US and Canada 800-247-4747; New Zealand 0800 73 33 39; UK 0800 12 38 00) handles express mail services from most home countries to Italy; for example, they can get a letter from New York to Italy in four to five days for US$39.

RECEIVING MAIL IN ITALY

There are several ways to arrange pick-up of letters sent to you by friends and relatives while you are abroad. Mail can be sent via **Poste Restante** (General Delivery; **Fermo Posta** in Italian) to almost any city or town in Italy with a post office, although this service is not always reliable. Address *Fermo Posta* letters like so:

Jane DOE, Fermo Posta, Ufficio Postale Centrale di Piazza Cordusio 4, Milano 20100, Italia.

The mail will go to a special desk in the central post office, unless you specify a post office by street address or postal code. It's best to use the largest post office, since mail may be sent there regardless. It is usually safer and quicker, though more expensive, to send mail express or registered. Bring your passport (or other photo ID) for pick-up; there may be a **small fee.** If the clerks insist that there is nothing for you, have them check under your first name as well. *Let's Go* lists post offices in the **Practical Information** section for each city and most towns.

American Express travel offices throughout the world offer a free **Client Letter Service** (mail held up to 30 days and forwarded upon request) for cardholders who contact them in advance. Address the letter in the same way shown above. Some offices will offer these services to non-cardholders (especially AmEx Travelers Cheque holders), but call ahead. *Let's Go* lists AmEx office locations for most large cities in **Practical Information** sections; for a free list, call ☎ 800-528-4800.

SENDING MAIL WITHIN ITALY

Domestic postal service is poor. A letter mailed less than 90 miles may take as many as three weeks to arrive. Items of value often do not reach their intended destination.

TELEPHONES

CELL TOTIN'. Both convenient and inexpensive, a cellular phone may be worth obtaining for longer visits. While the phones themselves are relatively expensive, starting at €50-€80, text messages are only €0.12 each, calls to other phones on the same company's plan are around €0.15 per min. on most plans (calls to cellular phones on other systems vary by plan), and **incoming calls cost you nothing.** The three main phone companies, **Vodafone Omnitel** (from Italy ☎ 800 19 01 90 or 800 20 82 08, from abroad 349 200 0190; www.omnitel.it), **Wind** (☎ 06 8311 4600 or 02 3011 6055; www.wind.it) and **Tim** (from Italy ☎ 800 55 53 33 or 800 61 96 19, from abroad 39 339 9119; www.tim.it), sell phone plans. Stores around the country sell phones and pre-paid cards (*schede*) with a fixed number of minutes. When your card runs out, simply head to a station (see web sites for locations) and refill.

CALLING HOME FROM ITALY

A **calling card** is probably your cheapest bet. Calls are billed collect or to your account. You can frequently call collect without even possessing a company's calling card just by calling their access number and following the instructions. **To obtain a calling card** from your national telecommunications service before leaving home, contact the appropriate company listed below. *Let's Go* has recently formed a partnership with ekit.com to provide a calling card that offers a number of services, including email and voice messaging services. Before purchasing any calling card, always be sure to compare rates with other cards, and to make sure it serves your needs (a local phonecard is generally better for local calls, for instance). For more information, visit www.letsgo.ekit.com. To **call home with a calling card,** contact the operator for your service provider in Italy by dialing the appropriate toll-free access number.

COMPANY	TO OBTAIN A CARD, DIAL:	TO CALL ABROAD, DIAL:
AT&T (US)	800-361-4470	172 1011
British Telecom Direct	800 34 51 44	800 17 24 42
Canada Direct	800-668-6878	800 79 00 74
Ireland Direct	323 1661 4808	172 0353
MCI (US)	800-444-2222	172 1022
New Zealand Direct	617 3806 2055	800 87 68 07
Sprint (US)	800-449-6060	172 1877
Telkom South Africa	10 219	172 1027
Telstra Australia	13 22 00	172 1061

You can usually also make direct international calls from pay phones. Prepaid phone cards and major credit cards can be used for direct international calls, but they are still less cost-efficient. Placing a **collect call** through an international operator is even more expensive, but may be necessary in case of emergency. You can typically place collect calls through the service providers listed above even if you don't possess one of their phone cards. If you will be making frequent international calls, it may be worthwhile to purchase a cell phone (*telefonino*; see box).

PLACING INTERNATIONAL CALLS.
To call Italy from home or to place an international call from Italy, dial:

1. The **international dialing prefix**. To dial out of **Australia,** dial 0011; **Canada** and the **US,** 011; **the Republic of Ireland, Italy, New Zealand,** or the **UK,** 00; **South Africa,** 09.
2. The **country code** of the country you want to call. To call **Australia,** dial 61; **Canada** or the **US,** 1; the **Republic of Ireland,** 353; **Italy,** 39; **New Zealand,** 64; **South Africa,** 27; **UK,** 44.
3. The **city** or **area code.** *Let's Go* lists the phone codes for cities and towns in Italy opposite the city or town name, next to a ☎. For most countries, if the first digit is a zero (e.g., 04 for Nice), omit the zero when calling from abroad. Italy, however, is the exception. Dial the number as written with the zero.
4. The **local number.**

CALLING WITHIN ITALY

While there are still coin-operated phones, the most common type takes **prepaid phone cards.** Phone card vendors and *tabacchi* carry a certain amount of phone time depending on the card's denomination (€5, €10, and €20), and they usually save time and money in the long run. Italian phone cards are a little tricky to maneuver; rip off the marked corner, and insert the card into the appropriate section of the pay phone. Watch your money click away in €.10-.50 units. Even when dialing within a city, the city code is required; for example, when dialing from one place in Milan to another, the (02) is still necessary. International calls start at €1 per minute and vary depending on where you are calling from.

TIME DIFFERENCES

Italy is one hour ahead of **Greenwich Mean Time (GMT).** Daylight-saving time starts on the last Sunday in March, when clocks are moved ahead one hour. Clocks are put back an hour on the last Sunday in September.

4AM	7AM	12PM	1PM	8PM	10PM
Vancouver	Toronto		Italy	China	Sydney
Seattle	Ottawa	London	Paris	Hong Kong	Canberra
San Francisco	New York	(GMT)	Munich	Manila	Melbourne
Los Angeles	Boston		Madrid	Singapore	

EMAIL AND INTERNET

Though Italy had initially lagged behind in the information superhighway, it's now playing the game of catch-up like a pro. While Internet cafes are still rare in rural and industrial cities, "Internet points" such as bars and even laundromats appear at an alarming rate in well-touristed areas. Rates range from €5-8 per hour. For free Internet access, try local universities and libraries.

Though in some places it's possible to forge a remote link with your home server, it's faster and cheaper to use a free **web-based email account** (e.g., www.hotmail.com and www.yahoo.com). *Let's Go* includes the major locations to surf the web and check email in each city. The following web sites offer comprehensive listings: www.ecs.net/cafe/#list and www.cybercaptive.com.

GETTING TO ITALY

BY PLANE

When it comes to airfare, a little effort can save you a bundle. If your plans are flexible enough to deal with the restrictions, courier fares are the cheapest. Tickets bought from consolidators and standby seating are also good deals, but last-minute specials and charter flights often beat these fares. The key is to hunt around, to be flexible, and to ask persistently about discounts. Students, seniors, and those under 26 should never pay full price for a ticket.

AIRFARES

Airfares to Italy peak between mid-June and early September; holidays also bring higher fares. Flights early in the week (M-Th morning) run US$40-50 cheaper than weekend flights, but they are generally more crowded and less likely to permit frequent-flier upgrades. Not fixing a return date ("open return") or arriving in and departing from different cities ("open-jaw") can be pricier than round-trip flights. Patching one-way flights together is the least economical way to travel. Flights into large cities such as Milan and Rome will offer the most competitive fares.

If Italy is only one stop on a more extensive globe-hop, consider a round-the-world (RTW) ticket. Tickets usually include at least 5 stops and are valid for about a year; prices range US$1200-5000. Try Northwest Airlines/KLM (US ☎800-447-4747; www.nwa.com) or Star Alliance, a consortium of 22 airlines including United Airlines (US ☎800-241-6522; www.star-alliance.com). Round-trip flights to Rome from the US or Canadian east coast start at US$600. In the off-season, late fall through early spring (excluding the holidays), flights can drop to US$400. From the US or Canadian west coast US$900/US$600; from the UK, UK£140/UK£120; from Australia AUS$1100/AUS$900; and from New Zealand NZ$1100/NZ$950.

BUDGET AND STUDENT TRAVEL AGENCIES

While knowledgeable agents specializing in flights to Italy can make your life easy and help you save, they may not spend the time to find you the lowest possible fare—they get paid on commission. Travelers holding **ISIC and IYTC cards** (see p. 38) qualify for big discounts from student travel agencies. Most flights from budget agencies are on major airlines, but in peak season some may sell seats on less reliable chartered aircraft.

usit world (www.usitworld.com). Over 50 **usit campus** branches in the UK. 52 Grosvenor Gardens, **London** SW1W 0AG (☎0870 240 1010); **Manchester** (☎0161 273 1880); and **Edinburgh** (☎0131 668 3303). Nearly 20 **usit NOW** offices in Ireland, including 19-21 Aston Quay, O'Connell Bridge, **Dublin** (☎01 602 1600; www.usitnow.ie), and **Belfast** (☎02 890 327 111; www.usitnow.com). Offices also in Athens, Auckland, Brussels, Frankfurt, Johannesburg, Lisbon, Luxembourg, Madrid, Paris, and Warsaw.

Council Travel (www.counciltravel.com). Countless US offices, including branches in Atlanta, Boston, Chicago, L.A., New York, San Francisco, Seattle, and Washington, D.C. Check the web site or call 800-226-8624 for the office nearest you. Also an office at

28A Poland St. (Oxford Circus), **London**, W1V 3DB (☎0207 437 7767). As of May 2002, Council had declared bankruptcy and was subsumed under STA. However, their offices are still in existence and transacting business.

CTS Travel, 44 Goodge St., **London** W1T 2AD, UK (☎0207 636 0031; fax 0207 637 5328; ctsinfo@ctstravel.co.uk).

STA Travel, 7890 S. Hardy Dr., Ste. 110, Tempe AZ 85284, USA (24hr. reservations and info ☎800-781-4040; www.sta-travel.com). Over 150 offices worldwide (check their web site for a listing of all their offices), US offices in Boston, Chicago, L.A., New York, San Francisco, Seattle, and Washington, D.C. They offer ticket booking, travel insurance, railpasses, and more. In the UK, walk-in office at 11 Goodge St., **London** W1T 2PF (☎0207 436 7779). In New Zealand, Shop 2B, 182 Queen St., **Auckland** (☎09 309 0458). In Australia, 366 Lygon St., **Carlton Vic** 3053 (☎03 9 349 4344).

Travel CUTS (Canadian Universities Travel Services Limited), 187 College St., **Toronto,** ON M5T 1P7 (☎416-979-2406; fax 979-8167; www.travelcuts.com). 60 offices across Canada. Also in the UK, 295-A Regent St., London W1R 7YA (☎0207 255 1944).

Wasteels, Skoubogade 6, 1158 Copenhagen K. (☎ 3314-4633; fax 7630-0865; www.wasteels.dk/uk). A huge chain with 165 locations across Europe. Sells Wasteels BIJ tickets discounted 30-45% off regular fare, 2nd-class international point-to-point train tickets with unlimited stopovers for those under 26 (sold only in Europe).

FLIGHT PLANNING ON THE INTERNET. Many airline sites offer special last-minute deals on the Web, where there are sites to do the legwork and compile the deals for you—try www.bestfares.com, www.flights.com, www.hotdeals.com, www.onetravel.com, and www.travelzoo.com. ■ **StudentUniverse** (www.studentuniverse.com), **STA** (www.sta-travel.com), and **Orbitz.com** provide quotes on student tickets, while **Expedia** (www.expedia.com) and **Travelocity** (www.travelocity.com) offer full travel services. **Priceline** (www.priceline.com) allows you to specify a price, and obligates you to buy any ticket that meets or beats it; be prepared for odd hours and routes. **Skyauction** (www.skyauction.com) allows you to bid on both last-minute and advance-purchase tickets. An indispensable resource on the Internet is the *Air Traveler's Handbook* (www.cs.cmu.edu/afs/cs/user/mkant/Public/Travel/airfare.html), a comprehensive listing of links to everything you need to know before you board a plane.

COMMERCIAL AIRLINES

The commercial airlines' lowest regular offer is the **APEX** (Advance Purchase Excursion) fare, which provides confirmed reservations and allows "open-jaw" tickets. Generally, reservations must be made seven to 21 days ahead of departure, with seven- to 14-day minimum-stay and up to 90-day maximum-stay restrictions. These fares carry hefty cancellation and change penalties (fees rise in summer). Book peak-season APEX fares early; by May you will have a hard time getting your desired departure date. Use **Microsoft Expedia** (msn.expedia.com) or **Travelocity** (www.travelocity.com) to get an idea of the lowest published fares, then use the resources outlined here to try and beat those fares. Low-season fares should be appreciably cheaper than the **high-season** (mid-June to early Sept.) ones listed here. Basic round-trip fares to Italy range from roughly US$200-750. Standard commercial carriers like **American** (US ☎800-433-7300; www.aa.com) and **United** (US ☎800-241-6522; www.ual.com) offer the most convenient flights to Rome and Milan, but they may not be the cheapest (unless you manage to grab a special promotion or airfare war ticket). You might find a better deal on one of the following airlines, if any of their limited departure points is convenient for you.

Icelandair: (☎800-223-5500; www.icelandair.com). Stopovers in Iceland for no extra cost on most transatlantic flights. New York to Frankfurt May-Sept. US$500-730; Oct.-May US$390-$450. For last-minute offers, subscribe to their email Lucky Fares.

Finnair: (☎800-950-5000; www.us.finnair.com). Cheap round-trips from San Francisco, New York, and Toronto to Helsinki; connections throughout Europe.

Martinair: (☎800-627-8462; www.martinair.com). Fly from California or Florida to Amsterdam mid-June to mid-Aug. US$880; mid-Aug. to mid-June US$730.

TRAVELING FROM THE UK AND IRELAND

Because of the many carriers flying between the British Isles to the continent, we only include discount airlines or those with cheap specials here. The **Air Travel Advisory Bureau** in London (☎020 7636 5000; www.atab.co.uk) provides referrals to travel agencies and consolidators that offer discounted airfares out of the UK.

Aer Lingus: (Ireland ☎0818 36 50 00; www.aerlingus.ie). Round-trip tickets from Dublin, Cork, Galway, Kerry, and Shannon to Milan and Rome (IR£102-244).

British Midland Airways: (UK ☎0870 607 0555; www.flybmi.com). Departures from throughout the UK. London to Brussels (UK£68), Madrid (UK£98), Paris (UK£71), and Frankfurt (UK£172).

buzz: (UK ☎0870 240 7070; www.buzzaway.com). A subsidiary of KLM. From London to Berlin, Frankfurt, Hamburg, Helsinki, Milan, Paris, and Vienna (UK£50-80). Tickets cannot be changed or refunded.

Go-Fly Limited: (UK ☎09 063 02 01 50, elsewhere call UK 44 1279 66 63 88; www.go-fly.com). A subsidiary of British Airways. From London to Naples, Rome, and Venice (round-trip UK£53-180).

KLM: (UK ☎0870 507 4074; www.klmuk.com. Cheap round-trip tickets from London and elsewhere to Amsterdam, Brussels, Frankfurt, Düsseldorf, Milan, Paris, and Rome.

Ryanair: Ireland ☎0818 30 30 30, UK 0870 156 9569; www.ryanair.ie). From Dublin, London, and Glasgow to destinations in Italy. Deals from as low as UK£9 on weekends.

TRAVELING FROM ELSEWHERE IN EUROPE

Most European carriers, including **Air France** (☎ 011 880 8040; www.air-france.com), **Alitalia** (☎800-223-5730 or UK 44 870 544 8259; www.alitalia.it/eng), **KLM** (see above), **Lufthansa** (see below), and **Sabena** (Belgium ☎3202 723 2323; www.sabena.com) have frequent flights to Rome, Milan, and Venice from many European cities. The sheer number of European airlines ensures reasonable fares.

TRAVELING FROM AUSTRALIA AND NEW ZEALAND

Air New Zealand: New Zealand ☎0800 73 70 00; www.airnz.co.nz. Auckland to Italy.

Qantas Air: (Australia ☎13 13 13, New Zealand ☎0800 808 767; www.qantas.com.au). Flights from Australia and New Zealand to Rome and Milan.

Singapore Air: (Australia ☎13 10 11, New Zealand ☎0800 80 89 09; www.singaporeair.com). Flies from Auckland, Sydney, Melbourne, and Perth to Western Europe.

Thai Airways: (Australia ☎1300 65 19 60, New Zealand ☎09 377 0268; www.thai-air.com). Auckland, Sydney, and Melbourne to Amsterdam, Frankfurt, and London.

TRAVELING FROM SOUTH AFRICA

Air France: (☎011 770 1601; www.airfrance.com/za). Connections throughout Europe.

British Airways: (☎0860 01 17 47; www.british-airways.com/regional/sa). Cape Town and Johannesburg to the UK and the rest of Europe from ZAR3400.

Lufthansa: (☎0861 84 25 38; www.lufthansa.co.za). From Cape Town, Durban, and Johannesburg to Germany and elsewhere.

Virgin Atlantic: (☎011 340 3400; www.virgin-atlantic.co.za). Flies to London from both Cape Town and Johannesburg.

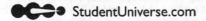

AIR COURIER FLIGHTS

Those who travel light should consider courier flights. Couriers help transport cargo on international flights by using their checked luggage space for freight. Generally, couriers must travel with carry-ons only and deal with complex flight restrictions. Most flights are round-trip only, with short fixed-length stays (usually one week) and a limit of a one ticket per issue. Most of these flights also operate only out of major gateway cities, mostly in North America. Generally, you must be over 21 (in some cases 18). In summer, the most popular destinations usually require an advance reservation of about two weeks (you can usually book up to two months ahead). Super-discounted fares are common for "last-minute" flights (three to 14 days ahead).

FROM NORTH AMERICA

Round-trip courier fares from the US to Italy run about US$200-500. Most flights leave from New York, Los Angeles, San Francisco, or Miami in the US; and from Montreal, Toronto, or Vancouver in Canada. The organizations below provide members with lists of opportunities and courier brokers for an annual fee. Prices quoted below are round-trip.

Air Courier Association, 350 Indiana St. #300, Golden, CO 80401, USA (☎800-282-1202; www.aircourier.org). Ten departure cities throughout the US and Canada to Rome and cities throughout Western Europe (high-season US$150-360). 1-year membership US$49.

International Association of Air Travel Couriers (IAATC), P.O. Box 980, Keystone Heights, FL 32656, USA (☎352-475-1584; fax 475-5326; www.courier.org). From 9 North American cities to Western European cities, including Rome. 1-year membership US$45.

Global Courier Travel, P.O. Box 3051, Nederland, CO 80466, USA (www.globalcourier-travel.com). Searchable online database. 6 departure points in the US and Canada to Milan and Rome. Lifetime membership US$40, 2 people US$55.

NOW Voyager, 315 W 49th St., New York, NY 10019, USA (☎212-459-1616; fax 262-7407). To Milan and Rome (US$499-699). Usually one-week max. stay. 1-year membership US$50. Non-courier discount fares also available.

FROM THE UK, IRELAND, AUSTRALIA, AND NEW ZEALAND

The minimum age for couriers from the **UK** is usually 18. **Brave New World Enterprises,** P.O. Box 22212, London SE5 8WB (www.courierflights.com) publishes a directory of all the companies offering courier flights in the UK (UK£10, in electronic form UK£8). The **International Association of Air Travel Couriers** (www.courier.org; see above) often offers courier flights from London. Global Courier Travel (see above) also offers flights from London and Dublin to continental Europe. **British Airways Travel Shop** (☎0870 240 0747; www.batravelshops.com) arranges some flights from London to destinations in continental Europe (specials may be as low as UK£60; no registration fee). From **Australia** and **New Zealand, Global Courier Travel** (see above) often has listings from Sydney and Auckland to London and occasionally Frankfurt.

STANDBY FLIGHTS

Traveling standby requires considerable flexibility in arrival and departure dates and cities. Companies dealing in standby flights sell vouchers rather than tickets, along with the promise to get to your destination (or near your destination) within a certain window of time (typically 1-5 days). You call in before your specific window of time to hear your flight options and the probability that you will be able to board each flight. You can then decide which flights you want to try to make, show up at the appropriate airport at the appropriate time, present your voucher, and board if space is available. Vouchers can usually be bought for both one-way and round-trip travel. You may receive a monetary refund only if

every available flight within your date range is full; if you opt not to take an available (but perhaps less convenient) flight, you can only get credit toward future travel. Carefully read agreements with any company offering standby flights, as tricky fine print can leave you in the lurch. To check on a company's service record in the US, call the Better Business Bureau (☎212-533-6200). One established standby company in the US is **Whole Earth Travel,** 325 W. 38th St., New York, NY 10018, USA (☎800-326-2009; fax 212-864-5489; www.4standby.com) and Los Angeles, CA, USA (☎888-247-4482), which offers one-way flights to Europe from the northeast (US$169), west coast and northwest (US$249), midwest (US$219), and southeast (US$199). Intracontinental connecting flights within the US or Europe cost US$79-139.

TICKET CONSOLIDATORS

Ticket consolidators, or **"bucket shops,"** buy unsold tickets in bulk from commercial airlines and sell them at discounted rates. The best place to look for their tiny ads is in the Sunday travel section of any major newspaper. Call quickly, as availability is typically extremely limited. Not all bucket shops are reliable; insist on a receipt that gives full details of restrictions, refunds, and tickets, and pay by credit card so you can stop payment if you never receive your tickets. For more information, see www.travel-library.com/air-travel/consolidators.html.

TRAVELING FROM THE US AND CANADA

Travel Avenue (☎800-333-3335; www.travelavenue.com) searches for best available published fares and then uses several consolidators to attempt to beat that fare. **NOW Voyager,** 74 Varick St., Ste. 307, New York, NY 10013, USA (☎212-431-1616; fax 219-1793; www.nowvoyagertravel.com) arranges discounted flights, mostly from New York, to Milan and Rome. Other consolidators worth trying are **Interworld** (☎305-443-4929; fax 443-0351); **Pennsylvania Travel** (☎800-331-0947); **Rebel** (☎800-227-3235; www.rebeltours.com); **Cheap Tickets** (☎800-377-1000; www.cheaptickets.com); and **Travac** (☎800-872-8800; fax 212-714-9063; www.travac.com). Yet more consolidators on the web include the **Internet Travel Network** (www.itn.com); **Travel Information Services** (www.tiss.com); **TravelHUB** (www.travelhub.com); and **The Travel Site** (www.thetravelsite.com). Keep in mind that these are just suggestions to get you started; *Let's Go* does not endorse any of these agencies. As always, be cautious, and of plenty of company research.

TRAVELING FROM THE UK, AUSTRALIA, AND NEW ZEALAND

In London, the **Air Travel Advisory Bureau** (☎0207 636 5000; www.atab.co.uk) can provide names of discount flight specialists.

CHARTER FLIGHTS

Charters are flights a tour operator contracts with an airline to fly extra loads of passengers during peak season. While charter flights are cheaper, they also fly less frequently than major airlines, make refunds particularly difficult, and are almost always fully booked. Schedules and itineraries may also change or be cancelled at the last moment (as late as 48 hours before the trip, and without a full refund), and check-in, boarding, and baggage claim are often much slower.

   Discount clubs and **fare brokers** offer members savings on last-minute charter and tour deals. Study contracts closely; you don't want to end up with an unwanted overnight layover. **Travelers Advantage,** Trumbull, CT, USA (☎203-365-2000; www.travelersadvantage.com; US$60 annual fee includes discounts and cheap flight directories) specializes in European travel and tour packages.

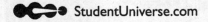

FURTHER READING: BY PLANE.
The Worldwide Guide to Cheap Airfare, Michael McColl. Insider Publications (US$15).
Discount Airfares: The Insider's Guide, George Hobart. Priceless Publications (US$14).
Air Traveler's Handbook (www.cs.cmu.edu/afs/cs/user/mkant/Public/Travel/airfare.htm).

TRANSPORTATION WITHIN ITALY

Unless stated otherwise, *Let's Go* lists one-way fares. In general, Italian trains are more efficient, economical, and romantic than other transportation alternatives.

BY TRAIN

The Italian State Railway, **Ferrovie dello Stato** or **FS** (national information line ☎848 88 80 88; www.fs-on-line.com), offers inexpensive and efficient service, although it is commonly plagued by strikes. The southern Italy offspring of FS, **Ferrovie Sud-Est (FSE)**, operates cars that are hot, crowded, and uncomfortable, and may be closer to cattle freights than trains; it may be worth the extra euro to take a classier train.

Several types of trains ride the Italian rails. The **locale** stops at every station along a particular line, often taking twice as long as a faster train. The **diretto** makes fewer stops than the *locale*, while the **espresso** just stops at major stations. The air-conditioned, more expensive **rapido**, an **InterCity (IC)** train, travels only to the largest cities. No *rapidi* have second-class compartments, and a few require reservations. Tickets for the fast, comfy, and pricey Eurostar trains (a first- and second-class train) require reservations. Eurail passes are valid without a supplement on all trains except Eurostar.

Trains are not always safe (for **safety tips,** see p. 43). For long trips, make sure you are on the correct car, as trains sometimes split at crossroads. Towns listed in parentheses on European train schedules require a train switch at the town listed immediately before the parentheses.

> If you're under 26 or over 60 and plan to travel extensively in Italy, your first purchase should be a **Cartaverde** or **Carta d'argento,** offering a year-long 20% discount on all train tickets (see p. 68).

RESERVATIONS. While seat reservations are only rarely required, you are not guaranteed a seat without one (€2.50 and up, depending on the ticket price). Reservations are available for two months in advance on major trains, and Europeans often reserve far ahead of time; you should strongly consider reserving during peak holiday and tourist seasons (at the very latest a few hours ahead). If you reserve a seat, be prepared to (politely) ask its occupant to move. To say, "Excuse me, but I have reserved this seat," try *"Mi scusa, ma ho prenotato questo posto."* It will be necessary to purchase a **supplement** (€3-15.50) or special fare for faster or higher-quality trains such as ETR500 and Pendolino. All InterRail holders must also purchase supplements (€3-20) for trains like EuroCity and InterCity.

OVERNIGHT TRAINS. Night trains have their advantages: you won't waste valuable daylight hours traveling, and you will be able to forego the hassle and considerable expense of securing a night's accommodation. However, night travel has its drawbacks as well: discomfort, sleeplessness, and lack of visibility. On overnight trips, consider paying extra for a **cuccetta,** one of six fold-down bunks within a compartment (€18); private **sleeping cars** offer more privacy and comfort, but are considerably more expensive (€25) and are not widely available in

ESSENTIALS

Italy. If you're not willing to spend the money on a *cuccetta*, consider taking an *espresso* train overnight—they usually have compartments with fold-out seats. If you are using a railpass valid only for a restricted number of days, inspect train schedules to maximize the use of your pass: an overnight train or boat journey uses up only one of your travel days if it departs after 7pm (you need only write in the next day's date on your pass).

DOMESTIC RAILPASSES

Railpasses theoretically allow you to jump on any train in Europe, go wherever you want whenever you want, and change your plans at will. In practice, it's not so simple. You still must stand in line to validate your pass, pay for supplements, and fork over cash for reservations. More importantly, railpasses don't always pay off. For estimates of pass prices, contact Rail Europe (see p. 69).

ITALIAN KILOMETRIC TICKET. A railpass may be a practical option only if you are planning to travel to other European countries, rather than solely within Italy. The Italian State Railway offers passes valid on all Italian trains but these are seldom cost-effective since regular fares are cheap. One option, the Italian Kilometric Ticket, is good for 20 trips or 3000km of travel, whichever comes first, and can be used for two months by up to five people traveling together. While it is virtually impossible for one person to break even on the Kilometric Ticket, it can be efficient for a couple or family. Children under 12 are charged for half the distance traveled, and kids under four travel free. A first-class Kilometric Ticket costs €174.41 (US$224), second-class €103.29 (US$132). For more information or tickets call the **North American hotline** (☎847-730-2121). You can also purchase this pass from the **Italian State Railway Representative,** in New York (☎212-730-2121) or in Italy (where the prices are slightly lower) at major train stations and offices of the **Compagnia Italiana Turismo (CIT).** When buying the ticket, make sure the sales agent stamps it with the date of purchase. As you travel, have your mileage stamped at the ticket booth or face buying another ticket on the train.

CARTAVERDE. *Cartaverde* are available to people aged 12 to 26. The card (€20.66) is valid for one year and entitles travelers to a 20% discount on any state train fare. If you're under 26 and plan to spend at least €103.29 on train tickets in Italy, this pass should be your first purchase upon arrival. Families of four or more and groups of up to five adults traveling together qualify for discounts on Italian railways. Persons over 60 get the same year-long 20% discount at the same price (€20.66) when they buy a **carta d'argento** ("silver card").

MULTINATIONAL PASSES

EURAILPASS. Eurail is valid in most of Western Europe: Austria, Belgium, Denmark, Finland, France, Germany, Greece, Hungary, Italy, Luxembourg, The Netherlands, Norway, Portugal, the Republic of Ireland, Spain, Sweden, and Switzerland. It is not valid in the UK. Standard **Eurailpasses,** valid for a consecutive given number of days, are most suitable for those planning on spending extensive time on trains every few days. **Flexipasses,** valid for any 10 or 15 (not necessarily consecutive) days in a two-month period, are more cost-effective for those traveling longer distances less frequently. **Saverpasses** provide first-class travel for travelers in groups of two to five (prices are per person). **Youthpasses** and **Youth Flexipasses** provide parallel second-class perks for those under 26.

Passholders receive a timetable for major routes and a map with details on possible ferry, steamer, bus, car rental, hotel, and Eurostar (see p. 62) discounts. Passholders often also receive reduced fares or free passage on many bus and boat lines. **Eurail freebies** (excepting surcharges such as reservation fees and port taxes) include: ferries between the Italian mainland and Sardinia (Civitavecchia-Golfo Aranci), Sicily (Villa S. Giovanni-Messina), and Greece (Brindisi-Patras).

EUROPASS. The Europass is a slimmed-down version of the Eurailpass: it allows five to 15 days of unlimited travel in any two-month period within France, Germany, Italy, Spain, and Switzerland. **First-Class Europasses** (for individuals) and **Saverpasses** (for people traveling in groups of 2-5) range from US$348/296 per person (5 days) to US$688/586 (15 days). **Second-Class Youthpasses** for those aged 12-25 cost US$244-482. For a fee, you can add **additional ferry zones** including the ADN/HML ferry between Italy and Greece; $62 for one associated country, $102 for two (pay less with the Saverpass). You are entitled to the same **freebies** afforded by the Eurailpass, but only when they are within or between countries that you have purchased. Plan your itinerary before buying a Europass: it will save you money if you only go to three, four, or five adjacent Western European countries, or if you only want to go to large cities, but would be a waste if you plan to make lots of side-trips.

INTERRAIL PASS. If you have lived for at least six months in one of the European countries where InterRail Passes are valid, they prove an economical option. There are eight InterRail **zones:** A (Great Britain and the Republic of Ireland),

EURAILPASSES	15 DAYS	21 DAYS	1 MONTH	2 MONTHS	3 MONTHS
1st class Eurailpass	US$710	US$740	US$918	US$1298	US$1606
Eurail Saverpass	US$604	US$630	US$780	US$1106	US$1366
Eurail Youthpass	US$497	US$518	US$644	US$910	US$1126

EURAIL FLEXIPASSES	10 DAYS IN 2 MONTHS	15 DAYS IN 2 MONTHS
1st class Eurail Flexipass	US$674	US$888
Eurail Saver Flexipass	US$574	US$756
Eurail Youth Flexipass	US$473	US$622

SHOPPING AROUND FOR A EURAIL OR EUROPASS. Eurailpasses and Europasses are designed by the EU itself and are purchasable only by non-Europeans almost exclusively from non-European distributors. These passes must be sold at uniform prices determined by the EU. However, some travel agents tack on a US$10 handling fee, and others offer certain bonuses with purchase, so shop around. Also, keep in mind that pass prices usually go up each year, so if you're planning to travel early in the year, you can save cash by purchasing before January 1 (you have three months from the purchase date to validate your pass in Europe).

It is best to buy your Eurailpass or Europass before leaving; only a few places in major European cities sell them, and at a marked-up price. Eurailpasses are non-refundable once validated; if your pass is completely unused and invalidated and you have the original purchase documents, you can get an 85% refund from the place of purchase. You can get a replacement for a lost pass only if you have purchased insurance on it under the Pass Protection Plan (US$10). Eurailpasses are available through travel agents, student travel agencies like STA and Council (see p. 59), and **Rail Europe,** 500 Mamaroneck Ave., Harrison, NY 10528, USA (US ☎ 888-382-7245, fax 800-432-1329; Canada ☎ 800-361-7245, fax 905-602-4198; UK ☎ 08705 84 88 48; www.raileurope.com) or **DER Travel Services,** 9501 W. Devon Ave. #301, Rosemont, IL 60018, USA (US ☎ 888-337-7350; fax 800-282-7474; www.dertravel.com).

ESSENTIALS

B (Norway, Sweden, and Finland), C (Germany, Austria, Denmark, and Switzerland), D (Croatia, Czech Republic, Hungary, Poland, and Slovakia), E (France, Belgium, the Netherlands, and Luxembourg), F (Spain, Portugal, and Morocco), G (Greece, Italy, Slovenia, and Turkey, including a Greece-Italy ferry), and H (Bulgaria, Romania, Yugoslavia, and Macedonia). The **Under 26 InterRail Card** allows either 14 days or one month of unlimited travel within one, two, three, or all of the eight zones; the cost is determined by the number of zones the pass covers (UK£119-249). A card can also be purchased for 12 days of travel in one zone (119£). The **Over 26 InterRail Card** (UK£169-355) provides the same services as the Under 26 InterRail Card, as does the new **Child Pass** (ages 4-11;UK£85-178). Passholders receive **discounts** on rail travel, Eurostar journeys, and most ferries to Ireland, Scandinavia, and the rest of Europe. Most exclude **supplements** for high-speed trains. For info and ticket sales in Europe contact **Student Travel Centre,** 24 Rupert St., 1st fl., London W1V 7FN (☎ 020 7437 8101; fax 7734 3836; www.student-travel-centre.com). Tickets are also available from travel agents, at major train stations throughout Europe, or through online vendors (www.railpassdirect.co.uk).

EURO DOMINO. Like the InterRail Pass, the Euro Domino pass is available to anyone who has lived in Europe for at least six months; however, it is only valid within the country that you designate upon buying the pass, which cannot be your country of residence. The Euro Domino pass is available for first- and second-class travel for 28 European countries plus Morocco, with a special rate for those under 26. It can be used for three to eight days of unlimited travel within a one-month period, but is not valid on Eurostar or Thalys trains. Supplements for high-speed trains (e.g., French TGV, German ICE, and Swedish X2000, but not Spanish AVE) are included, though you must still pay for **reservations** where they are compulsory. The pass must be bought within your country of residence; each destination has a different price. Inquire with your national rail company for more information.

RAIL-AND-DRIVE PASSES. In addition to simple railpasses, many countries (as well as Europass and Eurail) offer rail-and-drive passes, which combine car rental with rail travel—a good option for travelers who wish both to visit cities accessible by rail and to make side trips into the surrounding areas. Rail Europe (see **Shopping Around for a Eurail or Europass,** p. 69) offers a EurailDrive Pass with four trains days and two rental days for between US$439 and US$529, depending on the car.

> **FURTHER READING: BY TRAIN.**
> *Thomas Cook European Timetable,* updated monthly, covers all major and many minor train routes in Europe. In the US, order from Forsyth Travel Library (☎ 800-367-7984; www.forsyth.com. US$27.95). In Europe, find it at any Thomas Cook Money Exchange Center. Alternatively, buy directly from Thomas Cook (www.thomascook.com).
> *Guide to European Railpasses,* Rick Steves. Online and by mail. (US ☎ 425-771- 8303; fax 425-771-0833; www.ricksteves.com.) Free; delivery $8.
> *On the Rails Around Europe: A Comprehensive Guide to Travel by Train,* Melissa Shales. Thomas Cook Ltd. US$18.95.
> *Eurail and Train Travel Guide to Europe.* Houghton Mifflin US$15.

DISCOUNTED TICKETS

For travelers under 26, **BIJ** tickets (Billets Internationaux de Jeunesse; a.k.a. **Wasteels, Eurotrain,** and **Route 26**) are an alternative to railpasses. Available for trips within Europe and most ferry services, they knock 20-40% off regular second-class fares.

Tickets, good for 60 days after purchase, allow a number of stopovers along a train route. Issued for a specific international route between two points, they must be used in the direction and order of the designated route and must be bought in Europe. The equivalent, **BIGT** tickets provide a 20-30% discount on first- and second-class international tickets for over 26 business travelers, temporary European residents, and their families. Both types of tickets are available from European travel agents, Wasteels, or Eurotrain offices (in or near train stations). For more information, contact Wasteels (see p. 59). Other branches are at: Stazione Centrale, Naples (☎ 081 20 10 71; fax 20 69 03); Stazione Centrale, Milan (☎ 02 669 0020; fax 669 0500); and Stazione Maria Novella, Florence (☎/fax 05 52 80 63).

BY BUS

Although Italian trains are popular and inexpensive, the bus networks go on strike much less frequently and are thus worth getting to know. In Italy, buses serve many points inaccessible by train and occasionally arrive in more convenient places in larger towns. All tickets must be validated using the orange machines on-board immediately upon entering the bus. Failure to do so will result in large fines, up to US$140. International bus passes are sometimes cheaper than railpasses, and they typically allow unlimited travel on a hop-on, hop-off basis between major European cities. The following networks are popular among non-US backpackers:

Eurolines, 52 Grosvenor Gardens, London SW1W 0AU (UK ☎1582 40 45 11; www.eurolines.com; **Eurolines Italy** ☎27 20 01 30; www.eurolines.it). The largest operator of Europe-wide coach services, Eurolines offers unlimited peak-season 30-day (UK£229, under 26 UK£186) or 60-day (UK£279/205) travel between 30 major European cities in 16 countries; off-season prices are lower. Euroexplorers mini-passes offer stops at select cities across Europe (UK£55 to UK£69).

Busabout, 258 Vauxhall Bridge Rd., London SW1V 1BS (UK ☎207 950 1661; fax 950 1662; www.busabout.com) covers 60 cities and towns in Europe. Consecutive-Day Passes and Flexi Passes both available. Consecutive-Day standard/student passes range from US$269/239 for 2 wk. to US$1069/959 for a season pass. Flexi Pass standard/student passes range from US$259/229 for 6 days out of 1 month to US$839/759 for 25 days out of 4 months.

BY CAR

DRIVING PERMITS AND CAR INSURANCE

INTERNATIONAL DRIVING PERMIT (IDP)

If you plan to drive a car while in Italy, you must be over 18 and ought to have an International Driving Permit (IDP), though it is not always necessary to have one in Italy. It may be a good idea to get one anyway in case you're in a situation (e.g., an accident or stranded in a small town) where the police do not know English; information on the IDP is printed in Italian, French, Spanish, Russian, German, Arabic, Scandinavian, and Portuguese. Your IDP, valid for one year, must be issued in your own country before you depart. An application for an IDP usually requires two passport photos, a valid local license, and a fee (about US$10). To apply, contact the national or local branch of your country's Automobile Association. For more information on the driving permit and driving in Italy, contact "In Italy Online," at www.initaly.com/travel/info/driving.htm. **EU citizens do not need an international driving permit; in emergencies, use your passport to prove citizenship.**

Australia: Contact your local Royal Automobile Club (RAC) or the National Royal Motorist Association (NRMA) if in NSW or the ACT (☎08 9421 4444; www.rac.com.au/travel). Permits AUS$15.

Canada: Contact a Canadian Automobile Association (CAA) branch office or write to CAA, 1145 Hunt Club Rd., #200, K1V 0Y3. (☎613-247-0117; www.caa.ca/Cernet/travelservices/internationaldocumentation/idptravel.htm). Permits CDN$13.

Ireland: Contact the nearest Automobile Association (AA) office or write to the UK address below. The Irish Automobile Association, 23 Suffolk St., Rockhill, Blackrock, Co. Dublin (☎01 677 9481; 24hr. breakdown and road service ☎800 66 77 88, toll-free in Ireland).

New Zealand: Contact your local Automobile Association (AA) or the main office at Auckland Central, 99 Albert St., Auckland City, Auckland(☎09 377 4660; www.nzaa.co.nz). Permits NZ$12.

South Africa: Contact the Travel Services Department of the Automobile Association of South Africa at P.O. Box 596, 2000 Johannesburg (☎011 799 1000; fax 799 1960; www.aasa.co.za). Permits ZAR28.50.

UK: Contact the **AA Headquarters** (☎0870 600 0371), or write to: The Automobile Association, International Documents, Fanum House, Erskine, Renfrewshire PA8 6BW. For more info, see www.theaa.co.uk/motoringandtravel/idp/index.asp. Permits UK£4.

US: Visit any American Automobile Association (AAA) office or write to AAA Florida, Travel Related Services, 1000 AAA Drive (mail stop 100), Heathrow, FL 32746 (☎407-444-7000; fax 444-7380; www.aaa.com). You don't have to be a member to buy an IDP. Permits US$10. AAA Travel Related Services (☎800-222-4357) provides road maps, travel guides, emergency road services, travel services, and auto insurance.

ESSENTIALS

CAR INSURANCE

Liability and collision insurance are generally included in rental rates (ask to make sure). Rental agencies may require you to purchase theft insurance in countries that they consider to have a high risk of auto theft. If you plan to drive in Italy for more than 45 days, you will need a regular Italian insurance policy.

CAR SAFETY

Garages are usually the safest bet for parking in the city, but be sure to check rates before agreeing to anything. Parking can be extremely expensive, up to €10 per hour in city centers. To save money, park in the outskirts and take a bus or Inter-City train in to the city center. To avoid fines for street parking, ask your rental agency to equip your car with a dashboard timer. Most already do.

! **DRIVING PRECAUTIONS.** When traveling in the summer, bring substantial amounts of water (5L of **water** per person per day) for drinking and for the radiator. For long distances, make sure tires are in good repair and have enough air. Good maps, a **compass,** and a **car manual** can also be very useful. You should always carry a **spare tire** and **jack, jumper cables, extra oil, flares,** a **torch (flashlight),** and **heavy blankets** (in case your car breaks down at night or in the winter). If you don't know how to **change a tire,** learn before heading out, especially if you are planning on traveling in deserted areas. Blowouts on dirt roads are exceedingly common. If you do have a breakdown, **stay with your car;** if you wander off, there's less likelihood that trackers will find you.

DRIVING IN ITALY

If you are using a car, learn local driving signals. There are four different kinds of roads: *Autostrade* (Superhighways; most charge tolls, 110km per hr. speed limit, U-turns prohibited), *Strade Statali* (State Roads), *Strade Provinciali* (Provincial Roads), and *Strade Comunali* (Local Roads). The Italian highway code was formed at the Geneva Convention, so Italy uses international road signs. Always drive on the right and pass on the left. Violations of highway code bring fines and imprisonment in serious cases. For more driving rules and regulations, consult "In Italy Online" at www.initaly.com/travel/info/driving.htm.

The **Automobile Club Italiano (ACI)** is ready and willing to come to your aid with offices located throughout Italy. The main office is at V. Marsala 8, 00185 Rome (☎ 06 49 981; fax 499 8234). In case of **breakdown** on any Italian road, dial ☎ 116 at the nearest telephone. On superhighways, use the emergency telephones placed every two kilometers. For long drives in desolate areas, invest in a cellular phone and a roadside assistance program.

RENTING A CAR

You can rent a car from a US-based firm (Alamo, Avis, Budget, or Hertz) with European offices, from a European-based company with local representatives (Europcar), or from a tour operator (Auto Europe, Europe By Car, and Kemwel Holiday Autos) that will arrange a rental for you from a European company at its own rates. Multinationals offer greater flexibility, but tour operators often strike better deals. Expect to pay €50 per day for a teensy car. Due to large-scale wholesale contracts, it is generally cheaper to reserve a car from the US than from Europe. Some credit card companies cover the deductible on collision insurance, allowing their customers to decline the collision damage waiver.

Ask airlines about special fly-and-drive packages; you may get up to a week of free or discounted rental. Minimum age in Italy for car rental is usually 21, but can be as low as 18. At most agencies, all that's needed to rent a car is a license from home and proof that you've had it for a year.

Auto Europe, 39 Commercial St., P.O. Box 7006, Portland, ME 04112, USA (US and Canada ☎888-223-5555 or 207-842-2000; www.autoeurope.com).

Avis (US and Canada ☎800-230-4898; UK ☎0870 606 0100; Australia ☎800 13 63 33; New Zealand ☎6495 26 28 47; www.avis.com).

Budget (US ☎800-527-0700; elsewhere call US ☎800-472-3325; www.budget.com).

Europe by Car, One Rockefeller Plaza, New York, NY 10020, USA (US ☎800-223-1516 or 212-581-3040; fax 246-1458; www.europebycar.com).

Europcar, 145 av. Malekoff, 75016 Paris (France ☎03 31 30 44 90 00; US ☎877-506-0070; www.europcar.com).

Hertz (US ☎800-654-3131; Canada ☎800-263-0600; UK ☎870 844 8844; Australia ☎613 9698 2555; www.hertz.com).

BY FERRY

The islands of Sicily, Sardinia, and Corsica, as well as the smaller islands along the coasts, are connected to the mainland by ferries *(traghetti)* and hydrofoils *(aliscafi)*; international trips are generally made by ferries only. See www.traghetti.com for detailed listings of companies. Italy's largest private ferry service, **Tirrenia** (www.gruppotirrenia.it), runs ferries to Sardinia, Sicily, and Tunisia. Other major ferry companies (**Moby Lines, Grandi Navi, Tiremar, Saremar, Siremar,** and **Caremar**) and the **SNAV** (www.snavali.com) hydrofoil services travel to major ports such as Ancona, Bari, Brindisi, Genoa, Livorno, La Spezia, Naples, and Trapani. Ferry services also depart for the Tremiti, Pontine, and Lipari (Aeolian) Islands. Ferries from Italy's ports of Bari and Brindisi travel to Greece and Turkey (although you can only get a ferry to Corfu from Brindisi); ferries from Ancona go to Greece and Croatia. International ferry crossings leaving from Brindisi are generally covered by railpasses (p. 589).

For major trips reserve ferry tickets at least one week in advance. Ferry schedules change unpredictably—confirm your departure one day in advance. Some ports require that you check-in two hours before the departure or your reservation will be cancelled. **Posta ponte** (deck class; preferable in warm weather) is cheapest. It is, however, often only available when the **poltrone** (reclining cabin seats) are full. Port taxes often apply. Ask for student and Eurail discounts; some unscrupulous travelers have been known to ask locals to buy them heavily discounted resident tickets.

ADDITIONAL INFORMATION

SPECIFIC CONCERNS

WOMEN TRAVELERS

Women exploring on their own inevitably face some additional safety concerns, but it's easy to be adventurous without taking undue risks. The Italian art of *machismo* is well cultivated, and almost all foreign women will be hit on. In cities, you may be harassed no matter how you're dressed. Your best answer to verbal harassment is no answer at all; feigning deafness or the inability to speak either English or Italian, sitting motionless, and staring straight ahead at nothing in particular will do a world of good. The extremely persistent can sometimes be dissuaded by a firm *"Vai Via!"* (Go away!), *"Sono fidanzata"* (I'm engaged), or *"Ho un ragazzo. Italiano. Molto geloso."* (I have a boyfriend. Italian. Very jealous.) Wearing a conspicuous **wedding band** may also help prevent unwanted overtures. Some travelers report that carrying pictures of a "husband" or "children" is extremely useful to help document marriage status. Dress conservatively. "Modest dress" usually constitutes a long skirt (at least several inches past the knee) and a shirt with sleeves and a high neckline. Absolutely no bare shoulders or midriffs are allowed in most cathedrals or churches.

If you are concerned about hostel safety, you might consider staying in hostels that offer single rooms that lock from the inside or in religious organizations that offer women-only rooms. Communal showers in some hostels are safer than others; check before settling in. Avoid solitary late-night treks or metro rides. When traveling, always carry extra money for a phone call or taxi. **Hitchhiking** is never safe for lone women, or even for women traveling together.

All travelers to Italy should, however, be aware that conceptions of personal space is different from what they're probably used to. The guy crowded next to you on the bus or the woman gesticulating wildly in your face is not necessarily threatening you; it is acceptable and normal to stand close to the person you're addressing, to gesture forcefully, and to shout. Don't hesitate, however, to seek out a police officer or a passerby if you are being harassed. *Let's Go: Italy* lists emergency numbers in the Practical Information listings of most cities. An **IMPACT Model Mugging** self-defense course will not only prepare you for a potential attack, but will also raise your level of awareness of your surroundings as well as your confidence (see **Self Defense,** p. 43).

> **FURTHER READING: WOMEN TRAVELERS.**
> *A Journey of One's Own: Uncommon Advice for the Independent Woman Traveler,* Thalia Zepatos. Eighth Mountain Press (US$16.95).
> *Adventures in Good Company: The Complete Guide to Women's Tours and Outdoor Trips,* Thalia Zepatos. Eighth Mountain Press (US$8).
> *Active Women Vacation Guide,* Evelyn Kaye. Blue Panda Publications (US$18).

TRAVELING ALONE

As a lone traveler, you may find that Italians are more inclined to help you. On the other hand, any solo traveler is a more vulnerable target of harassment and street theft. Lone travelers need to be well organized and look confident at all times. Never admit that you are traveling alone. Maintain regular contact with someone at home who knows your itinerary. For more tips, pick up *Traveling Solo* by Eleanor Berman (Globe Pequot, US$17) or subscribe to **Connecting: Solo Travel Network,** 689 Park Road, Unit 6, Gibsons, British Columbia, V0N IV7 Canada (☎604-886-9009; fax 626-608-2139; www.cstn.org; membership US$35). **Travel Companion Exchange,** P.O. Box 833, Amityville, NY 11701, USA (☎631-454-0880 or in the U.S. 800-392-1256; www.whytravelalone.com; US$48), will link solo travelers with companions with similar travel habits and interests.

TRAVELING BY THUMB

Let's Go strongly urges you to consider the risks before you choose to hitchhike. We do not recommend hitchhiking as a safe means of transportation.

OLDER TRAVELERS

Senior citizens are eligible for a wide range of discounts on transportation, museums, movies, theaters, concerts, restaurants, and accommodations. If you don't see a senior citizen price listed, ask, and you may be delightfully surprised. The books *No Problem! Worldwise Tips for Mature Adventurers*, by Janice Kenyon (Orca Book Publishers; US$16) and *Unbelievably Good Deals and Great Adventures That You Absolutely Can't Get Unless You're Over 50*, by Joan Rattner Heilman (NTC/Contemporary Publishing; US$13) are both excellent resources. Generally, senior citizens in the mother country are treated with respect. They are often entitled to discounts. For the eternally young of heart, there are many senior travel groups to help you on your road to adventure.

ElderTreks, 597 Markham St., Toronto, ON M6G 2L7 Canada (☎800-741-7956; www.eldertreks.com). Adventure travel programs for 50+ travelers in Italy.

Elderhostel, 11 Ave. de Lafayette, Boston, MA 02111, USA (☎877-426-8056; www.elderhostel.org). Organizes 1- to 4-wk. "educational adventures" in Europe on varied subjects for those 55+.

The Mature Traveler, P.O. Box 15791, Sacramento, CA 95852, USA (☎800-460-6676). Discounts and travel packages for 50+ travelers. Subscription $30.

Walking the World, P.O. Box 1186, Fort Collins, CO 80522, USA (☎800-340-9255; www.walkingtheworld.com), organizes trips for 50+ travelers to Europe.

BISEXUAL, GAY, AND LESBIAN TRAVELERS

Italians are notoriously homophobic, a reputation rightly earned in many respects. The Vatican perennially opposes the gay pride parade in Rome. In 2000, The Vatican was joined by a majority of Italians who felt that WorldPride 2000 should not coincide with Jubilee 2000. Many, regardless of their disposition toward homosexuality, opposed the provocative invitations depicting a naked man and inviting participants to "Come in Rome." Nonetheless, Titti De Simone, a member of the Communist Refoundation Party, became the first out lesbian in Parliament when she was elected in March 2001. Her platform included extending equal rights to same sex couples and gay parents under common law. The resurgence of the Catholic rightist parties, heralded by the June 2001 election of conservative media magnate **Silvio Berlusconi,** may be a setback for the progress of gay rights in Italy.

Rome, Florence, Milan, and Bologna all have easily accessible gay scenes. Away from the larger cities, however, same-sex relationships may be less open, and gay social life may be difficult to find. Moreover, in smaller towns in the South, explicit public displays of affection will evoke shock.

The monthly *Babilonia* and annual *Guida Gay Italia*, the national homosexual magazines, are at most newsstands. The magazines, along with confronting gay issues, also list social events. Expect the larger cities to have gay *discoteche* and bars (listed in *Let's Go* where they exist). The **Italian Gay and Lesbian Yellow Pages** (www.gay.it/guida/italia/info.htm) lists gay bars, hotels, and shops. **Out and About** (www.outandabout.com) is a gay-oriented site with helpful travel links.

ARCI-GAY and ARCI-Lesbica, P. di Porta Saragozza, 2, 40123 Bologna (☎051 644 7054; www.malox.com/arcigay/link.htm), and V. Orvinio, 2, 00199 Roma (☎06 8638 5112); or V. dei Mille, 23, Roma (☎06 446 58 39). The national organizations for homosexuals holds group discussions, dances, and many special events. Their web site contains addresses and phone numbers of many city centers.

Gay's the Word, 66 Marchmont St., London WC1N 1AB, UK (☎44 20 7278 7654; www.gaystheword.co.uk). The largest gay and lesbian book shop in the UK, with both fiction and non-fiction titles. Mail-order service available.

ESSENTIALS

International Gay and Lesbian Travel Association, 4331 N. Federal Hwy., #304, Fort Lauderdale, FL 33308, USA (☎954-776-2626; fax 776-3303; www.iglta.com). An organization of over 1350 companies serving gay and lesbian travelers worldwide.

 FURTHER READING: BISEXUAL, GAY, & LESBIAN.
Spartacus International Gay Guide 2001-2002. Bruno Gmunder Verlag (US$33).
Damron Men's Guide, Damron's Accommodations, and *The Women's Traveller.* Damron Travel Guides (US$14-19). For more info, call ☎800-462-6654 or visit www.damron.com.
Ferrari Guides' Gay Travel A to Z, Ferrari Guides' Men's Travel in Your Pocket, and *Ferrari Guides' Inn Places.* Ferrari Publications (US$16-20). Purchase the guides online at www.ferrariguides.com.

TRAVELERS WITH DISABILITIES

Those with disabilities should inform airlines and hotels when making arrangements for travel; some time may be needed to prepare special accommodations. Few Italian hotels and hostels have adapted rooms. Call ahead to restaurants, hotels, and other facilities to find out about the existence of ramps, the widths of doors, the dimensions of elevators, etc. Many of the museums and famed landmarks are inaccessible. Venice is especially difficult to navigate.

Rail is probably the most convenient form of travel for disabled travelers in Europe: many stations have ramps, and some trains have wheelchair lifts, special seating areas, and specially equipped toilets. In general, Italy's Pendolino and many Eurostar and InterCity trains are wheelchair-accessible. For those who wish to rent cars, some major **car rental** agencies (Hertz, Avis, and National) offer hand-controlled vehicles.

Guide dog owners should inquire as to the specific quarantine policies of each destination country. At the very least, they will need to provide a certificate of immunization against rabies. In the wake of Foot and Mouth Disease, travelers from Great Britain and Ireland may still meet resistance if attempting to bring a guide animal into Italy and most other European countries.

USEFUL ORGANIZATIONS

Accessible Italy, with 2 main offices in Italy: **Promotur-Mondo Possibile,** P. Pitagora 9, 10137 Turin (☎011 309 6363; fax 309 1201); and **La Viaggeria,** V. Lemonia 161, 00174 Roma (☎06 7158 2945; fax 7158 3433). A travel agency for the disabled and aged, Accessible Italy is a member of SATH (see below) and more than ready to help out in any way possible. See www.tour-web.com/accitaly for more info.

Mobility International USA (MIUSA), P.O. Box 10767, Eugene, OR 97440, USA (☎541-343-1284 voice and TDD; fax 343-6812; www.miusa.org). Sells *A World of Options: A Guide to International Educational Exchange, Community Service, and Travel for Persons with Disabilities* (US$35).

Moss Rehab Hospital Travel Information Service, 1200 West Tabor Rd., Philadelphia, PA 19141-3099, USA (www.mossresourcenet.org). An information resource center on travel-related concerns for those with disabilities.

Society for the Accessible Travel & Hospitality (SATH), 347 Fifth Ave., #610, New York, NY 10016, USA (☎212-447-7284; www.sath.org). Publishes *Open World* (free for members, US$13 for nonmembers). Also publishes a wide range of info sheets on disability travel facilitation and destinations. Annual membership US$45, students and seniors US$30. Order a free copy of *Open World* online.

TOUR AGENCIES

Contiki Holidays (888-CONTIKI; www.contiki.com) offers a variety of European vacation packages designed for 18- to 35-year-olds. For an average cost of $60 per day, tours include accommodations, transportation, guided sightseeing and some meals.

Directions Unlimited, 720 N. Bedford, Bedford Hills, NY 10507, USA (☎ 800-533-5343; www.travel-cruises.com). Specializes in arranging individual and group vacations, tours, and cruises for the physically disabled.

The Guided Tour Inc., 7900 Old York Rd., #114B, Elkins Park, PA 19027, USA (☎800-783-5841 or 215-782-1370; fax 215-635-2637; www.guidedtour.com). Rome travel programs for persons with physical and mental challenges.

FURTHER READING: DISABLED TRAVELERS.
Resource Directory for the Disabled, Richard Neil Shrout. Facts on file (US$45).
Wheelchair Through Europe, Annie Mackin. Graphic Language Press (US ☎ 760-944-9594; niteowl@cts.com; US$13).

MINORITY TRAVELERS

In certain regions, particularly in the South, tourists of color or members of non-Christian religious groups may feel unwelcome. If you encounter discriminatory treatment, please let us know so that we can research the establishment and, if appropriate, warn other travelers. **Jewish tourists** may appreciate the *Italy Jewish Travel Guide* (US$15) from Israelowitz Publishing, P.O. Box 228, Brooklyn, NY 11229, USA, which provides information on sites of religious interest.

In terms of safety, there are no easy answers. Women of color may be seen as exotic but not unwelcome. Travel in groups and take a taxi whenever uncomfortable. The best answer to verbal harassment is often no answer at all.

TRAVELERS WITH CHILDREN

Family vacations often require that you slow your pace, and always require that you plan ahead. If you rent a car, make sure the rental company provides a car seat for younger children. **Be sure that your child carries some sort of ID** in case of an emergency or in case he or she gets lost. Museums, tourist attractions, accommodations, and restaurants often offer discounts for children. Children under two generally fly for 10% of the adult airfare on international flights (this does not necessarily include a seat). International fares are usually discounted 25% for children from two to 11. For more information, consult one of the following books:

Backpacking with Babies and Small Children, Goldie Silverman. Wilderness Press (US$10).

Take Your Kids to Europe, Cynthia W. Harriman. Cardogan Books (US$18).

How to take Great Trips with Your Kids, Sanford and Jane Portnoy. Harvard Common Press (US $10).

Have Kid, Will Travel: 101 Survival Strategies for Vacationing With Babies and Young Children, Claire and Lucille Tristram. Andrews McMeel Publishing (US$9). *Adventuring with Children: An Inspirational Guide to World Travel and the Outdoors,* Nan Jeffrey. Avalon House Publishing (US$15).

Trouble Free Travel with Children, Vicki Lansky. Book Peddlers (US$9).

DIETARY CONCERNS

While there are only a few specifically vegetarian restaurants sprinkled throughout Italy, it is not hard to find vegetarian meals. The Italian diet is not centered around meat; pasta and vegetables are plentiful. For veggie-based eateries around the country, check out the web site of **World Guide to Vegetarianism,** www.old.veg.org/Guide/Italy/index.htm, or that of the **A.V.I. Italian Vegetarian Association,** www.vegetariani.it/vegetarismo/ristoranti.htm. **The North American Vegetarian Society,** P.O. Box 72, Dolgeville, NY 13329, USA (☎518-568-7970; www.navsonline.org), publishes information about vegetarian travel, including *Transformative Adventures, a Guide to Vacations and Retreats* (US$15), and *The Vegetarian Journal's Guide to Natural Food Restaurants in the US and Canada* (US$12). For more information, visit your local bookstore, health food store, or library, and consult *The Vegetarian Traveler: Where to Stay if You're Vegetarian Vegan, Environmentally Sensitive,* by Jed and Susan Civic (Larson Publications; US$16).

Travelers who keep kosher should contact synagogues in larger cities for information on kosher restaurants. Your own synagogue or college Hillel should have access to lists of Jewish institutions across the nation. If you are strict in your observance, you may have to prepare your own food on the road. A good resource is the *Jewish Travel Guide,* by Michael Zaidner (Vallentine Mitchell; US$17).

OTHER RESOURCES

TRAVEL PUBLISHERS & BOOKSTORES

Hippocrene Books, Inc., 171 Madison Ave., New York, NY 10016, USA (☎718-454-2366; www.hippocrenebooks.com). Publishes foreign language dictionaries and language learning guides.

Hunter Publishing, 470 W. Broadway, fl. 2, South Boston, MA 02127, USA (☎617-269-0700; www.hunterpublishing.com). Has an extensive catalog of travel guides and diving and adventure travel books.

Rand McNally, P.O. Box 7600, Chicago, IL 60680, USA (☎847-329-8100; www.randmcnally.com). Publishes road atlases.

Adventurous Traveler Bookstore, P.O. Box 2221, Williston, VT 05495, USA (☎800-282-3963; www.adventuroustraveler.com).

Bon Voyage!, 2069 W. Bullard Ave., Fresno, CA 93711, USA (☎800-995-9716, from abroad 559-447-8441; www.bon-voyage-travel.com). They specialize in Europe but have titles pertaining to other regions as well. Free newsletter.

Travel Books & Language Center, Inc., 4437 Wisconsin Ave. NW, Washington, D.C. 20016, USA (☎800-220-2665; www.bookweb.org/bookstore/travelbks/). Over 60,000 titles from around the world.

WORLD WIDE WEB

Almost every aspect of budget travel is accessible via the web. With 10min. at a keyboard, you can make hostel reservations, get advice on travel hotspots, or find out exactly how much that train from Naples to Palermo costs. These are some budget travel sites to start you off; other relevant web sites are listed throughout the book.

OUR PERSONAL FAVORITE

Let's Go: www.letsgo.com. Our recently revamped web site features photos and streaming video, info about our books, a travel forum buzzing with stories and tips, and links that will help you find everything you could ever want to know about Italy. Be sure to check out our new *First Timer's Guide to Europe,* which features suggested itineraries, general info about Europe and individual European countries, and a section on travel documents and formalities.

THE ART OF BUDGET TRAVEL

How to See the World: www.artoftravel.com. A compendium of great travel tips, from cheap flights to self-defense to interacting with local culture.

Rec. Travel Library: www.travel-library.com. A fantastic set of links for general info and personal travelogues.

Lycos: http://travel.lycos.coom. General introductions to cities and regions throughout Italy, accompanied by links to applicable histories, news, and local tourism sites.

Backpacker's Ultimate Guide: www.bugeurope.com. Tips on packing, transportation, and where to go. Also tons of country-specific travel information.

INFORMATION ON ITALY

CIA World Factbook: www.odci.gov/cia/publications/factbook/index.html. Tons of vital statistics about Italy: geography, government, economy, and people.

Foreign Language for Travelers: www.travlang.com. Provides free online translating dictionaries and lists of phrases in Italian, as well as language courses at cost. **www.systransoft.com** is another translating web site.

MyTravelGuide: www.mytravelguide.com. Country overviews, with everything from history to transportation to live web cam coverage of Italy.

Geographia: www.geographia.com. Describes the highlights, culture, and people of Italy.

Atevo Travel: www.atevo.com/guides/destinations. Detailed introductions, travel tips, and suggested itineraries.

TravelPage: www.travelpage.com. Links to official tourist office sites throughout Italy.

ALTERNATIVES TO TOURISM

If you're looking for a rewarding and interactive travel experience, consider alternatives to tourism. Working, volunteering, or studying abroad can be a meaningful and educational adventure, one that the average traveler often misses.

STUDYING ABROAD

Study abroad programs range from basic language and culture courses to college-level classes for credit. Italy's popularity among study abroad students means you'll have many programs from which to choose. Programs vary greatly in expense, quality of academic program and living arrangements, and degree of exposure to local culture. Most are sponsored by American universities.

Those who speak Italian well can enroll directly in a university abroad. Direct enrollment is a less expensive option, although getting college credit at a home institution may be more difficult. Some American schools require students to pay them for credits they obtain elsewhere. University-level study-abroad programs are usually conducted in Italian, but most offer classes in English and multilevel language courses. A good resource for finding programs is **www.studyabroad.com.**

To choose a program that best fits your needs, you'll want to find out what kind of students participate in the program and what sort of accommodations are provided. You may feel more comfortable in programs that have large groups of students who speak English, but you won't have the same opportunity to practice Italian or to befriend the locals. For accommodations, dorm life provides a better opportunity to mingle with international students, though you're less likely to be immersed in the local culture. A homestay is conducive to lifelong friendships with natives and experiencing day-to-day Italian life.

PRE-DEPARTURE: DO YOUR HOMEWORK

EU citizens do not need to have a visa to study in Italy. Non-EU citizens wishing to study in Italy must obtain a student visa at least one week prior to departure from their nearest Italian embassy or consulate. As of August 2002, the visa fee for US citizens was US$28, payable in money order or cash only, for Australian citizens AUS$52, and for New Zealand citizens NZ$60. Upon arrival in Italy, students must register with the Foreigners' Bureau *(Ufficio degli Stranieri)* of the local *questura* in order to receive the *permesso di soggiorno per studio* (permit of stay). To obtain both the visa prior to departure and the permit of stay once in Italy, you will need to provide your passport, proof of enrollment from your home institution and/or the school or university in Italy, documentation of financial wherewithal, and proof of medical insurance for the duration of your stay in Italy. Americans may require a statement that they will purchase an additional Italian health insurance policy in Italy as a supplement to their domestic insurance.

Unless otherwise noted, the following programs are for college undergraduates, although many organizations also sponsor programs for graduate students. Prices listed generally include tuition, housing, and school-sponsored field trips, but do not include food, airfare, or books except where noted. Estimated credit hours vary on the basis of each college's academic policies. All prices are in US dollars, unless otherwise noted.

> **VISA INFORMATION.** Italy will throw loads of confusing paperwork at you before allowing you to stay. Unfortunately, Italian bureaucracy is not quite as well-oiled as one would wish. Many of the organizations listed throughout this chapter can provide advice on how to minimize red tape.
>
> **Long Term Visa:** All non-EU citizens are required to obtain a visa for any stay longer than 3 months, even if they are tourists. For information and applications, contact the Italian embassy or consulate in your country.
>
> **Permit to Stay:** All non-EU citizens are also required to obtain a *permesso di soggiorno* (permit of stay) within 8 days of arriving in Italy. If you are staying in a hotel or hostel, this requirement is generally waived, but otherwise, you must apply at a police station or the foreigner's office in main police stations. EU citizens must apply for a *permesso di soggiorno* within 3 months.
>
> **Residency:** Once you find a place to live, bring your permit to stay (it must have at least one year's validity) to a records office *(circoscrizione).* This certificate, which confirms your registered address, will expedite such procedures as clearing goods from abroad through customs and making large purchases.

AMERICAN PROGRAMS IN ITALY

John Cabot University, V. della Lungara, 233, 00165 Rome (☎39 06 681 9121; fax 683 2088; www.johncabot.edu). Offers a 4-year Bachelor of Arts degree and semester and summer courses. Tuition from $5500 per semester.

American University of Rome, V. Pietro Roselli, 4, 00153 Rome (☎39 06 5833 0919; fax 5833 0992; www.aur.edu). Offers courses in English on international business, international relations, and Italian civilization and culture. $4911 per semester; $2830 for housing.

American Institute for Foreign Study: Richmond in Florence/Rome, College Division, River Plaza, 9 W. Broad St., Stamford, CT 06902, USA (☎800-727-2437, ext. 5163; www.aifsabroad.com). Programs in Florence and Rome. Meals and homestay or student apartment included. 9-13 credits per semester. Semester $11,495; year $21,415.

Arcadia University for Education Abroad, 450 S. Easton Rd., Glenside, PA 19038, USA (☎866-927-2234; www.arcadia.edu/cea). *Accademia Italiana* in Florence: summer, 3 credits $2750; semester, 15 credits $9290; full academic year $15,990. Umbra Institute in Perugia: summer $3200; semester, 15-16 credits $9975; full academic year $17,995. Includes health insurance.

Art School in Florence, Studio Art Centers International, c/o Institute of International Education, 809 United Nations Plaza, New York, NY 10017-3580, USA (☎212-984-5548; fax 984-5325; www.saci-florence.org). Associated with Bowling Green State University. Humanities and studio arts courses. Apartment housing. Summer, 6 credits $4500; semester, 15 credits $9600.

Boston University International Programs, 232 Bay State Rd., 5th fl., Boston, MA 02215, USA (☎617-353-9888; fax 353-5402; www.bu.edu/abroad). Padua language program, 16 credits. Venice Studio Arts Program (www.scuolagrafica.it), up to 18 credits. Summer $5500; semester, airfare and stipend $18,010.

CET Academic Programs: History of Art Program in Siena, 1920 N St. NW, Ste. 200, Washington, D.C. 20036, USA (☎800-225-4262; www.cetacademicprograms.com). Classes taught in English. Medical insurance included. Summer $5690; semester $11,990.

Duke University: The Intercollegiate Center for Classical Studies in Rome, Office of Study Abroad, 2016 Campus Dr., Box 90057, Durham, NC 27708-0057, USA (www.aas.duke.edu/study_abroad/iccs/iccs.html). Located on the Gianiculum, the center houses 36 students. Semester, 16-20 credit hours and board $14,190.

Middlebury College: The Italian School in Italy, Middlebury, VT 05753, USA. (Undergraduate program: ☎802-443-5745; www.middlebury.edu/~msa, Graduate program: ☎802-443-5510; www.middlebury.edu/~ls.) Programs in Florence and Ferrara. School housed in Palazzo Giugni in old Florence. Students find own housing. Arranges internship opportunities. Year, 15-16 credits per semester $12,540.

New York University in Florence, NYU Study Abroad, 7 E. 12th St., 6th fl., New York, NY 10003, USA (☎212-998-4433; www.nyu.edu/studyabroad). Students may stay in apartments in Florence proper or in villas at the academic center La Pietra, a 57-acre Tuscan estate. Students provide own health and travel insurance. Semester $16,190-$17,090, depending on lodgings.

School for International Training, Experiment in International Living, Admissions, Kipling Rd., P.O. Box 676, Brattleboro, VT 05302, USA (☎800-345-2929; fax 802-258-3428; www.usexperiment.org). 3- to 5-wk. summer programs offer high school students cross-cultural homestays and language training in Tuscany and other parts of Italy. Late June-early Aug. $4600.

Trinity College: Rome Campus, Office of International Programs, Goodwin Lounge, 300 Summit St., Hartford, CT 06106, USA (☎860-297-2005; fax 297-5218; www.trincoll.edu/depts/rome). Located on the Aventine, close to Ancient City. Dormitory-style housing. Health insurance, meals, and weekend trips included in tuition. Summer $4750; semester $15,750.

ENROLLMENT IN ITALIAN UNIVERSITIES

Brown University: Study Abroad in Bologna, Office of International Programs, Brown University, Box 1973, RI 02912, USA (☎401-863-3555; fax 863-3311; www.brown.edu/Administration/OIP). Year-long program in which students take classes at the University of Bologna & *Accademia delle Belle Arti.* 4 full-year university classes required. Apartments with Italian students. Semester $13,900; year $27,000.

Institute for the International Education of Students: Study Abroad Italy, 33 N. LaSalle St., 15th fl., Chicago, IL 60602-2602, USA (☎800-995-2300; www.IESabroad.org). Milan-based program provides 15-19 credit hours (with option to take 1-2 courses at a local Italian university), housing (apartments with Italian students as well as homestays), and a cell phone. Semester $10,500.

Study Abroad Italy, 7151 Wilton Ave., Ste. 202, Sebastopol, CA 95472, USA (☎707-824-0198; fax 824-0198; www.studyabroad-italy.com). Arranges enrollment in schools in Florence, Sicily, and Perugia, as well as travel, student visas, housing, and academic advising. Semester $8000-10,000.

LANGUAGE SCHOOLS

Unlike American universities, language schools are frequently independently-run organizations or divisions of foreign universities that rarely offer college credit. They're a good alternative to university study if you want to take intensive Italian or have a less rigorous courseload, and they generally cost less.

Centro Fiorenza, V. S. Spirito, 14, 50125 Florence (☎39 055 239 8274; fax 28 71 48; www.centrofiorenza.com). Accommodations are homestays or student apartments (€16-67 per day). Also offers courses (with hotel accommodations) on the island of Elba, although these are considerably more expensive. 2- to 4-wk. courses, 20 lessons per wk., start at €270. €52 enrollment fee.

Eurocentres, 101 N. Union St., Ste. 300, Alexandria, VA 22314, USA (☎703-684-1494; www.eurocentres.com) or in Europe, Head Office, Seestr. 247, CH-8038 Zurich, Switzerland (☎411 485 5040; fax 481 6124). Center in Florence. Language programs for beginning to advanced students from €310 for 2 wk. (40-50min. lessons) basic language instruction. €75 enrollment fee. Housing arrangements additional (homestay half-board €200 per wk.).

ALTERNATIVES TO TOURISM

Istituto Zambler Venezia, Dorsoduro, 3116A, Campo S. Margherita, Venice (☎39 041 522 4331; fax 528 5628; www.istitutovenezia.com). 1- to 12-wk. language courses based in a 16th-century *palazzo* in the heart of Venice. €160-1240.

Italiaidea, P. della Cancelleria, 85, Rome (☎39 06 6830 7620; www.italiaidea.com). Italian language and culture courses, from €450. 4-wk. program, 60 total hr.

Koinè, V. de Pandolfini, 27, I-50122 Florence (☎39 055 21 38 81; fax 21 69 49; www.koinecenter.com). Language lessons (group and individual intensive), cultural lessons, wine tastings, and cooking lessons. Courses offered year-round in Florence, Lucca, and Bologna, summer programs in Cortona and Orbetello. Rates from €195 per wk. of 20 hr. group language lessons. Housing additional per wk.: €145 per person (single in a private home) to €372 (in a hotel).

Language Immersion Institute, 75 South Manheim Blvd., SUNY-New Paltz, New Paltz, NY 12561-2499, USA (☎845-257-3500; www.newpaltz.edu/lii). Instruction through the Scuola Leonardo da Vinci (www.scuolaleonardo.com) in Florence, Rome, and Siena; Viareggio and Portico in the summer. 2-wk. language courses from $475 (30 lessons per wk.); 2-wk. home-stay with half-board from $425 additional.

WORKING

Some travelers want long-term jobs that allow them to get to know another part of the world in depth (e.g. teaching English or working in the tourist industry). Others seek out short-term jobs to finance their travel. They usually work in the service sector or in agriculture, working for a few weeks at a time to finance the next leg of their journey. Foreigners should try securing harvest, restaurant, bar, and household work in the tourism industry, which need English speakers. **Enjoy Rome** (☎06 445 1843; www.enjoyrome.com) often has tourism employment.

VISAS FOR WORKING. EU passport holders do not require a visa to work in Italy. They must have a workers registration book *(libretto di lavoro)*, available at no extra cost upon presentation of the *permesso di soggiorno*. If your parents were born in an EU country, you may be able to claim dual citizenship, or at least the right to a work permit. Non-EU citizens seeking work in Italy must apply for an Italian work permit *(Autorizzazione al lavoro in Italia)* before entering the country. Permits are authorized by the Provincial Employment Office and approved by the *questura* before being forwarded to the employer and then the prospective employee. The prospective employee must then present the document, along with a valid passport, in order to obtain a work visa. Normally a three-month tourist permit is granted, and upon presentation of an employer's letter the permit can be extended for a period specified by the employment contract. In some sectors (like agricultural work), permit-less workers are rarely bothered by authorities.

American Chamber of Commerce in Italy, V. Cantù, 1, 20123, Milan (☎39 02 869 0661; fax 05 77 37; www.amcham.it). Lists employment opportunities and allows job seekers to post resumes. Membership (US$400 for non-residents) gives access to networking, trade fairs, economics information, and professional discounts.

Italian Chambers of Commerce Abroad (www.italchambers.net). Australia: Adelaide, Brisbane, Melbourne, Perth, Sydney. Canada: Toronto, Winnipeg, Vancouver. UK: London. US: Chicago, Houston, Los Angeles, and New York.

Recruitaly (www.recruitality.it). Directory of Italian corporations seeking to employ foreign college graduates. Useful information about labor laws and documentation.

LONG-TERM WORK

If you're planning on spending a substantial amount of time (more than three months) working in Italy, search for a job well in advance. International placement agencies are often the easiest way to go, especially for teaching English. **Internships,** usually for college students, are a good way to segue into working abroad, although they are often unpaid or poorly paid (many say the experience is well worth it). Note that many intern placement services charge fees. If you speak Italian, job web sites like **www.jobonline.it** and **www.manpower.it** may be useful. Many positions may be difficult for non-Italian or non-EU citizens to obtain.

American Institute for Foreign Study, River Plaza, 9 West Broad St., Stamford, CT 06902, USA (☎800-727-2437; www.aifs.org/college/InternAbroad/Italy.htm). Offers social science and business administration internships for credit in Florence, taken concurrently with an Italian language class and 1 other course. Business internship is part-time at a local company, with an application and interview process; working knowledge of Italian required. Social Science internship involves volunteering in elementary education or healthcare, or assisting the elderly or handicapped.

Center for Cultural Interchange, 17 N. Second Ave., St. Charles, IL 60174, USA (www.cci-exchange.com/intern.htm). Volunteer internships in Florence in General Business, Accounting/Finance, Travel/Tourism, or Social Services. At least 2 years of college-level study in Italian required. 3 wk. $1596; 4 wk. $1870.

Institute for the International Education of Students. 33 N. LaSalle St., 15th fl., Chicago, IL 60602, USA (☎800-995-2300; fax 312-944-1448; www.iesabroad.org). Intern placements in Milan, based on availability, background, skills and language ability. Must be for academic credit.

Intern Abroad, 8 E. 1st Ave., Ste. 102, Denver, CO 80203, USA (☎720-570-1703; fax 720-570-1702; www.internabroad.com). Internship listings for Rome and Florence. Search by country or type of job.

TEACHING ENGLISH

Teaching jobs abroad are rarely well-paid, although some elite private American schools can pay somewhat competitive salaries. Volunteering as a teacher is also a popular option. In almost all cases, you must have at least a bachelor's degree to be a full-fledged teacher, though college students can often get summer positions.

Italy abounds with English-language schools, but the supply of applicants is plentiful, and positions are competitive. Finding a teaching job is even harder for non-EU citizens, as some schools prefer or, in some cases, require EU citizenship. Nearly all schools in Italy require teachers to have a **Teaching English as a Foreign Language (TEFL)** certificate. Many, such as **International House in Rome** (www.ihro-mamz.it), also offer intensive and semi-intensive courses that provide teaching certification. Also consider advertising **English conversation** by the hour in a university town. You may be able to build a clientele from Italian students who are required to take English and are eager to practice with a native speaker.

Generally, the best option for finding a formal position is to contact a school directly; consult the **Italian Yellow Pages** (www.paginegialle.it) for listings. The **Associazione Italiana Scuole di Lingue,** V. S. Rocchetto, 3, 37121, Verona (www.eaquals.org/aisli/aisli.htm), is an organization of more elite English-language schools. Consult their list of member schools to make contacts.

International Schools Services, Educational Staffing Program, P.O. Box 5910, Princeton, NJ 08543 (☎609-452-0990; www.iss.edu). Recruits teachers and administrators for American and English schools in Italy. Bachelor's degree and 2 years of relevant experience required. Nonrefundable US$50 application fee. US$100 for establishing a profile on their web site. Publishes *The ISS Directory of Overseas Schools.*

Office of Overseas Schools, US Department of State, Room H328, SA-1, Washington, D.C. 20522, USA (☎202-261-8200; www.state.gov/www/about_state/schools/). Comprehensive list of schools abroad and teaching abroad agencies.

The schools listed below employ native English speakers. Smaller companies list in the Yellow Pages and in local Italian newspapers.

Wall Street Insititute, V. Maniago 2, Udine (☎39 0432 48 14 64; www.wsi.it).

British Institutes, Sede Centrale Milano, Cadorna (☎39 0243 90 041 or 480 11 149; www.britishinstitutes.org).

The Cambridge School, V. Rosmini, 6, Verona 37123 (☎39 0458 00 31 54; fax 01 49 00 00; www.cambridgeschool.it).

Associazione Culturale Linguistica Educational (ACLE), V. Roma 54, San Remo 18038 (☎/fax 39 018 450 6070; www.acle.org). English-language immersion summer camps for children.

AU PAIR WORK

Au pairs are typically women, aged 18-27, who work as live-in nannies, caring for children and doing light housework in foreign countries in exchange for room, board, and a small spending allowance or stipend. Most former au pairs speak favorably of their experience, and of how it allowed them to really get to know the country without the high expenses of traveling. Drawbacks, however, often include long hours, and the somewhat mediocre pay. Much of the au pair experience depends on the family you're placed with and the quality of the agency. Be sure to ask your agency for references from au pairs they have placed in the past. The agencies below are a good starting point.

Au Pair in Europe, P. O. Box 68056, Blakely Postal Outlet, Hamilton, Ontario, Canada L8M 3M7 (☎905-545-6305; fax 544-4121; www.princeent.com). Contracts in Italy from 3 months-1 year. Wages $75-120 per week.

ALTERNATIVES TO TOURISM

Au Pair Italy, V. Demetrio Martinelli, 11/d, Bologna 40133 (☎39 05 138 3466; www.aupairitaly.com). Stays from 3 months-2 years. Knowledge of Italian not required, but coursework while in Italy recommended. Stipends start at €60 per wk.

Mix Culture Au Pair Service, V. Nazionale 204, Rome 00184 (☎39 06 4788 2289; fax 4782 6164; web.tiscali.it/mixcultureroma/index.htm). Minimum stay of 6 months-1 year. Requires enrollment in a language school in order to obtain a student visa. €65 registration fee.

SHORT-TERM WORK

Many travelers try their hand at odd jobs for a few weeks at a time to defray the costs of long-term travel. Romantic images of picking in a sun-soaked vineyard may be dancing in your head, but in reality, casual agricultural jobs are hard to find in Italy, given the number of foreign migrant workers who may be willing to work for less pay. Your best bet for agricultural jobs is to look in the northwest; the harvest is usually in September and October.Another popular option is to work several hours a day at a hostel in exchange for free or discounted room and/ or board. These short-term jobs are often found by word of mouth, or simply by talking to the owner of a hostel or restaurant. Given the high turnover in the tourism industry, many places are eager for temporary help. *Let's Go* lists these temporary jobs whenever possible; check the practical information sections. Below are some in popular destinations.

Ostello La Primula (HI), V. IV Novembre, 86, Menaggio (☎034 43 23 56; fax 43 16 77; www.menaggiohostel.com). Work in return for room and board (p. 140).

Youth Info Center (Informagiovani), C. Porto Borsari, 17, Verona (☎045 801 0796). Provides info on work regulations and finds travelers local employment (p. 253).

Deck-hand work. In Viareggio, inquire at the yacht brokerages around V. Coppino (p. 411).

Summer jobs in Bari, the Lavoro Temporaneo Office, P. Aldo Moro, in Bari near the FAL station, can find jobs lasting a couple of months (p. 583).

FURTHER READING ON WORKING IN ITALY

Live and Work in Italy, by Pybus. Vacation-Work, 1999 (US$18).

Living and Working in Italy, by Daws. Survival Books, 2001 (US$22).

Living, Studying and Working in Italy: Everything You Need to Know to Fulfill Your Dreams of Living Abroad, by Neighbor and Larner. Henry Holt, 1998 (US$16).

Passport Italy: Your Pocket Guide to Italian Business, Customs and Etiquette, by Gioseffi and Szerlip. World Trade Press, 1997 (US$7).

VOLUNTEERING

Many volunteer services charge you a participation fee that can be surprisingly hefty, though they often cover airfare and most living expenses. Try to do research on a program before committing: talk to former participants, as conditions can vary greatly. Most volunteers go through a parent organization that takes care of logistical details and provides a group environment and support system. There are two main types of organizations: religious (often Catholic) and non-sectarian, although there are rarely restrictions on participation for either.

SHORT-TERM WORK

Concordia International Volunteer Projects, Heversham House, 20-22 Boundary Rd., Hove, England, BN3 4B (☎440 127 342 2218; fax 127 342 1182; www.concordia-iye.org.uk). 2- to 4-wk. environmental, archaeological, cultural, social, and arts-related volunteer opportunities throughout Italy for British volunteers ages 16-30. Work ranges from sculpting recycled material in Bolsena to maintaining paths on the island of Ustica. Applicants from UK only. Food and accommodations provided. £200-800.

Council on International Educational Exchange, International Volunteer Projects, 633 Third Ave., New York, NY 10017, USA (☎888-268-6245; fax 212-822-2649; www.councilexchanges.org). 2-4-wk. projects in construction/renovation, nature conservation, the arts, archaeology, and social work for 18+ volunteers. Offered primarily June-Sept.; check online calendar for new program schedule at end of Mar. No special skills required. US$300 includes placement, contact information, pre-departure support, accommodations and group activities.

Global Volunteers, 375 E. Little Canada Rd., St. Paul, MN 55117, USA (☎800-487-1074; fax 651-482-0915; www.globalvolunteers.com). Economic and human development projects offered year round, for 10 days-3 wk. Open to all ages, though typical age is 50+. Activities range from teaching English to constructing village water systems and group homes. No specific skills required. US$450-2395 includes accommodations, food, in-country support, project materials, and team leader.

LONG-TERM WORK

American Field Service (AFS), 310 SW 4 Ave., Ste. 630, Portland, OR 97204-2608, USA (☎800-237-4636; fax 503-248-4076; www.afs.org). The Community Service Program connects 18+ volunteers with teaching, environmental, and social service jobs in Italy for 4 months to 1 year. Fee covers round-trip airfare, orientation, language training, food and accommodation. Cost varies depending on destination. Fee does not cover the mandatory AFS health insurance.

Associazione Culturale Linguista Educational (ACLE), V. Roma 54, 18038 San Remo (☎/fax 3901 8450 6070; edu@rasenet.it). This nonprofit organization works to bring theater and the arts to Italian schools. Volunteer 6hr. a day, for a min. 2 wk. year-round, renovating a medieval house into a student art center in the beautiful village of Baiardo. Free board and cooking facilities. Alternatively, volunteer for 3-6 months as an ACLE recruitment officer for their projects, traveling between international universities and the San Remo central office. Italian useful. Accommodations and pocket money provided. Applicants accepted year round, write for more information.

Elderhostel, Inc., 11 Avenue de Lafayette, Boston, MA 92111-1746, USA (☎877-426-8056; fax 426-2166; www.elderhostel.org). Sends volunteers ages 55+ around the world to work in construction, research, and teach. Responsibilities may include manual labor, teaching English, archaeological preservation, and sanitation projects. Costs average $100 per day, plus airfare.

THE GREAT OUTDOORS

Archaeological Institute of America, c/o IA Placement Service at the University of Pennsylvania, 291 Logan Hall, 249 S. 36th St. Philadelphia, PA 19104-6304, USA (☎215-898-4975; fax 573-7874; www.aaclassics.org). *The Archaeological Fieldwork Opportunities Bulletin,* at www.archaeological.org, lists field sites throughout Europe where volunteers can participate in excavation archaeology. Site listings and job opportunities in Italy change frequently.

Earthwatch, 3 Clocktower Pl. Ste. 100, Box 75, Maynard, MA 01754, USA (☎800-776-0188 or 978-461-0081; www.earthwatch.org). Arranges 1 to 3-wk. programs in Italy for 16+ volunteers to promote conservation of natural resources. No special skills required. Fees vary based on program location and duration; costs average $1700, plus airfare.

Habitat for Humanity International, 121 Habitat St., Americus, GA 31709, USA (☎229-924-6935, ext. 2551; www.habitat.org). Volunteers aged 18-80 build houses for anywhere from 2 wk. to 3 years. Short-term programs in Italy cost US$1200-1800, including airfare, room and board, travel insurance, and a donation toward the construction in your assigned community.

Italian League for the Protection of Birds (LIPU), V. Trento, 9-43100 Parma (☎0521 27 30 43; fax 27 34 19; www.lipu.it). Places 350-400 volunteers ages 18+ in data collection and research, conservation, nesting site surveillance, and environmental education work camps. Also offers 1000 administrative positions in 100 divisions throughout Italy. Programs from 1 wk. to 1 month in Apr., May, Sept., and Oct. Knowledge of Italian is useful. Required skills vary depending on assignment.

Service Civil International Voluntary Service (SCI-IVS), SCI USA, 3213 W. Wheeler St., Seattle, WA 98199, USA (☎/fax 206-350-6585; www.sci-ivs.org). Places 18+ volunteers in 2- to 3-wk. work camps for construction, environmental, and social service projects. Camps run primarily June-Oct., but longer options available. See the *International Workcamp Directory* (US$20) or the SCI-IVS web site. Free room and board, but volunteers pay travel costs and US$125 registration fee.

Volunteers for Peace, 1034 Tiffany Rd., Belmont, VT 05730, USA (☎802-259-2759; www.vfp.org). Arranges placement in 2- to 3-wk. work camps in Italy for 18+ volunteers. Membership (US$20) required. US$200 provides food, accommodations and materials. Transportation not covered. No special skills required; volunteers working with children must submit a written application and a letter of recommendation.

Willing Workers on Organic Farms, 109 V. Casavecchia, Castagneto Carducci, 57022 (www.wwoof.org/italy). For a €24 fee, provides a list of organic farms that welcome volunteers.

HUMANITARIAN WORK

Agape Centro Ecumenico, 10060 Prali, Turin (☎3912 180 7690; fax 180 7514; www.chiesavaldese.org//agape). 12 volunteers age 18+ help run this international and national Christian conference center in the Italian Alps. Clean, cook, and maintain the center 6hr. per day, 6 days per wk. for at least 1 month. Work available June-Sept., Christmas, and Easter. Knowledge of Italian and any other languages a benefit. Free lodging provided. Travel costs not covered.

Italian Association for Education, Exchanges and Intercultural Activities (AFSAI) Viale Luigi Ronzoni, 91 - C/5, 00151 Rome (☎3906 537 0332; fax 5820 1442; www.afsai.it). The European Voluntary Service program, financed by the European Union, arranges for volunteers ages 16-25 to complete 6-12 month service projects in Italy. 2-wk. language course. Knowledge of Italian strongly encouraged.

Doctors Without Borders (Medicins Sans Frontieres/Medici Senza Frontiere), V. Volturno, 58, 00185 Rome (☎3906 448 6921; fax 448 6920; www.msf.it). The Italian branch coordinates 18+ volunteers to provide health care for immigrants and asylum seekers. Project length from 6 months to 1 year. Brindisi center provides immigrants with shelter and health care. Rome center registers Italians with national health care system and free medical consultations. Emergency medical training provided for volunteers. Basic living expenses, round-trip airfare, health insurance, and other travel costs covered. First-time volunteers offered a US$700 stipend. In-person interview required.

International Christian Youth Exchange, 134 West 26th St., New York, NY 10001, USA (☎212-206-7307; icyeio@igc.apc.org). Places high school graduates in short- and long-term social service projects. Long-term projects include working with homeless youth, the disabled, and elderly. Volunteers must pay a fee that covers all expenses.

Mobility International USA (MIUSA), P. O. Box 10767, Eugene, OR 97440, USA (☎541-343-1284; fax 343-6812; www.miusa.org). Coordinates exchange programs abroad for people with disabilities. Homestay and 3- to 4-wk. service project. Youth delegations ages 16-25; adult and professional delegations 25+. Costs vary greatly.

NORTHWEST ITALY

LOMBARDY (LOMBARDIA)

Ever since the Gauls took this region from the Etruscans, the fertile land and strategic location of Lombardy have made it highly sought-after by the Romans, Goths, Spaniards, Austrians, and Corsicans. The disputing European powers failed to rob Lombardy of her prosperity, and the region remains the wealthiest in Italy. Economic preeminence has allowed *Lombardesi* to cultivate an appreciation for the finer things in life. Historically, their luxury of choice has been opera—leading to the opening of theaters like **La Scala** (p. 102) and **Teatro Grande** (p. 133), as well as the cultivation of the first great operatic composer, Claudio Monteverdi. Financial wherewithal enticed great artists like Da Vinci and Bramante to design some of the region's civic spaces and ornate private residences. Critics claim that *Lombardesi* cultural sophistication is grounded in a desire to distance themselves from the comparatively underdeveloped southern regions and the international immigrants that flock to their powerful industrial cities, as evinced by the strong presence of secessionist political party **Lega Nord.**

HIGHLIGHTS OF LOMBARDY

REVEL in the best clubbing city in Europe; bar-hop in the **Navigli** (p. 110) after a hard-hitting cultural day at the **Last Supper** (p. 105) and the **Museo Poldi Pezzoli** (p. 103).

SCALE the steps of **La Scala,** the world's premier opera house (p. 102). Then see an actual opera at the Acrimboldi (p. 107).

VIEW the city of Milan from atop the **duomo** (p. 103).

FIDDLE the day away at Cremona's **Museo Stradivariano** (p. 118).

STAND agape beneath the dazzling ceiling of Bergamo's **Basilica di Santa Maria Maggiore** (p. 129).

MILAN (MILANO)   ☎02

Once served the capital of the Cisalpine Republic and the western half of the Roman empire, Milan is now the center of Italian style, financial markets, and industry. Car tire-producing giant Pirelli and fashion house Armani ensure business-minded *Milanesi* economic prowess. The pace of life is quicker here, and *il dolce di far niente* (the sweetness of doing nothing) is an unfamiliar taste. Milan's great works of art, including its ornate duomo, Da Vinci's *Last Supper*, and La Scala's stunning operas, must therefor be all the more dramatic to make a lasting impression. The city's pace quickens twice a year when local soccer teams AC Milan and Inter Milan face-off in matches on par with religious holidays. The *Milanesi* move fast and they do it with style, changing their fashions and those of the rest of the world four times a year.

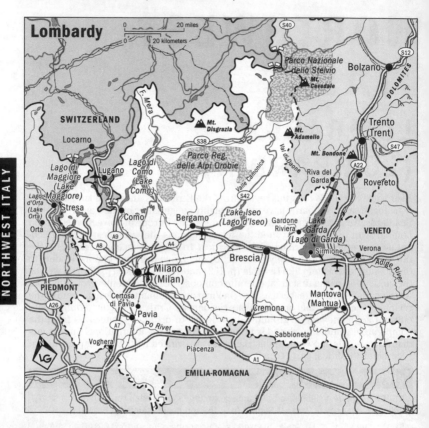

NORTHWEST ITALY

✈ INTERCITY TRANSPORTATION

Flights: Malpensa Airport, 45km from town. Intercontinental flights. **Luggage storage** and lost property services available (p. 97). **Malpensa Express** leaves from Cadorna metro station to airport (45min.; 5:50am-8pm; €9, if bought on train €11.50) and returns 6:45am-9:45pm. Express shuttle **buses** run to and from Stazione Centrale (50min, 6:20am-10:45pm, €4.50). **Linate Airport,** 7km from town, is easier logistically. Domestic/European flights and intercontinental flights with European transfers. **STAM bus** (☎02 71 71 06) runs from Linate to Stazione Centrale (every 20min.). City bus #73 also operates between the Linate and Milan's San Babila Metro station (€1, but more inconvenient and less secure). **General Flight Info** for both airports (☎02 7485 2200). International arrivals (☎02 2680 0619). International departures (☎02 2680 0627).

Trains: Stazione Centrale (☎01 4788 8088), in MM2: P. Duca d'Aosta. **Tourist office** opposite platforms. Open M-Sa 9am-6pm, Su 9am-12:30pm and 1:30pm-6pm. **Luggage storage** and lost property services available (p. 97). To: **Florence** (2½hr., every hr., €21.69); **Genoa** (1½hr., every hr., €7.90); **Rome** (4½hr., every hr., €27.37); **Turin** (2hr., every hr., €7.90); and **Venice** (3hr., 21 per day, €12.34). **Stazione Nord** is part of the local railway system and offers connections from Milan to **Como** and **Varese**

(every 30min., 6am-9pm). **Porta Genova** (at P. Le Stazione di Porta Genova) lies on the western line to **Vigevano, Alessandria,** and **Asti. Porta Garibaldi** (at P. Sigmund Freud) links **Milan** to **Lecco** and **Valtellina** to the northwest.

Buses: At **Stazione Centrale.** Signs for bus destinations, times, and prices posted outside. Tickets purchased inside. **Intercity** buses tend to leave from less convenient locales on the periphery of town. **SAL, SIA, Autostradale,** and many others depart from P. Castello (MM1: Cairoli) for Turin, the lake country, Bergamo, Certosa di Pavia, and points as far away as Rimini and Trieste.

■ ORIENTATION

The layout of the city resembles a giant target, divided by a series of ancient concentric city walls. In the outer rings lie suburbs built during the 50s and 60s to house southern immigrants. Within the inner circle are four central squares: **Piazza Duomo,** at the end of V. Mercanti; **Piazza Cairoli,** near the Castello Sforzesco; **Piazza Cordusio,** connected to Largo Cairoli by V. Dante; and **Piazza San Babila,** the business and fashion district along C. V. Emanuele. The **duomo** and **Galleria Vittorio Emanuele** comprise the bull's eye, roughly at the center of the downtown circle. To the northeast and northwest lie two large parks, the **Giardini Pubblici** and the **Parco Sempione. Stazione Centrale,** Milan's major transportation hub, lies northwest of the city's center in a commercial district filled with skyscrapers like the Pirelli tower. To reach P. Duomo at the city's center, take Metro line #3 (yellow) to **MM: Duomo.** By foot from Stazione Centrale, walk straight ahead from the platforms through the Stazione's main entrance into **Piazza Duca d'Aosta.** Follow **Via Pisani** through several name changes until you reach **Largo Cairoli,** just off the **Castello Sforzesco.** A short walk down **Via Dante** will bring you to **Piazza Duomo.** From here, the **Galleria Vittorio Emanuele** opens into **Piazza della Scala.** On the far side of the piazza is the **Via Manzoni** and **Manzoni Theater.** From V. Manzoni, take a left onto **Via della Spiga** to reach the fashion district. To the south lies the hopping nightlife district, the **Navigli,** which can be reached directly from Stazione Centrale by way of Metro line #2 to **MM: Porta Genova. Via Vito Pisani** leads from the station to downtown through **Piazza della Repubblica,** continuing through the wealthy business districts as **Via Turati.** Most of Milan's budget accommodations lie east of Stazione Centrale around **Piazza Loretto,** and southeast of the station towards **Corso Buenos Aires.**

▐ LOCAL TRANSPORTATION

The jumbled, winding lay-out of Milan's streets makes them difficult to navigate. Pick up the **Michelin map** (with street index; €6.20) at the tourist office. The streets are generally safe at night, but women are advised not to walk alone. An efficient public transportation system includes the metro, trams, and buses.

Public Transportation: The **Metropolitana Milanese** ("MM") operates 6am-midnight and is by far the most useful branch of Milan's public transportation network. Be wary of occasional strikes. **Line #1** (red, "MM1") stretches east to west from the *pensioni* district east of Stazione Centrale, through the center of town, and west to the youth hostel (Molino Dorino fork). **Line #2** (green, "MM2") links Milan's 3 train stations and crosses MM1 at Cadorna and Loreto. **Line #3** (yellow, "MM3") runs from north of Stazione Centrale to the southern sprawl of the city, crossing with MM2 at Stazione Centrale and MM1 at the duomo. Use the **bus system** for trips outside the city proper. **Trams #29** and **30** travel the city's outer ring road, while **buses #96** and **97** service the inner road. **Tickets** for 1½hr. worth of metro or bus use are €1. Tickets and 24hr. and 48hr. bus/metro passes are available at *tabacchi* and ticket booths. Metro tickets can also be bought at station machines (press the "Rete urbana di milano" button). Keep extra tickets with you, as *tabacchi* close at 8pm and ticket machines can be unreliable.

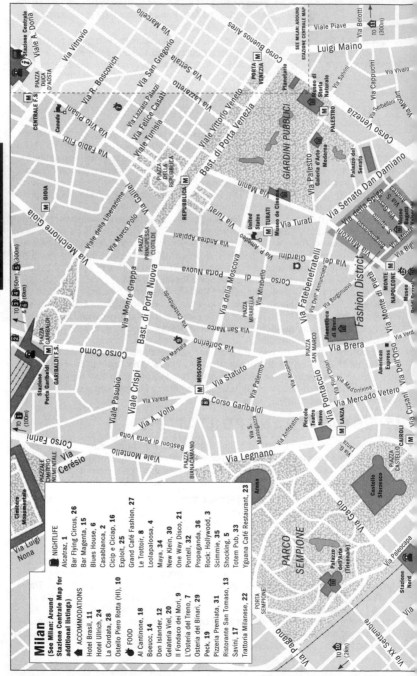

NORTHWEST ITALY

Milan

(See Milan: Around Stazione Centrale Map for additional listings)

★ ACCOMMODATIONS
Hotel Brasil, 11
Hotel Ullrich, 24
La Cordata, 28
Ostello Piero Rotta (HI), 10

♦ FOOD
Al Cantinone, 18
Boeucc, 14
Don Islander, 12
Gelateria Viel, 20
Il Fondaco dei Mori, 9
L'Osteria del Treno, 7
Osteria del Binari, 29
Peck, 19
Pizzeria Premiata, 31
Ristorante San Tomaso, 13
Savini, 17
Trattoria Milanese, 22

■ NIGHTLIFE
Alcatraz, 1
Bar Flying Circus, 26
Bar Magenta, 15
Blues House, 6
Casablanca, 2
Cicip e Ciciap, 16
Exploit, 25
Grand Café Fashion, 27
Le Trottoir, 8
Loolapaloosa, 4
Maya, 34
New Klein, 30
One Way Disco, 21
Pontell, 32
Propaganda, 36
Rock: Hollywood, 3
Scimmie, 35
Shocking, 5
Totem Pub, 33
Yguana Café Restaurant, 23

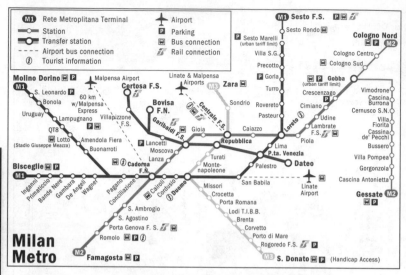

Milan Metro

Taxis: White taxis are omnipresent. If you can't find one, call the 24hr. **Radio Taxi** (☎02 53 53, 85 85, 83 83, 40 00, 40 40, or 52 51). Nighttime surcharge €3.10.

Car Rental: All have offices built into Stazione Centrale on the side facing P. Duca d'Aosta. An economy car with insurance from **Europcar** (☎02 6698 1589 or 800 01 44 10; open M-F 8am-7pm, Sa 8:30am-12:30pm) starts at €48 per day; from **Hertz** (☎02 669 0061; open M-F 8am-7pm, Sa 8am-2pm) at €60 per day; and from **Avis** (☎02 669 0280 or 670 1654; open M-F 8am-8pm, Sa 8am-4pm) at €74 per day.

Bike Rental: A.W.S. Bici Motor, V. Ponte Seveso, 33 (☎02 6707 2145). Exit Stazione Centrale to right. From the park, take V. S. Chiaparelli on right. After 3 blocks go left onto V. P. Seveso. Mountain bikes €10.50 per day. Open M-Sa 9am-1pm and 3-7pm.

🛈 PRACTICAL INFORMATION

TOURIST AND FINANCIAL SERVICES

Tourist Office: APT, V. Marconi, 1 (☎02 7252 4300; fax 7252 4350; www.milanoinfotourist.com), in "Palazzo di Turismo" in P. Duomo, to the right as you face the duomo. Comprehensive local and regional info. Useful map and museum guide (in Italian). €8 gets you the worthwhile info packet, "Welcome Card," with discount cards, maps, sights descriptions, a 24hr. bus/train pass, and a CD of Milan's best opera, all stowed neatly in a pouch that can also be used for your airline tickets. They will help with accommodations. Pick up the comprehensive *Milano e Milano* and *Milano Mese* for info on activities and clubs. Open M-F 8:30am-8pm, Sa 9am-1pm and 2-7pm, Su 9am-1pm and 2-5pm. **Branch office** at Stazione Centrale (☎02 7252 4370 or 7252 4360), off main hall on 2nd fl., through neon archway to left between 2 gift shops. Open M-Sa 9am-6pm, Su 9am-12:30pm and 1:30-6pm.

Consulates: US, V. P. Amedeo, 2/10 (☎02 29 03 51). MM3: Turati. Open M-F 9am-noon. **Australia,** V. Borgogna, 2 (☎02 77 70 41; fax 7770 4242). MM1: S. Babila. Open M-Th 9am-noon and 2-4pm, F 9am-noon. **Canada,** V. V. Pisani, 19 (☎02 67 581), MM2/3: Centrale F.S. Open M-F 9am-noon. **New Zealand,** V. d'Arezzo, 6 (☎02 4801 2544). Open M-F 9am-noon. **UK,** V. S. Paolo, 7 (☎02 72 30 01; emergency ☎03 358 10 68 57). MM1/3: Duomo. Open M-F 9:15am-12:15pm and 2:30pm-4:30pm.

Currency Exchange: Banks are everywhere and most are open M-F 8:30am-1:30pm and 2:30-4:30pm. **ATMs** also abound.

American Express: V. Brera, 3 (☎02 87 66 74), on the corner of V. dell'Orso. Walk through the Galleria, across P. Scala, and up V. Verdi. Servies for AmEx card members: **holds mail** free for 1 month (for non-members, US$5 per month) and offers Moneygram international **money transfer** (fees vary; €500 wire costs €30.99). Also **exchanges currency.** Open M-F 9am-5:30pm.

LOCAL SERVICES

Luggage Storage: In the Malpensa Airport: €2 per bag per day. Open 24hr. In the Stazione Centrale: €2.58 per 12hr. Open 4:30am-1:30am.

Lost Property: Ufficio Oggetti Smarriti Comune, V. Friuli, 30 (☎02 546 8118). Open M-F 8:30am-4pm. **Malpensa Airport** (☎02 58 58 00 69). **Linate Airport** (☎02 7012 4451). **Stazione Centrale** (☎02 6371 2667). Open daily 7am-1pm and 2-8pm.

English-Language Bookstores: The American Bookstore, V. Camperio, 16 (☎02 87 89 20; fax 7202 0030), at Largo Cairoli. Open Tu-Sa 10am-8pm, M 1-8pm. **Hoepli Libreria Internazionale,** V. Hoepli, 5 (☎02 86 48 71), off P. Media near P. Scala. Open M 2-7pm, Tu-Sa 10am-7pm. MC/V. **Rizzoli's** (☎02 8646 1071), Galleria Vittorio Emanuele. Open M-9am-8pm, Tu-Sa 9am-9pm, Su 12:30-7:30pm. AmEx/MC/V. Also try **street vendors** along Largo Mattioli for cheaper options.

Gay and Lesbian Resource: ARCI-GAY "Centro D'iniziativa Gay," V. Bezzeca, 3 (☎02 5412 2225; fax 5412 2226; www.arcigaymilano.org). Friendly staff speaks some English. Open M-F 3pm-8pm.

Handicapped/Disabled Services: Direzione Servizi Sociali, Largo Treves, 1 (☎02 6208 6954). Open 8:30am-noon and 1-5pm.

Laundromat: Acqua Dolce, V. B. Marcello, 32 (☎02 2952 5820). €3.10 wash, €3.10 dry. Open M-Su 8am-8pm. **Washland,** V. Porpora, 14 (☎340 335 5660). €3.10 wash, €3.10 dry. Open M-Su 8am-10pm.

EMERGENCY AND COMMUNICATIONS

Emergency: ☎118. **Police:** ☎113. **Carabinieri:** ☎112.

Tourist Police: SOS Turista, V. C.M. Maggi, 14 (☎02 3360 3060). Open daily 9:30am-1pm and 2:30-6pm.

First Aid: Pronto Soccorso (☎02 38 83) or **Red Cross** (☎02 34 567).

Late-Night Pharmacies: Stazione Centrale *galleria* 24hr. pharmacy (☎02 669 0735 or 669 0935). P. Duomo, 21 (☎02 8646 4832). Open M-Sa 9:30am-1pm and 3-7pm. All pharmacy doors list late-night pharmacies.

Hospital: Ospedale Maggiore di Milano, V. Francesco Sforza, 35 (☎02 55 031), 5min. from the duomo on the inner ring road.

Internet Access:

■**Manhattan Lab,** in Università Statale on V. Festa del Perdono. Use entrance opposite V. Bergamini. Take stairs to 3rd fl. At the end of the corridor, turn left and follow the signs to the Manhattan Lab. Try not to draw attention to yourself. Open Tu-Sa noon-8pm, Su 10:30am-3:30pm.

Gr@zia, P. Duca d'Aosta, 14 (☎02 670 0543). To the left of the station's main door. Internet cafe with good connection and rates. €1 per 15 min. Open M-Su 8am-12am.

!net, V. Torricelli, 9 (☎02 4549 0267). MM2: Porta Genova. 5 computers with good connection in the heart of the Navigli district. €1.30 per 15min. Open M-F 9am-10pm and Sa 10am-11pm.

Cafenet Dolphin Navigator, V. Padova, 2 (☎02 284 7209). MM1/2: Loreto. 3 computers with a great connection and food served. €1.30 per 15 min. €5 per hour. Open Tu-Su 9am-8pm.

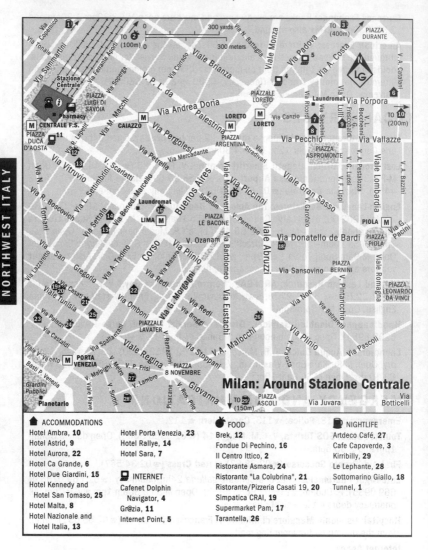

Milan: Around Stazione Centrale

♠ ACCOMMODATIONS
Hotel Ambra, **10**
Hotel Astrid, **9**
Hotel Aurora, **22**
Hotel Ca Grande, **6**
Hotel Due Giardini, **15**
Hotel Kennedy and
  Hotel San Tomaso, **25**
Hotel Malta, **8**
Hotel Nazionale and
  Hotel Italia, **13**

Hotel Porta Venezia, **23**
Hotel Rallye, **14**
Hotel Sara, **7**

🖥 INTERNET
Cafenet Dolphin
  Navigator, **4**
Gr@zia, **11**
Internet Point, **5**

🍴 FOOD
Brek, **12**
Fondue Di Pechino, **16**
Il Centro Ittico, **2**
Ristorante Asmara, **24**
Ristorante "La Colubrina", **21**
Ristorante/Pizzeria Casati 19, **20**
Simpatica CRAI, **19**
Supermarket Pam, **17**
Tarantella, **26**

🎵 NIGHTLIFE
Artdeco Café, **27**
Cafe Capoverde, **3**
Kirribilly, **29**
Le Lephante, **28**
Sottomarino Giallo, **18**
Tunnel, **1**

Internet Point, V. Padova, 38 (☎02 2804 0246). MM1/2: Loreto. 10 computers. Wire money, print and fax. €4 per hr. Open M-Su 10am-10pm.

Terzomillenio, V. Lazzaretto, 2 (☎02 205 2121). MM1: Porta Venezia. Take V. V. Veneto 4 blocks to V. Lazzarretto. €3 per 30min. Open M-F 8:30am-9pm, Sa 8:30am-6pm.

Post Office: V. Cordusio, 4 (☎02 7248 2223), near P. Duomo toward castle. Stamps, *Fermo Posta*, and **currency exchange.** Open M-F 8:30am-7:30pm, Sa 8:30am-1pm. There are 2 post offices at **Stazione Centrale.**

Postal Code: 20100.

🖍 ACCOMMODATIONS & CAMPING

Milan has a remarkably high standard of living; its accommodations are priced accordingly. Advanced booking is strongly advised.

NEAR STAZIONE CENTRALE

🏨 **Hotel Sara,** V. Sacchini, 17 (☎02 20 17 73; www.hotelsara.it). MM1/2: Loreto. From Loreto take V. Porpora; the 2nd street on the right is the peaceful V. Sacchini. Recently renovated. Bath and TV in every room. Free Internet. 24hr. reception. Singles €42-48; doubles €65-72; triples €88-93. AmEx/MC/V. ❹

🏨 **Hotel Ca Grande,** V. Porpora, 87 (☎/fax 02 2614 4001 or 2614 5295; www.hotelca-grande.lt). MM1/2: Loreto. 6 blocks from P. Loreto in a yellow house with a green fence. Take tram #33 from Stazione Centrale; it runs along V. Porpora and stops at V. Ampere, 50m from the front door. The traffic below can be noisy, but the windows block most of it out. Spacious rooms with TV. English and Croatian spoken. Breakfast included. Internet available. Reception 24hr. Singles €41, with bath €51; doubles €61.97/€72. AmEx/MC/V. ❹

Hotel Malta, V. Ricordi, 20 (☎02 204 9615 or 2952 1210; www.hotelmalta.it). MM1/2: Loreto. Take V. Porpora 1 block to V. Ricordi. Or from Stazione Centrale, take tram #33 to V. Ampere and backtrack along V. Porpora to V. Ricordi. 15 rooms, all with bath and TV, many with balconies overlooking a quiet rose garden. Reservations suggested. Pets allowed. 24hr. reception. Singles €47; doubles €73. ❹

Hotel Ambra, V. Caccianino, 10 (☎02 266 5465; fax 7060 6245). MM1/2: Loreto. V. Caccianino is about a block up on the right from Hotel Ca' Grande. Hotel is set off on a quiet side street and offers 19 rooms, all with bath, TV, telephone, and balconies. Breakfast €2.50. 24hr. reception. Reserve ahead. Singles €42; doubles €68; triples €91. Inquire about student discounts. ❹

Hotel Astrid, V. Lulli, 22 (☎/fax 02 236 1271). MM1/2: Loreto. From the P. Loreto, take V. Porpora for 3 blocks, then turn left onto V. Lulli. Well-priced rooms with TV. Singles €41.32; doubles €61.97, with bath €72; triples with bath €93. ❹

NEAR GIARDINI PUBBLICI

Hotel San Tomaso, V. Tunisia, 6, 3rd fl. (☎/fax 02 2951 4747; http://web.tin.it/hotel-santomaso). MM1: Porta Venezia. Take the C. Buenos Aires metro exit (a short walk to the opposite end of the station) and turn left at the McDonald's on V. Tunisia. Clean, simple rooms, some overlooking a courtyard, with TV. English spoken. Request keys if going out at night. Singles €35; doubles €62. AmEx/DC/MC/V. ❸

Hotel Aurora, C. Buenos Aires, 18 (☎02 204 7960; fax 204 9285; www.hotelitaly.com/hotels/aurora/index.htm). MM1: Porta Venezia. Exit the station onto C. Buenos Aires, walk straight ahead for 5min., and it's on the right. Just off the hectic C. Buenos Aires lie spotless modern rooms with phone, TV, and silence. Reception 24hr. Reserve ahead. Singles €41-46, with shower €46-54; doubles with bath €69-82. AmEx/DC/MC/V. ❹

Hotel Due Giardini, V. B. Marcello, 47 (☎02 2952 1093 or 2951 2309; duegiardiniho-tel@libero.it). MM1: Lima. Walk along V. Vitruvio 2 blocks to V. Marcello; take a left on the far side of the street. Minty green decor. 11 rooms with bath and TV. Some English spoken. Internet access. Breakfast €4. Singles €50.50; doubles €85-110. MC/V. ❹

Hotel Kennedy, V. Tunisia, 6, 6th fl. (☎02 2940 0934; raffaelo.bianchi@galactica.it). MM1: Porta Venezia. 3 floors above Hotel San Tomaso (elevator available). 16 clean rooms with TV in this recently refurbished hotel. Ask for the room with view of the duomo. Beware that the street below can be noisy. Check-out 10am. Reservations recommended. Ask for keys if going out at night. Singles €36.15, with bath €38; doubles €70/€75; triples €85; quads €95-105. *Let's Go* discount. AmEx/D/MC/V. ❹

Hotel Brasil, V. G. Modena, 20 (☎/fax 02 749 2482; hotelbrasil@libero.it). Just west of city. MM1: Palestro. From Stazione Centrale, take bus #60 to V. G. Modena. From Palestro, take V. Serbelloni and then a quick left onto V. Cappuccini, which crosses 2 larger roads, becoming V. F. Bellotti and finally V. G. Modena. Large rooms with TV and romantic view of the boulevard. Close to several clubs. Breakfast €4, served in bed. Reception closes 12:30am; ask for keys to enter later. Singles €39, with shower €44, with bath €57; doubles €52/€57/€72. AmEx/DC/MC/V. ❹

Hotel Rallye, V. B. Marcello, 59 (☎/fax 02 2953 1209; h.rallye@tiscalinet.it). MM1: Lima. Walk along V. Vitruvio 2 blocks to V. Marcello and turn left. 20 simple, quiet rooms with phone and TV. Breakfast included. Singles €30; doubles €51, with bath €67. AmEx/D/MC/V. ❸

Hotel Porta Venezia, V. P. Castaldi, 26 (☎ 02 2941 4227; fax 2024 9397). MM1: P. Venezia. Walk down C. Venezia for 2 blocks, then turn right onto V. P. Castaldi. Simple and clean rooms with phone and TV. Friendly staff with some English. Singles €31-42, with bath €36-47; doubles €52-77/€41-62. MC/V. ❹

Hotel Italia and **Hotel Nazionale,** V. Vitruvio, 44/46 (☎02 669 3826 or 02 670 5911; fax 670 9819; nazionaleitalia@tiscali.it). From Stazione Centrale, walk straight ahead from the platforms onto the P. Duca D'Aosta; turn left onto V. Vitruvio and walk 3 blocks. The 2 adjacent hotels are on the left-hand side. Run by the same family, the hotels offer the same prices and use the same reception on the ground floor of Hotel Italia. Simple, clean rooms in an ultra-convenient location. Reception closed 1am-6:30am. Reservations recommended. Singles €33, with bath €52; doubles €49/€70; triples with bath €93. AmEx/MC/V. ❸

NEAR THE CITY PERIPHERY

La Cordata, V. Burigozzo, 11 (☎02 5831 4675; fax 5830 3598; www.lacordata.it). MM3: Missori. From P. Missori, take C. Italia for 10 blocks; then turn left on V. Burigozzo. The entrance is just around the corner from the camping store that shares its name. Or go to MM1: S. Babila and take #65 bus towards Agrippa; get off at the S. Lucia stop and walk about a block in the same direction to V. Burigozzi. Hostel popular among backpackers. Most rooms have bath. Some English spoken. Kitchen use. Reception 9am-1pm and 2pm-12:30am. Dorms €15.50. ❶

Hotel Ullrich, C. Italia, 6. 6th fl. (☎02 8645 0156; fax 80 45 35). MM3: Missori. On C. Italia on the right-hand side a couple blocks from P. Missori. 5min. walk from the duomo. Clean rooms with TV. Communal bath. Breakfast included. Singles €50-70; doubles €70-90. MC/V. ❹

Ostello Piero Rotta (HI), V. Salmoiraghi, 1 (☎02 3926 7095). Northwest of city. MM1: QT8. From Metro, turn right and keep going right as you leave the station. The large hostel, with 350 dorm beds, will be on your right after about 300m. English spoken. Breakfast, lockers, and sheets included. Internet access €5.16. Laundry €5.50. 3-night max. stay. Reception daily 7-9:30am and 3:30pm-midnight. No morning check-in. Daytime lockout, with no exceptions. Curfew midnight. Lights out 12:30am. HI membership required. Mostly 6-bed rooms, but some family rooms available. No reservations. Closed Dec. 23-Jan. 13. Dorms €16. ❷

Camping Città di Milano, V. G. Airaghi, 61 (☎02 4820 0134; fax 4820 2999). From Stazione Centrale take metro to MM1/3: Duomo or MM1/2: Cadorna, then take bus #62 towards D'Angelli and get off at Vittoria Caldera. Laundry €4.50. €13 per person includes plot and electricity. Closed Dec.-Jan. ❶

🖸 FOOD

McDonald's restaurants gleam on practically ever street corner in Milan, catering to tourists and fast-paced Milanese businesspeople. The old-style *trattorie* still follow Milanese culinary traditions with *risotto a la Milanese* (rice with saffron), *cotoletta alla milanese* (breaded veal cutlet with lemon), and the infamous *osso buco* (shank of lamb, beef, or veal). *Panettone,* traditional holiday fruitcake, is sold at every *pasticcerie*. The **Fiera di Sinigallia**, a 400-year-old bargaining extravaganza, occurs on Saturdays on Darsena banks, a canal in Navigli (V. d'Annunzio). **Peck,** off V. Orefici near the P. Duomo, V. Cantu, 3, has sold delectables like *foie gras* and black forest ham since 1883. (☎02 869 3017. Open Tu-Sa 8:45am-7:30pm.) **Supermarket Pam,** V. Piccinni, 2, is off C. Buenos Aires. (☎02 2951 2715. Open Tu-Su 8:30am-9pm, M 3-9pm.) There's also a **Simpatica CRAI,** V. F. Casati, 21. (☎02 2940 5821. Open M 8am-1pm, Tu-Sa 8am-1pm and 4-7:30pm.) From P. Duomo, head past the tourist office down V. Marconi to **Viel,** V. G. Marconi, 3, for a huge cone of exotic fresh fruit *gelati* for €3.50. (☎02 869 2561. Open M-Sa 7am-7:30pm.)

ITALIAN RESTAURANTS AND TRATTORIE

▨ **Savini,** Galleria Vittorio Emanuele II (☎ 02 7200 3433; fax 7202 2888; www.thi.it). Opposite the McDonald's—in every way. Italian writer Castellaneta once said, "Savini is as much a part of Milan as the Galleria and La Scala." Since its founding in 1867, this internationally renowned *ristorante* has maintained the same decor and clientele: extravagant and well-dressed. *Primi* €13-20, *secondi* €21-29. Cover €7. Service 12%. Open M-Sa 12:30-2:30pm and 7:30-10:30pm. AmEx/DC/MC/V. ❺

▨ **Trattoria Milanese,** V. S. Marta, 11 (☎02 8645 1991). MM1/3: Duomo. From P. Duomo, take V. Torino; turn right onto V. Maurilio, and then right again onto V. S. Marta. Setting the standard in traditional *Milanese* cuisine in the same location since 1933. *Osso buco* (*risotto*; €18) and *costolette alla Milanese* (ribs; €14) are served the way they should be. *Primi* €5-8, *secondi* €6-18. Open W-M 12:30-3pm and 7pm-midnight. Cover €2. Service 11%. AmEx/DC/MC/V. ❸

▨ **Osteria del Binari,** V. Tortona, 1 (☎02 8940 9428). MM2: Porta Genova. Head to the C. Colombo side of P. Stazione Porta Genova. Cross the train tracks (by the overpass) to V. Tortona. The minute you walk through the door, you'll be greeted by warm smells from the refined del Binari kitchen. Superb food and exquisite desserts. *Primi* €6, *secondi* €12. Open M-Sa 7pm-2am. MC/V. ❸

Boeucc, P. Belgioso, 2 (☎02 7602 0224). MM3: Montenapoleone. From the metro, walk down V. Manzoni towards the duomo; turn left onto V. Morone, and take it to P. Belgioso. Boeucc has provided *Milanese* businesspeople with sustenance to brave the gritty world of high finance since 1696. *Primi* €11-13, *secondi* €19-24. Cover €5. Open M-F 12:40-2:30pm and 7:40-10:30pm, Su 7:40-10:30pm. AmEx. ❺

Don Islander, V. Manzoni, 12/A (☎02 7602 0130). MM3: Montenapoleone. As you exit the metro, walk down V. Manzoni towards the duomo. The restaurant is on your left, just before Museo Poldi-Pezzoli. Exceptional food and beautiful garden dining in the summer. *Primi* €11.50-13.50, *secondi* €18-20. Open M-Sa 12:30-2:30pm and 7:30-10:30pm. AmEx/MC/V. ❺

Al Cantinone, V. Agnello, 19 (☎02 8646 1338). MM1/3: Duomo. From the duomo, take C. V. Emanuelle II and then turn left onto V. Agnello. Antique furnishings dating from 1800. Excellent food. *Primi* € 5.68-€7.27, *secondi* €9.80-28.92. Open M-F noon-2:30pm and 7-11pm, Sa 7-11pm. AmEx/MC/V. ❸

L'Osteria del Treno, V. S. Gregorio, 46/48 (☎02 670 0479). MM2/3: Centrale F. S. From P. Duca d'Aosta, walk down V. Pisani and turn left onto V. S. Gregorio. Started as a railway laborers' club in the mid-1800s, it is still owned by a train workers' cooperative. Hearty, self-service lunch: *primi* €4.20, *secondi* €6.50. Sit-down dinner prices rise by a few euros. Cover €1.30. Open Su-F noon-2:30pm and 7-10:30pm. ❸

Il Centro Ittico, V. F. Aporti, 35 (☎02 2614 3774). MM2/3: Centrale F. S. 10-15min. walk down V. F. Aporti, which runs up the left-hand side of P. Duca d'Aosta. Once a fish market, it was converted into a restaurant that serves the finest of Neptune's bounty. Pick your dinner from a selection of fresh fish displayed in refrigerated cases. Market-determined prices: *primi* from €7, *secondi* from €10. Open M-Sa 12:30-2:30pm and 8pm-midnight. Cover €2.58. DC/MC/V. ❸

Tarantella, V. Abruzzi, 35 (☎02 2940 0218), just north of V. Plinio. MM1: Lima. Fresh produce makes up the decor and fills your plate. *Primi* €5.50-8, *secondi* €11.50-20. Open Sept.-July M-F noon-2:30pm and 7-11:30pm, Su 7-11:30pm. AmEx/MC/V. ❸

Ristorante San Tomaso, V. S. Tomaso, 5 (☎02 87 45 10). MM1: Cairoli. Take V. Dante and turn left onto V. S. Tomaso; the restaurant is on the left. Wrought-iron candelabras and stainless steel goblets create a medieval theme; Andrew Lloyd Webber showtunes strangely enhance the theatrical atmosphere. *Primi* €7.50, *secondi* €14. Cover €2. Open M-Sa noon-3pm and 7:30-11pm. AmEx/MC/DC/V. ❹

Ristorante "La Colubrina," V. Felice Casati, 5 (☎02 2951 8427). MM1: Porta Venezia. Mosaic stone floors. Social, neighborhood-oriented environment. Pizza €3.50-7, lunch *menù* from €10, daily specials €5.50-12. Cover €1.30. Open Sept.-July W-Su noon-2:30pm and 7-11:30pm, Tu 7-11:30pm. MC/V. ❸

Pizzeria Premiata, V. Alzaia Naviglio Grande, 2 (☎02 8940 0648). MM2: Porta Genova. From the metro, take V. Vigevano, and then take 2nd right onto V. Corsico. From there, take a left on V. Alzaia Naviglio Grande. Very popular with *Milanese* students. Hearty portions. Expect some delays at night. Pizzas from €4.50, *primi* €7.75. Open daily noon-2am. AmEx/MC/V. ❸

Pizzeria/Ristorante Casati 19, V. F. Casati, 19 (☎02 204 7292). MM1: Porta Venezia. Go up C. Buenos Aires 4 blocks, and then take a left onto V. F. Casati. Near Hotels San Tomaso and Kennedy. Good place to relax with a glass (or bottle) of wine. Pizza €5.20-6.80, *primi* €5.20-15, *secondi* €4.14-15.50. Open Tu-F and Su noon-2:30pm and 7-11:30pm, Sa 7-11:30pm. AmEx/DC/MC/V. ❷

Brek, V. Lepetit, 20 (☎02 670 5149), near Stazione Centrale. Very popular self-service chain restaurant. A/C, non-smoking room, and English-speaking staff. *Primi* €3.25, *secondi* €4.25. Open M-Sa 11:30am-3pm and 6:30-10:30pm. Other locations: **P. Cavour** (☎02 65 36 19; off V. Manzoni; MM3: M. Napoleone) and **Porta Giordano** (☎02 7602 3379; MM1: S. Babila). ❷

NON-ITALIAN ALTERNATIVES

▨ **Il Fondaco dei Mori,** V. Solferino, 33 (☎02 65 37 11). From MM2: Moscova, walk east on V. della Moscova and turn left onto V. Solferino; the restaurant is on the left. Limited menu, but all dishes are exquisite. Particularly exceptional is the *chawerma* (€11). Ask to dine under a tent, richly furnished with carpets, cushions, and tapestries. All food is *halal*. Lunch and dinner buffet €12, appetizers €2.10-4.20, main courses €10-12. Cover €1.60. Open M-Su noon-3pm and 7:30pm-midnight. DC/MC/V. ❹

Fondue di Pechino, V. Tadino, 52, (☎02 2940 5838). MM1/3: Centrale F. S. From the metro, take V. Vitruvio and then turn left onto V. Tadino. Beijing beckons at this quality Chinese restaurant. Traditional Pekingese food, including but not limited to the infamous duck. Lunch *menù* €7.50, *primi* €1-3.50, *secondi* €3.50-8. Open M-Su noon-3pm and 6pm-midnight. MC/V. ❶

Ristorante Asmara, V. Lazzaro Palazzi, 5 (☎02 2952 2453). MM1: Porta Venezia. Walk down C. Buenos Aires; V. L. Palazzi is 3rd on left. Eritrean food, eaten with thin, spongy flatbread (*injera*) and your hands. Sit on the balcony. To sample all vegetarian options, ask for *"Un po' di tutto vegetariano."* A/C. Vegetarian meals €9.30, large *piatti* €8.52-18.08. Open Th-Tu noon-3pm and 6pm-midnight. AmEx/MC/V. ❷

◉ SIGHTS

▨ **TEATRO ALLA SCALA.** Since its founding in 1778, La Scala has established Milan as the opera capital of the world. Through the years, this rather simple Neoclassical building has hosted the premiers of works by Rossini, Puccini, Mascagni, and Verdi, performed by virtuosos like Callas and Caruso. Although the theater is currently closed for renovation (and will be until 2004), the exterior of the building, only partially surrounded by scaffolding, can be viewed from P. della Scala. *(Through the Galleria Vittorio Emanuele from P. Duomo.)* Visitors can soak up La Scala's historical glow at the **Museo Teatrale alla Scala.** From poster art to a plaster cast of Toscanini's hand, the museum offers a glimpse into the opera house's past. *(C. Magenta, 71. MM1: Conciliazione. Directly opposite the Chiesa S. Marie delle Grazie. From P. Conciliazione, take V. Ruffini for 2 blocks. ☎02 805 3418. Open Tu-Su 9am-7:30pm. €5.)* Interim Teatro degli Arcimboldi (see opera section in **Entertainment,** p. 107) is hosting the La Scala troupe for the duration of the renovations. *(www.teatroallascala.org.)*

■ **DUOMO.** The looming Gothic cathedral is the geographical and spiritual center of Milan and makes a good starting point for any walking tour of the city. The duomo is the 3rd-largest church in the world, after St. Peter's at the Vatican and the Seville Cathedral. **Gian Galeazzo Visconti** founded the cathedral in 1386, hoping to flatter the Virgin into granting him a male heir. Construction proceeded sporadically over the next four centuries and was finally completed at Napoleon's command in 1809. In the meantime, the cathedral accumulated more than 3400 statues, 135 spires, and 96 gargoyles. The facade juxtaposes Italian Gothic and Baroque elements under a delicate crown. Inside, the 52 columns rise to canopied niches with statues as capitals. The church is a five-aisled cruciform shape, capable of seating 4000 worshipers. Narrow side aisles extend to the grand stained glass windows, among the largest in the world. The imposing 16th-century marble tomb of **Giacomo de Medici,** in the south transept, was inspired by the work of Michelangelo. ■**Climb** (or ride) to the top of the cathedral from outside the north transept, where you will find yourself surrounded by a fantastical field of turrets, spires, and statues. A Madonna painted in gold leaf crowns this rooftop kingdom. Scholars interested in early conceptions of human anatomy frequent the statue of St. Bartholomew. Sculpted by **Marco d'Agrate** in 1562, the statue depicts the saint wearing his own skin as a coat as a reminder that he was flayed alive. The roof walkway allows for a stroll of the perimeter, allowing tourists to view white marble statues and the ongoing restoration of the roof. On a clear day, the city opens in wide relief, with the striking Alps as a backdrop. *(MM1: Duomo. Cathedral open daily 9am-5:45pm; Nov.-Feb. 9am-4:15pm. Modest dress strictly enforced. Roof open daily 9am-5:30pm. €3.50, with elevator €5.)* The recently renovated **Museo del Duomo** displays artifacts relating to duomo's construction. *(P. del Duomo, 14, to the right as you face the duomo. ☎02 86 03 58. Open M-Su 10am-1:15pm and 3-6pm. €6.)*

■ **PINACOTECA AMBROSIANA.** The 23 tiny but lovely rooms of the Ambrosiana display exquisite works from the 14th through 19th century, including Botticelli's round M*adonna of the Canopy*, Leonardo's captivating *Portrait of a Musician*, Raphael's cartoon for *School of Athens,* Caravaggio's *Basket of Fruit* (the first still-life painting in Italy), Titian's *Adoration of the Magi,* works by Brueghel and Bril, and several large portraits by Hayez. The courtyard is full of statues and busts and the marble staircase is decorated with mosaics. *(P. Pio XI, 2. Follow V. Spadari off V. Torino and make a left onto V. Cantù. ☎02 8646 2981. Open Tu-Su 10am-5:30pm. €7.50.)*

■ **MUSEO POLDI PEZZOLI.** The museum contains an outstanding private art collection bequeathed to the city by Poldi Pezzoli in 1879. The museum's masterpieces hang in the Golden Room, overlooking a flower garden. Famous paintings include Andrea Mantegna's *Virgin and Child,* Botticelli's *Madonna and Child,* Bellini's *Ecce Homo,* Guardi's magical *Gray Lagoon,* and the museum's signature piece, Antonio Pollaiuolo's *Portrait of a Young Woman.* A number of smaller collections fill rooms on both floors. Particularly impressive is a tiny but sublime display of Italian military armaments. *(A few minutes from La Scala. V. Manzoni, 12. ☎02 79 48 89. Open Tu-Su 10am-6pm. €6, under 10 or over 60 €3.60.)*

PALAZZO REALE. An impressive structure that served as the residence for Milanese royalty since the 12th century, its exterior was graced with understated Neoclassical touches by Giuseppe Piermarini, the architect behind La Scala. Today it houses the Museo d'Arte Contemporanea, a series of exhibitions of art drawn from around the world. *(Located just south of the duomo. ☎ 02 6208 3219. Wheelchair-accessible. Open Tu-Su 9:30am-7:30pm. €6.20-9.30, depending upon exhibition.)*

GALLERIA VITTORIO EMANUELE II. A monumental glass barrel vault with an imposing glass and steel cupola (48m) covers a five-story arcade of overpriced cafes, shops, and offices. Mosaics representing different continents sieged by the Romans adorn the floors and the central octagon's upper walls. Once considered the drawing room of Milan, the Galleria is now a very old and very pretty mall. *(On the left, facing the duomo. ☎ 06 46 02 72. Open M-Sa 10am-11pm, Su 10am-8pm. Free.)*

MUSEO BAGATTI VALSECCHI. This beautifully preserved 19th-century aristocrat's house contains a collection of antique ceramics, *frescoes*, mosaics, ivory and weapons. *(At V. Santo Spirito, 10. MM3: Napoleone. From V. M. Napoleone, V. Santo Spirito is 2nd on the left. ☎ 02 7600 6132. Open Tu-Su 1-5:45pm. W €3, Th-T €6.)*

NEAR CASTELLO SFORZESCO

■ **CASTELLO SFORZESCO.** Restored after heavy bomb damage in 1943, the Castello Sforzesco is one of Milan's best-known monuments. Constructed in 1368 as a defense against Venice, it was used as an army barrack, a horse stall, and a storage house before da Vinci converted it into a studio. Inside are the **Musei Civici** (Civic Museums), which include the **Musical Instruments Museum** and the **Applied Arts Museum**. The ground floor contains a sculpture collection most renowned for Michelangelo's unfinished *Pietà Rondanini*, his last work. The tomb of Visconti in the center of the hall sets the duke's image atop a set of marble pillars, riding his beloved horse into eternity. At the Applied Arts Museum, filled primarily with ornate household furnishings, the *Automa contesta di demonio* stands out. The wooden fellow with winged ears and red eyes and tongue moves upon cranking from below. *(MM1: Cairoli. ☎ 02 8846 3703. Open Tu-Su 9:30am-7:30pm. Free.)*

■ **PINACOTECA DI BRERA.** The Brera Art Gallery presents a superb collection of 14th- to 20th-century paintings, with an emphasis on the Lombard School. Works include Bellini's *Pietà* (1460), Hayez's *The Kiss* (1859), Andrea Mantegna's brilliant *Dead Christ* (1480), Raphael's *Marriage of the Virgin* (1504), Caravaggio's *Supper at Emmaus* (1606), and Piero della Francesca's 15th-century *Sacra Conversazione* (1474). The vibrant, animated frescoes by Bramante from the Casa dei Panigarola provide comic relief from the dramatic intensity of other works. A limited collection of works by modern masters includes pieces by Modigliani and Carlo Carrà, and *Testa di Toro* by Picasso. *(MM2: Lanza. Immediately after V. G. Verdi when approaching from La Scala. V. Brera, 28. ☎ 02 72 26 31. Wheelchair-accessible. Open M-Su 8:30am-7:30pm. €6.20, EU citizens 18-25 €3.10.)*

■ **STADIO GIUSEPPE MEAZZA.** Even in a country where *calcio* (soccer) is always taken seriously, nothing comes close to the rivalry between Milan's two major clubs, Inter and A.C. Whenever the two teams face off in their shared stadium, the city reaches a fever pitch heightened by political overtones: Inter fans are often left-wing, while A.C. fans tend to be right-wing. The situation is further complicated by the fact that Inter is currently owned by ultra right-wing Prime Minister Silvio Berlusconi. A tour (offered in English) through the facilities will walk you through a museum of memorabilia, allow you to sit in the VIP seats, and take you into the locker rooms. *(MM2: Lotto. Walk along V. Fed. Caprilli; the stadium is on the left. Entrance at gate 4. V. Piccolomini, 5. Tours M-Sa 10am-6pm. €10, under 18 or over 65 €7. Tickets to A.C. games available at V. Turati, 3. ☎ 02 6228 5660. MM3: Turati. Inter fans can buy tickets at the Inter office, V. Durini, 24. ☎ 02 77 151. MM1: S. Babila. Tickets for either team are available at all Ticket One offices; call ☎ 02 39 22 61 for locations.)*

■ **CHIESA DI SANTA MARIA DELLA GRAZIE.** The church's Gothic nave is dark and elaborately patterned with frescoes, contrasting with the splendid, airy tribune Bramante added in 1492. The extensive interior renovations allow for a before and after view of the frescoes. Next to the church entrance is the *Cenacolo Vinciano* (Vinciano Refectory, or the convent dining hall), one of Milan's most famous sites and home to one of the most well-known pieces of art in the world: **Leonardo da Vinci's Last Supper.** The fresco captures the apostles' reaction to Jesus' prophecy: "One of you will betray me." *(MM1: Conciliazione. From P. Conciliazione, take V. Ruffini for about 2 blocks. P. di S. Maria delle Grazie, 2. ☎ 02 8942 1146 or 199 19 91 00. Reservations are strongly recommended. Arrive early or late in the day to avoid the 1hr. wait. Wheelchair-accessible. Open Tu-Su 8am-7:30pm, Sa 8am-11pm. Entrance to Last Supper €6.50, EU residents under 18 or over 65 €3.25. Audio guide €2.50.)*

LEONARDO DA VINCI'S HORSE. This bronze, based more on surmise of da Vinci's intentions than actual, documented designs, is a monument to one American's appreciation of Renaissance sculpture. *(MM1: Lotto. From Lotto, walk down V. Fed. Caprilli until the stadium is in view on your left. The statue is on your right, behind a large gate. V. Fed. Caprilli, 6-16. Free.)*

MUSEO NAZIONALE DELLA SCIENZA E DELLA TECNICA "DA VINCI". To further your study of da Vinci, explore this museum, which provides a historical view of the precursors of modern technology. The hall of computer technology features an interesting hybrid: a piano converted to a typewriter by Edoardo Hughes of Turin in 1885. The keys have letters pasted to them, and a ribbon receives the letters from a spinning wheel. Another section focuses on applied physics, while wooden models of Leonardo's most visionary inventions fill another room. *(MM2: San Ambrogio. V. San Vittore, 21, off V. Carducci. ☎ 02 48 55 51. Open Tu-F 9:30am-4:50pm, Sa-Su 9:30am-6:20pm. €6.20, under 12 or over 60 €4.20.)*

BASILICA DI SANT'AMBROGIO. A prototype for Lombard-Romanesque churches throughout Italy, Sant'Ambrogio is the most influential medieval building in Milan. Ninth-century reliefs in brilliant silver and gold decorate the high altar. St. Ambrose presided over this building between AD 379 and 386. Now you may preside over

A HORSE, OF COURSE. For nearly two decades, Renaissance great Leonardo da Vinci dreamt of fashioning the largest horse statue in the world. He even made a clay model four times life-size, unveiling it to acclaim at the wedding of Ludovico Sforza. While Leonardo sought funding to cast the statue, the model was left outside his studio. It went unmolested until September 10, 1499, when it attracted the notice of invading Gascon archers. Intrigued by the supple, humongous horse, they commenced target practice, bringing the venture in equestrian grandiosity to an end. A half-millennium later, in 1977, *National Geographic* ran an article on the subject, entitled "The Horse That Never Was." The article caught the attention of former United Airlines pilot Charles Dent, who was so inspired that he spent the rest of his life fundraising to finish da Vinci's noble endeavor. Dent died shortly before the September 10, 1999 unveiling of the 24 ft.-high, 15-ton bronze statue in the center of Milan.

him: go behind the altar, on either side, and descend into a dim sarcophagus, where you will find the skeletal remains of the saint (340-397) and his bedmate, St. Protasio. The 4th-century **Cappella di San Vittore in Ciel D'oro**, with exquisite 5th-century mosaics adorning its cupola, lies through the 7th chapel on the right; enter, walk a few paces, and then turn left. *(MM1: Sant'Ambrogio. Open M-Sa 7:30am-noon and 2:30-7pm, Su 3-7pm. Free. Audio guide €1.)*

FROM NAVIGLI ALONG THE CORSO DI PORTA TICINESE

■ **NAVIGLI DISTRICT.** The Venice of Lombardy, the Navigli district boasts canals, small footbridges, open-air markets, cafes, alleys, and trolleys. The Navigli are part of a medieval canal system (the original locks were designed by Leonardo da Vinci) that transported thousands of tons of marble to build the duomo and linked Milan to various northern cities and lakes. *(Outside the MM2: Porta Genova station, through the Arco di Porta Ticinese.)*

■ **BASILICA DI SANT'EUSTORGIO.** Founded in the 4th century to house the bones of the Magi, the church lost its original function when the dead wise men were spirited off to Cologne in 1164. The present building (erected in 1278) has a Lombard-Gothic interior of low vaults and brick ribs supported by substantial columns. The triumph of this church, and one of the great masterpieces of early Renaissance art, is the Portinari Chapel (1468), attributed to the Florentine Michelozzo. The Gothic tomb of St. Eustorgius (1339) rests in the center of the chapel. The ornate casket hovers, supported only by the soft, white marble shoulders of devotees, one of whom has three faces on one head. Near the front of the church is the 12th-century **Porta Ticinese**. *(Farther down C. Ticinese from San Lorenzo Maggiore. Tram #3. P. S. Eustorgio, 3. Open W-M 9:30am-noon and 3:30-6pm. Free.)*

CHIESA DI SAN LORENZO MAGGIORE. The oldest church in Milan, San Lorenzo Maggiore testifies to the city's 4th-century greatness. Begun as an early Christian church with an octagonal plan, it was rebuilt later and includes a 12th-century *campanile* and 16th-century dome. To the right of the church sits the 14th-century **Cappella di Sant'Aquilino.** Inside is a 5th-century mosaic of a beardless Christ among his apostles. A staircase behind the altar leads to the remains of an early Roman amphitheater. *(MM2: Porta Genova, then tram #3 from V. Torino. On C. Ticinese. Open daily 7:30am-6:45pm. Capella €1.)*

IN THE GIARDINI PUBLICI

GALLERIA D'ARTE MODERNA. Napoleon lived here with Josephine when Milan was the capital of the Napoleonic Kingdom of Italy (1805-1814). The gallery, reminiscent of Versailles, displays important modern Lombard art as well as works by Impressionists. Of special note are Modigliani's *Beatrice Hastings* (1915), Picasso's *Testa*, Klee's *Wald Bau*, and Morandi's *Natura Morta con Bottiglia*. Also see pieces by Matisse, Mondrian, and Dufy. *(MM12: Palestro. Gallery is at V. Palestro, 16, in the Villa Reale, not to be confused with the Palazzo Reale. ☎ 02 7600 2819. Open Tu-Su 9am-5:30pm. Free.)* Adjacent is the **Padiglione D'Arte Contemporanea (PAC),** an extravaganza of video, photographs, multimedia, and painting. *(Across P. Cardorna to Paleocapa, which becomes V. Alemagna. M1: Cardorna. Wheelchair-accessible. €8.)*

MUSEO CIVICO DI STORIA NATURALE. Milan's Museum of Natural History holds extensive geological and paleontological collections. *(C. Venezia, 55, in Giardini Pubblici. ☎ 02 78 13 02. Open M-F 9am-6pm, Sa-Su 9:30am-6:30pm. Free.)*

🎵 ENTERTAINMENT

Much of Milan's active cultural scene is sponsored by the city and therefore free. Events are detailed in the tourist office's free brochure *Milano Mese*.

OPERA

Although La Scala is currently closed for renovations, Milan remains the best place in the world to see an opera. Audience enthusiasm here is unparalleled, as is the La Scala troupe, who will be performing a full 2002-2003 season at their new home, the **Teatro degli Arcimboldi**. The season's official start is December 7 (St. Ambrose's Day), but operas are performed year-round. The new theater's excellent acoustics ensure full appreciation, cheap seats notwithstanding. A shuttle leaves for the theater from P. Duomo in front of the McDonald's on performance nights (6:45pm-7:15pm, €1), as well as from MM1: Precotto. Tickets are available in La Scala's new ticket office, in the Metro station at the Duomo stop. (☎02 7202 3339; www.teatroallascala.org. Tickets €10.32-154.93. At noon on the day of the performance, any remaining tickets are sold at half-price. Open M-Su noon-6pm.)

THEATER

The **Piccolo Teatro**, V. Rovello, 2, near V. Dante, was founded after WWII as a socialist theater. Owned by the city, it specializes in small, classical, off-beat productions. (☎02 7233 3222. Performances Tu-Sa 8:30pm, Su 4pm. €20, students €12.) The organization Teatri d'Italia sponsors **Milan Oltre** in June and July, a festival of drama, dance, and music. Call the **Ufficio Informazione del Comune** (☎02 8646 4094). Milan's **Carnevale** is the longest lasting in Italy and is increasingly popular. *Carnevale* occurs annually the Thursday, Friday, and Saturday after Ash Wednesday, centering around the duomo and spread throughout the city.

MUSIC

Milan lays claim to being the jazz capital of Italy, evinced no better than at the **Brianza Open Jazz Festival**, a series of performances scattered around the city in the first two weeks of July. (Information ☎02 237 2236; www.brianzaopen.com.) Free classical music concerts are organized by the city year-round, held in the city's aquarium, planetarium, and various churches. Ask at the tourist office or see *Milano Mese* for details.

FILM

Milan offers the usual slew of blockbusters; listings can be found in any major paper, particularly the Thursday editions. Wednesday shows are €3.75 instead of the normal €5. Many cinemas screen English films: Mondays at **Anteo**, V. Milazzo, 9 (MM2: Moscova; ☎02 659 77 32), Tuesdays at **Arcobaleno**, V. Tunisia, 11 (MM1: Porta Venezia; ☎02 2940 6054), and Thursdays at **Mexico**, V. Savona, 57 (MM2: Porta Genova; ☎02 4895 1802).

🛍 SHOPPING

Every year, thousands of fashion devotees make the pilgrimage to Italy's style capital. Even if you won't be paying major financial homage to deities Giorgio, Donatella, or Miuccia, the fashion district is worth a visit. Take the metro to MM1: S. Babila and then walk up V. Montenapoleone, being sure to note the two **Prada** stores within 100m of each other. Resist temptation and proceed past V. Sant'Andrea and the **Versace** store, turning right onto V. Gesù. Although distinctly less impressive, V. Gesù allows for a better approach to the inner sanctum along V.

FROM THE ROAD

ASTROLOGICAL OOPS

I often ask people I've just met for their astrological sign, secretly hoping that there is some truth to the signs' attributed characteristics. One night while researching a bar, I attempted to insert my query into a conversational lull. My question was met with delirious laughter.

Embarrassed, I asked what was so funny. After several minutes of convulsive laughter, a cigarette, and more laughter, my conversation partner explained.

Evidently, when I asked "Oroscopo?" ("Horoscope?"), I had placed the accent on the second-to-last syllable, so that it sounded like I was saying "Ora, scopo." "Ora" means "now" in Italian. "Scopo" is the first-person form of "scopare," Italian for "to sweep." But it has another, eh, less clean slang signification—I had essentially said, "Now I copulate."

Needless to say, I have since kept a lid on my astrological curiosities.

—Laura Nevison

Sant'Andrea. Toward the end of V. Gesù is a **Moschino** store, on V. della Spiga. Turn right, pass the **Dolce e Gabbana, Cerruti 1881,** and **Armani** stores, emerging on V. Sant'Andrea. This saint of a street has it all: **Fendi, Hermès, Chanel, Ferre,** another **Moschino, Armani, Prada,** and even **Armani Jr.** V. Sant'Andrea becomes V. Verri, with **Yves Saint Laurent.**

 PLACES OF WORSHIP. Show the same respect for Milan's fashion houses as you would for its cathedrals. This means nice pants for men and skirts or dresses for women. Leave those jeans at the hotel. Your credit cards, too.

If you can tolerate the stigma of being a season behind the trends, buy your designer duds from wholesale clothing outlets known as *blochisti* (stocks). Try **Monitor** on V. Monte Nero (MM3: Porta Romana, then tram #9 or 29) or the well-known **Il Salvagente,** V. Bronzetti, 16, off C. XXII Marzo (bus #60 from MM1: Lima or MM2/3: Stazione Centrale). If you're willing to go that extra mile, **Gruppo Italia Grandi Firme,** V. Montegani 3 (MM2: Famagosta) and **"Quel che c'e,"** V. Orobia, 11 (MM3: Lodi T.T.I.B.), are worth the trip. *Milano e Milano* has a great list of markets and second-hand stores. Shop around the area of C. di Porta Ticinese, the Navigli district, and C. Garibaldi for second-hand attire (MM2: Porta Genova, then bus #59). **Eliogabalo,** P. Eustorgio, 2 (☎ 02 837 8293), named after a Roman emperor renowned for his preoccupation with aesthetics, offers the latest in *haute couture*. True Milanese bargain hunters attack the bazaars on **V. Fauché** (MM2: Garibaldi) Tuesdays and Saturdays, and **Viale Papinian** (MM2: Agostino) Saturdays. The famous 400-year-old **Fiera di Sinigallia** on V. d'Annunzio is also great for bargains (Sa only). Another fabulous option is the classy Italian department store **La Rinascente,** where Armani began his infamous career, to the left of the duomo as you face it. (Open until 10pm.)

♞ NIGHTLIFE

Check any Milanese paper on Wednesday or Thursday for information on clubs and weekend events. *Corriere Della Sera* publishes an insert called *Vivi Milano* on Wednesdays, and *La Repubblica* produces *Tutto Milano* on Thursdays. *Milano Magazine* is a monthly publication by the Ufficio Informazione del Comune with information on bars, films, and seasonal events. The best guide to nightlife, however, is *Pass Milano*, published only

WALK LIKE AN ITALIAN. Italians have an uncanny ability to pick the tourists out of a crowd. Perhaps it's because every American tourist is wearing khaki shorts, a white t-shirt, and a pair of Tevas. If you want to avoid this phenomenon, and you're ready to make the leap into Euro-chic, add this simple starter kit of must-haves to your wardrobe.

Adidas shirt: Preferably one size too small and black with fluorescent stripes. For the full warm-up suit effect, buy the matching pants with chrome buttons.

See-through plastic straps: These bras and tops aren't strapless, but clearly trying.

Asymmetrical tanks: Don't want to bare it all? Revealing one shoulder is even better.

Really tight cargo pants: Thus negating the utility of all those pockets.

Capri pants: Skin-tight for women, loose and flowing for men.

Invicta backpack: Who knew that neon yellow went with hot pink? It does when the Invicta logo is plastered across the back in bright blue and mint green.

Telefonino: A mobile phone is essential; pretend with a fake.

in Italian, available in most bookstores (€12.50). The APT tourist office provides *Milano e Milano*, which has a comprehensive list of every entertainment option in the city, divided by type; **discoteche** are dance clubs, **cabaret** implies live music of all kinds (not necessarily with dancers), and **bar** means only that the venue *looks* like a bar, since many are otherwise indistinguishable from dance clubs. **Pubs** are Irish/English/Australian-themed places to drink and occasionally to eat, but almost never to dance. **Dancing** refers to ballroom dancing; **night club** translates into erotic dancing. Milan parties Thursday through Sunday nights and rests during the beginning of the week. Many clubs have "theme nights" (70s, 80s, hard rock, dance/house, electronica/trance, leather, gay, and bi) with varying cover charges. Remember that everything shuts down in August, and clubs are often reincarnated in totally different forms in September. During the summer there are numerous music festivals in Monza, north of Milan, advertised in the paper and on street posters.

A safe, attractive, and chic district lies near **V. Brera** northwest of the duomo and east of MM1: Cairoli; here you'll find art galleries, small clubs, restaurants, and an older, upscale crowd. In the early evening, Milan's youth migrate to the areas around **C. Porta Ticinese** and **Piazza Vetra** near Chiesa San Lorenzo, 15min. southwest of the duomo by foot. Lounge on the grass in the parks or grab a beer at one of the many *birrerie* (pubs). The highest concentration of bars and university-age youth can be found into the wee hours of the morning in the **Navigli** district.

The metro closes around midnight, and cabs are expensive, so plan the location of your evening activities with a walk home in mind or, better yet, think ahead and find a place to stay near your club or bar of choice. Milan is relatively safe to walk through at night, though the suburbs and the areas around Stazione Centrale and C. Buenos Aires deserve an extra dose of caution.

CORSO DI PORTA TICINESE AND PIAZZA VETRA

■ **Exploit, V. Piopette,** 3 (02 8940 8675), on your right just before La Chiesa di S. Lorenzo Maggiore. A trendy bar and restaurant with cheap beer (pint of Tennent's; €3). Join the crowd of locals around the colonnade. No cover. Open daily noon-3pm and 6pm-3am.

■ **Yguana Cafe Restaurant,** V. P. Gregorio XIV, 16 (☎02 8940 4195). Walk down C. di Porta Ticinese and turn left at P. Vetra. Embrace the stylish vibe. Beautiful natives sipping cocktails next to their scooters. Happy hour daily 5:30pm-9pm. No cover. Sunday brunch 12:30-3pm. Open daily 5pm-2am.

Grand Café Fashion, C. di Porta Ticinese, 60 (☎02 8940 0709). For music and food served late, try this bar/restaurant/dance club. Select, stunningly beautiful crowd, and velour leopard-print couches. Mandatory first drink €7.75. Happy hour F 6:30pm-10pm. No cover. Open Tu-Su 6pm-4am.

Bar Flying Circus, P. Vetra, 21 (☎02 5831 3577), facing rear of church. Cocktails and an assortment of 50 whiskeys. €4.50 for a pint. No cover. Open Su-F 9am-2am.

THE NAVIGLI

From C. Porta Ticinese, walk south until the street ends. Veer right through the P. XXIV Maggio to V. Naviglio Pavese and V. A. Sforza, two parallel streets bordering a canal. Alternatively, take the metro to MM2: Porta Genova. Walk along V. Vigevano until it ends and veer right onto V. Naviglio Pavese.

■ **Scimmie,** V. A. Sforza, 49 (☎02 8940 2874). A legendary bar with the best atmosphere in Navigli. Different theme every night and frequent concerts (10:30pm). Fusion, jazz, soul, and reggae. Open daily 8pm-3am.

■ **Pontell,** V. Naviglio Pavese, 2 (02 5810 1982). First bar on your right as you walk down V. Naviglio Pavese. Faux black-and-white leopard-skin furniture and lively atmosphere in a fairly traditional bar. Be sure to try the *bierre a la pression* (glass vessel that, when tilted, sends a thin stream of beer out at high pressure, €8). Open M-Su 6pm-2am.

Maya, V. A. Sforza, 41 (☎ 02 5810 5168). A lively bar and restaurant serving its own brand of Tex-Mex cuisine. Highly entertaining drinks (€5) include the flame-boyant *cuccaracha de toro*...Stand back or become part of the show. Open M-Su 8pm-2am.

New Klein, V. Vigevano, 8 (☎347 934 0124). From Porta Genova metro stop, walk 3 blocks down V. Vigevano. The diffused blue glow of New Klein is on the left. Try a Vodka Klein or Virgin Klein for €4.50. F-Sa DJ spins. No cover. Open Tu-Su 7:30pm-4am.

Totem Pub, V. E. Gola, 1 (☎02 837 5098). V. E. Gola branches off the left-hand side as you head down V. Naviglio Pavese. For the alternative sort. Beware the evil cow skull as you enter, and be prepared to hear anything from reggae to jungle. Huge Oktoberfest mug of beer for €8. Open daily 8:30pm-2:30am.

Propaganda, V. Castelbarco, 11 (☎02 5831 0682). From V. A. Sforza, walk east on V. Lagrange (next to Cafe Baraonda), which morphs into V. Giovenale. When you reach the end, the club will be on the left side of the farthest branch on the right. Some of the biggest dance floors in Milan (occasionally with live music). Caters mostly to a well-dressed, university-age crowd. Cover for ladies €13, men €16. Open Th-Su 11pm-4am.

AROUND CORSO COMO

■ **Loolapaloosa,** C. Como, 15 (☎02 655 5693). From MM2: Garibaldi, head south on C. Como. The club is on the right. A vigorous alternative to the hipper-than-thou scene. This bar is owned by the captain of the Italian football team. Energetic crowd may have you tipsy and dancing on the tables. Great rock'n'roll. Cover €6. Open M-Su 6pm-3am.

Rock: Hollywood, C. Como, 15 (☎02 659 8996), next door to Loolapaloosa. One of the the only discos in the city exclusive enough to choose from the crowd at the door. Slip into your nicest leather pants and pout for the bouncer. The ■ **mirror** in the women's restroom is said to have a view of the men's restroom. Gentlemen: smile for the ladies. Hip-hop, house, and pop. Cover Tu-W €13 and Th-Su €16. Open Tu-Su 11pm-4am.

Casablanca, C. Como, 16 (☎ 02 6269 0186). In a big white building just across from Rock: Hollywood and Loolapaloosa. Favorite among the ultra-trendy and ultra-hot. The crowd walking through the doors could just as easily be strutting down a runway. Cocktails €10. No cover. Open Tu-Su 6pm-3am.

Shocking, V. B. di Porta Nuova, 12 (☎02 659 5407). Head farther down C. Como. More down-to-earth than Hollywood, and minus the zaniness of Lollapaloosa. House/dance (€13, includes a drink); underground techno (€16, includes a drink). Open F-Sa 10:30pm-4am. Closed June-Aug.

AROUND LARGO CAIROLI

▨ **Le Trottoir,** C. Garibaldi, 1 (☎02 80 10 02). From MM2: Lanza, take V. Tivoli to C. Garibaldi intersection. One of the city's best bars. Live bands play nightly, but the bar is all about atmosphere. Pints and mixed drinks €8. No cover. Open daily 7pm-2:30am.

Bar Magenta, V. Carducci, 13 (☎02 805 3808). A short walk from MM1/2: Cardona. A traditional Guinness bar. No cover. Open M-Su 8pm-2am.

EAST OF CORSO BUENOS AIRES

▨ **Cafe Capoverde,** V. Leoncavallo, 16 (☎02 2682 0430). From MM1/2: Loreto, head down V. Costa, which becomes V. Leoncavallo (10min.). Walk through the flower shop to this heavenly, unique cafe that feels like a jungle full of natives. Cocktails dominate, but they also serve decent food. *Primi* or pizza around €6. Restaurant open M-Sa 12:30-2:30pm and 7:30pm-midnight, Su 12:30-2:30pm and 6pm-midnight. Bar open M-Su 11pm-2am.

▨ **Artdeco Cafe,** V. Lambro, 7 (☎02 2952 4760). From MM1: Porta Venezia, walk 3 blocks up C. Buenos Aires and take a right on V. Melzo. The bar is 3 blocks down on the left, across from Le Lephante. Modern and hip. Each table is decorated in a different style, though the predominant theme is Art Deco. House, hip-hop, and acid jazz. Dancing begins after midnight. Happy hour daily 6-9pm. No cover. Open M-Su 6pm-2am.

Kirribilly, V. Castelmorrone, 7 (☎02 7012 0151). From MM1: Porta Venezia take V. Regina Giovana from C. Buenos Aires. When you reach the P. Maria Adelaide di Savoia turn right down V. Castelmorrone. Kirribilly is on your right. A cheery Australian pub with good beer and a giant shark's head on the wall. M happy hour, Tu student night, Th pop quiz. No cover. Open M-F noon-3pm and 6pm-3am, Sa-Su 6pm-3am.

GAY BARS AND CLUBS

Le Lephante, V. Melzo, 22 (☎02 2951 8768). From MM2: Porta Venezia, walk up C. Buenos Aires 3 blocks; turn right on V. Melzo. Le Lephante is across from the Artdeco Cafe. Vaguely 60s interior with lava lamps and bizarre furniture. Mixed drinks €7-8. Happy hour 6:30pm-9:30pm, all drinks €5. No cover. Open Tu-Su 6:30pm-2am.

Sottomarino Giallo, V. Donatello de Bardi, 2 (☎02 2940 1047). MM1/2: Loreto. From P. Loreto, take V. Abruzzi to the corner of V. Donatello de Bardi. The biggest lesbian club in town. Open Tu-Su 10:30pm-3:30am.

Cicip e Ciciap, V. Gorani, 9 (☎02 86 72 02). From MM1: Cairoli, take V. S. Giov. sul Muro, which turns into V. Brisa. V. Gorani is the 2nd left. A bar/restaurant with a women-only crowd. Open Sa 8:30pm-3am.

One Way Disco, V. Cavallotti, 204 (☎02 242 1341). MM1: San Babila. From the station take C. Europa and turn left onto V. Cavallotti. A *discoteca* famed for the predominance of leather. Membership required. Open F-Sa 10:30pm-3:30am, Su 3:30-7pm.

LIVE MUSIC

▨ **Tunnel,** V. Sammartini, 30 (☎02 6671 1370), near V. Giuseppe Bruscetti, bordering Stazione Centrale. Post-punk, hardcore, ska, reggae, sci-fi surf, kraut rock, rockabilly, and various indie bands frequent this train-tunnel-turned-bandshell. Live music nightly. Double show F and Sa. Annual membership card necessary. Cover €3-10. Hours vary; check the paper.

Alcatraz, V. Valtellina, 25 (☎02 6901 6352). MM2: Porta Garibaldi. Take V. Ferrari and go right on C. Farni. After train tracks, turn left on V. Valtellina. Biggest club and indoor concert venue. Cover €13 (includes a drink). Open F-Sa 11pm-3am.

Blues House, V. S. Uguzzone, 26 (☎02 2700 3621). MM1: Villa S. Giovanni. Take V. Vipacco; turn right onto V. A. Soffredini and then a left onto V. S. Uguzzone. Good jazz and blues. Open W-Su 9pm-2:30am.

PAVIA
☎ 0382

Ever since Attila the Hun's forces unsuccessfully attacked Pavia in 452 BC, legions upon legions have sought admission to this the wealthiest of Milanese satellite towns. Those vying for entry today sport Prada and a penchant for academics. Pavia's prestigious university brings bustling student activity to the city. Romanesque churches fill the historic section, the da Vinci canals (an astounding achievement of contemporary engineering) run all the way from Navigli, and the nearby **Certosa di Pavia** is one of Italy's premier monastic structures.

▛ TRANSPORTATION

Trains: At the end of V. V. Emanuele. To **Genoa** (1½hr., every hr., 6:33am-10:45pm, €5.73) and **Milan** (30min., every hr., 6:08am-11:40pm, €2.75). Change at Codogno for **Cremona** (2hr., every hr., 6:37am-7:39pm, €4.66).

Buses: SGEA. Turn left out of train station. Buses depart from the enormous, modern brick building on V. Trieste. Tickets may be purchased at the office (painted green) under the terminal cover. To **Milan** (30min., 2 per hr., €2.60) via **Certosa di Pavia** (10min, €2.25).

Taxis: (☎ 0382 27 439) at the train station or (☎ 0382 29 190) at the center.

▟ ᐧ ORIENTATION AND PRACTICAL INFORMATION

Pavia sits on the banks of the Ticino River not far from where it merges with the Po. The train station overlooks **Piazzale Stazione** in the west end of the modern town. To get from the station to the historic center of town, walk down **Viale Vittorio Emanuele II** to **Piazzale Minerva.** Continue on Pavia's main street, **Corso Cavour,** to the city's narrow central square, **Piazza della Vittoria,** a block away from **Piazza Duomo.** Past P. Vittoria, the main street changes to **Corso Mazzini.**

Tourist Office, V. Filzi, 2 (☎ 0382 22 156). From train station, turn left on V. Trieste and then right on V. Filzi. Pleasant, knowledgeable, and English-speaking staff provides a good map. Open M-Sa 8:30am-12:30pm and 2-6pm.

Currency Exchange: Try **Banca Commerciale Italiana,** C. Cavour, 12, or **Banco Ambrosiano Veneto,** C. Cavour, 7d. Also try the 2nd floor of the **post office.**

English-Language Bookstore: Fox Books, C. Mazzini, 2c (☎ 0382 30 39 16), off P. Vittoria. Open Su-M 3-7:30pm, Tu-Sa 9am-1pm and 3-7:30pm.

Laundromat: Lavanderia Self-Service. Locations at S. Maria D. Pertiche, 22; V. Flarer, 22; and V. dei Mille, 56. Wash from €3.50, dry €3.50. Open M-Su 6am-10pm.

Emergency: ☎ 113.

First Aid/Ambulance: ☎ 118 or ☎ 0382 52 76 00 on nights and holidays.

Late-Night Pharmacy: Vippani, V. Bossolaro, 31 (☎ 0382 22 315), at corner of P. Duomo and V. Menocchio, has a list of pharmacies with night service. The staff provides emergency night services for surcharge. Open M-F 8:30am-12:30pm and 3:30-7:30pm.

Hospital: Ospedale S. Matteo, P. Golgi, 2 (☎ 0382 50 11).

Internet Access: University, from P. Vittoria, turn left on Strada Nuova. Walk past the intersection with V. Mentana and take 1st right. Continue through courtyard (bearing right) toward a large, seated statue with a long sword. On the right (behind the statue) is a door with the words *"Dipartimento di Scienza della Letteratura e dell'Arte Medievale e Moderna."* Have a student ID ready. Open M-F 9am-noon and 2-8pm.

Post Office: P. della Posta, 2 (☎0382 29 765), off V. Mentana, a block from C. Mazzini. Open M-F 8am-6pm, Sa 8am-1pm.
Postal Code: 27100.

☎ ACCOMMODATIONS & CAMPING

A dearth of reasonably priced places to stay makes Pavia unappealing as anything but a daytrip. Consider staying in Milan, or take advantage of Pavia's well-organized *agriturismo* program. Ask the tourist office for a complete pamphlet.

Locanda della Stazione, V. V. Emanuele II, 14 (☎0382 29 321), straight ahead from train station on your right. Great location and friendly staff. Simple, well-furnished rooms, many with A/C. Communal bath. Singles €21; doubles €31. ❷

Hotel Aurora, V. V. Emanuele, 25 (☎0382 23 664), straight ahead from train station on your left. With its white walls and Warhol-esque paintings, this hotel resembles a trendy art gallery. All 19 rooms with bath (showers only), TV, and A/C. Reserve ahead. Singles €45; doubles €68. MC/V. ❹

Hotel Excelsior, P. Stazione, 25 (☎0382 28 596). A more traditionally decorated hotel with bath, A/C, and TV in every room. Breakfast €6. Parking €8. Singles €50; doubles €73. AmEx/DC/MC/V. ❹

Camping: Ticino, V. Mascherpa, 10 (☎0382 52 70 94) From station, take bus #4 (dir.: Sora) for 10min. to Mascherpa stop. Up the road is a sign pointing to the campsite to the left. Restaurant next door. Entrance to pool: adults €6, children €4. Laundry €3.10 (wash). Campgrounds open Mar.-Oct. €5.20 per person, ages 5-12 €2.60, over 65 €4. €3.60 per tent, €8.30 per camper, €7.80 per caravan, €2.10 per car. ❶

☎ FOOD

Coniglio (rabbit) and *rana* (frog) are the local specialties, but if you don't eat things that hop and jump, wander to the *tavole calde* on C. Cavour and C. Mazzini. Try the well-loved *zuppa alla pavese*, piping-hot chicken or beef broth served with a poached egg floating on top and sprinkled with grated *grana* cheese. **Esselunga,** between V. Trieste and V. Battisti, at the far end of the mall complex, is a monolithic supermarket. (☎0382 26 210. Open M 1-9pm, Tu-Sa 8am-9pm.)

Ristorante Bardelli, V. Lungoticino Visconti, 2 (☎0382 53 10 77). Located right on the banks of the river Ticino, this restaurant offers excellent views and fine dining. The menu changes by season, with a focus upon Lombardian cuisine. *Primi* €10, *secondi* €13-16. Open Tu-Su noon-2:30pm and 7-10:30pm. AmEx/DC/MC/V. ❺

Antica Trattoria Ferrari, V. dei Mille, 111 (☎0382 53 90 25). The wood panelling bespeaks Swiss chalet, but the cuisine is strictly Italian. Fine Pavian cuisine and attentive service at this most inviting of local eateries. *Primi* €6.50, *secondi* €9.50. Cover €3. Service 10%. Open Tu-Sa 12:30-2pm and 7:30-9:45pm. MC/V. ❹

Ristorante-Pizzeria Marechiaro, P. Vittoria, 9 (☎0382 23 739). A warm interior and outside porch sheltered by white stucco. Delicious pizza (€3.50-9.50) served the way Neapolitan Mamas intended it. *Primi* €5-15, *secondi* €5-20. Cover €1.50. Open Tu-Su noon-2:30pm and 6pm-3am. AmEx/D/MC/V. ❷

Ristorante-Pizzeria Regisole, P. Duomo, 4 (☎0382 24 739), under the arcade with the duomo in clear view. Interior (with A/C) or outdoor seating. Relax to Baroque classical music. Pizzas from €4.50. *Profiteria* (chocolate cake; €2) is a must. Open Sept.-July W-M noon-2:15pm and 6:15pm-12:15am. AmEx/D/MC/V. ❶

NORTHWEST ITALY

◎ SIGHTS

▨ BASILICA DI SAN MICHELE. As the oldest building in town, this sandstone Romanesque church has witnessed many coronations, including that of Charlemagne in 774, Frederick Barbarossa in 1155, and various members of the Savoy family later on. It is said that when the crown was placed on Charlemagne's head, light shone down through one of the windows onto his newly crowned head. The Romanesque exterior dates from the 12th century, when the church was rebuilt following an earthquake. A 1491 fresco of the *Coronation of the Virgin* and 14th-century low-relief sculpture decorate the chancel, while an 8th-century crucifix of Theodore graces the *cappella. (Take C. Strada Nuova to C. Garibaldi and turn right onto V. S. Michele. Open daily 8am-noon and 3-8pm.)*

UNIVERSITY OF PAVIA. Founded in 1361, this beacon of higher education claims famous alumni Petrarch, Columbus, Venetian playwright Goldoni, and physicist Alessandro Volta (inventor of the battery), whose experiments are now on display. The university's patron and renowned sadist, Galeazzo II of the Visconti family, earned notoriety for his research on human torture. Three towers on P. da Vinci are the remnants of more than 100 medieval towers that once punctuated the skyline. The story of the university is laid out at the **Museo per la Storia dell'Università di Pavia**. *(From P. Vittoria, turn left onto V. Calatafimi and then right onto C. Stradivari; take the first entrance on the right. Museum open M 3:30pm-5pm, F 9:30am-noon. Free.)*

DUOMO. An all-star team of visionaries including Bramante, da Vinci, and Amadeo began work on the **Cattedrale Monumentale di Santo Stefano Martiro** in the 15th century. The **Torre Civica**, adjoining the duomo, collapsed in the spring of 1989, killing several people and taking a much of the left chapel with it. To the left of the duomo, you can see the remnants of the tower, surrounded by a metal fence. The duomo's shaky brick exterior, recently reinforced with concrete columns, conceals an impressive interior modified under Mussolini. *(Duomo diagonally across from P. San Michele.)*

CASTELLO VICONTEO. This colossal medieval castle (1360) is set in a beautifully landscaped park. Richly colored windows and elegant terra cotta decorations border three sides of the castle's vast courtyard; the 4th wall was destroyed in 1527 during the Franco-Spanish Wars. Pavia's **Museo Civico** resides here, featuring a formidable gallery of paintings and an extensive Lombard-Romanesque sculpture collection. On the second floor, there is a model of Pavia's duomo in rich, burnished wood. *(At the end of Strada Nuova. Castle ☎0382 33 853. Museum ☎0382 30 48 16. Open Tu-Sa 9am-1:30pm, Su 9am-1pm. €4.10, under 18 or over 65 €2.60.)*

BASILICA DI SAN PIETRO IN CIEL D'ORO. From the grounds of the castle, you can see the low, rounded forms of the Lombard-Romanesque *chiesa* of "St. Peter in the Sky of Gold" (1132). Inside, piercing rays of light stream down from tiny windows. On the high altar, an ornate, 14th-century Gothic tomb is said to contain the remains of St. Augustine. Intricate frescoes adorn the ceiling of the sacristy, to the left of the altar. *(Open daily 7am-noon and 3-7pm.)*

◪ NIGHTLIFE

Pavia's large student population makes for far better nightlife than one would expect from a city of its size. The eclectically decorated **▨Nice One,** Strada Nuova, 26, has a cocktail menu with 1200 drinks from €4.50 to €6. (☎0382 30 34 54. Open Tu-Su 5pm-2am.) A taste of the islands awaits in the fresh fruit cocktails (€4.15) at **Morgan's Drink House,** C. Cavour, 30C. (☎0382 26 880. Open W-M 7pm-2am.) Tribal rhythms beat on at **Malaika "Bar and Soul,"** V. Bossolaro, 21, off C. Cavour. Enjoy *panini* and fruit desserts (from €2) on leopard skin-covered stools. Happy-hour (7-9pm) cocktails go for €4.50. (☎382 30 13 99. Open Tu-Su 6am-2am.) **Il Broletto,** P. Vittoria 14E, is an Irish pub near the duomo. (☎382 67 541. Open 8pm-2am.)

▶ DAYTRIP FROM PAVIA: CERTOSA DI PAVIA

Buses from Milan-Famagosta (MM2) to Certosa (20min.; 2 per hr.; first from Milan 5:40am, last from Certosa 8pm; €2.25) and then to Pavia's Trieste Station (10min., €1.20). Exiting the bus in Certosa, turn right towards town; continue in this direction for a few blocks, and then turn right up the long, tree-lined V. Certosa. The monastery lies at the end of it. (☎0382 92 56 13. Open May-Aug. Tu-Su 9-11:30am and 2:30-6pm; Sept. Tu-Su 9-11:30am and 2:30-5:30pm; Apr. and Oct. Tu-Su 9-11:30am and 2:30 5pm; Nov.-Mar. Tu-Sa 9-11:30am and 2:30-4:30pm, Su 9-11:30am and 2:30-5pm. Appropriate dress required. Free.)

Eight kilometers north of Pavia stands the ◨**Certosa di Pavia** (Carthusian Monastery). It was built as a mausoleum for the Visconti family, who ruled the area from the 12th through the 15th centuries. Started in 1396 by the Viscontis and finished by the Sforzas in 1497, the monastery contains an eclectic array of four centuries of Italian art, from early Gothic to Baroque. More than 250 artists worked on the elaborate facade during the 15th-century Lombard Renaissance, embellishing it with inlaid marble and sculptures of saints. The old sacristy houses a Florentine triptych carved in ivory; 99 sculptures and 66 bas-reliefs depict the lives of Mary and Jesus. The beautiful backyard contains 24 houses, one for each Carthusian monk. In accordance with St. Benedict's motto *ora et labora* (pray and work), the monks are active in agriculture and distill excellent liquors, sold on the premises. The monks lead **group tours** (usually in Italian).

CREMONA   ☎0372

Muted earth-tone buildings and white stucco walls adorn the quiet streets of Cremona, suggesting to the unsuspecting visitor that this is just another sleepy Italian town that happens to be located north of the river Po. Underneath the light conversational buzz in the Piazza del Comune flows a tangible ardor for rich local history and traditions. Claudio Monteverdi was born here, and Andrea Amati created the first modern violin in Cremona in 1530, establishing the Cremonese violin-making dynasty. After learning the fundamentals as apprentices in the Amati workshop, Antonio Stradivarius (1644-1737) and Giuseppe Guarneri del Gesu (1698-1744) raised violin-making to a new art form. Students still come to the city's International School for Violin-Making to learn the legendary craft. Today, the city pays homage to its noble music-making tradition with perennial jazz, dance, opera, and classical music festivals at the Ponchielli Theater. Despite Cremona's claims on tourists' attentions, it remains a native-oriented town, with few English speakers but many a neighborly *"buona sera."*

▛ TRANSPORTATION

Trains: V. Dante, 68. Bus stop: P. Stazione. Info and ticket office (☎848 88 80 88, call daily 7am-9pm) open daily 6am-7:30pm. To: **Brescia** (45min., every hr., 5:24am-6:58pm, €3.75); **Mantua** (1hr., every hr., 6:24am-8:34pm, €4.15); **Milan** (1¼hr., 13 per day, 5:02am-7:24pm, €5); **Pavia** (2hr., 1 per day, 5:15am, €4.60). Trains also depart for **Bergamo, Bologna, Brescia, Codogno, Fidenza, Parma, Piacenza,** and **Pisa.** Check the newsstand in the station for schedules and prices, or ask at the ticket booth.

Buses: Autostazione di V. Dante (☎0372 29 212), 1 block to the left of train station. Ticket office open daily 7:40am-12:10pm and 2:30-6:30pm. To **Brescia** (every hr.; M-Sa 6:10am-6:55pm, Su less frequently; €4.10). Check at the station for scheduling information. For travel within Cremona, take the orange buses located just outside the train station. Schedules change frequently; pick one up at the information booth.

Taxis: (☎0372 21 300 or 26 740). At train station and piazzas, such as P. Stradivari.

Bike Rental: Bitibi, Brescia, 77 (☎347 982 6161). Bicycle and tandem rental. Call for prices and hours. Newly opened.

◄✳ 🔁 ORIENTATION AND PRACTICAL INFORMATION

As you leave the train station, bear to the left of the small stretch of grass. The road straight ahead is **Via Palestro,** which becomes **Corso Campi,** then **Via Verdi,** ending in **Piazza Stradivari.** Turn left at P. Cavour to **Piazza del Comune,** where the tourist office, duomo, and tower are located.

Tourist Office: Azienda Di Promozione Turistica, P. del Comune, 5 (☎0372 23 233). Ask for general info brochure on hotels, museums, and restaurants. Open daily 9am-12:30pm and 3-6pm.

Currency Exchange: Banco Nazionale del Lavoro, C. Campi, 4-10 (☎0372 40 01), on the left corner next to post office, when walking away from P. Stradivari on V. Verdi. Open M-F 8:20am-1:20pm and 2:30-4pm, Sa 8:20-11:50am. 24hr. **ATM.**

Emergency: ☎113. **Carabinieri:** ☎112. **Ambulance and First Aid:** ☎118.

Police: V. Tribunali, 6 (☎0372 40 74 27).

Hospital: Ospedale (☎0372 40 51 11), in Largo Priori. Past P. IV Novembre to the east, take V. B. Dovara and go right on V. Giuseppina.

Post Office: V. Verdi, 1 (☎ 0372 59 35 02). Open M-Sa 8:30am-7pm. **Currency exchange** for €2.58. Bring passport.

Postal Code: 26100.

🏠 ACCOMMODATIONS AND CAMPING

Albergo Touring, V. Palestro, 3 (☎0372 36 976). Heading out of train station, walk straight ahead to V. Palestro. 4 blocks ahead on your left. Great location, less than a 5min. walk from P. del Comune. Basic rooms, bright and very clean, with high ceilings. Some have balconies overlooking the street. Doors lock at 12am. Singles €21; doubles €37, with bath €48. ❷

Servizi per L'Accaglienza, V. Fuoco, 11 (☎/fax 0372 21 562). Walk down V. Trento e Trieste towards the P. Libertà. Take a right on V. Fuoco; Servizi will be on the left. Only travelers 18-65. Tranquil rooms with bath surround a central courtyard. No curfew. Singles €19, half-pension €21, full-pension €23.50; doubles €15.50/€18.10/€21. ❷

Hotel Duomo, V. Gonfalonieri, 13 (☎0372 35 242). Located in P. del Comune. Clean, bright rooms with bath, TV, and A/C. Reception area and hallways are tastefully and simply decorated. Adjacent restaurant with tables outside. Breakfast included. Parking garage for patrons. Singles €42; doubles €67; triples €82. AmEx/MC/V. ❹

La Locanda, V. Pallavicino, 4 (☎0372 457 8354; fax 45 78 34). From P. del Comune, walk up V. Solferino, turn right on C. Mazzini, bear left on C. Matteotti, and V. Pallavicino is a few blocks down on the right. 3-star hotel with clean rooms and friendly management. 9 rooms with carpeting, bath, TV, and phone. Some English spoken. Restaurant downstairs features homemade pasta. Breakfast included. Reception 24hr. Reservations recommended. Singles €38.73; doubles €56.83; triples €74.55. AmEx/MC/V. ❹

Giardino di Giada, V. Brescia, 7 (☎0372 43 46 15). From station, turn left down V. Dante and left again at P. Libertà, or take bus #5. Rooms are noisy, but tall French doors, balconies, and high ceilings almost make up for it. 2 communal bathrooms. No English. Singles €25; doubles €31; triples €36. AmEx/MC/V. ❷

Camping: Parco al Po, V. Lungo Po Europa, 12a (☎0372 212 68). From P. Cavour, walk 20min. down C. V. Emanuele. Located next to the River Po. Open Apr.-Sept. €7 per person and car, €2.50 per child 4-12, €1 per tent. €4.50 per each additional person. Parked caravans available: doubles €18, triples €26, quads €35. Showers and electricity free. AmEx/MC/V. ❶

⌂ FOOD

The city's *mostarda di Cremona*, first concocted in the 16th century, consists of cherries, figs, apricots, and melons preserved in a sweet mustard syrup. *Mostarda* can be found in most local *trattorie* and is traditionally served on boiled meats. Bars of *torrone* (an egg, honey, and nut nougat), another Cremonese specialty, are available in every sweet shop (most are closed on S and M mornings). Hours change frequently, so call or ask at your hotel. **Sperlari,** at V. Solferino, 25 (☎0372 22 346), has been keeping dentists in business since 1836. **Negozio Vergami Spelta e Generali,** C. Giacomo Matteotti, 112 (☎0372 23 67), at the P. della Libertà, on the corner of C. Matteotti and Trento e Trieste, has a similar assortment of goodies. The delicious *Grana Padano*, similar to parmesan cheese, is available in the local *salumerie*. On Wednesday and Saturday from 8am to 1pm, there is an open-air market in P. Stradivari that sells farm-fresh vegetables, fruits, and a wide variety of dried and cured meats in addition to aromatic cheeses. You can replenish your closet as well as your pantry—the market also sells clothes, bags, and household items. For supermarkets, **Il Punto,** at P. Risorgimento, 30 (☎0372 337 34), is near the train station. (Open M 8:30am-12:30pm, Tu-Sa 8:30am-12:30pm and 5-7:30pm.) **GS** at V. S. Tommaso, 9, is close to P. del Comune. (Open M 9am-8:15pm, Tu-Sa 8am-8:15pm, Su 9am-1pm.) You can also try **Colmark** on V. Dante, just left of the train station. (Open M 1:30-7:30pm, Tu-Sa 8:30am-7:30pm.)

La Piedigrotta, P. Risorgimento, 14 (☎0372 22 033). Convenient location 2 blocks to the right of train station, on the far side of the piazza. Sparklingly clean, with classic look, homey atmosphere, and hospitable staff. Extensive menu includes fish, pasta, risotto, and vegetarian options. Pizza for 2 starts at €4. The *pizza marechiaro* (€7) is especially delicious and impressively garnished with a completely intact fried crawfish. The fixed menù with *primi, secondi,* and *contorni* costs €10.50. Open F-W 11:30am-3pm and 6:30pm-1:30am. AmEx/MC/V. ❶

Ristorante Pizzeria Marechiaro, C. Campi, 49 (☎0372 26 289). Do your window shopping at their outdoor tables while the jolly staff serves you, or help yourself at the plentiful buffet of risotto, fish, and pasta dishes, available any time. Pizzas from €5.20. Cover €1.30. Open daily noon-3pm and 8pm-2am; Oct.-Apr. closed Tu. AmEx/MC/V. ❷

Ristorante Pizzeria Vesuvio, P. Libertà, 10 (☎0372 43 48 58). Opposite C. Matteotti. Take a seat outdoors or in a bright, airy room sporting a wood burning stove. Pizzas €4-8.50, *primi* from €4.50. Open Th-Tu noon-2pm and 7-10pm. AmEx/MC/V. ❷

Ristorante Dordoni, V. del Sale, 58 (☎0372 22 703). A 5min. walk from P. Cadorna and Parco al Po. A surplus of shrubbery outside gives way to A/C and chic decor within. Try the back room for a more intimate setting. Cover €2.50. Entrees €7-21. Reservations recommended. Open M noon-3pm, W-Su noon-3pm and 8pm-midnight. Don't miss the adjoining **Gelateria Dordoni** outside open W-M 2-8pm. AmEx/MC/V. ❹

NORTHWEST ITALY

SIGHTS

TEATRO PONCHIELLI. This lavishly decorated Baroque theater is one of Cremona's highlights. The 250-year-old masterpiece provided the testing ground for the Stradivari and Amati violins. In addition to having one of the largest stages in Italy, it stands as one of the most beautiful and undiscovered opera houses worldwide. Red velvet chairs offer sumptuous seating. Call in advance for free morning tours, which are difficult to arrange in August. Visit the ticket office for an up-to-date schedule of performances. *(Go to P. Stradivari and take C. V. Emanuele to 25. ☎ 0372 407 2745; www.rccr.cremona.it/doccomu/tea/teaindex.htm. Ticket office open June-Sept. M-Sa 4:30-7:30pm; Oct.-May M-Sa 4-7pm.)*

CHURCH OF SAN SIGISMONDO. A prime example of Cremonese Mannerism, the church was built to honor the union of the powerful Sforza and Visconti families in 1441, only to be rebuilt in 1463 after a ravaging fire. Mannerist masters Boccaccino, Giulio, and Antonio and Bernardino Campi revealed their talent in fresco on every pillar, arch, and vault. In this case, too many cooks failed to spoil the broth—the church is marked by a harmonious mixing of architecture and fresco work. Take a gander at *The Adulterous Woman Before Christ;* Boccaccino's subjects would have had no such privilege, as he failed to give their eyes pupils. *(Largo B. Visconti, off V. Giuseppina. From P. Libertà, 20min. walk down V. Ghisleri. Follow signs for the church. Or take bus #1, 2, 4. ☎ 0372 43 19 19. Open daily 8am-noon and 3-6pm. Free.)*

PIAZZA DEL COMUNE. The second floor of the **Palazzo Comunale** houses the lavish *Saletta dei Violini* (Violin Room), showcasing seven masterpieces attributed to Andrea Amati, Nicolò Amati, Stradivari, Gerolamo, Sacconi, and Guarneri. The guards will unlock the room and give you a personal tour in Italian. English information booklets are available. *(P. del Comune. With your back to the church, enter the courtyard; stairs are on the left and elevator is in front. Open Apr.-Sept. M-Sa 9am-6pm, Su 10am-6pm. Closed M Oct.-Mar. €6; students, over 60, and violin-makers €3.50.)* Directly facing the *palazzo*, the pink-marble duomo **Santa Maria Assunta** is a fine example of a Lombard-Romanesque cathedral, built in the 12th century. The interior displays a cycle of 16th-century frescoes. *(Open M-Sa 7:30am-noon and 3:30-7pm, Su 7:30am-1pm.)* To the left of the duomo stands the late 13th-century ■**Torrazzo.** Made completely of bricks and standing at 111m, it is the tallest *campanile* in Italy. A climb up 487 steps will reward you with a close-up view of the world's oldest known astrological clock. *(Closed for restoration, the Torrazzo is set to reopen September 2002. Check with the tourist office for current times and prices. Open Easter-Oct. M-Sa 10:30am-noon and 3-6:30pm, Su 10:30am-12:30pm and 3-7pm; Nov.-Easter Sa-Su 10:30am-12:30pm and 3-6pm. €4.13.)* The dome of the **baptistery** (1167) rises in a perfect, unadorned octagonal pattern. The Gothic **Loggia dei Militia,** located across from the baptistery, was the meeting point for the military in the 1200s. *(☎ 0372 27 386. Make a reservation with the priest to see both baptistery and loggia.)*

MUSEO CIVICO AND MUSEO STRADIVARIO. The newly restored **Palazzo Affaitati** (1561) flaunts an impressive Renaissance marble staircase that leads to the museum's extensive and diverse collection, well displayed in a light, airy gallery. The collection includes paintings by Bembo and Caravaggio and a collection of portraits of the Ala Ponzone family, the museum's benefactors in 1842. One room is dedicated solely to the enormous (up to 20ft. long) paintings and frescoes recovered from the destroyed church of San Domenico in Cremona. Other noteworthy pieces include Caravaggio's *San Francesco in Meditazione*, Genovesino's *Amore dormiente* (featuring a nude cupid sitting atop a book, leaning closed-eyed on a skull with bow in hand), and a curious painting by Arcimboldi.

Seen right side up, the painting is a remarkably detailed face made from vegetables, but upside down it looks like a pot of broccoli and carrots. The **Museo Stradivario** has no actual Stradivarius violins but has a room of his molds, models, drawings, and collection of other famous violins. A video tour in English explains the production of violins. The **Biblioteca Statale** features a large reading room with a fresco of Cremona on the far wall and an admirable collection of Olivetti typewriters from the 1950s. *(Palazzo Affaitati: V. Ugolani Dati, 4. ☎ 0372 46 77 70. Museo Civico and Stradivario: Open Tu-Sa 8:30am-6pm, Su 9am-noon and 3-6pm. €7, €4 for students and handicapped. Biblioteca: Open M 8:10am-2pm, Tu-F 8:10am-6pm, Sa 8:10am-2pm.)*

PALAZZO FODRI. Dating from 1499, the Fodri is another of Cremona's fine Renaissance buildings. The columns in the courtyard bear the French royal insignia in homage to Louis XII of France, who occupied the duchy of Milan in 1499. Frescoes and terracotta friezes adorn the rooms upstairs. *(C. Matteotti, 17. ☎ 0372 21 454. Call to make an appointment for viewing.)*

 MORE FOR YOUR MONEY. If your aim is to see all Cremona has to offer, consider a *biglietto cumulativo*, which covers admission to the **Museo Civico** and **Stradivario** and the **Palazzo Comunale** (€10, students €5). Or purchase the city card for discounts to all sights, some restaurants and fairs, and bus rides (€7.75). Both options are available at the tourist office.

🎵 ENTERTAINMENT

Music and festivity is in the Cremona air year-round. The **Monteverdi Festival,** the most well-known and widely attended spectacle, is held in May and June. The **Cremona Jazz,** running from April through May, introduces the summer season with a series of concerts throughout the city. **La Danza Festival,** festival of dance, is held in in July, and the opera season goes from October through December. Check with the tourist office for info on other fairs that spotlight antiquities, violin making, cattle, and wedding gowns. *(Teatro Ponchielli ticket booth at C. V. Emanuele, 52. ☎ 0372 407 2745; www.rccr.cremona.it/doccomu/tea/teaindex.htm. Open June-Sept. M-Sa 4:30-7:30pm; Oct.-May M-Sa 4-7pm. Tickets around €15.)*

MANTUA (MANTOVA) ☎ 0376

Mantua owes its literary fame to its most renowned son, the poet Virgil. The driving force that built the city's *centro storico*, however, was not the weaver of epics but the Gonzaga family that held sway over Mantua from 1328 to the mid-18th century. As patrons of the arts, the Gonzagas transformed a small village into a bustling cultural and literary haven. Giuseppe Verdi found inspiration here for his opera *Rigoletto*. You can see the legendary **House of Rigoletto** (see p. 124) in the Piazza Sordello. Today fragments of Mantegna and Pisanelli frescoes are juxtaposed with chic Italian shops. The countryside around Mantua is replete with small towns; **Castellaro, Cavriana,** and **Solferino** are famous for their historic architecture and inexpensive Mantuan wine. Mantua may be used as a base to explore the vineyards of the 3rd-largest wine-producing province in Lombardy; inquire at the tourist office about winery routes.

🚆 TRANSPORTATION

Trains: (☎ 0376 848 8088), in P. Don Leoni, end of V. Solferino. Ticket office open daily 7am-9pm. To: **Cremona** (1hr., every hr., 5:25am-8:50pm, €4.15); **Milan** (2hr., 9 per day, 5:25am-6:36pm, €7.90); and **Verona** (40min., 19 per day, 6:10am-10:20pm, €2.27).

Buses: APAM (☎0376 32 72 37), in P. Mondadori. Turn right and cross the street out of the train station. Cross C. V. Emanuele to V. Caduti. (1½hr., every hr., 5:45am-7:45pm, €5.25).

Taxis: ☎0376 36 88 44.

Bike Shop and Rental: Viale Piave, 22. €1.60 per hr. or €8 per day. Bike rental contingent upon weather. M-Sa 8:30am-12:30pm and 2:30-7:30pm. Check at the tourist office for bike itineraries around Mantua and the surrounding countryside.

✦🔢 ORIENTATION AND PRACTICAL INFORMATION

From the train station in P. Don E. Leoni, head left on **Via Solferino** and then right on Via Bonomi to the main street, **Corso Vittorio Emanuele II.** Follow it into P. Cavallotti to pick up C. Umberto I. **Piazza Marconi** is at the end, and **Piazza Mantegna** is on your left.

Tourist Office: P. Mantegna, 6 (☎0376 32 82 53; fax 36 32 92; www.aptmantova.it), adjacent to Sant'Andrea's church. From train station, turn left onto V. Solferino and follow it straight as it turns into V. Fratelli Bandiera. Right onto V. Verdi. Free brochures and city map. Open M-Sa 8:30am-12:30pm and 3-6pm, Su 9:30am-12:30pm.

Luggage Storage: Train station, right near the tracks. Open 7:30am-8:30pm. €3.87 per bag for 5 days.

Boat Excursions: Motonavi Andes, V. S. Giorgio, 10 (☎0376 32 28 75; fax 36 08 69).

Emergency: ☎113. **Ambulance:** ☎118.

Police: P. Sordello, 46 (☎0376 20 51).

Pharmacy: V. Roma, 24. Open Tu-Sa 8:30am-12:30pm and 4-8pm. Pharmacies located all over the city. Hours change weekly. Check any one to find rotating late-night service.

Hospital: Ospedale Civile Poma, V. Albertoni, 1 (☎0376 20 11).

Post Office: P. Martiri Belfiore, 15 (☎0376 32 64 03), up V. Roma from the tourist office. Open M-F 8:30am-7pm, Sa 8:30am-7pm. **Currency exchange** available.

Postal Code: 46100.

🛏 ACCOMMODATIONS

Those willing to stay in smaller nearby towns like Castellaro and Monzambano will be able to find less expensive accommodations. Ask at the tourist office for an up-to-date pamphlet of *agriturismo* options—farms offer accommodations for around €30 per person per night.

Albergo Giulia Gonzaga, V. Vespasiano Gonzaga, 65, Sabbioneta (☎0375 52 81 69). Well-kept hotel with large checkered floors in the quiet city of Sabbioneta, 45min. from Mantua by bus. Painted pastel woodwork gives a rustic-cottage effect. All 13 rooms with TV and bath. No curfew. Singles €30-35; doubles €50; triples €60. MC/V. ❸

Hotel Mantegna, V. Filzi, 10 (☎0376 32 80 19; fax 36 85 64), 2min. from P. Belfiore. In the heart of Mantua's historic district. Very relaxing lounge with bar and leather couches. 37 elegant, modern, carpeted rooms, all with bath, TV, telephone, and A/C. Breakfast extra. Singles €67; doubles €110; triples €130. AmEx/MC/V. ❺

Hotel ABC, P. Don Leoni, 25 (☎0376 32 33 47; fax 32 23 29), across from station. Small, clean, modern rooms, all with bath, fan, TV, and telephone. The outdoor patio is lit at night for reading. Buffet breakfast included. Seasonal variations in price. All rooms with bath. Singles €40-67; doubles €65-88; triples €90-118. ❹

Albergo Maragò, V. Villanova De Bellis, 2 (☎/fax 0376 37 03 13), at the Locanda Virgiliana. Take bus #25, which runs from P. Cavallotti or P. Sordello into Virgiliana (10min., every 30min.). The hotel is on the left, just past P. S. Isidro. If you don't mind

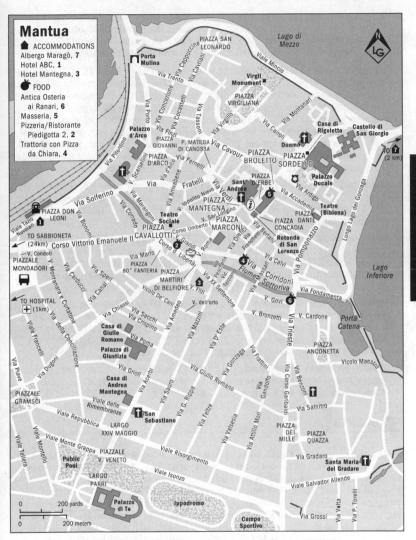

Mantua

🏠 ACCOMMODATIONS
Albergo Maragò, **7**
Hotel ABC, **1**
Hotel Mantegna, **3**

🍎 FOOD
Antica Osteria
  ai Ranari, **6**
Masseria, **5**
Pizzeria/Ristorante
  Piedigotta 2, **2**
Trattoria con Pizza
  da Chiara, **4**

the 2km journey from the center or the industrial setting, this hotel-restaurant's quiet, clean, dormitory-style rooms are a bargain. No TV or A/C. Singles without bath €21; doubles €32, with bath €42. Closed Aug. 20-Sept. 1. AmEx/DC/MC/V. ❷

🍴 FOOD

Mantuan cuisine is renowned for its famous *tortellini zucca* (pumpkin-filled ravioli) and its strict reliance upon locally grown produce and livestock. Homegrown gastronomical delights include parmesan cheese, truffles, river-bound fish, and risotto (rice fields abound in the region). *Risotto alla pilotta*, a specialty made with pork, is one of the staples in Mantua, where pigs outnumber people four to one. The pig is so revered that every December, the people of Mantua celebrate *Festa dell'Osso*, or festival of the bone, in which every part of the pig (including the face, ears, tail, and feet) is consumed by a carnivorous, pork-loving crowd.

▨ **Ristorante Corte Bondeno,** V. Mezzana Loria, Sabbioneta (☎348 775 9007). Exit the city north from P. Ducale. Follow marked signs. V. Mezzana Loria turns into dirt as you approach a large stone farmhouse, the restaurant. Most easily accessible by car, but the 30min. walk to this pastoral retreat is worth it. Sit back in the large country dining room to enjoy your bottle of *Lambrusco Mantovano*, a sparkling red wine, while the waiter brings you huge quantities of the freshest and most delicious food in Mantua. The *tortellini zucca* is sweet and dripping with butter and parmesan. Set *menù* €22, excluding wine. Open Tu-Th noon-2pm and 8pm-1am, F noon-2pm and 8pm-2am, Sa noon-3pm and 8pm-2am, Su noon-4pm and 8pm-2am. MC/V. ❹

Masseria, P. Broletto, 8 (☎/fax 0376 365 303). This romantic, candlelit restaurant with seating in the outdoor piazza is a perfect spot for people-watching. Masseria makes a great *risotto alla pilotta* (€8). Delicious pizza from €6.50. Open Tu-Su noon-3pm and 7:30pm-midnight. AmEx/MC/V. ❷

Antica Osteria ai Ranari, V. Trieste, 11 (☎0376 32 84 31; fax 32 84 31), at the intersection of V. Pomponazzo and V. Trieste. The 200-year-old building has rustic wooden beams and old-fashioned windows. The friendly proprietor serves authentic regional dishes in this tavern-style *trattoria*. *Primi* €4.50-6, *secondi* €4.50-9. Cover €1.50. Open Tu-Su noon-2:30pm and 7:15-11:30pm; closed July 15-Aug. 6. AmEx/MC/V. ❶

Trattoria con Pizza da Chiara, V. Corridoni, 44 (☎0376 22 35 68), right off V. Pomponazzo onto V. Corridoni. 1st street before the river. Unusual *trattoria* with a winding staircase that leads to 3 charming, distinct eating areas with stone floors. Bottom level has A/C. €5 buffet available any time. Pizza from €4, *primi* from €5, *secondi* from €8. Open W-M noon-3pm and 7pm-midnight. AmEx/MC/V. ❷

Pizzeria/Ristorante Piedigrotta 2, C. Libertà, 15 (☎0376 32 70 14). Great deals on pizza and delicious seafood dishes. Friendly, fish-loving staff. Pizza €2.50-8.50, *primi* €4.50, *secondi* from €6.50. Open T-Su noon-3pm and 6:30pm-12:30am. MC/V. ❷

⊙ SIGHTS

▨ **PALAZZO DUCALE. Piazza Sordello** lies beside what was once the largest palace in Europe, with 500 rooms and 15 courtyards. The 14th to 17th centuries saw the Gonzaga family's construction and decoration of the *palazzo*, in the company of the best architects and artists of the day. Throughout its history, the *palazzo* has spread its tentacles in all directions, absorbing all buildings in its path, including the Gothic **Magna Domus** and **Palazzo del Capitano.** Begin your tour of the *palazzo* at the **Hall of Dukes,** where evocative sections of Antonio Pisanello's frescoes (1439-44) were discovered in 1969 under thick layers of plaster. Especially beautiful is the *Zodiac Room*, containing a painting of Diana in her chariot and a mammoth lobster. The frescoes by Giulio Romano in the *Room of Troy* are also impressive. After passing through rooms draped with tapestries from Raphael's designs, the tour descends upon the Gonzagas's *sala dei fiumi*. Frescoed with vines and flowers, the room looks out on a garden bordered on three sides by a splendid portico. Formerly a fortress, the **Castello di San Giorgio** (1390-1406) was later consumed by the *palazzo* and turned into a wing. Inside the *castello*, the **Camera degli Sposi** (Marriage Chamber) contains Andrea Mantegna's famed frescoes of the Gonzaga family (1474). Call ahead, as occupancy can be limited. *(Palazzo Ducale: P. Sordello. ☎ 0376 38 21 50. Ticket office located under the porticoes facing the piazza. Open Tu-Su 8:45am-7:15pm. €6.50, students €3.25, under 18 or over 65 free.)*

▨ TEATRO (BIBIENA). The theater, one of the only ones in northern Italy not modeled after Milan's La Scala, looks like a miniature fairy tale castle. It was inaugurated by Mozart in 1796. Separate little balconies with small, velvet love couches are decorated in rose with stone gray trimming. Statues of Virgil and Pompanazzo sit in niches in the back wall of the stage. *(At the corner of V. Accademia and V. Pomponazzo. V. Accademia, 4. ☎ 0376 32 76 53. Open Tu-Su 9:30am-12:30pm and 3-5pm. €2.07; students, under 18 or over 60 €1.07.)*

PALAZZO DI TE. Built by Giulio Romano in 1534 as a suburban retreat for Federico II Gonzaga and his mistress Isabella, the opulent Palazzo di Te is widely considered the finest Mannerist building. It demonstrates the late Renaissance fascination with the Roman villa, nudity, and bending the rules of proportion. Idyllic and exotic murals of Psyche line Federico's banquet hall. The *Room of Giants* displays a continuous fresco of giants in various tortured positions, as Zeus punishes them for their insurrection with lightning bolts flung from the ceiling. Less monumental, though no less interesting, is the 16th-century graffiti decorating the walls. Another wing of the palace features regular shows of modern Italian works alongside a collection of Egyptian and Impressionist art. *(At far south end of the city down V. P. Amedeo through P. Veneto and down Largo Parri. ☎ 0376 32 32 66. Open M 1-6pm, Tu-Su 9am-6pm. €8, students and 12-18 €2.50, under 11 free, groups of 20 €4.50 per person.)*

ROTUNDA DI SAN LORENZO AND CHIESA DI SANT'ANDREA. This 11th-century Romanesque church is described as "La Matildica" because it was built in the time of Matilda di Canossa, the powerful noblewoman who bequeathed the rotunda to the pope. *(In the Piazza dell' Erbe, just south of P. Sordello. Open daily 10am-12:30pm and 2:30-4:30pm. Free.)* Opposite the rotunda rises Mantua's most important Renaissance creation, Leon Battista Alberti's **Chiesa di Sant'Andrea** (1472-1594). Its facade combines the classic triumphal arch motif—barrel-vaulted portal and flanking pilasters—with an antique pedimented temple front. The gargantuan interior was the first monumental space constructed in the Classical style since imperial Rome. The plan, including multiple side chapels, served as a prototype for ecclesiastical architecture for the next 200 years. Giorgio Anselmi painted the dome's frescoes. The painter Andrea Mantegna's tomb rests in the first chapel on the left as you enter the door. The church's holy relic, a piece of earth supposedly soaked in Christ's blood, parades the streets in a religious procession each Good Friday. The rest of the year, the relic of the Precious Blood is kept in a crypt beneath the nave. *(Open daily 8am-noon and 3-6:30pm. Free.)*

PALAZZO D'ARCO. Each of the *palazzo's* 14 small rooms has a theme and is furnished as it would have been in the 17th century. A separate wing contains a snow-colored library and the palace kitchen, complete with pots, pans, and dilapidated staircase. Across the gardens dotted with antique statues and blooming roses is the highlight of the *palazzo:* Falconetto's extraordinary zodiac chamber, a room with ornate frescoes of the astrological signs. *(Off V. Pitentino. Take V. Fernelli. ☎ 0376 32 22 42. Open Mar.-Oct. Tu-Su 10am-12:30pm and 2:30-5:30pm; Nov.-Feb. Sa-Su 10am-12:30pm and 2-5pm. €3.)*

CASA DI ANDREA MANTEGNA. Earthy red brick dating from 1476 contrasts sharply with the surrounding colorful homes and the grayish marble facade of the neighboring church of San Sebastiano (1460). The circular courtyard, approximately 20 ft. in diameter, is enclosed by soaring walls. The inside rooms are modern and host traveling art exhibitions. *(V. Acerbi, 47. ☎0376 36 05 06. Gallery open for exhibitions M-F 10am-12:30pm and 3-6pm. Exhibitions almost always free. Ask the tourist office for listings and prices.)*

CASA DI RIGOLETTO. This supposed dwelling of Verdi's legendary opera hero serves as offices for the Association Guide. The small but pretty gardens in the back with a balcony and statue of Rigoletto are open to the public. *(P. Sordello, 23. ☎0376 36 89 17. Gardens open daily 9:30am-12:30pm and 3:30-6:30pm.)*

🎵 ENTERTAINMENT

The **Teatro Sociale di Mantova,** P. Cavallotti (☎0376 36 27 39), off C. V. Emanuele, stages operas and occasional plays from October to December. The **Teatro Bibiena** (☎0376 32 76 53) on V. Accademia hosts purely musical events. Two classical concert seasons run from October to April and from April to June. Jazz performances span from April to June. **Grazie,** accessible by bus, holds its annual **Festa della Madonnari,** an international competition among street vendor painters on Ferragosto (August 15th). In early September, Italian speakers and scholars should check out **Festivaletteratura,** which attracts hordes of literary scholars from all over the world. Every first weekend of December, the town of Castel D'Ario celebrates the pig at the **Festa dell'Osso.**

🔁 DAYTRIP FROM MANTUA: SABBIONETA

Sabbioneta is 33km southwest of Mantua and easily accessible by bus from the Mantua bus station (45min, 8 per day, 6:35am-7:50pm, €6.40). Get off at the stop P. Gonzaga. Main tourist office: P. D'Armi, 1. Take a right around the building. Office is at the end. (☎0375 22 10 44; www.comune.sabbioneta.mn.it. Apr.-Sept. office open Tu-Su 10am-1pm and 2-5pm, sites open Tu-Su 10:30am-1pm and 2:30-6pm; Oct.-Mar. tourist office and sites open Tu-Su 9:30am-12:30pm and 2-5:30pm. Hours change frequently. Tours in English, French, or German €7.20, groups €5.70 per person. €5.70 for tickets without tour, €2.60 single monument. Free tours in Italian.)

Sabbioneta was founded by Vespasiano Gonzaga (1532-91) to rival his extended family's success in transforming Mantua into a center of art and culture. He succeeded in establishing a bustling feudal town which earned the title "Little Athens of the Gonzagas" for its importance as an artistic center in the late Renaissance. Inside the well-preserved 16th-century city walls lie Vespasiano's creations. An excellent guided tour from the tourist office starts at the **Palazzo del Giardino,** which has intricately decorated alcoves, one with the head of Medusa on the ceiling surrounded by rosettes in stucco relief. The long gallery is lined with windows and bright frescoes. The **Palazzo Ducale** has fewer surviving frescoes but is to be admired for its architecture and mahogany ceilings. The tiny **Teatro Olimpico** has a colorful mural along the back wall of the balcony as well as a decorated stage.

If you prefer to meander around the quiet streets, be sure to admire the most ancient gate in the town, the **Porta Vittoria,** and the more elaborate **Porta Imperiale** to the east. Tickets to the **Sinagoga** are available at Sabbioneta's other tourist office on V. Vespasiano Gonzago, 27. (☎0375 52 039. Open Tu-Sa 9:30am-noon and 2:30-5pm. Tickets €2.50, groups €1.50.) To see any of Sabbioneta's four churches, contact the priest 10 days in advance (☎0375 52 035). The Baroque interior of **Chiesa di Villa Pasquali** is open for viewing (daily 9am-noon and 3-6pm). A map at the tourist office outlines the scenic route, past farmhouses and fields of corn, to the parish church. On the first Sunday of each month, antique aficionados arrive in Sabbioneta for the exhaustive **Mercato dell'Antiquariato.** During September and October, traveling music, theater, and ballet groups also stop here.

BERGAMO ☎ 035

Every city should have a castle in the clouds. This one does. Glimmering in the distance, a medieval town sits on a bluff, presiding over the rest of Bergamo. Palaces, churches, and a huge stone fortification used to defend Venetian-controlled Venice from Spanish-ruled Milan characterize the *città alta* (high city), as do narrow, cobblestoned streets, lined by houses little touched by the march of time. Below, the *città bassa* (low city) is a modern metropolis whose Galleria dell'Accademia Carrara is packed with quintessential Renaissance artwork.

▐ TRANSPORTATION

Trains: (☎035 24 76 24) in P. Marconi. At the juncture of the Brembana and Seriana valleys. **Luggage storage** available (p. 125). To: **Brescia** (1hr., every hr., 6:14am-8:40pm, €3.25); **Cremona** (1½hr., every hr., 8:58am-5:30pm, €5); **Milan** (1hr., every hr., 5:46am-11:02pm, €3.65); and **Venice** (2hr., 8:22am, €11.21).

Buses: To right from train station. To: **Como** (6:25am-7:45pm, 7 per day, €4.15) and **Milan** (every 30min., 5:35am-9:35pm, €4.10).

▐█ ▐ ORIENTATION AND PRACTICAL INFORMATION

The train station, bus station, and numerous budget hotels are in the *città bassa*. There are three ways to reach *città alta:* take bus #1 (€0.90) to the *funicolare di città alta,* which ascends from **Via Vittorio Emanuele** to the Mercato delle Scarpe (8 per hr, €0.90, free if you still have your bus ticket). Bus #1a runs to the Colle Aperto, stopping at the top of the *città alta*. Or take the stairs on **Via Salità della Scaletta,** which starts to the left of the funicular on V. V. Emanuele. Turn right at the top to enter *città alta* on **Via San Giacomo** through **Porta San Giacomo** (10-15min. walk).

Tourist Offices: In *città alta:* **APT,** V. Aquila Nera, 2 (☎035 24 22 26; fax 24 29 94; www.apt.bergamo.it). Take bus #1 or 1a to the funicular; from the funicular, follow V. Gombito to P. Vecchia, and turn right just before the P. Vecchia onto V. Aquila Nera; office is 1st door on right. Open daily 9am-12:30pm and 2-5:30pm. In *città bassa:* **APT,** V. V. Emanuele, 20 (☎035 21 02 04 or 21 31 85; fax 23 01 84). From the train station, head straight up V. Papa Giovanni, which after about 8 blocks and 2 name changes will bring you to V. V. Emanuele and the tourist office, set off the road inside a large, brown building with a black, wrought iron fence. Press the buzzer to the left of the 1st gate and all the maps in Bergamo will be yours. Open M-F 9am-12:30pm and 2-5:30pm.

Currency Exchange: Banca Nazionale del Lavoro, V. Petrarca, 12 (☎035 23 80 16), off V. V. Emanuele, near P. della Libertà. Good rates. Open M-F 8:30am-1:20pm and 2:45-4:15pm. Also on 2nd fl. of the **post office.** Open M-F 8:30am-5pm.

ATM: Can be found in the train station near the *tabacchi* and outside **Banca Popolare di Milano,** on V. P. Paleocapa off V. Papa Giovanni XXIII.

Money Transfers: World Center Agenti, V. Quarenghi, 37/d (☎035 31 31 24; fax 32 13 63), off V. P. Paleocapa. Open daily 10:30am-8pm.

Luggage Storage: In train station. €2.58 per 12hr. Open daily 7am-9pm.

Laundromat: "Speedy Wash," V. A. Mai, 39/b (☎0335 425 9971). Open M-Su 7:30am-8pm. Wash €3.50 per 8kg, dry €1 per 10min.

Emergency: ☎113. **Ambulance:** ☎118.

First Aid: ☎035 26 91 11; nights and Su ☎035 25 02 46.

Police: V. Galagerio, 25 (☎035 23 82 38).

Hospital: Ospedale Maggiore, Largo Barozzi, 1 (☎035 26 91 11).

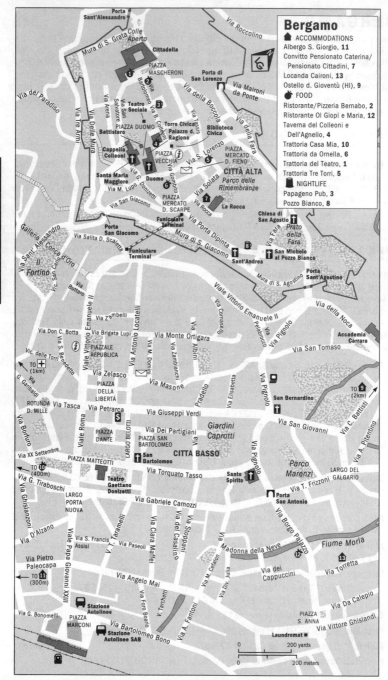

Bergamo

ACCOMMODATIONS
Albergo S. Giorgio, **11**
Convitto Pensionato Caterina/
 Pensionato Cittadini, **7**
Locanda Caironi, **13**
Ostello d. Gioventù (HI), **9**

FOOD
Ristorante/Pizzeria Bernabo, **2**
Ristorante Ol Giopi e Maria, **12**
Taverna del Colleoni e
 Dell'Agnello, **4**
Trattoria Casa Mia, **10**
Trattoria da Ornella, **6**
Trattoria del Teatro, **1**
Trattoria Tre Torri, **5**

NIGHTLIFE
Papageno Pub, **3**
Pozzo Bianco, **8**

Internet Access: For Bergamo's HI hostel guests (€5.16 per hr.), or at the **Centro Giovenile e Universitario Diocesano,** V. Pignolo, 73/a, in *città bassa*. From Largo Porta Nuova, walk along Gabriele Camozzi, turn left on V. Pignolo, and look for an archway with dark wooden doors on the right. Walk to the end of the entrance hallway and through the doorway on the right, and then walk up 2 flights of steps to the 1st floor Enter 2nd door on the left. €1.50 per hr. Open M-Sa 9am-12:20pm and 3-6:45pm.

Post Office: V. Locatelli, 11 (☎035 24 32 56). Take V. Zelasco from V. V. Emanuele. Open M-F 8:30am-1:40pm, Sa 8:30-11:40am. Packages are handled at V. Pascoli, 6 (☎035 23 86 98). Same hours.

Postal Code: 24122.

ACCOMMODATIONS

Prices rise with altitude; the most affordable *alberghi* are found in the *città bassa*. The tourist office has information on cheaper *agriturismo* options.

Ostello della Gioventù di Bergamo (HI), V. G. Ferraris, 1 (☎/fax 035 36 17 24; www.sottosopra.org/ostello). From train station take #9 bus to Comozzi, then bus #14 to Leonardo da Vinci. From there, backtrack about 50m and take the flight of stairs up the hill. The hostel will be to your right. Modern and clean. Each dorm has a private full bath. HI members only. Gates close at midnight. Lockout 10am-2pm. No morning check-in, strictly enforced. Breakfast included. Laundry for guests (€8 for wash, dry, and detergent). Internet access €5.16 per hr. Dorms €13.50. MC/V. ●

Locanda Caironi, V. Torretta, 6B/8 (☎035 24 30 83). From train station, walk straight ahead (on V. Papa Giovanni XXIII) to V. Angelo Maj, make a right, then continue for several blocks until you reach V. Borgo Palazzo; make a left. Turn right at 2nd block. Accessible by bus #5 or 7 from V. Angelo Maj. A family affair, replete with exquisite courtyard. Quiet residential neighborhood. The rooms of the 18th-century building overlook a secluded garden *trattoria,* one of Bergamo's best-kept culinary secrets. Reservations recommended. Shared bath. Singles €15.50; doubles €28.50. MC/V. ●

Albergo S. Giorgio, V. S. Giorgio, 10 (☎035 21 20 43; fax 31 00 72). Bus #7, or a short walk from train station: walk straight on V. Papa Giovanni XXIII to V. P. Paleocapa, make a left; this street becomes V. S. Giorgio. Train tracks and a construction site nearby, but fairly quiet inside. Neat, modern rooms with TV and sink. Some English spoken. 68 beds. 2 rooms wheelchair-accessible. Door closes at midnight but 24hr. access possible; ask at desk. Singles €27, with bath €39; doubles €39/€57. DC/MC/V. ●

Convitto Pensionato Caterina Cittadini, V. Rocca, 10 (☎035 24 39 11), off P. Mercato delle Scarpe (V. Rocca is the small, narrow street on right after exiting top of the funicular) in *città alta*. Women only. The orange-hued walls of this *pensione* give a warm glow to the open-air courtyard and sun-lit rooftop terraces. The nuns in charge are happy to give foreigners a home, although little English is spoken. Reception on 2nd floor Breakfast and dinner included. Curfew 10pm; if going out later, ask for a key. Singles €25, with bath €30; doubles €40. ●

FOOD

Casonsei, meat-filled ravioli dishes, are a typical *primo* in Bergamo, while the *branzi* and *taleggio* cheeses are part of a traditional *formaggio* course that concludes the meal. Try them with the local *Valcalepio* red and white wines. The typical meal includes horse *(cavallo)* or donkey *(asino)* with a side of polenta, a staple dish made from corn meal and water. Streets in the *città alta* are lined with *pasticcerie* selling yellow polentina confections, topped with chocolate blobs intended to resemble birds. These sweet treats are primarily pricey tourist bait; many natives have never sampled one. For meal necessities, shop at **Compra Bene**

Supermercato, on the right side of V. V. Emanuele, past the *città bassa* tourist office at the bottom of the hill heading to the *città alta.* (Open M 8:30am-1pm, Tu-Sa 8:30am-8pm. MC/V.) Most *Bergamese* shops are closed Monday mornings.

CITTÀ BASSA

In comparison to their loftier cousins, restaurants in the *città bassa* are often less traditionally *Bergamesco*, and the quality can be less cloud-nine.

> **Trattoria Casa Mia,** V. S. Bernardino, 20A (☎035 22 06 76). From train station walk straight ahead to Porta Nuova. Turn left onto V. G. Tiraboschi, which becomes V. Zambonate. Then turn left onto V. Bernadino. Full home-style meal with *primo, secondo, contorno,* and drink €11, at lunch €8.50. Open M-Sa noon-2pm and 7-10pm. Closed 1 week in the middle of Aug. ❷

> **Ristorante Ol Giopi e Maria,** V. Borgo Palazzo, 27 (☎035 42 366). From the train station, turn right onto V. B. Bono, then left onto V. Borgo Palazzo. The restaurant is about 1½ blocks past P. Sant'Anna. Popular with excellent Bergamescan food. Lunch *menù* €25.82, dinner *menù* €36.15. Open Tu-Sa noon-3:30pm and 7:30pm-midnight. ❺

CITTÀ ALTA

Many of Bergamo's best restaurants are located here on the main tourist drag, V. Bartolomeo, and its continuations V. Colleoni and V. Gombito. The romantic Venetian alcove at the **Vineria Cozzi,** V. B. Colleoni, 22 (☎035 23 88 36), appeals to tourists as do their low-priced bottles of wine. (Open Th-Tu 10:30am-2am. MC/V.)

> **Taverna del Colleoni & Dell'Agnello,** P. Vecchia, 7 (☎035 23 25 96). Great views and excellent local cuisine more than compensate for steep prices at this 300-plus-year-old restaurant. *Primi* €12-14, *secondi* €13-24. Open Tu-Sa noon-2:30pm and 7:30-10:30pm, Su noon-2:30pm and 7:30-10pm. AmEx/DC/MC/V. ❹

> **Trattoria del Teatro,** P. Mascheroni, 3a (☎035 23 88 62). At the start of V. Bartolomeo. An understated restaurant, offering exceptional local fare at moderate prices. *Primi* €7-8, *secondi* €12-14. Open Tu-Su 12:30-3:30pm and 7:30-11:30pm. ❸

> **Trattoria Tre Torri,** P. Mercato del Fieno, 7a (☎035 24 43 66). Take a left off V. Gombito when heading away from P. Vecchia. Less ornate then its more expensive counterparts, but off-the-beaten path and with authentically *Bergamasco* cuisine. *Antipasti* and *primi* €6.50, *secondi* €9. Cover €1.50. Open M-Su noon-3pm and 7:30-10:30pm; closed W in winter. MC/V. ❸

> **Ristorante-Pizzeria Bernabo,** P. Mascheroni, 11 (☎ 035 23 76 92). About the best non-*Bergamasco* restaurant you'll find in the *città alta.* Pizza and pasta extraordinaire. *Primi* €8.50-10.50, *secondi* €6-12. Open F-W 12:30-2:30pm and 7:30-10:30pm. AmEx/DC/MC/V. ❹

> **Trattoria da Ornella,** V. Gombito, 15 (☎035 23 27 36). Popular place specializing in rich *polenta taragna,* made with butter and local cheeses. *Primi* €6-8, *secondi* €10-14. Open F-W noon-3pm and 7-11pm. AmEx/DC/MC/V. ❸

◉ SIGHTS

CITTÀ BASSA

The newer of the two parts of the city, situated at the base of the bluff, *città bassa* compensates for its generally lackluster appearance with the Galleria dell'Accademia Carrara, which brims with some of Italy's most important artworks.

■ **GALLERIA DELL'ACCADEMIA CARRARA.** Housed in a glorious Neoclassical palace, this is one of the most important art galleries in Italy. The works displayed start from 13th-century Gothic art, with an emphasis on Florentine humanism. Fifteen rooms are hung with canvasses by the Dutch School and *Bergameschi* greats like Fra' Galgario, as well as canvases by Boticelli *(Ritratto di Giuliano de Medici)*, Lotto *(Ritratto di Giovinetto)*, Tiepolo, Titian, Rubens, Brueghel, Bellini, Mantegna, Goyen, van Dyck, and El Greco. There are several pieces by Rizzi (in **gallery VI**), including a diptych *Maddalena in Meditazione*, which finds Mary Maddalena looking upon a crucified Christ while trying to hold up her shirt; and, in *Maddalena Penitente*, still intent on the cross, she covers her breasts with a Bible. The Rizzis are beside several Lottos, including *Nozze Mistiche di Santa Caterina*. **Gallery IX** is dominated by the works of Moroni. *(P. dell'Accademia 82a. From Largo Porta Nuova, take V. Camozzi to V. Pignolo, turn left to V. San Tomaso, then right. ☎ 035 39 96 43. Open Oct.-Mar. Tu-Su 9:30am-1pm and 2-5:45pm, Apr.-Sept. Tu-Su 9:30am-1pm and 2:30-6:45pm. €2.58, over 60 or under 18 free.)*

OTHER SIGHTS. Piazza Matteotti, in the heart of *città bassa*, was redesigned by the Fascists in 1924 and is a favorite meeting place for both tourists and native *passeggiatori*. In the **Chiesa di San Bartolomeo**, at the far right of the piazza, you will find a superb altarpiece of the Madonna and Child by Lorenzo Lotto. *(Open daily 9am-4pm. Free.)* To the right of San Bartolomeo, V. Tasso leads to the **Chiesa del Santo Spirito**, marked by its strangely sculpted facade. The fine Renaissance interior (1521) houses paintings by Lotto, Borgognone and Previtali. *(Open Sept.-June M-Sa 7-11:30am and 4-6:30pm, Su 8am-noon and 4-7pm; July-Aug. M-Sa 7-11am and 5-6:30pm, Su 8:30am-noon and 5-7pm.)* On the left, V. Pignolo connects bassa to alta, winding past a succession of handsome 16th- to 18th-century palaces. Along the way is the tiny **Chiesa di San Bernardino**, whose colorful interior pales behind a splendid painting by Lotto. *(Open W-Th 10am-1pm. Free.)*

CITTÀ ALTA

The *città alta*, perched above the modern city, is a wonderfully preserved medieval town with a fountain, panoramic view, and archway around every corner. The town is accessible by funicular, bus, and foot. From the Carrara gallery, the terraced V. Noca ascends from the lower city to Porta S. Agostino, a 16th-century gate built by the Venetians as a fortification. After passing through the gate, V. Porta Dipinta leads to V. Gombito, which ends in P. Vecchia.

■ BASILICA DI SANTA MARIA MAGGIORE. Despite a dim, stark Romanesque exterior, this 12th-century basilica, joined to the Cappella Colleoni, possesses a breathtakingly elaborate and bright Baroque interior. Lavish, iridescent ceilings frame dark paintings beneath an octagonal dome. Tapestries with various biblical stories hang on several walls, surrounding the Victorian tomb of 19th-century composer Gaetano Donizetti, Bergamo's most famous son. *(Left of Cappella Colleoni. ☎ 035 22 33 27. Open Apr.-Oct. M-Su 9am-12:30pm and 2:30-6pm; Nov.-Mar. M-Sa 9am-12:30pm and 2:30-5pm, Su 9am-noon and 3-6pm. Free.)*

■ CAPPELLA COLLEONI. The patterned, pastel marble facade of this chapel was designed in 1476 by G. A. Amadeo (also behind the Certosa di Pavia) as a tomb and chapel for the celebrated *Bergamesco* mercenary Bartolomeo Colleoni. Notable are the 18th-century ceiling frescoes by Tiepolo. Look up as you exit for a gruesome decapitation of John the Baptist. *(Head through archway flanking P. Vecchia to reach P. del Duomo; the Cappella is to the right. Open Apr.-Oct. M-Su 9am-12:30pm and 2-6:30pm; Nov.-Mar. Tu-Su 9am-12:30pm and 2:30-4:30pm. Free.)*

PIAZZA VECCHIA. This piazza houses a majestic ensemble of medieval and Renaissance buildings flanked by restaurants and cafes in the heart of the *città alta*. Rest your legs as you sit with locals on the steps of the white marble **Biblioteca Civica** (1594), repository of Bergamo's rich collection of manuscripts. Across the piazza is the massive Venetian Gothic **Palazzo della Ragione** (Courts of Justice, 1199) and a 300-year-old sundial (on the ground beneath the arched portico). To the right, connected to the *palazzo* by a 16th-century covered stairway, stands the 12th-century ▨**Torre Civica** (Civic Tower), whose 15th-century bell rings 180 times each night at 10pm in memory of the medieval curfew. *(Open May to mid-Sept. M-Th and Su 10am-8pm, F-Sa 10am-10pm; mid-Sept. to Oct. M and F 9:30am-12:30pm and 2-7pm, Sa-Su 10am-7pm; Nov.-Feb. Sa 10:30am-12:30pm and 2-4pm, Su 10:30am-4pm; Mar.- Apr. Tu and Th-Sa 10:30am-12:30pm and 2-6pm, Su 10:30am-6pm. €1, under 18 or over 65 €0.50.)*

BAPTISTERY. This octagonal structure, in white and red stone, just to the left of the Cappella in P. del Duomo, holds several small, marble relief depictions of Jesus's life. The baptistery is a reconstruction of its 14th-century predecessor that was once a part of the basilica. *(Between Cappella Colleoni and the Basilica.)*

CHIESA DI SAN MICHELE AL POZZO BIANCO. Built in the 8th century and renovated during the 15th, the church's real attraction is a fresco by Lotto, located in the chapel of the Madonna. *(Near the intersection of V. P. Dipinta and V. Osmano. ☎ 035 25 12 33. Open daily 8am-6pm.)*

PARCO DELLE RIMEMBRANZE. Located on the site of a Roman military camp, this park's shady paths are dedicated to Italian battle casualties, but are currently overrun with the youth of Bergamo. Climb **La Rocca**, the distinguished fort standing in the middle of the park; it provides a stunning panoramic view of the Po Valley and the *città alta*. *(At the end of V. Solata. P. Brigate Legnano, 12. ☎ 035 24 71 16. Park: Apr.-Sept. M-Su 9am-8pm; Oct. and Mar. M-Su 10am-6pm; Nov.-Feb. M-Su 10am-4pm. Free. La Rocca: ☎ 035 22 47 00. Open May-Sept. Sa-Su 10am-8pm; Sept. 16-Oct. 31 Sa-Su 10am-6pm; Nov.-Feb. Sa-Su 10:30am-12:30pm and 2-4pm; Mar.-Apr. 10:30am-12:30pm and 2-6pm. €1, under 18 or over 60 €0.50.)*

♫ ENTERTAINMENT

The arts thrive in Bergamo. The opera season lasts from September to November and is followed from November through April by the drama season at the **Donizetti Theater,** P. Cavour, 15, in the *città bassa.* (☎035 416 0602.) In May and June, the spotlight falls on the highly acclaimed **Festivale Pianistico Internazionale,** co-hosted by the city of Brescia. In September, Bergamo celebrates its premier native composer with a festival of Gaetano Donizetti's lesser-known works. Contact the tourist office or the theater at P. Cavour, 14 (☎035 24 96 31) for info. During summer, the tourist office provides a program of free events, *Viva La Tua Città.*

The *città alta* transforms at night. Though many locals head to discos in surrounding towns, masses of twentysomethings pack the eateries, pubs, and *vinerie* to socialize. Head down to ▨**Pozzo Bianco,** V. Porta Dipinta, 30/b; going up will be easier after a few good beers. A *birreria* with a kitchen and character is by far the liveliest hangout for local youth. (☎035 24 76 94. Open daily 7am-3pm and 6pm-3am. AmEx/MC/V.) The nearly 200 types of Belgian beer at the **Papageno Pub,** V. Colleoni, 1b should keep you busy. (☎035 23 66 24. Open F-W 7am-2am.)

BRESCIA ☎030

When observed from afar, Brescia's glass high rises sparkle in the afternoon sun, reflecting the green of the duomo, the red terracotta roofs of the residential districts, and the skeletons of the *centro storico*'s Roman ruins in an explosion of Italian color. The city once owed its prosperity to the estates of wealthy aristocrats; it now exports the less-than-glamorous Beretta weaponry and sink fixtures. But the soul of this industrial town, surprisingly, is its thriving fashion industry. Reminiscent of smaller, less glamorous Milan, the streets are illuminated with names like Ferragamo and Versace.

⌐ TRANSPORTATION

Trains: Brescia lies between Milan and Verona on the Torino-Trieste line. **Luggage storage** available (p. 131). To: **Bergamo** (1hr., 10 per day, 5:25am-10:28pm, €3.25); **Cremona** (1¾hr., 11 per day, 6:29am-9:25pm, €3.65); **Milan** (1hr., every hr., 5:55am-11:38pm, €6.92); **Padua** (1¾hr., every hr., 6:15am-9:13pm, €10.90); **Venice** (2¼hr., every hr., 4:13-9:13pm, €13.53); **Verona** (45min., 10 per day, 7:23am-1:34am, €5.53); and **Vicenza** (1¼hr., every hr., 5:58am-9:13pm, €9.19). Info office (☎ 147 88 80 88). Open 7am-9pm.

Buses: (☎ 030 44 915). Eastbound buses, including destinations on the Western shores of Lake Garda, leave from the station to your right as you depart train station. To: **Cremona** (1¼hr., every hr., 6:30am-6:55pm, €4.25); **Mantua** (1½hr., every hr., 5:45am-7:15pm, €4.95); and **Verona** (2¼hr., every hr., 6:45am-6:15pm, €5.27). Westbound buses leave from the **SAIA** station (☎ 030 377 4237), to the left as you exit the train station. To **Milan** (1¾hr., 8:32am-6:32pm, €5.98). Ticket office open M-F 7am-12:30pm and 1:30-6:25pm, Sa 7am-12:30pm and 1:30-3:10pm.

Taxis: (☎ 030 35 111). 24hr.

◢▮ ◨ ORIENTATION AND PRACTICAL INFORMATION

The city's architectural gems are concentrated in the rectangular *centro storico*. To reach the *centro* from the train station, take **Via Foppa** to **Via V. Emanuele II**, and then turn left. Take another left onto **Via Gramsci**. As you head up V. Gramsci, a right onto **Via Moretto** will take you to the Pinacoteca Civica Tosio Martinengo, while a right onto **Corso Zanardelli** will take you to the magnificent Teatro Grande, the tourist office, and some of the best shopping in the city. Less than a block after the Teatro Grande on the left is **Via Mazzini**. Up V. Mazzini lies both of Brescia's duomos, as well as **Via dei Musei**, the Museo della Città, and Tempio Capitolino to the right; the **Piazza della Loggia** is to the left. A quick jaunt up the path at the end of the V. Mazzini leads to the **Via del Castello** and the castle itself.

Tourist Office: APT, C. Zanardelli, 34 (☎ 030 43 418; fax 375 6450). English spoken. Helpful event fliers, maps, and walking guides. Open M-F 9am-12:30pm and 3-6pm, Sa 9am-12:30pm. **City Tourist Office,** P. Loggia, 6 (☎ 030 240 0357; www.comune.brescia.it). Open Oct.-Mar. M-F 9:30am-12:30pm and 2-5pm, Sa 9:30am-12:30pm; Apr.-Sept. M-Sa 9:30am-6:30pm.

Paragliding School: Brixia Flying, V. S. Zeno, 117 (☎ 030 242 2094; www.spidernet.it/bresciafly).

Car Rental: Avis, V. XX Settembre, 2/f (☎ 030 29 54 74). **Europcar Italia,** V. Stazione, 49 (☎ 030 28 04 87). **Hertz,** V. XXV Aprile, 4c (☎ 030 45 32).

Luggage Storage: In train station. €4. Open 10am-8pm. Self-storage also available, from €2.50 per 24hr.

Emergency: ☎ 113. **Police:** ☎ 112. **First Aid:** ☎ 118.

Hospital: Ospedale Civile (☎ 030 39 951).

Internet Access: Black Rose, V.Cattaneo, 22/A (☎ 030 280 7704). Two computers in a cozy bar. €5 per hr. Open M-Sa 7am-midnight.

Bank: Banco di Brescia. C. Zanardelli, 54. 2 24hr. **ATMs** face the street (just to left of tourist office). M-F 8:25am-1:25pm and 2:40-4:10pm.

Post Office: P. Vittoria, 1 (☎ 030 44 421). Open M-F 8:15am-5:30pm, Sa 8:15am-1pm.

Postal Code: 25100.

⚓ ACCOMMODATIONS

Brescia's lodgings are reasonably priced, but they fill up weekends in the summer. Call a week ahead. Ask at the tourist office about *agriturismo* options.

Albergo San Marco, V. Spalto, 15 (☎030 304 5541). From station, take V. Foppa to its end, then turn right onto V. V. Emanuele, which will turn into V. Spalto. 10-15min. walk. Busy street, which means plenty of noise. Breakfast €1.65. Communal baths. Singles €22; doubles €37. AmEx/DC/MC/V. ❷

Albergo Regine, C. Magenta, 14 (☎030 375 7881; fax 45 400). From V. Emanuele, make a left onto V. Cavour, then a left onto V. Magenta; hotel is on your left. A wood-finished lobby leads to 30 clean and quiet rooms. Shared living room area with TV. Breakfast included. Singles €31; doubles with bath €62. MC/V. ❸

Albergo Stazione, V. Stazione, 15-17 (☎030 377 4614; fax 377 3995). From the station, head left and take the V. le Stazione. The hotel is down the Vicolo Stazione after about 150m. 36 clean rooms with TV and A/C. At night, women should exercise caution in this area. Singles €30, with bath €40; doubles €50/€60. MC/V. ❸

🍴 FOOD

Brescian cuisine is similar to that of neighbor Bergamo, but with original dishes *manzo all'olio* (beef prepared in olive oil) and *tortelli di zucca* (zucchini tort). Whatever and wherever you choose to eat, be sure to sample some of the local wines. *Tocai di San Martino della Battaglia* (a dry white wine), *groppello* (a medium red), and *botticino* (a dry red of medium age) are all Brescian favorites. There is a street market with produce on Saturday mornings at P. Loggia. For inexpensive staples, seek out the open-air vendors in P. Mercato. (Open Tu-F 8:30am-6pm, M and Sa 8:30am-11am.) **Supermercato PAM,** V. Porcellaga, 26, is on a continuation of C. M. della Libertà. (Open M 2-8pm, Tu-Sa 9am-8pm.)

▨ Trattoria G.A. Porteri, V. Trento, 52 (☎030 38 09 47). From the train station, take V. Foppa to its end; turn right onto V. V. Emanuele II, and then left onto V. Gramsci. After passing through P. della Vittoria and P. della Loggia, you will emerge onto V. Solferino. Take it straight, passing through P. Trento. Walk along V. Trento for 12 blocks. The restaurant will be on your left. Ring the buzzer for admission. Locals make the long walk from the town center for a taste of Brescian cuisine at its very best. *Primi* €8, *secondi* €10-12. Reservations essential. Open Tu-Sa noon-2pm and 8-10pm. MC/V. ❸

Al Frate, V. Musei, 25 (☎030 377 0550). Brescian food with a twist. Fresh, exciting dishes, like *coniglio ai fichi* (rabbit with figs). *Primi* €7.50-8.30, *secondi* €8.50-16.50. Cover €2. Open Tu-Su 12:30-2:30pm and 7:30-11:30pm. MC/V. ❸

Trattoria Due Stelle, V. S. Faustino, 46 (☎030 42 370). Follow directions for Porteri to V. Solferino. The restaurant will be on your right after about 2 blocks. 150-year-old Due Stelle is the oldest *trattoria* in Brescia, reflected in the decor and the upholding of time-honored Brescian culinary traditions. The *tripe, casonsei,* and *zuppe di verdura* (vegetable soup) are all wonderful. *Primi* €6-7, *secondi* €8-10. Open Tu-Sa noon-3pm and 7:30-10:30pm, Su noon-3pm. DC/MC/V. ❷

Ristorante/Pizzeria Cavour, C. Cavour, 56 (☎030 240 0900). Take V. V. Emanuele II to C. Cavour and make a left. Great pizza and pasta dishes. Try the *pizza cavour,* with tomatoes, mozzarella, *pancetta,* and basil. Pizza from €3.75, *primi* €6.71. Cover €1.50. Open W-M 11am-3pm and 6:30pm-1am. DC/V. ❶

◉ SIGHTS

DUOMO NUOVO AND ROTONDA. Not to be content with just one duomo, the Brescians built two. The **Duomo Nuovo** (1604-1825) stands adjacent to the smaller **Rotonda** (old duomo, or Cathedral of Santa Maria Assunta). The newer church is a gargantuan Rococo structure with Corinthian columns and the third highest dome in Italy. The detail here is almost entirely sculptural; there is very little color and only a few paintings. The 11th-century *rotonda* is a simple Romanesque structure with a squat, round tower, a tile roof, and a dark interior. *(In P. Paolo IV, or P. del Duomo. From P. della Vittoria, take path through the archways and under clocktower. Appropriate dress required. Old duomo: Apr.-Oct. Tu-Su 9am-noon and 3-7pm, Nov.-Mar. Sa-Su 9am-noon and 3-7pm. New duomo: open daily M-Sa 7:30am-noon and 4-7:30pm, Su 8am-1pm and 4-7:30pm.)*

TEATRO GRANDE. Fresh on the heels of the smash hit *Tosca*, Puccini's *Madame Butterfly* premiered in 1904 at Milan's La Scala. Unbeknownst to the *maestro*, some of his worst enemies (including librettist Alberto Franchetti, who Puccini had tricked out of the rights to *Tosca*), had bought up large sections of the theater and filled them with hecklers, who catcalled throughout the first act. Later that year *Butterfly* opened for a second time in Brescia to a far more receptive audience in this Baroque theater glittering with gold *stuccato*. *(From P. della Vittoria, go down V. Gramsci 2 blocks and take a left onto C. Zanardeli. C. Zanardeli, 9. ☎030 297 9311. Closed for construction in summer 2002, but visits can still be arranged; call ahead.)*

PIAZZA DELLA LOGGIA. Venetian mayor Marco Foscari had his hand in the construction of this piazza in 1433, and it shows. **Torre dell'Orologio** (1544), the piazza's centerpiece, was modeled on the clock tower in Venice's P. San Marco and features a full zodiacal face and two bronze-covered wooden figurines who have been striking the time since 1581. Opposite stands the lead-domed **Loggia** (arcade), begun in 1492 under the direction of architects Sansovino and Palladio.

PINACOTECA TOSIO-MARTINENGO. The Pinacoteca is one of Brescia's principal artistic attractions. This unadorned, 22-room *palazzo* displays a fine collection of works by Bresciani masters (notably Moretto), as well as Raphael's *Cristo Benedicente*. The collection is enriched with works by Ferramola, Romanino, Foppa, and Lotto. *(From P. Vittoria, take V. A. Gramsci to V. Moretto, and turn left; the Pinacoteca is at end of the street. Enter through center of the piazza (behind statue). V. Martinengo da Barco, 1. ☎030 377 4999. Open June-Sept. Tu-Su 10am-5pm; Oct.-Mar. Tu-Su 9:30am-1pm and 2:30-5pm. €3, 14-18 or over 65 €1.)*

TEMPIO CAPITOLINO. Fragments of Brescia's classical roots are sprinkled on V. dei Musei. The Roman colony of Brixia lies buried beneath the overgrown greenery in the **Piazza del Foro.** Between the large, dark buildings stand the remaining pieces of Emperor Vespasian's vast Tempio Capitolino. *(From P. Paolo VI, with your back to the duomo, take V. Mazzini to the left, and turn right on V. dei Musei. Closed for renovation, the temple is visible from behind the gates.)*

MUSEO DELLA CITTÀ DI SANTA GIULIA. This former monastery, Monasterio di San Salvatore e Santa Giulia, served as the final retreat for Charlemagne's ex-wife Ermengarda and now houses artistic and archaeological representations of the history of Brescia. The museum's Oratorio de S. Maria in Solario displays a bronze *Winged Victory* and the precious 8th-century *Cross of Desiderius*, encased in silver, jewels, and cameos. *(A few paces farther down from the Tempio Capitolino. V. dei Musei, 14. ☎030 297 7834. Open Oct.-Mar. Tu-Su 10am-6pm; Apr.-May Tu-Th and Sa-Su 9am-7pm, F 9am-9pm. €6, 14-18 or over 65 €2.)*

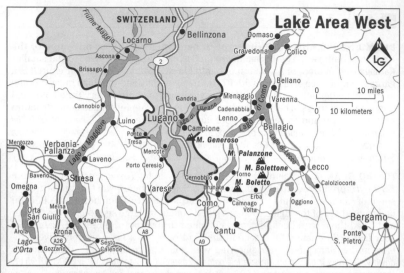

CASTELLO. Although construction took place from the 13th to the 16th centuries, the most prominent and striking features of the castle date from the time of the Viscontis, notably the fortified keep built in 1343. During the Risorgimento, Austrian troops bombarded the town from within the castle walls in an attempt to quash the Brescian rebellion, known as "Ten Days." The castle comes complete with ramparts, underground tunnels, and a drawbridge. It also houses a **weapons museum,** which contains over 500 items of armor and weaponry made in Europe and especially Italy between 1300 and 1700, and the **Museo Civico del Risorgimento,** which details the town's involvement in the Risorgimento. The Castello is periodically used in the summer as a restaurant featuring live music. *(V. del Castello. En route to the castle, be sure to stick to the residential streets and main road, as secluded paths on the hillside are known to harbor drug users and dealers. Open Tu-Su 8am-8pm. Free. Weapons museum ☎ 030 29 32 92; Civic Museum ☎ 030 44 176. Both open Oct.-May Tu-Su 9:30am-1pm and 2:30-5pm; June-Sept. Tu-Su 10am-5pm. €3 for each, 14-18 or over 65 €1 each. Inquire at tourist office for details about events in the castle.)*

🎵 ENTERTAINMENT

In addition to a gamut of high-brow cultural events, Brescia hosts the infamous **Mille Miglia** (thousand miles), a car race that runs from Brescia to Rome and back. The event attracted some of race car driving's bests during what many would call the golden age of motor racing, notably Stirling Moss, who clinched the title in 1955. An accident involving the driver Portago brought the race to an end in 1957. Although the race cannot be run at full speed, a leisurely re-run takes place every year in early May. The only entry requirement is that the car date from the period during which the original race was run (1927-1957), ensuring a fine showing of Ferraris, Maseratis, Alfa Romeos, Porsches, and Astin Martins. The annual **Stagione di Prosa,** a series of dramatic performances, runs from December to April. From April to June, the focus shifts to the **Festivale Pianistico Internazionale,** co-hosted by nearby Bergamo. The **Brescia Jazz Festival** is a three-day celebration at the end of July. (☎ 030 353 1947; www.bresciaonlinel.it. Outdoor performances free; those in the castle €10.) From June to September, the city hosts an open-air cinema, concerts, dance recitals, and opera. (Find schedules at the tourist office, or call ☎ 035 377 1111 for more information.)

THE LAKE COUNTRY

When Hollywood director George Lucas was looking for an idyllic setting for his love story *(Star Wars Episode 2: Attack of the Clones)*, he could find nowhere more romantic or visually stunning than the Italian Lake Country. Other artistic visionaries like Liszt, Longfellow, and Wordsworth occasioned to retreat into the serenity of the lake shores, drawn by the quiet murmur of clear water lapping at the foot of snow-capped mountains. Summertime attracts droves of tourists who paint the lush scenery into landscapes of their own making: a young, mostly German crowd descends upon the more affordable Lake Garda, enjoying water sports by day and gyrating across the dance floor at night. Only an hour north of Milan by train, Lake Como produces the silk sported by sophisticated Milanese, who in turn lend their urbane influence to the thriving city of Como, the lake's southern transportation hub. Long a playground for the rich and famous, Lake Como's mountainous shoreline also harbors well-run and inexpensive hostels. Palatial luxury hotels dot Lake Maggiore's sleepy shores, where tourism is the least obtrusive and the scenery the most tranquil; and romance abounds in the Borromean Islands, renowned for their palaces, gardens, and wandering peacocks.

LAKE COMO (LAGO DI COMO)

The well-to-do have been using Lake Como as a refuge since before the Roman Empire, as the numerous luxury villas on the shores of the Lake will attest. You don't need a *palazzo* to appreciate the beauty that surrounds Europe's deepest lake (410m). Many struggling artists, including Rossini, Bellini, Wordsworth, and Shelley relied upon this lake for inspiration. An unworldly aura lingers around the lavish villas that adorn Lake Como's backdrop, warmed by the sun and cooled by lakeside breezes. Three long lakes form the forked Lake Como, joined at the three towns of Centro Lago: Bellagio, Menaggio, and Varenna. These make for a more relaxing stay than their industrial neighbor Como, the largest city on the lake, which should be used largely as a transportation hub. Villages cover the dense green slopes—drop your baggage, hop on a bus or ferry, and step off whenever a villa, castle, garden, vineyard, restaurant, or small town beckons.

COMO ☎ 031

Situated on the southwest tip of the lake, at the receiving end of the Milan rail line, Como is the lake's token semi-industrial town, where Alessandro Volta was born and where Terragni immortalized his fascist architectural designs. Although famous for silk manufacturing, the town now mainly serves as a launch point for tourists arriving from Milan to explore the lakes. Mediocre beaches, impeccably dressed

---

HIGHLIGHTS OF THE LAKE COUNTRY

SMOOCH on the same **Villa del Balbianello** balcony as Annakin and Amidala in *Star Wars Episode 2* (p. 141).

JUMP into Villa D'Este's floating lake pool in **Cernobbio** (p. 138).

IDLE AWAY an afternoon on the tranquil shores of **Lago Maggiore** (p. 146) or take a bike trip around any of the lakes.

STRUT with peacocks in the exotic gardens of the **Borromean Islands** (p. 149).

HOBNOB with Northern Italy's elite in **Bellagio** (p. 141).

NORTHWEST ITALY

businessmen, and zipping scooters don't inspire visitors to linger, but there are attractions enough to keep those passing through entertained. Como has excellent hiking, many beautiful buildings and fine restaurants within the walls of the old city, and wisteria-draped 18th-century villas along the waterfront that make for lovely after-dinner *passeggiate*.

▐ TRANSPORTATION

Trains: Stazione San Giovanni (☎0147 88 80 88). Ticket window open daily 6:40am-8:25pm. To **Milan** Centrale (1hr., every 30min., 4:45am-11:35pm, €4.85) and **Venice** S. Lucia (4hr., every hr., 4:45am-7:55pm, €21.33) via **Milan**. **Ferrovia Nord (Como Nord)** (☎031 30 48 00), by P. Matteotti, serves Stazione Nord (Cadorna) in **Milan** (1hr., 2 per hr., 5am-10:35pm, €3.72), via **Saronno** (€1.96).

Buses: SPT (☎031 24 72 47), on P. Matteotti. Ticket office open daily 6am-8:15pm. Info booth open M-F 8am-noon and 2-6pm, Sa 8am-noon. To: **Bellagio** (**C30**; 1hr., every hr., 6:34am-8:14pm, €2.72); **Bergamo** (**C46**; 2hr., every hr., 6:45am-6:30pm, €4.30); **Domaso** (**C10**, 2hr., every hr., 7:10am-6:40pm, €4.75); **Gravedona** (**C10**; 2hr., every hr. 7:10am-6:40pm, €3.56); and **Menaggio** (1hr., every hr., 7:10am-8:30pm, €2.43).

Ferries: Navigazione Lago di Como (☎031 57 92 11). The most convenient and enjoyable way to travel the lake. Departs daily to all lake towns from the piers along Lungo Lario Trieste in front of P. Cavour. Ferries run as often as every 15min. One-way to Mennagio €7.40. Numerous day passes covering various regions of the lake €6.80-17.10. Pick up the booklet *Orario* for a schedule, including summer night service.

Public Transportation: Tickets at *tabacchi*, bus station, or the hostel (€0.77).

Taxis: Radio Taxi (☎031 26 15 15).

Bike Rental: Montagna Sport (☎031 24 08 21), on V. Regina, rents mountain bikes for €20.66 per day. Ask about multi-day discounts. Open daily 9:30am-12:30pm and 2:30-7pm. AmEx/MC/V. The **hostel** rents mountain bikes for €11 per day.

✦ ❔ ORIENTATION AND PRACTICAL INFORMATION

From Como's **Stazione San Giovanni,** head down the stairs, straight ahead, and through the little park. Take **Via Fratelli Ricchi** on your left and then take a right on **Viale Fratelli Rosselli,** which turns into **Lungo Lario Trento,** which in turn winds its way around the mouth of the lake toward the main square, **Piazza Cavour.** To get to the commercial center from P. Cavour, take **Via Plinio** to **Piazza Duomo,** where it becomes **Via Vittorio Emanuele.** To reach the **bus station** and **Stazione Ferrovia Nord** near P. Matteotti, turn right when facing the lake from P. Cavour.

Tourist Office: P. Cavour, 16 (☎031 26 97 12; fax 24 01 11; www.lakecomo.org), in the large lakeside piazza near the dock. Maps and extensive info. Ask the multilingual staff about hiking and hotels. Open M-Sa 9am-1pm and 2:30-6pm, Su 9:30am-1pm.

Currency Exchange: Banca Nazionale del Lavoro, P. Cavour, 33 (☎031 31 31), across from the tourist office, has dependable rates and a 24hr. **ATM.** Open M-F 8:30am-1:20pm and 2:30-4pm. Currency exchange also available at the tourist office, train station, post office, and numerous other banks.

Emergency: ☎113. **Ambulance:** ☎118. **Police:** ☎112.

Late-Night Pharmacy: Farmacia Centrale, V. Plinio, 1 (☎031 42 04), off P. Cavour. Open Tu-Su 8:30am-12:30pm and 3:30-7:30pm. Lists of night pharmacies posted.

Hospitals: Ospedale Valduce, V. Dante, 11 (☎031 32 41 11). **Ospedale Sant'Anna,** V. Napoleana, 60 (☎031 58 51 11). **Ospedale Villa Aprica,** Castel Carnasino (☎031 57 94 11).

Internet Access: Bar Black Panther, V. Garibaldi, 59 (☎031 26 65 35). From P. Cavour, walk through V. Fontana to P. Volta and take V. Garibaldi straight ahead. €3.10 per hr.; 30min. free Internet access with drink purchase. Open Tu-Su 7am-12pm. **Como Bar,** V. Volta, 51 (☎031 26 20 51). €3.60 per hr. Open Tu-Su 7:30am-9:30pm. **Clic Zone,** V. Volta, 29 (031 24 30 70). €3.10 per hr. Open M 1pm-3pm, Tu-Sa 10am-2pm.

Post Office: V. V. Emanuele II, 113 (☎031 26 02 10), in town center. Open M-F 8:10am-5:30pm, Sa 8:10am-1pm.

Postal Code: 22100.

ACCOMMODATIONS

▧ **Hotel Funicolare,** V. Coloniola 8/10 (☎031 30 42 77; fax 30 16 06). Head up from P. Matteoti and turn left. Beautiful and reasonably priced 2-star hotel with friendly staff and an excellent location. All rooms come with bath and A/C. Singles €38-47 depending on size. Extra beds €24.50. AmEx/DC/MC/V. ❹

In Riva al Lago, P. Matteotti, 4 (☎031 30 23 33), behind bus stop. Centrally located and with a good pub. English spoken. Internet €1.03 per hr. Breakfast €2-4. Laundry service €2.60. Reserve ahead. Singles €24, with bath and TV €39; doubles €47-52. Flats available for 2-11 people at similar rates. AmEx/DC/MC/V. ❷

Ostello Villa Olmo (HI), V. Bellinzona, 2 (☎/fax 031 57 38 00; ostellocomo@tin.it), behind Villa Olmo. From Stazione S. Giovanni, walk down the steps and past the giant hands. Then turn left and walk 20min. down V. Borgo Vico. Or take bus #1, 6, or 11 to Villa Olmo (€0.77). Lively, fun, and down-to-earth. Run by a wonderful, multilingual staff. Offers a bar, bag lunches (€11), and hefty 3-course dinners (€13). Breakfast included. Crowded rooms come with personal locker and sheets. Self-service laundry €3; ironing €0.85. Lockout 10am. Strict curfew 11:30pm. Reserve ahead. Open daily Mar-Nov. 7-10am and 4-11:30pm. Dorms €11.50. ❶

Protezione della Giovane (ISJGIF), V. Borgovico, 182 (☎031 57 43 90 or 57 35 40), on the way to the youth hostel, on the right side. Take bus #1, 6, or 11. Run by nuns. 18+ women only. 52 clean rooms, with crucifixes everywhere. Free kitchen use. Laundry €3.70 per load. Curfew 10:30pm. Singles or doubles €11 per person for the first 3 nights, €10.33 thereafter. ❶

Albergo Piazzolo, V. Indipendenza, 65 (☎031 27 21 86). From P. Cavour, take V. Bonta, which becomes V. Boldini and V. Luni. Pedestrian only V. Indipendenza is on the right. Airy, breezy rooms, all tastefully furnished and with modern bathrooms. 3 large doubles with bath €51.65; 1 quad €82.73. AmEx/DC/MC/V. ❹

Albergo Sociale, V. Maestri Comacini, 8 (☎031 26 40 42), on the right side of the duomo. Unadorned rooms and small beds. Central location. Call ahead. 1 single without bath €20.66; 4 doubles €38, 1 with bath €48; triples €51. AmEx/DC/MC/V. ❷

FOOD

Since Como is a tourist center, dining out can be an expensive proposition. Picnicking is the best way to experience regional culinary specialties on the cheap; lakeside benches provide all the *al fresco* ambiance you could ask for. *Resca* (sweet bread with dried fruit) and the harder, cake-like *mataloc* are great Como-specific treats sold at **Beretta Il Fornaio,** V. Fratelli Rosselli, 26a. (Open M 7:30am-1pm, Tu-Sa 7:30am-1pm and 2-7:30pm.) Local cheeses *semuda* and *robiola* are available at

THE BIG SPLURGE

THE LAKE OF LUXURY

The world-famous **Villa d'Este,** once the vacation home of the Este family of Ferrara, is now the most opulent of luxury accommodations. The lush ⧫ **gardens** of the Villa alone merit a trip to Cernobbio. You might get to dine with the Queen of England, and there's an even better chance that your room will have a view of the Villa's swimming pool, a unique contraption floating in the middle of a lake that was voted one of the top five pools in the world by *Gourmet* magazine. (In 2000, the magazine also ranked the hotel #1 for "grand ambiance.")

Occupying one of the uniquely-furnished rooms in the hotel entitles you to the use of 8 tennis courts, an indoor pool, a children's pool, a squash court, a gym, a sauna, Turkish baths, as well as canoeing and windsurfing, and of course, the famous pool.

The hotel offers sumptuous packages, including *Italian Cooking with Luciano Parolari* (head chef and author of the Villa d'Este cookbook series; €2125 per person for 5 nights) and beauty spa retreats.

Don't feel like spending the night? Drop €15.50 for a cup of espresso and enjoy the scenery. You can even land your ride on the hotel's private helipad. Those disinclined to fly can take the C10 motor coach from Como (6:55-10:30pm, €2.13), though it's frightfully common.

V. Regina, 40. ☎ *031 3491; fax 348 844; www.villadeste.com. High season singles €355; doubles €560; exclusive suite €1540.*

most local supermarkets, including **G.S. supermarket** on the corner of V. Fratelli Recchi and V. Fratelli Roselli, across from the park (☎ 031 57 08 95; open M 9:30am-8:30pm, Tu-F 8am-8:30pm, Sa 8am-8pm), and **Gran Mercato,** P. Matteotti, 3 (open M 8:30am-1pm, Tu-F 8:30am-1:30pm and 3:30-7:30pm, Sa 8am-8pm, Su 8:30am-1pm). An **outdoor market** is held Tuesday and Thursday mornings and all day Saturday in P. Vittoria. When dining out, keep in mind that a small increase in price brings a huge increase in quality.

Scalda Sole, V. Volta, 41 (☎ 031 26 38 89), off P. Volta. Expect a sea of collared shirts of a local professional crowd eating very professional food. *Primi* €8, *secondi* €13. The vegetarian *pasticcio di melanzane e patate* (potato and eggplant pie; €13) is remarkable. Open Tu-Su 1-8:30pm. ❸

Il Solito Posto, V. Lambertenghi, 9 (☎ 031 26 53 40). From P. Duomo, head down V. V. Emanuele and turn right onto V. Lambertenghi. A beautiful restaurant frequented by crowds of locals. Try the *terine* of asparagus (€9.50) and *bresaola* with artichoke and grain noodles (€9.30). Open Tu-Su noon-3:30pm and 6-9:30pm. AmEx/MC/V. ❹

Il Carrettiere, V. Colonnia, 18 (☎ 031 30 34 78), off P. A. d. Gasperi, near P. Matteotti. Seafood is this local haunt's specialty, its decor decidedly pirate, and its music of choice Ella Fitzgerald. For the briny deep's finest flavors, try the *spaghetti all'astrice* or *allo scoglio* (€12.91). Open Tu-Su noon-3pm and 7:30-11pm. AmEx/MC/V. ❹

Osteria del Gallo, V. Vitani 16 (☎ 031 27 25 91). From P. Cavour take V. B. Perretta, turn right onto V. Juvara, and take it to V. Vitani. Stuffed tomatoes and other hearty rustic foods at an informal eatery in the heart of the old town. Prices vary on the basis of how much you eat, but it's cheap. Open M 9am-3:30pm and Tu-Sa 9am-7:30pm. ❷

🔆 SIGHTS

DUOMO AND ENVIRONS. Dating from 1396, Como's newly restored duomo houses a magnificent octagonal dome and harmoniously combines Romanesque, Gothic, Renaissance, and Baroque elements. The Rodari brothers' life-like sculptures of the Exodus from Egypt animate the church's exterior. Statues of Como residents Pliny the Elder and Pliny the Younger flank the door. *(Near P. Cavour. Open daily 7am-noon and 3-7pm.)* Just behind the duomo and across the rail tracks, Giuseppe Terragni's Casa del Fascio—now called **Palazzo Terragni**—was built between 1934 and 1936 to house the local Fascist government.

Uncharacteristically light designs have made it a world-famous icon of Modernist Italian architecture. Near the back walls of the city, a gathering of museums includes the **Silk museum.** *(V. Vallegio, 3. ☎031 30 31 80. Open T-Sa 9am-noon and 3-6pm. €7.75; €5.16 group rate. Call ahead to arrange group visits.)* The **Museo Buco del Piombo** is a collection of materials collected in a Jurassic cave. *(V. Cantu, 15. ☎031 62 95 99. Open Apr.-Oct. Sa 2-6pm and Su 10am-6pm. Adults €4, children €3. Groups can visit with a booking.)* The cave itself is near Erba and is worth a trip in itself. *(See hiking.)*

LAKE AREA. The pantheon-like **Tempio Voltiano** was dedicated to the inventor of the battery, Alessandro Volta. *(From P. Cavour, go left along the waterfront. ☎031 57 47 05. Open Apr.-Nov. Tu-Su 10am-noon and 3-6pm; Dec.-Mar. 10am-noon and 2-4pm. €2.07, groups and under 6 €1.29.)* Volta's tomb is located at **Camnago Volta.** *(Take bus #4 from the bus stop or Stazione S. Giovanni; 15min., every 30min., 6:20am-8:20pm, €0.77.)* The villas lining the lake include **Villa "La Rotonda,"** with Rococo stuccato and chandeliers. *(Open M-Th 9am-noon and 3-5pm, F 9am-noon.)* Farther north is the ambassadorial **Villa Olmo** in the romantic, statue-lined park of the same name. *(Villa open Apr.-Sept. M-Sa 9:30am-noon and 3-6pm. Gardens open Apr.-Sept. daily 8am-11pm; Oct.-Mar. 9am-7pm.)*

◪ HIKING

To avoid a long uphill climb, take the ◪**funiculare** from P. dei Gasperi, 4, at the far end of Lungo Lario Trieste, to **Brunate** for an excellent hike back down to Como. *(☎031 30 36 08. June-Sept. every 15min., 6am-midnight; Oct.-May every 30min., 6am-10:30pm, €2.25, under 12 €1.50, round-trip €3.95, adult round-trip €2.80 if purchased through the hostel.)* For even better panoramas, hike up toward **Faro Voltiano** (906m, 20min. walk). a lighthouse dedicated to Volta. It's easy to find; just keep heading up until you hit the summit. On your way, be sure to take note of Santa Rita, Europe's smallest sanctuary. At the top, enjoy a breathtaking view of the Alps and Switzerland, and on a clear day, of both Milan and the Matterhorn. Even with cloudy skies, Como's majestic villas are visible.

From Faro Voltiano, another 15min. of hiking brings you to **San Maurizio,** and another 1hr. should be enough time to reach **Monte Boletto** (1236m). There is a bus that runs from Brunate to approximately 1km past S. Maurizio and stops by Faro Voltiano (every 30min., 8:15am-6:45pm, €0.77). If the hike to M. Boletto hasn't left you exhausted, stroll for another hour to **Monte Bolettone** (1317m).

Another option is to head northwest between S. Maurizio and M. Boletto after the restaurant Baita Carla, on a path leading to lakeside **Torno,** 8km north of Como, and a good place to catch a boat ride back to Como (every hr., 7:23am-8:21pm, €1.90). In Torno, check out the opulent Chiesa di San Giovanni or the Villa Pliniana, 15min. north of the boat dock, closed to visitors but worth a look from afar.

If you're up for more extensive exploration of the mountains east of Como, take bus **C40** from the Como bus station to Erba (30min.; every hr.; 7:05am-10:35pm, last bus back to Como at 10:51pm; €2.53). From Erba, make the beautiful hike to Caslino D'Erba, which leads to Monte Palanzone (1436m). Head into the cool recesses of Buco del Piombo for an encounter with prehistory.

IL CENTRO LAGO

Numerous towns line the beautiful central lake. Although they can all be reached by bus, the out-of-the-way trips often take more than two hours. A more direct (and far more romantic) mode of travel is by ferry. **Navigazione del Lago** offers an all-day pass for €6.80 that covers travel to Bellagio, Varenna, Menaggio, Cadenabbia, Tremezzo and Lenno. Most journeys last no more than 5 min., with boats arriving roughly every 15 min., 8:45am-7:45pm daily.

MENAGGIO   ☎0344

On Lake Como's Western shore, Menaggio is home to cobblestone streets, stunning hillside scenery, and a constant procession of Yamaha-bound motor tourists. You can explore Lake Como while staying in Menaggio's youth hostel for a fraction of the cost (and double the character) of any other establishment on the lake.

▣ � TRANSPORTATION AND PRACTICAL INFORMATION. Buses and **ferries** link Menaggio to the other lake towns. In the town center at P. Garibaldi, 4, the helpful and multilingual **tourist office** has information on lake excursions. (☎0344 32 924; infomenaggio@tiscalinet.it. Open M-Sa 9am-noon and 3-6pm.) In an **emergency**, dial ☎113, or reach the **police** at ☎112 or an **ambulance** at ☎118. P. Garibaldi also houses a **pharmacy**. (☎0344 32 10 51. Open 8:30am-12:30pm and 3-7pm.) Menaggio's **hospital** is on V. Cadorna (☎0344 33 111). **Internet** access costs €1.50 per 15min. at **Video Mix**, across from the creperie. (☎0344 34 110. Open Tu-Sa 9:30am-12:30pm and 4-7pm.) The **post office** is at V. Lusardi, 48, and has **currency exchange**. (Open M-F 8:20am-6:30pm, Sa 8:20-11:30am.) **Postal Code:** 22017. The folks at Ostello la Primula have been known to offer short-term **work opportunities** in return for room board and a small stipend, but require a face-to-face interview.

▮ ACCOMMODATIONS AND CAMPING. ▨**Ostello La Primula (HI) ❶**, V. IV Novembre, 86, offers the best budget value in the lake district, as well as a warm and welcoming atmosphere. From the ferry dock, walk straight until you reach the road, turn left, and stick to the upward path that clings to the right side of the road. A helpful newsletter lists activities, including guided hikes, cooking classes, and horseback riding. The hostel provides guests with home-cooked native cuisine (dinner €9.30), family suites, a washing machine (€3.50 per load), bike and kayak rental (€10.50 per day for guests), picnic lunch (€5), Internet access (€2 per 15min.), and free beach access. (☎034 43 23 56; fax 43 16 77; www.menaggiohostel.com. Breakfast included. Lockout 10am-5pm. Curfew 11:30pm. Call ahead to reserve. Open Mar.-Nov. Dorms €11.50; family rooms with 4 or 6 beds and private bath €12 per person.) **Albergo il Vapore ❸**, P. T. Grossi, 3, just off Piazza Garibaldi, another inexpensive alternative, has small, warmly decorated rooms, some with bath. (☎0344 32 229; fax 34 850; ilvapore@usa.net. Breakfast €6.50. Reserve ahead. Singles €26; doubles €45, €48.50 with lake view.) **Camping Europa ❶** is a healthy trek up the lake from the city center. (☎0344 31 187. €4.50 per person, €7.50 per tent. Bungalows from €25 per 1 person to €55 per 6.) Campers should consider traveling farther up the lake to the more scenic Domaso sites.

◻ FOOD. While the fabulous hostel dinner ought to satisfy even the pickiest diners, there are plenty of pizzerias and restaurants in the town proper if you want to stretch your legs. Head left at the junction near Banca San Paolo for **Pizzeria Lugano ❸**, V. Como, 26, where a *quattro stagione* pizza is €5.25. (☎0344 31 664. Open Tu-Su noon-2:30pm and 7-11pm.) For a splurge, **Il Ristorante ❹**, Largo Cavour, 3, located just off P. Garibaldi, has over 300 wines and a lake view to write home about. Try the *carre de agnello seibacola* (€20) and *taglietelle* with fresh lake fish (€8.50) for a delightful meal. (☎0322 32 133. Open M-Su 12:30-10:30pm; closed T in winter.) **Tanamana Pub ❷**, V. IV Novembre, 79, is right next to the ferry stop. (☎0344 32 558. Open daily 9am-3am). **Hotel du Lac's cafe ❶**, V. Mazzini, 21, has the best *tiramisù* (€3 per slice) in town. (☎0344 35 281. Open M-Su 8am-1am.)

◪ ◪ SIGHTS AND HIKING. The **Rifugio Menaggio** (☎034 43 72 82) stands 1400m above the lake. From the top, hikers can make trips to **Monte Grona** and the **Chiesa di S. Amate.** There are a number of shorter hikes starting in Como, such as the 2hr. hike (each way) to the picturesque **Sass Corbee Gorge,** just outside of town.

Another low-commitment option is the 2hr. hike to **Lago di Piano,** a small nature reserve in Val Menaggio (from which you can ride the **C12** bus back). The less hiking-happy can make a half-hour walk up to the panorama at **La Crocetta.** Inquire at the tourist office or at the hostel for detailed directions and maps, as some of these treks are complicated.

BELLAGIO
☎ 031

Favored by the upper-crust of Milanese society, Bellagio is one of the loveliest and most heavily visited central lake towns. Its name is a compound of *bello* (beautiful) and *agio* (comfort), and its fame stretches to Las Vegas, home of the famous Bellagio Hotel. You won't find Elvis impersonators or technicolor frescoes here, however; its lakeside promenades, steep streets, and sidewalk cafes lead to silk shops and the villas of Lombard aristocrats.

⬛ 🔁 TRANSPORTATION AND PRACTICAL INFORMATION. To reach Bellagio from Milan, take a **ferry** from the train station in nearby **Varenna. Buses** also run from **Como.** The tourist office is at P. Mazzini; when you get off the ferry, go into the little hut on your left. The English-speaking staff has detailed information about daytrips to various parts of the lake. (☎ 031 95 02 04. Open M, W-Sa 9am-12pm and 3-6pm, Tu and Su 10am-12:30pm and 3-5:30pm.) In an emergency, dial ☎ 113 for the **police,** ☎ 112 for the **carabinieri,** or ☎ 118 for an **ambulance.** The **pharmacy** at V. Roma, 12, has nighttime service—ring the bell. (☎ 031 95 01 86. Open Th-Tu 9am-12:30pm and 3:30-8pm.) Bellagio's **post office,** on Lungo Lario Manzoni, 4, offers **currency exchange.** (☎ 031 95 19 42. Open M-F 8:10am-1:30pm, Sa 8:10am-11:40pm.) **Postal Code:** 22021.

⬛⬛ ACCOMMODATIONS, CAMPING, AND FOOD. Expect higher rates in Bellagio than in other lake towns. **Albergo Giardinetto ❸,** V. Roncati, 12, just off P. della Chiesa, is by far the best deal in town, with simple rooms and quiet atmosphere. (☎ 031 95 01 68. Open Mar.-Nov. Singles €29; doubles €42, with bath €52.) Quality restaurants are high-priced. **⬛Ristorante Barchetta ❹,** S. Mella, 13 (☎ 031 95 13 89) is located in the heart of the old town and features creative Lombardy cuisine. Try their specialty gnocchi with shrimp and asparagus tips (€10.50). The gastronomic *menù* (€20 per person) serves two. (Open Mar.-Oct. Su-M, W-Sa noon-2:30pm and 7-10:15pm.) **Ristorante La Punta ❸,** V. Eugenio Vitali, 19 (from the dock walk straight to P. della Chiesa, and then turn left and walk for about 400m), has a fabulous lake view and good food. The cheese and spinach ravioli in a cream walnut sauce (€8) is among the vegetarian options. (☎ 031 95 18 88. Open M-Su 8am-12pm.) **Ditta Negrini M. Rosa ❶,** V. Centrale, 3, near P. della Chiesa, provides great *panino* fixings and wine (€3.50-115.50 per bottle).

⬛ SIGHTS. The **Villa Serbelloni** (not to be confused with the stately five-star Grand Hotel Villa Serbelloni down the hill—entrance price €240 per night) offers spectacular views from the fortifications on the promontory and a lovely cyprus-lined garden. (☎/fax 031 95 15 51. Villa open Apr.-Oct. Tu-Su 9am-6pm. ½hr. tours €5, Tu-Su 11am and 4pm. Buy tickets in the tourist office 15min. before the tour.) The lakeside gardens of **Villa Melzi** blossom at the other end of town. Turn right at the ferry dock and follow the road that winds along the waterfront. The villa is still Duke Lodovico Galarati Scoti's private residence, but the **grounds,** including a chapel and museum with Roman and Napoleonic art, are open to the public. (Open Mar.-Oct. daily 9am-6pm. €5, under 12 €3.) Only a short ferry ride away lies Lenno (included in the €6.80 Centro Lago all-day ferry pass). From Lenno, a motorboat leaves for the ◾Villa del Balbianello, where Annakin and Amidala smooched in *Star Wars Episode 2*. The 18th-century villa is the lake's most gorgeous. (☎0344 56 110. Open Apr.-Oct. Tu and Th-Su 10am-12:30pm and 3:30-6:30pm. Entry to the gardens €5, children 4-12 €2.50. Call for info on guided group tours.)

VARENNA   ☎0341

Only a short ferry ride away from Bellagio, Varenna is a decidedly less polished version of its more famous cousin. The low-key atmosphere warrants a daytrip; the prohibitively high prices require one. Numerous gardens and churches rival those elsewhere on the lake in splendor, and steps down dark cobblestone streets appear to drop off into nowhere.

⊞⊡ TRANSPORTATION AND PRACTICAL INFORMATION. Varenna's railway station links the eastern side of the lake to Milan, easing journeys from Milan to the central lake region. (☎0341 36 85 84. Trains depart Milan for Varenna every hour, 5:40am- 9:10pm, €2.10.) From the ferry dock, turn right and then left at Nilus Bar to get to the **tourist office** in P. S. Giorgio. A non-English-speaking staff is nonetheless accommodating, with an excellent selection of maps. (☎0341 83 03 67. Open May-Sept. Tu-Su 10am-12:30pm.) Also located in P. S. Giorgio are a **bank** (open M-F 8:20am-1:20pm and 2:45-3:45pm); a **pharmacy** (open Th-Tu 9am-12:30pm and 3:30-7:30pm, W 9am-12:30pm); and a **post office** (on the water side; open M-F 8:30am-2pm and Sa 8:30am-12:30pm). In an **emergency**, dial ☎113, or the **police** (☎0341 82 11 21). **Postal Code:** 23829.

⊡ ⊡ ACCOMMODATIONS AND FOOD. Albergo Olivedo ❺, P. Martiri, 4, has air-conditioned rooms with bathrooms, some of which offer great lake views. (☎0341 83 01 15; www.olivedo.it. Open mid-Dec. to mid-Nov. Double with breakfast €80-110.) Two **alimentari** grace P. S. Giorgio. (Open Tu-Su 8am-12:30pm and 4-6:30pm.) The pizza (€4.20-7.30), crepes (€4-5.70), and *panini* (€4.20-7.30) at **Nilus Bar ❷**, Riva Garibaldi, 4, provide a filling lunch. (Open daily 10am-1am. AmEx/MC/V.) **Vecchia Varenna ❹**, Contrada Scoscesa, 10, is a superb restaurant located on the most tranquil part of the waterfront. The *robiola* cheese ravioli with pear and *grappa* sauce (€11) is delicious. (☎0341 83 07 93. Open T-Su noon-3:30pm and 6:30-11pm.)

◾ SIGHTS. A scenic passageway beside the water connects both sides of Varenna and offers incredible lake vistas. Varenna's finest church is the 14th-century **Chiesa di S. Giorgio,** which looms above the town with late Romanesque simplicity. (Open daily 7am-noon and 2-7pm.) Varenna's most famous sights, however, are the two lakeside gardens of nearby 13th-century villas: **Villa Monastero,** 150m to the right of the church, and the proud **Villa Cipressi,** weekend home of Lombard aristocrats, another 100m along. (Gardens open Mar.-Oct. daily 9am-7pm. €2 for either, combined ticket €3.50.) Turn left at the ferry dock and head uphill a couple blocks for **La Sorgente del Fiumelatte.** At 250m, the river has the rather dubious distinction of being the shortest in Italy. A 20min. ascent past the piazza and uphill leads to the 12th-century **Castello Vezio,** linked to its small tower by a drawbridge. (Open daily Mar.-Sept. 10am-7pm. €1.55.)

DOMASO   ☎0344

The breezes in this unspectacular, tiny town on the north lake create perfect windsurfing. Surfers and wake boarders flock to the relaxing **Ostello della Gioventù: La Vespa (HI) ❶**, V. Case Sparse, 12. Turn left from the ferry dock and follow the road across the river to the hostel sign on your right. This modern, festive hostel lies 50km (2hr.) from Como by bus and is also accessible by boat. (☎0344 97 449;

www.ostellolavespadomaso.it. Breakfast included. Low windsurfing and mountain biking rates offered through the hostel. Wheelchair-accessible. Reception open 8am-midnight.Curfew midnight. Open Mar.-Oct. Dorms €11. AmEx/MC/V.)

The **tourist office** in the Villa Camilla, on your left as you head to the youth hostel, provides information on sights. (☎0344 96 044. Open Tu-Sa 10am-noon and 3-5pm.) Sights include the 13th-century church **S. Bartolomeo.** (Open M-Su 9am-9pm.) The town's **villa** was built in the 18th century. Local restaurants specialize in *missoltini*, dried and salted fish contained in small barrels. Culinary alternatives include *gelato* at the waterfront **Gelateria Pochintesta ❶.** (Head right from the ferry dock. ☎344 97 473. €1.80 for a large. Open Tu-Su 6:30am-12am.)

7 Italy's **international dialing prefix** is 00. Switzerland's **country code** is 41, and the **city code** for both Lugano and Locarno is 091. Remember to drop the zero when calling internationally. Exchange rates for the **Swiss Franc (SFr)** are as follows: 1SFr=€0.66; €1=1.50SFr.

NEAR LAKE COMO

LUGANO, SWITZERLAND   ☎091

Lugano, Switzerland's third-largest banking center, rests in a crevassed valley between the peaks of San Salvatore and Monte Brè. Warmed by a Mediterranean climate, Lugano's shaded streets are lined with climbing vines and wildflowers. The city has a definite Teutonic streak: the streets are clean, the buses run that much closer to schedule, and the local teenagers are afflicted with heavy dose of *Welterschmerz* (a world-weariness typically experienced by privileged youth).

█ ⚄ TRANSPORTATION AND PRACTICAL INFORMATION. Frequent buses run to **Lugano** from **Menaggio** (2hr., 8 per day, €4.20). Trains arrive at P. della Stazione from **Locarno** (1hr., every 30min., 5:30am-12:05pm, 16.60SFr; change in Giubiasco or Bellinzona) and **Milan** (1½hr., every hr., 7:14am-9:48pm, 21SFr). **Luggage storage** in underground passageways is 4-7SFr. The 15min. downhill walk from the train station to the arcaded **Piazza della Riforma**, the town's center, winds through Lugano's large pedestrian zone. For those who would rather avoid the walk, a cable car runs between the train station and the waterfront **Piazza Cioccaro** (about every 3min., 5:20am-11:50pm, 1.10SFr.). The **tourist office** is in the Palazzo Civico, Riva Albertolli, at the corner of P. Rezzonico. From the station, cross the footbridge labeled "Centro" and proceed down V. Cattedrale straight through P. Cioccaro as it turns into V. Pessina. Turn left on V. dei Pesci and left on Riva via Vela, which becomes Riva Giocondo Albertolli. The office is past the fountain on the left, across from the ferry launch. (☎091 913 3232; fax 922 7653; www.luganotourism.ch. Open Apr.-Oct. M-F 9am-6:30pm, Sa 9am-12:30pm and 1:30-5pm, Su 10am-2pm; Nov.-Mar. M-F 9am-12:30pm and 1:30-5:30pm.)

⌂ ACCOMMODATIONS. Travelers flock to Lugano's two extraordinary youth hostels, both built from luxury villas. Try **▨Hotel and Hostel Montarina ❷**, V. Montarina, 1, just behind the train station. Facing the back left exit of the station, walk up the mimosa-covered incline, heading left. When you hit the road, turn left and follow it until you see a collection of pink buildings on your right. This palm-tree-enveloped hostel/hotel attracts young families and students with its swimming pool, groomed grounds, ping-pong, chandeliered reading room, and terrace with a view. If sharing a room with strangers, be forewarned that some rooms have a sleeping arrangement that entails three mattresses with only one frame.

(☎ 091 966 7272; fax 966 0017; www.montarina.ch. Buffet breakfast 12SFr. Sheets 4SFr. Dorms 25SFr; singles 50-65SFr; doubles 100SFr, with bath 120SFr.) The ▓**Ostello della Gioventù (YHI) ❶**, Lugano-Savosa, 13 V. Cantonale, is just as popular. Note that there are two streets called V. Cantonale, one in downtown Lugano and one in Savosa, where the hostel is. Take bus #5 (walk 350m to the left as you exit the station, then cross the street to get to the bus stop) to "Crocifisso" (6th stop), backtrack a bit, and turn left up V. Cantonale. A former luxury villa, this hostel has secluded gardens, a pool, and an elegant atmosphere. (☎ 091 966 2728; fax 968 2363. Breakfast 8SFr. Kitchen use 1SFr. Internet 5SFr for 20min. Laundry 5SFr. Reception 7am-12:30pm and 3-10pm. Curfew 10pm; keys available upon request. Reserve ahead. Open mid-Mar. to Oct. Dorms 23SFr; singles 35SFr, with kitchenette 45SFr; doubles 56SFr/70SFr.) A non-hostel option is the friendly **Hotel Pestalozzi ❸**, P. Indipendenza, 9, in a central, lake-level location that is free of long, uphill climbs. The pine-accented rooms are clean and fairly simple, but some offer the ever-coveted lake view. (☎ 091 921 4646. Single without bath 60SFr, with bath or shower 92SFr; double 100SFr/144-154SFr.)

◖❚ **FOOD.** Lugano's many outdoor restaurants and cafes pay homage to the province's Italian heritage, serving up plates of *penne* and *gnocchi* and freshly spun pizzas. There is a **public market ❶** in P. della Riforma that sells seafood, produce, and veggie sandwiches for 4SFr. (Open Tu and F 7am-noon.) For some quick *al fresco* shopping and eating, **V. Pessina,** off P. Riforma, livens up at midday with outdoor sandwich and fruit shops. **Salumeria ❶**, V. Pessina, 12, is one of the better ones—selling thick, crusty, oregano-rich pizza (4.15SFr per 0.125kg), as well as sandwiches for 5SFr. (Open daily 8am-6:30pm, Sa 8am-5pm.) **Migros ❶**, V. Pretoria, 15, is two blocks left of the post office, down V. Pretorio in the center of town, and offers fresh pasta and delicious *ciabatta* (a crusty bread). The food court on the ground floor saves the near-penniless with huge slices of thin-crusted pizza from 2.90SFr and sandwiches from 4.50SFr. (Open M-F 8am-6:30pm, Sa 7:30am-5pm.) Romance awaits at ▓**La Tinèra ❸**, V. dei Gorini, 2, behind Credit Suisse in P. della Riforma. Tucked away in an alley off a cobblestone road, this low-lit underground restaurant has great daily specials for 12 to 18SFr. (☎ 091 923 52 19. Open M-Sa 11am-3pm and 6:30-11pm. AmEx/DC/MC/V.) If, for some reason, Swiss efficiency has failed and there has been an ATM error in your favor, **Ristorante Orologio ❸**, V. Nizzola 2, is an elegant little place. From P. Riforma, head to the P. Dante then turn right and head straight to try the *galatina di stinco di maiale con gamberi di fiume a portulaca* (18SFr), hard to say and to forget. (☎ 091 923 2338. Open M-Sa 9:30am-2:30pm and 6:30pm-midnight.)

◙ 🏛 **SIGHTS AND MUSEUMS.** The frescoes of the 16th-century **Cattedrale San Lorenzo,** just south of the train station, gleam with colors that are still vivid despite time. The frescoes on the west wall date from the 13th century. Lugano's most spectacular fresco is Bernardio Luini's gargantuan **Crucifixion** (1529), now in the **Chiesa Santa Maria degli Angioli,** to the right of the tourist office on the waterfront. Aside from the churches, art museums are Lugano's best-known cultural attractions. The **Museo Civico di Belle Arti,** located in the Villa Ciani (the large pink building inside the Parco Civico), houses the permanent collection of the city of Lugano. This highly impressive collection emphasizes the Impressionists and features works by Matisse, Monet, and Rousseau, along with natives Bossoli, Ciseri, Vela, and Rinaldi. (Open Apr.-Aug. Tu-Su 10am-noon and 2-6pm. 5SFr, groups 3SFr per person, under 14 free.) The city also runs the **Museo d'Arte Moderna,** which puts on two exhibitions a year at its gallery just up from the Belvedere. (Open Tu-Su 9am-7pm. 11SFr, students 8SFr.) The **Museo delle Culture Extraeuropee,** V. C. Cattaneo, 4, is located in the **Villa Helenum,** which is a 2km walk along the water from the tourist office; you can also get there by ferry (see below). The *Museo* showcases indigenous art from Africa, Asia, and Oceania. (Open Tu-Su 10am-5pm. 5SFr, students 3SFr.) The **Museo Cantonale d'Arte,** V. Canova, 10, across from Chiesa San Rocco, houses a few sketches by Picasso, Modigliani, and Derain. (☎ 091 910 4780. Open Tu 2-5pm, W-Su 10am-5pm. Permanent collection 7SFr, students 5SFr; special exhibits 10SFr, students 7SFr. MC/V.)

↖ OUTDOOR ACTIVITIES. Lugano is replete with public spaces, many of which are used by the city to display modern art as part of its Sculpture in the City program. The largest of these is **Parco Civico,** which stretches from the Corso Elevezia to the Viale Castagnola. To get there, turn left as you exit the tourist office and follow the road that hugs the waterfront until you reach the park. Its paths are brightened by flower beds and trees that reach down with willowy, long arms to touch the lake below. Backpackers have been known to illegally crash here. *Let's Go* does not recommend breaking the law. (Open Mar.-Oct. 6:30am-11:30pm; Nov.-Feb. 7am-9pm.) The **Piazza della Riforma** is another public art display site. Turn right from the tourist office and follow the curve of the lake until you reach the twisted metal at the **Belvedere,** which has a permanent collection of metalwork and a small memorial to Giorgio Washington at its easternmost point.

Those tired of the lakeside views can take advantage of the park-side views offered by the lake. **Boat tours** leave from the Società Navigazione del Lago di Lugano, to the left of the tourist office. The Società offers six different tours of the lake, some with meals. (One of each tour a day, 10am-9:15pm. 26.20-34.80SFr). Also offered is a ferry service between Lugano and the other lake towns. (☎ 091 923 1779; lake.lugano@bluewin.ch. 8:30am-9:15pm. All day pass 34SFr.) Various vendors along the lake rent **pedal boats** (8SFr per 30min.), and **Boat Saladin,** V. Motta 28, to the right of the tourist office, rents **motor boats** for as little as 25SFr for half an hour. (☎ 091 92 35 73. Open M-Su 9-12am, subject to weather conditions.)

When Lugano's perfection becomes irritating, head to the hills. Lugano offers superb hiking opportunities for those with a sturdy foot and reliable map. The tourist office and Hotel Montarina have excellent topographical maps and trail guides in stock. The cheapest and most rewarding hike is to the peak of **Monte Boglio,** a five-hour round-trip that can be extended over two days by staying at the Pairolhütte (ask at hostels or tourist office for more information). *Funiculari* take those lacking energy and enthusiasm directly to the peaks of **Monte Brè** and **San Salvatore.** The **Monte Brè funiculare** (☎ 091 971 3171) can be reached by turning left as you exit the tourist office and following the road that winds along the river until V. Pico. Turn left; the #1 bus runs from the center of town to the ACT Cassarate/Monte Brè stop (every 30 min.; 9:15-11:45am and 1:45-6:15pm, in summer 8:15am-6:15pm; one-way 13 SFr). The 110-year old San Salvatore funicular (☎ 091 985 2828), can be reached by turning right as you leave the tourist office then right again when you reach the V. E. Bosia, and then right one last time onto the V. delle Scuole. The summit, which offers a restaurant, a world-class conference center, and a splendid view of the lake, can be reached by tram (every 30 min., 8:30am-11pm, 17SFr during high season).

🎵 ENTERTAINMENT. The arcades of the town piazzas fill at night with people enjoying after-dinner coffee and maybe even an aperitif. For the best *tiramisù* in town try **Ristorante Comercianti,** P. Dante 1 (☎ 091 921 3306), where impressive slabs are a mere 8SFr. (Open M-Su 6pm-midnight. 9am-midnight on holidays.) For the closest thing to a hot night on the town in demure Lugano, set the dance floor on fire at the **Discoteca Prince,** Riva Albertolli, 1, located inside the Lugano casino. (☎ 091 923 3281. Cover 25SFr. Open W-Su midnight-4am.)

LAKE MAGGIORE (LAGO MAGGIORE)

Cradling similarly temperate mountain waters and idyllic shores, but without the tourist frenzy of its eastern neighbors, Lago Maggiore has many faces. A stroll past any of the grandiose shore-side hotels reveals Maggiore as the preferred watering hole of the elite. Steep green hills punctuate the shoreline, and to the west, the dark, glaciated outline of Monte Rosa (4634m) peers down the valley toward Maggiore. Don't be discouraged by Maggiore's reputation as the most expensive lake; many modest *pensioni* offer reasonable rates. Stresa is the most convenient base for exploring the Borromean Islands and Lago di Orta, while its cross-lake relative, Verbania-Pallanza, has a terrific hostel.

STRESA
☎0323

Stresa retains much of the manicured charm that lured visitors during the 19th and early 20th centuries. Blooming hydrangeas and art nouveau hotels line the waterfront, giving the little town a romantic, old-fashioned appearance. Splendid vistas of the mountain lake-country await around each bend of the cobblestone streets. Stresa is a resort town, filled with Italian, French, English, American, and German tourists; there is little to do but hop the boats to the Borromeans with the rest of the vacationing masses, or while away the day admiring lakeside villas with more than a touch of envy. Of course, if you've seen enough conspicuous consumption for the day, you can always explore the hillside of nearby Motterone.

E⁊ TRANSPORTATION AND PRACTICAL INFORMATION. Stresa lies only an hour from Milan on the Milan-Domodossola train line (every hr., 7:30am-10:15pm, €5.10). The ticket is office open M-F 6:10am-12:10pm and 12:50-8:10pm, Sa 7am-2pm, Su 12:50-8:10pm. The **local IAT tourist office** is in the ferry building at the ferry dock, in P. Martini. (☎/fax 0323 30 150 or 31 308. Open daily 10am-12:30pm and 3-6:30pm.) For **currency exchange** and a 24-hour **ATM**, try **Banca Popolare di Intra,** C. Umberto 1, just off P. Marconi. (☎0323 30 330. Open M-F 8:20am-1:20am and 2:35-4pm.) Stresa's pharmacy, **Farmacia Internazionale,** C. Italia, 40 (☎0323 30 326), posts the list of rotating late-night pharmacies. In case of **emergency,** contact **police** (☎112 or 0323 30 118), **first aid** (☎113 or ☎0323 31 844), an or an **ambulance** (☎118 or 0323 33 360). The **post office** is at V. A. Bolongaro, 44, near P. Rossi. (☎0323 30 065. Open M-F 8:15am-6pm, Sa 8:15am-noon.) **Postal Code:** 28838.

⫙ ACCOMMODATIONS. The modern and friendly **Albergo Luina ❸,** V. Garibaldi, 21, is conveniently located near the town center, but call several weeks in advance for reservations as they are consistently booked throughout the summer. There are only a few rooms, but all have bath and TV. (☎/fax 0323 30 285; luinastresa@yahoo.it. 10% discount with *Let's Go.* Singles €31-46; doubles €47-68.) **Hotel Mon Toc ❹,** V. Duchessa di Genova, 67/69, can be reached by taking a right out of the station and another at the intersection under the tracks. It has very well-maintained, breezy rooms, all with bath, TV, and telephone. (☎0323 30 282; fax 93 38 60; info@hotelmontoc.com. Breakfast included. Singles €45; doubles €78. AmEx/DC/MC/V.) Reach **Orsola Meublé ❸,** V. Duchessa di Genova, 45, from the station by turning right, walking downhill to the intersection, and turning left. A far cry from lakeside luxury, Orsola Meublé nonetheless features affordable blue-tiled rooms with cement balconies decked with plastic chairs and a breakfast room adorned with golf trophies. The cramped showers and short beds leave something to be desired. (☎0323 31 087; fax 93 31 21. Breakfast included. Singles €30.90, with bath €36.15; doubles €51.55/ €61.96. AmEx/DC/MC/V.)

🞖 **FOOD.** Stresa boasts one truly unique local dish: *Le Margheritine*, a buttery cake dripping with icing sugar. Hidden behind the pricier hotels are surprisingly good restaurant deals, such as the **Taverna del Pappagallo ❷**, V. P. Margherita, 46, which serves delicious pasta and brick-oven pizza in the warm interior or outside in the lovely garden. Try the *omelette al prosciutto* for €6, or *cannelloni alla "Pappagallo"* for €7.32. (☎ 0323 304 11. *Primi* €3.62-7.32; *secondi* €9.30-11.36. Cover €1.30. Open Th-M 11:30am-2:30pm and 6:30-10:30pm.) At **Pizza D.O.C. ❶**, C. Italia, 60, busy waiters serve up inexpensive food while you take in the panoramic lakeside view on the balcony of the old Hotel Ariston. 72 inventive kinds of pizza (€3-9.30) and free delivery make this place a winner. Dessert pizzas, available *alla nutella and alla mele*, are €5.20-10.30. (☎ 0323 30 000; fax 31 195. *Primi* €5.50-6.70; *secondi* €6.50 to 10.30. Open daily 11:30am-2pm and 6:30-11pm. AmEx/MC/DC/V.) Stock up on necessities at the **GS supermarket**, V. Roma, 11. Pizza slices start at €1.20. (Open M-Sa 8:30am-1pm and 3-7:30pm, Su 8:30am-12:30pm.)

🞖🞖 **SIGHTS AND ENTERTAINMENT.** Stresa boasts hiking and villas galore, but what makes this town truly exceptional is **Il Museo dell'Ombrello e del Parasole**, V. Golf Panorama, 2, the world's only umbrella museum. Over 1000 items are exhibited, proof of the town's heritage as the resort of choice during La Belle Epoque, when the esplanade was graced with the presence of well-to-do ladies shading themselves from the harsh Mediterranean sun. (☎ 0323 20 80 64. Open Apr.-Sept. 10am-noon and 3-6pm.) **Villa Pallavicino** not only boasts 20 hectares of gardens for your strolling pleasure, but also scores of exotic animals and birds including llamas and zebras. (☎ 0323 31 533. Open daily Mar.-Oct. 9am-6pm. €6.40). Otherwise, head for the hills on the **Stresa-Mottarone Funivia**, P. Lido, 8, and explore Mottarone's extensive hiking and mountain-bike trails. (Turn right out of the tourist office and follow the road that winds along the waterfront. When it splits into two take the far left road and turn right onto the Viale Lido.(☎ 0323 303 99. Open 9:30am-5:30pm. Every 20 min.; €6.20, round-trip €11. Mountain bike rental next door.)

The **L'Idrovolante Cafe**, P. Lido, 6, next to the Funivia, is a major local hangout and offers live soul, R&B, and blues. Check your email there at €7.80 per hour. (☎ 0323 313 84. Open Tu-Th 8am-midnight, F-Sa 8am-2am, Su 8am-midnight.) From the last week in August to the 3rd week in September, classical musicians and fans gather for the internationally acclaimed **Settimane Musicali di Stresa e del Lago Maggiore**, a celebration of the full canon of classical music. (Various ticket packages start €20. Those under 26 may purchase a limited number of tickets for €10.) Contact the ticket office at V. Carducci, 38 (☎ 0323 31 095 or 30 459; fax 33 006).

NEAR STRESA

VERBANIA ☎ 0323

Verbania, an amalgamation of the smaller communities of Intra and Pallanza, lies on the **Milan-Domodossola** line. The line is part of the national or FS train network and runs up one side of Lago Maggiore. To arrive at Verbania by train, you must first arrive at Milan or Domodossola. The first is extremely easy, but the second will most likely require a train from Locarno. Alternatively, if you have more of a nautical edge, Verbania can be easily reached by ferry from any city bordering the lake. Farther north, the service may be infrequent. You can combine the two by taking a train to towns on the other shore (such as **Laveno**, which is part of the regional network and easily reached from Como), and taking a ferry across the lake to Verbania.

The town has a significantly less touristed feel than other lake towns with similar sights and entertainment. The **tourist office**, C. Zanitello, 8, a 5min. walk to the right when facing inland from the port, has extensive information on all the major sites. (☎ 0323 50 32 49; fax 55 66 69; turismo@comune.verbania.it. Open M-Sa 9am-12:30pm and 3-6pm, Su 9am-noon.) **Banca Popolare di Intra,** P. Garibaldi, 20, with a 24hr. **ATM,** is just to the right as you exit the boat. (Open M-F 8:20am-1:20pm, Sa-Su 8:20-11:50am.) **Farmacia dott.nitals,** in P. Gramsci, lists the night pharmacies in an electronic box outside. (Open M-Sa 8:30am-12:30pm and 3-7pm.) In an **emergency,** dial ☎ 113, the **police** ☎ 112 or an **ambulance** ☎ 118. Pallanza's **post office** is also in P. Gramsci. (Open M-F 8:15am-1:40pm, Sa 8:15am-noon.) **Postal Code:** 28922.

Only a few years old, **Ostello Verbania Internazionale (HI) ❶,** V. alle Rose, 7, in a quiet old villa 10-15min. from the Borromean Island ferries, offers extremely modern and clean facilities with ping-pong, pool, foosball, arcade games, TV room, and gigantic bathrooms. After exiting the ferry, turn right and walk for 5min. along the water to V. V. Veneto, just past the tourist office. Take a left on V. Panoramica, keep walking up the hill, continue around the bend, and take your last right. The hostel is 50m on the left. (☎ 0323 50 16 48; fax 50 78 77. Breakfast included. Lunch and dinner €8. Lockout 11am-4pm. Curfew midnight. Reception 8-11am, 4-5:30pm, and 10-11pm. Dorms with sheets and locker €12.50; 3 family rooms with bath €14 per person.) **Hotel Novara ❸,** P. Garibaldi, 30, has 16 immaculate rooms above a restaurant; all rooms have TV and telephone. Facing the water, turn left from the dock and walk 2min. to P. Garibaldi. (☎ 0323 50 35 27; fax 50 35 28. Singles €18-28.50; doubles with bath €39-57. AmEx/DC/MC/V.)

From the hostel toward Intra lies the beautiful **Villa Taranto.** The Villa and gardens were the life's work of Captain Neil McEacharn, who dreamt of creating a world-class botanical garden in the heart of the Italian lakes. The result is a systematic collection of flora biodiversity, including a particularly lovely specimen of the genus *Pinus Sabiniana.* (☎ 0323 55 66 67; fax 55 66 67. Open daily Apr.-Oct. 8:30am-7:30pm. The ticket office closes at 6:30. €7, children under 6 free.)

Pizzeria Emiliana ❶, P. Giovanni XXIII, 24, offers brick-oven pizzas from €3.60-7.80. (☎ 0323 50 35 22. *Primi* €4.40-9.50, *secondi* €6.80-13.50. Open Th-Tu noon-2:30pm and 6:45pm-midnight.) For something a little more substantial, head to **Hostaria il Cortile ❷,** V. Albertazzi, 14. The courtyard, though slightly run-down, creates old world ambiance. Try the *penne gorgonzola* at €4.65, or the *scaloppine vino bianco al limone* €6.20. (☎ 0323 50 28 16. Open Th-Tu 11:30am-3:30pm and 5:30pm-2am. *Primi* from €4.10-4.65, *secondi* from €5.10-6.20. DC/MC/V.)

LOCARNO, SWITZERLAND   ☎ 091

On the shores of **Lago Maggiore,** Locarno (pop. 30,000), has been a resort town since Imperial Rome, and was a major spot until at least the 11th century. The Dark Ages were bad for business, though, and it has since fallen behind towns like Stresa. In 1925 the Locarno Treaty was signed here, earning it the appellation of the Town of Peace and creating street names like V. della Pace. A world-famous 11-day **film festival,** held each August, brings over 150,000 big-screen enthusiasts. The centerpiece of the festival is a giant 26m by 14m outdoor screen set up in P. Grande for big name premieres, while smaller screens throughout the city highlight young filmmakers and ground-breaking experimentation. (☎ 091 756 2121; fax 756 2149; www.pardo.ch.) Locarno also serves as an excellent starting point for mountain hikes along the Verzasca and Maggia valleys and regional skiing.

Take an **FS train** from **Pallanza** to **Locarno** (2¼hr., change at Domodossola; M-Sa 8 per day, 8am-8pm; Su 1 per day; 36SFr); **Lugano** (1hr., change in Giubiasco or Bellinzona, every 30min., 5:30am-12:05pm, 16.60SFr); and **Milan** (2½hr., 6:30am-8:30pm, 63SFr). The **tourist office** is on Largo Zorzi in P. Grande. From the main exit of the train station, walk diagonally right, cross V. della Stazione and continue on V. alla Ramogna, the pedestrian walkway. Cross Largo Zorzi to your left; the tourist office is in the same building as the casino. (☎091 791 0091; fax 751 9070; www.maggiore.ch. Open M-F 9am-6pm, Sa 9am-5pm, Su 10am-noon and 1-3pm.)

All the worldly languor of Locarno coexists in relative peace with the piety of the worshipers in the churches of the **Città Vecchia** (old city). For centuries, visitors have journeyed to Locarno just to see the church of **Madonna del Sasso** (Madonna of the Rock). Its orange-yellow hue renders it immediately recognizable from anywhere in town. The church is accessible by a *funicular* that leaves every 11min. from a small station on the V. alla Romagna, which is to your right as you exit the station from the front, where there are no bus stops (one-way 4.50SFr, round-trip 6.60SFr). You can also make the 20min. walk up the smooth stones of V. al Sasso. (Off V. Cappuccini in the Città Vecchia. Grounds open daily 7am-7pm. 2.50SFr, students 1.50SFr. Free English guidebook at the entrance.)

The **Verzasca Dam** has brought scores of visitors dizzying adrenaline rushes courtesy of its famous **bungee jump**, the highest in the world. The 255m jump, conquered with panache by James Bond in *Goldeneye*, costs 244SFr the first time (with training, drink, and diploma) and 195SFr for subsequent leaps. For information, contact **Trekking Team.** (☎0848 80 80 07; www.trekking.ch. Open Apr.-Oct.) Hidden among the chestnut trees, waterfalls, and dozens of lakes in Ticino's largest valley, Valle Maggia is the village of **Aurigeno.** Come here to take a "vacation from your vacation" at ◙**Baracca Backpacker ❷**, a tiny hostel with ten beds amidst the peaceful outdoors. From the train station in Locarno, take bus #10 (dir.: Valle Maggia) to Ronchini (25min., every hr., 5:30am-11:35pm, 6.80SFr). Cross the street, turn right from the bus stop, and follow the hostel signs into the forest (15min.), crossing the suspension bridge. When you reach the town, continue straight and turn right. The hostel is before the church and to its right. With a waterfall in the back garden to lull you to sleep and a full herbarium at your disposal, this has to be one of the best hostels you'll encounter. If, for some inexplicable reason, you should want to leave, the couple that runs the hostel can rent you a bike and give you extensive information on the **hiking, climbing,** and **swimming** possibilities in the area. (☎079 207 1554. Call ahead. Sleepsack 2SFr per day. Reception 9-11am and 5-8pm. Open Apr.-Oct. Dorms 25SFr; doubles 28SFr). **Palagiovani (HI) ❸,** V. Varenna 18, is an great hostel just 15min. from the train station. Along the well-marked path to the hostel are the music school and Radio Ticino (the local youth radio station). Also easily reached by bus, take #31 or 36 from the train station towards Ascona/Losone, to the Cinque Vie stop. (☎091 756 1500. Reception 8-10am and 3-11:30pm. Curfew 10:30pm, but guests are given the access code. Internet 14SFr per hr. Beds from 32SFr with breakfast and sheets.)

THE BORROMEAN ISLANDS (ISOLE BORROMEE) ☎0323

Beckoning to visitors with promises of dense green thickets and stately old villas, the lush beauty of the three Borromean Islands is the major attraction of the southern and central lake. Ferries run to all three islands from both Stresa and Pallanza every half hour (9am-7pm), and a day's ticket, covering the islands, Stresa Palanza and the Villa Taranto, goes for just €10. The entrance fees to the sights on each island can be pricey. It's cheaper to buy your tickets at the ferry ticket window in Stresa or Pallanza than on the island.

The opulent ◙**Palazzo e Giardini Borromeo** is set on the pearl of Maggiore, **Isola Bella.** The Baroque palace, built in 1670 by Count Borromeo, features six meticulously designed rooms with priceless masterpieces, tapestries, sculptures by

Canova and paintings by van Dyck. The ten terraced gardens, punctuated with statues and topped by a unicorn, rise up like a large wedding cake. The Borromeo family's motto, *"Humilitas"?* Not here. (☎ 0323 30 556. Open daily Mar.-Sept. 9am-noon and 1:30-5:30pm; Oct. 9am-noon and 1:30-5pm. €8.50, ages 6-15 €4).

Take the ferry from aristocratic Isola Bella to mingle with the fishermen of the **Isola Superiore (dei Pescatori).** In addition to a free beach, charming paths, and a children's park, the only garden-free island offers you the chance to interact with fishermen who make a simple living selling kitschy souvenirs.

Isola Madre is the longest and quietest of the three islands. Its elegant 16th-century **villa** was started in 1502 by Lancelotto Borromeo and finished by the Count Renato 100 years later, after Lancelotto met his unfortunate end in the mouth of a dragon. It contains stage sets, a vast collection of portraits, and Princess Borromeo's *bambini* marionette collection. Even if you choose to skip the house, the botanical garden's stupendous array of exotic trees, the tallest palms in Italy, and strutting peacocks are worth the entrance fee. (☎ 0323 31 261; fax 50 18 41. Open Mar.-Sept. daily 9am-noon and 1:30-5:30pm; Oct. 9am-12:30pm and 1:30-5:30pm. €8, ages 6-15 €4.) Do not stop on the island unless you plan to see the garden, or you'll be forced to wait on the lone sidewalk (the only admission-free place on the island) until the next boat arrives. Off Isola Madre, you will be able to see the 4th island, **Isolino San Giovanni,** revered by Arthur Toscanini, who frequently visited the villa. Unfortunately, the *isolino* is not open to public.

LAKE ORTA (LAGO DI ORTA)
ORTA SAN GIULIO ☎ 0322

Orta San Giulio is the gateway to Lake Orta, by far the least touristed of the lakes. The high houses that line the narrow cobblestone streets evoke the very best of old Italy. Without a car, the town is difficult to reach; most tourists are Italian. Its seclusion is precisely what drew Nietzsche here in May 1882, with his young love Lou Salome, to escape the watchful eye of her mother. Nietzsche claimed he couldn't remember whether or not the two had kissed, because the views had sent him into a state of grace.

▛ TRANSPORTATION. Orta lies on the Novara-Domodossola **train** line and as such can be reached from **Stresa** (1½hr., €2.62). Change at either Cuzzago or Premosello, and take one of the buses run by the railway. Buy train tickets for Orta from the conductor on board. Get off at **Orta Miasino,** 3km above Orta, and walk down to the left until you reach the intersection. Turn left on V. Fava, and the town of Orta San Giulio is a 10min. walk away. A twisting road connects Orta to nearby Lake Maggiore. On weekdays, **buses** leave from Stresa's P. Marconi (next to the phones and the little white food hut), traveling to Orta (1hr., in summer M-F 9am noon and 4pm, €5), via **Baveno.** The return trip from Orta to Stresa is a bit tricky (1hr.; in summer M-F 10am, 1pm, and 5pm; €5). Those with a car can try the nearby lake towns of **Alzo** and **Arola;** contact the Orta tourist office for details.

▟ PRACTICAL INFORMATION. Orta's tourist office is on V. Panoramica, across the street and down from the ornate Villa Crespi tower. From the train station, turn left and walk for 10 min. straight through the intersection. (☎ 0322 90 56 14; fax 90 58 00; infoorta@jumpy.it. Open M-F in summer 9am-1pm and 2-6pm.) There is a **pharmacy** on V. Corina Care Albertolletti, 6, off the main piazza. (☎ 0322 90 117. Open M-Sa 8:30am-noon and 3:30-7:30pm.) In case of an **emergency,** call an **ambulance** (☎ 118 or 0322 90 114) or the **police** (☎ 0322 82 444). **Banca Popolare di Novara,** V. Olina, 14, has **currency exchange** and outdoor **ATMs.** (Open M-F 8:20am-1:20pm and 2:35-3:35pm, Sa 8:20-11:20am.) The **post office** is in P. Ragazzoni. (☎ 0322 90 157. Open M-Sa 8:15am-5:30pm.) **Postal Code:** 28016.

REST IN PEACE. St. Giulius, after whom the island was named, arrived in Orta in AD 319. Like most right-thinking Christians of his day, he decided to build a church. Legend has it that the natives of the region distrusted the man, exiling him to the island for fear that his construction project would attract snakes and devils (the bane of developers and contractors everywhere). Ever-persistent Giulio continued with the construction of the church, and eventually the locals, realizing that he was a good man, helped him build one of the smallest (and prettiest) basilicas in the world. The island is still known as an Eden of silence, and its narrow streets are full of signs (in numerous languages) with pearls of wisdom like, "Silence is the language of love," or "In silence you receive all." San Giulio himself rests in decaying peace in a glass sarcophagus in the crypt of the basilica. Be prepared, or your scream might wake up all 47 nuns (and 3 families) on the island. The natives left him visible to scare away creatures of evil (and hordes of tourists). So far, he seems to be doing a pretty good job.

⚑ ACCOMMODATIONS AND CAMPING. "Affordable" accommodations start at €64.56 for a double, so you might also consider staying in Stresa and coming just for the day. **Piccolo Hotel Olina ❹**, V. Olina, 40, offers beautiful rooms with private baths. Family rooms with kitchens are also available. (☎ 0322 90 56 56. Breakfast included. Singles €52; doubles €72. AmEx/DC/MC/V.) Outside of town, but only a few minutes from the train station, is **Hotel-Meublé Santa Caterina ❺**, V. Marconi, 10. Recently renovated, it has spacious, sleek rooms. (☎ 0322 91 58 65; fax 90 377. Singles €57; doubles €77. AmEx/MC/V.) Rooms with a balcony or private garden cost slightly more. **Camping Orta ❶**, V. Domodossola, 28, offers lakeside camping. From the train station, turn left, go down to the intersection, and turn right. (☎/fax 0322 90 267. €4.75 per person, €7.50 per tent, €9 per lakeside site.)

❐ FOOD. Lago d'Orta is known as the home of *tapulon* (donkey meat, minced, well-spiced, and cooked in red wine). Fruit cake San Giulio, creative pasta, and bottles of alcohol, among other goodies, are available at the unparalleled ▨**Salumeria Il Buongustaio**, V. Olina, 8 (☎ 0322 90 56 26). English, French, German, and Spanish are spoken. Chat with Lucca, who will gladly sell you Italy's only peanut butter, as well as 150 proof alcohol. An **open-air market** on Wednesday mornings in P. Motta sells fruit, vegetables, and dry goods.

If you don't fancy the more traditional local fare, head to **Pizzeria La Campana ❷**, V. Giovanetti, 41, the continuation of V. Olina after P. Motta. (☎ 0322 90 211. Pizzas €5.15-8.25, *primi* €5.20-6.20, *secondi* €7-13; desserts €3.10-3.65. Open Tu-Su 11am-3:30pm and 6-11pm.) Visitors are drawn upstairs to **Taverna Antico Agnello ❸**, V. Olina, 18, by the fabulous food and attentive service. (☎ 0322 90 25 92. *Primi* €6.50-8.20; *secondi* €8.60-13.20. Open W-M noon-2:30pm and 7-11pm. AmEx/DC/MC/V.) On Isola di San Giulio, head to the most inexpensive (and only) restaurant on the island, **Ristorante San Giulio ❷**, V. Basilica, 4. Munch brunch in the 18th-century dining room. (☎ 0322 90 234. *Primi* €3.62-5.16; *secondi* €4.32-8.26. Cover €1.55.) A return boat to the island runs after the public ones have stopped.

◙ SIGHTS. Walk around ▨**Isola di San Giulio** (pop.: 59), across from Orta. The island is as beautiful as the Borromeans, but much quieter. Its 12th-century **Romanesque basilica,** with interesting Baroque ornaments and frescoes inside, was built on 4th-century foundations. The church's masterpiece is the **pulpit,** built out of black marble (representative of the Evangelists). Downstairs, the

skeleton of San Giulio, dressed in brocade robes, rests in a glass sarcophagus. (Basilica open M 11am-12:15pm, Tu-Sa 9:30am-12:15pm and 2-6:45pm, Su 8:30-10:45am and 2-6:45pm. Free. Appropriate dress required.) Small **motorboats** weave back and forth during the summer (every 10min., €2.60 round-trip; tickets sold on board). The boat is €1.81, but only departs every hour (9:45am-5:40pm). Ask the tourist office for a schedule of music and sporting events.

A short hike above Orta proper in the cool, verdant hills, the **Sacro Monte** monastic complex is devoted to St. Francis of Assisi, patron saint of Italy. The sanctuary, founded in 1591, has 20 chapels with 376 life-size statues and 900 frescoes. (Open daily 8:30am-7pm. Free.) The **Mercato Antiquariato** (antique market) is held in P. Motta on the first Saturday of the month. (Apr.-Oct. 9am-6pm.)

LIGURIA (ITALIAN RIVIERA)

Like a black pearl nestled in the mouth of a flawless white oyster shell, dark and dreary Genoa divides the largely luminescent Ligurian coastal strip into the **Riviera di Levante** (rising sun) to the east and the **Riviera di Ponente** (setting sun) to the west. The Italian Riviera stretches 350km along the Mediterranean between France and Tuscany, forming the most famous and touristed area of the Italian coastline. Protected from the north's severe weather by the Alps, Liguria still receives its fair share of tumultuous summer storms. Rainwater streams down the terraced hillsides, irrigating crops on high and smoothing the beach sands at sea level. Along the less congested Levante, rain renews the smell of blossoming flowers among the mighty Apennine mountains and pebble beaches. Meanwhile, heat evaporates from crowded Ponente beachside *discoteche* and medieval villages.

In remote villages as in major cities, Ligurians are known for their cultural isolation. They claim Nordic, not Roman, ancestry and have their own vocabulary and accent, often incomprehensible to other Italians. Their distinctive character, however, doesn't make them any less Italian, and nor did it stop them from playing a leading role in unifying the Italian peninsula. Giuseppe Mazzini, the father of the Risorgimento, and Giuseppe Garibaldi, its most popular hero, were both Ligurians.

HIGHLIGHTS OF LIGURIA

EXPLORE the *palazzi* and study fine Flemish art in Genoa (p. 158).

GET WET in the stunning fountain in **Genoa's Piazza dei Ferrari** (p. 160).

SAVOR a *gelato*-filled cone from one of **Finale Ligure's** many *gelaterie* (**p. 177**).

CATCH a flower flung in **Ventimiglia's Battagli dei Fiori** (**p. 188**).

LOSE your money and curse your luck while gambling at **San Remo's casino** (p. 180).

DANCE the night away at a beachside *discoteca* off **Genoa's Corso Italia** (p. 161).

GAPE at marine life at **Genoa's Aquarium** (p. 159).

STROLL the bewitching **Via dell'Amore** (p. 171) in **Cinque Terre** and add your name to its list of lovers.

Italian Riviera

NORTHWEST ITALY

GENOA (GENOVA) ☎010

City of grit and grandeur, Genoa has little in common with the villages that dot the rest of the Riviera. As any Ligurian will tell you, "*Si deve conoscerla per amarla*"— you have to know Genoa to love her. Many travelers flee to nearby beach towns, but those who linger in this once wealthy port may find themselves bewitched. From the 12th through the 17th century, the sweeping boulevards and arcane twisting *vicoli* (alleyways) were home to Genoa's leading families, who had amassed great wealth in international trade. These riches were lavished on extravagant palaces and churches. Genoa has made no secret of its many celebrated historical heroes, among them Christopher Columbus, the Risorgimento ideologue Giuseppe Mazzini, and the virtuoso violinist Nicolò Paganini. In the 18th century, the city fell out of renown and into decline. Genoa's great wall, second in length only to China's, now encircles a coarse yet cosmopolitan city that continues its struggle to unearth bygone grandeur.

⌐ TRANSPORTATION

Flights: C. Colombo Internazionale (☎010 60 151), in Sesti Ponente. Services European destinations. Take **Volabus #100** from Stazione Brignole (every 30min., 5:30am-9:30pm, €2) and get off at the Aeroporto stop.

Trains: Stazione Principe in P. Acquaverde and **Stazione Brignole** in P. Verdi. Buses #18, 19, 33, and 37 connect the 2 stations (25min., €0.80). **Luggage storage** available (see p. 154). Open daily 6am-10pm. Trains run from the stations to points along the Ligurian Riviera and to major Italian cities including **Rome** (5hr., 14 per day,· €23.50) and **Turin** (2hr., 19 per day, €8.70).

Ferries: At the Ponte Assereto arm of the port. Walk 15min. from Stazione Marittima or ride bus #20 from Stazione Principe. Purchase tickets at a city travel agency or **Stazione Marittima.** Arrive at Ponte Assereto at least 1hr. before departure. Destinations include **Barcelona, Olbia, Palau, Palermo, Porto Torres,** and **Tunisia. TRIS** (☎010 576 2411) and **Tirrenia** (☎081 317 2999) run to Sardinia only. **Grandi Traghetti** (☎010 58 93 31) heads to Palermo.

Local Buses: AMT, V. D'Annunzio, 8r (☎010 558 2414). One-way tickets within the city (€0.80) valid for 1½hr. All-day tourist passes €3 (foreign passport necessary). Tickets and passes can also be used for funicular and elevator rides.

Taxis: ☎010 59 66.

Bike Rental: Nuovo Centro Sportivo 2000, P. dei Garibaldi, 18r (☎010 254 1243; fax 254 2639). €6 per day. Open Tu-Sa 9:15am-12:30pm and 3:30-7:30pm, M 3:30-7:30pm. AmEx/MC/V.

⚔❓ ORIENTATION AND PRACTICAL INFORMATION

Most visitors arrive at one of Genoa's 2 train stations: **Stazione Principe**, in P. Acquaverde, or **Stazione Brignole**, in P. Verdi. From Stazione Principe take bus #18, 19, 20, 30, 32, 35, or 41, and from Stazione Brignole take bus #19 or 40 to **Piazza dei Ferrari** in the center of town. If walking to P. de Ferrari from Stazione Principe, take **Via Balbi** to **Via Cairoli** (which becomes **Via Garibaldi**), and at **Piazza delle Fontane Marose**, turn right on **Via XXV Aprile**. From Stazione Brignole, turn right out of the station to **Via Fiume,** and then right onto **Via XX Settembre.** Genoa's streets can stump even a native—don't leave home without a map!

The *centro storico* (historic center) contains many of Genoa's monuments. Unfortunately, it is also the city's most dangerous quarter, and its shadowy, labyrinthine streets are riddled with drugs and prostitutes at night. While locals may tell you that Genoa is worth getting acquainted with, they will also tell you never to get chummy with the *centro storico* after dark, on Sundays (when shops are closed), or in August (when the natives leave). Even at other times, only venture into the *centro storico* with a clear plan and route in mind and good map in hand.

Tourist Offices: APT (☎010 24 87 11), on Porto Antico, near Aquarium, in Palazzina S. Maria. Find the aquarium directly on the water, face the water, then walk toward the complex of buildings 30m to left. Limited English spoken. Decent maps. Open daily 9am-1pm and 2-6pm. **APT** has **branches** at Stazione Principe (☎010 246 2633) and airport (☎010 601 5247). Both open M-Sa 9:30am-1pm and 2:30-6pm. **Informagiovani,** Palazzo Ducale, 24r (☎010 557 4320; fax 557 4321), in P. Mateotti, is a youth center offering info on apartment rentals, jobs, and concerts, and free Internet access. Reserve 1wk. in advance, or fill a cancellation. Open Sept.-June M-F 9am-12:30pm and 3-6pm; July-Aug. M-Tu and Th-F 9am-12:30pm, W 9am-12:30pm and 3-6pm.

Budget Travel: CTS, V. San Vincenzo, 117r (☎010 56 43 66 or 53 27 48), off V. XX Settembre near Ponte Monumentale. Walk up the flight of stairs on the shopping complex to the left. Student fares available. Open M-F 9am-1pm and 2:30-6pm.

Consulates: UK, V. XX Settembre, 2, 5th fl., #37/38 (☎010 56 48 33). Open Tu-Th 9am-noon. **US,** V. Dante, 2, 3rd fl., #43 (☎010 58 44 92, emergency 335 652 1252). Open June-Sept. M-Th 11am-2pm; Oct.-May M noon-2pm, Tu-W 10am-noon, Th 10am-noon and 3-5pm.

Luggage Storage: In both train stations. €3 per 12hr.

English-Language Bookstore: Mondovori, V. XX Settembre, 210r (☎010 58 57 43). Huge bookstore with a full wall of English-language classics and some bestsellers. Choose from a lovely selection of *Let's Go* travel guides in the basement. Open M-F 9:30am-10pm, Sa 9:30am-11pm, Su 10:30am-1pm and 2-10pm.

Emergency: ☎113. **Police:** ☎112. **Ambulance:** ☎118.

Late-Night Pharmacy: Pescetto, V. Balbi, 185r (☎010 246 26 97 or 25 27. 86), near Stazione Principe. List of late-night pharmacies posted.

Hospital: Ospedale San Martino, V. Benedetto XV, 10 (☎010 55 51).

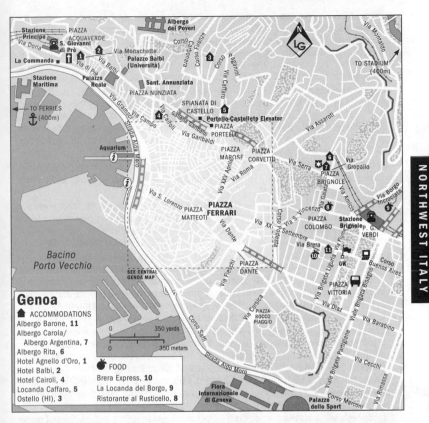

Genoa

🏠 ACCOMMODATIONS
Albergo Barone, **11**
Albergo Carola/
   Albergo Argentina, **7**
Albergo Rita, **6**
Hotel Agnello d'Oro, **1**
Hotel Balbi, **2**
Hotel Cairoli, **4**
Locanda Caffaro, **5**
Ostello (HI), **3**

🍴 FOOD
Brera Express, **10**
La Locanda del Borgo, **9**
Ristorante al Rusticello, **8**

Internet Access: Internet Village (☎010 570 4878), at intersection of V. Brigata Bisagno and C. Buenos Aires, across from P. Vittoria. €7.75 per hr. Open M-Sa 9am-1pm and 3-7pm. MC/V. **A.P.C.A.,** V. Colombo, 35r (☎/fax 010 58 13 41). Internet €5.35 per hr., €1.55 per 15min. Open M-F 9am-noon. Also, see **Informagiovani** (above) for the possibility of free Internet.

Post Office: Main office, P. Dante, 4/6r (☎010 259 4687), 2 blocks from P. de Ferrari. *Fermo Posta.* Open M-Sa 8am-7pm. Most branches open 8am-1:30pm.

Postal Code: 16121.

ACCOMMODATIONS & CAMPING

Rooms in Genoa are scarce only in October, when the city hosts a wave of nautical conventions. Almost without exception, budget lodgings in the *centro storico* and near the port prefer to rent rooms by the hour. Try the hostel, if you're willing to take a long bus ride up the hillside, or stick around Stazione Brignole, where the establishments are more refined.

Ostello Per La Gioventù (HI), V. Costanzi, 120 (☎/fax 010 242 2457). From Stazione Principe, take bus #35 and tell the driver that you want to transfer to #40 at V. Napoli; once you get off there, take #40 to hostel. From Stazione Brignole, pick up bus #40 (every 15min.) and ride it all the way up the hill—ask the driver to let you off at the *ostello*. Facility offers 213 beds and plenty of amenities: cafeteria, elevator, free lockers, parking, TV, wheelchair access, and a view of the city that lies far, far below. Multilingual staff. Breakfast, hot showers, and sheets included. Laundry €6.50 per 5kg. Reception 7-11am and 3:30pm-12:30am. Check-out 9am. No curfew. HI card required (available at the hostel). Dorms €13; family accommodations €14-18 per person. ❶

Albergo Argentina, V. Gropallo, 4/4 (☎/fax 010 839 3722). From Stazione Brignole, turn right on V. de Amicis and continue into P. Brignole. When facing Albergo Astoria, turn right and walk 15m. Look for the big wooden doors with bronze lion heads on the left hand side of the street and ring the buzzer. 9 large, clean, elegantly furnished rooms overlook a quiet garden in a well-maintained and secure building. Singles €26; doubles €42; 1 triple €56; 1 quad €68. ❸

Albergo Carola, V. Gropallo, 4/12 (☎010 839 1340). 2 flights up from the Argentina (see above). Proprietor can give you directions to a laundromat in Italian or Spanish. Singles €26; doubles €42. ❸

Hotel Balbi, V. Balbi, 21/3 (☎/fax 010 25 23 62; hotelbalbi@inwind.it). Though you will have trouble finding a room with a view, Balbi's wonderful staff and proximity to Stazione Principe make it a great place to stay. Breakfast €4. Singles €25, with bath €32; doubles €45/€55; triples and quads add 30% per person. AmEx/DC/MC/V. ❷

Locanda di Palazzo Cicala, P. San Lorenzo, 16 (☎010 251 8824 or 348 584 8481; fax 010 246 7414; www.palazzocicala.it). If you're royalty, or just spend money like you are, your *palazzo* awaits. Ideal location in the heart of the city, with restaurants and tourist sights just steps away from the front door. Relax in funky red chairs and couches in the big, spacious sitting room. 9 huge, newly renovated rooms, each with A/C, bath, phone, and computer with Internet connection. Rooms from €150. AmEx/MC/V. ❺

Locanda Caffaro, V. Caffaro, 3 (☎/ fax 010 247 2362), off P. Portello, midway between Stazione Principe and Stazione Brignole. Take bus #18 from Stazione Principe and get off at P. Portello (3rd stop). 8 clean rooms and management that's eager to please. Check out their terrace for a view of cupolas and spires sloping their way down to the waterfront. Singles €24; doubles €42; triples €55; quads €65. AmEx/DC/MC/V. ❷

Albergo Barone, V. XX Settembre, 2/23 (☎/fax 010 58 75 78). From Stazione Brignole, veer to the right and walk down V. Fiume to V. XX Settembre. 12 clean rooms with spacious beds and windows that look out on Genoa's lively shopping district. Some English spoken. Reception 8:30am-midnight. Call ahead for reservations (credit card required). Singles €31, with shower €39; doubles €40/€46; triples with shower €52-60, with full bath €69; quads with shower €68-76. AmEx/DC/MC/V. ❸

Albergo Rita, V. Gropallo, 8C (☎/fax 010 87 02 07). Homey atmosphere pervades all 9 rooms. Singles €31; doubles €45, with bath €52; triple €60. MC/V. ❸

Hotel Cairoli, V. Cairoli, 14, 4th fl. (☎010 246 1454; fax 246 7512), on a relatively quiet street that connects V. P. Bensa and V. Garibaldi. Lovely terrace with flowers. All rooms with bath, mini-fridge, and TV. Breakfast €6. Singles €47-77; doubles €67-88; triples €78-83; quads €88-93. AmEx/DC/MC/V. ❹

Hotel Agnello d'Oro, V. Monachette, 6 (☎010 246 2084; fax 246 2327; www.hotelagnellodoro.it), off V. Balbi, a 2min. walk from Stazione Principe. 20 rooms, with bath and TV. Some with terrace and A/C. Fans available. Breakfast included. Singles €70; doubles €85-95; triples €100-105. AmEx/DC/MC/V. ❺

Camping: The Genoa area is teeming with campgrounds, but many are booked solid during July and August. The tourist office is your best source of info. **Genova Est** (☎010 347 2053) is on V. Marcon Loc Cassa. Take the train from Stazione Brignole to the suburb of Bogliasco (10min., 6 per day, €1.08). A free bus (5min., every 2hr., 8:10am-6pm) will take you from Bogliasco to the campsite. Washing machines €3.50 per load. €4.65 per person, €9.30 per large tent. Electricity €1.60 per day. ❶

Central Genoa

🍴 FOOD

Blue Jamaica Cafe, 5
Caffè degli Specchi, 6
Da Vittorio, 1
I Tre Merli, 2
Ristorante Napoleon, 4
Trattoria da Maria, 3

NORTHWEST ITALY

🍴 FOOD

In culinary terms, a dish prepared *alla Genovese* is served with Genoa's pride and joy, pesto—a green sauce made from ground basil, pine nuts, garlic, Parmesan cheese, and olive oil. The *Genovese* put it on almost everything, so don't be afraid to experiment. Other delectable edibles include *farinata* (a fried pancake of chick-pea flour) and *pansotti* (ravioli stuffed with spinach and ricotta and served with a creamy walnut sauce). Stop by a *macelleria* and try a fresh slice of Genoa's world-famous salami. Don't forget to sample the seafood. **Mercato Orientale,** off V. XX Settembre south of the Ponte Monumentale, is the place to go for fresh fruit and vegetables. (Open M-Sa 7:30am-1pm and 3:30-7:30pm.) Another option is **Supersconto,** V. di San Pietro, 76r. (Walk south from P. Bianchi marketplace to the intersection of V. San Pietro and Vico delle Compere.)

🏆 **Trattoria da Maria,** V. Testa d'Oro, 14r (☎010 58 10 80), off V. XXV Aprile near P. Marose. Red-checkered tablecloths, clinks and clanks from the kitchen, and friendly waiters yelling orders down a dumbwaiter chute all contribute to the vivacious charm of this classic Italian restaurant. The menu changes daily, but the dishes are always delicious. *Pranzo turistico* lunch *menù* €6.71. Open Tu-F and Su noon-2:30pm and 7-9:30pm, M noon-2:30pm. ➋

▨ **Da Vittorio,** V. Sottoripa, 59r (☎010 247 2927). Ask a local where to find the best seafood in the city, and he will likely name Vittorio. The throngs of people crowding the entrance agree. The catch-of-the-day is displayed in the front window (you'll see waiters periodically carting trays of seafood from the ice back to the kitchen). *Primi* from €6, *secondi* from €8, lobster around €22. Reservations recommended. Open daily noon-4pm and 7pm-1:30am. ❸

▨ **Ristorante Napoleon,** V. XXV Aprile, 33r (☎010 54 18 88 or 56 29 80), on your left as you go toward P. dei Ferrari. Elegant yet friendly restaurant; lovely place for a delicious meal. Try the *"tre moschettiere"* pasta—the "three musketeers" at work in this dish are tomatoes, finely ground meat, and pesto. *Primi* €7.20-9.30, *secondi* €13.40-20.60. Open M 7:15-10:15pm, Tu-Sa 12:15-3:15pm and 7:15-10:15pm. ❸

Pizzeria Vittorio al Mare, V. Belvedere E. Firpo, 1 (☎010 376 0141), in Boccadasse on the water below its more classy incarnation, the Ristorante Vittorio al Mare. Try a pizza (€4-8), or drop a little more cash on *primi* (€9-15) and *secondi* (€13-22), as you enjoy the seaside view. Have your *dolce della casa* (€3.50) to go and finish up the meal watching the water (and couples stealing kisses) on the rocks outside. Open Tu-F noon-3pm and 7:30-11pm, Sa-Su noon-3pm. AmEx/DC/MC/V. ❹

Blu Jamaica Cafe, P. dei Ferrari, 34/36r (☎010 247 4548). Easy-to-find spot for a reasonably priced meal. 28 kinds of pizza (€3.87-6.72), *primi* (€3.63-5.16), *secondi* (€4.14-6.20). Grab a *panino* or *gelato* to go. Open Su-F 7am-9pm. AmEx/MC/V. ❷

I Tre Merli, Vico della Maddalena, 26r (☎010 247 4095; fax 247 4042), on a narrow street off V. Garibaldi. A hidden gem of a restaurant with brick walls, soft music, and mellow atmosphere. Wine connoisseurs take note—the wine list is 16 pages long! *Primi* €8-9, *secondi* €7-9. Open M-Tu and Th-F 12:30-3pm and 7:30pm-midnight, Sa 7:30pm-1am, Su 7:30pm-midnight. ❹

Caffè degli Specchi, Salita Pollaiuoli, 43r (☎010 246 8193). Walk down Salita Pollaioli from P. Matteotti. The cafe will appear on your left, with umbrellas shading outdoor seating in the summer. Inside, the bar is lined with mirrors and marble, and a sophisticated crowd pleads for a *bicchierino di vino* (glass of wine; €3.60), a *piccolo panino* (€1.30), or a frozen *forza cappuccino* (€0.98). Upstairs, fresh salads (including chicken and apple) run €7.75. Open M-Sa 7am-8:30pm. ❷

Ristorante al Rusticello, V. S. Vicenzo, 59r (☎010 58 85 56), not far from Stazione Brignole. Al Rusticello is perfect for the budget traveler fed up with plastic tables and paper tablecloths. Dress up a little—and spend a tad more than you might otherwise—to enjoy good food and romantic atmosphere. *Primi* €5.20-9.30, *secondi* €4.70-15.50. Open daily noon-2:30pm and 6:30pm-midnight. MC/V. ❸

La Locanda del Borgo, V. Borgo Incrociati, 47r (☎010 81 06 31), behind Stazione Brignole. Exit the station, turn right and go through the tunnel—V. Borgo Incrociati is straight ahead. Clean, friendly, and popular. Delicious food at great prices. *Primi* €4-8; *secondi* €7-13. Lunch *Menù* M-Th €8. Open daily 8am-4pm and 8pm-12:30am. AmEx/DC/MC/V. ❸

Brera Express, V. di Brera, 11r (☎010 54 32 80), just off V. XX Settembre near Stazione Brignole. The best deal at this cafeteria-style joint is the *menù* for €8.80 (includes *primo, secondo,* fruit, and a drink), but all entrees are cheap and fresh. *Primi* €3.10-3.40, *secondi* €5.20-5.70. Don't waste your money on the full-service pizzeria on the right side of the restaurant—you'll pay twice the price for the same meal. Open daily 11:45am-3pm and 7pm-midnight. Self-service closes 10pm. ❷

👁 SIGHTS

FROM STAZIONE PRINCIPE TO THE CENTRO STORICO

Outside of the winding alleyways of the *centro storico*, Genoa boasts a multitude of *palazzi* built by its famous merchant families. These are best glimpsed along **Via Garibaldi,** which skirts the edge of the *centro storico*, and **Via Balbi,** which runs through the heart of the university quarter from Stazione Principe to P. Nunizia. On both streets, the *palazzi* line up cheek to jowl, dwarfing the passersby who walk through the shadows below. Once home to Genoa's gentry, these mansions are now open to the public and showcase 16th- and 17th-century Flemish and Italian works of art. If you're planning on visiting a lot of museums, ask the tourist office or one of the museums themselves about the fixed-price pass.

■ **PALAZZO REALE.** Built between 1600 and 1700, this *palazzo* was originally home to the Balbi family, for which the street was named, and then later to the Durazzo family, both powerful in maritime Genoa. The *palazzo* only became the Royal Palace in the 18th century, and the structural setup installed for the Savoy rulers persists for the most part into the present day. The Rococo throne room, covered in red velvet and gold paint, remains untouched, along with the royal waiting room and sleeping quarters. See yourself framed in gold thousands of times in the **Galleria degli Specchi**, modeled after the Hall of Mirrors at Versailles, and watch the moon on the **queen's clock** move across the night sky (to be lit from behind by a candle). Paintings crowding the walls include works by Tintoretto, van Dyck, and Bassano. After buying your ticket, ascend the red-carpeted stairs on the left. *(10min. west of V. Garibaldi. V. Balbi, 10. ☎010 271 0272. Open M-Tu 9am-3:30pm, W-Su 8:15am-6:45pm. €4, ages 18-25 €2, under 18 or over 65 free.)*

■ **PORTELLO-CASTELLETO ELEVATOR.** Ride the elevator up with all the locals who find it no more special than taking the bus (it's considered part of Genoa's public transportation system). The 30 second ride rewards you with one of the best panoramic views of the city, particularly of the port. *(Through the tunnel entrance on P. Portello. Open daily 6:40am-midnight. €3.50.)*

AQUARIUM. Genoa may be practically beach-free, but that doesn't mean you can't still go under the sea. Bask in frigid air-conditioning, gaze at ocean-dwelling fauna cavorting in huge tanks (this aquarium has the largest volume of water of any in Europe), check out the 3-D movie, and start to feel a little cold-blooded. Still not wet enough? Check out the *Grande Nave Blu* (Big Blue Boat) for exhibits that extend above and beyond the sea and an interactive tank where you can grab slithery sea rays and get splashed by slippery pre-teens, all for the noble cause of engendering "harmony with the sea." *(On Porto Antico, across from the tourist office. ☎010 248 1205 for recorded info. Open M-F 9:30am-7:30pm, last entry at 5:30pm; Sa-Su 9:30am-8:30pm, last entry 6:30pm. In the summer, open Th until 11pm, last entry 9:30pm. Closed M Nov.-Jan. €12; cheaper rates for groups and kids.)*

VIA GARIBALDI. Also known as Via Aurea (Golden Street), Via Garibaldi remains the most impressive street in Genoa. Lined with elegant *palazzi*, it was constructed during the 17th century by wealthy families seeking to flaunt their prominence. A glance inside the courtyards reveals fountains, frescoes, and leafy gardens. **Galleria Palazzo Rosso,** V. Garibaldi, 18 (☎010 247 6351), built in the 16th century, earned its name when it was painted red in the 17th. Red carpeting also covers the floors of exhibit halls that feature lavishly frescoed ceilings and a display of several hundred years' worth of Genovese ceramics. The second floor now holds several full-length van Dyck portraits and Bernardo Strozzi's masterpiece, *La Cuoca.* Across the street, the **Galleria di Palazzo Bianco** (1548, rebuilt 1712) exhibits one of the city's largest collections of Ligurian art, as well as some Dutch and Flemish paintings. *(V. Garibaldi, 11. ☎010 247 6377. Both galleries open Tu-Sa 9am-7pm, Su 10am-6pm. One gallery €3.10, both €5.16, under 18 or over 60 free. Su free.)*

CHIESA DI GESÙ. Also known as **S. Ambrogio e Andrea** (1549-1606), the church features over-the-top *trompe l'oeil* effects and two Rubens canvases, *The Circumcision* (1605), over the altar, and *St. Ignatius Healing a Woman Possessed of the Devil* (1620), in the 3rd alcove on the left. *(From P. de Ferrari, take V. Boetto to P. Matteotti. Open daily 7:15am-12:30pm and 4-7:30pm, except when there is a mass. Free.)*

PALAZZO MUNICIPALE. Built from 1554 to 1570, the Palazzo Municipale (city hall) showcases Nicolò Paganini's violin, the **Guarneri del Gesù.** The sound of this instrument broke the hearts of some, drove others to suicide, and convinced the rest that they were hearing angels sing. The violin is still used on rare occasions to perform Paganini's works. To see the violin, go upstairs to the left, and ask the secretary. *(V. Garibaldi, 9. Open M-F 8:30am-6pm. Free.)*

SAN GIOVANNI DI PRÈ. This Romanesque church, built in 1180, is one of Genoa's oldest monuments. The vaulted stone roof and filtered light create a cavernous weight and contemplative feel. A left turn around the church leads to the 12th-century **La Commenda,** which housed the Knight Commanders of St. John. *(Head away from the Stazione Principe toward V. Balbi and turn right on Salita di San Giovanni.)*

VILLETTA DI NEGRO. The beautiful park is spread out along a hill, and boasts waterfalls, grottoes, and statues of patriots amidst terraced gardens. *(From P. delle Fontane Marose, take Salita di S. Caterina to P. Corvetto. Open daily 8am-10pm.)*

HARBOR CRUISES. Boats depart at least every hour from Porto Antico next to the aquarium, across from the tourist office. Prices depend on trip duration.

THE CENTRO STORICO

The eerie, beautiful, and sometimes dangerous historic center is a mass of narrow winding streets and cobbled alleyways bordered by the port, V. Garibaldi, and P. de Ferrari. It's home to some of Genoa's most memorable monuments: the **duomo, Palazzo Spinola,** and the medieval **Torre Embriaci,** whose Guelph battlements jut out among the buildings to the left when facing the **Chiesa di Santa Maria di Castello.** Due to a high crime rate, the center is only safe for tourists during weekdays, when stores are open. At night, the quarter's seedy underground emerges, and not even the police venture here.

■ **CHIESA DI SANTA MARIA DI CASTELLO.** This 15th-century church, with foundations that date to 500 BC, is a labyrinth of chapels (added onto the original structure during the 16th-18th centuries), courtyards, cloisters, and crucifixes. In the chapel directly to the left of the high altar, you'll find the spooky **Crocifisso Miracoloso.** According to legend, this wooden Jesus once moved its head to attest to the honesty of a young damsel betrayed by her lover; Jesus's beard is said to grow longer every time a crisis hits the city. As you stroll around, watch your step: the floor is paved with 18th-century tombs. To see the painting of **S. Pietro Martire di Verona,** complete with a halo and a large cleaver conspicuously thrust into his cranium, go up the stairs to the right of the high altar, turn right, and right again. The painting is above the door. Incensed locals are said to have turned poor Pietro's head into a butcher block. *(From P. G. Matteotti, head up V. S. Lorenzo toward the water and turn left on V. Chiabrera. A left on serpentine V. di Mascherona leads to the church in P. Caricamento. Open daily 9am-noon and 3-6pm, except Su, when there is morning mass. Free.)*

DUOMO (SAN LORENZO). Though it was already in existence by the 9th century, the duomo was enlarged and reconstructed between the 12th and 16th centuries after religious authorities deemed it "imperfect and deformed." The result may have been more perfect, but it sure wasn't symmetrical—the church has a lopsided appearance because only one of the two planned bell towers was completed. The striped Gothic facade (the stripes are designed to make it look bigger) flaunts copiously carved main entrances and 9th-century lions and sirens and vines (oh, my!) that give way to an incongruous interior, a mix of Roman, Gothic, Renaissance, Baroque, and Neoclassical architectures. The front part, holding the altar, was added during the 17th and 18th centuries. *(P. San Lorenzo, off V. San Lorenzo, which emerges from P. Matteotti. Open M-Sa 8am-7pm, Su 7am-7pm. Guided tour every 30min. Free.)*

The adjoining **Museo del Tesoro** showcases of some of the church's treasures, including the beautiful emerald-colored *Sacro Catino* (sacred bowl), ornate goblets, and arks. *(Open M-Sa 9am-noon and 3-6pm. €5.16, group and family discounts.)*

PORTA SOPRANA. The historical centerpiece of P. Dante (and today the passageway from the modern piazza into the *centro storico*), this medieval structure was built in 1100 to intimidate enemies of the Republic of Genoa. Would-be assailant Emperor Frederico Barbarossa took one look at the mighty arch, whose Latin inscription welcomes the passing of those who come in peace but threatens doom to enemy armies, and decided to terrorize elsewhere. The bastion of strength that was the Porta would come to serve as the portal onto the world for **Christopher Columbus.** His reputed boyhood home lies to the right of the gate, alongside the Cloister of Sant'Andrea, the remains of a 12th-century convent. *(From P. G. Matteotti, head down V. di Porta Soprana. Columbus's home open Sa and Su 9am-noon and 3-6pm.)*

PALAZZO SPINOLA DI PELLICCERIA. Built at the close of the 16th century to flaunt Genovese mercantile monies, this *palazzo* Peter Paul Rubens, who described it warmly in his 1622 book on pleasing palaces. It is now home to the **Galleria Nazionale,** a collection of art and furnishings. most of which were donated by the family of Maddalena Doria Spinola, who owned the palace during the first half of the 18th century. The building shows its age; different sections represent the variety of styles that shaped it through the centuries, including an 18th-century kitchen. Van Dyck's four portraits of the evangelists reside in the *Sala da Pranzo.* Be sure to visit the *terrazzo* on the top of the building for a great view of the city's rooftops and outlying hills. *(P. di Pelliceria, 1, between V. Maddalena and P. S. Luca. ☎ 010 270 5300. Open Tu-Sa 8:30am-7:30pm, Su 1-8pm. €4. 18-25, over 65, and students €2.)*

CHIESA DI SAN SIRO. Majestic vaulted ceilings aside, Genoa's first cathedral (rebuilt 1588-1613) may remind you of grandma's house: layers of dusty trinkets represent a worthwhile history, if you're willing to sort through the clutter. *(Where V. S. Siro branches to the right. Open M-F 4-6pm. Free.)*

PIAZZA SAN MATTEO. This tiny square contains the houses and chapel of the medieval rulers of Genoa, the Doria family. The animal reliefs above the first floor are the trademarks of the masons who built the houses, and the striped Romanesque stonework is reminiscent of many of Genoa's other well-aged buildings. Chiseled into the facade of the small but elaborately decorated **Chiesa di San Matteo,** founded by the Dorias in 1125, are descriptions of the aristocrats' great deeds. The church was rebuilt in 1278 and raised above street level as a reflection of the power of the Dorias in religious as well as civic affairs. *(Behind the duomo, off Salita all'Arcivovato. Open M-Sa 8am-noon and 4-6:30pm, Su 9am-noon and 4-6:30pm. Free.)*

MUSEO DI SANT'AGOSTINO (MUSEO DELL'ARCHITETTURA E SCULTURA LIGURE). The old city's newest addition occupies the former monastery of S. Agostino. The museum surveys Genoa's history through its surviving art (many pieces have been plucked from buildings for preservation). Giovanni Pisano carved the outstanding though piecemeal funerary monument for Margherita of Brabant (1312). Also noteworthy is the Neoclassic Penitent Magdalena in the Desert, so sensuous it borders on sacrilege. *(Follow directions to Porta Soprana and head toward the port on V. Ravecca. ☎ 010 20 60 22. Open Tu-Sa 9am-7pm, Su 9am-12:30pm. €3.50.)*

🎬 ENTERTAINMENT

The **Carignano D'Essai** shows English-language movies from October through June at V. Villa Glori, 8, near P. dei Ferrari. (☎010 570 2348. Shows W-Th 3pm and 9pm, Su 7pm.) Bus #31, a 20min. ride down C. Italia takes you to **Boccadasse,**

NORTHWEST ITALY

a seaside playground of wealthy Genovese. Sea breezes thin out cigarette smoke and soft promises of undying love overwrite graffiti threatening anarchy. Here seaside mansions tower over remnants of stone piers washed away by the waves, and the dining *salas* (halls) of extravagant restaurants jut out over the cove. The road that runs from Genoa to Boccadasse, Corso Italia, is also the *V. Balbi, 10*.home to much of Genoa's nightlife.

■ **Mako,** on Corso Italia, is the place to see, be seen, and get your groove on. To get there, take a taxi (€9.30) or bus #31. The young, beautiful and suntanned clientele begins arriving around 12:30am, and the place is packed by 1:30 or 2am. Be forewarned: prices are steep—cover is €11 and a mere wine cooler will cost you €8. Open 12:15-4am. Get there no later than 12:30am to avoid tedious lines.

Estoril, C. Italia. Come to this *discoteca* for expensive drinks with priceless karaoke. Sing and dance the night away. Open F-Sa 11pm-4am. Karaoke daily until 1:30am.

Britannia Pub, Vico Casana, 76r (☎010 247 4532), on a little street to your right as you enter P. dei Ferrari from V. XXV Aprile. An international watering hole open late. Pints €3.90, cocktails €3.70-4.70. Open M-Sa 4:30pm-3am.

Al Parador, P. della Vittoria, 49r (☎010 58 17 71). Late-night bar frequented by the likes of Uma Thurman and Claudia Schiffer. This is the place to go when the *discoteche* have closed and you still want to party. M-Sa open 24hr.

Le Corbusier, V. S. Donato, 36/38 (☎010 246 8652). Smoke rises from the crowd of students and artists gathered in this self-consciously hip place. The music and the atmosphere are more thoughtful, intense, and—dare we say—avant-garde than in most other bars. With art showings and the occasional literary lecture, Le Corbusier feels like a Renaissance salon. Commence your philosophizing and drink yourself into oblivion. Open M-F 8am-1am, Sa-Su 6pm-1am.

RIVIERA DI LEVANTE

CAMOGLI   ☎0185

Camogli is a postcard-perfect town with peach-colored houses crowding the hilltop, lively red and turquoise boats knocking in the harbor, fishing nets draped over graying docks, and dark stone beaches dotted with bright umbrellas. What Dickens once called a "piratical little place" has since mellowed into a peaceful resort town of 6000. Less ritzy and more youth-friendly than nearby Portofino and Santa Margherita, Camogli is the place to go for a relaxing stroll down the boardwalk or up steep streets.

▢ TRANSPORTATION

Trains: On Genoa-La Spezia line. Open M-F 6am-noon, Sa-Su 1-7:15pm. Ticket counter open M-F 5:50am-12:40am, Sa-Su 12:50-7:40pm. Tickets also sold at tourist office. Luggage storage available (p. 163). To: **Genoa** (20min., 32 per day, 6:26am-10:06pm, €1.50); **La Spezia** via **Santa Margherita** (1½hr., 21 per day, 5:27am-11:49pm, €3.50); and **Sestri Levante** (30min., 20 per day, 1:03am-11:50pm, €2).

Buses: Tigullio buses leave P. Schiaffino, near tourist office, for nearby towns. Buy tickets at tourist office or at the *tabacchi* at V. Repubblica, 25. To **Santa Margherita** (30min., 14 per day, €1.03). Buses also run to **Rapallo, Ruta,** and **San Lorenzo.**

Ferries: Golfo Paradiso, V. Scalo, 3 (☎0185 77 20 91; fax 77 12 63; www.golfoparad-iso.it). Look for the "Servizi Batelli" sign near P. Colombo by the water. Buy tickets at dock or on the ferry. To: **Cinque Terre** (Portovenere at Vernazza; June 15-July 1 Su; July 1-Aug. 1 Tu and Sa-Su; Sept. 1-15 Th and Su; 9:30am, returns 5:30pm; €12); **Portofino** (Sa-Su 3pm, return 5:30pm; round-trip €8); and **San Fruttuoso** (30min., May-Sept. 7-11 per day, round-trip €8).

■■ ORIENTATION AND PRACTICAL INFORMATION

Camogli extends uphill from the sea into pine and olive groves overlooking the beach and harbor below. To get to the center of town, go right as you exit the **Camogli-San Fruttuoso station.** About 100m from the station, turn left down the stairs to **Via Garibaldi.** From V. Garibaldi, turn right into the alley to the beaches.

Tourist Office: V. XX Settembre, 33 (☎0185 77 10 66). Turn right as you leave station. Helps with accommodations. English spoken. Open M-Sa 9am-12:30pm and 3:30-7pm, Su 9am-1pm. Closes 30min. earlier in winter.

Currency Exchange: Banco di Chiavari della Riviera Ligure, V. XX Settembre, 19 (☎0185 77 51 13). Reasonable rates. **ATM** outside. Open M-F 8:20am-1:20pm and 2:35-4pm.

Luggage Storage: In the train station. €3 per bag

Medical Emergency: ☎118.

Police: ☎0185 77 07 25. **Carabinieri:** V. Cuneo, 30/f (☎112 or 0185 77 00 00).

Late-Night Pharmacy: Dr. Machi, V. Repubblica, 4-6 (☎0185 77 10 81). Sign lists late-night pharmacies. Open Tu-Sa July-Aug. 8:30am-12:30pm and 4-8pm; Sept.-June 3:30-7:30pm.

Hospital: S. Martino (☎0105 55 27 94) in Genoa. In Recco, V. Bianchi, 1 (☎0185 74 377).

Post Office: V. Cuneo, 4 (☎0185 77 43 32). Exit train station and turn left. Open M-F 8am-1:30pm, Sa 8am-noon.

Postal Code: 16032.

▌ ACCOMMODATIONS

▨ **Albergo La Camogliese,** V. Garibaldi, 55 (☎0185 77 14 02; fax 77 40 24; info@lacamogliese.it). Exit train station and walk down the long stairway to right, where you'll see a big blue sign. Large, well-decorated rooms are a joy. Bath, TV, and phone in every room. Steps away from the beach. Singles €51-59; doubles €69-75. 10% *Let's Go* discount on cash payments. AmEx/D/MC/V. ❶

Albergo Augusta, V. Schiaffino, 100 (☎0185 77 05 92; fax 77 05 93; hotelaugusta@galactica.it), at other end of town. 15 recently renovated rooms have bath, TV, and phone; some with harbor view and balcony. Get free 15min. Internet use with *Let's Go* in hand. Breakfast €5.16. Singles €40-50; doubles €55-78. AmEx/MC/V. ❹

Albergo Selene, V. Cuneo, 16 (☎0185 77 01 49; fax 77 01 95). Exit train station and take a left past the post office. Rooms are clean and simple; some have balconies. Breakfast included. Singles €35; doubles €60; triples €85. AmEx/MC/V. ❸

Pensione Faro, V. Schiaffino, 116-118 (☎0185 77 14 00), above the restaurant of the same name, down the street from the Augusta. 8 beds. Pension required in summer: half-pension doubles €48 per person; full-pension doubles €60 per person. In winter doubles €50. AmEx/MC/V. ❹

☐ FOOD

The numerous shops on V. Repubblica (one block up from the harbor) and **Picasso supermarket,** V. XX Settembre, 35, supply picnickers. (Open M-Sa 8am-12:30pm and 4:30-7:30pm, Su 8:30am-noon.) An **open-air market** in P. del Teatro offers clothes, food, and fishhooks. (Open W 8am-noon.)

Pizzeria Il Lido, V. Garibaldi, 133 (☎0185 77 01 41), on the boardwalk. Expensive pizza, served and consumed by bronzed *Camogliesi.* Great view of sunbathers and the ocean. Pizza €5.50-8, *primi* from €8.50. Cover €1.55. Open W-M 12:30-3pm and 7:30-11pm. ❶

La Rotonda, V. Garibaldi, 101 (☎0185 77 14 02), on the boardwalk. Great view of the harbor. Pasta and seafood. *Primi* from €7, *secondi* from €10. Open daily 12:30-2:45pm and 7:30-11:45pm. AmEx/MC/V. ❸

Il Bar Teatro, P. Matteotti, 3 (☎0185 77 25 72). Serving 60 types of pizza for over 40 years (€4.20-8), Il Teatro ought to elicit a "Bravo!" Cover €1.60. Open F-W 7am-2pm and 7:30-11:30pm. AmEx/MC/V. ❶

La Creperie Bretonne, V. Garibaldi, 162 (0185 77 50 17). Charming nook for a quick snack or small meal. Crepes €3-5. Apr.-Sept. open daily noon-midnight. ❶

☉ ♫ SIGHTS AND ENTERTAINMENT

If you tire of the beach and boardwalk, you might make the 3hr. hike to **San Fruttuoso** (see below). The Camogli tourist office has a useful trail map. Blue dots mark the well-worn path, which starts at the end of V. Cuneo (near the *carabinieri* station). Ferry or snorkeling trips also make interesting (but more costly) diversions. **Band B Diving Center,** V. S. Fortunato, 11/13, off P. Colombo, sails boats for scuba diving and snorkeling (€10-50 per person) to 18 immersion spots along the coast. (☎0185 77 27 51. 10-person boat capacity. Open daily 9am-7pm.)

On the second Sunday in May, tourists descend on the town for an enormous fish fry, the **Sagra del Pesce.** The frying pan, constructed in 1952, measures 4m in diameter and holds over 2000 fish. If you miss the sardine-rush, you may still see the pans, as they adorn a city wall for the remainder of the year. They hang to the right on V. Garibaldi as you descend the stairs to the beaches.

Camogli doesn't have spectacular nightlife, but listen for thudding disco-house from the bar **Il Barcollo,** V. Garibaldi, 92. (☎0185 77 33 22. Open 5pm-3am.) Down the street, **Captain Hook,** V. al Porto, 4 (☎0185 77 16 95), is decorated like a ship's cabin and serves food well after 10pm. (Open daily 8am-3am.) Both have outdoor seating overlooking the beach.

☒ DAYTRIP FROM CAMOGLI: SAN FRUTTUOSO

You can hike to San Fruttuoso from Portofino Mare (1½hr.), Portofino Vetta (1½hr.), or Camogli (3hr.). Golfo Paradiso (☎0185 77 20 91) runs boats from Camogli (9 per day; 8am-5pm, last return from San Fruttuoso 6pm; €8 round-trip). Servizio Marittimo del Tigullio (☎0185 28 46 70) runs ferries from Camogli to Portofino (every hr., 9:30am-4:30pm, €12 round-trip) and Santa Margherita (every hr, 9:15am-4:15pm, €6).

If you approach tiny San Fruttuoso by sea, the 16th-century *torre di Doria* (tower of Doria) will appear as a lone gladiator surrounded by an arena of green. The town is named after the Benedictine **Abbazia di San Fruttuoso di Capodimonte,** constructed from the 10th to the 13th century. The monastery houses a cloister, archaeological artifacts, and a tower that you can climb for a panoramic view.

(☎0185 77 27 03. Open June-Sept. daily 10am-6pm; Oct. and Mar.-May Tu-Su 10am-4pm; Dec.-Feb. Sa-Su and holidays 10am-4pm. €6, children €4. Prices vary for special exhibitions.) Fifteen meters offshore and 17m underwater, the bronze *Christ of the Depths* stands with arms upraised in memory of the sea's casualties. The statue now serves as protector of scuba divers. A replica of the statue stands in **Chiesa di San Fruttuoso,** next to the abbey. Think about the ferry ride home before you pass on making an offering to the *Sacrario dei Morti in Mare.* Avoid the expensive, touristy restaurants that outnumber the houses here by bringing a picnic lunch. **Da Laura ❷** serves lunch noon-3pm. (*Primi* from €5.)

SANTA MARGHERITA LIGURE ☎0185

From its founding in the 12th century, Santa Margherita Ligure led a calm existence as a fishing village far from the Levante limelight. In the early 20th century, Hollywood stars discovered it, and its popularity grew after a *National Geographic* feature in the 1950s. Glitz paints the beachfront and palm trees line the harbor, but the serenity of Santa Margherita's early days lingers, making it a peaceful, affordable base for exploring the Riviera di Levante.

▐▀ TRANSPORTATION

Trains: P. Federico Raoul Nobili at top of V. Roma. Intercity trains on the Pisa-Genoa line stop at Santa Margherita. **Luggage storage** available (p. 166). To **Genoa** (40min., 2-3 per hr., 6:16am-10pm, €2) and **La Spezia** (1-2 per hr., 5:34am-10:55pm, €3.80), via **Cinque Terre** (1½hr.).

Buses: Tigullio buses (☎0185 28 88 34) depart from P. V. Veneto at the small green kiosk on the waterfront. Ticket office open 7:10am-7:40pm. To **Portofino** (20min., 3 per hr., €1.50) and **Camogli** (30min., every hr., €1.20).

Ferries: Tigullio, V. Palestro, 8/1b (☎0185 28 46 70). Boats leave from the docks at P. Martiri della Libertà. To: **Cinque Terre** (July-Sept. W and Sa-Su 1 tour per day, €20); **Portofino** (every hr., €3.20); and **San Fruttuoso** (every hr., €6.80).

Taxis: (☎0185 28 65 08), in P. Stazione.

Bike and Moped Rental: Noleggio Cicli e Motocicli, V. XXV Aprile, 11 (☎330 87 86 12). Motorscooter driving license required for tandems. Under 18 must have guardian's signature to rent mopeds. Bikes €3.62 per hr., €10.33 per day; tandems €7.75/€15.50; motor scooters €15.50/€41.32. Open daily 10am-12:30pm and 3-7pm.

◢◣ ▐ ORIENTATION AND PRACTICAL INFORMATION

To get to the waterfront from the train station, take **Via Roma,** or take the stairs to the right of the stop sign in front of the station and follow **Via della Stazione** directly to the water. Two main squares lie on the waterfront: **Piazza Martiri della Libertà** and the smaller **Piazza Vittorio Veneto,** both lined with palm trees. **Via Gramsci** winds around the port and **Via XXV Aprile** leads to the tourist office, becoming **Corso Matteotti** alongside the other main square in town, **Piazza Mazzini.**

Tourist Office: Pro Loco, V. XXV Aprile, 2/b (☎0185 28 74 85; fax 28 30 34). Turn right from train station onto V. Roma, follow it to C. Rainusso, and turn left. V. XXV Aprile is a hard right up from Largo Giusti. Staff provides maps and accommodations advice. Open M-Sa 9am-12:30pm and 3-7:30pm, Su 9:30am-12:30pm and 4:30-7:30pm.

Luggage Storage: At Hotel Terminus, in front of train station. €6 per bag.

Emergency: ☎113. **Guardia Medica:** ☎118.

Police: Polizia Municipale, C. Matteotti, 54 (☎0185 20 54 50).

Late-Night Pharmacies: Farmarcia A. Pennino, V. V. Veneto, 2 (☎0185 28 70 77). Open daily 8:30am-12:30pm and 4-8pm. **Farmacia di Turno,** V. Partigiani d'Italia, 31/ 32 (☎0185 28 84 84). Open 8:30am-1pm and 4-10pm.

Hospital: (☎0185 68 31), V. F. Arpe.

Post Office: V. Gruncheto, 46, near train station. Open M-F 8am-6pm, Sa 8am-1:15pm. *Fermo Posta.* **Currency exchange** €3.

Postal Code: 16038.

▐ ACCOMMODATIONS

Ritzy waterfront accommodations are by no means the only options. Santa Margherita is small enough that there's no such thing as a long walk to the ocean.

▨ **Hotel Nuova Riviera,** V. Belvedere, 10 (☎0185 28 74 03; www.nuovariviera.com), in a garden near P. Mazzini. Spacious, elegant rooms in a beautiful old villa built at the turn of the 20th century. Warm, welcoming proprietors. Breakfast included. Internet access €9 per hr. Singles €55-75; doubles €62-92; triples €90-120; 1 quad €120-145. *Affittacamere* (rooms to rent) available for rental by the week. Cash discount €5. MC/V. ❹

Hotel Terminus, P. Nobili, 4 (☎0185 28 61 21; fax 28 25 46), to left as you exit station. Rumble of trains will keep light sleepers awake. Owner Angelo speaks perfect English and is very attentive. Buffet breakfast included. 4-course dinner on the garden terrace €18. Singles €50; doubles with bath €82.60. AmEx/MC/V. ❹

Hotel Europa, V. Trento, 5 (☎0185 28 71 87; fax 28 01 54; info@hoteleuropa-sml.it). Tucked behind the harbor glitz, this modern hotel offers 18 rooms with bath, TV, and phone. Breakfast included. Parking available. Singles €41-71; doubles €66-96; triples €80-110; quads €100-125. AmEx/D/MC/V. ❹

Hotel Helios, V. Gramsci, 6 (☎0185 28 74; fax 28 47 89; www.hotelhelios.com). Well-financed visitors to the Riviera flock here for sun-worshiping on the hotel's private beach. All rooms with bath, A/C, and TV. Breakfast included. Singles €85-135; doubles €100-180; triples €130-210. Parking €17-21. AmEx/MC/V. ❺

▐ FOOD

Markets, bakeries, and fruit vendors line C. Matteotti. The **COOP supermarket,** C. Matteotti, 9/c, off P. Mazzini, stocks basics. (☎0185 28 43 15. Open M-Sa 8:15am-1pm and 3:30-8pm. V.) The day's catch is sold at the morning **fish market** on Lungomare Marconi. (Open daily 8am-12:30pm; boats arrive Th-Tu 4-6pm.)

▨ **La Piadineria and Crêperia,** V. Giuncheto, 5, off P. Martiri della Libertà. Escape from the traditional into the subtly hip. This nook-in-the-wall serves 30 types of *piadine* (heaping sandwiches on soft, thin bread; €5.56), crepes (€4.50-5.50), and *taglieri* (generous plates of assorted meats and cheeses; €11). Wine (€3 per glass), beer (€3), and cocktails (€3.50-6.50) complete a small meal or late-night snack. Open daily 5pm-3am. ❶

Trattoria Da Pezzi, V. Cavour, 21 (☎0185 28 53 03). Skip the pizza and load up on some real food. *Prosciutto* and melon €6.20, pasta from €3.70, *secondi* from €3.70, beer from €1.55. Finish off the meal with a whiskey on the rocks—make that whiskey on *gelato* (€3.87). MC/V. ❶

Trattoria Baicin, V. Algeria, 9 (☎0185 28 67 63), off P. Martiri della Libertà. Papà Piero is the master chef, but Mamma Carmela rolls the pasta and simmers the sauces. Try the homemade *trofie alla genovese* (*gnocchi* with string beans and pesto; €5.50). *Menù* €22. *Primi* from €4.50. Cover €1.50. Open Tu-Su noon-3pm and 7pm-midnight. Kitchen closes 10:30pm. AmEx/MC/V. ❷

🎦 🎵 SIGHTS AND ENTERTAINMENT

If lapping waves aren't sufficiently invigorating your spirit, there's always the holy water at the Rococo **Basilica di Santa Margherita** at P. Caprera; it's held in basins shaped liked scallops. Dripping with gold and crystal, the church also contains fine Flemish and Italian works. At P. Martiri della Libertà, 32, a crowd guzzles beer and watches European football at **Sabot American Bar.** (☎0185 28 07 47. Open W-M 10am-2am.) The tribute to drinking U.S. of A.-style continues right down the street at **Miami,** P. della Libertà, 29. Neon blue lights, white vinyl booths, and €6.20 Manhattans set the high-rollin' scene. (☎0185 28 34 24. Open daily 5pm-3am.) For something a little more low-key, go to **La Piadineria,** which is just a few doors down, for a glass of wine or some dessert.

▶ DAYTRIP FROM SANTA MARGHERITA: PORTOFINO

Take a bus to Portofino Mare (not Portofino Vetta). From Portofino's P. Martiri della Libertà, Tigullio buses run to Santa Margherita (3 per hr., €1). Tickets sold at the green kiosk in P. Martiri della Libertà. Portofino is also accessible by ferry from Santa Margherita (every hr. 9am-7pm, €3.50) and Camogli (2 per day, €7).

Yachts fill Portofino's harbor, chic boutiques and art galleries line the cobbled streets, and luxury cars fill the parking lots. Nonetheless, princes and paupers alike can enjoy the shore's curves and tiny bay, and the town is a perfect half-day outing from Santa Margherita. A 1hr. walk along the main road passes small rocky beaches like **Njasca,** where you can rent boats in the summer. (☎347 175 7682. Wind-surfing €8 per hr.; kayaks €6-8; pedal boats €8; tiny sailboats €13.) **Paraggi** is the area's only sandy beach, and only a small strip is free. A **nature reserve** surrounds Portofino and Paraggi; treks through the hilly terrain, past ruined churches and voluptuous villas, lead to Santa Margherita (1½hr.) and San Fruttuoso (2hr.).

In town, as you face the water, head right around the port and climb the stairs up to the cool, stark white interior of the **Chiesa di San Giorgio.** Behind the church lies a small cemetery—outcast Protestants were laid to rest just outside these walls. A few minutes up the road outside the 16th-century **castle** is a serene garden. The castle was once a fortress, but was converted to a summer home in the 19th century. (Open daily 9am-7pm; in winter Sa-Su 10am-5pm. €2.50.) Back in town, **Alimentari Repetto,** on P. Martiri dell'Olivetta, the main square in front of the harbor, fortifies hikers with Gatorade (€2), sandwiches (from €2), and *foccaccia* (€1). (☎0185 26 90 56. Open daily 8am-10pm; in winter 9am-6pm.) **Trattoria Concordia ❸,** V. del Fondaco, 5 (☎0185 26 92 07), makes up for the absence of a water view with authentic atmosphere. (*Primi* from €7.78, *secondi* from €10.33. AmEx/DC/MC/V.) A drink at one of the numerous bars along the harbor costs upward of €6.50, though watching twilight descend on the harbor is worth it.

At the **tourist office,** V. Roma, 35, on the way to the waterfront from the bus stop, the English-speaking staff has maps and brochures. (☎0185 26 90 24. Open M-Tu 10:30am-1:30pm and 2:30-7:30pm, W-Su 10:30am-1:30pm and 2-7pm.) **Exchange currency** at the Banco di Chiavari, V. Roma, 14/16. (☎0185 26 91 64. Open M-F 8:20am-1:20pm and 2:35-4pm.) In an **emergency,** call the **police,** V. del Fondaco, 8 (☎0185 26 90 88). The **pharmacy** is at P. Martiri della Libertà, 6. (☎0185 26 91 01. Open daily 9am-1pm and 4-8pm; closed Su in winter. AmEx/MC/V.) The **post office** is at V. Roma, 32. (☎0185 26 91 56. Open M-F 8am-1:30pm, Sa 8am-noon.)

NORTHWEST ITALY

CINQUE TERRE
☎ 0187

Eugenio Montale, Italian poet and Nobel laureate, wrote of his hometown of 30 years: *"Qui delle divertite passioni per miracolo tace la guerra"* ("Here the passions of pleasure miraculously quiet conflict"). The five bright fishing villages of Cinque Terre will bring your spirit sweet silence. A vast expanse of dazzling turquoise sea laps against the *cittadine* that cling to a stretch of terraced hillsides and steep crumbling cliffs. Through a trick of perspective and sea mist, each town, when glimpsed from the next, appears both distant and proximate, as if an unreachable mountain village in one moment might become a handful of pastels and pebbles in the next. You can hike the string of five towns end-to-end in several hours. The Five Lands of Monterosso, Vernazza, Corniglia, Manarola, and Riomaggiore are the poet's mystical muse—and fodder for a booming tourist industry. Reserve a room in advance, or consider day-tripping in from Levanto.

▐ TRANSPORTATION

Trains: The towns lie on the Genoa-La Spezia (Pisa) line. Schedules available at tourist office. 24hr. **Cinque Terre Tourist Ticket** (€4.20) allows unlimited trips among the five towns and to La Spezia or Levanto. Available at the 5 train stations—ask at ticket window. **Monterosso** is the most accessible. From the station on V. Fegina, the north end of town, trains run to: **Florence** (3½hr., every hr., €8), via **Pisa** (2½hr., every hr., 8:30am-4:24pm, €4.39); **Genoa** (1½hr., every hr., 5:31am-11:03pm, €3.62); **La Spezia** (20min., every 30min., €1.19); and **Rome** (7hr., every 2hr., €26.60). Frequent trains connect the 5 towns (5-20min., every 50min., €1-1.50). Make sure the train is local.

Ferries: Monterosso can be reached by ferry from **La Spezia** (1hr., 2 per day, €18). Ferries from Monterosso also connect the towns. **Navigazione Golfo dei Poeti** (☎0187 77 77 27), in front of the **IAT** office at the port (in the old part of town). To: **Manarola** (5 per day, €8); **Portovenere** (€15); **Riomaggiore** (8 per day, €8); and **Vernazza** (9 per day, €2.25). **Motobarca Vernazza** also goes from Monterosso to **Vernazza** (5min., 1 per hr., 9:30am-6:45pm, €2.58).

Taxis: ☎0335 616 5842 or 616 5845.

Boat Rental: Along the beach. Pedal boats €8-9 per hr.; kayaks €5.75-8.50 per hr., €26 per day; motorboats €16-24 per hr., €80-115 per day.

◼✴ ▐ ORIENTATION AND PRACTICAL INFORMATION

The villages are connected by trains and footpaths that traverse the terraced vineyards and rocky shoreline. **Monterosso,** the beach bum's town of choice, is the most commercially developed, and has three sandy beaches and spirited nightlife. From this hub, the four other villages are easily accessible by train as well as by foot, ferry, and kayak, depending on your inclination and stamina. **Vernazza** is graced by a large seaside piazza, surrounded by colorful buildings and a harbor full of parked boats. Its sheltered cove has a pebble beach and a pier covered with swimmers and sunbathers. **Corniglia** hovers high above the sea, and hundreds of steps connect it to its train station. Without the beachside glitter of the other towns, it offers a nude beach, peaceful solitude, and an amazing vantage-point for viewing romantic sunsets. **Manarola** has quiet streets, an excellent new hostel, plenty of quality eateries, and a swimming cove. In **Riomaggiore** there are a bunch of rooms for rent around the tiny harbor, where you're as likely to see a fisherman swabbing varnish on a boat hull as a tanner smoothing on oil. **All listings are for Monterosso unless otherwise indicated.**

Tourist Office: Pro Loco, V. Fegina, 38 (☎0187 81 75 06), below the train station. Info on boats, hikes, and hotels. Accommodations service. Staff speaks English. Open Apr.-Oct. M-Sa 10am-12:45pm and 2:15-6:45pm, Su 10am-12:45pm. In **Riomaggiore,** an office in the train station (☎0187 92 06 33) provides info on trails, hotels, and excursions. Open daily June-Sept. 10am-6pm.

Tours: Navigazione 5 Terre (☎0187 81 74 52) offers tours (€3, €5 round-trip) departing from Monterosso (9 per day, 10:30am-6pm) and Vernazza (9 per day, 10:40am-6:10pm).

Currency Exchange: At the post office (cash exchange €3). For traveler's check transactions, head to **Banca Carige,** V. Roma, 69, or **Casa di Risparmio della Spezia,** V. Roma, 47. **ATMs** also at **Bancomat,** V. Fegina, 40, under the train station.

Laundry: Las Vegas, V. Mazzini, 4. €11 to wash, soap, and dry 7kg of clothes. Hit the beach between loads. Open daily 9am-9pm.

Emergency: ☎113. **Police:** ☎112. **Medical Emergency:** ☎118.

Carabinieri: ☎0187 81 75 24. In Riomaggiore (☎0187 92 01 12).

First Aid: In **Corniglia** (☎338 853 0949); **Manarola** (☎0187 92 07 66); **Monterosso** (☎0187 81 76

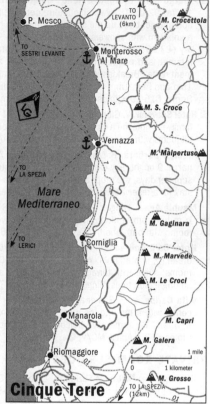

87); **Riomaggiore** (☎0187 80 09 73); and **Vernazza** (☎0187 82 10 84).

Pharmacies: V. Fegina, 44, under train station. Open M-Sa 9am-12:30pm and 4-8pm, Su 9:30am-12:30pm and 4-7:30pm. Also at V. Roma, 2 (☎0187 81 23 96), in Vernazza. Open M-W, F-Sa 8am-12:30pm and 4-7:30pm, Th 8am-12:30pm.

Internet Access: The Net, V. V. Emanuele, 55 (☎/fax 0187 81 72 88). 10 computers. Fast connection. €2 for 1st 15min., €1 per 10min after that. **Bar Centrale,** V. C. Colombo, 144, in Riomaggiore. €0.10 per min., €6 per hr. **Ostello "Cinque Terre,"** V. B. Riccobaldi, 21, in Manarola. €1.50 per 15min.

Post Office: V. Loreto, 73 (☎0187 81 83 94). *Fermo Posta* and telephone cards. Open M-F 8am-1:30pm, Sa 8am-noon. **Another branch** at V. Discovolo, 216 (☎0187 92 01 98), in Manarola. Open M-F 8am-1:30pm, Sa 9am-noon.

Postal Code: 19016.

🏠 ACCOMMODATIONS

Reserve at least several weeks in advance. The few budget **hotels** (all in Monterosso and Vernazza) fill at the beginning of the season in June. If you're still looking for a room when you arrive, gamble on the cheaper and more plentiful *affittacamere* (private rooms) in Riomaggiore, Monterosso, or Vernazza.

■ **Albergo Della Gioventù-Ostello "Cinque Terre,"** V. B. Riccobaldi, 21 (☎0187 92 02 15; fax 92 02 18; www.cinqueterre.net/ostello), in Manarola. Turn right from train station and continue up the hill 300m. The new hostel is across from the church. 48 beds, a solarium with showers, an outdoor terrace, music systems on each co-ed floor, laundry (€3.50 wash, €2.50 dry), a glass elevator, wheelchair access, photocopying, fax, Internet, and phones. Incredible views. Ask about kayak, bike, and snorkeling equipment rental. Breakfast €3.50. Sheets and 5min. shower included. Reception daily 7am-1pm and 5pm-1am. Curfew 1am, in winter midnight. Reserve at least 1 wk. in advance. Dorms €16-19. Quads with bath €64-76. AmEx/MC/V. ❷

■ **Hotel Souvenir,** V. Gioberti, 24 (☎/fax 0187 81 75 95; hotel_souvenir@yahoo.com). Quiet, family-run hotel on a charming street, with 30 beds, a friendly staff, and an outdoor garden. All rooms with modern bath. Breakfast €5. Rooms €35 per person, students €30. ❸

Albergo Barbara, P. Marconi, 30, top fl. (☎/fax 0187 81 23 98), at the port in Vernazza. 9 bright, airy rooms, some with fantastic views of Vernazza's colorful port. On hot summer days, the proprietors sit outside at a make-shift receptionist desk. 2-night min. stay for a reservation. Doubles €43-55; triples €65; quads €70. ❹

Meublè Agavi, Lungomare Fegina, 30 (☎0187 81 71 71 or 80 16 65; fax 81 82 64). Turn left from station onto boardwalk. Convenient location and good views. 10 airy rooms with bath and fridge. Reception until 6pm. Singles €45; doubles €83. ❹

Hotel Ca'D'Andrean, V. A. Disocolo, 101 (☎0187 92 00 40; fax 92 04 52; www.candrean.it), in Manarola. Walk uphill on V. A. Discovolo from the train station. Spacious rooms, some with terrace. In the summer, eat breakfast (€6) outside in the garden among lemon trees. Singles €55; doubles €73. ❺

Villa Caribe, V. P. Semeria, 49 (☎0187 81 72 79). Escape the heavily touristed city center with a trip into the hills. Free taxi transport; call ahead. All 5 rooms have bath, A/C, and TV; some have balconies. Reception 7am-1pm. Singles €60; doubles €80; triples €120. AmEx/MC/V. ❺

PRIVATE ROOM SERVICES

Riomaggiore: ■ **Robert Fazioli,** V. Colombo, 94 (☎0187 92 09 04). Singles, doubles, and apartments with harbor views. €20.60-50, depending on number of people and room type. Open daily 9am-8pm. **Edi,** V. Colombo, 111 (☎/fax 0187 92 03 25; edivesigna@iol.it), has comparable prices. Doubles €52. **Ivana** (☎0187 92 01 96) has breezy rooms up the hill from train station. Alberto or Ivo at **Bar Centrale,** V. Colombo, 144 (☎0187 92 02 08), can help find accommodations. The folks at the **Bar Stazione** (☎0187 92 00 46), right outside the train station, might be able to help you, as might **Trattoria Via Dell'Amore** (☎0187 92 08 60), **Locando dalla Compagnia** (☎0187 76 00 50), or **Roberta Veneziani** (☎0187 92 07 89).

Monterosso: The **tourist office** (☎0187 81 75 06) has a list of rooms, and the agents will mediate with home owners.

Vernazza: Trattoria Gianni Franzi, P. Marconi, 5 (☎0187 82 10 03; fax 81 22 28). Singles from €35; triples with bath €86. **Anna Maria,** V. Carattino, 64 (☎0187 82 10 82), rents doubles from €45.

Manarola: Da Baranin, V. Rollandi, 35/a (☎0187 92 05 95). Clean rooms and apartments up road from the hostel. Breakfast included. Doubles from €73.

Corniglia: Ristorante Cecio (☎0187 81 20 43), on the small road that leads from Corniglia to Vernazza. From train station, follow the signs at the top of stairs that lead to town. From main piazza, take a right up the hill and walk 150 yd. A wonderful restaurant that also rents 13 rooms with bath and postcard views. Doubles €55. *Affittacamere* also on V. della Stazione (☎0187 81 22 93). You can also try the *affittacamere* associated with La Posada (see **Food,** below) at ☎0187 81 23 84.

🍴 FOOD

If you're on a tight budget in Cinque Terre, consider romantic picnics. Wash your beach or cliffside meal down with the locally made, sweet *Sciacchetrà* wine; or opt for the cheaper and dry *Cinque Terre* white.

SUPERMARKETS AND ENOTECHE

Cantina di Sciacchetrà, V. Roma, 7 (☎0187 81 78 28), in Monterosso, has free wine tastings, delicious *antipasti,* and deals on souvenirs. Jovial Gian Luigi will proudly point out all of the finest from the **Cinque Terre Farming Cooperative,** including lemons, olive oil, and wine (*Cinque Terre bianco* €11, *sciacchetrà* €25). Open daily Mar.-Oct. 9am-11pm; Dec.-Feb. open only weekends. MC/V.

Superconrad Margherita, P. Matteotti, 9, in Monterosso. Open June-Sept. M-Sa 8am-1pm and 5-7:30pm, Su 8am-1pm.

Punto Market, V. Molinelli, 21, in Monterosso. Open daily 7:45am-1pm and 5-8pm; closed Su afternoon.

Focacceria Il Frantoio, V. Gioberti, 1 (☎0187 81 83 33), in Monterosso. The wood-burning oven bakes mouth-watering *focaccia* stuffed with olives, onions, herbs, and other fillings. Slices €1-2. Open F-W 9am-2pm and 4-7:30pm. ❶

RISTORANTI, TRATTORIE, AND PANINOTECHE

Il Ciliegio, Località Beo (☎0187 81 78 29), near P. Garibaldi. Free taxi service from the historical city center (call ahead). Fantastic food, made fresh daily with ingredients from the owners' gardens. Savor your meal and the view of the mountains and sea from the terrace outside. Lunch *menù* €27. *Primi* €6-8, *secondi* €7-11. ❹

Marina Piccola, V. lo Scalo, 16 (☎0187 92 01 03), in Manarola. Little marina, big meals (along with a sizeable bill). Marina occupies a prime location on the edge of Manarola's rocky cove. Savor *tagliatelle ai granchi* (linguini with crab; €8.50) and *penne agli scampi* (with shrimp; €8.50). *Primi* from €8, *secondi* from €10. Open daily noon-3pm and 7-11pm. MC/V. ❹

FAST, V. Roma, 13 (☎0187 81 71 64). Beneath hanging electric guitars, FAbio and STefano toss together fresh sandwiches (from €3.50) and mixed drinks. By 11pm, beer consumption outpaces that of *panini.* Open daily 8am-1am; in winter Tu-Su 8am-noon. MC/V. ❶

La Posada, V. Alla Stazione (☎0187 82 11 74), in Corniglia. Climb the staircase from the train station. Take a right on the road at the top; follow about 150m. The food is delicious, and the sweeping seaside view is priceless. *Primi* €8, *secondi* €7-11. Cover €2. Lunch starts daily at noon, dinner at 7pm. MC/V. ❸

Trattoria Il Porticciolo, V. R. Birolli, 92 (☎0187 92 00 83), in Manarola. Standard *trattoria* that serves reasonably priced meals. *Primi* €3.62-7.75, *secondi* €5.16-15.49. Try their superb homemade *torta nocciola* (nut cake; €3). Cover €2. Open Th-Tu 7am-4pm and 6:30pm until the last guest says a sleepy *buona notte.* AmEx/MC/V. ❷

Ristorante Cecio, in Corniglia. (See **Private Room Services,** above, for directions and contact info.) Swill your *vino* and twirl your spaghetti as you watch the sunset through the dangling grape vines that drape the outdoor terrace. Delicious food, and a fabulous view of cultivated gardens sloping into the unruly sea. *Primi* €6-8, *secondi* from €7. Cover €2. Open daily noon-3pm and 7pm-1am. MC/V. ❸

🥾 HIKING AND SIGHTS

Nature created Cinque Terre's best sights. Savage cliffs and lush tropical vegetation surround the stone villages. Enjoy the best views from the narrow goat paths that link the towns, winding through vineyards, streams, and dense foliage dotted with cacti and lemon trees. If you have a good pair of walking shoes, you can cover the distance between Monterosso and Riomaggiore in about five hours. The best and most challenging hike lies between Monterosso and Vernazza (1½hr.), while the trail between Vernazza and Corniglia (2hr.) passes through spectacular scenery. The road between Corniglia and Manarola (1hr.) offers a pleasant hike. The final stretch, the famous **Via dell'Amore** that links Manarola and Riomaggiore (20min.), is a leisurely paved path with great views and access to the rocky coves.

To avoid scaling rocks, start at Riomaggiore and end with Vernazza or Monterosso. It's always best to start in the morning to avoid the scorching sun. Walk the leisurely V. dell'Amore to the #2 hike at Manarola's Punta Bonfiglio. Follow it to the end, or branch off onto the #7 from Manarola to Corniglia. The #7 goes uphill to the highway, which levels off and then finally starts downhill. The highway rejoins the hiking trail into Vernazza. Take a moment to jump in the water and refresh yourself before tackling the last leg to Monterosso. If you ever tire of hiking, simply hop on the train and return to your base town.

In Monterosso, visit the **Convento dei Cappuccini** (built 1618-1622), perched on a hill in the center of town. The convent contains an impressive Crucifixion by Flemish master Anthony van Dyck, who sojourned here during his most productive years. (Open daily 9am-noon and 4-7pm.) In Vernazza, the remains of the 11th-century **Castello Doria**, up a staircase on the left of P. Marconi (when facing the port), offer yet another spectacular view. (Open daily 10am-6:30pm. €1.)

BEACHES

The *spiaggie* (beaches) of Cinque Terre are predominantly private beaches. Use of a private beach will cost you €3 entrance, €14 to 16 for an umbrella, *cabina*, and two deck chairs, and €6.50 to 7.50 for a deck bed, with prices subject to increase during July and August. Many establishments insist you rent a chair and umbrella to be admitted, and as many beaches fill up, it's best to arrive early. A free day at the beach is possible if you're willing to expand your definition of beach beyond the typical image of flat stretches of sand.

The largest **free beach** lies directly below the train station in Monterosso. Alternatively, follow V. Fegina through the tunnel to get to another free beach in front of the old town. Other small patches open to the public are on the southern and northernmost tips of town. Vernazza also has a small free beach and lots of sunbathing room on the pier. Manarola, Corniglia, and Riomaggiore's rocky coves are covered with towels and human bodies on sunny days. These makeshift beaches are less crowded and add a bit of character to your sunbathing experience.

Boys and girls in their birthday suits await at **Guvano Beach** in Corniglia (tunnel open June and Sept. Sa-Su 9am-7pm, July-Aug. daily 9am-7pm). When you depart from the train station, proceed as you would to get to the town, but bypass the stairs and go left down the ramp on the other side of the tracks. When you get to a tunnel, press the button; the gate will open. A 15min. walk through the dark, spooky tunnel (don't walk it by yourself) and a €3 toll will reward you with a less-populated beach than the pebbly strip south of the station. Be wary of the all-but-nonexistent steps on the way down.

Coopsub Cinqueterre Diving Center, on V. S. Giacomo in Riomaggiore, offers snorkel and scuba equipment as well as chaperoned dives anywhere along the coast. In June and September when there's less traffic, you're likely to see dolphins in addition to coral and schools of fish. A license is required for scuba dives, but lessons are also offered. (☎0187 92 00 11. Open daily Easter to late Sept. 9am-7pm. Snorkeling off the coast along V. dell'Amore €5.50 per day. Dives €30-50. Night dives €36 per hr. Boat trips include a stop to frolic in the natural waterfalls of Caneto Beach. Kayaks €2-4 per hr.) **Sea Adventures,** V. Rollandi, 35/a (☎0187 92 05 95 or 62 74 87), in Manarola, also offers cruises along the coast with snorkeling.

♫ ENTERTAINMENT

Bar Centrale, V. C. Colombo, 144, in Riomaggiore. If young Americans are not to your liking, this bar won't be either. Energetic Ivo serves a nice cold one and then turns up swingin' Motown. Internet access. Beer €3-4. *Bruschetta* €2. Open daily 7:30am-1am.

Il Bar Sopra il Mare (☎0187 76 20 58), on Punta Bonfiglio, in Manarola. Enjoy the incredible view of Manarola at night. Sit under the stars watching the waves crash at Manarola's rocky base. *Cappuccino* €1, beer €2.50-3, mixed drinks €3.60-4.15. Open daily mid-June to Oct. 6pm-1am.

Il Casello, V. Lungo Ferravia, 70. Follow V. Fegina through the tunnel to old town. In a pink building overlooking the water. The menu says it all: "don't complain for delays...let's have fun." *Focaccia* €3.50, mozzarella and tomato salad €5, beer and liquor from €3. Internet access €1.55 per 15min. Easter-Oct. open daily 10pm-2am

NEAR CINQUE TERRE

LEVANTO ☎0187

Quiet and untouched by tourists in comparison to the nearby Cinque Terre, Levanto is the place to go for a place to stay.

⚟ 🔁 ORIENTATION AND PRACTICAL INFORMATION. Levanto lies on the Genoa-La Spezia line, 6km away from **Cinque Terre** (5min. to Monterosso, 20 per day 8:02am-10:08pm). The **tourist office, I.A.T.,** on P. Mazzini, 1, provides maps and information on hotels, private rooms, and *agriturismi*. (☎0187 80 81 25. Open M-Sa 9am-1pm and 3-6pm, Su 9am-1pm. Hours vary in winter.) In an **emergency,** call the **police** (☎113), **carabinieri** (☎0187 80 81 05), **medic** (☎118), **Red Cross** (☎0187 80 85 35), **Green Cross** (☎0187 80 87 60), **Guardia Medica** (☎0187 80 09 73), or **hospital** (☎0187 80 04 09). Levanto has **Farmacia Cimitan,** V. Dante, 2. (☎0187 80 83 46. Open M-Sa 8:30am-12:30pm and 4-8pm.) The **post office,** V. Jiacopo, 31, holds *Fermo Posta* and **exchanges currency.** (☎0187 80 82 04. Open M-F 8am-6pm, Sa 8am-1pm.)

🔒 📑 ACCOMMODATIONS AND FOOD. For a bite to eat, your best bet is the **Supermercato Corner,** V. Martiri della Libertà, 26. (☎0187 80 86 66. Open daily 8am-1pm and 5-8pm. MC/V.) Levanto's star attraction, **Ospitalia del Mare ❷,** V. San Niccolo, 1, is 15min. from the train station. Walk down to the river and cross the bridge to V. Garibaldi, which turns into V. Guanti. At P. Popolo, go left to V. Cantarana. Housed in a 12th-century Augustinian friary, this hostel offers brand-new facilities, including two elevators, wheelchair-accessible dorm rooms, and one family room. Each room has four, six, or eight beds and an attached bathroom. (☎0187 80 25 62; fax 80 36 96; www.ospitaliadelmare.it. Internet €2 per 15min. Fax available. 63 beds. Dorms €19-21 per person including breakfast. Doubles €28 per person. Ask about 10% discount at local restaurants and group rates. AmEx/MC/V.) **Campeggio Acqua Dolce ❶** is up the road from the hostel, 200m from the beach; follow the signs from V. Cantarana. Well-tended grounds overflow with tents, campers, and flowering vines. (☎/fax 0187 80 84 65. Reception open 8am-1pm and 3-10pm. No reservations accepted. €4.50-5.50 per small tent, €5.50-7 per person. Electricity €1.50.)

LA SPEZIA ☎0187

In the summer of 2000, an unsuspecting gardener was digging in his backyard and turned up more than sticks and stones; a bomb lay beneath his tomato plants. Heavily attacked during WWII because of its naval base and artillery, La Spezia has since recovered from its wartime woes. With careful tending of its nautical roots (and the occasional evacuation of the city for the deployment of unexploded artillery), it has evolved into a major commercial port, as a departure point for Corsica and an unavoidable transfer stop to and from Cinque Terre. Situated in *Il Golfo dei Poeti* (The Gulf of Poets), La Spezia makes a great base for daytrips to the small fishing village of Porto Venere, the beach resorts of San Terenzo and Lerici, and the beautiful coves of Fiascherino. Though La Spezia boasts none of the majestic architecture, cobblestone passageways, or charm that grace these neighboring villages, it does have affordable lodgings and a few impressive, palm-lined shopping boulevards.

TRANSPORTATION. La Spezia lies on the Genoa-Pisa train line. A ticket from Monterosso costs €1.95; from Manarola, €1.25. **Happy Lines,** with a ticket kiosk on V. Italia (☎0187 65 12 73; open daily 6:30am-noon and 3:30-7:30pm), near the *Molo Italia* deck, sends ferries to **Corsica** (round-trip €64.04, low-season €43.38). **Navigazione Golfo dei Poeti,** V. D. Minzoni, 21 (☎0187 21 010 or 73 29 87), offers ferries that stop in each village of **Cinque Terre** and **Portovenere** (Easter-Nov. 4; €11, €19 round-trip); **Capraia** (July-Aug., 5 hr., round-trip €41); and **Elba** (July-Aug. W and Sa, 3½ hr., €41 round-trip). Be sure to call ahead for ferries; schedules change. For **taxis,** call ☎0187 52 35 22 or 52 35 23.

ORIENTATION AND PRACTICAL INFORMATION. From the train station, turn left and walk down **Via XX Settembre,** then turn right down any street to **Via Prione,** the city's main drag. Turn right and continue on V. Prione until its hits **Via Chiode. Via Mazzini** runs parallel to V. Chiodo, closer to the water. Spezia's main **tourist office** is beside the port at V. Mazzini, 45. (☎0187 77 09 00. Open daily 9am-1pm and 3-6pm.) **CTS Travel,** V. Sapri, 86, helps with ferry tickets (to Greece and Yugoslavia), student airfares, and car rentals. (☎0187 75 10 74; fax 75 27 53; cts.laspezia@tin.it. English spoken. Open M-Sa 9:30am-12:30pm and 3:30-7:30pm.)

In an **emergency,** dial ☎113 or contact the **police** (☎112) or a **medic** (☎118). **Farmacia dell'Aquila,** V. Chiodo, 97 (☎0187 23 162), is open M-F 8:30am-12:30pm and 4-8pm. A list of other pharmacies is posted outside. **Phone Center,** P. S. Bon, 1, just 5min. from the train station, has **Internet access** and UPS and Western Union services. (☎0187 77 78 05; fax 71 21 11. €5 per hr. Open M-Sa 9:15am-12:30pm and 3-10pm.) The **post office** is a few blocks from the port at P. Verdi. (☎0187 79 61. Open M-F 8am-6:30pm and Sa 8am-12pm.) **Postal Code:** 19100.

ACCOMMODATIONS AND FOOD. Close to the port, try **Albergo Teatro ❹,** V. Carpenino, 31, near the Teatro Civico. Newly renovated, the seven rooms here are bright and have bathrooms. (☎/fax 0187 73 13 74; albergoteatro@libero.it. Doubles €60.) On the next street over, **Albergo Spezia ❹,** V. Cavalloti, 31, off V. Prione, offers 11 rooms with couches and high ceilings. (☎0187 73 51 64. Doubles €39, with bath €47; triples €52-62. MC/V.) Via del Priore is lined with reasonably priced *trattorie* and *paninoteche.* Savor La Spezia's local specialty, *mesciua* (a thick soup of beans, corn-meal, olive oil, and pepper), at any of the city's *antiche osterie.* For groceries, try the **Coop supermarket,** in P. J. F. Kennedy, on V. Saffi. Pick up a loaf of bread, *pesto genovese,* and some mozzarella cheese for less than €6. (☎0187 51 81 43. Open M-Sa 8:30am-8pm.) **Dino ❸,** V. Cadorna, 18, has good prices. (*Primi* €4-9, fish *secondi* €6-15. Closed Su night and M. AmEx/DC/MC/V.) **Pizzeria Il Comera ❶,** C. Cavour, 326, is an excellent place for a quick lunch, with pizza and *focaccia* to go. (☎0187 74 32 36. Open Tu-Su 8:30am-11pm.) **Antico Sacrista ❶,** C. Cavour, 276, prepares 39 varieties of pizza (€2.60-5.70) and *testaroli al pesto,* a dainty pasta produced only in Liguria. (☎0187 71 33 84. Open Tu-Su noon-2:30pm and 7:30-10:30pm, takeout all day. AmEx/MC/V.)

◙ **SIGHTS.** La Spezia is one of Italy's classiest and cleanest ports, with regal palms lining the Morin promenade, sailors strolling **Via del Prione,** and parks brimming with citrus trees. La Spezia also has an eclectic collection of museums, many of them related to the sea and its long impact on the history of this area.

The unique collection of the **Museo Navale,** in P. Chiodo next to the entrance of the Arsenale Militare Marittimo (Maritime Military Arsenal) built in 1860-1865 and destined to catalyze the growth of the city, features marshmallow-man diving suits dating from WW II, carved prows of 19th-century ships (including a huge green salamander), gargantuan iron anchors, and tiny replicas of Egyptian, Roman, and European vessels. (☎ 0187 78 30 16; fax 78 29 08. Open M-Sa 8:30am-6pm, Su 10:45am-3:45pm. €1.55.)

The **Museo Amadeo Lia,** V. Prione, 234, in the ancient church and convent of the Friars of St. Francis from Paola, houses a beautiful collection of paintings spanning the 13th to 17th century, including some works attributed to Raphael. Room VII has a small collection of works from the 16th century, including Titian's *Portrait of a Gentleman* and Bellini's *Portrait of an Attorney.* (☎ 0187 73 11 00; fax 72 14 08; www.castagna.it/mal. Open Tu-Su 10am-6pm. €6, students €4.)

The **Castello di San Giorgio,** built in the 14th century when Genoa ruled La Spezia, houses an archaeological museum and offers expansive views of the port. (Open M-W 9:30am-12:30pm and 5-8pm. €2.58.) The **Museo Civico Entografico,** V. Curtatone, 9, has clothes, furniture, jewelry and popular art from the 18th to 20th century. (Open M-Sa 8am-noon.) There is also the **Museo del Sigillo,** V. Priore 236, in the **Palazzina delle Arti,** with one of the largest collection of seals in the world. (☎ 0187 77 85 44. Open W-Su 10am-noon and 4:30-7:30pm and Tu 4:30-7:30pm.)

RIVIERA DI PONENTE

SAVONA ☎019

This Ligurian metropolis is a clean, comfortable, manageable alternative to Genoa. Because of its strategic position between the Po Valley and the Ligurian Coast, the Genovese ransacked the harbor in 1528 and built a fortress on the Priamar promontory. Savona is notable largely for its two hostels and busy port.

▐ TRANSPORTATION

Trains: From the train station, take bus #2 or any utilibus (€0.80) to the city center and the fortress hostel. To **Genoa** (30min., 1-3 per hr., 4:42am-10:12pm, €2.75) and **Ventimiglia** (2hr., 1-2 per hr., 6am-10:58pm, €6.15).

Buses: ACTS buses to **Finale Ligure** (every 20min., 5:02am-10:22pm) stop outside train station. Buses #4 and 5 leave P. Mamelli for train station (every 15min., 5:15am-midnight, €0.80). Buy ticket at train station, or pay an extra €0.40 to buy on the bus.

Bike Rental: Noleggio Biciclette, in Public Gardens. Take V. Dante down to P. Heroe dei Due Mondi. Bikes for kids and grown-ups. €2.50 per hr., €9 per day. Open M-F 11am-midnight, Sa-Su 3-7pm.

▨ ▐ ORIENTATION AND PRACTICAL INFORMATION

The 16th-century fortress lies toward the water off **Piazza Priamar.** The medieval *centro storico,* with churches and *palazzi,* is bounded by **Via Manzoni** and **Via Paleocapa.** Across the harbor (by means of Calata Sbarbaro) lies **Piazza Mancine** and Savona's summer social scene.

Tourist Office, Corso Italia, 157/r (☎019 840 2321; fax 840 3672). Maps and bus schedules. Open M-Tu, Th 10am-12:30pm and 3-6pm; W, F-Sa 10am-12:30pm.

English-Language Bookstore: Libreria Economica, V. Pia, 88/r (☎019 838 7424). Eclectic blend of classics and bestsellers. Open M-Sa 9:15am-12:30pm and 3:30-7:30pm. MC/V.

Police: ☎ 112. **Medical Emergency:** ☎118.

Ambulance: Croce Bianca ☎019 827 2727. **Guardia Medica** ☎800 55 66 88.

Pharmacy: Farmacia della Ferrera, C. Italia, 153/r (☎019 82 72 02). Posts a list of other pharmacies. Open daily 8:30am-12:30pm and 3:30pm-8am.

Hospital: Ospedale San Paolo, V. Genova, 30 (☎019 84 041).

Post Office: P. Diaz, 9 (☎019 841 4547). Phone cards, *Fermo Posta,* and **currency exchange** available 8:15am-5:30pm. Open M-Sa 8am-6:30pm.

Postal Code: 17100.

ACCOMMODATIONS & CAMPING

Ostello Fortezza del Piramar, C. Mazzini (☎019 81 26 53; priamarhostel@iol.it). From train station, either take bus #2 or walk 5-10min. down C. Mazzini until you see the ramp. Walk up ramp to fortress and follow signs through the labyrinth of dark tunnels to the hostel. With cell-like rooms, you're sure to receive an authentic fortress experience. Reception 7-10am and 4:30-11:30pm. Reservations recommended. Dorm with breakfast €12; 1 person in a double room €14. ❶

Ostello Villa de Franceschini, Villa alla Strà, 29, Conca Verde (☎019 26 32 22; concaverd@hotmail.com). No public transportation to hostel. 3km away from train station; call hostel and hope for a ride (larger groups have better chances). Pick-ups 9am-8pm; scheduled pick-ups at 5 and 7pm. Breakfast included. Reception open 7am-10pm and 4pm-12:30am. Dorm €10, family rooms €12 per person. ❶

Hotel Savona, P. del Popolo, 53r (☎019 82 18 20; fax 82 18 21). Conveniently located with light, spacious rooms. All rooms with bath. Breakfast included. Singles €26-42; doubles €42-62. Half-pension €21-47 per person; full-pension €31-62. MC/V. ❸

Camping Vittoria, V. Nizza, 111 (☎019 88 14 39). Catch the #6 (5am-11pm) on the V. Baselli side of P. Mamelli. Campgrounds are on the water with a small beach. €6 per person, €9 per tent, €4 per car. Electricity €3. Prices higher in summer. ❶

FOOD

Vino e Farinata, V. Pia, 15/r. Typical Ligurian fare. *Farinata* (€3.80) abounds, as do fish dishes. Servings of salmon, shrimp, or swordfish cost only €7. *Primi* from €3.70, *secondi* €5.50-8. Cover €1.15. ❷

Pizzeria Ristorante Mario, V. XX Settembre, 11/r (☎019 81 26 00). Near P. del Popolo. Food is straightforward and simple. Pizza €3-6.50, *primi* €4.50-8, *secondi* €5.50-10.50. Open Th-Tu 10am-3pm and 6pm-1am. AmEx/MC/V. ❷

Trattoria Mordi e Funghi, P. Marconi, 13/r (☎019 838 6648). Pizza from €3.10. Cover €0.52. Open Tu-Sa 11:30am-2:30pm and 7-11pm, M 11:20am-2:30pm. ❶

BEACHES AND NIGHTLIFE

A **public beach** lies along the water in front of the public gardens. Take C. Italia to V. Dante. Walk past the statue of a gallant Garibaldi to a small stretch of sand taken over by pick-up games of soccer. Many bars line the water on the far side of the harbor, but for Italians with dreads, **Birrò,** V. Baglietto, 42r, is really the only option. Expect lots of reggae, as well as a live DJ every night at 11pm. Strut your stuff down the dock past all the hipper-than-thou spots for a €2.50 bottle of beer or €4.50 cocktails. (Open daily 8pm-1am.)

FINALE LIGURE

☎019

At the base of a statue along the promenade, a plaque claims that Finale Ligure is the place for *"Il riposo del popolo,"* or "the people's rest." Whether your idea of *riposo* involves bodysurfing in the choppy waves, browsing through chic boutiques, or scaling Finalborgo's looming 15th-century Castello di San Giovanni, you shouldn't run out of ways to occupy your time. Since *riposo* should definitely include experiencing the delights of *gelato*, in Finale Ligure *gelaterie* almost outnumber the suntanned travelers who stroll the tree-lined boardwalk.

TRANSPORTATION

Trains: In P. V. Veneto. To **Genoa** (1hr., every hr., 5:37am-3:31pm, €3.70) and **Ventimiglia** (2½hr., every hr., 6:40am-11:14pm, €4.80). Most trains to Genoa stop at **Savona** and most trains to Ventimiglia stop at **San Remo**.

Buses: SAR departs from the front of train station. Buy tickets from *tabacchi* nearby. To **Finalborgo** (5min., every 20min., €0.80). Catch the bus for **Borgo Verezzi** across the street (10min., 8 per day, €0.80).

Bike Rental: Oddonebici, V. Colombo, 20 (☎019 69 42 15). Jealous of the Italians on their Vespas? You too can zoom, or at least pedal. Adult bicycles €15.50 per day. Open Tu-Sa 8:30am-12:30pm and 3-8pm. MC/V.

ORIENTATION AND PRACTICAL INFORMATION

The city is divided into three sections: **Finalpia** to the east, **Finalmarina** in the center, and **Finalborgo**, the old city, inland to the northwest. The train station and most of the listings below are in Finalmarina. The main street winds through the town between the station and **Piazza Vittorio Emanuele II**, changing its name from **Via de Raimondi** to **Via Pertica** to **Via Garibaldi**. From P. V. Emanuele, **Via della Concezione** runs parallel to the shore. To reach the old city, far behind the train station, turn left from the station, cross under the tracks, and continue walking left on **Via Domenico Bruneghi** for about 10-15min.

Tourist Office: IAT, V. S. Pietro, 14 (☎019 68 10 19; fax 68 18 04), on the main street overlooking the sea. Open M-Sa 9am-12:30pm and 3:30-6:30pm, Su 9am-noon.

Currency Exchange: Banca Carige, V. Garibaldi, 4, at corner of P. V. Emanuele. €4.13 service charge. Open M-F 8:20am-1:20pm and 2:30-4pm. On Sa **post office** has lower rates (€3) and longer waits. **ATMs** are in Banca Carige, V. Garibaldi, 4, and Banca San Paolo, V. della Concezione, 33.

Bookstore: Piccardo, V. Pertica, 35 (☎019 69 26 03). Steele, King, Shakespeare. Open M-Sa 8:30am-12:30pm and 3:30-7:30pm; in summer also open Su 9am-12:30pm and 4-7:30pm.

Police: V. Brunanghi, 67 (☎112 or ☎019 69 26 66).

Ambulance: ☎118. **P.A. Croce Bianca,** V. Torino, 16 (☎019 69 23 33), in Finalmarina. **Guardia Medica:** ☎118. Open M-F 8pm-8am, Sa 2pm-8am.

Late-Night Pharmacy: Comunale, V. Ghiglieri, 2 (☎019 69 26 70), at intersection where V. Raimondi becomes V. Pertica. Posts late-night locations. Open M-Sa 8:30am-12:30pm and 4-11pm.

Hospital: Ospedale Santa Corona, V. XXV Aprile, 128 (☎019 62 301), in Pietra Ligure.

Internet Access: Net Village Internet Cafe, V. di Raimondi, 21 (☎0184 681 6283), right across from the train station—cross 2 streets and it's right there. 3 computers. Open daily 8am-midnight.

Post Office: V. della Concezione, 29 (☎019 681 5331). Open M-F 8am-6pm, Sa 8am-1:15pm. Phone cards and fax. **Currency exchange** €2.58.

Postal Code: 17024.

↑ ACCOMMODATIONS & CAMPING

The youth hostel has the best prices, not to mention the best view. In July and August, it may be the only place that's not booked solid (they don't take reservations). For all other accommodations listed, reservations are strongly recommended. The tourist office will help find rooms for rent in private houses.

Castello Wuillerman (HI), V. Generale Caviglia, 46 (☎/fax 019 69 05 15; hostelfinaleligure@libero.it). From train station, cross the street and turn left onto V. Raimondo Pertica, then left onto V. Rossi. After passing a church on the left, take a left onto V. Alonzo. Go up 222 stairs (called "Gradinate delle Rose"). At the top, more stairs mark the way to the red-brick castle overlooking the sea. Beautiful courtyard and renovated baths. Internet access €4.50 per hr. Dinner €7.50 (vegetarian meals available). HI card-holders only; HI cards available for purchase. Breakfast and sheets included. Laundry €4 per load. Reception 7-10am and 5-10pm. Curfew 11:30pm. Reservations only by email or in person. Dorms €11. MC/V. ●

Pensione Enzo, Gradinata delle Rose, 3 (☎019 69 13 83). Take a break from never-ending staircase on the way to the hostel (see above) and take an early left. Charming owner, great view. Breakfast available. All rooms with bath and TV. 7 doubles €40-50. Open mid-Mar. to Sept. ●

Albergo Oasi, V. S. Cagna, 25 (☎019 69 17 17; fax 681 5989; albergooasi@libreo.it). From train station, bear left on V. Brunenghi, and walk through underpass to V. Silla and turn right. Walk uphill, about 100m, and it's on the left. Closer to train station than the hostel. Provides 12 tidy rooms (some with bathrooms and balconies), garden patio, a sitting room with TV, and a restaurant (dinner €12). Free Internet. Breakfast included. Singles €25; doubles €50; extra bed €25. ●

Albergo Carla, V. Colombo, 44 (☎019 69 22 85; fax 68 19 65). Conveniently located in the center of town. All rooms with bath. Bar and restaurant. Breakfast €3.70. Singles €23-29; doubles €44-49. AmEx/DC/MC/V. ●

Albergo San Marco, V. della Concezione, 22 (☎019 69 25 33; fax 681 6187). From train station, walk straight ahead down V. Saccone, and turn left on V. della Concezione. Enter through restaurant. 14 spotless rooms have bath (with basic shower) and phone; many include balcony and ocean view. Easy access to waterfront. Minimal English spoken. Breakfast included. Reservations recommended. Open Easter-late Sept. Singles €33-38.50; doubles €45-56.80. Extra bed €10. AmEx/DC/MC/V. ●

Camping: Camping Tahiti (☎/fax 019 60 06 00), on V. Varese. Take bus for Calvisio from stop in P. V. Veneto. Get off at Bar Paradiso and cross bridge at V. Rossini. Turn left and walk along river to V. Vanese. Hillside site features 8 terraces, 90 lots, and 360-person capacity. Reception 8am-8pm. Open Easter-Oct. 15. High season €6.50 per person, €5 per tent. Hot showers €0.50. Electricity €2.50. AmEx/MC/V. ●

Del Mulino (☎019 60 16 69), on V. Castelli. From station, take the Calvisio bus to Boncardo Hotel, and follow brown, then yellow, signs to campsite entrance. Bar, restaurant, and mini-market. Laundry €5. Office open Apr.-Sept. 8am-8pm. €7 per person, €7 per tent. Hot showers free. ●

◩ FOOD

Trattorie and pizzerias line the streets closest to the beach. If you want to stock up at a supermarket, pay a visit to **Coop,** V. Dante Alighieri, 7. To reach it, walk up V. Brunenghi toward Finalborgo, and take a left on V. Saggitario. At the end of this little street take a right; the supermarket is on your right. (Open M-Th 8:30am-1pm and 2:30-7:30pm, F-Sa 8:30am-7:30pm, Su 9am-1pm. MC/V.)

▨ **Spaghetteria Il Posto,** V. Porro, 21 (☎019 60 00 95). Fill your stomach with mountains of well-priced pasta. Oodles of vegetarian options. *Penne quattro stagioni* (with bacon, mushrooms, tomatoes, artichokes, and mozzarella; €6.50); *penne pirata* (with shrimp and salmon; €7); spaghetti marinara (with capers, clams, and olives; €7.50). Cover €1. Open Tu-Su 7-10:30pm. Closed first 2 weeks of Mar. ❷

▨ **Il Dattero,** on the fork where V. Pertica splits into V. Rossi and V. Garibaldi. Though every other shop in Finale Ligure seems to be a *gelateria,* ignore them and make a beeline for Il Dattero. At night, the lines in front of the door demonstrate this *gelateria's* well-earned popularity. Those feeling especially decadent can get a pastry with their choice of *gelato* inside it (2 flavors; €2.20). A cone or a cup with 2 flavors €1.30, with 3 flavors €1.80. Open daily 11am-midnight. ❶

Farinata e Vino, V. Roma, 25 (☎019 69 25 62). Small, popular *trattoria* bills itself as *"una trattoria alla vecchia maniera"* (old school). Enjoy homestyle cooking (especially the fish) at excellent prices. Menu changes daily. *Primi* €5.50-8, *secondi* €7.50-15. Open 12:30-2pm and 7:30-9pm. Call for reservations in summer. MC/V. ❸

Da Badabin, V. Garibaldi, 75 (☎019 69 43 66). Stop here for thicker pizzas with mushrooms or eggplant (€1.40 per slice). You can also get lasagna or crepes. Open daily 8am-2pm and 4:30-8:30pm. ❶

Bei Gisela, V. Colombo, 2 (☎019 69 52 75), at the intersection of V. Alonzo and V. Colombo. Travelers tired of red-checked tablecloths can appreciate the chic ambiance of this restaurant. The decor will make even the most footsore traveler feel serene. *Primi* €8.50-8.80, *secondi* €7.30-10.30. Open M-Tu and Th 7:30-10:30pm, F-Su 12:30-2pm and 7:30-10:30pm. On Th check out the wine bar 7-12:30pm. ❸

◎ SIGHTS

The towns surrounding Finale Ligure are worth extra exploration. SAR buses run to tiny **Borgio Verezzi** (every 15min., 6:35am-1:41am, €1.50), or hike up the winding V. Nazario Sauro (about an hour), and delight in the far-reaching vistas. The cool, tranquil streets, caves, and artificial rock formations of the tiny medieval village at the top make the trip worthwhile. Stop at **A Topia ❶**, V. Roma, 16, for a wood-burning oven-baked pizza *quattro stagioni* for €5. (☎019 61 69 05. Open daily 7pm-1am; in winter closed Tu.) If you end up in Verezzi after dark, do not take a short-cut down the hillside. Guard dogs run rampant off the main road.

Enclosed within ancient walls, Finalborgo, the historic quarter of Finale Ligure, is a 1km walk or short bus ride up V. Bruneghi from the station. Past the **Porto Reale,** the Chiostro di Santa Caterina, a 14th-century edifice, houses the **Museo Civico del Finale,** dedicated to Ligurian history. (☎019 69 00 20; museoarcheofinale@libero.it. Open Tu-Su 9am-noon and 3-6pm; in winter Tu-Sa 9am-noon and 2:30-5pm, Su 9am-noon. Free.) Up a tough but fulfilling trail, ▨**Castel Govone,** a small ruined castle behind the larger ruins of San Giovanni, lends a spectacular view of Finale. For further rock climbing in the area, the **Rock Store,** P. Garibaldi, 14, in Finalborgo, provides maps and necessary gear. (☎019 69 02 08. Open Tu-Su 9am-12:30pm and 4:30-7:30pm.)

◤ BEACHES

Spray-painted on the inner wall of the tunnel that leads to the prime free beach in Finale Marina is *"Voglio il sole/Cerco nuova luce/nella konfusione"* ("I want the sun/I look for new light/in the confusion"). Watch out, Dante. If you empathize with this graffiti poet, you've come to the right place. Be adventurous and forget the narrow strip of free beach in town, where you'd feel like a beached sardine. Instead, walk east along V. Aurelia through the first tunnel. The beach before you, cradled by overhanging cliffs, is an ideal spot to sunbathe away from the crowds.

NORTHWEST ITALY

🎵 ENTERTAINMENT

A bar popular among young tourists and locals alike, **Pilade,** V. Garibaldi, 67, features live music on some Friday nights, ranging from blues to jazz to soul. The wooden statue of the horn player in the red tux on the sidewalk and a real live saxophonist inside will draw you in like the Pied Pipers of Ligure-Lin. Just be willing to do a little shouting above the music to order a mixed drink (€5) or a beer (€3 and up). In the wee hours the rest of the week, you'll find drinkers nodding their heads in unison to rock and Italian techno, eyes glazed over from one too many a Peroni. Pizza, burgers, and delicious *panini* are always available. (☎019 69 22 20. Open daily 10am-2am. Closed Th in winter.) As the sun sets, boogie down to V. Torino and the bass-beats emanating from **Cuba Libre.** It's complete with multiple dance floors and bars, fog machine, and political message. (☎019 60 12 84. Cover €13 for men, €10 for women. Open F-Sa 10pm-sunrise.) If you're traveling with kids or fun-loving adults, check out the merry-go-rounds and other carnival-style diversions that line the waterfront.

SAN REMO ☎0184

Once a glamorous retreat for Russian nobles, czars, *literati*, and artists, San Remo is the largest resort town on the Italian Riviera. Recently, it served as the backdrop for Matt Damon's more murderous machinations in *The Talented Mr. Ripley*. These days, San Remo upholds its glamorous profile with finely-dressed couples gambling and bikini-clad women gamboling along the palm-lined promenade of Corso Imperatrice. As befits its location on the Riviera dei Fiori (Riviera of Flowers), San Remo blooms with carnations year-round. Admittedly, this town isn't teeming with deals to make the budget traveler drool, but the winding alleys of La Pigna, the historic district, provide a quieter ambiance and more reasonable prices. While many might be drawn to San Remo for the click of dice and the clink of poker chips, San Remo is most famous in Italy for its annual music festival, featuring classic Italian tunes.

🚆 TRANSPORTATION

The **train** station faces C. F. Cavalotti. Trains run to: **Genoa** (3hr., every 2hr., 5:30am-10:05pm, €7.20); **Milan** (3½hr., every 2hr., 5:30am-7:40pm, €13.22); **Turin** (4½hr., every 45min., 2:37-7:18pm, €11); and **Ventimiglia** (15min., every hr., 7:18am-11pm, €1.50).

✴🔃 ORIENTATION AND PRACTICAL INFORMATION

The city is formed by three main parallel streets, running from west to east, parallel to the beach. The new train station faces **Corso F. Cavalotti.** To get to the center of town, turn right onto C. F. Cavalotti. When you reach **Rondo G. Garibaldi** (a rotary), cross it and veer slightly to your left down **Corso Giuseppe Garibaldi.** Once you reach the next piazza, **Piazza Colombo,** either turn left down **Via Manzoni** to reach the intersection of **Via Roma** and **Via Nino Bixio,** or continue straight, veering slightly left as you cross the piazza onto the swanky **Corso G. Matteotti.**

> **Tourist Office: APT Tourist Office,** V. Nuvoloni, 1 (☎0184 59 059; fax 50 76 49; www.sanremonet.com). Turn right out of the train station. From P. Colombo, veer left onto C. G. Matteotti, and follow this all the way to the end. Helpful maps and brochures are worth the hike from the train station. Open M-Sa 8am-7pm, Su 9am-1pm.

> **Bank: Banco Ambrosiano,** V. Roma, 62 (☎0184 59 23 11). Offers **currency exchange** and **ATM.** Open M-F 8:20am-1:20pm and 2:35-4:05pm, Sa 8:20-11:50am. There are a few other banks on V. Roma. **Banca di Genova San Giorgio** is right across the street.

Bookstore: Libreria Beraldi, V. Cavour 8 (☎0184 54 11 11). Reasonable collection of bestsellers in English, French, German, and Spanish. Also sells language dictionaries. Open daily 8:30am-12:30pm and 3:30-7:30pm. MC/V.

Laundromat: Blu Acquazzura, V. A. Volta, 131. Wash and dry €5 each. Open daily 6am-7:30pm.

Emergency: ☎118. **Police:** ☎113.

Pharmacy: Farmacia Centrale, V. Matteotti, 190 (☎0184 50 90 65). Open M-Sa 8:30am-10pm, Su 9am-1pm.

Hospital: Ospedale Civile, V. G. Borea, 56 (☎0184 53 61).

Internet Access: Mailboxes, Etc., C. Cavallotti, 86 (☎0184 59 16 73). 3 computers. €4 per 30min., €7.50 per hr. Photocopier, fax, scanner, and CD burner also available. Open M-F 9am-6:30pm, Sa 9am-1pm.

Post Office: V. Roma, 156. Open M-Sa 8am-6pm.

Postal Code: 18038.

ACCOMMODATIONS

Albergo De Paoli, C. Raimondo, 53, 2nd fl. (☎0184 50 04 93). From the train station, take a right onto C. F. Cavalotti and a left onto V. Fiume. When V. Fiume hits C. Orazio Raimondo, take another left. De Paoli will be on your left, surrounded by the more expensive, 3-star Hotel Esperia. The owners are lovely, the rooms are well-kept, and the common baths are very clean. Singles €18; doubles €30.50. ❷

Metropolis Terminus, V. Roma, 8 (☎0184 5771 0010). Turn right down V. Roma out of the train station. Rooms feature high ceilings and attractive wood floors and furniture. Restaurant run by same proprietors. Singles €30; doubles €50. Add €10 in Aug. ❸

Hotel Mara, V. Roma, 93, 3rd. fl. (☎0184 53 38 60). From train station, go right on C. F. Cavalotti, left on V. Fiume, and right onto C. O. Raimondo until it becomes V. Roma. The hotel will be on your right. Simple and spacious rooms. No private baths. No singles. Doubles €36-€51. ❹

Albergo Al Dom, C. Mombello, 13, 2nd fl. (☎0184 50 14 60). From train station, take a left off C. G. Matteotti onto C. Mombello; it's on your left after you cross V. Roma. Owned by a very friendly family and located in the middle of the city center. Grand, old-style rooms with baths and high ceilings. Singles €25-40; doubles €40-60. ❷

Hotel Graziella, Rondo Garibaldi, 2 (☎0184 571 0321; fax 57 00 43). From train station, turn right on C. F. Cavalotti. Turn right to go around Rondo Garibaldi, and you'll see it set back from the road on your right. Though not huge, rooms are beautifully decorated and clean, with high ceilings and windows. All rooms have fridge and TV; rooms on 2nd fl. have A/C. Breakfast €4.13. Singles €35; doubles €55. ❸

FOOD

San Remo's restaurants are generally overpriced, but affordable options do exist. C. N. Sauro, which runs along the waterfront across the train tracks from V. N. Bixio, has several decent pizzerias.

Dick Turpin's, C. N. Sauro, 15 (☎0184 50 34 99). Follow C. N. Sauro until it meets the beach. Casual atmosphere and teenage waiters. Serves crepes from €5 as well as pizza and pasta. Open daily noon-4pm and 7pm-1am. ❷

Ristorante Pizzeria delle Palme, V. N. Sauro, 31 (☎0184 50 34 55). Serves up pizza (€5-8), fish (€8 and up), and more. Open Th-Tu noon-3pm and 7:30pm-midnight. ❸

Pizzeria Napoletana da Giovanni, V. C. Pesante, 7 (☎0184 50 49 54), off V. XX Settembre. Casual atmosphere and the quiet side-street location make Napoletana a nice change of pace from the crowded restaurants near the water. 41 kinds of pizza (€4.50-8.50). *Primi* €5.50-10.50, *secondi* €5.50-7.50. There are also 3 tourist *menùs* for €13, €15, and €23.50. Open F-W noon-2:30pm and 7-11pm. AmEx/DC/MC/V. ❸

Pizzeria Ai 4 Amici, V. XX Septembre, 28 (☎0184 50 26 27). Turn left where V. Roma and C. N. Bixio merge. Inexpensive *pizzeria* with delicious and hearty portions. Try the pizza *quattro stagione* with ham, artichokes, mushrooms, and olives (€6.50). Pizza €5.50-8. Open M-Sa for lunch starting at noon, for dinner 6-7pm. MC/V. ❷

Ristorante Pizzeria Italia (☎0184 50 02 78), on the corner of V. XX Settembre and C. G. Raimondo. Elegant dining setting, with wood-paneled walls and welcoming waiters. Pizza about €6, *primi* from €9.30, *secondi* from €13. Tourist *menù* €15.50. Open Th-Tu 12:15-2:30pm and 7:15pm-1:30am. AmEx/DC/MC/V. ❹

👁 🎵 SIGHTS AND ENTERTAINMENT

The Russian Orthodox **Chiesa di Cristo Salvatore,** across the street from the tourist office, is a church with intricate onion-domes, blue vaulted ceilings that soothe sun-struck eyes, and Russian religious art. (Open Tu-Su 9:30am-noon and 3-6pm, M 9:30am-noon. Donation of €0.50 required.)

Gamblers frequent the **Casino Municipale di San Remo,** C. Inglesi, 18, a dazzling example of Belle Epoque architecture. No sneakers, jeans, or shorts are allowed; coat and tie are required in winter. (☎0184 59 51. 18+. Cover F-Su €7.50. Open daily 2:30pm-2am, Sa-Su open until 3 or 4am.) The "American Room," featuring the "American" games of blackjack and slot machines, has neither a strict dress code nor an entrance fee. Much of San Remo's nightlife is centered around the casino. After dark, however, well-to-do couples meander along the swanky **Corso Matteotti,** window shopping, enjoying *gelato*, or sipping liquors at wayside bars.

At one end of C. Matteotti is the casino, and at the other end is a piazza; all along the way are cafes and bars. One such bar is **🛑Zoo Bizarre,** V. Gaudio, 10, on a little side street off C. Matteotti, to your left as you walk toward the casino. This trendy spot has colored tables and chairs and a ceiling decorated with an overlapping mishmash of movie posters. The hip, twentysomething crowd kicks off their weekend evenings here around 9pm with drinks (€4-6.50; gin and tonic €5) and free tiny appetizers. (☎0184 50 57 74. Open M-F 8pm-2am, Sa-Su 8pm-3am.) After whetting your whistle here, head over to nightclub **Disco Ninfa Egeria,** V. Matteotti, 178, which promises to be happening if you're willing to pay the hefty cover to get past the hefty bouncers. (☎0184 59 11 33. Cover €13. Open Sa from 11pm, dancing begins well after midnight.)

Italian-speakers can see an Italian or dubbed foreign movie at the **Theatre Ariston,** also along C. Matteotti. Beach-lovers should try the shore to the right of the casino as you face the water. You'll find plenty of Speedo- and bikini-clad company, both at the stretches of free beach and the numerous *bagni* that line the water. There's real sand (no pebble beaches here), rocky jetties, and sparkling water. This is common knowledge, though, so get down there fairly early to snag a spot.

BORDIGHERA ☎0184

When Italian writer Giovanni Ruffini crafted the plot line for his 1855 melodrama, *Il Dottor Antonio,* he unknowingly laid the foundation for the development of both Bordighera and the Italian Riviera's tourism industry. The novel tells the story of a young English girl brought to the brink of death by illness, but miraculously revived by Bordighera's sultry sands and warm wisps of summer air. Within a decade, the novel's devoted English readers clamored for the real thing, leading to the construction of the first of several huge hotels, the Hotel d'Angleterre, and the subsequent growth of Bordighera into one of the Riviera's foremost resort towns. In the latter half of the 19th century, tourists, among them Queen Margaret and Claude Monet, outnumbered natives by as much as five to one. Although the town still fills up in July and August, the ratio is a little less extreme these days, leaving all the more room for seaside sallying among the palm-lined streets.

TRANSPORTATION

Trains: In P. Eroi Libertà (☎848 88 80 88). To: **Genoa** (3hr., €7.20); **San Remo** (every hr., €1.30); and **Ventimiglia** (every hr., €1).

Buses: Riviera Transporte buses stop every 300m along V. V. Emanuele and run to **San Remo** (20min., €1.25) and **Ventimiglia** (20min., €1.14).

ORIENTATION AND PRACTICAL INFORMATION

The bus from Ventimiglia stops on the main street, **Via Vittorio Emanuele,** which runs parallel to the train station one block in front of it. Behind the station, set apart from the rest of the town, the scenic **Lungomare Argentina,** a 2km beach promenade, runs parallel to the *città moderna* (new town), where most offices and shops are found. To get from the town to the Lungomare, use one of the many tunnels that go underneath the train tracks.

Tourist Office: V. V. Emanuele, 172 (☎0184 26 23 22; fax 26 44 55). From the train station walk along V. Roma, turn left on V. V. Emanuele, and take a right just after the park. Open M-Sa 8am-7pm, Su 9am-1pm (closed on Su in the winter).

Currency Exchange: Banca Commerciale Italiana, V. V. Emanuele, 165 (☎0184 26 36 54). **ATM** outside bank, one of many along V. V. Emanuele. Open M-F 8:20am-1:25pm and 2:50-4:15pm.

Emergency: ☎113. **Ambulance:** ☎118.

Police: V. Prima Maggio, 49 (☎112 or 0184 26 26 26).

24-Hour Pharmacy: Farmacia Centrale, V. V. Emanuele, 145 (☎0184 26 12 46). List of 24hr. pharmacies posted. Open M-F 8:30am-12:30pm and 3:30-7:30pm.

Hospital: V. Aurelia, 122 (☎0184 27 51).

Post Office: V. V. Veneto, 3 (☎0184 26 91 51). Open M-Sa 8am-6pm.

Postal Code: 18012.

ACCOMMODATIONS

During the high season many hotels require that clients accept full-pension, half-pension, or at least breakfast.

Villa Miki, V. Lagazzi, 14 (☎0184 26 18 44). Take an immediate left out of the station; walk until you hit V. V. Emanuele, and then turn left. V. Lagazzi is several blocks down on the right. This family-run *pensione* is in a serene, residential area. Small rooms with balconies over a garden. 16 beds. Breakfast and showers included. Prices go down €3.62 without breakfast. With a reservation: singles €26-28; doubles €34-44. Full-pension low season €39 per person, high season €49. ❸

Albergo Nagos, P. Eroi della Libertà, 7 (☎0184 26 04 57), across from the train station on the left. A word to the wise: don't leave your window open all night, because mosquitoes abound. No English spoken. Communal bathrooms. Breakfast €8.45-9.45. Singles €23.24; doubles €38.22. Half-pension €30.99-33.57; full-pension €37.18-38.22. ❷

🛈 FOOD

Budget restaurants are few and far between, but a few exceptions can be found. Some *trattorie* in the *città alta* offer traditional Ligurian cuisine at reasonable prices. At Christmas time, try *cubaite* (elaborately decorated wafers filled with caramel cream), a Bordighera specialty. Rossese, a deliciously sweet red wine from Dolceacqua and other nearby towns, is available year-round. The **covered market**, P. Garibaldi, 46-48, has picnic supplies. (Open daily 8am-7:30pm.) There is also a **STANDA supermarket** at V. Libertà, 32. (Open M-Sa 8am-8pm, Su 9am-1pm and 4-8pm. AmEx/DC/MC/V.) To get there, walk east down V. V. Emanuele and cross Piazza Ruffini, bearing left, to V. Libertà.

Creperie-Caffè Giglio, V. V. Emanuele, 158 (☎0184 26 15 30). Popular local hangout. Large selection of inexpensive *panini* (€3) and delicious crepes (€4.50). The proximity of the French-Italian border inspired the mozzarella, tomato, and oregano crepe (€3.90). Sweet crepes are terrific desserts. Open Tu-Sa 7pm-3am, Su 3pm-3am. ❷

Pizzeria Napoletana, V. V. Emanuele, 250 (☎0184 26 37 22). Delicious, reasonably priced food. Pizza €4.60-8.30, *primi* €5.20-8.50, *secondi* €5.50-9.50. Open W-M noon-3pm and 6pm-1am. ❸

Gastronomia and Rosticceria Marisa, V. V. Emanuele, 319 (☎0184 26 16 57). For something a little more substantial than pizza or pasta, try the rotisserie chicken or lasagna (€4.90 per kg). Ask for a plastic spoon at one of the *gelaterie*. Open Tu-Sa 8:30am-1pm and 4:30-7:30pm. ❶

Ristorante Stella, V. V. Emanuele, 106 (☎0184 26 37 15). Stop in here for quiet, pleasant atmosphere and delicious pasta, such as *penne al salmone*. 4-course *menùs* (either €14 or €18) for the very hungry. *Primi* €5.68-8.26, *secondi* €7.75-12. Open W-M noon-3pm and 7:15pm-late. AmEx/MC/V. ❸

🄶 SIGHTS

The **Giardino Esotico Pallanca** (exotic garden) contains over 3000 species of cacti and rare South American flora. Walk 1km down V. Aziglia to V. Madonna della Ruota, 1, or grab a bus on V. V. Emanuele in the direction of San Remo and ask the driver where to get off. (☎0184 26 63 47. Open M 3-7pm, Tu-Su 9am-12:30pm and 2-6:30pm. €5.50.) A stroll east from the town center along V. Romana provides a view of the many hotels constructed during the 19th century for the fans of *Il Dottor Antonio*. Past P. de Amicis, the road becomes C. F. Rossi. Meander through the park, which leads to downhill steps to the **Chiesa di Sant'Ampelio,** built overlooking the sea around the grotto where Ampelio, the town hermit (later the town patron) holed up. Preferring *pesce* to prayers, fishermen and tanners congregate on the rocks below the church. (Open Su at 10am. Otherwise knock.) On May 14, the church hosts the **Festival of Sant'Ampelio** with a procession and ritual pomp. From September to May, the **Chiosco della Musica** on the boardwalk offers concerts. Every year, Bordighera or *la città dell'umorismo*, hosts the **International Salon of Humor,** a juried contest of humorous drawings and cabaret-style comedy.

🎜 ENTERTAINMENT

Graffiti Pub, V. V. Emanuele, 122 (☎0184 26 15 90). The bulldog statue may have a faceguard, but that doesn't keep friendly bar bums from boisterous yapping and frenzied lapping. Raucous 25+ crowd fills blue lounges inside and tables along street. *Panini* €2.58. Beer on tap €2.07-3.62, liquor €3.10. Open M-Sa 5pm-3am. MC/V.

Disco Kursaal, Lungomare, 7 (☎0184 26 46 85). Walk through tunnel to left of the train station. Wide variety of music, both live and recorded. Underground, house, and industrial. Open Sept.-July F-Su midnight-5am; Aug. daily midnight-5am. AmEx/MC/V.

Chica Loca (☎0184 26 35 10), down the beach from the disco. *Paella* for 2 €15; *panini* €4. Margarita €6. Dancing after midnight. Open daily 11:30am-6:30am.

VENTIMIGLIA   ☎0184

Around 2000 years ago, the final stages of the expansion of the Empire brought the Romans to the mouth of the Roya River, near the present-day border between France and Italy. Augustus and his cohorts took hold of the area by ruthlessly conquering a local tribe, the Intemeli. To boost Augustus's sagging ego, the town was named Venti Intemelian (boasting that this was his 20th such conquest), which later evolved into Ventimiglia. Today, with the colossal remains of a Roman theater, winding 11th-century streets, and Romanesque religious sites, Ventimiglia makes an agreeable starting point for those who want to explore the Italian Riviera and the French Côte d'Azur.

▐ TRANSPORTATION

Trains: In P. Stazione (☎848 88 80 88). **Luggage storage** available (p. 185). To: **Genoa** (3hr., every 1¼hr., €12.65); **Marseilles** (€26.10); and **Nice** (45min., every hr., €5.30).

Buses: Agenzia Viaggi & Turismo Monte Carlo, V. Cavour, 57 (☎0184 35 75 77), left from the tourist office. Office open M-Sa 9am-12:30pm and 2:30-7pm. To **Bordighera** (15min., 4 per hr., €1.14) and **San Remo** (15min., 4 per hr., €1.70).

Bike Rental: Eurocicli, V. Cavour, 70b (☎0184 35 18 79). €1 per hr., €5 per day, €15 per week, €50 per month. Open M-Sa 8:30am-12:30pm and 3-7:30pm. AmEx/MC/V.

▐ ORIENTATION AND PRACTICAL INFORMATION

Upon arriving in Ventimiglia by train, cross the street and walk down **Via della Stazione** to the center of town. The second crossroad is **Via Cavour,** where Via della Stazione becomes **Corso Repubblica** as it continues toward the waterfront. To visit France, hop on a train or a blue **Riviera Transporte** bus. Remember your passport.

Tourist Office: V. Cavour, 61 (☎0184 35 11 83). City maps and info on neighboring attractions. Open M-Sa 9am-12:30pm and 3-7pm. The travel agency next door, **Agenzia Viaggi & Turismo Monte Carlo,** V. Cavour, 57c (☎0184 35 75 77; fax 35 26 21), has **currency exchange** and bus and hotel info. Some English spoken. Open M-Sa 9am-12:30pm and 2:30-7pm.

Luggage Storage: In train station (€3.87). Open daily 6am-7pm.

English-Language Bookstore: Libreria Casella, V. della Stazione, 1d (☎0184 35 79 00). Small selection. Open M-Sa 8:30am-12:30pm and 3-7:30pm. MC/V.

Emergency: ☎113.

Police: V. Aprosio, 12 (☎112 or 0184 23 82 61).

Ambulance: Croce Rossa Italiana, V. Dante Alighieri, 12 (☎0184 23 20 00) or **Croce Verde,** P. XX Settembre 8 (☎0184 35 11 75).

Pharmacy: Farmacia Internazionale, V. Cavour, 28a (☎0184 35 13 00). Open M-F 8:30am-12:30pm and 3:30-7:30pm, Sa 8:30am-12:30pm.

Hospital: Ospedale, V. Basso, 2, off C. Genova. V. Cavour becomes C. Genova as you go east toward Bordighera. **Saint Charles** (☎0184 27 51).

Internet Access: Mail Boxes, Etc., V. V. Veneto, 4b (☎0184 23 84 23), just past the Giardini Pubblici from C. Repubblica. €4.50 per 30min., €7.75 per hr. Open M-F 8:30am-12:30pm and 3-7pm, Sa 8:30am-12:30pm.

Post Office: C. Repubblica, 8 (☎0184 35 13 12), on your right after crossing V. Roma. Phonecards and **currency exchange** (€2.58). *Fermo Posta.* Open M-Sa 8am-6:30pm.

Postal Code: 18039.

⌐ ACCOMMODATIONS & CAMPING

Ventimiglia is one of the Riviera's cheapest options, but unsurprisingly, it fills up in July and August. Reservations are strongly recommended in the summer, but if you can't find a room, consider traveling to nearby Menton, France.

▨ **Hotel XX Settembre,** V. Roma, 16 (☎0184 35 12 22). Spacious rooms are meticulously cleaned. **Restaurant** downstairs (*menù* €16.50; open Tu-Su 10am-3pm and 6:30-11pm). Single rooms have double beds. Communal bath, unless you get 2 rooms with bath (€80). Breakfast €4. Singles €30; doubles €50; triples €65. ❸

Auberge de Jeunesse (HI), plateau St. Michel, Menton, FA (☎00 334 9335 9314 from Italy or ☎04 9335 9314 within France). Take bus #6 from Menton (4 per day, €1.22), or call the hostel for minibus service (€3.05 per person for 1-2 people, €1.53 per person for 3 or more). Friendly, English-speaking staff, eager to share traveling tales. Great seaside view. Breakfast included. Dinner €8. Laundry €6. Sleepsack €2.70. Reception 7am-noon and 5pm-midnight. Dorms €12. Open Feb.-Nov. ❶

Hotel Villa Franca, C. Repubblica, 12 (☎0184 35 18 71), next to the waterfront and public park. Clean, small rooms, with friendly management and a parrot in the lobby who says "ciao." Quality meals at restaurant. Breakfast included. Singles €30; doubles €44, with bath €52; triples €72. AmEx/MC/V. ❸

Calypso Hotel, V. Matteotti, 8G (☎0184 35 15 88; fax 35 27 42). Clean, fairly spacious rooms. Breakfast included. Reception 7am-midnight. 2 singles €37.70 each; doubles €58.36, with bath and TV €71.27; triples €80. Closed Jan. ❹

Camping Roma, V. Peglia, 5 (☎0184 23 90 07; fax 23 90 35), across the river and 400m from the waterfront. From the station, follow V. della Stazione (which changes into V. della Repubblica) and go right on V. Roma until you reach the river at Lungo Roia Girolamo Rossi. Cross the bridge, and make an immediate right on C. Francia. After 50m it becomes V. Peglia, which has a pedestrian pathway alongside it. Well-maintained campsites and hillside panoramas. Market and bar nearby. €10 per person, €9 per tent. Bungalows for 4 €65 with electricity. Showers free. Open Apr.-Sept. MC/V. ❶

⌐ FOOD

The **covered market** unfolds Monday to Thursday mornings until 1pm, and occasionally all day on Friday and Saturday, displaying a staggering array of fruit and vegetables along V. della Repubblica, V. Libertà, V. Aprosio, and V. Roma. The vendors along V. Aprosio near the fake flower stands tend to be small, in-town gardeners and have the freshest produce. A **STANDA supermarket** is at the corner of V. Roma and V. Ruffini. (Open M-Sa 8am-8pm, Su 9am-1pm and 4-8pm.) Along the beach on the Bassa side, there are five or six *pizzerie* in a row, offering similar fare for €8-12. Head over to the Alta shore for a bit more variety.

NORTHWEST ITALY

Pasta and Basta, V. Marconi, 20A (☎0184 23 08 78). On the Alta side of the river, shortly before the Galleria Scoglietti. The *ristorante* offers refreshing A/C, a view of the water, and an affordable change from *pizzeric*. 22 delicious sauces (€4-8.50) and 9 freshly made pastas (€1-3). You'll be saying *"Basta!"* with plenty still on your plate. Open Tu-Sa after 7:30pm. ❷

Ristorante "Il Salto," V. Mazzini, 13d (☎0184 23 86 70). Sit outside on the terrace or inside. Cozy but modern, "Il Salto" offers quality standard fare at reasonable prices (*primi* €5.50-7, *secondi* €6.50-9), as well as different types of pizza (night only) and a 4-course *menù turistico* (€11). Open for lunch and dinner. AmEx/MC/V. ❸

Ristorante Nanni, V. Milite Ignoto, 2c (☎0184 33 230). Dine across the street from the *giardini publicci*. A fantastic view of the sunset awaits 50 paces down the road. Dine inside or outside. 4-course *menù turistico* €11.86-14.46. AmEx/DC/MC/V. ❸

The Buffet Stazione (☎0184 35 12 36), in the train station, is a fastidiously clean option for a quick bite. Pizza and *focaccia* €0.70, *panini* €2.80. If you want to sit down (most people stand) there will be an additional service charge (about 10%). You can also buy cookies, chips, breadsticks, or candy for the road. Open daily 5am-1am. Bar open daily 5am-11pm. ❶

La Vecchia Napoli, V. Trossarelli, 28 (☎0184 35 24 71), conveniently located just off the footbridge on the Alta side of town. Try typical Neapolitan food, made in a wood-burning oven. Offers 25 different kinds of pizza (€4.20-8.20) and a wide variety of *primi* and *secondi* (€7.50-14.50). Open daily 10am-midnight. MC/V. ❸

🧭 SIGHTS

Blue Riviera Trasporti buses leave from the corner of V. Cavour and V. Martiri della Libertà (dir.: Ponte San Luigi, 15min., 12 per day, first bus leaves at 9:05am, €1.14), and stop at La Mortola, home of the internationally renowned ▨**Botanical Hanbury Gardens.** Here, terraces of exotic flora from three continents cascade down the summit of Cape Mortola to the sea. Elegant marble gazebos and nudes tucked into rocky niches lie along the twisting pebble or cobblestone paths. Near the bottom is a church with a lily pad-covered pond in front of it; sit here and rest a minute before going down to the seaside cafe at the bottom. The comprehensive course mapped out in the brochure takes about two hours. A stretch of the ancient **Strada Romana** lies directly under the bridge just before the bathrooms; it was used by the Romans to travel to Provence and by St. Catherine to fetch the Pope from Avignon back to Rome. (☎0184 22 95 07. Open in summer daily 9am-6pm. €4.38, ages 6-14 and groups €2.32.)

A short trip through some of the old town's winding, ancient streets will reward you with a view of the **Romanesque cathedral.** Walk across the footbridge to Ventimiglia Alta and turn right on V. Trossarelli; 50m ahead you'll find Discesa Marina; climb to V. Galerina and then V. Falerina. The cathedral melds classic simplicity with ancient grandeur. Nestled on the other side of the old town, off V. Garibaldi at P. Colleta, is the 11th-century church of **San Michele.** Its **crypt** was constructed using pilfered Roman columns. (Crypt open Su 10:30-noon.)

The **Museo Archeologico,** V. Verdi, 41, sits on the hill overlooking the sea. It's quite a hike, but the bus to Ponte San Luigi stops nearby; ask the driver where to get off. Roman artifacts found in the area, including a dozen marble heads, are on display. (☎0184 35 11 81. Open Tu-Sa 9:30am-12:30pm and 3-5pm, Su 10am-12:30pm. €3.) Taking the bus all the way to Ponte San Luigi will leave you a 10min. walk from the **Balzi Rossi** (red cliffs), which Cro-Magnon man used to call home. Spectacular skeletons reside in Balzi Rossi's **Prehistoric Museum.** (☎0184 38 113. Open Tu–Su 8:30am-7:30pm. €2, €2.50 for groups.)

Clean, quiet beaches lie across the river in Alta, along **Passeggiata Marconi.** If you're willing to travel a little to reach the best beach in Ventimiglia, take the Ponte San Luigi bus to the archaeological museum.\ On your left is an inconspicuous set of stairs. A 10min. hike down a cliffside overrun with grass opens up to **Spiaggia Le Calandre,** a surprisingly natural sandy beach. Frolicking on the smooth sands with Italian boys and girls won't cost you anything. If you want to play grown-up, two chairs and an umbrella on the rocks will run you €15.50. *Let's Go* does not recommend staying past sundown, as the trek back could be dangerous in the dark. (☎0347 431 5393. Open daily 8am-9pm.)

🎵 ENTERTAINMENT

Frenzied activity during daylight hours compensates for the largely non-existent nightlife in Ventimiglia. Mid- to late June brings the 43rd annual **Battaglia de Fiori,** which consists of floats and flower flinging. On Fridays, the **Mercato Settimanale,** around the Giardini Pubblici and along the river, is the biggest market on the Riviera and the Côte d'Azur. The humming *mercato* is just the place to heckle over slinky French slips, suede coats, and salami. Just keep an eye on your wallet.

📍 DAYTRIP FROM VENTIMIGLIA: DOLCEACQUA

To make this scenic daytrip, catch a bus (20min., 10 per day, 6:10am-7:07pm) from V. Cavour across from the tourist office.

A string of villages rose up along the Roya River during the Middle Ages to accommodate journeymen along an essential trade route between Ventimiglia and the rest of northern Italy. Dolceacqua, graced with a medieval castle, was one of these tiny *cittadini.* Even for the history buff, Dolceacqua (9km from Ventimiglia) will suffice as a survey of the historical passageway from Piedmont to France. During your bus ride, take note of the spattering of greenhouses planted along the hillsides of the valley; exotic flowers grown here are exported worldwide.

As it does in Ventimiglia, the Roya divides the new city from the medieval town on the hill. Cross the stunning Roman footbridge, turn right, and walk along the river to reach the Easter egg-colored **Rococo cathedral, San Antonio Abate.** On the left, take any one of the snarled, narrow cobblestone streets uphill to the **Castello dei Doria.** Here breezes swirl through the ruins, water trickles over rocks in a stream below, and a roguish rooster occasions to upset the stillness. (☎0184 20 64 19. Open Sa-Su 10am-5pm. €3 for entrance and guided tour.)

Chances are when you come back down you'll be up for a sampling of Dolceacqua's tastiest pizza at **Pizzeria La Rampa ❸,** V. Barberis Colomba, 11, on the left side of P. Garibaldi in the new town. (☎0184 20 61 98. Open Tu-Su 7pm-midnight.) Then have a glass of Rossese, Dolceacqua's infamous "sweet water," made for over a century at the Arcagne Vineyards, high above the new part of town. If you're interested in staying longer than a day, there are no hotels in Dolceaquea, but a 5min. bus ride to the outskirts of **Isolabona** brings you to **Albergo Da Adolfo ❸.** (☎0184 20 81 11. Reception Tu-F 7am-9pm, Sa-Su 7am-1pm. Singles with bath €30.99.) Try the **IAT tourist office** in P. Garibaldi (☎0184 20 66 66; open Sa-Su 10am-1pm and 3-6pm) for information on **Ferragosto,** which fills the piazza with swirling regional *balletti,* traditional costumes, and mouth-watering pastries in August.

PIEDMONT (PIEMONTE)

More than just the source of the Po River, Piedmont has long been a fountainhead of nobility and fine food and wine. The region falls into three zones: the **Alpine,** the **Pianura,** and the **Colline.** The Alpine, with the peaks of Monviso and Gran Paradiso, contains ski resorts and a national park that spills into Valle d'Aosta. The Pianura includes Turin, the vineyards of Asti, and the beginning of the Po valley. The Colline is dotted with many of the region's isolated castles.

Piedmont's political history is tumultuous. Obscure during the Roman era, the region rose to prominence in 1861 when the Savoys, having dominated the region since the 11th century, selected Turin as capital of their re-united Italy. Though the capital relocated four years later, Piedmont remained a hive of political activity, home to both the latter-day monarchists and the Red Brigades.

Today, the *Piedmontese* show a more languid side, favoring gentle strolls through the countryside and indulging the palate. Although most *Piedmontese* grudgingly accept their place after Bologna and Emilia-Romagna as culinary capital of Italy, they nonetheless insist on the superiority of their wine (in Italy and thus internationally) and scoff at such pretenders to the throne as Tuscany. The region's fine wines complement local specialties *agnololotti* and *bolliti* (boiled

NORTHWEST ITALY

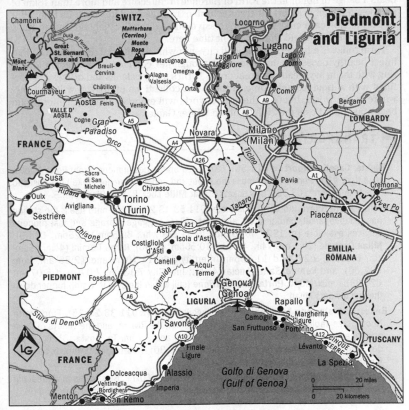

Piedmont and Liguria

HIGHLIGHTS OF PIEDMONT

AUTHENTICATE Christianity's most famous relic, the **Holy Shroud of Turin** (p. 195).

SIP fine regional wines **Freşa** and **Barolo** and feel the zing of the Alpine herbs in vermouths **Carpano** and **Martini.**

GAPE at **Asti's** dazzling **Gothic churches** (p. 200).

CLUB all night at the **Murazzi** (p. 199) in **Turin**'s underground scene.

---

meats). No meal is complete without an aperitif; it was here that Bendedetto Carpano invented Vermouth (the main ingredient in the Martini) in 1786. No matter what political intrigues come the *Piedmontesi* way, excellent cuisine and fine wines ensure they will be shaken and never stirred.

TURIN (TORINO) ☎011

Turin's status as the fourth-largest city in Italy does not do justice to its once prominent position on the Italian political landscape. It was here that Vittorio Emanuele II and Camillo Cavour forged a nation, and it was here that the Red Brigades threatened to tear it apart again. The city that sparked the Risorgimento bears a badge of honor in the form of Baroque architecture and more than 18km of arcades in the city center. Its architectural extravagance dates from its brief stint as Italy's showcase city, when progressive-minded intellectuals on tour in Italy, including Nietzsche and Dumas, spent time here.

Turin today is a modern, well-oiled city into which industrial titans such as Fiat inject healthy doses of employment. Although her corridors of power no longer ring with the heavy tread of bureaucrats, Turin's many palaces and offices are now filled with antiquities and some of the finest collections of art you will find anywhere in the world. In 2006, the whole world will embrace the city's energy and beauty as Turin hosts the 20th Olympic Winter Games.

▆ TRANSPORTATION

Flights: Caselle Airport (☎011 567 6361). European destinations. From Porta Nuova, take tram #1 to Porta Susa. Across the street and under the arcade, take blue buses to "Castelle Airport" (€3.36). Buy tickets at **Bar Mille Luci**, P. XVIII Dicembre, 5.

Trains: Porta Nuova, on C. V. Emanuele (011 53 13 27). A city onto itself, the station has a supermarket, barber shop, and **post office. Luggage storage** and lost property services available (p. 192). To: **Genoa** (2hr., every hr., 6:25am-10:25pm, €7.90); **Milan** Centrale (2hr., every hr., 4:50am-10:50pm, €7.90); **Rome** Termini (4½hr.; Eurostar 6:15am, 9:27, and 11:30pm; InterCityNight 11:10pm and 12:55 am; from €32.60); and **Venice** Santa Lucia (4½hr.; InterCity 7:13am, 2:07, and 5:07pm; €27.68). AmEx/MC/V. **Porta Susa Stazione** (still within the city) is 1 stop further down the line towards Milan.

Buses: Autostazione Terminal Bus, C. Inghilterra, 3 (☎011 33 25 25). From Porta Nuova, take cable car #9 or 15. Serves ski resorts, the Riviera, and the valleys of Susa and Pinerolo. Ticket office open daily 7am-noon and 3-7pm. To: **Aosta** (3½hr., 6 per day, €6.28); **Chamonix, FA** (4hr., 1 per day, €8.30); **Courmayeur** (4hr., 6 per day, €7.49); and **Milan** (2hr., every hr., €5.68).

Public Transportation: City buses and **cable cars** cost €0.77. Buy tickets at a *tabacchi* before boarding. The system is easy to navigate. Buses run daily 5am-1am.

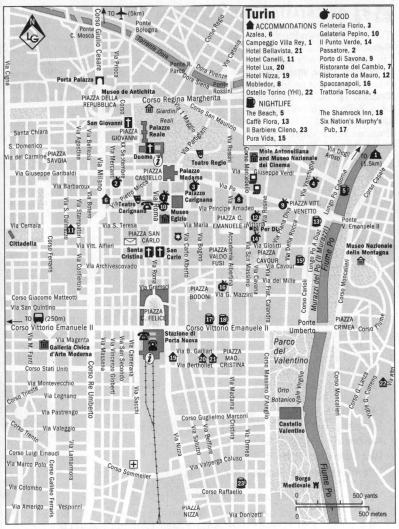

Turin 🍎 FOOD

🏠 ACCOMMODATIONS
Azalea, **6**
Campeggio Villa Rey, **1**
Hotel Bellavista, **21**
Hotel Canelli, **11**
Hotel Lux, **20**
Hotel Nizza, **19**
Mobledor, **8**
Ostello Torino (YHI), **22**

Gelateria Fiorio, **3**
Gelateria Pepino, **10**
Il Punto Verde, **14**
Passatore, **2**
Porto di Savona, **9**
Ristorante del Cambio, **7**
Ristorante da Mauro, **12**
Spaccanapoli, **16**
Trattoria Toscana, **4**

🎵 NIGHTLIFE
The Beach, **5**
Caffè Flora, **13**
Il Barbiere Cileno, **23**
Pura Vida, **15**

The Shamrock Inn, **18**
Six Nation's Murphy's
Pub, **17**

NORTHWEST ITALY

Taxis: ☎011 57 37, 011 57 30, or 011 33 99.

Bike Rental: Parco Valentino Noleggio Biciclette (☎347 413 4728 or 339 582 9332), one of many city-run bike rentals in parks, is on V. Ceppi in Parco Valentino. Walk east (heading toward the Po River) down C. V. Emanuele; just before the Ponte Umberto I Bridge, make a right. €3.61 per 12hr., €5.16 per 24hr. Open Tu-Su 9am-12:30pm and 2:30-7pm.

Car Rental: Maggiore (011 650 3013), in the Porta Nuova Station, on the right hand side by the platforms. From €78 per day (100km). Call ahead. Open M-F 8am-12pm and 3-6pm, Sa 8am-noon.

⊞ 🛈 ORIENTATION AND PRACTICAL INFORMATION

Turin lies in the Po River valley, flanked by the Alps on three sides. **Stazione Porta Nuova,** in the heart of the city, is the usual place of arrival. The city itself is an Italian rarity: its streets meet at right angles, making it easy to navigate either by bus or on foot. **Corso Vittorio Emanuele II** runs past the station to the river. **Via Roma,** which houses the principal sights, runs north through **Piazza San Carlo** and **Piazza Castello.** The other two main streets, **Via Po** and **Via Garibaldi,** extend from P. Castello. V. Po continues diagonally through **Piazza Vittorio Veneto** (the university center) to the river. V. Garibaldi stretches to **Piazza Statuto** and **Stazione Porta Susa.** Stazione Porta Nuova, Stazione Porta Susa, and Piazza della Repubblica are **dangerous areas;** don't walk alone.

Tourist Office: ATL, P. Castello, 161 (☎011 53 51 81 or 53 59 01; www.turismotorino.org), under the arcade on the left of the piazza as you face Palazzo Reale (a large white "i" on a blue post marks where to enter for info). English, German, French, and Spanish spoken. Excellent map of Turin with street index. Info regarding museums and historic cafes. Ask about the daily sightseeing tram and tour bus routes (M, W-Su 2:30pm, €7). **Info booth** at Porta Nuova train station (☎011 53 13 27), opposite platform 17. Both open M-Sa 9:30am-7pm, Su 9:30am-3:30pm.

Currency Exchange: The convenient exchange office with a big "change" sign in the Porta Nuova Station offers a decent rate. Open daily 7:30am-7:35pm. MC/V. Otherwise try the **ATM** or the APT office or the **banks** along V. Roma and V. Alfieri (generally open M-F 8:20am-1:20pm and 2:20-4:20pm).

Luggage Storage: €2.58 per 12hr. in both **Porta Nuova Train Station** (open daily 4:30am-2:30am) and **Porta Susa Train Station** (open daily 7am-11pm).

English-Language Bookstore: Libreria Internazionale Luxembourg, V. Accademia delle Scienze, 3 (☎011 561 3896; fax 54 03 70), across from P. Carignano. English-speaking staff of this 3-floor bookstore can help you find English, French, German, and Spanish books, newspapers, and magazines. Open M-Sa 8am-7:30pm. MC/V.

Laundromat: Lavanderia Vizzini, V. S. Secondo, 1F (☎011 54 58 82). When facing Stazione P. Nuova, walk 2 blocks to the right to V. S. Secondo. Wash and dry €7.75 per 4kg. Open M-F 8:30am-1pm and 3:30-7:30pm.

Emergency: ☎112 or 113. **Ambulance:** ☎118. **Police:** ☎112.

Red Cross: ☎011 28 03 33.

First Aid: ☎011 508 0370.

Late-Night Pharmacy: Farmacia Boniscontro, C. V. Emanuele, 66 (☎011 54 12 71 or 53 82 71). When facing Stazione P. Nuova, walk 3 blocks to the right. Schedule of other pharmacies' hours on the door. Open 3pm-12:30am.

Hospital: San Giovanni Battista, commonly known as Molinette, at C. Bramante, 88 (☎011 633 1633). **Mauriziano Umberto,** C. Turati, 62 (☎011 508 0111).

Internet Access:

Università degli Studi di Torino Infopoint, V. Po 29 (☎011 670 3020 or 011 670 3021). From P. V. Veneto (on the banks of the R. Po by I Murazzi), head up the right hand side of the V. Po, which runs perpendicular to the river. 30min. Internet access free. Open 9am-6:50pm.

1pc4you, V. Verdi 20G (☎011 83 59 08), just around the corner from the Mole. The biggest Internet cafe in northern Italy; 72 top-of-the-line machines. Rates start at €2 per hour. Open M-F 9am-10pm, Sa-Su noon-10pm.

Telecom Italia Internet corners, at V. Roma 18, just off P. Castello, and 1 inside the Porta Nuova station on the left hand side near the main exit. Both filled with phone-card based web stations and phones. €0.10 per 70sec. Open 8am-10pm.

Post Office: V. Alfieri, 10 (☎011 53 58 94 or 562 8100), off P. S. Carlo. Facing north (toward P. Reale), head left. Two blocks down on the right. Fax and telegram service. Open M-F 8:15am-7:20pm, Sa 8:15am-1pm, last day of the month 8:15am-noon. *Fermo Posta* open M-Sa 9am-noon and 3-7pm.
Postal Code: 10100.

✂ ACCOMMODATIONS & CAMPING

Despite being relatively under-touristed, Turin's accommodations are by no means cheap. While some of the more reasonably priced establishments are clustered around the P. Nuova station, along with some of Italy's finest pick-pockets and a host of other unsavory characters, there are many reasonably priced rooms in the heart of the older (and safer) part of town.

Ostello Torino (YHI), V. Alby, 1 (☎011 660 2939; fax 660 4445; hostelto@tin.it). Take bus #52 from Stazione Porto Nuova (bus #64 on Su). Get off the bus just after you cross the Po River (at P. Crimea, which has a tall sandstone obelisk at its center). Cross the piazza and turn right onto V. Crimea. When you reach C. Lanza, you should see an Ostello sign at the corner. Follow the signs, which lead you left to V. Gatti, and then a 200m climb up a winding road. The hostel, behind a large row of shrubs, offers an opportunity to live among the posh villas in the hills at a considerable discount. A clean and well-run hostel with beautiful views. 76 beds and TV room. Dinner at 8pm (book before 7pm, €8). Breakfast (7:30am-9am) included. Lockers (€10 deposit.) Sheets included. Laundry (wash and dry) with €4 tokens available at reception. Detergent €0.50. Reception 7-10:30am and 3:30-11:30pm. Curfew 11:30pm; ask for key if going out. Reserve ahead. Closed Dec. 20-Feb. 1. Dorms €12; doubles €13, with bath €16; triple with bath €14; quad with bath €13. Oct. 15-Apr. 15 €1 additional per day for heat. ●

Hotel Canelli, V. S. Dalmazzo 5b (011 53 71 66). When you exit Port Nuova, take bus #52 to Cernaia, turn right down V. Gianone, and then turn left onto V. S. Dalmazzo. Simple but clean rooms, all bath. Singles €22; doubles €30. ❷

Mobledor, V. Accademia Albertina, 1 (011 88 84 45). Leave Porta Nuova station by the front door and take bus 68 to Giolitti. From there, walk a block, take a left down V. S. Croce, and then turn left again down V. Accademia Albertina. All rooms with bath and TV. Singles €29.95; doubles €44.95; triples €56.80. MC/V. ❸

Azalea, V. Mercanti 16 (011 53 81 15). Exit Porta Nuova station on the right hand side and head for the yellow bus stop. From here take #58 or 72 to Garibaldi. Turn left up V. Garibaldi (away from P. Castello), and then turn left onto V. Mercanti. Immaculate rooms with bath in a very central location. Singles €31; doubles €52. DC/MC/V. ❸

Hotel Bellavista, V. B. Galliari, 15, 6th fl. (☎011 669 8139; fax 668 7989). Near the train station. As you exit Porta Nuova, turn right and then take the 2nd left on V. Galliari. Newly renovated. 46 large, airy rooms with TV and balconies with views. Breakfast €5. Singles €36, with bath €41; doubles €55/€65. ❹

Hotel Lux, V. B. Galliari, 9, 2nd fl. (☎011 65 72 57; fax 668 7482). Near the train station. From Stazione P. Nuova, walk down V. Nizza and take the 2nd left to V. Galliari. Basic, affordable rooms with TV. Singles €27; doubles with bath €42. ❸

Hotel Nizza, V. Nizza, 9, 2nd fl. (☎/fax 011 669 0516 or 650 5963). Near the station. Exit to the right from Porta Nuova on V. Nizza. Large, spacious rooms, all with bath, TV, and phone. Balcony has a bar. Breakfast included. Singles €45; doubles €70; triples €94.50; quads €113.62. AmEx/DC/MC/V. ❹

Camping: Campeggio Villa Rey, Strada Superiore Val S. Martino, 27 (☎/fax 011 819 0117). Exit from the right-hand side of Porta Nuova station with the tracks to your back. From the yellow bus stop take the #72 or #63 bus to Porta Palazzo, change to the #3, and ride it to the end of the line at Hermada. From there, it's a 1km walk uphill or a 5min. bus ride on the #54. Quiet hillside location. Bar, small supermarket, and restaurant (2-course meal €10). Laundry €3.10. €5-6 per person, €2.10-3 per 1-person tent, €4-5 per 2. Over 4-person campers €9-10 per person. Light €6. Showers €0.80. ❶

⬭ FOOD

Since the Savoy dynasty, the butchers, bakers, and confectioners of Turin have constantly sought new ways to satisfy the fickle tastes of the upper classes. The visiting gourmand should have an easy time finding a meal fit for a king. *Grissini,* crunchy bread sticks, and *bagna caôda,* a pungent mix of hot garlic and anchovies, grace restaurant tabletops. The real treat is the sweets; ever since the Savoys started taking an evening cup of *cioccolato* in 1678, Turin has grown into one of the great international centers of chocolate. Great Swiss chocolatiers picked up their techniques here. Napoleonic restrictions on buying chocolate brought Caffarel-Prochet's hazelnut chocolate substitute *gianduiotti,* now the key ingredient in a distinctly Turinese ice cream flavor known as *gianduia.* It's done best at the **Gelateria Fiorio,** V. Po, 8 (011 817 32 25), which was once frequented by so many officers and aristocrats that it became known as "the pony-tail cafe." (Open W and F-Su 8am-2am and T and Th 8am-1am.) **Gelateria Pepino,** P. Carignano, 8 (011 54 20 09), reputed favorite of the house of Savoy, claims credit for the 1880s invention of the eskimo pie; they still serve the *Pinguino.* (Open daily 8am-1am. Closed M in winter.) *Gelaterie* are everywhere in Turin; look for the *produzione propria* (made on premises) sign. For something a more substantial, try the **Di Per Di** supermarket chain. (Branches at V. Maria Vittoria, 11 and V. S. Massimo, 43.) P. della Repubblica hosts Europe's largest open-air market every morning until noon.

> **MONEY TO MANGIA.** *Piemontese* cuisine is a sophisticated blend of northern Italian peasant staples and elegant French garnishes. Butter replaces olive oil, and cheese, mushrooms, and white truffles are used more than tomatoes, peppers, or spices. *Agnolotti* (ravioli stuffed with lamb and cabbage) is the local pasta specialty, but polenta, a cornmeal porridge often topped with fontina cheese, is the more common starch. The three most outstanding (and expensive) red wines in Italy, *Barolo, Barbaresco,* and *Barbera,* are available in Turin's markets and restaurants. To sample the true flavors of *Piemontese* cuisine, be ready to pay—restaurants that specialize in regional dishes are expensive.

🍽 **Ristorante del Cambio,** P. Carignano, 2 (011 53 52 82), opposite the Palazzo Carignano. Founded in 1757, this restaurant once wined and dined Cavour. The distinctly *Piedmontese* menu changes 4 times a year in tune with the seasons. The *menù di tradizione* (€60 for a minimum of 2) includes 5 beautifully interlaced courses and an invitation to the bar for one of del Cambio's signature cigars and a dram of their private stock. *Primi €13-16, secondi €20-42.* Cover €5. Service 15%. Open M-Sa 12:30-2:30pm and 8-10:30pm. AmEx/DC/MC/V. ❺

🍽 **Ristorante da Mauro,** V. M. Vittoria, 21 (011 817 06 04). After 40 years in the same location, Signore Mauro is known for his exquisite and affordable Tuscan and Piedmontese cuisine, with a following that includes soccer players Del Piero and Galante. *Bue del piemonte ai ferri* (€9.30) and *castellana al prosciutto* (€7.50) are what you'd call, er, a scoooore. *Primi €6.20, secondi €5-13.* Open Tu-Su noon-2pm and 7:30-10pm. ❸

Passatore, V. Barbaroux, 10 (011 55 88 18). Situated just off P. Castello. Serves up cheap yet filling Emilia-Romagna specialty *piadina* (€2.10-3.90). A tortilla-like shell is heaped with ingredients from *prosciutto crudo* to Nutella. Open M-Sa 11am-7:30pm. ❶

Brek, Italy's line of refined fast-food Joints, offers extensive variety and reasonable prices. *Primi* from €3.36, *secondi* from €4.65. Open M-Su 11:30am-3pm and 6:30-10:30pm. AmEx/DC/MC/V. Branches at P. Carlo Felice, 22 (☎011 53 45 56) off V. Roma; off P. Solferino at V. S. Teresa, 23 (☎011 54 54 24; open until 11pm); and at C. Comm. "Le Gru" Grugliasco (☎011 70 72 58). ❶

Porto di Savona, P. V. Veneto, 2 (☎011 817 3500). A Turinese institution. Lunch-time *monopiatti* (large platters of pasta, salad, dessert, and coffee; €8-20.50) are a great deal. Best bets are *gnocchi al gorgonzola* and *fusilli alla diavola* (a spicy delight made with tomato, pesto, and cream sauce), both €5.50. Huge portions. *Primi* from €5.50, *secondi* from €7.50. Open Tu 7:30-10:30pm, W-Su 12:30-2:30pm and 7:30-10:30pm. Closed 1st 2 weeks of Aug. MC/V. ❸

Spaccanapoli, V. Mazzini, 19 (☎011 812 6694). V. Mazzini has the best pizza joints in town, and this is the cream of the crop. Be sure to try the Kraft (€5.80), topped with buffalo mozzarella, bacon, and gorgonzola. Pizza €4-11.50, *primi* €5.30-6.30, *secondi* €9.50-15. Cover €2. Open M, W-Sa noon-2pm and 7pm-1am. AmEx/DC/MC/V. ❸

Il Punto Verde, V. S. Massimo, 17 (☎011 88 55 43), off V. Po near P. C. Emanuele II. California juice bar and traditional Italian *trattoria* had a baby and named it Punto. Vegetarian dishes at prices that attract a large and trendy crowd. *Primi* €4.50-7, *secondi* €5.50-8.50, giant *monopiatti* €11.50. Cover €1.50. Open M-F noon-2:30pm and 7-10:30pm, Sa 7-10:30pm. Closed Aug. MC/V. ❸

Trattoria Toscana, V. Vanchiglia, 2 (☎011 812 2914), off P. V. Veneto near the university. Hearty, unpretentious fare. Try the *bistecca di cinghiale* (wild boar steak; €5.68). Open Sept.-July W-Su noon-2pm and 7-10pm, M noon-2pm. DC/MC/V.

👁 SIGHTS

In addition to the second finest museum collection of Egyptian antiquities outside of Cairo, the visitor to Turin can look forward to excellent exhibitions covering everything from cinema to modern art. Checking out all the sights can be costly; the **Turin Card** (€14), good for 48hr. of admission to Turin's 82 museums, plus public transport, makes it more affordable.

CATTEDRALE DI SAN GIOVANNI. A Renaissance cathedral dedicated to John the Baptist, this house of worship is best known for its enigmatic Christian relic, the ▨**Holy Shroud of Turin,** transferred to Turin from Chambéry, France in 1578. The shroud, 3 by 14ft., now rests in a covered glass and aluminium case inside the Cappella della Santa Sindone to the left of the altar. Above it hangs a 3m photograph of the shroud which, unless you're the pope, is as close as you'll get to the real thing. Two lateral figures are visible, head to head; the left is the top of the body (with face and arms clearly distinguishable), and the right is the back of the body.

SHROUD OF MYSTERY. The Holy Shroud of Turin, preserved in the Basilica di S. Giovanni Battista since 1578, is called a hoax by some and a miracle by others. The piece of linen was supposedly wrapped around Jesus's body in preparation for burial. Radiocarbon dating suggests the piece is from the 12th century AD. Visible on the cloth are outflows of blood: around the head (from the Crown of Thorns?), all over the body (from scourging?), and most importantly, around the wrists and feet (where the body was nailed to the cross?). Scientists agree that the shroud was wrapped around the body of a 5'7" man who died by crucifixion, but whether it was the body of Jesus remains a mystery. For Christian believers, however, the importance of this relic is best summed up by Pope Paul VI's words: "The Shroud is a document of Christ's love written in characters of blood."

THE LOCAL STORY

UNREAL RELICS?

Dr. Luigi Garlaschelli is an organic chemist at the University of Pavia who investigates the authenticity of religious blood relics in his spare time.

Q: Why are relics everywhere in Italy?

A: In the Middle Ages, it was believed that they would protect the city from its enemies. [Relics include] the last breath of St. Joseph, the feather of the Archangel Michael, the milk of the Virgin Mary, and the fingernails and blood of Christ.

Q: What was your first project?

A: My first work was on the blood of St. Januarius, which is contained in a small vial kept in the duomo in Naples. St. Januarius was beheaded in 305 AD. The relic only appeared in the Middle Ages, 1000 years later, contemporary to the appearance of the shroud of Turin. Normally blood taken from a living body will clot only once; the "miracle" of this blood is that it turns from solid to liquid and back again twice a year during religious ceremonies.

Q: How does that work?

A: Well, using only ferric chloride (an iron salt), which exists naturally near active volcanoes (like Vesuvius, near Naples, active at the time of the discovery of the blood), calcium carbonate (for example, crushed eggshells), kitchen salt, and techniques available in the Middle Ages, we were able to make a substance of the same color and properties as the reputed blood of St. Januarius. The matter would be closed were we to open the vial and take a sample. But, of course, the vial is sealed. *(See http://chifis.unipv.it/garlaschelli for more information on Dr. Garlaschelli's research.)*

Reputed to be Christ's burial shroud, it was carbon-dated to early this millennium and now represents one of the clearest confrontations between science and faith. *(Behind Palazzo Reale where V. XX Settembre crosses P. S. Giovanni. ☎011 436 1540. Open daily 7am-12:30pm and 3-7pm. Free.)*

■ **MUSEO EGIZIO & GALLERIA SABAUDA.** The **Palazzo dell'Accademia delle Scienze** houses two of Turin's best museums. Crammed onto two floors is the Museo Egizio, with the second-largest collection of Egyptian artifacts in any museum outside of Cairo. The collection includes several copies of the Egyptian Book of the Dead and the intact sarcophagus of Vizier Ghemenef-Har-Bak, which stands out among the large sculptures and architectural fragments on the ground floor. Upstairs lies the fascinating, well-furnished tomb of 14th-century BC architect Kha and his wife, one of the few tombs spared by grave-robbers. On the first floor, the body of the 6th-century BC Egyptian courtier Rei Harteb lies about 4ft. in the air, with skin, including eyelids, ears, and nose, intact. Even his original teeth remain in place after 27 centuries. *(V. Accademia delle Scienze, 6, 2 blocks from P. Castello. ☎011 561 7776; fax 53 46 23. Open Tu-F, Su 8:30am-7:30pm, Sa 8:30am-11pm. €6.50, ages 18-25 €3, under 18 or over 65 free.)* The 3rd and 4th floors hold the **Galleria Sabauda,** which houses art collections from Palazzo Reale and Palazzo Carignano in Turin and Palazzo Durazzo in Genoa. The gallery is renowned for its Flemish and Dutch paintings, including van Eyck's *St. Francis Receiving the Stigmata,* Memling's *Passion,* van Dyck's *Children of Charles I of England,* and Rembrandt's *Old Man Sleeping.* The Sabauda is also home to several Mannerist and Baroque paintings, including a Poussin, several Strozzis, and Volture's *Decapitation of John the Baptist.* *(☎011 54 74 40. Hours same as Egyptian Museum. €4, ages 18-25 €2, under 18 or over 65 free. Combined ticket for both museums €8. Both covered by Turin card.)*

■ **MOLE ANTONELLIANA.** Begun as a synagogue in 1863, the Mole ended a Victorian eccentricity. It was only intended to be 47m, but by the time it was inaugurated in 1908, the Mole had reached a towering 167m. The largest structure in the world built with traditional masonry, the Mole dominates Turin's skyline. The glass elevator that runs through the middle of the building will take you as far as the observation deck, where you can enjoy a panoramic view. The Mole now boasts the **Museo Nazionale del Cinema,** which catalogues the origins and development of cinema. Highlights include several 19th-century shorts by Thomas Edison and the very bizarre phenakistiscope. In the open space at the center of the museum is a series of exhibitions dedicated to the artistic development of cinema. A wide range of movies, from *Robocop* to *JFK*, have been dubbed into Italian and are shown in idiosyncratic settings—a 1960s living room, a neolithic cave, and a giant fridge with a man holding a potted plant standing on top—that bear no apparent correlation to the clips being shown. You haven't lived until you've heard Arnold Schwarzenegger say "*Ritornerò*." *(A few blocks east of P. Castello. V. Montebello, 20. ☎ 011 815 4230. Museum €5.20, elevator €3.62, combined ticket €6.80. Both covered by Turin card. Open Tu-F and Su 10am-8pm and Sa 10am-11pm.)*

PALAZZO CARIGNANO. One of Guarini's grandiose Baroque palaces, the *palazzo* that housed the Princess of Savoy and the first Italian parliament, was built in 1679. The elegant and ornate building contains the only museum devoted entirely to Italian national history, the **Museo Nazionale del Risorgimento Italiano,** commemorating the unification of Italy (1706-1946). Non-Italian speakers will have a difficult time sorting through stacks of documents and other historical paraphernalia. *(Enter from P. Carlo Alberto on the other side of the palazzo opposite the Biblioteca Nazionale. V. Accademia delle Scienze, 5. ☎ 011 562 3719. Open Tu-Su 9am-7pm. Free guided tour Su 10-11:30am. €4.25, students €2.50, under 10 or over 65 free.)*

TEATRO CARIGNANO. Just across from the Palazzo is a theater that the *Turinesi* claim rivals Milan's **La Scala** (p. 102). As La Scala is currently closed, the Teatro may just accomplish this. The gleaming gold and rose Baroque music hall was manicured with attention to every detail and is graced with a Neoclassical ceiling fresco. *(☎ 011 54 70 54. No set hours. Call ahead. Free.)*

GALLERIA CIVICA D'ARTE MODERNA E CONTEMPORANEA. This premier modern and contemporary art museum covers Divisionism, Dadaism, and Pop Art. The museum's collection is mostly Italian, including some Modiglianis and de Chiricos, but also has Andy Warhol's gruesome *Orange Car Crash* and works by Picasso, Ernst, Leger, Chagall, Twombly, Klee, Courbet, and Renoir. *(On the corner of C. G. Ferraris, off Largo Emanuele. V. Magenta, 31. ☎ 011 562 9911; www.gam.intesa.it. Open Tu-Su 9am-7pm. €5.20, under 26 €2.80, under 10 or over 65 free. Free with the Turin Card.)*

PALAZZO REALE. Home to the Princes of Savoy from 1645 to 1865, the palace consists mostly of ornate apartments. Its red and gold interior houses an outstanding collection of Chinese porcelain vases. Louis le Nôtre (1697), more famous for his work on the gardens of Versailles, designed the *palazzo's* grounds. Although the city owes its glory to political rather than ecclesiastical leadership, unadulterated splendor blesses the interior of the **Chiesa di San Lorenzo,** next to the Palazzo Reale. Constructed between 1668 and 1680, it is Guarini's most unique creation, with a dynamic, swirling dome. *(In Piazzetta Reale, at the end of P. Castello. ☎ 011 436 1455. Palazzo open Tu-Su 9am-7pm. 40min. guided tours in Italian Tu-Su 9am-1pm and 2-7pm. 1st fl. €4.50, entire Palazzo €5.25; ages 18-25 €2.65; under 18 or over 65 free. Gardens open 9am-1 hr. before sunset. Church open 8am-12:30pm and 3:30-6pm. Free.)*

In the right wing of the Royal Palace lies the **Armeria Reale** (Royal Armory) of the House of Savoy, containing the world's best collection of medieval and Renaissance war tools. The Beaumont gallery, which houses most of the collection, is now closed for restoration. All that remains open is one small and moderately impressive room full of weapons and stuffed horses. *(P. Castello, 191. ☎ 011 54 38 89. Open Tu-Su 9am-7pm. €4.50, under 18 or over 65 free.)*

BASILICA DI SUPERGA. When the French attacked Turin on September 6, 1706, King Vittorio Amedeo II made a pact with the Virgin Mary to build a magnificent cathedral in her honor should the city withstand the invasion. Turin stood unconquered, and this structure was the result. The basilica stands on a 672m summit outside of Turin, described by Le Corbusier as "the most enchanting position in

NORTHWEST ITALY

the world." Indeed, it offers panoramic views of the city, the Po valley below, and the Alps rising beyond. A Neoclassical portico and high drum create a spectacular dome. *(Take tram #15 (€0.77) from V. XX Settembre to Stazione Sassi. From the station, take bus #79 or board a small cable railway for a clanking ride uphill (20min.; every hr. on the hr.; M, W, Th, F 9am-noon and 2-8pm, Tu 7pm-12am, Sa and holidays 9am-8pm; round-trip €3.10, Su and holidays €6.15.) Basilica: ☎011 898 0083. Open Apr.-Sept. 9:30am-noon and 3-6pm; Oct.-Mar. 10am-noon and 3-5pm. Free. €1.55 for tombs. Railroad and tombs free with Turin Card.)*

PARCO DEL VALENTINO. One of Italy's largest parks on the banks of the Po, Valentino's lush and romantic grounds provide haven for whispering lovers and running children. Upon entering the park from C. V. Emanuele, **Castello del Valentino** will be on the left. Once the home of the designer of the same name, and now the home of the Facoltà di Architettura. Farther south along the river, beside the calm, manicured **Giardino Roccioso**, is **Borgo e Rocca Medievale**, a "medieval" village built for the 1884 World Exposition. *(Park and castle at V. Virgilio, 107, along the Po. ☎011 817 7178. Open Aug. 15-Oct. 25. Phone reservations required for castle. Free.)*

PIAZZA SAN CARLO. Between P. Felice and P. Reale, formal Baroque grandeur takes over; the equestrian statue of Duke Emanuele Filiberto sits proudly on a horse over the crowds. In addition to the Baroque buildings, the piazza features the opulent twin churches of **Santa Cristina** and **San Carlo Borromeo**, on the right and left, respectively, upon entering the piazza from V. Roma. Santa Cristina has the more formidable statuary on its facade. *(Santa Christina open 8am-1pm and 3-8pm. San Carlo open 7am-noon and 3-7pm. Free.)*

MUSEO DELL'AUTOMOBILE. The museum documents the evolution of the automobile, exhibiting prints, drawings, leaflets, more than 150 original cars, and the first models by Ford, Benz, Peugeot, Oldsmobile, and homegrown Fiat. The focus is on Italian cars and car racing. *(Head south along V. Nizza from Stazione Porta Nuova. C. Unità d' Italia, 40. ☎011 67 76 66. Open Tu-Su 10am-7pm. €2.70. Free with Turin Card.)*

🎵 ENTERTAINMENT

For the skinny on happening spots, inquire at the tourist office for a copy of *News Spettacolo*. On Fridays, check out Turin's newspaper, *La Stampa*, which publishes *Torino Sette*, an excellent section on current cultural events. Music of all genres enlivens Turin between June and August, when the city invites international performers to the **Giorni d'Estate Festival.** For information, programs, and venues, contact the tourist office or the **Vetrina per Torino,** P. S. Carlo, 154 (☎800 01 54 75. Open M-Sa 11am-7pm.) From September 5-25, the **Settembre Musica** extravaganza features over 40 classical concerts performed throughout the city. Contact the Vetrina or the tourist office for programs (available by the beginning of July). **Cinemas** all over Turin offer the latest blockbusters, obscure art films, and even pornography. Try **Lux,** on V. Roma between P. San Carlo and P. C. Felice, on the left when facing P. Reale; **Cinema Vittoria,** on V. Antonio Gramsci where it meets V. Roma; or **Multisala Ambrosio,** to the right as you exit Porta Nuova on C. V. Emanuele. During the academic year, a number of foreign films are shown in their original languages. A list of films is in the leaflet **Arena Metropolis** at the tourist office.

🛍 SHOPPING

One of Turin's unique events is the **Gran Balon flea market,** held every other Sunday behind the Porta Palazzo. Here, junk sellers rub shoulders with treasure-hunting dealers of antiques and valuable rarities. Though clothing stores line Turin's streets, the chic, designer shops on **Via Roma** are best for window shopping. The department store **La Rinascente**, at the corner of V. Lagrange and V. Teofilo Rossi, sells traditional attire. **Musy Padre e Figli**, V. Po 1, just off the P. Castello, claims to be the world's oldest jewelry shop. Still in the Musy family today, the shop was founded in 1707 after the Musy's relocation from France. The shop maintains the same 18th-century facade and taste for silver as the day it opened. (☎011 812 5582. Open M-Th 9am-12pm and 3-5pm.)

🎵 NIGHTLIFE

Despite being the birthplace of such quality music groups as Eiffel 65, Turin will never be one of the great clubbing capitals of the world. *Torinesi* are happier just getting together with a group of friends and going out for a few drinks. Occasionally Turin does manage to attract major international acts, such as at the **Turin Extra Festival** in the second week of July. Contact Vetrina per Torino (see **Entertainment**) or picking up *News Spettacolo* at the tourist office for more information.

I MURAZZI

The center of Turin's social scene, *I Murazzi*, consists of two stretches of boardwalk, one between Ponte V. Emanuele II and Ponte Umberto and another smaller, adjacent stretch downstream from the Ponte V. Emanuele II. *Murazzi del Po* attracts everyone from yuppies to goths. Most turn up around 11pm, any and every night of the week, and spend the next 4 hours sitting outside the fairly homogeneous clubs that line the waterfront, sipping drinks at €2-4 a pop. Inside **The Beach**, in the smaller section towards the end, you'll find a "sleepy chill-out zone," deck chairs, and the best techno music anywhere along the Po. (☎011 18 20 22. €10.33 cover includes a drink. Open daily midnight-3am.)

NORTH OF I MURAZZI, LUNGO PO CADORNA

Pura Vida, C. Cairoli, 14 (☎0348 420 5231). Always packed with a university-age crowd hungry for Latin and reggae music. Feed your tummy with a *tortilla* (€2.70) or *torta de pollo* (€3.25). Open M-F, Su 10am-3am, Sa 10am-4am.

Caffè Flora, P. V. Veneto, 24 (☎011 817 15 30). A chill session—20 to 30 people hangin' in comfortable chairs. Lots of drinks (€5), but no food. Open Tu-Su 12pm-3am.

CORSO VITTORIO EMANUELE

Several excellent English and Irish pubs line C. V. Emanuele from Stazione Porta Nuova to the Po River.

Six Nations Murphy's Pub, C. V. Emanuele, 28 (☎011 88 72 55). Make a right out of Porta Nuova; it's a few blocks down on your left. Back smoking area. Pint of Murphy's €4.20. Open daily 6pm-3am.

The Shamrock Inn, C. V. Emanuele, 34 (☎011 817 49 50), further toward the river. Offers lively rumba dancing, decent sandwiches, and desserts. Several beers on tap. Nice window seat with a view of the tree-lined street. Open daily 8:30pm-3am.

ACROSS THE RIVER AND LINGOTTO

Hiroshima Mon Amour, V. Carlo Bossoli, 63 (☎011 317 6636). Take bus #1 or 34 to Lingotto Centro Fiere. The name: a reference to Resnais's 1959 film about metropolitan love. The place: almost certainly the best club in town. Excellent music, often live, creates a dancer's paradise. The genre changes nightly from reggae to rock 'n' roll, as does the cover, ranging from free to €10. Plan on taking a taxi back to the city. Open nightly 11pm until late.

Il Barbiere Cileno, V. Ormea 78 (388 200 1980). From Porta Nuova station take the #34 to Valpergo Caluso. Keep the same direction until you reach the Angolo Corso Raffaello and then turn left; it branches off from there. Very young, hip crowd and an excellent place to hang out. Music varies from house to Latin. Try the *papas alla huangaina* (€3.10). Open M-Sa 8:30pm-3:30am and Su 11:30pm-3:30am.

AEIOU, V. Spanzotti 24 (347 925 7826). From Porta Nuova take the #15 bus towards Brissogne and get off at S. Paolo. Live music and an excellent bar; one of Turin's better night spots. Cuba Day on Su features the finest in Latin flavah. Open M-Su 8pm-3am.

☂ OLYMPICS

In 2006, Turin will be in the global spotlight when it hosts the XX Olympic Winter Games. The games will mark the first Winter Olympics in Italy since the 1956 Winter Olympics in Cortina d'Ampezzo. Turin's bid-winning presentation to the International Olympic Committee focused on their blend of Alpine ski lodge and thriving metropolis. To join the winter fun, hit the slopes at **Alagna Valsesia, Macugnaga,** or **Sestriere.** For more information about the Games, contact the **Torino Organizing Committee** at V. Nizza, 262 (☎ 011 631 0511; www.torino2006.it.).

◢ DAYTRIP FROM TURIN: ▨ SACRA DI SAN MICHELE

Be sure to call ahead and make a reservation for your visit; the monastery is open sporadic hours. To reach the monastery from Turin, take a train to Avigliana (15 per day, €1.76). Without a car, getting to the monastery is difficult, as there are no public buses. The 14km day's hike from Avigliana (around 3hr.) will make you feel like a proud pilgrim; if you're not looking to boast, a taxi cab (☎ 011 93 02 18) ride can be arranged. Expect to pay around €30; decide upon the rate with the driver before you take the ride. Otherwise, from the station in Avigliana, turn left and follow the main road, C. Laghi, through town and around Lago Grande for about 30min. This part runs along the shoulder of a busy road and is not very pleasant. Turn right on the green street Sacra di S. Michele, which winds its way slowly up the mountain. The way is clearly marked. Wear sturdy shoes, and bring plenty of water. For a map of the arduous trek, head to Avigliana's Informazione Turistico, P. del Popolo, 2, a 5-10min. walk straight ahead from the station. (☎ 011 932 8650. Open M-F 9am-noon and 3-6pm.) Restaurants cluster halfway up the hill and before the end of the climb. (Monastery ☎ 011 93 91 30. Open M-F 9am-noon and 3-6pm. Su 9am-1pm and 3pm-5pm. Adults €3.50, children €2.)

On a bluff 1000m above the town of Avigliana, the massive stone monastery of Sacra di San Michele seems to grow out of the very rock on which it was built. *The Name of the Rose* was not filmed here but probably should have been. Umberto Eco based the plot of his book on the monastery, and even in the summer, there is a haunting cinematic quality about the place. Founded in 1000 by an Alevernian pilgrim named Ugo di Montboissier, the monastery perches atop Mt. Pirchiriano (877m) with sweeping and spectacular views in all directions. Upon entering the structure, the impressive **Stairway of the Dead,** an immense set of steps helping to buttress the building, leads outside to the beautifully carved wooden doors that depict the arms of St. Michael with the Serpent of Eden. The shrine of St. Michael is down the small steps in the middle of the nave, where there are three tiny chapels. In 966, St. John Vincent built the largest, with a back wall of solid rock; today, it holds the tombs of medieval members of the Savoy family. Although the building is undergoing restoration, it remains open to the public.

ASTI ☎ 0141

Asti sparkles, just like its popular, intoxicating progeny. Asti has bustled with activity since Roman times, when it bore the name "Hasta." Few ancient buildings remain, though many structures eked through the turbulent times under Savoy rulership (1300-1700), when the town was repeatedly sacked and burned during struggles with local princes. The medieval city is known for locally born 18th-century poet Vittorio Alfieri, but is notorious more for the sparkling wines that bear its name. Limestone-rich soils on gentle south-facing slopes produce grapes destined for the bottles of *Barolo*, *Barbera*, and *Asti Spumanti* that line the cellars of wine connoisseurs world-wide.

TRANSPORTATION

Trains: P. Marconi, where V. Cavour meets C. L. Einaudi. Info open M-F 6am-12:40pm and 1:10-7:45pm. To: **Alessandria** (30min., every hr., 5:22am-7:50pm, €2.25); **Milan** Stazione Centrale (1½hr., 6:48am, €6.82); and **Turin** P. Nuova (1hr., 2 per hr., 4:30am-11:14pm, €3.10).

Buses: P. Medaglie d'Oro, across from the train station. Tickets (€1.55-2.07) on the bus. To: **Canelli** (every 1½ hr., 7:10am-6:40pm); **Castagnole** (every 2hr., 7:20am-6:40pm); **Costigliole** (7:15, 11am, and 12:50pm); and **Isola d'Asti** (6 per day, 10am-6:50pm).

Taxis: In P. Alfieri (☎0141 53 26 05) or at the station in P. Marconi (☎0141 59 27 22).

ORIENTATION AND PRACTICAL INFORMATION

The center of town lies in the triangular **Piazza Vittorio Alfieri**. Most historical sights are slightly to the left of the piazza when facing the statue, down **Corso V. Alfieri**.

Tourist Office: P. Alfieri, 29 (☎0141 53 03 57; fax 53 82 00). Assists in finding (but not reserving) accommodations, including *agriturismo* options. Info on daytrips to wineries and castles. Pick up indispensable map and free *Guide to Asti and its Province*. English, French, and German. Open M-Sa 9am-1pm and 2:30-6:30pm, Su 10am-1pm.

Currency Exchange: Cassa di Risparmio di Asti, on the corner of P. 1 Maggio and V. M. Rainero. Open M-F 8:20am-1:20pm and 2:30-3:50pm, Sa 8:20-11:20am. Also try the post office. 24hr. **ATMs** in the train station and along V. Dante.

Emergency: ☎113.

Police: C. XXV Aprile, 19 (☎0141 41 81 11).

Red Cross Ambulance: ☎0141 41 77 41.

Hospital: Ospedale Civile, V. Botallo, 4 (☎0141 39 21 11).

Internet Access: Ufficio Relazioni il Pubblico, P. Alfieri 34, (☎014 43 32 25), at the end of the building near tourist office. 3 computer terminals. Free. Open 8am-5:30pm.

Post Office: C. Dante, 55 (☎0141 35 72 51), off P. Alfieri. Open M-F 8:30am-5:30pm, Sa 8:15am-noon.

Postal Code: 14100.

ACCOMMODATIONS & CAMPING

Hotel Cavour, P. Marconi, 18 (☎/fax 0141 53 02 22). As you exit the train station, it's across the piazza and slightly to your left. Friendly management. Modern, immaculate rooms with TV, bath, and phone. Reception daily 6am-1am. Closed Aug. Singles €38.45; doubles €55.27. AmEx/DC/MC/V. ❹

Hotel Genova, C. Alessandria, 26 (☎0141 59 31 97). From P. Alfieri, take C. V. Alfieri until it turns into C. Alexandria; it is on your left. All rooms have TV and sink in this simple but reasonably priced hotel. Breakfast €1.80-6.20. Reception open until midnight. Singles €31, with bath €39; doubles €47/€57. DC/MC/V. ❸

Campeggio Umberto Cagni, V. Valmanera, 152 (☎0141 27 12 38). From P. Alfieri, turn onto V. Aro, which becomes C. Volta, and then take a left onto V. Valmanera. The camp is popular with Italian vacationers, and features playground, restaurant, and bar. Electricity €2. Open Apr.-Sept. €3.50 per person, €4-4.50 per tent. Showers free. ❶

🍴 FOOD

Astigiano cuisine is known for its simplicity, using only a few crucial ingredients and pungent cheeses like gorgonzola to create culinary masterpieces. Classic *Piemontese* dishes are composed of rabbit and boar, and gently flavored with truffles and mountain herbs. The extensive fruit and vegetable **market** at Campo del Palio provides great snacks. (Open W and Sa 7:30am-1pm.) The P. Alfieri market sells clothes, shoes, bags, and other durable goods. (Same hours as Campo del Palio.) At **Mercato Coperto Alimentari**, in P. della Libertà between P. Alfieri and Campo del Palio, separate kiosks vend fresh meats, fruits, and vegetables. (Open M-W and F 8am-1pm and 3:30-7:30pm, Sa 8am-7:30pm.) The **Super Gulliver Market**, V. Cavour, 77, could feed an army of Lilliputians; despite its "super" name, it is tiny. (Open M-W and F-Sa 8am-7:30pm, Th 8:30am-1pm.)

🦞 **Ristorante Aldo di Castiglione**, V. Giobert, 8 (☎0141 35 49 05). From P. Alfieri, turn left onto C. V. Alfieri, then left onto V. Giobert. Aldo has been dazzling the residents of Castiglione with his inventive *Piedmontese* cuisine for the last 30 years. Now relocated, he promises to wow Asti residents and visitors. A 3-course dinner will cost €20-€30. Open F-W noon-2:30pm and 7:30-10pm. DC/MC/V. ❹

L'Altra Campana, V. Q. Sella, 2 (☎0141 43 70 83). From P. Marconi, take V. Cavour to its end, then turn left and head through the arch. Exceptional selection of local cheeses like *robbiola*, *toma*, and gorgonzola. *Agnolotti*, boar, and truffles are all done well here. *Primi* €6.20-8, *secondi* €6.50-8. Open W-M noon-3pm and 7-11pm. Their *enoteca* (wine store) across the street keeps the same hours. DC/MC/V. ❸

L'Angolo del Beato, V. Guttari, 12 (☎0141 53 16 68). From P. Marconi, take V. Cavour; V. Guttari will be on your left. Exceptional fresh pasta and other regional specialties guarantee this restaurant a place in Asti's line-up of fine restaurants. The *agnolotti* should be complemented with a glass of Barbera or Barolo. *Primi* €8, *secondi* €13. Open M-Sa 12:15-2:15pm and 7-10:30pm. AmEx/DC/MC/V. ❸

Pizzeria Francese, V. dei Cappelli, 15 (☎0141 59 87 11). From P. Alfieri, turn left onto V. Garibaldi, and then cross P. S. Secondo to V. dei Cappelli. Signore Francese is rather particular about his pizza, so much so that he's written a 692-page guide to the best *pizzerie* in Italy. His own pies are true taste sensations, with light crusts, flavorful marinara, and rich buffalo mozzarella. Pizza €4.91-7.23, *primi* €6.20, *secondi* €7.75. Open Th-Tu noon-3pm and 6pm-2am. DC/MC/V. ❷

🎟 SIGHTS

CATTEDRALE D'ASTI. This duomo, begun in 1309, is one of Piedmont's more noteworthy Gothic cathedrals. The piazza entrance has several well-preserved statues of monks and priests. The clock tower, toward the back of the duomo, rings just before and just after the hour. A sun dial is set into the side facing the piazza, about mid-way up the tower. Throughout the 16th and 17th centuries, local artists, including native son Gandolfino d'Asti, covered every inch of the walls with frescoes; even the columns are painted to appear as if there are vines climbing up them. The remains of 11th-century mosaics blanket the floor around the altar. Three circular stained glass windows brighten the front; just to your right, a life-size terracotta scene depicts the death of Jesus. (*In P. Cattedrale. Walk down C. Alfieri and turn right on V. Mazzini. Open daily 7am-12:30pm and 3-7pm.*)

CHIESA DI SAN PIETRO IN CONSAVIA. A 15th-century church with a 12th-century octagonal baptistery, this structure served as an army hospital in WW II. Romans, friars, and war casualties share burial space beneath the courtyard. On the first floor, the **Museo Paleontologico** has a minimal collection of fossils and bones from the Astiano area. On the second floor, the **Museo Archeologico** showcases 4th-century BC Greek vases and jugs. A number of Roman pieces line the halls, primarily from the Asti area and the Ligurian region. *(On the far end of C. Alfieri. Open Tu-Sa 10am-1pm and 4-7pm, Su 10am-noon. Free.)*

OTHER SIGHTS. P. S. Secondo is home to the 18th-century **Palazzo di Città** (City Hall) and the medieval **Collegiata di San Secondo.** The Romanesque tower now stands on the very spot where Secondo, Asti's patron saint, was decapitated. *(From P. Vittorio Alfieri, a short walk west on V. Garibaldi leads to the piazza.)* **Piazza Medici** boasts the 13th-century **Torre Toyana o Dell'Orologio.** At the end of C. Alfieri is Asti's oldest tower, the 16-sided **Torre Rossa** (Red Tower), where San Secondo was imprisoned before his execution. The tower, with foundations dating to the time of Augustus, adjoins the elliptical Baroque **Chiesa di Santa Caterina.** *(Directly north of P. S. Secondo, across C. Alfieri. Open daily 7:30am-noon and 3-7pm.)* The **Giardini Pubblici** (public gardens) are a pleasant place for a picnic or stroll. *(Between P. Alfieri and Campo del Palio.)*

🎵 ENTERTAINMENT

From the last week of June through the first week of July, **Asti Teatro** puts on performances of drama, music, and dance. (☎0141 39 93 41. €8-13, children under 12 €5-9. Reserve tickets and hotel room in advance.) Beginning on the second Friday in September, agricultural Asti revels in the **Douja d'Or,** a week-long fair and exposition of rare local wines, with competitions and tastings. During this week, on the second Sunday in September, is the **Paisan,** or the **Festivale delle Sagre,** with traditional costumes, parades, and feasts. On the 3rd Sunday in September, the Douja d'Or comes to a close with the **Palio di Asti.** A procession commemorating the town's liberation in 1200 is followed by bareback horse races. (☎0141 53 52 11.) On the first Sunday in July, the area's biggest **donkey race** is held 4km from Asti in the village of Quarto, ending with a town-wide *ravioli* banquet.

🏃 DAYTRIP FROM ASTI: CANELLI

Buses run to Canelli (30min., every 1½hr., 7:10am-5pm, €2.07) from the bus station in Asti. Trains also run from Asti (5:28am-7:08pm, €2.25) via Castagnole.

The sparkling *Asti Cinzano* and *Asti Spumante,* as well as the super-sweet *Moscato,* bubble forth from the countryside vineyards surrounding Asti, providing both an economic base and a source of widespread renown. Many wineries remain under family control, and a warm reception awaits visitors who take the time to explore these less touristed areas. **Casa Contratto,** V. G.B. Giuliani, 56, is a family-owned cellar dating from 1867. Tours take visitors through the entire wine-making process. The cellar, carved 32m into a hill, contains about 500,000 bottles of wine. Bottles are kept upside down in racks and are turned 90 degrees by hand daily, until the cellar master declares them to have reached maturation. Tours are in Italian, but the visuals speak for themselves. (☎0141 82 33 49. Open M-F 8am-12pm and 2-6pm. Sa-Su by appointment only. Call ahead to book a tour.)

ACQUI TERME ☎0144

Acqui Terme, like most small towns, has something bubbling beneath its placid surface. Sulfuric springs at temperatures of 75°C (167°F) gurgle just underneath the ground, attracting those in need of holistic treatment. The mineral-rich water and *fanghi* (mud baths) provide relaxation and, according to some, healing.

🖪 TRANSPORTATION AND PRACTICAL INFORMATION. From Genoa, catch a **train** (1½hr., every hr., €3.36) via **Ovada.** Acqui Terme's train station (☎0144 32 25 83) is in P. V. Veneto. Trains also run from **Asti** (1hr., 13 per day, €2.65). To reach the town center from the station, turn left on **Via Alessandria**, and continue as it becomes **Corso Vigano** and ends in **Piazza Italia**. To reach the **IAT Tourist Office**, V. Maggiorino Ferraris, 5, walk down C. Dante, turn right on C. Cavour and left on V. Ferraris. (☎0144 32 21 42; fax 32 90 54. Open in summer M 10:30am-12:30pm and 3:30-6:30pm, Tu-Sa 9:30am-12:30pm and 3:30-6:30pm, Su and holidays 9:30am-3pm. In winter M 10:30am-12:30pm, Tu-F 9am-noon and 3-6pm, Sa-Su and holidays 10am-12:30pm and 3-6pm.) For **currency exchange**, there are banks on C. Dante, including **Cassa di Risparmio di Torino**, C. Dante, 26 (☎0144 57 001). There is free **Internet access** at **Acqui Terme Biblioteca Civica**, V. Ferraris, 15, just around the corner from the tourist office. (Open M, Th 8:30am-1:30pm and 4-6pm, Tu, W, F 8:30am-1:30pm, Sa 9am-noon.) Take V. XX Settembre from P. Italia to the **post office** (☎0144 32 29 84), on V. Truco, off P. Matteotti. (Open M-F 8am-6:30pm, Sa 9am-12:30pm.) **Postal Code:** 15011.

⚏⚏ ACCOMMODATIONS AND FOOD. For a centrally located, well-staffed, and comfortable hotel, try **Albergo San Marco ❷**, V. Ghione, 5. From P. Italia, take C. Bagni about 15m and make the first right onto V. Ghione. (☎0144 32 24 56; fax 32 10 73. Closed Dec. 24-Jan., mid-July to mid-Aug. Singles €23, with bath €28; doubles with bath €44.) The **restaurant ❷** downstairs is said to have some of the best wine in town. Try the excellent *Spumone al Torrone* (€3) for dessert. (*Primi* €4-6.50, *secondi* €6.50-9.) Beyond the town center (15min. by foot), many hotels, budget and otherwise, surround the mineral baths across the river. **Albergo VIP ❹**, V. Einaudi, 15, has gloriously furnished rooms, all with bath, TV, minibar/fridge, and Internet access. From P. Italia, take C. Bagni over the river. V. Einaudi is the first left. (☎0144 35 27 23; fax 32 54 95. Singles €41.31; doubles €72.30; palatial suites with massage service €103.)

Acqui Terme offers a wide selection of excellent, well-priced restaurants. For a fine dining experience, take C. Dante (which becomes V. Don Bosco) from P. Italia until you see the white awnings of **Il Nuovo Ciarlocco ❸**, V. Don Bosco, 1. Average prices are charged for excellent food and service. The menu changes daily. (☎0144 57 720. *Primi* €6-8, *secondi* €8-18. Open Th-M noon-2pm and 7:30-10pm, Tu noon-2pm. AmEx/MC/V.) Traditional local fare like *trippa in umido* (moist tripe; €5.20) and Ligurian specialty *farinata* (€2.60) are served at local favorite **Antica Osteria di Bigat ❶**, V. Mazzini, 30/32 (☎0144 32 42 83. Open Th-Sa, M-Tu noon-2pm and 5-9pm, Su 5-9pm. DC/MC/V.) **Supermarket Di per Di**, V. Garibaldi, 50, offers a wide selection of cheap groceries. (Open W 8:30am-12:30pm, M-Tu and Th-Sa 8:30am-12:30pm and 3:45-7:45pm.)

◙ SIGHTS. Even if you're in perfect health, no trip to Acqui Terme would be complete without at least dipping your finger in the steamy **sulfuric water**. At the romantic **Piazza Bollente**, the hot water pours out of a fountain, sending up steam even in summer. Take V. Manzoni up the hill to **Castello dei Paleogi**, constructed in the 11th century, which houses the **Museo Civico Archeologico**. The museum displays a small but evocative collection of Roman tombs and mosaics. (☎0144 57 555. Open W-Sa 9:30am-12:30pm and 3:30-6:30pm, Su 3:30-6:30pm. €5, 18-25 €2, under 18 or over 65 free.) The Romanesque **duomo**, down V. Barone from the Museo Archeologico in P. Duomo, is home to Rubens's famous *Trittico (Madonna and Child)*, now locked away in the sacristy. Ask at the tourist office about viewing possibilities. (Open M-F 7am-9pm, Sa-Su 8am-noon and 6-8pm.) From the river, the four intact arches of the **Acquedotto Romano** are visible.

In the **zona bagni**, the **Reparto Regina**, V. Donati, 2, gives you a chance to soak and spend. From the city center, walk down C. Bagni over the river, and turn left onto

V. le Einaudi. The *reparto* is part of the Hotel Regina, the first hotel you'll pass on your left. Lung ventilation (€13.76) and a mud bath supreme (€34.50) are among an array of health and relaxation options. (☎0144 32 14 22. Call ahead.)

For a different kind of treatment, head to the ☒**Enoteca Regionale di Acqui Terme,** P. A. Levi, 7. From P. Italia, take C. Italia, turn left on V. Garibaldi, and take the first right into P. Levi. The cavernous winery features 230 different kinds of wine, including the sweet domestics *Dolcetto* and *Bracchetto,* realizing its slogan *dove l'aqua è salute, e il vino è allegria* ("where the water is healthy, and wine is happiness"). (☎0144 77 02 73; fax 35 01 96. Open Tu and F-Su 10am-noon and 3-6:30pm, Th 3-6:30pm. DC/MC/V.)

VALLE D'AOSTA

Italy's least populated and highest region, Valle d'Aosta is rich with valleys, pine forests, waterfalls, and international cable cars. Close to their Swiss and French neighbors, the *Valdostani* have taken on much of their continental cousins' cultural character. The Valle is a key transportation hub; Hannibal and his elephants once crossed Aosta's **St. Bernard Pass,** and today an even greater stampede of heavy goods vehicles (HGV or *TIR* in Italian) barrels through the Monte Bianco tunnel. Italian locals who display "No ai TIR!" placards and hold frequent protests believe that Aosta's new status as a trade gateway threatens to damage nature splendor and destabilize the tourist economy, which for centuries has provided most of Aosta's non-agricultural wealth. Before there were Gore-tex clad snow warriors battling the *piste* (trails) on ski and board, the wealthy and weak filled ski chalets to soak in the hot springs and Alpine air.

☒ HIKING

The scenic trails of Valle d'Aosta are a hikers' paradise. July, August, and the first week of September, when much of the snow has melted and the public buses are running on a full schedule, are the best times to hike. In April and May, thawing snow often causes avalanches. Monte Bianco and surrounding peaks may be classic climbs, but only pros should attempt to conquer them. Talk to the staff at a tourist office or Alpine information office about the difficulty and condition of hikes—they often speak English. For information on safety see **Essentials,** p. 43.

Despite these warnings, don't be scared of venturing into the Alps. Each area's tourist office offers assistance to hikers of all levels. The tourist offices in Aosta and those in the smaller valleys provide information on routes as well as lists of campgrounds, bagged lunch *(pranzo al sacco)* vendors, **rifugi alpini** (mountain huts), and **bivacchi** (public refuges)—ask for *Mountain Huts and Bivouacs in Aosta Valley.* Some mountain huts lie only a cable-car ride or 30min. walk away from roads, and many offer half-pension for around €30. Public refuges tend to be empty and free; those run by caretakers cost about €16 per night. For information, call **Società Guide,** V. Monte Emilius, 13 (☎/fax 0165 444 48), or **Club Alpino Italiano,** P. Chanoux, 15 (☎0165 409 39; fax 36 32 44; www.guidealpine.com), both in Aosta. They offer insurance and refuge discounts.

Most regional tourist offices also carry *Alte Vie* (High Roads), with maps, photographs, and helpful advice pertaining to the two serpentine mountain trails that circumvent the valley and link the region's most dramatic peaks. Long stretches of these trails require no expertise and offer adventure with panoramic views.

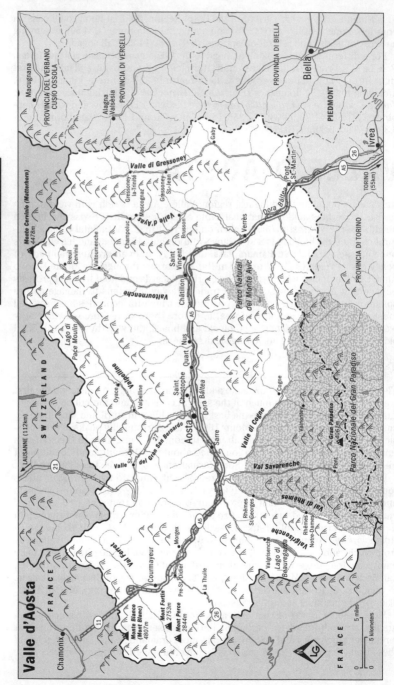

Valle d'Aosta

⚜ SKIING

Skiing Valle d'Aosta's mountains and glaciers is fantastic; unfortunately, it is not a bargain. **Settimane bianche** ("white weeks") packages for skiers are one source of discounts. For information and prices, call **Ufficio Informazioni Turistiche**, P. Chanoux, 8 (☎ 0165 23 66 27), in Aosta, and request the pamphlet *White Weeks: Aosta Valley*. Accommodations for a week in March runs €230-360 per person, with discounted fares in the early and late season. A 6-day lift pass costs about €150.

Courmayeur and **Breuil-Cervinia** are the best-known ski resorts in the 11 valleys. **Val d'Ayas** and **Val di Gressoney** offer equally challenging terrain for lower rates. **Cogne** and **Brusson**, halfway down Val d'Ayas, have cross-country skiing and less-demanding downhill trails. In Courmayeur and Breuil-Cervinia, die-hards tackle the slopes in bathing suits for extensive **summer skiing**. Arrange summer package deals through the tourist office in either Breuil-Cervinia or Courmayeur.

✎ OTHER SPORTS

A host of other sports—rock climbing, mountain biking, hang-gliding, kayaking, and rafting—will keep non-skiers' adrenaline pumping. For white water enthusiasts, the most navigable and popular rivers are the **Dora Baltea,** which runs across the valley, the **Dora di Veny,** which branches south from Courmayeur, the **Dora di Ferre,** which meanders north from Courmayeur, the **Dora di Rhêmes,** which flows through the Val di Rhêmes, and the **Grand Eyvia,** which courses through the Val di Cogne. Centro Nazionale Acque Bianche (Rafting 4810), Fenis, Vale d'Aosta, about an hour from Aosta, runs the most affordable rafting trips. (☎ 0165 76 46 46; www.rafting4810.com. 1-3hr.; €22.90-37.25 per person.) For a complete list of recreational activities, including bike rental, ask for *Attrezzature Sportive e Ricreative della Valle d'Aosta* at any tourist office.

AOSTA ☎ 0165

Aosta is a town perched on the fence between Italian and French *Valdostana* border culture. Street signs alternate from French to Italian (with the town hall known as L'hôtel du Ville), and most residents are bilingual. This half-hearted compromise generally favors the southern side, however, as their best language is Italian, and pizza and *gelato* shops abound. For many years Aosta was Rome's outpost on the Italian frontier and a launching point for military expeditions. To this day, it serves as a geographic and financial center, and as a departure point for hiking trips. Inside the crumbling walls that once defended Rome's Alpine outpost, swanky boutiques and gourmet food shops are packed into a dense *centro storico;* outside, a commercial and industrial minefield stretches across the valley. Valley-bound Aosta's prices soar like the nearby peaks of Monte Emilius (3559m) and Becca di Nona (3142m), and the distant glacial expanses of Grand Combin (4314m), and Becca du Lac (3396m).

Although Aosta has dazzling views, they prove mere shimmering powder when compared to those that await further up the valley. Aosta makes a good starting point for explorations into the Italian Alps, but be aware that daytrips to the surrounding valleys often require tricky train and bus connections—if you hope to return before nightfall, plan ahead.

⬛ TRANSPORTATION

Trains: The station is in the pink building at P. Manzetti. Ticket window open daily 4:50-11:25am and 1:45-8:30pm. To: **Chivasso** (1½hr., every hr., 5:12am-8:40pm, €4.65) via **Châtillon** (15min., every hr., 6:12am-8:40pm, €1.80); **Milan**'s Centrale (4hr., 12 per day, 6:12am-8:40pm, €10.12); **Pont St. Martin** (50min., every hr., 5:12am-8:40pm, €3.10); **Turin's** P. Nuova (2hr., every hr., 5:15am-8:40pm, €6.82); and **Verrès** (30min., every hr., 6:12am-8:40pm, €2.45).

Buses: SAVDA (☎0165 26 20 27), on V. Carrel off P. Manzetti, to the right of the train station. Open 4:30am-1:30am. To: **Courmayeur** (1hr., every hr., 6:45am-9:45pm, €2.48) and **Great St. Bernard Pass** (2hr., 9:40am and 2:25pm, €2.70). **SVAP** serves closer towns. To: **Cogne** (1hr., 7 per day, 8:05am-8:35pm, €2.07) and **Fenis** (1hr., 4 per day, 9:50am-7pm, €1.55). Buses to **Breuil-Cervinia** (2hr., 7 per day, €3.10) and **Valtournenche** leave from the Châtillon train station.

Taxis: P. Manzetti (☎0165 26 20 10). P. Narbonne (☎0165 35 656 or 31 831).

Car Rental: Europcar, P. Manzetti, 3 (☎0165 41 432), left of the train station. 18+. Economy car daily rate from €55 (100km or less per day) to €69 (unlimited mileage). Open M-F 8:30am-12:30pm and 3-7pm, Sa 8:30am-12:30am. MC/V.

◪ ⁊ ORIENTATION AND PRACTICAL INFORMATION

Trains stop at **Piazza Manzetti**. From there, walk straight down **Av. du Conseil des Commis** until it ends in the enormous **Piazza Chanoux**, Aosta's center. The main street runs east-west through P. Chanoux and suffers a number of name changes. From Av. du Conseil des Commis, **Via J. B. de Tiller**, which then becomes **Via Aubert**, is to the left; to the right is **Via Porta Praetoria**, which leads to the historic gate, **Porta Praetoria**, where it becomes **Via Sant'Anselmo**.

Tourist Office: P. Chanoux, 8 (☎0165 23 66 27; fax 34 657; www.regione.vda.it/turismo), straight down Av. du Conseil des Commis from train station. Ask for *Aosta, Monument Guide* and the *Annuario Alberghi*, which has a listing of all the hotels in the region with prices and telephone numbers. English, German, and French spoken. Open M-Sa 9am-1pm and 3-8pm, Su 9am-1pm.

Alpine Information: Club Alpino Italiano, C. Battaglione, 81 (☎0165 40 194). Off the Piazza della Repubblica. Open M, Tu, Th 6pm-7:30pm, F 8pm-10pm. Or try **Società Guide,** V. Monte Emilius, 13 (☎0165 40 939; fax 44 448; www.guidealpine.com). For **weather conditions,** try **Protezione Civile** in V. St. Christophe (☎0165 44 113) or ask at the tourist office.

Currency Exchange: Monte dei Paschi di Siena, P. Chanoux, 51 (☎0165 27 68 88). **ATM** outside. Open M-F 8:20am-1:20pm and 2:40-4:10pm.

Outdoor Gear and Apparel: Meinardi Sport, V. Aubert, 27 (☎0165 41 432). A moderately priced, extensive selection of gear and clothing, including maps and guides to the Italian Alps. Open daily 9am-12:30pm and 3-7:30pm; in late July closed Su; closed Aug. **Ski rental** is available in the numerous hangars by the chair lift behind the station.

Laundromat: Onda Blu, V. Chambery, 60. Wash €3.50, dry €3.50. Open daily 8am-10pm.

Work Opportunity: Old Distillery Pub (p. 210) hires workers seasonally.

Police: C. Battaglione Aosta, 169 (☎113).

First Aid: ☎118.

Mountain Rescue: ☎0165 34 983.

Pharmacy: Farmacia Chenal, V. Croix-de-Ville, 1 (☎0165 26 21 33), at the corner of V. Aubert. Open M-Tu, Th-Su 9am-12:30pm and 3-7:30pm. Displays all-night openings.

Hospital: V. Ginevra, 3 (☎0165 30 41).

Internet Access: Bar Snooker: V. Lucat, 3 (☎0165 23 63 68). From the station, turn right onto V. Giorgio Carrel and left on V. Lucat. Pool hall, video poker, and a card-playing salon. Internet access €5 per hr. Open M-Tu, Th-Su 8am-3am, W 1pm-3am.

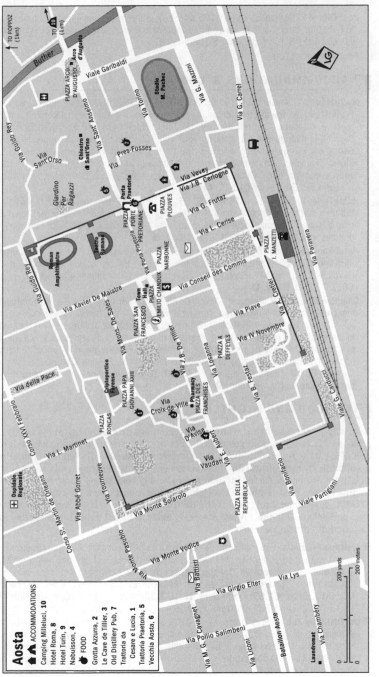

NORTHWEST ITALY

Aosta

▲ ACCOMMODATIONS
Camping Milleluci, 10
Hotel Roma, 8
Hotel Turin, 9
Nabuisson, 4

🍴 FOOD
Grotta Azzurra, 2
Le Cave de Tillier, 3
Old Distillery Pub, 7
Trattoria da
  Cesare e Lucia, 1
Trattoria Praetoria, 5
Vecchia Aosta, 6

Post Office: P. Narbonne, 1A (☎0165 44 138), in the huge semi-circular building. Open M-F 8:15am-6pm, Sa 8:15am-1pm. *Fermo Posta* is across town on V. Cesare Battisti, 10. Open M-F 8:15am-6pm, Sa 8:15am-1pm.

Postal Code: 11100.

⌂ ACCOMMODATIONS & CAMPING

Nabuisson, V. Aubert, 50 (0165 36 30 06 or 339 609 0332; www.bedbreakfastaosta.it). As you exit the station, walk straight down V. Conseil des Commis until you reach P. Chanoux. Turn left down V. De Tiller, which turns into V. Aubert. The yellow building is through the iron gate on your right. Charming, spacious rooms off a small courtyard. The owner also works in the tourist office and can answer questions in English, French, German, and Italian. All rooms with bath and TV. Breakfast €10. Reservations recommended. Open June-Oct. and Dec.-Apr. Doubles €40; apartment with full kitchen €50. Extra beds €10-15. ❹

Hotel Turin, V. Torino, 14 (0165 44 55 93; fax 36 13 77; www.hotelturin.it). As you exit the train station, turn left down V. Giorgio, then right onto the V. Vevey, and then right onto V. Torino. Centrally located. All rooms with TV. Singles €21-30, with bath €37-48; doubles with bath €62.20-72.20. DC/MC/V. ❷

Hotel Roma, V. Torino, 7 (0165 41 00; fax 32 404; hroma@libero.it). Just a few short minutes from the station and the center of town, around the corner from the Hotel Turin. All rooms with bath and TV. Friendly management is a plus. Singles €37-48.30; doubles €62.20-72.20. MC/V. ❹

Camping Milleluci, V. Porossan, 15 (☎0165 23 52 78; fax 23 52 84; www.hotelmilleluci.com). 1km hike from station. Turn right when you leave the train station onto V. Carrel, and then left onto V. Garibaldi. When you reach the Arc of Augustus (in the middle of piazza of same name), cross the river and turn left onto V. Pasquettaz, which will then fork to the left, changing to V. Porossan. Take it V. des Seigneurs de quart. Each plot has a small cabin connected to a trailer. Friendly staff. Parking €10.30. Laundry €5. Showers €0.50. Adults €5; ages 1-10 €3.50. 10% discount for 7-night or more stay, 2-night or more on the weekend. ❶

◖▮◗ FOOD AND NIGHTLIFE

Normally, if you asked your waiter for a recommendation and he told you to go eat a piece of lard, this would grounds for not tipping. Not so in Aosta, where lard is one of the most revered items in the *Valdostana* kitchen. The colder climate and predominantly agricultural lifestyle has generated a wholesome and hearty cuisine rich in fat. Other delicacies include *fonduta*, a cheesy sauce made from the local fontina cheese, that is put on everything in great quantities. Pick up a can at the **STANDA supermarket,** on V. Festaz, 10. (☎0165 35 757. Open M-Sa 8am-8pm, Su 9am-1pm and 3:30pm-7:30pm.) Aosta's weekly **outdoor market** is held on Tuesday in P. Cavalieri di Vittorio Veneto.

▨ **Trattoria Praetoria,** V. S. Anselmo, 9 (☎0165 443 56), just past the Porta Praetoria. The best Aostan food you'll find. With classy, arched stucco ceilings and warm staff, the atmosphere is unbeatable. Try the *salsiccette in umido* (local sausages braised in tomato sauce). Expect a ½hr. wait on weekend evenings. *Primi* €6-7.50, *secondi* €6.50-12. Cover €1.50. Open daily 12:15-2:30pm and 7:15-9:30pm; in winter F-W 12:15-2:30pm and 7:15-9:30pm. V. ❸

▨ **Old Distillery Pub,** V. Pres Fosses, 7 (☎0165 23 95 11). From Porta Pretoria, walk down V. Ansemo and go right through a small archway onto the winding V. Pres Fosses. Pub is on the left. Manned entirely by Brits, this place is usually packed, especially when local acts rock it out downstairs. Pint of Guinness €4.50. *Weissbier* of the week €3.50. Open daily 6pm-2am. ❷

Trattoria Da Cesare e Lucia, V. Martinet, 4. From P. Chanoux, head down V. de Tillier and turn right onto the V. Croix de Ville. It's opposite the Carabinieri building. While the dining room at this wonderful *trattoria* is informal, the food most certainly is not. *Primi* €4.13-5.16, *secondi* €6.20-8.26. Open M-Sa 12:15-2pm and 7:30-10pm. ❷

Vecchia Aosta, P. Porta Praetoria, 4 (0165 36 11 86). Just inside the Praetorian gate, in a truly wonderful location. Fine *Valdastano* food. *La mocetta ed il lardo di Arnad con castagne al miele* (€7.50) is particularly good. If the idea of eating large chunks of fat is enough to turn you vegetarian, try *la crepe di asparaghi con vellutata di fonduta* (€7.50) instead. Open Th-Tu 12:30-2:30pm and 7:30-10pm. MC/V. ❸

La Cave De Tillier, V. De Tillier, 40 (0165 23 01 33). Just off P. Chanoux, the restaurant is set off the street in an alleyway to your right. Just when you were starting to find cobblestone streets a little passé, prepare to be dazzled by this restaurant's cobblestone walls. The food's not bad either. *Primi* €6-10.50, *secondi* €7-16. Open Tu-Su 12:30-2:30pm and 7:30-10:30pm. DC/MC/V. ❸

Grotta Azzurra, V. Croix-de-Ville (Croce di città), 97 (☎0165 26 24 74), uphill from V. de Tillier as it becomes V. Aubert. Antiqued decor lends this *pizzeria* a medieval feel. Pizza from €5, pasta with *pesce* €8. Cover €1. Open Th-Tu noon-2:30pm and 7-10:30pm. Closed 2nd and 3rd wk. of June. ❸

◉ SIGHTS

ROMAN RUINS. Empires rise and fall, but sometimes the buildings they leave behind stick around. Aosta bears traces of the empire that was Rome, particularly in the partially intact walls that still skirt the center of town. The marble fluted columns that were stylish in the Augustan period are absent; Aosta's ruins distinguish themselves as an example of a more practical architecture in a decadent age. The **Porta Pretoria,** now on the street bearing its name, once stood at the edge of the walled city and served as a guard house. To its left lies the sprawling remains of the massive **Roman Theater,** now under repair. Visits are possible only with a court-appointed guide *(☎334 1674 7994. July-May tours every 30min., 10am-5pm; €5.15. June-July tours for groups of 4-12 must be booked 12hr. in advance; adults €3, under 12 free.)* Through Porta Pretoria, V. S. Anselmo leads to the **Arco d'Augusta.** The monument appears modern but dates from Roman times. The forum, or **Criptoportico Forense,** is off P. Papa Giovanni XXIII. *(Open M and W-Su 9am-6pm. Free.)*

SANT'ORSO. Within this unassuming church are some ornate 15th-century choir stalls and the amazing wood-carved **Chiostro di Sant'Orso.** Imaginatively carved columns and ceiling decorate the tiny cloister with bestial and biblical scenes. The **Fiera di Sant'Orso,** the region's most famous crafts fair, takes place January 30-31 and the Sunday before *Ferragosto* (mid-Aug.). The traditional fair dates to the 9th century and is known for Valdostan handicrafts. *(From the Porta Pretoria, take V. S. Anselmo and turn left on V. S. Orso. Open daily 7am-7pm. Free.)*

◪ OUTDOORS

VALLE DEL GRAN SAN BERNARDO. A valley with more medieval towers than tourists, Valle del Gran San Bernardo links Aosta to Switzerland via the Great St. Bernard Pass. Motor-tourists and intrepid cyclists tackle this winding mountain road in summer. Come snow, they retreat to a more highly trafficked 5854m tunnel through the mountain. Tourists follow the footsteps of Hannibal and his elephants, as well as Napoleon, who trekked through the pass with 40,000 soldiers in 1800. This region is best known for the **Hospice of St. Bernard,** dating from 1505 and home to the patron saint of dogs. The legendary life-saver was stuffed for posterity and can still be seen as you drive through the pass. The hospice (just across the Swiss border—remember your passport) offers great views of international peaks and is just a tail-wag away from the dog museum, where you can see St. Bernard puppies in training. A smaller, more serene branch of the valley leads to the communes of **Ollomont** and **Oyace,** where hiking trails, valleys, and pine forests await exploration. Easier hiking is above the hospice on a trail that skirts the ridge. *(For information call the Aosta tourist office or the ski-lift office ☎ 0165 78 00 46 at St. Rhémy.)*

THE MATTERHORN AND BREUIL-CERVINIA. The highest mountain in Switzerland, the **Matterhorn (Il Cervino)** looms majestically over the town of Breuil-Cervinia in Valtournenche. The buildings of **Breuil-Cervinia** differ only in purpose; some serve expensive food, others offer expensive accommodations, and the rest rent expensive sports equipment. In spite of the cost, many fresh-air fiends consider these man-made deterrents a small price to pay for the chance to climb up and glide down the glaciers of one of the world's most famous mountains. A cable car provides service to **Plateau Rosà** (round-trip €25), where summer skiers tackle the slopes in lighter gear. Hikers can forgo the lift tickets and attempt the 3-hr. ascent to **Colle Superiore delle Cime Bianche** (2982m), with tremendous views of Val d'Ayas to the east, and the Cervino glacier to the west. A shorter trek (1½hr.) on the same trail leads to the emerald waters of **Lake Goillet.** The tourist office hands out a good hiking map detailing these hikes and more. The **Società Guide** (☎ 0166 94 81 69), across from the tourist office, arranges group outings. Don't forget your **passport;** a number of trails cross into Zermatt, Switzerland.

Buses run to Breuil-Cervinia (6 per day, 6:10am-7:15pm, €2.30) from Châtillon on the Aosta-Turin train line. Direct buses also arrive daily from P. Castello in **Milan** (5hr.). Buses run to **Turin** (4hr.; M-Sa 6:45am, 1:25, 5pm; Su 6pm; €7.80). The English-speaking staff of the Tourist Info Center, V. Carrel, 29, provides visitors with information on White-week Packages and Settimane Estive, the summer equivalent. (☎ 0166 94 91 36; fax 94 97 31; www.montecervinia.it. Open daily 9am-noon and 3-6:30pm.) Students should inquire about the University Card, which reduces the price of passes by 10-20%.

VAL D'AYAS. Budget-minded sports enthusiasts should consider visiting the gently sloping Val d'Ayas. Under the shadow of the glaciated Monte Rosa, this wide valley offers the same activities as its flashy neighbors—skiing, hiking, and rafting. Try the town of **Champoluc** for some excellent hiking, including the 45min. hike up **trail #14** to the tiny hamlet of **Mascognoz,** a cluster of wood chalets home to a farming population of ten. **Trains** run to **Verrès** from Aosta (40min., 17 per day, 6:35am-8:40pm, €2.60) and Turin (1½hr.). **Buses** run from the train station at Verrès to **Champoluc** (1hr., 4 per day, 9:30am-6pm, €2.17). The **tourist office** in **Brusson** (☎ 0125 30 02 40; fax 30 06 91) has branches in Champoluc, V. Varase, 16 (☎ 0125 30 71 13; fax 30 77 85) and **Antagnod** (☎ 0125 30 63 35). They speak English and have trail maps and hotel information. (Branches open daily 9am-12:30pm and 3-6pm.)

VAL DI COGNE. When Cogne's mines failed in the 1970s, the townspeople resorted to a more genteel pursuit, delicately parting cross-country skiers from their money. In winter, Cogne heads an 80km entanglement of **cross-country trails** (daily pass €4.13). Cogne is also one of the world's premier places to ice climb (inquire at Aosta's guide office). A cable car transports alpine addicts to the modest **downhill skiing** facilities (€5.16 round-trip; daily pass €18.08; 7-day pass including cable car €100). In summer, the pastoral community serves as the gateway to the wild, unspoiled expanse of Italy's largest nature reserve, **Gran Paradiso National Park.** In addition to an endless network of hiking trails, waterfalls, and a population of 5000 ibex, the park has the highest **glacier** (4061m) fully contained within Italian borders, aptly named Gran Paradiso. Cogne and its characteristic dry, rocky valley dotted with pine trees, is a scenic **bus** ride from Aosta (1hr., 6 per day, 8:15am-8:30pm). The bus stops in front of the **AIAT tourist office,** P. Chanoux, 36, which distributes regional maps and helps find accommodations. (☎0165 74 040 or 74 056; fax 74 91 25. Open daily 9am-12:30pm and 3-6pm; in winter M-Sa 9am-12:30pm and 2:30-5:30pm, Su 9am-12:30pm.)

VALNONTEY. This hamlet affords an unobstructed view of the towering Gran Paradiso. Lodged in a narrow valley in the midst of a national park, it is an exceptional 45min. walk along the river from Cogne on **trail #25**, which leaves from the river-side tourist office. June-Aug. buses run from Cogne to **Valnontey** (every 30min., 7:30am-8pm, €1.10; buy tickets on bus), notable for its convenient *alimentari*, 2-star hotels, access to trails, and a botanical garden, **Giardino Alpino Paradisia.** The inspiration to construct a botanical garden came during the Cogne Mountain Festival in 1955, and the gardens boast over 1000 species of rare Alpine vegetation—mostly lichen. (☎0165 74 147. Open June 8–Sept. 8 daily 10am-6:30pm. Adults €2.10, 11-15 €1.10, under 10 free.) Beyond the botanical garden, a 15min. hike on **trail #6** is a stunning waterfall. From June to September, campers can choose between the rolling hills of **Camping Gran Paradiso ❶** (☎0165 74 92 04; self-service laundromat; €5.16 per person, ages 7-16 €3.62, under 6 free; €5.06 for tent, car, and electricity) and **Lo Stambecco ❶** (☎0165 74 152; €4.91 per person; tent and electricity €3.10-3.62; free showers).

COURMAYEUR ☎0165

In the spectacular shadows of Europe's highest peak, Italy's oldest alpine resort town still lures tourists in droves. Monte Bianco, with its jagged ridges and unmelting snow fields, perfect for hiking and skiing, is, of course, the attraction. Unfortunately for budget travelers who seek Alpine serenity, prices are high, rooms are booked year-round, and streets are saturated with manicured boutiques and obtrusive tour buses. Quiet falls in May and June when shopkeepers go on vacation.

⌧⏎ TRANSPORTATION AND PRACTICAL INFORMATION. One building in **P. Monte Bianco** houses almost everything a traveler needs. The **bus station** at P. Monte Bianco offers frequent service to larger towns. (☎0165 84 20 31. Open daily 7:30am-8:30pm.) Buses go to **Aosta** (1hr., every hr., 4:45am-8:45pm, €2.48) and **Turin** (3½hr., 4 per day, 8am-4pm, €7.49). To the right of the bus station, the **AIAT tourist office** offers maps and has staff that speak English, German, French, and Spanish. (☎0165 84 20 60; www.courmayeur.net. Open M-Sa 9am-12:30pm and 3-6:30pm, Su 9:30am-12:30pm and 3-6pm.) The bus ticket office has a **currency exchange** with the same hours. 24 hr. **taxis** (☎0165 84 29 60; night ☎84 23 33) are at P. M. Bianco. In an **emergency**, call ☎113, or an **ambulance,** Strada delle Volpi, 3 (☎118). There is a **pharmacy** at V. Roma, 33. (Open M-Sa 9am-12:30pm and 3-7:30pm.) **Internet access** is at **Ziggy**, V. Marconi, 15, which is just off V. Roma, which is just off P. A. Henry (☎0165 84 37 52. 45min. €5.20. Open daily 3pm-2:30am. May-June closed M, Tu, W.) The **post office** is in P. M. Bianco. (☎0165 84 20 42. Open M-F 8:15am-1:15pm, Sa 8:15-1:30am.) **Postal Code:** 11013.

⌧⌧ ACCOMMODATIONS AND FOOD. For winter accommodations, you can't book far enough in advance. In the summer, finding accommodations remains challenging because many places are closed. The trouble is worth it, however, for those interested in hiking, as Courmayeur is far closer to mountain paths than Aosta. **Pensione Venezia ❸** is at V. delle Villete, 2. From P. Monte Bianco, head up hill, then turn left on V. Circonvallazione, to this basic, clean, convenient hotel. (☎/fax 0165 84 24 61. Breakfast included. Singles €28.91; doubles €41.32.)

Picnicking is the best way to appreciate all Alpine freshness. At **Pastificio Gabriella ❶**, Passaggio dell'Angelo, 2, toward the end of V. Roma, you'll find excellent cold cuts, pasta salads, crepes, and a line out the door. (☎0165 84 33 59. Th-Tu 8am-1pm and 4-7:30pm; closed 2 weeks in June. MC/V.) **Il Fornaio ❶**, V. Monte Bianco, 17, serves scrumptious breads and pastries. Particularly good are the local specialty *tegole* (€19.36 per kg), round cookies made from egg whites. (☎0165 84 24 54. Open Th-F and Su-Tu 8am-12:30pm and 4-7:30pm, Sa 8am-12:30pm.) On Wednesdays, the **market** is 1km away in Dolonne. (Open daily 8:30am-2pm.)

Courmayeur has some reasonable restaurants, offering hearty portions that fulfill the most gnawing of appetites. Most close for the summer, but **La Terraza ❸**, V. Circonvallazione, 73, is open year-round. Just uphill from the P. Monte Bianco, this restaurant specializes in *Valdostano* food. They serve fondue and lard lightly garnished with warm chestnuts and honey (€12.91). The real attraction is the *menù*, with 3 large courses for €12. (☎0165 84 33 30. *Primi* from €9.30, *secondi* from €13.43. Open Tu-Su noon-2:15pm and 7:30-10pm.) If sweeping vistas are starting to overwhelm, try the cloistered **La Boite ❹**, S. Margherita, 14 (0165 84 67 94). To your right as you face uphill from the P. Monte Bianco, it offers wonderful food at decent prices. (*Primi* €8-9.50, *secondi* €10.50-21. Fish on F if reserved by W. Open daily 11:45am-3pm and 6:45pm-1am.)

◪ OUTDOOR ACTIVITIES. Ski passes are priced on a complex rotating schedule—check at the tourist office for details. (6-day pass in high season Oct. 26-Dec. 20, Jan. 7-24, and Mar. 30 until the snow melts: €126.75-169; low season €114-152. The brochures *White Weeks*, *Aosta Valley* (English), *Settimane Bianche*, and *Courmayeur* list rental and pass prices.

Nineteenth-century English gentlemen brushed off the **Giro del Monte Bianco** as a two- or three-day **climbing** excursion for "less adventurous travelers." These days, guides suggest that travelers take a week or more to complete the trip. The trail leads around Monte Bianco, past Chamonix and Courmayeur, and then into Switzerland. *Rifugi* and hostel dormitories are 5 or 6hr. apart along the route (€15.50-18.08 per person). One section of the trail makes an ideal daytrip, and two can fill a weekend. This is difficult mountaineering; be sure you are equipped and trained. Inquire at the guide office (see below) for more information.

For less rigorous excursions, take the beautiful 6hr. hike on the road up the valley past **Rifugio Elisabetta,** where the path (actually an *alta via*, marked by a "2" in a triangle) branches to the left and clambers up to the **Chavannes Pass** (2603m). There is no bus, so rent or borrow a car. The trail runs along **Mont Perce,** beneath the crest, to **Mont Fortin** (2758m), then down to Lake Combal. Courmayeur's two smaller valleys, Val Veny and Val Ferret, fork the base of Monte Bianco and are filled with day-long hikes. **SAVDA** buses serve both valleys; inquire at the tourist office for more information, including the brochure *Seven Itineraries around Mont Blanc, Val Veny, and Val Ferret.* A map is crucial; buy one at the **Libreria La Buona Stampa,** V. Roma, 4. (☎0165 84 67 71. Open daily 9am-1pm and 3:30-7:30pm.) A good place to ask questions and find a guide is the **Ufficio delle Guide,** P. Abbe Henri, 2, to the left behind the church. (☎0165 84 20 64. Open daily 9am-12:30pm and 3pm-7:30pm; in winter Tu-Su 9am-7pm.) The office includes a unique **mountaineering museum** with old equipment, photographs, and expedition histories. (Open Tu-Su 9am-7pm. €2.58, ages 8-12 €1.55.) The office finds guides for all the major hikes and climbs. They arrange ascents like the famous like *Dente del gigante* (286.25-315m, depending on which face you want to try) and the challenging 1½-day climb to Aiguille Noire Cresta Sud (prices given by guide).

The **◪Funivie Monte Bianco** cable cars head first to the **Punta Helbronner** (3462m) and then to **Chamonix.** The top affords unparalleled views of Monte Bianco's expansive, windswept ice sheet, as well as the spectacular **Matterhorn, Monte Rosa,** and **Gran Paradiso.** *Funivie* depart from La Palud near the Val Ferret (10min. bus ride from Courmayeur, €1.55). The cable cars make several stops on the mountain, so you can get off before Chamonix. (☎0165 89 925 or 89 196; www.montebianco.com. Round-trip to Punta Hellbronner €29.50-32.50. Summer only.) For **guided nature excursions** (*accompagnatori della natura*), contact English-speaking Cristina Gaggini (☎368 734 5407 or 0165 84 28 12).

VENICE
(VENEZIA)

From her salmon-colored buildings to her crooked lanes and stone bridges, Venice emanates romance. Her lavish palaces stand proudly on a network of wood that has been sinking since the time of Attila the Hun, and the emerald-clouded waters of her age-old canals lap at the feet of ancient doorways. When the city founded by Roman fisherman swapped its gondolas for seabound ships in the 11th century, it soon gained a monopoly on Eastern trade. The world depended on Venetian merchants for gold, silks, spices, and coffee. With the conquest of Constantinople in 1203, Venice gained control of lands throughout the Adriatic, the Greek islands, modern Turkey, and mainland Italy, becoming the envy of the world. Over the next century, however, jealous European powers in the west and the Turks in the east robbed Venice of its trade monopoly and whittled away its wealthy empire.

But Venice is adept at utilizing its resources. Throughout the centuries, the city kept itself well preserved and switched its means of livelihood from trade to tourism. People flock year-round to the churches, museums, and palaces that store priceless works by artists such as Titian and Giorgione. Visitors meander through labyrinthine streets, admiring the beauty and artistry of Gothic and Byzantine buildings. Native Venetians recline on the bridges yelling "Gondola, gondola ride!" to passing tourists. Every year, the indigenous population decreases, and *La Serenissima* (the Most Serene One) is left to the tourists (see **Behind the Mask,** p. 230).

HIGHLIGHTS OF VENICE

BUY a journal at **Rivoaltus** (see p. 233), where Wanda Scarpa sits daily in her attic making leatherbound portfolios by hand. Then, sit atop the **Rialto Bridge** to sketch.

MOUNT the steps of winding **Scala del Bovolo** (see p. 235), the impressive staircase of the snails.

CLIMB to the top of the **campanile** in San Marco (see p. 235) for a panoramic view of the city. On a clear day, look for Slovenia and Croatia across the Adriatic Sea.

BLOW glass at the **Murano Gallery** (see p. 240) and see their galleries of delicate chandeliers and drinking vessels handmade with centuries-old tools.

SIT in Attila the Hun's stone throne on the **Island of Torcello** (see p. 241).

VISIT **Squero di San Trovaso** (see p. 237), the last local gondola workshop.

ADMIRE Tintoretto's mysticism in the **Scuola Grande di S. Rocco** (see p. 236); then head to the Basilica dei Frari (see p. 236) to see rival Titian's sensual works.

RIDE a *vaporetto* to the tiny fishing village of **Burano** (see p. 240) and marvel at its rows of pastel facades and age-old lace industry.

WANDER among the quiet streets and still canals of **Dorsoduro** (see p. 228).

FEAST your eyes on the afternoon sun streaming into the **Basilica di S. Marco** (see p. 233), setting fire to its gold mosaics. At night, **waltz** to golden oldies in the piazza.

VENICE

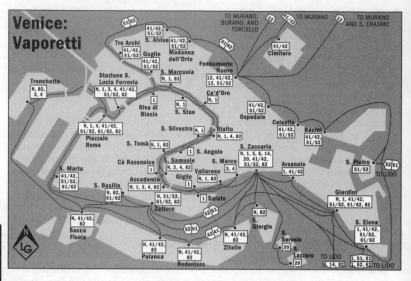

Venice: Vaporetti

■ **INTERCITY TRANSPORTATION**

Flights: Aeroporto Marco Polo (☎041 260 6111; www.veniceairport.it), 10km north of the city. The **ATVO** shuttle bus (☎041 520 5530) links the airport to Piazzale Roma on the main island (30min.; 5am-9am, 1 per hr.; 10am-8:40pm, 1 per hr.; €2.70). Shuttle bus ticket office open daily 6:40am-7:30pm.

Trains: Stazione Santa Lucia, Venice's main station in northwest corner of city. If arriving by train, disembark at Santa Lucia, not Mestre on the mainland. Open daily 3:45am-12:30am. Info office on the left as you exit the platforms. Open daily 7am-9pm. **Trains** to: **Bologna** (2hr., 1 per hr., 6:07am-8:07pm, €7.90-18.33); **Florence** (3hr., every 2hr., 6:33am-8:07pm, €26.60); **Milan** (3hr., 1-2 per hr., 5:12am-9:12pm; €12.40); **Padua** (30min., 1-3 per hr., 7:48am-9:12pm, €2.32); **Rome** (4½hr., 5 per day, 6:33am-6:33pm, €45); **Trieste** (2hr., every hr., 7:13am-11:44pm, €8). Some trains require a reservation. Check the information booth for info on your train. **Lost and found** ("*ogetti rinvenuti;*" ☎041 78 52 38; open M-F 8am-5pm) and **luggage storage** (open daily 3:30am-12:30am; 6hr. storage €1.60-2.10) by platform 14. Luggage storage also at **Deposito Pullman Bar,** P. Roma, 497 (☎041 523 1107). Open daily 6am-9pm. 24hr. storage for €2.58.

Buses: ACTV (☎041 528 7886), in P. Roma. Local line for buses and boats. **ACTV long-distance carrier** runs buses to **Padua** (1½hr., 6:15am-10:11pm, €3.10, round-trip €5.16) and **Treviso** (1hr., 2 per hr., 6:37am-9:40pm, round-trip €2.17). Ticket and info office open daily 6:30am-11:30pm.

■ **ORIENTATION**

Venice is 118 bodies of land in a lagoon, connected to the mainland city of Mestre by a thin causeway. The city is divided into six *sestieri* (sections): **Cannaregio, Castello, San Marco, Dorsoduro, San Polo,** and **Santa Croce** with the **Canal Grande** snaking throughout.

In the north, **Cannaregio** encompasses the *ferrovia*, the Jewish ghetto, and the Cà d'Oro. **Castello** continues east from there toward the Arsenale and the Giardini Publici. **S. Marco**, bounded to the north by the Ponte di Rialto, to the east by Ponte Accademia, and to the west by Piazza S. Marco, fills in the remaining area below Cannaregio. **Dorsoduro**, on the other side of the bridge, stretches the length of the Canal della Giudecca and extends north to Campo S. Pantalon. Farther north is **S. Polo**, which runs from the Chiesa S. Maria dei Frari to the Ponti di Rialto. **S. Croce** is west of S. Polo, directly across the Canal Grande from the *ferrovia*, and includes Piazzale Roma. *Sestiere* boundaries are rather vague, but they will help you orient yourself once you learn their general location. Accept that you will get lost, though the below information will help minimize the damage.

Venice's layout consists of a labyrinth of *calli* (narrow streets), *campi* (squares), *lista* (large streets), and *ponti* (bridges). The most confusing to navigate are the *calli*. Thousands criss-cross among buildings. Street names are often indistinguishable or not even listed, and street numbers do not form a contiguous set. Number 2300 could be located right next to 2400, with number 2301 at the other end of the block.

It is useless to try to follow a detailed map of the city. If you do, you will spend all of your time trying to make out the worn name of the back alley you're standing in and pinpoint it on a map whose streets are as thin as horsehairs. Instead, learn to navigate like a true Venetian. Locate the following sights on the map: **Ponte di Rialto** (in the center), **Piazza S. Marco** (central south), **Ponte Accademia** (southwest), **Ferrovia** (or Stazione Santa Lucia, the train station, northwest), **Ponte Scalzi** (in front of the station), and **Piazzale Roma** (southwest of the station). These are the main **orientation points** of Venice.

There are a plethora of **yellow signs** posted throughout the city with arrows directing you to each of these points. When trying to find a destination, first locate *sestiere*. Then depending on where you are, find a landmark that will lead you in that direction. As a general rule, follow the arrow of the sign as precisely as possible. If a street suddenly leads into a *campo* and branches in five different directions, pick the street that follows the original direction of the arrow as closely as possible until you come to the next sign. As you get closer, narrow down your search by locating the *campo* or main street near your destination and aim for that. All of the listings in the following pages are posted on the map with icons so you can spot the orientation points near each one. While directions in listings may seem vague, they are actually the simplest way to go.

To get to **Piazza S. Marco** or the **Rialto Bridge** from the train station or P. Roma, *vaporetto* #82 is the most direct, but most congested, with people sometimes queuing in lines for 30min. *Vaporetto* #1, with its 10min. extra journey, ends up being faster than #82, is never crowded, and offers better views. Or, if you prefer going on foot, follow the signs for the 30min. walk to P. S. Marco, starting left of the station on Lista di Spagna. For a more scenic route, take the Ponte Scalzi and head straight to Santa M. dei Frari and San Polo, following signs for Rialto.

⌐ LOCAL TRANSPORTATION

The cheapest (and often fastest) way to see the city is to walk through it. The Grand Canal can be crossed on foot at the *ponti* Scalzi, Rialto, and Accademia. ■*Traghetti* (gondola ferry boats) cross the canal at eight locations, including Ferrovia, San Marcuola, Cà d'Oro, and Rialto (€0.40). *Vaporetti* (water buses) provide 24hr. service around the city, although after midnight they run less frequently. Tickets cost €3.10 one way, but if you plan to move longer distances around the city or are staying on an island, an extended pass is more economical (24hr. €9.30; 3-day €15.50; 7-day €30.99). Schedules, route maps, and tickets are available at any ACTV or APT office (see Information Offices, p. 222). If you want to buy extra tickets for later, make

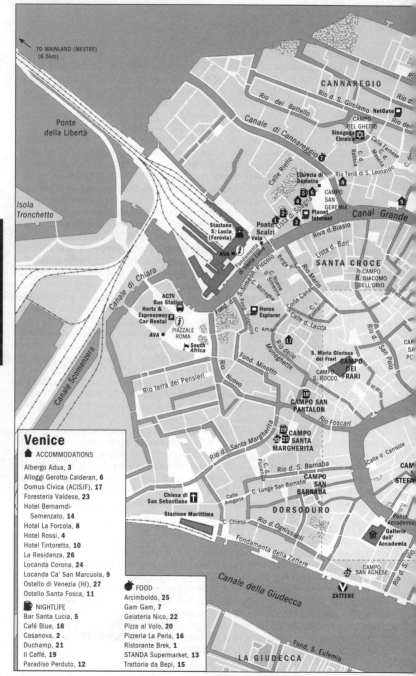

TO MAINLAND (MESTRE)
(6.5km)

Ponte
della Libertà

*Isola
Tronchetto*

CANNAREGIO

Rio del Battello

Rio d. S. Girolamo

NetGate

Rio de

Canale di Cannareggio

CAMPO
DEL GHETTO

Sinagoga
Ebraica

Calle Farnese

*C. d.
Rabbia*

Maseña d

C. tip

Calle Riello

Libreria di
Demetra

Rio Terra di S. Leonardo

CAMPO
SAN
GEREMIA

Planet
Internet

Lista di Spagna

Stazione
S. Lucia
(Ferovia)

Ponte
Scalzi

Canal Grande

Vela

Riva d. Biasio

AVA

Lista d. Bari

*Fondamenta
di Santa Lucia*

Canale di Chiara

Fond. d. S. Simeon Piccolo

Berga ma

Rio Marin

SANTA CROCE

CAMPO
S. GIACOMO
DELL'ORIO

S. C. Shneone

S. C. Munette

C. Nuova

Corte Canal

*C. I.
Contarina*

ACTV
Bus Station
Hertz &
Expressway
Car Rental

Horus
Explorer

Fond. d. S. Simeon

Fond. Tolentini

C. Amai

Calle d. Lacca

Rio d. San Polo

AVA

PIAZZALE
ROMA

South
Africa

*Rio delle
Muneghette*

S. Maria Gloriosa
dei Frari

CAMPO
DEI
FRARI

CAN
SA
PO

Fond. Minotto

CAMPO
S. ROCCO

Rio terra dei Pensieri

*Rio
Nuovo*

CAMPO SAN
PANTALON

Rio Foscari

CAMPO
SANTA
MARGHERITA

Rio di Santa Margherita

Calle d. Carrozze

CAM
S
STEFA

Pazienta

*C. d.
Pazienza*

Rio d. S. Barnaba

CAMPO
SAN
BARNABA

C. Lunga San Barnaba

*Calle
Avogaria*

Chiesa di
San Sebastiano

DORSODURO

Ponte
Accademia

Gallerie
dell'
Accademia

Stazione Marittima

C. Chiesa

Rio d. Ognissanti

Fondamenta della Zattere

CAMPO
SAN AGNESE

Rio d. S. Vio

Canale della Giudecca

ZATTERE

Fond. S. Eufemia

LA GIUDECCA

Venice

ACCOMMODATIONS

Albergo Adua, **3**
Alloggi Gerotto Calderan, **6**
Domus Civica (ACISJF), **17**
Foresteria Valdese, **23**
Hotel Bernarndi-
Semenzato, **14**
Hotel La Forcola, **8**
Hotel Rossi, **4**
Hotel Tintoretto, **10**
La Residenza, **26**
Locanda Corona, **24**
Locanda Ca' San Marcuola, **9**
Ostello di Venezia (HI), **27**
Ostello Santa Fosca, **11**

NIGHTLIFE

Bar Santa Lucia, **5**
Café Blue, **18**
Casanova, **2**
Duchamp, **21**
Il Caffé, **19**
Paradiso Perduto, **12**

FOOD

Arcimboldo, **25**
Gam Gam, **7**
Gelateria Nico, **22**
Pizza al Volo, **20**
Pizzeria La Perla, **16**
Ristorante Brek, **1**
STANDA Supermarket, **13**
Trattoria da Bepi, **15**

VENICE

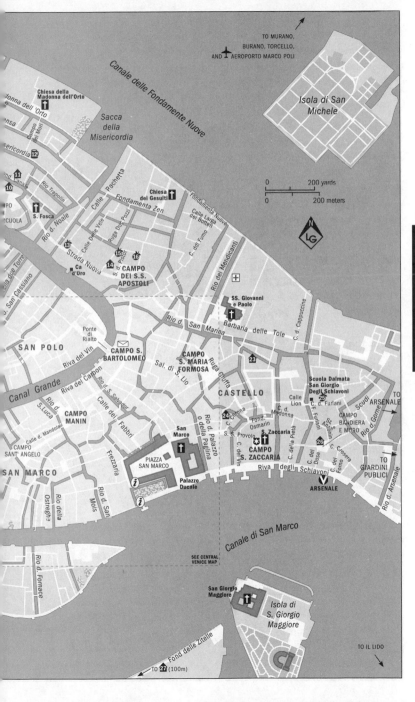

TO MURANO,
BURANO, TORCELLO,
AND ✈ AEROPORTO MARCO POLI

Isola di San
Michele

Canale delle Fondamente Nuove

Chiesa della
Madonna dell'Orto

Sacca
della
Misericordia

onna dell 'Orto

nsa

ericordia 12

11

10

PO

S. Fosca

CUOLA

Rio Trapolin

Rio di Noale

Chiesa
del Gesulti

Fondamenta Zen

Calle Pacherta

Calle Delle Vele

Ruga Due Pozzi

Calle Larga
del Botteri

Fondamenta Nuove

C. dei Fumo

0   200 yards
0   200 meters

N
LG

13

15   16

14

Ca
d'Oro

CAMPO
DEI S.S.
APOSTOLI

Strada Nuova

sta due Torre

J. San Cassiano

Rio del Mendicanti

SS. Giovanni
e Paolo

Rio d. San Marina

Barbaria delle Tole

C. d. Cappuccine

VENICE

SAN POLO

Ponte
di
Rialto

Riva del Vin

Riva del Carbon

Canal Grande

Rio di
S. Luca

CAMPO
MANIN

Calle d. Mandola

CAMPO
SANT' ANGELO

SAN MARCO

CAMPO S.
BARTOLOMEO

Sal. di S. Lio

Rio d. S. Salvador

Calle dei Fabbri

Frezzaria

Rio della
Ostregh?

Rio d. San

Mois

CAMPO
S. MARIA
FORMOSA

Ruga Giuffa

23

CASTELLO

Calle
Lion

C. d. Furlani

Scuola Dalmata
San Giorgio
Degli Schiavoni

25

TO
ARSENALE

Scudi

Rio d. Gorne

CAMPO
BANDIERA
E MORO

C. Crosera

TO
GIARDINI
PUBLICI

Rio d. Palazzo
o della Paglina

24 C. Corona

Fond.
Osmarin

S. S. Provolo

C. del Vin

S. Zaccaria

CAMPO
S. ZACCARIA

C. della Pieta

C. d.
Madonna

C. Furlani

C. S.
Antonin

C. del
Dose

26

C. del
Forno

Rio d. Arsenale

San
Marco

PIAZZA
SAN MARCO

Palazzo
Ducale

ⓘ

ⓘ

Riva degli Schiavoni

V
ARSENALE

Canale di San Marco

SEE CENTRAL
VENICE MAP

San Giorgio
Maggiore

Isola di
S. Giorgio
Maggiore

Rio d. Fornace

Fond delle Zitelle

TO 27 (100m)

TO IL LIDO

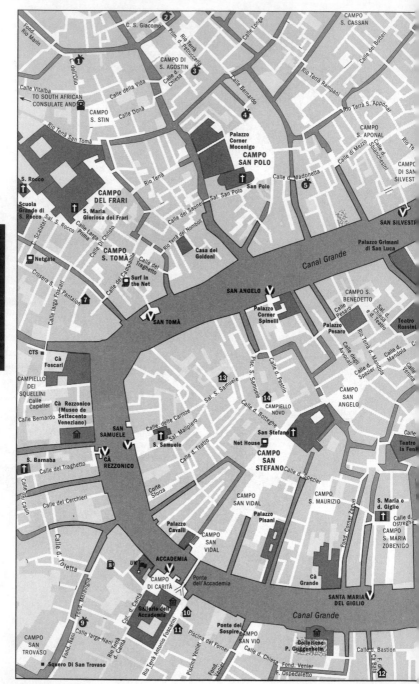

VENICE

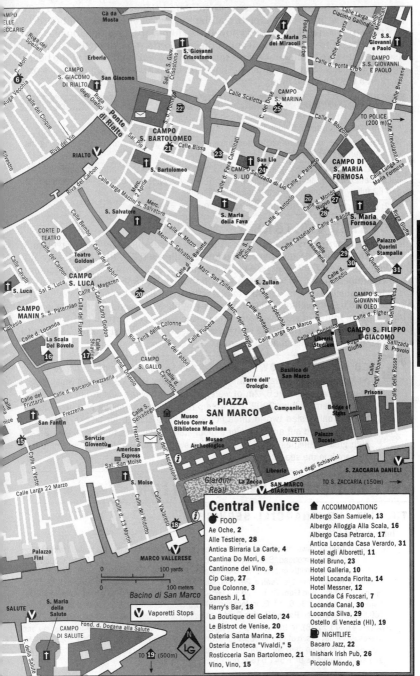

VENICE

Central Venice

🍴 FOOD

Ae Oche, **2**
Alle Testiere, **28**
Antica Birraria La Carte, **4**
Cantina Do Mori, **6**
Cantinone del Vino, **9**
Cip Ciap, **27**
Due Colonne, **3**
Ganesh Ji, **1**
Harry's Bar, **18**
La Boutique del Gelato, **24**
Le Bistrot de Venise, **20**
Osteria Santa Marina, **25**
Osteria Enoteca "Vivaldi," **5**
Rosticceria San Bartolomeo, **21**
Vino, Vino, **15**

🛏 ACCOMMODATIONS

Albergo San Samuele, **13**
Albergo Alloggia Alla Scala, **16**
Albergo Casa Petrarca, **17**
Antica Locanda Casa Verardo, **31**
Hotel agli Alboretti, **11**
Hotel Bruno, **23**
Hotel Galleria, **10**
Hotel Locanda Fiorita, **14**
Hotel Messner, **12**
Locanda Cá Foscari, **7**
Locanda Canal, **30**
Locanda Silva, **29**
Ostello di Venezia (HI), **19**

🍷 NIGHTLIFE

Bacaro Jazz, **22**
Inishark Irish Pub, **26**
Piccolo Mondo, **8**

V Vaporetti Stops

sure you specify that you want an unvalidated ticket *(non timbrato)*. To avoid paying a fine, remember to validate your ticket before you board by inserting it into one of the little yellow boxes found at each stop. You may also buy your ticket from booths in front of the *vaporetto* stops or on the *vaporetto* itself. But be sure to announce your intent to buy a ticket onboard at the beginning of the ride rather than at the end—the "confused foreigner" act won't work in a town with so many tourists.

MAIN VAPORETTO LINES
#82: Runs from the station, down the Grand Canal, up the Giudecca Canal, and back to the station. Always crowded with long lines.
#1: Has the same route as #82, but less crowded, with a great view of the *palazzi* along the canal. 10min. slower than #82, and with more stops.
#52, 51; 62, 61: Circumnavigate Venice. #51 and 61 run from the station, through the Giudecca Canal to Lido, along the northern edge of the city, and back to the station, while #52 and 62 follow the same route in the opposite direction.
#12: Runs from Fondamente Nuove to Murano, Burano, and Torcello.

DISABLED VISITORS

Informa Handicap offers an information hotline for disabled and deaf travelers in Italy. (June-Sept. M-F 9am-6pm and Sa-Su 9am-1pm: ☎ 167 17 91 79. Oct.-May M-F 9:30am-1pm and Tu 3-6pm: ☎ 041 97 64 35; fax 041 97 44 57; informahandicap@comune.venzia.it.) The **S. Lucia Train Station** (☎ 041 78 55 70) also has information for disabled travelers. The **APT tourist office** has a list of lodgings in Venice that are wheelchair accessible. Additionally, they publish a free map of the city outlining handicap routes in each *sestiere* and on the islands of Murano and Lido. Keys for wheelchair lifts at the bridges are available from the tourist office. Vaporetti lines #1 and 82 are wheelchair accessible.

GO WITH THE FLOW. Spring high tides and winter rain cause *acque alte*, periodic floods that swamp parts of Venice (notably P. S. Marco) with waist-high levels of water. In 1966, 2m of water covered the piazza, destroying priceless pieces of art. In June 2002, the waters rose again. The *acque alte*, in typical fashion, only lasted two to three hours—just long enough for planks and platforms to be laid out across major thoroughfares, Venetians to unpack their 3ft.-high green galoshes, and for rumors to swirl anew about Venice's eminent descent into the sea.

◪ PRACTICAL INFORMATION

TOURIST AND FINANCIAL SERVICES

Information Offices:

APT Tourist Offices (www.tourismovenezia.it), are located all over the city. Avoid the **train station** office, as it is always mobbed. Seek out offices in: **Piazzale Roma** (☎/fax 041 241 1499; open daily 9:30am-3:30pm); directly opposite the Basilica at **P. S. Marco,** 71/F (☎/fax 041 529 8740; open daily 9:30am-3:30pm); the **Venice Pavilion, Giardini Ex Reali,** in San Marco (☎041 522 5150; open 10am-6pm); and **Lido,** Gran Viale, 6a (☎041 526 5721; fax 529 8720; open June-Sept. daily 9am-12:30pm and 3:30-6pm). Every location sells *vaporetto* tickets (€3.10 one-way) and schedules (€0.50), as well as the **Rolling Venice Card** (see below) and theater and concert tickets.

AVA (☎041 171 5288), in train station, to right of tourist office. Finds available hotel rooms and makes same-day reservations for €5.20. Advance reservations by phone (☎041 522 2264 or 800 84 30 06. Open daily 9am-10pm in summer.) Offices in **Piazzale Roma** (☎041 523 1379) and at the **airport** (☎041 541 5133) book rooms for €2.07.

Rolling Venice Card: Offers discounts at over 200 select restaurants, cafes, hotels, museums, and shops for people aged 14-29. Tourist office provides list of participating vendors. Cards cost €2.58 and are valid for 1 year from date of purchase. A 3-day vaporetto pass with the card costs €12.91 as opposed to the undiscounted €15.50. The card is sponsored by ACTV and can be purchased at the **ACTV VeLa** office (☎ 041 274 7650) in P. Roma, open daily 8:30am-6pm. The card is also available at all APT tourist offices and ACTV VeLa kiosks next to the **Ferrovia, Rialto, S. Marco,** and **Vallaresso** vaporetto stops.

Budget Travel: CTS, Fondamenta Tagliapietra, Dorsoduro, 3252 (☎ 041 520 5660; www.cts.it). From Campo S. Barnaba, cross bridge closest to church and follow the road through the small piazza. Turn left at foot of large bridge. Sells discounted student plane tickets and issues ISIC cards. English spoken. Open M-F 9:30am-1:30pm and 2:30-6pm.

Consulates: US (☎ 02 29 03 51) and **Australian** consulates in Milan; **Canadian** consulate (☎ 049 878 1147) in Padua; **New Zealand** citizens should contact their embassy in Rome. **South Africa,** S. Croce, 466/G (☎ 041 524 1599), in P. Roma, just to the left of Garage Venezia. Cross Accademia Bridge from S. Marco and turn right for the **UK,** Dorsoduro, 1051 (☎ 041 522 7207; open M-F 10am-noon and 2-3pm).

Currency Exchange: Money exchangers charge high prices. Use banks whenever possible and inquire about fees beforehand. The streets around S. Marco and S. Polo are full of banks and **ATMs.** Many 24hr. automatic change machines, outside banks and next to ATMs, offer low commissions and decent rates.

American Express: Calle S. Moise, S. Marco, 1471 (☎ 800 87 20 00 or 041 520 0844). Exit the P. S. Marco with your back to the basilica and walk for 2min. Currency exchange with average rates, but no commission. Mail service with AmEx card or AmEx traveler's checks only. Office open for **currency exchange** M-F 9am-8pm, Sa-Su 9am-5:30pm. Member services daily 9am-1pm and 2-5:30pm.

LOCAL TRANSPORT

Car Rental: Expressway, P. Roma, 496/N (☎ 041 522 3000; fax 520 0000; www.expressway-online.com). 18+. Free car delivery to/from airport. From €65 per day and €300 per wk. Show *Let's Go* or student card for discount. Open daily 8am-12:30pm and 1:30-6pm. AmEx/MC/V. **Hertz,** P. Roma, 496/F (☎ 041 528 4091; fax 520 0614). 23+. Credit card required. €71.70 per day, €252.98 per wk. Open in summer M-F 8am-6pm, Sa-Su 8am-1pm; in winter M-F 8am-12:30pm and 3-5:30pm, Sa 8am-1pm.

24hr. Parking at **P. Roma** (☎ 041 523 2213) and island of **Tronchetto** (☎ 041 520 7555). Around €20 per day. Parking is considerably cheaper on the mainland. Consider leaving your car in **Mestre** (1st train stop out of Venice).

LOCAL SERVICES

English-Language Bookstores: Libreria Studium, S. Marco, 337A (☎/fax 041 522 2382). From P. S. Marco, head left on C. delle Canonico between basilica and clock tower; it's the last shop on the right. Novels and guidebooks about Venice. 10% discount with Rolling Venice card. Open M-Sa 9am-7:30pm. AmEx/MC/V. **Libreria Al Ponte,** Calle della Mandola, S. Marco 3717/D (☎ 041 522 4030), on the bridge. Follow C. Cortesia out of Campo Manin. Open daily 10:30am-12:30pm and 1-7:30pm. **La Libreria di Demetra,** Campo S. Geremia, 283a (☎ 041 275 0152). Open M-Sa 9am-midnight, Su 10am-midnight.

Religious Services: Anglican: Chiesa Anglicana St. George's, Campo S. Vio, Dorsoduro, 870 (☎ 041 520 0571). Su 10:30am, evening song daily at 6pm. **Jewish: Sinagoga Ebraica,** Ghetto Vecchio, Cannaregio (☎ 041 71 50 12). F 7:30pm and Sa 9am.

Gay and Lesbian Resources: ARCI-GAY Venezia, V. A'Costa 38/A, Rm 21, 2nd fl., Mestre (☎ 041 72 11 97; www.gay.it/arcigay/venezia). Meetings Tu 9-11pm.

VENICE

Laundromat: Self-Service, Calle della Chioverette, S. Croce, 665B. From the Scalzi Bridge, turn right onto Fondamenta S. Piccolo, then left down the alley after the church. Wash €3.50, dry €5.50, and detergent €0.50. Open daily 7am-10pm.

Public Toilets: AMAV W.C. Marked by white signs throughout the city. €0.52. Open daily 8am-9pm.

EMERGENCY AND COMMUNICATIONS

Police: ☎113 or 112. **First Aid:** ☎118. **Fire:** ☎115.

Carabinieri, Campo S. Zaccaria, Castello, 4693/A (☎041 520 4777). **Questura,** V. Nicoladi, 24, Marghera (☎041 271 5511).

Complaint Line: Venezia No Problem (☎800 35 59 20) is a 24hr. daily service for hotel complaints.

Pharmacy: Farmacia Italo Inglese, Calle della Mandola, S. Marco, 3717 (☎041 522 4837). Follow C. Cortesia out of Campo Manin. Open M-F 9am-12:30pm and 3:45-7:30pm, Sa 9am-12:30pm. Late-night and weekend pharmacies rotate; check the list posted in the window of any pharmacy.

Hospital: Ospedale Civile, Campo SS. Giovanni e Paolo, Castello (☎041 529 4111).

Internet Access:

▧ **The NetGate,** Crosera S. Pantalon, Dorsoduro, 3812/A (☎041 244 0213). From Santa Frari, take C. Scalater to C. Pantalon and follow signs for Campo Margherita. 1hr. session €3.99; 1hr. session split €4.99, students and Rolling Venice card-holders €3.99. Open M-F 10:15am-8pm, Sa 10:10am-10pm, Su 2:15-10pm. AmEx/MC/V.

Surf In the Net, Calle del Campanile, S. Polo, 2898a (☎041 244 076). From *vaporetto:* S. Tomà, take Calle del Traghetto, and turn left. €6.20 per hr., students €4.65. Open M-Sa 11am-9pm.

Net House, in Campo S. Stefano, S. Marco, 2967-2958 (☎041 227 1190). €9 per hr., with ISIC or Rolling Venice €6. Open 24hr.

Horus Explorer, Fondamenta Tolentini, S. Croce, 220 (☎041 71 04 70; fax 275 8399). With your back to the Ponte Scalzi, head right and take a left on F. Tolentiai immediately before the bridge. €5.16 per hr., 10% Rolling Venice discount. Fax and photocopy services. Open M, F 9am-6pm; Tu-Th 8:30am-1pm and 2:30-7pm.

Planet Internet, Lista di Spagna, Cannaregio, 1519 (☎041 524 4188). €5 per 30 min., €8 per hr. Sells international calling cards. Open daily 9am-midnight.

Post Office: Poste Venezia Centrale, Salizzada Fontego dei Tedeschi, S. Marco, 5554 (☎041 271 7111), off Campo S. Bartolomeo. *Fermo Posta* at window #17. Open M-Sa 8:30am-6:30pm. **Branch office** (☎041 528 5949), through the arcades at the end of P. S. Marco and opposite the basilica. Open M-Sa 8:30am-6pm.

Postal Codes: S. Marco: 30124; Castello: 30122; S. Polo, S. Croce, and Canareggio: 30121; Dorsoduro: 30123.

▐ ACCOMMODATIONS AND CAMPING

Plan to spend more for a room in Venice than you would elsewhere in Italy. Always agree on what you will pay before you take a room, and if possible, make reservations at least one month in advance. Dormitory-style arrangements are sometimes available without reservations, even during the months of June through September. If you cannot find a vacancy, the **AVA** (see **Information Offices,** p. 222) will find you a room with same-day availability, but it will not be cheap.

Religious institutions around the city offer both dorms and private rooms during the summer for about €25-70. Options include **Casa Murialdo,** Fondamenta Madonna dell'Orto, Cannaregio, 3512 (☎041 71 99 33); **Casa Capitania,** S. Croce, 561 (☎041 520 3099; open June-Sept.); **Patronato Salesiano Leone XIII,** Calle S. Domenico, Castello, 1281 (☎041 240 3611); **Domus Cavanis,** Dorsoduro, 896 (☎041

528 7374), near the Accademia Bridge; **Ostello Santa Fosca,** Cannaregio, 2372 (☎041 71 57 75); **Istituto Canossiano,** F. delle Romite, Dorsoduro, 1323 (☎041 240 9711); and **Istituto Ciliota,** Calle Muneghe S. Stefano, S. Marco, 2976 (☎041 520 4888).

CANNAREGIO AND SANTA CROCE

The station area, around the Lista di Spagna, has some of Venice's best budget accommodations. Although a 20min. *vaporetto* ride and a 30min. walk from most major sights, at night the streets bustle with young travelers and students.

▨ **Alloggi Gerotto Calderan,** Campo S. Geremia, 283 (☎041 71 55 62; fax 71 53 61; www.casagerottocalderan.com). 34 bright, big rooms. 4 clean common bathrooms/ showers per floor. Internet €3.10 per 30min. Check-out 10am. Curfew 12:30am for dorms, 1am for private rooms. Reserve at least 15 days in advance. Dorms €21; singles €31-41; doubles €46-72, with bath €78-108; triples €78-108/€120. ❷

▨ **Locanda Cà San Marcuola,** Campo S. Marcuola, Cannaregio, 1763 (☎041 71 60 48; fax 275 9217; www.casanmarcuola.com). From the Lista di Spagna, follow signs for S. Marcuola. The hotel is the salmon-colored building with 2 stone lions flanking the entrance, next to the *vaporetto* stop. This homey 17th-century Venetian house's rooms are impeccably clean and completely refurbished. 3rd fl. rooms, with exposed wooden beams, have lots of character; some have canal view. For a real treat, the *doppia superiore* has a soaring ceiling with a chandelier and balcony view of canal. All rooms with bath, A/C, and TV. Free Internet. Wheelchair accessible. Breakfast included. Singles €51-80; doubles €100-130; triples €140-180; *doppia superiore* €140-180 for 2, €180-200 for 3. AmEx/MC/V. ❹

Hotel La Forcola, Cannaregio, 2353 (☎041 524 1484; fax 524 5380; www.laforcola-hotel.com). From the station, turn left on Lista di Spagna, directly on the left after the 2nd bridge. Once a Venetian palace, this modern hotel has 23 stately and elegant rooms dressed in cream and mahogany. All rooms with bath, A/C, and TV. Wheelchair accessible. Elaborate buffet breakfast included. Singles €64-130; doubles €78-200; triples €94-238. AmEx/MC/V. ❺

Hotel Tintoretto, Santa Fosca, 2316 (☎041 72 15 22; fax 72 17 91; www.hoteltintoretto.com). Heading down Lista di Spagna from the station, follow the signs for the hotel. Cheery, large rooms, all with bath, A/C, TV, and minibar, some with views of the canal. Breakfast included. Singles €41-114; doubles €74-163; triples €200. AmEx/MC/V. ❹

Ostello Santa Fosca, Fondamenta Canal, Cannaregio, 2372 (☎/fax 041 71 57 75; www.santafosca.it). From Lista di Spagna, turn into Campo S. Fosca. Cross 1st bridge and turn left onto Fondamenta Canal. Student-operated, church-affiliated, and quiet. July-Sept. 140 beds available; Oct.-June 31 beds. July-Sept. reception daily 7am-noon and 6-11pm; no curfew. Oct.-June reception 8am-noon and 5-8pm; curfew 1am. Dorms €18; singles and doubles €21 per person. €2 discount with ISIC or Rolling Venice. ❷

Hotel Bernardi-Semenzato, Calle dell'Oca, Cannaregio, 4366 (☎041 522 7257; fax 522 2424; mtpepoli@tin.it). From *vaporetto*: Cà d'Oro, turn right onto Strada Nuova, left onto tiny Calle del Duca, then right onto Calle dell'Oca. Venetian antiques decorate a newly renovated annex. 25 rooms. TV €2.58 per day and A/C €5.16. Check-out 10:30am. Curfew 1am; exceptions made. Breakfast included. Singles €36.15, with bath €54.23; doubles €51.60/€72.30; triples €67.14/€87.80; quads €82.63/ €98.13. 15% Rolling Venice discount on larger rooms. AmEx/MC/V. ❹

Hotel Rossi, Lista di Spagna, Cannaregio, 262 (☎041 71 51 64; ☎/fax 71 77 84; rossi-hotel@interfree.it). 14 rooms with high ceilings and fans in older hotel. Breakfast included. June-Sept. reserve at least 1 month in advance. Singles €50, with bath €65; doubles €73/€89; triples with bath €103.29; quads with bath €121.37. 10% Rolling Venice discount. MC/V. ❹

VENICE

Albergo Adua, Lista di Spagna, Cannaregio, 233a (☎041 71 61 84; fax 244 0162). 22 basic rooms with A/C and TV come at a price. Singles €70, with bath €100; doubles €78/€114; triples €95/€150. Breakfast €6. AmEx/MC/V. ❹

Ostello di Venezia (HI), Fondamenta Zitelle, Giudecca, 87 (☎041 523 8211; fax 523 5689; www.hostelbooking.com). Check web site for room availability and reservations, rather than calling. Can be reached only by *vaporetto* #82, 41, or 42 to Zitelle. Turn right alongside canal. Institutional, but sweeping view of the water. 250 beds (men and women bunk on separate floors), Internet free, and a snack bar. Breakfast included. Dinner €8. Sheets free. Reception 7-9:30am and 1:30-11:30pm. Lock-out 9:30am-1:30pm. Curfew 11:30pm. Reservations through IBN from other HI hostels or online at www.hostelbooking.com. HI members only; temporary and full HI cards available. Dorms €16. MC/V. ❷

Istituto Canosiano, Ponte Piccolo, Giudecca, 428 (☎/fax 041 522 2157). Take *vaporetto* #82, 41 to Palanca, and walk left over the bridge. Women only. 35 beds. Lockout noon-3pm. Strict curfew 10:30pm; winter 10pm. Large dorms €13. ❶

SAN MARCO AND SAN POLO

Surrounded by exclusive shops, souvenir stands, scores of *trattorie* and *pizzerie*, and many of Venice's most popular sights, these accommodations are pricey options for those in search of Venice's showy, tourist-oriented side.

▣ **Albergo San Samuele,** S. Marco, 3358 (☎/fax 041 522 8045). Follow Calle delle Botteghe from Campo S. Stefano and turn left on Salizzada S. Samuele. A crumbling stone courtyard leads to this charming, wonderfully priced hotel. Tapestry-print wallpaper and Italian art decorate colorful, clean rooms with sparkling bathrooms. 8 rooms with gorgeous balcony view of S. Marco's red roof-tops. 2 rooms downstairs without view are more spacious. Reserve 1-2 months ahead. Singles €26-45; doubles €36-70, with bath €46-100; triples €62-135. ❸

Albergo Casa Petrarca, Calle Schiavine, S. Marco, 4386 (☎/fax 041 520 0430). From Campo S. Luca, follow C. Fuseri and take your 2nd left and then a right. A tiny hotel with 7 small, clean, white rooms. Bright and cheery sitting room with rows of books in English. Fans in each room. 4 rooms with bath. Breakfast €7 extra. Singles €44; doubles €88. Discounts for extended stays. ❹

Hotel Locanda Fiorita, Campiello Novo, S. Marco, 3457 (☎041 523 4754; ☎/fax 522 8043; www.locandafiorita.com). From Campo S. Stefano, take Calle del Pestrin and then climb onto the raised piazza. A beautiful vine-covered courtyard and terrace lead to large doubles decorated with oriental rugs and couches. All rooms with A/C and TV. The nearby annex has a few ground-floor accommodations and satellite TV. Breakfast included. Singles without bath €78; doubles €90-145. Extra bed 30% more. AmEx/MC/V. ❺

Albergo Alloggia Alla Scala, Corte Contarini del Bovolo, S. Marco, 4306 (☎041 521 0629; fax 522 6451). From Campo Manin, facing the bridge, take a left down the alley and look for signs leading to La Scala del Bovolo. Superb location. Plain but simple rooms, reminiscent of the 1950s, all with bath. Singles €55; doubles €77-87; triples €117. Breakfast €18. MC/V. 6% discount for cash. ❹

Domus Civica (ACISJF), Campiello Chiovere Frari, S. Polo, 3082 (☎041 72 11 03; fax 522 7139). From station, cross Scalzi Bridge and turn right. Turn left on Fondamenta dei Tolentini and then left through the courtyard onto Corte Amai. The hostel's rounded facade is to the right, after the bridge. Simple student housing. 75 beds. TV room and piano. Check-in 7:30am-2pm. Strict curfew 11:30pm. Open mid-June to Sept. Singles €28.50, Rolling Venice and ISIC €23; doubles and triples €26/€21 per person. ❸

CASTELLO

Castello is arguably the most beautiful part of the city, and as it houses the largest number of native Venetians, it is also the most authentically Italian. A room on the second or 3rd floor with a view of red rooftops and breathtaking sights is worth the inevitability of losing your way among some of the narrowest and most tightly clustered streets in Venice.

Foresteria Valdese, Castello, 5170 (☎041 528 6797; fax 241 6238; www.chiesavaldese.org/venezia). From Campo S. Maria Formosa take Calle Lunga S. Maria. Housed in the *Palazzo* Cavagnis, immediately over the 1st bridge. This stunning building was once the 18th-century guest house of Venice's largest Protestant church and is a 2min. walk from Venice's major sights. Frescoed ceilings grace the dorms (with 33 beds) and the private rooms (all with TV). Breakfast included. Reception daily 9am-1pm and 6-8pm. Lock-out 10am-1pm. No curfew. Closed 3 wk. in Nov. Dorms €20 1st night, €19 each additional night; doubles €54-70; quads €98. Also has 2 apartments with bath and kitchen €99-110. €1 Rolling Venice discount. MC/V. ❷

La Residenza, Campo Bandiera e Moro, Castello, 3608 (☎041 528 5315; fax 523 8859; www.venicelaresidenza.com). From the Arsenal *vaporetto* stop: take a left on Riva degli Schiavoni and turn right on C. del Dose into the *campo*. 15th-century *palazzo* converted into an elaborately decorated, luxurious hotel complete with stone sculpture and billowing drapes. All rooms with bath, A/C, TV, and minibar. Breakfast included. Singles €60-90; doubles €100-155. Extra bed and breakfast €35. MC/V. ❺

Antica Locanda Casa Verardo, Castello, 4765 (☎041 528 6127; fax 523 2765; www.casaverardo.it). From the Basilica, walk down C. Canonica and take a right before the bridge and then left over the bridge on Ruga Giuffa into S. Filippo e Giacomo. Follow C. della Chiesa left out of the *campo* until you come to a bridge. The hotel is directly on the other side. Elegant and richly colored rooms in a newly refurbished 15th-century *palazzo*, still with original floor and ceiling. Magnificent rooftop sitting area has a view to rival that of the *campanile*. Some bathrooms have rooftop views as well. Private terrace for breakfast. All rooms with bath, A/C, and TV. Deluxe rooms have bathtubs. Possible 3-night min. stay. Singles €78-93; doubles €104-156, deluxe €130-197; triples €156-205/€197-233. AmEx/MC/V. ❺

Hotel Bruno, Salizzada S. Lio, Castello, 5726/A (☎041 523 0452; fax 522 1157; www.hoteldabruno.it). From Campo S. Bartolomeo, take the Salizzada S. Lio, crossing the bridge. High-ceilinged, beautiful rooms decorated in the original elaborate Venetian style. All rooms with bath and A/C. Breakfast included. Singles €60-155; doubles €80-210; triples €120-260. MC/V. ❺

Locanda Silva, Fondamenta del Rimedio, Castello, 4423 (☎041 522 7643; fax 528 6817; albergosilva@libero.it). From P. S. Marco, walk under clock tower, turn right onto Calle Larga S. Marco, left on Calle d. Angelo before the bridge, and then right onto Calle d. Rimedio before the next bridge. Follow straight to the end. This hotel, with its odd mixture of Asian and 1950s decor, has 24 sparse, clean rooms, and 2 resident cats. All rooms with phone. Breakfast included. Open Feb. to mid-Nov. Singles €46.50; doubles €77.50-104; triples €140. ❹

Locanda Canal, Fondamenta del Rimedio, Castello, 4422c (☎041 523 4538; fax 241 9138), next to Locanda Silva. A warm waiting room leads to 7 clean, sparsely decorated rooms in a converted 14th-century *palazzo*, some overlooking the canal. Family-like atmosphere. Breakfast included. Some rooms without shower. Doubles €87-115; triples €130-150. ❺

Locanda Corona, Calle Corona, Castello, 4464 (☎041 522 9174). From S. Maria Formosa, take Calle Rugagiuffa and turn right on Calle Corona. Well-worn, 3rd fl. hotel has 8 pricey, no-frills rooms. Wheelchair lift. Breakfast €10. Open Feb.-Dec. Singles €45; doubles €60; triples €65. ❹

VENICE

DORSODURO

Spartan facades and still canals trace the quieter, wider streets of Dorsoduro. Here, numerous art museums draw visitors to canal-front real estate, while the interior remains a little-visited residential quarter. Most hotels in Dorsoduro tend to be pricey, and are situated toward the Canal Grande, between the Chiesa dei Frari and the Accademia Bridge.

Hotel Galleria, Rio Terra Antonio Foscarini, Dorsoduro, 878/A (☎041 523 2489; fax 520 4172; www.hotelgalleria.it), on the left as you face the Accademia museum. Sumptuous oriental rugs and tasteful art prints lend the Galleria an elegance appropriate to its location on the Grand Canal. Stunning views in some of the 10 rooms compensate for their small size. Breakfast, served in rooms, included. Singles €62; doubles €88-135. Extra bed 30% more. AmEx/MC/V. ❺

Locanda Cà Foscari, Calle della Frescada, Dorsoduro, 3887b (☎041 71 04 01; fax 71 08 17; valtersc@tin.it), in a quiet neighborhood. From *vaporetto:* San Tomà, turn left at the dead end, cross the bridge, turn right, and then take a left into the little alleyway. Murano glass chandeliers and Venetian Carnival masks embellish this simple hotel operated by a warm older couple. Breakfast included. Curfew 1am. Book 2 or 3 months in advance. Closed 1st wk. of Aug., and end of Nov.-Jan. 1. Singles €60; doubles €70-90; triples €87-110; quads €108-130. MC/V. ❹

Hotel agli Alboretti, Accademia, 884 (☎ 041 523 0058; fax 521 0158; www.aglialboretti.com). From Accademia *vaporetto,* turn left off the landing, then right along the avenue. Typical Venetian house completely renovated. All rooms with bath, A/C, and TV. Breakfast included. Singles €93-134; doubles €100.50-145; triples €174. MC/V. ❺

Hotel Messner, Fondamenta di Cà Bala, Dorsoduro, 216 (☎041 522 7443; fax 522 7266; messner@doge.it). From *vaporetto:* Salute, walk up F. della Salute and turn right over the last bridge. The street ends at F. di Cà Bala. 31 rooms range from institutional singles to a quad with bath and kitchenette. All rooms with bath and phone. Annex has no TV or A/C and is less expensive. Buffet breakfast included. Open June to mid-Nov. Singles €102; doubles €155; triples €170. Annex singles €90; doubles €118; triples €147. AmEx/MC/V. ❺

CAMPING

If camping, plan on a 20min. boat ride to Venice. In addition to these listings, the **Litorale del Cavallino,** on the Lido's Adriatic side, has endless beach campsites.

Camping Miramare, Lungomare Dante Alighieri, 29 (☎041 96 61 50; fax 530 1150; www.camping-miramare.it). A 40min. boat ride (*vaporetto* #14) from P. S. Marco to Punta Sabbioni. Campground is 700m along the beach to your right. Plan on a 3-night min. stay in high season. Open mid-Mar. to Dec. €3.60-5.85 per person, €3.25-14.20 per tent. Bungalows €23.20-58.50. 15% Rolling Venice discount. ❶

Camping Fusina, V. Moranzani, 79 (☎041 547 0055; www.camping-fusina.com), in Malcontenta. From Mestre, take bus #1. Call ahead. €6 per person, €8-13 per tent and car, €11 to sleep in car. ❶

◖ FOOD

In Venice, dining well requires exploration. Beware the hordes of restaurants lining the canals around S. Marco and advertising *menù turistico*. You will pay heavily for white Christmas lights and mediocre cuisine. With a few exceptions, the best restaurants lie along less-traveled alleyways. There you can sample an authentic Venetian *pesce* (fish) dish. *Nero di seppie* (cuttlefish) is a soft, squid-like creature coated with its own ink and usually served with *polenta,* the Veneto's cornmeal staple. *Sarde in saor* (sardines in vinegar and onions) is available only in Venice. *Pesce fritta mista* (mixed fried seafood) usually includes shrimp, *calamari* (squid), and *polpo* (octopus). *Spaghetti alle vongole* (pasta with fresh clams) is on nearly every menu. A less famous, but still highly appreciated specialty in Venice is the asparagus. Every year at the *Festa dell'asparago di Giare* people flock to taste the thin stalks of white and green asparagus. Another favorite is *fegato alla veneziana* (liver and onions). *Panino con gelato* is a delicious desert of ice cream sandwiched between thin slices of flaky, buttery brioche.

The Veneto and Friuli regions produce an abundance of excellent **wines.** Good local whites include the sparkling *prosecco della Marca*, the dry *tocai*, and the savory *bianco di Custoza*. For reds, try a *valpolicella*. The least expensive option is by no means inferior: a simple *vino bianco* or *vino rosso* is usually the delicious locally produced merlot or chardonnay.

For an inexpensive and informal alternative to traditional restaurants, visit any *osteria* or *bacaro* in town for meat- and cheese-filled pastries, seafood, rice, or *tramezzini* (triangular slices of soft white bread with any imaginable filling). These snacks are known as **cicchetti** (chee-KET-ee) and usually go for about €3 each. Generally, you pay extra for table service, so standing at the bar is much cheaper than sitting down. Venetians generally drift from *bacaro* to *bacaro*, stopping in for a quick snack or just a glass of wine in the late afternoon (although *grappa* consumption often starts as early as 9am). Traditional *bacari* (see **Do Mori,** p. 233) fill the streets between the Rialto Bridge and Campo S. Polo.

The internationally renowned **Rialto Markets,** once the center of trade for the Venetian Republic, fill the area between the Grand Canal and the S. Polo foot of the Rialto Bridge every morning from Monday to Saturday. Fruit stands sell Sicilian blood oranges in the winter and Treviso cherries in the summer; a bit farther back, eels squirm on icy beds in the fish markets. Smaller fruit and vegetable markets set up in Cannaregio, on Rio Terra S. Leonardo by the Ponte delle Guglie, and in many of the city's *campi*.

STANDA Supermarket, Strada Nuova, Cannaregio, 3650, is near Campo Apostoli. (Open M-Sa 8:30am-7:20pm, Su 9am-7:20pm. AmEx/MC/V.) Smaller **FULL Alimentari,** Calle Carminati, 5989, Castello, is just north of P. S. Marco. (Open M-Sa 9am-1pm and 4-7:30pm. MC/V.)

CANNAREGIO

Trattoria da Bepi, Cannaregio, 4550 (☎041 528 5031; fax 241 7245). From Campo SS. Apostoli, turn left onto Salizzade del Pistor. This traditional Venetian restaurant, family-run for 38 years, has a charmingly rustic interior, with copper pots dangling from the ceiling. Outdoor patio dining. Huge bread baskets and authentic Venetian cuisine. *Primi* €7-10.50, *secondi* €9.50-18. Open F-W noon-2:30pm and 7-10pm. MC/V. ❹

Pizzeria La Perla, Rio Terra dei Franceschi, Cannaregio, 4615 (☎041 528 5175). From Strada Nuova, turn left onto Salizzade del Pistor in Campo SS. Apostoli. Follow it to the end, and then follow the signs for the Fondamente Nuove. Offers no less than 90 types of pizza and pasta, each served in heaping portions by friendly staff. Informal and spacious, it is perfect for families. Pasta €6.10-8.20, pizza €4.65-7.90. Wheelchair accessible. Cover €1.10. Open Sept.-July M-Sa noon-2pm and 7-9:45pm. AmEx/MC/V. ❸

Gam Gam, Canale di Cannaregio, Cannaregio, 1122 (☎041 71 52 84). From Campo S. Geremia, cross the bridge and turn left. The only Jewish restaurant with Kosher food in Venice. *Schnitzel* €11.50, falafel platter €8.75, and pasta €7.50-9. Outdoor seating by canal. Join Shabbat service on Friday night and enjoy a free Shabbat dinner after; all are welcome. 10% *Let's Go* discount. Open Su-F noon-10pm. ❹

Ristorante Brek, Lista di Spagna, Cannaregio, 124A (☎041 244 0158). From the station, turn left. Italian fast food chain whips up pasta and salad dishes from an extensive array of ingredients that you choose. Perfect for a meal on the go. Menu and prices change daily. About €2-8. Open daily 8-10:30am and 11:30am-10:30pm. ❷

BEHIND THE MASK
Venice Struggles to Preserve Itself

The sweep of the Rialto Bridge, stoic under a swarm of Americans and Germans. The glittering Piazza San Marco, an elegant backdrop for weary French parents and screaming Japanese children. The riot of the Grand Canal, indifferent to Venetian commuters pushing past British amateur photographers.

"Where is the real Venice?" a visitor wonders despairingly, dodging pigeons, photographers, and guides. "Away from the tourists?"

There is no Venice apart from the tourists. Venice is theater; every action is meant to be observed, from the gondolier's flourish to the bickering in the Rialto Markets. Where they couldn't be sure of spectators, residents carved them—watchful faces smiling down from every *palazzo*—or filled shop windows with them—rows of reproachfully staring masks.

Venice has always been vested in maintaining its stream of observers. In 828 AD the city stole the body of St. Mark, the city's newly adopted patron, from Egypt. This relic made Venice a major pilgrimage site with enough clout to declare its independence; Venice gained statehood only by becoming a tourist destination. In the 13th and 14th centuries, the republic, with a monopoly on trade routes between Europe and the East, attracted buyers, sellers, and curious travelers from around the world to its renowned Rialto Markets. Tourism stayed strong for centuries, and when Venice lost its trade monopoly, tourism became its main revenue source. By the 1700s the city had become the premiere playground for Europe's rich, and the city of masks and illusion gave itself completely to the revelry.

Today, Venice desperately looks to recapture that former financial glory. In the 1950s, new industry on the mainland drew away many of the city's young families, leaving a permanent population of only 50,000 and a people with an average age of 50 (New York's, in contrast, is 34; Sydney's is 38). Over half the islands' buildings are now abandoned. The city continues to sink (though more slowly), creating floods of at least 4 inches 100 times a year and causing brick-eroding salt from lagoon water to seep into the lowered buildings.

Venetian officials have turned once again to Venice's specialty—tourism. Although proposals for attracting permanent residents have been made, actual accomplishments have focused on attracting more tourists for longer stays, such as the Biennale International Art Exhibition and the annual Film Festival.

The city is also looking to change the type of tourists who visit. The majority of the 10 million who arrive each year currently spend little money in the city, doing the rounds in a few hours then leaving for less-expensive Padua or Florence. Rather than encouraging more affordable hotels or restaurants in Italy's most expensive city, however, former Mayor Massimo Cacciari preferred discouraging the Polaroid crowd altogether. In 1999 he commissioned a series of Benetton ads called "Against Venice/For Venice," which depicted such scenes as a tourist being mauled by pigeons. Other officials want to charge admission to the city, increase airport and train taxes, or issue tickets to limit the number of daytrippers. The new mayor, Paolo Costa, has so far eschewed such radical Keep Out signs, instead proposing new development that would create jobs during construction and house modern businesses once completed. He has also suggested trademarking Venice, presumably a response to Las Vegas's Venetian casino, which has created a well-publicized feud between the two cities.

Once the meeting place of the world's cultures, Venice now hovers at the point where many of Europe's major problems converge. As those who love the city cry for help with its restoration and protection, it remains to be seen whether the city of illusions will sink beneath her popularity, or whether she will choose a new mask and reinvent herself once more.

Lisa Nosal was a Researcher-Writer for Let's Go: Italy 2000, *a Managing Editor in 1999, and the editor of* Austria & Switzerland 1998. *She led guided tours of Venice for the Enjoy Venice cultural association, and now works for an educational travel company in Boston.*

CASTELLO

Alle Testiere, Calle del Mondo Novo, Castello, 5801 (☎/fax 041 522 7220). From Campo S. Maria Formosa, take the Calle Mondo Nuovo. Tiny restaurant mixes old tradition with *nuovo* decor and cuisine. Black and white photos line the walls, and guests sit at highly polished wooden tables selecting delicious fish entrees from a small but carefully compiled menu. *Primi* €13, *secondi* €20-23. Reservations suggested. Open Tu-Sa noon-2pm and 7-10:30pm. MC/V. ❺

Pizzeria/Trattoria Al Vecio Canton, Castello, 4738/a (☎041 528 5176). From Campo S. Maria Formosa, with the church on your right, cross the bridge and follow Rugagiuffa. Take a right at the end. This farm-house like *trattoria* is famous for its specialty pizza *Al Vecio Canton* (topped with tomatoes, cheese, olive oil, garlic, and a spritz of lemon; €6.20). Open W-M noon-11pm. ❸

Arcimboldo, Calle dei Furlani, Castello, 3219 (☎ 041 528 6569). From Riva Schiavoni, take C. Dose up to Campo Bandiera, and follow Sal. S. Antonin straight up to Furlani. Take a right at the Scuola S. Giorgio onto Calle dei Furlani. Tucked away from local tourist haunts, along the canal. Colorful paintings by Arcimboldo and romantic atmosphere. Try the specialty *pesce al forno con verdure di stagione* (baked fish with vegetables; €26 serves 2). *Primi* €13. Open W-M noon-3:30pm and 7-10:30pm. MC/V. ❺

Cip Ciap, Calle Mondo Novo, 5799a (☎041 523 6621). From Campo S. Maria Formosa, follow Calle Mondo Novo. Huge, delicious pizzas from €3.65. The *disco volante* (literally, flying saucer) is made like a calzone and stuffed with mushrooms, eggplant, ham, egg, and salami (€6.20). Open W-M 9am-9pm. ❸

Osteria Santa Marina, Campo S. Marina, Castello, 5911 (☎/fax 041 528 5239). Take C. Bartolomeo to C. Lio; then take your 1st left after the bridge onto Calle Carminati. Take a right at the end. At that end, take a left. For a splurge, enjoy traditional Venetian cuisine with well-dressed locals, or stop by for some *cicchetti* and a glass of *prosecco*. The restaurant specializes in fish. *Primi* €14, *secondi* €18. Cover €2.50. Open Tu-Sa 7:30-10pm and 12:30-2:30pm, Su-M 7:30-10pm. MC/V. ❺

SAN MARCO

🔲 **Le Bistrot de Venise,** Calle dei Fabbri, S. Marco, 4685 (☎041 523 6651; www.bistrotdevenise.com). From P. S. Marco, head through the 2nd *sottoportego* dei Dai under the awning. Follow the road around and over a bridge and go right. Scrumptious, beautifully presented meals prepared solely from 14th-century recipes in an elegant and relaxing setting. The ravioli (€13) is a specialty, as is the risotto with eel. The homemade pasta dishes are superb, and the wine list extensive (€4-5 a glass); try the Bisol *prosecco,* a sparkling white wine. From Oct. to May, Le Bistrot's frequent afternoon arts and literature exhibitions draw local artisans, poets, and musicians. Open daily noon-3pm and 7pm-1am. *Secondi* from €17. Service 15%. AmEx/MC/V. ❺

Vino, Vino, Ponte delle Veste, S. Marco, 2007a (☎041 241 7688). From Calle Larga XXII Marzo, turn onto Calle delle Veste. Dark, no-frills wine bar has over 350 varieties of wine. Seafood-focused menu changes daily. *Primi* €5, *secondi* €9. Cover €1. Open W-F, Su-M 10:30am-midnight, Sa 10:30am-1am. 15% Rolling Venice discount. ❸

Rosticceria San Bartomoleo, Calle della Bissa, S. Marco, 5424/A (☎041 522 3569). From Campo S. Bartolomeo, follow the Sottoportego de la Bissa to the neon sign. Offers a smorgasbord of sandwiches, pasta, and *cicchetti* to be enjoyed on the go or at a window booth. The full-service restaurant upstairs is open for lunch. Entrees start at €4.90. Cover €1.30. Open Tu-Su 9:30am-9:30pm. AmEx/MC/V. ❶

VENICE

Harry's Bar, Calle Vallaresso, S. Marco, 1323 (☎041 528 5777), around the corner from the Venice Pavilion. Founded in 1931 by a Bostonian named Harry who felt that Venice suffered a lack of bars, this cafe has been pouring pricey drinks (including his famous *bellini*) to tourists and notables like Ernest Hemingway, Katharine Hepburn, Robert DeNiro, and Tom Cruise ever since. *Bellini* €13. Service 15%. Open daily 10:30am-10:55pm. MC/V. ❹

DORSODURO

Pizza al Volo, Campo S. Margherita, Dorsoduro, 2944 (☎041 522 5430). Hang-out spot for students and locals who come for delicious, cheap pizza. The tasty house specialty *al volo* is a sauceless pie topped with *mozzarella* and *melanzane* (eggplant). Slices from €1.30. Large pizzas from €3.40. Gigantic pizzas, large enough for 2, from €6.30. Takeout only. Open daily 11:30am-4pm and 5:30pm-1:30am. ❶

Cantinone del Vino, Fondamente Meraviglie, Dorsoduro, 992 (☎041 523 0034). From Frari, follow the signs for the Accademia bridge. Just before the Ponte Meraviglie, turn right toward the church of S. Trovaso. Cross the 1st bridge. A spectacular display of wines line the walls, ranging from €3 to 200 a bottle. Enjoy a glass at the bar with some *cichetti* (from €1). Open M-Sa 8am-2:30pm and 3:15-8:30pm. ❷

SAN POLO AND SANTA CROCE

Ae Oche, Santa Croce, 1552a/b (☎041 524 1161). From Campo S. Giacomo da L'orio, take Calle del Trentor. Join Venetians at their local hangout. Choose from 100 different types of huge pizzas (€4-7). Open daily noon-3pm and 7pm-midnight. MC/V. ❷

Osteria Enoteca "Vivaldi," San Polo, 1457 (☎041 523 8185). From the C. S. Polo, opposite the church, go over the bridge to Calle della Madonnetta. Let Sigfrido and Massimiliano serve you their version of the Venetian specialty *sarde in saor,* in what is appropriately called Venice's "Friendliest Restaurant." *Primi* €8, *secondi* €10. Open daily 11:30am-2:30pm and 6:30-10:30pm. Reserve for F-Sa nights. AmEx/MC/V. ❸

Ristorante Ribò, Fondamenta Minotto, S. Croce, 158 (☎041 524 2486). With your back to the station, cross the Scalzi Bridge and turn right. Left on F. dei Tolentini just before the bridge, then left on F. Minotto. Canal view in an elegant setting with traditional Venetian cuisine. Outdoor dining also available. Bright, friendly atmosphere, not ideal for a romantic evening. *Primi* from €12, *secondi* €14. Cover €3. Open Tu-Su 12:30-2:15pm and 7:30-10:15pm. Closed Sa for lunch. AmEx/MC/V. ❺

Ganesh Ji, Calle dell'Olio, S. Polo, 2426 (☎/fax 041 71 98 04). From the station, cross the Scalzi Bridge, continue straight, and turn left on Calle della Bergama. Take a right on Fondamenta Rio Marin and then another right on Calle dell'Olio. Delicious Indian food, served outside on the terrace with a canal view, or indoors among the elephant statues and candy-stripe poles. Vegetarian lunch €11, regular €12. Cover €1.70. 10% Rolling Venice discount. Takeout available. Open W-Th 7-11pm, F-Tu 12:30-2pm and 7-11pm. In winter closed W. MC/V. ❸

Antica Birraria La Carte, Campo S. Polo, S. Polo, 2168 (☎041 275 0570). Housed in a former brewery, the Birraria stays true to its roots with an extensive selection of German beers and a lively youth scene. Accordion players often just outside. Beer €1.50-4.30, pizzas €4-8. Open Tu-Su noon-3pm and 6pm-midnight. AmEx/MC/V. ❷

Due Colonne, Campo S. Agostin, S. Polo, 2343 (☎041 524 0685). Cross the bridge away from the Frari, turn left, and cross into Campo S. Stin; then turn right on Calle Donà and cross the bridge. Students, families, and tourists crowd the large indoor booths and the *campo* seating to sample a variety of pizzas (€3.50-7.50). Elegant charcoal sketches of Venice cover the dark wood walls. Cover €0.80. Service 10%. Open Sept.-July M-Sa 8am-3pm and 7-11pm. Kitchen closes 10pm. ❶

Cantina Do Mori, Calle due Mori, S. Polo, 429 (☎041 522 5401). From the Rialto Bridge, follow signs to C. S. Giacomo. Follow Orefici out straight; it turns into R. dei Speziali. Take a left on C. Mori. Aging copperware lining the walls and an uneven stone floor give Venice's oldest wine bar a charming antique feel to which tourists gravitate. Still an elegant place to grab a a few *cicchetti* (from €1.50) or a superb glass of local wine. No seating. Open M-Sa 9am-9pm. ❷

GELATERIE AND PASTICCERIE

La Boutique del Gelato, Salizzada S. Lio, Castello, 5727 (☎041 522 3283). From Campo Bartolomeo, walk under the Sotoportego de la Bissa, go straight, and cross the bridge into Campo S. Lio. Follow Salizada S. Lio; it's on the left. Large cones and the cheapest prices. Single scoop €0.80. Open daily 10am-8pm.

Gelateria Nico, Fondamenta Zattere, Dorsoduro, 922 (☎041 522 5293). Near *vaporetto*: Zattere, with a great view of the Giudecca Canal. *Gelato* €0.80-6.50. Try the Venetian specialty *gianduiotto al passagetto* (a slice of dense chocolate-hazelnut ice cream dunked in whipped cream; €2.30). Open daily 6:45am-11pm.

🄶 SIGHTS

AROUND THE RIALTO BRIDGE

THE GRAND CANAL. The grand canal loops through Venice, passing the splendid facades of the *palazzi* that crown its banks and testifying to the city's history of immense wealth. Although their external decorations vary, the palaces share the same basic structure. The most decorated floors, the *piani nobili* (noble floors; second and third stories), housed luxurious salons and bedrooms. The rich merchant families stored their goods on the ground floor, and the servants slept in the tiny rooms below the roof. The candy cane-like posts used for mooring boats on the canal are called *bricole,* and they are decorated with the colors of the family owning the adjoining *palazzo. (To see the facades of these buildings, ride vaporetto #82 or the slower #1 from the train station to P. S. Marco. A nighttime ride reveals the floodlit facades, a dazzling play of reflections and light.)*

THE RIALTO BRIDGE. This impressive architectural construct was named after Rivo Alto, the first colony built in Venice. It was originally built of wood, but after its collapse in the 1500s, Antonio da Ponte designed the current stone spectacle (1588-91). Today, shops and vendors crowd the top of the bridge offering their wares. Beware terrifying tourist prices.

RIVOALTUS LEGATORIA. Step into Rivoaltus on any given day and you will hear Wanda Scarpa shouting greetings from the attic, where she has been sewing leatherbound reproductions of antique journals and portfolios for more than 30 years. Giorgio Scarpa jokes that he chains her there to make her work. This delightful, reasonably priced shop is cluttered with the results of her diligent toiling. Buy an album and sketch a view of Venice from the bridge. Although Venice is now littered with a plethora of shops advertising handmade journals, Rivoaltus was the first to open, and products are of such high quality that movie stars have been known to send their agents specifically to this shop to buy a portfolio before their movie shoots. *(Ponte di Rialto. ☎041 523 6195. Open daily 10am-7:30pm.)*

AROUND PIAZZA SAN MARCO

BASILICA DI SAN MARCO. The crown jewel of Venice is a spectacular fusion of gold and marble that graces the piazza with its symmetry and frescos. As the city's largest tourist attraction, it also has the longest lines. Visit in the early morning for the shortest wait, or in the late afternoon for the best natural illumination of the interior mosaics and exterior frescos.

Construction of the basilica began in the 9th century, when two Venetian merchants stole St. Mark's remains from Alexandria and packed them in pork in order to sneak them past Arab officials. After the first church dedicated to St. Mark burnt down in the 11th century, Venice set out to erect a church that would not only house the Evangelist but also rival the magnificent houses of worship in Rome and Constantinople. During construction, the city snubbed the Roman Catholic Church's standard architectural structure, choosing to build the basilica according to a Greek-cross plan crowned by five bulbous domes.

The interior of the church sparkles with gold mosaics from both the 13th-century Byzantine and 16th-century Renaissance periods. Christ Pantocrator (Ruler of All) sits in judgment above the high altar, surrounded by his Evangelists. The floor is composed of magnificent 12th-century stone mosaics. Nine centuries of uneven sinking of the foundations have given the floor its sea-like waviness. Behind the altar screen, decorated with Renaissance statues of the Apostles, the Virgin Mary, and Mary Magdalene, is the **Pala D'Oro,** a gem-encrusted relief covering the tomb of St. Mark. To the right of the altar is the **Tesoro** (treasury) of gold and relics from the Fourth Crusade. Steep stairs in the atrium lead to the **Galleria della Basilica,** which offers a staggering perspective of the interior mosaics, a tranquil vista of the piazza, and an intimate view of the original bronze Horses of St. Mark. *(Basilica open daily 9:30am-4:30pm. Illuminated 11:30am-12:30pm. Dress code enforced; shoulders and knees must be covered. Free. Pala D'Oro open daily 9:45am-5pm. €1.50, reduced €1. Treasury open M-Sa 9:45am-5pm. €2, reduced €1. Galleria open daily 9:45am-5pm. €1.50, reduced €1.)*

> **MINI-SKIRTS, MINI-PASSES, AND MINI-DISCOUNTS.** Mini-skirts are verboten in many Venetian churches, which enforce a strict dress code that calls for coverage of shoulders and knees. Mini-passes to visit Venice's churches are sold by the Foundation for the Churches of Venice. A three-day mini pass (€8, students €5) for all 15 of Venice's churches, including S. Maria dei Miracoli, S. Maria Gloriosa dei Frari, S. Polo, Madonna dell'Orto, Il Redentore, and S. Sebastiano, is available at all participating churches (except S. Maria Gloriosa dei Frari). For information call ☎041 275 0462.

■ **PALAZZO DUCALE (DOGE'S PALACE).** Once the home of Venice's mayor, or Doge, the Palazzo Ducale is now a museum that reveals history in light of the spectacular artwork, including Veronese's *Rape of Europa*, of the Doge's public and private rooms. When the city enlarged the palace in the 15th century, it maintained the original 14th-century building's graceful, light design (despite opposition from Renaissance architects who claimed the building looked "upside-down"). In the courtyard, Sansovino's enormous sculptures, *Mars* and *Neptune,* flank the *Scala dei Giganti* (Stairs of the Giants), upon which new Doges would be crowned. On the balcony stands the *Bocca di Leone* (Lion's Mouth), into which the Council of Ten (the Doge's assistants, who acted as judges and administrators) would drop the names of those they suspected guilty of crimes. Within the palace lie the Doge's private apartments and the magnificent state rooms of the Republic. Climb the richly decorated *Scala d'Oro* (Golden Staircase) to reach the *Sala del Maggior Consiglio* (Great Council Room), dominated by Tintoretto's *Paradise*, the largest oil painting in the world. More stairs lead to the *Sala delle Quattro Porte* (Room of the Four Doors) and the *Sala dell'Anticollegio* (Antechamber of the Senate), decorated with, amongst other things, masterful allegories by Tintoretto. Passages lead through the courtrooms of the much-feared Council of Ten and the even-more-feared Council of Three, crossing the underground *Ponte dei Sospiri* (Bridge of

Sighs) and continuing into the prisons. The infamous Casanova was among those condemned by the Ten to walk across this bridge, which gets its name from 19th-century Romantic writers' references to the mournful groans of prisoners descending into dank cells. (☎041 520 9070; mkt.musei@comune.venezia.it. Open Nov.-Apr. daily 9am-3:30pm, Apr.-Oct. 9am-5:30pm. Wheelchair accessible. €9.50, student €5.50, ages 6-14 €3. Includes entrance to Museo Correr, Biblioteca Nazionale Marciana, Museo Archeologico, Museo di Palazzo Mocenigo, Museo del Vetro di Murano, and Museo del Merletto di Burano. Pass for above museums and Casa Rezzonico and Casa di Goldoni €15.50, students €10. Audio guides €5.50.)

▨**PIAZZA SAN MARCO.** Unlike the narrow, labyrinthine streets that wind through most of Venice, P. S. Marco (Venice's only official piazza) is a magnificent expanse of light and space, and palatial architecture. Enclosing the piazza are the 16th-century Renaissance **Procuratie Vecchie** (Old Treasury Offices), the more ornate 17th-century Baroque **Procuratie Nuove** (New Treasury Offices), and the smaller Neoclassical **Ala Napoleonica** (also Treasury Offices). The **Basilica di San Marco** stands majestically over the open end of the piazza.

Between the basilica and the Procuratie Vecchie perches the **Torre dell'Orologio (Clock Tower)**, constructed between 1496 and 1499 according to Coducci's design. The 24-hour clock indicates the hour, lunar phase, and ascending constellation. Unfortunately, this time-keeping treasure has been hidden from view for several years now by restoration scaffolding.

The brick **campanile** (96m bell tower), which stands on Roman foundations, and was designed by Bartolomeo Bon (1511-1514), provides one of the best aerial views of the city. Though it originally served as a watchtower and lighthouse, Venice later took advantage of its location, creating a medieval tourist attraction by dangling state prisoners in cages from its top, a practice that continued well into the 18th century. In a 1902 restoration project, the tower collapsed into a mere pile of bricks. It was reconstructed in 1912, with the practical addition of an elevator. On a clear day, you can see the coast of Croatia and Slovenia from the top. (Campanile open daily 9am-9pm. €6. Audioguide €3, 2 for €4.)

PIAZZA SAN MARCO'S MUSEUMS. Beneath the arcade at the short end of P. S. Marco lies the entrance to a trio of museums. The **Museo Civico Correr** contains artifacts from Venice's imperial past such as intricately decorated plates, and curiosities of Venetian life, like the platform shoes worn by sequestered noblewomen. The first part of the museum shows the Neoclassical French influence on Venetian art, then progress to a medley of works by Bellini and some by Carpaccio. The **Museo Archeologico** houses a modest but beautiful collection of ancient Greek and Roman sculpture and medallions. There is even a fragment of a colossal foot with a big toenail larger than the average hand. Gorgeous paintings by Veronese, Titian, and Tintoretto adorn the main reading room of the **Biblioteca Nazionale Marciana.** The library was built by Jacopo Sansovino from 1537 to 1560. (☎041 522 4951; mkt.musei@comune.venezia.it. Open daily 9am-7pm. Tickets €9.50, students €5.50. Includes entrance to Palazzo Ducale, Museo Vetrario di Murano, and Museo del Merletto di Burano. Or free with pass; see above. Free guided tours for the Archeologico M-F 2pm, Sa-Su 2:30pm, and for the Biblioteca Sa-Su 10am, noon, 2 and 4pm.)

LA SCALA DEL BOVOLO. This snow-white marble "staircase of the snails," as it translates into English, is a magnificent architectural creation. Legend has it that the staircase was designed by Leonardo da Vinci himself, and constructed by his assistants. It once led to the top floors of a now-destroyed palace. The top only affords views of the interior of the next-door neighbor's kitchen. (From the Campo Manin, facing the bridge, take a left down the alley looking for the signs. Open Apr.-Oct. daily 10am-6pm; Nov.-Feb. 10am-5pm. €2.50. Groups of 10 or more €2.)

VENICE

WHERE IT'S @. The "@" symbol reputedly originated in Venice. When Venetian merchants exported goods, they would write "@" in front of the package's address to distinguish the destination from the shipping point. La Scala del Bovolo is reputedly in an "@"-like spiral shape because it was once attached to the palace of a wealthy merchant.

SAN POLO

■ **SCUOLA GRANDE DI SAN ROCCO.** Venice's most illustrious *scuola*, or guild hall, stands as a monument to Jacopo Tintoretto. The painter, who left Venice only once in his 76 years (and refused to take that trip without his wife), set out to combine "the color of Titian with the drawing of Michelangelo." To achieve effects of depth, he often built dioramas in which he placed models so that he could portray the figures with spatial accuracy. The *scuola* commissioned Tintoretto to complete all of the paintings in the building, a task that took 23 years. The *Crucifixion* in the last room upstairs is the building's crowning glory. Lined with intricately carved columns and richly colored marble, the *scuola* is itself quite a masterpiece. If you step outside to admire it, you will often find yourself surrounded by street musicians performing classical music. *(Behind Basilica dei Frari in Campo S. Rocco. ☎041 523 4864. Open Nov.-Mar. M-F 10am-1pm, Sa-Su 10am-4pm. €5.50, students €3.75, under 18 free. Audio guides free.)*

CAMPO SAN POLO. The second-largest *campo* in Venice (only P. S. Marco is larger), S. Polo once hosted bull-baiting matches. During the *carnevale*, authorities would release a wild bull into the crowds and then set dogs after it. After ripping and tearing the bull's flesh, the exhausted animal would finally be decapitated amidst the cheering throngs of people. A painting depicting the ensuing chaos hangs in the Museo Correr in P. S. Marco. Today, its benches, trees, and frolicking children give the field a relaxed quality. *(Between the Frari and Rialto Bridges. Vaporetto: "S. Silvestro." Straight back from the vaporetto. Or from in front of the Frari, cross the bridge and turn right, then left on Rio Terà, right on Calle Seconda d. Saoneri, and left at the dead end.)*

DORSODURO

■ **GALLERIE DELL'ACCADEMIA.** This gallery houses the most extensive collection of Venetian art in the world. Room I, with a ceiling full of cherubim, houses the colorful Venetian Gothic art. Among the enormous altarpieces in Room II, Giovanni Bellini's *Madonna Enthroned with Child, Saints, and Angels* stands out for its lush serenity. Rooms IV and V display more Bellinis, including the magnificent *Madonna and Child with Magdalene and Saint Catherine* and two works by Giorgione. Giorgione defied contemporary convention by creating works that apparently told no story. Attempts to find plot or moral in *The Tempest* have been fruitless. An X-ray of the pictures reveals that Giorgione originally painted a bathing woman where the young man now stands. Other Venetian Renaissance works line the rooms leading to Room X, home to Veronese's colossal *Supper in the House of Levi*. Originally painted as a Last Supper, the infuriated Inquisition council tried to force Veronese to modify his unorthodox interpretation of the memorable event which depicts a Protestant German, a midget, dogs, and fat men. Instead, Veronese cleverly changed the title, saving his artistic license and his life. Hanging on the wall facing the entrance are several Tintorettos, displaying his virtuosity at painting swooping, diving figures. On the opposite wall is Titian's last painting, *a Pietà*, intended for his tomb. In Room XX, works by Gentile Bellini and Carpaccio display Venetian processions and cityscapes so accurately that scholars use them as "photos" of Venice's past. *(Vaporetto: "Accademia." ☎041 522 2247. Open M 8:15am-2pm, T-Su 9:15am-7:15pm. €6.50. Guided tours free for groups.)*

■ **COLLEZIONE PEGGY GUGGENHEIM.** Guggenheim's elegant, water-front Palazzo Venier dei Leoni, once a gathering place for the world's artistic elite, now displays a private modern art collection. The museum includes wonderful and eclectic works by Brancusi, Marini, Kandinsky, Picasso, Magritte, Rothko, Ernst, Pollock, and Dalí. In the peaceful sculpture garden, the late Guggenheim and her beloved pets (14 Shih Tzu dogs) are buried. The Marini sculpture *Angel in the City*, which stands triumphantly on the terrace, was designed with a detachable penis. Ms. Guggenheim occasionally modified this sculpture so as not to offend her more prudish guests. The flowering terrace offers unobstructed views of the Grand Canal. The temporary exhibit "Turner: Romantic Landscapes in Venice" is expected in May 2003. *(Calle S. Cristoforo, Dorsoduro, 710. Vaporetto: "Accademia." Turn left and follow the yellow signs. ☎041 240 5411; fax 520 6885. Open Su-M and W-F 10am-6pm, Sa 10am-10pm. €8, ISIC or Rolling Venice €5, under 12 free. Audioguide €4.)*

SQUERO DI SAN TROVASO. The last remaining gondola shipyard in Venice (built in the 17th century), this *squero* displays the boats in various stages of development (and decay). The buildings are in the style of Cadore mountain dwellings. (Cadore is the native region of the boat makers, as well as the wood source for the boats.) To see gondolas in the process of assembly even if the main door is closed, cross the canal and look into the back of the yard. *(Vaporetto: "Zattere." Follow signs for the Accademia Bridge. Go up Fond. Nani, where you'll see the boats. Cross the 1st bridge to reach the entrance on Campo S. Trovaso. Open sporadically. Free.)*

CÀ REZZONICO. Longhena's great 17th-century Venetian palace houses the newly restored **Museo del Settecento Veneziano (Museum of 17th Century Venice).** Known as the "Temple of Venetian Settecento," this grand palace showcases a truly regal ballroom, complete with flowing curtains and Crosato's frescoed ceiling depicting Phoebus with the continents. Other rooms display elaborate Venetian Rococo decor. The upstairs contains two extensive portrait galleries. Reserve at least 2hr. in advance to take in works by Tiepolo, Guardi, and Longhi and Tintoretto. *(Vaporetto: "Cà Rezzonico." Go straight into Campo S. Barnaba, take the 1st bridge on the right, and turn right on Fond. Rezzonico. ☎041 241 0100. Open Apr.-Feb. W-M 10am-6pm. €6.50, students €4.50. Audioguide €5.50.)*

CASTELLO

SCUOLA DALMATA SAN GIORGIO DEGLI SCHIAVONI. Carpaccio decorated the ground floor of this modest early 16th-century building with some of his finest paintings, depicting episodes from the lives of St. George, Jerome, and Tryfon. *(Castello, 3259/A. Vaporetto: S. Zaccaria. From the Riva Schiavoni, take Calle Dose up to Calle Bandiera e Moro. Follow it to S. Antonin and then to Fond. Furlani. Open Tu-Sa 9:30am-12:30pm and 3:30-6:30pm, Su 9:30am-12:30pm. Shoulders and knees must be covered. €2.)*

GIARDINI PUBLICI AND SANT'ELENA. Longing for trees and grass? Stroll through the Public Gardens, installed by Napoleon, or bring a picnic lunch to the shady lawns of Sant'Elena. *(Vaporetto: "Giardini" or "S. Elena." Free.)*

GONDOLAS GONE GOTH. Gondolas were once floating displays of multicolored brilliance. The lavish reds and purples turned to somber black, however, when the plague struck in 1700s. To seal out the disease-infected canal waters, and stop potential contamination, the bare wooden boats were covered in black tar and pitch. The morbid color was also a sign of respect for Venice's dying. While plague was eradicated from the canals, the color stuck.

VENICE

CANNAREGIO

JEWISH GHETTO. In 1516, the Doge forced Venice's Jewish population into the old cannon-foundry area, creating the first Jewish ghetto in Europe. *(Ghetto* is the Venetian word for foundry.) At its height, the ghetto housed 5000 people in buildings up to seven stories, making them among the tallest tenements in Europe at the time. The oldest synagogue, or *schola*, the **Schola Grande Tedesca (German Synagogue)**, shares a building with the **Museo Ebraica di Venezia (Hebrew Museum of Venice)** in the Campo del Ghetto Nuovo. In the adjoining Campiello d. Scuole stand the opulent **Schola Levantina (Levantine Synagogue)** and the **Schola Spagnola (Spanish Synagogue)**, both at least partially designed by Longhena. *(Cannaregio, 2899/B. Vaporetto: "S. Marcuola." Follow the signs straight ahead and then turn left into Campo del Ghetto Nuovo. ☎041 71 53 59. Hebrew Museum open June-Sept. Su-F 10am-7pm. €3, students €2. Entrance to synagogues by guided tour only (40min.). English tours leave from the museum every hr. 10:30am-4:30pm. Museum and tour €8, students €6.50.)*

CÀ D'ORO AND GALLERIA GIORGIO FRANCHETTI. The most spectacular facade on the Grand Canal and a premiere example of Venetian Gothic, the Cà d'Oro (1425-1440) now houses the Giorgio Franchetti collection of art. Highlights include Andrea Mantegna's *Saint Sebastian*, the last example of a subject that Mantegna frequently portrayed, and Bonaccio's *Apollo Belvedere*, one of the most important bronzes of the 15th century. For the best ▨view of the Cà D'Oro's "wedding cake" facade, take the *traghetto* across the canal to the Rialto Markets. *(Vaporetto: "Cà d'Oro." ☎041 523 8790. Open M-Su 9am-2pm. €3.50.)*

CHURCHES

▨**CHIESA DI SAN ZACCARIA (SAN MARCO).** Dedicated to the father of John the Baptist and designed by Coducci (among others) in the late 1400s, this Gothic-Renaissance church holds one of the masterpieces of Venetian Renaissance painting, Giovanni Bellini's *Virgin and Child Enthroned with Four Saints*. With rich tones and shadows, it's a prime example of Venetian artists' meticulous attention to detail. *(Vaporetto: "S. Zaccaria." From P. S. Marco, turn left along the water, cross the bridge, and turn left on Calle Albanesi. Take a right and go straight. ☎041 522 1257. Open daily 10am-noon and 4-6pm. Free.)*

CHIESA DI SAN GIACOMO DI RIALTO (SAN MARCO). Between the Rialto Bridge and surrounding markets stands Venice's first church, diminutively called "San Giacometto." An ornate clock-face adorns its *campanile*. Across the piazza, a statue called *il Gobbo* (the hunchback) supports the steps; it once served as a podium from which officials made announcements and at whose feet convicted thieves, forced to run naked from P. S. Marco and lashed all the way by bystanders, could finally collapse. *(Vaporetto: "Rialto." Cross bridge and head right. Church open daily 10am-5pm. Free.)*

BASILICA DI SANTA MARIA GLORIOSA DEI FRARI (I FRARI) (SAN POLO). The Franciscans started construction on this enormous Gothic church in 1340. Now, two paintings by Titian as well as the Renaissance master himself lie within the cathedral's cavernous terra-cotta walls. His ▨*Assumption* (1516-18) on the high altar marks the height of the Venetian Renaissance. Like contemporary Roman and Florentine painters Titian created balanced, harmonious compositions, while adding the Venetian love of color and sensuality. Titian's other work, *the Madonna and Child with Saints and Members of the Pesaro Family* (1547) is on the right as you enter. The work is revolutionary because of Titian's unorthodox placement of the Virgin Mary and Child to the right of center and his forthright depiction of the Madonna's humble facial expression. Titian's elaborate tomb, a triumphal arch, stands diagonally across from the Pesaro altar and directly across from the enormous pyramid in which the sculptor Canova (1757-1822) rests. An extraordinary work by Bellini, *Virgin and Child with Saints Nicholas, Peter, Benedict, and Mark* (1488) hangs in the sacristy. In the Florentine chapel to the right of the high altar is Donatello's *St. John the Baptist* (1438), a wooden sculpture. *(Vaporetto: "S. Tomà." Follow signs back to Campo dei Frari. Open M-Sa 9am-6pm, Su 1-6pm. €2 or free with chorus pass.)*

CHIESA DI SANTA MARIA DELLA SALUTE (DORSODURO). The theatrical *Salute* (Italian for "health"), poised at the tip of Dorsoduro, is a prime example of the Venetian Baroque, a style designed to pull the spectator into the space and make him central to the architecture. In 1631, the city commissioned Longhena to build the church for the Virgin, whom they believed would return the favor by ending the plague. These days, Venice celebrates the third Sunday in November by building a wooden pontoon bridge across the Canal and lighting candles in the church (see **Entertainment,** p. 241). Next to the *Salute* stands the *Dogana*, the old customs house, where ships sailing into Venice were required to stop and pay appropriate duties. Upon leaving the *Dogana*, walk along the *fondamenta* to the tip of Dorsoduro, where a marvelous ■view of the city awaits you. *(Vaporetto: "Salute." ☎ 041 522 5558. Open daily 9am-noon and 3-5:30pm. The inside of the Dogana is closed to the public. Free. Entrance to sacristy with donation.)*

CHIESA DI SAN SEBASTIANO (DORSODURO). The Renaissance painter Veronese took refuge in this 16th-century church when he fled Verona in 1555 after allegedly killing a man. By 1565 he had filled the church with an amazing cycle of paintings and frescoes. His breathtaking *Stories of Queen Esther* covers the ceiling, while the man himself rests in peace under the gravestone by the organ. Also displayed are works by Paris Bordone and Titian. *(Vaporetto: "S. Basilio." Continue straight ahead. Open M-Sa 10am-5pm, Su 3-5pm. €2 or free with chorus pass.)*

CHIESA DI SANTISSIMI GIOVANNI E PAOLO (SAN ZANIPOLO) (CASTELLO). The monumental walls of cream stone and salmon-colored brick hold the tombs and monuments of past Doges for the benefit of the common people. The terra-cotta structure is primarily Gothic, though it has a Renaissance-style portal, with an arch supported by columns of Greek marble. On the right as you enter stands a gory relief depicting the agonizing death of Marcantonio Bragadin. Bragadin valiantly defended Cyprus from the Turks in 1571, only to be skinned alive after surrendering—his remains now rest in the little urn above the monument. Next to Bragadin is an altarpiece by Giovanni Bellini, showing St. Christopher, Sebastian, and Vincent Ferrar. Off the left transept is the **Cappella del Rosario.** After a fire destroyed the chapel in 1867, works by Veronese were brought in to replace the lost paintings. Outside the church stands the bronze equestrian **statue of Bartolomeo Colleoni,** a mercenary who left his inheritance to the city on the condition that a monument in his honor would be erected in front of S. Marco. The city, unwilling to honor anyone in such a grand space, decided to place the statue in front of the Scuola di S. Marco, thus satisfying the conditions of the will and laying claim to the money. The statue was designed in 1479 by da Vinci's teacher, the Florentine Verrochio. *(Vaporetto: "Fond. Nuove." Turn left and then right onto Fond. dei Mendicanti. ☎ 041 523 5913. Open M-Sa 7:30am-12:30pm and 3:30-7pm, Su 3-6pm. Free.)*

CHIESA DI SANTA MARIA DEI MIRACOLI (CASTELLO). The Lombardi designed this Renaissance jewel in the late 1400s, and it remains one of the prettiest churches in Venice, elegantly faced with polychrome marble and inside brimming with lavish color, gold reliefs, and sculpted figures. *(From S. S. Giovanni e Paolo, cross Ponte Rosse continue straight. Open M-Sa 10am-5pm, Su 1-5pm. €2 or free with chorus pass.)*

CHIESA SANTA MARIA ASSUNTA (CHIESA DEI GESUITI). An excessive amount of green-and-white marble awaits within this extravagant 18th century church, capped by an equally lavish Baroque facade—its gilded stucco work is unparalleled in Venice. Titian's *Martyrdom of Saint Lawrence* hangs in the altar to the left as you enter the church. *(Vaporetto: "Fond. Nuove"; turn right and then left on Sal. dei Specchieri. ☎ 041 623 1610. Open daily 10am-noon and 4-6pm.)*

CHIESA DELLA MADONNA DELL'ORTO. Tintoretto painted some of his most moving works for his parish church, another quintessential example of Venetian Gothic architecture. Inside, gaping wood ceilings accommodate 10 of his largest paintings. Near the high altar hang his *Last Judgment,* a spatially intense mass of souls, and *The Sacrifice of the Golden Calf.* On the right apse is the splendidly colored *Presentation of the Virgin at the Temple.* A light switch for illuminating the works is at each of the far corners. *(Vaporetto: "Madonna dell'Orto." Open M-Sa 10am-5pm, Su 1-5pm. €2 or free with chorus pass.)*

SAN GIORGIO MAGGIORE AND GIUDECCA

BASILICA DI SAN GIORGIO MAGGIORE. Standing on its own monastic island, S. Giorgio Maggiore contrasts sharply with most other Venetian churches. Palladio ignored the Venetian fondness for color and decorative excess and constructed an austere church. Light fills the enormous open space inside, although it unfortunately does not hit Tintoretto's *Last Supper* by the high altar; you'll have to put €0.30 in the light box if you want to see the wraith-like angels hovering over Christ's table. The beautiful nearby courtyard, to the right of the church, is closed to the public, but Palladio's architecture is visible through the gates. Ascend the elevator to the top of the **campanile** for a marvelous view of the city. *(Vaporetto: "S. Giorgio Maggiore." ☎ 041 522 7827. Open M-Sa 10am-12:30pm and 2:30-4:30pm. Basilica free. Campanile €3. Pay the Brother in the elevator.)*

TEMPIO DEL S. S. REDENTORE. Palladio's true religious masterpiece, this longitudinally immense Renaissance church, like the *Salute,* commemorates a deal that Venice struck with God to end a plague. Every year the city still celebrates with a fireworks display. Paintings by Veronese and Bassano hang in the sacristy. *(Vaporetto: "Redentore." Ask to enter the sacristy. Open M-Sa 10am-5pm, Su 1-5pm. €2 or free with chorus pass.)*

ISLANDS OF THE LAGOON

■ **BURANO.** In this traditional fishing village, fishermen haul in their catch every morning while woman sit in the doorways of the fantastically colored houses, creating unique knots of Venetian lace. See their handiwork in the small **Scuola di Merletti di Burano (Lace Museum).** *(A 40min. boat ride from Venice. Vaporetto #12: "Burano" from either "S. Zaccaria" or "Fond. Nuove." Museum in P. Galuppi. ☎ 041 73 00 34. Open W-M 10am-5pm. €4. Included on combined Palazzo Ducale ticket or full museum pass.)*

MURANO. Famous for its glass since 1292 (when Venice's artisans were forced off Venice proper because their kilns started fires), the island of Murano affords visitors the opportunity to witness the glass-blowing process. Don't be fooled by the vendors near the train station or P. S. Marco who will try to sell you a ticket to see a glass demonstration—the studios in Murano are free. Look for signs directing you toward *fornace,* concentrated near the "Colona," "Faro," and "Navagero" vaporetto stops. The speed and grace of these artisans will leave you in awe, and some studios will let you blow your own glass creation. The **Museo Vetrario (Glass Museum)** houses a splendid collection that includes pieces from Roman times. Farther down the street stands the exceptional 12th-century **Basilica di Santa Maria e San Donato,** which contains the bones of the dragon slain by Saint Donatus. *(Vaporetto #12 or 52: "Faro" from either "S. Zaccaria" or "Fond. Nuove." Museo Vetrario, Fond. Giustian, 8. ☎ 041 73 95 86. Open Th-Tu 10am-5pm. €5, students €3. Included on combined Palazzo Ducale ticket or with the complete museum pass. Basilica ☎ 041 73 90 56. Open daily 8am-noon and 4-7pm. Free.)*

TORCELLO. Torcello, a safe haven for early fishermen fleeing barbarians on the mainland, was the most powerful island of the lagoon before Venice usurped its inhabitants and its glory. Torcello is today a less-visited locale whose lush vegetation and simple natural beauty draw those seeking a respite from the whirl of shops and tourists on the mainland. The island's cathedral, **Santa Maria Assunta,** contains 11th- and 12th-century mosaics depicting the Last Judgment and the Virgin Mary. The *campanile* affords splendid views of the outer lagoon. *(A 45min. boat ride from Venice. Vaporetto #12: "Torcello" from either "S. Zaccaria" or "Fond. Nuove." Cathedral ☎ 041 73 00 84. Open daily 10:30am-12:30pm and 2-6:30pm. €2 or free with chorus pass.)*

LIDO. Venice's Lido was the setting for Thomas Mann's classic 14th-century novel *Death in Venice.* Visonti's film version was also shot here at the famous Hotel des Bains *(Lungomare Marconi, 17).* Now people flock to Lido to enjoy the water at the crowded, noisy, and somewhat dirty public beach with an impressive shipwreck at one end. The island also has a casino, horseback-riding stables, and Italy's finest putting green, the Alberoni Golf Club. *(Vaporetto: Lido.)*

ISOLA DI SAN MICHELE. Venice's cemetery island, S. Michele, is home to Coducci's tiny Chiesa di S. Michele in Isola (1469), the first Renaissance church in Venice. Entrance to the cyprus-lined grounds is gained through the church's right-hand portal, over which sits a relief depicting St. Michael slaying the dragon. Poet, Fascist sympathizer, and enemy of the state Ezra Pound was laid to rest here in the Protestant cemetery, as were Russian composer Igor Stravinsky and Russian choreographer Sergei Diaghilev. Both are found in the Orthodox cemetery. *(Vaporetto: "Cimitero," from "Fond. Nuove." Church and cemetery open Apr.-Sept. daily 7:30am-6pm; Oct.-Mar. 7:30am-4pm. Free.)*

🎵 ENTERTAINMENT

The weekly booklet *A Guest in Venice*, free at hotels and tourist offices or online at www.unospitedivenezia.it, lists current festivals, concerts, and gallery shows.

GONDOLAS

Venice was built to be traveled by gondola, and admiring the front doors of houses and *palazzi* via their original pathways is an experience only a gondola can provide. Gondola rides are most romantic if taken about 50min. before sunset and almost affordable if shared by six people. The rate that a gondolier quotes is negotiable and the most bargain-able gondoliers are those standing by themselves, rather than those in groups at the "taxi-stands" throughout the city. (Rides start at €62 per group for 50min.)

ORCHESTRAL MUSIC

Venice swoons for **orchestral music,** from the outdoor chamber orchestras in P. S. Marco to costumed concerts. **Vivaldi,** the red-haired priest and one-time choirmaster in the Chiesa di S. Maria della Pietà (a few blocks along the waterfront from P. S. Marco), was forgotten for centuries after his death. Today, his music, especially *The Four Seasons,* can be heard almost nightly in the summer and regularly during the winter. The **Church of S. Vidal,** right next door to C. S. Samuele in S. Marco, has classical concerts with instruments from the 15th century. (Purchase tickets at the church: open daily 9am-5pm. Concerts at 9pm every night except Su. €21, students €16.)

THEATER, CINEMA, AND ART EXHIBITIONS

The 2002-2003 season at **Teatro Goldoni,** Calle del Teatro, S. Marco 4650/B (☎041 520 5422 or 240 2011; teatrogoldini@libero.it), near the Rialto Bridge, showcases *commedia dell'arte* plays; even non-Italian speakers will appreciate this native Italian art form. The **Mostra Internazionale di Cinema (Venice International Film Festival),** held annually from late Aug. to early Sept., draws such luminaries as Steven Spielberg. Movies are shown in the original language. (☎041 520 0311. Tickets are €20 and are sold throughout the city. Some late-night outdoor showings are free.) Venice's main cinemas include: the **Accademia,** Calle Gambara, Dorsoduro, 1019 (☎041 528 7706), right of the museum, showing original language films; the **Giorgione,** C. S. Apostoli, Cannaregio (☎041 522 6298); and the **Rossini,** S. Marco, 3988 (☎041 523 0322), off Campo Manin, generally showing films only in Italian. The famed **Biennale di Venezia** (☎041 521 1898; www.labiennale.org), a world-wide contemporary art exhibition, drowns the Giardini Publici and the Arsenal in provocative international art every odd-numbered year.

FESTIVALS

Banned by the church for several centuries, Venice's famous **Carnevale** was successfully reinstated in the early 1970s. During the 10 days before Ash Wednesday, masked figures jam the streets, and outdoor concerts and street performances spring up throughout the city. On **Mardi Gras,** the population of the city doubles. Contact the tourist office in January for details, and be sure to make lodging arrangements well in advance. Venice's second-most colorful festival is the **Festa del Redentore** (3rd Su in July), originally held to celebrate the end of a 16th-century plague. The city kicks off the festival with a magnificent fireworks display at 11:30pm the night before. The next day the military builds a bridge of boats across the Giudecca Canal, connecting Il Redentore to the Zattere. On the first Saturday in September, Venice stages its classic **regata storica,** a gondola race down the Grand Canal. During the religious **Festa della Salute** (3rd Su in Nov.), which also originated as a celebration of the end of a plague, the city celebrates with another pontoon bridge, this time over the Grand Canal.

SHOPPING

Be wary of shopping in the heavily touristed P. S. Marco or around the Rialto Bridge (excluding Rivoaltus). Shops outside these areas often have better quality products and greater selection for about half the price. Interesting clothing, glass, and mask boutiques line the streets leading from the Rialto Bridge to Campo S. Polo and Strada Nuova and from the Rialto Bridge toward the station. The map accompanying the Rolling Venice card lists many shops that offer discounts to card holders. The most concentrated and varied selections of Venetian glass and lace require trips to the nearby islands of Murano (p. 240) and Burano (p. 240), respectively.

▨ NIGHTLIFE

Venetian nightlife is quieter and more relaxed than that of other major Italian cities. Most locals spend the evening sipping wine or beer, or listening to string quartets in P. S. Marco, rather than gyrating in a disco, but Venice does have a few hot dance spots. Student nightlife is concentrated around **Campo Santa Margherita** in Dorsoduro and the areas around the **Lista di Spagna** in Cannaregio.

▧ **Paradiso Perduto,** Fond. della Misericordia, Cannaregio, 2540 (☎041 72 05 81). From Strada Nuova, cross Campo S. Fosca, cross bridge, and continue in same direction, crossing 2 more bridges. Students and locals flood this unassuming bar, while the young waitstaff doles out large portions of *cichetti* (mixed plate, €11.36). Live jazz Su 9pm. Open Th-Su 7pm-2am.

Piccolo Mondo, Accademia, Dorsoduro, 1056/A (☎041 520 0371). With your back to the canal, facing the Accademia, turn right and follow the street around. Join in with the dance-happy students, locals, and tourists at this small, but pumping *discoteca* where notables like Shaquille O'Neil, Mick Jagger, and Prince Albert of Monaco have strutted their stuff. Drinks start €7. No cover. Open nightly 10pm-4am. AmEx/MC/V.

Duchamp, C. Santa Margherita, 3019 (☎041 52 86 255). Lively place with students and tourists noisily congregating. Outdoor seating. Pint of beer €4.30. Wine €1.10. Open Su-F 9pm-2am, Sa 5pm-2am.

Casanova, Lista di Spagna, Cannaregio, 158/A (☎041 275 0199; www.casanova.it). Modest crowds mean there's always plenty of room on the floor for the tourists and locals to dance to the perpetual strobe light and beats of house and techno music. Enthusiastic dance lovers make up for the lack of numbers, shaking things up until closing. F-Sa €10 cover includes free drink. Open daily 10pm-4am. AmEx/MC/V.

Inishark Irish Pub, Calle Mondo Novo, Castello, 5787 (☎041 523 5300), off C. S. Maria Formosa. Most creative Irish pub in Venice, with themed decorations. Guinness €4.65; Harp €4.50. Open Tu-Su 6pm-1:30am.

Il Caffè, Campo S. Margherita, Dorsoduro, 2963 (☎041 528 7998). Music pumps at the door and people stuff inside this tiny, non-descript bar. Outdoor seating. Wine €0.80, beer €1.36. Open M-Sa 8am-2am.

Bacaro Jazz, Campo S. Bartolmeo, S. Marco, 5546 (☎041 528 5249). From post office, follow red lights and sounds of jazz across the street. At this chic restaurant and evening haunt, 20- and 30-somethings share big, expensive plates of *cichetti* (€13). Jazz paraphernalia lines the walls. Drinks more affordable during happy hours, 3-7pm, when drinks are 2 for 1. Fun atmosphere and open late, sometimes until 4am. Open Th-Tu 11am-2am.

Café Blue, S. Pantalon, Dorsoduro, 5778 (☎041 71 02 27). From S. Maria Frari, take Calle Scalater and turn right at the end. Bright, noisy, and crowded American bar with droves of expats and exchange students. Free email kiosk. Afternoon tea in winter 3:30-7:30pm. All drinks half price 8:30-9:30pm. Bar open M-Sa 9:30pm-2am.

Bar Santa Lucia, Lista di Spagna, Cannaregio 282/B (☎041 524 2880), near the train station. This tiny bar stays crowded and noisy long into the night with American travelers and the locals who want to meet them. Good selection of Irish beers. Pint of Guinness €5. Wine €2.10. Open M-Sa 6pm-2am.

VENICE

NORTHEAST ITALY

THE VENETO

From the rocky foothills of the Dolomites to the fertile valleys of the Po River, the Veneto region has a geography as diverse as its historical influences. Once loosely linked under the Venetian Empire, these towns retained their cultural independence, and visitors are more likely to hear regional dialects than standard Italian when neighbors gossip across their geranium-cloaked windows. Culinary influences marched in with the Austrians and swim in with the day's catch. In the smaller northern towns, German influences trickle down through the foothills and dishes such as *Wurstel* appear on restaurant menus. The pervasiveness of local culture and custom will surprise and delight visitors who come to the region expecting only Venetian canals and *gondole*.

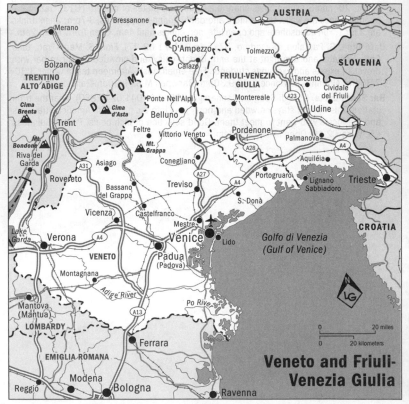

Veneto and Friuli-Venezia Giulia

PADUA (PADOVA)   ☎049

Padua was a wealthy center of commerce in ancient times, but centuries of barbarian attacks and natural disasters left few of its architectural glories intact. Luminaries such as Dante, Petrarch, Galileo, Copernicus, Mantegna, Giotto, and Donatello all contributed to the city's reputation as a center of learning. Padua's university, founded in 1222 and second in seniority only to Bologna's, brings booktoting students and an air of liberal individualism to statue-lined piazzas.

▄ TRANSPORTATION

Trains: In P. Stazione, at the northern end of C. del Popolo, the continuation of C. Garibaldi. Open 5am-midnight. **Luggage storage** available (see p. 246). To: **Bologna** (1½hr., 1-2 per hr., 4:22am-10:41pm, €5.73); **Milan** (2½hr., 1-2 per hr., 5:49am-11pm, €16.77); **Venice** (30min., 3-4 per hr., 4:42am-11pm, €2.32); and **Verona** (1hr., 1-2 per hr., 5:49am-11pm, €6.90).

Buses: SITA (☎049 820 6811), in P. Boschetti. From train station, walk down C. del Popolo, turn left on V. Trieste, and bear right at V. Vecchio. Open M-Th 8:30am-1pm and 3-6:30pm, F 8:30am-1pm and 3-5:30pm. To: **Bassano del Grappa** (1¼hr., 2 per hr., €3.85); **Montagnana** (1hr., 1-2 per hr., €3.35); **Venice** (45min., 2 per hr., €3.25); and **Vicenza** (1hr., 2 per hr., €3.25).

Local Buses: ACAP (☎049 824 1111), at the train station. Buses #8, 12, and 18 run downtown. €1.85 for 1hr., €2.70 for 1 day.

Taxis: Radio Taxi (☎049 65 13 33). Available 24hr.

Car Rental: Europcar, P. Stazione, 6 (☎049 875 8590). 21+. Open M-F 8:30am-12:30pm and 3-7:30pm, Sa 8:30am-12:30pm. **Maggiore Budget,** P. Stazione, 15 bis (☎049 875 2852). Must have had license for 1 year. Open M-F 8:30am-12:30pm and 2:30-6:30pm, Sa 9am-noon.

◤◢ ▛ ORIENTATION AND PRACTICAL INFORMATION

The train station is on the northern edge of town, outside the 16th-century walls. A 10min. walk down **Corso del Popolo,** which becomes **Corso Garibaldi,** leads to the heart of town and the university.

Tourist Office: In the **train station** (☎049 875 2077; fax 875 5088). Open M-Sa 9am-7pm, Su 8:30am-12:30pm. **Main office** (☎049 876 7927), P. Pedrocchi, 11, to the right of Cafe Pedrocchi, off P. Cavour. Open M-Sa 9am-12:30pm and 3-7pm. **Branch office,** P. del Santo (☎049 875 3087), a small outdoor stand. Open M-F 9am-7pm, Sa 9:30am-1pm and 1:30-6pm, Su 9am-1pm.

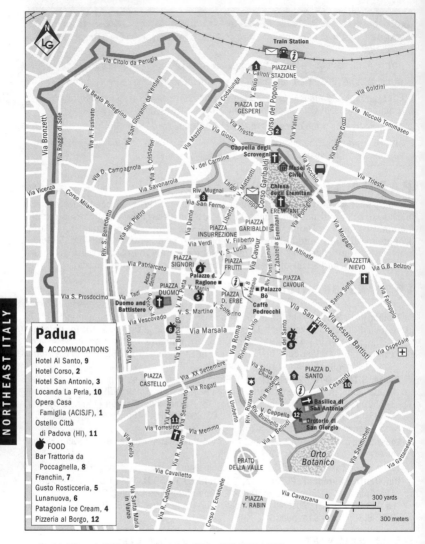

Padua

📍 ACCOMMODATIONS
Hotel Al Santo, **9**
Hotel Corso, **2**
Hotel San Antonio, **3**
Locanda La Perla, **10**
Opera Casa
  Famiglia (ACISJF), **1**
Ostello Città
  di Padova (HI), **11**

🍴 FOOD
Bar Trattoria da
  Poccagnella, **8**
Franchin, **7**
Gusto Rosticceria, **5**
Lunanuova, **6**
Patagonia Ice Cream, **4**
Pizzeria al Borgo, **12**

Budget Travel: CTS, Riviera Mugnai, 22 (☎049 876 1639), near the post office. Student IDs and train tickets. Open M-F 8:45-11:45am and 3:45-6:45pm, Sa 8:45-11:45am.

English-Language Bookstore: Feltrinelli International, V. S. Francesco, 14 (☎049 875 0792). From V. Cavour, take a left. Novels and travel guides in English. Open M-F 10am-7:30pm, Sa 9am-1pm and 2:30-7:30pm.

Laundromat: Fastclean, V. Ognissanti, 6 (☎049 77 57 59), off V. del Portello. Take bus #9. €3.50 wash. Open M-F 9am-12:30pm and 3:15-8pm, Sa 9am-12:30pm.

Luggage Storage: At the train station. €3.87 per bag. Open daily 8am-12:30pm and 2-6:30pm.

Emergency: ☎112 or 113. **Ambulance:** ☎118.

Police: Carabinieri (☎049 21 21 21), on Prato della Valle.

Hospital: Ospedale Civile, V. Giustiniani, 1 (☎049 821 1111), off V. Ospedale.

Post Office: C. Garibaldi, 33 (☎049 820 8511). Open M-Sa 8:30am-6:30pm. **Branch** at train station. Open M-F 8:30am-2pm, Sa 8:30am-1pm.

Postal Code: 35100.

ACCOMMODATIONS & CAMPING

Padua's accommodations can be fairly inexpensive, but reservations in the summer are essential.

Locanda la Perla, V. Cesarotti, 67 (☎049 8755 8939). Near the Prato della Valle. From the center of town, take V. San Francesco to the end and turn right. Great location right next to the *basilica*. 8 small, tidy rooms. 1 room with a beautiful view of the *basilica*. Communal bath. Singles €25.82; doubles €36.15. ❸

Ostello Città di Padova (HI), V. Aleardi, 30 (☎049 875 2219; fax 65 42 10; pdyhtl@tin.it), near Prato della Valle. Take bus #18 from train station to the stop after Prato della Valle. Walk 2 blocks, make a right onto V. Marin, and go straight through the rotary while keeping the church to your right. Turn left on V. Torresino. Well used, but fairly clean. Women and men on the same floor. TV room. Internet €0.10 per min. Wash and dry €5. Wheelchair-accessible. Breakfast, shower, and sheets included. Reception 7-9:30am and 4-11pm. Room lockout 9:30am-4pm. Shower and common rooms open after 2:30pm. Curfew 11pm. Reserve 1 wk. in advance. 16-bed dorms €13; 4-5 person family rooms €52. MC/V. ❶

Hotel Al Santo, V. del Santo, 147 (☎049 875 2131; fax 878 8076), near the basilica. 20 small but airy, pretty rooms. All rooms with bath, fans, and TV. Breakfast included. Lunch or dinner with *primo, secondo,* drink, and coffee in the downstairs restaurant €15. Singles €52; doubles €90; triples €130. AmEx/MC/V. ❹

Hotel S. Antonio, V. S. Fermo, 118 (☎049 875 1393; fax 875 2508). Clean, simple rooms with large windows, A/C, and TV; some with river view. All rooms with AC and TV. Buffet breakfast €6.70. Singles €37-57; doubles €57-74; triples €69-93. MC/V. ❹

Hotel Corso, C. del Popolo, 2 (☎049 875 0822; fax 66 15 76). At the intersection of C. del Popolo and V. Trieste. Small rooms with modern decoration and great views overlooking the street. All rooms with bath, AC, and TV. Buffet breakfast included. Singles €78-93; doubles €103-13; triples €145. AmEx/MC/V. ❺

Opera Casa Famiglia (ACISJF), V. Nino Bixio, 4 (☎049 875 1554), off P. Stazione. Leave station, walk to right, and turn left on the street just before Hotel Monaco. Women under 30 only. Study and kitchen open at night. 36 beds. Curfew 10:30pm. Modern and tidy doubles, triples, and quads €16 per bed. ❷

Camping: Sporting Center, V. Roma, 123/125 (☎049 79 34 00). Take the train to Montegrotto; from station, walk out the front and follow signs. Tennis and beach volleyball. Restaurant discounts for guests. Open Mar. to early Nov. €5.16-7.02 per person, €7.02-13.01 per car with tent. ❶

FOOD

Morning **markets** are held in P. delle Erbe and P. della Frutta from 8am to 2pm, but sidewalk vendors also sell fresh produce, meats, and cheeses. **Supermarket PAM** is downtown in P. Cavour. (Open M-Sa 8am-8pm.) For an inexpensive lunch, visit **Franchin,** V. del Santo, which has fresh gourmet meats, cheeses, and bread, as well as wine. (☎049 875 0532. Open Th-Tu 10:30am-1:30pm and 5-8pm. MC/V.) Wine lovers may sample a glass from the nearby **Colli Euganei** wine district or try the sparkling *Lambruschi* from Emilia-Romagna. Visitors to the Basilica di Sant'Antonio can nibble on the *dolce del santo* in nearby *pasticcerie*.

■ **Pizzeria Al Borgo,** V. Luca Belludi, 56 (☎049 875 8857), near the Basilica di S. Antonio, just a few steps off P. del Santo (heading toward Prato della Valle). Join a rollicking crowd for dinner on the terrace. Large pizzas from €3.50, *primi* from €6. Open W-M noon-2pm and 7pm-midnight. AmEx/MC/V. ❷

■ **Patagonia Ice Cream,** P. dei Signori, 27 (☎049 875 1045). On the side closest to V. Dante. Serves delicious, creamy *gelato* (€0.80 per scoop). Open daily 9am-7pm. ❶

Alexander Birreria Paninoteca, V. S. Francesco, 38 (☎049 65 28 84). Take V. del Santo to V. S. Francesco and make a left onto the street. Wide range of sandwiches €3.14-5.16. Open M-Sa 8:30am-2am. ❶

Bar Trattoria da Paccagnella, V. del Santo, 113 (☎049 875 0549). An antique, quiet restaurant with Paduan cuisine. *Primi* from €5, *secondi* €7-13. Open daily noon-3pm and 7-10pm. MC/V. ❸

Lunanuova, V. G. Barbarigo, 12 (☎049 875 8907). The street leads out of P. Duomo. Vegetarian pasta and Middle Eastern dishes from €5-8. Open Tu-Sa 12:30-2:15pm and 7:30pm-midnight. ❷

Gusto Rosticceria, V. Manin, 33 (☎049 66 08 78). The street runs out of P. Erbe towards the duomo. This *rosticceria* serves quick, wholesome, inexpensive food. Pizza starts at €1.50. Open M-Sa 9am-12:30pm and 1:30-8pm. ❶

⊙ SIGHTS

Padua has a wealth of sights that are best visited with the **Padova Card,** which covers entrance to the Scrovegni Chapel, Musei Civici Erimitani, Palazzo della Ragione, Caffè Pedrocchi's Piano Nobile, and Oratorio di San Michele. It also provides free transport on local buses and discounts at participating stores. To purchase and for more information, visit the tourist office.

■ **CAPELLA DEGLI SCROVEGNI (ARENA CHAPEL).** Enrico Scrovegni dedicated this chapel to the Virgin Mary in an attempt to save the soul of his father Reginald, a usurer. Ironically, he used his father's pilfered money to build and decorate it. The Florentine master Giotto frescoed the stunning walls of this chapel with scenes from the lives of Mary, Jesus, and Mary's parents Joachim and Anne. Completed between 1305 and 1306 this 38-panel cycle jump-started the Italian Renaissance by bringing depth and realism to painting. The attached **Musei Civici Erimitani** contains an overwhelmingly extensive art collection. It also conserves a beautiful crucifix by Giotto that once adorned the Scrovegni Chapel. (*P. Eremitani, 8.* ☎049 820 4550. Entrance to the chapel only through the museum. Open daily Feb.-Oct. 9am-7pm, Nov.-Jan. 9am-6pm. Tickets must be booked in advance for a €1 fee through the tourist office (☎049 876 7927), or online at www.cappelladegliscrovegni.it. Chapel €7.50. Museum €9, students €4. Combination ticket €11, handicapped free.)

■ **BASILICA DI SANT'ANTONIO (IL SANTO).** Bronze sculptures by Donatello grace the high altar, surrounded by the artist's *Crucifixion* and several earlier Gothic frescoes. St. Anthony's remains are separated into various containers and lie scattered around the church. The final resting place of his bones, the **Tomba di Sant'Antonio,** to the left of the altar, is the final destination for thousands of pilgrims who visit the basilica each year. A **multimedia show** (follow "Mostra" signs) in the attached courtyard details St. Anthony's life. The adjoining **Oratorio di San Giorgio** houses examples of Giotto-school frescoes, and the **Scuola del Santo** includes three by the young Titian. *(P. del Santo. ☎049 824 2811. Cathedral open daily Apr.-Sept. 6:30am-8pm; Nov.-Mar. 6:30am-7pm. Dress code enforced. Mostra open daily 9am-12:30pm and 2:30-6pm. Audio tour in English available at front desk. Oratorio and Scuola ☎049 875 5235. Open daily 9am-12:30pm and 2:30-7pm. Wheelchair-accessible. €2, students €1.)*

PALAZZO DELLA RAGIONE (LAW COURTS). This *palazzo* overlooks the lively market stalls of P. della Frutta. Astrological signs line the walls. The original ceiling, once painted as a starry sky, survived a 1420 fire only to topple in a 1756 tornado. The damage is still being fixed. To the right of the entrance sits the **Stone of Shame.** Inspired by St. Anthony in 1231 to abolish debtors' prisons, Padua adopted the more humane practice of forcing the partially clad debtor onto the stone to repeat before a crowd of at least one hundred hecklers, *"Cedo bonis"* ("I renounce my property"). At the end of the hall stands a massive wooden horse falsely attributed to Donatello. *(Enter through city hall on V. Febbraio, 8. ☎049 820 5006. Closed for restoration in summer 2002. Check tourist office for times and prices.)*

PALAZZO BO AND ENVIRONS. The university campus is scattered throughout the city but is centered in Palazzo Bò. The **Teatro Anatomico** (1594), the first of its kind in Europe, hosted medical pioneers like Vesalius and Englishman William Harvey. Almost all Venetian noblemen received their mandatory law and public policy instruction in the **Great Hall.** The chair of Galileo is preserved in the **Sala dei Quaranta,** where the physicist once lectured. Across the street, **Caffè Pedrocchi** served as the headquarters for 19th-century liberals who supported Risorgimento leader Giuseppe Mazzini. When it was first built, the cafe's famous Neoclassical facade had no doors and was open around the clock. A battle between students and Austrian police exploded here in February 1848, a turning point in the revolutionary movement. The upstairs **Piano Nobile** is a tiny museum of prettily decorated rooms. Capture the spirit for the price of a *cappuccino. (Palazzo Bò, in P. delle Erbe. ☎049 820 9773. Guided tours M, W, and F at 3, 4, and 5pm; Tu, Th, and Sa at 9, 10, and 11am. Tours €2.58, students €1.03. Caffè Pedrocchi, V. VIII Febbraio, 15. Open Tu-Su 9:30am-12:30pm and 3-7pm. Piano Nobile €3, students €2.)*

DUOMO. Michelangelo reputedly participated in the design of this church, erected between the 16th and 18th centuries. The interior is entirely white, with just the capitals of the columns in gray. There are no frescoes and just a few paintings. Next door the 12th-century **Battistero,** a jewel of Padua, was dedicated to St. John Baptist. Abstract and impersonal representations of the apostles adorn the ceiling and area over the chapel. *(P. Duomo. ☎049 66 28 14. Duomo open M-Sa 7:30am-noon and 3:45-7:45pm, Su 7:45am-1pm and 3:45-8:30pm. Free. Baptistery open daily 10am-6pm. €2.50, students €1.50.)*

GATTAMELATA STATUE. In the center of P. del Santo stands Donatello's bronze equestrian statue of Erasmo da Narni (*Gattamelata* or Calico Cat), a general remembered for his agility and ferocity. Donatello modeled his work on the equestrian statue of Marcus Aurelius at the Campidoglio in Rome. Compare Erasmo's serenity with the ferocity of Colleoni in Venice (p. 239), completed 10 years later.

ORTO BOTANICO. A veritable oasis of magnolias and palm trees in the middle of the congested city. This oldest university botanical garden in Europe tempts visitors with water lilies, medicinal herbs, and a 1585 palm tree that still offers shade. *(From the basilica, follow signs to V. Orto Botanico, 15. ☎049 827 2119. Open daily 9am-1pm and 3-6pm; in winter M-F 9am-1pm. €2.58, students €1.55.)*

PRATO DELLA VALLE. This verdant ellipse was once a Roman theater and now is the largest square in Europe after the Red Square in Moscow. Water and bridges divide the ground into four separate avenues, lined with 78 statues of famous Padovan men. At night, the Prato is brilliantly lit as students stroll or race around the natural track on in-line skates.

♫ ENTERTAINMENT

Restaurant terraces begin drawing boisterous crowds around 9pm. **Lucifer Young,** V. Altinate, 89, is a hip bar whose decorator took lessons from the lowest circle in Dante's *Inferno*. (☎049 66 55 31. Open Su-Tu and Th 7pm-2am, F-Sa 7pm-4am.) The tourist office pamphlet *Where Shall We Go Tonight?* lists restaurants and nightlife spots. Pilgrims pack the city on June 13, as Padua remembers the death of its patron St. Anthony with a procession of the saint's statue and jawbone. An **antique market** assembles in the Prato della Valle on the 3rd Sunday of each month. Every Saturday the area holds an **outdoor market** selling food and clothing.

VICENZA ☎0444

Vicenza was settled by the Romans a few centuries before Christ, destroyed by barbarians in the middle ages, and finally welcomed into the Veneto as a member province in the 15th century. Under the influence of neighboring cultural epicenter Venice and with the help of Andrea Palladio's multiple architectural masterpieces, Vicenza grew in importance. Today it is a successful, bustling city, with one of the highest average incomes in Italy. The impressive rolling landscape draws tourists to the surrounding countryside for golf, horseback riding, tennis, and relaxation.

▉ TRANSPORTATION

Trains: P. Stazione, at the end of V. Roma. Across from Campo Marzo. Info open daily 7:30am-8:30pm. Ticket office open M-Sa 6am-9:15pm, Su 6am-10pm. **Luggage Storage** available (p. 251). To: **Milan** (2½hr., 17 per day, 6:08am-10:16pm, €9.50-15.25); **Padua** (30min., 9 per day, 8:35am-6:48pm,€2.35-4.85); **Verona** (40min., 16 per day, 6:20am-10:17pm, €2.74-4.85); and **Venice** (1½hr., 40 per day, 5:52am-11:36pm, €3.30-6.60).

Buses: FTV, V. Milano, 7 (☎0444 22 31 15), to your left as you exit train station. Office open daily 6am-7:45pm. To: **Bassano** (1hr., 26 per day, 5:50am-9:30pm, €3); **Montagnana** (1¼hr., 7 per day, 7:20am-5:30pm, €3.40); and **Padua** (30min., 30 per day, 6am-8:20pm, €3).

Taxis: Radiotaxi (☎0444 92 06 00). Usually available at either end of C. Palladio.

▉ ▉ ORIENTATION AND PRACTICAL INFORMATION

Vicenza lies in the heart of the Veneto. The train station and the adjacent intercity bus station are in the southern part of Vicenza. Glance at the map outside the station before walking into town on **Viale Roma.** At the Giardino Salvi, take a right under the Roman archway onto **Corso Palladio.** Walk straight several blocks to the old Roman wall that serves as a gate to the Teatro Olimpico. The tourist office is the door just to the right. **Piazza Matteotti** lies in front, at the end of Corso Palladio.

Tourist Office: P. Matteotti, 12 (☎0444 32 08 54; fax 32 70 72; www.vicenzae.org), next to Teatro Olimpico. Free city map and info on wheelchair access. Open daily 9am-1pm and 2-6pm.

Budget Travel: AVIT, V. Roma, 17 (☎0444 54 56 77), before you reach supermarket PAM. BIJ and Transalpino tickets. **Avis** and **Hertz** rental cars. Also a Hertz at train station. English spoken. Open M-F 9am-1pm and 3-7pm, Sa 9:30am-12:30pm. **CTS,** Contra Ponta Nova, 43 (☎0444 32 38 64), near the Chiesa dei Carmini. Discount flights, tours, and ISICs. English spoken. Open M-F 9am-12:30pm and 3-7pm.

Currency Exchange: At train station and post office (see below). **ATMs** in the train station, on Contra del Monte, and throughout the downtown area.

Luggage Storage: In train station. €3 for 24hr. Open daily 6am-10pm.

Emergency: ☎ 113. **Ambulance:** ☎ 118.

Police: V. Muggia, 2 (☎ 0444 50 40 44).

Night, Weekend, and Holiday Doctor: ☎ 0444 56 72 28.

Hospital: Ospedale Civile, V. Rodolfi, 8 (☎ 0444 99 31 11).

Internet Access: Gala 2000, on V. Roma across from supermarket PAM. Closed Aug.

Post Office: Contrà Garibaldi, 1 (☎ 0444 33 20 77), between the duomo and P. Signori. Open M-Sa 8:10am-6:30pm. **Currency exchange** M-Sa 8:10am-6pm.

Postal Code: 36100.

ACCOMMODATIONS AND CAMPING

Hotel Vicenza, Strada dei Nodari, 9 (☎/fax 0444 32 15 12), off P. Signori in the alley across from Ristorante Garibaldi. Make a fast left at the patio of Ristorante Garibaldi. Meticulously clean, with rustic tile floor and high ceilings. Prices vary by season. Singles €36.15, with bath €43.90; doubles €49.58, with bath €59.39. ❹

Hotel Giardini, V. Giuriolo, 10 (☎/fax 0444 32 64 58), off P. Matteoti, turn right away from the tourist office. Brand-new hotel with modern decor and hard wood floors. All 18 rooms are large and have satellite TV, A/C, bath, and minibar. Singles €82.63-98.13; doubles €113.62; triples €118.79. AmEx/MC/V. ❺

Ostello Olimpico Vicenza, Viale Giuriolo, 9 (☎ 0444 54 02 22; fax 54 77 62), to the right of the Teatro Olimpico and across from Museo Civico, in a bright yellow building. 84 beds. Bright walls complemented by large windows and 3 terraces. Wheelchair-accessible. Breakfast €1.75. Lunch or dinner €9.50. Reception 7-9am and 3:30-11:30pm. Singles €17; family-size rooms €15. ❷

Camping: Campeggio Vicenza, Strada Pelosa, 239 (☎ 0444 58 23 11; fax 58 24 34; www.ascom.vi.it/camping). Only accessible by car: take SS11 toward Padua, turn left on Strada Pelosa, and follow signs. Showers included. TV, bar, tennis, and mini golf. Laundry €5.50. Open Mar.-Sept. €2.60-6.20 per person, €5.20-13.50 per tent with car. ❶

FOOD

Vicenza's regional specialties include dried salted cod with polenta, asparagus with eggs, and *torresani* (pigeon). A produce market is held daily in P. delle Erbe behind the basilica. On Thursdays from 7:30am-1pm in the city center (P. Erbe, P. Signori, and Viale Roma), there is a market with cheese, chicken, fish, produce and clothing. Supermarket PAM, V. Roma, 1, is open M-F 8:30am-8pm.

Zi' Teresa, Contrà S. Antonio, 1 (☎ 0444 32 14 11), right off P. Signori. Elegant, contemporary decor mixed with old wood. Accommodating, friendly owner lets you mix and match from an extensive array of dishes. Pizza from €4. *Menù* with *primo, secondo,* and *contorno,* €25. Baked sea bass *menù* is a real treat, with antipasto for €35. Cover €1.50. Open Th-Tu noon-3pm, 6pm-midnight. AmEx/MC/V. ❹

Righetti, P. del Duomo, 3 (☎ 0444 54 31 35), with another entrance at Contrà Fontana, 6. Offers self-service fare and outdoor seating. Menu changes daily. *Primi* from €2.50; *secondi* from €4. Cover €0.30. Open Sept.-July M-F 9am-3pm and 5:30pm-1am. ❷

◉ SIGHTS

For an elevated view of Vicenza and many of Palladio's works, **Piazzale Vittoria** on **Monte Berico** is a short hike uphill from the train station toward V. Risorgimento.

▨ TEATRO OLIMPICO. This theater is the last structure planned by Andrea Palladio, although he died before its completion. The intricate Vicenzian streets and alleyways unfolding off the stage, coupled with the detailed statues cluttering the theater's walls, make quite an impression. *(P. Matteotti. ☎ 0444 32 37 81. www.olimpico.vicenza.it. Open M-Sa 9:30am-12:20, 3-5:30pm. Tickets €7, includes entrance to Museo Civico.)* Every year from June to Sept., the city hosts productions in the Teatro Olimpico, showcasing both local and imported talent. *(☎ 0444 54 00 72. €11-20, students €8-15.50.)*

▨ PIAZZA DEI SIGNORI. This piazza was Vicenza's showpiece when the town was controlled by Venice. Palladio's reworking of the **Basilica Palladiana** brought the young architect his first fame. In 1546, Palladio's patron, the wealthy Giovan Giorgio Trissino, agreed to fund his proposal to shore up the collapsing Palazzo della Ragione, a project that had frustrated some of the foremost architects of the day. Palladio applied pilasters on twin *loggie* of the basilica to mask the Gothic structure beneath. The **Torre di Piazza** (to the left) reflects the basilica's former appearance. The **Loggia del Capitano,** across from the Torre di Piazza, illustrates Palladio's later renovations. *(☎ 0444 32 36 81. Basilica open Tu-Sa 10am-7pm. Entrance fee €3-5 during art exhibitions in the basilica.)*

MUSEO CIVICO. Housed in Palladio's **Palazzo Chiericati,** this extensive collection includes Montagna's *Madonna Enthroned,* a Memling Crucifixion, Tintoretto's *Miracle of St. Augustine,* Van Dyck's *Le Tre Eta Dell'Uomo* (The Three Ages of Man), Veneto's *Ritratto Virile,* and works by Veronese. *(Directly across from the tourist office. ☎ 0444 32 13 48. Open Tu-Su 10am-7pm. Buy tickets at the Teatro Olimpico. Entrance included with ticket for theater.)*

▣ PALLADIAN VILLAS

Vicenza's countryside is studded with Palladio's works. Venetian expansion to the mainland began in the early 15th century and provided infinite opportunity for Palladio to display his talents. As Venice's maritime supremacy faded, its nobles turned their attention to the acquisition of real estate on the mainland. The Venetian senate decreed that nobles build villas rather than castles to preclude the possibility of petty fiefdoms. The Veneto is now home to hundreds of the most splendid villas in Europe. Some offer classical music concerts during June and July. Check with the tourist office for details.

Most of the Palladian villas scattered throughout Veneto are difficult to reach, but luckily, some of the most famous lie in range of Vicenza. The **Villa Valmarana "ai Nani"** (of the dwarfs) is a 5min. walk from Monte Berico's Piazzale Vittoria. Keep heading straight with the mountains on your right. Bear left, following the signs for the small but beautifully kept villa, set in the middle of a series of circular flower gardens. Dwarf statues line the top of its surrounding walls. *(☎ 0444 54 39 76. Open May-Sept. M, Tu, F 10am-noon, Tu-Su 3-6pm; Mar.-Apr. and Oct.-Nov. Tu-Su 2:30-5:30pm. €6.)*

Continue from Villa Valmarana down Stradella Valmarana, or take bus #8 to the **▨ Villa Rotonda.** Considered one of history's most magnificent architectural achievements, this villa became a model for buildings in France, England, and the US, most notably Thomas Jefferson's Monticello. *(☎ 0444 32 17 93. Open Mar. 15-Oct. 15: exterior grounds Tu and Th 10am-noon and 3-6pm, €3; interior open W 10am-noon and 3-6pm, €6.)*

VERONA   ☎ 045

In Roman times, the white marble, Medusa's-head-bearing **Porta Borsari** served as the main entrance into the prestigious colony of Verona. Now the gate, at Via Catullo, acts as a portal from the car-ridden part of the city to the pedestrian shopping areas, welcoming visitors to a delightful blend of the new and the old. During the summer, well-dressed Italians emerge from exclusive high-fashion shops and head to the Arena to hear Verona's renowned opera. The city's medley of monuments, fine wines, and natural beauty inspired Shakespeare to choose it as the setting of *Romeo and Juliet*, and tourists today come in search of a tangible remnant of Shakespeare's well-known tragic romance.

▄ TRANSPORTATION

Trains: (☎045 800 0861) on P. XXV Aprile. Ticket office open daily 5:45am-10:45pm. Info open daily 7am-9pm. **Luggage storage** available (see below). To: **Bologna** (2hr., every 2hr., €5.72); **Cinque Terre** (4½hr., 4 per day, €17.40); **Milan** (2hr., every hr., €6.82); **Naples** (8hr., 4 per day, €50); **Rome** (5hr., 5 per day, €35); **Trent** (1hr., every 2hr., €4.65); and **Venice** (1¾hr., every hr., €5.73).

Buses: APT (☎045 800 4129), on P. XXV Aprile, in the gray building in front of the train station, to the right of the AMT bus platforms. To: **Brescia** (2hr., every hr., €5.50); **Montagnana** (2hr., 4 per day, €3); **Riva del Garda** (2hr., 12 per day, €5.20); and **Sirmione** (1hr., 13 per day, €2.75).

Taxis: Radiotaxi (☎045 53 26 66). Available 24hr.

Car Rental: Hertz (☎045 800 0832), **Avis** (☎045 800 0663), and **Europcar** (☎045 59 27 59) share the same office at the train station. From €48 per day. Discounts on longer rentals. Open M-F 8am-noon and 2:30-7pm, Sa 8am-noon. AmEx/MC/V.

Bike Rental: El Pedal Scaligeri (☎045 33353 67770), in the booth outside the tourist office. €4 per hr., €12 per day. 10% student discount. Also rents tandem bikes and rickshaws. Free rental with receipt of purchase from the wine bar *Oreste dal Zovo*. Open daily Apr.-Sept. 9am-7pm.

▄▐ ORIENTATION AND PRACTICAL INFORMATION

From the train station in P. XXV Aprile, walk 20min. up **Corso Porta Nuova,** or take bus #11, 12, 13, 72, or 73 (weekends take #91, 92, or 93) to Verona's heart, the **Arena** in **Piazza Brà** (tickets €0.93, full-day €3.10). Most sights lie between P. Brà and the Adige River. **Via Mazzini** connects the Arena to the monuments of **Piazza della Erbe** and **Piazza dei Signori.** The **university,** the **Teatro Romano,** and the **Giardino Giusti** lie across the Ponte Pietra.

Tourist Office: (☎045 806 8680; fax 800 3638; info@tourism.verona.it) on V. D. Alpini. English spoken. Open M-Sa 9am-7pm, Su 9am-3pm. **Airport branch** (☎/fax 045 861 9163). **Train station branch** is open M-Sa 9am-6pm. **Budget Travel: CIT** (☎045 59 06 49 or 59 17 88; fax 800 2199), P. Brà, 2. At V. Mazzini. Currency exchange. Open M-F 9am-1pm and 3-6:30pm; Sa 9am-1pm and 5:30-8:45pm.

Luggage Storage: At the train station. €2.58 per bag for 12hr. Open 24hr.

Lockers: At the train station. €1.60-3.70.

Lost and Found Property Office, V. del Pontiere, 32 (☎045 807 84 58), in police station.

English-Language Bookstore: The Bookshop, V. Interrato dell'Acqua Morta, 3a (☎045 800 7614), Ponte Navi. Classics in English and a small selection in French, Spanish, and German. Open Su, W-F 9:15am-12:30pm and 3:30-7:30pm, M 3:30-7:30pm, Sa 9:15am-12:30pm.

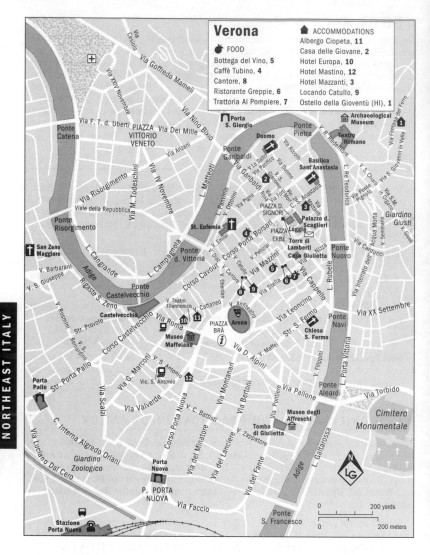

Verona

🍴 FOOD
Bottega del Vino, 5
Caffè Tubino, 4
Cantore, 8
Ristorante Greppie, 6
Trattoria Al Pompiere, 7

🏠 ACCOMMODATIONS
Albergo Ciopeta, 11
Casa delle Giovane, 2
Hotel Europa, 10
Hotel Mastino, 12
Hotel Mazzanti, 3
Locando Catullo, 9
Ostello della Gioventù (HI), 1

Laundromat: Onda Blu, V. XX Settembre, 62A (☎0336 52 28 58). Take bus #11, 12, and 13. Wash €3.10. Dry €3.10. Open 24hr.

Work Opportunity: Youth Info Center (Informagiovani), C. Porto Borsari, 17 (☎045 801 0796). Genial staff speaks English. Provides info on regulations for working in Italy. Helps travelers find employment or study opportunities in Verona. Open M, W, F 9am-1pm and 4-7pm; Tu and Th 4-7pm.

Emergency: ☎113. **Ambulance:** ☎118. **First Aid:** ☎118.

Police: Questura: ☎045 809 0411. **Ufficio Stranieri:** ☎045 809 0500.

Late-Night Pharmacy: Farmacia Due Campane, V. Mazzini, 52 (☎045 800 6660). Open M-F 9:10am-12:30pm and 3:30-7:30pm, Sa 9:10am-12:30pm. Check the *L'Arena* newspaper for 24hr. pharmacy listings.

Hospital: Ospedale Civile Maggiore (☎045 807 1111), on Borgo Trento, in P. Stefani.

Internet Access: Internet Train, V. Roma, 17/a (☎045 801 3394). From P. Brà turn right onto V. Roma. 2 blocks ahead on left. €2.50 per 30min. First-time users €5 for 2hr. Open M-F 10am-10pm. Telefon Piu', Vicolo Antonio, 6. (☎045 803 3355). From P. Borsa walk down V. Roma and take your 3rd right onto V. Antonin. Vicolo Antonio is ahead on the left. €1.50 per 30min. 2 computers; arrive before it opens to avoid a line. Also has good rates for international phone calls, shipping, fax, and money transfer. Photocopies €0.03 per page. Open daily 9:30am-10pm.

Post Office: P. Viviani, 7 (☎045 805 9311). Follow V. Cairoli from P. delle Erbe. Open M-Sa 8:10am-7pm. **Branch office**, V. C. Cattaneo, 23 (☎045 805 9911). **Postal Code:** 37100.

ACCOMMODATIONS

Budget hotels are sparse in Verona, and existing ones fill quickly. Make reservations, especially during the opera season (June-Sept.).

Ostello della Gioventù (HI), "Villa Francescatti," Salita Fontana del Ferro, 15 (☎045 59 03 60; fax 800 9127). Take bus #73 or night bus #90 to P. Isolo. By foot from the Arena, cross the Ponte Nuovo onto V. Carducci. Turn left onto V. Giusti just before the piazza, and follow it straight towards Teatro Romano. Turn right onto Vicolo Borgo Tascherio and follow the yellow signs for the hostel up the hill. This 16th-century villa has spotless dorms, several pleasant patios, and a communal feel. Hot showers until 11pm. Sheets and breakfast included. Dinner with a vegetarian option €7.50. Max. 5-night stay. Check-in 5pm. Checkout 7-9pm. Lockout 9am-5pm. Gates lock at 11:30pm, though opera-goers may make arrangements. No reservations except for family rooms. 36 dorm beds €12.50 each. Family rooms (strictly for families) €13.50 per person. ❶

Casa delle Giovane (ACISJF), V. Pigna, 7 (☎045 59 68 80; fax 800 5449; info@casa-dellegiovane.com). From P. della Erbe, turn right at Palazzo Maffei by the Azienda Promozione Turistica onto C. S. Anastasia and take your 1st left onto V. Rosa. The 3rd street on the right is V. Pigna; the hostel is down on the left at the corner of V. Pigna and V. S. Giacomo alla Pigna. Bright rooms surround a quiet courtyard, some with view of Verona's rooftops. Women only. Reception 8:30am-10:30pm. Curfew 11pm, except for opera-goers. 11 bed dorms €11.50; singles €16.50; doubles €13-15.50 per person; triples €13 per person. Make reservations by fax or email. ❶

Albergo Ciopeta, V. L. Teatro Filarmonico, 2 (☎045 800 6843; fax 803 3722). With your back to Castelvecchio, head down V. Roma, turn left on V. Teatro Filarmonico and then right on Vicolo T. Filarmonico. Small 5-room hotel with adjoining restaurant run by effervescent owner. All rooms with A/C, none with private bath. Breakfast included. Reservations required. Singles €44; doubles €72.30; triples €100. MC/V. ❹

Locanda Catullo, Vco. Catullo, 1 (☎045 800 2786; fax 59 69 87). At V. Mazzini, 40, turn onto V. Catullo, then turn left onto Vco. Catullo. Old-style decor and homey feel. July-Sept. 3-night min. stay. Singles €37; doubles €52-62; triples €78-93. ❹

Hotel Mazzanti, V. Mazzanti, 6 (☎045 59 13 70; fax 801 1262). From P. delle Erbe, walk down C. S. Anastasia and take the 1st right. Older hotel with modern comforts and great prices. All 23 rooms with A/C and TV. Breakfast included. Singles €35-72; doubles €55-104; triples €95-130. AmEx/MC/V. ❸

Hotel Mastino, Corso Porta Nuova, 16 (☎045 59 53 88; fax 59 77 18; hotelmastino@alinet.it). Brand-new, with modern amenities. All rooms with bath, A/C, TV, minibar. Breakfast included. Singles €123; doubles €155; triples €185. AmEx/MC/V. ❺

Hotel Europa, V. Roma, 8 (☎045 59 47 44; fax 045 800 18 52; www.veronahoteleuropa.com). Modern rooms with bath, A/C, TV, and minibar. Unusual green marble baths, some with tubs. Breakfast included. Singles €100-127; doubles €155; triples €185. AmEx/MC/V. ❺

◻ FOOD

Verona is famous for its wines—the dry white *soave* or the red *valpolicella*, *bardolino, recioto,* and *amarone.* For a large sampling try **Oreste dal Zovo,** Vicolo S. Marco in Foro, 7/5, off C. Porta Borsari. (☎045 803 4369. Open Tu-F 8:30am-1:30pm and 2:30-10pm.) Veronese culinary specialties include *gnocchi,* pasta with beans, *risotto* from nearby *isole,* and asparagus from Rivoli. *Pandoro,* a Christmas cake, is available year-round. A **daily market** in P. della Erbe sells produce and fresh fruit. **Pam supermarket,** V. dei Mutilati, 3, is open M-Sa 8:30am-8pm and Su 9am-1pm.

■ **Cantore,** V. A. Mario, 2 (☎045 803 1830), at the corner of V. Mazzini and V. Catullo near P. Brà. Cantore boasts some of the best pizza in Verona. Tables are full by sunset and remain so into the night. The sauce is tangy, the cheese ample, and the crust delectable. Pizza €4.30, *primi* €6.80, *secondi* €8. The house specialty, *spaghetti scoglio con frutti di mare* (shell fish), is €11.70. AmEx/MC/V. ❸

Ristorante Greppie, V. lo Samaritana, 3 (☎045 800 4577). The street links V. Mazzini and V. Cappello; follow the signs from Casa Giulietta. Tucked into a romantic back alley, this elegant restaurant serves traditional Veronese cuisine. *Primi* €6.50, *secondi* €11.50. Open Tu-Su noon-2:30pm and 7-10:30pm. AmEx/MC/V. ❸

Trattoria Al Pompiere, V. lo Regina d'Ungheria, 5 (☎045 803 0537), around the corner from Ristorante Greppie, off V. Cappello. A quaint, 90-year-old *trattoria* with dark wood interior, decorated with photographs of the owner's friends. *Primi* €8-11, *secondi* €8-18. Open Tu-Sa noon-2pm and 7:40-10:30pm, Su-M 7:40-10:30pm. AmEx/MC/V. ❹

Bottega del Vino, V. Scudo di Francia, 3 (☎045 800 4535), off V. Mazzini. Turn left at Banco Nazionale Lavoro; it's the 1st door on your left. Classy antique *trattoria* has nearly 3000 bottles of wine and over 100 different types of wine by the glass. The cheapest is a glass of local white (€0.80). Delicious appetizers available at the bar, or wait until 7:30pm, when it becomes a sit-down restaurant, to take a spot at the little tables crowded with locals. *Primi* €6.50-16, *secondi* €8-21. AmEx/MC/V. ❹

Caffè Tubino, C. Porta Borsari, 15d (☎045 803 2296), near the large arch at the intersection of Porta Borsari and V. Fama. Housed in a 17th-century *palazzo,* this tiny cafe has a wide selection of tea and coffee. Take home a tin of biscuits or caramels to complement Tubino's specialty coffee. Drinks from €1.19. Open daily 7am-midnight. ❶

◻ SIGHTS

If you plan to see all of the city's sights, the **Verona card** (€8 for 1 day, €12 for 3 days) is an excellent money-saving option, covering entry to all museums, churches, and sights, excluding the Giardino Giusti and the Scavi Scaligeri. Purchase it at any participating museum or church. Churches also offer their own pass (€5 for entrance to the *basilica,* duomo, San Fermo, S. Zeno and S. Lorenzo).

■ **THE ARENA.** The first-century AD Roman amphitheater, at the heart of the city, is Verona's modern-day **opera house.** The pink marble arena survived a 12th-century earthquake that toppled much of its outer wall. The view of its 44 seating tiers is worth the fee. For performance listings, see **Entertainment.** *(In P. Brà. Info ☎045 800 3204; www.arena.it. Wheelchair-accessible. Open Tu-Su 8:30am-7:30pm, M 1:45-7:30pm. During opera season, opening times vary and are shortened. €3.10, students €2.10.)*

⬛ PIAZZA DELLA ERBE AND ENVIRONS. Eclectic markets and stunning architecture reminiscent of an earlier empire fill this square. At the far end, the Baroque **Palazzo Maffei** overlooks the piazza. **Madonna Verona's Fountain** stands in the center of the market. Vendors' awnings nearly hide the four-columned **Berlina**, a platform on which convicts were pelted with fruit in medieval days. The winged lion perched above the **Column of St. Mark,** built in 1523, recalls centuries of Venetian domination. P. della Erbe lies near **Via Mazzini,** where pink marble, extracted from quarries in nearby Valpolicella, paves the city's famous fashion row.

PIAZZA DEI SIGNORI. The **Arco della Costa** (Arch of the Rib) connects P. della Erbe to P. dei Signori. From the arch hangs a whale rib, prophesied to fall on the first passing person who has never told a lie. A severe statue of a contemplative Dante Alighieri stands in the center of the piazza. Though they were brutish warlords, the della Scalas avidly patronized the arts. The **Palazzo degli Scaglieri,** once the family's primary residence, is opposite the Arco della Costa (to the right of the statue of Dante). The 15th-century Venetian Renaissance **Loggia del Consiglio** also sits in the piazza. The view of Verona from the 83m-high **⬛Torre dei Lamberti** (1172) is stunning; stone belfries and church spires rise from a sea of red-shingled roofs. *(☎ 045 803 2726. Open Tu-Su 8:30am-7:30pm. Elevator €2.60, students €2.10; stairs €2.10.)* Through the arch in P. dei Signori along V. Arche Scaligere lie the medieval **Tombs of the Scaligeri,** visible only from the outside.

SHAKESPEAREAN HUBRIS. Verona's most prized attraction is the Casa di Giulietta, a vine-encrusted brick house. Although most of the rooms are empty, paintings and frescoes depicting the lovers dot the walls. A balcony overlooks a courtyard full of camera-happy tourists waiting to rub the bronze statue of Juliet. Modern-day lovers scrawl odes in the entrance, making the bricks a kind of international hall of love graffiti. Contrary to popular belief, the del Cappello (Capulet) family never lived here. *(V. Cappello, 23. ☎ 045 803 4303. Open Tu-Su 8:30am-7:30pm, M 1:30-7:30pm. €3.10, students €2.10.)* The most interesting part of the Museo Degli Affreschi is the wishing tree in the front, said to be from the magical forest of the fairy kingdom Brecheliant. The underground Tomba di Giulietta (Juliet's Tomb) adjoins the museum. *(V. del Pontiere, 5. ☎ 045 800 0361. Open Tu-Su 8:30am-7:30pm, M 1:30-7:30pm. €2.60, students €1.50.)* The **Casa di Romeo,** reputedly once the home of the Montecchi (Montague) family, is around the corner from P. dei Signori at V. Arche Scaligeri, 2. The villa is privately owned and closed to the public.

BASILICA OF SANT'ANASTASIA AND ENVIRONS. This Gothic church, the largest in Verona, boasts impressive works of art, including Pisanello's *St. George Freeing the Princess* (in the left transept of the Giusti Chapel) and frescoes by Altichiero and Turone. To the right of the altar is the **Capella Pellegrini,** Michele da Firenze's series of 24 terracotta reliefs depicting the life of Christ. *(At the end of C. S. Anastasia. M-Sa 9am-6pm, Su 1-6pm. €2.)* The **Biblioteca Capitolare,** behind the cathedral in P. Duomo, maintains a priceless medieval manuscript collection. *(☎ 045 59 65 16. Open M-W, F-Sa 9:30am-12:30pm; Tu, 4-6pm. Free.)*

DUOMO. Thermal baths occupied the areas beneath and surrounding the duomo during the Roman period. The current 12th-century church rests on the remains of two previous *basiliche*. The excavated area is called the Church of St. Elena, and is accessible through the duomo, at the front of the church. The duomo itself has been recently restored, and with pink columns, chandeliers and bright frescoes is Verona's most elegant church. Titian's *Assumption of the Virgin* is located in the first chapel on the left. *(At the end of V. Duomo. From the basilica turn onto V. Massalongo, which turns into V. Duomo. M-Sa 10am-5:30pm and Su 1:30-5:30pm. €2.)*

TEATRO ROMANO AND GIARDINO GIUSTI. A crumbling stone Roman theater leads to the **archaeological museum.** Today the outdoor theater stages Shakespeare productions in Italian. The museum, once a Jesuit monastery, was built in 1480 and houses Roman and Greek artifacts excavated from Verona. The collection includes a room full of headless statues, colorful glass vessels, and an impressive display of bronze votive offerings. *(V. R. Redentore, 2. Cross the Ponte Pietra from the city center and turn right.* ☎ *045 800 0360. Open Tu-Su 8:30am-7:30pm, M 1:45-7:30pm. €2.60, students €1.50.)* Just down the street lies the **Giardino Giusti,** a stunning 16th-century garden with mythological statues, fountains, and one of the oldest labyrinths in Europe. The cypress-lined avenue gradually rises upwards, leading to a breathtaking view of the city. Mozart, Goethe, and Cosimo de'Medici were among the garden's admirers. *(Down V. S. Chiara from Teatro Romano.* ☎ *045 803 4029. Open daily Apr.-Sept. 9am-8pm; Oct.-Mar. 9am-sunset. €4.50, under 18, €3.50.)*

CASTELVECCHIO AND ENVIRONS. The castle was built in the 14th century by the della Scala family. The Veronese added *"Vecchio"* (old) to its title to distinguish it from a castle later built by the Visconti. Inside a **museum** features a collection of sculptures and paintings, including Pisanello's *Madonna and Child* and Luca di Leyda's *Crucifixion*. Be sure to cross the **Ponte Castelvecchio** to the left of the castle. The steps halfway across provide a balcony view of Verona along the river. *(At the end of V. Roma from P. Brà.* ☎ *045 59 47 34. Open Tu-Su 8:30am-7:30pm, M 1:30-7:30pm. €4.20, students €3.10.)* The nearby **Museo Maffeiano** contains one of Europe's oldest collections of Greek, Roman and Etruscan art (1675), and inscribed tablets galore. *(Down from Castelvecchio at the corner of V. Roma and C. Porta Nuova.* ☎ *045 59 00 87. Open Tu-Su 9am-7:30pm, M 1:30-7:30pm. €2.10, students €1.50.)*

SAN ZENO MAGGIORE. This massive brick church, fronted by bronze doors, is one of Verona's finest examples of Italian Romanesque architecture. Verona's black patron Saint Zeno Maggiore converted the city to Christianity in the 4th century. The two-story apse contains a famous Renaissance triptych by Mantegna. An urn in the stone crypt holds Zeno's remains. *(From Castelvecchio, walk up Rigaste S. Zeno and turn left at the piazza onto V. Barbarani, which leads to the church. Open daily Nov.-Feb. 8:30am-1pm and 1:30-5pm; Mar.-Oct. daily 8:30am-6pm. €2.)*

SAN FERMO. This 11th-century church rests on the spot where Saints Fermo and Rustico were tortured to death in AD 304. It has a rustic upper interior with Gothic design and mostly wooden architecture. A staircase on the right leads to the Romanesque marble lower church, with a forest of columns and remains of the saints. *(Walk down V. Cappello towards P. Navi. The church is at the end on the corner of Str. S. Fermo. Open daily 10am-6pm and Su 1-6pm. €2.)*

🎵 ENTERTAINMENT

Every year, droves of opera lovers flock to Verona for the world-famous **Verona Opera Festival.** Verdi's *Aida* and *Rigoletto* have been performed in recent years. (☎ 045 800 5151; fax 801 3287. General admission on the Roman steps Su-Th €19.50, F-Sa €21.50. General admission ticket-holders should arrive 1hr. before showtime. Reserved seats €70-154.) From June to September, the Teatro Romano stages dance performances and Shakespeare productions (in Italian). June brings a one-week jazz festival known as **Verona Jazz.** (Info ☎ 045 807 7205 or 806 6485. Tickets for both €10.33-20.66.) If you don't like opera (or its prices), there is a **movie theater** at V. Poloni, 16 (☎ 045 800 6777). Verona's nightclubs lie beyond walking distance of the city. You can take bus #92 or 94 from the station or Castelvecchio to **Berfi's Club,** V. Lussemburgo, 1, one of the city's hotter spots, but you'll need a cab to return. (☎ 045 50 80 24. Open 11pm-4am.) **Alter Ego,** V. Torricelle, 9, is so fashionable that buses don't run to it. (☎ 045 91 51 30. Open 11pm-4am.)

TREVISO

☎ 0422

Treviso, the provincial capital of the Veneto, is known by two other names, *Città d'acqua* (City of Water) and *Città Dipinta* (Painted City). The town's watery name is derived from the numerous canals which loop through the town, offshoots of the rivers Sile and Botteniga. The painted reference comes from the frescoed facades of Treviso's buildings. However, a third aspect of Treviso's self-image is its wealth. In this birthplace of Benetton, fashion is at the forefront. Beautiful people sport clothes and shoes that seem to drop straight from the Italian fashion gods. Come to this glitzy spot to window-shop; bring credit cards at your own risk.

▐ TRANSPORTATION

Trains: Station at Piazza Duca d'Aosta, just south of city center. From bus station, turn right down V. Roma. Ticket counter open 6am-9pm. Station open 4:30am-12:30am. Main stop on heavily trafficked Venice-Udine line. To: **Trieste** (2½hr., 12 per day, 7:21am-10:14pm, €8.99); **Udine** (1½hr., 26 per day, 7:21am-11:17pm, €5.73); **Venice** (30min., 42 per day, 7:10am-11:41pm, €1.91). To reach **Milan** or **Padua,** make a connection in Venice.

Buses: Lungosile A. Mattei, 21 (☎0422 57 73 60), is off Corso del Popolo, where it crosses river. Offices open 6:50am-1pm and 1:30-7:45pm. La Marca (☎0422 41 22 22) bus line services the Veneto region and the Palladian Villas. To: **Bassano del Grappa** (1hr., every hr., 6:35am-6:10pm, €3.35); **Padua** (1½hr., 31 per day, 6am-8:15pm, €3.35); **Venice, Mestre station** (30min., 45 per day, 4:10am-10:45pm, €2.15); **Vicenza** (1½hr., 9 per day, 6:15am-6:30pm, €3.90).

✴ ▐ ORIENTATION AND PRACTICAL INFORMATION

Treviso lies 30km inland from Venice. Traced by the flowing waters of the Sile, the old city walls encompass Treviso's historic city center (and most points of interest). From the train station, the **ACTT** (intracity) bus hub is directly across from the busy **Piazza Duca d'Aosta.** Just left of the buses, **Via Roma** leads from between the crumbling walls into the city center. It then becomes **Corso del Popolo,** crosses the river, and drains into **Piazza della Borsa.** From there, a short walk up **Via XX Settembre** is rewarded by splendid **Piazza dei Signori,** Treviso's main square and showcase for **Palazzo dei Trecento.** Pedestrian-dominated **Via Calmaggiore** leads to the duomo.

Tourist Office: APT, P. Monte di Pietà, 8 (☎0422 54 76 32; fax 41 90 92; www.provincia.treviso.it), on the side of Palazzo dei Trecento from P. dei Signori. Has city maps and a list of walking tours that follow the Sile River. Open M 9am-12:30pm, Tu-F 9am-12:30pm and 2-6pm, Sa-Su 9am-12:30pm and 3-6pm.

Emergency: ☎113. **Ambulance:** ☎118.

Carabinieri: V. Cornarotta, 24 (☎112). **Questura,** V. Carlo Alberto, 37 (☎0422 59 91).

Hospital: Ospedale Civile Ca' Foncello, Piazzale Ospedale, 1, (☎0422 32 21 11).

Internet Access: Attrazione Las Vegas, V. Roma, 39 (☎0422 59 02 47), upstairs in a smoky video game arcade. €6.50 per hr. Open daily 10am-1am.

Post Office: P. Vittoria, 1 (☎0422 317 2111). Housed in a palatial building at the end of V. Cadorna, off C. del Popolo. Open M-S 8:10am-6pm.

Postal Code: 31100.

ACCOMMODATIONS AND FOOD

Most of Treviso's in-town accommodations are expensive. **Hotel Carlton ⑤**, Largo Porta Altinia, 15, right off of V. Roma, 2 min. from the train station will serve you with 4 star elegance. The extensive buffet breakfast, including eggs, yogurt, cereal, cheese, meat, bread, and an array of baked goods, is almost worth the price. Singles €82-103, doubles €134-165. AmEx/MC/V. **Albergo Campeol ④**, P. Ancilotto, 4, conveniently situated behind Palazzo dei Trecento, offers some of the least expensive rooms in town, all with bath, TV, phone, and a cheery yellow motif. (☎/fax 0422 566 01. Breakfast €6. Singles €52; doubles €83. AmEx/MC/V.) **Da Renzo ④**, V. Terragio, lacks the allure of city center accommodations, but is only a bus ride from the station (#7, 8, or 11 and ask the driver for Da Renzo, or the Borgo Savoia stop; €0.74). All rooms have bath, A/C, phones, and breakfast. (☎ 0422 40 20 68; fax 54 68 82; www.sevenonline.it/darenzo. Singles €43-48; doubles €63-71. MC/V.)

The city is famous for its radicchio, *ciliege* (cherries) and 🖾tiramisù, a heavenly combination of espresso-and-liquor-soaked cake layered with the delectable, mild cheese, mascarpone. Cherries ripen in June, radicchio peaks in December, and tiramisù is always in season. (In the summer, *gelateria* offer *tiramisù gelato*.) To taste these delights, head to the daily morning **produce market** at the Stiore stop of the #2 or 11 bus. The **pescheria**, or fish and vegetable market, located on the tiny Isola dell'Pescheria surrounded by the canals, is open Tu-Sa 7:30am-12:30pm. For basics, shop at the **PAM supermarket**, P. Borso, 12. (☎ 0422 58 39 13. Open M-Sa 8:30am-7:30pm.) **All'Oca Bianca**, V. della Torre, 7, on a side street off central V. Calmaggiore, is a casual *trattoria* that serves excellent fish dishes. If you missed cherry season, try the *grappa*-steeped version, *ciliege sotto grappa*. (☎ 0422 54 18 50. *Primi* €6.20; *secondi* and *pesce* €7.32-8.26. Cover €1.55. Open Tu 12:30-2pm, Th-M 9am-3pm and 6pm-midnight. AmEx/MC/V.) If *primi* seems a merely an inconvenient delay, begin with dessert at **Nascimben**, V. XX Settembre, 3. (☎ 0422 59 12 91. Open Tu-Su 7am-6pm.)

SIGHTS

PALAZZO DEI TRECENTO. Dominating P. dei Signori, this palace proudly recalls Treviso's successful reemergence from a 1944 air raid on Good Friday that demolished half the town. The post-bombing restoration blends perfectly with the original frescoes, though the original position of the stairs and outer wall are clearly labeled. (☎ 0422 65 82 35. Open occasionally for groups. Call to make a reservation.)

DUOMO. Calmaggiore's *passeggiata* flows beneath the arcades of the piazza to this seven-domed church complete with Neoclassical facade. The duomo's **Cappella Malchiostro** dates from 1519 and contains works by sworn enemies, Titian (*Annunciation*) and Pordenone. (Open M-Th 9am-noon, Sa-Su 9am-noon and 3-6pm.)

MUSEO CIVICO. Also called the Museo Bailo, this museum is home to Titian's Sperone Speroni and Lorenzo Lotto's *Portrait of a Dominican*. The ground floor showcases Treviso's archaeological finds, which include 5th century BC bronze discs from Montebelluna. (Borgo Cavour, 24. ☎ 0422 59 13 37. Open Tu-Sa 9am-12:30pm and 2:30-5pm, Su 9am-noon. €3, students €2.)

PALLADIAN VILLAS. Palladio's penchant for building villas (see **Palladian Villas**, p. 252) spilled into the Treviso area. Among them is **Villa** (1560) on the Treviso-Bassano line at the small village of Maser. (☎ 0423 92 30 04. Open Mar.-Oct. Tu, Sa, Su and holidays 3-6pm; Nov.-Feb. Sa-Su and holidays 2:30-5pm. €5, students €2.50.) The nearby **Villa Elmo** is a bit more difficult to reach, requiring first a bus or train ride from Treviso to Vastelfrance, then a bus ride from there to Fanzolo. The villa is considered to be one of the most characteristic Palladian works. *(Open Apr.-Oct. M-Sa 3-7pm, Su 10:30am-12:30pm and 3-7pm; Nov.-Mar. Sa-Su and holidays 2-6pm. €5.50.)*

BASSANO DEL GRAPPA   ☎ 0422

Bassano del Grappa is a tiny hill-side town situated before rising mountain peaks and the tranquil river Brenta, over which Palladio designed the monumental wooden *Ponte degli Alpini* (Alpine Bridge), commonly referred to today as the *Ponte Vecchio*. The slanted cobblestoned streets show traces of Roman and medieval architecture, while cluttered antique shops provide one of Bassano's greatest attractions. The other is *grappa*, a fiery hard liquor once used as a medieval elixir, distilled from the skins and seeds of grapes (the leftovers of the second wine pressing). The varieties of *grappa* have grown exponentially over the centuries; today there are sweet *grappe* flavored with blueberries or strawberries. Bassano's mild climate allows for the prolific cultivation of grapes, as well as *broccoletti* (broccoli) in autumn, *bisi di Borso* (native grown peas), and regional specialty *asparagi bianchi* (white asparagus; dating back to the 16th century) from April to May. It is also famous for its honey and pottery. The people of Bassano are proud of their traditional agriculture, arts and crafts, and if you pause on one of the sloping streets to admire the view of the Brenta and the imposing mountains, a friendly native will eagerly stop to tell you all about it.

■ ⚐ **TRANSPORTATION AND PRACTICAL INFORMATION.** Bassano's principal piazze lie between the train station and the **Fiume Brenta.** The **train station** is at the end of V. Chilesotti. (Ticket counter open M-Sa 6:05am-7:30pm, Su 6:30am-8:45pm.) **Trains** to: **Padua** (1hr., 12 per day, 5:35am-10:45pm, €2.79); **Trent** (2hr., 9 per day, 5:40am-8:46pm, €4.65); and **Venice** (1hr., 18 per day, 5:30am-9:15pm, €3.62). The **bus station** is in P. Trento, off V. delle Fosse. FTV (☎ 0424 30 850) serves **Vicenza** (1hr., 24 per day, 5:30am-7:50pm, €2.63). La Marca Line (☎ 0422 41 22 22) runs to **Treviso** (1hr., 10 per day, 7am-7:18pm, €3). Buy tickets at Bar Trevisani in P. Trento.

As you exit the train station, **Via Chilesotti** will be directly in front of you. To reach the heart of town, take a right on **Viale delle Fosse** and left on **Via da Ponte.** To reach the **tourist office,** Largo Corona d'Italia, 35, cross V. delle Fosse, and enter the shopping complex through the opening in the stone wall. Make an immediate right and head to the older, separate building against the wall. They provide a town map and information and pamphlets on local festivals, canoeing, skiing, biking, hiking, and routes for picturesque walks though the countryside. (☎ 0424 52 43 51; fax 52 53 01. Open M-F 9am-12:30pm and 2-5pm, Sa 9am-12:30pm.) For info on the city before your arrival, call the **Bassano Città Murato.** (☎ 0424 22 82 41.)

⚐ ⚑ **ACCOMMODATIONS AND FOOD.** The **Istituto Cremona,** V. Chini, 6. part elementary school, part hostel, is currently closed for restoration. Try **Hotel Victoria ❹,** Viale Diaz, 33, which is about a 5min. walk from the center of town. From P. Liberta, take V. Marinali straight into Piazzale Cadorna. Follow it through and cross the Ponte Nuovo. Viale Diaz is directly after the bridge and the hotel is down on the left. Pristine and comfortable rooms have phone, bath, satellite TV, A/C, and minibar. (☎ 0424 50 36 20. Breakfast included. Singles €52; doubles €82. MC/V.) To get to **Hotel Al Castello ❹,** V. Bonamigo, 19, from P. Liberta, turn down V. Matteotti, which turns into V. Bonamigo. The hotel is plain but clean; all rooms come with bath, A/C and TV. (☎ 0424 22 86 65. Breakfast €6. Singles €45; doubles €82; triples €100. AmEx/MC/V.)

To get the *grappa* out of Bassano, buy a bottle at **Nardini's,** Ponte Vecchio (☎ 042 27 741), the oldest and best producer of *grappa* in town. Other distilleries surround

TRAVELIN' ITALY: LACTOSE-INTOLERANT STYLE.

You've watched with envy as your friends scarfed down pizza and ice cream. You are lactose intolerant. All your life, you've pondered one question: How can I travel in Italy? Have no fear, gentle traveler. *Let's Go* will show you the way.

Step One: Learn the Early Warning Signs. Study these four critical names: *latte* (milk); *crema* (cream); *formaggio* (cheese); and *burro* (butter). Practice these crucial phrases: *"Si potrebbe farlo senza crema?"* (Could you make that without cream?); *"C'è latte?"* (Is that made with milk?); and *"Potrei avere una bella, forte pompa stomaco?"* (May I please have a good, hard stomach-pumping?).

Step Two: The Truth About Pizza. Ever taken slack for scraping the cheese off your pizza ("Dude, that's not pizza! That's like...bread with sauce.")? Well in Italy, not only is this acceptable, but it's on the menu. Ask for *pizza marinara*: pizza without cheese, just the way Mother Nature intended it.

Step Three: The Gelato Question. Cities crumble, stomachs growl, but hope survives. Though you can't eat ice cream, you may be able to eat the tastier *gelato*. Fruit flavors, especially lemon and strawberry, have a smaller milk content than flavors like vanilla. Some *gelaterie* even carry soy-based *gelato*.

Step Four: The After-Dinner Coffee. You've long stared longingly at the fluffy sophistication of Italian *cappuccino*, and yet one sip of the lactose-free version (espresso) left you up and shaking half the night. Jitter no more, for in the lovely and culinarily ingenious land of Italia there's *caffè di orto*, a "coffee" made of roasted barley that's caffeine-free and never taken with milk. Who would have thought that a drink made from barley could taste so good...oh, wait.

the bridge, and some will even provide free tastes upon request. For dinner, try local favorite **Birreria Ottone ❸**, V. Matteotti, 50, just off the P. Libertà. The restaurant is elegantly decorated, with an intricate set of cables suspending a tiny lamp over each table. Try the Hungarian goulash (€10.40), as well as the famous apple pie or iced *zabayone* with caramel, a frozen drink. (☎0424 22 206. Cover €1.80. Open Sept.-July M 11:30am-3:30pm, W-Su 11am-3pm and 7-11pm. MC/V.) For healthy food, check out **Un Punto Macrobiotico ❷**, V. Roma, 45/B. From the P. Libertà, turn down V. Roma; the restaurant is in an alcove to your left. This vegetarian, all-natural restaurant is dressed in dark wood and yellow in a nuovo-eclectic style. Soups and pizzas are €2.10-6.20. A shop selling all-natural condiments and pastas is adjacent. (☎0242 22 71 52. Open Tu-Su 12:30-2pm and 7:30-9pm.) The **open-air market** in P. Garibaldi sells local produce. (Open Th and Sa 8am-1pm.)

◧ **SIGHTS.** The █**Ponte Vecchio,** besides being an architectural delight on its own, provides a beautiful view of Bassano's ancient, colorful buildings with their red roofs, dwarfed by the looming Dolomites. For a closer look at the river, cross the bridge and take a left on the first street, descending gradually to the **Veduta Panoramica,** where you can walk along the shore. For another elevated view, cross back over the bridge and turn left up **P. Terraglio.** Also off the Ponte Vecchio, at V. Gamba 6, is the **Museo della Grappa,** a modern-day distillery run by the Polli family, housed in a 15th-century *palazzo*. The small, bright white and copper museum explains the origins and evolution of the *grappa*-making process. Their own *grappa* sells for about €4 per tiny bottle. Ask to sample the *grappa aromatizzata al mirtillo*, sweet *grappa* flavored with blueberries. (☎0424 52 44 26. Open Tu-Su 9am-1pm and 2:30-7:30pm, M 2:30-7:30pm. Free.)

The majestic **Piazza della Libertà** contains the imposing statue-topped facade of the **Chiesa di San Giovanni Battista,** and the sculpted Venetian winged lion to the right.

In the adjacent P. Garibaldi, the **Chiesa di San Francesco** sits next door to the **Museo Civico,** one of the oldest museums in the Veneto. It features over 500 works dating back to the Middle Ages. A highlight is the collection of Jacopo Bassano's paintings of dark worlds split open by divine light, such as the famous *Flight into Egypt* and *St. Valentine Baptizing St. Lucilla.* The Museo also shows the Chini Collection of Greek artifacts from southeast Italy (6th-3rd centuries BC) and works by contemporary artists. (☎ 0424 52 22 35. Open Apr.-Oct. Tu-Sa 9am-12:30pm and 3:30-6:30pm; June-Sept. same hours and Su 10am-12:30pm. €4.50, students and seniors €3. Ticket includes entrance to Pottery Museum.) The **Pottery Museum,** located in the Palazzo Storm, close to the Ponte Vecchio on V. Ferracina, preserves the detailed craftsmanship of generations of Bassano's ceramic artisans. (☎ 0424 82 98 07. Open same hours as Museo Civico. €4.50, students and seniors €3, or free with ticket to Museo Civico.) Every July and August, the **Opera Estate Festival Veneto** comes to Bassano, bringing lively and eclectic performances of dance, theatre, opera, and open-air cinema.

DOLOMITES (DOLOMITI)

Somewhere between Trent and Innsbruck lies a land of shattered rose-colored peaks, etched smooth by the passage of turquoise streams. This surreal landscape takes its name from the mineral of which it is largely composed. Dolomite is a carbonate interlaced with magnesium, the latter of which gives this sedimentary rock an off-pink color and pearlescent luster. Because the rock is unusually hard, it has formed jagged peaks, difficult to traverse. Their impassibility has isolated the Dolomites, ensuring the continued existence of groups such as the Ladins, who speak a 2000-year-old linguistic hybrid of Latin and Celtic. To this day, poor transport networks impede the area's economic growth and protect the beauty that prompted Le Corbusier to call the Dolomites "the most beautiful natural architecture in the world." **Belluno** (p. 263) and **Cortina d'Ampezzo** (p. 266) are good starting points for exploring the Dolomites; Trentino Alto-Adige's **Bolzano** (p. 283) and **Bressanone** (p. 286), while not in the Dolomites proper, are in their vicinity.

BELLUNO ☎ 0437

For much of the summer, the dramatic spires of Dolomitic rock that hover over Belluno are just visible through the blanket of humid air settling in the valley. But it is the extensive public transportation network, inexpensive lodging, and proximity to the high country that draw serious outdoorsmen and intrepid budget travelers to Belluno. The town is an ideal entry point for dayhikes or multi-day treks in the Dolomites, including the famous *alte vie*, or high routes. With a few splendid *palazzi* and glossy arcades, Belluno is a city more or less undiscovered by the tourists that crowd other, more famous mountain towns (see Cortina, p. 266).

◪ TRANSPORTATION. Belluno sits in an easily accessible region in the southern Dolomites, 50km north of Venice and 70km west of Udine. Trains run directly to Belluno from **Padua** (2hr., every hr., 6am-10:33pm, €5.73) via **Conegliano** (1hr., 8 per day, 6:39pm-8:43pm, €2.69), a stop on the Venice-Udine line. From Conegliano, some scheduled trains run directly to Belluno, but many require you to change in nearby Ponte nelle Alpi. (☎ 0437 72 77 91. Ticket office open daily 6am-7:25pm.) Belluno's **bus station,** across **Piazza della Stazione** from the train station, is a regional hub for **Dolomiti Bus,** which services the pre-Alps to the west and the eastern Dolomites. Buses run to directly to: **Calazo** (1hr., 12 per day, 6:15am-8:05pm, €3); **Cortina** (2hr., 10 per day, 6:25am-6:50pm, €3.70); and **Feltre** (40min., 16 per day, 6:20am-7:10pm, €2.50). For more information, stop by or call **Dolomiti Bus.** (☎ 0437 94 11 67, 94 12 37, or 21 72 00. Open M-Sa 6:50am-6:25pm and 7-7:15pm.) The orange **local** buses all stop in P. della Stazione, and service the greater city area for €0.77 per ride.

NORTHEAST ITALY

The Dolomites

0   5 miles
0   5 kilometers

TO INNSBRUCK, AUSTRIA

Brunico

Val Pusteria

Dobbiaco

Bressanone

Val di Luson

Chiusa

Pedracès

San Candido   Sesto

Val di Landro

Val di Funes

La Villa   Ospitale

Susi   Ortisei

Selva di Val Gardena   San Cassiano   Missurina

Auronzo

Val Gardena

Corvara

Cortina d'Ampezzo   Lozzo di Cadore   S. Stefano di Cadore

Bolzano

Arabba   *Ampezzo*

Cadore

Nova Levante   Canazei   San Vito di Cadore   Calalzo di Cadore   Forni di Sopra

Nova Ponente   Vigo   Caprile   Borca di Cadore   Pieve di Cadore   TO UDINE

TO TRENTO   Moena   *Val di Fassa*   Canale d'Agordo   Alleghe   Zoldo Alto

Predazzo   Cenceniga   Cibiana

Caralese   Falcade   Forno di Zoldo   Ospitale di Cadore

Agordo   *Val di Zoldo*

Molina   *Val di Flemme*   *Valle Travignolo*   San martino di Castrozza   Longarone

Imer   Fiera di Primiero   Mezzano

Belluno

TO VENICE

NORTHEAST ITALY

■✦🛈 ORIENTATION AND PRACTICAL INFORMATION. From the train and bus stations, the city center, **Piazza dei Martiri**, is only a 5min. walk. Follow **Via Dante,** opposite the train terminal, and cross the small **Piazzale Battisti** onto **Via Loreto.** When V. Loreto ends after 50m, turn left onto **Via Matteotti.** P. dei Martiri, with its long arcade overlooking several fountains and sculpted gardens, is now in sight. The **APT tourist office** is on the opposite side of the piazza, at P. dei Martiri, 8. (☎0437 94 00 83; www.infodolimiti.it. Open M-Sa 9am-12:30pm and 3-6pm, Su 10am-12:30pm and 3:30-6:30pm.) **Pitta S. Francesco** lies on the other side of C. Italia from the station. From the duomo, take the stairs to your left, turn right at the bottom of the stairs, and cross the street. Turn left, and the office is on your right. (☎0437 32 31; fax 32 35. Open daily 9am-12:30pm and 4-7pm.) No less than six **banks** line the piazza, all with similar **currency exchange** rates and 24hr. **ATMs.**

In case of an **emergency,** call ☎113, the **police** (☎0437 94 55 08), on V. Volontari d. Libertà, or an **ambulance** (☎118). 24hr. pharmacies rotate (check pharmacy windows); **Farmacia Chiarelli,** V. Matteotti, is a good option. (☎0437 94 18 91. Open M-Sa 8:30am-12:30pm and 4-7:30pm.) Belluno's **hospital** is on V. Europa (☎0437 16 111). **The Hotel Astor,** P. dei Martiri, 26/E, offers **Internet** use for €6 per hr. (☎0437 94 20 94. Open M-Sa 9am-11pm.) A **Telecom Italia calling center** at V. Caffi, 7, also has Internet for €5.16 per hr. (Open M-Su 8am-11pm.) Belluno's **post office,** with fax and photocopy services, sits on V. Roma, off P. Emanuele. (☎0437 95 32 11. Open M-F 8:10am-7pm, Sa 8:15am-1:50pm.) **Postal Code:** 32100.

CLUB ALPINO ITALIANO. If you're intending to do a serious amount of hiking in Italy, consider purchasing a **CAI** (Club Alpino Italino) membership. CAI runs many mountain *rifugi*, and members pay half-price for lodgings. *Rifugi* (which generally operate from late June to early October) may also rent out *vie ferrate* hiking equipment essentials. CAI membership is €35, under 18 €11.50, with a €5.50 supplement for new members and €15.50 surcharge for non-Italians. It can be purchased at a CAI office (see the office in Belluno); bring a passport photo.

◪◧ ACCOMMODATIONS AND FOOD. Cheap, central accommodations add to Belluno's allure. **La Cerva B&B ❶**, V. Paoletti, 7/B, boasts free use of mountain bikes and unlimited fridge privileges with free access to soft drinks and beer. To find the B&B, cross the piazza and, as you exit the train station, turn left onto the V. le Volantari Libertà, and then turn left again onto the V. Fantuzzi. Cross the main road to reach V. Col di Lana and turn right after 15m. (☎338 825 3608. Communal bath. Breakfast €2.50. Singles €15.50; doubles €26. Extra bed €8.50.) For **Albergo Cappello e Cadore ❹**, V. Ricci, 8, take V. le Volontari Libertà from the station. Turn right onto V. Fantuzzi, which changes to V. J. Tasso, off of which branches V. Ricci. Built in 1864, this beautifully renovated, centrally-located three-star hotel offers rooms with bath, A/C, satellite TV, and minibar. (☎0437 94 02 46; fax 0437 29 23 19; www.albergocappello.com; albergo.cappello.bl@libero.it. Breakfast included. Singles €50; doubles €92. AmEx/DC/MC/V.) **Albergo Centrale ❸**, V. Loreto, 2, in the city center as its name suggests, has 12 clean, affordable rooms. (☎0437 94 33 49. Breakfast included. Reserve ahead. Singles €31; doubles with bath €52.) Inquire at the tourist office about other cheap accommodations.

Dining in Belluno is inexpensive, but not particularly outstanding. Serving local specialties like *galletti alla diavola* (devil's chicken) is **Ristorante Taverna ❸**, V. Cipro, 7. (☎0437 25 192. *Primi* €5.20-6, *secondi* €7-10. Cover €1. Open M-Sa noon-2:30pm and 7:30-10pm. MC/V.) **La Buca ❷**, V. Carrera, 15c, has pizzas for €3.10-9.30, as well as other standard fare. (☎0437 94 01 91. *Primi* €4.80-8.50, *secondi* €6.50-10.30. Open M-Su noon-2:30pm and 6pm-1am; in winter closed M.) **Supermarket per Dolomiti**, P. dei Martiri, 9/10, next to the tourist office, stocks food for excursions. (Open Th-Tu 8:30am-1pm and 4:30pm-7:30pm, W 8:30am-1pm.)

◙ SIGHTS. Belluno's Piazza del Duomo is its masterpiece. From P. dei Martiri, follow signs to the duomo. Three *palazzi* (Palazzo Rettori, Palazzo Rosso, and Palazzo dei Giuristi) cry Venetian Renaissance, and the nearby **Museo Civico** showcases Caffi's enchanting *Venice in the Snow* and Ricci's startling *Fall of Fetonte*. (☎0437 94 48 36; www.comune.belluno.it. Open Apr. 8-Sept. 30 Tu-Sa 10am-noon and 4-7pm, Su 10:30am-12:30pm.; Oct.-Apr. 7 M-Sa 10am-noon and Tu-F 3pm-6pm. €3.50.) While you're in the vicinity, head down the *Scala Mobile* (a three-tiered escalator that leaves from Palazzo Rosso), or walk down the nearby stairs for some nice views of the valley. There's a bike-borrowing stand at the foot of the *Scala Mobile*. (Open daily 9am-6pm. Small deposit required.)

Belluno's biggest attractions loom on the horizon. The impressive Dolomitic rock faces and grassy peaks that tower over town are only the tip of the iceberg. To the North, where the Dolomites proper begin, the vast, wild expanse of the **Parco Nazionale di Dolomiti Bellunese** (Bellunese Dolomites National Park) is only 30min. away by car or bus. The less challenging **Botanical Garden of the Eastern Alps** rests at the top of a chairlift on the western slope of nearby **Monte Favaghera**. From July 1-Sept. 15, buses from Belluno service a chairlift to whisks visitors up 1500m in the air. (☎0437 94 48 30. Inquire at the tourist office for bus and chairlift schedules.)

▨ HIKING. For Alpine information, visit the **CAI** (Club Alpino Italiano), P. S. Giovanni Bosco, 11. From the tourist office, cross the piazza and turn right onto P. Vittorio Emanuele. Continue straight ahead and down the stairs. Cross the river and take V. San Antonio. When the road forks, take the V. S. Giuseppe to P. S. Giovanni Bosco. The office is straight ahead, on the opposite side of the piazza. Buy a membership card for a reduced price at mountain *rifugi*. (☎/fax 0437 93 16 55; http:// digilander.iol.it/caibelluno. Open Nov.-Apr. Tu 6pm-8pm and F 8:30pm-10:30pm; Apr.-Oct. F 8:30pm-10:30pm.)

Belluno offers a lot of excellent hikes; one of the best is along the *altavia*, stretching north and south from Braies and Belluno, respectively. To hike the entire *altavia* would probably take from 8 to 15 days. The hike along the first stretch, from Belluno to *rifugio* #7, can be done in a day. From Belluno's P. Martiri, take V. J. Tasso, which changes to V. Fantuzzi, and then V. Col di Lana. Follow this for about 1km until a sign points right, directing you to Bolzano; walk uphill for about 9km. The paved road can be easily cycled or walked in about 3hr., ending in Casa Bortot (707m). Stock up on food here—it's your last chance before the *rifugio* #7. Follow the small gravel path to your left, leading to the **Parco Nazionale Dolomiti Bellunesi,** or the start of **altavia #1.** The route is well-marked and sticks fairly close to the river gorge, with views of waterfalls and deep pools etched out of the dolomite rock. A 3-4hr. hike will bring you to a small meadow and **rifugio no. #7** at **Pils Pilon.** (☎0437 94 16 31 or 0445 66 11 28 in winter. Call ahead to confirm availability. Serves hot meals. Members of CAI €8 per night, nonmembers €16. Inquire about the more difficult surrounding *vie ferrate*.) For more information on *altavia* #1, visit www.dolomiti-altevie.it.

CORTINA D'AMPEZZO   ☎0436

Come snowfall, glitzy Cortina draws skiers from across Europe to the craggy peaks far above its streets. The aristocrats of the Hapsburg empire had the same idea, but were shut down by the onset of WWII, when Cortina saw some of Italy's bloodiest battles. Hikes in the mountains showcase not only Tyrolean natural splendor, but also afford close-up views of old trenches and war tunnels. The not-so-athletically-inclined beware: there is little to do in the town but spend money at the outrageously-priced boutiques and German pastry shops.

⬛ TRANSPORTATION. Cortina lies near the Austrian border, north of Belluno and east of Bolzano. The nearest **train station** is in Calazo, from which buses take a steep road to reach Cortina (1hr., every hr., 6:30am-8:35pm, €2.41). Cortina is most easily reached by car, but if you're relying on public transportation, trains run to Calazo from Belluno (1hr., 9 per day, 8:15am-9:17pm, €2.85), Milan (8hr.), and Venice (3hr.). **Buses** run directly from Cortina to Belluno (2hr., 10 per day, 6:15am-6:55pm, €3.70); **Milan** (7hr., F-Sa June-Aug., €22.56); and **Venice** (5hr.; Sept.-June 22 Sa-Su, June 23-Aug. daily; €13.45). The orange **urban bus** services Cortina and the Ampezzo Valley, and is useful for reaching hotels and *funivie* (cable cars) outside town. (Tickets sold at newsstands, *tabacchi*, and bars near bus stops. €0.72.) For more information on all buses, call or stop by the Dolomiti Bus information desk, in the Cortina **bus station.** (☎0436 86 79 21. Open M-Sa 8:15am-12:30pm and 2:30-5pm.) For **RadioTaxi,** dial ☎0436 86 08 88 (24hr. service.)

⬛▨ ORIENTATION AND PRACTICAL INFORMATION. The center of town is the pedestrian-only **Corso Italia,** lined with expensive shops and punctuated by the duomo's 75m *campanile*. From the bus station, cross the street, head left, and take **Largo Poste** to the *centro*. The **APT tourist office** is on Piazzetta S. Francesco, 8, off V. Mercato, on the opposite side of the duomo from the station. (☎0436 32 31; fax 32 35;

www.apt-dolomiti-cortina.it. Open daily 9am-12:30pm and 4-7pm.) There's another office at P. Roma, 1. (☎0436 27 11; fax 32 35; www.infodolimiti.it. Open daily 9am-12:30pm and 3:30pm-6:30pm.) **Banks** with similar high exchange rates and 24hr. **ATMs** line C. Italia. In an **emergency,** dial ☎113, or the **police** (☎0436 86 62 00), on V. Marconi. The town **hospital,** Ospedale Cortina, is at V. Roma, 121 (☎0436 88 51 11). 24hr. **pharmacies** rotate with lists posted in their windows, but **Farmacia Internazionale,** C. Italia, 151, offers long hours. (☎0436 22 23. Open M-Sa 9am-12:45pm and 3-7pm.) **Dolomiti Multimedia,** L. Poste, 59, charges €6.20 per hr. of **Internet access.** (☎0436 86 80 90. Open M-F 8:30am-12:30pm and 3-7:30pm.) The **post office** is at L. Poste. (☎0436 29 79. Open M-F 8:10am-6pm, Sa 8:10am-12:30pm.) **Postal Code:** 32043.

⚑ ACCOMMODATIONS AND FOOD. Cortina hosted the 1956 Winter Olympics, but abundant and overpriced accommodations prove that Olympic spirit is still in the air. For the tragically urban, the cheapest option in Cortina *centro* is **Hotel Montana ❸,** C. Italia, 94, near the duomo. (☎0436 86 21 26; fax 0436 86 82 11. Singles €34-50; doubles €62-90. MC/V.) **Hotel Fiames ❹,** Località Fiames, 13, books rooms and serves meals in Fiames, 5km north of town. Take bus #1 (expect sporadic service; 10min., 1 per hr., 7:35am-6:50pm, €2.35) from the station to the last stop. (☎0436 23 66; fax 57 33. Breakfast included; lunch or dinner €15.50. Singles with bath €42-54; doubles with bath €52-65.) **International Camping Olimpia ❶,** Località Fiames, is north of town, before Hotel Fiames. Bus #1 stops at the access road; ask the driver for the Olimpia stop. (☎0436 50 57. €13.50 per person.)

Pizzeria Il Ponte ❶, V. B. Franchetti, 8, offers a view of the mountains and delicious pizzas from €3.50. Head behind the duomo on C. Italia, then make a left onto V. B. Franchetti. (☎0436 86 76 24. Open T-Su 10am-3pm and 6pm-midnight. AmEx/MC/V.) Across the street is the inexpensive **Kanguro supermarket,** V. B. Franchetti, 1. (Open M-Sa 8:30am-12:30pm and 3:30-7:30pm. MC/V.)

◐ SIGHTS. Cortina's tourist office has a wealth of advice and information on local skiing, hiking, water sports, and nature walks. Not every excursion is physically demanding—a flat *passeggiata,* or pedestrian and bike path, traverses 7km of the town, from the ski-jump platform to Fiames. The views of **Croda del Pomogagnon,** a series of towering rock spires to the east, are striking. Look for the *passeggiata* signs at both ends of V. Marconi.

FRIULI-VENEZIA GIULIA

Overshadowed by the touristed cities of the Veneto and the mountains of Trentino-Alto Adige, Friuli-Venezia Giulia traditionally receives less than its fair share of recognition. Trieste, a long-standing exception to this rule, attracts increasing numbers of beach-goers searching for the least expensive resorts on the Adriatic. The area's towns, which owe their charm to their small size, offer an untainted slice of local life and culture absent from Italy's larger cities.

Friuli-Venezia Giulia derives its name from several distinct provinces. Unified by the clergy between the 6th and 15th centuries, the region was appropriated by the Venetian Republic and later swallowed, Venetians and all, by Austria-Hungary. Historical differences and the area's vulnerability to eastern forces give Friuli-Venezia Giulia a hybrid character. The splash of political intrigue and coffee-culture elegance brought by the Austro-Hungarian Empire attracted turn-of-the-century intellectuals to Friuli. James Joyce lived in Trieste for 12 years, during which time he wrote the bulk of *Ulysses;* Ernest Hemingway drew part of his plot for *A Farewell to Arms* from the region's role in WWI; and Sigmund Freud and Rainer Maria Rilke both worked and wrote here.

TRIESTE
☎ 040

Trieste's position on a narrow strip of land, sandwiched between the Balkans and the Adriatic Sea, hasn't always been one of peaceful coexistence. From the 9th through 15th centuries, the city was Venice's main rival on the Adriatic. In the post-Napoleonic real estate market, Austria snatched the city, and when she did, she proceeded to rip out its medieval heart, replacing it with Neoclassical bombast. In the years that followed, the Hapsburgs' heavy-handed style of government alienated the city's large Italian majority, breeding fervent *irredentisti* who clamored for unification with the new Italian Republic. At the end of WWII, when Allied troops liberated the city from Nazi occupiers, the ownership dispute resurfaced, this time between the Slavs and the Italians. Though Trieste finally became part of Italy in 1954, the city still remains divided between its Slavic and Italian origins.

▐ TRANSPORTATION

Trieste is a direct train ride from both Venice and Udine. Several trains and buses also cross daily to Slovenia and Croatia. In summer, ferries make trips to Croatia's Istrian Peninsula, with less frequent service to the Dalmatian Coast and Greece.

Flights: Aeroporto Friuli-Venezia Giulia/Ronchi dei Legionari, V. Aquileia, 46 (☎0481 77 32 24 or 77 32 25). To get to the airport, take the public **SAF bus** (1hr., M-Sa every hr., €3.10). Ticket counter (☎0481 77 32 32) open daily 7am-noon and 1-7pm. Daily **British Airways** (☎0652 49 15 71) flights to **London.** Open M-F 8am-8pm, Sa 9am-5pm. Alitalia (☎1478 65 643) flights to: **Genoa, Milan, Munich, Naples, and Rome.**

Trains: P. della Libertà, 8 (☎040 379 4737), down C. Cavour from quays. Ticket counter (☎040 41 86 12) open daily 5:40am-9:30pm. Info office open daily 7am-9pm. To: **Budapest** (12hr., 2 per day, €71.32); **Ljubljana** (3hr., 3 per day, €18.56); **Udine** (1½hr., every hr., €5.55); and **Venice** (2hr., 2 per hr., €8.12).

Regional Buses: P. della Libertà, 11 (☎040 42 50 01), next to train station. Turn left at end of C. Cavour. **SAITA** (☎040 42 50 01) to **Rijeka/Fiume** (2-2½hr., 2 per day, €7.87) and **Udine** (1½hr., 18 per day, €4.27). Smaller lines to: **Duino, Miramare, Muggia, and Opiciao.**

Ferries: Adriatica di Navigazione, P. Unità, 7 (☎040 6702 7211), off C. Cavour, sails to: **Albania, Croatia, Greece, and Slovenia. Anek Lines,** Molo Bersaglieri, 3 (☎0403 22 05 61), off R. D. Mandracchio, runs ferries to Greece. **Agemar Viaggi,** P. Duca degli Abruzzi 1/a, (☎0403 63 32 22), off C. Cavour, has detailed departure schedules and sells tickets for both lines. Open M-F 9am-12:30pm and 3-6pm.

Public Transportation: A.C.T. orange buses travel city and provincial routes to the Carso, Miramare, and Opicina. Buy your ticket at *tabacchi* shops and bars near bus stops (€0.90).

Tram: Europe's only **funicular** links P. Oberdan with Opicina, a city on the Carso Plateau above Trieste. From P. Oberdan (25min., every 20min., 7:11am-8:11pm, €0.90).

Taxis: Radio Taxi (☎040 30 77 30). Available 24hr.

Car Rental: Maggiore/Budget/Alamo (☎040 42 13 23), in train station. €68 per day; €250 per week. Open M-F 8:30am-12:30pm and 3-7pm, Sa 8:30am-12:30pm.

▰▰ ORIENTATION AND PRACTICAL INFORMATION

From the city center, the industrialized quays serving ferries, fishermen, and sailing regattas taper off north into the **Barcola,** Trieste's excuse for a beach—a stretch of tiered concrete populated with bronzed bodies that runs 7km from the edge of town to the castle at Miramare. The center of Trieste is organized as a grid,

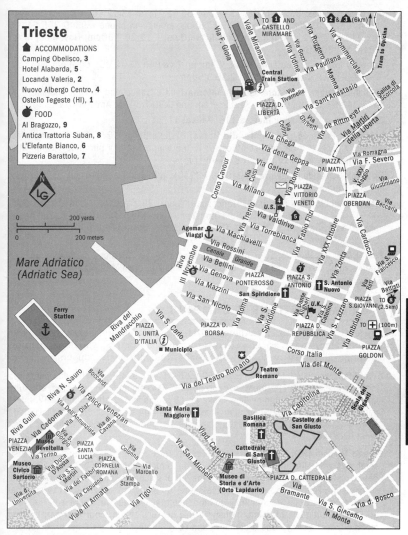

Trieste

⌂ ACCOMMODATIONS
Camping Obelisco, **3**
Hotel Alabarda, **5**
Locanda Valeria, **2**
Nuovo Albergo Centro, **4**
Ostello Tegeste (HI), **1**

♦ FOOD
Al Bragozzo, **9**
Antica Trattoria Suban, **8**
L'Elefante Bianco, **6**
Pizzeria Barattolo, **7**

0 — 200 yards
0 — 200 meters

Mare Adriatico
(Adriatic Sea)

NORTHEAST ITALY

bounded to the east by **Via Carducci**, which stretches south from **Piazza Oberdan**. To the west, boutique-heavy **Corso Italia** runs south from the spectacular **Piazza dell'Unità d'Italia,** a vast, uncluttered square with one edge along the harbor. The two streets intersect at the busy **Piazza Goldoni.** Steps from P. Unità, along C. Italia, lies the **Piazza della Borsa,** where the *Triestini* come to strut their stuff.

Tourist Office: APT, P. dell'Unità d'Italia, 4/e (☎040 347 8312; fax 347 8320). A wealth of info, including lists of *manifestazioni* (artistic events) and a James Joyce walking tour itinerary. Another office in **train station** (☎040 44 114), on the left as you exit platforms. Open M-Sa 9am-7pm for both. English spoken at both offices.

Consular Services: US, V. Roma, 15 (☎040 66 01 77; fax 63 12 40). Open M-F 10am-noon. **UK,** V. D. Alighieri, 7 (☎040 347 8303; emergency phone ☎0349 355 8110; fax 040 347 8311). Open Apr.-Oct. Tu 8-10am, F 12:30-2:30pm; Nov.-Mar. Tu 9-11am, F 1:30-3:30pm.

Currency Exchange: Deutsche Bank, V. Roma, 7 (☎040 63 19 25). Cash advances on Visa. Open M-F 8:15am-1pm and 2:35-3:50pm.

English-Language Bookstore: Libreria Internazionale Transalpina, V. Torre Bianca, 21/a (☎040 63 12 88). Open Tu-Sa 9am-1pm and 3:30-7:30pm. AmEx/MC/V.

Emergency: ☎113. **Ambulance:** ☎118. **Police:** 112.

Late-Night Pharmacy: Farmacia alla Borsa, P. della Borsa, 12/a. 24hr. pharmacies rotate. Check with the tourist office, or in the window of any pharmacy. Open M-F 8:30am-1pm and 4-7:30pm, Sa 8:30am-1pm.

Hospital: Ospedale Maggiore (☎040 399 2210), in P. dell'Ospedale, up V. S. Maurizio from V. Carducci.

Internet Access: One Net, V. S. Francesco d'Assisi, 28/c (☎040 77 11 90; fax 372 6154). €6.50 per hr. Open M-Sa 10am-1pm and 4-9pm. **Interland,** V. Gallina, 1 (☎040 372 8635; fax 372 5413). €1.29 per 15min. Open M-F 10:30am-8:30pm and Sa 2:30-8:30pm.

Post Office: P. V. Veneto, 1 (☎040 676 4111; fax 77 19 72), along V. Roma. From the train station, take 2nd right off V. Ghega. Fax machine. Open M-Sa 8:15am-7pm.

Postal Code: 34100.

ACCOMMODATIONS & CAMPING

Cheap and clean rooms aren't a dime a dozen in Trieste, but some exist outside the city center. Many rooms are geared toward seasonal workers, who book them by the month, while others are filled with Croatian and Slovenian shoppers.

▨ **Hotel Alabarda,** V. Valdirivo, 22 (☎040 63 02 69; fax 63 92 84; www.hotelalabarda.it), in the city center. From P. Oberdan, head down V. XXX Ottobre, near tram stop, and turn right onto V. Valdirivo. High ceilings make all 18 rooms feel palatial. Satellite TV. Internet access €5.16 per hr. Wheelchair-accessible. Parking available. Breakfast included. Singles €31-33, with bath €46; doubles €43-48/€66. 10% discount with *Let's Go.* AmEx/MC/V. ❸

Ostello Tegeste (HI), V. Miramare, 331 (☎/fax 040 22 41 02), on the seaside, just south of Castle Miramare. 6km from city center. From station, take bus #36 (€0.90), departing from V. Miramare, the street to the left of station as you exit. Ask driver for the Ostello stop. From there, walk along the shore, following the seaside road toward the castle. Other accommodations may be more centrally located, but the view of the Adriatic from the terrace adds enormously to this hostel's charm. Courtyard bar, bicycle rental (€2 for half day), and a dinner option (€8). Internet access €4 per hr. Breakfast and hot shower included. Reception daily 8am-11:30pm. Lockout 10am-1pm. Curfew midnight. Dorms €12 for HI members, nonmembers €14.58. MC/V. ❶

Nuovo Albergo Centro, V. Roma, 13 (☎040 347 8790; fax 347 5258; www.hotelcentrotrieste.it). New and centrally located. All rooms have satellite TV and telephone with external line. Parking available. Reception M-Su 8am-midnight. Singles €29, with bath €40; doubles €42/€62; triples €57/€84; quad €70/€106. AmEx/DC/MC/V. ❸

Locanda Valeria, Strada per Vienna, 156 (☎040 21 12 04), in Opicina, 7km east of Trieste. From P. Oberdan, take the tram to the last stop (see **Transportation,** p. 268); or take bus #39 from P. Libertà to S. Per Vienna. Valeria is 3 blocks from tram/bus stop.

Though hardly the chic scene you'd find in downtown Trieste, the hotel has a friendly atmosphere and a restaurant filled with animated Italian and Slovenian locals. Breakfast €3.50. Singles €23.24; doubles €41.32. ❷

Camping Obelisco, S. Nuova per Opicina, 37 (☎040 21 16 55; fax 21 27 44), in Opicina. Take the tram from P. Oberdan; ask for the Obelisco stop. Follow the yellow signs. Nice facilities with bar. €3.10-3.62 per person, €5.68-7.23 per tent. ❶

▄ FOOD

Although many dishes in Trieste's restaurants have Eastern European overtones, the selection of fresh seafood from the Adriatic rivals that of Venice. The city is renowned for its *frutti del mare*, especially *sardoni in savor* (large sardines marinated in oil and garlic). Other local specialties are *cevap cici* (spicy Serbian sausages infused with garlic) and *jota* (a hearty sauerkraut, bean, and sausage stew). The **Osmizze** are informal restaurants that date from 1784, when a decree allowed peasants on the Carso (outside Trieste) to sell local produce for only eight days a year. Today, families in the Carso open their terraces to the public for two weeks, serving their own produce and wine (like the regional *terrano del Carso*, a dry red wine valued for its therapeutic properties). The proprietors of *osmizze* agree amongst themselves who will open and when, and then announce in *Primorski*, a Slovenian-language paper. Inquire as to schedules at the tourist office.

For basics, V. Carducci is home to several **alimentari,** or small, permanent markets. For lower prices and continuous hours, try **Euro Spesa supermarket,** V. Valdirivo, 13/f, off C. Cavour. (Open M-Sa 8am-8pm.) It wouldn't be Italy without a **STANDA**—Trieste's branch is at V. Battisti, 15. (Open M 3:30-7:30pm, Tu-F 9am-1pm and 3:30-7:30pm, Sa 9am-7:30pm.) Trieste has a **covered market** with fruit, vegetable, meat, and cheese vendors at V. Carducci, 36/d, on the corner of V. della Majolica. (Open M 8am-2pm, Tu-Sa 8am-7pm.) Also stroll through the **open-air market** in P. Ponterosso by the canal. (Open Tu-Sa 8am-5:30pm.) Most shops in Trieste close on Mondays, and maintain strict siesta hours from 12:30 to 3:30pm.

RESTAURANTS

▨ **L'Elefante Bianco,** Riva III Novembre, 3 (☎040 36 26 03). A local inn during the Hapsburg era, l'Elefante has since grown into a chic restaurant serving predominantly Mediterranean cuisine. Trendy crowd and delicate flavor fusions, but still reasonable prices—a full dinner runs about €30 per person. Open M-F 12:30pm-2:30pm and 7:30pm-10:30pm and Sa 7:30pm-10:30pm. AmEx/DC. ❺

▨ **Antica Trattoria Suban,** V. Comici, 2 (☎040 54 368). Opened in 1865 by a tailor in the Hapsburg court, this *trattoria* still serves up superb Hungarian-, Austrian-, and Italian-influenced dishes such as honey strudel and veal croquettes with *parmigiano* and egg yolks. The heavenly food has been appreciated by the likes of Pope John Paul II. Dinner €25-30 per person. Open W-Su 12:30-2:30pm and 7:30-10pm. Reservations recommended. Closed 1st 2 weeks in Aug. AmEx/DC/MC/V. ❺

Al Bragozzo, Riva Nazario Sauro, 22 (☎040 30 30 01). Serves pasta and creative seafood dishes, making the most of Trieste's proximity to the sea. The braised monkfish in white wine and artichokes is exceptional. Full meal €30 per person. Open Tu-Sa 11am-3pm and 7-10pm. Closed June 22-July 10 and Dec. 25-Jan. 10. AmEx/DC/MC/V. ❺

Pizzeria Barattolo, P. S. Antonio, 2 (☎040 63 14 80), along the canal. Canopied seating with a view of P. S. Antonio. A sweet pizza crust draws mostly young crowds at lunch time. Bar and *tavola calda* offerings. Pizza €4.30-9.20, *primi* €4.20-5.50, *secondi* €5.80-€10.50. Cover €1. Service 15%. Open daily 8:30am-midnight. ❶

> **ℹ️ TRIESTE FOR YOU (T FOR YOU)!** This card, available free at hotels throughout the city when you stay for two nights or more, entitles visitors to discounts at hotels, restaurants, sights, and stores throughout the city. For more information, contact the local tourist office (see above).

👁 SIGHTS

CITY CENTER

CITTÀ NUOVA. In the 1700s, Empress Maria Theresa of Austria commissioned a "Città Nuova" plan for Trieste, which 19th-century Viennese urban planners implemented between the waterfront and the Castello di San Giusto. The resulting grid-like pattern of streets lined with Neoclassical palaces centers around the Canale Grande. Facing the canal from the south is the Serbian Orthodox Chiesa di San Spiridione, a neo-Byzantine church with pale blue domes and a lush interior. *(Open Tu-Sa 9am-noon and 5-8pm. Shoulders and knees must be covered.)* The **Municipio** at the head of Piazza dell'Unità d'Italia complements the largest piazza in Italy. An allegorical fountain with statues representing four continents sits in the center.

CASTELLO DI SAN GIUSTO. The 15th-century Venetian **Castello di San Giusto** presides over **Capitoline Hill**, the city's historic center. The ramparts of the castle enclose a **museum** that has temporary exhibits and a permanent collection of 13th-century weaponry, furniture, and tapestries. Within the castle walls, a huge outdoor theater is host to festivals in August. If you're up for the walk, ascend the hill from P. Goldoni by way of the daunting 265 **Scala dei Giganti** (Steps of the Giants). *(South of P. dell'Unità. Take bus #24 from the station to the last stop. ☎ 040 31 36 36. Castle open daily 9am-sunset. Museum open T-Su 9am-1pm. €1.55.)*

PIAZZA DELLA CATTEDRALE. This hilltop piazza overlooks the sea and downtown Trieste. Directly below lie the remains of the old Roman city center, and across the street is the restored **Cattedrale di San Giusto.** The church was originally comprised of two separate basilicas, one dedicated to S. Giusto, the other to S. Maria Assunta. They were joined in the 14th century, creating the cathedral's irregular shape. Inside, two splendid mosaics decorate the chapels directly to the left and right of the altar.

MUSEO DI STORIA ED ARTE. This art history museum provides archaeological documentation of the history of Trieste and the upper Adriatic, dating from before Roman times. It also holds a growing collection of Egyptian and Greek art and artifacts. Outside, the **Orto Lapidario** (Rock Garden) showcases fragments of pillars and buildings from the Roman period. *(P. Cattedrale, 1. ☎ 040 31 05 00 or 30 86 86. Open Th-Su 9am-1pm, Tu-W 9am-7pm. €1.55.)*

TEATRO ROMANO. The crumbling *teatro* was built under the auspices of Trajan in the first century AD. Crowds hooted at gladiatorial contests and later wept at the passion of Greek revival tragedy. *(On V. del Teatro, off C. Italia. From the Orto Lapidario, descend the hill and head toward P. Unità.)*

MUSEO REVOLTELLA. This museum brings many temporary modern art exhibits to Trieste. Combining the neo-Renaissance 18th-century home of Baron Revoltella and the Galleria d'Arte Moderna, the Revoltella also has a permanent collection of art from the Neoclassical period to the present day. *(V. Diaz, 21. ☎ 040 31 13 61 or 30 09 38. Open W-M 9am-1:30pm and 4-7pm.)*

CITY ENVIRONS

▨ CASTELLO MIRAMARE. The **Barcola** (city beach) ends at the stunning castle of Archduke Maximilian of Austria, who ordered its construction in the mid-19th century. The lavishly decorated apartments feature huge crystal chandeliers, intricately carved furniture, rich tapestries, Asian porcelain, and good explanations of everything in English. Legend has it that the ghost of Carlotta, Maximilian's wife, who went mad after losing her husband to a firing squad, haunts the castle. Poised on a high promontory over the gulf, Miramare's white turrets are easily visible from the Capitoline Hill in Trieste. Its extensive parks and gardens are free. *(To reach Miramare, take bus #36 (15 min., €0.90) to the hostel and walk along the water. ☎040 224 7013. Open daily 9am-7pm, ticket office closes 1hr. earlier. €4. English tours €2.)*

BARCOLA. Had enough Neoclassicism to last you a lifetime? Grab your tanning oil and hit the cement. On the **Barcola,** the cafe-lined boardwalk that extends for 7km north of town, you'll find yourself in the company of sunbathers, in-line skaters, joggers, and *bocci* players. Each year, on the second Sunday in October, Trieste stages the *Barcolana*, a regatta that attracts mariners worldwide and saturates the harbor with thousands of billowing sails.

MARINE PARK. Sponsored by the World Wildlife Fund, the marine park is serviced out of **Castelletto Miramare,** a small aquatic museum within the gardens of Castel Miramare. Museum entrance is by guided tour only, so call ahead. From the gardens, the yellow buoys marking the park are visible, but to get closer you have to go on a snorkel or scuba tour. *(☎040 22 41 47. Tours Winter Sa-Su 10am, noon, and 3pm, summer M-Su 9:30am, 11:30am, 2:30pm, and 4:30pm. Call to reserve. Free. You must have certification to scuba dive. Snorkel, fins, and mask included. Reservations required. Must be in groups of 10; ask to be grouped with others if your group is less than 10. Scuba tours at 9am and 2pm. Office open M-F 9am-7pm, Sa 9am-5pm. €14.50, children €10.50.)*

KUGY PATH AND GROTTA GIGANTE. The tram to Opicina from P. Oberdan is one of the longest running funiculars in Europe. After a steep climb, the tram runs past local vineyards and provides breathtaking views of the Adriatic coastline. Hop off at the Obelisk stop to meet up with the Kugy Path, a popular trail that cuts along the sides of the Carso cliffs. There are benches along the path; stop to admire the views of the Adriatic and the coastline of Slovenia and Croatia. At the end of the tram route is the Grotta Gigante, the world's largest touristed cave. Staircases wind in and around the 107m high interior. *(V. Machiavelli, 17. Bus #45 (€0.90) arrives in the small parking lot across V. Nazionale from the tram stop. ☎040 32 73 12; www.ts.cam.com.it/english/grotta/htm. Open Apr.-Sept. Tu-Sa 10am-6pm, tours every 30min.; Mar. and Oct. Tu-Sa 10am–4pm, every hr.; Nov.-Feb. 10am-noon and 2-4pm, every hr. €8.)*

RISIERA DE SAN SABBA. One of Italy's two WWII concentration camps occupied an abandoned rice factory outside Trieste. The *risiera* houses a museum detailing Trieste's role in the Slovenian-born resistance movement that confronted the Nazi occupation. *(Ratto della Pileria, 43. Take bus #8. ☎040 82 62 02. Open May 16-Mar. Tu-Su 9am-1pm; Apr.-May 15 Tu-F 9am-6pm, Sa-Su 9am-1pm. Free.)*

FARO DELLA VITTORIA. Built on the foundations of the Austrian Fort Kressich, the Faro della Vittoria lighthouse is a tribute to those who gave their lives at sea in WW I. Inaugurated in 1927 in the presence of King Vittorio Emanuele III, the 70m tower incorporates the anchor of the first Italian ship to enter Trieste harbour during the 1918 liberation. *(S. del Friuli, 141. ☎040 41 04 61. Open Apr.-Sept. M-Sa 9:30-12:30am and 3:30-6:30pm; Oct.-Mar. Sa-Su 10am-3pm. Free.)*

🎜 ENTERTAINMENT

The opera season of the **Teatro Verdi** runs November to May, but the theater holds a six-week operetta season from July to mid-August. Buy tickets or make reservations at **Riva III**, Novembre, 1. (☎040 672 2298 or 672 2299; www.teatroverditrieste.com. Open Tu-Su 9am-noon and 4-7pm. €8-36.) The liveliest *passeggiate* take place along Capo di Piazza, a traffic-free avenue on the pedestrian shopping street connecting P. della Borsa to P. dell'Unità.

Bar Unità, on the southwest corner of P. dell'Unità, weathers the winter to see its outdoor tables packed with students in summer. (☎040 36 80 63. Open M-Sa 6:30am-3:30am.) **Juice,** V. Madonnina, 10, is always packed, with twentysomethings crowding over menus written on old vinyl records. Warm up with crepes filled with Nutella (€2), or try a **scivelo** (€5), a local drink made from strawberry Keglevich vodka and lemon soda. (☎040 760 0341. Open daily Sept.-June 7:30pm-2am.)

AQUILEIA
☎0431

When the streaming landscape of cornfields and grapevines suddenly gives way to a cluster of half-standing columns and neatly-arranged limestone bricks, you've arrived. Two minutes and several dozen buildings later, the cultivated landscape returns, and you have already left. To the hundreds of tourists who pass through this pocket-size town on their way to the seaside resort of Grado, this is Aquileia. By staying on the main road, they neglect a sleepy village with a proud history and impeccably preserved artifacts dating from AD 200 to 452, when Aquileia was a flourishing Roman city and the Eastern Empire's gateway to the Adriatic.

🖈 **PRACTICAL INFORMATION.** Aquileia can be reached by **bus** from **Udine** (1hr., 16 per day, 6:10am-9:40pm, €2.69). From Cervignano, a **train station** on the Trieste-Venice line, buses leave to Aquileia *centro*. (15min., every 30min., 6am-8:30pm, €1.35). For a list of budget accommodations and camping in the area, including the resort island of Grado (just 15km south on **Via Beligna,** the main thoroughfare that cuts through town), consult Aquileia's helpful **APT tourist office,** P. Capitolo, 4. From the bus stop, cross the street and head up **Via Popone.** The basilica is straight ahead, and the APT office is on your left as you enter the piazza. (☎0431 91 087. Open Apr.-Oct. daily 9am-7pm, Nov.-Mar. 9am-noon.) In an **emergency,** dial ☎113, or call the **police station,** V. Semina (☎0431 91 03 34). **Farmacia,** the largest local pharmacy, is on Corso Gramsci, two blocks from Albergo Aquila Nera. (☎0431 91 00 01. Open M-F 8:30am-12:30pm and 3:30-7:30pm, Sa 8:30am-12:30pm.) For **currency exchange** and **postal services** July through September, walk two blocks along V. Augusta (toward Cervignano) to the **Poste Italiane** kiosk. (Open M-F 9am-12:30pm and 3:30-5pm.) Otherwise, the central post office is in P. Cervi, off Corso Gramsci. (☎0431 91 92 72. Open M-Sa 8:25am-1:40pm.) **Postal Code:** 33051.

🏠 **ACCOMMODATIONS AND FOOD.** Aquileia has few accommodations, but one terrific hostel, **Domus Augustus (HI) ❶,** V. Roma, 25. (☎0431 91 024; fax 91 71 05; www.ostelloaquileia.it. Breakfast included. Internet access €5.16. Reception and check-in 2-11:30pm. Check-out 7:30-10am. Lockout 10am-2pm. Curfew 11:30pm. Dorms €13-17. MC/V.) **Albergo Aquila Nera ❸,** P. Garibaldi, 5, a 5min. walk up V. Roma from V. Beligna, has simple but clean rooms in a convenient location. (☎0431 91 045. Breakfast included. Communal bath. Singles €28; doubles €46; triples €60.) **Camping Aquileia,** V. Gemina, 10, a tranquil spot with a swimming pool, lies up the street from the forum. (☎0431 91 042; ☎/fax 91 95 83; www.campingaquileia.it. €5.25 per person, under 12 €3.25. Tent sites €9. 3-person bungalow €42, 4-person bungalow €51.90. Open May 15-Sept. 20.) From the tourist office, cut across the fields towards the bus parking lot, then turn right on the first road you reach, and follow it as it bends round; **La Colombara ❹**, V. S. Zilli, 42, will be on your left. Specializing in delights like *calamari ai sedani* (squid with celery), Colombara also offers occasional Roman-themed dinners. (☎ 0431 91 513; info@lacolombara.it. Dinner €20-40 per person. Open Tu-Su 12:30-2:30pm and 7:30-10:30pm. MC/V.) From the tourist office, exit the piazza back to the main road to Cervignano. Turn left towards Grado (away from Cervignano), and **La Pergola ❷**, V. Beligna, 4, will be on your left after about two blocks. A delicious, locally grown meal of *agnello* (lamb) is the house specialty. (☎ 0431 91 306. *Primi* €4.20-6.50, *secondi* €6.40-9.30. Open M, W-F 10am-3pm and 5-11pm, Sa-Su noon-4pm and 5-11pm.) The **Desparo supermarket** is on V. Augusta, across from the bus parking lot. (Open Tu and Th-Sa 8:30am-1pm and 4-7pm, W 8:30am-1pm, Su 8am-1pm.)

🟥 **SIGHTS.** Although Aquileia's basilica officially retains a religious function, the hordes of tourists have driven away all but the most God-fearing of Christians. The floor, a remnant of the original church, is a mosaic animating over 700 square meters with geometric designs and bestial images. Beneath the altar, the crypt's 12th-century frescoes illustrate the trials of Aquileia's early Christians as well as scenes from the life of Christ. In the **Cripta degli Scavi**, to the left upon entering, excavations have uncovered three layers of flooring, including mosaics from a first-century Roman house. (☎ 0431 91 067. Basilica open daily 8:30am-7pm. Free. Crypt open M-Su 8:30am-6:30pm. €2.60.) From the nearby **campanile** (constructed in 1031 using the remains of the Roman amphitheater), enjoy unobstructed views of the Slovenian Alps to the north, Trieste to the east, the Adriatic to the south, and the lagoon to the west. (Open daily 9:30am-1pm and 3-6pm. €1.10.)

Porto Fluviale, the cypress-lined alley behind the basilica, was the dockyard of Aquileia's thriving Roman river harbor from 100 BC to AD 300, and is a pleasant alternative to V. Augusta as a path to the ruins of the **forum.** From there, continue to the **Museo Paleocristiano** to view moss-covered mosaics documenting the transition from classical paganism to Christianity. (☎ 0431 91 131. Open M 8:30am-1:45pm, Tu-Su 8:30am-7:30pm. Free.) Artifacts from numerous excavations reside in the **Museo Archeologico** at the corner of V. Augusta and V. Roma. The ground floor houses Roman portrait busts; upstairs are terracotta, glass, and gold pieces. (☎ 0431 91 016. Open M 8:30am-2pm, Tu-Su 8:30am-7:30pm. €4.50.)

UDINE ☎ 0432

Udine's Piazza della Libertà, split into tilting, elevated levels and with looming statues and Moorish figures, is 60 square meters of pure Renaissance. Aside from this design marvel, Udine's tourist offerings are few. Fervent Giovanni Battista Tiepolo fans will appreciate the city's otherwise uninteresting churches and museums. Udine's volatile history includes being conquered by Venice in 1420, appropriated by Austria in the late 18th century, and bombed severely in WWII. Today, tourists are scarce in the quiet streets, as expensive accommodations put Udine's peaceful atmosphere beyond the reach of many budget-minded travelers.

📮 **TRANSPORTATION**

Trains: On V. Europa Unità. Info office (☎ 1478 88 088) open 7am-9pm. Tickets and reservations 7am-8:30pm. To: **Milan** (4½hr., 5:45am and 6:49pm, €24.79); **Trieste** (1½hr., 1-3 per hr., 5:12am-11:29pm, €5.55); **Vienna, Austria** (7hr., 5 per day, 9:52am-1:45am, €54.87); and **Venice** (2hr., 1-3 per hr., 5:50am-10:29pm, €7.84.)

Buses: V. Europa Unità. Cross the street from the train station and walk 1 block to the right. **SAF** (☎0432 60 81 12) runs to: **Aquileia** (every hr., 6:50am-9pm, €2.69); **Cividale** (every hr., 6:40am-7:15pm, €1.92); **Palmanova** (every 2hr., 6:50am-9pm, €2.07); and **Trieste** (2 per hr., 5:10am-10:55pm, €4.27).

Taxi: Radio Taxi (☎0432 50 58 58).

✴❷ ORIENTATION AND PRACTICAL INFORMATION

Udine's train and regional bus stations are both on **Via Europa Unità**, in the southern part of town. All local bus lines pass the train station, but only buses #1, 3, and 8 run from V. Europa Unità to the center, passing by **Piazza della Libertà** and **Castle Hill**. To walk from the station (15min.), go right to **Piazza D'Annunzio**, then turn left under the arches to **Via Aquileia**. Continue up **Via Veneto** to P. della Libertà.

Tourist Office: P. 1° Maggio, 7 (☎0432 29 59 72 or 29 97 74; fax 50 47 43; arpt_ud1@regione.fvg.it). From the southern end of P. della Libertà, turn right onto V. Manin and left onto P. 1° Maggio. Look for the pink-arched facade. Otherwise, take bus #2, 7, or 10 to P. 1° Maggio. English spoken. Open M-Sa 9am-1pm and 3-6pm; in winter 9am-1pm and 3-5pm.

Currency Exchange: Banks line the streets around P. della Libertà, all offering comparable rates. Also in the **post office** (on left as you enter).

Mountain Information: The bulletin board of the **Club Alpino Italiano** (☎0432 50 42 90) is at V. Odorico, 3. Info on skiing and mountain excursions for all of Italy. For hikes in the pre-Alps of Friuli-Venezia Giulia, contact **Società Alpina Friulana,** V. Odorico, 3 (☎0432 50 42 90). Alpine info and excursions. Open M-F 5-7:30pm.

Emergency: ☎113. **Ambulance:** ☎118. **Carabinieri,** V. D. Prefettura, 16 (☎112).

Late-Night Pharmacy: **Farmacia Beltrame,** P. della Libertà, 9 (☎0432 50 28 77). Open M-Sa 8:30am-12:30pm and 3:30-11pm. Ring the bell 11pm-8am.

Hospital: Ospedale Civile (☎0432 55 21), in P. Santa Maria della Misericordia. Take bus #1 north to the last stop.

Post Office: V. Veneto, 42 (☎0432 51 09 35). *Fermo Posta,* stamps, and fax. Open M-Sa 8:30am-7pm. **Branch** office at V. Roma, 25 (☎0432 22 31 11), straight ahead from train station. Open M-Sa 8:30am-7pm.

Postal Code: 33100.

▗ ACCOMMODATIONS

The good news is that Udine's hotels are clearly marked on the large map outside the train station. The bad news is that the cheapest spots may already be occupied.

Hotel Quo Vadis, P. le Cella, 28 (☎0432 21 091; fax 21 092; hoteluovadis@libero.it). Located in a major automotive hub, this well-maintained hotel's rooms have bath and TV, some with A/C. Singles €37; doubles €60. V. ❹

Al Bue, V. Pracchiuso, 75 (☎0432 29 90 70; fax 29 98 39). Take bus #4 from the station, get off at P. Oberdan, and walk down V. Pracchiuso on the far side of the piazza. Upscale, well-appointed rooms (all with bath, TV, and phone) open onto a terraced courtyard. Quiet location. Restaurant downstairs serves lunch and dinner. Singles €47-57; doubles €73-103. ❹

Hotel Europa, V. L. Europa Unità, 47 (☎0432 50 87 31 or 29 44 46; fax 51 26 54). As you exit the train station, turn right, cross the street, and walk 2 blocks. Small elevator takes you to the bar downstairs. Clean rooms with bath, A/C, and TV. Breakfast included. Singles €57; doubles €83. MC/V. ❹

Albergo Al Vecchio Tram, P. Garibaldi, 15 (☎0432 50 25 16). Simple rooms in a central location. Communal baths. Singles €18; doubles €29. ❷

◘ FOOD

Udinese cuisine is a mix of Italian, Austrian, and Slovenian influence. A typical regional specialty is *brovada e museto*, a stew made with marinated turnips and boiled sausage. Shop for produce weekday mornings in the **markets** at P. Matteotti near P. della Libertà, at V. Redipuglia, and at P. 1° Maggio. (Open Sa 8am-1pm.) The centrally-located **Dimeglio supermarket** is on V. Stringer, off P. XX Settembre. (Open M-Sa 9am-1:30pm and 4-7:45pm. Closed W 1-5pm.)

▨ **Ristorante Vitello d'Oro,** V. E. Valvason, 4 (☎0432 50 89 82). The guiding light in classical Udinese cooking for at least as far back as 1849. *Primi* €6.50-10.50, *secondi* €15.50-18. Cover €2.60. Open daily noon-3pm and 7-11pm; closed Su in summer, W in winter. AmEx/DC/MC/V. ❹

▨ **Trattoria al Chianti,** V. Marinelli, 4 (☎0432 50 11 05), near police station. A *trattoria* whose decor is almost as delicate and tasteful as the food it serves. The menu is a mixture of Italian and Slovenian cooking. *Primi* €4.10-4.60, *secondi* €5.10-9.30. Cover €1. Open M-Sa 8:30am-3:30pm and 6pm-midnight. ❷

Al Vecchio Stallo, V. Viola, 7 (☎0432 21 296). A very informal restaurant with classic Italian dishes. Lunch menù with *primo, secondo,* and side €10. *Primi* €4.50-5.50, *secondi* €4.50-9. Cover €1. Open July-Aug. M-Sa 11am-3:30pm and 5pm-midnight. ❷

Ristorante da Brando, P. le Cella, 16 (☎0432 50 28 37). Family-run restaurant in operation for the last 50 years. The *Friuliano* cuisine is of high quality, and the prices low. The fixed menù, with *primo, secondo,* side, and a ¼L bottle of wine, costs €10. *Primi* from €3.62, *secondi* from €4.65. Cover €1.55. Open M-Sa 8am-midnight. ❷

◉◪ SIGHTS AND ENTERTAINMENT

From June to September, P. 1° Maggio becomes the fairgrounds for **Estate in Città,** a series of concerts, movies, and guided tours of the city. **Bar Americano,** in P. della Libertà, is one of the many cafes that tend to be the center of *Udinese* nightlife. (☎0432 24 80 18. Open daily 6:30am-midnight.) **Taverna dell'Angelo Osteria,** V. della Prefettura, 3c, is a throwback to the old Venetian wine culture. **The Black Stuff,** V. Gorghi, 3a, draws a young crowd. (☎0432 29 78 38. Open W-M 5:30pm-2am.)

PIAZZA DELLA LIBERTÀ. This asymmetrical, partitioned, tilting square marks the center of old Udine. Along the raised edge, the **Arcado di San Giovanni** creates a covered walkway overlooking the action below. Directly above, the bell tower features automated Moorish figures that swivel to strike the hour. Across from the arcade, the **Loggia del Lionello** (1488) serves as a public gathering place. In the highest corner of the square, through the **Arco Bollani,** a cobblestone road winds ethereally up alongside an arched promenade to the **castello** above. Once home to Venetian governors, today the castle holds the **Civici Musei e Galleria di Storia ed Arte Antica,** featuring notable though not necessarily exciting works. (☎0432 50 18 24 or 0432 50 28 72. Open Tu-Sa 9:30am-12:30pm and 3-6pm, Su 9:30am-12:30pm. €2.58, students or over 60 €1.81.)

DUOMO. The Roman-Gothic cathedral has several Tiepolos on display (on the first, second, and fourth altars on the right side). The squat brick **campanile** houses a small **museum** with 14th-century frescoes by Vitale da Bologna. (In P. del Duomo, 50m from P. della Libertà. ☎0432 50 68 30. Open daily 7am-noon and 4-8pm. Free.)

ORATORIA DELLA PURITÀ. Udine has been called the city of Tiepolo, and some of this Baroque painter's finest works adorn the Oratorio della Purità. The *Assumption* (1759) on the ceiling and the *Immaculate Conception* on the altarpiece show Tiepolo's love of light and air. (Across from duomo. ☎0432 50 68 30. Free.)

NORTHEAST ITALY

MUSEO DIOCESANO E GALLERIA DEL TIEPOLO. Besides housing the sacred art of the Udinian diocese, this 16th-century *palazzo* contains a sampling of earlier Tiepolo frescoes. From 1726 to 1730, the artist executed a series of Old Testament scenes here. The museum also displays Romanesque maple sculptures from the Friuli region. *(P. Patriarcato, 1, at the head of V. Ungheria. Entrance beneath the ornate coat of arms. ☎ 0432 25 003. Open W-Su 10am-noon and 3:30-6:30pm. €4, under 10 €3.)*

CIVIDALE DEL FRIULI ☎ 0432

You can wind through Cividale's serpentine medieval streets, around corners, and under archways only to arrive meters from where you started. The city, founded by Julius Caesar in 50 BC as Forum Iulii, became the capital of the first Lombard duchy in AD 568, and flourished as a hot spot for artists and nobility in the Middle Ages. The arrival of Venetian conquerors in 1420 stunted Cividale's growth, leaving quality *cucina friuliana* (Friulian cooking) as its main tourist draw.

🖪 **PRACTICAL INFORMATION.** Cividale is best reached from Udine by **train** (15min., every half hr., 6am-8:05pm, €1.60). **Buses** from Udine (€1.47) are less frequent. The train station, which opens onto V. Libertà, is close to the center of town. (☎ 0432 73 10 32. Open M-Sa 5:45am-8pm, Su 7am-8pm.) From the train station, head onto Via Marconi and turn left through the **Porta Arsenale Veneto** when the street ends. Bear right into Piazza Dante, then left onto Largo Boiani. The duomo is straight ahead. The **tourist office,** Calle P. d'Aquileia, 10, is across from the duomo. (☎ 0432 73 14 61; fax 73 13 98. Open M-F 9am-1pm and 3-6pm.) Banca Antoniana Popolare Veneto, Largo Boiani, 20, has an ATM. In case of **emergency,** dial ☎ 113, seek out the **police** (☎ 0432 70 61 11), on P. A. Diaz, off P. Dante, or contact the **hospital** (Ospedale Civile), in P. dell'Ospedale (☎ 0432 73 12 55). **Farmacia Minisini,** is at Largo Bioani, 11. (Open Tu-F 8:30am-12:30pm and 3:50-7:30pm, Sa 8:30am-12:30pm.) The **post office,** at Largo Boiani, 31, offers AmEx traveler's check exchange. (☎ 0432 73 12 55. Open M-Sa 8:30am-6pm.) **Postal Code:** 33043.

🖪🖪 **ACCOMMODATIONS AND FOOD.** As you exit the tourist office, turn right and then left down S. Matteoti, to **Casa Il Gelsomino ❷,** S. Matteoti, 11/2, a beautiful, post-and-beam house with a friendly proprietor. Large breakfast (included) is straight from the local bakery. (☎ 0432 73 19 62. €20 per person for rooms without bath.) The centrally-located, two-star **Al Pomo d'Oro ❹,** P. S. Giovanni, 20, is the cheapest hotel in town. All rooms with bath and TV. (☎ 0432 73 14 89; fax 70 12 57. Breakfast included. Full- and half-pension available. Wheelchair-accessible. Rooms held until 6pm. Singles €41.32; doubles €61.98. AmEx/DC/MC/V.)

Regional culinary specialties are *picolit* (a dessert wine), *frico* (a cheese and potato pancake), and *gubana* (a fig-and prune-filled pastry laced and sometimes doused with *grappa*). Most bars stock pre-packaged *gubana*, but for a freshly made treat, look for **Gubana Cividalese** at Corso P. D'Aquileia, 16, on the right as you near the Ponte del Diavolo. Ask for a *gubanetta* (€0.62), unless you want the whole cake. P. Diacono hosts Cividale's **open-air market** every Saturday from 8am to 1pm. **Coopca supermarket,** V. A. Ristori, 17, accommodates those on the tightest of budgets. (☎ 0432 73 11 05. Open T-Su 8:30am-12:45pm and 4-7:30pm.) **Antica Trattoria Dominissini ❷,** Stretta Stellini, 18, serves regional dishes like *frico* and *polenta* in a lively bar setting. (☎ 0432 73 37 63. *Primi* €4.70-6.20, *secondi* €4.70-13. Cover €1. Open Tu-Su 9:30am-4pm and 6-11pm.) **Alla Frasca ❸,** S. B. De Rubeis 8/a, offers a fine selection of local fare in a relaxed environment. (☎ 0432 73 12 70. *Primi* €5-10, *secondi* €10-15.50. Cover €1.50. Open Tu-Su 12:30pm-3pm and 6:30pm-midnight. DC/MC/V). **Antica Trattoria alla Speranza ❸,** Foro Giulio Cesare, 6, off Largo Bioani, dishes out similar regional fare, but with an emphasis on locally-produced cheeses. (☎ 0432 73 11 31. *Primi* €6.20, *secondi* €9-11. Cover €1. Open W-M 8am-3pm and 6pm-midnight.)

◙ **SIGHTS.** Expanded over the centuries, Cividale's **duomo** is an odd melange of architectural styles, but Pietro Lombardo completed the bulk of the construction in 1528. The 12th-century silver altarpiece of Pellegrino II features 25 saints and a pair of archangels. The Renaissance sarcophagus of Patriarch Nicolò Donato lies to the left of the entrance. Annexed to the duomo is the **Museo Cristiano.** This display includes the marvelously sculpted **Baptistery of Callisto,** commissioned by the first Aquileian patriarch in Cividale and the **Altar of Ratchis,** a carved work from 740. (☎ 0432 73 11 44. Duomo and museum open M-Sa 9:30am-noon and 3-6pm, Su 3-5:30pm. Both free.) Down the hill lies the **Tempietto Longobardo,** an 8th-century sanctuary built on the remains of Roman homes. As you exit the duomo, turn right, then head straight through the piazza and turn right again onto Riva Pozzo di Callisto. At the bottom of the stairs, turn left and follow the signs. Inside, a sextet of stucco figures, called *The Procession of Virgins and Martyrs,* lines the wall. (☎ 0432 70 08 67. Open daily 9am-1pm and 3-6:30pm; in winter 10am-1pm and 3:30-5:30pm. €2, students €1.) For a stunning view, head down the road from the tourist office to the **Ponte del Diavolo,** an impressive 15th-century stone bridge. Local legend has it that Lucifer himself threw down the great stone beneath the bridge.

TRENTINO-ALTO ADIGE

At the foot of the Italian Alps, peaks sharpen, rivers run crystalline, and natural blonde becomes the predominant local color. The Mediterranean groove of the southern provinces gradually fades under Austrian influences in Trentino-Alto Adige. In the beginning of the 19th century, Napoleon conquered this integral part of the Holy Roman Empire, only to relinquish it to the Austro-Hungarians. A century later, at the end of WW I, Trentino and the Südtirol fell under Italian rule. Though Germany cut short Mussolini's brutal efforts to Italianize the region, Mussolini managed to give every German name an Italian equivalent. While southern Trentino is predominantly Italian-speaking, Südtirol (South Tirol), encompassing most of the northern mountain region known as the Dolomites, still resounds with German. Here, street signs, architecture, and even cuisine blend Austrian and Italian traditions. Practice your German—you'll need it to order fine Italian food at one of the region's many *Spaghettihäuser.*

NORTHEAST ITALY

HIGHLIGHTS OF TRENTINO-ALTO ADIGE

GO WILD in the white-peaked **Dolomite** (p. 263) frontier.

AUSTRIA-CIZE YOURSELF in a Habsburg cafe in **Bolzano** (p. 283).

BE AN AMPHIBIAN at **Lake Garda** (p. 288)—explore both land and water.

TRENT (TRENTO, TRIENT)   ☎ 0461

When you arrive in Trent, find a cozy *pasticceria* in the center of town and order *Apfel Strudel* and a *cappuccino.* Before your eyes, you'll find an edible metaphor for the city itself—a harmonious and tasty mix of Germanic and Mediterranean flavors. Inside the Alpine threshold but connected to the Veneto by a deep valley, Trent became the Romans' strategic gateway to the north. For centuries to follow, fortresses such as the Castello del Buonconsiglio proliferated in the region. Cultural and political ownership of the city, contested in the 19th century, was finally settled at the end of WWI, when Trent became Italy's.

Trentino Alto-Adige

⌐ TRANSPORTATION

Trains: (☎0461 98 36 27) on V. Dogana. Ticket window open daily 5:40am-8:30pm; info office 9am-noon and 2:30-6pm. **Luggage storage** available (see below). To: **Bologna** (3hr., 13 per day, 5:37am-1:05am, €10.12); **Bolzano** (45min., 2 per hr., 1:40am-11:22pm, €2.89); **Venice** (3hr., 5 per day, 4:15am-6:19pm, €10.12); and **Verona** (1hr., every hr., 2:28am-10:14pm, €4.65).

Buses: Atesina (☎0461 82 10 00), on V. Pozzo next to train station. To **Rovereto** (25min., every hr., 6:28am-6:34pm, €2.12) and **Riva del Garda** (1hr., every hr., 5:57am-8:12pm, €2.79).

Local Buses: Atesina also operates an extensive local bus system. Tickets on sale at *tabacchi* for €0.77 and good for 1hr.

Cableways: Funivia Trento-Sardegna (☎0461 38 10 00), on V. Lung'Adige Monte Grappa. From bus station, turn right onto V. Pozzo and take 1st right onto Cavalcavia S. Lorenzo. Cross bridge over train tracks and head across the intersection to the unmarked building. Open M-F 7am-10pm, Sa 7am-9:25pm, Su 9:30am-7pm. To **Sardegna** on Mt. Bondone (every 30min., €0.77).

Taxis: Radio Taxi (☎0461 93 00 02).

Bike Rental: Cicli Moser, V. Calepina, 37 (☎0461 23 03 27). Mountain bikes €14 per day.

⬛ 🛈 ORIENTATION AND PRACTICAL INFORMATION

The bus and train stations are on the same street, between the **Adige River** and the **public gardens.** The center of town lies east of the Adige. From the stations, walk right to the intersection with **Via Torre Vanga.** Continue straight as **Via Pozzo** becomes **Via Orfane** and **Via Cavour** before reaching **Piazza del Duomo** in the town's center. Numerous **ATMs** are found nearby. For **Castello del Buonconsiglio,** follow **Via Roma** eastward, away from the river, as it becomes **Via Manci,** then **Via S. Marco.**

Tourist Office: Azienda di Promozione Turistica di Trento, V. Manci, 2 (☎ 0461 98 38 80; fax 23 24 26; www.apt.trento.it). Turn right as you exit the train station. An excellent tourist office with information on excursions, including all-day dairy tours with tastings (July-Aug., €5-22). Open daily 9am-7pm.

Luggage Storage: In train station. €2 per day. Open M-F 7:15am-5:45pm.

English-Language Bookstore: Libreria Disertori, V. M. Diaz, 11 (☎ 0461 98 14 55), near Piazzale C. Battisti. Carries literature and romance titles in English, as well as an assortment of hiking maps. Open M 3:30-7pm, Tu-Sa 9am-noon and 3:30-7pm. MC/V.

Emergency: ☎ 113. **Ambulance:** ☎ 118.

Police: (☎ 112 or 0461 89 95 11) on P. Mostra.

24-Hour Pharmacy: Farmacia dall'Armi, P. Duomo, 10 (☎ 0461 23 61 39). Serving the city since 1490. Open M-Sa 8:30am-12:30pm and 3:30-7pm. Check the late-night pharmacy schedule posted in any pharmacy's window.

Hospital: Ospedale Santa Chiara, Largo Medaglie d'Oro, 9 (☎ 0461 90 31 11), up V. Orsi past the swimming pool.

Internet Access: Call Me, V. Belenzani, 58 (☎ 0461 98 33 02), near the duomo. €4 per hr. Open M-F 9am-9pm and Sa 9am-1pm and 2-9pm, Su 9am-1pm and 2-7pm.

Post Office: V. Calepina, 16 (☎ 0461 98 72 70), at P. Vittoria. Open M-F 8:10am-6:30pm, Sa 8:10am-12:20pm. Another **branch** next to train station on V. Dogana (☎ 0461 98 23 01). Open M-F 8:10am-6:30pm, Sa 8:10am-12:20pm.

Postal Code: 38100.

🏠 ACCOMMODATIONS

▨ **Ostello Giovane Europa (HI),** V. Torre Vanga, 11 (☎ 0461 26 34 84; fax 22 25 17). As you exit the train station, turn right. White building on the corner, just past the bus station. Turn right to enter. New rooms with clean bathrooms. Basic breakfast, showers, and sheets included. Full buffet breakfast with meats, cheeses, cereals, and pastries for €3. Lockers €1.50 per day. Wash €4, dry €2. Reception 7:30am-11pm. Check-out 10am. Curfew 11:30pm, but entry possible all night; ask for the code. Internet access €5.16. Reserve ahead. Dorms €12.91; singles €20.66. ❶

▨ **Hotel Venezia,** P. Duomo, 45 (☎/fax 0461 23 41 14). Large, pleasant rooms, some with a view of the duomo. Great location and surprisingly low prices. All rooms with bath. Singles €40; doubles with bath €59. MC/V. ❹

Hotel Paganella, V. Aeroporto, 27 (☎/fax 0461 99 03 55). From the Stazione, cross the street and turn left. From the corner bus stop, take the #14 bus to P. della Chiesa, which features a small church and the closed hotel Aquila Nera. From here back-track, and then turn right down V. Aeroporto. The hotel is on your left after about 50m. Out-of-the-way, but cheap and clean. Communal bath. Singles €30; doubles €50. MC/V. ❸

☐ FOOD

Trentino cuisine owes much to area dairy farmers' production of exceptional cheeses Nostrano, Tosela, and the highly prized Vezzena. *Piatti del Malgaro* (Herdsman's plates) include creamy *formaggi* (cheeses), polenta, mushrooms, and sausage. Another hearty favorite is *minestrone trippe* (tripe soup). A subtle Germanic undercurrent shows itself in the town's exceptional *Apfel Strudel.* Cheeses, fruits, and vegetables are sold at the open-air **market** every Thursday 8am-1pm behind P. del Duomo. The **Trentini supermarket,** P. Lodron, 28, lies across P. Pasi from the duomo. (☎0461 22 01 96. Open Tu-Sa 8:30am-12:30pm and 2:30-7:30pm, M 2:30-7:30pm.) The **Poli supermarket,** at V. Roma and V. delle Orfane, is near the station. (☎0461 98 50 63. Open M and Sa 8:30am-12:30pm, Tu-F 8:30am-12:30pm and 3:15-7:15pm.)

▨ **Ristorante Il Capello,** P. Lunelli, 5 (☎0451 23 58 50). From the station, turn right and then left onto V. Roma. After 4 blocks, turn right. The tranquil setting, delicate and subtle flavors, and attentive service makes for a delightful Trentino-Tuscan dinner. *Primi* €7-7.50, *secondi* €10-14.50. Cover €1.50. Open Tu-Sa noon-2pm and 7:30-10pm, Su noon-2pm. DC/MC/V. ❸

Ristorante Al Vo, Vicolo del Vo, 11 (☎ 0461 98 53 74). From the station, turn right until you reach V. Torre Vanga. Turn left and the restaurant is on your right after about 200m. Classic Trentino cooking. Ultra-traditional *bolliti* (mustard-flavored meats) and *stincho di agnello* (shank of lamb) at great prices. Lunch with *primo, secondo,* and a side around €12. Open M-Sa 11:30am-3pm, Th-F 7-9:30pm. AmEx/DC/MC/V. ❸

Cantinota, V. San Marco, 22/24 (0461 23 85 27). From the station, turn right and then left onto V. Roma. Take a left after about 3 blocks. Part piano bar, part *trattoria.* Mixing of local and standard Italian fare, best exemplified in the horse pizza (€10). *Primi* €6.50-7.50, *secondi* €12-13. Open F-W 11am-3pm and 7-10pm. MC/V. ❸

Antica Trattoria Due Mori, V. San Marco, 11 (☎0461 98 42 51). Down and across the street from Cantinota. Decor and classic *Trentino* cuisine at this fine *trattoria* are indeed *antica. Primi* €4.10-€6.20, *secondi* €7.20-€23.80. Cover €1.60. Open Tu-Sa noon-2:30pm and 7-10:30pm, Su noon-2:30pm and 7-10pm. MC/V. ❷

ⓖ ♫ SIGHTS AND ENTERTAINMENT

PIAZZA DEL DUOMO. The piazza, Trent's center of gravity and social heart, contains the city's best sights. The **Fontana del Nettuno** stands in the center of the piazza, trident in hand. Its steps offer a good view of the stretch of frescoes tattooing the **Cazuffi houses.** Nearby stands the **Cattedrale di San Vigilio,** named for the patron saint of Trent. *(Open daily 6:40am-12:15pm and 2:30-7:30pm. Free.)*

MUSEO DIOCESANO. Housed in a slender, tall castle of fading red and white stone, this museum holds a collection of sacred paintings, altarpieces, and garments related to the cathedral and the famed Council of Trent. *(P. del Duomo, 18.* ☎0461 23 44 19. Museum open M-Sa 9:30am-12:30pm and 2:30-6pm. €3, ages 12-18 €0.50. Entrance includes access to the archaeological excavations beneath the church.)

CASTELLO DEL BUONCONSIGLIO. This fusion of intricate stone-work and stout turrets is Trent's largest and most characteristic attraction. The castle houses everything from woodwork and pottery to 13th-century art. The *Locus Reflections* room is where the Austrians condemned Cesare Battisti to death during WW I. For more information on Trent's hometown nationalist hero, and the city's role in Europe's modern wars, stop into the **Museo Storico di Trento,** on the castle grounds and included on your ticket. If you want to see *Buonconsiglio's* famous frescoes, ask the janitor in the *Loggia del Romanino* to show you to the Torre dell'Aquila. *(Walk down V. Belenzani and head right on V. Roma. ☎ 0461 23 37 70. Open daily 10am-6pm. €5, students and under 18 or over 60 €2.50. Ticket price includes admission to Tridentum, an excavation of Roman ruins under P. Battisti.)*

BOLZANO (BOZEN) ☎ 0471

In the tug-of-war between Austrian and Italian influence, Austria pulls harder on Bolzano. Here, Italy is dipped in pastel paint and decorated with top-heavy Gothic spires, pointed arches, and lacy trim. Bolzano's duomo does not recall Renaissance harmony, but has a thunderous Gothic presence; the city's museum showcases a partially decayed man who was encased in ice during the Copper Age rather than restored paintings and sculptures. The best sights in Bolzano, however, aren't the sort for which you pay admission; head to the crystal-green Talvera River, catch the afternoon sun on Castel Roncolo, and gaze at the steep green hills, resplendent with neat rows of ripening vines.

▗ TRANSPORTATION

Trains: (☎ 0471 97 42 92) in P. Stazione. Info office open M-Sa 8am-5:30pm, Su 9am-1pm and 2:30-5:30pm. **Luggage storage** available. To: **Bressanone** (30min., every hr., 6am-9:31pm, €3.25); **Merano** (45min., every hr., 6:58am-10pm, €3.25); **Milan** (3½hr., 3 per day, 11:31am-3:44am, €21); **Trent** (45min., 1-2 per hr., 5:15am-9:40pm, €2.89); and **Verona** (2hr., 1-2 per hr., 5:15am-9:40pm, €6.80). More frequent service to Milan via Verona.

Buses: SAD, V. Perathoner, 4 (☎ 0471 45 01 11), between train station and P. Walther. Bus station and tourist office distribute schedules detailing the extensive service to the western Dolomites. Less frequent service Su and after 6pm. To: **Bressanone** (1hr., every hr., 4:19am-9:31pm, €4.65); **Cortina d'Ampezzo** (4hr., every hr., 5:45am-8:35pm, €13.65); and **Merano** (1hr., every hr., 6:50am-8:35pm, €3.60).

Local Buses: SASA (☎ 0471 45 01 11 or 800 84 60 47). Bus service throughout the city. All lines stop in P. Walther. Buy your ticket (€0.90) at *tabacchi* stands, or from the machines near some bus stops.

Cableways: 3 cableways, located at the edges of Bolzano, whisk you up 1000m or more over the city to the nearest trailhead or bike path. The tourist office is happy to advise you on potential routes, and publishes *Bolzano a Passeggio,* a guide to 14 easy walks in the surrounding hills. They also distribute the *funivia* schedule in booklet form.

Funivia del Colle (☎ 0471 97 85 45), the **world's oldest cableway,** leads from V. Campiglio to Colle or Kohlern. (9min.; 1-2 per hr., 7am-7pm; €2.60 round-trip; bikes €2.10.)

Funivia del Renon (Rittner Seilbahn; ☎ 0471 97 84 79) heads from V. Renon, a 5min. walk from the train station, to Renon or Ritten. (12min.; 3 per hr., 7:10am-8:20pm; €3.50 round-trip, bikes €2.)

Funivia San Genesio (☎ 0471 97 84 36), on V. Sarentino, across the Talvera River near Ponte S. Antonio, connects Bolzano to Salto's high plateaus. (9min.; 2-3 per hr., 7:05am-12:30pm and 2:15-7:30pm; €3.40 round-trip, bikes €2.58.)

Taxi: Radiotaxi (☎ 0471 98 11 11), V. Perathoner, 4. 24hr. service.

Car Rental: Budget-National-Maggiore, V. Garibaldi, 32 (☎ 0471 97 15 31). 21+. From €69.72 per day. Open M-F 8am-noon and 3-7pm, Sa 8am-noon. **Hertz,** V. Garibaldi, 34 (☎ 0471 98 14 11; fax 30 37 15). From €51.65 per day.

FROM THE ROAD

TABLE FOR ONE

Working as a researcher-writer means that you spend a lot of time by yourself, including meal time. One evening, while dining alone at a *trattoria*, I noticed yet again the questioning stares from fellow patrons and raised eyebrows from the waitstaff.

Italians are a naturally affable people. Wherever you go, you're likely to find them in a large group, gesticulating madly and speaking at high decibel levels. This is precisely what makes them so wonderful. At the same time, the members of a culture so firmly based in community have a hard time believing that anyone would voluntarily choose solitude. Instead, Italians assume that those with the misfortune of being alone must either be looking for someone (this is why single women traveling in Italy will often invent a partner with an extended life history), or must have something so fundamentally wrong with them that they can't find anyone who would tolerate them.

Rose sellers steer clear of folks alone, and fiddlers never ask the loners if they can play their song. That night, not one but two hearing-impaired vendors passed through, placing items on tables in hopes of a sale. Did they offer their wares to me? They did not. They had the only visual cue they needed: I was eating alone. I asked a diner at the adjoining table why I'd been ignored.

He responded, "They probably think that you have bigger problems than they do."

—Hunter Maats

Bike Rental: Sportler Velo, V. Grappoli, 56 (☎0471 97 77 19), near P. Municipale (Rathausplatz). Mountain bikes €15.50 per day, €23.24 per 2 days, and €77.47 per week. Big selection of retail bikes and equipment. Open M-F 9am-12:30pm and 4:30-7pm, Sa 9am-12:30pm.

🛈 PRACTICAL INFORMATION

Bolzano's **historic center** lies between the train station and the **Talvera River** (Talfer Fluss), with all major piazzas within walking distance. Street and place names are listed in Italian and German, and most maps will mark both. A brief walk through the park on **Via Stazione** (Banhofsallee) from the train station, or **Via Alto Adige** (Sudtirolerstr.) from the bus stop, leads to **Piazza Walther** (Waltherplatz), and the duomo. Beyond P. Walther, **Piazza del Grano** leads left to **Via Portici** (Laubenstr.), home to Bolzano's swankiest district, where German and Italian merchants traditionally set up shop on opposite sides of the arcade. To reach **Ponte Talvera,** follow V. Portici beyond **Piazza Erbe.**

Tourist Office: Azienda di Soggiorno e Turismo, P. Walther, 8 (☎0471 30 70 00; fax 98 01 28; www.bolzano-bozen.it). Provides a city map and a list of accommodations, including hotels, campgrounds, and *agriturismo.* Open M-F 9am-6:30pm, Sa 9am-12:30pm.

Currency Exchange and ATM: At **Banca Nazionale del Lavoro,** in P. Walther, next door to tourist office, or at post office. Good rates. Open M-F 8:20am-1:20pm and 3-4:30pm. ATMs are omnipresent in the city center.

Alpine Info: Club Alpino Italiano (CAI), P. Erbe, 46 (☎0471 97 81 72). Ring the bell; office is on the 2nd fl. Hiking and climbing info, as well as guided excursions. Little English spoken. Open Tu-F 11am-1pm and 5-7pm.

Laundromat: Lava e Asciuga, V. Rosmini, 81, near the Ponte Talvera. Wash €3.10, dry €3.10, detergent €1. Open daily 7:30am-10:30pm.

Emergency: ☎113. **Police:** 112. **First Aid:** ☎118.

24-Hour Pharmacy: Farmacia all'Aquila Nera, V. Portici, 46/b. Open M-F 8:30am-noon and 3-7pm, Sa 8:30-noon. 24hr. pharmacies rotate; check window for postings.

Hospital: Ospedale Regionale San Maurizio (☎0471 90 81 11), on V. Lorenz Böhler. Hop on the #10 bus, last stop.

Internet Access: Telecom Italia calling center, P. Parrocchia, 21. From the tourist office, cross P. Walther, and turn left after about a block. The standard phone-card-operated booths cost €5.16 per hr. Open M-Su 8am-11pm.

Post Office: V. della Posta, 1 (☎0471 97 94 52), by the duomo. Open M-F 8:05am-6:30pm, Sa 8:05am-1pm.

Postal Code: 39100.

ACCOMMODATIONS & CAMPING

Bolzano's handful of inexpensive accommodations fill up quickly in the summer, so book ahead. The tourist office also has information on *agriturismo*. Unfortunately, private transportation to these hillside *pensioni* is usually necessary.

Croce Bianca, P. del Grano, 3 (☎0471 97 75 52; fax 97 22 73). From P. Walter, head past the tourist office until you emerge in P. del Grano (or Kornplatz). The hotel is 50m to your right. Homey rooms with thick mattresses. Most centrally-located budget beds in town. Breakfast €4.13. Reserve in advance. Singles €28; doubles €47, with bath €55; triples with bath €72. MC/V. ❸

Schwarze Katz, Stazione Maddalena di Sotto, 2 (☎0471 97 54 17; fax 32 50 28), near V. Brennero, 15min. from *centro*. From train station, head right on V. Renon, past *funivia*, and look for signs that lead 20m up a steep hill on the left. Family-run, friendly place with a garden restaurant popular with locals. 9 rooms with bath. Breakfast included. Reserve ahead. Singles €25.82; doubles €45.45-53.71. ❷

Garni Thiulle, V. Thiulle, 5 (☎0471 26 28 77). 15min. walk from train station. Cross Ponte Talvera, heading away from city center. Head left on V. S. Quirino, take 1st right, and walk left onto V. Thiulle. Simple, quiet rooms, some with views of a garden. Little English spoken. Singles €25.82-41.32; doubles €51.65-67.14. ❷

Camping: Moosbauer, V. S. Maurizio, 83 (☎0471 91 84 92; fax 20 48 94). Take SAD bus to Merano and ask driver for Moosbauer stop. €5.50 per person, €4.25 per tent. Showers included. ❶

FOOD

In Bolzano, pizza and *gelato* take a back seat to *Knödel*, *Strudel*, and other Austrian fare. *Rindgulasch* is a delicious beef stew; *Speck* is tasty smoked bacon. *Knödel* (dumplings) come in dozens of rib-sticking varieties. The three types of *Strudel*—*Apfel* (apple), *Topfen* (soft cheese), and *Mohn* (poppyseed)—make delicious snacks. The week-long *Südtiroler Törgelen* tasting spree in the fall is celebrated in the local vineyards. There's an all-day market in P. delle Erbe and along V. della Roggia, vending fine local produce. For a snack (sausage; €3.60), try the market **Wurst stand ❶.** (Open M-Sa 8am-7pm.) A **Despar supermarket** is at V. della Rena, 40. (☎0471 97 45 37. Open M-F 8:30am-12:30pm and 3-7:30pm, Sa 8am-1pm.) Numerous *alimentari* are scattered around P. Erbe.

Casa al Torchio, V. Museo, 2C, just off P. Erbe. Italian locals crowd this Gothic house, a labyrinth of low-ceilinged rooms decked with wood carvings and antlers. Fast service. Try the pizza, piled high with fresh tomatoes, cheeses, and *Speck* (€7.50). Cover €1. Service 10%. Open M-F noon-2pm and 7-11pm, Su 6:30-11pm. ❷

Hopfen & Co., V. Argentieri, 36 (☎0471 30 07 88). Offers a smorgasbord of regional specialties. Sample a tall *birra oscura* (dark beer) or *chiaro* (light) for a mere €3.40, or dine in the elegant rooms upstairs. The savory, stew-like *goulasch* is pricey (€11), but makes for a filling meal. Open M-Sa 9:30am-1am. MC/V. ❸

Hostaria Argentieri, V. Argentieri, 14 (☎0471 98 17 18). As Italian as you'll find this close to the border. *Primi* €7.50-15.50, *secondi* €8.50-19.30. Cover €1.50. Open M-Sa noon-2:30pm and 7-10:30pm. MC/V. ❹

◉ SIGHTS

DUOMO AND CHIESA DEI FRANCESCANI. With its prickly spined tower and a diamond-patterned roof, the Gothic duomo is a dark sight. For the most part, the beauty of Bolzano is in the facades—some of the most eye-pleasing architecture is unveiled near the P. Erbe and V. Museo. The exception is Chiesa dei Francescani, where a simple triangular exterior hides a splendid interior. At the proper distance, the cross seems to float in front of three dazzling stained-glass windows, in bright slivers of gold, red, and purple. *(Duomo in P. Walther. Chiesa off P. Erbe. Both open M-F 9:45am-noon and 2-5pm, Sa 9:45am-noon. Free.)*

SOUTH TYROL MUSEUM OF ARCHAEOLOGY. Exhibits here trace the evolution of human life in the Sudtirol region from the Stone Age to the early Middle Ages. See an actual Ice Man, a 5000-year-old body discovered by Germans trekking in the Alps. *(V. Museo, 43, near Ponte Talvera.* ☎ *0471 98 20 98; fax 98 06 48; www.iceman.it. Open Tu-W and F-Su 10am-6pm, Th 10am-8pm. Audio guides €1.60. €6.70, students €3.60.)*

CASTEL RONCOLO. Perched on the vine-covered hills above town, this is the most accessible of Bolzano's medieval fortresses. Catch a spectacular view of the city from the winding path that leads to the castle. Inside, devil masks, demonic statues, and hollow-eyed mannequins are juxtaposed with lavish frescoes. *(Up V. Weggerstein to V. San Antonio. Take city bus #12 (€0.90) or the free shuttle bus from P. Walther.* ☎ *0471 32 98 08. Open July-Sept. Tu-Su 10am-8pm and Oct.-June 10am-6pm. Gates for frescoes close 5pm. €3.)*

◪ HIKING

Bolzano is technically located in the pre-Alps, despite local allegiance to the Dolomites. Hiking here pales in comparison to that in the Alps to the west or the Dolomites proper to the east. The **CAI** (Club Alpino Italiano; see p. 284) **office** is likely to be far more helpful than the tourist office with information on hikes. The best hikes can be accessed by the three *funivie* that surround the town, which will allow you to get straight to vista level. While the **funivia del Renon** and **funivia del Colle** have limited marked trails, the **funivia San Genesio** offers extensively marked trails of moderate difficulty. All three *funivie* offer free maps that should be sufficient for the easier hikes. The gentle walk from the San Genesio *funivia* to the Edelweiss rest house, and then to the Tachaufenhaus and back to the San Genesio *funivia* via the Locher rest house, makes for a pleasant hike (4½hr.). Even for the easiest hikes, take precautions against dehydration and exposure.

BRESSANONE (BRIXEN) ☎ 0472

Northwest of the Dolomites and south of Austria, Bressanone's Alpine valley spoils visitors with unimpeded views of green mountains, crystalline rivers, and neat rows of pastel houses. The town's medieval heritage has bestowed a number of artistic treasures upon Bressanone, most notably the 14th-century *chiostro* (cloister). Bressanone is smaller and less popular than Bolzano. Nonetheless, tourists arrive by the busload in the summer, so prepare your escape to the mountains.

▣◪ TRANSPORTATION AND PRACTICAL INFORMATION. Bressanone is an easy daytrip by train or bus from Bolzano or Trent. **Trains** run to: **Bolzano** (30min., every hr., 6:27am-9:09pm, €3.25); **Munich, Germany** (5hr., 3-4 per day, 8:33am-6:57pm, €42.53); **Trent** (1-1½hr., every 2hr., 6:27am-9:09pm, €6.15); and **Verona**

(2hr., 3-4 per day, 6:27am-9:09pm, €14.15). **Buses** run to **Bolzano** (1hr., every hr., 7am-8:15pm, €2.68). The center of town is **Piazza del Duomo.** From the train station and bus stop, follow **Viale Stazione** left 500m to past the glass-encased **tourist office** (on your right, at the corner of Viale Stazione and V. Cassiano). At the intersection, take **Via Bastioni Min.**, and turn right through the flower-covered arch on your right to enter the courtyard of the **Palazzo Vescovile.** The **tourist office,** Viale Stazione, 9, distributes town maps and info on suggested hikes. (☎0472 83 64 01; fax 83 60 67; www.brixen.org. Open M-F 8:30am-12:30pm and 2:30-6pm, Sa 9am-12:30pm.) In an **emergency,** dial ☎113, the **police** (☎112 or ☎0472 83 34 55), or an **ambulance** (☎118). There is a **pharmacy** at Kl. Lauber, 2/a; check the sign posted in the window for the weekly nighttime pharmacy. (Open M-T, Th-Su 8am-12:30pm and 3-9pm, W 8am-12:30pm.) The **hospital** (☎0472 81 21 11) is on V. Dante, toward Brenner. **ATMs** line V. Bastioni Magg., one block north of P. del Duomo. **Change money** at Bressanone's **post office,** behind the tourist office. (Open M-F 8:05am-6:30pm, Sa 8:05am-1pm.) **Postal Code:** 39042.

ꕯꕯ ACCOMMODATIONS AND FOOD. Accommodations in Bressanone are surprisingly affordable; three-star accommodations go for €40-50 per night. **Ostello della Gioventù Kassianeum ❷,** V. Bruno, 2, off the duomo, has lightly finished pine and whitewashed walls that lend themselves well to the mountain setting. The rooms promise spectacular vistas. (☎0472 27 99 99; fax 27 99 98; jukas@jukas.net. Buffet breakfast and sheets included. Dorms €19-27.) From the train station, turn left onto Viale Stazione; about a block after the tourist office is **Hotel Croce d'Oro ❹,** V. Bastioni Minori, 8. Besides a central location, this gorgeous three-star offers sauna, hot tub, Turkish bath, and solarium. (☎0472 83 61 55; fax 83 42 55; hotel.goldenes.kreuz@rolmail.it. Singles €45-70, doubles €70-120.) From the station, head straight up the V. le Mozart then take the first left onto V. Vittorio Veneto. Follow this road as it changes into the V. Dante, V. Peter Mayr and the V. Brennero until you reach the river. Cross the bridge and **Garni Schonruh ❹,** V. dei Vigneti, 1, will be on your left (10min. walk). This quiet three-star hotel has bath and TV. (☎/fax 0472 83 65 48; schoenruh@rolmail.com. Singles €41; doubles €77. MC/V.) **Cremona ❸,** V. Veneto, 26, offers friendly service and 12 clean rooms, most with bath, outside the town center. (☎0472 83 56 02; fax 20 07 94. Breakfast included. Singles €27; doubles €52.)

Finsterwirt ❸, Vicolo Duomo, 3 (☎0472 83 23 44), just off P. Duomo, is a very sedate restaurant offering Italian food with a Tyrolean twist. (*Primi* €6.20-9.30, *secondi* €14.50-18. Open Tu-Su 12:30pm-2:30pm and 6:30pm-10:30pm. MC/V.) **Torre Bianca ❶,** V. Torre Bianca, 6 (☎0472 83 29 72), serves a wide variety of pizzas as well as traditional Tyrolean fare. Pizzas start at €3.50; pizza *al cacciatore* (hunter's pizza; €6.80) is garnished with forest mushrooms and venison. (Open W-M 9:30am-10pm. MC/V.) At the century-old **Restaurant Fink ❷,** Kl. Lauben, 4, local crafts decorate the windows, and waitresses in traditional dress serve up Austrian and Italian cuisine. (☎0472 83 48 83. *Rosti* of potatoes and veggies €6.55, *insalata grande con mozzarella e pane d'olive* €6.40. Cover €1. Open M-Sa 11am-11pm.) Dining on a more limited budget? Try the ever-present **STANDA supermarket,** Viale Stazione, 7, next to the tourist office. (Open M-Sa 8am-7pm.)

◪ꕦ SIGHTS AND HIKING. Most sights are concentrated around P. del Duomo. A few yards south of the piazza, at P. Palazzo, the richly ornamented **Palazzo Vescovile,** originally constructed in 1595, houses the **Museo Diocesano.** The building itself has a stunning interior courtyard, while the museum traces the development of Western Christianity amidst evolving European social structures and technological advances such as the printing press. A number of medieval and Renaissance portraits are also on display, including copies of works by Hans Klocker and Albrecht

Dürer. Explanatory information is in Italian and German only. (☎0472 83 05 05. Open Mar. 15-Oct. Tu-Su 10am-5pm. €5, reduced €4.)

The **duomo,** in the center of the piazza, was originally constructed in the Romanesque style, but it acquired Baroque and Neoclassical detailing during renovations in 1595, 1754, and 1790; the gilded ceiling and marble walls are dazzling. The nearby **chiostro,** to the left as you exit the duomo, dates from the 14th century and highlights the evolution of medieval painting through a series of frescoes. (Duomo and *chiostro* open M-Sa 6am-noon and 3-6pm, Su 3-6pm. Free.)

One of the most enjoyable activities in Bressanone is simply strolling the pleasant streets of the city. From Ponte Aquila behind the duomo, cross the bridge to the tiny **Altstadt** (old town), where flowerboxes decorate the windows of pastel houses situated along winding cobblestone lanes.

The Plose Plateau, towering over Bressanone to the East at heights of over 2000m, is a popular and accessible alpine area, thanks to the **Santa Andrea Cable Car** (10min., 2 per hr., 9am-6pm, €6.20 round-trip, bike transport €2.50), which operates from the nearby hillside town of **S. Andrea.** SAD **bus #126** departs from the Bressanone train station to S. Andrea daily at 7:54am, 9:13am, and 12:13pm, with return service at 5:11pm and 6:45pm. Buy tickets at the train station (€2 round-trip). From the upper cable-car station, **trail #30** leads along the smooth terrain of the Plose's west slope, and **trail #17** follows the meadows on the Plose's southern slope. For a longer, more strenuous hike, **trail #7** traverses the three summits of the Plose massif: Monte Telegrafo, Monte Fana, and Monte Forca, reaching altitudes of 2600m. Two alpine *rifugi*, **Plose** and **Rossalm,** offer hot meals and overnight stays. A tourist office brochure details three easy hikes on the Plose, ranging from three to six hours. Don't forget to verify bus and lift schedules, and be prepared to face rough terrain and high altitudes (2000m).

LAKE GARDA (LAGO DI GARDA)

In centuries past, Milan and Venice competed for Lake Garda's freshwater fish, olives, citrus fruit, and white and black truffles. In 1426, Venice won, subsequently gaining economic prestige (the tides have since turned). Stretching 52km into the regions of the Veneto, Lombardy, and Trent, Lake Garda's shores wash up historical bounty as well as exotic produce, including the world's oldest wooden plough (2000 BC) and the remains of a Bronze Age civilization. Every summer, German, Dutch, and Italian tourists crowd its pebbly beaches to bask in the hot sun and windsurf, hang-glide, and kayak. Renting a scooter will allow you to tour Garda's towns quickly, zipping through mountain tunnels and past staggering lake views.

SIRMIONE   ☎030

Isolated on a peninsula from the other surrounding lakeside towns, little Sirmione is elegant and relaxing. The healing powers of its spa waters, renowned in ancient times, today still constitute one of Sirmione's main draws. Its peace and tranquility are heightened by the fact that the old town is only accessible by foot. The heavy tread of European tourists has not worn away the charm of a quiet beach town with winding medieval streets and architecture, and modern, trendy boutiques and restaurants that satisfy the tastes of its sophisticated vacationers.

🖃🔁 TRANSPORTATION AND PRACTICAL INFORMATION. Sirmione is a thin peninsula at the southern end of the lake. Buses run every hour from **Desenzano** (20min., €1.45), which has the closest train station, to **Brescia** (1hr., €3.10) and **Verona** (1hr., €2.65). Buy tickets from the blue machine near the bus stop, or inside the Atesina kiosk during business hours. **Navigazione Lago Garda** (toll-free

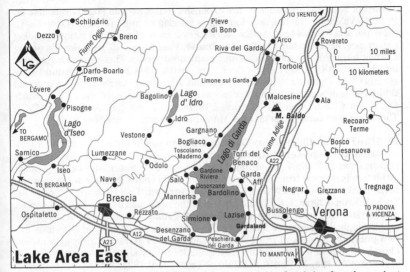

Lake Area East

☎ 800 55 18 01 or 030 914 9511) may be more expensive, but it is often the easiest way to reach places along and across the lake. **Battelli** (water steamers) run until 8pm to: **Desenzano** (20min., €3); **Gardone** (1¼hr., €6); and **Riva** (4hr., €8.50). For **taxis,** dial ☎ 030 91 60 82 or 91 92 40. The **tourist office**, V. Guglielmo Marconi, 2, is in the disc-shaped building. (☎ 030 91 61 14. Open Apr.-Oct. daily 9am-9pm; Nov.-Mar. M-F 9am-12:30pm and 3-6pm, Sa 9am-12:30pm.) Sirmione's major attractions are concentrated in the north end of the peninsula, in the old town, across the street from the tourist office. **Via Marconi** leads to **Via Vittorio Emanuele** and Sirmione's historic castle, **Rocca Scaligera**. The **Banca Popolare di Verona**, P. Castello, 3-4, across from the castle, has an **ATM**. (Open daily 8:25am-1:20pm and 2:40-6:10pm.) Rent **bikes** at **Adventure Sprint**, V. Brescia, 9 (☎ 030 91 90 00; €8-19 per day). In **emergencies,** dial ☎ 113, the **Assistenza Sanitaria Turistica**, V. Alfieri, 6 (☎ 030 990 9171; open June 15- Sept. 15), or the **police** (☎ 030 990 6777). The **post office** is near the tourist office. (Open M-F 8:10am-1:30pm, Sa 8:10am-11:40am.) **Postal Code:** 25019.

☎🏠 ACCOMMODATIONS AND FOOD. Though a thorough exploration of Sirmione takes only an afternoon, it does have a large selection of fairly pricey hotels. Reserve rooms in the summer, as accommodations fill quickly. **Hotel Meridiana ❺,** V. Catullo, 5, has spacious rooms with hardwood floors. All come with bath, A/C, TV, and full buffet breakfast. (☎ 030 91 61 62; fax 91 62 14. Singles €70-78; doubles €88-103; triples €110-120. AmEx/MC/V.) **Corte Regina ❹,** V. Anticha Mura, 11, has simpler rooms with bath, A/C, and TV. (☎ 030 91 61 47; fax 919 6470. Breakfast included. Singles €50-70; doubles €75-90; triples €90-120. MC/V.) **Albergo Grifone ❸,** V. Bocchio, 4, offers rooms with bath and views of the lake. (☎ 030 91 60 14; fax 91 65 48. Reservations necessary. Singles €32; doubles €55. Extra bed €15.) Sirmione also has a campground, **Campeggio Sirmione ❶,** V. Sirmioncino, 9, 2km from town behind Hotel Benaco. Take the Servizio Urbano bus. (☎ 030 990 4665; fax 91 90 45. Open Mar. 15-Oct. 15. €5.50-8.50 per person, €8.50-13.50 per site. 2-person bungalows €45-65; 4-person €65-95; each additional person €5.50-8.50.)

Most of Sirmione's restaurants are expensive, but **Ristorante Pizzeria Valentino ❷**, P. Porto Valentino, 13, has delicious pizza ranging from €4.65-8.80. (Open Sa-Th 9am-3pm and 5:30pm-1am. AmEx/MC/V.) For a more elegant and intimate dining experience, **Antica Trattoria La Spe Ran Zina ❺**, Viale Dante, 16, has lakeside dining on their terrace and in their beautifully manicured garden. There is also a spacious interior with A/C. Reservations necessary. (☎030 990 6292. *Primi* around €15, *secondi* €18. Open Tu-Su noon-2:30pm and 7-10:30pm. AmEx/MC/V.) **Ristorante Grifione ❸** is downstairs from the *albergo* of the same name. (*Primi* €7, *secondi* €9. Cover €2.50. Open Th-Tu noon-2:15pm and 7-10:15pm. AmEx/DC/MC/V.) There is also an **outdoor market** in P. Montebaldo. (Open F 8am-1pm.)

🄖 **SIGHTS.** The 13th-century **Castello Scaligero** sits in the center of town as a testament to the power of the della Scala family, who controlled the Veronese region from 1260-1387. Completely surrounded by water, the castle's main attraction is its view from the turrets; the inside is empty save for some cannonballs, bricks, and dirt. (☎030 91 64 68. Open Apr.-Oct. Tu-Su 9am-7pm; Nov.-Mar. Tu-Su 8:30am-4:30pm. €4.) At the far end of the peninsula lies the best-preserved aristocratic villa in Northern Italy, **Grotte di Catullo.** There is also an adjacent archaeological museum (☎031 91 61 57). Between the castle and the ruins are two public beaches and the **Chiesa di San Pietro in Mavino,** Sirmione's oldest church. Eighth- and 16th-century frescoes adorn the walls. Sirmione also boasts a year-round **spa,** V. Punto Staffalo, 1 (☎030 990 4923; www.termedisirmi-one.com), with a thermal swimming pool, underwater massages (€24.90), beauty treatments, and mud baths (€13.30-27.50). See the tourist office for spa information and **summer event** listings, including musical and dance performances, theater, art exhibitions, and trout tastings.

GARDONE RIVIERA   ☎0365

Once a fashionable tourist destination among the European elite, the Gardone Riviera is now a retired hotspot. Gracefully aging villas, lush gardens, and a tranquil lifestyle have replaced the boisterous routs of wealthy *Great Gatsby* types. Enchanting memories of times long past seem to seep through the streets and walls of the old town. As the town lacks the energy of Sirmione, a visit to Riviera is peaceful and self-indulgent.

🄴🄷 **TRANSPORTATION AND PRACTICAL INFORMATION.** Gardone's two main thoroughfares, **Gardone Sotto** and **Corso Zanardelli,** intersect near the bus stop. **Buses** (☎0365 21 061 or 800 4125) run to: **Brescia** (1hr., 2 per hr., €2.80); **Desenzano** (30min., 6 per day, €2.40); and **Milan** (3hr., 2 per day, €8). You can purchase bus tickets at the **Molinari Viaggi Travel Agency,** P. Wimmer, 2, near the ferry stop. (☎0365 21 551. Open daily 8:30am-2:15pm and 3-6:30pm.) The **APT tourist office,** V. Repubblica, 8, in the center of Gardone Sotto, provides maps and accommodations information. (☎/fax 0365 20 347. Open M-Sa 9am-1pm and 3:30-6:30pm, Su 9am-1pm.) For **currency exchange,** head to the **Banco di Brescia,** across from the Grand Hotel. From the ferry dock, turn right and climb the stairs. (☎0365 20 081. Open M-F 8:25am-1:25pm and 2:40-3:40pm.) In case of an **emergency,** dial ☎113, contact the **police** (☎112 or 0365 54 06 10), or call the **hospital** (☎0365 29 71). For **first aid** at night and on holidays, dial ☎0365 29 71. The **post office,** V. Roma, 8, is next door to the bank. (☎0365 20 862. Open M-F 8:30am-2pm, Sa 8:30am-12:30pm.) **Postal Code:** 25083.

🄵🄲 **ACCOMMODATIONS AND FOOD.** Budget travelers should explore Gardone as a daytrip, as inexpensive accommodations are scarce. **Locanda Trattoria agli Angeli ❺**, P. Garibaldi, 2, has 10 rooms furnished with antiques and with bath, A/C, and TV. (☎0365 20 832. Open May-Sept. Breakfast included. Singles €75; doubles €80. AmEx/MC/V.) **Pizzeria Ristorante Emiliano ❶**, V. Repubblica, 57, right by the ferry station, serves enormous, inexpensive pizzas from €3.90. (☎0365 21 517. Cover €1.10. Open daily noon-2:30pm and 6-11pm.) **La Stalla ❷**, V. dei Colli, 14, off V. Roma, has romantic outdoor dining. The *trata alla griglia* (grilled fresh fish; €8) will melt in your mouth. (☎0365 21 038. Open daily 7-11pm. AmEx/MC/V.)

🎥 🎵 SIGHTS AND ENTERTAINMENT. Off of V. Roma and V. dei Colli lies **ll Vittoriale**, the sprawling estate of Gabriele D'Annunzio, poet, novelist, and latter-day Casanova. His ultra-nationalistic stunts ranged from single-handedly piloting a plane to drop propaganda over Vienna in 1918, to seizing Fiume from infant Yugoslavia with an army of poetry-lovers. Mussolini found D'Annunzio's energetic escapades an embarrassment, and gave him this rural villa to distract him from politics. D'Annunzio occupied himself by erecting monuments to his own achievements, displaying on his vast estate the bow of the battleship Puglia, a speedboat which he used for the "Buccari Escapade," and the famous airplane that traversed Austria. Also on the grounds are D'Annunzio's tomb, mausoleum, and shaded avenues lined with the urns of his wartime companions. The villa's interior immortalizes D'Annunzio's eccentric penchant for collecting—with thousands of knick-knacks, paintings, and sculptures. The bathroom is strewn with 2000 fragments and fixtures. Visit the house early, before crowds arrive. (☎0365 29 65 11; www.vittoriale.it. Villa open Apr.-Sept. Tu-Su 8:30am-8pm. Gardens open Oct.-Mar. Tu-Su 9am-5pm. House €6, house and gardens €11. Audio guide €4.50 for 1, €6 for 2.)

The **Giardino Botanico**, at the corner of V. Roma and V. Disciplina, was planted in 1900 by Arturo Hruska, doctor to the Tsar. More than 8000 varieties of plants and flowers in a 10,000-square-meter space drop petals over tiny platform bridges criss-crossing rivulets. (☎0365 336 410 877. Open daily 9am-7pm. €6. €2 discount at Vittoriale with ticket to gardens.) The **Fondazione "al Vittoriale"** sponsors a summer program of plays, concerts, and dance performances in the outdoor **Teatro del Vittoriale**. (Ticket info ☎0365 29 65 06. Performances mid-July to early Aug. Tickets from €15.50.) The Riviera's parish **Church of St. Nicolas**, next to Vittoriale, dates to 1391, though little of the original construction remains. After the church was demolished in 1730, Paolo Soratini, a Camoldolite monk, reconstructed it in the Baroque style, with an elaborately painted green and white

THE BIG SPLURGE

GRAND FINALE

Follow in the footsteps of one-time guests Winston Churchill and Vladimir Nabokov down the path that winds from the exquisite four-star **Grand Hotel**, V. Zanardelli, 74, to a beach-chair-coated pier and gently lapping waves. This *Belle Epoque palazzo* embodies the quintessential Lake Garda resort experience. Located directly on the lake, with awe-inspiring water and mountain views, the Grand has been coaxing guests into pampered relaxation since 1888.

The hotel's long history, manicured grounds, lake-sailing arrangements, and high thread-count sheets make it the embodiment of Gardone Riviera's aged and yet ever-youthful elegance. Luxuriate in the heated outdoor swimming pool, jacuzzi, private beach, or Turkish bath; take your afternoon caffè in the vine- and rose-entwined garden; and dance after dinner at the piano bar.

Rooms have bathtubs, A/C, TV, minibar, and balconies overlooking the lake. The elaborate buffet breakfast, large enough to pass as a five-course brunch, is in itself quite nearly worth the price of a room.

V. Zanardelli, 74. ☎0365 20 261; fax 22 695; www.grangardone.it. Open Oct.-Apr. Singles €92-112; doubles €132-205; suites €192-245. AmEx/MC/V.

interior. Frescoes depicting the life of St. Nicolas of Bari and by Paolo Veronese's son, Carlo Caliari (1570-1596), adorn the walls and ceiling. Note the two wooden caskets in the altar of relics. Found in the Roman catacombs, they are said to contain the bones and congealed blood of Christian martyrs Feliciano and Zosimo. (Open M-Sa 10am-6pm and Su 1-6pm.) A walk around the outside of the church offers a panoramic view of the lake.

RIVA DEL GARDA ☎0464

With lake waters lapping at the foot of the mountains, Riva is a spot for those who love *belle viste* (beautiful views) and outdoor activities, but who are traveling on a budget. The gentle mountain winds make Garda the second-best lake in the world for windsurfing, and Riva's windsurfing schools are internationally renowned. The area is also a prime locale for hiking, canoeing, whitewater rafting, kayaking, bicycling, and swimming. The youth hostel here makes it all affordable.

TRANSPORTATION

Buses: Viale Trento, 5 (☎0464 55 23 23). From: **Rovereto** (1hr., every hr., 5am-7:05pm, €2.20); **Trent** (2hr., 6 per day, 5:50am-6:15pm, €3.20); and **Verona** (2hr., 11 per day 5am-8:30pm, €5).

Ferries: Navigazione Lago di Garda (☎030 914 9511), in P. Catena. Services **Gardone** (€6.60) and **Sirmione** (€3.90). Also offers sightseeing tours from €10.60 from 8am-6pm.

Bike Rental: Fiori e Bike, Viale dei Tigli, 24 (☎0464 55 18 30). Mountain and city bikes €8-13 per day. Ask for multiple-day discounts and free guided tours. **Nautic Club Riva,** Lungolago dei Pini, 7 (☎0464 55 24 53). Mountain bikes €3-11 per hr., €24 per day; city bikes €5/€10.

Scooter Rental: Santorum Autonoleggio, Viale Rovereto, 76 (☎0464 55 22 82). 1hr. €13, 5hr. €29, 1 day €44, 2 days €75, 1 wk. €160. Open M-Sa 9am-12:30pm and 2:30-7pm, Su 9am-noon. AmEx/MC/V.

ORIENTATION AND PRACTICAL INFORMATION

To reach the town center from the station, walk straight onto **Viale Trento** and then take **Via Roma** to **Piazza Cavour.**

Tourist Office: Giardini di Porta Orientale, 8 (☎0464 55 44 44; fax 52 03 08), near the water's edge, behind a small playground on V. della Liberazione. Lists hotel vacancies and offers a variety of inexpensive tours of the region. Ask for a city map and hiking routes. Open M-Sa 9am-noon and 3-6pm, Su 10am-noon and 4-6:30pm.

Emergency: ☎113. **Police:** ☎112. **First Aid:** ☎118.

Late-Night Pharmacy: V. Dante Alighieri, 12c (☎0464 55 25 08), and V. Maffei, 8 (☎0464 55 23 02), in P. della Erbe. Both open M-Sa 8:30am-12:30pm and 3:30-7:30pm, Su 9am-12:30pm and 4:30-7pm.

Internet Access: Clem's Bowling Club, Viale D. Chiesa, 4 (☎0464 55 35 96). €0.13 per min., €8 per hr. F-Sa 7pm-1am, Su 3pm-1am. **Sunrise Cafe,** Viale Trento, 66, (☎0464 553 008). €2 per 20 min., €5 per hr. Open Tu-Su 6am-midnight.

Post Office: V. Francesco, 26 (☎0464 55 23 46). Issues traveler's checks and changes money. Open M-F 8am-6:30pm, Sa 8am-12:30pm.

Postal Code: 38066.

▐ ACCOMMODATIONS & CAMPING

Riva is one of Lake Garda's few affordable destinations. Book ahead for July and August.

Hotel Benini, V. S. Alessandro, 25 (☎0464 55 30 40; fax 52 10 62). This sparkling, modern hotel, 1km from the city center, provides bicycles for all of its guests. Garden and brand-new swimming pool. Rooms have bath, A/C, and TV. Singles €43; doubles €70; triples €105. Buffet breakfast included. AmEx/MC/V. ❹

Ostello Benacus (HI), P. Cavour, 9 (☎0464 55 49 11; fax 55 65 54; www.garda.com/ostelloriva), in the center of town. From the bus station, walk down V. Trento, take V. Roma, turn left under the arch, and follow the signs. The hostel has hot showers, satellite TV with VCR, cabinets with locks, and a dining hall. Breakfast, sheets, and shower included. Reception daily 7-9am and 3pm-midnight. Book a few days ahead. 100 beds. Dorms €12. AmEx/MC/V. ❶

Locanda La Montanara, V. Montanara, 20 (☎/fax 0464 55 48 57). Off V. Florida. 9 bright and comfortable rooms, some with bath. The one communal bath has a bathtub. Breakfast €5. Singles €16; doubles €32-35.50; triples €48.50. Reserve one month ahead in summer. MC/V. ❷

Albergo Ancora, V. Montanara, 2 (☎0464 52 21 31; fax 55 00 50). White antique furniture and elegantly embroidered drapes adorn sunny, white rooms. All rooms with bath and TV. Buffet breakfast included. Wheelchair-accessible. Double rooms as singles €52-57; doubles €39-44 per person. Discount with extended stay. AmEx/MC/V. ❹

Villa Maria, V. dei Tigli, 19 (☎0464 55 22 88; fax 56 11 70; www.garnimaria.com). Removed from the square and in a less-than-attractive area, this hotel has clean rooms with bath, A/C, and TV. Rooftop terrace has view of mountains and industrial-looking apartments. Singles €33; doubles €46.48. MC/V. ❸

Camping: Bavaria ❶, V. Rovereto, 100 (☎0464 55 25 24; fax 55 91 26), on road toward Torbole. Excellent location on the water. Filled with die-hard windsurfing families, it has its own windsurfing school and rental, as well as sailing, canoeing, and swimming options. Pizzeria on premises. Hot showers €0.80. Open Apr.-Oct. €6.60 per person, €8.60 per site. **Monte Brione ❶,** V. Brione, 32 (☎0464 52 08 85; fax 52 08 90), has a swimming pool, washing machine, electricity, and free hot showers. €6.70 per person, €10.35 per site.

◖ FOOD

A small **open-air market** sells fruit and vegetables in P. della Erbe. (Open M-Sa mornings.) The **Orvea supermarket,** Giardino Verdi, 12, is across the street from the post office. (Open M-Sa 8:30am-12:30pm and 3:30-7pm, Su 8:30am-12:30pm.)

Ristorante Ancora, V. Montanara, 2 (☎0464 52 21 31). Guests at their hotel receive a 10% discount. Enjoy a wide range of dishes upstairs on the outdoor terrace or in the elegant restaurant. *Spaghetti allo scoglio* (spaghetti with shellfish and tomato sauce; €12.50) is delicious. *Primi* start at €8, *secondi* €9.50. Open daily noon-2:30pm and 7pm-midnight. Closed in the afternoon June-Sept. AmEx/MC/V. ❸

Leon d'Oro, V. Fiume, 20 (☎0464 55 23 41). Delicious and affordable local wines and food served in low-arched rooms. *Primi* from €6.50, *pesce* from €8. Cover €1.30. Open daily noon-3pm and 7-11pm. AmEx/MC/V. ❷

Ristorante-Pizzeria La Leonessa, V. Maffei, 24 (☎0464 55 27 77), just off P. della Erbe. A delightful respite from harborside prices. Outdoor tables and Mediterranean fare. House specialty is *Sorpresa della Casa* (pasta with capers, olives, and tomatoes wrapped inside pizza dough; €6). Open Th-Tu noon-2:30pm and 6-10pm. MC/V. ❷

NORTHEAST ITALY

Bireria Spaten, in P. della Erbe. An unrepentant beer hall, where long wooden tables, checkered tablecloths, high ceilings, and noisy patrons make for a raucous feast. *Wurstel* €7.50, *Goulasch* from €8, *birra grande* €3.70. Open daily 11am-3pm and 5:30pm-midnight. AmEx/MC/V. ❷

👁 🏔 SIGHTS AND OUTDOOR ACTIVITIES

For freshwater swimming, pebbly sunbathing, or stunning lake views, follow the lakeside path behind the tourist office and head away from the mountains.

WATERFALL. Just outside Riva (3km), the 20,000-year-old waterfall at **Cascato Varone** has chiseled a huge gorge in the mountain, falling at a height of 100 meters. *(Take bus #1 or 2 from V. Martiri. ☎0464 52 14 21. Open May-Aug. daily 9am-7pm; Oct. and Mar. 10am-12:30pm and 2-5pm; Apr. and Sept. 9am-6pm. €4.)*

GARDALAND. An hour from Riva del Garda, this amusement park has medieval jousting, ice shows, rollercoasters, shops, restaurants and gardens and a safari ride. *(From Riva, hourly APT buses head to Peschiera del Garda, from which a Gardaland-run bus service heads to the park (every hr., 8:50am-10:15pm). Direct bus service from Riva to Gardaland Tu and Th 8:45am and 4:05pm, round-trip €30. Gardaland info and buses ☎045 644 9777. €20.50, children less than 1m tall free. Open late Mar. to late Oct.; hours vary.)*

PADDLE BOATS. Noleggio Rudderboat Rental, on Lungalago Marinai d'Italia, right on the waterfront, offers hourly rentals (2 people €7, 4 people €8).

HIKING AND OTHER ACTIVITIES. A steep, one-hour hike leads to **Chiesetta Santa Barbara,** a tiny chapel, lit at night, and with a breathtaking view of the entire valley during the day. On the other side of town, follow V. Dante up to the mountains and take trail #404. The tourist office dispenses pamphlets on other hiking, climbing, canoeing, riding, and golfing opportunities.

🎵 NIGHTLIFE

Pub All'Oca, V. Santa Maria (☎0464 55 34 57), is always crowded with the young and fashionable. Sip wine (€2.50) and listen to swing music. Open daily 6pm-2am.

Cafe Latino, V. Oro, 15 (☎0464 55 57 85). A fun, young crowd converges at this swanky *discoteca* overlooking the lake. Bartenders are recognizable by glitter tattoos on their faces. 3 floors of dancing, with an outdoor terrace and seating area on the top floor. €8 for club admission and 1 drink. Get a drink card to punch the drinks you have, but lose it and pay €70. Open F-Sa 11pm-4am, although things don't start up until 12:30am. AmEx/MC/V.

Discoteca Tiffany, Giardini di Porta Orientale (☎0464 55 25 12), across from the tourist office, is less pretentious. Students, travelers, and natives dance to techno and house music, while others enjoy the comfy bar stools and panoramic view of the beautifully lit harbor. Open Th-Su 10pm-4am, July 10-Aug. open daily 10pm-4am. AmEx/MC/V.

Party Boats (☎0464 914 9511). Cruise across the lake to Latin techno beats. Ask at the tourist office for a listing of free musical concerts. Cover €12.50, includes 1 drink. Cruises July 27-Aug.

ROVERETO   ☎0464

Because the tiny town of Rovereto is nestled deep in the Dolomites, far from the attentions of camera-toting tourists, you may be able to enjoy its charms in relative solitude. Cobblestoned streets wind among the elegantly frescoed buildings. Decorative stone fountains dot the piazzas and side streets. Cool mountain breezes course down *strade* both serene and majestic. The surrounding countryside offers countless opportunities for biking, hiking, walking, and horseback-riding. In addition to the city's pastoral pleasures, Rovereto is replete with cafes, restaurants, and fashionable shops.

◪🄿 TRANSPORTATION AND PRACTICAL INFORMATION.

The **train station** is located at V. Rosmini, 41-45. **Trains** to: **Bologna** (3hr., every hr., 7:15am-8:30pm, €10.15); **Bolzano** (1hr., 1-2 per hr., 6:30am-9:45pm, €4.30); **Milan** (2½hr., 3 per day, 7am-7pm, €10.31); **Trent** (15min., 1-2 per hr., 6:35am-10:45pm, €2.40); and **Verona** (1hr., 1-2 per hr., 6:25am-9:27pm, €3.20). **Luggage storage** is at platform #1. (€3 for 6hr. Open 24hr.) The **bus station** is farther down the road on V. Rosmini. **Buses** run frequently to **Riva** (1hr., every hr., 6:44am-8:32pm, €2.20) and **Trent** (30min., 18 per day, 6:37am-8:40pm, €4.15). The **tourist office**, V. Dante, 63, next to the central park, provides a town map and info about trekking, biking, rock climbing, and skiing in the area. (☎ 0464 43 03 63; www.apt.rovereto.tn.it. Open daily 9am-noon and 2:30-6pm.) An **ATM/change machine** is in the train station. ATMs are also located throughout the town. To reach the **police station,** V. Sighele, 1, follow signs directly across the street from the train station. A **pharmacy** lies conveniently between the bus and train station at V. Dante, 3. (☎ 0464 42 10 30. Open M-F 8:30am-noon and 3-7pm.) The **post office** is uphill from the bus station. **Postal Code:** 38068.

🄵🄲 ACCOMMODATIONS AND FOOD.

The city's only hostel, the ▧**Ostello della Gioventu (HI),** V. delle Scuole, 16/18, is currently closed for remodeling. It is set to reopen next year. For ▧**Fox Dansyl ❷,** V. della Terra, 14, walk from P. Battisti up V. Rialto to V. della Terra, on the left near the stone fountain, or call to be picked up from the train station. This American-owned and Irish-run bed and breakfast is housed in a rustic, 500 year-old villa. Amenities include Internet connection, satellite TV, a washing machine, and a superb breakfast. In the summer they host neighborhood parties in their outdoor garden, for which Colin prepares the food from his collection of Belfast recipes. (☎ 0464 43 61 71. Doubles €50, €25 for one person; €25 to rent upstairs kitchen and sitting area.) **Vecchia Trattoria Birrara Scala della Torre ❸,** V. Scala della Torre, 7, serves tavern-style food with a German flair. (☎ 0464 43 71 00. *Primi* from €5.20, *secondi* from €6.70. Cover €1. Open daily noon-2:30pm and 7:30-9:30pm.) There is also a grocery store, **Supermercati Trentini,** on V. Mazzini. (Open M 8:30am-1:30pm, Tu-Sa 8:30am-12:30pm and 3:15-7:15pm.)

IN RECENT NEWS

MUSEO OR MONSTROSITY?

In January 2003, the Polo Museale will open in Rovereto as the largest modern art museum in Italy. Its imminent completion is mired in community discontent. *Roveretesi* regard the museum not as a graceful bestower of enlightenment, but as a rarefied force of destruction.

Residents of the small town of Rovereto believe that the museum will not attract enough visitors to compensate for the financial drain and physical toll its construction has taken.

Rovereto's tourist economy is small and its hotels limited enough, some say, that the venture is destined to be an unsuccessful and colossally wasteful one. Rovereto's siphoning of funds into construction has meant that little is left for the maintenance of its crumbling historic buildings.

While remnants of a colorful past deteriorate, reckless digging has left local real estate worthless. After digging out earth from the side of a hillside in preparation for the pouring of the museum's foundation, the hill and over 200 neighborhood houses that sat upon it began to sink.

One of the displaced inhabitants expressed her frustration: *"Che cazzo. Chi è Chirico? No mi importa per niente"* ("Why do I care? Nothing matters if I don't have a home"). With the homes unliveable and lawsuits pending, Rovereto has offered to buy the homes—at a reduced price.

◙ **SIGHTS.** The **Castello di Rovereto,** V. Castelbarco, 7, was the first building to be erected during Venice's construction of the city. The **Museo della Guerra** (Museum of War), inside the castle, opened in 1921 and showcases armor and weapons. (☎ 0464 43 81 00. Open July-Sept. Tu-F 10am-6pm, Sa-Su 9:30am-6:30pm; Mar.-June and Oct.-Nov. Tu-Su 8:30am-12:30pm and 2-6pm. Castle and museum €5.20.) A 20min. walk or a short car or bike ride from town, the **Bell of Peace,** on V. Miravalle, is the largest ringing bell in the world. It was cast in 1924 from 226.39 tons of bronze recycled from the canons of the 19 nations involved in WWI, and later blessed by Pope Paul VI. (☎ 0464 43 44 12. Open daily 9am-noon and 2-4pm. From June 15 to Sept. 15 you can attend the nightly ringing of the bell 9-9:30pm. €1.03.) The **Civic Museum,** Borgo Santa Caterina, 41, provides guided tours to the **Dinosaur Tracks** in the southern part of Rovereto. Three hundred and fifty tracks left by herbivores and carnivores over 200 million years ago are visible along a steep slope of an ancient landslide. (☎ 0464 43 90 55. Call to arrange a tour.)

EMILIA-ROMAGNA

Go to Florence, Venice, and Rome to sightsee, but come to Emilia-Romagna to eat. Italy's wealthiest wheat- and dairy-producing region covers the fertile plains of the Po River Valley and fosters the finest culinary traditions on the Italian Peninsula. Gorge yourself on Parmesan cheese and *prosciutto*, Bolognese fresh pasta and *mortadella*, and Ferrarese *salama* and *grana* cheese. Complement these dishes with fine regional wines like Parma's sparkling red *Lambrusco*.

Although the Romans originally settled this region, most of the visible ruins are remnants of medieval structures. Outside the towns, the uninterrupted plains seem to stretch forever, and the cold gray fog of winter—replaced in summer by silver haze and stifling heat—magnifies the illusion of distance. Emilia-Romagna, a stronghold of the left since the 19th-century rise of the Italian Socialist movement, has a look, feel, and taste unique in Italy.

HIGHLIGHTS OF EMILIA-ROMAGNA

EAVESDROP on impassioned political arguments among the intellectuals of **Bologna** (see below).

FEAST on palatable *prosciutto* and *parmigiano* in **Parma** (p. 317).

GO TO PIECES over the spectacular golden **Byzantine mosaics** in **Ravenna** (p. 319).

LOUNGE on **Rimini's** snow-white **beaches** (p. 323).

TASTE the richness of **Modena's balsamic vinegar** (p. 313).

BOLOGNA
☎ 051

Bologna has been known since ancient times as the *grassa* (fat) and *dotta* (learned) city. Wheat, grain, and wine from the surrounding countryside are transformed into rich, flavorful dishes. The city houses Europe's oldest university, founded in 1088 as a law school by a group of scholars trying to settle the disputes between the Holy Roman Empire and the papacy. Academic liberalism drives political activism—minority groups, student alliances, and the national gay organization all find a voice (and listening ears) in Bologna. All eyes, however, are on Bologna's art. Painterly treasures inhabit numerous museums and churches, whose 700-year-old porticoes line wide, straight streets.

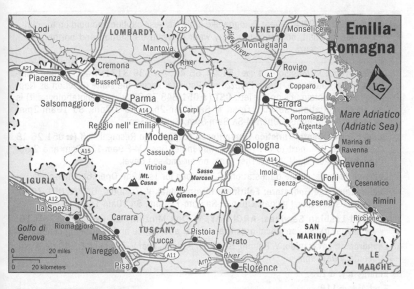

TRANSPORTATION

Flights: Aeroporto G. Marconi (☎051 647 9615), at Borgo Panigale, northwest of city center. The **Aerobus** (☎051 29 02 90) runs to airport from Track D outside train station (every 15min., 5:30am-11:57pm, €4.50).

Trains: Info office open daily 7am-9pm. **Luggage storage** available (see below). To: **Florence** (1½hr., every 2hr., 4:03am-10:48pm, €5-7.10); **Milan** (3hr., 2-3 per hr., 2:53am-10:16pm, €10.10); and **Rome** (4hr., 1-2 per hr., 12:32am-8:48pm, €21.41); and **Venice** (2hr., every hr., 6:02am-11pm, €10.12).

Buses: ATC (☎051 29 02 90), in P. XX Settembre. To reach the piazza, turn left as you exit train station. To **Ferrara** (1hr., 1-2 per hr., 6:35am-8pm, €3.30). **Terminal Bus** (☎051 24 21 50), next to ATC ticket counter, provides Eurolines bus service. Open M-F 9am-1pm and 3-6:30pm, Sa 9-1 and 3-5pm, Su 3-5:30pm.

Public Transportation: ATC (☎051 29 02 90). ATC's efficient buses get crowded in the early afternoon and evening. Intracity tickets (€1) are good 1hr. after validation on board. Purchase at newsstands, self-service machines, or *tabacchi*. Buses #25 and 30 run up V. Marconi and across V. Ugo Bassi and V. Rizzoli from train station.

Car Rental: Hertz, V. Amendola, 16 (☎051 25 48 30; fax 25 48 52), straight ahead when exiting the train station. Open M-F 8am-1pm and 2-6pm, Sa 8am-1pm.

Taxis: C.A.T.: ☎051 53 41 41. **Radiotaxi:** ☎051 37 27 27. Available 24hr.

ORIENTATION AND PRACTICAL INFORMATION

From the station, turn left on **Viale Pietro Pietramellara** until you come to **Piazza XX Settembre**. From the piazza, take **Via dell'Indipendenza,** which leads straight into **Piazza del Nettuno;** behind it is **Piazza Maggiore**, the city center. V. dell'Indipendenza intersects **Via Ugo Bassi,** which runs west, and **Via Rizzoli,** which runs east to **Piazza Porta Ravegnana**. **Via Zamboni** and **Strada Maggiore** lead out of this piazza.

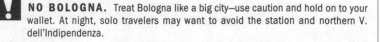

NO BOLOGNA. Treat Bologna like a big city—use caution and hold on to your wallet. At night, solo travelers may want to avoid the station and northern V. dell'Indipendenza.

Tourist Office: P. Maggiore, 1 (☎051 24 65 41; fax 639 3171; www.comune.bologna.it/bolognaturismo), in the Palazzo del Podesta. Facing the same direction as Neptune in the fountain, it's on the left. **CST** (☎051 648 76 07; www.prenotabologna.it) is an accommodations service. Open M-Sa 10am-2pm and 3-7pm, Su 10am-2pm. **Branch office** at airport. Open M-Sa 8am-8pm, Su 9am-3pm.

Budget Travel: Centro Turistico Studentesco (CTS), Largo Respighi, 2/f (☎051 26 18 02 or 23 48 62), next to the Teatro Communale. Open M-F 9am-12:30pm and 2:30-6pm. BIJ tickets and HI cards. Discounts on air and sea travel.

Luggage Storage: At the train station. €3 per bag for 1st 12hr. Open 6am-midnight.

English-Language Bookstore: Feltrinelli International, V. Zamboni, 6/7 (☎051 26 82 10). Novels and travel guides. Open M-Sa 9am-7:30pm, Su 10am-1:30pm.

Gay and Lesbian Services: ARCI-GAY, V. Don Minzoni, 18 (☎051 649 4416; www.arcigay.it). Sociopolitical organization with a reference and counseling center.

Laundromat: Lavarapido, V. Petroni, 38/b, off P. Verdi, near V. Zamboni. €3.40 per wash. Open daily 9am-9pm.

Emergency: ☎113.

First Aid: ☎118.

Police: P. Galileo, 7 (☎051 640 1111).

Pharmacy: P. Maggiore, 6/b (☎051 23 85 09).

Hospital: Ospedale Policlinico Sant'Orsola, V. Massarenti, 9 (☎051 636 3111).

Internet Access: Comune di Bologna, P. Maggiore, 6 (☎051 20 31 84), 3 DSL-equipped computers. Booked weeks ahead in high season. Sign up at the office. Free. Open M-F 8:30am-7pm, Sa 8:30am-2pm. **Bar College,** Largo Respighi 6/d (☎051 22 96 24) next to the Teatro Communale. €3.10 for 30min. Open daily 8am-midnight.

Post Office: (☎051 23 06 99), P. Minghetti, southeast of P. Maggiore, off V. Farini. Open M-F 8am-6:30pm, Sa 8:30am-7pm. **Currency exchange.** Also in train station (☎051 24 34 25). Open M-F 8am-1pm, Sa 8:15am-12:20pm.

Postal Code: 40100.

ACCOMMODATIONS

Bologna's hotels are rather pricey; reservations are recommended.

Albergo Panorama, V. Livraghi, 1, 4th fl. (☎051 22 18 02; fax 26 63 60; panorama.hotel@libero.it). Take V. Ugo Bassi from P. del Nettuno, then take the 3rd left. Prime location and sparklingly clean hotel. Enormous rooms with high ceilings, hardwood floors, and lots of sunshine, all with TV. Communal bathroom is huge and pristine. Singles €47; doubles €62, with bath €78; triples €78. AmEx/MC/V. ➍

Ostello due Torre San Sisto (HI), V. Viadagola, 5 (☎/fax 051 50 18 10), off V. San Donato, in Località di San Sisto, 6km northeast of the center of town. Tourist office has map with directions. Take bus #93 from Marconi St. (available M-Sa) or #301 from the *autostazione* (only a few trips per day). Ask the driver for the San Sisto stop. Exit bus and cross street; hostel is yellow building on right with yellow-and-green metal fence. Large building in a tranquil setting. Laundry service, basketball court, and reading room. Wheelchair-accessible. Reception 7am-noon and 5-11:30pm. Curfew midnight. Dorms €12, €3.50 extra for nonmembers. Family rooms €13-14 per person. ➊

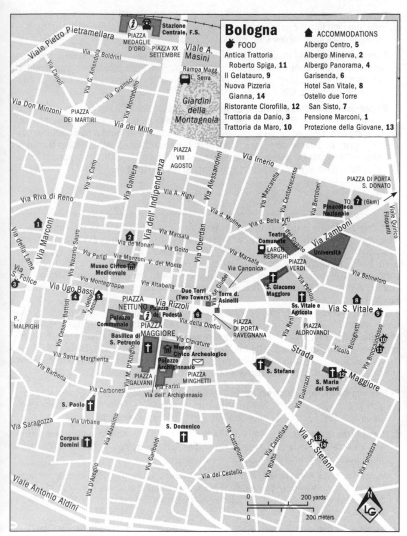

Bologna

🍴 FOOD

Antica Trattoria
  Roberto Spiga, **11**
Il Gelatauro, **9**
Nuova Pizzeria
  Gianna, **14**
Ristorante Clorofilla, **12**
Trattoria da Danio, **3**
Trattoria da Maro, **10**

🏠 ACCOMMODATIONS

Albergo Centro, **5**
Albergo Minerva, **2**
Albergo Panorama, **4**
Garisenda, **6**
Hotel San Vitale, **8**
Ostello due Torre
San Sisto, **7**
Pensione Marconi, **1**
Protezione della Giovane, **13**

NORTHEAST ITALY

Hotel San Vitale, V. S. Vitale, 94 (☎051 22 59 66; fax 23 93 96). Follow V. Rizzoli past the towers onto V. S. Vitale. 17 simple, clean rooms with TV and bath. Wheelchair-accessible. Beautiful outdoor garden in back with benches. Singles €52-57; doubles €68-78; triples €84-96. ❺

Albergo Centro, V. della Zecca, 2, 3rd fl. (☎051 22 51 14; fax 23 51 62; werterg@tin.it). Take V. Ugo Bassi from P. Nettuno and take 2nd left onto V. della Zecca. Elegant, spacious rooms, all with bath, dark drapery, and wood floors. A/C on request. Breakfast €8. Singles €49-67; doubles €72-88; triples €114. AmEx/MC/V. ❺

Albergo Minerva, V. dé Monari, 3 (☎/fax 051 23 96 52), off V. dell'Indipendenza. A bit past its prime. Large rooms, all without bath. Doubles €52; triples €62. MC/V. ❹

Garisenda, Galleria Leone, 1, 3rd fl. (☎051 22 43 69; fax 22 10 07). Down V. Rizzoli and turn right into the gallery mall. Homey and comfortable. Breakfast included. Singles €42; doubles €62; triples €83. AmEx/MC/V. ❹

Pensione Marconi, V. Marconi, 22 (☎051 26 28 32). Turn right from station and then left onto V. Amendola, which becomes V. Marconi. The large rooms are reminiscent of empty office spaces—high ceilings and squeaky clean gray floors. Singles €34-43; doubles €53-68; triples €90 (all with bath). ❹

Protezione della Giovane, V. S. Stefano, 45 (☎051 22 55 73). Just past the church on the right-hand side. Ring the buzzer and climb the large back staircase. Beautiful old building with frescoed ceilings and large French windows overlooks a quiet but inaccessible garden. 1 large dormitory. Most rooms are partitioned into doubles with new wooden furnishings. Well-used bathrooms. Continental breakfast included. Curfew 10:30pm. Women only. Dorms €13, per month €336.70. ❶

◪ FOOD

Bologna's cuisine centers on fresh, handmade pasta in all shapes and sizes. The best of the stuffed pastas are *tortellini*, made with ground meat, or *tortelloni*, made with ricotta and spinach. Try Bologna's namesake dish, *spaghetti alla bolognese*, pasta with a hefty meat and tomato sauce. Bologna is renowned for its large variety of salami and ham, including *mortadella*, the Italian version of "bologna," but with no resemblance to the processed American version.

Restaurants cluster on side streets minutes away from the town center; try the areas around V. Augusto Righi, V. Piella, and V. Saragozza for traditional *trattorie*. **Mercato delle Erbe,** V. Ugo Bassi, 27, is a vast indoor market that sells produce, cheeses, meats, and bread. (Open M-W 7am-1:15pm and 5-7pm, Th and Sa 7am-1:15pm, F 7am-1:15pm and 4:30-7:30pm.) A **PAM supermarket,** V. Marconi, 26, is by the intersection of V. Riva di Reno. (Open daily 7:45am-8pm.)

▧ **Trattoria Da Maro,** V. Broccaindosso, 71B (☎051 22 73 04), between Strada Maggiore and V. San Vitale. Locals chatter over plates of *tagliatelle. Primi* €5-6, *secondi* €5-7. Open M 8-10:15pm, Tu-Sa noon-2:30pm and 8-10:15pm. AmEx/MC/V. ❸

▧ **Nuova Pizzeria Gianna,** V. S. Stefano 76A (☎051 22 25 16). Known to loyal fans simply as "Mamma's." Chat with Gianna as she crafts incomparable pizza (€2.90-6.70). Open M-Sa 9am-midnight. Closed Aug. ❶

Antica Trattoria Roberto Spiga, V. Broccaindosso, 21A (☎051 23 00 63). Between Strada Maggiore and V. San Vitale. Family-run restaurant serves hearty food. Menu changes daily. Bologna specialty €13 (W only). *Primi* €6-8, *secondi* €8-10. Open M-Sa noon-2:30pm and 8-11pm, Su noon-2:30pm. Closed Aug. MC/V. ❸

Trattoria Da Danio, V. S. Felice, 50A (☎051 55 52 02). Casual *trattoria* specializes in fish but has an extensive menu. 3-course meal with drinks €10.33. *Primi* €5.50-8, *secondi* €4.50-10.50. Open daily noon-3pm and 7-11pm. AmEx/MC/V. ❸

Ristorante Clorofilla, Strada Maggiore, 64C (☎051 23 53 43). A hip, almost exclusively vegetarian restaurant. Imaginative salads €5-6, hot dishes about €5-8. Open M-Sa 12:15-2:45pm and 7:30pm-11pm. In winter, tea served 4-6:30pm. MC/V. ❷

Il Gelatauro, V. S. Vitale, 82B (☎051 23 00 49). Tame the mythical half-man, half-monster, all-*gelato* beast. Fresh fruit *gelato,* served as a sandwich in a brioche for the daring. Those under 14 can spin the Wheel-of-Gelatauro for a free cone. Cones around €2. Open Tu-Su 11am-11pm. Closed Aug. ❶

👁 SIGHTS

Twenty-five miles of porticoed buildings line the streets of Bologna, the answer to a housing crisis that started in the 14th century. The building boom lasted several centuries, resulting in a mix of Gothic, Renaissance, and Baroque styles.

PIAZZA MAGGIORE. A display wall of photographs of victims to violence behind the fountain of Neptune, is a chilling reminder of Italy's struggle in WWII and of more recent right-wing attacks, including the 1980 bombing of the Bologna train station. The Romanesque **Palazzo de Podestà** was remodeled by Aristotle Fioravanti, the designer of Moscow's Kremlin. The columns of the vault, rather than the ground, support this 15th-century feat of architectural engineering. Directly across from the *palazzo* is the **Basilica di San Petronio,** designed by Antonio da Vincenzo in 1390. The *Bolognese* originally plotted to make their basilica larger than St. Peter's in Rome, but the jealous Church ordered that the funds be used instead to build the nearby Palazzo Archiginnasio. The cavernous Gothic interior played host to both the Council of Trent (when it was not meeting in Trent) and the 1530 ceremony in which Pope Clement VII gave Italy to the German emperor Charles V. The **zodiac sundial** on the floor of the north aisle is the largest in Italy. The tiny museum in back has a beautiful collection of chalices and illuminated books. *(P. Maggiore, 3. Basilica and museum open daily 7:15am-1:30pm and 2:30-6:30pm.)*

PALAZZO ARCHIGINNASIO. This *palazzo*, formerly a university building, now houses the town library. The upstairs theater was constructed in 1637 by Antonio Levanti in order to teach anatomy to local students. The walls are decorated with statues of pompous-looking university doctors lecturing. In the center of the ceiling, Apollo watches over the dissection table below. Notice the two statues to the right as you enter. These skinless "anatomical" men illustrate 17th-century conceptions of musculature. *(V. della Archiginnasio, right after the Museo Archeologico. Follow the signs from P. Maggiore. ☎ 051 23 64 88. Open daily 9am-1pm. Closed 2 wk. in Aug. Free.)*

PINACOTECA NAZIONALE. The *Pinacoteca* traces the progress of Bolognese artists from the Roman Age to Mannerism with works by Giotto, Titian, and Giovanni Battista. It also contains a well-preserved frescoed room depicting courtly life from the 1500s. In **Gallery 26,** there is a beautiful portrait by Francesco Albani of the *Madonna e Bambino.*

IN RECENT NEWS

OLD GUARD

They stand motionless, two at a time, for up to six hours. Clad in black capes and somber expressions, an estimated 400 skinheads from around Italy have been keeping vigil in a *Guardia D'Onore* at the grave of Benito Mussolini since 2001.

"We're trying to recreate a sense of identity which is lacking among young people in Italy nowadays," ███ told the BBC. "People are ███ to study the many positive things this man did for the Italian peninsula."

In the tiny northern town of Predappio, where the Italian dictator was born, a recent resurgence of Fascist sentiment draws an estimated 70,000 visitors a year. Souvenir shops peddle ashtrays and cufflinks emblazoned with the face of *Il Duce,* and sympathizers and tourists alike flock to the October 28 parade marking the 1922 Fascist march on Rome.

While most Italians harbor little nostalgia for the 20 years of iron-fisted Mussolini rule, some historians argue that their reluctance to come to terms with their past has partially enabled the revival of Fascist sentiment. Others see the right's mainstream comeback as bolstering the fringes.

Meanwhile, in Predappio, the town's leftist mayor has opened Mussoli's birthplace to the public in an effort to replace nostalgic memory with historical, and to encourage debate about the Fascist past and its political future.

Gallery 22 has several large, impressive canvases, among them Giorgio Vasari's *Christ in Casa di Marta*. *(V. delle Belle Arti, 56, off V. Zamboni. ☎ 054 24 32 22. Open Tu-Su 9am-6:30pm. €7, students €3.50.)*

PIAZZA DEL NETTUNO. This piazza contains Giambologna's famous 16th-century bronze fountain *Neptune and Attendants*. Affectionately called "The Giant," Neptune reigns over a collection of water-babies and sirens. This statue was designed with a spiral progression, enticing viewers to walk in a circle around it.

PALAZZO COMMUNALE. Nicolò dell'Arca's terra-cotta *Madonna* and a Menganti bronze statue of Pope Gregory XIV adorn the outside of this *palazzo*. The upstairs houses one of Bologna's prettiest museums, the **Collezioni Comunali d'Arte.** The impressive art collection is displayed among period furniture and elaborate frescoes. The adjoining **Museo Morandi** is dedicated to the early 20th-century painter, Morandi. Many of his works are still lifes, influenced by the artists Cezzanne and Piero della Francesca. *(P. Maggiore, 6. Collezioni Comunali ☎ 051 20 36 29. Open Tu-Sa 9am-6:30pm, Su 10am-6:30pm. €4, students €2. Museo Morandi ☎ 051 20 33 32. Open Tu-Su 10am-6pm. €4, students €2.)*

MUSEO CIVICO ARCHEOLOGICO. This collection houses fascinating ancient artifacts. On the first floor are Bronze and Stone Age tools, and an overwhelming collection of Greek vases, statues, and Roman inscriptions. There's a stuffed crocodile in the Egyptian section downstairs. *(V. Archiginnasio, 2. Follow the signs from P. Maggiore. ☎ 051 23 52 04. Open Tu-Sa 9am-6:30pm, Su 10am-6:30pm. €4, students €2.)*

THE TWO TOWERS. A land shift botched an attempt to build an observation tower for the civic defense system (the lower, tilting Garisendi tower), so the city tried again with greater success. Today, you can climb the 498 steps of the **Torre degli Asinelli,** for an amazing view. The **Torre degli Garisenda** is closed to the public. *(P. Porta Ravegana, at the end of V. Rizzoli. Open May-Aug. 9am-6pm; Sept.-Apr. 9am-5pm. €3.)*

MUSEO CIVICO MEDIOEVALE. This extensive museum contains an interesting assortment of objects from mosaics and shoes to stone sculptures and sarcophagi. There are also curiosities from later centuries, including a collection of miniature bronze figurines from the Renaissance. *(V. Manzoni, 4. Off V. dell'Indipendenza, near P. Maggiore. ☎ 051 20 39 30. Open Tu-Su 9am-6:30pm, Su 10am-6:30pm. €4, students €2.)*

CHURCHES

CHIESA SANTO STEFANO. The present church sits atop the remains of a group of seven basilicas once used by ancient Egyptian monks. The Benedictines later built the collection of buildings into a monastery. A stone tablet found here proves this land was once the site of a temple to the goddess Isis. *(In P. Santo Stefano. Follow V. S. Stefano from V. Rizzoli. ☎ 051 22 32 56. Open daily 9am-noon and 3:30-6pm.)* Only four of the seven churches of the original Romanesque **basilica** remain. Bologna's patron saint, San Petronio, is buried in the **Chiesa di San Sepolcro** in the center of the group. In the rear courtyard is the **Basin of Pilate,** where the governor absolved himself of responsibility for Christ's death. *(Modest dress required.)*

CHIESA DI SANTA MARI DEI SERVI. In this well-preserved Gothic construction, columns support an unusual combination of arches and ribbed vaulting. Cimabue's *Maestà* hangs behind the altar of a chapel on the left. Giovanni Antonio Montorsoli, a pupil of Michelangelo, executed the exquisitely sculptured altar. *(Take Strada Maggiore to P. Aldrovandi. ☎ 051 22 68 07. Open daily 7am-1pm and 3:30-8pm.)*

CHIESA DELLE SANTISSIME VITALE E AGRICOLA. The facade of this church incorporates shards of capitals and columns from Roman temples. Below lies an 11th-century crypt, with paintings by Francia and Sano di Pietro. There is also a sculpture of Christ based on the anatomical clues suggested by the Holy Shroud of Turin. *(V. S. Vitale, 48. ☎ 051 22 05 70. Open daily 7:45am-noon and 3:45-7:30pm.)*

CHIESA DI SAN GIACOMO MAGGIORE. A melange of Romanesque and Gothic styles, this church adjoins **Oratorio di Santa Cecilia,** containing a cycle of frescoes showing the marriage and martyrdom of St. Cecilia. *(Follow V. Zamboni to P. Rossini. ☎ 051 22 59 70. Open daily 6:30am-noon and 3:30-6:30pm. Enter the oratorio from V. Zamboni, 15. Open daily 10am-1pm and 3-7pm.)*

CHIESA SAN DOMENICO. The inside houses the tomb of St. Dominic—an elaborate marble carving by Nicolò Pisano, adorned with an angel by the young Michelangelo. *(From P. Maggiore, follow V. dell'Archiginnasio to V. Farini and turn right on V. Garibaldi. ☎ 051 22 32 56. Open daily 7:30am-1pm and 2:30-8pm.)*

🎭 🎵 NIGHTLIFE AND ENTERTAINMENT

Every year from mid-June to mid-September, the city *comune* sponsors an **entertainment festival** of dance, theatre, music, cinema, and art shows. Many events are free, or cost around €5. If you visit Bologna during the summer, contact the tourist office for a program of events. The **Teatro Comunale,** Largo Respighi, 1, hosts operas, symphony concerts, and ballet performances with world-class performers. To order tickets in advance, send a fax, email, or sign up outside the ticket office two days before performances. (☎ 051 52 99 99; fax 32 99 95; boxoffice@comunale-bologna.it; www.comunalebologna.it. 10% surcharge for pre-order. Tickets €5-200. Box office open M-F 3:30-7pm and Sa 9:30am-12:30pm and 3:30-7pm.)

Bologna's student population accounts for the large number of bars, pubs and clubs in the city. During June and July, most nightclubs shut down and the party scene moves outdoors. Always call ahead for hours and cover; info changes frequently, especially in summer. The tourist office provides an extensive list of temporary, outdoor summer music venues. But don't expect much livelihood in August—the outdoor *discoteche* shut down, and the city heads to the beach.

▨ Cassero, V. Don Minzoni, 18 (☎ 051 649 4416). Take V. Marconi to P. dei Martiri and turn left on the street. The breezy rooftop terrace offers beautiful vistas. Dance the night away catch one of the weekly shows in the coolest club in town. Open daily 10pm-2am.

Cluricaune, V. Zamboni, 18B (☎ 051 26 34 19). An old Irish bar packed with students. Pints €3.10-4.20. W night happy hour until 10:30pm. Open daily Su-F 11am-3am, Sa 4pm-3am.

Cantina Bentivoglio, V. Mascarella, 4B (☎ 051 26 54 16), near Largo Respighi and the Teatro Comunale. Upscale bar with food and wine (from €5). Live jazz and a relaxed atmosphere under an umbrella-covered patio. Walls are lined with wine bottles. Open Tu-Su 8pm-2am; closed 1½ months in summer. AmEx/MC/V.

Made in Bo, Parco Nord-V. Stalingrado (☎ 051 53 38 80; www.madeinbo.it), accessible by bus #25. No bus service back; cabs €10-20. Open-air disco and multiple bars on a floodlit hillside. One of Bologna's best summer clubs, this disco gets moving around 11pm. Open May to mid-July.

SPORTS

See the pride of Bologna play *calcio* (soccer) at **Stadio Comunale,** V. Andrea Costa, 174. Take bus #21 from the train station or 14 from Porta Isaia. The season runs from September to June, with games on Sunday afternoons. Tickets for games against popular clubs such as Juventus or AC Milan tend to sell fast. Call the Bologna Football Club (☎ 051 57 74 51) for tickets and information.

FERRARA ☎ 0532

Rome has its mopeds, Venice its boats, and Ferrara its *biciclette*. For a city that boasts 160,000 bicycles and 135,000 inhabitants, it's no wonder that a biker is a more common sight than a pedestrian. Businessmen sporting suits and toting briefcases, old ladies with grocery bags, and fashionable Gucci-wearing girls with short skirts and spiked sandals pedal through Ferrara's jumble of thoroughfares and twisting medieval roads, off-limits to automobiles. The result is a city center that's friendlier to pedestrian traffic, with buildings free from the heavy veneer of diesel exhaust. Ferrara was ruled by the Este dynasty from 1208 to 1598. When not murdering relatives, these enlightened rulers founded a university that attracted Petrarch, Mantegna, and Titian. Grab a bike and pedal through the open, harmoniously designed city they left behind.

⌐ TRANSPORTATION

Trains: Ticket office open 7am-9pm. **Luggage storage** (see below). Trains to: **Bologna** (30min., 1-2 per hr., 1:42am-9:38pm, €2.75); **Padua** (1hr., every hr., 3:52am-11:07pm, €4.03); **Ravenna** (1hr., 1-3 per hr., 6:12am-8:15pm, €4.10); **Rome** (3-4hr., 7 per day, 7:47am-7:25pm, €30.73); and **Venice** (2hr., 1-2 per hr., 3:52am-10:11pm, €5.73).

Buses: ACFT (☎0532 59 94 92) and **GGFP.** Main terminal on V. Ramparti S. Paolo. Most buses also leave from the train station. From the bus #2 stop, turn onto V. S. Paolo and head to the building labeled *biglietteria.* Open daily 6:15am-8pm. To Ferrara's **beaches** (1hr., 12 per day, 7:30am-6:50pm, €4.05-4.80), **Bologna** (1½hr., 17 per day, 5:15am-7:35pm, €3.30), and **Modena** (1½hr., every hr., 6:22am-7:05pm, €4.50). Buses run less frequently on Su.

Taxi: Radiotaxi (☎0532 90 09 00). Open 24hr.

Bike Rental: Pirani e Bagni, P. Stazione, 2 (☎0532 77 21 90). Open M-F 6:30am-1pm and 3:30pm-7:30pm, Sa 7am-2pm. €7 per day.

✴ 🔋 ORIENTATION AND PRACTICAL INFORMATION

To get to the center of town, turn left out of the train station onto **Viale Costituzione.** This road becomes **Viale Cavour** and runs to the **Castello Estense** (1km). Alternatively, take bus #2 to the Castello stop or bus #1 or 9 to the post office (every 15-20min., 7am-8:20pm, €0.83). Turn right after the *castello* onto **Corso Martiri della Libertà,** which leads up to the duomo.

Tourist Office: (☎0532 20 93 70), in Castello Estense, near P. Cattedrale. Open daily 9am-1pm and 3-5:30pm.

Currency Exchange: Banca Nazionale de Lavoro, C. Porta Reno, 19. Open M-F 8:30am-1:30pm and 3:15-4:35pm, Sa 8:30am-noon.

Luggage Storage: In train station. €1.55-2.07 per 6hr. Open 24hr.

Emergency: ☎ 113 or 0532 20 31 31. **Ambulance:** ☎ 118.

Police: C. Ercole I d'Este, 26 (☎0532 29 43 11), off Largo Castello.

Red Cross: ☎0532 20 94 00.

Pharmacy: Fides, C. Giovecca, 125 (☎0532 20 25 24). **Comunale #1,** C. Porta Mare, 114 (☎0532 75 32 84).

Hospital: Ospedale Sant'Anna, C. Giovecca, 203 (☎0532 23 61 11). Across from Palazzina Marfrissa near P. Medaglie D'Oro, a gateway to the old town.

Internet Access: Speedy Internet Club, C. Porta Po, 37 (☎0532 24 80 92), across the street from the youth hostel. €3.10 per 30min., €4.65 per 45min. Also has photocopy and fax service. Open M-F 9am-1pm and 2:30-7:30pm, Sa 10am-1pm.

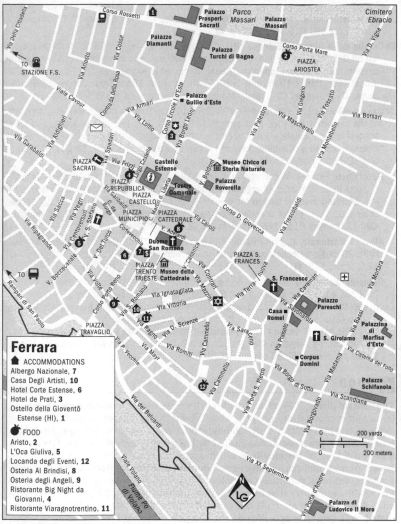

Ferrara

🏠 ACCOMMODATIONS
Albergo Nazionale, **7**
Casa Degli Artisti, **10**
Hotel Corte Estense, **6**
Hotel de Prati, **3**
Ostello della Gioventõ
  Estense (HI), **1**

🍴 FOOD
Aristo, **2**
L'Oca Giuliva, **5**
Locanda degli Eventi, **12**
Osteria Al Brindisi, **8**
Osteria degli Angeli, **9**
Ristorante Big Night da
  Giovanni, **4**
Ristorante Viaragnotrentino, **11**

Post Office: V. Cavour, 29 (☎ 0532 20 75 12), a block toward train station from the *castello. Fermo Posta.* Also **exchanges currency.** Open M-Sa 8am-6:30pm.

Postal Code: 44100.

🏠 ACCOMMODATIONS & CAMPING

Ferrara is an easy daytrip from Bologna or Modena, but it also has a wealth of inexpensive accommodations.

🏨 **Hotel de Prati,** V. Padiglioni, 5 (☎ 0532 24 19 05; fax 24 19 66). From Viale Cavour, turn onto C. Ercole d'Este and take your 1st right. New 3-star hotel with excellent rates. Yellow hallways artfully decorated with colorful abstract paintings. 12 rooms with bath,

A/C, TV, fridge, and authentic 18th-century wooden armoires. Internet available. Buffet breakfast included. Wheelchair-accessible. Singles €47-65; doubles €68-105; suites €130. Extra bed €16. AmEx/MC/V. ❹

■ **Ostello della Gioventù Estense (HI),** C. B. Rossetti, 24 (☎/fax 0532 20 42 27). Turn left off C. Ercole I d'Este from the *castello*, or take bus #4c from station and ask for the *castello* stop. New and sparkling clean. Comfortable sitting area and Internet and TV room. Reception 7-10am and 5-10:30pm. Lockout 10am-5pm. Curfew 11:30pm. Dorms €13; doubles €29; family rooms €14.50 per person. AmEx/MC/V. ❶

■ **Casa degli Artisti,** V. Vittoria, 66 (☎0532 76 10 38). From C. Martiri d. Libertà, turn left at the cathedral and then right onto V. S. Romano. Turn left onto V. Ragno and take another left immediately. Hotel is on the left, in a bright yellow building. Large, clean, simple rooms in a very quiet, central location, for a fabulous price. Singles €21; doubles €38, with bath €55. ❷

Hotel Corte Estense, V. Correggiari, 4 (☎0532 24 21 76; fax 24 64 05). Turn right off C. Porta Reno right after Albergo Nazionale. Refurbished 17th-century palace is charming. Enclosed outdoor terrace for breakfast. All rooms with bath, A/C, and TV. Wheelchair-accessible. Buffet breakfast and parking included. Singles €62-72.50; doubles €98-124; triples €130-166. AmEx/MC/V. ❺

Albergo Nazionale, C. Porta Reno, 32 (☎/fax 0532 20 96 04). The hotel is on your right. 20 clean, eclectically decorated rooms with bath and TV. Singles €40; doubles €65; triples €78. ❹

Camping: Estense, V. Gramicia, 76 (☎/fax 0532 75 23 96), 1km from the city center. Take bus #1 to P. S. Giovanni (€0.83). From the church next to the bus stop another bus heads straight to the campground (every 20min., 2-8:20pm). Bus route is temporary, so check with the ACFT office in the train station before you head off. If driving from the castle, take C. Ercole I d'Este, make a right onto C. Porta Mare, and then a left onto V. Gramicia. It's ahead on the right, just past V. Pannonio. Open year-round 8am-10pm. €4.50 per person, €6.50 per car. MC/V. ❶

🗘 FOOD

The verdant plains of Ferrara provide a wholesome store of staples, which *cuoche* (cooks) incorporate into recipes passed down through generations. The *salama da sugo* is a 15th-century dish combining pork meats, spices, and wine. *Pasticcio alla ferrarese* is a sweet bread stuffed with macaroni and meat sauce. *Passatelli,* a flavorful type of vermicelli, is a thin spaghetti made from a mixture of eggs, bread crumbs, and parmesan cheese, cooked in chicken broth. Herring, clams, scallops, sea-bass, and mullet are integral to a diet dependent upon seafood. Corpus Domini nuns invented Ferrara's most famous dessert, the *pampepato* (rich chocolate cake with almonds and candied fruit, coated with a thick layer of chocolate icing), centuries ago. *Mandurlin dal pont,* dry, hard biscuits of eggs, sugar, and almonds were first made by *Ferraresi* fishermen's wives for their daily damp journey along the river Po. For wine, try the slightly sparkling *Uva D'Oro* (Golden Grape), compliments of Renata di Francia, who is said who have brought the grapes from France to ferment into a wine suitable for her 16th-century marriage to Duca Ercole II d'Este. The **Mercato Comunale** is on V. Garibaldi. (Open daily 7am-1:30pm and 4:30-7:30pm; closed Th and Sa afternoon.)

■ **Osteria Al Brindisi,** V. G. degli Adelardi, 11 (☎0532 20 91 42). V. Adelardi is through the arch on left side of duomo. This *Osteria* dating from 1435 has wined or dined Copernicus, Cellini, and Pope John Paul II. Hip crowds enjoy inexpensive, traditional dishes at tables inside and out. *Primi* from €4.50. Open Tu-Su 9am-1am. MC/V. ❸

L'Oca Giuliva, V. di S. Stefano, 38 (☎0532 20 76 28). Classy restaurant in a 15th-century structure hung with 20th-century artwork. *Primi* €7-10, *secondi* around €13. Open W-Su 12:30-2pm and 8-10pm, Tu 8-10pm. AmEx/MC/V. ❹

Osteria degli Angeli, V. delle Volte, 4 (☎0532 76 43 76). From the *basilica*, take C. Porta Reno and turn left under the arch onto V. delle Volte. Cozy, quaint, and housed in a 16th-century building. Hospitable service. Try their specialty *Segreto degli Angeli* (beef secret). *Primi* €7, *secondi* €8-11. Open Tu-Su noon-2pm and 7-10pm. MC/V. ❸

Ristorantino Viaragnotrentino, V. Ragno, 31a (☎0532 76 90 70). Turn left off V. S. Romano. Swanky restaurant serves eclectic Italian cuisine, like whole-wheat, thin *tagliatelle* with fried *lourgette*. Few menu options. *Primi* from €8, *secondi* €13. Open F-W 12:45-3pm and 7:50-10:30pm. MC/V. ❹

Locanda degli Eventi, V. Carlo Mayr, 21 (☎0532 76 13 47). Serves traditional local cuisine in a relaxing and comfortable setting. *Primi* €6.20, *secondi* €10. Open from Th-Tu 11am-3pm and 5-11:30pm. MC/V. ❸

Ristorante Italia Big Night da Giovanni, V. Largo Castello, 38 (☎0532 24 23 67). The name of this restaurant was inspired from the movie *Big Night*, the story of 2 Italian brothers struggling to "make it big" in America with their authentic Italian restaurant. Elegant dining and high quality fare. *Primi* €8-17, *secondi* €15-23. Open M-Sa 12:30-1:45pm and 8:15-10pm. MC/V. ❺

Aristo: Bar, Gelateria, Pasticceria, Paninoteca, P. Ariostea, 13, 15, 19 (☎0532 20 76 00). From the castle, walk down C. Ercole I D'Este, turn right onto C. Porta Mare, and walk 2 blocks. This eatery with patio seating offers several varieties of pizza, pastry, and *gelato*. Also has a bar and a video arcade. Open daily. MC/V. ❶

👁 SIGHTS

Under the tutelage of Leonello d'Este, humanist ruler and patron of the arts, Ferrara became an important artistic center with its own school of painting, called the *Officina Ferrarese*. Works by famous artists like Pisanello, Leon Battista Alberti, Piero della Francesca, and Titian grace the walls of the city's palaces. If you're yearning for more arboreal beauty, ride or walk down the tranquil 9km concourse that runs along the well-preserved medieval wall of the city. Any road out of Ferrara will lead you to the path.

▨CASTELLO ESTENSE. Towered, turreted, and moated, this 14th-century *castello* stands precisely in the center of town. Marquis Nicolo II knocked down houses and churches to build the fortress as protection against the disgruntled tax-paying masses. The castle balconies offer a panoramic view of the city. The dungeons, with 10ft. thick walls of stone and cement and three layers of barred windows, are not for the claustrophobic. *(☎0532 29 92 33. Open Tu-Su 9:30am-5pm. €4.10, students €3. Supplement for tower €1.)*

DUOMO SAN ROMANO. Dedicated to the city's patron saints, George and Maurelius, the cathedral is the sum product of numerous artists and architects' contributions throughout the centuries. Rosetti designed the tall slender arches and terracotta ornamented apse and Alberti executed the pink *campanile*. Across the street, the **Museo della Cattedrale** displays precious works from the church, including the *Officina Ferrarese* statues by Jacopo della Quercia and Cosmè Tura's 15th-century *San Giorgio* and *Annunciation*. *(Enter museum across the street from the duomo through the courtyard on V. S. Romano. Duomo open M-Sa 7:30am-noon and 3-6:30pm, Su 7:30am-12:30pm and 3:30-7:30pm. Museum ☎0532 76 12 99. Museum open daily 9am-1pm and 3-6pm. €4.20, students €2.)*

PALAZZO DIAMANTI. Built in 1493 by Biagio Rossetti, the palace has more than 800 stones polished in diamond shapes adorning the exterior facade. The *palazzo* hosts the **Galleria d'Arte Moderna e Contemporanea,** to the right as you enter, an extensive series of diverse, permanent modern art exhibitions. To the left is the **Pinacoteca Nazionale** which contains many massive Ferrarese school paintings. Most impressive are Carpaccio's *Passing of the Virgin* (1508) and Garofalo's incredibly detailed *Massacre of the Innocents.* Also noteworthy are two works by Bastianino of Ferrara in the first room as you enter: The *Last Judgement* and *Resurrection. (Down C. Ercole I d'Este just before the intersection of C. Rossetti. Open Tu-Su 9:30am-1:30pm and 3-6pm. Galleria ☎ 0532 20 99 88. €7.23, students €6.20. Pinacoteca ☎ 0532 20 58 44. €4, students €2. Combination ticket €8.30.)*

PALAZZO MASSARI. Once a 16th-century residence, the palace now houses a museum complex. On the first floor, the **Museo d'Arte Moderna e Contemporanea Filippo de Pisis** showcases early 20th-century art but primarily focuses on the progression of artist Filippo de Pisis, who made multiple nude male sketches. Upstairs, the lavish **Museo Ferrarese dell'Ottocento/Museo Giovanni Boldini** contains Boldoni's portraits of the early 20th century's most glamorous women, including his not-to-be-missed *A Woman in Pink. (C. Porta Mare, 9. Turn right off C. Ercole I d'Este. ☎ 0532 20 99 88. Museums open Tu-Su 9am-1pm and 3-6pm. Pisis €2. Ottocento/Boldini €4.20, students €2. Combination ticket €6.70, students €4.20.)*

SINAGOGHE E MUSEO EBRAICO. The city's Jewish museum is located in the heart of the ghetto, and contains art and documents that reflects religious traditions and tell the history of the Jews of Ferrara. The tourist office also has a map of Jewish itineraries throughout the city. *(V. Mazzini, 95. From the duomo, on the left side of the street. ☎ 0532 21 02 28. Guided tours Su-Th 10, 11am, and noon. €4, students €2.)*

CASA ROMEI. Giovanni Romei was an ambitious 15th-century merchant. His shrewd business sense funded his marriage into the d'Este family and the construction of this immense house, a typical Renaissance upper-class dwelling. The rooms and walls lack decoration, but it contains a pleasant courtyard. *(V. Savonarola, 30. From P. Cattedrale, take V. Adelardi left of the duomo and follow it straight until it becomes V. Savonarola. ☎ 0532 24 03 41. Open Tu-Su 8:30am-7:30pm. €2, students €1.)*

PALAZZINA MARFISA D'ESTE. This late Renaissance palace in miniature belonged to Francesco d'Este and features spectacularly frescoed ceilings. *(C. Giovecca, 170. Follow C. Gioveca from Largo Castello, or take bus #9. ☎ 0532 20 74 50. Open Tu-Su 9am-1pm, 3-6pm. €2, students €1.60. Combination with Schifanoia €6.70, students €4.20.)*

PALAZZO SCHIFANOIA. This *palazzo* was the d'Este family's retreat. Its main attraction is the faded Hall of the Months, with a renowned Renaissance fresco series. *(V. Scandiana, 23. From P. Cattedrale, follow V. Adelardi to V. Savonarola. Turn right onto V. Madama and left onto V. Scandiana. ☎ 0532 64 178. Open Tu-Su 9am-1pm and 3-6pm. €2, students €1.60. Combination with Palazzina Marfisa €6.70, students €4.20.)*

PALAZZO DI LUDOVICO IL MORO. A two-sided courtyard leads to this spacious palace, constructed in 1495 as a d'Este court official's residence. A Renaissance garden lies behind the palace, and some rooms still contain ceiling frescoes by Garofalo. Inside, the **Museo Archeologico Nazionale** showcases artifacts from Spina, the Greek-Etruscan city that disappeared under Adriatic waters 2,000 years ago. *(V. XX Settembre, 124. From Palazzo Schifanoia, it's a short walk down V. Porta d'Amore. From P. Trento Trieste, follow V. Mazzini, which turns into V. Saraceno, to the end; turn left onto V. Mayr and then right onto V. Borgovado. ☎ 0532 66 299. Open Tu-Su 9am-2pm. €4, students €2.)*

CIMITERO EBRAICO (JEWISH CEMETERY). Most of Ferrara's 19th- and 20th-century Jewish community is buried here. A monument commemorates the Ferrarese Jews murdered at Auschwitz. *(From the castello, head down C. Giovecca. Turn left on V. Montebello and continue to end of V. Vigne. ☎ 0532 75 13 37. Open Su-F 9am-4:30pm.)*

♫ ENTERTAINMENT

Each year on the last Sunday of May, Ferrara recreates the ancient **Palio di San Giorgio.** This event, dating from the 13th century, begins with a lively procession of delegates from the city's eight *contrade* (districts), followed by a series of four races in P. Ariostea: the boy's race, the girl's race, the donkey race, and finally, the great horse race. On Ferrara's seafood-heavy *tavola,* the eel is the "queen of cuisine." Appreciate the countless methods of eel-preparation at the annual **Eel Festival,** celebrated at the beginning of October in the province of Comacchio. During the 3rd or 4th week of August, street musicians and performers display their talents at the **Busker's Festival** (☎ 0532 24 93 37; www.ferrarabuskers.com). A free **Discobus** service sporadically runs between Ferrara and the hottest clubs. Check at the train or bus station for information.

MODENA ☎ 059

Modena boasts Luciano Pavarotti, the Ferrari and Maserati factories, and internationally-renowned balsamic vinegar. There are few sights or ancient structures, but the city abounds with colorful buildings and tantalizing food.

⬛ TRANSPORTATION

Trains (☎ 1478 88 088) depart from P. Dante Alighieri (info office open daily 8am-7pm) to **Bologna** (30min., every hr., €2.32); **Milan** (2hr., every hr., €8.90); and **Parma** (30min., 2 per hr., €3.15). **ATCM** buses (☎ 199 11 11 01) leave from V. Fabriani, off V. Monte Kosica, to the right of the train station, to **Ferrara** (every hr., €4.65) and **Maranello** (every 1-2hr., €2). Call a **taxi** at ☎ 059 37 42 42.

⬛⬛ ORIENTATION AND PRACTICAL INFORMATION

From the train station, take bus #7 or 11 (€1) to **Piazza Grande** and the center of town, or walk out of the station on **Via Galvini** and turn right on **Via Monte Kosica.** Turn left on **Via Ganaceto,** which leads directly to **Via Emilia.** Turn left on V. Emilia and walk several blocks to **Piazza Torre,** which opens into **Piazza Grande** on the left. V. Emilia changes names from **Via Emilia Ovest** on the west side of the center, to **Via Emilia Centro** in the center, and then to **Via Emilia Est** on the east.

> **Tourist Office:** V. Scudari, 12 (☎ 059 20 66 60; fax 20 66 59; iatmo@comune.modena.it). From P. Grande, take V. Castellaro and make the 1st left. Open M 3-6pm, Tu-Sa 9am-1pm and 3-6pm, Su 9am-1pm. **Informagiovani,** P. Grande, 17 (☎ 059 20 65 83), geared specifically to young people; computers also available. Open M-Sa 9am-1pm and 3-7pm.

> **Currency Exchange: Credito Italiano,** V. Emilia Centro, 102 (☎ 059 41 21 11), across from V. Scudari. Take a ticket at the door. Open M-F 8:20am-1:20pm and 3-4:30pm, Sa 8:20-12:45pm. **ATMs** in the Rolo Banca 1473 building, in P. Grande.

> **Emergency:** ☎ 118.

> **Police:** ☎ 113.

> **Ambulance: Blue Cross** (☎ 059 34 24 24).

> **First Aid:** ☎ 059 36 13 71 or 43 72 71.

> **Pharmacy:** Urgent care number (☎ 059 24 43 20). Look for the green sign outside any pharmacy to see which has late night service.

> **Hospital: Ospedale Civile** (☎ 059 43 51 11), in P. S. Agostino.

ACID TRIP. The art of balsamic vinegar production is one the *Modenese* take seriously. *Aceto balsamico* can be traced back to Roman times, although regular production didn't begin until a millennium later. In the 1400s, the Duke of Modena used it to ward off the plague; Italians soon came to appreciate the sweet and tangy vinegar for culinary rather than medicinal purposes. A few drops can be used to enhance foods like strawberries, cheese, and ice cream. Well-aged vinegars approach the consistency of port, and are sometimes sipped as *aperitivi*. The fresh base and careful aging process of Modenese vinegar set it apart. Instead of being fermented from an alcohol base, it is made directly from Trebbiano grapes. After simmering for hours, the juice is stored for up to a century in 500-year-old barrels. During this period, the vinegar is transferred several times to caskets made of different wood. The result is a smooth, rich-flavored vinegar that is unique and expensive—a 3½ oz. bottle can sell for €160. So precious is balsamic in Italy that it is often included in wedding dowries.

Internet Access: Informagiovane, P. Grande, 17. ID required. Registration €1.29. €2.58 per 2hr. Open M-Sa 9am-1pm and 3-7pm. **Netgate,** V. Berengano, 72/74 (☎059 23 64 83). Take V. Emilia to V. Emilia Ovest and turn right down the street. €4 per hr. Open Sept.-July M, W, and F 10am-9pm; Tu, Th 10am-8pm; Sa 2-8pm.

Post Office: V. Emilia Centro, 86 (☎059 24 35 09 or 24 21 37). Open M-F 8am-6:30pm, Sa 8am-12:30pm.

Postal Code: 41100.

ACCOMMODATIONS & CAMPING

Ostello San Filippo Neri, V. S. Orsola 48-52 (☎/fax 059 23 45 98). Take V. Ganaceto from the station and make your 1st left. New, multi-level hostel with modern amenities: clean bathrooms, sturdy closets with locks, vending machines, Internet access, public phone, TV, VCR, several large patio spaces, and an elevator. Lockout 10am-2pm. Curfew midnight. Dorms €14.50. AmEx/MC/V. ❶

Albergo Bonci, V. Ramazzini, 59 (☎059 22 36 34). From the station, turn left down V. Ganaceto, right onto V. Cerca, and keep going straight. Dimly lit but clean rooms with high ceilings. Communal bath. Singles €32; doubles €47; triples €65. AmEx/MC/V. ❸

Locanda Sole, V. Malatesta, 45 (☎059 21 42 45). From V. Ganaceto, turn right on V. Emilia and left on V. Malatesta. Clean rooms, some with TV and extra-springy mattresses. Communal bath. Closed 1st 3 wk. in Aug. Singles €25; doubles €43. ❸

Camping: International Camping Modena, V. Cave Ramo, 111 (☎059 33 22 52), in Località Bruciata. Take bus #19 (dir.: Rubiera, 6:20am-8:30pm) and ask driver for the stop. Open Mar.-Sept. €7 per person, €9 per tent. ❶

FOOD

The area around Modena has some of the most fertile soil on the Italian peninsula, which results in bountiful fresh produce. Modena, like nearby Bologna and Parma, produces *prosciutto crudo* and the sparkling *lambrusco* red wine. Modenese sprinkle fragrant and full-bodied balsamic vinegar liberally over salads, vegetables, and fruit. The **Mercato Albinelli** is a few steps down V. Albinelli from P. XX Settembre. Locals come to this food bazaar for fruit, vegetables, squid, and snails. (Open June-Aug. M-Sa 6:30am-2pm; Sept.-May daily 6:30am-2pm and 4:30-7pm.) There is also a weekly **market** in the Parco Novi Sad. (Open M 7:30am-1:30pm.)

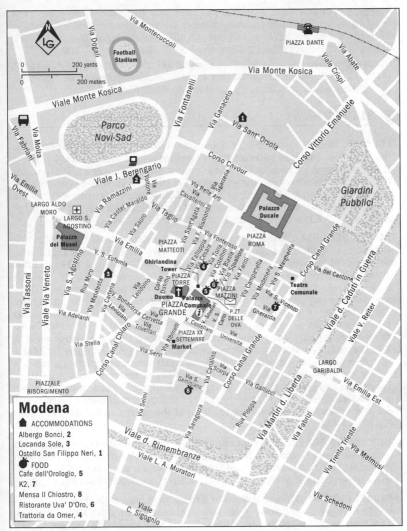

Modena

🔺 ACCOMMODATIONS
Albergo Bonci, **2**
Locanda Sole, **3**
Ostello San Filippo Neri, **1**
🔺 FOOD
Cafe dell'Orologio, **5**
K2, **7**
Mensa Il Chiostro, **8**
Ristorante Uva' D'Oro, **6**
Trattoria da Omer, **4**

▨ **Mensa Il Chiostro,** V. S. Geminiano, 3 (☎059 23 04 30), in the courtyard of an antique cloister. From P. XX Settembre, take V. Mondatora and turn left down the street. Self-service restaurant offers generous portions to a local crowd. *Primi* from €2.20, *secondi* €4-6. Open M-F 11:45am-2:30pm, Sa noon-2pm. ❷

▨ **K2,** C. Canal Grande, 67 (☎059 21 91 81), off V. Emilia. Experience the pinnacle of scrumptious *gelato*. Each cone is sculpted into a flower-shaped treat. Cones from €1.60. Open Th-Tu 9am-midnight. ❶

Ristorante Uva' D'Oro, P. Mazzini, 38 (☎059 23 91 71). Enjoy outdoor, candlelit seating in the piazza, or feast on your large, elaborate vegetable salad (€7-8) in the elegant interior. *Primi* €9.50, *secondi* €12.50. Open M-F noon-2:30pm and 7:30-10:30pm, Sa-Su 7:30-10:30pm. AmEx/MC/V. ❹

Trattoria da Omer, V. Torre, 33 (☎ 059 21 80 50), off V. Emilia across from P. Torre. Very casual decor, but with meticulously prepared delicacies. Try the *tortelloni fiocchi di neve* (with fresh ricotta, butter, and sage; €6.80). Vegetable buffet €2-8, *primi* €7.23, *secondi* €7.23. Open M-Sa 1-2:15pm and 7:30-10:30pm. AmEx/MC/V. ❸

Cafe dell'Orologio, Piazzetta delle Ova, 4 (☎ 059 387 256 608). Cross V. Emilia from P. Mazzini. Great place for an evening drink outside. Classy atmosphere inside. Jazz music. Cocktails start €6, *cappuccino* €3. Open W-M 9:30am-10pm. ❷

👁 SIGHTS

🏛 DUOMO. Modena's Romanesque duomo dates from the early 12th century. The church houses a relic of patron saint S. Geminiano. His arm, encased in silver (1178), takes to the streets in a religious procession on January 31. The sculptor Wiligelmo and his school decorated most of the duomo with stylized carvings that draw on local, Roman, Biblical, and Celtic themes; carvings around the doors depict scenes from the Old Testament and S. Geminiano's travels to Asia. *(P. Grande. ☎ 059 21 60 78. Open daily 6:30am-12:30pm and 3:30-7pm.)*

PALAZZO DEI MUSEI. Inside the *palazzo*, the **Biblioteca Estense** has a collection of exquisitely illuminated books, including masterpieces such as a 1501 Portuguese map of the world; the library's **Sala Campori** houses the **Biblia di Borso d'Este**, a 1200-page Bible partially illustrated by the 15th-century Emilian painter Taddeo Crivelli. Large glass cases contain musical instruments, wall-paper patterns, 19th-century scientific instruments, ceramics, fabric, and cultural anthropology collections from the Americas, Asia, and Africa. Matteo Campori's art collection includes the remarkable *Testa di Fanciulla con Turbante* by Francesco Stringa. *(In Largo S. Agostino at the western side of V. Emilia. Biblioteca ☎ 059 22 22 48. Call the library 1 wk. in advance for an appointment to see the Sala Campori and Biblia di Borso d'Este. Free.)* Above the library, the **Galleria Estense** stores gigantic canvases in modern, enormous rooms. Keep an eye out for Francesco Botticini's *Adoration of the Child* and Cosme' Tura's *St. Antonio of Padova.* The jewels of the collection are Velázquez's *Portrait of Francesco d'Este* and Bernini's magnificent bust of the same subject, found at the head of the gallery. *(☎ 059 439 5711. Open Tu-Su 8:30am-7:30pm. €4, students €2.)*

GHIRLANDINA TOWER. This 95m tower was built in the late 13th century, and incorporates both Gothic and Romanesque elements. A memorial to those who died fighting the Nazis and Fascists during WWII stands at the base. Climb to the top for a view of the city. *(Open daily 9:30am-12:30pm and 3-7pm. Closed Aug. €1.50.)*

FERRARI FACTORY. Modena's claim to international fame is the Ferrari automobile. The factory is southwest of Modena in **Maranello.** After the Maranello stop, buses head straight to the factory. Although you're not allowed to sniff around the inner workings of this top-secret complex, you can view antique and modern Ferraris, Formula One racers, and trophies at the nearby company museum, **Galleria Ferrari,** in an oversized glass-and-steel structure. *(Galleria at V. Dino Ferrari, 43. To reach museum from Ferrari factory bus stop, continue along road in same direction as bus for 200 yards, then turn right at Galleria Ferrari sign. ☎ 0536 94 32 04. Open daily 9:30am-6pm. €9.50.)*

PAVAROTTI'S PAD. If you're on a Three Tenors pilgrimage, Pavarotti's house is a necessary stop along the way. Don't get your hopes up to hear Luciano belt out *"La donna è mobile"* from his balcony—not only is his house far outside the city center, he's also known to be something of a recluse. *(The big villa hidden at the corner of Stradello Chiesa and V. Giardini. Not open to the public.)*

FOOD TOURS. If you're curious about the legends and lore of Modenese cuisine, food tours can show you the secrets behind **prosciutto** and **balsamic vinegar** production, and take you **vignola cherry** picking or **wine-tasting.** Some tours are close to the *centro*, others are in surrounding hamlets. *(Tourist information center with general information:* ☎ *059 22 00 22; fax 20 66 88. Most tours require a minimum of 4-5 people; contact at least 2 wk. in advance.)* Consider visiting one of the many local foundations specializing in regional cuisine. Most require a written request 15-20 days in advance for reservations. For information on **prosciutto,** contact the Consorzio del Prosciutto di Modena at V. Corassori, 72 *(*☎ *059 34 34 64).* For local **balsamic vinegar,** call the Consorzio Produttori di Aceto Balsamico at the Chamber of Commerce, V. Ganaceto, 134 *(*☎ *059 24 25 65).* For **vignola cherries,** send request to the Consorzio della Cigliegia Tipica di Vignola, V. Barozzi, 2 *(*☎ *059 77 36 45),* in the hamlet of Savignano sul Parano. For **wine-tasting** possibilities, contact the Consorzio Tutela del Lambrusco di Modena, V. Schedoni, 41 *(*☎ *059 23 50 05).*

🎵 ENTERTAINMENT

Every year, towards the end of May or first week in June, Modena hosts the one-night **Pavarotti and Friends,** a benefit concert featuring the Three Tenors. For tickets, contact the tourist office in May. For one week—usually late June to early July—the **Serate Estensi** enlivens Modena with exhibits, art shows, street vendors, and a costumed bonanza in which residents dress up in Renaissance garb for a *corteo storico* (historic parade). Perhaps the most important tradition is **Balsamica,** the festival that reflects the Modenese people's dedication to their balsamic vinegar. The event hosts exhibitions, tastings and cooking classes and lasts three weeks from the middle of May. (Info ☎ 059 22 00 22.)

PARMA   ☎0521

The name Parma conjures up visions of platters overflowing with aged *parmigiano* cheese and rosy-pink, cured pig *(prosciutto).* A trip to this city will never leave your taste buds disappointed. Parma's artistic excellence is not confined to the kitchen. 16th-century Mannerist painting came into full bloom under native artists Parmigianino and Correggio. The city was the birthplace of Giuseppe Verdi, who resided in Parma while composing some of his greatest works. His music lured Napoleon's second wife Marie-Louise here. Pervasive French influences inspired Stendhal to choose it as the setting of his 1839 novel, *The Charterhouse of Parma.* The city cultivates a mannered elegance, recalling the artistic airs of the 16th century and the refinement of the 19th, only slightly unnerved by the impious youthful energy of the nearby university.

🚍 TRANSPORTATION

Flights: G. Verdi Airport, V. dell'Aeroporto, 44/a (☎0521 98 26 26).

Trains: P. Carlo Alberto della Chiesa. Parma lies about 200km northwest of Bologna, served by the Bologna-Milan train line. To: **Bologna** (1hr., 2 per hr., €4.15); **Florence** (3hr., 7 per day, €14.16); and **Milan** (1½hr., every hr., €6.82).

Buses: V. P. Toschi, 7B (☎0521 28 27 56). To the right as you exit the train station. To: **Bardi** (6:20am-5:30pm, €3.65); **Busseto** (7:13am-7:50pm, €3.50); **Colorno** (7:15am-7:32pm, €1.55); **Fontanellato** (7:13am-6:43pm, €2.10); and **Torrechiara** (6:25am-7:20pm, €1.45).

Taxis: ☎0521 25 25 62.

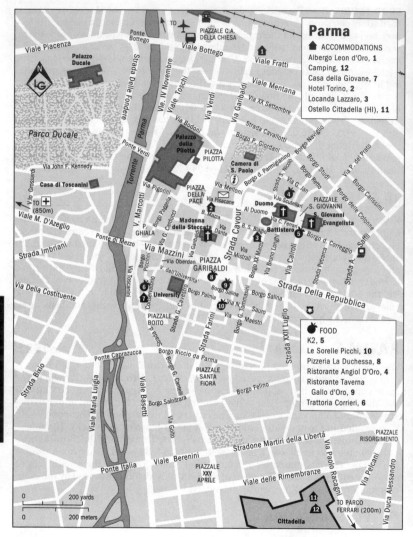

Parma

🏠 ACCOMMODATIONS
Albergo Leon d'Oro, **1**
Camping, **12**
Casa della Giovane, **7**
Hotel Torino, **2**
Locanda Lazzaro, **3**
Ostello Cittadella (HI), **11**

🍎 FOOD
K2, **5**
Le Sorelle Picchi, **10**
Pizzeria La Duchessa, **8**
Ristorante Angiol D'Oro, **4**
Ristorante Taverna
  Gallo d'Oro, **9**
Trattoria Corrieri, **6**

❖ ᔿ ORIENTATION AND PRACTICAL INFORMATION

To get to the city, exit the station, keeping the park to the right. Turn left on **Via Bottego,** right on **Via Garibaldi,** and follow it 1km into the town center. Turn left on **Via Mazzini** to reach **Piazza Garibaldi,** the town center. **Via della Repubblica, Strada Cavour,** and **Strada Farini,** the city's main streets, all branch out of the piazza.

   Tourist Office: V. Melloni, 1/a (☎0521 21 88 89; ☎/fax 23 47 35). From train station, walk left and turn right down V. Garibaldi, then left onto V. Melloni. M-Sa 9am-7pm, Su and holidays 9am-1pm. Next door, **Informagiovani,** V. Melloni 1 (☎0521 21

87 49), has daytrip advice and **job listings** in Italian. English spoken. Open F-W 9am-1pm and 3-7pm, Th 9am-7pm.

English-Language Bookstore: Feltrinelli, V. della Repubblica, 2 (☎0521 23 74 92), on the corner of P. Garibaldi. English classics and bestsellers. Open M-Sa 9am-8pm, Su 10am-1pm and 3:30-7:30pm.

Emergency: ☎ 113.

Ambulance: ☎ 118.

Police: Questura (☎0521 21 94), on Borgo della Posta.

First Aid: ☎0521 28 58 30.

Pharmacy: Farmacia Guareschi, Strada Farini, 5 (☎0521 28 22 40). Night service list posted outside all pharmacies.

Hospital: Ospedale Maggiore, V. Gramsci, 14 (☎0521 99 11 11 or 25 91 11), over the river past the Parco Ducale.

Internet Access: Informagiovani (see above) offers free 2hr. blocks. Book in advance.

Post Office: Strada Piscane (☎0521 23 75 54). Turn left off of Strada Cavour, heading away from P. Garibaldi. Open M-Sa 8am-6:30pm. Another **branch** at V. Verdi, 25 (☎0521 20 64 39), across from train station. Open M-F 8am-6:30pm, Sa 8:30am-11:30am.

Postal Code: 43100.

ACCOMMODATIONS & CAMPING

Ostello Cittadella (HI) (☎0521 96 14 34), Parco della Citadella. From station, take bus #9 (last bus leaves 7:55pm, €0.75). Get off when the bus turns left on Str. Martiri della Libertà. Alternatively, take Str. Farini from P. Garibaldi for 7 blocks and turn left on Str. Martiri della Libertà. Turn right onto V. Passo Buole, and enter the large white portico surrounded by ancient walls. Modern building with plate glass and rubber floors in the corner of a 15th-century fortress. Simple, spacious rooms with 5 beds, hot showers, and squat-style toilets. HI members only, but may accept student ID. 3-night max. stay. Call for availability. Lockout 9:30am-5pm. Curfew 11pm. Open Apr.-Oct. Dorms €9. ❶

Locanda Lazzaro, Borgo XX Marzo, 14 (☎0521 20 89 44), off V. della Repubblica. Upstairs from the pricey but welcoming restaurant of the same name. 8 rooms. Reserve 1 wk. in advance during the summer. Singles €34-42, doubles €57-75; triples €78 (all with bath). AmEx/MC/V. ❹

Albergo Leon d'Oro, V. Fratti, 4 (☎0521 77 31 82), off V. Garibaldi. From train station, go left 2 blocks. Old but clean hotel. No private baths. Singles €30; doubles €47; triples €70. Restaurant downstairs (see below). AmEx/MC/V. ❸

Casa della Giovane, V. del Conservatorio, 11 (☎0521 28 32 29). From V. Mazzini, turn left on V. Oberdan and follow as it winds around. It's on your right. Women under 25 only. An upbeat atmosphere and comfortable rooms. Breakfast and large, tasty dinners included. €21 per person. ❷

Hotel Torino, V. Mazza, 7 (☎0521 28 10 46; fax 23 07 25; www.hotel-torino.it). From P. Garibaldi, take V. Cavour and turn left on V. Mazza. Beautiful, elegant hotel with an extensive buffet breakfast. All rooms with bath, A/C, and TV. Singles €72; doubles €102; triples €130. AmEx/MC/V. ❺

Camping: The only campground near Parma is at the **Ostello Cittadella** (see above), in the Cittadella public park beside the hostel. Electrical outlets. 3-night max. stay. Open Apr.-Oct. €6 per person, €11 per car. ❶

◘ FOOD

Parma's cuisine is rich, delicious, and affordable. Crumbly *parmigiano* cheese and silky-smooth *prosciutto crudo* fill the windows of the *salumerie* along V. Garibaldi. *Malvasia* is the wine of choice. When exported, this sparkling white loses its natural fizz, so carbon dioxide is usually added—here's your chance to sample the real thing. Of the sparkling red wines, *lambrusco* is a favorite. An **open-air market** is at P. Ghiaia, off V. Marcotti past Palazzo Pilotta, and P. della Pace. (Open W and Sa 8am-1pm.) There is also a **Supermarket** on V. XXII Luglio, 27/c. (☎ 0521 28 13 82. Open M-W and F-Sa 8:30am-1pm and 4:30-8pm, Th 8:30am-1pm.)

Trattoria Corrieri, V. Conservatorio, 1 (☎ 0521 23 44 26). From V. Mazzini, take V. Oberdan; V. del Conservatorio is to the right. Whitewashed arches, red-checked tablecloths, and hanging hams and wheels of cheese. Not cheap, but worth it. Try *Tris* (tortelli filled with asparagus; €7.30). *Primi* €6-7, *secondi* €6.20-7.80. Open M-Sa noon-2:30pm and 7:30-10:30pm. AmEx/MC/V. ❸

Le Sorelle Picchi, Strada Farini, 27 (☎ 0521 23 35 28). The street begins at P. Garibaldi. Walk in the direction toward which the Signor Garibaldi faces, left of the bank. A traditional *salumeria*, and one of the best *trattorie* in town. *Primi* €5.50-6, *secondi* €6.50-8. Open M-Sa noon-3pm for lunch. *Salumeria* open 8:30am-7pm. MC/V. ❸

Ristorante Taverna Gallo d'Oro, Borgo della Salina, 3 (☎ 0521 20 88 46). From P. Garibaldi, take Str. Farini and turn left onto the street. 14th-century building houses a cozy *trattoria* with an impressive wine collection. Outdoor dining in summer, removed from the noise of the busy street. *Primi* €6.50, *secondi* €7.50. Open M-Sa noon-4:30pm and 7:30-10:30pm. AmEx/MC/V. ❸

Ristorante Leon d'Oro, V. Fratti, 4 (☎ 0521 77 31 82), off V. Garibaldi. See accommodations above. Sunny and newly remodeled. Open daily 12:30-3:30pm and 7:30pm-midnight. €20 for an extensive, full-course meal. Make reservations on weekends. AmEx/MC/V. ❹

Ristorante Angiol D'Oro, Vicolo Scutellari, 1 (☎ 0521 28 26 32). Directly across from the baptistery heading away from P. Garibaldi. Impressively prepared food is served with quiet pomp and circumstance. *Primi* €9.50-10.50, *secondi* €13-15. Open M-Sa 12:30-2:30pm and 7:30-10:30pm. AmEx/MC/V. ❹

Pizzeria La Duchessa, P. Garibaldi, 1/B (☎ 0521 23 59 62). An excellent *trattoria* with a large variety of thick-crust pizzas. Be prepared to wait for a seat. Outdoor patio dining in summer. Pizzas €4.20-9.50, *primi* €5.50-8, *secondi* €6.50-15. Open Tu-Su 10am-2:30pm and 7pm-12:30am. MC/V. ❸

K2, Strada Cairoli, 23 (☎ 0521 28 55 42), on the corner next to the Chiesa di San Giovanni Evangelista. The creamiest *gelato* in Parma, deftly sculpted into a flower atop the mountainous cone by workers in pink-and-white uniforms. Try their new flavor *Amarenada,* or the classic *Fiordinutella*. Cones from €1.50. Open Th-Tu 11am-midnight. ❶

◉ SIGHTS

▨ **DUOMO AND BAPTISTERY.** Parma's 11th-century Romanesque duomo has vibrant paintings of *putti*, balanced by austere masterpieces including the Episcopal throne and Benedetto Antelami's bas-relief *Descent from the Cross* (1178). The pink-and-white marble **baptistery** has a dark interior adorned with well-preserved medieval wall frescoes. *(In P. del Duomo. From P. Garibaldi, follow Strada Cavour and turn right on Strada al Duomo. ☎ 0521 23 58 86. Duomo open daily 9am-12:30pm and 3-7pm. Baptistery open daily 9am-12:30pm and 3-6:45pm. €2.70, students €1.50.)*

CHIESA DI SAN GIOVANNI EVANGELISTA. The dome inside was frescoed by Correggio. Along the left nave, over the first, second, and fourth chapels are frescoes by Parmigianino. The 3rd chapel's frescoes were stolen by a nasty amateur Byzantine thief named Alfonso, who tried to ransom from the Parmigiani family. *(In P. S. Giovanni, behind the duomo. ☎ 0521 23 55 92. Open daily 9am-noon and 3-6pm.)*

CAMERA SAN PAOLO. Highlights include a wonderfully intricate wooden bench along with several rooms containing detailed ceiling frescoes. The most impressive are the tiny but very muscular *putti* engaged in various activities adorning the ceiling of one room. *(From P. Garibaldi, head up Strada Cavour, turn left on V. Melloni and follow the signs. ☎ 0521 23 33 09. Open Tu-Su 8:30am-1:45pm. €2.)*

PALAZZO DELLA PILOTTA. Constructed in 1602, the palace suggests the authoritarian ambitions of the Farnese dukes, who were behind the Pilotta and the Cittadella (now a park on the other side of town). Today, the Palazzo houses several museums. The elegant, wooden **Farnese Theater** (1615) flanks the entrance to the art museum. The rooms leading out of the theater contain miniature models of scenes from past performances. The **Galleria Nazionale** contains numerous romantic 18th-century portraits with mythological themes. An entire gallery is devoted to Parmigiano and Correggio. The collection also includes Leonardo da Vinci's *Testa d'una Fanciulla* (Head of a Young Girl). *(From Strada Cavour, turn left on Strada Piscane and cut across P. della Pace to P. Pilotta. ☎ 0521 23 33 09. Open Tu-Su 8:30am-1:45pm. Gallery and theater €6. Theater only €2, students €1.)* Downstairs, the **Museo Archaeologico Nazionale** houses displays of coins, bronzes, and sculptures of Greek, Etruscan, Roman, and Egyptian origin. *(☎ 0521 23 37 18. Open Tu-Su 8:30am-2pm. €2.)*

PARMIGIANO AND PROSCIUTTO FACTORIES. *Parmigiano* cheese fans should contact the **Consorzio del Parmigiano-Reggiano** to arrange a tour of the factory, with free samples. *(V. Gramsci, 26/c. ☎ 0521 29 27 00; fax 29 34 41.)* To arrange a visit to a *prosciutto* factory, contact the **Consorzio del Prosciutto di Parma.** *(V. M. dell'Arpa, 8/b. ☎ 0521 24 39 87; fax 24 39 83. Factories lie in the Province of Parma, outside the city walls. At least 10 people required for tour.)*

FRENCH GARDENS AND COMPOSERS. Many of the French *palazzi* were blasted to pieces during WWII. Marie-Louise's lush, French gardens thrive by the Baroque palace in Parco Ducale. *(West of Palazzo Pilotta over the Ponte Verdi. Open May-Sept. daily 7am-midnight, Oct.-Apr. 7am-8pm.)* **Casa Natale e Museo di Aurturo Toscanini** (1867-1957) houses *maestro* memorabilia. *(☎ 0521 28 54 99. South of the park at Borgo Rodolfo Tanzi, 13. Ask for a tour in English. Open Tu-Su 9am-1pm and 2-6pm. €1.50.)*

❒ ENTERTAINMENT

The **Teatro Regio** is one of Italy's premier opera houses. Check with the tourist office for the prices of standing-room tickets. The opera season runs from December to April. *(V. Garibaldi, 16, next to P. della Pace. ☎ 0521 21 89 10.)* **E'grande Estate** classical music, opera, jazz, and tango concerts are held in Piazzale della Pilotta in July. *(Info ☎ 0521 21 86 78. Tickets from €10-15.)*

❒ DAYTRIP FROM PARMA: BUSSETO

No composer conveys love more poignantly (and at greater length) than opera giant Giuseppe Verdi. His native hamlet of **Roncole Verdi** is on the Parma plain, 3½km outside the city of **Busseto** (35km drive or a 1hr. bus ride from Parma). To see where this son of a poor innkeeper received his earliest inspiration, visit the house and museum at **Verdi's birth site.** *(☎ 0524 97 450. Open 9:30am-12:30pm and 3-7pm. €4.)* In Busseto proper, within the walls of the ancient Rocca, the famous

Teatro Verdi opened in 1868. (☎0524 91 864. Guided tours Tu-Su every 30min. 9:30am-noon and 3-6:30pm. €4.) Busseto's gossip about Verdi's affair with a premier diva drove him to secluded Sant'Agata. The **Villa Sant'Agata** lies 3km from Busseto (on the same bus line). Parts of this mansion, unaltered since Verdi's death in 1901, are open to the public. (☎0523 83 00 00. Open Tu-Su 9-11:40am and 3-6:45pm. €6. Reservations required. For maps and directions, contact the tourist office in Bussetto at ☎0524 92 487.)

PIACENZA   ☎0523

Piacenza was one of the first Roman colonies in northern Italy, and the longtime headquarters of Julius Ceasar. After 2000 years, the city hasn't expanded much, housing only a few noteworthy monuments of the Renaissance and the Middle Ages. Although the quiet hamlet abstains from a tourist economy, Piacenza was recently voted one of Italy's most hospitable cities. It is an ideal stopover on a trip to Parma, Bologna, or Milan.

▐ TRANSPORTATION

Trains (☎0523 32 12 63 or 39 91 11) leave from P. Marconi. Locker storage available. To: **Bologna** (1½hr., every hr., €7.35); **Milan** (1hr., every hr., €4.60); and **Turin** (2½hr., 9 per day, €8.99). For a **taxi** call ☎0523 59 19 19.

◼▐ ORIENTATION AND PRACTICAL INFORMATION

From the train station, walk along the left side of the park on **Via dei Mille** and turn right on **Via Giulio Alberoni.** Follow it onto **Via Roma,** and then turn left onto **Via Daveri,** which leads to **Piazza Duomo.** From there, **Via XX Settembre** leads straight to **Piazza dei Cavalli.**

Tourist office: IAT, P. Cavalli, 7 (☎/fax 0523 32 93 24; iat@comune.piacenza.it), in the large building behind the horse statues, Il Gotico. Open Tu-Sa 9:30am-12:30pm and 3-6pm. **Ufficio Relazione con il Pubblico,** P. Cavalli, 2 (☎0523 49 22 24). Open M-Sa 9am-1pm and M-Th 3-8pm.

Lockers: At the train station. Self-service 24hr.

Ambulances: ☎118.

Emergency: ☎113.

Police: Viale Malta, 10 (☎0523 39 71 11).

Hospital: Ospedale Civile da Piacenza, V. G. Taverna, 49 (☎0523 30 11 11).

Post Office: V. Sant'Antonino, 38-40 (☎0523 31 64 11). Open M-F 8:15am-5:30pm, Sa 8:15-1pm.

Postal Code: 29100.

▐ ◖ ACCOMMODATIONS AND FOOD

Hotel Astra ❸, V. R. Boselli, 19, has 10 simple but spotless rooms above a neat street cafe. From the station, turn left on V. La Primogenita to Piazzale Roma. Follow Viale dei Patrioti out, stay straight, and bear left onto V. Passerini; then walk around to the intersection of V. Rodolfo. (☎0523 45 70 31. Reserve ahead. Singles €20.66-23.24; doubles €30.99-33.57.) **Protezione delle Giovane ❷,** V. Tempio, 26, has immaculate rooms, well tended by the nuns. From P. Cavalli take C. Vittorio Emanuele and turn right on V. Tempio. (☎0523 32 38 12. Women only. Curfew 10:30pm. Singles and doubles €23, with breakfast €25.)

An **open-air market** is held every Wednesday and on Saturday mornings in P. Duomo and P. dei Cavalli. Local specialties include *tortelli* filled with spinach and ricotta, and *pisarei e faso*, a hearty mix of beans and small balls of dough. **Osteria Del Trentino ❸**, V. del Castello, 71, off P. Borgo, serves delicious meals like the specialty *tortelli ricotta e spinaci* (€6.50) in a garden as charming as its staff. (☎0523 32 42 60. *Primi* from €5.50, *secondi* from €6.50. Open M-Sa noon-3pm and 8pm-midnight. AmEx/MC/V.) **Trattoria/Pizzeria dell'Orologio ❸**, P. Duomo, 38, serves delicious pizza (from €4.50), and traditional *piacentina* cuisine in the shadow of the duomo. (☎0523 32 46 69. *Primi* €6.50-8, *secondi* €10.50-13. Open F-W noon-12:30pm and 6:30pm-midnight. AmEx/DC/MC/V.)

🅖 SIGHTS

PIAZZA DEI CAVALLI. This central square is named for the two 17th-century equestrian statues that grace the piazza. Although the statues were intended as tributes to the riders, Duke Rannucio I and his father Duke Alessandro Farnese, the huge horses overpower their masters. The masterpiece of the piazza is the Gothic **Palazzo del Comune,** called **Il Gotico.** The building was constructed in 1280, when Piacenza led the Lombard League, a powerful trading group of city-states in northern Italy. From P. dei Cavalli, follow V. XX Settembre to the **duomo,** constructed between 1122 and 1233 with an unadorned, three-aisle nave. The **crypt,** a maze of thin columns, is one of Italy's spookiest. A vigil is kept over the bones of S. Giustina at its center. To the right of the altar on the main level, find the body of Giovanni Battista Scalabrini. *(Open daily 7:30am-noon and 4-7pm.)*

MUSEUMS. Palazzo Farnese houses the **Museo Civico,** the **Pinacoteca,** and the **Museo delle Carrozze.** The most notable work in the Pinacoteca is a Botticelli fresco depicting Christ's birth. *(In P. Cittadella, at the end of C. Cavour opposite P. dei Cavalli. Take V. Cavour from P. dei Cavalli and turn left on V. Bacchiochi. ☎0523 32 82 70. Open Tu-Th 9am-1pm, F 10-11am and 1-5pm, Sa-Su 9:30am-noon and 3-5:30pm. Museo Civico and Pinacoteca €4.20, students €3.15. Museo delle Carrozze €2.10, students €1.60. All the museums €5.25, students €4.20.)* The **Galleria Ricci Oddi,** V. S. Siro, 13, holds a collection of modern art, including works by F. Hayez. *(Take C. V. Emanuele from P. dei Cavalli; turn left on V. S. Siro. ☎0523 32 07 42. Open Tu-Sa 10am-noon and 3-6pm. €4.)*

RAVENNA   ☎0544

During the decline of the Roman Empire, Ravenna rose from the chaos, a grand finale of sparkling, mosaic-bedecked edifices. Justinian and Theodora, rulers of the Byzantine Empire, were responsible for the city's growth, choosing Ravenna as headquarters for an effort to restore order to the anarchic West. Today, while art fanatics come to see the mosaics, literary pilgrims come for Dante's tomb, to the ire of Florentines, who maintain an (empty) tomb for their estranged native.

🮱 TRANSPORTATION

Trains: (☎0544 21 78 84). Ticket counter open daily 6am-8pm. Info office in P. Farini open daily 7am-8:30pm. To **Bologna** (1hr., every 1-2hr., 5:05am-7:34pm, €4) and **Rimini** (1hr., every hr., 5am-9:35pm, €4.30) with connections to **Ferrara, Florence,** and **Venice** (1hr., every 2hr., 6:20am-9:33pm, €4.50).

Buses: ATR (regional) and ATM (municipal) buses (☎0544 68 99 00) depart outside train station for coastal towns **Lido di Classe** (€2) and **Marina di Ravenna** (€1). Info and tickets (3-day tourist pass €3) at the booth marked "PUNTO" across from station. Buy a return ticket; they're difficult to find outside Ravenna. Office open M-Sa 6:30am-8:30pm, Su 7am-8:30pm; in winter M-Sa 6:30am-7:30pm, Su 7:30am-7:30pm.

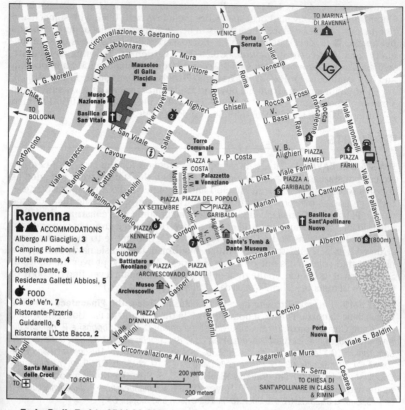

Ravenna

▲▲ ACCOMMODATIONS
Albergo Al Giaciglio, **3**
Camping Piomboni, **1**
Hotel Ravenna, **4**
Ostello Dante, **8**
Residenza Galletti Abbiosi, **5**

🍎 **FOOD**
Cà de' Ve'n, **7**
Ristorante-Pizzeria
  Guidarello, **6**
Ristorante L'Oste Bacca, **2**

Taxis: Radio Taxi (☎ 0544 33 888), in P. Farini, across from the train station. Open 24hr.

Bike Rental: In P. Farini to left as you exit train station. €1.03 per hr., €7.75 per day. Mountain bikes €1.55 per hr. Open M-Sa 6:15am-8pm.

🔧 ❷ ORIENTATION AND PRACTICAL INFORMATION

The train station is in **Piazza Farini** at the east end of town. **Viale Farini** leads from the station to **Via Diaz,** which runs to **Piazza del Popolo,** the center of town.

Tourist Office: V. Salara, 8 (☎ 0544 35 404). From P. Garibaldi, turn left into P. del Popolo, walk to the end. Turn right onto V. Matteotti and follow signs. Open Apr.-Sept. M-Sa 8:30am-7pm, Su 10am-4pm; Oct.-Mar. M-Sa 8:30am-6pm, Su 10am-4pm.

Emergency: ☎ 113. **First Aid:** ☎ 118. **Questura:** V. Berlinguer, 20 (☎ 0544 29 91 11).

Hospital: Santa Maria delle Croci, Viale Randi, 5 (☎ 0544 28 511). Take minibus #2 or 4 or from the station.

Internet Access: Biblioteca Classense, V. Baccarini, 3 (☎ 0544 48 21 14). From P. del Popolo, take a left onto V. Cairoli and bear right into P. Caduti. Head straight on V. Baccini. 5 new computers. €2.07 per hr. Open M-F 8:30am-7pm, Sa 8:30am-1:30pm. Closed July 23-Aug. 17. Access also at the **tourist office** and **hostel.**

Post Office: P. Garibaldi, 1 (☎ 0544 24 33 11), off V. Diaz before P. del Popolo. Open M-F 8am-6:30pm, Sa 8am-12:30pm. **Currency exchange** available. **Postal Code:** 48100.

ACCOMMODATIONS & CAMPING

Albergo Al Giaciglio, V. Rocca Brancaleone, 42 (☎ 0544 39 403). Walk along V. Farini and turn right across P. Maneli. Recently renovated budget hotel is the best deal in town. 18 carpeted rooms with wood-paneled walls and TVs. Restaurant downstairs. Breakfast €2-5. Singles €28-32; doubles €35-45; triples €45-60. MC/V. ❸

Residenza Galletti Abbiosi, V. Roma, 140 (☎ 0544 21 51 27; fax 21 11 96; info@ostellora.org). Church-like orphanage-turned-hotel. Singles, doubles, and triples with A/C and bath. €28 per person. AmEx/MC/V. ❸

Ostello Dante (HI), V. Nicolodi, 12 (☎/fax 0544 42 11 64). Take bus #1 or 70 from V. Pallavicini, at the station (every 15min.-1hr., 6:30am-11:30pm). A clean, simple hostel east of the city center, offering satellite TV, soda machines, and Internet access. Wheelchair-accessible. Breakfast included. Reception 7-10am and 5-11:30pm. Strict lockout 10am-5pm. Curfew 11:30pm. Dorms €12.50, family rooms €14 per person. MC/V. ❶

Hotel Ravenna, V. Maroncelli, 12 (☎ 0544 21 22 04; fax 21 20 77), to the right as you exit the station, on the left side of the street. 26 clean rooms with tile floors and TV. Cozy TV room downstairs. Wheelchair-accessible. Complimentary off-street parking. Singles €37-42; doubles €50-62; triples €84-105. MC/V. ❹

Camping Piomboni, Viale della Pace, 421 (☎ 0544 53 02 30), in Marina di Ravenna, 8km from Ravenna Centro. Take bus #70, across the street from train station, to stop #34 (15-20min., every 30min., 5:35am-11:30pm). 3-star camping near the beach. Reception daily 8am-10:30pm. Open May to mid-Sept. €3.90-6.20 per person, €6.80-9.70 per tent. MC/V. ❶

FOOD

Ravenna's hearty cuisine of homemade pasta and barbecued meat are made especially flavorful with *Ravennese* salt, extra virgin olive oil, chestnuts, and Alpine herbs. Accompany a filling meal with a glass of the full-bodied *Albana* or *Trebbiano* wine. The tourist office provides a listing of wine and food routes throughout the province. For dessert, try the *zuppa inglese*, a combination of biscuits and custard enlivened by a splash of sweet cordial. Or head to **Gelateria Nuovo Mondo,** Viale Forini, 60, for a gigantic and cheap scoop of delicious ice cream. Hostel guests benefit from the **Coop Supermarket,** across the street at V. Aquileia, 110. (Open M 3:30-8pm, Tu-Sa 8am-8pm.) Also try the **Mercato Coperto,** up V. IV Novembre from P. del Popolo. (Open M-Sa 7am-2pm, F 7am-2pm and 4:30-7:30pm.)

▩ **Cà de' Ve'n,** V. Corrado Ricci, 24 (☎ 0544 30 163). From P. Garibaldi, turn right on V. Gordini and left on V. Ricci. This 16th-century apothecary-turned-*osteria* reflects the influence of the Byzantine era with an elaborately decorated domed roof. Wines from €1.80 a glass. *Primi* €4-7. Open Tu-Su 11am-4:15pm and 6-10pm. AmEx/MC/V. ❸

Ristorante L'Oste Bacca, V. Salara, 20 (☎ 0544 35 363). Traditional *Ravennese* cuisine. The scrumptious specialty of the house is *tortellaci di ortica* (fresh pasta stuffed with cheese accompanied by fish and tomatoes). *Piadina*—hot, triangular pieces of flat bread—are dipped in *squaquerone*, a melted mild cheese native to the region. *Primi* €5-7, *secondi* from €8.50. Open W-M 12:15-2:30pm and 7:15-10:30pm. AmEx/MC/V. ❸

Ristorante-Pizzeria Guidarello, V. Gessi, 9, off P. Arcivescovado beside the duomo. Feast on the *Fantasia della Casa* (3 meats with mixed vegetables; €9.80). Pizza €4-5, *primi* €5.70-7.20, *secondi* €6.70-10. Open M-Sa noon-4:30pm and 7-9pm. MC/V. ❸

⊙ SIGHTS

The **Ravenna Card** is a single ticket that provides admission to the Archiepiscopal Museum, Neonian Baptistery, Basilica dello Spirito Santo, Basilica of Sant'Apollinare Nuovo, Basilica of San Vitale, and the Mausoleum of Galla Placidia. There is no single ticket for any one of the monuments. The price varies according to the season, but averages around €6. Purchase it at any participating site.

■ **BASILICA DI SAN VITALE.** The 6th-century **Basilica di San Vitale** is an architectural marvel and an artistic masterpiece. Multiple arches, glittering with golden mosaics, support the soaring domes of the immense church. The decor is unusual, but the church harmoniously combines Renaissance and Byzantine art: graceful Renaissance wall paintings depicting passionate Greeks recline next to rigid mosaics of saints. *(V. S. Vitale, 17. Take V. Argentario from V. Cavour. ☎0544 21 62 92. Open daily 9am-7pm and 9:30am-4:30pm.)* Mosaics cover the interior of the **Mausoleo di Galla Placidia.** A representation of Jesus as Shepherd, leaning against his cross-shaped staff and petting a sheep, decorates the upper wall above the door. *(Behind S. Vitale. Same hours as basilica.)* Every Friday night in July and August, the city of Ravenna bustles with illuminated brilliance. All of the shops remain open until midnight, and the monuments are open to the public.

■ **CHIESA DI SANT'APOLLINARE IN CLASSE.** Astounding mosaics decorate the interior of this 6th-century church. The mosaic of Christ sitting on his throne among angels rivals the stunning gold cross on an azure background in the main apse. St. Apollinare is located in the lower portion. *(In Classe, south of the city. Take bus #4 or 44, which stops across the street from train station. ☎0544 47 36 61. Open M-Sa 8:30am-7:30pm, Su 1-7pm. €2, combination with National Museum €6.50.)*

MUSEO NAZIONALE. This collection, housed in a former Benedictine monastery, features works from the Roman, early Christian, Byzantine, and medieval periods. Highlights include intricate ivory carvings, ivory inlaid weapons, and recent excavations from a burial ground in Classe. *(On V. Fiandrini. Ticket booth at the entrance of the Basilica di San Vitale to the right. Museum is through the courtyard. ☎0544 34 424. Open Tu-Su 8:30am-7:30pm. €4, students €2. Combination ticket with basilica €5, reduced €2.50.)*

DANTE'S TOMB AND THE DANTE MUSEUM. Much to Florence's dismay, Ravenna's most popular monument is the Tomb of Dante Alighieri. The adjoining Dante Museum holds 18,000 scholarly volumes. *(V. Dante Alighieri. From P. del Popolo, cut through P. Garibaldi to V. Alighieri. Tomb open daily 9am-7pm. Free. Museum ☎0544 30 252. Museum open Apr.-Sept. Tu-Su 9am-noon and 3:30-6pm, Oct.-Mar. Tu-Su 9am-noon. €2.)*

BASILICA DI SANT'APOLLINARE NUOVO. Poised beside a round brick tower, this 6th-century *basilica*, which passed into the hands of the Roman Catholics 40 years after it was built, features arched windows and mortar made with crushed seashells. Lengthy mosaic strips of saints and prophets line the sides of the central aisle, and the central apse recounts miracles performed by Jesus. *(On V. di Roma. ☎0544 21 99 38. Open daily 9am-7pm.)*

BATTISTERO NEONIANO. This mosaic-laden baptistery of the duomo is thought to have once contained a Roman bath. The central dome features Jesus submerged in the Jordan River, with John the Baptist to his right and a personification of the river to his left. The baptismal font is at the center of the room; the duomo is next door. *(From P. del Popolo follow V. Cairoli, turn right on V. Gessi, and head toward P. Arcivescovado. Open daily 9:30am-4:30pm. Duomo open daily 7:30am-noon and 3:30-6:30pm. Free.)*

MUSEO ARCIVESCOVILE. Adjoining the baptistery, this small *museo* displays a collection of mosaics from the duomo and a number of impressive fragments of engraved stone. Don't miss the lovely mosaics in the ■**Cappella di S. Andrea** or the

Throne of Maximilian, an exemplary piece of ivory carving. *(In P. Duomo. Walk to the right of the Battistero Neoniano.* ☎ *0544 21 99 38. Open daily 9:30am-4:30pm.)*

🎵 ENTERTAINMENT

Ravenna bustles with cultural vivacity. Since 1990, some of the most famous classical performers from around the world, including at least two of the Three Tenors, have gathered in the city each June and July for the internationally renowned **Ravenna Festival.** (Information office at V. D. Alighieri, 1. ☎ 0544 24 92 44; www.ravennafestival.org. Open M-Sa 9am-1pm and 3-6pm. Tickets start around €10-15. Reservations necessary for popular events. For tickets ☎ 0544 32 577; fax 21 58 40.) An annual **Dante Festival,** organized by the Chiesa di S. Francesco (☎ 0544 30 252), brings the poet to life with exhibits and theatricals during the second week in September. The **Organ Music Festival** is held in the Church of San Vitale. From June to September the city streets are crowded with spectators of the *Bella di Sera,* the festival of street theater shows. ▨**Fuschini Colori-Belle Arti,** P. Mameli, 16, off of Viale Farini, sells *tesserae* of all shapes and sizes to make your own mosaic. (☎ 0544 37 387. Open daily 9am-12:30pm and 4:30-7:30pm. Closed Sa afternoons.)

RIMINI ☎ 0541

Rimini is the party town of choice for young, fashionable vacationers. Vitality flows through the streets, which never seem to quiet. By day, crowds flock to the beach to enjoy the powder-fine, light brown sand. By night, scantily-clad Europeans head to the *discoteche* that keep pumping till the wee hours. Still, Rimini offers much more than beach and music. Especially popular among families for its carefree, fun atmosphere, it offers a medley of entertainment opportunities, including innumerable water sports, shopping boutiques, and water and amusement parks. Along the *lungomare,* stiletto-heeled mothers push baby strollers past caricature artists, *gelateria,* and clothing shops that close well past midnight. Inland, the historic center preserves the Roman influence with an alluring jumble of streets overshadowed by the Malatesta Temple and the Augustan Arch.

🚍 TRANSPORTATION

Flights: Miramare Civil Airport (☎ 0541 71 57 11), on V. Flaminia. Mostly charter flights. Serves many European cities. Bus #9, across the street from train station, travels to the airport (every 30min., 5:45am-12:40am).

Trains: Piazzale C. Battisti and V. Dante. To: **Ancona** (1hr., 1-2 per hr., 5:45am-10:41pm, €4); **Bologna** (1½hr., 1-3 per hr., 12:38am-10:25pm, €5.50); **Milan** (3hr., 1-2 per hr., 1:34am-8:23pm, €15.70); and **Ravenna** (1hr., 1-2 per hr., 1:28am-10:57pm, €3.20).

Buses: TRAM intercity bus station (☎ 0541 30 05 33), at V. Roma on P. Clementini, near the station. From train station, follow V. Dante Alghieri and take 1st left. Service to many inland towns (1hr. €0.88, 24hr. €2.84). Ticket booth open M-Sa 7:15am-12:30pm and 2:30-6:30pm. Buying tickets on the bus is more expensive and not always possible. Pick up a schedule or ask at the station for longer passes. **Fratelli Benedettini** (☎ 0549 90 38 54) and **Bonelli Bus** (☎ 0541 37 34 32) run the most convenient buses to **San Marino** (50min., 11 per day, 7:30am-7pm, €3.36). Buses depart from the train station and fill quickly, so arrive 15min. before departure for a seat.

Car Rental: Hertz, V. Trieste, 16a (☎ 0541 53 110), near the beach, off V. Vespucci (bus #11: stop 12). Open M-Sa 8:30am-1pm and 3-7:30pm.

Bike Rental: On V. Fiume at V. Vespucci (bus #11: stop 12). €3 per hr. for bikes and mountain bikes.

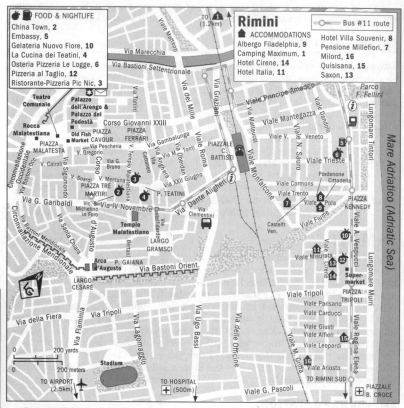

FOOD & NIGHTLIFE
China Town, **2**
Embassy, **5**
Gelateria Nuovo Fiore, **10**
La Cucina dei Teatini, **4**
Osteria Pizzeria Le Logge, **6**
Pizzeria al Taglio, **12**
Ristorante-Pizzeria Pic Nic, **3**

Rimini

⬡── Bus #11 route

ACCOMMODATIONS
Albergo Filadelphia, **9**
Camping Maximum, **1**
Hotel Cirene, **14**
Hotel Italia, **11**

Hotel Villa Souvenir, **8**
Pensione Millefiori, **7**
Milord, **16**
Quisisana, **15**
Saxon, **13**

Scooter Rental: Noleggio Ambra N. 21, Piazzale Kennedy, 6 (☎0541 27 016). On your right off V. le Vespucci, keeping the water on your right. Best prices in town and friendly service. Rentals starting at €13 per hr. Also has the *ciclocarrolzzelle*. Open Mar.-Oct. daily 8:15am-1am.

✳ 🛈 ORIENTATION AND PRACTICAL INFORMATION

To reach the beach from the train station in **Piazzale Cesare Battisti,** turn right out of the station, take another right into the tunnel at the yellow arrow indicating *al mare,* and follow **Viale Principe Amadeo.** To your right, **Viale Vespucci,** runs one block inland along the beach. The hub of Rimini's action, it features countless hotels and restaurants. Bus #11 (every 15min., 5:30am-2am) runs to the beach from the train station and continues along V. A. Vespucci and V. R. Elena. Bus stops are conveniently numbered. Buy tickets (€0.88, 24hr. €2.84) at the kiosk in front of the station or at *tabacchi.* To reach the historic center, take **Via Dante Alighieri** from the station and follow it to **Piazza Tre Martiri.** The center of Rimini is called **Marina Centro. Rimini Sud** (South) branches out from the main city along the coast and comprises the neighborhoods of **Bellariva, Marebello, Rivazzurra and Miramare. Rimini Nord** (North) goes toward the less-visited Rivabella, Viserba, and Viserbella.

Tourist Offices: IAT, Piazzale C. Battisti, 1 (☎0541 51 331; fax 27 927; www.riminiturismo.it), left as you exit train station. Open M-Sa 8:30am-7pm, Su 9am-noon. **Branch office,** P. Fellini, 3 (☎0541 56 902 or 56 598), at the beginning of V. Vespucci (bus #11: stop 10). Open daily 8am-7pm; in winter 9am-noon and 3-8pm. **Hotel Reservations-Adria** (☎0541 69 36 28; www.iperhotel.com) in the train station, finds rooms for free. Open M-Sa 8:30am-12:30pm and 3-6pm, Su 8:30am-12:30pm.

Budget Travel: CTS, Grantour Viaggi, V. Matteuci, 4 (☎0541 55 525; fax 55 966), off V. Principe Amadeo. Tickets, ISICs, and info on group tours. Open M-W and F 9am-noon and 3:30-6:30pm, Th 9am-4pm, Sa 9:30am-noon.

Luggage Storage: In train station. €3.87 for 24hr. Open June-Sept. daily 7am-10pm.

Laundromat: Lavanderia Trieste Exspress, V. le Trieste, 16 (☎0541 26 764), off V. Vespucci. €5 per wash, €5 per dry. No self-service. Open M-Sa 8:30am-12:30pm and 3-7:30pm.

Emergency: ☎ 113. **Ambulance:** ☎ 118.

Police: C. d'Augusto, 192 (☎0541 353 1111).

First Aid: (☎0541 70 77 04), on beach at the end of V. Gounod (bus #11: stop 16). Open in summer daily 8am-8pm.

Hospital: Ospedale Infermi, V. Settembrini, 2 (☎0541 70 51 11).

Internet Access: Central Park, V. Vespucci, 21 (☎0541 37 44 50). 9 computers. €1 per 10min., €2 per 25min. Open daily 9am-2am.

Post Office: C. d'Augusto, 8 (☎0541 78 16 73), off P. Tre Martiri, near the Arch of Augustus. Open M-F 8am-6:30pm, Sa 8am-12:30pm. **Currency exchange.**

Postal Code: 47900.

▮ ACCOMMODATIONS & CAMPING

Reservations are always necessary. The tourist office provides a complete list of hotels and campgrounds. Countless hotels line the smaller streets off V. Vespucci and V. R. Elena, many between stops 12 and 20 of bus #11. Prices peak in August.

▨ **Hotel Villa Souvenir,** V. Trento, 16 (☎/fax 0541 24 365). Bus #11: stop 12. Turn left from the bus and then right onto Viale Trento. Large, sunny, airy, and spotlessly clean rooms in a fabulous location. Let Gianni serve you *cappuccino* in the morning in his brightly-lit plant filled breakfast room. Buffet breakfast included. Open June to mid-Sept. Singles €13-20; doubles €26-40. AmEx/MC/V. ❷

▨ **Hotel Cirene,** V. Cirene, 50 (☎0541 39 09 04; fax 30 41 89; www.hotelcirene.com). Bus #11: stop 13. From V. Tripoli, heading towards P. Tripoli, turn left onto V. Cirene. Beautiful, antique-style hotel run by a kindly couple. Neat rooms, some with balconies, all with bath and TV. Buffet breakfast included. Singles €31; doubles €46.50; triples €53. Full- and half-pension available. AmEx/MC/V. ❸

▨ **Saxon,** V. Cirene, 36 (☎/fax 0541 39 14 00). Bus #11: stop 13. Exit the bus to left, turn right on V. Misurata then left on V. Cirene. A small, 3-star hotel on a quiet street. 30 soothing blue rooms with TV, phone, and fridge. Breakfast included. Singles €27.89-45.45; doubles €51.65. AmEx/MC/V. ❸

Albergo Filadelphia, V. Pola, 25 (☎0541 23 679). Bus #11: stop 12. From V. le Trento, take a left onto V. le Sauro. Hospitable owner. 1st fl. doubles have balconies. Some rooms with bath. Open Apr.-Sept. Singles €21; doubles €42. AmEx/MC/V. ❷

Hotel Italia, V. Misurata, 13 (☎0541 39 09 94; fax 38 14 87; hotelitaliarimini@virgilio.it). Bus #11: stop 13. From V. le Tripoli, turn onto V. le Cirene. V. Misurata intersects it. 23 clean, white rooms, all with bath. Buffet breakfast included. €25-33 per person. Full-pension available. During Aug. €45 per person. MC/V. ❸

Pensione Millefiori, V. Pola, 42 (☎0541 25 617; fax 43 33 16; hpeonia@libero.it). Bus #11: stop 12. A family-oriented *pensione* with large rooms and soft beds. Buffet breakfast included. €21 per person. ❷

Milord, V. Ariosto, 19 (☎0541 38 17 66; fax 38 57 62). Bus #11: stop 16. Exit the bus to right and head left on V. Ariosto. Right off of V. le Regina Elena. 38 spacious rooms with bath, TV and phone right next to the train track. A/C available upon request. Has beach cabins. Restaurant downstairs. Buffet breakfast included. €26-37 per person. Half- and full-pension available. AmEx/MC/V. ❸

Quisisana, V. R. Elena, 41 (☎0541 38 13 85; fax 38 78 16). Bus #11: stop 15. Minimum stay 3 days. 10% surcharge for single room. All rooms with TV. Buffet breakfast included. Full- and half-pension available from restaurant on 1st fl. €23.25-33.57 per person; full-pension €27.89-45.45 per person. MC/V. ❸

Camping: Maximum, V. le Principe di Piemonte, 57 (☎0541 37 26 02; fax 37 02 71). Bus #11: stop 33. Reception daily 9am-noon and 4-10pm. Open June-Sept. €4-9 per adult, €9-16 per tent. Bungalows from €41. MC/V. ❶

🔆 FOOD

Rimini's **covered market,** between V. Castelfidardo and the *Tempio,* provides a wide array of food. (Open M, W, and F-Sa 7:15am-1pm and 5-7:30pm, Tu and Th 7:15am-1pm.) The **rosticceria** in the market has inexpensive seafood. The **STANDA supermarket,** V. Vespucci, 133, is between P. Kennedy and P. Tripoli. (Open June-Sept. M-Sa 8am-11:30pm.)

Pizzeria al Taglio, V. Misurata, 5 (☎0541 39 28 78). Turn onto it from V. le Vespucci. Close to P. Kennedy. Large, fresh pizzas cooked while you wait. Try the *pizza caprese* (cheese, olive oil, basil, and raw tomatoes) or the *pizza diavoli* (mozzarella, tomatoes and salami). Pizza €4-6. Open daily noon-3pm and 5:30pm-2am. ❷

Osteria Pizzeria Le Logge, V. le Trieste, 5 (☎0541 55 978). Gigantic pizzas, generous portions, and outdoor seating make up for slow service. Delicious risotto dishes such as *risotto alla asparagi* (with asparagus, €5.20). Pizza €3.20-7.30, *primi* €4.20-7.80. Open daily 7pm-1:30am. AmEx/MC/V. ❸

Ristorante-Pizzeria Pic Nic, V. Tempio Malatestiano, 30 (☎0541 21 916). From V. IV Novembre heading towards P. Tre Martiri, turn right at the sign and go straight. Local favorite with eclectic decor. Try the *pizza bianco e verde* (baked cheese and herbs, €5.20). *Primi* €6-8, *secondi* €8. Open daily noon-3pm and 7pm-1am. AmEx/MC/V. ❷

La Cucina dei Teatini, Piazzetta Teatini, 3 (☎0541 28 008). Just off V. IV Novembre, close to the temple. Removed from the bustle of the *centro.* Romantic outdoor seating under a covered awning. Eclectic but classy decor. Lots of pottery, subdued but colorful tones, and modern art. *Primi* €8.50, *secondi* €11.50-13. Open M-Sa 12:30-2:30pm and 7:30-10:30pm. AmEx/MC/V. ❹

China Town, V. lo S. Michelino in Foro, 7 (☎0541 25 412). From V. IV Novembre heading towards P. Tre Martiri, turn right on V. lo S. Michelino right after the temple. Enjoy your Chinese *gnocchi* (€2.32), in a softly-lit, red room. Open daily 10am-3pm and 7pm-midnight, closed M morning. AmEx/MC/V. ❶

Gelateria Nuovo Fiore, V. Vespucci, 7 (☎0541 23 602), with a 2nd location at V. Vespucci, 85 (☎0541 39 11 22). Skip this bar's rather unremarkable *gelato* and go instead for their specialty concoctions. Try the sinfully delicious *tartufo affogato alla Kalua* (truffle *gelato* drowned in Kahlua). Elaborate *gelato* mixed with fruit, whipped cream, and chocolate €6.50. Open Mar.-Oct. daily 8am-3am; Jan.-Feb. Sa-Su 8am-3am. ❷

👁 🏖 SIGHTS AND BEACHES

▧ THE BEACH. Rimini's most coveted sight is its remarkable beach of finely sifted sand, wild umbrellas, and mild Adriatic waves. More expensive hotels reserve strips of beach with chairs and umbrellas for their guests. If you're not their guest, make sure you're on the public beach. **Beach 26,** Fabrizio-Gabriele (☎0541 68 00 41; www.bagno26rimini.com), provides amenities such as chairs and umbrellas, Internet access, whirlpools, a gym, volleyball courts, and lockers. Fees vary but average €5 per day. At night, it has a fun atmosphere, with a bar, live music and Caribbean theme. Vendors along the beach offer countless water sports, including kayaking, jet skiing, parasailing, and deep-sea diving.

TEMPIO MALATESTIANO. A tour of the historic center should begin with this Renaissance masterpiece constructed in Franciscan Gothic style. In the 1440s the ruler Sigismondo Malatesta (Sigmund Headache) made the church a monument to himself and his fourth wife Isotta. His image remains atop the black elephants in the first chapel on the left. Sigismondo Malatesta was the only person in history canonized to hell as a guilty heretic by the pope. A soldier, patriot, and avid patron of the arts, Sigismondo ruled Rimini at its height (1417-1468), employing artists like Piero della Francesca and Leon Battista Alberti. Alberti designed the facade of the new church after the Roman **Arch of Augustus,** which still stands at the gates of Rimini. The interior and wooden-trussed roof recall the temple's original Franciscan design. *(On V. IV Novembre. Follow V. Dante Alighieri from train station. ☎0541 51 130. Open M-Sa 7:50am-12:30pm and 3:30-6:30pm, Su 9am-1pm and 3:30-7pm.)*

PIAZZA CAVOUR. Rimini's medieval and contemporary center contains one of the oddest ensembles of buildings in Italy. The tall Renaissance arcade of the **Palazzo Garampi,** the first building on the right when facing away from the Pescheria, contrasts dramatically with the adjoining fortress-like **Palazzo dell'Arengo** and the smaller **Palazzo del Podestà,** in the middle when facing away from the Pescheria. Perpendicular to the municipal building lies the pink brick **Teatro Comunale** (1857), which lost its auditorium to WWII bombs. A motley collection of shops, bars, and offices surrounds the Renaissance **Pescheria** (fish market). The four stone fish, located in each corner of the interior arcade space, once spouted water into the small canals for cleaning fish (visible under the benches). There are two statues in the center of the piazza: an eccentric, mossy fountain (1543) engraved with an inscription about Leonardo da Vinci, and a seated Pope Paul V (1614) brandishing ferocious eagles. *(From the train station follow V. D. Alighieri to V. IV Novembre. At P. Tre Martiri turn right on C. d'Augusto. Palazzo del Podestà open for exhibitions. Check with tourist office.)*

ARCH OF AUGUSTUS. This triumphal arch, built in 27 BC in honor of the Emperor Augustus, is the oldest surviving Roman archway. Along with the Tiberian Bridge (located just outside of the city), the arch reflects the town's importance to the Romans. Construction makes it impossible to see the arch up close, but there is an inscription to the Emperor on the upper part, and depictions of the gods Jupiter, Neptune, Apollo, and Minerva. The arch serves as a bold gateway into P. Tre Martitiri, one of the busiest areas of the *centro storico. (Follow V. IV Novembre to P. Tre Martiri and turn left on C. d'Augusto.)*

NORTHEAST ITALY

♫ ENTERTAINMENT

Rimini is notorious for its nonstop partying, be it on the beach by day, or in the *discoteche* by night. On the first weekend of September of even numbered years, Rimini hosts a festival on the beach. A pontoon bridge is built of boats in the water, and there are classical concerts, parties and a fireworks display. If dancing isn't your thing, there is also a bustling nightlife scene in the historic center by the old fish market. From P. Cavour, follow **V. Pescheria,** which is lined with countless pubs and bars that are lively until 3am.

All of Rimini's clubs lie along or near the *lungomare* in Rimini sud and surrounding areas. The only nightclub within easy walking distance of Rimini *centro* is **Embassy** (see below). Clubs change their hours and prices frequently, and many shut down during the winter. For exact entrance fees and opening times, call before going. Prices can be exorbitant, so hang on to the discount passes that you are likely to pick up along V. Vespucci and V. Regina Elena.

Many clubs offer free bus services (check at the travel agency in P. Tripoli for schedules; open M-Sa 8:30am-7pm and Su 9am-noon), but there is also a **Blue Line** bus service (€3 per night) that runs from mid-July to August for disco-goers. Lines originate at the station and travel the bus #11 route up V. Vespucci and Viale Regina Elena to the nearby beach towns (every 20min.) and back. Buy tickets on the bus. The last bus is generally around 5:30am. Be careful not to miss it; cab rides back to Rimini are expensive.

L'Altro Mondo Studio's, V. Flaminia, 328, Mirimare (☎0541 37 31 51; www.altromondo.com). Free bus service drop-off at the door, or take bus #11 to stop 31 and walk 10-15min. One of Rimini's best, though little-discussed nightclubs. Mix of house and techno. Don't miss the amazing laser show around midnight. International crowd is young and stylish. Cover about €20. Open daily 11pm-5am.

Cocorico, V. Chietti, 44, Riccione (☎0541 60 51 83), 10km south of Rimini, take bus #11. From the outside, Cocorico looks like a suburban house, surrounded by a white picket fence. Here, though, the trees sway not from the wind but from the bass coming from one of Rimini's most fashionable parties. 4 dance floors play house and techno. Cover of about €20 includes 1 drink. Open F-Sa. Call for schedule.

Embassy, V. Vespucci, 33 (☎0541 23 934 or 335 815 6340), 5min. walk from P. Kennedy. Reminiscent of a homey Italian villa, this club is slightly pretentious, but as the only disco in *marina centro,* how could it not be? One indoor techno room and a mix of house, techno and hip hop in the outdoor garden. 18-25 year-old crowd doesn't get going until 1am, picking up when the foam machines start. Cover around €10-16. Drink cards. Open daily 11pm-4am.

Life, V. le Reg. Margherita, 11, Bellariva (☎0541 37 34 73), free bus service, or take bus #11. A little grungy, but a lot of fun. Join the party-loving staff in taking tequila body shots and playing pass-the-ice-cube. Free drink from the bar at 2:30am. Cover about €9. Open daily 11pm-4am.

Walky Cup by Aquafa'n, V. Pistoia, Riccone. (☎0541 60 30 50). Use the free bus service or take bus #11 to Riccione and then #45 to Aquafa'n. Multiple dance floors spinning house, techno and hip hop. Themes change nightly, but the crowd is always well-dressed. Amusement park inside. Water park open until midnight. Cover about €20. Open F-Sa 11pm-4am. Call for hours during the week.

Byblo's Disco Dinner Club, V. P. Castello, 24 (☎0541 69 02 52; www.byblo-sclub.com). Misano, follow signs from Aquafan. No bus service available. House and

Latin music. Sophisticated club caters to BMW-driving late-20-somethings. Outdoor dance floor surrounded by palm trees and candlelit tables. Cover about €15-35. Open W and F-Su 9:30pm-6am.

Carnaby, V. Brindisi, 20, Rivazzurra (☎0541 37 32 04; www.carnaby.it). Free bus service, or bus #11: stop 26. Teenagers in scanty jeans and tank tops eye each other under a crashed yellow Volkswagen bug. 3 levels play house, hip hop, and classic rock/ oldies. Cover about €8-18. Open daily 10pm-4am.

SAN MARINO   ☎0549

San Marino was founded in AD 301 by Marinus, a pious stone-cutter, when the unwanted attentions of an amorous woman drove him to take refuge on Mount Titano. Legend has it that the son of the noblewoman who owned Mt. Titano despised Christians. When he tried to attack Marinus, God paralyzed him. The noblewoman promised to convert to Christianity and give Marinus and his followers Mt. Titano if he healed her son. 1700 years later, San Marino is still a 26 sq. km republic boasting brightly-garbed troops and UN recognition. In proportion to its population of 28,000, San Marino is also the most visited country in the world. The cobblestoned streets, winding around the mountain and the three fortresses, are lined with trinket stands and packed with tourists. The view of the countryside from atop the Rocca Guaita alone is worth the trek to this tiny country.

▆ TRANSPORTATION

Trains: The closest station is in Rimini, connected to San Marino by bus.

Buses: Fratelli Benedettini (☎0549 90 38 54) and **Bonelli Bus** (☎0541 37 24 32) leave from San Marino's historical center (50min., every hr., €3.36) to Rimini's train station and to V. Calzecchi in Rimini Sud (South), Rivazzurra. Arrive 15min. before bus departs; they fill quickly.

Cableways: (☎0549 88 35 90) San Marino's *funivia* runs from Borgo Maggiore to the historical center (every 15min.; 7:50am-8pm; €2.07, €3.10 round-trip).

Taxis: (☎0549 99 14 41), in P. Lo Stradone.

▌▌ ORIENTATION AND PRACTICAL INFORMATION

San Marino's streets wind around **Mount Titano,** and signs lead pedestrians from one attraction to the next. From the bus, exit to the left, climb the staircase and pass through the **Porta San Francesco** to begin the ascent. From the *porta,* **Via Basilicus** leads up to **Piazza Titano.** From there, **Contrada del Collegio** leads through **Piazza Garibaldi** to **Piazza della Libertà.**

Tourist Office: Contra Omagnano, 20 (☎0549 88 24 00 or 88 24 10; fax 88 25 75; statoturismo@omniway.sm). From P. Garibaldi, follow C. del Collegio to P. della Libertà. Open M and Th 8:15am-2:15pm and 3-6pm; Tu, W and F 8:15am-2:15pm. **Branch office** (☎0549 88 29 14), in Contrada del Collegio, near P. della Libertà. Open W and F 9am-1pm and 2-6:30pm. Tourist **info booth** in Piazzale Stradone, just before P. S. Francesco. Rents listening guides €2.75. Open daily 8:30am-noon and 2:30-5pm.

Border Controls: None, but the tourist office will stamp your passport for €1.03.

Currency Exchange: San Marino mints its own coins in the same denominations as the euro, but they are mostly saved as collector's items. If you should chance to get a San Marino coin, it is used interchangeably with the euro.

Emergency: ☎113 or 115. Ambulance: ☎118.

Police: ☎0549 88 77 77

Post Office: Viale Onofri (☎0549 88 29 09). Open M-F 8:30am-6pm, Sa 8:30am-noon.

Coin and Stamp Office: P. Garibaldi, 5 (☎0549 88 23 70). Open M-F 8:15am-6:15pm, Sa-Su 8:15am-6:15pm.

COUNTRY CODE	San Marino's country code is 00378. It's only necessary to dial when calling from outside Italy.

⌂ ☐ ACCOMMODATIONS AND FOOD

San Marino's hotels are small and overpriced, but the Republic is an easy daytrip from Rimini or Ravenna. The **Diamond Hotel ❹**, Contra del Collegio, 50 (☎0549 99 10 03), across from Basilica di San Marino, has five breezy rooms which overlook the crowded streets below. (Breakfast included. Doubles €54. **Restaurant ❸** downstairs. *Primi* €7.50-8.50, *secondi* €9-12. MC/V.) **Hotel La Rocca ❸**, Salita alla Rocca, 37 (☎0549 99 11 66), under the castle, offers 10 spotless rooms with TV, bath, and great views. Singles €31-51; doubles €23-34 per person; triples €19-30 per person. AmEx/MC/V.)

The food scene in San Marino is similarly overpriced. Snack bars and generic tourist fare are abundant. Many restaurants offer balcony seating, but the view will not hide your small portion of overcooked pasta. For more affordable food, try the fruit and vegetable **market**, Contra Omereli, 2, just off P. Titano (open daily June-Sept. 9:30am-8pm; Oct.-May 8am-noon and 3:30-6:30pm), or the supermarket **Alimentari Chiaruzzi**, Contra del Collegio, 13, between P. Titano and P. Garibaldi. (Open June-Sept. daily 8am-midnight, Oct.-May daily 8am-8pm. AmEx/MC/V.)

◉ ♫ SIGHTS AND ENTERTAINMENT

ROCCA GUAITA. One of San Marino's best vista points, 11th-century Rocca Guaita, is reachable by a steep climb. This structure once served as the principal defense bulwark of Mt. Titano and San Marino. Stroll around the tower ramparts, a chapel, and a prison. Peer over the tower walls to see how the fortress is cut out of the side of the mountain. *(Follow signs from Piazza Libertà. ☎0549 99 13 69. Open Apr.-Sept. daily 8am-8pm, Oct.-Mar. 8:50am-5pm. €2.07, combined ticket with Rocca Cesta €3.10.)*

ROCCA CESTA AND ROCCA MONTALE. Farther along the castle trail stands the less popular but still impressive Rocca Cesta. It houses an arms museum with chain mail, spears, rifles, and other weaponry. At the top, there is another view of the countryside and of Rocca Guaita. Follow the trail outside Rocca Cesta to the 3rd tower, Rocca Montale, which can only be seen from outside. *(☎0549 99 12 95. Open Apr.-Sept. daily 8am-8pm, Oct.-Mar. 8:50am-5pm. €2.07, cumulative ticket €3.10.)*

MUSEO DELLA TORTURA. A museum dedicated to over 100 original instruments used for human torture. Listen to soothing classical music as you read about how to flay or impale a human body. Descriptions in English. *(☎0549 99 12 15. Museum is just to right after entering main gate, near the porta S. Francesco. Open July-Aug. daily 9am-midnight, Sept.-May daily 10am-7pm. €6, students €4.)*

MUSEO DELLE CURIOSITÀ. This museum is rather like taking a tour through the oddities section of the Guinness Book of World Records. The collection of unique objects includes sandals worn by a Grecian prostitute. *(Salita alla Rocca, 26. ☎0549 99 24 37. Open daily 9am-midnight. €5.50.)*

PALAZZO PUBLICO. Francesco Azzuri erected this white beacon (1884-1894) atop the ruins of the *Parva Domus Commuis*. The exterior is far more interesting than the inside, except for the anachronistic meeting room upstairs adorned with frescoes, painted woodwork, and large-screen TVs. The changing of the guard takes place in front of the palace in the spring, summer, and fall at half past the hour from 8:30am to 6:30pm. Arrive 10min. before to secure a place, as droves of tourists flock to the front of the palace to see one brightly-dressed guard replace another. *(P. della Libertà. ☎ 0549 88 53 70. Open Apr.-Sept. daily 8am-8pm, Oct.-Mar. 8:50am-5pm. €2.07 includes Chiesa San Francesco.)*

MEDIEVAL FESTIVAL. From August 3 to September 3, the republic stages a medieval festival with parades, food, musicians, and jugglers. There is an additional celebration on September 3, the **Palio delle Balestre**, or crossbowman's show, which commemorates the establishment of the Republic. Increased bus service allows those not staying in San Marino to participate. *(Call the tourist office for the exact dates and other info. www.omniway.sm/medieval.)*

FLORENCE (FIRENZE)

Shortly after his public debut as a clerk in 1494, the political fortunes of Niccolo Machiavelli skyrocketed when he acquired the pompous title "secretary to the chancery of the commune of Florence." The list of people he served as an envoy reads like a 16th-century *Who's Who*, but his connections were not enough to save his infant republic from collapse and the man himself from torture and exile when Cosimo de' Medici brought Machiavelli up on conspiracy charges. His masterpiece of domination and statecraft, *The Prince*, was penned in an attempt to regain favor with the Medici clan, and so he praised their cold brutality and willingness to torture. Charles V's sack of Rome and the downfall of the Medici Pope Clement VII ended Machiavelli's hopes of re-gaining office, however; he died while still in exile.

Machiavelli's life is a window onto what was arguably Florence's greatest century, when the city became the European capital of art, architecture, commerce, and political thought. Machiavelli was a typically political-minded and ambitious Florentine, albeit a slightly more controversial one. Florentine students today quote Marx and Malcolm X in street graffiti, and children brashly kick soccer balls against the side of the duomo. When the Arno flooded its banks in 1966, swamping Santa Croce and the Uffizi in 6m of water, Florentines and foreigners alike braved the waters to rescue paintings, sculptures, and books. Be prepared to swim through crowds of tourists and undulating entrance fees to see the emblems of Florence's one-time intellectual and artistic preeminence.

HIGHLIGHTS OF FLORENCE

EXPERIENCE David-hopping, from Michelangelo's formidable hunk in the **Accademia** (p. 359) to Donatello's supple bronze boy in the **Bargello** (p. 355).

CLIMB to the top of **Brunelleschi's dome** to reach **Michelangelo's cupola** (p. 351) and a 360-degree panorama of Florence.

RELISH the works of **Botticelli, Giotto, Raphael,** and just about any other Renaissance grandmaster in the unparalleled art collection of the **Uffizi** (p. 354).

ESCAPE the hordes and heat of Florence in the Arno Valley's **Fiesole** (p. 364).

SINK into a juicy cut of *bistecca fiorentina* at a traditional **Tuscan trattoria** (p. 347).

ADMIRE **Ponte Vecchio**'s late-afternoon light sparkling off waves and wares (p. 355).

PICNIC at the crest of **Boboli Hill** in the hedge-rowed gardens (p. 361).

✈ INTERCITY TRANSPORTATION

Flights: Amerigo Vespucci Airport (☎055 31 58 74), in the Florentine suburb of Peretola. Mostly domestic and charter flights. The orange **ATAF** bus #62 connects the train station to the airport (€1). Buy tickets from the *tabacchi* on the upper level of the departure side of airport.

SITA, V. S. Caterina da Siena, 157 (☎800 3737 6046 or 055 28 46 61), runs regular buses (€4) to airport from station.

Galileo Galilei Airport (☎050 50 07 07), in Pisa. Take airport express from Florence train station (1¼hr., 10 per day, €4.85). In Florence, ask for info at the "air terminal" (☎055 21 60 73) halfway down platform #5 in train station. Open daily 7:30am-5pm.

Trains: Santa Maria Novella Station, across from S. Maria Novella. Florence's only modern-style building. Info office open daily 7am-9pm; after hours call national train info ☎ 848 88 80 88. **Luggage storage** and lost property services available (p. 339). Trains depart every hr. to: **Bologna** (1hr., 4:33am-10:34pm, €7.75); **Milan** (3½hr., 5:44am-9:13pm, €22); **Rome** (3½hr., 5:55am-10:55pm, €15-22); **Siena** (1½hr., 10 per day, 8:33am-8:30pm, €5.30); and **Venice** (3hr., 4 per day, €19).

Buses: 3 major bus companies serve Tuscany's towns. Offices near P. della Stazione.

SITA, V. S. Caterina da Siena, 15r (☎800 3737 6046 or 055 28 46 61). To: **Arezzo** (2½hr., 3 per day, €4.10); **Poggibonsi** (1 hr., 11 per day, €4.20); **San Gimignano** (1½hr., 14 per day, €5.70); **Siena** (1½hr., 2 per day, €6.50); **Volterra** via **Colle Val D'Elsa** (2hr., 6 per day, €6.66).

LAZZI, P. Adua, 1-4r (☎055 35 10 61). To: **Lucca** (every hr., 6:50am-8:15pm, €4.50); **Pisa** (every hr., 6:50am-6:15pm, €5.80); **Pistoia** (6:50am-6pm, €2.60); and **Prato** (6am-11pm, €2).

CAP, Largo Alinari, 9 (☎055 21 46 37). To **Prato** (50min., 6am-8pm, €2).

✦ ORIENTATION

From Stazione S. Maria Novella, a short walk on **Via de'Panzani** and a left onto **Via de'Cerrentari** leads to the **duomo**, the heart of Florence. Just as all roads lead to Rome, all streets in Florence lead to the instantly recognizable dome, soaring high above every other building. **Via de'Calzaiuoli,** dominated by throngs of pedestrians, leads south from the duomo to the **Piazza Signoria,** the statue-filled plaza in front of the **Palazzo Vecchio** and the world-famous **Uffizi Gallery.** The other major piazza is the **Piazza della Repubblica,** a vast plaza the size of an entire city block. Major streets run from this piazza north back toward the duomo and south toward the shop-lined **Ponte Vecchio** (literally, "Old Bridge"). The Ponte Vecchio is one of five bridges that cross from central Florence into the **Oltrarno,** the district south of the Arno River. When navigating in Florence, note that most **streets change names unpredictably,** often every few blocks. For guidance through Florence's tangled center, grab a **free map** (one with a street index) from the tourist office, *Informazione Turistica,* across the piazza from the train station (see **Practical Information,** p. 338).

☰ LOCAL TRANSPORTATION

Public Transportation: Orange **ATAF** city buses will take you almost anywhere from 6am to 1am. Buy tickets at any newsstand, *tabacchi,* or coin-operated ticket dispenser before boarding. €1 per 1hr. of unlimited use, €3.90 for 4 such tickets; €1.80 per 3hr.; €4 per 24hr.; €7.20 per 3 days; €12 per week. Validate ticket on board using orange machine or risk €50 fine. Once validated, ticket allows travel on any bus for 1hr. From 9pm to 6am tickets sold on bus (€1.55). As you exit the train station, **ATAF info and ticket office** (☎800 424 500) will be on your left. Open daily 6:30am-8pm. Free bus map. #7 to Fiesole, #10 to Settignano, #17 to Villa Camerate (€1).

Car Rental: Hertz, V. Finiguerra, 17 (☎055 239 8205). 25+. Open M-F 8am-11pm, Sa 8am-7pm, Su 8am-1pm. **Maggiore** (☎055 31 12 56), at airport. 19+. Open daily 8:30am-10:30pm. At V. Finiguerra, 13 (☎055 21 02 38). Open daily 8:30am-10:30pm. **Avis** (☎055 31 55 88), at airport. 25+. Open 8am-11:30pm. Also at Borgo Ognissanti, 128r (☎055 21 36 29). Open M-F 8am-1pm and 3-6pm, Sa 8am-4pm.

FLORENCE

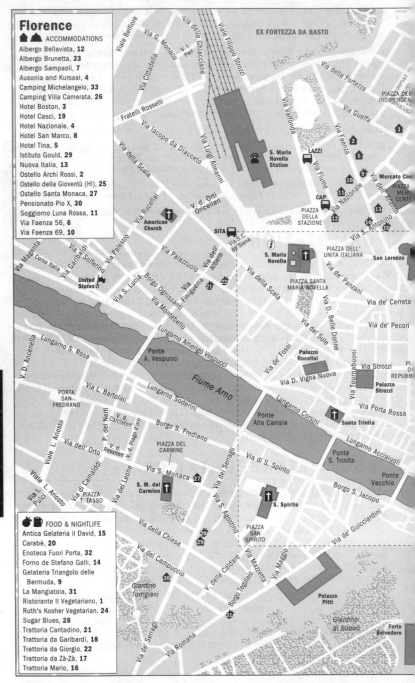

Florence

🏠🏕 ACCOMMODATIONS

Albergo Bellavista, 12
Albergo Brunetta, 23
Albergo Sampaoli, 7
Ausonia and Kursaal, 4
Camping Michelangelo, 33
Camping Villa Camerata, 26
Hotel Boston, 3
Hotel Casci, 19
Hotel Nazionale, 4
Hotel San Marco, 8
Hotel Tina, 5
Istituto Gould, 29
Nuova Italia, 13
Ostello Archi Rossi, 2
Ostello della Gioventù (HI), 25
Ostello Santa Monaca, 27
Pensionato Pio X, 30
Soggiorno Luna Rossa, 11
Via Faenza 56, 6
Via Faenza 69, 10

🍎🍷 FOOD & NIGHTLIFE

Antica Gelateria il David, 15
Carabè, 20
Enoteca Fuori Porta, 32
Forno de Stefano Galli, 14
Gelateria Triangolo delle
  Bermuda, 9
La Mangiatoia, 31
Ristorante Il Vegetariano, 1
Ruth's Kosher Vegetarian, 24
Sugar Blues, 28
Trattoria Cantadino, 21
Trattoria da Garibaldi, 18
Trattoria da Giorgio, 22
Trattoria da Zà-Zà, 17
Trattoria Mario, 16

FLORENCE

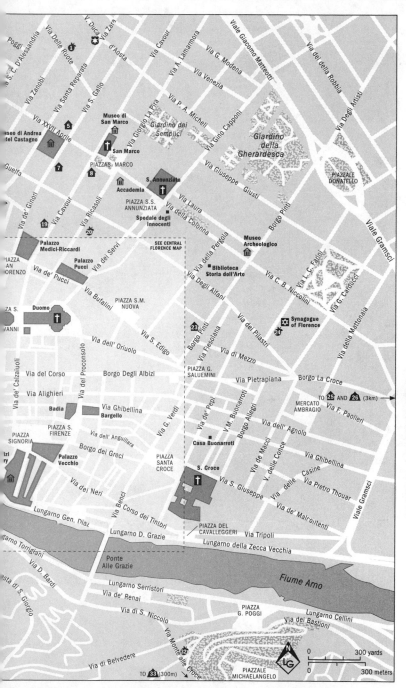

FLORENCE

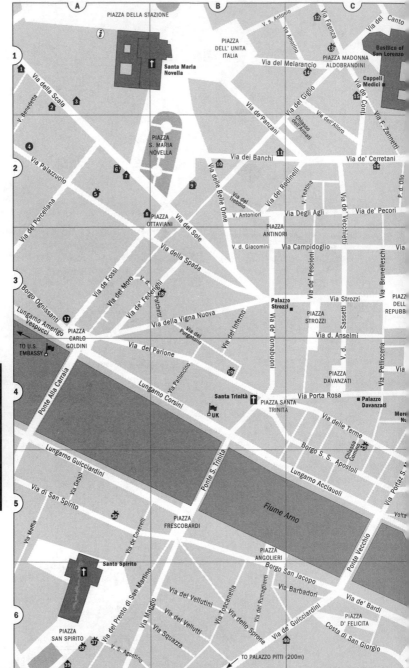

FLORENCE

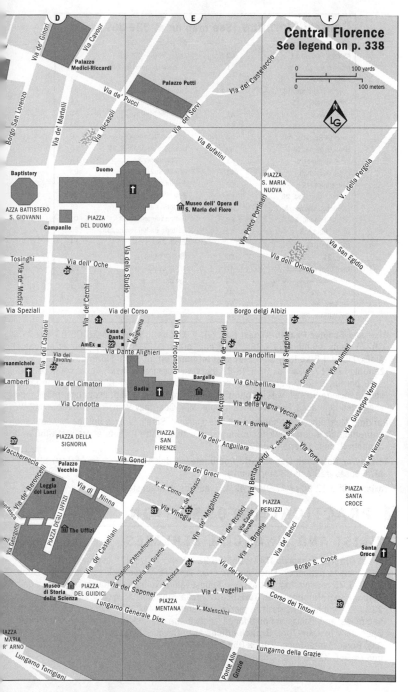

Central Florence
See legend on p. 338

FLORENCE

Central Florence (See map on p. 336-337)

♠ ACCOMMODATIONS		🍅 FOOD	
Albergo Firenze, **21**	D3	Acqua al Due, **27**	E4
Albergo Margaret, **2**	A1	Al Lume di Candela, **29**	C4
Hotel Abaco/		Amon, **5**	A2
Hotel Giappone, **11**	B2	Enoteca Alessi, **20**	D3
Hotel Bellettini, **15**	C1	Il Borgo Antico, **38**	A6
Hotel Elite, **3**	A1	Il Cantinone, **36**	A5
Hotel il Perseo, **16**	C2	Il Latini, **18**	B3
Hotel La Scaletta, **40**	B6	Oltrarno Trattoria Casalinga, **37**	A6
Hotel Le Vigne, **10**	B2	La Loggia degli Albizi, **25**	F3
Hotel Montreal, **1**	A1	Le Colonnine, **34**	F6
Hotel Visconti, **8**	A3	Perchè No?, **23**	D4
Katti House, **12**	C1	Ristorante de' Medici, **14**	C1
Locanda Orchidea, **26**	F3	Rose's Cafe, **19**	B4
Pensione Ottaviani, **8**	A2	Trattoria Anita, **32**	E5
Sorelle Bandini, **39**	A6	Trattoria Antellesi, **13**	C1
Tourist House, **7**	A2	Trattoria da Benvenuto, **33**	E5
🍷 NIGHTLIFE		Vivoli, **28**	F4
Blob, **31**	E5	● SERVICES	
The Chequers Pub, **6**	A2	BM Bookstore, **17**	A3
The Fiddler's Elbow, **9**	B2	Gymnasium, **4**	A2
May Day, **22**	D3		
Tabasco, **30**	D4		
The William, **35**	F6		

Bike and Scooter Rental: Alinari Noleggi, V. Guelfa, 85r (☎055 28 05 00; fax 271 7871), rents scooters for €28-55 per day; bikes €12-18 per day, helmet included. AmEx/MC/V. **I Bike Italy** (see **Practical Information,** p. 338). **Florence by Bike,** V. S. Zanobi, 120/122r (☎/fax 055 48 89 92; www.florencebybike.it), rents bikes (€2.50-3.50 per hr., €12-32 per day) and **scooters** (50-650cc, €30-92 per day). Bike rental should include helmet, water bottles, locks, spare tubes, pump, insurance, maps, and suggested itineraries. Reserve ahead. Open Mar.-Oct. daily 9am-7:30pm. AmEx/MC/V.

Parking: Most city center hotels don't offer parking. Small garages dot the city but keep unpredictable hours—look for a blue sign with a white P. Lots at train station and beneath P. della Libertà open 24hr.

Towed-Car Retrieval: Depositeria Comunale, V. dell'Arcovata, 6 (☎055 30 82 49). ATAF buses #23 and 33 stop nearby.

Taxis: (☎055 43 90 or 47 98 or 42 42), outside the train station.

🛈 PRACTICAL INFORMATION

TOURIST AND FINANCIAL SERVICES

Tourist Offices: Consorzio ITA (☎055 28 28 93 and 21 95 37), in train station by track #16, next to pharmacy. Lines can be quite long. Finds rooms if you come in person. €2.50-7.75 commission; not always the best value. No maps or tourist info. Open daily 8:45am-8pm. **Informazione Turistica,** P. della Stazione, 4 (☎055 21 22 45; ☎/fax 238 1226), directly across the piazza from station's main exit. Info on cultural events, free maps, and listings of hours for all sights in the city. Ask for a map with street index. Open daily 8:30am-7pm. **Branch offices** at V. Cavour, 1r (☎055 29 08 32 or 29 08 33); Borgo Santa Croce, 29r (☎055 234 0444); V. Manzoni, 16 (☎055 23 320); airport (☎055 31 58 74). Similar hours.

Walking Tours:

Enjoy Florence (☎055 167 274 819; www.enjoyflorence.com). Guides give fast-paced, informative tours to small groups. Old city center tours focus on history of medieval and Renaissance Florence. Tours leave daily at 10am in front of Thomas Cook office at the Ponte Vecchio. €15.50, under 26 €12.91.

Walking Tours of Florence, P. Santo Stefano, 2b (☎055 264 5033; www.artviva.com), 1 block north of Ponte Vecchio. A theater company offers leisurely walks around Florence, accompanied by an anecdotal history. €25, students under 26 €20. Also offers a tour of the Uffizi (€35, pre-booked gallery ticket included); Tuscan wine country (€49); and nearby Siena and San Gimignano (€75). Tours available in German, French, and Russian. Open daily Apr.-Nov. 8am-6:30pm; Jan.-Feb. 8:30am-1:30pm; Mar. 8:30am-3:30pm.

Biking Tours: Florence by Bike, V. S. Zanobi, 120/122r (☎/fax 055 48 89 92; www.florencebybike.it). Gives bike tours of historic Florence, the Chianti region, and Florentine hills (€23.24-60.43). Reserve ahead. Open daily 9am-7:30pm. **I Bike Italy** (☎055 234 2371; www.ibikeitaly.com). Offers 1- and 2-day bike tours of varying difficulty, through Fiesole, the Chianti, and the Tuscan vineyards. Call ahead.

CTS, V. Ginori, 25r (☎055 28 95 70). Provides Transalpino tickets, discount airfares, car rentals, organized trips, and ISIC cards. Arrive early and take a number. Open M-F 9:30am-1:30pm and 2:30-6pm, Sa 9:30am-12:30pm.

Consulates: UK, Lungarno Corsini, 2 (☎055 28 41 33). Open M-F 9:30am-12:30pm and 2:30-4:30pm. Can be reached by phone M-F 9am-1pm and 2-5pm. **US,** Lungarno Amerigo Vespucci, 38 (☎055 239 8276), at V. Palestro, near the station. Open M-F 9am-12:30pm. **Canadians, Australians,** and **New Zealanders** should contact their consulates in Rome or Milan.

Currency Exchange: Local banks offer the best exchange rates. Most open M-F 8:20am-1:20pm and 2:45-3:45pm. 24hr. **ATMs** all over the city.

American Express: V. Dante Alighieri, 22r (☎055 50 981). From duomo, walk down V. dei Calzaiuoli, turn left onto V. dei Tavolini, and continue to the small piazza. Cashes personal checks for cardholders. Also holds mail for card- and traveler's check-holders at no cost; all others €1.55 per inquiry. €1.55 to leave messages. Open M-F 9am-5:30pm. Open for financial services only Sa 9am-12:30pm.

LOCAL SERVICES

Luggage Storage: In train station at track #16. €2.58 for 12hr. Open daily 4:15am-1:30am.

Lost Property: Ufficio Oggetti Rinvenuti (☎055 235 2190), next to the baggage deposit, for objects left on trains.

English-Language Bookstores: ▓ **Paperback Exchange,** V. Fiesolana, 31r (☎055 247 8154; www.papex.it). Swaps books. Special *Italianistica* section features novels about Brits and Americans in Italy. Open M-F 9am-7:30pm, Sa 10am-1pm and 3:30-7:30pm. Closed 2 weeks in mid-Aug. AmEx/MC/V. **BM Bookstore,** Borgo Ognissanti, 4r (☎055 29 45 75). English-language books on every subject imaginable. Stocks textbooks for American study abroad programs. Open Mar.-Oct. M-Sa 9:30am-7:30pm, Su afternoons; Nov.-Feb. M-Sa 9:30am-7:30pm.

RED AND BLACK ATTACK. Florence's streets are numbered in red and black sequences. Red numbers indicate commercial establishments and black (or blue) numbers denote residential addresses (including most sights and hotels). Black addresses appear here as a numeral only, while red addresses are indicated by a number followed by an "r." If you reach an address and it's not what you're looking for, you've probably got the wrong color.

FROM THE ROAD

FLORENCE TICKET TYRANTS

I thought I had the Italian public transportation system all figured out. Having never encountered a ticket check on Tuscany's trains, I decided that buying one was probably optional. Not five minutes into my first ticket-less ride on Florence's intracity bus systems (ATAF), two blue-shirted men with badges and clipboards boarded the rear of the bus and started their ticket check—with me.

I put on my best "I'm not from around these parts" look and tried to illustrate, through a flurry of upturned hands and shrugged shoulders, my innocent ignorance.

The official waved my invalidated ticket warily.

ATAF: "Ticket. No good."

Me: "Uhhhh... *Non lo sapevo* (I didn't know)... *Mi dispiace* (Sorry)?"

The official irately produced a laminated blue card, which read: "If riding with invalidated ticket, you will be fined €50. IGNORANCE IS NO EXCUSE!"

There was no way out. The door was blocked by the agent's person. With heavy hand and irrational anger rising, I handed over a crisp €50 bill.

Lesson learned: forget the dumb tourist routine—and validate your ticket.

—Paul Guilianelli

Library: Biblioteca Marucelliana, V. Cavour, 43 (☎055 27 221 or 26 062), 2min. from the duomo. Open M-F 8:30am-7pm, Sa 8:30am-1:45pm.

Religious Services: Anglican: St. Mark's Church of England, V. Maggio, 16 (☎055 29 47 64). Su 9am and 10:30am. **Catholic:** In English at the duomo. Sa 5pm. **Episcopal: The American Church,** V. B. Rucellai, 9 (☎055 29 44 17). Su 9am and 11am. **Jewish (Orthodox): Tempio Israelito,** V. Farini, 4 (☎055 24 52 52). F sunset, Sa 8:45am. **Muslim: Centro Culturale Islamico,** P. degli Scarlatti, 1 (☎055 71 16 48).

Bulletin Boards: Lists of people seeking roommates, English teachers, babysitters, and religious and cultural activities conducted in English. Open Tu-F 9am-1pm. **The American Church,** V. B. Rucellai, 9 (☎055 29 44 17), off V. della Scala, near train station.

Ticket Agency: The Box Office, V. Alamanni, 39r (☎055 21 08 04; fax 21 31 12), sells tickets for Florence's theatrical and musical performances, including rock concerts. Advance booking service. Open M-F 10am-7:30pm. Pick up a listing of events in any tourist office or buy the city's entertainment monthly, *Firenze Spettacolo* (€1.55).

Laundromats:

Wash and Dry Lavarapido, V. dei Servi, 105r, 2 blocks from the duomo. **Other locations:** V. della Scala, 52-54r; V. del Sole, 29r; V. Ghibellina, 143r; V. dei Serragli, 87r; V. Morgagni, 21r; V. Nazionale, 129r. Self-service wash and dry €7. Laundry soap €0.80. Open daily 8am-10pm.

Ondo Blu, V. degli Alfani, 24r. Self-service wash and dry €6. Open daily 8am-10pm.

Swimming Pool: Bellariva, Lungarno Colombo, 6 (☎055 67 75 21). Bus #14 from the station or a 15min. walk upstream along the Arno. €6. Open June-Sept. W and F-M 10am-6pm, Tu and Th 10am-6pm and 8:30-11pm.

Everfit SRL, V. Palazzuolo, 49r (☎055 29 33 08). Workout equipment and daily step aerobics. €11 per day; €68 per month.

EMERGENCY AND COMMUNICATIONS

Emergency: ☎113. **Carabinieri:** ☎112. **Medical Emergency:** ☎118. **Road Assistance (ACI):** ☎116. **Fire:** ☎115.

Police Central Office (Questura), V. Zara, 2 (☎055 49 771). Another branch at P. del Duomo, 5. Open M-Th 8:15am-6pm, F-Sa 8:15am-2pm. **Tourist Police: Ufficio Stranieri,** V. Zara, 2 (☎055 49 771), for visa or work-permit problems. Open M-F 8:30am-noon. To report lost or stolen items, go around corner to **Ufficio Denunce,** V. Duca D'Aosta, 3 (☎055 49 771). Open M-Sa 8am-8pm, Su 8am-2pm.

Tourist Medical Service, V. Lorenzo il Magnifico, 59 (☎055 47 54 11). Group of general practitioners and specialists. Doctor on call 24hr. Office visits €45; house calls €65 during day, €80 at night. AmEx/MC/V.

24-Hour Pharmacies: Farmacia Comunale (☎055 28 94 35), at the train station by track #16. **Molteni,** V. dei Calzaiuoli, 7r (☎055 28 94 90).

Internet Access: Walk down any busy street and you're sure to find an Internet cafe. **Internet Train.** 15 locations throughout Florence listed on www.internettrain.it/citta.isp. Offers telnet, email, and web-cruising. Adults €4 per hr., students €3 per hr. Hours vary slightly depending on location. Most open M-F 9am-midnight, Sa 10am-8pm, Su noon-9pm. AmEx/MC/V.

Post Office: (☎055 21 61 22), on V. Pellicceria, off P. della Repubblica. To send packages, go behind the building to V. dei Sassetti, 4. Open M-F 8:15am-7pm, Sa 8:15am-12:30pm. Telegram office in front open 24hr.

Postal Code: 50100.

◪ ACCOMMODATIONS & CAMPING

Florence's large number of budget accommodations make it likely you'll find a room even if you arrive without a reservation. The **Consorzio ITA** in the train station (see **Tourist and Financial Services,** above) can inform you of available rooms and going rates in the one-star *pensioni* and private *affittacamere* that flood Florence. Another option is to check your bag at the train station (see **Intercity Transportation,** above) and start pounding the pavement. Reasonable options should present themselves. Hotel owners are often willing to refer you to others if their establishment has no vacancies; don't hesitate to ask.

Because of the constant stream of tourists, it is best to make reservations *(prenotazioni)* at least 10 days in advance, especially if you plan to visit during Easter or the summer. If you make reservations, the majority of *pensioni* prefer them in writing with at least one night's deposit in the form of a money order; others simply ask that you call to confirm a few days before you arrive.

If you have any complaints, first talk to the proprietor and then to the **Ufficio Controllo Alberghi,** V. Cavour, 37 (☎055 27 601). The municipal government strictly regulates hotel prices; proprietors can charge neither more nor less than the approved range for their category. Rates uniformly increase around 10% every year; the new rates take effect in March or April.

Long-term housing in Florence is easy to secure. If you plan on staying a month or more, check **bulletin boards** (see p. 340), classified ads in *La Pulce,* published three times weekly (€2), or **Grillo Fiorentino,** a free monthly local paper, for apartment, sublet, and roommate listings. Reasonable prices range from €200-600 per month.

FLORENCE

⚠ Each day at Santa Maria Novella Station, **boosters** assail unwitting travelers with offers of rooms at ridiculously cheap prices. These fly-by-night operations are illegal and best avoided. The police routinely evacuate **illegal** *pensioni* during the night, leaving bleary-eyed backpackers to fend for themselves in the wee hours of the morning. As they are unregulated by the government, they may also be dangerous. All legitimate hotels, hostels, campsites, and *affittacamere* in Tuscany are subject to annual government inspections and must post their official rating outside their establishment (from one to five stars). Make sure to look for the stars when securing accommodations, or better yet, just stick with us—*Let's Go* would never leave you searching for a park bench at 4am.

HOSTELS

▩ **Ostello Archi Rossi,** V. Faenza, 94r (☎055 29 08 04; fax 230 2601), 2 blocks from train station. Exit left from station onto V. Nazionale. Take 2nd left onto V. Faenza. Look for blue neon *ostello* sign. Floor-to-ceiling murals, ceramic tiles, and brick archways. Courtyard patio and dining/TV room brimming with travelers. Expansion in the works. Breakfast options range from continental to crepes and omelettes (€1.60-2.60). Dinner €3.60-4.20. Laundry €5.20. Free Internet. **Luggage storage.** June-Sept. arrive before 8am for a room—earlier if in a large group. Room lockout 9:30am-2:30pm; hostel lockout 11am-2:30pm. Curfew 1am. No reservations. 4- to 9-bed dorms €17-23. Reserved rooms for handicapped travelers €26. ❷

▩ **Istituto Gould,** V. de' Serragli, 49 (☎055 21 25 76), in Oltrarno. Take bus #36 or 37 from station to the 2nd stop across the river. Spotless rooms, some overlooking noisy street. Large colonnaded courtyard. Reception M-F 9am-1pm and 3-7pm, Sa 9am-1pm. Su check-out only. No lockout or curfew. 88 beds. All rooms with multiple beds may be rented out dorm-style. Singles €30, with bath €35; doubles €44/€50; triples €56/€63; quads €72/€80. MC/V. ❸

Ostello Santa Monaca, V. S. Monaca, 6 (☎055 26 83 38; fax 28 01 85; www.ostello.it). Follow the directions to the Istituto Gould, but go right off V. dei Serragli onto V. S. Monaca. Crowds up to 20 beds into high-ceilinged rooms. Helpful management and friendly clientele. Minimal kitchen facilities—bring utensils. No meals. Use of clean showers and sheets included. Self-service laundry €6.50 per 5kg. Internet access €4 per hr. June-Sept. arrive before 9am for a room. 7-night max. stay. Reception 6am-1pm and 2pm-1am. Curfew 1am. Reservations must be made by email 3 days in advance. 114 beds. Dorms €16. AmEx/MC/V. ❷

Ostello della Gioventù Europa Villa Camerata (HI), V. Augusto Righi, 2-4 (☎055 60 14 51; fax 61 03 00), northeast of town. Take bus #17 from outside train station (near track #5), or from P. dell'Unità across from station; get off at the Salviatino stop. (Ask the bus driver when to get off.) Walk 8-10min. from the street entrance past a vineyard. Tidy and popular, in a beautiful (if inconveniently located) villa with *loggia* (lodge). Breakfast and sheets included. Dinner €8. Self-service laundry €5.20. 3-night max. Reception daily 7am-12:30pm and 1pm-midnight. Check-out 7-10am. Lockout 10am-2pm. Strict midnight curfew. Make reservations in writing. 4, 6, or 8 beds per room. 322 beds. Dorms €15. €2.58 extra per night without HI card. ❶

Pensionato Pio X, V. de'Serragli, 106 (☎/fax 055 22 50 44). Follow directions to Istituto Gould, and walk a few blocks farther. On right in a courtyard. Full in summer. Quiet, with 3-5 beds per room. Clean, functional rooms. 4 basic lounges. 2-night min. stay, or pay extra €1. 5-night stay max. Arrive before 9am for a room. Check-out 9am. Curfew midnight. No reservations. 54 beds. Dorms €15, with bath €17. ❶

> ⚠ Hotel prices in Florence change regularly; by summer 2003, rates will be **at least** 10-20% higher than those listed here.

HOTELS

PIAZZA SANTA MARIA NOVELLA AND ENVIRONS

The budget accommodations that cluster around this piazza in front of the train station offer a prime location near the duomo and town center. What more could you ask for than stepping out of a cozy *pensione* to be confronted by Alberti's masterful facade on Santa Maria Novella? Ask for a room overlooking the piazza.

Hotel Elite, V. della Scala, 12 (☎055 21 53 95; fax 21 38 32). Follow directions to Albergo Margaret. Engaging service enhances this 2-star hotel's well-maintained rooms. Cozy breakfast and sitting room. All rooms have TV, phone, and A/C. Quieter rooms in the rear. Breakfast €6. Singles with shower €52, with toilet €70; doubles €70/€85; triples with shower €95. ❹

Hotel Abaco, V. dei Banchi, 1 (☎/fax 055 238 1919; abacohotel@tin.it). Follow directions to Hotel Giappone. Reproduction 17th-century antique headboards, noise-proof windows, and free Internet access. Seven rooms, each named after a Renaissance great, include reproductions of artist's most famous work on the walls. All rooms have A/C, phone, and TV. Breakfast included. Laundry €7 per load. Singles €63; doubles €70, with bath €85. Extra bed €10. AmEx/MC/V. ❺

Hotel Visconti, P. Ottaviani, 1 (☎/fax 055 21 38 77). Exit train station and cross to the back of Santa Maria Novella church. Walk past church into P. S. Maria Novella, then across the left side of the piazza until you reach the tiny P. Ottaviani. Bar, TV lounge, and 10 rooms. Breakfast included. Singles €40; doubles €60, with bath €90; triples €80/€100; quads €90. ❹

Hotel Montreal, V. della Scala, 43 (☎055 238 2331; fax 28 74 91; www.hotelmontreal.com). Follow directions to Albergo Margaret. 22 modern, wood-furnished rooms. Helpful reception. Flexible curfew 1:30am. Singles €40; doubles €65, with bath €75; triples €85/€105; quads with bath €120. ❹

Albergo Margaret, V. della Scala, 25 (☎/fax 055 21 01 38). Exit train station to right onto V. D. Orti Oricellari, which leads to V. della Scala; take a left. Plush decor, with small statues on pedestals in the hallway. Kind staff and 7 beautiful rooms, some with balconies. TV, A/C in all rooms. Curfew midnight. June-Aug. singles €50; doubles with shower €70, with full bath €90. Lower prices Sept.-May and for longer stays. ❹

Pensione Ottaviani, P. Ottaviani, 1 (☎055 23 962; fax 29 33 55), upstairs from Hotel Visconti. 20 simple, comfortable rooms on 2 floors. Friendly reception and sunny dining area. Singles €40; doubles with shower €60, with full bath €70; extra bed €25. ❹

Soggiorno Luna Rossa, V. Nazionale, 7 (☎055 230 2185; fax 28 25 52; www.touristhouse.com). Exit train station to left onto V. Nazionale. Small *pensione* with large, high-ceilinged rooms with TVs. Breakfast included. Doubles €63, with bath €78; triples €63/€100; quads or larger €23 per person. ❺

Albergo Bellavista, Largo F. Alinari, 15 (☎055 28 45 28; fax 28 48 74; bellavistahotel@iol.it). Exit train station and cross the piazza diagonally to the left. On 5th floor of an old *palazzo*, just steps from the train station. Comfortable old-fashioned furnishings and accommodating owners. All rooms have beautiful views, balconies, phone, A/C, and bath. Breakfast included. Doubles €98; triples €139. AmEx/MC/V. ❺

Hotel Giappone, V. dei Banchi, 1 (☎055 21 00 90; fax 29 28 77; info@hotelmontreal.com). From train station, cross to the back of Santa Maria Novella church. Walk past church into P. S. Maria Novella and go left onto V. dei Banchi. 8 clean rooms in a central location. All rooms with phone, TV, A/C, Internet jacks, and shower. Singles €42; doubles €67.14, with bath €82.63; triples €98/€103; quad €125. MC/V. ❹

Tourist House, V. della Scala, 1 (☎055 26 86 75; fax 28 25 52; www.touristhouse.com). Follow directions to Albergo Margaret. Extremely friendly proprietors also run Hotel Giappone. Comfortable rooms with bath, TV, and Internet jacks. Some with A/C. Take your breakfast (included) on the adjoining terrace. Singles €67; doubles €83; quads €124. AmEx/MC/V. ❺

Hotel Le Vigne, P. Santa Maria Novella, 24 (☎055 29 44 49; fax 230 2263; www.hotellevigne.it). Large rooms with dark wood furniture, telephone, TV, and A/C; some with views of Santa Maria Novella. Elevator will soon be installed. Check if the rooms on the 4th fl. are cheaper. Singles €72.50, with bath €98; doubles €87/€114; triples with bath €142. AmEx/MC/V. ❺

OLD CITY (NEAR THE DUOMO)

Flooded by tourists, this area tends to be more expensive than elsewhere. Many accommodations provide great views of Florence's monuments, while others lie hidden in Renaissance *palazzi*. Follow V. de' Panzani from the train station and take a left on V. de' Cerretani to reach the duomo.

■ **Locanda Orchidea**, Borgo degli Albizi, 11 (☎/fax 055 248 0346; hotelorchidea@yahoo.it). Take a left off V. Proconsolo from the duomo. Dante's wife was born in this 12th-century *palazzo*, built around a still-intact tower. Newly tiled lobby adorned with canine-themed print cycle. Friendly and helpful management. Book exchange. 7 graceful rooms, some of which open onto a garden. Singles €45; doubles €65; triples €90. ❹

■ **Hotel Il Perseo**, V. de Cerretani, 1 (☎055 21 25 04; fax 28 83 77; www.hotelperseo.com). Exit the train station and walk down V. de' Panzani, which becomes V. de' Cerretani. Aussie-Italian couple welcome travelers to 19 bright, immaculate rooms. All with fans; some with breathtaking views. Cozy bar and TV lounge decorated with proprietor's art. Breakfast included. Internet access €4 per hr. Parking €15.50 per day. Singles €50; doubles €70, with bath €88; triples €93/€115. MC/V. ❹

Albergo Brunetta, Borgo Pinti, 5 (☎/fax 055 247 8134). Exit P. del Duomo on V. dell' Oriuolo behind the duomo. After 2 long blocks, take a left on Borgo Pinti. Good prices for central location. Take advantage of the roof-top terrace that offers a spectacular panorama of Florence. 12 rooms, all without bath. Ask for the *Let's Go* discount. Singles €51.60; doubles €82; triples €103. ❹

Albergo Firenze, P. dei Donati, 4 (☎055 21 42 03 or 21 33 11; fax 21 23 70), off V. del Corso, 2 blocks south of the duomo. Centrally located in a beautiful *palazzo*. 60 modern rooms with tile floors, TV, and bathrooms. Wheelchair accessible. English spoken. Breakfast included. Singles €67; doubles €88; triples €126; quads €156. ❺

Hotel Bellettini, V. de Conti, 7 (☎055 21 35 61; fax 28 35 51; www.firenze.net/hotelbellettini). Located on a side street a stone's throw from the Medici Chapels and the duomo, Bellettini allows you to see it all without having to hear it. Nicely furnished rooms have soft beds, bathroom, A/C, telephone, and TV. Awash in late-afternoon sunlight, the sitting area is a great place to relax after a day of sightseeing. Free Internet and continental buffet breakfast included. Singles €72, with bath €93; doubles €97/€124; triples with bath €155; quads with bath €180. AmEx/MC/V. ❺

VIA NAZIONALE AND ENVIRONS

From P. della Stazione, V. Nazionale leads to budget hotels that are a short walk from both the duomo and the train station. The buildings on V. Nazionale, V. Faenza, V. Fiume, and V. Guelfa are filled with inexpensive establishments, but rooms facing the street may be noisy due to throngs of pedestrians.

■ **Katti House**, V. Faenza, 21 (☎055 21 34 10; www.kattihouse.com). Exit train station onto V. Nazionale; walk 1 block and turn right onto V. Faenza. A jewel among Florence's travel lodgings, it was lovingly renovated by the proprietors and now features hand-made drapes, 400-year-old antiques, and attentive staff. Large rooms with A/C, TV, and bath. Doubles €95; triples €105; quads €105. Prices drop significantly Nov.-Mar. ❺

■ **Via Faenza, 56**, V. Faenza, 56. 6 *pensioni* among the best deals in the city. Same directions as Katti House. Azzi, Anna, and Paola have the same prices and amenities; reception for all 3 is at Azzi.

Pensione Azzi (☎055 21 38 06; fax 264 8613) styles itself as a *locanda degli artisti* (an artists' inn), but all travelers, not just bohemians, will appreciate the friendly management, 12 large, immaculate rooms, and relaxing terrace. Wheelchair accessible. Breakfast included. Singles €41; doubles €62, with bath €77.50. AmEx/MC/V. ❹

Albergo Anna (☎055 239 8322). 8 lovely rooms with frescoes and antique wooden furniture. ❹

Locanda Paola (☎055 21 36 82). 7 minimalist, spotless double rooms, some with views of Fiesole and the surrounding hills. Flexible 2am curfew. ❹

Albergo Merlini (☎055 21 28 48; www.hotelmerlini.it). Murals and red geraniums adorn the lounge/solarium. Handsome polished stone floors throughout. Some rooms offer great views of the duomo. Simple breakfast €5. Flexible 1am curfew. Doubles €69, with bath €80; triples €80/€98; quads €98. AmEx/MC/V. ❺

Albergo Marini (☎055 28 48 24). A polished wood hallway leads to 10 inviting, spotless rooms. If you're staying in a double, ask for the room with the large terrace (#7). Breakfast €5.16. Flexible 1am curfew. Singles €46.48; doubles €61.97, with bathroom €72.30; triples €82.63/€92.96; quads €103.29/€113; quints €123.95/€134.28. ❹

Albergo Armonia (☎055 21 11 46). Posters of American films bedeck 7 clean rooms. Communal bathrooms. Prices drop 25% in winter. Singles €42; doubles €65; triples €90; quads €100. ❹

▨ **Via Faenza, 69,** V. Faenza, 69. 2 comfortable, no-frills accommodations under the same roof. Same directions as above.

Hotel Nella/Pina, 1st and 2nd fl. (☎055 265 4346; fax 2728 3621; www.hotelnella.net). 14 basic rooms and good prices, not to mention free Internet. Recently renovated Nella rooms have A/C, phone, and satellite TV. Ask for the *Let's Go* discount. Nella: singles €52, with bath €57; doubles €83. Pina: singles €47; doubles with bath €62. AmEx/MC/V. ❹

Locanda Giovanna (☎/fax 055 238 13 53). 7 fair-sized, well-kept rooms, some with garden views. Singles €37.40; doubles €57, with bath €67; triples €77/€87. ❹

Hotel Nazionale, V. Nazionale, 22 (☎055 238 2203; fax 238 1735; www.nazionaleho-tel.it). Exit train station and turn left onto V. Nazionale. 9 sunny rooms with comfy beds, all with bath and A/C. Breakfast is included and brought to your room between 8 and 9:30am. Singles €50, with bath €60; doubles €78/€88; triples €97/€110. MC/V. ❹

Ausonia and Kursaal, V. Nazionale, 24 (☎055 49 65 47; www.kursonia.com). Follow directions to Hotel Nazionale. Divided into "regular" rooms (phone) and "superior" rooms (A/C, TV, bathroom). English library and book exchange. Currency exchange. Wheelchair accessible. Breakfast included. Laundry €9. Doubles €82, "superior" doubles €116; triples €109/€143; quads (superior only) €170. MC/V. ❺

Hotel Boston, V. Guelfa, 68 (☎055 47 03 84; fax 47 09 34). Exposed wooden-beamed ceilings, intricate tiled floors, and yellow bedspreads spruce up this hotel's 14 comfortable rooms, all with A/C, TV, and telephone. Enjoy breakfast in the beautiful antique-style dining room or outside in the soothing patio garden. Singles €51.65, with bath €87.80; doubles €134.28. ❹

Nuova Italia, V. Faenza, 26 (☎055 26 84 30; fax 21 09 41; hotel.nuova.italia@dada.it). Prints and posters crowd this 2-star hotel's lobby and hallways. The 24hr. bar is the perfect place to wash down late-night gelato. All rooms have A/C and TV. Breakfast included. Singles €99.16; doubles €139.44; triples €186. AmEx/MC/V. ❺

NEAR PIAZZA SAN MARCO AND THE UNIVERSITY

This area is considerably calmer and less tourist-ridden than its proximity to the center might suggest, and offers some of the best values in the city. All accommodations listed are within a few blocks of the delicate beauty of San Marco, one of Florence's less touristed churches. To reach this neighborhood, exit the train station and take a left onto V. Nazionale. Take a right on V. Guelfa, which intersects V. S. Gallo and V. Cavour.

■ **Hotel Tina,** V. S. Gallo, 31 (☎055 48 35 19; fax 48 35 93; hoteltina@tin.it). Small *pensione* with high ceilings, blue carpeting, and bright bedspreads. Cozy sitting room with complimentary Herald Tribune. Beautiful prints. 18 rooms, all with A/C; some with hair dryers. Singles €44; doubles €62, with shower €67.14, with bath €77.47; triples with shower €82.63; quads €103.29. MC/V. ❹

■ **Albergo Sampaoli,** V. S. Gallo, 14 (☎055 28 48 34; fax 28 24 28; www.hotelsampaoli.it). Helpful reception and a large common area with patterned tile floors and wooden furniture. Some rooms with balconies, all with fans; many with antique furniture. Refrigerators available. Free Internet (30min.). Singles €45, with bath €54; doubles €58/€80; triple with bath €110. AmEx/MC/V. ❹

Hotel San Marco, V. Cavour, 50 (☎055 28 18 51; fax 28 42 35; San_marco@inwind.it). 2 floors with 15 modern, airy rooms. Elegant breakfast room. Breakfast included. Key available by request. Singles (available Sept.-Mar. only) €41.32, with bath €51.62; doubles €56.81/€72.30; triples with bath €103.29; quads with bath €134.28. MC/V. ❹

Hotel Casci, V. Cavour, 13 (☎055 21 16 86; fax 239 6461; www.hotelcasci.com). The accommodating Lombardi family operates this 25-room hotel situated in a 15th-century *palazzo* halfway between the duomo and P. San Marco. Comfortable rooms include bath, minibar, TV, telephone, safe, and A/C. Free Internet in the lobby. All-you-can-drink *cappuccino* at the breakfast buffet. Singles €100; doubles €135; triples €175; quads €220. AmEx/MC/V. ❺

IN THE OLTRARNO

Only a 10min. walk across the Arno from the duomo, this area and its *pensioni* offer a respite from Florence's bustling hubs. From San Spirito to Palazzo Pitti to the Boboli gardens, there are still enough sites nearby to make this an ideal location for a stay.

■ **Hotel La Scaletta,** V. de' Guicciardini, 13b (☎055 28 30 28; fax 28 95 62; www.lascaletta.com). Turn right onto V. Roma from the duomo. Cross the Ponte Vecchio and continue onto V. Guicciardini. Look for candy on your pillow in one of the 13 gorgeous rooms filled with antique furniture and connected by stairways and alcoves. Most rooms with A/C. Rooftop terrace with spectacular view of Boboli Gardens. Welcoming breakfast room. Breakfast included. Singles €51, with bath €93; doubles €100/€129; triples with bath €154; quads with bath €170. 10% *Let's Go* discount for those paying in cash. MC/V. ❹

Sorelle Bandini, P. Santo Spirito, 9 (☎055 21 53 08; fax 28 27 61; pensionebandini@tiscali.it). From Ponte S. Trinità, continue down V. Maggio and take the 3rd right into P. S. Spirito. 12 rooms on the top 2 floors of a beautiful 500-year-old *palazzo*. Spectacular views of the Oltrarno from the huge, wrap-around *loggia* (lodges). Heavy, worn wood furniture fills spacious rooms that show their age. Some have frescoed ceilings and fireplaces. Breakfast included. Doubles €103; triples €141; quads €168. ❺

CAMPING

Campeggio Michelangelo, V. Michelangelo, 80 (☎055 681 1977), beyond Piazzale Michelangelo. Take bus #13 from the station (15min., last bus 11:25pm). Extremely crowded, but offers a spectacular panorama of Florence and a chance to doze under olive trees. Well-stocked food store and bar. Rents tents €10.50 per night. Reception daily 6am-midnight. Open Apr.-Nov. €7.50 per person, €4.65 per tent, €4.30 per car, €3.20 per motorcycle. ❶

Villa Camerata, V. A. Righi, 2-4 (☎055 60 03 15; fax 61 03 00), same entrance as HI hostel on #17 bus route (see HI directions, p. 342); same reception as well. Breakfast at hostel €1.55. Open daily 7am-12:30pm and 1pm-midnight; if closed, stake your site and return before midnight to register and pay. 6-night max. stay. Check-out 7-10am. €6 per person, €4.80 with camping card; €5-€10.50 per tent., €10.50 per car. ❶

◻ FOOD

Florentine cuisine arose from the peasant fare of the surrounding countryside. Characterized by rustic dishes created with fresh ingredients and simple preparations, Tuscan food ranks among the world's best. White beans and olive oil are two staple ingredients. Famous specialties include *bruschetta* (toasted bread doused with olive oil and garlic, usually topped with tomatoes and basil and anchovy or liver paste). For *primi*, Florentines favor the Tuscan classics *minestra di fagioli* (a delicious white bean and garlic soup) and *ribollita* (a hearty bean, bread, and black cabbage stew). Florence's classic *secondo* is *bistecca alla Fiorentina* (thick sirloin steak). Florentines order it *al sangue* (very rare; literally "bloody") but you can order it *al puntito* (medium) or *ben cotto* (well-done). The best local cheese is *pecorino*, made from sheep's milk. No Tuscan meal is complete without wine, and a genuine *chianti classico* commands a premium price. A liter of house wine costs €3.50-6 in Florence's *trattorie*; stores sell bottles for as little as €2.50. The local dessert is *cantuccini di prato* (hard almond cookies made with many egg yolks) dipped in *vinsanto* (a rich dessert wine made from raisins).

For lunch, visit a *rosticceria, gastronomia,* or *pizzeria,* or stop by the **students' mensa ❷**, at V. dei Servi, 52, where a filling meal costs only €8. (Open M-Sa noon-2:15pm and 6:45-9pm. Closed mid-July to Aug.) Buy your own fresh produce and meat (or stock up on that tripe you've been craving) at the **Mercato Centrale**, between V. Nazionale and S. Lorenzo. (Open June-Sept. M-Sa 7:30am-2pm; Oct.-May Sa 7am-2pm and 4-8pm.) For basics, head to the **STANDA supermarket**, V. Pietrapiana, 1r. Take a right on V. del Proconsolo and the first left on Borgo degli Albizi. Continue straight through P. G. Salvemini; the supermarket is on the left. (☎ 055 223 478 569. Open M-Sa 8am-9pm, Su 9:30am-1:30pm and 3:30-6:30pm.)

Vegetarians can find several health-food markets in the city. The two best stores are named after the American book **Sugar Blues**. One is a 5min. walk from the duomo up V. de Martelli (which turns into V. Cavour) at V. XXVII Aprile, 46r. (☎ 055 48 36 66. Open M-F 9am-1:30pm and 4-7:30pm, Sa 9am-1:30pm.) The other is next to the Instituto Gould (see **Accommodations**, p. 342), in the Oltrarno at V. dei Serragli, 57r. (☎ 055 26 83 78. Open Su-Tu and Th-F 9am-1:30pm and 4:30-8pm, Sa and W 9am-1:30pm.) Also try **La Raccolta**, V. Leopardi, 2r. (☎ 055 247 9068. Open daily 8:30am-7:30pm.) **Ruth's Kosher Vegetarian**, V. Farini, 2, serves **kosher** fare on the second floor of the building that is to the right of the synagogue. (Open Su-Th 12:30-2:30pm and 8-10:30pm.) You can get information on **halal** vendors from **Centro Culturale Islamico** (see p. 340).

OLD CITY (NEAR THE DUOMO)

▨ **Trattoria Anita**, V. del Parlascio, 2r (☎ 055 21 86 98), just behind the Bargello. Dine by candlelight, surrounded by expensive wine bottles on wooden shelves. Traditional Tuscan fare, including filling pastas and an array of meat dishes from roast chicken to *bistecca alla Fiorentina. Primi* €4.70-5.20, *secondi* from €5.20. Fantastic lunch *menù* €5.50. Cover €1. Open M-Sa noon-2:30pm and 7-10pm. AmEx/MC/V. ❷

▨ **Acqua al Due**, V. della Vigna Vecchia, 40r (☎ 055 28 41 70), behind the Bargello. Florentine specialties in a snug, air-conditioned place popular with young Italians and foreigners alike. The *assaggio* (a selection of 5 pasta dishes, €8) demands a taste. *Primi* €6.71, *secondi* from €7-19, excellent *insalate* from €5. Cover €1.03. Open daily 7:30pm-1am. Don't show up without reservations. AmEx/MC/V. ❸

Al Lume di Candela, V. delle Terme, 23r (☎ 055 265 6561), halfway between P. S. Trinità and P. di Signoria. Candlelit tables illuminate the bright yellow walls of this brand new restaurant. Chef Ottaviano prepares Tuscan, Venetian, and Southern Italian favorites on golden platters. *Primi* €5.90-7.90, *secondi* with *contorni* €9.60-11.90. Open daily noon-2:30pm and 7-10:30pm. AmEx/MC/V. ❸

Trattoria da Benvenuto, V. della Mosca, 16r, (☎055 21 48 33). Pastel decor and linen table cloths make for elegant dining. *Spaghetti alle vongole* (with clams) €5.50. *Penne* with mushrooms and olives €5.50. *Primi* €4.50-8.50, *secondi* €6-13. Cover €1.50. 10% service charge. Open M-Sa 11am-3pm and 7pm-midnight. AmEx/MC/V. ❸

Le Colonnine, V. de' Benci, 6r (☎055 23 46 47), near Ponte alle Grazie. Outdoor tables seat a mostly Italian crowd. *Primi* €6, *secondi* from €7, pizza from €4.70. For a real treat, bring a friend or cute stranger to conquer a skillet of their famous paella (€18 for 2). Open daily noon-3:30pm and 6:30pm-midnight. MC/V. ❸

La Loggia degli Albizi, Borgo degli Albizi, 39r (☎055 247 9574). From behind the duomo, go right on V. del Proconsolo and take the 1st left onto Borgo degli Albizi. Head 2 blocks down and look right. A hidden treasure, this bakery/cafe offers escape from the tourist hordes. Pastries from €0.80, coffee from €0.80. Open M-Sa 7am-8pm. ❶

SANTA MARIA NOVELLA AND ENVIRONS

▧ **Trattoria Contadino,** V. Palazzuolo, 71r (☎055 238 2673). Filling, home-style meals. Offers fixed price *menù* option only–but this is not a *menù turistica*. It's the real deal, served to an almost exclusively Italian crowd in an informal setting. *Menù* includes *primo, secondo,* bread, water, and ¼L of house wine. Lunch *menù* €8.50; dinner *menù* €9. Open M-Sa noon-2:30pm and 6-9:30pm. AmEx/MC/V. ❷

▧ **Trattoria da Giorgio,** V. Palazzuolo, 100r (☎055 28 43 02). Crowded setting for full meal, with *primo, secondo,* bread, water, and house wine. Expect a wait. Lunch *menù* €8.50, dinner *menù* €9. Open M-Sa noon-3:30pm and 7pm-12:30am. AmEx/MC/V. ❷

Il Latini, V. dei Palchetti, 6r. From the Ponte alla Carraia, walk up V. del Moro; V. dei Palchetti is on the right. Tuscan classics such as *ribollita* (€5.50). *Primi* €5.50-6.50, *secondi* €9.50-15.50. Open Tu-Su 12:30-2:30pm and 7:30-10:30pm. AmEx/MC/V. ❸

Trattoria Antellesi, V. Faenza, 9r (☎055 21 69 90). Classic Tuscan *trattoria* tucked just off P. Madonna Aldobrandini. A good place to sample regional favorites such as *pecorino antipasto* and *bistecca alla Fiorentina* (€16). *Primi* €5.50-7.50, *secondi* €9.50-16. Cover €2. Open noon-2:30pm and 7-10:30pm. AmEx/MC/V. ❸

Rose's Cafe, V. del Parione, 26r (☎055 28 70 90). This hip Japanese restaurant prides itself on its chic atmosphere. Noodle and rice dishes such as *tempura udon* (€8-12). Extensive sushi bar (€12-31). Open Sept.-July Su-Th 8-1am, F-Sa 8-2am. Sushi bar open Tu-Su 7-11pm. AmEx/MC/V. ❺

Amon, V. Palazzuolo, 28r (☎055 29 31 46). Cheerful Egyptian owner cooks his own bread and serves scrumptious Middle Eastern food. Try the *mousaka* (pita filled with baked eggplant) or *foul* (spiced beans). The falafel is spicy and quite good. English menu. Stand-up or takeout only. Falafel €2.60-3.20, *shish kebab* €3.10. Open Tu-Su noon-3pm and 6-11pm. ❶

THE STATION AND UNIVERSITY QUARTER

▧ **Trattoria da Zà-Zà,** P. del Mercato Centrale, 26r (☎055 21 54 11). Wooden beam ceilings, brick archways, and wine racks on the wall. Filled with Italians and foreigners. Try the *tris* (a mixed bean and vegetable soup, €6) or the *tagliata di manzo* (cut of beef, €12-15.50). Finish with *vinsanto e cantucci* (€3.50). Outdoor seating available. Cover €1.55. Open M-Sa noon-3pm and 7-11pm. Reservations suggested. AmEx/MC/V. ❹

▧ **Trattoria Mario,** V. Rosina, 2r (☎055 21 85 50), right around the corner from P. del Mercato Centrale. Informal lunch spot with incredible pasta and cheap meat dishes. *Primi* €3.10-3.40; *secondi* €3.10-10.50. Cover €0.50. Open M-Sa noon-3:30pm. ❷

▧ **Ristorante de' Medici,** V. del Melarancio, 10r (☎055 29 52 92), 1 block off P. dell'Unità Italia. Classy place with pink table cloths and portraits of the Medici, frequented by an almost exclusively Italian clientele. Calzones (€7) and *gnocchi al pesto* (€6). *Primi* €5-8; *secondi* €7-10. AmEx/MC/V. ❸

Trattoria da Garibardi, P. del Mercato Centrale, 38r (☎ 055 21 22 67). Locals fill outdoor seating and formal indoor dining room with good reason. *Penne ai quattro formaggi* (4 cheese) and *pesto alla genovese* are delicious. *Primi* €4.20-10.50, *secondi* from €5.20. Fixed-price *menù* €12.40. €1.50 cover for meals outside the *menù*. Open June-Aug. daily noon-11pm, Sept.-May M-Sa noon-3pm and 7-11pm. MC/V. ❸

Ristorante Il Vegetariano, V. delle Ruote, 30r (☎ 055 47 50 30), off V. S. Gallo. Look closely for the address, as there's no sign. Self-service restaurant with fresh, inventive dishes and vegetarian wonders. Outdoor tables in a peaceful bamboo garden. Brown rice *risotto al pesto* €4.65. Ask to be seated in the smoke-free room. Salads €3.62-4.65, *primi* from €4.65, *secondi* from €5.68. Open Sept.-July Tu-F 12:30-3pm and 7:30pm-midnight, Sa-Su 8pm-midnight. ❸

Forno di Stefano Galli, V. Faenza, 39r (☎ 055 21 53 14). Wondering where to go to get that bread you enjoyed so much at dinner last night? Wide variety of fresh breads and pastries sold here. Pastries €0.80-2.30; loaves of bread €0.80. Open 7:30am-4:30am. Other locations at V. delle Panche, 91 and V. Bufalini, 31-35r. ❶

THE OLTRARNO

Il Borgo Antico, P. S. Spirito, 6r (☎ 055 21 04 37). *Mangia* inside or out. Test the wonderful *antipasto* (tomato and basil salad, €7). The bread comes with black olives in oil with a touch of hot pepper. *Spaghetti alle vangole* (with clams, €6), *antipasti* €5-10, *primi* €6, *secondi* €10-15. Cover €2. Open June-Sept. daily 1pm-12:30am, Oct.-May daily 12:45-2:30pm and 7:45pm-1am. Reservations recommended. AmEx/MC/V. ❹

La Mangiatoia, P. S. Felice, 8r (☎ 055 22 40 60). Continue straight on V. Guicciardini from Ponte Vecchio, passing P. dei Pitti. Quality Tuscan fare. Grab a table in back dining room, or sit at stone counter in front to watch them make pizza in the brick oven. Try the *gnocchi al pesto* (€4). *Primi* €3.50-5.50, *secondi* €3-9, pizza €4-7.50. Cover €1 in dining room. Open Tu-Su noon-3pm and 7-10pm. AmEx/MC/V. ❷

Oltrarno Trattoria Casalinga, V. Michelozzi, 9r (☎ 055 21 86 24), near P. S. Spirito. Delicious Tuscan specialties. Excellent pesto. Great quality for the price. *Primi* €4-6, *secondi* €5-9. Cover €1.50. Open M-Sa noon-2:30pm and 7-10pm. ❸

Il Cantinone, V. Santo Spirito, 6r (☎ 055 21 88 98). From the Ponte S. Trinità, pass through P. Frescobaldi, and then go right onto V. S. Spirito. Descend into this *enoteca's* red-brick, vaulted wine cellar to sample rustic Tuscan fare. *Primi* €7.50-9.50, *secondi* €7.50-31. Cover €2. Open Tu-Su 12:30-2pm and 7:30-10:30pm. AmEx/MC/V. ❹

GELATERIE

Gelato is said to have been invented centuries ago by Florence's Buontalenti family. Before shelling out €1.50 for a *piccolo* cone, assess the quality of an establishment by looking at the banana *gelato:* if it's bright yellow, it's been made from a mix—keep on walking. If it's slightly gray, real bananas were used. Most *gelaterie* also serve *granite*, flavored ices that are easier on the waistline.

Vivoli, V. della Stinche, 7 (☎ 055 29 23 34), behind the Bargello. The self-proclaimed "best ice cream in the world." The crowd that spills out on the street each night is proof that the public agrees. Huge selection includes fruit flavors, hazelnut, and chocolate mousse. Cups from €1.50. Open T-Sa 7:30am-1am, Su 9:30-1am. AmEx/MC/V.

Antica Gelateria Il David, V. San Antonino, 28r (☎ 055 21 86 45), off V. Faenza. A hidden gem that's short on variety but long on quality. Hand-crafted, basic flavors make this place a real triumph of substance over image. Large scoops at low prices. Cones from €1.60. Open daily 11am-midnight. ❶

Gelateria Triangolo delle Bermuda, V. Nazionale, 61r (☎055 28 74 90). With *gelato* this good, you'll never want to escape. Blissful *crema venusiana* blends hazelnut, caramel, and merengue. Try the strawberry and rose sorbets. Owner even travels to the US every year to get Oreos for his *gelato*. Cones from €1.60. Open daily 11am-midnight. ❶

Perchè No?, V. Tavolini, 19r (☎055 239 8969), off V. dei Calzaiuoli. Why not indeed. This place answers with some of Florence's finest *gelato*. It serves heavenly pistacchio, mouth-watering chocolate, and chunky *nocciolosa*. Cones €2. Open Apr.-Oct. daily 11am-12:30am, Nov.-Mar. W-M 10am-8pm. ❶

Carabè, V. Ricasoli, 60r (☎055 28 94 76). Amazing *gelato* with ingredients shipped from Sicily. Pistacchio, *limone*, *nocciola*, and the more unusual flavors like *susine* (plum) are outstanding, as are the *granite* (ices), particularly *mandorle* (almond) and *more* (blackberries). Cups from €1.55, *granite* from €2.10. Open May-Sept. daily 10am-midnight; Oct., Mar., and Apr. noon-midnight. ❶

ENOTECHE (WINE BARS)

Check out an *enoteca* to sample some of Italy's finest wines. A meal can often be made out of the exquisite complementary side-dish sensations (cheeses, olives, toast-and-spreads, and salami).

Enoteca Alessi, V. della Oche, 27/29r (☎055 21 49 66; fax 239 6987), 1 block from the duomo. Among Florence's finest. Boasts over 1000 wines. Also offers delicious nibbles between sips. Enter through cavernous wine and chocolate shop in front. Spacious, high-ceilinged, and cool. Open M-F 9am-1pm and 4-8pm. AmEx/MC/V. ❷

Enoteca Fuori Porta, V. Monte alle Croce, 10r (☎055 234 2483), in the shadows of S. Miniato. This more casual and off-the-beaten-track *enoteca* serves reasonable meals of traditional Tuscan pasta and *secondi* (from €5.70) in addition to the complimentary snacks. Open daily 10am-2pm and 5-9pm. ❷

SIGHTS

With the views from Brunelleschi's dome, the perfection of San Spirito's nave and the overwhelming array of art in the Ufizzi, it's hard to go wrong in Florence. There's enough to see in the center of Florence alone to keep a visitor occupied for years; if you're in the city for only a few days, hit the highlights. Plan well, as the city's art museums are spectacular, but exhausting and expensive.

BLAME IT ON THE MEDICI. Florentine museums have recently doubled their prices. Most major venues now charge €3.10-8.50, so breezing in and out of each place that strikes your fancy will quickly become a costly endeavor. Sadly, capital letters at most museum entrances remind you that there are **no student discounts.** The price of a ticket should not discourage you from seeing the best collections of Renaissance art in the world. Choose your itinerary carefully and plan to spend a few hours at each landmark. Additionally, many of Florence's churches are free treasuries of great art. In the summer, inquire at the tourist office about **Sere al Museo,** evenings when certain museums are free from 8:30 to 11pm. Note that most museums stop selling tickets 30min.-1hr. before closing. You can now make reservations for the Uffizi, Accademia, Medici Chapels, Galleria Palatina, Museum of San Marco, Bargello, and Encounter with Giorgio Vasari on the web at **www.florenceart.it.**

PIAZZA DEL DUOMO AND ENVIRONS

THE DUOMO (CATTEDRALE DI SANTA MARIA DEL FIORE). In 1296, the city fathers commissioned Arnolfo di Cambio to erect a cathedral "with the most high and sumptuous magnificence" so that it would be "impossible to make it either better or more beautiful with the industry and power of man." Arnolfo succeeded, completing the massive nave by 1418. One problem remained—no one had the engineering skills necessary to construct the Cathedral's dome. Finally, Filippo Brunelleschi devised the ingenious technique for building the duomo's sublime crown, now known simply as **Brunelleschi's Dome.** Drawing upon his knowledge of classical methods, the architect designed a revolutionary double-shelled structure, using self-supporting, interlocking bricks. During the construction, Brunelleschi, an obsessive task master, built kitchens, sleeping rooms, and lavoratories between the two walls of the cupola so the masons would never have to descend. The **Museo del Opera del Duomo** (see below) chronicles Brunelleschi's engineering feats. A 16th-century Medici rebuilding campaign removed the duomo's incomplete Gothic-Renaissance facade. The front of the duomo remained naked until 1871, when Emilio de Fabris, a Florentine architect, won the commission to create a colorful facade in the Neo-Gothic style.

Today, the duomo claims the world's 3rd-longest nave after St. Peter's in Rome and St. Paul's in London. Brunelleschi's dome rises 100m into the air, making it instantly recognizable from afar and providing unparalleled vistas of Florence. The duomo is ornately decorated on the outside with inlaid green and white marble, but is visually unexciting on the inside, except for the visions of the apocalypse painted on dome's ceiling. Also notice Paolo Uccello's celebrated *trompe l'oeil* (trick-of-the-eye) monument to the mercenary captain Sir John Hawkwood on the cathedral's left wall, and his **orologio** on the back wall. The orologio won't give you the time of day—this 24hr. clock runs backward, starting its cycle at sunset, when the *Ave Maria* is traditionally sung. *(Duomo open M-Sa 10am-4:45pm, Su 1:30-4:45pm; 1st Sa of every month 10am-3:30pm. Shortest wait at 10am. Masses daily 7am-12:30pm and 5-7pm. Ask inside the entrance, to the left, about free guided tours in English.)* Climb the 463 steps inside the dome to Michelangelo's **lantern** for an unparalleled view of the city from the 100m high external gallery. *(Entrance on south side of duomo. ☎ 055 230 2885. Open M-F 8:30am-7pm, Sa 8:30am-5:40pm. €6.)* The cathedral's **crypt** contains Brunelleschi's tomb. *(Open M-Sa 9:30am-5pm. €3.)*

BAPTISTERY. Although it was built between the 5th and 9th centuries, in Dante's time the baptistery was believed to have originated as a Roman temple. These days, the exterior has the same green and white marble patterning as the duomo, and the interior contains magnificent 13th-century Byzantine-style mosaics. Dante was christened here and later found inspiration for the *Inferno* in the murals of the devil devouring sinners.

Florentine artists competed fiercely for the commission to execute the baptistery's famous **bronze doors,** depicting scenes from the Bible in exquisite detail. In 1330, Andrea Pisano left Pisa to cast the first set of doors, which now guard the south entrance (toward the river). In 1401, the cloth guild announced a competition to choose an artist for the remaining doors. The field was narrowed to two artists, Brunelleschi (then 23 years old) and Ghiberti (then 20). They were asked to work in partnership, but the uncompromising Brunelleschi left in an arrogant huff, leaving Ghiberti to complete the project. The competition panels are displayed side by side in the Bargello. Ghiberti's project, completed in 1425, was so admired that he immediately received the commission to forge the last set of doors. The **Gates of Paradise,** as Michelangelo reportedly called them, are nothing like the two earlier portals. Originally intended for the north side, they so impressed the

Florentines that they placed them in their current honored position facing the cathedral. The doors have been under restoration since the flood of 1966 and will eventually reside in the Museo dell'Opera del Duomo. *(Opposite the duomo. Open M-Sa noon-7pm, Su 8:30am-2pm. Mass M-F 10:30am and 11:30am. €3. Audioguide €2.)*

CAMPANILE. The 82m high *campanile* next to the duomo has a pink, green, and white marble exterior that matches the duomo and *battistero*. Giotto drew the design and laid the foundation in 1334, but died soon after. Andrea Pisano added two stories to the tower, and Francesco Talenti completed it in 1359. The original exterior decoration is now in the Museo dell'Opera del Duomo. The 414 steps to the top lead to beautiful views. *(Open daily 8:30am-7:30pm. €6.)*

MUSEO DELL'OPERA DEL DUOMO. Most of the duomo's art resides in this modern-looking museum, including a late *Pietà* by Michelangelo, up the first flight of stairs. According to legend, Michelangelo severed Christ's left arm with a hammer in a fit of frustration. Soon after, an overly eager apprentice touched up the work, leaving visible scars on parts of Mary Magdalene's head. Also in this museum are Donatello's wooden ▨St. Mary Magdalene (1455), Donatello and Luca della Robbia's **cantorie** (choir balconies with bas-reliefs of cavorting children), and four frames from the baptistery's **Gates of Paradise**. A huge wall displays all of the paintings submitted by architects in the 1870 competition for the facade of the duomo. *(P. del Duomo, 9, behind the duomo. ☎ 055 264 7287. Open M-Sa 9am-6:30pm, Su 9am-1pm. €6. Audioguide €4.)*

ORSANMICHELE. Built in 1337 as a granary, the Orsanmichele was converted into a church after a great fire convinced city officials to move grain operations outside the city walls. The *loggia* (lodge) structure and ancient grain chutes are still visible from the outside. Secular and spiritual concerns mingle in the statues along the facade. Within these niches, look for Ghiberti's *St. John the Baptist* and *St. Stephen*, Donatello's *St. Peter* and *St. Mark*, and Giambologna's *St. Luke*. Inside, a Gothic tabernacle designed by Andrea Orcagna encases Bernardo Daddi's miraculous *Virgin*, an intricately wrought, expressive marble statue of Mary at her most beatific. The top floor occasionally hosts special exhibits. Across the street, the **Museo di Orsanmichele** exhibits numerous paintings and sculptures from the original church. *(V. Arte della Lana, between duomo and P. della Signoria. ☎ 055 28 49 44 for church and museum. The church was closed for renovations in summer of 2002; scheduled to reopen in 2003. Museum open daily 9am-noon. Closed 1st and last M of the month. Free.)*

MUSEO FIRENZE COM'ERA. This small, amusing museum provides a welcome escape from the crowds. Florence is depicted through the ages, starting with a large model of the town during imperial Roman times. A room of charming street scenes by Della Gatta leads to the final piece—a detailed, 5 ft. by 10 ft. aerial view of 13th-century Florence. *(V. delle Oriuolo, 3 blocks from duomo. ☎ 055 261 6545. Open F-W 9am-2pm. €2.60.)*

PIAZZA DELLA SIGNORIA AND ENVIRONS

From P. del Duomo, **V. dei Calzaiuoli,** one of the city's oldest streets, leads to P. della Signoria. Built by the Romans, V. dei Calzaiuoli now bustles with crowds, chic shops, *gelaterie*, and vendors.

PIAZZA DELLA SIGNORIA. The blank-walled, turreted Palazzo Vecchio (see below) and the corner of the Uffizi gallery dominate this 13th-century piazza. The space is filled with crowds, drawn here at night by street performers. The piazza indirectly resulted from the struggle between the Guelphs and the Ghibellines. Many of the Ghibelline families' homes were destroyed by the Guelphs in the 13th century, creating the open space. With the construction of the Palazzo Vecchio, the square was transformed into Florence's civic and political center. In 1497, religious zealot Girolamo Savonarola convinced Florentines to light the **Bonfire of the Vanities** in the piazza, a grand roast that consumed some of Florence's best art, including, according to legend, all of Botticelli's secular works held in public collections. A year later, disillusioned citizens sent Savonarola up in smoke on the same spot, marked today by a commemorative disc. Monumental sculptures cluster around the Palazzo Vecchio, including Donatello's *Judith and Holofernes*, a copy of Michelangelo's *David*, Giambologna's equestrian *Cosimo I*, and Bandinelli's *Hercules*. The awkward *Neptune*, to the left of the Palazzo Vecchio, so revolted Michelangelo that he decried the artist: "Oh, Ammannato, Ammannato, what lovely marble you have ruined!" Apparently most Florentines share his opinion. Called *Il Biancone* (the Big White One) in derision, *Neptune* is regularly subject to attacks of vandalism by angry aesthetes. The graceful 14th-century **Loggia dei Lanzi** (adjacent to the Palazzo), built as a stage for civic orators, is now one of the best places in Florence to see world-class sculpture free of charge.

PALAZZO VECCHIO. Arnolfo del Cambio designed this fortress-like *palazzo* (1299-1304) as the seat of the *comune's* government. The massive brown stone facade has a square tower rising from its center, and turrets along the top. Its apartments once served as living quarters for members of the *signoria* (city council) during their two-month terms. The building later became the Medici family home, and in 1470, Michelozzo decorated the █**courtyard** in Renaissance style. He filled it with religious frescoes and placed ornate stone pediments over every door and window. The courtyard also has stone lions and a copy of Verrocchio's 15th-century *Putto* fountain. *(Same hours as Monumental Apartments, see below.)*

The tour offerings at the Palazzo Vecchio have recently expanded; in addition to the Monumental Apartments (see below), there are "Secret Routes," "Activities," and "An Encounter with Giorgio Vasari" tours. They must be booked in advance, are generally conducted in groups of eight to 10, and can be given in English upon request.) Tours of the **Secret Routes** visit staircases hidden in walls, Duke Cosimo I de'Medici's secret chambers, and the roof cavity above the Salone del Cinquecento (see below). The **Activities** tour includes re-enactments of Medici court life, displays of architectural models, and demonstrations of science experiments by Galileo and Torricelli, both Medici court mathematicians. The **Encounter with Giorgio Vasari** is a tour through the Monumental Apartments, with a guide playing the part of Vasari, Duke Cosimo I de' Medici's court painter and architect. *(☎ 055 276 8224 or 276 8558; www.museoragazzi.it. Booking office open daily 9am-1pm and 3-7pm. Reservations required, make them online, by phone, or at the booking office. "Secret Routes" and "Activities": Sept. 16-June 14 daily; June 15-Sept. 15 M and F. "Encounter with Giorgio Vasari": Sept. 16-June 14 Tu, Th, Sa, and Su; June 15-Sept. 15 F through M. All tours included with entrance ticket. €9.30.)*

The Monumental Apartments, which house the *palazzo's* extensive art collections, are accessible as a museum. There are now 12 interactive terminals in various rooms, where there are virtual tours of the building's history that feature detailed computer animations. The city commissioned Michelangelo and Leonardo da Vinci to paint opposite walls of the **Salone del Cinquecento,** the meeting room of the Grand Council of the Republic. Although they never completed the frescoes, their preliminary cartoons, the *Battle of Cascina* and the *Battle of Anghiari*, were studied by Florentine artists for years afterward for their powerful depiction of humans and horses in strenuous motion. The tiny **Studio di Francesco I,** built by Vasari, is a treasure trove of Mannerist art, with paintings by Bronzino, Allori, and Vasari and bronze statuettes by Giambologna and Ammannati. The **Mez-**

zanino houses some of the *palazzo*'s best art, including Bronzino's portrait of the poet Laura Battiferi and Giambologna's *Hercules and the Hydra.* (☎055 276 8465. *June 15-Sept. 15 Tu-W and Sa 9am-7pm, M and F 9am-11pm, Th and Su 9am-2pm; Sept.-May M-W and F-Sa 9am-7pm, Th and Su 9am-2pm. Palazzo €5.70; courtyard free.*)

■**THE UFFIZI.** From P. B.S. Giovanni, go down V. Roma past P. della Repubblica, where the street turns into V. Calimala. Continue until V. Vacchereccia and turn left. The Uffizi is straight ahead. Giorgio Vasari designed this palace in 1554 for Duke Cosimo and called it the Uffizi because it housed the offices *(uffizi)* of the Medici administration. Today it holds more great art per square inch than any other museum in the world. An impressive walkway between the two main branches of the building leads, in grim colonnaded fashion, from the Piazza della Signoria to the Arno River. Vendors hawking trinkets and prints of the fabulous art inside abound along the *loggia* of this massive building. Before visiting the main gallery on the second floor, stop to see the exhibits of the Cabinet of Drawings and Prints on the first floor. Upstairs, in a U-shaped corridor, is a collection of Hellenistic and Roman marble statues. Arranged chronologically in rooms off the corridor, the collection promises a thorough education on the Florentine Renaissance, as well as a choice sampling of German and Venetian art.

Room 2 features three 13th- and 14th-century *Madonne* of the great forefathers of the Renaissance: Cimabue, Duccio di Buoninsegna, and Giotto. **Room 3** features works from 14th-century Siena (including works by the Lorenzetti brothers and Simone Martini's *Annunciation*, notable for their palpable emotion). **Rooms 5** and **6** contain examples of International Gothic art, popular in European royal courts.

The most awe-inspiring gallery in the museum, **Room 7** houses two Fra Angelico (referred to as Beato Angelico in Italian museums) paintings and a *Madonna and Child* by Masaccio. Domenico Veneziano's *Madonna with Child and Saints (Sacra Conversazione)* is one of the first paintings of Mary surrounded by the saints. Piero della Francesca's double portrait of Duke Federico and his wife Battista Sforza stands out for its translucent color and honest detail. (A jousting accident gave the Duke his unusual nose shape.) Finally, the rounded warhorses distinguish Paolo Uccello's *Battle of San Romano.* **Room 8** has Filippo Lippi's touching *Madonna and Child with Two Angels.* Works by the Pollaiuolo brothers and an allegedly forged Filippino Lippi occupy **Room 9.**

Rooms 10-14 are a shrine to Florence's cherished Botticelli—the resplendent *Primavera, Birth of Venus, Madonna della Melagrana,* and *Pallas and the Centaur* glow from recent restorations. **Room 15** moves into the High Renaissance with Leonardo da Vinci's *Annunciation* and the more remarkable unfinished *Adoration of the Magi.* Leonardo and the other painters of the high Renaissance create a more realistic ideal beauty than the almost cartoon-like image in many works by Lippi and Botticelli. **Room 18,** designed by Buontalenti to hold the Medici treasures, has a mother-of-pearl dome and a collection of portraits, most notably Bronzino's *Bia de'Medici* and Vasari's *Lorenzo il Magnifico.* Also note Rosso Fiorentino's often-duplicated *Musician Angel.*

Room 19 features Piero della Francesca's students Perugino and Signorelli. **Rooms 20** and **22** detour into Northern European art. Note the contrast between Albrecht Dürer's life-like *Adam and Eve* and Cranach the Elder's haunting treatment of the same subject. **Room 21** contains 15th century Venetian artwork. Bellini's *Sacred Allegory* and Mantegna's *Adoration of the Magi* highlight **Room 23.**

Rooms 25-27 showcase Florentine works, including Michelangelo's only oil painting *(Doni Tondo),* a string of Raphaels (check out the detail on the rings of his portrait of Julius II), Andrea del Sarto's *Madonna of the Harpies,* and Pontormo's *Supper at Emmaus.* **Room 28** displays Titian's beautiful *Venus of Urbino.* Parmigianino's *Madonna of the Long Neck* is in **Room 29.** Works by

Paolo Veronese and Tintoretto dominate **Rooms 31** and **32**. The staircase vestibule **(Rooms 36-40)** contains a Roman marble boar, inspiration for the brass *Porcellino* that sits in Florence's New Market. **Rooms 41 and 43-45** are currently undergoing restoration, so many works by Rembrandt, Rubens, and Caravaggio are currently not on display, though visitors can see Caravaggio's famous *Bacchus* in **Room 16**.

Vasari's designs for the Medici included a **secret corridor** running between the Palazzo Vecchio and the Medici's Palazzo Pitti. The corridor runs through the Uffizi and over the Ponte Vecchio, housing more art, including a special collection of artists' self-portraits. Sadly, these works can't be viewed because of damage from the flood of 1966. *(Open Tu-Su 8:15am-6:50pm. ☎ 055 29 48 83. €8.50, save hours of waiting by purchasing advance tickets for €1.55 extra. Audioguide €4.65.)*

THE PONTE VECCHIO. The nearby Ponte Vecchio (Old Bridge) is indeed the oldest bridge in Florence. Built in 1345, it replaced a Roman version. In the 1500s, butchers and tanners lined the bridge and dumped pig's blood and intestines in the river, creating an odor that, not surprisingly, offended the powerful bankers as they crossed the Arno on their way to their *uffizi* (offices). In an effort to improve the area, the Medici kicked out the lower-class shopkeepers, and the more decorous goldsmiths and diamond-carvers moved in; their descendants now line the bridge selling their beautiful wares from medieval-looking boutiques that cantilever precariously off the sides of the bridge. While technically open to traffic, the bridge is completely swamped by tourists and street musicians.

The Ponte Vecchio was the only bridge to escape German bombs during WWII. A German commander who led his retreating army across the river in 1944 couldn't bear to destroy it, choosing instead to make the bridge impassable by toppling nearby buildings. From the neighboring ▨**Ponte alle Grazie** *(towards P. Santa Croce)*, the view of Ponte Vecchio melting in the setting sun is nothing less than heart-stopping. *(From Uffizi, turn left onto V. Georgofili and right at the river.)*

THE BARGELLO AND ENVIRONS

▨**BARGELLO.** In the heart of medieval Florence, this 13th-century fortress was once the residence of Florence's chief magistrate. It later became a brutal prison that held public executions in the courtyard. In the 19th century, the Bargello's one-time elegance was restored, and it now gracefully hosts the **Museo Nazionale,** a treasury of Florentine sculpture. From the outside, the Bargello looks like a three-story fortress, but the arched windows of the inner courtyard offer glimpses of sculpture-lined colonnades. Upstairs to the right in the **Salone di Donatello,** Donatello's bronze *David*, the first free-standing nude since antiquity, eroticizes and androgynizes the adolescent male figure. The artist's marble *David*, completed about 30 years earlier, stands near the left wall. On the right are two beautiful bronze panels of the *Sacrifice of Isaac*, submitted by Ghiberti and Brunelleschi to the baptistery door competition (see **Baptistery**, p. 351). The *loggia* on the first floor displays a collection of bronze animals made by Giambologna for a Medici garden grotto. Michelangelo's early works, including a debauched *Bacchus*, a handsome bust of *Brutus*, an unfinished *Apollo*, and a *Madonna and Child*, dominate the ground floor. Cellini's models for *Perseus* and *Bust of Cosimo I* occupy the same room. Giambologna's *Oceanus* reigns in the Gothic courtyard outside, while his *Mercury* poses in the Michelangelo room. *(V. del Proconsolo, 4, between duomo and P. della Signoria. ☎ 055 238 8606. Open daily 8:15am-1:50pm; closed 2nd and 4th M of each month. Hours and closing days vary by month. €4. Audioguide €3.62.)*

BADIA. This was the site of medieval Florence's richest monastery. Buried in the interior of a residential block, and with no facade, one would never guess the treasures that lie within. Filippino Lippi's stunning *Apparition of the Virgin to St.*

Bernard, one of the most famous paintings of the late 15th century, hangs in eerie gloom to the left of the entrance to the church. Note the beautiful, if dingy, frescoes and Corinthian pilasters. *(Entrance on V. Dante Alighieri, just off V. Proconsolo. ☎ 055 26 44 02. Open to worshipers daily 7:30am-12:30pm and 1-6pm, to tourists M 3-6pm.)*

MUSEO DI STORIA DELLA SCIENZA. After pondering great Italian artists and writers for hours, head over to this museum to be awed by the greats of science. This impressive collection boasts scientific instruments from the Renaissance, including telescopes, astrological models, clock workings, and wax models of anatomy and childbirth. The highlight of the museum is **Room 4,** where a number of Galileo's tools are on display, including his embalmed middle finger and the objective lens through which he first observed the satellites of Jupiter in 1610. Detailed English guides are available at the ticket office. *(P. dei Giudici, 1, behind Palazzo Vecchio and the Uffizi. ☎ 055 29 34 93. Open M, W-F 9:30am-5pm; Tu, Sa 9:30am-1pm. Oct. 1-May 31 also open 2nd Su of each month, 10am-1pm. €6.50.)*

CASA DI DANTE. The Casa di Dante is reputedly identical to the house Dante inhabited. Anyone who can read Italian and has an abiding fascination with Dante will enjoy the displays. Nearby is a facsimile of the abandoned and melancholy little church where Beatrice, Dante's unrequited love and spiritual guide (in *Paradiso*), attended mass. A plaque commemorates the many days he silently watched her pass. *(Corner of V. Dante Alighieri and V. S. Margherita within 1 block of the Bargello. ☎ 055 21 94 16. Open M and W-Sa 10am-5pm, Su 10am-2pm. €3, groups over 15 €2 per person.)*

PIAZZA DELLA REPUBBLICA AND FARTHER WEST

After hours of contemplating great Florentine art, visit the area that financed it all. In the early 1420s, 72 banks operated in Florence, most in the area around the Mercato Nuovo and V. Tornabuoni. With a much lower concentration of tourist sights, this area is quieter and more residential.

■ **CHIESA DI SANTA MARIA NOVELLA.** The wealthiest merchants built their chapels in this church near the train station. Santa Maria Novella was home to the order of Dominicans, or *Domini canes* (Hounds of the Lord), who took a bite out of sin and corruption. Built between 1279 and 1360, the *chiesa* boasts a green and white Romanesque-Gothic facade, considered one of the greatest masterpieces of early Renaissance architecture. The facade is geometrically pure and balanced, a precursor to the classical revival of the high Renaissance. Thirteenth-century frescoes covered the interior until the Medici commissioned Vasari to paint new ones. Fortunately, Vasari spared Masaccio's powerful ■*Trinity*, the first painting to use geometric perspective. This fresco, on the left side of the nave, creates the illusion of a tabernacle. The **Cappella di Filippo Strozzi,** to the right of the high altar, contains cartoon-like frescoes by Filippo Lippi, including a rather green Adam, a woolly Abraham, and an excruciating *Torture of St. John the Evangelist.* A cycle of Ghirlandaio frescoes covers the **Tournabuoni Chapel** behind the main altar. *(☎ 055 055 210 113. Open M-Th and Sa 9:30am-5pm, F and Su 1-5pm. €2.50.)* The **cloister** next door has Paolo Uccello's *The Flood* and *The Sacrifice of Noah.* The adjoining **Cappella Spagnola** (Spanish Chapel) harbors 14th-century frescoes by Andrea di Bonaiuto. *(☎ 055 28 21 87. Open M-Th and Sa 9am-4:30pm, Su 9am-2pm. €2.60.)*

PIAZZA DELLA REPUBBLICA. The largest open space in Florence, this piazza teems with crowds and street performers in the evenings. An enormous arch filling in the gap over V. Strozzi marks the western edge of the square. The rest of the piazza is lined with overpriced coffee shops, restaurants, and *gelaterie.* In 1890, the piazza replaced the Mercato Vecchio as the site of the city's market. The inscription *"Antico centro della città, da secolare squalore, a vita nuova res-*

tituito" ("The ancient center of the city, squalid for centuries, restored to new life") makes a derogatory reference to the fact that the piazza is the site of the old Jewish ghetto. The ghetto slowly disappeared as a result of the "liberation of the Jews" in Italy in the 1860s that allowed members of the Jewish community to live elsewhere. An ill-advised plan to demolish the city center's historic buildings and remodel Florence sought the destruction of the Old Market. Fortunately, an international campaign successfully thwarted the razing.

CHIESA DI SANTA TRINITÀ. To spend an eternity in the company of society's elites, most fashionable *palazzo* owners commissioned family chapels here. The facade, designed by Bernardo Buontalenti in the 16th century, is an exquisite example of late-Renaissance architecture that verges on Baroque in its ornamentation. The interior shows its Romanesque origins, displaying beautiful proportions with less ornament. The 4th chapel on the right houses the remains of *Scenes From the Life of a Virgin*, and a magnificent *Annunciation*, both by Lorenzo Monaco. Scenes from Ghirlandaio's *Life of St. Francis* decorate the **Sassetti chapel** in the right arm of the transept. The famous altarpiece, Ghirlandaio's *Adoration of the Shepherds*, resides in the Uffizi—this one is a convincing copy. *(In P. S. Trinità. ☎ 055 21 69 12. Open M-Sa 8am-noon and 4-6pm, Su 4-6pm.)*

MERCATO NUOVO. The *loggie* of the New Market have housed gold and silk traders since 1547 under their Corinthian-columned splendor. Today, vendors sell purses, belts, clothes, fruit, and vegetables, as well as some gold and silk. Pietro Tacca's pleasantly plump statue, *Il Porcellino* (The Little Pig; actually a wild boar), appeared some 50 years after the market first opened. Reputed to bring good luck, its snout is polished from tourists' rubbing. *(Off V. Calimala, between P. della Repubblica and the Ponte Vecchio. Sellers hawk their wares from dawn until dusk.)*

PALAZZO DAVANZATI. As Florence's 15th-century economy expanded, its bankers and merchants flaunted their new wealth by erecting grand palaces. The great *quattrocento* boom began with construction of the Palazzo Davanzati. Today, the high-ceilinged *palazzo* finds life as the **Museo della Casa Fiorentina Antica.** With reproductions and original furniture, restored frescoes, and wooden doors and ornaments, this museum recreates the 15th-century merchants' life of luxury. *(V. Porta Rossa, 13. ☎ 055 238 8610. Open daily 8:30am-1:50pm. Closed 1st, 3rd, and 5th M and 2nd and 4th Su of each month. Videos 10am, 11am, and noon, on 4th fl.)*

PALAZZO STROZZI. The modesty of the Palazzo Davanzati's facade gave way to more extravagant *palazzi*. The Palazzo Strozzi, begun in 1489, may be the grandest of its kind, occupying an entire block. Its regal proportions and three-tiered facade, made of bulging blocks of brown stone, embody the Florentine style. The *palazzo* now shelters several cultural institutes, not open to the public, and occasionally hosts art exhibits that are open to all. The courtyard is open to the public and worth a look. *(On V. Tornabuoni at V. Strozzi. Enter from P. della Strozzi. ☎ 055 28 53 95.)*

MUSEO SALVATORE FERRAGAMO. If you've seen too much Renaissance art and have always felt a certain kinship to Imelda Marcos, pop into this free museum, on the sumptuous second floor of the Ferragamo Store. View a history of all the shoes designed by the master and check out silent movie clips featuring his earliest work. *(V. Tornabuoni, 2, near the Arno. ☎ 055 336 0456. Open M-F 9am-1pm and 2-6pm.)*

SAN LORENZO AND FARTHER NORTH

BASILICA DI SAN LORENZO. In 1419, Brunelleschi designed this spacious basilica, another Florentine example of early-Renaissance simple lines and proportion. Because the Medici lent the funds to build the church, they retained artistic control over its construction. Their coat of arms, featuring five red balls, appears all over the nave, and their tombs fill the two sacristies and the **Cappella dei Principi** (see below) behind the altar. The family cunningly placed Cosimo dei Medici's grave in front of the high altar, making the entire church his personal mausoleum. Michelangelo designed the church's exterior but, disgusted by the murkiness of Florentine politics, abandoned the project to study architecture in Rome. The basilica still stands unadorned. *(Open M-Sa 10am-5pm. €2.50.)*

The ▨**Cappelle dei Medici** (Medici Chapels) consist of dual design contributions by Matteo Nigetti and Michelangelo. Intended as a grand mausoleum, Nigetti's **Cappella dei Principi** (Princes' Chapel) emulates the baptistery in P. del Duomo. Except for the gilded portraits of the Medici dukes, the decor is a rare glimpse of the Baroque in Florence. Michelangelo's simple architectural design of the **Sacrestia Nuova** (New Sacristy) reveals the master's study of Brunelleschi. Michelangelo sculpted two impressive tombs for Medici dukes Lorenzo and Giuliano. On the tomb of the military-minded Giuliano lounge the smooth, female *Night* and the rising, male *Day*. Michelangelo personified the hazier states of *Dawn* and *Dusk* with slightly more androgynous figures for the milder-mannered Lorenzo. In both cases, the paired figures represent life and death. Some of Michelangelo's sketches are in the basement. *(Walk around to the back entrance on P. Madonna degli Aldobrandini. In summer 2002, distracting scaffolding partially blocked some of the artwork. Open daily 8:15am-5pm; closed the 2nd and 4th Su and the 1st, 3rd, and 5th M of every month. €6.)*

The adjacent **Laurentian Library** houses one of the world's most valuable manuscript collections. Michelangelo's famous entrance portico confirms his virtuosity; the elaborate *pietra serena* sandstone staircase is one of his most innovative architectural designs. *(☎055 21 07 60. Open daily 8:30am-1:30pm. Free.)*

▨**MUSEO DELLA CHIESA DI SAN MARCO.** Remarkable works by Fra Angelico adorn the Museo della Chiesa di San Marco, one of the most peaceful and spiritual places in Florence. A large room to the right of the lovely courtyard contains some of the painter's major works, including the church's altarpiece. The second floor houses Angelico's most famous *Annunciation*, across from the top of the stairwell, as well as the monks' quarters. Every cell in the convent contains its own Fra Angelico fresco, each painted in flat colors and with sparse detail to facilitate the monks' somber meditation. To the right of the stairwell, Michelozzo's library, modeled on Michelangelo's work in S. Lorenzo, is a fine example of purity and vigor. After visiting, you may want to follow in the footsteps of the convent's patron, Cosimo I, who retired here. (His cell is the largest.) Look also for Savonarola's cell, where you can see some of his relics. On your way to the exit, you will pass two rooms housing the **Museo di Firenze Antica**, worth a quick visit. On display are numerous archeological fragments, most of them pieces of stone work from Etruscan and Roman buildings in the area. *(Enter at P. di San Marco, 3. ☎055 238 8608 or 238 8704. Open daily 8:15am-6:50pm. Closed 1st, 3rd, and 5th Su and 2nd and 4th M of every month. €4, EU citizens 18-25 €2, over 65 or under 18 free.)*

MALATA NOTTE (SICKLY NIGHT).

Art historian Jonathan Nelson and oncologist James Stark made a rather startling discovery while examining the left breast of Michelangelo's *Night*, the female statue adorning Giuliano Medici's tomb in the Medici Chapels: the nude sculpture exhibits signs of cancer. Nelson and Stark reasoned that Michelangelo may have used a corpse as his model, and that *Night* is a true-to-life portrayal of a 16th-century breast cancer victim. Their supposition imbues the figure of *Notte* with a particularly sobering sense of *mortalità*.

ACCADEMIA. Michelangelo's triumphant ▨**David** stands in self-assured perfection under the rotunda designed just for him. He was moved here from P. della Signoria in 1873 after a stone hurled during a riot broke his left wrist in two places. If the real *David* looks different to you than the slightly top-heavy copy in front of the Palazzo Vecchio, there's a reason—even though the statues are practically identical, in the Accademia, David stands on a higher pedestal. Michelangelo exaggerated his head and torso to correct for distortion from viewing far below. In the hallway leading up to the *David* are Michelangelo's four *Slaves*. The master left these intriguing statues intentionally unfinished. Remaining true to his theories of living stone, he chipped away only enough to show their figure emerging from the stone. Don't miss the impressive collection of Gothic triptychs on the second floor in **Room 2.** Also on the second floor, in **Room 3,** is an astounding collection of Russian icons. *(V. Ricasoli, 60, between the churches of San Marco and S. S. Annunziata. ☎ 055 29 48 83. Most areas wheelchair accessible. Open Tu-Su 8:15am-6:50pm. €6.50.)*

PALAZZO MEDICI RICCARDI. The palace's innovative facade is the work of Michelozzo—it stands as the archetype for all Renaissance *palazzi*. The private chapel inside features Benozzo Gozzoli's beautiful, wrap-around fresco of the ▨*Three Magi* and several Medici family portraits. The *palazzo* hosts rotating exhibits ranging from Renaissance architectural sketches to Fellini memorabilia. *(V. Cavour, 3. ☎ 055 276 0340. Open daily 9am-7pm. €4, children €2.60.)*

OSPEDALE DEGLI INNOCENTI. Brunelleschi designed the right-hand *loggia* of the Hospital of the Innocents in the 1420s. It opened in 1444 as the first orphanage in Europe. On the left side of the portico stands the rotating stone cylinder on which mothers would place their unwanted children. They would then ring the bell as a signal for those inside to rotate the stone and receive the child. An equestrian statue of Ferdinando de Medici presides over the piazza. The bright and airy **Galleria dello Spedale degli Innocenti** contains Botticelli's *Madonna e Angelo* and Ghirlandaio's *Adoration of the Magi*, along with many lesser-known Renaissance paintings. *(Around P. Annunziata. ☎ 055 203 7308. Open Th-Tu 8:30am-2pm. €2.60.)*

MUSEO ARCHEOLOGICO. Unassuming behind its bland, yellow plaster facade and small sign, the archeological museum has a surprisingly diverse collection. Inside, you'll find notable collections of statues and other monuments of the ancient Greeks, Etruscans, and Egyptians. A long, thin, two-story gallery devoted to Etruscan jewelry runs along the length of the plant- and tree-filled courtyard. In almost any other city in the world, this museum would be a major cultural highlight, but in Florence, its possible to enjoy it without large crowds. Don't miss the *chimera d'Arezzo* in **Room 14.** *(V. della Colonna, 38. ☎ 055 23 575. Open M 2-7pm, Tu and Th 8:30am-7pm, W and F-Su 8:30am-2pm. €4.)*

MERCATO CENTRALE. Just two blocks from San Lorenzo, the Central Market is home to butchers and cheese and wine vendors on the first floor and a vegetable and fruit market on the second floor. The market was built in the 1920s, with wrought iron railing and intertwining staircases between the open levels. It's a great place to buy cheap fixings for an afternoon picnic in the Boboli Gardens (see p. 361). The Piazza Mercato Centrale and surrounding streets are filled with vendors selling the usual leather goods and clothing. *(Open daily 8am-2pm.)*

PIAZZA SANTA CROCE AND ENVIRONS

▨**CHIESA DI SANTA CROCE.** The Franciscans built this church as far as possible from their Dominican rivals at S. Maria Novella. The ascetic Franciscans ironically produced what is arguably the most splendid church in the city. A fresco cycle by

Andrea Orcagna originally adorned the nave. Never heard of Orcagna? That may be because Vasari not only destroyed the entire cycle but also left Orcagna out of his famous *Lives of the Artists*. To the right of the altar, the frescoes of the **Cappella Peruzzi** vie with those of the **Cappella Bardi**. Giotto and his school painted both, but unfortunately, the works are badly faded. Among the famous Florentines buried in this church are Michelangelo, who rests at the front of the right aisle in a tomb designed by Vasari, and humanist Leonardo Bruni, shown holding his precious *History of Florence* farther down the aisle. To the right of Bruni's tomb sits Donatello's gilded *Annunciation*. The Florentines, who banished Dante, eventually prepared a tomb for him here. Dante died in Ravenna, however, and the literary necrophiles there have never sent him back. Florence did manage to retain the bodies of Machiavelli and Galileo, who both rest here. You win some, you lose some. Be sure to note the high water mark about 8 ft. up on the walls and pillars, an enduring reminder of the flood of 1966. (☎ 055 24 46 19. Open Mar. 15-Nov. 15: M-Sa 9:30am-5:30pm, Su and holidays 3-5:30pm; Nov. 16-Mar. 14: M-Sa 9:30am-12:30pm and 3-5:30pm, Su and holidays 3-5:30pm.)

The **Museo dell'Opera di Santa Croce** was hard-hit by the 1966 flood, which left Cimabue's *Crucifixion* in a tragic state. The museum forms three sides of the church's peaceful courtyard with gravel paths and cyprus trees. The former dining hall contains Taddeo Gaddi's imaginative fresco of *The Tree of the Cross*, and beneath it, his *Last Supper*. Intricate stone pilasters, Luca della Robbia's *tondi* of the apostles, and statues of the evangelists by Donatello are among the profusion of colorful decorations that grace Brunelleschi's small ▓**Cappella Pazzi**, at the end of the cloister next to the church. *(Enter museum through the loggia in front of Cappella Pazzi. Open Th-Tu 10am-7pm. €2.58.)*

SYNAGOGUE OF FLORENCE. This synagogue, also known as the **Museo del Tempio Israelitico,** lies hidden behind gates and walls, waiting to reveal its Sephardic temple's domes, horseshoe arches, and patterns. David Levi, a wealthy Florentine Jewish business man, donated his fortune in 1870 for the construction of "a monumental temple worthy of Florence," in recognition of the fact that Jews were newly allowed to live and worship outside the old Jewish ghetto. Architects Micheli, Falchi, and Treves created one of Europe's most beautiful synagogues. *(V. Farini, 4, at V. Pilastri. The museum includes free, informative tours every hour; book in advance. ☎ 055 24 52 52 or 24 52 53. Open Su-Th 10am-6pm and 2-5pm, F 10am-2pm. €4)*

CASA BUONARROTI. This unassuming little museum houses Michelangelo memorabilia and two of his most important early works, *The Madonna of the Steps* and *The Battle of the Centaurs*. Both pieces are to the left of the second floor landing. He completed these panels, which illustrate his growth from bas-relief to sculpture, when he was only 16 years old. *(V. Ghibellina, 70. From P. S. Croce, follow V. de' Pepi and turn right onto V. Ghibellina. ☎ 055 24 17 52. Open W-M 9:30am-2pm. €6.50.)*

IN THE OLTRARNO

The far side of the Arno is a lively, unpretentious quarter. Though you'll likely cross over the Ponte Vecchio on the way to the Oltrarno, consider coming back along V. Maggio, a street lined with Renaissance *palazzi*, many of which have markers with historical descriptions. Head over the Ponte S. Trinità, which affords excellent views of the Ponte Vecchio, or dally a bit in Piazza San Spirito, where markets are held during the day and street artists perform at night.

▓ **PALAZZO PITTI.** Luca Pitti, a 15th-century banker, built his *palazzo* east of S. Spirito against the Boboli hill. The Medici family acquired the *palazzo* and the hill in 1550 and enlarged everything possible. During Italy's brief experiment with monarchy, the structure served as a royal residence. Today the **Palazzo Pitti** is fronted with a vast uninhabited piazza and houses a gallery and four museums. *(Ticket office/info ☎ 055 29 48 83. Ticket to gallery, museums, and Boboli Gardens €10.50.)*

The ◼**Galleria Palatina** was one of only a few public galleries when it opened in 1833. Today it houses Florence's second-most important collection (behind the Uffizi). An overwhelming array of Renaissance works, including a number of works by Raphael, Titian, Andrea del Sarto, Rosso, Caravaggio, and Rubens fill its 30 rooms. Flemish works dominate the Neoclassical Music Room and the Putti Room. While admiring the collection, remember to look up at the frescoes on the ceilings. *(Open Tu-Su 8:30am-6.50pm. €6.50. Informative official guides €7.50.)*

The **Museo degli Argenti** (Silver Museum), on the ground floor, exhibits the Medici family treasures, including cases of precious gems, ivories, silver pieces, and Lorenzo the Magnificent's famous collection of vases. *(€2, combined with Museo della Porcellana and Boboli Gardens €3.)* The **Museo della Porcellana**, hidden in back of the gardens, exhibits fine ceramics from the Medici collection. *(Admission included in Boboli Gardens ticket.)* Find out if the clothes make the Medici in the **Galleria del Costume**, a decadent display of the family's finery. In the last museum, the **Galleria d'Arte Moderna**, lies one of Italian art history's big surprises, the early-19th century proto-Impressionist works of the Macchiaioli school. The collection also includes Neoclassical and Romantic pieces, like Giovanni Dupré's sculptural group *Cain and Abel*. *(Same ticket office as Galleria Palatina. All museums open daily 8:30am-1:50pm; closed 1st, 3rd, 5th M and the 2nd and 4th Su of every month. Combined ticket for both galleries €5.)* The **Appartamenti Reale** (Royal Apartments) house lavish reminders of the time when the palazzo served as the royal House of Savoy's living quarters. *(Open Tu-Su 8:30am-6:30pm. Appartamenti included in Galleria Palatina ticket.)*

◼ **BOBOLI GARDENS.** This elaborately landscaped park, an exquisite example of a stylized Renaissance garden, provides teasing glimpses of Florence and wonderful views of the surrounding countryside. A large oval lawn sits just up the hill from the back of the palace, marked by an Egyptian obelisk and lined with a hedge dotted by marble statues. Labyrinthine avenues of cypress trees lead eager meanderers to bubbling fountains with nudes and shaded picnic areas. *(Pass through courtyard of Palazzo Pitti to ticket office and entrance. ☎ 055 265 1816. Open Nov.-Feb. daily 9am-4:30pm; Mar-Apr. and Sept.-Oct. 9am-5:30pm; May 9am-6:30pm; and June-Aug. 9am-7:30pm. Closed 1st and last M of each month. €2, EU citizens with passport €1.)*

CHIESA DI SANTA MARIA DEL CARMINE. Inside this church, the ◼**Brancacci Chapel** holds Masaccio's stunning 15th-century frescoes, declared masterpieces in their own time. 50 years later, a respectful Filippino Lippi completed the cycle. Masolino's *Adam and Eve* and Masaccio's *Expulsion from the Garden* stand face to face, illustrating the young Masaccio's innovative depiction of imperfect human forms. With such monumental works as the *Tribute Money*, this chapel became a school for artists, including Michelangelo. Visitors are not allowed in the nave of the church, but can peer from the roped-off chapel into the gloomy, but beautifully frescoed main aisle. *(Open M and W-Sa 10am-5pm, Su 1-5pm. €3.10.)*

CHIESA DI SANTO SPIRITO. This church has a simple and well-proportioned Renaissance interior. Brunelleschi's design was significantly ahead of its time. He envisioned a barrel-vaulted, four-aisled nave surrounded by round chapels, which would have created a softly undulating outer wall. Brunelleschi died when the project was only partially completed, however, and the plans were altered to be more conventional, yielding the standard flat roofed, three-aisled nave. Tall, thin columns make the church feel airy and light, while the unusually high clerestory admits shafts of sunlight to illuminate the church. *(☎ 055 21 00 30. Open M-Tu and Th-F 8:30am-noon and 4-6pm, W 8:30am-noon, Su 8am-noon and 4-7pm.)*

SAN MINIATO AL MONTE AND ENVIRONS

■ **SAN MINIATO AL MONTE.** One of Florence's oldest churches gloriously surveys all of Florence. The inlaid marble facade and 13th-century mosaics provide a prelude to the incredible pavement inside, patterned with lions, doves, and astrological signs. Inside, the **Chapel of the Cardinal of Portugal** holds a collection of superlative della Robbia terra-cottas. Be sure to circle the church and spend a moment in the cemetery, an overwhelming profusion of tombs and mausoleums in many architectural styles. *(Take bus #13 from the station or climb the stairs from Piazzale Michelangelo.* ☎ *055 234 2731. Church open daily 7:30am-7pm.)*

PIAZZALE MICHELANGELO. Laid out in 1860, Piazzale Michelangelo offers a fine panorama of the entire city. Sunset provides the most spectacular lighting of the city. Now, the piazza doubles as a large parking lot, home to hordes of tour buses during summer days. It occasionally hosts concerts as well. The stunning photoop, in addition to the copy of Michelangelo's *David* on an ornate pedestal in the center, make this parking lot worth the trek. *(Cross Ponte Vecchio and turn left, walk through the piazza, and turn right up V. de' Bardi. Follow it uphill as it becomes V. del Monte alle Croci, where a staircase to the left heads to the Piazzale.)*

⚐ ENTERTAINMENT

Florence disagrees with England over who invented modern soccer, but every June, the various *quartieri* of the city turn out in costume to play their own medieval version of the sport, known as **calcio storico.** Two teams face off over a wooden ball in one of the city's piazzas. These games often blur the line between athletic contest and riot. A make-shift stadium in P. Santa Croce hosts three nights of games in June. Check newspapers or the tourist office for the exact dates and locations of historic or modern *calcio.* The **stadio,** north of the city center, is home to the modern soccer games. Tickets (around €16) are sold at the **Box Office** and at **Marisa,** the bar across the street from the stadium.

The most important of Florence's traditional festivals celebrating the patron saint, **San Giovanni Battista,** on June 24, features a tremendous fireworks display in Piazzale Michelangelo that starts around 10pm and is easily visible from the Arno. The summer also swings with music festivals, starting in late April with the classical **Maggio Musicale.** The **Estate Fiesolana** (June-Aug.) fills the Roman theater in Fiesole with concerts, opera, theater, ballet, and film.

In the summer, the **L'Europa dei Sensi** program hosts **Rime Rapanti,** nightly cultural shows with music, poetry, and food from a chosen European country. Call the information office (☎ 348 580 4812; www.rimerampanti.it) to make reservations. The same company also hosts the more modern and lively **Le Pavoniere,** with live music, pool, bar, and pizzeria, in the Ippodromo delle Cascine (along the river past the train station). Call the office (☎ 055 321 7541) for information and reservations. In September, Florence hosts the **Festa dell'Unità,** a music and concert series at Campi Bisenzia (bus #30). The **Festa del Grillo** (Festival of the Cricket) is held the first Sunday after Ascension Day (40 days after Easter)—crickets in wooden cages are hawked in the Cascine park to be released into the grass.

⌐ SHOPPING

The Florentines design their window displays (and their wares) with flair. V. Tornabuoni's swanky **boutiques** and the well-stocked goldsmiths on the Ponte Vecchio serve a sophisticated clientele. Florence makes its contribution to *alta moda* with a number of fashion shows, including the biannual **Pitti Uomo show** (in Jan. and June), Europe's most important exhibition of menswear.

The city's artisan traditions thrive at the open markets. **San Lorenzo,** the largest, cheapest, and most touristed, sprawls for several blocks around P. S. Lorenzo. High prices are rare, as are quality and honesty. (Open M-Sa 9am-after sunset.) For everything from potholders to parakeets, visit **Parco delle Cascine,** which begins west of the city center at P. V. Veneto and stretches along the Arno River. The market at the Cascine sells used clothing and shoes. (At night, commodities of a different sort go up for sale as transvestite prostitutes prowl the piazza in search of customers.) For a flea market specializing in old furniture, postcards, and bric-a-brac, visit **Piazza Ciompi,** off V. Pietrapiana from Borgo degli Albizi. (Open Tu-Sa.) Even when prices are marked, don't be afraid to haggle. Generally, you should start with half of the price offered, but never ask for a price you're not willing to pay. Bargaining is often impossible if you are using a credit card.

Books and **art reproductions** are the best Florentine souvenirs. **Alinari,** L. Alinari, 15, stocks the world's largest selection of art prints and high-quality photographs, from €25. (☎ 055 23 951. Open M-F 9am-1pm and 2:30-6:30pm, Sa 9am-1pm. AmEx/MC/V.) **Abacus,** V. de'Ginori, 30r, sells beautiful photo albums, journals, and address books, all made of fine leather and *carta fiorentina*, paper covered in an intricate floral design. (☎ 055 21 97 19. Open M-Sa 9:30am-1:30pm and 3-7:30pm.) Florentine **leatherwork** is affordable and usually of high quality. Some of the best leather artisans in the city work around P. S. Croce and V. Porta S. Maria. The **Santa Croce Leather School,** in Chiesa di Santa Croce, offers some of the city's best products with prices to match. (On Su, enter through V. S. Giuseppe, 5r. ☎ 055 24 45 33 and 247 9913; www.leatherschool.it. Open Mar. 15-Nov. 15 M-Sa 9am-6:30pm, Su 10:30am-12:30pm and 3-6pm; Nov. 16-Mar. 14 M-Sa 9am-12:30pm and 3-6pm.)

◪ NIGHTLIFE

For reliable information, consult the city's entertainment monthly, *Firenze Spettacolo* (€2). Street performers draw crowds to the steps of the duomo, the arcades of the Mercato Nuovo, Piazza della Signoria, and Ple. Michelangelo. **Piazza Santo Spirito** in Oltrarno has regular live music in the summer and a good selection of bars and restaurants. Take the #25 bus from the station to the **Giardini del Drago** (Gardens of the Dragon) for a pick-up game of soccer.

BARS

May Day Lounge, V. Dante Alighieri, 16r. Artists display their work on walls of this eclectic lounge. Play pong on the 1980s gaming system or sip mixed drinks (€4.50-6.50) to the beat of the funk. Draft beer €4.50. Happy hour 8-10pm. Open daily 8pm-2am.

Eby's Latin Bar, V. dell' Oriuolo, 5r (☎ 338 650 8959). Eby blends tasty fresh fruit cocktails, with only seasonal ingredients. Fantastic Mexican wraps and the best nachos in Florence are 2 more reasons to visit. Cocktails €5.50. Beer €3. Happy hour 6-9pm (drinks €3). Open M-Sa noon-3pm and 6pm-3am.

The William, V. Magliabechi, 7/9/11r (☎ 055 263 8357). Plenty of outdoor seating. Comfortable brick-walled interior. Rowdy and packed on weekends; calm and brooding during the week. One of the few English pubs in Florence serving Bass Ale. Pints of all draft beer €4.50. Open Su-Th 12:30pm-1:30am, F-Sa until 2:30am. AmEx/MC/V.

Montecarla, V. dei Bardi, 2 (☎ 055 234 0259), in the Oltrarno, off P. de' Mozzi. 3-tiered wonder-world of jaguar-print upholstery with a plastic flower motif. Deliciously plush club is mellow in summer but stuffed in winter. If you're lucky, you'll meet Carla, the famous owner. Mixed drinks €7. Membership card to enter €5. Open Su-Th 9pm-3:30am, F-Sa 9pm-5:30am.

The Chequers Pub, V. della Scala, 7/9r (☎ 055 28 75 88). Of all the pubs in Florence, this one attracts the liveliest Italian crowd. Wide range of beers (pints €4.50). Happy hour daily 6:30-8pm (pints €2.50). Open daily Apr.-Oct. Su-Th 12:30pm-1:30am, F-Sa until 2:30am; Nov.-Mar. 6pm-1:30am, F-Sa until 2:30am. AmEx/MC/V.

The Fiddler's Elbow, P. S. Maria Novella, 7r (☎ 055 21 50 56). Authentic Irish pub serves cider, Guinness, and other beers for €4.20 per pint. Crowded with convivial foreigners. Happy hour until 8pm. Open daily Su-Th 3pm-1am, F-Sa 2pm-2am.

DISCOS

Rio Grande, V. degli Olmi, 1 (☎ 055 33 13 71), near Parco delle Cascinè. This is the most popular of Florence's discos among locals and tourists alike. €16 cover includes 1 drink; each subsequent drink €7. Special nights include soul, hip-hop, house, and reggae. Call for their weekly schedule. Open Tu-Sa 11pm-4am. AmEx/MC/V.

Central Park, Parco delle Cascinè. Open-air dance floors pulse with hip-hop, jungle, reggae, and Italian "dance rock." A cinema, *pizzeria*, *creperia*, and Internet bar are all vaguely attached to the dance complex. Mixed drinks €8. Open Th-Sa and M-Tu 11pm to late, W 9pm to late. AmEx/MC/V.

Yab, V. Sassetti, 5 (☎ 055 21 51 60). Another dance club seething with American students, as well as locals. Classic R&B and reggae on M, and other music specialties on a rotating basis other nights. A very large dance floor, mercifully free of strobe lights, is packed come midnight. Mixed drinks €5. Open winter daily 9pm-1am.

Blob, V. Vinegia, 21r (☎ 055 21 12 09), behind the Palazzo Vecchio. From mellow evenings to boisterous nights (to early mornings), this little club has much to offer, including DJs, an open mic, movies in original sound, and foosball. Mixed drinks €5.50-6.50. 2-for-1 happy hour 6-10pm. Open daily 6pm-3:30am. AmEx/MC/V.

Tabasco Gay Club, P .S. Cecilia, 3r (☎ 055 21 30 00), in tiny alleyway across P. della Signoria from Palazzo Vecchio. Smoke machines, strobe lights and low vaulted ceilings in this dark basement club. Caters primarily to gay men. 18+. Cover €10 before 1am, €13 later on, includes 1st drink. Open Tu-Su 10pm-4am. AmEx/MC/V.

⊡ DAYTRIP FROM FLORENCE: FIESOLE

The town is a 25min. bus ride away; catch the ATAF city bus #7 from the train station near track #16 or P. S. Marco. It drops passengers at P. Mino da Fiesole in the town center. The tourist office, V. Portigiani, 3, is next to the Teatro Romano, a half a block off P. Mino da Fiesole, directly across the piazza from the bus stop. The office provides a free map with museum and sights listings. ☎ 055 59 87 20. Open M-Sa 8:30am-7:30pm, Su 10am-7pm.

Older than Florence itself, Fiesole is the site of the original Etruscan settlement. Florence was actually colonized and settled as an off-shoot. Fiesole has long been a welcome escape from the sweltering summer heat of the Arno Valley and a source of inspiration for numerous famous figures—among them Alexander Dumas, Anatole France, Marcel Proust, Gertrude Stein, Frank Lloyd Wright, and Paul Klee. Leonardo da Vinci even used the town as a testing ground for his famed flying machine. Fiesole's location provides incomparable views of Florence and the rolling countryside to the north.

With the bus stop at your back, walk half a block off P. Mino da Fiesole, to the entrance gate of the **Museo Civico**. One ticket gains admission to three constituent museums. The **Teatro Romano** is used intermittently for concerts in summer and includes Etruscan thermal baths, temple ruins, and wonderful countryside views.

The amphitheater grounds lead into the **Museo Civico Archeologico,** which houses an extensive collection of Etruscan artifacts, well-preserved Grecian urns, and vases from *Magna Graecia* (modern-day Southern Italy under the Greek Empire). Hop across the street to breeze through the **Museo Bandini,** which houses a collection of 15th-century Italian paintings. (Open Apr.-Oct. daily 9:30am-6:30pm; Sept.-Mar. W-M 9:30am-6:30pm. €6.20, students or over 65 €4.13.)

Accommodations in Fiesole are expensive, but the town is a great place to sit down for a leisurely afternoon lunch. To grab a bite to eat, head to the **Pizzeria Etrusca ❷,** in P. Mina da Fiesole, near the bus stop. (☎ 055 59 94 84. *Primi* from €4.65, *secondi* from €8.26. Open noon-3pm and 7pm-1am.) If you're looking for something lighter, ponder the fantastic view of the Arno Valley over coffee (from €0.80) or *gelato* (€1.55-2.60) at **Blu Bar ❷,** right behind the bus stop. (P. Mino, 39. Open Apr.-Oct. daily 8-1am, Nov.-Mar. W-M 8-1am.) Up the hill on your left, with your back to the bus stop, you will find the **Convento Francesco** and the public gardens. It's a steep, mercifully short climb, well worth the effort for the breathtaking panorama of Florence and the surrounding hills. The monastery contains a frescoed **chapel** and a bite-size **museum** of exquisite Chinese pottery, jade figurines, and Egyptian artifacts (including a mummy) brought back by Franciscan missionaries. (Open June-Sept. M-F 10am-noon and 3-6pm, Sa-Su 3-6pm; Oct.-Mar. M-F 10am-noon and 3-5pm, Sa-Su 3-5pm.)

CENTRAL ITALY

TUSCANY (TOSCANA)

In Tuscany, Renaissance masterpieces seem to occupy every corner, perfectly preserved hilltop citadels dot the countryside, and fields of sunflowers bow in the perpetual sunlight. Tuscany's beauty is dazzling. It's also no secret. Every summer, Tuscany's unparalleled concentration of art, architecture, world-renowned wine, and sinfully simple cuisine lure millions of tourists. Tour groups shuffle from duomo to *pinacoteca*, clogging narrow medieval streets. As a result, prices and wait times for many of the more popular sights are ever-rising, and booking accommodations in advance is often a necessity during high season.

While it's nearly impossible to get completely off-the-beaten-path in Tuscany, a little effort can still yield moments of perfect solitude. No art history degree is needed to stroll through the silent sanctuary of a hidden 15th-century Romanesque church, to meander atop a bike through the mesmerizing clay hills of La Crete, or to take a shaded walk atop Lucca's *baluardi* (city walls). So go ahead and lean with all the other vacationers on the tower in Pisa, gaze open-mouthed at the Botticellis in the Uffizi, and loiter in Siena's Il Campo; these classic tourist sights should not be missed. Just remember, patience and a bit of wanderlust will bring full enjoyment of Tuscany's captivating piazzas and rolling hills.

HIGHLIGHTS OF TUSCANY

CHOOSE your own hill town. You can't go wrong in the **Chianti** region (p. 382), where blankets of sunflowers are interspersed with medieval towers.

WAIT for hours and hours in the hot sun with the teeming masses only to go wild for 30 seconds during Siena's world-famous **Palio** (p. 381).

STEP into Pisa's **Field of Miracles** and help support its faulty **tower** (p. 406).

EXILE yourself to **Elba** at **Napoleon's villa** in Portoferraio or the wind-warped **coastal cliffs** near Chiusi (p. 413).

VIEW two regions at once from the lofty bastions of the **Medici Fortress** (p. 369).

CIRCLE Lucca's *centro* on perfectly preserved **medieval walls** (p. 398).

WINCE at the graphic displays of medieval torture devices at the **Museo della Tortura** in San Gimignano (p. 394).

CORTONA ☎ 0575

The ancient town of Cortona regally surveys Tuscany and Umbria from its mountain peak. Stunning hills and rich farmland, punctuated by the shimmering Lake Trasimeno, make for spectacular sunsets. Though currently peaceful, the city once rivaled Perugia, Arezzo, and even Florence in power and belligerence. When Cortona finally lost its autonomy in 1409, it was auctioned off to the rival Florentines. For all its grumbling, Cortona enjoyed peace and prosperity under Florentine rule. The paintings of Luca Signorelli and Pietro Lorenzetti, signs of this prosperity, are now exhibited in Cortona's Museo Diocesano.

Tuscany and Umbria

TRANSPORTATION

Trains: Florence (every hr., €6.20) and **Rome** (every 1-2hr., €8.99) arrive at **Camucia-Cortona.** LFI bus to Cortona's P. Garibaldi leaves from the station (15min., €1). Despite what the smiling old man outside the station says, do not walk from the station to town.

Buses: Buses run to P. Garibaldi from **Arezzo** (1hr., 12 per day, €2.50). Buy LFI bus tickets from the tourist office, a bar, or *tabacchi*.

Taxis: ☎335 819 6313.

ORIENTATION AND PRACTICAL INFORMATION

Buses from neighboring cities stop at **Piazza Garibaldi** just outside the city wall. Enter the city by turning left uphill following **Via Nazionale.** Pass the tourist office immediately on the left, and you'll reach **Piazza della Repubblica,** the center of town. Diagonally across the piazza lies **Piazza Signorelli,** Cortona's main square.

Tourist Office: V. Nazionale, 42 (☎0575 63 03 52; fax 63 06 56). English-speaking staff provides maps, rail and bus schedules, and tickets. Open May-Sept. M-Sa 9am-1pm and 3-7pm, Su 9am-1pm; Oct.-Apr. M-F 9am-1pm and 3-6pm, Sa 9am-1pm.

Currency Exchange: Banca Populare, V. Guelfa, 4. Open M-F 8:20am-1:20pm and 2:35-3:35pm. 24hr. **ATM,** V. S. Margherita, 2/3.

Emergency: ☎113. **Medical Emergency:** ☎118.

Police: V. Dardano, 9 (☎0575 60 30 06).

Misericordia: ☎0575 60 30 83.

Pharmacy: Farmacia Centrale, V. Nazionale, 38 (☎/fax 0575 60 32 06). Open M-Sa 9am-1pm and 4:30-8pm.

Hospital: (☎0575 63 91), on V. Maffei.

Post Office: V. Santucci, 1, 15m uphill from P. della Repubblica. Open M-F 8:15am-1:30pm, Sa 8:15am-12:30pm.

Postal Code: 52044.

ACCOMMODATIONS

▓ **Ostello San Marco (HI),** V. Maffei, 57 (☎0575 60 13 92 or 60 17 65; www.cortonahostel.com). From bus stop, walk 5min. uphill on V. S. Margarita and follow signs to hostel. 13th-century mansion. Breakfast, showers, and sheets included. Complete dinner €8. Reception daily 7-10am and 4pm-midnight. Lockout 9:30am-3pm. Dorms €10.33 per person. Open mid-Mar. to Nov., year-round for groups. ❶

Istituto Santa Margherita, V. Cesare Battisti, 15 (☎0575 63 03 36). Walk down V. Severini from P. Garibaldi. Istituto on corner of V. Battisti, on the left. Get thee to this nunnery with marble hallways and rooms with baths. Breakfast €3.50. Flexible midnight curfew. Singles €26; doubles (no unmarried couples) €41; triples €52; quads €62. ❸

Albergo Italia, V. Ghibellina, 5 (☎0575 63 02 54 or 63 05 64; fax 60 57 63), off P. Repubblica. 16th-century *palazzo* with 3-star rooms, A/C, antique furniture, firm beds, satellite TV, and pristine bathrooms. Buffet breakfast included. Singles €67.14; doubles €100; triples €115; quads €145. AmEx/MC/V. ❺

Hotel San Luca, P. Garibaldi, 1 (☎0575 63 04 60; fax 63 01 05; www.sanlucacortona.com). Wide, blue-carpeted hallways lead to refined rooms. The rooms facing the valley have balconies, offering sweeping vistas of the Val di Chiena. All rooms include bath, satellite TV, A/C, phone, minibar, and continental breakfast. Singles €67; doubles €98; triples €134; quads €170; quints €201. AmEx/MC/V. ❺

FOOD

Cortona's *trattorie* serve Tuscan dishes for reasonable prices. Have dinner with a glass of the fine local wine, *bianco vergine di Valdichiana*. Penny-pinchers can pick up a €2.50 bottle at the **Despar Market,** P. della Repubblica, 23, which also makes *panini* with fresh ingredients for €3. (☎0575 63 06 66. Open Apr.-Oct. M-Sa 7:30am-1:30pm and 4:30-8pm, Su 7:30am-1:30pm; Nov.-Mar. M-Tu and Th-Sa 7am-1:30pm and 4:30-8pm, W 7am-1:30pm. AmEx/MC/V.) On Saturday **Piazza Signorelli** hosts an **open-air market.** (8am-1pm.)

Trattoria Toscana, V. Dardano, 12 (☎0575 60 41 92). The charming Santinos runs this classic Tuscan restaurant. Try local speciality *bistecca di Valdichiana*. Primi €5-6.20, secondi €7.30-13. Cover €1.50. Open W-M noon-2:30pm and 7-9:45pm. MC/V. ❷

Trattoria La Grotta, P. Baldelli, 3 (☎0575 63 02 71), off P. della Repubblica. Delectable fare served in a secluded courtyard. Sample the homemade *gnocchi alla ricotta e spinaci* (ricotta and spinach dumplings; €6.50). Primi €5.50-7.50, secondi €5.50-16. Cover €1.60. Open W-M noon-2:30pm and 7-10pm. AmEx/MC/V. ❷

Pizzeria Fufluns, V. Ghibellina, 3 (☎ 0575 76 41 40), off P. della Republica. Pizza and more dished out in cozy, stone-walled interior. Limited seating outdoors on the sloping street. Try the enigmatic *antipasto Fufluns* (€7). Pizza €4-5.50, *primi* €5-7.50, *secondi* €13. Open W-M 12:30-2:30pm and 7:30pm-12:30am. MC/V. ❷

Trattoria Etrusca, V. Dardano, 37/39 (☎ 0575 60 40 88), next to the Porta Colonia. Specializes in *primi* like the *gnocchi al pesto* (€4.13-5.16). The only *secondo* is *bistecca "Cortonese"* (slab of steak; €2.58 per 100g). Outdoor seating available. Open F-W noon-2pm and 7:30-10pm. MC/V. ❷

◉ SIGHTS

▧ MUSEO DIOCESANO. The upstairs gallery of this small Renaissance art museum houses the stunning *Annunciation* by Fra Angelico (Room 3). Christ's pain-wrenched face looks down from Pietro Lorenzetti's fresco of *The Way to Calvary.* The collection also includes Luca Signorelli's masterpiece, *The Deposition,* a vivid portrayal of Christ's death and resurrection, in Room 1. *(From P. della Repubblica, pass through P. Signorelli and follow the signs. ☎ 0575 62 830. Open Apr.-Sept. Tu-Su 9:30am-1pm and 3:30-7pm; Oct.-Mar. 10am-1pm and 3-5pm. €5.)*

FORTEZZA MEDICEA. Views of the Val di Chiena, all the way to Lake Trasimeno, are more breathtaking at this fortress than from P. Garibaldi. The courtyards and turrets contain temporary art installations. *(A thigh-burning 15min. walk up V. S. Margherita from P. Garibaldi and the bus stop. Continue past the church and climb the small road on the far side of the parking lot. Open May-Sept. Tu-Su 10am-6pm. €3, under 18 €1.50.)*

MUSEO DELL'ACCADEMIA ETRUSCA. This museum features a varied collection of carvings, coins, paintings, and furniture from the first through 18th centuries, not to mention a couple of genuine Egyptian mummies and sarcophagi. In the first hall, a 5th-century BC circular bronze chandelier, weighing 58kg, hangs from the ceiling. In the third gallery, you'll find 12th- and 13th-century Tuscan art. The museum's final room exhibits 20th-century lithographs, and collages. *(Inside the courtyard of Palazzo Casali, near P. della Repubblica. ☎ 0575 63 04 15. Open Nov.-Mar. Tu-Su 10am-5pm; Apr.-Oct. Tu-Su 10am-7pm. €4.20, groups of 15 or more €2.50.)*

PALAZZI AND PIAZZAS. In P. della Repubblica stands the 13th-century **Palazzo Comunale,** with a clock tower and monumental staircase. **Palazzo Casali,** to the right and behind the Palazzo del Comune, dominates P. Signorelli. Only the courtyard walls, lined with coats of arms, remain from the original structure; the facade and interlocking staircase were added in the 17th century. **Piazza del Duomo** lies to the right and downhill from the Palazzo Casali. Inside the duomo rests an impressive Baroque-canopied high altar, completed in 1664 by Francesco Mattioli. *(Duomo open May-Sept. 7:30am-1pm and 3-6:30pm; Oct.-Apr. 8am-12:30pm and 3-5:30pm.)*

◘ FESTIVALS

For **Sagra della Bistecca** (Aug. 14-15), the town's most important festival, the town converges on the public gardens behind the church of S. Domenico to feast upon superb local steak (about €20). Following closely on its heels during the third weekend in August is the superb **Festa dei Porcini,** when the public gardens fill with mushroom-lovers. Tickets are available at the garden entrance. Various musical and theatrical events clustering mainly in July, when Cortona absorbs the spillover from the Perugia Jazz Festival. Relax in the gardens or join in the evening *passeggiata* in the park, where Cortona's residents screen Italian movies from mid-June through early September. (Films start around 9:30pm. Buy ticket at gardens. €6.)

CENTRAL ITALY

AREZZO ☎0575

Arezzo is often overlooked on tours of central Italy. As a result, there are no tourist throngs shuffling through overpriced sights in this living, breathing provincial town. Arezzo and its neighboring valleys were once home to Renaissance titans Piero della Francesco and Michelangelo, the poet Petrarch, the humanist Leonardo Bruni, and the artist and historian Giorgio Vasari; it is also the hometown of Roberto Benigni, who wrote and starred in the award-winning film *Life is Beautiful* (1997). Many vestiges of past genius remain in the delightful historical district, from Vasari's stunning architecture in P. Grande, to Francesco's unparalleled *Legend of the True Cross* in the Basilica di San Francesco. Outside the walls, the four valleys of Arezzo radiate from the city, offering further opportunities for exploration in this often forgotten corner of Tuscany.

⌷ TRANSPORTATION

Trains: P. della Repubblica. Info open M-F 8am-noon and 3-6pm, Sa 9am-noon. To **Florence** (1½hr.; 2 per hr.; 4:30am-9:50pm; €5, InterCity €8) and **Rome** (2hr.; every 1-2hr.; 6:30am-10:11pm; €11/€18).

Buses: ☎0575 38 26 51. **TRA-IN, SITA,** and **LFI** buses stop at P. della Repubblica, to left of train station. To: **Cortona** (1hr., every hr., €2.50); **Sansepolcro** (1hr., SITA every hr., €2.90); and **Siena** (1½hr., 7 per day, €4.60). Buy tickets at ATAM *biglietteria*, ahead and to left from train station exit. Open daily 6am-noon and 1:30-7:45pm.

Taxis: Radio Taxi (☎0575 38 26 26). Open 24hr.

Car Rental: Autonoleggi Ermini, V. Perrenio, 21 (☎0575 35 35 70). €55-105 per day. 21+. Open M-F 8:30am-12:30pm and 3:30-7:30pm, Sa 8:30am-12:30pm.

◼✳ 🛈 ORIENTATION AND PRACTICAL INFORMATION

Arezzo lies on the Florence-Rome train line. **Via Guido Monaco,** which begins directly across from the train station at **Piazza della Repubblica,** parallels **Corso Italia;** together they form the backbone of Arezzo's commercial district. To get to the city's historic center, follow V. Guido Monaco from the station to the traffic circle at **Piazza Guido Monaco.** Turn right on **Via Roma** and then left onto the pedestrian walkway, Corso Italia, which leads to the old city. **Piazza Grande** lies to the right, 250m up Corso Italia.

Tourist Office: APT, P. della Repubblica, 28 (☎0575 37 76 78; fax 20 839), to the right as you leave the station. English-speaking staff. Free maps and info on surrounding valleys. Open Apr.-Sept. M-Sa 9am-1pm and 3-7pm, Su 9am-1pm; Oct.-Mar. M-Sa 9am-1pm and 3-6:30pm.

Budget Travel: CTS, V. V. Veneto, 25 (☎0575 90 78 09 or 90 78 08). Sells Eurail passes and plane tickets. Open M-F 9am-1pm and 3-7:30pm, Sa 9am-1pm.

Currency Exchange: Banca Nazionale del Lavoro, V. G. Monaco, 74. 24hr. **ATM.** Open M-F 8:20am-1:35pm and 2:45-4:05pm.

Emergency: ☎113. **Medical Emergency:** ☎118.

Police: V. Dardano, 9 (☎113 or 0575 90 66 67), off V. Fra Guittone by the train station. **Carabinieri:** ☎112.

24-Hour Pharmacy: Farmacia Comunale, Campo di Marte, 1 (☎0575 90 24 66), faces V. V. Veneto.

Hospital: Ospedale S. Donato, on V. Fonte Veneziana. **Misericordia:** ☎0575 24 242.

Internet Access: ⬛ **InformaGiovani,** P. G. Monaco, 2 (☎199 44 09 99; informagiovanni.arezzo@plugit.it). 30min. free. Open M-Sa 9:30am-7:30pm.

Post Office: V. G. Monaco, 34. **Currency exchange** (€0.50 commission) at *sportello* #1 (same hours). Open M-F 8:15am-7pm, Sa 8:15am-12:30pm.

Postal Code: 52100.

▐ ACCOMMODATIONS

Hotels fill to capacity during the **Fiera Antiquaria** (Antique Fair) on the first weekend of every month. Otherwise, you should have little trouble finding a room.

Ostello Villa Severi, V. Redi, 13 (☎0575 29 90 47), a bit of a hike from town. Take bus #4 (€0.80) from P. G. Monaco to 2 stops after Ospedale Vecchio (7min.); disembark when you see the town park on your left. The hostel is surrounded by this park. Spacious, with high ceilings and wood-beam detail. Breakfast €1.70. Lunch or dinner, including several courses and wine, €10. Reserve ahead for meals. Reception daily 9am-1pm and 6-11:30pm. Lockout 1-6pm. Dorms €13. ❶

Hotel Astoria, V. G. Monaco, 54 (☎/fax 0575 24 361 or 24 362). From train station, walk straight up V. G. Monaco, through the piazza, and look left. Basic, comfortable rooms. Wheelchair-accessible. Small breakfast €5. Singles €28.41, with bath and TV €38.74; doubles €46.48/€61.97. AmEx/MC/V. ❸

Albergo Cecco, C. Italia, 215 (☎0575 20 986; fax 35 67 30). Follow V. G. Monaco from train station, take a right onto V. Roma and another right onto C. Italia (5min.). Large, clean rooms. Restaurant downstairs. Breakfast €3. Singles €28, with bath €39; doubles €42/€57; triples €54/€72; quads with bath €88. AmEx/MC/V. ❸

Hotel Continentale, P. G. Monaco, 7 (☎0575 20 251; fax 35 04 85; www.hotelcontinentale.com). Tasteful, modern rooms all have bath, A/C, and satellite TV. Knowledgeable reception offers sightseeing and dining suggestions. Spacious lobby downstairs and panoramic view of the sloping historical quarter on the roof terrace. Buffet breakfast €8. Singles €67; doubles €98; triples €132; quads €165. AmEx/MC/V. ❺

◖ FOOD

The **Conad Supermarket,** on the corner of V. V. Veneto and V. L.B. Alberti, behind the train station, is large and well stocked. (Open M-Tu, Th-Sa 8am-8:30pm, W 8am-1:30pm.) An **open-air market** takes place in P. Sant'Agostino on weekdays and on V. Niccolò Aretino on Saturdays. For all your cheese needs, head over to **La Mozzarella,** V. Spinello, 25. (Open M-Sa 8am-1pm and 4-8pm.)

⬛ **Antica Osteria L'Agania,** V. Mazzini, 10 (☎/fax 0575 29 53 81), off C. Italia. A mix of tourists and locals feast on homemade pasta (€4-8) and delicious *secondi* (€5-8). Open Tu-Su noon-3pm and 7:30-11:30pm. AmEx/MC/V. ❷

Un Punto Macrobiotico, P. San Gemignano, 1 (☎0575 30 24 20). Turn right on V. G. Oberdan from C. Italia and follow it to P. di S. Gemignano. Veggie heaven. A soup and selection of 5 mini entrees (like brown rice *risotto* and simple salads) make a filling meal (€6.20). Open M-Sa 12:30-2pm and 7:30-9pm. ❷

Bruschetteria Toscana, V. di Tolletta, 14/16/20 (☎0575 29 98 60). Walking up V. G. Monaco, take your 2nd right after P. G. Monaco, onto V. di Tolletta. It's ahead on the left. *Primi* €5.50-7, *secondi* €8.50-12. Cover €1.50. Open W-M 12:30am-2:45pm and 7:30-10:45pm. AmEx/MC/V. ❸

Le Taste Vin, V. de' Cenci, 9 (☎0575 28 304). Continue down the street past Bruschetteria Toscana. The French name alludes to the chic, antique-styled interior, rather than the traditional Tuscan cooking. *Primi* €6-10, *secondi* €9-11. Open Tu-Su 12:30-3pm and 8-11:30pm. Closed Aug. 5-20. AmEx/MC/V. ❸

Paradiso di Stelle, V. G. Monaco, 58 (☎0575 27 448). 1st-rate homemade *gelato*. The *nocciola* (hazelnut) and *tiramisù* are superb (from €1.30). Open Mar.-Sept. Tu-Su 10:30am-midnight; Oct.-Feb. Tu-Su 10:30am-9pm. ❶

👁 SIGHTS

BASILICA DI SAN FRANCESCO. This extraordinary 11th-century basilica houses a number of frescoes, including Piero della Francesca's ▨*Leggenda della Vera Croce* (Legend of the True Cross), which portrays the story of the crucifix and its role in the Catholic church. The narrative begins with the death of Adam and proceeds to major events such as Emperor Constantine's conversion. The figure kneeling at the foot of the cross is St. Francis, to whom the church is dedicated. *(Up V. G. Monaco from train station, right at P. San Francesco. Basilica open daily 8:30am-noon and 2-7pm; free. Chapel containing della Francesca's frescoes open M-F 9am-7pm, Sa 9am-6pm, Su 1-6pm. Visitors admitted in groups of 25 every 30min.; last visit begins 30min. before chapel closes. Reservations required. Call ☎ 0575 90 04 04 or visit the office to the right of the church. €5.03, students 18-25 €3.03, art students or those under 18 €1.03. You can see the upper portion of the fresco cycle without paying entrance fee.)*

PIAZZA GRANDE. The piazza contains the **Chiesa di Santa Maria della Pieve,** Arezzo's most important architectural monument. The spectacular Pisan-Romanesque church dates from the 12th century. On the elevated presbytery sits Pietro Lorenzetti's brilliantly restored polyptych, depicting the *Annunciation* and *Madonna and Child.* Below lies the 9th-century *chiesa* upon which the Pieve was built. The adjoining tower is known as the "Tower of a Hundred Holes." Arezzo's best architecture surrounds the *chiesa* in P. Grande. Rotating counterclockwise from the church reveals the 14th-century Romanesque **Palazzo della Fraternità dei Laici,** and the hulking 16th-century Baroque **Loggiato dei Vasari.** The piazza also hosts the monthly **antique fair,** and the semiannual **Giostra del Saraceno** (see **Festivals**) each summer. *(P. Grande is down C. Italia, on the right. Chiesa open M-Sa 8am-noon and 3-7pm, Su 8:30am-noon and 4-7pm.)*

THE DUOMO. The massive cathedral, built in spooky Tuscan Gothic, houses Bishop Guido Tarlati's **tomb,** on the left side of the nave near the altar. Carved reliefs relate stories about the iconoclast's unconventional life. Light filters into the Gothic interior through the six 20 ft. circular stained glass windows designed by Gugliemo de Marcillat. The *Capella della Madonna del Conforto*, off the severe nave, holds a terra-cotta *Crucifixion* by Andrea della Robbia. *(Up V. Andrea Cesalpino from P. S. Francesco. Cathedral open daily 7am-12:30pm and 3-6:30pm.)*

CHIESA DI SAN DOMENICA. As was often the case, the Dominicans built their church on the end of town opposite the Franciscan establishment. The church contains a superb Cimabue crucifix (1265), Spinello Aretino's *Annunciation*, and the Marcillat rose window. *(Take V. Andrea Celaspino from P. S. Francesco, turn left at P. Libertà onto V. Ricasorli, and then right onto V. di Sassoverde, leading to the Chiesa. Open daily 8am-noon and 2:30-7:30pm, although hours vary. Closed during Mass.)* Near the church lies **Vasari's house,** which the historian built for himself and decorated with impressive frescoes depicting his peers. He even painted himself contemplating the view from one of the windows. *(V. XX Settembre, 55, just off V. San Domenico. ☎ 0575 30 03 01. Open M and W-Sa 9am-7pm, Su 9am-1pm. Free.)*

◙ FESTIVALS

Arezzo's **antique fairs** take place in and around P. Grande on the first Sunday and preceding Saturday of every month. Beautiful antique furniture and religious paraphernalia are sold alongside bric-a-brac. The **Giostra del Saraceno,** a medieval joust, is performed on the third Sunday of June and the first Sunday of September. In a ritual recalling the Crusades, "knights" representing the four quarters of the town charge a wooden effigy of a Turk with lances drawn.

▷ DAYTRIP FROM AREZZO: SANSEPOLCRO

Sansepolcro is most easily accessible by the hourly SITA bus from Arezzo (1hr., 15 per day, €2.90). Some routes require a change in Le Villel; ask the driver. The bus arrives just outside the walls of the old city. From the bus stop, enter the old city on V. N. Aggiunti. Follow the street for five blocks, until you pass the Museo Civico on your right. Take a right under an arch onto V. G. Matteotti, and an immediate left into P. Garibaldi. Sansepolcro's tourist office, P. Garibaldi, 2 (☎/fax 0575 74 05 36), is one block ahead on the left. Open daily 9:30am-1pm and 3:30-6:30pm.

Nestled in the valley of the Tiber, at the foot of the densely forested Appenines, Sansepolcro's claim to fame is as the birthplace of painter Piero della Francesca. The ◙**Museo Civico,** V. Aggiunti, 65, displays some of della Francesca's finest works. *The Resurrection* features a triumphant Jesus towering above the sleeping guards, bearing a red and white banner. A muscular Christ rests one foot on his coffin and meets the viewer's eyes with an intense, disconcerting gaze. The polyptych *Madonna della Misericordia* depicts a stern Madonna. (☎0575 73 22 18. Open June-Sept. daily 9am-1:30pm and 2:30-7:30pm, Oct.-May 9:30am-1pm and 2:30-6pm. €6.20, ages 10-16 €3, and over 65 or groups €4.50.) The left chapel of the Romanesque-styled **duomo** shelters the town's other cherished sight, the mysterious **Volto Santo,** V. Matteoti, just off P. Torre di Berta. Believed by some to be much older than its 12th-century attribution, the Holy Face's Assyrian features suggest Oriental origins. Scholars conjecture that the same artist produced the much-celebrated Volto Santo in Lucca. (Open 8am-noon and 3-7pm.) Sansepolcro is best seen as a daytrip, but the comfortable **Albergo Fiorentino ❹,** V. Luca Pacioli, 60, two blocks from the Museo Civico, has well-furnished, welcoming rooms and a fantastic English-speaking staff. Aromas waft from the elegant but affordable restaurant downstairs. (☎0575 74 03 50; fax 74 03 70. Breakfast included. Singles €46.48; doubles €67.14; triples €82.63; quads €92.96.)

SIENA ☎0577

Many travelers rush directly from Rome to Florence, neglecting beautiful medieval Siena. During the 13th century, Siena's wool traders, crafty bankers, and politicians fashioned the city into a sophisticated European metropolis. But Siena's rise threatened Florence. In 1230, Florentines catapulted feces over Siena's walls, in the hopes that it might trigger a plague. The plot failed, and 30 years later Siena routed the mighty Florentines at the Battle of Montaperti. The century of grandiose construction that followed endowed the city with its flamboyant architecture. Siena lost its preeminence in 1348, when the Black Death claimed half the city's population. But from the destruction, Siena produced St. Catherine (1347-1380), an ecstatic illiterate whose fanatical following and interventions in church politics prompted the church to return to Italy from Avignon; and St. Bernadino (1487-1564), a wanderer who revived the teachings of St. Francis. These days, the Sienese proudly celebrate their rich past with events like the semiannual Palio, a wild horse race between the city's 17 competing *contrade* (districts). An intoxicating display of pageantry, the Palio is the main attraction of Siena's tourist industry.

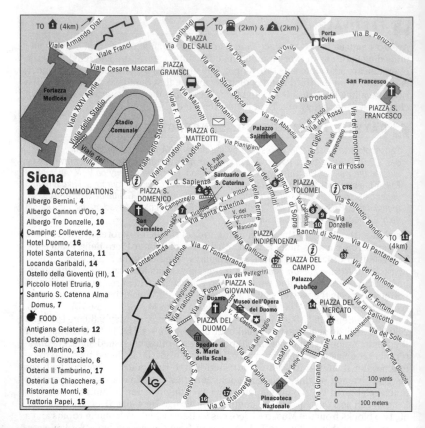

Siena

🏠 🏠 ACCOMMODATIONS

Albergo Bernini, **4**
Albergo Cannon d'Oro, **3**
Albergo Tre Donzelle, **10**
Camping: Colleverde, **2**
Hotel Duomo, **16**
Hotel Santa Caterina, **11**
Locanda Garibaldi, **14**
Ostello della Gioventù (HI), **1**
Piccolo Hotel Etruria, **9**
Santurio S. Catenna Alma
  Domus, **7**

🍴 FOOD

Antigiana Gelateria, **12**
Osteria Compagnia di
  San Martino, **13**
Osteria Il Grattacielo, **6**
Osteria Il Tamburino, **17**
Osteria La Chiacchera, **5**
Ristorante Monti, **8**
Trattoria Papei, **15**

📇 TRANSPORTATION

Trains: in P. Rosselli, several km from city center. Ticket office open daily 5:50am–8:20pm. To Siena from Rome and points south, change at Chiusi; from points north, change at Florence. **Luggage storage** available (p. 375). Departures to **Florence** (1¾hr., 12 per day, €5.30) and **Rome** (3hr., 16 per day via Chiusi, €16.14).

Buses: TRA-IN/SITA (☎0577 20 42 45) ticket office in P. Gramsci, near heart of the city; take the stairs that go under the piazza. Buses are the easiest and most convenient way to reach Siena. Frequent buses link Siena to the rest of Tuscany, making Siena an ideal base for exploring. Some intercity buses leave from P. Gramsci and others from the train station. Schedule and destinations listed on a large display in the underground terminal in P. Gramsci. Open daily 5:45am–8:15pm. To: **Arezzo** (7 per day, €4.60); **Florence** (express bus every hr., €6.50); **Montalcino** (7 per day, €2.50); **Montepulciano** (4 per day, €4.30); **San Gimignano** (8 per day, €5); and **Volterra** (12 per day, €2.50; get off at Colle Val d'Elsa and buy tickets at newsstand for a **CPT** bus to Volterra). **TRA-IN** also runs the bus network within Siena. Buy tickets (1hr., €0.77) at the office in P. Gramsci or any commercial center that displays a TRA-IN sign.

Taxis: Radio Taxi (☎0577 49 222). Open daily 7am–9pm.

Car Rental: Intercar, V. Mentana, 108 (☎0577 41 148). Suzuki cars available from €80.57 per day. €0.21 extra for every km over 200. 10% discount for rentals of 3 days or more. 21+. Open M-Sa 9am-1pm and 3:30-8pm. MC/V.

Bike and Moped Rental: DF Moto, V. Gazzani, 16-18 (☎0577 28 83 87). Mountain bikes €10 per day; student discount €7 per day. 50cc scooters €26 per day, 100cc €37 per day. Open daily 9:30am-7:30pm. AmEx/MC/V. **Automotocicli Perozzi,** V. del Romitorio, 5 (☎0577 28 08 39). Bikes €8 per day; scooters 50cc €24 per day, 100cc €34 per day. Open M-Sa 8:30am-12:30pm. AmEx/MC/V.

✳ 🛈 ORIENTATION AND PRACTICAL INFORMATION

From the train station, cross the street and take bus #3, 4, 7, 8, 9, 10, 14, 17, or 77 to the town center. These buses stop in either **Piazza del Sale** or **Piazza Gramsci.** Some buses stop just before P. Gramsci, making it difficult to know when to get off; ask the bus driver. From either piazza, follow the numerous signs to **Piazza del Campo** (a.k.a. Il Campo), Siena's historic center. Buy local bus tickets from vending machines by the station entrance or at the *biglietteria* window for bus tickets (€0.77). From the bus station in P. S. Domenico, follow the signs to P. del Campo. **Piazza del Duomo** lies 100m west of Il Campo.

Tourist Office: APT, Il Campo, 56 (☎0577 28 05 51; fax 27 06 76), provides snappy brochures on sights in and around Siena. Open Mar. 16-Nov. 14 daily 9:30am-1pm and 2:30pm-6pm; Nov. 15-Mar. 15 M-Sa 8:30am-1pm and 3-7pm, Su 9am-1pm. **Prenotazioni Alberghiere** (☎0577 28 80 84; fax 28 02 90), in P. S. Domenico, finds lodgings for €2. Also books reservations for **walking tours** of **Siena** and **San Gimignano.** (2hr. Siena tour M-F at 4:30pm; book by 1pm; €20). Open Apr.-Oct. M-Sa 9am-8pm; Nov.-Mar. M-Sa 9am-7pm.

Budget Travel: CTS, V. Sallustio Bandini, 21 (☎0577 28 58 08). Student travel services. Open M-F 9am-12:30pm and 3:30-7pm.

English-Language Bookstore: Libreria Ticci, V. delle Terme, 5/7 (☎0577 28 00 10). Extensive selection of books. Open M-F 9am-7:45pm, Sa 9am-2:30pm. **Feltrinelli,** V. Banchi di Sopra, 52 (☎0577 27 11 04). Large selection of English language classic and popular fiction in paperback, and some English language magazines and newspapers. Open M-Sa 9am-9:30pm, Su 11am-7:30pm.

Laundromat: Lavorapido, V. di Pantaneto, 38. Wash €3 per 8kg. Dry €3. Open daily 8am-9pm. **Onda Blu,** Casato di Sotto, 17 (☎0800 86 13 46). Wash €3 per 6½kg. Dry €3. Open daily 8am-10pm.

Luggage Storage: At TRA-IN ticket office beneath P. Gramsci. €2-3.50. No overnight storage. Open 7am-7:45pm.

Emergency: ☎113. **Police: Questura** (☎112) on V. del Castoro near the duomo.

Medical Assistance: ☎118.

Ambulance: Misericordia, V. del Porrione, 49 (☎0577 43 111).

Late-Night Pharmacy: Farmacia del Campo, P. del Campo, 26. Pharmacies rotate late-night shifts. Open daily 9am-noon and 4-8pm; in winter 9am-noon and 3:30-7:30pm.

Hospital: V. Le Scotte, 14 (☎0577 58 51 11). Take bus #77 from P. Gramsci.

Internet Access: Internet Train, V. di Città, 121 (☎0577 22 63 66). €5.16 per hr. Open M-Sa 10am-8pm, Su noon-8pm. V. Pantaneto, 54 (☎0577 24 74 68). Open M-F 10am-9pm, Su 4-9pm. **Engineering Systems,** V. Stalloreggi, 8 (☎0577 27 47 52). €4.13 per hr., student €3.62 per hr. Open daily 10am-8pm.

Post Office: P. Matteotti, 36. Exchanges currency. €2.58 fee for amounts over €5.16. Open M-Sa 8:15am-7pm.

Postal Code: 53100.

ACCOMMODATIONS & CAMPING

Finding a room in Siena can be difficult in the summer months. Book months ahead for **Palio** (see p. 381). For visits of a week or longer, rooms in private homes are an attractive option. The APT and Prenotazioni Alberghiere tourist offices can provide a list of private rooms.

Albergo Tre Donzelle, V. Donzelle, 5 (☎0577 28 03 58; fax 22 39 33). Basic rooms with tasteful wood furnishings. Dining area and sitting room. Close to Il Campo, but often noisy as a result. Curfew 1am. Singles €31; doubles €44, with bath €57. Additional bed €18 in rooms without bath, €19 in those with bath. AmEx/MC/V. ❸

Piccolo Hotel Etruria, V. Donzelle, 3 (☎0577 28 80 88; fax 28 84 61). Immaculate, modern rooms with floral bedspreads, phones, TVs, and hair dryers. Breakfast €6. Curfew 12:30pm. Singles €40, with bath €46; doubles with bath €76; triples with bath €100. AmEx/MC/V. ❹

Ostello della Gioventù "Guidoriccio" (HI), V. Fiorentina, 89 (☎0577 52 212), in Località Lo Stellino, a 20min. bus ride from the *centro*. Take bus #15 or 10 from P. Gramsci. Su evening bus service is infrequent. Bus #15 stops at front door of the hostel. Ask driver when to get off bus #10. From stop, continue in the direction bus was traveling and take 1st right on winding uphill road. Look for small sign on right side pointing to the left. Good value. €2 key deposit. Breakfast €1.55; dinner €8.78. Lockout 9:30am-3pm. Curfew midnight. Reservations recommended. Dorms €12.90 per person. ❶

Santuario S. Caterina Alma Domus, V. Camporeggio, 37 (☎0577 44 177; fax 47 601), behind S. Domenico. Spotless rooms with antique metal-frame beds, polished stone floors and crucifixes. All rooms with bath. Curfew 11:30pm. Breakfast €6. Singles €42; doubles €55; triples €70; quads €85. ❹

Albergo Bernini, V. della Sapienza, 15 (☎/fax 0577 28 90 47; www.albergobernini.com). Antique-laden rooms have picture windows with views of the duomo. Outdoor breakfast patio is lined with plants and full of exotic birds. Breakfast €7. Curfew midnight. July-Sept. enormous single €78; double €62, with bath €82; triples with bath €107; quads with bath and A/C €132. Off-season prices drop 20%. ❺

Albergo Cannon d'Oro, V. Montanini, 28 (☎0577 44 321; fax 0577 28 08 68), near P. Matteotti. Classy green neon welcomes you to the marble-filled lobby. Luxurious rooms with wood furniture, TV, and phone. All rooms with bath. Wheelchair-accessible. Breakfast €6. Singles €62; doubles €76.50; triples €101; quads €119. AmEx/MC/V. ❺

Locanda Garibaldi, V. Giovanni Dupré, 18 (☎0577 28 42 04), behind the Palazzo Pubblico and P. del Campo. Whitewashed walls and exposed, wood-trussed ceilings. Funky, low-vaulted sitting area. Most rooms with bath. Restaurant downstairs. Curfew midnight. Reservations recommended. Doubles €62, with bath €70; triples €90; quads €110. ❸

Hotel Santa Caterina, V. E.S. Piccolomini, 7 (☎0577 22 11 05; fax 0577 27 10 87; info@hscsiena.it), just outside Porta Romana. Exposed brick and wood-beamed ceilings in split-level rooms on 1st floor. Stone-floored rooms 1 flight up feature fantastic views of Monte Amiata. Buffet breakfast (included) served in garden or on embroidered white tablecloths in the solarium. All rooms have bath, satellite TV, minibar, and A/C. Singles €98; doubles €144; triples €195. AmEx/MC/V. ❺

Hotel Duomo, V. Stalloreggi, 38 (☎0577 28 90 88; fax 0577 43 043; hduomo@comune.siena.it). Many of the rooms in this 17th-century mansion have sublime views of the duomo. Bath, satellite TV, and A/C. Breakfast included. In the summer reserve well in advance. Singles €104; double €130; triples €171; quads €184. AmEx/MC/V. Prices drop 30% Nov.-early Mar. ❺

Camping: Colleverde, Strada di Scacciapensieri, 47 (☎0577 28 00 44). Take bus #3 or 8 from P. del Sale; ask to be sure you are on the right route. Buses run every ½hr.; late #8 buses (10:37 and 11:57pm) run from P. del Sale. Well-kept, with grocery store, restaurant, and bar nearby. Open late Mar. to mid-Nov. Pool €1.55, children €1.03. €7.75 per person, ages 3-11 €4.13. MC/V. ❶

🍴 FOOD

Siena specializes in rich pastries. The most famous is *panforte*, a dense concoction of honey, almonds, and citron, first baked as trail mix for the Crusaders. For a lighter snack, try *ricciarelli*, soft almond cookies with powdered vanilla on top. Sample either (€1.90 per 100g) at the **Bar/Pasticceria Nannini,** the oldest *pasticceria* in Siena, with branches at V. Banchi di Sopra, 22-24, and throughout town. **Enoteca Italiana,** in the Fortezza Medicea near the entrance off V. Cesare Maccari, sells fine Italian wines (from €1.60 per glass), including *Brunello, Barolo, Asti Spumante,* and *Vernaccia.* (☎0577 28 84 97. Open M noon-10pm, Tu-Sa noon-1am. MC/V.) Siena's **open-air market** fills P. La Lizza each Wednesday 8am-1pm. For groceries, try the **Consortio Agrario supermarket,** V. Pianigiani, 5, off P. Salimberi. (Open M-Sa 8am-7:30pm.) The **COOP supermarket** is a couple of blocks from the train station—with your back to the station turn left, then left again one block down at the overpass; the supermarket is in the shopping complex immediately to your right. (Open M-Sa 8am-7:30pm.)

■ **Ristorante Monti,** V. Calzoleria, 12 (☎0577 28 90 10), a few blocks from P. del Campo. Don't let the takeout *rosticceria* downstairs fool you—upstairs, an intimate dining area awaits. Fantastic dishes transcend the bounds of traditional Tuscan fare. Try the *tagliata rucola* (sliced steak with rucola and chickpeas; €12.50). If time is tight, the takeout roast chicken earns raves. *Primi* €5.50-7.50, *secondi* €10.50-12.50. Cover €2. Open Tu-Sa 10am-3pm and 6:30-11pm, Su 10am-3pm. MC/V. ❸

■ **Trattoria Papei,** P. del Mercato, 6 (☎0577 28 08 94). P. del Mercato is on the far side of Palazzo Pubblico from Il Campo. This delicious *trattoria* has both outdoor tables and a stone-arched dining room. Try one of a huge range of homemade pasta dishes (€6.20) as well as traditional *secondi* (€6.20-9.30). The *coniglio all arrabbiata* (rabbit with sage and rosemary; €7.50) is scrumptious, as is the house red (€6 per liter). Cover €1.55. Open Tu-Su 12:30-3pm and 7-10:30pm. AmEx/MC/V. ❸

■ **Osteria La Chiacchera,** Costa di S. Antonio, 4 (☎0577 28 06 31), next to Santuario di Santa Caterina. Eat in the tiny dining room or perch precariously at outdoor tables propped up with blocks on the steep street. Hearty homemade pasta dishes (€4.20-5.50) like the *tagliatelli* with wild boar (€5.20). Divine house wine (€2.60 per ½L). *Secondi* €4.80-7. Open W-M noon-3:30pm and 7-midnight. AmEx/MC/V. ❷

Osteria Il Grattacielo, V. dei Pontani, 8 (☎0577 28 93 26). Between V. dei Termini and Banchi di Sopra on a tiny street. Olives, stewed baby artichokes, sun-dried tomatoes in oil, hunks of salami and pecorino cheese, and many other culinary delights. No menu means the pricing system is a mystery, but a sampling of 5 or 6 of their exquisite dishes (quite a lot of food), plus bread and a ¼L of the delicious house red will run you about €7.71. Open May-Sept. M-Sa 8am-7pm; Oct.-Apr. 8am-2:30pm and 5-10pm. ❷

Osteria Compagnia di San Martino, V. Porrione, 25 (☎0577 493 06). Just off Il Campo, this *osteria* serves Tuscan cuisine on the quiet street or in the A/C upstairs dining room. The homemade pasta with wild boar sauce (€6.50) is fantastic. *Primi* €6-7, *secondi* €7-13. Cover €1.50. Open M-Sa noon-3pm and 7-10:30pm. AmEx/MC/V. ❸

Osteria Il Tamburino, V. Stalloreggi, 11 (☎0577 28 03 06). From P. del Duomo, follow V. del Capitano to P. della Postierla; turn right on V. di Stalloreggi. *Primi* €5-8, *secondi* 5.80-13. House red €6 per liter. Cover €0.70. Open M-Sa noon-2:30pm and 7-9:30pm. MC/V. ❸

FROM THE ROAD

GOOD TO GO

I needed to get away. Shoved into a rack of postcards by a stampeding tour group, I stood face-to-face with a winged angel, the poster child for the piles of Renaissance art I had become numb to after several weeks on the road. Overexposed to map-toting, sandal-wearing, *gelato*-slurping tourists, I wanted to find a place where I could tote my maps, wear my sandals, and slurp my *gelato* in relat   itude. The only masterpiece I'd fi   uld be peace of mind.

Picking up the scattered postcards, one caught my eye. A single, gnarled tree was silhouetted on the horizon amid rolling, amber hills. "La Crete," it said, and I knew I had to get there.

The next day, I rode toward the hills on a scooter, leaving crucifixes, audio guides, and fanny packs behind. Following the signs toward Asciano, I entered La Crete* ("the clay"). The rich, clay hillsides, cultivated for centuries, framed a panoramic tableau of soft lines. I didn't even mind when a car-full of German tourists pulled over next to me, interrupting a reflective moment. I would take the long shadow cast by a stone granary in the late afternoon light, and they could have the darkened furrow of a receding hillside. No one makes the exact same journe   gh these hills. I turned back to Siena reeling like I could even take in a few *Annunciations* before dinner.

—*Paul Guilianelli*

La Crete, southeast of Siena, includes Asciano, Buonconvento, Monteroni d'Arbia, Rapolano Terme, and San Giovanni d'Asso.

Antigiana Gelateria, V. d. Città, 31 (☎0577 28 80 76), off P. del Campo. High quality *gelato* at reasonable prices. Cones from €1.50. Open Mar.-Sept. daily 8am-midnight; Oct.-Feb. 8am-10pm. ❶

👁 SIGHTS

SIEN-ANY SIGHTS? Siena offers two *biglietto cumulativi* (cumulative tickets). The 1st allows 5 days of entry into the Museo dell'Opera Metropolitana, the baptistery, and the Piccolomini Library (€7.50). The second covers those 3 monuments and museums plus 4 others, including the Museo Civico, and is valid for 7 days (€16). Both tickets can be bought at any of the included sights.

IL CAMPO. Siena radiates from the **Piazza del Campo,** the shell-shaped brick square designed specifically for civic events. The piazza's brick paving is divided into nine sections, representing the city's medieval Council of Nine. Dante referred to the square in his account of the real-life drama of Provenzan Salvani, the heroic Sienese merchant who panhandled in Il Campo to pay for a friend's ransom. Later, Sienese mystics such as San Bernadino used the piazza as a public auditorium. Now it has the dubious honor of entertaining local teenagers, wide-eyed tourists, and souvenir carts by days; in the evening, when the elegant cafes pull back their awnings and the Sienese strut in a ritual *passeggiata*, the piazza glitters with decadence. Twice each summer, the **Palio** reduces the sublimely mellow Campo to mayhem as horses race around its outer edge (see p. 381).

At the highest point of Il Campo's sloping plane is the **Fonte Gaia,** surrounded by reproductions of native Jacopo della Quercia's famous carvings (1408-1419). The originals are in the **Spedale di S. Maria della Scala** (see p. 380). The water here emerges from the same 25km aqueduct that has refreshed Siena since the 14th century. Closing the bottom of the shell-shaped piazza is the graceful castle-like **Palazzo Pubblico,** with its imposing 102m high clock tower, the **Torre del Mangia.**

In front of the *palazzo* is the **Cappella di Piazza,** which was started in 1348 but took 100 years to complete, due to the untimely interruption of the Black Death. The transition from Gothic to Renaissance architecture is evinced in the movement from pointed arches to graceful rounded ones.

⊠PALAZZO PUBBLICO. This impressive medieval building was home to Siena's Council of Nine in the Middle Ages. It still houses city government offices, but the main touristic draw is the **Museo Civico.** Although the Sienese art collection pieces range from medieval triptychs to 18th-century landscapes, the greatest treasure is its collection of late medieval to early Renaissance painting in the distinctive Sienese style. The **Sala del Mappamondo,** named for a lost series of astronomical frescoes, displays Simone Martini's *Maestà (Enthroned Virgin),* which combines an overt religious quality with civic and literary awareness; the parchment the Christ Child holds is inscribed with the city motto of upholding justice, and the steps of the canopied throne are engraved with two stanzas from Dante's *Divine Comedy.* In the next room, the **Sala dei Nove** exhibits Pietro and Ambrogio Lorenzetti's famous frescoes, the *Allegories of Good and Bad Government and their Effects on Town and Country.* The well-preserved fresco on the right shows the Utopia created by good government. The fresco on the left, flaking away, depicts thieves, devils, and lost souls in the land of bad government. *(Open Nov.-Feb. daily 10am-4pm; Mar.-Oct. 10am-7pm. €6.50, students €4, under 11 free.)*

The Palazzo Pubblico's other star attraction is the **Torre de Mangia,** named for gluttonous bell-ringer Giovanni di Duccio, or "Mangiaguadagni" ("Eat the profits"). At 102m, the tower was the second highest in medieval Italy, after Cremona's. *(Same hours as Museo Civico. €5.50 or €9.50 combined ticket with Museo Civico.)*

⊠THE DUOMO. The city's dark green-and-white-striped duomo, atop one of its seven hills, is one of the few full Gothic cathedrals south of the Alps, and is one of Italy's finest. Civic pride demanded that the 13th-century duomo combine enormous scale with a prominent position, but the limited size of the hill posed a design problem. The apse would have hung in mid-air over the edge of the hill. The Sienese, doubting a miraculous solution to the problem, turned to more earthly preventative measures and built the **baptistery** (see p. 381). A huge arch, part of a striped wall to your right facing the front of the cathedral, is the sole remnant of Siena's 1339 plan to construct a new nave, which would have made this duomo the largest church in all Christendom. The grandiose effort ended when the plague decimated the working populace. One of the duomo's side aisles has been enclosed and turned into the **Museo dell'Opera Metropolitana** (see below). Statues of philosophers, sibyls, and prophets, all by Giovanni Pisano, hold sway beneath impressive spires.

The bronze sun symbol on the facade of the duomo was the brainchild of St. Bernadino of Siena, who wanted the feuding Sienese to relinquish their loyalty to emblems of nobility and unite under this symbol of the risen Christ. Not too surprisingly, his efforts were futile; the Sienese continue to identify with the animal symbols of their *contrada* (districts). The **marble pavement** on the floor is, like the rest of the duomo, richly ornate, and depicts such widely varying themes as alchemy and the Slaughter of the Innocents. Most of the pieces are covered for preservation purpose, except in September when visitors can look for the works by Machese d'Adamo, perhaps the most spectacular in the entire building. Halfway up the left aisle is the **Piccolomini altar,** designed by Andrea Bregno in 1503. Although it appears to be the facade of an entire building unto itself, the altar contains niches that house life-like statues of St. Peter and St. Paul, sculpted by Michelangelo early in his career. In the neighboring chapel, Donatello's bronze statue of St. John the Baptist is graceful even in his emaciation. The lavish **Libreria Piccolomini,** commissioned by Pope Pius III, houses the elaborately illustrated books of his uncle Pius II. The library also contains a Roman copy of the Greek statue, *The Three Graces,* 15th-century illuminated scores, and a fresco cycle by Pinturicchio. *(Duomo open Mar. 15-Oct. 31 daily 9am-7:30pm; Nov. 1-Mar. 14 10am-1pm and 2:30pm-5pm. Modest dress required. Free, except when floor is uncovered in Sept., €4-5.50. Library, same hours, €1.50.)*

MUSEO DELL'OPERA METROPOLITANA. The cathedral museum holds all the art that won't fit in the church. The first floor contains some of the foremost Gothic statuary in Italy, all by Giovanni Pisano. Upstairs is the magnificent 700-year-old ◨*Maestà*, by Duccio di Buoninsegna, originally the screen of the cathedral's altar. Dismembered in 1771 by voracious art collectors, most of the narrative panels have been returned to the Sienese, except for a handful held by the National Gallery in London, the Frick Gallery in New York, and the National Gallery of Art in Washington. Other noteworthy works in the museum are the Byzantine *Madonna degli Occhi Coressi*, paintings by Lorenzetti, and two altarpieces by Matteo di Giovanni. Find the **Scala del Falciatore,** off one of the upper levels of the museum (follow the signs for the panorama), to climb onto a balcony over the nave. A very narrow spiral staircase leads to a tiny tower for a breathtaking view of the duomo and the entire city. *(Museum housed in part of the unfinished nave on the right side of the duomo. Open Mar. 15-Oct. 31 daily 9am-7:30pm; Nov. 1--Mar. 14 9am-1:30pm. €5.50.)*

SPEDALE DI S. MARIA DELLA SCALA. Originally a hospital dating from the 13th century, the Spedale is now a museum, displaying its original frescoes, chapels and vaults, as well as beautiful paintings and statuary. The **Sala del Pellegrinaio,** used as a ward until the late 20th century, contains a fresco cycle by Vecchietta, often considered to be his masterpiece. In the first panel, the pregnant mother of the legendary founder of the hospital, Beato Sorore, dreams of the future good deeds of her son. The most artistically interesting room, the **Sagrestia Vecchia** or **Cappello del Sacro Chiedo,** houses masterful 15th-century Sienese frescoes. Downstairs from the entrance you can peer out curtained windows for a view of a shallow valley before ducking into the underground chapels and vaults—a somewhat startling descent until you remember the hospital was built on a hillside. The dim little vaults were the site of rituals and "acts of piety for the dead" performed by various *contrada* fraternities. One level down is the entrance to the **Museo Archeologico,** included in admission to the Spedale. Established in 1933 to collect and preserve Etruscan artifacts from the Siena area, the museum is now almost entirely in the eerie medieval underground water works of the city. Signs lead you through the dank, labyrinthine brick-and-concrete-vaulted passageways before you emerge into rooms of well-lit glass cases of Etruscan pottery and coins. *(Open Mar.-Nov. daily 10am-6pm; Dec.-Feb. 10:30am-4:30pm. €5.20, students €3.10.)*

PINACOTECA NAZIONALE. Siena's superb art gallery features works by every major artist of the highly stylized Sienese school. The masters represented include the seven followers of Onccio—Simone Martini, the Lorenzetti brothers, Bartolo di Fredi, Da Domenico, Sano di Pietro, and Il Sodoma—as well as many others. The museum is refreshingly free of the tourist hordes that can make it difficult to appreciate many of Florence's prime collections. *(V. S. Pietro, 29, in the Palazzo Buonsignori down V. del Capitano from the duomo. Open Tu-Sa 8:15am-7:15pm, Su 8:15am-1:15pm, M 8:30am-1:30pm. €4, EU citizens 18-26 €2, EU citizens under 18 or over 65 free.)*

SANTUARIO DI SANTA CATERINA. The sanctuary honors the daughter of Siena, a simple girl who had a vision of herself as Christ's bride. She had the ear of popes and became the patron saint of Italy. The building, converted into a Renaissance *loggia*, opens onto many Baroque chapels. The **Chiesa del Crosifisso** is impressive. *(Entrance at the intersection of Costa di S. Antonio and V. dei Pittori, down from P. S. Domenico. Open Mar.-Nov. daily 9am-7pm. Dec.-Feb. 9am-1pm and 3-6pm. Free.)*

BAPTISTERY. Lavish and intricate frescoes, depicting the lives of Christ and St. Anthony, decorate the baptistery. The centerpiece of the baptistery, however, is the hexagonal Renaissance **baptismal font** (1417-30). Ghiberti's *Baptism of Christ* and *John in Prison* stand next to Donatello's *Herod's Feast*. *(Behind the duomo. Open Mar. 15-Oct. 31 daily 9am-7:30pm; Nov. 1-Mar. 14 9am-1pm and 2:30-5pm. €2.50.)*

OTHER SIGHTS. Like in many Italian towns, the Franciscans and the Dominicans have rival basilicas at opposite ends of town. The **Chiesa di San Domenico** contains Andrea Vanni's portrait of St. Catherine and a number of other dramatic frescoes, which render the saint in a state of religious fervor. The exquisite *cappella* inside, dedicated to St. Catherine, was built in 1460 to store her preserved head (no longer on the premises). *(P. S. Domenico. Open Nov. 1-Apr. 31 daily 9am-12:55pm and 3-6pm; May 1-Oct. 31 7am-12:55pm and 3-7pm.)* The **Chiesa di San Francesco** houses two frescoes by Pietro and Ambrogio Lorenzetti, moved into the church after a fire in the last century. *(Open daily 7:30am-noon and 3:30-7pm.)* Those interested in the Palio may enjoy one of Siena's 17 **contrade museums.** Each neighborhood organization maintains its own collection of costumes, artifacts, banners, and icons, ranging from the eagle and caterpillar to the she-wolf and tortoise. *(Most require an appointment— ask at the tourist office. Schedule visits at least 1 week in advance.)*

◪ ENTERTAINMENT

Siena's ◪**Palio** occurs twice a year, on July 2 and August 16. As the bare-backed horse races approach, Siena's emotional temperature rises. Ten of the 17 *contrade* make elaborate preparations. Young partisans sporting the colors of their *contrada* chant in packs on the street, singing often obscene lyrics to the tune of "Twinkle, Twinkle, Little Star." Five trial races take place over the three days leading up to the race, and a final trial runs the same morning. On the eve of the race, revelry concludes around 3am. At 2:30pm on the day of the race, the horses are led into the churches of their respective *contrade* and blessed. A two-hour parade of heralds and flag-bearers prefaces the anarchy to come with regal pomp. The last piece in the procession is the *Palio* itself, a banner depicting the Madonna and Child, drawn in a cart by white oxen (the race is called *Il Palio* because a *palio* is given to the winner). The start of the race can be the most exciting part. Riders battle for position at the start until the announcer is satisfied that all is in order and he drops the rope without warning. The race begins at 7:30pm and it takes the jockeys about 90 seconds to tear around Il Campo three times. During the race, they have free rein, according to the age-old, barbaric set of rules that guide the event, to whip their opponents. The straps they use are no ordinary pieces of leather; they are made from the skin of a bull's penis, especially durable and said to leave deep welts and psychological scars.

To stay in Siena during the *Palio*, book rooms at least four months in advance— especially budget accommodations. Contact the APT in March or April for a list of companies and individuals that rent rooms. Inquire about reserving seats in the grandstands for the best view of the race (seating prices can be prohibitively expensive). Otherwise, you can stand in the "infield" of the piazza for free if you stake out a spot early. From there, you may only be able to see the frenzied sea of fans surrounding you. For information on *Il Palio*, ask at the tourist office and pick up the excellent program (available in English).

In late July, the **Accademia Chigiana** (☎0577 22 091; www.chigiani.it) sponsors a music festival, the **Settimana Musicale Sienese.** Siena hosts a **jazz festival** in July, featuring internationally known musicians. For information, call ☎0577 27 14 01.

CENTRAL ITALY

🔁 DAYTRIPS FROM SIENA

SAN GALGANO

Get a car or scooter; 26km southwest of Siena. Follow No. 73 from Siena, after 20km look for the signs. For more information and maps, contact Siena's tourist office.

Slightly removed from a winding country pass between Siena and Massa Marittima, the decaying 13th-century **Cistercian Abbey of San Galgano** was once one of the richest and most powerful in Tuscany. Its monks served as treasurers and judges for the communes of Siena and Volterra, helped construct the duomo in Siena, and became bishops and saints (but only after extensive lobbying). But by the mid-16th century, widespread corruption spelled the church's decline. The derelict abbey, the foremost specimen of Cistercian Gothic architecture in Italy, lies hidden in dense woodland. It stands without a roof, utterly exposed to the elements. As nature slowly undoes the Gothic church, the absence of a vaulted ceiling gives view to blue skies and tiny birds that chirp lightly in the stony nooks.

THE CHIANTI REGION

Buses connect Siena to Castellina and Radda, major bases for exploring vineyards (45min.-1hr., 6 per day, €2.43). 3 buses a day also connect Radda with Florence (1½hr.; last bus to Florence 6:10pm, last bus to Siena 6:40pm).

Siena lies within easy reach of the Chianti region, whose wines of the same name have become famous throughout the world. The Castellina private **tourist office,** V. della Rocca, 12, just off **Piazza del Comune,** can help find accommodations and provide information. (☎0577 74 60 20; info@collinverdi.it. Open in summer M-Sa 9am-1pm and 3-6pm; in winter 10am-1pm.)

Numerous shops sell the trademark Chianti; one good choice is **Le Volte Enoteca,** V. Ferruccio, 12, a block from P. del Comune, where you can buy a bottle starting at €5. (☎0577 74 13 14; fax 74 28 91; enotecalevolte@libero.it. Open Mar.-Oct. daily 9:30am-7:30pm; Nov.-Dec. 10am-noon and 4-7:30pm. MC/V.) For a huge variety of pizza slices starting at €0.95, head to **Pizza Chiantigiana ❶,** V. Chiantigiana, 7, just off the main intersection where the bus stops. (☎0577 74 12 91. Open Tu-Su 11am-2:30pm and 4-9:30pm.)

While Castellina has a few nice blocks in the center of town, it's not nearly as attractive as many other Tuscan hill towns. Rather than spend all your time here, consider heading to **Radda in Chianti,** just 9km away, on the same bus (#125) from Siena. Radda's **tourist office,** P. Ferrucci, 1, in the town's main square, has a multilingual staff willing to help you find accommodation. Ask here about the few wineries within walking distance of the town center. To reach the tourist office, walk two blocks from the bus stop with the city walls on your left. Take a left toward the public gardens and then a left into the city onto V. Roma, the main street in town, which leads to P. Ferrucci. (☎0577 73 84 94; proradda@chiantinet.it. Open Mar.-Oct. M-Sa 10am-1pm and 3-7pm, Su 10am-1pm.) For more info on touring the nearby wineries, inquire at **ChiantiMania,** V. Trento e Trieste, 12 (☎0577 73 89 79; chmania@tin.it. Open M-Sa 10am-1pm and 3-6pm.) Since many wineries give free tastings, consider getting a map of local wineries and exploring them on your own.

It's hard to beat the clean, modern rooms of **Le Camere di Giovannino ❹,** V. Roma, 6-8, a few meters from the tourist office. All rooms have bath. (☎/fax 0577 73 56 01. Singles €42; doubles €52-55; triples €75.)

Like Castellina, Radda is home to numerous *enoteche;* try **Porciatti Alimentari,** P. IV Novembre, 1-3, within the town's 14th-century walls. Bottles start at €7. They also sell homemade pork sausages and cheese. (☎0577 73 80 55; fax 73 82 34; www.casaporciatti.it. Open May-Oct. M-Sa 7:45am-1pm and 5-8pm, Su 7:45am-

CENTRAL ITALY

1pm; Nov.-Apr. M-Sa 8am-1pm and 4:30-7:30pm.) The cheapest place to get wine is the **Coop Market,** V. Roma, 26, with bottles from €3.10. (Open M-Tu and Th-Sa 8am-1pm and 4:30-8pm, W 8am-1pm.) **Ristorante Il Giarrosto ❷,** V. Roma, 41, has a lunch tourist *menù* for €6.10, including *primo, secondo,* dessert, coffee, wine, and water. (☎ 0577 73 80 10. Open Th-Tu for lunch and dinner.)

A cheap, delicious option with takeout or table service is **Enoteca Dante Alighieri ❹,** P. Dante Alighieri, 1, opposite the bus stop. They specialize in *bruschette* and *crostini* (from €2.25), and have an extensive wine list. (☎ 0577 73 88 15. Open Su-F 7am-10pm.) After a hard day of wine tasting, relax in the shaded public gardens just outside the city walls. Through the gardens is a terrace with stone benches and beautiful views of the countryside.

MONTALCINO ☎ 0577

Montalcino has changed little since medieval times, when it was a Sienese strong-hold. The foremost activity in this tiny town is its production of the heavenly **Brunello di Montalcino,** a wine acknowledged as Italy's finest red. Sample the local Brunello in the numerous wine shops that line the town's narrow streets, or head outside the city walls to one of the wineries for a tour and a free taste.

🛈 PRACTICAL INFORMATION. To reach Montalcino, take one of the daily **TRA-IN buses** from **Siena** (1¼hr., 7 per day, €2.84). The buses leave from the train station, not P. Gramsci, but tickets can be bought at the TRA-IN ticket window in either place. (See Siena **Transportation,** p. 373. Last bus to Montalcino departs at 10:15pm; last bus back to Siena departs at 8:30pm.) If coming from **Montepulciano** (1¼hr., €3.62), change buses at **Torrenieri.** Contact the **tourist office** (Associazione Pro-Loco Montalcino), Costa del Municipio, 8, for information about tours of the local vineyards, free maps and hotel booking, and **currency exchange.** From P. Cavour, where the bus stops, walk up V. Mazzini into P. del Popolo. The tourist office is under the clock tower. (☎ 0577 84 93 31; www.prolocomantalcino.it. Open Apr.-Oct. daily 10am-1pm and 2-5:40pm; Nov.-Mar. Tu-Su same hours.) Rent a **mountain bike** (€13 per day) or **scooter** (from €26 per day) at **Minocci Lorenzo Noleggio,** V. P. Strozzi, 31, in the gas station. (☎ 0577 84 82 82; montalcinolmnoleggio@libero.it. Open daily 7am-7:30pm.)

🛏🍴 ACCOMMODATIONS AND FOOD. Hotel rooms tend to be expensive and scarce in Montalcino; try to find a bed in one of the many *affittacamere* (private lodgings), which are generally well kept and run €42-52 for a double with bath. The tourist office can provide a list of all hotels and *affittacamere* in the area. **🏨Albergo Il Giardino ❹,** P. Cavour, 4, is a reasonably priced option in the heart of the town that offers modern, tasteful rooms. The cozy lounge has leather couches and a stone fireplace. (☎ 0577 84 82 57. Singles €45; doubles €53; triples €72.) **Affittacamere Mariuccia ❹,** P. del Popolo, 28, offers three white-walled, well-appointed rooms with immaculate private bath and TV. Reception is across the street in Enotecha Pierangioli. (☎ 0577 84 91 13. Singles €38; doubles €44.) The oldest hotel in town, **Albergo Il Giglio ❹,** V. S. Saloni, 5, features rooms with fantastic views. All rooms have bath, phone, and satellite TV. (☎/fax 0577 84 81 67; hotelgiglio@tin.it. Singles €52; doubles €72; triples €83. AmEx/MC/V.)

You'll find the best deals on Brunello (€16-27) at the **COOP supermarket,** on the corner of V. Sant'Agostino and V. della Libertà. (Open M-Tu and Th-Sa 8am-1pm and 4-8pm, W 8am-1pm.) V. Mazzini, the main street through the heart of town, is absolutely littered with *enoteche* (wine bars), all nearly identical in their huge selection of Brunello, offering sophisticated snacks from *bruschette* (€4-6) to cheese and meat plates (€3-6). Many city center restaurants offer full meals as well

CENTRAL ITALY

as huge selections of wine. Near the *fortezza*, the **Osteria di Porta al Cassero ❸**, V. Ricasoli, 32, dishes out *scottiglia di cinghiale* (wild boar stew) for €7.25 and *coniglio arrosto* (roast rabbit) for €6.70. (☎0577 84 71 96. Open Th-Tu noon-3pm and 7-10pm.) **Taverna Il Grappolo Blu ❸**, Scale di V. Moglio, 1, down a small staircase off of V. Mazzini, offers pasta (€6-7.50). The garlicky homemade pasta with truffle sauce (€7) must be eaten to be believed. (☎0577 84 71 50. Cover €1.50. Open Sa-Th noon-3pm and 7-10pm. AmEx/MC/V.) For delicious *sfogliatine ripiene di stracchino e pere* (ravioli with cheese and pears; €11.50) stop off at Maria Pia's **Re di Macchia ❹**, V. S. Saloni, 21. (☎0577 84 61 16. Cover €2.50. Open F-W 12:30-2pm and 7:30-10pm. AmEx/MC/V.) Head to **Sapori di Napoli ❶**, V. Mazzini, 34/36, for pizza slices or hot sandwiches. (☎0347 621 6148. Open daily 10am-8pm.)

🄶 **SIGHTS.** To appreciate the local vineyards, head past the *fortezza* on V. P. Strozzi, and follow the signs out of town toward "Castelnuovo dell'Abate" and "Abbazia di S. Antimo." Just 3km down this scenic, winding road is the entrance to the **Tenuta Greppo,** which produced the first *Brunello* in 1888. (☎0577 84 80 87; www.biondisanti.it. Open for tours M-F 9-11am and 3-5pm.) It's an easy walk (10-15min.) or bike ride from the *fortezza;* watch for occasional traffic. Up a straight cyprus-lined gravel drive awaits the sprawling stone complex housing the cellars and tasting room. Tours and tastings are by appointment only, geared toward those with an interest in buying their fabulous but expensive wines. Two km further down the road lies **Fattoria dei Barbi,** a winery for the rest of us. It is an easy walk (30min.) or bike ride from the *fortezza*. Look for the sign on the left side of the road pointing to a gravel road and follow the signs from there. Tours of the extensive cellars are followed by a tasting of three of their delicious wines (one *Brunello*, one blend, and one dessert wine). Tasting can be done any time during their opening hours; ring bell for service. The winery also includes a restaurant, open for lunch and dinner. (☎0577 84 11 11; www.fattoria deibarbi.it. Open M-F 10am-1pm and 2:30-6pm, Sa 2:30-6pm. Free tours given every hour M-F 11am-noon and 3-5pm.) The **Palazzo Comunale,** in the P. del Popolo, hosts wine exhibitions.

Apicoltura Ciacci, V. Ricasoli, 26, up the street from the Chiesa di S. Agostino, stocks every honey product imaginable, including honey soap, honey biscuits, honey milk, honey candies, and honey *grappa*. (☎0577 84 80 19. Open Nov.-Mar. daily. Ring the bell for assistance. MC/V.)

Montalcino's most inspiring sight, the 🆂**Abbazia di Sant'Antimo,** lies 10km from Montalcino down the same road as the wineries. Check times at the bus stop in P. Cavour, or ask at the tourist office. Make sure that there is a return bus from Castelnuovo. Keep in mind the walk from Castelnuovo to the abbey takes about 8min. With its rounded apse and carved alabaster capitals, this early 12th-century abbey is one of Tuscany's most beautiful Romanesque structures. Moreover, it is surrounded by sloping hills, vineyards, and cypresses in quintessential Tuscan countryside. Inside, monks perform Mass in **Gregorian chant** seven times a day (during which time the church is closed to the public). Recorded chants float through the church the rest of the day. (☎0577 83 56 69. Open M-Sa 10:30am-12:30pm and 3-6:30pm, Su 9-10:30am and 3-6pm.) Buses leave from Montalcino for the abbey and stop at Castelnuovo (€2). It is a 15min. ride by scooter or car (follow signs to the right when you near the tiny village of Castelnuovo dell'Abate), and an easy trip by bike, though it's a long, hard uphill ride back.

Montalcino's 14th-century **fortezza** sheltered a band of republicans escaping the Florentine siege of Siena in 1555. The fortress is almost perfectly preserved, with five towers and part of the town walls incorporated into the structure. Two courtyards beckon inside the fortress, one sunny and cheered by geraniums, the other shaded by foliage, making for a nice picnic spot. The fortezza's sophisticated **Eno-**

teca La Fortezza offers cheese plates (€7) and local wines (€3-9 per glass; *Brunello* €6-12). If the staff behind the counter is vigilant, you'll have to pay the €3 to climb the stairs through the turret onto the *fortezza* walls for a breathtaking view of the surrounding countryside. (Fort and Enoteca open Apr.-Oct. daily 9am-8pm; Nov.-Mar. Tu-Su 9am-6pm.)

MONTEPULCIANO   ☎0578

This small medieval hamlet, stretched along the crest of a narrow limestone ridge and enclosed by stone walls, is one of Tuscany's highest hilltop towns. Montepulciano was built in four phases, first to protect against belligerent neighbors and later to ward off disease-ridden pilgrims. Crammed within its fortifications lie Renaissance *palazzi* and churches. Montepulciano is best known for its local *Vino Nobile* wines. At many local wineries, the traveling epicurean can experience the garnet-colored wine that put the town on the map. Even if you skip the wine, the landscape and museums make Montepulciano an enlightening refuge.

▄ TRANSPORTATION

Trains: Lies on Siena-Chiusi line. Station 10km from town center. To **Chiusi** (20min., every hr., €2.50). **LFI** buses run to town from train station (Sept.-May 6am-9pm, €1). In June-Aug., the LFI bus service is infrequent, and the alternative is a €13-16 cab ride. Take the train to Chiusi, and then a bus.

Buses: TRA-IN buses run from **Siena** (1½hr., M-Sa 4 per day, €4.30), some via **Buonconvento**. 2 direct buses also run between Montepulciano and **Florence** (2hr., €7.50). **LFI** buses to Chiusi (1hr., every hr., 7am-9:50pm, €2). Tickets available at agencies displaying LFI Biglietti and TRA-IN signs.

Taxis: ☎0578 63 989. **24hr. taxi service and car rental:** ☎0578 71 60 81.

▄ ▄ ORIENTATION AND PRACTICAL INFORMATION

Buses stop at the bottom of the hill outside the town. Disembark at the *centro storico*, before the bus begins its descent. A short, steep climb leads to the **Corso**, the main street. Orange ATAF **buses** make the trip easier (€0.72). Divided nominally into four parts (V. di Gracciano nel Corso, V. di Voltaia nel Corso, V. dell'Opio nel Corso, and V. del Poliziano), the Corso winds languorously up a precipitous hill. At the end, the street starts to level off; from here, on **Via del Teatro,** another incline on the right leads to **Piazza Grande,** the main square.

Tourist Office: P. Grande, 7 (☎0578 71 74 84; fax 75 27 49; www.stradavinonobile.it). Gives out maps and makes free arrangements for *alberghi* and *affittacamere* in town and the surrounding countryside. Open M-Sa 10am-1pm and 3-6pm.

Currency Exchange: Banca Toscana, P. Michelozzo, 2. **ATM** outside. Open M-F 8:20am-1:20pm and 2:45-3:45pm. Currency exchange is also available at the **post office** and the 24hr. exchange machines in P. Savonarola.

Emergency: ☎113. **Medical Emergency:** ☎118. **Police:** P. Savonarola, 16 (☎112).

Pharmacy: Farmacia Franceschi, V. di Voltaia nel Corso, 47 (☎0578 71 63 92). Open Apr.-Sept. M-Sa 9am-1pm and 4:30-7:30pm; Oct.-May 9am-1pm and 4-7pm. **Farmacia Sorbini** (☎0578 75 73 52) on V. Calamandrei, fills urgent prescriptions.

Post Office: V. dell'Erbe, 12, uphill from the P. dell'Erbe and the Corso. **Currency exchange** (€0.50 commission). Open M-F 8:15am-7pm, Sa 8:15am-12:30pm.

Postal Code: 53045.

ACCOMMODATIONS

Most lodgings in Montepulciano cost as much as three- or four-star hotels elsewhere. *Affittacamere* (rooms for rent) are the best option. The tourist office can help you find a place to stay if Montepulciano becomes more than a daytrip.

Affittacamere Bellavista, V. Ricci, 25 (☎ 347 823 2314 or 338 229 1964), downhill from the tourist office. Rents small, lovely rooms, some with fantastic views. Call ahead to reserve room and get the key. Doubles with bath €46.48. ➍

Albergo La Terrazza, V. Piè al Sasso, 16 (☎/fax 0578 75 74 40; www.laterrazzadimontepulciano.com). From P. Grande, take V. del Teatro downhill, left of the duomo. In Piazeta del Teatro, turn left on V. di Cagnano. On right, 4 blocks ahead. Engaging owners. Reserve ahead. Singles €56; doubles €83; triples €108.50; quads €124. MC/V. ➍

Meuble Il Riccio, V. Talosa, 21 (☎/fax 0578 75 77 13; www.ilriccio.net), just off P. Grande. Stunning views from the rooftop terrace survey the Val di Chiana and its lakes, Montepulciano, Chiusi, and Trasimeno. Reservations recommended. Breakfast €8. Singles €70; doubles €80; triples €96. AmEx/MC/V. ➎

Ristorante Cittino, V. della Nuova, 2 (☎0578 75 73 35), off V. di Voltaia del Corso. Rooms above a popular restaurant with superb food (full meals €15). 2 clean doubles (€50) and 1 single (€25). Prices negotiable. Open Th-Tu. ➌

FOOD

Minimarkets line the Corso. A **Conad Supermarket** is near P. Savonarola, outside the city walls. (Open M-Tu and Th-Sa 8:30am-7pm, W 8:30am-noon.) Thursday brings an **open-air market** to the lot behind the bus station. (Open 8am-1pm.)

Osteria dell'Acquacheta, V. del Teatro, 22 (☎0578 75 84 43 or 71 70 86), off the Corso. Juicy *bistecca alla fiorentina.* Exotic *pecorino miele e noci* (cheese with honey and nuts) or *pecorino di peinza al tartufo* (with truffles; €5.20). *Primi* €5.20, *secondi* by weight. Open W-M July-Sept. noon-4pm and 6pm-2am; Oct.-June noon-4pm and 7pm-1am. MC/V. ➌

Trattoria Diva e Maceo, V. Gracciano nel Corso, 92 (☎0578 71 69 51). Locals dine on *cannelloni* (stuffed with ricotta and spinach; €7) and *ossobuco* (beef stew; €7.50). Open W-M 12:30-2pm and 7:30-9:30pm. Closed 1st week of July. AmEx/MC/V. ➋

Il Cantuccio, V. delle Cantine, 1-2 (☎0578 75 78 70), off V. di Gracciano nel Corso. Specializes in classic Tuscan fare with an Etruscan twist. Try the *bistecca alla fiorentina* or the *pollo e coniglio all'Etrusca* (Etruscan-style chicken and rabbit; €11.36). *Primi* €6.20-9.30, *secondi* €7.23-15.49. Open Tu-Su noon-2pm and 8-10pm. Closed 1st 2 weeks of July. MC/V. ➌

Caffè Poliziano, V. del Voltaio nel Corso, 27 (☎0578 75 86 15). Marble tabletops and a brass-accented bar complete this classy cafe and its delectable pastries (from €0.70). 2 tiny terraces offer splendid views. Formal dining room next door open for dinner (M-Sa 7-10:15pm). Cafe open daily 7am-1am. AmEx/MC/V. ➊

Pub Grotta di Nano, V. Gracciano del Corso, 11 (☎0578 75 60 23). Inexpensive and quick. Offers sandwiches, pizza by the slice, a *gelato* bar, and a small menu. Wine and *panzanella* €5.50. *Crostini* and wine €8.50. Beer €2.40-4.50. Open daily 10:30am-9:30pm. AmEx/MC/V. ➊

🔎 SIGHTS

CHIESA DI SAN BIAGIO. Built in an unusual Greek-cross shape, this church is a stunning example of high Renaissance symmetry and is Sangallo's masterpiece. The cavernous interior was redone in the 17th century in overwrought Baroque, but the simple skeleton is still visible. *(From P. Grande, follow V. Ricci to V. della Mercenzia. Turn left down staircase before Piazzeta di S. Francesco. Follow signs on switchbacks, through the city walls, and along V. di San Biagio. Open daily 9am-1pm and 3:30-7pm.)*

VIA DI GRACCIANO QUARTER. Noteworthy *palazzi* line this neighborhood. On the right, **Palazzo Avignonesi** (1507-1575) is attributed to Vignola. The elegant windows on the second floor contrast sharply with the bold protruding windows on the ground floor, displaying the *palazzo*'s different stages of construction. The lions' heads on either side of the door correspond to those on top of the **Marzocco Column**, in front of the *palazzo*. The lion, the heraldic symbol of Florence, replaced the she-wolf of Siena when Florence took over Montepulciano in 1511. The original statue now rests in the **Museo Civico.** Farther up the street rises the asymmetrical facade of **Palazzo Cocconi,** attributed to Antonio da Sangallo the Elder (1455-1534). Across the street, **Palazzo Bucelli** showcases Roman and Etruscan reliefs, urn slabs, and inscriptions collected by the 18th-century proprietor, Pietro Bucelli.

PIAZZA GRANDE. The unfinished duomo, the Palazzo Tarugi, the Palazzo Contucci, and the 14th-century Palazzo Comunale all surround this piazza. The construction of the duomo began in the 16th century when the town council deemed the existing cathedral unworthy. After several years of commissioning and firing architects, the town council settled on Ippolito Scalza, an architect

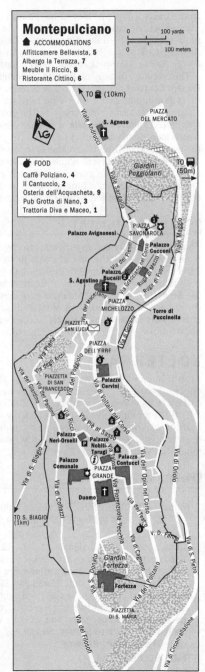

Montepulciano

| 0 | 100 yards |
| 0 | 100 meters |

▲ ACCOMMODATIONS
Affittcamere Bellavista, **5**
Albergo la Terrazza, **7**
Meuble Il Riccio, **8**
Ristorante Cittino, **6**

TO 🏠 (10km)

PIAZZA DEL MERCATO

Viale Andreuzzi

S. Agnese

🍴 FOOD
Caffè Poliziano, **4**
Il Cantuccio, **2**
Osteria dell'Acquacheta, **9**
Pub Grotta di Nano, **3**
Trattoria Diva e Maceo, **1**

TO 🚌 (50m)

Giardini Poggiofanti

Viale Sangallo

Viale Maggio

PIAZZA SAVONAROLA

Palazzo Avignonesi

Palazzo Cocconi

Via dei Fiemi

Via di Gracciano nel Corso

Rugapi Mezzo

Rugapi di Fuori

Palazzo Bucelli

S. Agostino

Via del Macellano

PIAZZA MICHELOZZO

Torre di Puccinella

PIAZZETTA SAN LUCIA

Via di Cagnano

PIAZZA DELL'ERBE

Via Piana

Via degli Archi

PIAZZETTA DI SAN FRANCESCO

Via del Poggiolo

Via del Paolino

Via del Giardino

Palazzo Cervini

Via di Voltaia nel Corso

Palazzo Neri-Orselli

Via Ricci

Via Pié di Sasso

Palazzo Nobili-Tarugi

Palazzo Contucci

Via del Teatro

Via dell'Opio nel Corso

Via di Oriolo

Palazzo Comunale

PIAZZA GRANDE

Duomo

Via di S. Biagio

Via di Collazzi

Via Fiorenzuola Vecchia

Via Florenzuola Vecchia

TO S. BIAGIO (1km)

V. D. Fanne

Giardini Fortezza

Via S. Donato

Via del Filosofi

Fortezza

Via del Poliziano

Via di S. Pietro

PIAZZETTA DI S. MARIA

Via di Circonvallazione

from Orvieto. The product of his painstaking process is an unaccountably stark duomo whose rustic, unfinished facade reflects its sparse interior. However unpretentious, the duomo does have Taddeo di Bartolo's poignant masterpiece, *Assumption of the Virgin*, in a triptych above the altar. *(In P. Grande, at the top of the hill. Walk up Il Corso. Open daily 9am-12:30pm and 3:15-7pm.)*

The elegant facade of **Palazzo de'Nobili-Tarugi** faces the duomo. The nearby **Palazzo Contucci** is a graceful, if eccentric, hybrid of architectural styles. The Contucci family has made fine wine here for well over a century and today runs a charming *enoteca* (wine store) on the ground floor. In the mid-1400s Michelozzo completed **Palazzo Comunale**, a smaller version of the Palazzo Vecchio in Florence, which took nearly a century to build. The *palazzo's* tower offers views of Siena to the north and of Gran Sasso Massif to the south. *(Tower open M-Sa 10am-6pm. €1.55.)*

The **Palazzo Neri-Orselli** houses the **Museo Civico**, one of Montepulciano's foremost attractions. The museum contains a collection of enameled terra cotta by della Robbia, Etruscan funerary urns, and more than 200 paintings. *(V. Ricci, 10. Open Tu-Su 10am-1pm and 3-7pm. €4.13, under 18 or over 65 €2.58.)*

🎵 ENTERTAINMENT

Tourists primarily occupy themselves by browsing wine stores and tasting free wine samples. Try the one at Porta di Bacco, on the left immediately after you enter the city gates. (Open daily 9am-8pm.) In the first half of August, the town fills with musicians who perform at **Cantiere Internazionale d'Arte.** Around August 15, the **Bruscello** (a series of amateur concerts and theatrical productions) occurs on the steps of the duomo. Visit Montepulciano the last Sunday in August to see the raucous **Bravio delle Botti** (Barrel Race), held to commemorate the eight neighborhood militias who fended off the Florentines and Sienese.

VOLTERRA ☎ 0588

Atop a huge bluff known as *Le Balze*, the town presides over a surrounding checkerboard of green and yellow fields. This one-time Etruscan settlement shrunk to its current size during the Middle Ages, when outlying parts of the town fell off the eroding hillside upon which it was built. Today, alabaster statues (memorabilia of Volterra's Etruscan past), medieval architecture, and superb views draw tourists, but it is outside the city gates, in semolina fields and distant mountains, that Volterra reveals its real appeal.

▣ TRANSPORTATION

Trains: (☎ 0588 86 150), 9km west in **Saline di Volterra.** Take the CPT bus to **Saline** (€1.50) for trains to **Pisa** (€6.35) and the **coast.**

Buses: (☎ 0588 86 150), in P. Martiri della Libertà. To **Florence** (1.5hr., €6.56). **TRA-IN** connects to **San Gimignano** (1.5hr., €3.87) and **Siena** (1.5hr., €4.40). All 3 destinations require a change at Colle Val d'Elsa. **CPT** runs between Volterra and Colle Val D'Elsa—buy tickets at **Associazione Pro Volterra,** a *tabacchi,* or at the vending machines near the bus stop. **TRA-IN** and **SITA** run buses from Colle Val d'Elsa to elsewhere in Tuscany. Buy tickets at travel agencies or at town offices, like the one in the square where buses arrive and leave in Colle Val D'Elsa. When buying your 1st ticket, be sure that the connection time at Colle Val D'Elsa is reasonable. **CPT** also runs to **Saline di Volterra** (6 per day, Su and Aug. 2 per day; €1.50) and **Pisa** (2hr., 10 per day, €4.91), via **Pontedera.**

Taxis: ☎ 0588 87 517.

⚡ ℹ ORIENTATION AND PRACTICAL INFORMATION

To get from the bus stop in **Piazza della Libertà** to the town center in **Piazza dei Priori**, walk into town, turn left onto **Via Ricciarelli**, and walk 40m.

Tourist Office: P. dei Priori, 20 (☎ 0588 87 257). English spoken. Provides maps, brochures, and makes hotel and taxi reservations for free. Rents recorded walking tours (€7 per person, €10 for 2). Open Apr.-Oct. daily 10am-1pm and 2-7pm; Nov.-Mar. 10am-1pm and 2-6pm.

Associazione Pro Volterra: V. Turazza (☎ 0588 86 150; fax 90 350), just off P. dei Priori. Sells CPT bus tickets, and provides schedule and fare information on **buses to Pisa, Saline di Volterra, San Gimignano, Florence,** and **Siena;** and **trains to Pisa.**

Currency Exchange: Cassa di Risparmio di Firenze, V. Matteotti, 1, has a 24hr. exchange machine and an **ATM** outside. Also in P. Martiri della Libertà.

Internet: 🖳**Web and Wine,** V. Porte all'Arco, 11/13 (☎ 0588 81 531; www.webandwine.com). After surfing the web, kick back with a glass of *chianti* with your eye on the Etruscan ruins visible through the glass floor. €5.20 per hr. Open Tu-Su 7am-1am.

SESHA, P. XX Settembre, 10. €6 per hr. Open daily 9am-1pm and 4-8pm. MC/V.

Emergency: ☎ 113. **Medical Emergency:** ☎ 118.

Pharmacy: Farmacia Amidei, V. Ricciarelli, 2 (☎ 0588 86 060). Open M-Sa 9am-1pm and 4-8pm; open Su in emergency situations.

Hospital: (☎ 0588 91 911), on Borgo S. Lazzaro.

Post Office: P. Priori, 14 (☎ 0588 86 969). Open M-F 8:15am-7pm, Sa 8:15am-12:30pm.

Postal Code: 56048.

🛏 ACCOMMODATIONS & CAMPING

Ask the tourist office for a list of *affittacamere*. Doubles begin at €36.

Seminario Sant'Andrea, V. V. Veneto, 2 (☎ 0588 86 028), in P. S. Andrea, next to the church. From P. della Libertà, jog left, then immediately right onto V. Matteotti. Take another right onto V. Gramsci, walk through P. XX Settembre, and take 1st left. Exit city through Porta Marcoli and follow the road, bearing left, until you reach Sant'Andrea. 2-4 person rooms with antique furniture off frescoed hallways. Reception 8am-midnight. Curfew midnight. Reservations required. Breakfast €3.10. €13.94 per person; €17.56 for rooms with bath. Half-pension €24.79; full-pension €29.95. MC/V. ❷

L'Etrusca, V. Porta all'Arco, 37/41 (☎/fax 0588 84 073). From the bus stop, turn left onto V. Marchesi and then left onto V. Porta all'Arco. Clean, modern flats, all with bath, TV, and kitchen facilities. Reserve ahead. Singles €39; doubles €65; triples €77. ❹

Albergo Etruria, V. Matteotti, 32 (☎ 0588 87 377). Exit P. Libertà to the left and take your 1st right onto V. Matteotti; the Etruria is a few blocks down. White-walled rooms with clean bath, TV, and high ceilings. Lounge and garden. Breakfast €6. Singles €42, with bath €46; doubles €52/€66; triples €62/€72; quads with bath €77. MC/V. ❹

Hotel La Locanda, V. Guarnacci 24/28 (☎ 0588 81 547; fax 81 541), just off P. San Michele. Sparkling new hotel newly opened in June 2002. Plush rooms adorned with matching bedspreads, curtains, and upholstered furniture, and hung with artwork from a local gallery. All include bath, satellite TV, fridge, and safe. Breakfast included. Doubles €85; triples €134; quads €165. Rooms with massage showers or whirlpools significantly more expensive. AmEx/MC/V. ❺

Camping: Le Balze, V. Mandringa, 15 (☎ 0588 87 880). Exit through Porta S. Francesco, and bear right on Strada Provincial Pisana. Turn left onto V. Mandringa (20 min.). Campground has pool and bar. Store sells tickets for bus into town (every hr., 8:18am-9:21pm). Showers included. Reception 8am-11pm. Cars must be parked by 11pm. Open Apr.-Oct. €6 per person, €4 per tent, €7 per camper. AmEx/MC/V. ❶

CENTRAL ITALY

▣ FOOD

An excellent selection of local cheeses and game dishes is available at any of the *alimentari* along V. Guarnacci or V. Gramsci. Sample *salsiccia di cinghiale* (wild boar sausage) and *pecorino* (sheep's milk cheese). For a sweet snack, try *ossi di morto* (bones of death), a rock-hard local confection made of egg whites, sugar, hazelnuts, and a hint of lemon, or *pane di pescatore*, a dense and delicious sweet bread full of nuts and raisins. Pick up groceries at the **Despar market,** V. Gramsci, 12. (Open M-F 7:30am-1pm and 5-8pm, Sa 7:30am-1pm.)

Ristorante Etruria, P. dei Priori, 6/8 (☎ 0588 86 064). The "temple of Volterra gastronomy" serves up rich soups and local game. Dine amid towers and *palazzi* in the large outdoor seating area. *Primi* €3.50-9, *secondi* €4.50-12. Tourist *menù* €12.50. Service 10%. Open daily noon-3pm and 7-10pm. AmEx/MC/V. ❸

Il Pozzo degli Etruschi, V. dei Prigioni, 30 (☎ 0588 80 60). Hearty *penne all'Etrusca* (pasta with tomato, mushroom, and cheese; €6.20) and *cinghiale alla maremmane* (wild boar; €8.26). *Primi* €3.10-8.26, *secondi* €3.26-12.91. Tourist *menù* €12.91. Cover €1.29. Service 10%. Open Sa-Th noon-3pm and 6:30-10pm. AmEx/MC/V. ❸

L'Ombra della Sera, V. Gramsci, 70 (☎ 0588 86 663), off P. XX Settembre. Volterran classics served in pink-walled dining room. *Primi* €4.90-7.80, *secondi* €9-12.90. Cover €1.30. Service 10%. Open Tu-Su noon-3pm and 7-10pm. AmEx/MC/V. ❸

Pizzeria/Birreria Ombra della Sera, V. Guarnacci, 16 (☎ 0588 85 274). Cross-vaulted ceilings and long wood benches at heavy, dark wood tables contribute to a subtly medieval ambiance. Pizza €4-7, salad €5.70, and pasta €4.70-6.80. Cover €0.80. Service 10%. Open Tu-Su noon-3pm and 7-10pm. MC/V. ❶

◉ ♫ SIGHTS AND ENTERTAINMENT

PIAZZA DEI PRIORI AND FORTEZZA MEDICEA. Volterra revolves around Piazza dei Priori, which is surrounded by sober, dignified *palazzi.* The **Palazzo dei Priori,** the oldest governmental palace in Tuscany (1208-1254), presides over the square. Inside, the council hall and the antechamber are open to the public. Jacopo di Cione Orcagna's damaged *Annunciation with Four Saints* occupies most of the right wall. The *sinopia* is displayed in the adjoining antechamber. *(Open M-Sa 10am-6:45pm, Su 10am-1pm and 2-6:45pm. €1.)* Across the piazza, **Palazzo Pretorio's** 13th-century buildings and towers house municipal offices. Volterra's most prominent structure is the elegant **Fortezza Medicea,** which now houses a state prison and is closed to the public. The neighboring **public park** affords a decent view of the fort and is a great picnic spot. *(Park open daily 8am-8pm. From the bus stop, walk into town and take the 1st right. The road will turn uphill; follow it to the park entrance.)*

DUOMO. Construction began on Volterra's Pisan-Romanesque cathedral in the 13th century, continuing for three centuries. Inside and on the left, the oratory houses a series of wooden statues depicting the life of Jesus from nativity to crucifixion. The chapel off the left transept holds frescoes by Rosselli, including the brilliant *Missione per Damasco.* Also note the spectacular use of perspective in the *Annunciation* by M. Albertinelli and Fra Bartolomeo on the left wall. *(Down V. Turazza from P. dei Priori to P. S. Giovanni. Open daily 8am-12:30pm and 3-6pm.)*

PINACOTECA COMUNALE. A graceful building with a courtyard contains Volterra's best art in understated, dimly lit rooms. Taddeo di Bartolo's elegant *Madonna and Saints* altarpiece will upset the expectations of anyone who has seen his gruesome *Last Judgment* in San Gimignano. In Rosso Fiorentino's spectacular first-floor work, the *Deposition* (1521), Christ's body seems to be painted green (most likely a result of aging and poor restoration). The work is mesmerizing, in part because the painting spills from the canvas onto the frame, creating the illusion that Fiorentino's subjects are not confined to the flat surface. *(V. dei Sartiri, 1. Up V. Buonparenti from P. dei Priori. ☎ 0588 87 580. Open daily 7am-7pm. A combination ticket including Pinacoteca, Museo Etrusco, and Museo dell' Opera del Duomo di Arte Sacra is available at any sight. €7, students €5.)*

MUSEO ETRUSCO GUARNACCI. The Etruscan museum displays over 600 finely carved funeral urns from the 7th and 8th centuries BC. A stylized figure representing the deceased tops each urn; below, dramatic bas-reliefs recreate various episodes from classical mythology. The pieces are not well displayed, and an audio tour will run you an additional €4.50. The first floor (Room XXII) holds the museum's most famous piece, the elongated bronze figure dubbed *l'Ombra della Sera* (Shadow of the Evening), which inspired the great modern Italian sculptor Giacommetti. The farmer who unearthed it used it for years as a fireplace poker until a visitor recognized it as an Etruscan votive figure. In Room XX, the famous urn *Urna degli Sposi* depicts an angry married couple. *(V. Minzoni, 15. From P. dei Priori, head down to V. Matteotti, turn right on V. Gramsci, and follow it to V. Minzoni. ☎ 0588 86 347. Gallery and museum open mid-Mar. to Oct. daily 9am-7pm; Nov. to mid-Mar. 9am-2pm.)*

MUSEO DELL'OPERA DEL DUOMO DI ARTE SACRA. Its inclusion on the cumulative ticket is the primary reason to visit this tiny, three-room museum, which holds much of the art originally in the duomo. Objects on display range from liturgical robes to impressive metallic sculptures. *(V. Roma, 1, near duomo. ☎ 0588 86 290. Open mid-Mar. to Oct. daily 9:30am-1pm and 3-6pm; Nov. to mid-Mar. 9am-1pm.)*

ROMAN AMPHITHEATER. These impressive ruins include partly grass-covered stone seating and Corinthian columns salvaged from the stage. Walk among the ruins, or admire them from a bird's-eye view for free on the road next to Porta Fiorentina. *(Just outside the city walls next to Porta Fiorentina. From P. dei Priori, follow V. delle Prigioni, take a right at the T-junction and your 1st left. Proceed down V. Guarnacci, out the Porta and through the parking lot to your left. Open daily 10am-1pm and 2-6pm. €2.)*

SAN GIMIGNANO ☎ 0577

The hilltop village of San Gimignano looks like an illustration from a medieval manuscript—towers, churches and *palazzi* of cartoonish proportion bulge out from within the city's walls. San Gimignano's famous 14 towers, which are all that survive of the original 72, date from a period when prosperous families fought battles within the city walls, using their towers to store grain for sieges. The towers were also convenient for dumping boiling oil on attacking enemies. After WWII, its towered horizon began to lure postwar tourists, whose tastes and wallets resuscitated production of the golden *Vernaccia* wine. With hordes of daytrippers, an infestation of souvenir shops, and countless restaurants, San Gimignano now has the feel of a Disney Medieval Land. Nevertheless, it's impressive and worth the packed bus rides.

▐▀ TRANSPORTATION

Trains: The nearest station is in **Poggibonsi;** buses connect the station to the town (M-F every 30 min., 6:10am-8:35pm; Sa-Su every hr., 7:40am-8pm; €1.35).

Buses: TRA-IN buses (☎ 0577 20 41 11 or 93 72 07) leave from P. Montemaggio, outside Porta S. Giovanni. Schedules and tickets at **Caffè Combattente,** V. S. Giovanni, 124, to the left as you enter the city gates. Tickets also available from *tabacchi* or at the tourist office. Change at **Poggibonsi** (20min., every hr., €1.35) for **Siena** (1hr., every 1-2hr., €5) and **Florence** (1½hr. with a good connection, every 1hr., €5.70).

Scooter/Bike/Car Rental: Jolly Pentacar, V. di Fugnano, 10 (☎0577 94 05 75; www.jolly-pentacar.com), 1km from Porta San Matteo. Bikes €10 per day and scooters from €23 per day. Small cars from €58 per day. Open daily 8am-8pm. **Bruno Bellini,** V. Roma, 41 (☎0577 94 02 01; www.bellinibruno.com), 200m down the hill from Porta S. Giovanni. Bikes €4-9 per hr., €11-21 per day. Scooters from €31 per day. Cars from €58 per day. Open daily 9am-1pm and 3-8pm. AmEx/MC/V.

■✴🛈 ORIENTATION AND PRACTICAL INFORMATION

Buses to San Gimignano stop in **Piazzale Martini Montemaggio,** the large square just outside the city walls. To reach the city center, pass through the *porta* and climb the hill, following **Via San Giovanni** to **Piazza della Cisterna,** which merges with **Piazza del Duomo.** Addresses in San Gimignano are marked in both faded black stencil and etched clay tiles; since most establishments go by the black, these are listed.

Tourist Office: Pro Loco, P. del Duomo, 1 (☎0577 94 00 08; fax 94 09 03; pro-locsg@tin.it). Has lists of hotels and rooms for rent as well as bus and train schedules and bus tickets. Offers 2½hr. tours of wineries on Tu at 11am and Th at 5pm. Includes multiple tastings (all with food) and transportation by bus for €26 (€18 if you drive yourself). Reserve by noon the day before. Office also makes private room reservations (if you visit in person). English spoken. Open Mar.-Oct. daily 9am-1pm and 3-7pm; Nov.-Feb. 9am-1pm and 2-6pm.

Accommodations Services: Siena Hotels Promotion, V. S. Giovanni, 125 (☎0577 94 08 09; fax 94 01 13), on the right as you enter the city gates; look for the *"Cooperativa Alberghi e Ristoranti"* sign. Reserves hotel rooms in San Gimignano and Siena for 5% commission. Open M-Sa 9:30am-7pm.

Associazione Strutture Extraberghiere, P. della Cisterna, 6 (☎/fax 0577 94 31 90). Patient staff makes reservations for private rooms without charge. Doubles with bath €50-60. Call a week in advance if you want to stay in the countryside; they can always find a place in the city center. Open Mar.-Nov. daily 9:30am-7:30pm.

Currency Exchange: Pro Loco tourist office and post office offer best rates. Rip-offs elsewhere. **ATMs** scattered along V. S. Giovanni, V. degli Innocenti, and P. della Cisterna.

Police: ☎112. **Carabinieri** (☎0577 94 03 13), on P. Martiri.

Medical Emergency: ☎118.

Late-Night Pharmacy: P. Cisterna, 8 (☎0577 94 03 69). Fills urgent prescriptions all night; call ☎0368 713 6675. Open M-Sa 9am-1pm and 4:30-8pm.

Post Office: P. delle Erbe, 8, behind the duomo. Open daily M-F 8:15am-7pm, Sa 8:15am-12:30pm. Currency exchange available.

Postal Code: 53037.

🛏 ACCOMMODATIONS & CAMPING

San Gimignano caters to wealthy tourists, and most accommodations are well beyond budget range. *Affittacamere* provide an alternative to overpriced hotels, with doubles from €50-60. The tourist office and the **Associazione Strutture Extralberghiere** (see above) have lists of budget rooms.

Albergo/Ristorante Il Pino, V. Cellolese, 6 (☎/fax 0577 94 04 15), off V. S. Matteo at Porta S. Matteo. Dark wood furnishings and quilted comforters adorn rustic rooms with bath and TV. Reservations recommended. Singles €45; doubles€55. AmEx/MC/V. ❹

Camere Cennini Gianni, V. S. Giovanni, 21 (☎347 074 8188; fax 0577 94 10 51; www.sangiapartments.com). From the bus stop, enter through Porta S. Giovanni. Reception is at the *pasticceria* at V. S. Giovanni, 88. Quaint, clean rooms with bath. Kitchens for groups of 4. Reserve ahead. Doubles €55; triples €65; quads €75. May, June, and Aug. prices €5-10 higher. MC/V. ❹

Hotel La Cisterna, P. della Cisterna, 24 (☎0577 94 03 28; fax 94 20 80; lacisterna@iol.it). Wrought iron headboards, flowing curtains, and floral designs complement the balcony's stunning pastoral panorama. All rooms have bath and satellite TV. Buffet breakfast €8. A/C €5. Singles €68; doubles €88, with view €100, with view and balcony €112. Additional beds €30. AmEx/MC/V. ❺

Camping: Il Boschetto (☎0577 94 03 52; fax 94 19 82; bpiemma@tiscalinet.it), at Santa Lucia, 2½km downhill from Porta S. Giovanni. Buses run from P. dei Martiri (€0.77). Ask the driver if the bus is going to the campgrounds; it's also not a bad hike. Bar and market on the premises. Reception daily 8am-1pm and 3-10pm. Open Apr.-Oct. 15. €4.70 per person, €5 per small tent. Hot showers included. ❶

🍴🍷 FOOD AND NIGHTLIFE

If you didn't guess from the sad glass eyes of stuffed tuskers across town, San Gimignano specializes in boar and other wild game. The town also caters to less daring palates with mainstream Tuscan dishes at fairly high prices. Whether you're looking to save or savor, try the **open-air market** in P. del Duomo on Thursday mornings. (Open 8am to noon.) Purchase the famous *Vernaccia di San Gimignano*, a light white wine with a hint of sweetness, from **La Buca,** V. S. Giovanni, 16. This cooperative also offers terrific sausages and meats, all produced on its own farm. The boar sausage *al pignoli* (€2.07 per hectogram) and the *salame con mirto* (with blueberry) are especially delicious. (☎0577 94 04 07. Open Apr.-Oct. daily 9am-9pm; Nov.-Mar. 9am-7pm. AmEx/MC/V.)

🍴 **Trattoria Chiribiri,** P. della Madonna, 1 (☎0577 94 19 48). From the bus stop, take your 1st left off V. S. Giovanni up a short staircase. Tiny restaurant serves amazing local fare at unusually affordable prices. The roast rabbit stuffed with vegetables (€7.80) is divine. *Primi* €5-7, *secondi* from €7.50. The dining room can get overheated when crowded, but the service is phenomenal. Open Mar.-Oct. Th-Tu 11am-11pm; Nov.-Feb. Th-Tu noon-2pm and 7-10pm. AmEx/MC/V. ❸

La Bettola del Grillo, V. Quercecchio, 33 (☎0577 94 18 44), off V. S. Giovanni, opposite P. della Cisterna. Serves up traditional Tuscan delights in a hip, plastic-tabled atmosphere, with a small garden with a view in back. Vegetarian options. *Primi* €5.20-8, *secondi* €6.50-11.30. Cover €1.30. Fixed-price *menù* (€13) includes wine and dessert. Open Tu-Su 12:30-3pm and 7:30-11pm. ❸

La Stella, V. San Matteo, 77 (☎0577 94 04 44). Delicious food made with produce from the restaurant's own farm. Delectable, homemade pasta with wild boar sauce, €7.80. *Primi* €4.95-8.75, *secondi* €7.75-11.95. Extensive wine list includes San Gimignano's famous *Vernaccia*. Cover €1.85. Open Apr.-Oct Th-Tu noon-2:30pm and 7-9:30pm; Nov.-Mar. Th-Tu noon-2pm and 7-9pm. AmEx/MC/V. ❸

Ristorante Perucà, V. Capassi, 16 (☎0577 94 31 36). Hidden behind V. San Matteo. Quieter spot away from the tourist bustle. *Primi* €4.50-12, *secondi* €10-16. Cover €2. Open F-W noon-2:30pm and 7-10:30pm. AmEx/MC/V. ❹

Birreria di Pietrafitta (☎0577 94 10 90), Località Cortennano, near San Gimignano. Set in a sunflower field, Birreria fills with attractive Italians and live music nightly. Also serves light meals. Open May-Oct. daily 11am-3am; Nov.-Apr. W-M 11am-3am, Tu 11am-4pm and 8pm-3am. ❷

👁 🎵 SIGHTS AND ENTERTAINMENT

Famous as the *Città delle Belle Torri* (City of Beautiful Towers), San Gimignano has always appealed to artists. During the Renaissance, they came in droves, and the collection of their works complement San Gimignano's cityscape.

> 👁 **TICKET FOR *TUTTO*.** Cumulative tickets for the town's museums are available at varying rates. *Biglietti interi* (€7.50) are full-priced adult tickets; *biglietti ridotti* (€5.50) are discounted tickets, available to students under 18 and children between the ages of 8 and 18. Children under 7 are allowed *ingresso gratuito* (free entrance). One ticket allows entry into nearly all of San Gimignano's sights. Tickets are available at nearly any tourist sight.

⛶ PIAZZA DELLA CISTERNA AND PIAZZA DEL DUOMO. Piazza Cisterna (1237) is surrounded by towers and *palazzi*. It adjoins P. del Duomo, site of the impressive tower of the **Palazzo del Podestà**. To its left, imposing tunnels and intricate *loggie* riddle the **Palazzo del Popolo** (see below). To the right of the *palazzo* rises its **Torre Grossa,** the highest tower in town and the only one visitors can ascend. Also in the piazza stand the twin towers of the Ardinghelli, truncated due to a medieval zoning ordinance that prohibited structures higher than the Torre Grossa.

⛶ MUSEO DELLA TORTURA. This disturbing museum (a sign near the entrance to the first room actually forbids the entrance of "sensitive people"), displays over 50 torture devices from Medieval times to the present. Among the items included in the nine rooms are axes, swords, chastity belts, spiked collars, guillotines, the rack, an Iron Maiden, and even an electric chair. Morbidly fascinating captions in multiple languages explain the history and mechanics of the devices. If that wasn't enough, diagrams accompany each display depicting the torture device in use— particularly helpful in the case of the rectal pear. *(V. del Castello 1, just off P. Cisterna. Open mid-July to mid-Sept. 10am-midnight; Apr. to mid-July and mid-Sept. to Oct. 10am-8pm; Nov.-Mar. 10am-6pm. Entrance €8, students €5.50.)*

PALAZZO DEL POPOLO. A frescoed medieval courtyard leads to the entrance to the **Museo Civico** on the second floor. The first room of the museum is the **Sala di Dante,** where Dante spoke on May 8, 1300 in an attempt to convince San Gimignano to side with the Florentines in their ongoing wars with Siena. On the walls, Lippo Memmi's sparkling *Maestà* blesses the accompanying 14th-century scenes of hunting and tournament pageantry. Up the stairs, Taddeo di Bartolo's altarpiece, *The Story of San Gimignano,* tells the story of the city's namesake, originally a bishop of Modena. Within the museum lies the entrance to the 218-step climb up **Torre Grossa.** The tower offers beautiful panoramas of San Gimignano's many towers, the Tuscan landscape, the ancient fortress, and several piazzas. The tower's bell rings daily at noon. *(Palazzo del Popolo, Museo Civico, and Tower open daily Mar.-Oct. 9:30am-7pm, Nov.-Feb. 10am-7pm. €5, students €4.)*

BASILICA DI COLLEGIATA. This 12th-century church is covered with a bare facade that seems unfit to shelter the exceptional frescoed interior. Off the right aisle, the **Cappella di Santa Fina** is covered in Ghirlandaio's splendid frescoes on the life of Santa Fina, patron saint of San Gimignano. Santa Fina saved the village from barbarian hordes. In the main church, Bartolo di Fredi painted beautiful frescoes of Old Testament scenes along the north aisle, while Barna da Siena provided the extremely impressive New Testament counterparts along the south aisle. *(In P. del Duomo. Church and chapel open Apr.-Oct. M-F 9:30am-7:30pm, Sa 9:30am-5pm, Su 1-5pm; Nov.-Mar. M-Sa 9:30am-5pm, Su 1-5pm. Closed Feb. €3.50, students €1.50.)*

FORTEZZA. Follow the signs past the Basilica di Collegiata from P. del Duomo to this tiny, crumbling fortress. The courtyard is often full of street artists and musicians, and the turret offers a beautiful view of the countryside. There are weekly screenings of movies in the courtyard at night during July and August. *(Schedule and info at the tourist office. Movies €6.20.)*

PISTOIA ☎ 0573

Most travelers know Pistoia only as a stop on the train line between Florence and Lucca. The tourist hordes skips over this small town and its tiny medieval center, stolid stone houses and churches, and crowded, narrow streets and open piazzas. Little do they know that Pistoia is the quintessential small Tuscan city, complete with a beautiful duomo, *campanile*, papistry, and checkered history. In 1177, Pistoia joined several other Italian city-states in declaring its independence. Despite its bold debut, the city was soon surpassed by its neighbors in military, political, and economic strength. Pistoia became a murderous backwater, whose inhabitants Michelangelo maligned as the "enemies of heaven." In 1254, one Pistoian allegedly chopped off a child's hand in retaliation for an injury the boy had caused his son, dragging the entire town into battle. Pistoia has lent its bloody name to the *pistole* dagger (the favored weapon of Pistoia assassins) and the pistol. Recently, residents have turned their attention to more peaceful endeavors—the city is home to one of the world's leading train manufacturers.

▐ TRANSPORTATION

Trains: (☎ 848 88 80 88). Info office open daily 6am-8:30pm. From P. Dante Alighieri to: **Florence** (40min., every hr., 4:40am-11pm, €2.55); **Pisa** (1hr., every 2 hr., 6:50am-11:30pm, €4); **Rome** via **Florence** (4hr., every hr., €25-32); and **Viareggio** (1 hr., every 2 hr., 6:15am-10:30pm, €4).

Buses: COPIT buses (☎ 0573 36 32 43) run from the train station. Open daily 7am-8:15pm. Buy tickets at the office across from the train station at V. XX Settembre, 71. To: **Empoli** (1¼hr., 6:20am-8pm, €2.79) and **Florence** (1hr., 5am-10:20pm, €2.79).

Taxis: Cooperative Pistoia Taxi (☎ 0573 21 237 or 24 291), at P. Garibaldi, P. San Francesco, and the train station. Night service available until 1am.

Bike Rental: Bencini, Corso Gramsci, 98 (☎ 0573 25 144), rents mountain bikes for €15 per day. Open M-Sa 9:15am-1pm and 3:30-7:30pm. AmEx/MC/V.

◤▌ ORIENTATION AND PRACTICAL INFORMATION

To reach the heart of town from the train station, walk up **Via XX Settembre** and continue straight as it changes names to **Via Vanucci,** and then to **Via Cino.** When the street becomes **Via Buozzi** (and bears slightly left), proceed one block and turn right onto the narrow **Via degli Orai,** which leads to the **Piazza del Duomo,** the heart of the town. Local **COPIT bus** #1 can drop you at Piazza Gavinana (€1, tickets at local *tabacchi*). From there, turn right onto **Via Cavour** and left onto **Via Roma,** which runs into P. del Duomo.

Tourist Office: APT tourist office, P. del Duomo, 4 (☎ 0573 21 622; fax 34 327), in Palazzo dei Vescovi. Friendly English-speaking staff distributes free maps and brochures. Internet service available (€5 per hr.). Open daily 9am-1pm and 3-6pm.

Currency exchange: Cassa di Risparmio di Pistoia e Pescia, V. Roma, 3 (☎ 0573 36 91), next door to the post office. Changes traveler's checks and cash. Open M-F 8:20am-1:20pm and 2:50-3:50pm. The **post office** itself also exchanges currency.

Police: ☎ 112. **Medical Emergency and Ambulance:** ☎ 118.

Pharmacy: V. Cino, 33 (☎ 0573 36 81 80). Open daily 8:30am-1pm and 3:30-8pm.

Hospital: ☎ 0573 35 21.

Internet: Telnet Internet Point, V. G. Carducci, 7, (☎ 0573 99 35 71). €4 per hr. Open M-F 9:30am-1pm and 3:30pm-midnight, Sa and 2nd and 4th Su of the month 3:30-8pm.

Post Office: V. Roma, 5 (☎ 0573 99 52 11). **Currency exchange** and AmEx traveler's checks. Open M-Sa 8:15am-7pm.

Postal Code: 51100.

░░ ACCOMMODATIONS AND FOOD

Rooms at reasonable prices are rare finds in Pistoia, but **Albergo Firenze ❹**, V. Curtatone e Montanara, 42, offers comfort and relative value. From the station walk down V. XX Settembre and continue straight as it goes through several name changes (see **Orientation**) until it becomes V. Curtatone e Montanara. The hotel, indicated by a blue neon sign, is near the end of the street on the right. Rooms have satellite TV and floral and lace decor. (☎/fax 0573 23 141. Breakfast and Internet use included. Singles €37, with bath €46; doubles €62/€72-79. AmEx/MC/V.) At P. Treviso, where V. XX Settembre becomes V. A. Vannucci, **Hotel Piccolo Ritz ❹**, V. A. Vannucci, 67, offers slightly larger rooms at slightly higher prices. From the train station, walk up V. XX Settembre to the first piazza; the hotel is on the right. Most rooms have showers, telephone, satellite TV, and minifridge. (☎ 0573 26 775. Singles €41.32, with bath €61.97; doubles €56.81/€82.63. AmEx/MC/V.)

Grocery stores and specialty shops line the side streets. Bargain hunters browse the **open-air market** in and around P. del Duomo. (Open W and Sa 7:30am-2pm.) There's a daily fruit and vegetable market in P. della Sala, site of food markets since medieval times. (Open daily 8am-7pm.) **Dimeglio supermarket** is on V. Veneto, opposite the train station and to the right. (Open Th-T 8am-10pm, W 8am-1:30pm.) Sample exquisite Italian cuisine and imported wines at **La Botte Gaia ❷**, V. Lastrone, 17/19, or try gourmet cheeses, *antipasti*, *crostini*, and salads. The *bruschette* (€4.70) with sundried tomato and *pecorino* (goat's milk) are small but heavenly. (☎ 0573 36 56 02. *Antipasti* from €4.20, *crostini* from €4. Reservations recommended. Open Tu-Sa 10:30am-3pm and 6:30pm-1am, Su 6:30pm-1am. AmEx/MC/V.) **Trattoria dell'Abbondanza ❷**, V. dell'Abbondanza, 10, serves excellent meals like *Panzanella di Farro* (summer salad with oil-soaked bread, basil, tomatoes, parsley, and garlic) and roasted rabbit. (☎ 0573 36 80 37. *Primi* from €5, *secondi* from €6. Open F-Tu 12:15-2:15pm and 7-10pm, Th 7-10pm). Menus in English, French, German, and Italian offer numerous options at **Ristorante San Jacopo ❸**, V. Crispi, 15. The owner recommends the *macceroni San Jacopo* (€5.50) and *tagliata con restarino* (T-bone steak grilled with rosemary; €10.50). (☎ 0573 27 786. Open W-Su noon-2:30pm and 7-10:30pm, Tu 7-10:30pm. AmEx/MC/V.)

⊙ SIGHTS

CATTEDRALE DI SAN ZENO. Life in Pistoia converges at the **Piazza del Duomo.** The green-and-white marbled duomo houses an impressive store of early Renaissance art, as well as San Zeno's greatest treasure, the ▩**Dossale di San Jacopo.** The tremendously ornate altarpiece, set off in the plain chapel along the right, was worked on by nearly every important Tuscan silversmith between 1287 and 1456, including the young Brunelleschi. (*☎ 0573 25 095. Open daily 8:30am-12:30pm and 3:30-7pm; altar open 11:20am-noon and 4-5:30pm. Modest dress required. Altar entry €2.*)

Designed by Andrea Pisano, the octagonal 14th-century **baptistery** across from the duomo presents a relatively modest interior, enlivened by Nino and Tommaso Pisano's sculpture, *Virgin and Child*. *(Open Tu-Sa 9:30am-12:30pm and 3-6pm, Su 9:30am-12:30pm.)* The **Campanile**, adjacent to the duomo, has been sounding the time since the 12th century. At 66m, the belltower offers a spectacular view; on a clear day, you can see all the way to Florence. *(☎ 0573 21 622. Open F-M 9am-1pm and 3-6pm. Tours must be booked beforehand at the tourist office. €5.)*

PISTOIA'S PALAZZI. Next to the duomo, facing the piazza, stands the 13th-century **Palazzo Comunale.** Left of the central balcony on the facade, about half-way up, an arm reaches out of the wall, brandishing a club above the black marble head below—a tribute to the 1115 Pistoian victory over the Moorish king Musetto. Inside, the Civic Museum houses artwork dating back to the 13th-century. With its Gothic windows and archways, the courtyard is also well worth a peek. *(☎ 0573 37 11 96. Open Tu-Sa 10am-7pm, Su 9am-12:30pm.)* The **Centro Marino Marini** in the **Palazzo del Tau** celebrates one of Italy's most renowned 20th-century artists, native Marino Marini. The collection's pieces are connected by a maze of stairs and include sculptures (many of the sensuous Pomono, ancient Roman fertility goddess), studies, and paintings. *(C. Silvano Fedi, 30. ☎ 0573 30 285. Open May-Sept. Tu-Sa 10am-1pm and 4-7pm, Su 9am-12:30pm. Oct.-Apr. Tu-Sa 10am-1pm and 3-6pm, Su 9am-12:30pm. €3.)*

CHIESA DI SANT'ANDREA. In this typically Pisan-Romanesque church, Giovanni Pisano carved the pulpit now considered his masterpiece. Supported by seven red marble columns, the pulpit's five white marble panels have delicately carved figures illustrating the *Nativity, Adoration of the Magi, Massacre of the Innocents, Crucifixion,* and *Last Judgment*. *(Exit P. del Duomo by V. del Duca, from the corner opposite the duomo, and continue as it changes to V. dei Rossi and then V. Sant'Andrea. ☎ 0573 21 912. Open daily 8:30am-12:30pm and 3:30-6pm; in summer until 7pm.)*

CHIESA DI SAN GIOVANNI FUORCIVITAS. The single-naved interior of this 12th-century church (St. John Outside the City) is a vast, box-like space with vibrant stained glass windows. The church contains Luca della Robbia's *Visitation* and a Romanesque relief of *The Last Supper* on the lintel. Giovanni Pisano's font and Guglielmo de Pisa's pulpit are both among the finest of the 13th-century carving revival. *(At the intersection of V. Cavour and V. Crispi. Open daily 9am-noon and 5-6:30pm.)*

▨ ◗ NIGHTLIFE AND FESTIVALS

With Staropramen, Hopf Weizen, and Bass on tap (€4 per pint), **Vecchia Praga,** P. della Sala, 6, is a beer-lover's haven in a sea of *vino*. Cocktails, liquor, wine, and light meal menu are also available. *(☎ 0573 31 155. Open daily 10-2am. MC/V.)*

Europe's remaining flower children converge annually in Pistoia for the **Pistoia Blues** concert series, held in July. Past performers include B. B. King, Bob Dylan, and David Bowie. *(☎ 0573 35 86; www.pistoiablues.com.)* During the festival, the city allows free camping in designated sites near the stadium. On July 25, Pistoia celebrates the **Giostra dell'Orso** (Joust of the Bear). In accordance with 13th-century custom, 12 contemporary knights from four competing districts joust a defenseless bear-shaped target, earning points for the accuracy of their lunges.

▨ DAYTRIP FROM PISTOIA: MONTECATINI TERME

Despite its fairly small size, Montecatini Terme has 2 train stations (2min. apart). Most trains stop at both. The Stazione Centrale, the farther station from Pistoia, is slightly more centrally located than the Stazione Monsummano. From the former, exit the station, and with your back to the front entrance, walk up V. Manzoni or through P. XX Settembre until you arrive at P. del Popolo. Walk through to Viale Verdi. From Stazione Monsummano, with your back to the station, walk left down C. Matteotti to Stazione Centrale and follow the above directions. Pick up a map and a list of spa locations at the tourist office, Viale Verdi, 66-68. (☎0572 77 22 44. Open M-Sa 9am-12:30pm and 3-6pm, Su 9am-noon.)

A mere 10min. train ride from Pistoia, Montecatini Terme offers budget travelers a taste of the affluent life, without draining too many euros. Famous for its thermal baths, Montecatini Terme is the classic spa town, where well-off Italians and European tourists spend their days relaxing under palm trees and in fancy boutiques.

If you plan to visit many spas, buy a cumulative ticket at Viale Verdi, 41. (☎0572 77 84 52. Open M-F 8am-1pm and 3:30-6:30pm, Sa 8am-noon.) The town's most famous spa is the Neoclassical **Tettuccio**, at the end of Viale Verdi. Bring your own cup, or pay €0.50 to drink the medicinal waters. (☎0572 77 85 01. Open May-Oct. 9am-noon and 4-7pm. €4-8.50.) If you arrive in winter, the **Excelsior** offers similar services year-round. (☎0572 77 85 11. Treatments open M-F 8am-12:30pm and 4-7pm, Sa 8am-12:30pm; thermal wellness open M-Sa 8:30am-7pm, Su 8am-1pm.)

Though Montecatini Terme has several hotels and restaurants, many establishments close during the off season. **Hotel Splendid ❸**, V. Mazzini, 36, is a comfortable year-round option with friendly management. (☎/fax 0572 70 148. Singles €31; doubles €42. Extra person €10). **Corsaro Verde ❷**, P. XX Settembre, 11, is a family-run restaurant that offers a large selection of Tuscan fare. (☎0572 91 16 50. *Primi* from €4.50, *secondi* from €5.20. Open May-Oct. daily 11:30am-3pm and 7-11pm; Nov.-Apr. Tu-Su 11:30am-3pm and 7-11pm. AmEx/MC/V.)

LUCCA   ☎0583

Although it once rivaled Florence and Siena in political and military might, today this charming Tuscan town's medieval wall defends only against traffic and the modern world. Tourists are more successful invaders, drawn to Lucca's winding, canyon-like corridors, amphitheaters, hidden churches, and medieval storefronts. A soothing promenade, with a double avenue of trees, runs along the top of the city walls, and bicycles are the transport vehicles of choice.

☐ TRANSPORTATION

Trains: (☎0583 47 013) in P. Ricasoli, just outside the city walls. Trains provide the most convenient transport to Lucca. Info open daily 8am-noon and 3-8:30pm. To: **Florence** (1½hr., every hr., 5:10am-10:19pm, €4.45); **Pisa** (30min., every hr., 6:40-12:17am, €2); and **Viareggio** (20min., every hr., 6:22am-11:11pm, €2). **Luggage storage** available.

Buses: Lazzi (☎0583 58 40 76), in P. Verdi, next to the tourist office. To **Florence** (1½hr., every hr., 6:25am-6:45pm, €4.50) and **Pisa** (50min., every hr., 5:55am-8pm, €2.10).

Taxis: (☎0583 95 52 00) in P. Verdi, (☎0583 49 49 89) in P. Stazione, (☎0583 49 26 91) in P. Napoleone, and (☎0583 49 41 90) in P. S. Maria.

Bike Rental: Promo Turist, P. S. Maria, 31 (☎348 380 0126), 2 doors down from the regional tourist office. Offers a large selection of bikes and multi-day rentals. Basic bikes €2.10 per hr., €9.30 per day; mountain and racing bikes €3.15/€19.90 per day; and tandem bikes €5.15 per hr. Open daily 9am-8pm. **Antonio Poli,** P. S. Maria, 42 (☎0583 49 37 87; www.biciclettepoli.com), on the other side of the regional tourist info office. Offers virtually identical services and prices. Open daily 8:30am-8pm.

Scooter Rental: Serchio Motori, V. Mazzini, 20 (☎0583 95 42 75). Take a right onto V. Mazzini from train station. 50cc scooters €31 per day. AmEx/MC/V.

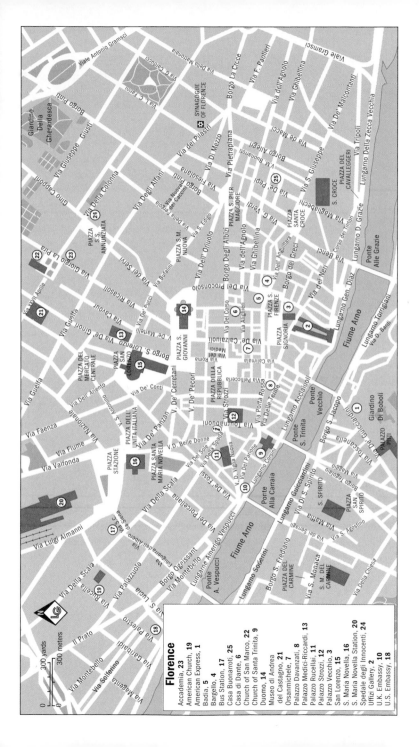

Florence

Accademia, **23**
American Church, **19**
American Express, **1**
Bargello, **4**
Badia, **5**
Bus Station, **17**
Casa Buonarroti, **25**
Casa di Dante, **6**
Church of San Marco, **22**
Church of Santa Trinita, **9**
Duomo, **14**
Museo di Andrea
  del Castagno, **7**
Orsanmichele, **7**
Palazzo Davanzati, **8**
Palazzo Medici-Riccardi, **13**
Palazzo Rucellai, **11**
Palazzo Strozzi, **12**
Palazzo Vecchio, **3**
San Lorenzo, **15**
S. Maria Novella, **16**
S. Maria Novella Station, **20**
Spedale degli Innocenti, **24**
Uffizi Gallery, **2**
U.K. Embassy, **10**
U.S. Embassy, **18**

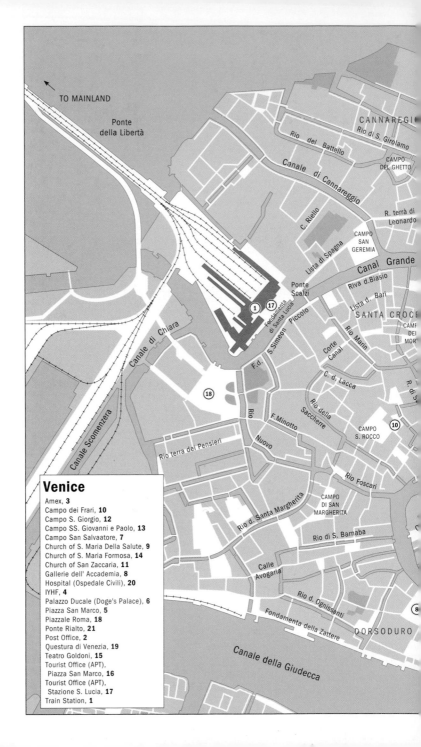

TO MAINLAND

Ponte
della Libertà

CANNAREGI

Rio di S. Girolamo

Rio del Battello

CAMPO
DEL GHETTO

Canale di Cannareggio

C. Riello

R. terrà di
Leonardo

Lista di Spagna

CAMPO
SAN
GEREMIA

Canal Grande

Riva d.Biasio

Ponte
Scalzi

Lista d. Bari

Fondamenta di Santa Lucia

S.Simeon Piccolo

SANTA CROCE

① ⑰

Rio Marin

CAMPO
DEI
MOR

Canale di Chiara

F.d.

Corte
Canal

C. d. Lacca

R. d. S

⑱

Rio della
Saccherre

CAMPO
S. ROCCO

⑩

Canale Scomenzera

Rio

F.Minotto

Nuovo

Rio Foscari

Rio terra dei Pensieri

Rio d. Santa Margherita

CAMPO
DI SAN
MARGHERITA

Rio di S. Barnaba

Calle
Avogaria

Rio d. Ognissanti

⑧

Fondamenta della Zattere

DORSODURO

Canale della Giudecca

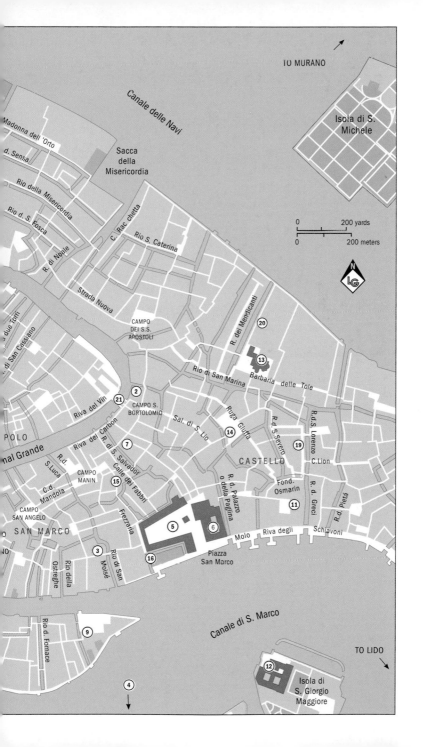

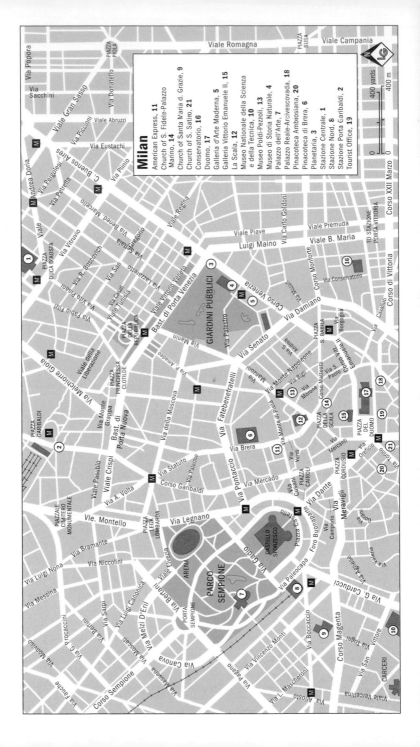

Milan

American Express, **11**
Church of S. Fidele-Palazzo Marino, **14**
Church of Santa Maria d. Grazie, **9**
Church of S. Satiro, **21**
Conservatorio, **16**
Duomo, **17**
Galleria d'Arte Moderna, **5**
Galleria Vittorio Emanuele II, **15**
La Scala, **12**
Museo Nazionale della Scienza e della Tecnica, **10**
Museo Poldi-Pezzoli, **13**
Museo di Storia Naturale, **4**
Palazzo dell'Arte, **7**
Palazzo Reale-Arcivescovada, **18**
Pinacoteca Ambrosiana, **20**
Pinacoteca di Brera, **6**
Planetaria, **3**
Stazione Centrale, **1**
Stazione Nord, **8**
Stazione Porta Garibaldi, **2**
Tourist Office, **19**

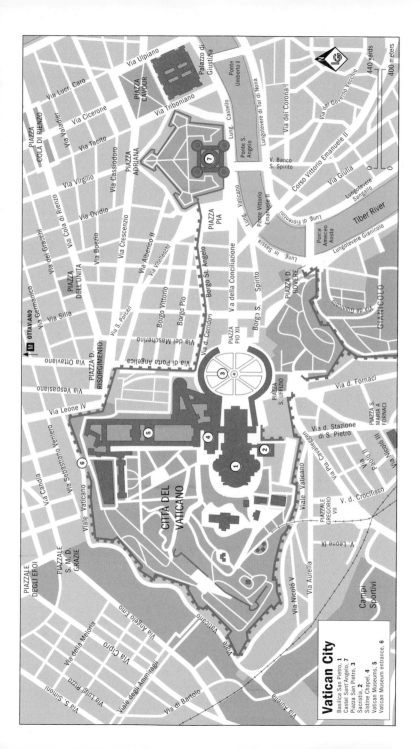

Vatican City

Basilica San Pietro, **1**
Castel Sant'Angelo, **7**
Piazza San Pietro, **3**
Sacristia, **2**
Sistine Chapel, **4**
Vatican Museums, **5**
Vatican Museum entrance, **6**

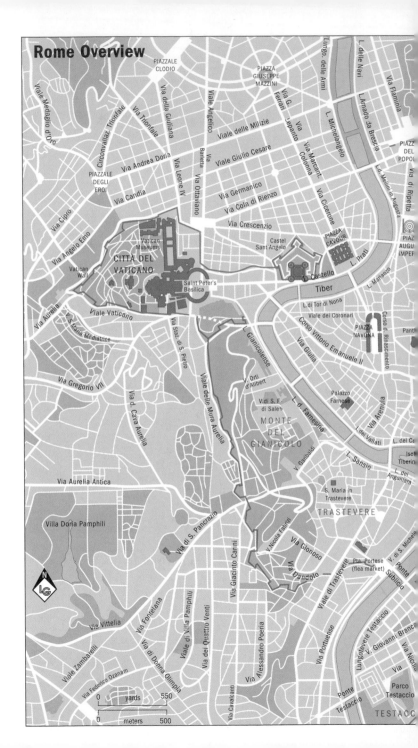

Rome Overview

PIAZZALE CLODIO

PIAZZA GIUSEPPE MAZZINI

Lungo. delle Armi

L. delle Navi

Viale Medaglio d'Oro

Circonvallaz. Trionfale

Via Trionfale

Via della Giuliana

Viale Angelico

Via G. Ferrari

Via Lepanto

Via Marcant. Colonna

Via Michelangelo

Ld. Arnaldo da Brescia

Via Flaminia

PIAZZ DEL POPOL

Viale delle Milizie

Via Andrea Doria

Via Leone IV

Via Barletta

Via Ottaviano

Viale Giulio Cesare

Via Cicerone

Via di Ripetta

PIAZZALE DEGLI EROI

Via Candia

Via Germanico

Via Cola di Rienzo

PIAZZA CAVOUR

Ld. Mellini in Augusta

Via Cipro

Via Angelo Emo

Via Crescenzio

Castel Sant'Angelo

L. Prati

PIAŻ AUGU IMPEF

Vatican Museums

Vatican Wall

CITTÀ DEL VATICANO

Saint Peter's Basilica

L. Castello

L. Marianzo

Tiber

Via Aurelia

V.S. Maria Mediatrice

Viale Vaticano

Via Staz. di S. Pietro

L. di Tor di Nona

Viale dei Coronari

Corso Vittorio Emanuele II

Corso d. Rinascimento

PIAZZA NAVONA

Pant

Via Gregorio VII

Via d. Cava Aurelia

Viale delle Mura Aurelia

L. Giancicolense

Via Giulia

V. Orti d'Alibert

Palazzo Farnese

L. Arenula

L. d. Farnesina

L. dei Vallati

L. del Ce

V.di S. F. di Sales

MONTE DEL GIANICOLO

V. Garibaldi

L. Sansio

Iso Tiberin

L. dei Anguillara

Via Aurelia Antica

S. Maria in Trastevere

Villa Doria Pamphili

TRASTEVERE

V.Nicola Fabrizi

Via Glorioso

V. di S. Michele

Via di S. Pancrazio

Via Giacinto Carini

Via Dandolo

Pta. Portese (flea market)

Ponte Subiglio

Via vitelia

Via Fontelana

Via di Villa Pamphili

Viale dei Quattro Venti

Via Alessandro Poeria

Viale di Trastevere

Via di S. Michele

Viale Zambarelli

Via Federico Ozanam

Via di Donna Olimpia

Via Cavalcanti

Via Portuense

Lungotevere Testaccio

V. Giovanni Branca

Via Nicola

Via

Ponte Testaccio

Parco Testaccio

TESTACC

N LG

0   yards   550

0   meters   500

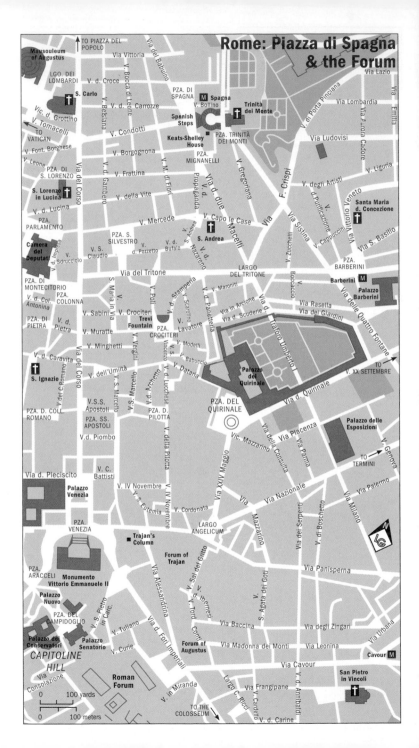

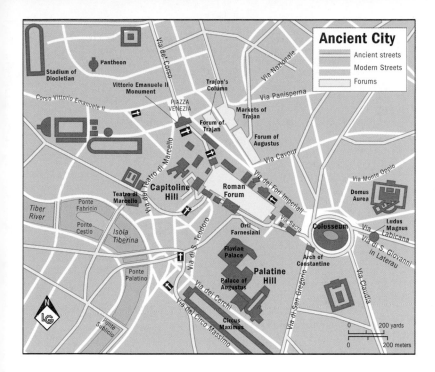

Ancient City

Ancient streets
Modern Streets
Forums

Stadium of Diocletian

Pantheon

Via del Corso

Vittorio Emanuele II Monument

Trajan's Column

Via Nazionale

Via Panisperna

Corso Vittorio Emanuele II

PIAZZA VENEZIA

Markets of Trajan

Forum of Trajan

Forum of Augustus

Via Cavour

Via Monte Oppio

Domus Aurea

Capitoline Hill

Roman Forum

Via dei Fori Imperiali

Ludus Magnus

Via Labicana

Teatro di Marcello

Via del Teatro di Marcello

Tiber River

Ponte Fabricio

Ponte Cestio

Isola Tiberina

Via di S. Teodoro

Orti Farnesiani

Via Sacra

Colosseum

Via di S. Giovanni in Laterau

Ponte Palatino

Flavian Palace

Arch of Constantine

Via Claudia

Palace of Augustus

Palatine Hill

Via San Gregorio

Via dei Cerchi

Ponte Sublicio

Via del Circo Massimo

Circus Maximus

0   200 yards
0   200 meters

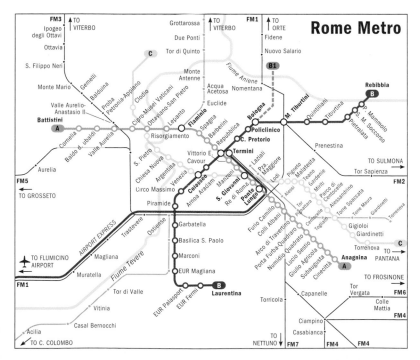

Rome Metro

FM3

TO VITERBO

Ipogeo degli Ottavi

Ottavia

S. Filippo Neri

Monte Mario

Valle Aurelio-Anastasio II

Battistini

Grottarossa

Due Ponti

Tor di Quinto

TO VITERBO

FM1

TO ORTE

Fidene

Nuovo Salario

Monte Antenne

Acqua Acetosa

Nomentana

Euclide

B1

Rebibbia

B

Gemelli

Balduina

Proba Petronia-Appiano

Clodio

Cipro-Musei Vaticani

Ottaviano-San Pietro

Lepanto

Flaminio

Spagna

Barberini

Repubblica

Bologna

M. Tiburtini

Quintiliani

Tiburtina

P. Mammolo

S. M. Soccorso

Pietralata

Cornelia

Baldo d. Ubaldi

Valle Aurelia

Risorgimento

Policlinico

C. Pretorio

Prenestina

Aurelia

S. Pietro

Chiesa Nuova

Argentina

Venezia

Vittorio E. Cavour

Termini

Laziali

Pza. Maggiore

Lodi

Pigneto

Malatesta

Teano

Gardenie

Parco di Centocelle

TO SULMONA

Tor Sapienza

FM2

FM5

TO GROSSETO

Circo Massimo

Colosseo

Manzoni

Arno Aradam

S. Giovanni

Re di Roma

Ponte Lungo

Furio Camillo

Colli Albani

Arco di Travertino

Porta Furba Quadraro

Numidio Quadrato

Lucio Sestio

Giulio Agricola

Subaugusta

Cinecittà

Alessi

Pigliatara

Togliatti

Mirti

Gigioli

Giardinetti

Torre Spaccata

Torre Maura

Giardinetti

Torrenova

C

TO PANTANA

Piramide

AIRPORT EXPRESS

Trastevere

Ostiense

Garbatella

Basilica S. Paolo

Marconi

EUR Magliana

Anagnina

A

TO FROSINONE

TO FLUMICINO AIRPORT

Magliana

Muratella

Fiume Tevere

EUR Palasport

EUR Fermi

Laurentina

B

Torricola

Capannelle

Tor Vergata

FM6

Colle Mattia

FM4

FM1

Tor di Valle

Vitinia

Casal Bernocchi

Acilia

TO C. COLOMBO

Ciampino

Casabianca

TO NETTUNO

FM7

FM4

FM4

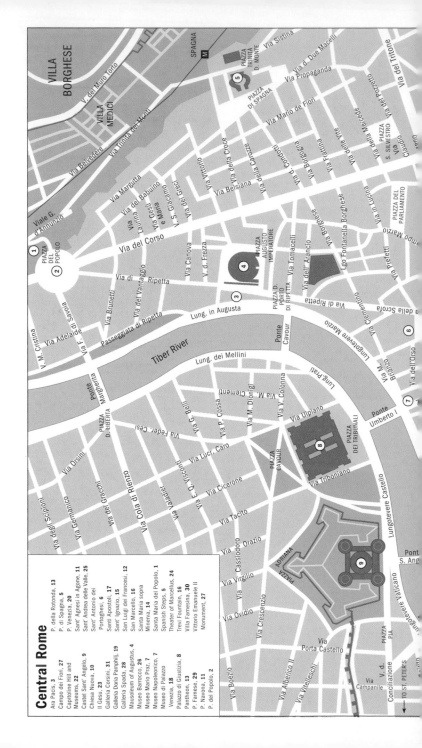

Central Rome

Ara Pacis, **3**
Campo dei Fiori, **27**
Capitoline Hill and Museums, **22**
Castel Sant' Angelo, **9**
Chiesa Nuova, **10**
Il Gesù, **23**
Galleria Corsini, **31**
Galleria Doria Pamphilj, **19**
Galleria Spada, **28**
Mausoleum of Augustus, **4**
Museo Barrocco, **26**
Museo Mario Praz, **7**
Museo Napoleonico, **7**
Museo di Palazzo Venezia, **18**
Palazzo di Giustizia, **8**
Pantheon, **13**
P. Farnese, **29**
P. Navona, **11**
P. del Popolo, **2**
P. della Rotonda, **13**
P. di Spagna, **5**
P. Venezia, **20**
Sant' Agnese in Agone, **11**
Sant' Andrea delle Valle, **25**
Sant' Antonio dei Portoghesi, **6**
Santi Apostoli, **17**
Sant' Ignazio, **15**
San Luigi dei Francesi, **12**
San Marcello, **16**
Santa Maria sopra Minerva, **14**
Santa Maria del Popolo, **1**
Spanish Steps, **5**
Theater of Marcellus, **24**
Trevi Fountain, **16**
Villa Farnesina, **30**
Vittorio Emanuele II Monument, **27**

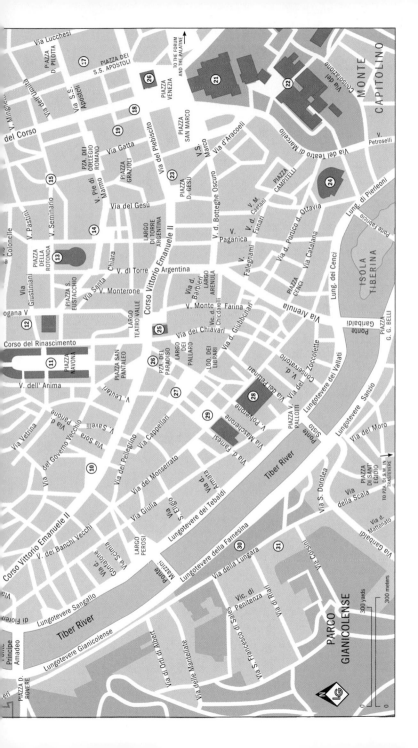

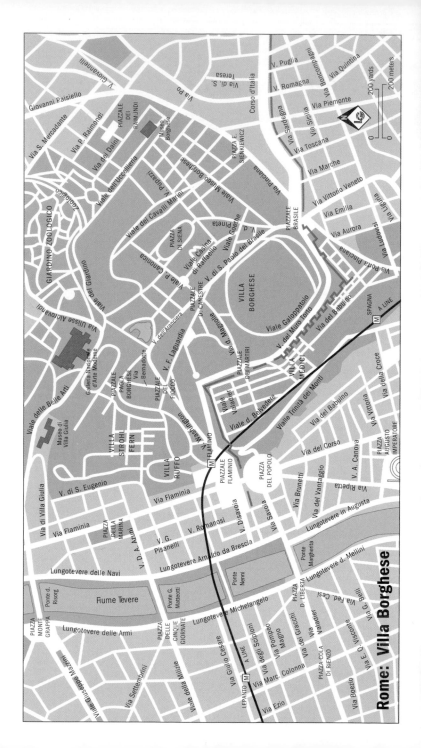

Rome: Villa Borghese

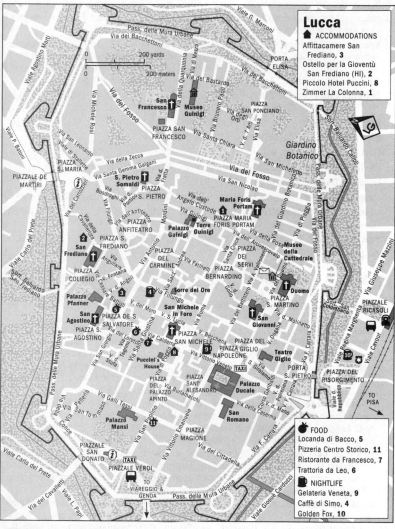

Lucca

🏠 ACCOMMODATIONS
Affittacamere San
  Frediano, **3**
Ostello per la Gioventù
  San Frediano (HI), **2**
Piccolo Hotel Puccini, **8**
Zimmer La Colonna, **1**

🍴 FOOD
Locanda di Bacco, **5**
Pizzeria Centro Storico, **11**
Ristorante da Francesco, **7**
Trattoria da Leo, **6**

🍷 NIGHTLIFE
Gelateria Veneta, **9**
Caffè di Simo, **4**
Golden Fox, **10**

CENTRAL ITALY

✦ 🛈 ORIENTATION AND PRACTICAL INFORMATION

To reach the center of town from the train station, cross the roadway and turn left.
Enter the city with the cars at **Porta San Pietro** to your right, then head left on **Corso Garibaldi**. Turn right on **Via Vittorio Veneto** and follow it one block to **Piazza Napoleone** (P. Grande), the hub of the city. If you arrive by bus, follow **Via San Paolino** toward the center of town and turn onto V. V. Veneto to reach the piazza.

  Tourist Office: Centro Accoglienza Turistica (☎0583 58 31 50), in Piazzale Verdi.
Walk into the city through Porta S. Pietro, turn left on V. Carrara and then right onto V.
Veneto. Turn left on V. S. Paolino and continue to P. Verdi. Office is on the right. English-

speaking staff provides maps, as well as train and bus info. Offers self-guided audio tours (€9 for one unit, €12 for two) and bike rental (€2.10 per hr.). Free room reservation service, but not for the cheaper hotels. Open daily 9am-7pm.

Agenzia per il Turismo, P. Santa Maria, 35 (☎0583 91 99 31). From V. Roma, take a left onto V. Fillungo. Follow V. Fillungo until it ends and take a left onto V. S. Gemma Galgani and a left into P. S. Maria. The office is on the left between the two bike shops. Detailed brochures and hotel reservation service. Open daily 9am-7pm.

Currency Exchange: Credito Italiano, P. S. Michele, 47 (☎0583 47 546). 24hr. **ATM** in front. Open M-F 8:20am-1:20pm and 2:45-4:15pm, Sa 8:20-11:50am.

Luggage Storage: In train station. €2-3.60 per 12hr. At tourist office, €0.50 per hr.

Emergency: ☎113. **Carabinieri:** ☎112.

First Aid: Misericordia, ☎118.

24-Hour Pharmacy: Farmacia Comunale, V. S. Girolamo, 16, off P. Napoleone.

Hospital: Campo di Marte (☎0583 97 01).

Laundry: Lavanderia Niagara, V. Michele Rosi, (☎0335 629 2055). Open daily 8am-10pm.

Internet Access: Internet Zone, V. Cesare Battisti, 58/60, (☎583 469 873). €2.50 per hr. Open daily 10-2am.

Post Office: (☎0583 43 351), on V. Vallisneri, off P. del Duomo. Open M-Sa 8:15am-7pm.

Postal Code: 55100.

ACCOMMODATIONS

Ostello per la Gioventù San Frediano (HI), V. della Cavallerizza, 12 (☎0583 46 99 57; www.ostellolucca.it). From P. Napoleone, turn onto V. Beccheria and walk for 2 blocks. Take a right onto V. Roma and your 1st left onto V. Fillungo. 6 blocks later, take a left onto P. S. Frediano and then a right at the church onto V. della Cavalleriza. The hostel is on your left (15min.). Good-sized rooms and immaculate modern bathrooms. HI card required. Breakfast €1.55, meals €8. Towels €1.50. Internet and laundry facilities available. Reception daily 10-1am. Check-in 3:30pm-1am. Lockout 9:45am-3:30pm. Curfew 1am. Dorms €15, with bath €16. Family rooms with bath €19.50 per person. ❶

Affittacamere San Frediano, V. degli Angeli, 19 (☎0583 46 96 30; sanfredianolu@onenet.it). Follow directions to HI hostel, but take a left onto arched V. degli Angeli, 2 blocks before P. S. Frediano. All rooms with TV. Basic breakfast included. Singles €36.15, with bath €46.50; doubles €46.50/€62. AmEx/MC/V. ❹

Zimmer La Colonna, V. dell'Angelo Custode, 16 (☎/fax 0583 44 01 70 or 339 460 7152), just off P. Maria Foris Portam. Spacious rooms with über-modern bathrooms and TV. Some rooms have enormous windows opening onto a quiet courtyard. Prices drop €5 per person in winter. Singles €47; doubles €62; triples €78. ❹

Piccolo Hotel Puccini, V. di Poggio, 9 (☎0583 55 421). Around the corner from Puccini's birthplace, each room is decorated with framed playbills from his operas. Attentive owner speaks English, Spanish, and French. Cozy, comfortable rooms have TV, telephone, and safe. Singles €55; doubles €80. AmEx/MC/V. ❹

FOOD

The **central market** occupies the large building on the east side of P. del Carmine. (Open M-Sa 7am-1pm and 4-7:30pm.) An **open-air market** overruns V. dei Bacchettoni. (W and Sa 8am-1pm.) The closest supermarket is **Superal**, V. Diaz, 124. Turn right from Porta Elisa, and take the first left onto V. Diaz. The supermarket is at the end of the block on the right. (☎0583 49 05 96. Open M-Tu and Th-Su 8am-8pm, W 8am-1:30pm.) You may have to hunt for Lucca's cheaper restaurants.

▨ **Pizzeria Centro Storico,** V. S. Paolina (☎ 0583 53 409), at the intersection with V. Galli Tassi. English and German-speaking owner Michele has many fans. Slices of pizza €1.70, *primi* €5, and *secondi* €4.95. Open daily 9am-midnight. AmEx/MC/V. ❶

▨ **Ristorante da Francesco,** Corte Portici, 13 (☎ 0583 41 80 49), off V. Calderia between P. S. Salvatore and P. S. Michele. Try the spaghetti with mussels and pesto (€4.70). *Primi* €4.10-5.70, *secondi* from €6.70. Wine €7.20 per liter. Cover €1.50. Open Tu-Su noon-2:30pm and 8-10:30pm. ❷

    Trattoria da Leo, V. Tegrimi, 1 (☎ 0583 49 22 36; www.trattoriadaleo.it), off P. del Salvatore— ask for it by name. A bustling local hangout specializing in *minestra di farro* (€4.70). *Primi* €4.70, *secondi* from €7.80. Cover €1.10. Open M-Sa noon-2:30pm and 7:30-10:30pm. ❷

    Locanda di Bacco, V. S. Giorgio, 36 (☎ 0583 49 31 36). Extensive menu makes this a nice place to splurge, so go ahead and order a few extra courses. Try the *petto d' anastra* (breast of duck; €8.80). *Primi* from €4.70, *secondi* from €7.50. Open W-M noon-2:30pm and 8-10:30pm. AmEx/MC/V. ❷

⚆ SIGHTS

PIAZZA NAPOLEONE. This piazza, in the heart of Lucca, is the town's administrative center. The 16th-century **Palazzo Ducale** now houses government offices. In the evening, P. Napoleone is packed with *Luccese* young and old, out for their *passeggiata*. **Piazza Anfiteatro** is also quite popular with locals and tourists alike. The surrounding buildings shoulder one another, creating a nearly seamless oval wall.

▨ **DUOMO DI SAN MARTINO.** The architects designed the facade of this ornate, asymmetrical duomo around its bell tower, constructed two centuries earlier. The 13th-century reliefs that decorate the exterior include Nicola Pisano's *Journey of the Magi* and *Deposition*. Matteo Civitali, Lucca's famous sculptor, designed the floor, contributed the statue of St. Martin to the right of the door, and designed his prized piece, the *Tempietto*, located half-way up the left aisle, housing the **Volto Santo** (Holy Face). Reputedly carved by Nicodemus at Calvary, this wooden crucifix is said to depict the true image of Christ. The statue passed into the hands of the bishop of Lucca, who set off in a boat without a crew or sails and miraculously landed safely at Luni. To settle the ownership dispute that arose between Lucca and Luni, the statue was placed on an ox-cart. The oxen turned toward Lucca. The Volto is taken for a ride through the town every September 13 to commemorate the oxen's wise choice. Don't miss Tintoretto's *Last Supper*, in the 3rd chapel on the right. The **sacristy** contains the well-preserved *Madonna and Saints* by Ghirlandaio and Jacopo della Quercia's masterly **sarcophagus**, adorned with a life-size sculpture of Ilaria del Carretto. The **Museo Della Cattedrale,** around the corner from the duomo, has glass cases of religious objects taken from the duomo. An enlightening guided audio tour is free with admission. *(P. S. Marino, between bell tower and post office. From P. Napoleone, take V. del Duomo. Duomo open M-F 9am-6pm, Sa 9am-7pm, Su 8:30am-6:30pm. Sacristy open M-F 9:30am-5:45pm, Sa 9:30am-6:45pm, Su 9-9:50am, 11:30-11:50am, and 1-5:45pm. €2. Museo della Cattedrale open Apr.-Oct. daily 10am-6pm; Nov.-Mar. M-F 10am-2pm, Sa-Su 10am-5pm. €3.50. Combination ticket for the Sacristy, Museo della Cattedrale, and Chiesa di S. Giovanni €5.50.)*

CHIESA DI SAN GIOVANNI. This unassuming church hides an archeological treasure trove. Under the large, simple plaster dome of the left transept is the entrance to a recently excavated, 2nd-century AD Roman complex. The ruins of a private house and bath (and the church's foundations), as well as some 12th-century graffiti, are exposed under the floor. *(Walk past San Giovanni from P. S. Martino and around the corner to the right. Open Apr.-Oct. daily 10am-6pm; Nov.-Mar. Sa-Su 10am-5pm. €2.50.)*

CHIESA DI SAN FREDIANO. Off P. Scalpellini rises this imposing Romanesque church, the facade of which is graced by Berlinghieri's spectacular *Ascension*, a huge polychromatic mosaic. Inside, the second chapel on the right holds the remains of S. Zita, the beloved Virgin of Lucca. Despite the myth that she lies untouched by time, she appears to be decaying in her glass-enclosed coffin. Amico Aspertini's frescoes of the *Legend of the Volto Santo* decorate the chapel on the left. *(From P. S. Michele, take V. Fillungo to P. S. Frediano. Open 8am-noon and 2:30-6:30pm.)*

CASA PUCCINI (BIRTHPLACE OF GIACOMO PUCCINI). Music lovers shouldn't miss the birthplace of Giacomo Puccini, composer of *La Bohème* and *Madame Butterfly*. This plain stucco house has airy, tiled rooms exhibiting the piano on which Puccini composed his last opera, *Turandot*. Admire his letters and manuscripts, while strains of his operas filter through the apartment. *(C. S. Lorenzo, 9, off V. Poggi. His apartment is on the 4th floor. ☎ 0583 58 40 28. Open June-Sept. daily 10am-6pm; Mar.-May and Oct.-Dec. Tu-Su 10am-1pm and 3-6pm; Jan.-Feb. closed. €3.)*

TORRE GUINIGI AND TORRE DELLA ORE. The **Torre Guinigi** tower rises above Lucca from the mute stone mass of Palazzo Guinigi. While the *palazzo* is not open to the public, the narrow tower is. At the top of 230 stairs, the 360-degree view of Lucca and the surrounding hills from behind the railings but in front of the large planters, is stunning. *(V. S. Andrea, 41. From P. S. Michele, follow V. Roma for 1 block and take a left onto V. Fillungo, and a right onto V. S. Andrea. Open daily June-Sept. 9am-midnight; Oct.-Jan. 9am-4pm; Feb.-May 9am-6pm. €3.10.)* For a similar view, you can climb the 207 steps of the **Torre della Ore** (clock towers), two of the 15 towers that remain of medieval Lucca's original 250. *(V. Fillungo, 22. Follow the directions to Torre Guinigi, and you'll pass it on V. Fillungo. Open daily 10am-8pm. €3.10.)*

■BALUARDI. No tour of Lucca is complete without a walk or bike ride around the perfectly intact city walls. The shaded 4km path, which remains closed to cars, passes grassy parks and cool fountains as it progresses along the *baluardi* (battlements). From here, appreciate the layout of the city and the beautiful countryside high above the moat; it's perfect for a breezy afternoon picnic and *siesta*.

■ ♫ NIGHTLIFE AND ENTERTAINMENT

Lucca's calendar bulges with artistic performances, especially during the summer. The **Summer Festival** takes place throughout July and has featured performances by pop stars such as Jamiroquai, Paul Simon, Rod Stewart, and Oasis. (☎ 0584 46 477; www.summer-festival.com.) Sample **Teatro Comunale del Giglio**'s opera season, starting at the end of September, or their ballet season, starting in January. The king of Lucca's festivals is the **Settembre Lucchese** (Sept. 13-22), a lively jumble of artistic, athletic, and folkloric presentations. The annual **Palio della Balestra,** a crossbow competition dating from 1443 and revived for tourists in the early 1970s, takes place here. Participants wear traditional costume on July 12 and September 14 for the competition. (www.luccavirtuale.it/rubriche/balestrieri/palio.htm.)

Gelateria Veneta, V. Vittorio Veneto, 74 (☎ 0583 46 70 37). For evidence that Lucca is, at its heart, a sleepy Tuscan town, look no further than this *gelateria* on a Saturday night. That's right, the place to see and be seen on the late night scene is an ice cream shop. Crowds throng on V. Vittorio Veneto, and Veneta serves as the epicenter of activity. Cones €1.60-3.50. Open Su-F 10-1am, Sa 10-2am.

Caffè Di Simo, V. Fillungo, 58 (☎ 0583 49 62 34). Chandeliers, marble tables, and a zinc bar. In the 19th century, the cafe was frequented by artists, writers, Risorgimento-plotters and musicians (like Puccini), but they probably didn't have to pay the €2.10 that customers are now charged for a cup of coffee. You will if you sit down. Instead, have your cup of joe while standing at the bar for just €0.90. Open Tu-Sa 8am-10pm.

Golden Fox, V. R. Margherita, 207 (☎0583 49 16 19). From train station, cross Piazzale Ricasoli and take a left on V. R. Margherita. Bar is on the left. Brass and dark wood adorn this spacious English-style pub. A mostly Italian crowd comes to hang out, drink beer (€4.50 per pint), and listen to loud American music. Open daily 8pm-2am.

PISA
☎050

Each year in the Campo dei Miracoli, millions of tourists arrive to marvel at the famous leaning tower, forming a T-shirt-buying, ice-cream-licking, photo-snapping mire. The tower is indeed remarkable, all the more so given its role in rescuing Pisa from obscurity. In the Middle Ages, when the Arno flowed continuously to the Mediterranean, the city earned its living as a port and had a trade empire that extended to Corsica, Sardinia, and the Balearics. But with time, the Arno filled with silt and Pisa's fortunes dried up. Luckily, the impressive tower brought tourist revenues to revive the cathedral, baptistery, museums, and cemetery that cluster in the same piazza. Today, Pisa also thrives as a university town, attested to by the innumerable copy shops and bookstores. Wander around the sprawling university neighborhood, through Piazzas Cavalieri and Dante Alighieri, and along picturesque alleys lined with elegant buildings and impassioned political graffiti.

▐ TRANSPORTATION

Flights: Galileo Galilei Airport (☎050 50 07 07). Trains that make the 5min. trip (€1) between the train station and the airport coincide with flight departures and arrivals. You can also take bus #3 from the airport, which will take you to the train station and other points in Pisa and its environs (10min. from the airport and the station, every 20min., €0.77). Charter, domestic, and international flights. To: **London** (2¼hr., 11 per day); **Munich** (1½hr., 3 per day); and **Paris** (2hr., 3 per day).

Trains: (☎147 80 888), in P. della Stazione, at southern end of town. Info office open daily 7am-9pm. Ticket booths open 6am-9:30pm; 24hr. self-service ticket machines available. To: **Genoa** (2½hr., 2:37am-7:03pm, €7.90); **Florence** (1hr., every hr., 4:12am-11:03pm, €4.85); **Livorno** (20min., every hr., €1.50); and **Rome** (3hr., 12 per day, €15.40-23.50). Local regional trains to **Lucca** (20min., every 30min., 6:24am-9:40pm, €1.76) stop at Pisa's **San Rossore,** closer to the duomo and the youth hostel. If leaving Pisa from S. Rossore, buy train tickets at *tabacchi,* as there is no ticket office in the station.

Buses: Lazzi, P. Emanuele, 11 (☎050 46 288). To: **Florence** (change at Lucca, 2½hr., every hr., €5.80); **La Spezia** (3hr., 4 per day, €5.80); **Lucca** (40min., every hr., €2.10); and **Pistoia** (1½hr., 3 per day, €4.50). **CPT** (☎800 01 27 73), in P. Sant'Antonio, near train station. To **Livorno** (45min., 5am-7:30pm, €2.17) and **Volterra** (1½hr., 7 per day, €4.91) via Pontederra.

Taxis: Radio Taxi (☎050 54 16 00 or 41 252) in P. Stazione, (☎050 56 18 78) in P. Duomo, and (☎050 28 542) at the airport.

Car Rental: Avis (☎050 42 028; 25+), **Hertz** (☎050 43 220; 23+), and **Maggiore** (☎050 42 574; 21+) have offices at the airport. From €61 per day.

◪ ▐ ORIENTATION AND PRACTICAL INFORMATION

Pisa lies on Italy's Tyrrhenian coast, near the mouth of the Arno, west of Florence. Most of Pisa's sights lie to the north of the Arno; the main train station lies to the south. To reach the **Campo dei Miracoli (Piazza del Duomo)** from the station, take bus #3 (tickets sold in *tabacchi,* €0.75). Alternatively, walk straight up **Viale Gramsci,** through **Piazza Vittorio Emanuele,** and stroll along **Corso Italia** across the Arno, where it becomes **Via Borgo Stretto.** From the university district, turn left on V. U. Dini to pass through P. dei Cavalieri, and head toward the duomo and tower.

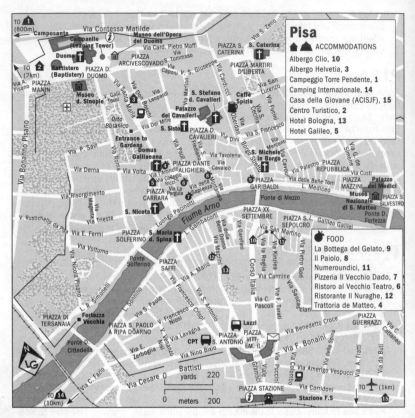

Pisa

▲ ▲ ACCOMMODATIONS

Albergo Clio, **10**
Albergo Helvetia, **3**
Campeggio Torre Pendente, **1**
Camping Internazionale, **14**
Casa della Giovane (ACISJF), **15**
Centro Turistico, **2**
Hotel Bologna, **13**
Hotel Galileo, **5**

🍎 FOOD

La Bottega del Gelato, **9**
Il Paiolo, **8**
Numeroundici, **11**
Pizzeria Il Vecchio Dado, **7**
Ristoro al Vecchio Teatro, **6**
Ristorante Il Nuraghe, **12**
Trattoria de Matteo, **4**

Tourist Office, (☎ 050 42 291; www.turismo.toscana.it), in P. della Stazione, to the left as you exit the station. English-speaking staff provides detailed maps. No accommodations service, but they do provide a very detailed listing of all the local hotels and campsites, including prices and locations. Open Apr.-Oct. M-Sa 9am-7pm, Su 9:30am-3:30pm; Nov.-Mar. M-Sa 9am-6pm, Su 9:30am-3:30pm. Another **branch** (☎ 050 56 04 64) is behind the leaning tower. Open M-Sa 9am-7pm, Su 10:30am-4:30pm.

Budget Travel: CTS, V. S. Maria, 12 (☎ 050 48 300 or 29 221; fax 45 431), by the Hotel Galileo. International tickets and boats to nearby islands. English spoken. Open M-F 9:30am-12:30pm and 4-7pm, Sa 9:30am-12:30pm.

Luggage Storage: At the airport. Drop-off available 10am-6pm, pick-up 8am-8pm. €6 per bag per day.

English-Language Bookstore: The Bookshop, V. Rigattieri, 33/39 (☎ 050 57 34 34). Best English-language selection in town. Classics, guide books, and some contemporary titles. Open Aug.-June Su-F 9am-8pm; July Su-F 9am-1pm and 4-8pm. V.

Gay and Lesbian Resources: ARCI-GAY "Pride!" V. S. Lorenzo, 38 (☎ 050 55 56 18; www.gay.it/pride). Open M-F 1:30-7:30pm.

Laundromats: Lavanderia, V. Corridoni, 100. Turn right from the train station. Wash €3 per 7kg, dry €3. Open daily 8am-10pm. **Speedy Wash,** V. Trento, 9 (☎ 050 48 353). Wash €3.50, dry €3.10. Soap €0.50. Open Tu-F 9am-8:30pm, Sa 2-8pm.

Emergency: ☎113. **Medical Emergency:** ☎118.

Police: ☎050 58 35 11.

24-Hour Pharmacy: Farmacia (☎050 54 40 02), V. Lugarno Mediceo, 51.

Hospital: (☎050 99 21 11), on V. Bonanno near P. del Duomo.

Internet Access: Pisa Internet Point, V. Colombo, 53 (☎050 220 0408), 2 blocks from the train station. €4.65 per hr., students €3.61. Open M-Sa 10am-10pm. **Internet Planet,** P. Cavolloti (☎050 83 97 92; info@internetplanet.it). From P. del Duomo, follow V. S. Maria and take 2nd left onto P. Cavolloti. €2 per 30min., €3.10 per hr. Open M-Sa 10am-midnight, Su 3pm-midnight.

Post Office: P. Emanuele, 8 (☎050 18 69), near the station. Open M-Sa 8:30am-7pm.

Postal Code: 56100.

ACCOMMODATIONS & CAMPING

Pisa has plenty of cheap *pensioni* and *locande*, always in high demand. Call ahead for reservations, or pick up the hotel booklet and map at the tourist office.

Albergo Helvetia, V. Don G. Boschi, 31 (☎050 55 30 84), off P. Archivescovado, 2min. from the duomo. Large, clean rooms. Most rooms face a quiet courtyard; all have TV. Bar downstairs. English spoken. Breakfast (must order the night before, served 8:30-11am) €4.50. Reception open 8am-midnight. Singles €32; doubles €42, with bath €57; triples with bath €72; quads with bath €92. ❸

Centro Turistico Madonna dell'Acqua, V. Pietrasantina, 15 (☎050 89 06 22), behind old Catholic sanctuary 2km from the Tower. Bus #3 from station (4 per hr., last 9:45pm); ask driver to stop at *ostello*. Board the bus across the street from 1st departure point in piazza, just outside the Hotel Cavalieri, to avoid making a detour to the airport. Located next to a creek where mosquitoes linger and crickets sing you to sleep. Kitchen available. Sheets €1. Reception daily 6-midnight. Check-out 9:30am. Dorms €15; doubles €42; triples €54; quads €64. MC/V. ❶

Albergo Clio, V. S. Lorenzino, 3 (☎050 284 46), off C. Italia, 1 block from the Ponte Mezzo. Vintage Hollywood dream of a lobby: pink chairs, black-and-white tiled floor, and mirrored moldings. Tiled hallways lead to modern rooms and tidy bathrooms. Singles €28.32; doubles €41.32, with bath €51.56; triples with bath €62.❸

Casa della Giovane (ACISJF), V. F. Corridoni, 29 (☎050 43 061), 10min. to the right from the station. Nuns kindly welcome travelers of any faith, provided they happen to be female. Large kitchen, dining facilities, Internet, and private bicycle parking. All rooms have baths. Reception daily 7am-10pm. Check-out 9am. Curfew 10pm. Singles €25.85; doubles €31. ❸

Hotel Galileo, V. S. Maria, 12 (☎050 40 621). A solar system of spacious rooms. Stellar proprietress. Don't be put off by the dark entryway—sunny skies are ahead. Groups of four should ask for the massive room. Singles with bath €42; doubles €42, with bath €55; triples €57/€70.❹

Hotel Bologna, V. Mazzini, 57 (☎050 50 21 20). If you dig complimentary shower caps, elevators, and front-desk service that extends beyond handing over the keys, this is the place for you. Rooms with wood floors, cherubic paintings, and bath. Breakfast included. English spoken. Internet €1 per hr. Check-out by 11am. Singles €65; doubles €85; triples €105; quads €125. AmEx/MC/V. ❺

Camping: Campeggio Torre Pendente, V. delle Cascine, 86 (☎050 56 17 04), 1km away from tower. Bus #3 to P. Manin. With city wall on right, walk 2 blocks and take left onto V. delle Cascine, following camping signs. Walk through long concrete underpass, emerge, and walk past industrial-looking buildings; campground on right, in a convenient location. Swimming pool and decent bathrooms. Open Easter-Oct. €6.75 per person, €3.20 per child, €4.20 per tent. Bungalows €32-82. ❶

Camping Internazionale (☎050 35 211), 10km away on V. Litoranea in Marina di Pisa, across from its private beach. Take CPT bus (intercity bus) from P. S. Antonio to Marina di Pisa (buy ticket in CPT office as you enter P. S. Antonio from P. V. Emanuele; €1.50). Open May-Sept. €5 per person, €4 per child, €6 per small tent, €7.50 per large tent. July-Aug. prices increase by €1-2. AmEx/MC/V. ❶

🍴 FOOD

For more authentic ambiance than that of the touristy *trattorie*, head toward the river. Cheap restaurants are plentiful in the university area. In **P. Vettovaglie**, produce and haggling from the open-air market spill into nearby streets. Bakeries and *salumerie* fill Pisa's residential quarter. For conveniently pre-packaged goods, try **Superal**, V. Pascoli, 6, just off C. Italia. (Open M-Sa 8am-8pm.)

Il Paiolo, V. Curtatone Montanara, 9 (☎050 42 528), near the university. Lively pub atmosphere. Order their hearty *bistecca* (steak with mushrooms, arugula, nuts and parmesan cheese), or try their heavenly *risotto*, with mussels, tiny calamari, and chunks of salmon (€5.20), with the light, sweet house white wine (¼ liter €2.10). *Primi* and *secondi* from €4.15-7.75. Open M-F noon-3pm and 7pm-1am, Sa 7pm-1am. ❷

Numeroundici, V. S. Martino, 47. Eat generous-sized sandwiches (€2.50) and superb vegetable *torte* (€2.30) in the airy dining area. *Primi* €4, *secondi* €6. Open M-F noon-10pm, Sa 5-10pm. ❷

Trattoria da Matteo, V. l'Aroncio, 46 (☎050 41 057), off V. S. Maria near Hotel Galileo. *Gnocchi al pesto* €5. *Scaloppina con funghi* (veal with mushrooms; €6.40). *Menù* €12. Cover €1. Open Su-F 9am-3pm and 6-11pm. Bar open noon-11pm. V. ❸

Ristoro al Vecchio Teatro, V. Collegio Ricci, 2 (☎050 20 210), off P. Dante. Delicious and innovative cuisine built around fresh vegetables. Try the *risotto mare* (rice with seafood, €6) or the buttery *sfogliata di zucchine* (zucchini tort; €7). *Primi* €6, *secondi* €7. Desserts €3. Open Su-Th 12:15-3pm, F-Sa 12:15-3pm and 8-10pm. Closed Aug. AmEx/MC/V. ❸

Pizzeria Il Vecchio Dado, Luongo Pacinotti, 21-22 (☎/fax 050 58 09 00). On the Arno, this restaurant offers excellent pizza (from €3.10). Other meal options available. Open F-Tu 12:30-3pm and 7:30pm-12:30am. In winter, closes at 10pm. MC/V. ❷

Ristorante Il Nuraghe, V. Mazzini, 58 (☎050 44 368), near the Hotel Bologna. Features Sardinian specialties. Pick from among the numerous seafood dishes or try *sa fregula* (pasta in broth with saffron). *Primi* from €4.50, *secondi* from €6. *Menù* €13-25. Open Tu-Su noon-2pm and 7:30-10:30pm. AmEx/MC/V. ❸

La Bottega del Gelato, P. Garibaldi, 11. Offers huge range of flavors, from Nutella to pistachio. Popular after sundown. Cones and cups €1.20. Open Th-Tu 11am-1am. ❶

👁 SIGHTS

Campo dei Miracoli (Field of Miracles) is an appropriate nickname for **Piazza del Duomo.** The **Leaning Tower, duomo, baptistery,** and **Camposanto** all rise improbably from manicured swaths of plush, emerald green grass that surround the field.

LEANING TOWER. A close inspection reveals that all the buildings in the Campo dei Miracoli are leaning at different angles, thanks to shifting soil. None lean quite so dramatically or famously as the *campanile* of the duomo. Bonanno Pisano began building the tower in 1173, and it had reached the height of 10m when the soil beneath unexpectedly shifted. The tilt intensified after WWII, when ever-more tourists were ascending; it continues to slip 1-2mm every year. In June of 2001, the steel safety cables and iron girdles that had imprisoned the tower during a multi-year stabilization effort were finally removed. One year later, the tower reopened, albeit in a tightly regulated manner. Guided tours of 40 visitors are permitted to ascend the 300 steps once every 40min. *(Make reservations at the ticket offices in the Museo del Duomo or next to the tourist information office. Tours 8:30am-7:50pm. Childen under 8 not permitted, under 18 must be accompanied by an adult. €15.)*

■ **DUOMO.** The dark green-and-white facade of the duomo is the archetype of the Pisan-Romanesque style; indeed, it is one of the most important Romanesque cathedrals in the world. Begun in 1063 by Boschetto (who had himself entombed in the wall), the cathedral was the Campo's first structure. Enter the five-aisled nave through Bonanno Pisano's bronze doors (1180). Although most of the interior was destroyed by fire in 1595, paintings by Ghirlandaio hang along the right wall, Cimabue's spectacular gilded mosaic *Christ Pantocrator* graces the apse, and bits of the Cosmati pavement remain. The cathedral's elaborate chandelier is rumored (falsely) to have inspired Galileo's theories of universal gravity. Giovanni Pisano's last and greatest pulpit, designed to outdo his father's in the baptistery, sits majestically at the heart of the cathedral. Relief panels depict classical and biblical subjects, including the Nativity, the Last Judgment, and the Massacre of the Innocents. Always up for good allegory, Pisano carved the pulpit's supports into figures symbolizing the arts and virtues. *(Open M-Sa 10am-7:30pm, Su 1-7:30pm. €2. Free for Su mass, but you must look very pious to get past the rigid guards.)*

■ **BAPTISTERY.** The baptistery, an enormous barrel of a building, was begun in 1152 by a man known as Deotisalvi ("God save you"). It measures 107m in girth and reaches up 55m into the Pisan sky. Its architecture is a blend of styles, incorporating typical Tuscan-Romanesque stripes with a stunning Gothic ensemble of gables, pinnacles, and statuary. Nicola Pisano's pulpit (1260), to the left of the baptismal font, recaptures the sobriety and dignity of classical antiquity and is one of the harbingers of Renaissance art in Italy. The dome's acoustics are astounding—an unamplified choir singing in the baptistery can be heard 2km away. A staircase, embedded in the wall, leads to an interior balcony; farther up you can catch glimpses of the town through the narrow windows. *(Open late Apr.-late Sept. daily 8am-7:30pm; Oct.-Mar. 9am-6pm. €6, plus free entrance to one other museum/monument on the combination ticket list.)*

CAMPOSANTO. The Camposanto, a cloistered courtyard cemetery covered with earth that the Crusaders brought back from Golgotha, holds the Roman sarcophagi whose reliefs inspired Nicola Pisano's pulpit in the baptistery. Fragments of frescoes shattered by

THE LOCAL STORY

PICTURE PERFECT

Pisa resident Massimo proudly proclaims himself one of the most famous Tuscans on the face of the planet, noting "My picture appears in photo albums all over the world."

While tourists snap photos of themselves holding up the leaning tower, Massimo, a jovial Lucchese who spent three years studying in Pisa, has made a game of strategically positioning himself in the background.

With a sly grin, he reasons, "It's good to give life to the typical tourist photos with a smiling Italian, no?"

Massimo has some advice for amateur photographers on how to avoid clichéd poses. "All tourists try to hold up the tower with just their hands, but the tower is heavy," he explains. "It's better to turn around and get your backside and legs into it. Or, better still, with so many people pushing it up, it could topple the other way. We need some counterbalance. Go ahead and push it down, gravity needs help too."

Allied bombs during WWII line the galleries. The **Cappella Ammannati** contains the haunting frescoes of Florence succumbing to the plague. The unidentified 14th-century artist is known as the "Master of the Triumph of Death." *(Open late Apr.-late Sept. daily 8am-7:30pm; Mar. and Oct. daily 9am-5:40pm; Nov.-Feb. 9am-4:40pm. €6.20, includes entrance to one other museum/monument on the combination ticket list.)*

MUSEO NAZIONALE DI SAN MATTEO. This converted convent's 30 rooms showcase spectacular panels by artists like Masaccio, Fra Angelico, Ghirlandaio, and Simone Martini. There are also sculptures by the Pisano clan and a bust by Donatello in this converted convent. *(Just off P. Mazzini on Lugamo Mediceo. Open Tu-Sa 9am-7pm, Su 9am-2pm. €4, ages 18-26 €2, under 18 and over 65 free.)*

MUSEO DELL'OPERA DEL DUOMO AND MUSEO DELLE SINOPIE. The Museo dell'Opera del Duomo displays artwork from the three buildings of P. del Duomo. The *Madonna del Colloquio* (Conversation) by Giovanni Pisano was named for the expressive gazes exchanged between mother and child. The display also includes an 11th-century crucifix, strangely resembling Picasso, works by Tino Camaino and Nino Pisano, and an assortment of Roman and Etruscan pieces tucked into the church during the Middle Ages. *(Behind the Leaning Tower. Open Apr.-late Sept. daily 8am-7:20pm; Mar. and Oct. 9am-5:20pm; Nov.-Feb. 9am-4:20pm. €6, plus free entrance to one other museum/monument on the combination ticket list.)* Across the square from the Camposanto, the **Museo delle Sinopie** houses a display of fresco sketches by Traini, Veneziano, and Gaddi, as well as other sketches discovered during the post-WWII restoration. *(Same hours and admission cost and conditions as Museo dell'Opera del Duomo.)*

> **TOWER SOLD SEPARATELY.** The city offers an all-inclusive ticket, with entrance to the duomo, baptistery, Camposanto, Museo delle Sinopie, and Museo del Duomo for €10.50; to 2 of the above monuments, €6; to the duomo and 2 other monuments, €7; to everything but the duomo, €8.50. Tickets to the tower must be purchased separately. Combination tickets can be bought at the door of any one of the sights.

PIAZZA DEI CAVALIERI. Designed by Vasari and built on the site of the Roman forum, this piazza held Pisa's town hall during the Middle Ages. Today, it is the seat of the **Scuola Normale Superiore**, one of Italy's premier universities. Though not open to the public, it merits a short walk about the exterior. Busts of the old Grand Dukes of Tuscany decorate the facade. The black wrought-iron baskets on either end of the **Palazzo dell'Orologio** (Palace of the Clock) were once receptacles for the heads of delinquent Pisans. In the *palazzo's* tower, Ugolino della Gherardesca, with all his sons and grandsons, was starved to death in 1208 as punishment for treachery. This murky episode in Tuscan politics is commemorated in both Dante's *Inferno* and Shelley's *Tower of Famine*.

OTHER SIGHTS. Of Pisa's many churches, three merit special attention. The **Chiesa di Santa Maria della Spina** (Church of Saint Mary of the Thorn), which faces Gambacorti near the river, is quintessentially Gothic. It was built to house a thorn taken from Christ's Crown of Thorns. Visitors can view the church's interior only during Italy's annual **Culture Week.** *(From the Campo, walk down V. S. Maria and over the bridge. Ask at the tourist office about Culture Week.)* The **Chiesa di San Michele in Borgo** is notable for the Latin scribblings found on its facade, which concern a 14th-century electoral campaign for University Rector. *(From the Chiesa di Santa Maria della Spina, walk with the river to your left, cross the 1st bridge, and continue straight one block.)* Another worthy sidetrack from P. del Duomo is the **Chiesa di San Nicola.** The famous altarpiece in the 4th chapel on the right shows St. Nicholas deflecting the arrows that a wrathful God aims at Pisa. The bell tower of the church inclines slightly, not unlike its more famous cousin. *(Between V. S. Maria and P. Carrara. Open daily 7:45-11:30am and 5-6:30pm.)* If you're maxed out on gray stone and culture, go to the **Orto Botanico** public garden for palm trees and fresh air. *(Entrance at V. L. Ghini, 5, between V. Roma and V. S. Maria. Open M-F 8am-5:30pm, Sa 8am-1pm. Last entrance 30min. before closing.)*

🔊 🎵 NIGHTLIFE AND ENTERTAINMENT

Occasional concerts are given in the duomo. Call **Opera della Primaziale** (☎ 050 56 05 47). The annual **Gioco del Ponte** revives the city's tradition of medieval pageantry. Pisans divide, pledging their allegiance to one side of the Arno or another. The opposing sides converge on a bridge to see which side's cart can claim the largest portion of the bridge. (☎ 050 92 91 11; last Su in June). The night before the holiday of the patron saint Nicholas in mid-June, the **Luminara di San Ranieri** brings the illumination of Pisa (including the tower) with 70,000 lights. The main street of the University District, which runs up from P. Garibaldi on the river, changing names from Borgo Stretto to V. Oberdan to V. Carducci, is lined with places to drink beer, sip coffee, or enjoy *gelato*, such as **Caffè Spizio ❶**, V. Oberdan, 54 (☎ 050 58 02 81).

LIVORNO ☎ 0586

Dwarfed by monstrous oceanliners awaiting departure for Sardinia, Corsica, Greece, and Spain, Livorno is a rough-and-ready port town that attracts tourists with its convenient ferry system. Henry James's assertion that Livorno "has neither a church worth one's attention, nor a municipal palace, nor a museum, and it may claim the distinction, unique in Italy, of being the city of no pictures" holds true. Nonetheless, those awaiting ferries will find excellent seafood, views of the surrounding countryside, a few sights, and a cheap hostel.

▐ TRANSPORTATION

Trains: Frequent service connects Livorno to: **Florence** (1½hr., €5.70); **Piombino** (1½hr., €4.85); **Pisa** (15min., €1.50); and **Rome** (3½hr., €14.31). **Luggage storage** available (p. 410).

Buses: ATL (☎ 0586 84 71 11) sends buses from P. Grande to **Piombino** (8 per day, €6) and **Pisa** (16 per day, €2). If you are facing the church in P. Grande, the office is around toward the back of the church on the left.

Ferries: At the Stazione Marittima. From train station, take bus #1 to P. Grande (buy ticket from *tabacchi*; €1). All ferry ticket offices open before and after arrivals and departures. From P. Grande, take PB 1, 2, or 3 bus, or walk down V. Logorano, cross P. Municipio, and take V. Porticciolo, which becomes V. Venezia and leads to the port and Stazione Marittima (10min.). At Stazione Marittima, there is **currency exchange, luggage storage,** and a **restaurant.** Check where and when your boat leaves—schedules vary. Prices increase in summer and on weekends. Port taxes €3-8. **Corsica Marittima** (☎ 0586 21 05 07) runs fast service to **Bastia, Corsica** (2hr., late Apr. to mid-Sept. 2-4 per day, €16-29), and **Porto Vecchio, Corsica** (10hr., June-Sept. 1-2 per week). **Moby Lines** (☎ 0586 82 68 25) runs to **Bastia** (3hr., June-Sept. 1 per day, €15-28) and **Olbia, Sardinia** (8-10hr., mid-Mar. to Sept. 1 per day, €20-46). **Corsica and Sardinia Ferries** (☎ 0586 88 13 80; fax 89 61 03) runs to **Bastia** (4hr., May-Sept. 1 per day, €16-28) and **Golfo Aranci, Sardinia** (6-8hr.; June-Aug. Tu-Su 2 per day, greatly reduced off-season service; €21-47).

Taxis: (☎ 0586 21 00 00) in P. XX Settembre; (☎ 0586 89 80 94) in P. Grande; and (☎ 0586 40 12 94) at train station.

■◢ ❷ ORIENTATION AND PRACTICAL INFORMATION

From the train station, take bus #1 to reach **Piazza Grande,** the center of town. Buses #2 and 8 also stop at P. Grande, but only after tripping along the suburban periphery. Buy tickets (€1) at the booth outside the station, at a *tabacchi*, or at one of the orange vending machines. If you prefer to walk, cross the park in front of the station and head straight down **Viale Carducci,** which becomes **Via dei Larderei,** to **Piazza Repubblica.** Cross the piazza and take **Via delle Galere** to P. Grande.

Tourist Office: P. Cavour, 6, 3rd fl. (☎0586 89 81 11; info@livorno.turismo.toscana.it), up V. Cairoli from P. Grande, in P. Cavour; on the left. Open M-F 9am-1pm and 3-5pm, Sa 9am-1pm. Reduced hours Sept.-May. **Branch office** (☎0586 89 53 20), in the Stazione Marittima. Open June-Sept. M 8am-1pm and 4-8pm, Tu and Th-Su 8am-1pm and 2-8pm, W 8am-noon and 4-8pm.

Currency Exchange: Fair rates at the **train station.** Open daily 8-11:45am and 3-5:45pm. Also at **Stazione Marittima,** the **post office,** and the **banks** on V. Cairoli.

Luggage Storage: Self-service, in the train station. €2.07-3.62 per 24hr.

Emergency: ☎113. **Medical Emergency:** ☎118.

24-Hour Pharmacy: Farmacia Comunale, P. Grande, 8 (☎0586 89 44 90).

Hospital: Pronto Soccorso (☎0586 22 33 29 or 88 33 33).

Post Office: V. Cairoli, 12/16 (☎0586 27 641). Open M-F 8:30am-7pm, Sa 8:30am-12:30pm. Offers **currency exchange.**

Postal Code: 57100.

▟ ACCOMMODATIONS

▨ **Ostello/Albergo Villa Morazzana,** V. Collinet, 40 (☎0586 50 00 76; fax 56 24 26), in countryside, just within city limits. Bus #1 to P. Grande (€1) and at P. Grande, 25, transfer to bus #3 (20min.). #3 buses run different routes on outskirts of town, so ask at info booth in P. Grande which goes to hostel. Weekdays 1 per hr. in each direction. Other #3 buses will drop you off on V. Popogna; from there turn left onto V. S. Martino and follow the signs to the hostel (15min.). Housed in a 17th-century villa, the hostel hosts exhibitions of Livornese artists. Some rooms have breathtaking views of the countryside and sea. Minutes from a quiet beach and lovely Tuscan walks. Breakfast included. Lockout 9:30am-5pm. Curfew 11:30pm. Wheelchair-accessible. Call ahead. Dorms €13; singles €26, with bath €42; doubles with bath €62. AmEx/MC/V. ❶

Hotel Cavour, V. Adua, 10 (☎/fax 0586 89 96 04). From the main tourist office (see above), cross P. Cavour, and follow V. Michon to V. Adua. Clean, simple rooms. Singles €24; doubles €36, with bath €47; triples €51/€65; quads with bath €83. ❷

Hotel Marina, C. Mazzini, 24 (☎0586 83 42 78). From the main tourist office (see above), continue straight through P. Cavour, follow V. Ricasoli 1 long block, and take a right onto V. Mazzini. Modern amenities include bath, TV, and A/C. Wheelchair-accessible. Singles €47; doubles €62; triples €72; quads €80. MC/V. ❹

Hotel Boston, P. Mazzini, 40 (☎0586 88 23 33; fax 88 20 44; www.hotelboston.it). From P. Grande, follow V. Grande to the harborfront, go left onto S. C. Cialdini, which becomes S. C. Novi Lena, and cross the park, when P. Mazzini appears on your left. 3-star hotel with sleek, white lobby. Green-accented rooms, all with bath. Breakfast €5.50. A/C €10 extra. Singles €67; doubles €85; triples €111. AmEx/MC/V. ❺

◻ FOOD

Livorno owes its culinary specialties to the sea. The city has its own variation of *bouillabaise:* a fiery, tomato-based seafood stew they called *cacciucco.* The **Central Market** is at P. Cavallotti. (Open M-F 5am-3pm, Sa 5am-8pm.) Fill your brown bag at the **STANDA supermarket,** V. Grande, 174, off P. Grande. (Open Mar.-Oct. M-Sa 8:30am-12:30pm and 4-8pm; Nov.-Feb. M-Sa 8:30am-12:30pm and 3:30-7pm.)

> **La Cantonata,** C. Mazzini, 222 (☎0586 88 14 42), 2 blocks from Hotel Marian (see above). Huge plates of *spaghetti ai frutti di mare* (with seafood; €4.13) and *riso nero* (rice turned black from squid ink; €4.13). *Primi* €3.26-6.20, *secondi* €4.13-10.33. Cover €1.29. Service 10%. Open Tu-Su noon-3pm and 6:30-11pm. MC/V. ❷

> **Trattoria Il Sottomarino,** V. dei Terrazzini, 48 (☎0586 88 70 25), off P. della Repubblica past the end of V. Pina d'Oro. *Cacciucco* €11.36. *Primi* from €6.20, *secondi* from €7.75. Open Aug.-June W-Su 12:30-2:30pm and 7:30-10pm. MC/V. ❸

> **Hostaria dell'Eremo,** Scali Cialdini, 39 (☎0586 88 14 87). Pink walls and pink tile floors. *Cacciucco* €12.91. *Cosimo terzo* (shrimp and prosciutto; €6.20). Open Su-F 7:30pm-midnight, Sa 12:30-3pm and 7:30pm-midnight. AmEx/MC/V. ❸

> **Ristorante Vecchia Livorno,** Scali delle Cantine, 34 (☎0586 88 40 48), across from Fortezza Nuova. This popular spot serves classic Livornese fare. *Antipasti* €4.65-7.50. *Primi* €5.15-9, *secondi* €7.75-14.50. Cover €1.50. Service 10%. Open W-M noon-2:30pm and 7-10pm. ❸

◎ ◪ SIGHTS AND ENTERTAINMENT

FORTRESSES. The **Fortezza Nuova,** circled by a large moat, is in the heart of **Piccola Venezia,** coursed by canals. **Fortezza Vecchia** sprawls out on the water. Down the waterfront in P. Micheli is the **Monumento dei Quattro Mori,** Bandini's marble figure of Duke Ferdinand I (1595), joined by Tacca's manacled bronze slaves (1626).

MUSEO CIVICO GIOVANNI FATTORI. Livorno made its mark on painting with the 19th-century "blotters" movement, *I Macchiaioli,* and the 20th-century portraitist Amadeo Modigliani. Livornese work crowds the museum. *(In Villa Mimbelli, on V. S. Iacopo in Acquaviva, off V. Montebello. ☎0586 80 80 01. Open summer Tu-Su 10am-1pm and 5-11pm; winter 10am-1pm and 4-7pm. €6.50, students €4.50.)*

FESTIVALS. In mid-July, rowers in the **Palio Marinaro** race traditional crafts toward the old port. At the end of the month, **Effeto Venezia** transforms Livorno's Piccola Venezia into an open-air theater with 10 days of concerts and exhibitions.

VIAREGGIO ☎0584

The resort town of Viareggio sits quietly at the foot of the Riviera, tucked between the colorful beach umbrellas of the Versilian coast and the olive and chestnut groves cloaking the foothills of the Apuan Mountains. Young Italians arrive each morning to soak up sunshine; by night, wealthy European tourists stroll along the shore's promenade, taking in grandiose 1920s architecture and glitzy boutiques.

◗ **TRANSPORTATION.** Viareggio lies on both the Rome-Genoa and the Viareggio-Florence train lines. Trains service **Florence** (2hr., 5:45am-10pm, €5.70); **Genoa** (2½hr., 5:51am-9:20pm, €11.26); **La Spezia** (1hr., 7:25am-11:25pm, €5.11); **Livorno** via Pisa (30min., 7am-11:21pm, €4.85); and **Rome** (3hr., 3 per day, €25.20). Lazzi buses (☎0584 46 233) connect Viareggio to: **Florence** (2¼hr., 4 per day, €6.50); **La Spezia** (2hr., 4 per day, €3.40); **Lucca** (45min., every hr., €2.40); and **Pisa** (20 per day, €2.40). All buses stop in P. Mazzini, the town's main square. **Taxis** (☎0584 45 454) are available at the train station.

⊠ PRACTICAL INFORMATION. The **tourist office** at the train station has good maps, local bus schedules, and information on hotels. (Open May-Sept. W-Sa 9:30am-12:30pm and 3-5:30pm, Su 9:30am-noon; Oct.-Apr. reduced hours.) To get to the **main tourist office,** V. Carducci, 10, from the main exit of the train station, walk directly across the piazza and head right. Take your first left and walk about a mile straight down V. XX Settembre to P. Mazzini. At the other end of the piazza, turn right onto V. Carducci and walk 2½ blocks. The personable, English-speaking staff supplies decent maps and brochures, as well as information on hikes and car tours. The adjoining office has hotel information and can reserve rooms. (☎0584 96 22 33; www.versilia.turismo.toscana.it. Open M-F 9am-1pm and 3-6:30pm, Sa 9:30am-12:30pm and 3:30-6:30pm, Su 10am-noon.) Several of their recommended itineraries require a car—you can rent one at **Avis,** on V. Aurelia Nord in front of the supermarket, only 200m from the station. (☎0584 45 620. 25+. Open M-Sa 9am-8pm.) **Currency exchange** is available at the post office or at any of the banks along V. Garibaldi. If you're hunting for **work opportunities,** try landing a berth on one of the yachts docked at the main port. Getting hired is a long shot, but it never hurts to ask. Inquire at the yacht brokerages on and around V. Coppino. EU citizens have a better chance of finding employment with one of the many private beach clubs that line the waterfront. In case of **emergency,** dial ☎113; for **first aid,** call ☎118. An all-night **pharmacy** is at V. Mazzini, 14. The **post office** is at the corner of V. Garibaldi and V. Puccini. (☎0584 30 345. Open M-F 8:15am-7pm, Sa 8:15am-12:30pm.) **Postal Code:** 55049.

⟨⟩ ACCOMMODATIONS AND FOOD. Amid the splendor and pretense of four-stardom hide budget accommodations. Many, however, turn into long-term *pensioni* in the summer, catering to Italians on holidays of a week or more. For clean, simple white-walled rooms with bath, try the **Hotel Albachiara ❸,** V. Zanardelli, 81. (☎0584 44 541. Doubles Sept.-June €56; July-Aug. €62. Full-pension Sept.-June €44 per person; July-Aug. €47-49.) All rooms at **Hotel Derna ❺,** V. Buonarroti, 73, have soft beds, balconies, and TV. Prices fluctuate with demand; prices listed are the maximum possible rates. (☎0584 94 11 87. Singles €77; doubles €93. Half-pension €83; full-pension €88. AmEx/MC/V.) **Hotel Rex ❹,** V. S. Martino, 48, has a common room with mirrors and plush couches, and small, clean rooms with bath, TV, and A/C. (☎0584 96 11 40. Breakfast included. Singles late June to Aug. €65; doubles €85. Prices €20 lower rest of year. AmEx/MC/V.)

Accustomed to catering to a wealthy clientele, Viareggio restaurants are none too cheap. To avoid the ubiquitous €1.50 cover and 15% service charge, head to **Lo Zio Pietro ❷,** V. S. Martino, 73, and savor *roticceria* fare from *calccio* (fish stew, €5) to slow-roasted chicken. (☎0584 96 21 83. Open M-Sa 9am-8pm.) Spend €4.50 enjoying coffee and dessert on the ritzy terrace of the **Gran Caffè Margherita ❷,** overlooking the sea. (From P. Mazzini, as you face the sea, take a left onto the main drag; the cafe is ahead about 5 blocks on the right.)

⟨⟩ BEACHES AND ENTERTAINMENT. Most of the shoreline has been ungraciously roped off by the owners of Viareggio's private beaches, but you can walk through these areas to the water as long as you've already left your stuff somewhere else. Walking to the left as you face the water, across the canal along Viale Europa, leads to the free beach *(spiaggia libera)* near the southern edge of town (30min. from train station). The *spiaggia libera* caters to the young, hip (and often more modest) crowd that is noticeably lacking from the private beaches. If waking up with sand in your pants isn't your idea of fun, head to the ultra-posh town of **Forte dei Marmi,** for some fascinating people-watching. You can grab one of the blue CLAP buses, at P. Mazzini, to get to the town (every hr., €1.80). Once there, stake out a table at one of the expensive outdoor cafes and watch as Armani-clad locals emerge from their secluded villas to shop at designer boutiques. When night falls, stroll along the promenade.

ELBA

According to legend, the enchanting island of Elba grew from a precious stone that slipped from Venus's neck into the azure waters of the Tyrrhenian Sea. This paradise has since drawn the likes of Jason and the Argonauts, Etruscan miners, and Roman patricians. Since Hellenic times, Elba, nicknamed "Sparks" *(Aethalia)* by the Greeks, has gained renown for its mineral wealth. Of course, the island derives its greatest fame from its association with Napoleon; the Little Emperor was sent into his first exile here in 1814, creating both a temporarily war-free Europe and the famous palindrome: "Able was I ere I saw Elba." All vanquished conquerors of Europe should be so lucky: Elba's turquoise waters, dramatic mountains, velvety beaches, and diverse attractions can accommodate almost any interest. Each zone of the island attracts a distinct variety of visitors—families lounge in **Marina di Campo** and **Marciana Marina,** party-hard beach fanatics waste away in **Capoliveri,** yacht-club members gallivant in **Porto Azzurro,** and nature lovers gravitate to the mountainous northeast tip between the beachfront **Cavi** and **Rio nell'Elba** in the interior.

⌚ TRANSPORTATION TO ELBA

Elba's **airport** (☎ 0565 97 60 11), in Marina di Campo, sends flights to **Milan, Munich, Parma, Rome, Vienna,** and **Zurich.** The best way to reach Elba is to take a **ferry** from **Piombino Marittima** (also called Piombino Porto) on the mainland to **Portoferraio,** Elba's largest city. Ferries also dock at **Porto Azzuro,** on the opposite side of the island. **Trains** on the Genoa-Rome line travel straight to Piombino Marittima but usually stop at Campiglia Marittima (from Florence, change at Pisa). From Campiglia Marittima, a connecting *pullman* (intercity bus; 30min., €1), timed to meet incoming trains, takes you to the ferries in Piombino Marittima. If you buy a ticket to Piombino at a train station, and your scheduled train makes the bus connection, the bus ticket will be included. Both **Toremar** (ferry 1hr., €5.70-7.51; hydrofoil in summer 30min., €6.74-9.84) and **Moby Lines** (1hr., €6.50-9.50) run about 16 trips to Elba per day, with the last ferry leaving around 11:30pm. The ticket offices of **Toremar** (☎ 0565 31 100) and **Moby Lines** (☎ 0565 22 52 11) are in the Stazione Marittima at the ferry docks. You can buy tickets for the next departing ferry at the **FS** booth in the train station in Campiglia Marittima, as well as at the offices in Piombino. Should you be stuck in Piombino Marittima, take a bus from the port to the city (5min., about every hr., €1) or walk (15min.). The bus to Campiglia Marittima also stops in the town of Piombino.

PORTOFERRAIO ☎ 0565

Portoferraio has two personalities: west of the Medici Fortress is a modern, rather unattractive port, while to the east lies a picturesque Tuscan city. As the main port of Elba, it is probably the island's liveliest city and contains most of its essential services. Though low on sights, the old city is charming.

⌐ TRANSPORTATION

Buses: ATL, V. Elba, 20 (☎0565 91 43 92), across from the Toremar landing. Hourly service to **Capoliveri, Cavo, Lacona Marciana, Marciana Marina, Marina di Campo, Pomonte, Porto Azzurro,** and **Rio Elba.** Tickets €1.20-3.10. Schedules, day passes (€6.50), and 6-day passes (€18). Open June-Sept. daily 8am-8pm; Oct.-May M-Sa 8am-1:20pm and 4-6:30pm, Su 9am-12:30pm and 2-6:30pm.

Ferries: Toremar, Calata Italia, 23 (☎0565 91 80 80). **Moby Lines,** V. Elba, 4 (☎0565 91 41 33; fax 91 67 58).

Taxis: ☎0565 91 51 12.

Car Rental: Rent Chiappi, Calata Italia, 38 (☎0565 91 66 87). Cars €42-60 per day. Helpful staff. Mopeds €18-40. Mountain bikes €10. Insurance included.

Bike/Moped Rental: TWN, V. Elba, 32 (☎0565 91 46 66; fax 91 58 99). 50cc scooters from €19 per day, 125cc scooters €31, mountain bikes €15, kayaks €19, and Fiats from €39. 10% more in Aug. Branches around Elba (**Porto Azzurro, Lacona, Bagnaia,** and **Marina di Campo**). €5 fee for returning rentals to different branch. 10% *Let's Go* discount. Open 9am-1pm and 4-7pm. AmEx/MC/V.

🛈 PRACTICAL INFORMATION

Tourist Offices: APT, Calata Italia, 32, 1st fl. (☎0565 91 46 71; www.aptelba.it). Follow the arrows along the waterfront until you see the brown sign with the info symbol. Accommodations info, maps, bus schedules. Open in summer daily 8am-8pm; in winter 8am-1pm and 4-8pm.

Associazione Albergatori, Calata Italia, 20 (☎0565 91 47 54), finds rooms for free. Open M-F 9am-1pm and 3:30-5pm, Sa 9:30am-12:30pm and 4-5pm. **Tourist Information for Camping,** V. Elba, 9 (☎/fax 0565 93 02 08). Open M-F 9am-1pm and 4-7pm, Sa 9am-1pm.

Boat Excursions: Linee di Navigazione Archipelago Toscano (☎/fax 0565 91 47 97; www.elbacrociere.com) offers tours of Elba's coast as well as excursions to nearby islands (€25.80-36.20).

Currency Exchange: There are countless rip-offs. Be smart—walk up to the banks on V. Manganaro, near Hotel Nobel, including **Banca di Roma,** V. Manganaro, 1 (☎0565 91 90 07), which also has an ATM. Open M-F 8:30am-1:30pm and 3:10-4pm.

Laundry: Self-service at V. Elba, 29, near the Hotel Nobel. €4 wash (30min.), €4 dry (20min.). Open daily 8am-10pm.

Emergency: ☎113.

Ambulance: ☎0565 91 40 09.

Hospital: (☎0565 926 1111), off V. Carducci.

Internet Access: Internet Train, V. Cairoli, 47 (☎0565 91 64 08), across from Albergo Le Ghiaie. €5 per hr. Open M-Sa 9:30am-12:30pm and 3:30-7:30pm.

Post Office: in P. Pietro Gori, off P. della Repubblica. Open M-F 8:15am-7pm, Sa 8:15am-12:30pm. There is **another branch** on V. Carducci, closer to the port. Open M-F 8:30am-1:30pm, Sa 8:15am-12:30pm.

Postal Code: 57037.

┏ ACCOMMODATIONS

Reserve ahead in the summer; the Associazione Albergatori (see above) can help.

Ape Elbana, Salita Cosimo de' Medici, 2 (☎0565 91 42 45; fax 94 59 85), overlooking the main piazza of the *centro storico*. English-speaking staff. Cheery rooms with bath; some with TV and A/C. Breakfast included. Singles €50; doubles €62. About €15 cheaper in winter. Summer half-pension €60; full-pension €70. MC/V. ❹

Albergo Le Ghiaie, V. A. de Gasperi (☎0565 91 51 78), on pleasant beach of same name. All rooms have private bath; many have balconies with views of the sea. Singles €50; doubles €82; triples €95. Off-season prices drop 10-20%. AmEx/MC/V. ❹

Hotel Nobel, V. Manganaro, 72 (☎0565 91 52 17; fax 91 54 15; Nobel@elbalink.it). Follow V. Elba from the port until it merges with V. Manganaro. The hotel is on the right. Somewhat run-down, but perfect for those on a tight budget. Singles €33.57, with bath €41.32; doubles €43.90/€62. AmEx/MC/V. ❸

Hotel Massimo, Calata Italia, 23 (☎0565 91 47 66; fax 93 01 17), on the port. Large rooms all have bath, TV, A/C, and phone. Restaurant terrace surveys entire harbor. Continental breakfast buffet included. Singles €55; doubles €99; triples €106; quads €119. Prices drop 20% in low season. MC/V. ❹

◖ FOOD

Schiaccia is an Elban bread cooked in olive oil and embedded with either onions or black olives, and *aleatico* is a sweet liqueur. Suffering from an infestation of overpriced tourist-trap restaurants, Portoferraio is ideal for budget dining. For groceries, head to the centrally located **Conad Supermarket,** P. Pietri, 2-4, off V. Elba and near the Hotel Nobel. (Open M-Sa 7:30am-9pm, Su 7:30am-1pm and 4-8pm.)

Trattoria-Pizzeria Napoletana da Zucchetta, P. della Repubblica, 40 (☎0565 91 53 31), in historic center. Neapolitan pizza €4.60-8.20, *primi* €5.20-9.30, and *secondi* €7.70-23. Open daily 11:30am-3pm and 6-11:30pm. AmEx/MC/V. ❸

Ristorante Frescantico, V. Carducci, 132 (☎0565 91 89 89). This charming wine bar prepares delicious meals, well worth every euro. Fresh homemade pasta from €7.50. *Secondi* €18. Cover and service 10%. Open May-Nov. daily 12:30-3pm and 7-11pm; Dec.-Apr. M-Sa 12:30-3pm and 7-10pm. MC/V. ❹

Ristorante Stella Marina, Banchina Alto Fondale (☎0565 91 59 83), across from Toremar dock. Specializes in seafood, particularly Elban lobster. *Primi* €6-11, *secondi* by weight. Open mid-Nov. to Dec. Tu-Su noon-2pm and 7:30-11pm. AmEx/MC/V. ❹

Ristorante Residence (☎0565 91 68 15), on Catala Italia. Affordable dishes (€2.07-6.20) for takeout or self-service. Bar open May-Oct. daily 6:30am-11pm, Nov.-Apr. F-W 6:30am-11pm. Self-service 11:30am-3:30pm. AmEx/MC/V. ❷

◉ SIGHTS

If you're in Portoferraio and aren't in the mood for the beach, stroll along the pleasant cobblestone streets of the old town; they're lined with pink-, yellow-, and orange-shuttered houses set into the mountainside.

NAPOLEONIC WHATNOTS. The **Napoleon museum** is located at his one-time residence, the **Villa dei Mulini.** Inside are Napoleon's personal library, furniture graced by the imperial derriere, a number of letters from exile, and the sovereign Elban flag that he designed and decorated with bees from his own imperial crest.

CENTRAL ITALY

(☎0565 91 91 08. Open M, W-Sa 9am-7pm, Su 9am-1pm. €3; cumulative ticket also allows entry to the Villa Napoleonica €5.) The **Villa Napoleonica di San Martino** is emblazoned with monogrammatic Ns, placed there after his death. Note especially the Sala Egizia, with friezes depicting his Egyptian campaign. (Take bus #1 6km out of Portoferraio. ☎0565 91 91 51. Same hours as Villa dei Mulini.) A block away from the museum, you can pay homage to the great man's death mask at the **Chiesa della Misericordia.** (Undergoing restoration in summer 2002; ask at tourist office for updated info. €0.50.)

NON-NAPOLEONIC WHATNOTS. The **Museo Archeologico** guides you through the history of Elba, with exhibits of archaeological finds from ancient trading boat wrecks. (Fortezza del Lingrella. ☎0565 91 73 38. Open Sept.-June daily 9am-1:30pm and 3-7pm; July-Aug. 9:30am-2pm and 6pm-midnight. €2, children and individuals in large groups €1.) The **Medici Fortress** overlooks the port. Cosimo de' Medici, Grand Duke of Tuscany, began the impregnable complex in 1548. So imposing was its structure that in 1553 the dread Turkish pirate Dracut declared the building impenetrable, calling off his planned attack on Portoferraio. (Open daily 9am-8pm. €2, children €1.)

MARINA DI CAMPO   ☎0565

Marina di Campo's white beaches wind their way for miles along the coast, attracting masses of vacationing families. Numerous campgrounds around Marina di Campo are popular with a younger crowd. Bake in the sun or rent sporting equipment like sailboards (€8 per hr.) or paddleboats (€6 per hr.) along the beach. **Biko's Bikes,** V. G. Donizetti, across from the tourist office, rents bicycles and scooters for €12-69 per day. (☎0565 97 61 94. Open 8:30am-12:30pm and 3-7pm.) The **tourist office,** across from the bus stop, offers information on beaches. (Open May-Sept. Tu-Su 8am-8pm.) In case of an emergency, call the **carabinieri** (☎0565 97 60 03) or the **Guardia Medica** (☎118; in summer ☎0565 97 60 61).

The clean and comfortable rooms of **Hotel Lido ❹,** V. Mascagni, 29, near the center of town (turn left from P. Torino), are only a minute from the beach. (☎0565 97 60 40. Breakfast included. Internet €5 per hr. Doubles €52, with bath €68; triples €78/€86. MC/V.) A few blocks farther down the street, **Hotel Barcarola 2 ❹,** V. Mascagni, 208, has large rooms with bath, A/C, and satellite TV. (☎0565 97 62 55; fax 97 77 47. Breakfast included. Open May-Sept. Singles €45-80; doubles €70-128. AmEx/MC/V.) For **camping,** walk straight toward the beach from the bus stop, turn left at P. Torino, and walk the length of V. degli Etruschi. Continue past the sign that marks the end of Marino di Campo and take an immediate right at the "La Foce" sign (20min.). **La Foce ❶** is directly on the beach, with two restaurants, a bike rental, and a store with basic goods. (☎0565 97 64 56; fax 97 73 85. €6-12.50 per person and €6-12 per tent.) Another camping option is **Del Mare ❶,** which shares the same grounds, and offers bungalows. (☎0565 97 62 37; fax 97 78 50. Open Apr.-Oct. €5.80-11 per person and €5.80-8 per tent, depending on season. 1-room bungalow €40-90; 2-room €52-118.)

In town, **CONAD,** V. R. Fucini, across from the tourist office, stocks essentials. (Open M-Sa 8am-11pm, Su 8am-1:30pm and 3:30-11pm.) Contrary to its name, the only things baked at the **Canabis Restaurant ❷,** V. Roma, 41/61, are the fabulous meals, including crepes stuffed with cheese and prosciutto (€3.10). A variety of large salads (€4-7.50) and fruit drinks diversify the typically Italian menu. (☎0565 97 75 55. Open daily 6am-2am. AmEx/MC/V.) **Ristorante La Vecchia Locanda ❹,** L. Garibaldi, 40, offers simple island fare. Menù with drink starts at €10.30. (☎0565 97 80 60. Open daily noon-2:30pm and 6pm-midnight, but you must call ahead to give the kitchen time to prepare for your particular needs.) Also in the centro storico, **Ristorante Bologna ❹,** V. Firenze, 27, serves a variety of menùs, including vegetarian (€20) and tipico Elbano (€25). (☎0565 97 61 05. Open Mar.-Nov. daily noon-2:30pm and 6-11:30pm. MC/V.)

PORTO AZZURRO   ☎ 0565

A favorite sunspot of the ultra-thin and the ultra-rich, Porto Azzurro shelters some of the island's finest beaches. But the beauty doesn't come cheap—if you intend to stay in Porto Azzurro, brace yourself for a major financial outlay. To escape the hedonism, take a bus to Portoferraio (1hr., 7am-8:55pm). In emergencies, call the **carabinieri** (☎ 112) or an **ambulance** (☎ 118).

Budget travelers should consider staying at one of the campgrounds at Località Barbarossa, near the beach. The largest is **Camping Rocian's ❶** (☎ 0565 95 78 03), followed by **Arrighi ❶** (☎ 0565 95 568), **Da Mario ❶** (☎ 0565 95 80 32), and **Il Gabbiano ❶** (☎ 0565 95 087). **Albergo Barbarossa ❸**, also at Località Barbarossa, offers charmingly old-fashioned rooms, all with bath. (☎ 0565 95 087. Singles €30; doubles €46.50; triples €51.50.) To reach Barbarossa, you can either take the bus headed toward **Marina di Campo** (be sure to ask the driver if it stops at Barbarossa), or walk. To do the latter, follow the signs for the *carabinieri* from the main square bordering the ocean, pass the *carabinieri* office, continue walking until you hit the main road, and then go right. Look for the camping signs along the 15min., partially uphill walk. For comfortable digs back in town, check out **Hotel Belmare ❹**, Banchina IV Novembre, 21, across from the ferry dock. Seaside rooms all have balconies and bath. (☎ 0565 95 012; fax 92 10 77; www.elba-hotelbelmare.it. Closed Dec.-Feb. Singles €55; doubles €85. AmEx/MC/V.)

If you're looking for a quick bite, don't miss **La Creperia ❷**, V. Marconi, 2, just off the main square. The Nutella and mascarpone crepe (€3.10) is a sweet sensation. (Open daily Apr.-Oct. 11am-midnight.) **The Grill ❷**, V. Marconi, 26, near the Blumarine Hotel, has decent food. (*Primi* from €4.50. Open Tu-Su 9am-2pm and 7-10pm), or try the more elegant **Ristorante Bella H'Briana ❸**, V. D'Alarcon, 29. (*Primi* €5.50-8, *secondi* €7-14. Cover €2. Open noon-3pm and 6-11pm.)

Bar Tamata, V. Cesare Battisti, 3, has a mellow late-night crowd. (☎ 0347 381 3986. Open Th-Tu 10am-2pm and 5pm-2am.) **Morumbi**, 2km down the road to Capoliveri, is one of the island's hottest discos, with dance floors, a *pizzeria*, and a pagoda. (☎ 0565 92 01 91. Weekend cover €13. Ladies free. Open June 30-Sept. 15.)

MARCIANA MARINA   ☎ 0565

The strip of pebbles that borders Marciana Marina's waterfront is just one of countless beaches hiding in isolated coves along the island. Numerous other stretches are accessible only by boat. The lesser known ones lie between Sant'Andrea and Fetovaia, an area rumored to have the island's clearest stretches of water. The coastline here varies from fine white-sand beaches to gentle outcroppings of flat-topped rocks, perfect for sunbathing and diving into the sea.

🛅 PRACTICAL INFORMATION. Reach Marciana Marina from Portoferraio by car, moped, boat, or **bus** (50min., €1.80). The **tourist office,** P. Vittorio Emanuele, 20, one block off the water, finds rooms. (☎ 0565 90 42 44. Open June to mid-Oct. Th-Tu 9:30am-12:30pm and 4:30-7:30pm.) In an **emergency**, call the **carabinieri** (☎ 112) or an **ambulance** (☎ 118). The **post office** is on V. Lloyd. (Open M-F 8:15am-1:30pm, Sa 8:15am-12:30pm.)

🛏🍴 ACCOMMODATIONS AND FOOD. Cheap *affittacamere* are all over; look for signs. In Marciana Marina, **Hotel Imperia ❸**, V. Amedeo, 12, offers comfortable rooms. The personable proprietor finagles discounts at local restaurants. All rooms have a TV; some have refrigerator and balcony. (☎ 0565 99 082; imperia@elbalink.it. Breakfast included. Singles and doubles €31-46 per person.) Follow V. Amedeo away from the beach 500m to **Casa Lupi ❹**, Loc. Ontanelli, 35. Clean rooms behind green shutters all have bath. Terrace overlooks a vineyard and the sea. (☎ 0565 99 143. Aug. singles €42; doubles €68. Sept.-July singles €27; doubles €58.) Located on the harborfront, **Hotel Marinella ❹**, V. Margherita, 38, provides large rooms with great views, bath, and TV. (☎ 0565 99 018; fax 99 895; hotel-marinella@elbalink.it. Prices per person: June €44, July €52, Aug. €72, lower in off season; half-board €49-83. AmEx/MC/V.) If finding a room in one of the main centers proves difficult, **Albergo dei Fiori ❸** in **Chiessi** (30min. from Marciana, 1½hr. from Portoferrario; some buses go directly, others change in Procchio) provides tranquility, beautiful views of the azure sea, and huge rooms with modern bathrooms for a great price. Ask for a balcony or patio facing the ocean. Check in at their family-run restaurant, **L'Olivo**, 20m uphill from the bus stop. (☎ 0565 90 60 13. July-Aug. singles €25; doubles €38, with bath €45.)

Back in Marciana, seek out **Pizzeria First Love ❸**, V. G. Dussel, 9/13, and fall for their tasty pasta dishes (€7) and *secondi* (€7.50-17) at first bite. (☎ 0565 99 355. Open daily 7pm-2am. MC/V.) A good option for quick eats are the takeout crepes (€2.70-4) and *panini* (€3-4) at **Bar L'Onda ❷**, V. Amedeo, 4.

◪ SIGHTS. A visit to **Monte Capanne**, Elba's highest peak, provides an uplifting excursion from Marciana Marina. The top of this 1019m mountain offers views of the entire island and Corsica. The strenuous uphill trek takes 2hr., but a cable car can shorten the trip. (Open 10:30am-12:15pm and 2:30-6pm. €12.) To reach Monte Capanne, take the bus from Marciana Marina to **Marciana**, a medieval town that clings to the mountainside, and get off at "Monte Capanne" (15min.). Not far from Marciana are the **Romitorio di San Cerbone** (40min. on foot from **Poggio**) and the **Santuario della Madonna del Monte** (1½hr. on foot from Marciana), two sanctuaries once described as "dense with mysticism." Nearby **Chiessi** has secluded beaches and rocky coves that make it a perfect place to relax.

UMBRIA

Umbria is known as the "green heart of Italy," a land rich in wild woods and fertile plains, craggy gorges and gentle hills, tiny cobblestoned villages and lively international educational centers. Three thousand years ago, Etruscans settled this region landlocked between the Adriatic and Tyrrhenian coasts, leaving burial grounds, necropoli, tombs, and ruins. Another conqueror, Christianity, transformed Umbria's architecture and regional identity, turning it into a breeding ground for saints and religious movements. St. Francis shamed the extravagant church with his legacy of humility, pacifism, and charity that persists in Assisi to this day. The region holds Giotto's greatest masterpieces and produced medieval masters Perugino and Pinturicchio. Umbria's artistic spirit gives life today to the internationally renowned annual Spoleto Festival and Umbria Jazz Festival.

HIGHLIGHTS OF UMBRIA

GRAB HOLD of something sturdy; Assisi's **Basilica di San Francesco** (p. 432) has frescoes so beautiful, they make the earth quake.

EXPLORE Orvieto's ancient subterranean **Etruscan city** (p. 446).

GET YOUR GROOVE ON at the world-renowned **Umbria Jazz Festival** (p. 425).

SPELUNK in Orvieto's ancient subterranean **Etruscan city** (p. 414).

GORGE yourself on **Perugia**'s celebrated **hazelnut chocolates** (p. 422).

TRAVERSE Spoleto's Ponte delle Torri, a marvel of medieval engineering (p. 438).

PERUGIA ☎075

Perugians may be the most polite people you'll meet in Italy—an odd fact, considering Perugia's long history of conflict with its neighbors. Periods of prosperity during peace time gave rise to stunning artistic achievement. Perugia was home to the great Pietro Vannucci "Perugino," teacher of Raphael, and served as a meeting ground for 13th- through 15th-century Tuscan and Umbrian masters. This legacy is preserved in one of Italy's most important art museums, the Galleria Nazionale dell'Umbria. A renowned jazz festival and a vibrant academic community only add to Perugia's overpowering draw.

▄ TRANSPORTATION

Trains: Perugia FS, in P. V. Veneto, Fontiveggio. Perugia lies on the Foligno-Terontola line. Info open M-Sa 8:10am-7:45pm. Ticket window open daily 6am-8:40pm. To: **Arezzo** (1½hr., 7 per day, €3.82); **Assisi** (25min., every hr., €1.60); **Foligno** (40min., every hr., €2.20); **Orvieto** via **Terontola** (2hr., 8 per day, €6); **Florence** (2½hr., 7 per day, from €7.90); **Passignano sul Trasimeno** (30min., every hr., €2); **Rome** via **Terontola** or **Foligno** (2½hr., 6 per day, 4:55am-6:10pm, from €10.12); and **Spoleto** via **Foligno** (1½hr., every hr., €3.50). **Secondary Station: Perugia Sant'Anna** in P. Bellucci Giuseppe. Commuter rail to **Sansepolcro** (1½hr., 14 per day, 6:18am-8:31pm, €3.90) and **Terni** (1½hr., 13 per day, 5:21am-8:07pm, €4.30) via **Todi** (1hr., €2.70).

Buses: P. dei Partigiani, down *scala mobile* from P. Italia. City bus #6 (€0.80) heads to train station. **APM** (☎075 573 1707), in P. dei Partigiani. To: **Assisi** (1hr., 7 per day, 9:30am-6:10pm, €2.80); **Chiusi** (1½hr., 5 per day, 6:30am-6:30pm, €4.80); **Gubbio** (1¼hr., 10per day, 7:40am-8pm, €4); and **Todi** (1½hr., 6 per day, 6:30am-6:25pm, €4.80). Reduced service Su. Additional buses leave from **Stazione Fontiveggio,** next to the main train station. Tickets at Radio Taxi Perugia, to the right of the train station as you face it. To **Siena** (every 2hr., €9).

Taxis: Radio Taxi Perugia (☎075 500 4888).

Car Rental: Hertz, P. Vittorio Veneto, 2 (☎337 65 08 37). Near train station. Cars from €82.73 per day. Open M-F 8:30am-12:30pm and 3-7pm, Sa 8:30am-1pm.

▄ ▜ ORIENTATION AND PRACTICAL INFORMATION

From the **Perugia FS train station** in **Piazza Vittorio Veneto,** Fontiveggio, buses #6, 7, 9, 13d, and 15 go to **Piazza Italia** (€0.80). Otherwise, it's a 2km trek uphill. To get to P. Italia from the **bus station** in **Piazza dei Partigiani** or from the nearby **Perugia Sant' Anna train station** at **Piazza Giuseppe,** follow the signs to the **escalator** *(scala mobile)* that goes underneath the old city to P. Italia. From P. Italia, **Corso Vannucci,** the main shopping thoroughfare, leads to **Piazza IV Novembre** and the duomo. Behind the duomo lies the university district. One block off C. Vannucci is **Via Baghoni,** which leads to **Piazza Matteotti,** the municipal center.

Tourist Office: P. IV Novembre, 3 (☎075 572 3327 or 573 6458; fax 573 9386). The friendly, knowledgeable staff provides maps and info on accommodations, restaurants, and cultural events. Open M-Sa 8:30am-1:30pm and 3:30-6:30pm, Su 9am-1pm.

Info Umbria, L. Cacciatori delle Alpi, 3/b (☎075 573 2933; fax 572 7235; www.guideinumbria.com), next to the bus station. Private office provides maps, free booking for many hotels and farmhouses, and sells tickets to concerts, shows, and sporting events. Internet €3 per hr. **Luggage storage** €1.30 for 1st hr., €0.80 each additional hr. Open M-Sa 9am-2pm and 2:30-6:30pm.

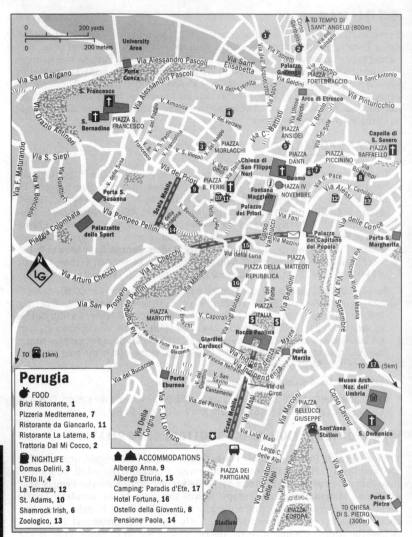

Perugia

🍎 **FOOD**
Brizi Ristorante, **1**
Pizzeria Mediterranea, **7**
Ristorante da Giancarlo, **11**
Ristorante La Laterna, **5**
Trattoria Dal Mi Cocco, **2**

🍸 **NIGHTLIFE**
Domus Delirii, **3**
L'Elfo II, **4**
La Terrazza, **12**
St. Adams, **10**
Shamrock Irish, **6**
Zoologico, **13**

🏠🏔 **ACCOMMODATIONS**
Albergo Anna, **9**
Albergo Etruria, **15**
Camping: Paradis d'Ete, **17**
Hotel Fortuna, **16**
Ostello della Gioventù, **8**
Pensione Paola, **14**

Budget Travel: CTS, V. del Roscetto, 21 (☎075 572 0284), off V. Pinturicchio toward the bottom of the street. Student travel service offers vacation deals to ISIC holders. Open M-F 10am-1pm and 3-6pm. **SESTANTE Travel,** C. Vannucci, 2 (☎075 572 6061). Books flights, sells train tickets, and rents cars. Open M-F 9am-1pm and 3:30-7pm, Sa 10am-1pm.

Currency Exchange: Banks have the best rates; those in P. Italia have 24hr. **ATMs.** The Perugia FS train station charges no commission for exchanges of less than €40.

Luggage Storage: Train Station, €3.87 per 24hr. Open daily 6am-9pm. **Info Umbria,** next to bus station. €1.30 1st hr., €0.80 each additional hr.

English-Language Bookstore: Libreria, V. Rocchi, 3 (☎075 753 6104). A variety of classics and a few recent bestsellers and travel guides. English-language books €10-15. Open M-Sa 10am-1pm and 3:30-8pm, Su 10:30am-1pm.

Laundromat: 67 Laundry, V. Fabretti, 7/a. Wash €3 per 7kg, dry €1. Open daily 8am-10pm. **Bolle Blu,** C. Garibaldi, 43. Wash €3 per 8kg, dry €3. Open daily 8am-10pm.

Medical Emergency: ☎118.

Police: ☎112.

Questura: V. Cortonese, 157 (☎075 50 621).

24-Hour Pharmacy: Farmacia S. Martino, P. Matteotti, 26 (☎075 572 2335).

Hospital: ☎075 57 81.

Internet Access: Centro TIM, V. Fabbretti, 1 (☎/fax 075 571 6041). From P. IV Novembre, walk past duomo on right and out left through P. Dante; follow V. Rocchi downhill to P. Braccio Fortebraccio. Cross the piazza and turn left on V. Fabretti. €1.80 per hr. Also provides fax and copy services. Open daily 9am-8pm.

Post Office: In P. Matteotti. M-Sa 8:10am-7:30pm, Su 8:30am-5:30pm. **Currency exchange** M-F 8:10am-5:30pm, Sa 8:10am-1pm, Su 8:30am-5:30pm.

Postal Code: 06100.

ACCOMMODATIONS & CAMPING

Make reservations well ahead of time in July, during the Umbria Jazz Festival.

▨ **Ostello della Gioventù/Centro Internazionale di Accoglienza per la Gioventù,** V. Bontempi, 13 (☎/fax 075 572 2880; www.ostello.perugia.it). From P. Italia, walk length of C. Vanucci to P. IV Novembre. Continue past duomo and P. Dante, staying right into P. Piccinino, and turn right onto V. Bontempi; hostel short way down on right. High, frescoed ceilings and great views. Kitchen, lockers, and TV room. Showers and kitchen use included. Sheets €1.50. 2 week max. stay. Lockout 9:30am-4pm. Curfew midnight, 1am during Jazz Festival. Open Jan. 16-Dec. 14. Dorms €12. MC/V. ❶

▨ **Albergo Anna,** V. dei Priori, 48 (☎/fax 075 573 6304), 152m off C. Vannucci. Climb 3 floors to clean, cool, and cozy 17th-century rooms. Some boast ceramic fireplaces and great views. Charming common area. Singles €40, with bath €45; doubles €46/€60; triples €70/€85. Extra 2% for credit cards. AmEx/MC/V. ❹

Albergo Etruria, V. della Luna, 21 (☎075 572 3730). Walking from P. Italia on C. Vannucci, take 1st left after P. della Republica onto C. della Luna. Many rooms with modern bathrooms, antiques, and balconies. Immense 13th-century sitting room. Showers €2.50. Singles €26; doubles €39, with bath €50; triples with bath €80. ❸

Pensione Paola, V. della Canapina, 5 (☎075 572 3816). From P. IV Novembre, follow V. dei Priori, take a left on V. della Cupa, take a right at the overlook, and go down the steps; it's ahead on the left. Comfortable rooms. Communal bath. Common terrace with love seat. Breakfast €3. Singles €30; doubles €46; triples €60; quads €76. ❸

Hotel Fortuna, V. Bonazzi, 19 (☎075 572 2845; fax 573 5040; www.umbriahotels.com), off P. della Repubblica. In a 13th-century *palazzo*, this hotel features a frescoed reading room, a rooftop terrace, free Internet access, and buffet breakfast. All rooms have bath, A/C, telephone, satellite TV, minibar, and hair dryer. Singles €79; doubles €114. Prices drop 20% in low season. AmEx/MC/V. ❺

Camping: Paradis d'Eté (☎075 517 3121), 8km away in Colle della Trinità. Take a city bus from P. Italia (dir.: Colle della Trinità; every 1-2hr.) and ask the driver to let you off at the campgrounds. Restaurant nearby. €6.20 per person, €5 per tent, €3 per car. Hot showers and pool use included. ❶

CENTRAL ITALY

BUT ALL I WANTED WAS A PIECE OF CHOCOLATE.

CHOCOLATE. From Etruscan to medieval times, Perugia never lost its zest for battle, constantly laying siege to surrounding villages. Its denizens once entertained themselves with the Battaglia de'Sassi (Battle of Stones), an annual festival involving two teams pelting each other to death with rocks. The city's reputation only improved when it played host to the Order of Flagellants in the 14th century, a group of religious fanatics who traveled Europe whipping themselves publicly. The city added defiance of papal rule, the imprisonment of the peace-loving St. Francis of Assisi, and the murders of two popes to its formidable record of heretical shenanigans.

▟ FOOD

Though renowned for its chocolate, Perugia also serves a variety of delectable breads and pastries. Both the *torta di formaggio* (cheese bread) and the *mele al cartoccio* (apple pie) are available at **Ceccarani,** P. Matteotti, 16. (☎075 572 1960. Open M-Sa 7:30am-8pm, Su 9am-1:30pm.) For local confections, such as *torciglione* (eel-shaped sweet almond bread; €1.85 per 100g) and *baci* (chocolate-hazelnut kisses; €0.40 per piece), follow your nose to **Pasticceria Sandri,** C. Vannucci, 32. This gorgeous bakery and candy shop doubles as a bar/cafe and is a great place for morning coffee. (Open Tu-Su 8am-10pm.)

On Tuesday and Saturday mornings, find delectable meats, cheeses, and vegetables at the **open-air market** in P. Europa. Other days, try the **mercato coperto** (covered market) in P. Matteotti; the entrance is below street level. (Open M-F 7am-1:30pm and Sa 7am-1:30pm and 4:30-7:30pm.) On summer nights, the market becomes an outdoor cafe. Buy essentials at the **COOP,** P. Matteotti, 15 (Open M-Sa 9am-8pm.) Complement your meal with 500mL of one of these two regional wines: *sagrantino secco*, a full-bodied, dry red, or *grechetto*, a light, dry white.

▦ Trattoria Dal Mi Cocco, C. Garibaldi, 12 (☎075 573 2511). Nothing pretentious about this local favorite, but the menu, written in Perugian dialect, is hard to read. *Menù* includes an *antipasto*, 2 *primi*, 2 *secondi*, a *contorno*, dessert, and a glass of liquor; €13. Reservations advised. Open Tu-Su 1-3pm and 8:45pm-midnight. MC/V. ❸

Brizi Ristorante, V. Fabretti, 75-79 (☎075 572 1386). From P. IV Novembre, walk to right of duomo, left through P. Danti, and right down V. Rocchi to P. Braccio Fortebraccio. On far side of piazza, take left on V. Fabretti. Mixed grill, with lamb, sausage, and chicken €6.20. *Primi* €3.62-4.65, *secondi* from €4.13. Complete tourist *menù* €10.50. Cover €1.30. Open W-M noon-2:30pm and 7-10:30pm. MC/V. ❷

Ristorante da Giancarlo, V. dei Priori, 36 (☎075 572 4314), 2 blocks off C. Vannucci. *Gnocchi alla pomodoro* melt in your mouth (€6.20). *Primi* €6.20-14, *secondi* €9.30-20.50. Cover €2. Open Sa-Th noon-3pm and 6-10pm. MC/V. ❹

Ristorante La Lanterna, V. Rocchi, 6, near the duomo. Enjoy *gnocchi lanterna* (ricotta and spinach dumplings with mushrooms, truffles, and cheese; €8), in inviting brick-vaulted dining rooms. *Primi* €8-11, *secondi* €10-14.50. Service 15%. Open daily May-Aug. 12:30-3:30pm and 6:30pm-midnight; Sept.-Apr. closed Th. AmEx/MC/V. ❹

Pizzeria Mediterranea, P. Piccinino, 11/12 (☎075 572 1322). From P. IV Novembre, walk to right of duomo and turn right. Upscale pizza for downscale prices (from €3.70). Try *pizza prosciutto crudo* (with mushrooms, prosciutto, *pecorino* cheese and basil; €5.16). Cover €1.10. Open daily 12:30-2:30pm and 7:30pm-11pm. AmEx/MC/V. ❶

🔵 SIGHTS

PIAZZA IV NOVEMBRE

The city's most visited sights frame Piazza IV Novembre on the north end of the city, and most other monuments lie no more than 15min. away. In the middle of the piazza sits the **Fontana Maggiore**, designed by Fra' Bevignate and decorated by Nicola and Giovanni Pisano. The bas-reliefs covering the double basin depict religious and Roman history; allegories explain the seasons and sciences in the lower basin and the saints and other historic figures in the upper basin.

▨ PALAZZO DEI PRIORI AND GALLERIA NAZIONALE DELL'UMBRIA. The 13th-century windows and sawtooth turrets of this *palazzo* are remnants of an embattled era. This building, one of the finest examples of Gothic communal architecture, shelters the impressive **Galleria Nazionale dell'Umbria**. The collection contains magnificent 13th- and 14th-century works by Duccio, Fra Angelico, Taddeo di Bartolo, Guido da Siena, and Piero della Francesca. Among these early masterpieces, Duccio's skillful rendering of the transparent garments in his *Virgin and Child and Six Angels* (Room 2) is worth a close look. Another highlight is Della Francesca's simply awesome *Polyptych of Saint Anthony* (Room 11). Native sons Pinturicchio and Perugina share Room 15. The former's *Miracles of San Bernardino of Siena* uses sumptuous colors, his rich tones contrasting with Perugino's soft pastels. *(In P. IV Novembre at C. Vanucci, 19. Gallery ☎ 075 572 1009. Open daily 8:30am-7:30pm. Closed Jan. 1, Dec. 25, and 1st M of every month. €6.50, EU citizens under 18 or over 65 free.)*

The **Sala dei Notari** was once the citizens' assembly chamber. Thirteenth-century frescoes portray scenes from the Bible and Aesop's fables. *(On the right of the Galleria, up the steps across from the fountain and across from the duomo. Open June-Sept. daily 9am-1pm and 3-7pm; Oct.-May Tu-Su 9am-1pm and 3-7pm.)*

DUOMO. Perugia's imposing Gothic duomo was begun in the 14th century, but the facade was never finished. Though not as ornate as other cathedrals in Tuscany and Umbria, the 15th- to 18th-century embellishments create a sense of balance and harmony within the church. The Virgin Mary's wedding ring, a relic snagged from Chiusi in the Middle Ages, is kept under lock and key, out of public view. *(P. IV Novembre. Open M-Sa 9am-12:45pm and 4-5:15pm, Su 4-5:45pm.)*

COLLEGIO DELLA MERCANZIA (MERCHANTS'S GUILD). In this building, Perugino suffused his frescoes with the gentleness that he later passed on to his great pupil Raphael. Raphael is said to have collaborated with his teacher on the *Prophets and Sibyls*. *(C. Vanucci, 15, next door to the Galleria Nazionale dell'Umbria. ☎ 075 573 0366. Open Mar.-Oct. and Dec. 20-Jan. 6 M-Sa 9am-1pm and 2:30-5:30pm, Su and holidays 9am-1pm; Nov.-Dec. 19 and Jan. 7-Feb. 28 Tu, Th-F 8am-2pm, W and Sa 8am-4:30pm, Su 9am-1pm. €1.03, combination ticket including Collegio Del Cambio €3.10.)*

COLLEGIO DEL CAMBIO (EXCHANGE GUILD). The 88 members of Perugia's merchant guild have met in this richly paneled structure to debate tax laws and local commerce since 1390. The books in the annexed archive contain the names of the guild's members dating back to the Middle Ages. On the walls of the **Sala dell'Udienza** (Audience Chamber), Perugino's frescoes portray heroes, prophets, sybils, and even the artist himself. Grotesque depictions of Roman Gods and the decapitation of John the Baptist are equally striking. *(Next to the National Gallery and Merchant's Guild at Corso Vannucci, 25. ☎ 075 572 8599. Open Mar.-Oct. and Dec. 20-Jan. 6 M-Sa 9am-12:30pm and 2:30-5:30pm, Su and holidays 9am-1pm; Nov.-Dec. 19 and Jan. 7-Feb. Tu-Su 9am-12:30pm. €2.60, groups or over 65 €1.60. Combined ticket with Merchant's Guild €3.10.)*

VIA DEI PRIORI

Don't be misled by the current calm gray face of *pietra serena* (rock-like serenity)—V. dei Priori was one of the bloodiest and goriest streets of medieval Perugia. Many midnight betrayals occurred here, and the spikes on the lower walls of the street were once used to impale the rotting heads of executed criminals. The attractive **Chiesa di Sant'Agata** has a number of 14th-century frescoes. *(One block off of Vannucci, hidden in a plain brick building on the left. Open daily 8am-12:30pm and 3:30-6:30pm.)* The Baroque **Chiesa di San Filippo Neri** (built in 1627) resides solemnly in P. Ferri; the heart of Santa Maria di Vallicella is kept here. *(Two blocks further from Chiesa di Sant'Agata. Open in summer daily 7am-noon and 4:30-7:30pm; winter 8am-noon and 4-6pm.)* **Piazza San Francesco al Prato** is a rare grassy square inviting lounging and bare feet. At its edge is the colorful **Oratorio di San Bernardino**, near the end of V. dei Priori. Built between 1457 and 1461 in early Renaissance style, its facade is embellished with finely carved reliefs and sculptures. *(A few blocks farther from Chiesa di San Filippo Neri, to the right down V. San Francesco. Oratorio open daily 8am-12:30pm and 3:30-6pm.)*

VIA ROCCHI AND THE NORTHEAST

From behind the duomo, medieval V. Ulisse Rocchi, the city's oldest street, winds through the north city gate to the **Arco di Etrusco**, a perfectly preserved Roman arch built on Etruscan pedestals and topped by a 16th-century portico. Walk straight through P. Braccio Fortebraccio and follow C. Guiseppe Garibaldi. The jewel-like **Tempio di Sant'Angelo** is a circular, 5th-century church, constructed with stone and wood taken from ancient pagan buildings. *(Past Palazzo Gallenga, off to the right near the end of C. Garibaldi. ☎ 075 572 2624. Open Tu-Su 9:30am-noon and 3:30pm-sunset.)* The **Capella di San Severo**, home to the *Holy Trinity and Saints*, a fresco painted in parts. The upper section is by Raphael and the lower section by his teacher Perugino . *(On your way back from Tempio di Sant'Angelo, veer to the left of P. B. Fortebraccio to a stairwell that winds up the hillside. Continue straight for one block from the top of the stairs, and then head right into P. Michelotti. Take V. Aquila on the left of the piazza and then take the 1st right into P. Raffaello. ☎ 075 57 38 64. Open Apr.-Oct. Tu-Su 10am-1:30pm and 2:30-6:30pm; Nov.-Mar. Tu-F 10:30am-1:30pm and 2:30-4:30pm, Sa-Su and holidays 10:30am-1:30pm and 2:30-5:30pm. €2.50, including Etruscan well.)* The **Pozzo Etrusco** (Etruscan well) is remarkably wide, with a depth of 36m. The well dates to the 3rd century BC, when it was the town's main water source. Climb down the stairs onto the footbridge spanning it just meters above the water. *(P. Danti, 18, across from the duomo. Follow V. Raffaello, jog left, and then right onto V. Bontempi. ☎ 075 573 3669. Open Tu-Su 10am-1:30pm and 2:30-6:30pm, daily in Aug. €2.50, including the Capella di San Severo.)*

THE EAST SIDE

■ **BASILICA DI SAN PIETRO.** This 10th-century *chiesa* consists of a double arcade of closely spaced columns leading to a choir, and is hung with solemn, majestic paintings and frescoes depicting saints and soldiers. Look for Perugino's *Pietà* along the north aisle. At the far end of the basilica is a medieval garden; its lower section offers a must-see view of the surrounding countryside. *(At the end of town on Borao XX Guigo, past the Port S. Pietro. Open daily 8am-noon and 3-6:30pm.)*

CHIESA DI SAN DOMENICO. This imposing cathedral is the largest church in Umbria. Its huge Gothic rose window contrasts with its sober, Renaissance interior. The magnificently carved **Tomb of Pope Benedict XI** (1325) rests in the chapel to the right of the high altar. *(On C. Cavour. Open daily 8am-noon and 4pm-sunset.)*

MUSEO ARCHAEOLOGICO NAZIONALE DELL'UMBRIA. Housed in the vast cloisters attached to the Chiesa di San Domenico, this museum has an extensive collection of Roman and Etruscan artifacts, including the *Cippu Perugino*, a memorial stone with one of the longest inscriptions in the Etruscan language. One hall includes a photo exhibit that takes you through the history of Umbria. The excavated Etruscan tomb of *Cai Cutu* lies near the entrance. A tunnel passes around the tiny cross-shaped chamber with windows looking over 50 stone burial urns. (☎075 572 7141. *Entrance in courtyard to left of entrance to Chiesa di San Domenico. Open M 2:30-7:30pm and Tu-Su 8:30am-7:30pm. €2.*)

GIARDINI CARDUCCI. These well-maintained public gardens are named after the 19th-century poet Giosuè Carducci, who wrote a stirring ode to Italy, inspired by Perugia's historic zeal for independence. From the garden wall, enjoy the panorama of the Umbrian countryside; a castle or an ancient church crowns every hill. (*At the far end of C. Vannucci, the main street leading from P. IV Novembre.*)

▣ ▧ FESTIVALS AND NIGHTLIFE

The glorious 10-day ▨**Umbria Jazz Festival** in July draws world-class performers. (Contact the tourist office or go to www.umbriajazz.com for information. €8-50, some events free.) Summer brings **Teatro è la notte,** a series of musical, cinematic, and dance performances. In September, the **Sagra Musicale Umbra** fills local churches with concerts of religious and classical music. Check Palazzo Gallenga for English films and event listings. Contact the tourist office about the internationally renowned **Eurochocolate Festival,** which lasts 10 days at the end of October.

Perugia has more nightlife options than any other Umbrian city, and its large university population keeps clubs packed nearly every night of the week from September to May, when school is in session. During the academic year, join the nightly bandwagon at **P. Fortebraccio,** where free buses depart (starting at 11pm) for several nearby clubs. A cover charge of €13-26 gets you deafening electronic music and an assortment of scantily clad club kids. Within the city, Perugia's two hottest dance clubs are **Domus Delirii,** V. del Naspo, 3, just off P. Morlacchi, and **St. Adams,** V. della Cupa, 6, left off V. dei Priori as you are walking from C. Vannucci. (Both open daily midnight-5am.)

Shamrock Irish, at P. Danti, 18, on the way to the Pozzo Etrusco, is home to the best Guinness in town—each pint (€4.50) includes a free shot of whiskey. (☎075 573 6625. Happy hour 6-9pm; open daily 6pm-2:30am.) **Zoologico,** V. Alessi, 64, usually has live music and carousing locals and travelers. (Open Tu-Su 7pm-2am.) Head to **La Terrazza,** in P. Matteotti, on the terrace behind the Mercato Coperto, for cheap drinks. It boasts excellent views, open-air movies, cabaret, and book readings. (Open daily 6pm-3am, closed in inclement weather.) **L'Elfo II,** V. del Verzaro, 39, off P. Morlacchi, has a candlelit interior across a gully in the University quarter. (Beer €3.50-3.80 per bottle, drinks €5.50. Open daily 9pm-2am.)

▣ DAYTRIPS FROM PERUGIA: LAKE TRASIMENO

Expansive Lake Trasimeno, 30km west of Perugia, is a tranquil and refreshing refuge from stifling heat and packed tourist centers. While a pleasant and peaceful daytrip destination today, Lake Trasimeno was once wracked with violence. In 217 BC, during the Second Punic War, Hannibal's elephant-riding army, fresh from the Alps, routed the Romans north of the lake. The names of the lakeside villages, **Ossaia** (place of bones) and **Sanguineto** (bloody), merrily recall the carnage of 16,000 Roman troops. The mass graves of these dead have recently been discovered under the battlefields of **Tuero,** between the two main towns guarding the lake, **Passignano sul Trasimeno** and **Castiglione del Lago,** easily accessible by train and bus. A system of ferries connects Passignano sul Trasimeno, Castiglione del Lago, Tuero, San Feliciano, and Lake Trasimeno's two largest islands— **Isola Maggiore** and **Isola Palvese.**

CASTIGLIONE DEL LAGO

Castiglione del Lago lies on the Florence-Rome train line. To get there from Perugia, change at Terontola to a train headed for Rome or Chiusi (1hr., depending on connection; 8 per day; €2.79). To reach the town center from the train station, take a left out of the station and follow the "centro" signs. Once on V. B. Buozzi, the modern town's main drag, follow it to its end, go up the broad flight of stairs facing you, and then go up the smaller flight of stairs, to the right through the city walls, and onto V. V. Emanuele, the main street of the tiny historical center (15min.). To reach the ferry dock, take a right downhill at the end of V. V. Emanuele and out the city walls. Take a left at the T-junction and then an immediate right down stone steps. Take a left, then a right (10min.).

The largest resort area on Trasimeno, Castiglione del Lago is nevertheless a sleepy-town. It is located on a limestone promontory covered in olive groves; solid medieval walls enclose its two main streets and single square. The **tourist office,** P. Mazzini, 10, in the main square, provides boat schedules, exchanges money, and helps find rooms in hotels or in private homes or apartments. (☎075 965 2484. Open Apr.-Sept. M-F 8:30am-1pm and 3:30-7pm, Sa 9am-1pm and 3:30-7pm, Su and holidays 9am-1pm; Oct.-Mar. M-F 8:30am-1pm and 3:30-7pm; Sa 8:30am-1pm.)

At the end of V. V. Emanuele, next to the hospital, stand the **Palazzo della Corgna** and the **Rocca Medievale.** The courtyard of the imposing, crumbling fortress is free and open to the public, and its sloping grass lawn is sometimes used as seating for open-air concerts. The view of the lake from the walls of the fortress is beautiful. The 16th-century *palazzo* is notable for its frescoes by Niccolò Circignani, or Il Pomarancio. (Open daily Apr. 9:30am-1pm and 3:30-7pm; May-June 10am-1:30pm and 4-7:30pm; July-Aug. 10am-1:30pm and 4:30-8pm; Sept.-Oct. 10am-1:30pm and 3:30-7pm; Nov.-Mar. 9:30am-4:30pm. Entrance to Palazzo and Rocca walls €2.60.)

Budget accommodations are scarce in the immediate vicinity of Castiglione del Lago, but the three-star **La Torre ❹,** V. V. Emanuele, 50, offers clean rooms with bath in the heart of the old town. (☎/fax 075 95 16 66. Breakfast €5. Singles €50; doubles €72; triples €85; quads €90. AmEx/MC/V.) The four-story **Hotel Miralago ❺,** P. Mazzini, 6, offers picturesque views of the lake and the town's main square. Rooms include bath, A/C, and satellite TV. (☎075 95 11 57; fax 95 19 24. Breakfast €5. Singles €61.92; doubles €72.30; triples €77.47. AmEx/MC/V.)

For food, try the shops lining V. V. Emanuele, or dine at **Paprika ❸,** V. V. Emanuele, 107, which serves local specialties; the *spaghetti ai sapori di Trasimeno* (with eel sauce) is €7.30. (*Primi* €6.50-7.50, *secondi* €7.80-13.40. Cover €1.70. Open W-M 12:30-3pm and 7-10:30pm. AmEx/MC/V.) **Ristorante L'Acquario ❸,** V. V. Emanuele, 69, offers a variety of lunch *menùs* (€12.50-16.40), featuring seafood fresh from the lake. (*Primi* €5.20-7.80, *secondi* €7.80-13. Cover €1.60. Open Th-Tu noon-2:30pm and 7-10:30pm. Nov.-Feb. closed M. AmEx/MC/V.)

PASSIGNANO SUL TRASIMENO

Passignano sul Trasimeno lies on the Foligno-Terontola train line. Trains run from Perugia (30min., 13 per day, €1.65). To reach the waterfront and ferry, turn right from the train station. Follow the road as it passes over the railroad tracks, curves right, and curves left into the main waterfront drag. The ferry dock is 5min. ahead on the right.

Passignano is the ferry point to Isola Maggiore easiest reachable from Perugia. There's not much to see here. While waiting for your ferry, browse the numerous ceramic shops that line the waterfront, or walk uphill through the tiny medieval center. The single street through the charming residential neighborhood ends in a beautiful panorama of the lake.

ISOLA MAGGIORE

A convenient ferry system connects the island to Passignano sul Trasimeno (25min.; every hr.; 7:15am-7:45pm; €3.20, round-trip €5.30) and Castiglione del Lago (30min.; every 1½hr.; 8:35am-7:10pm; €3.20, round-trip €5.80). Buy tickets on board when coming from the island, or at the docks in the towns.

Follow in St. Francis's footsteps and spend a delightful day on Isola Maggiore, Lake Trasimeno's only inhabited island. A **tourist information booth** sits by the dock. (Open daily 10am-6pm. No free map, but glossy guides to the island €3.) As you leave the dock, turn right and follow the path to the tip of the island and the ruined **Guglielmi castle**. All that is accessible is the decaying Baroque chapel, dimly lit with peeling plaster and fading frescoes. You may run into the sweet old caretaker who offers less-than-informative tours of the castle in Italian. (Open 9am-5pm.)

Down the castle to the right, make your way to the shore and follow the path around to the left, to find a clearing with a statue of St. Francis. On the far side of the clearing, take the stone stairs up to the left to see the tiny chapel enclosing the rock atop which St. Francis spent 40 days in 1211. From here, hike 5min. up to the Chiesa di San Michele Arcangelo for lovely 14th-century frescoes and a wonderful view of the island. (Open daily 10:30am-1pm and 3-6pm. €2.60.) On the side of the island opposite the castle, some have been known to sneak a dip at the island's small private beach, but *Let's Go* does not recommend trespassing.

TODI   ☎075

According to legend, an eagle flew to this rocky site, bringing with him the founders of Todi. Until a recent tourist boom, it had since seen few other visitors. This isolated town long remained untouched by historical change and still retains visible traces of its Etruscan, Roman, and medieval past. Though many areas of the modern city seem to have been transformed into parking lots, there's hardly room for cars (or any other 20th-century amenities) in the charming historic center. A number of antique shops have nonetheless squeezed their way in, catering to the busloads of daytrippers who unload in Piazza Jacopone each morning.

Ⓝ PRACTICAL INFORMATION. Todi is best reached by **bus** from Perugia. The bus station is in P. Consolazione, a short ride on city bus A or a winding, uphill 1km walk from the town center. **APM** (☎075 894 2939 or toll-free 800 51 21 41) runs buses to and from **Perugia** (1¼hr.; M-Sa 7 per day; last bus from Todi 5pm, last bus from Perugia 7:30pm; €4.80). Todi is also accessible by **train** on the Perugia-Trevi line from **Perugia Sant'Anna** (45min., 13 per day, €2.70). **Taxis** are available in P. Garibaldi (☎075 894 2375), P. Jacopone (☎075 894 2525), or by calling ☎0347 774 8321. The **IAT** tourist office, P. Umberto I, 5/6, provides maps, transportation schedules, and information about area restaurants and accommodations. (☎075 894 2526. Open M-Sa 9am-1pm and 3-7pm.) In case of **emergency**, call the **police** (☎112 or 075 895 6243), an **ambulance** (☎118), or the **hospital** (☎075 88 581). A pharmacy, **Farmacia Pirrami** (☎075 894 2320), is in P. del Popolo, 46. **Postal Code:** 06059.

Ⓝ Ⓒ ACCOMMODATIONS AND FOOD. Todi is short on budget options. The best values are a 20min. walk from the town center, just beyond Porta Romana. From Porta Romana, head straight down V. Cortesi, left on V. del Crocefisso, and right on V. Maesta dei Lombardi to find the three-star **Tuder ❹**. (☎075 894 2184; fax 894 3952. All rooms with bath. Singles €56.90; doubles €93. AmEx/MC/V.) Farther down on V. Cortesi, **Villa Luisa ❺**, V. Cortesi, 147, has a pool and a large garden area. (☎075 894 8571; www.villaluisa.it. All rooms with bath. Singles €66.50; doubles €101; triples €121. Pick up provisions at the **COOP** at the intersection of V. Cortesi and V. del Crocefisso. (Open M-Sa 9am-8pm.) **Ristorante Cavour ❸**, V. Cavour, 21/23, offers pizza (€3-6) and filling meals (€15). Their specialty is *tortellini al tartufo nero* (tortellini with black truffles) for €6. (☎075 894 3730. Open Th-Tu noon-3pm and 7:30pm-2am. AmEx/MC/V.) For a speedy bite, stop at **Pizzeria Italo ❶**, P. Bartolomeo d'Alviano, 1. Thin crust pizzas start at €2.60. (Open 9am-3pm and 6pm-midnight. MC/V.)

◙ **SIGHTS. Piazza del Popolo,** the town center and Todi's focal point since Roman times, remains the town's high point in altitude and architectural achievement. It is a stately ensemble of glowering *palazzi* and a somber duomo. In the piazza, the **Palazzo del Capitano** contains the **Pinacoteca Civica** and the **Museo Archelogico** in its upper floors. Fascinating frescoes, including Lo Spagna's *Incoronazione della Vergine e Santi,* are in the **Sala del Capitano del Popolo,** at the top of the exterior staircase. (Open daily 10:30am-1pm and 2:30-6pm. €3.10, under 15 €1.55, ages 15-25 €2.32.) The **duomo,** across from P. del Popolo, rests solidly atop a flight of broad stone steps. The central rose window and arched doorway attract attention with their intricate decoration. The Gothic side arcade, added in the 1300s, shelters an unusual altarpiece—Madonna's head emerges in high relief from the painting's flat surface. (Open daily 8:30am-12:30pm and 2:30-6:30pm.) Across from the duomo, the tower and facade of the **Palazzo dei Priori** (1297-1337) retain vestiges of medieval gloom despite rows of Renaissance windows carved in the early 16th century.

Neighboring P. Garibaldi has been reduced to little more than a municipal parking lot, but it still opens onto a superb vista. From the piazza, follow the signs leading off C. Cavour to the remaining walls of the **Foro Romano** and the nearby 12th-century **Chiesa di San Ilario.** The **Fonti Scannabecco's** 13th-century porticoes still house a working tap. Return to P. del Popolo and take V. Mazzini to the majestically angular **Tempio di San Fortunato.** Built by the Franciscans between the 13th and 15th century, the church features Romanesque portals, a Gothic interior, and the musky **tomb of San Jacopone.** To the right of S. Fortunato, a path bends uphill toward **La Rocca,** a ruined 14th-century castle that now fronts a quaint public park (Park open Apr.-Oct. 6:30am-10pm; Nov.-May 7am-7pm.) Next to the castle, follow a sinuous path, appropriately named **Viale della Serpentina,** to a breathtaking belvedere constructed on the remains of an old Roman wall. Follow the twisting paths down to the base of the hill and cross Viale della Consolazione to the Renaissance **Tempio di Santa Maria della Consolazione,** with its elegant domes. Inside are 12 enormous statues of the region's saints and a magnificent altar worth the trek.

ASSISI ☎079

> For it is in giving that we receive; it is in pardoning that we are pardoned; and it is in dying that we are born to eternal life.
> —St. Francis of Assisi

Assisi's serenity originates from the legacy of St. Francis, a 12th-century monk who founded the Franciscan order and sparked a revolution in the Catholic church. Young Franciscan nuns and monks still fill the city, dressed in their brown *cappucci* robes. Assisi is an important pilgrimage site, especially among Italian youth, who converge here for religious conferences and festivals. Fervent religiosity is hardly a prerequisite for adoring Assisi. The Basilica of St. Francis is perhaps the most visited sight in all Umbria, containing the saint's relics and Giotto's renowned fresco series of St. Francis's life. Ruins attest to Assisi's Etruscan and Roman roots. Grand palaces and majestic *rocce* (castles) from a later era tower above the orange roofs. The rose-colored town is beautifully preserved, and has great places to eat and stay. Earthquakes in 1997 devastated the city, but renovations have repaired most of the damage.

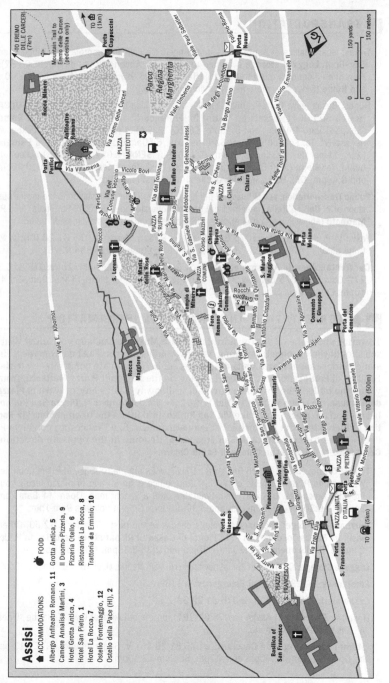

Assisi

▲ ACCOMMODATIONS

Albergo Anfiteatro Romano, **11**
Camere Annalisa Martini, **3**
Hotel Grotta Antica, **4**
Hotel San Pietro, **1**
Hotel La Rocca, **7**
Ostello Fontemaggio, **12**
Ostello della Pace (HI), **2**

🍴 FOOD

Grotta Antica, **5**
Il Duomo Pizzeria, **9**
Pizzeria Otello, **6**
Ristorante La Rocca, **8**
Trattoria da Erminio, **10**

▐ TRANSPORTATION

Trains: Near Basilica of Santa Maria degli Angeli. On Foligno-Terontola line. Office open 6am-8pm. **Luggage storage** available (p. 430). To: **Ancona** (8 per day, from €6.82); **Florence** (7 per day, more frequent via Terontola, €8.99); **Perugia** (1 per hr., €1.60); and **Rome** (5 per day, more frequent via Foligno, €8.99).

Buses: Buses leave from P. Unità D'Italia, near Basilica di San Francesco. Buy **SULGA** (☎075 500 9641) tickets on board. To: **Florence** (2½hr., 7am, €6.40) and **Rome** (3hr.; 1:45pm, 4:45pm, and 5:45pm; €8.26). Buy **APM** (☎075 573 1707) tickets at newsstand. To: **Foligno** (1hr., M-Sa 9 per day, 6:50am-6:10pm, €3.36) and **Perugia** (1hr., 11 per day, 6:35am-6:25pm, €2.70). Buy **SENA** (☎057 728 3208) tickets on board. To: **Siena** (2hr.; 5:35pm, from S. Maria degli Angeli near train station 10:25am and 8:45pm; €7). Bus schedules available at tourist info office.

Public Transportation: Local buses (2 per hr., €0.80) run from train station to the town's bus stops at **P. Unità d'Italia** (near basilica), **Largo Properzio** (near church of St. Chiara), and **P. Matteotti** (above P. del Comune). Buy tickets at *tabacchi* in train station, or on board.

Taxis: In P. del Comune (☎075 81 31 93), in P. San Chiara (☎075 81 26 00), in P. Unità d'Italia (☎075 81 23 78), and at the train station (☎075 804 0275).

Car Rental: Agenzia Assisiorganizza, V. S. Gabriele dell'Addolorata, 25 (☎075 81 23 27). Cars from €75 per day, €347 per week. 21+. Open M-Sa 11am-10pm, Su 4-10pm. Credit cards only. AmEx/MC/V.

◼✴🔃 ORIENTATION AND PRACTICAL INFORMATION

Towering above the city to the north, the **Rocca Maggiore** can help you orient yourself should you become lost among Assisi's winding streets. The bus from the train station stops first at **Piazza Unità d'Italia;** get off here if you are going directly to the Basilica di San Francesco. Otherwise, stay on the bus until **Piazza Matteotti,** from which the bulk of the town is a downhill walk away. The center of town is **Piazza del Comune.** To reach it from P. Matteotti, take **Via del Torrione** to **Piazza San Rufino,** bear left in the piazza, and take **Via San Rufino** until it hits the town center. **Via Portica** (which intersects V. Fortini, V. Seminario, and V. San Francesco) connects P. del Comune to the **Basilica di San Francesco.** Heading in the opposite direction, **Corso Mazzini** leads to the **Chiesa di Santa Chiara.**

Tourist Office: (☎075 81 25 34; fax 81 37 27; www.umbria2000.it), in P. del Comune. Walking into P. del Comune on V. S. Rufino, office is on far end of piazza facing you. Provides brochures, bus info, train timetable, and a decent map. Open M-F 8am-2pm and 3:30-6:30pm, Sa 9am-1pm and 3:30-6:30pm, Su and holidays 9am-1pm.

Currency Exchange: Exchange traveler's checks at the post office for €1-2.60. Otherwise, try **Banca Toscana,** on P. S. Pietro, or **Cassa di Risparmio di Perugia,** on P. del Comune. Banks open M-F 8:20am-1:20pm and 2:35-3:35pm. **ATMs** outside.

Luggage Storage: €2.58 per 12hr. at newsstand in train station. Open daily 6:30am-6:30pm.

Emergency: ☎113. **Medical Emergency:** ☎118.

Carabinieri: P. Matteotti, 3 (☎075 81 22 39).

Hospital: Ospedale di Assisi (☎075 81 391), on the outskirts of town. Take the "Linea A" bus from P. del Comune.

Internet Access: Agenzia Casciarri (☎075 81 28 15), V. Borgo Aretino, 39. €4.13 per hr. Open M-F 9am-12:30pm and 4-7pm, Sa 9am-12:30pm.

Internet World, V. S. Gabriele dell'Addolorata, 25 (☎075 81 23 27; internetworld@tiscali.it). ADSL line €3.20 per hr. Open M-Sa 11am-10pm, Su 4-10pm.

Post Office: Largo Properzio, 4, up the stairs to the left just outside of Porta Nuova. Open M-Sa 8:35am-1:25pm. **Secondary branch** at P. S. Pietro, 41. Open M-F 8:10am-7pm, Sa 8:10am-1:25pm. Same postal code.

Postal Code: 06081.

▐ ACCOMMODATIONS

Reservations are crucial around Easter and Christmas and strongly recommended for the **Festa di Calendimaggio** in early May. If you don't mind turning in around 11pm, ask the tourist office for a list of **religious institutions.** The tourist office also has a list of *affittacamere.*

▩ **Ostello della Pace (HI),** V. di Valecchi, 177 (☎/fax 075 81 67 67; www.assisihostel.com). From P. Unità d'Italia, walk downhill on V. Marconi and then left on V. Valecchie (10min.). From train station, go left on V. Carducci and then right on the main road for 500m. Signs will point you right and 250m later left onto V. Valecchi (30min.). Rooms with 4-6 beds and spotless bathrooms. Breakfast included. Dinner €8. Laundry €3.50. Reception daily 7-10am and 3:30-11:30pm. Check-out 9:30am. Lockout 9:30am-3:30pm. Communal areas locked at 11:30pm. Reserve ahead. HI card required; you can buy one at hostel. Dorms €14, with private bath €16. MC/V. ❷

▩ **Camere Annalisa Martini,** V. S. Gregorio, 6 (☎/fax 075 81 35 36). Follow V. Portico from P. del Comune and take 1st left onto V. S. Gregorio. *Affittacamere* at excellent prices. Outdoor picnic seating, washer, phone, and fax. If no room, Annalisa can refer you to her friends. Laundry €2.50-5. Singles €22, with bath €25; doubles €32/€36; triples €48-52; quads €57. Prices reduced for 3 days or longer. ❸

Ostello Fontemaggio, V. per l'Eremo delle Carceri, 8 (☎075 81 36 36; fax 81 37 49). V. Eremo begins in P. Matteotti and leads through Porta Cappuccini; follow 1km up the road and then bear right at the sign. Hostel, hotel, bungalows, campgrounds, and market. New hostel has 8-bed rooms. Delicious home-cooked fare. Breakfast €3. Check-out 10am. Curfew 11pm. Dorms €20. Singles €36; doubles €51.60; triples €72.50; quads €80. 4- to 8-person bungalows €50-139.50. ❸

Albergo Anfiteatro Romano, V. Anfiteatro Romano, 4 (☎075 81 30 25; fax 81 51 10), off P. Matteotti. Quiet, welcoming rooms with views of the Rocca. See **Food,** below. Singles €21; doubles €33, with bath €43. AmEx/MC/V. ❷

Hotel La Rocca, V. di Porta Perlici, 27 (☎/fax 075 81 22 84). From P. del Comune, follow V. S. Rufino up hill and cross piazza. Go up V. Porta Perlici until you hit the old arches; hotel on left. Rooms with great views of Rocca Minore and the Subasio Valley. All rooms with bath. Breakfast €4. Singles €33.50; doubles €40; triples €60. Closed Jan-Feb. AmEx/MC/V. ❸

Hotel Grotta Antica, Viccolo dei Macelli Vecchi, 1 (☎075 81 34 67). From P. del Comune, walk downhill on V. dell'Arco dei Priori (under arch); take a right onto Vicolo dei Macelli Vecchi. See **Food,** below. Simple, clean rooms, all with bathroom and TV. Singles €30; doubles €38; triples €49; quads €56. ❸

Hotel San Pietro, P. San Pietro, 5 (☎075 81 24 52; fax 81 63 32; www.hotel-sanpietro.it), just inside Porta San Pietro. Spacious, stone-floored rooms with new furniture, bath, A/C, satellite TV, minibar, safe, and hair dryer. Breakfast included. Singles €70; doubles €110; triples €120. Nov.-Mar. and June-Aug. 20% discount. AmEx/MC/V. ❺

Camping at Ostello Fontemaggio. €5 per person, €4.20 per tent, €2.50 per car. ❶

CENTRAL ITALY

◆ FOOD

Assisi will tempt you with a sinful array of nut breads and sweets, including mouth-watering *torrone* (a sweet nougat of almonds and egg whites; €2.90 per kg), and divine *brustengolo* (packed with raisins, apples, and walnuts; €21 per kg). **Pasticceria Santa Monica**, at V. Portica, 4, right off P. del Comune, sells these and other treats at low prices. (Open daily 9:30am-8pm.) On Saturday mornings, the **open-air market** takes over P. Matteotti. For fresh fruits and vegetables on weekdays, head to V. S. Gabriele.

Pizzeria Otello, V. San Antonio, 1 (☎075 81 24 15). Head downhill on V. dell'Arco dei Priori (under arch) and take 1st left. Centrally located *pizzeria* serves a variety of pies at good prices (€4.20-6.20). Focaccia sandwiches and large salads €4.40. *Primi* €5-6.80, *secondi* from €5-7.80. Open July-Aug. daily noon-3:30pm and 7-10:30pm; Sept.-June M-Sa noon-3:30pm. AmEx/MC/V. ❸

Trattoria da Erminio, V. Monte Cavallo, 19 (☎075 81 25 06). From P. del Comune, follow V. S. Rufino up through P. S. Rufino and onto V. Porta Perlici; take 1st right. Meat dishes grilled on an open fire in a corner of the dining room. *Primi* €4.70-8.30, *secondi* €5.20-10.90. Cover €1.30. Open F-W noon-2:30pm and 7-9pm. AmEx/MC/V. ❸

Il Duomo Pizzeria, V. di Porta Perlici, 11 (☎075 81 63 26). Large pizza oven is focal point of this brick cross-vaulted *pizzeria*. Open late. Diverse and well-priced *menù*. Wonderful pizza €3.10-6.20, *primi* €3.65-7, *secondi* €5.40-8.85. Cover €1.05. Open daily noon-3pm and 6:30pm-1am. Nov.-Mar. closed W. AmEx/MC/V. ❸

Ristorante Anfiteatro Romano, V. Anfiteatro Romano, 4 (☎075 81 30 25; fax 81 51 10), off P. Matteotti. The restaurant, downstairs from the hotel, serves large portions. *Primi* €4.20-7.80, *secondi* €5.20-8.30, *menù turistica* €12. AmEx/MC/V. ❷

Ristorante La Rocca, V. di Porta Perlici, 27 (☎/fax 075 81 22 84). In same building as the hotel (see above). Try the ravioli with black truffle sauce (€5.70). *Primi* €4.10-5.70, *secondi* €4.70-8.30. House wine €1.90 per 0.5L. Cover €1.55. Open daily 12:30-1:30pm and 7:30-8:30pm. MC/V. ❷

Hotel Grotta Antica Ristorante Caldrino, V. Macelli Vecchi, 1 (☎075 81 52 20). In same building as the hotel (see above). Mushroom and truffle dishes and over 1000 Umbrian wines. *Primi* €4.13-7.75, *secondi* €6.20-9.30. Cover €1.55. Open Apr.-Oct. daily noon-10pm. ❸

◉ SIGHTS

At age 19, St. Francis (b. 1182) abandoned military and social ambitions, rejected his father's wealth, and embraced asceticism. His love of nature, devoted humility, and renunciation of the church's worldliness earned him a huge European following, posing an unprecedented challenge to the decadent papacy and corrupt monastic orders. St. Francis continued to preach chastity and poverty until his death in 1226, when the order he founded was gradually subsumed into the Catholic hierarchy that it had criticized. Ironically, the Catholic church has glorified the modest saint through countless churches constructed in his honor.

BASILICA DI SAN FRANCESCO. When construction of the ▨**Basilica di San Francesco** began in the mid-13th century, the Franciscan order protested—the elaborate church seemed an impious monument to the conspicuous consumption that St. Francis had scorned. Brother Elia, the vicar of the order, insisted that a double church be erected, the lower level to be built around the saint's crypt, the upper level to be used as a church for services. The subdued art in the lower church commemorates Francis's modest life, while the upper church pays tribute to his sainthood and consecration. Although the basilica was damaged by an earthquake in 1997, the furious restoration efforts in preparation for Jubilee Year 2000 spurred a speedy reconstruction.

The walls of the upper church are covered with Giotto's renowned *Life of St. Francis* fresco cycle. The story starts on the right wall near the altar and runs clockwise, from a teenage Francis in courtly dress surprised by a prophecy of future greatness to an image of the saint passing through the agony of the "Dark Night." St. Francis's pictorial path of holy deeds is paralleled by the story of Jesus.

Cimabue's magnificent *Madonna and Child, Angels,* and *St. Francis* grace the right transept. Those who have been to Arezzo will recognize one of the images as an almost exact copy of his famous crucifix in the Chiesa di S. Domenico. Tragically, most of Cimabue's frescoes in the transepts and apse have so deteriorated that they now look like photographic negatives. Pietro Lorenzetti decorated the left transept with his outstanding *Crucifixion, Last Supper,* and *Madonna and Saints.* Also stunning are Simone Martini's frescoes in the first chapel off the left wall, which depict the life of St. Martin. Descend through a door in the right side of the apse to enter the room housing St. Francis's tunic and sandals.

St. Francis's tomb, the inspiration for the entire edifice, lies below the lower church. The coffin itself was hidden in the 15th century, for fear that the war-mongering Perugians would desecrate it. The rediscovery of the Neoclassical tomb was met with disdain from friars in 1818; a simplified version came in 1935. The stone coffin sits above the altar in the crypt, surrounded by the sarcophagi of four of the saint's dearest friends. (☎ *075 819 0084. Tours given by Franciscan monks daily 9am-noon and 2-5:30pm. Tours begin outside lower basilica. Arrange ahead for tours; call or visit info window across from entrance to lower basilica. €1 per person. Information window open daily 9am-12pm and 2-5pm. Lower basilica open daily 6:30am-7pm. Upper basilica open daily 8:30am-7pm. Museo Tesoro della Basilica ☎ 075 81 90 01. Open M-Sa 9:30am-6pm, Su 9:30am-noon and 2:30-6pm. Free.)*

OTHER SIGHTS

ROCCA MAGGIORE. The dramatic Rocca Maggiore looms uphill from the duomo. Check out the view down onto the town and the Basilica di S. Francesco from the sun-baked gravel lot outside the Rocca, or pay the nominal entrance fee to go inside the fortress and make like a mole through a 50m long tunnel to a lookout tower. The view is stunning in all directions, but the trip through the tunnel is not recommended for claustrophobes. *(From P. del Comune, follow V. S. Rufino to P. S. Rufino. Continue up V. Porta Perlici and take your 1st left up a narrow staircase, following signs for the Rocca. Open daily Apr.-Sept. 10am-7pm; Nov.-Mar. 10am-4:30pm. Closed in bad weather. €1.70, students €1. Prices may be higher when central courtyard renovations finish.)*

BASILICA DI SANTA CHIARA. The interior of the pink and white Basilica di Santa Chiara is a beautiful example of early Gothic architecture. It stands at the opposite end of Assisi on the site where St. Francis attended school. The church shelters not only the tomb (and hair) of St. Clare, but also tunics and shoes worn by St. Francis and the crucifix that revealed God's message to him. The nuns in this convent are sworn to seclusion. *(☎ 075 81 22 82. Open daily 9am-noon and 2-7pm.)*

DUOMO (CHIESA DI SAN RUFINO). V. S. Rufino climbs steeply up from P. del Comune between closely packed old houses, opening onto P. S. Rufino to reveal the squat duomo with its massive bell tower. The restored interior is quite spartan compared to its decorative facade. *(☎ 057 81 22 82. Open daily 8am-1pm and 2-6pm.)*

PIAZZA DEL COMUNE AND ENVIRONS. From the Basilica di San Francesco, V. S. Francesco snakes between medieval buildings and their 16th-century additions. Not far from the basilica, the wide, pink facade of the **Palazzo Vallemani** serves as temporary cover for the **Pinacoteca** while workers repair earthquake-inflicted

CENTRAL ITALY

wounds to its original home, the **Palazzo del Priore.** The museum has works by important Umbrian artists and a collection of Renaissance frescoes lifted from city gates and various shrines. Twenty meters up the street, the colorfully frescoed **Oratorio del Pelegrino** (Pilgrim Oratory) is worth a brief peek. At the end of the street, P. del Comune sits upon the old **Foro Romano.** Enter from the **crypt of St. Nicholas** on V. Portica and walk among the columns and statues of the old Roman forum, which stretches the length of P. del Comune. Back above ground sits the **Tempio di Minerva,** a majestic Roman relic with crumbling Corinthian columns. Rounding out the impressive buildings, just off the square is the **Chiesa Nuova,** with a rounded, central apse and a frescoed interior. *(Forum ☎ 075 81 30 53. Pinacoteca ☎ 075 81 52 92. Both open Mar. 16-Oct. 15 daily 10am-1pm and 2:30-7pm; Oct. 16-Mar. 15 10am-1pm and 2-5pm. €2.50 for each sight, students €2. The biglietto cumulativo (forum, La Rocca Maggiore, and Pinacoteca) €5.20, students €4. Tempio di Minerva open daily 6:30am-noon and 2:30-5pm. Chiesa Nuova ☎ 075 81 23 39. Same hours as Tempio di Minerva.)*

🎵 ENTERTAINMENT

All of Assisi's religious festivals involve feasts and processions. An especially long, dramatic performance marks **Easter Week.** On Holy Thursday, a mystery play reenacts the Deposition from the Cross. Traditional processions trail through town on Good Friday and Easter Sunday. Assisi welcomes spring with the **Festa di Calendimaggio** (first Thursday, Friday, and Saturday of May). A queen is chosen and dubbed *Primavera* (Spring), while the upper and lower quarters of the city compete in a clamorous musical tournament. Ladies and knights overtake the streets crooning amorous melodies in celebration of the young St. Francis, who wandered the streets of Assisi singing serenades at night. It was on one such night that he encountered a vision of the *Madonna della Povertà* (Lady of Poverty). Classical music concerts and organ recitals occur once or twice each week from April to October in the various churches. October 4 marks the **Festival of St. Francis,** which kicks off in Chiesa di Santa Maria degli Angeli, the site of St. Francis's death. Each year a different region of Italy offers oil for the cathedral's votive lamp, and the traditional dances and songs of that region are performed.

🚲 DAYTRIPS FROM ASSISI

EREMO DELLE CARCERI AND MT. SUBASIO
From P. Matteotti, exit the city through Porta Cappuccini and turn immediately left up the dirt road, parallel to the city wall. At the Rocca Minore, follow the trail uphill to the right. A little over ½ of the way up, the trail flattens and follows the flank of the mountain, giving spectacular views of the fertile valley below. Follow the paved road to the right, instead of crossing and taking the trail uphill. Loose rocks can make the descent difficult. For an easier walk (or drive) from Porta Cappuccini, follow the dirt trail next to the paved road uphill. ☎ 075 81 23 01. Open Easter-Oct. daily 6:30am-7pm; Nov.-Easter 6:30am-5:30pm.

A strenuous but gorgeous 1hr. hike up Mt. Subasio reveals the inspiring ▩**Eremo delle Carceri.** To explore Mt. Subasio, you can purchase a Kompass map (€6.20) or less detailed Club Alpino Italiano map (€4.65) in any bookshop or newspaper stand in Assisi. Those who follow the mountain trail may be startled by the line of parked cars and the kitschy souvenir stand outside the gate to the hermitage. But these are soon forgotten as you follow the path to the little complex of rough stone buildings. From the central courtyard, you can reach the **Grotta di San Francesco,** a series of tiny cells and chapels where St. Francis slept and prayed, connected by steep stairs and child-sized doorways. Trails run through the natural beauty to which St. Francis so often retreated.

Several churches associated with St. Francis and St. Clare stand in the immediate vicinity of Assisi. A 15min. stroll down the steep road outside Porta Nuova leads to the **Convent of San Damiano,** where St. Francis heard his calling and later wrote the *Canticle of the Creatures.* The chapel contains fine 14th-century frescoes and a riveting carving of Christ. (☎075 81 22 73. Open daily 6:30am-noon and 2-7pm.)

The train to Assisi passes **Basilica di Santa Maria degli Angeli,** a church inside a church. From Assisi, take the frequent bus to the train station (marked S. M. degli Angeli) from P. Matteotti, Largo Properzio, or P. Unità d'Italia and get off one stop after the train station. From the train station, exit left and take your first left, over the tracks, on Viale Patrono d'Italia. The basilica is ahead on the left (10min.). This church, with a Renaissance facade and Baroque interior, capped by a purple dome, houses two buildings that used to sit quietly in the woods until the church was built in the 15th century. **Porziuncola** is a chapel St. Francis built himself, and where he instituted the annual **Festa del Perdono** on August 2. In the right transept lies a small Benedictine cell, the **Cappella de Transito,** where St. Francis died. In order to overcome temptation, St. Francis supposedly flung himself on thorny rosebushes in the garden just outside the basilica, eternally staining the leaves red. Through the rose garden lies the **Museo di Santa Maria degli Angeli,** which houses holy relics from the Porziuncola. (☎075 805 1432. Basilica open daily 6:15am-8pm, July-Sept. until 9pm. Museum open daily 9am-noon and 3:30-6:30pm. Free.)

GUBBIO ☎075

A reminder of Gubbio's long, tumultuous history since its founding in the 3rd century takes form in the Eugabian Tables, records of the ancient town's alliance with the Romans against the Etruscans. Graceful portals and a well-preserved theater attest to the past grip of Roman emperors, and splendid *palazzi* recall years of subjugation under the powerful Dukes of Urbino. Gubbio has cobblestone streets and spectacular vistas, but its distinction lies in its school of painting, its ceramics tradition, and its favorite son Bosone Novello Raffaelli, Italy's first novelist.

▐ TRANSPORTATION

Trains: Nearest station is **Fossato di Vico's,** 19km away on Rome-Ancona line. To: **Ancona** (1½hr., 15 per day, from €4.23); **Rome** (2½hr., 10 per day, €10.12); and **Spoleto** (1¼hr., 10 per day, €3.36). Buses connect Gubbio to Fossato (M-Sa 12 per day, Su 6 per day; €2). Tickets at newsstand in P. Quaranta Martiri, at Perugia bus stop, and at newsstand in Fossato's train station. If stranded in Fossato without bus service, call a taxi at ☎075 91 92 02 or 033 5337 4871.

Buses: APM (☎075 50 67 81) runs to and from **Perugia** (1hr.; M-F 10 per day, Sa-Su 4 per day; €4) and are much more convenient than the train.

Taxis: (☎075 927 3800), in P. Quaranta Martiri.

◼◼ ⚄ ORIENTATION AND PRACTICAL INFORMATION

Gubbio is a tangle of twisting streets and medieval alleyways opening into the piazzas. Buses leave you in **Piazza Quaranta Martiri.** A short uphill walk on **Via della Repubblica,** the street ahead as you exit the bus station, leads to **Corso Garibaldi.** Signs point further uphill to **Piazza Grande,** the civic headquarters on the ledge of the hill. Some of Gubbio's best ceramics are sold on **Via dei Consoli** and P. Grande.

Tourist Office: IAT, P. Oderisi, 6 (☎075 922 0693), off C. Garibaldi next door to local Communist Party headquarters. Helpful English-speaking staff provides bus schedules, train times, and maps. Open Mar.-Sept. M-F 8:15am-1:45pm and 3:30-6:30pm, Sa 9am-1pm and 3:30-6:30pm, Su 8:30am-12:30pm; Oct.-Apr. M-F 8:15am-1:45pm and 3-6pm, Sa 9am-1pm and 3:30-6:30pm, Su 9am-1pm. July-Aug. also Su 3:30-6:30pm.

24hr. ATM: P. Quaranta Martiri, 48.

Emergency: ☎113. **Medical Emergency:** ☎118

Police: (☎075 22 15 42), on V. Leonardo da Vinci.

Late-Night Pharmacy: Farmacia Luconi, C. Garibaldi, 12 (☎075 927 3783). Open Apr.-Sept. M-Sa 9am-1pm and 4:30-8pm; Oct.-Mar. 9am-1pm and 4-7:30pm. 4 pharmacies rotate 24hr service.

Hospital: ☎075 23 94 67 or 23 94 69.

Post Office: V. Cairoli, 11 (☎075 927 3925). Open M-F 8am-6:30pm, Sa 8am-12:30pm.

Postal Code: 06024.

ACCOMMODATIONS

Residence di "Via Piccardi," V. Piccardi, 14 (☎075 927 6108). 6 large, comfortable rooms with bath overlook the outdoor garden. Friendly staff welcomes young backpackers. Breakfast included. Singles €30; doubles €45; triples €55; quads €72. ❸

Locanda del Duca, V. Piccardi, 3 (☎075 927 7753). From P. Quaranta Martiri, take a right onto V. Piccardi. Rooms with bath and TV. Restaurant below. Breakfast €2.58; dinner €14.46. Singles €37; doubles €52; triples €62; quads €72. AmEx/MC/V. ❹

Pensione Grotta dell'Angelo, V. Gioia, 47 (☎075 927 1747). Walk up from P. Quaranta Martiri on V. della Republica and take 1st right on V. Gioia. Spacious rooms. TV, phone, and bath. Dining in attached restaurant. Breakfast €3. Singles €30; doubles €46; triples €56. AmEx/MC/V. ❸

Hotel Gattapone, V. Beni, 11/13 (☎075 927 2489; fax 927 2417; www.mencarelligroup.com). Walk up V. della Repubblica, take 1st left across P. San Giovanni, and 1st right on V. Beni. Small, elegant hotel has 16 rooms, all with bath, minibar, telephone, and satellite TV. Buffet breakfast included. Singles €72.30; doubles €92.96; triples €129.11; quads 154.94. Prices 20% lower in Jan.-Mar. and June-July. AmEx/MC/V. ❺

FOOD

For a quick bite, try the sandwiches (€2.20) at the **alimentari,** P. Quaranta Martiri, 36, across from the bus station. (Open daily 8am-1pm and 4:30-8pm.) On Tuesday mornings, explore the **market** under P. Quaranta Martiri's *loggie.* Local delicacies await at **Prodotti Tipici e Tartufati Eugubini,** V. Piccardi, 17. Sample *salumi di cinghiale o cervo* (boar or deer sausage) and *pecorino* cheese, or indulge in truffle oil. (Open daily 10am-1pm and 2:30-8pm.)

Taverna del Buchetto, V. Dante, 30 (☎075 927 7034), near the Porta Romana off C. Garibaldi. Spicy *pollo alla diavola* (devil's chicken; €7.23). Pizza €3.62-7.23, *primi* €4.13-7.75. Cover €1.29. Open Tu-Su noon-2:30pm and 7:30-10pm. AmEx/MC/V. ❷

La Cantina Ristorante/Pizzeria, V. Francesco Piccotti, 3 (☎075 922 0583), off V. della Repubblica. This upscale *pizzeria* specializes in *funghi porcini e tartufi* (mushrooms and truffles). Pizza €4.50-7, *primi* €6.50-10.50, *secondi* €6.50-13. Cover €1. Open Tu-Su noon-2:30pm and 7-10pm; open for pizza noon-3pm. MC/V. ❷

San Francesco e il Lupo, at V. Cairoli and C. Garibaldi, (☎075 927 2344). Pizza €5.50-10.50, *primi* €4.65-12.40, *secondi* €7.23-11.88. *Menù* with *primo, secondo, contorno*, fresh fruit, and dessert €13. Cover €1.50 for meals outside the *menù*. Open W-M noon-2pm and 7-10pm. MC/V. ❸

Ristorante La Lanterna, V. Gioia, 23 (☎075 927 5594). High stone walls enclose 2 refined dining rooms where locals and tourists sample typical *Eugubbino* cuisine. Try the *frittata al tartufo di Gubbio* (€9.30). *Primi* €5.17-10.33, *secondi* €8.27-12.40. Open F-W noon-3pm and 7-10:30pm. MC/V. ❸

🎯 SIGHTS

PIAZZA QUARANTA MARTIRI. In the middle of the piazza stretches the **Giardino dei Quaranta Martiri** (Garden of the 40 Martyrs), a memorial to those shot by the Nazis in reprisal for the assassination of two German officials. **Chiesa di San Francesco,** one of several places where St. Francis reputedly experienced his powerful conversion, stands on one side of the square. The central apse holds the *Vita della Madonna* (Life of the Madonna), a partially destroyed 15th-century fresco series by Ottaviano Nelli, Gubbio's most famous painter. Across the piazza from the church is **Loggia dei Tiratoi,** where 14th-century weavers stretched their cloth so it would shrink evenly. V. Matteotti runs from P. Quaranto Martiri outside the city walls to the beautiful **Roman theater,** which still stages classical productions. *(Church open daily 7:15am-noon and 3:30 6:30pm.)*

PALAZZO DEI CONSOLI. This white stone palace was built in 1332 for the high magistrate of Gubbio. Within the *palazzo*, the **Museo Civico** displays a collection of Eugubine and Roman artifacts, beginning in the cavernous main room. Statues, pieces of marble friezes, and tablets are arrayed along the walls. Tacked in a room upstairs, to the left beyond the staircase, are the ▨**Tavole Eugubine (Eugabian Tables),** often compared to the Rosetta Stone. Discovered in 1444 near the Roman theater outside the city walls, five of these seven bronze tablets (300-100 BC) form one of the few remaining documents of the ancient Umbrian language (the last two are in Latin). A farmer discovered the tablets in an underground chamber of the Roman theater. The ritual texts spell out the social and political organization of early Umbria and provide the novice with advice on how to read omens from animal livers. *(☎075 927 4298. P. Grande. Palazzo and Museo open mid-Mar. to Oct. daily 10am-1pm and 3-6pm; Nov. to mid-Mar. 10am-1pm and 2-5pm. €4, ages 7-25 €2, under 7 free.)*

PALAZZO DUCALE AND THE DUOMO. Climb to the pinnacle of the town, where the 15th-century Palazzo Ducale and the 13th-century duomo face off. Federico da Montefeltro commissioned Luciano Laurana, designer of his larger palace in Urbino, to build this smaller but equally elegant version. The duomo, an unassuming pink Gothic building, has 12th-century stained-glass windows and Pinturicchio's *Adoration of the Shepherds*. *(Follow the signs uphill from P. Grande. Museum open M-Sa 9am-1pm and 2:30-6:30pm, Su 9am-12:30pm. Palazzo entrance €2, under 18 or over 60 free. Duomo open daily 9am-noon and 2-6pm.)*

MONTE INGINO. When the museums close for lunch, take the birdcage chairlift *(funivia;* 7min.) to the peak of Monte Ingino for a splendid view and prime picnicking. Visit the **basilica and monastery of Sant'Ubaldo,** Gubbio's patron saint. The basilica houses St. Ubaldo's pickled body in a glass case above the elaborate altar and the three *ceri*, large wooden candles carried in the **Corsa dei Ceri** procession each May (see **Entertainment,** p. 438). *(From the uphill entrance to the basilica, bear left and continue upward on a dirt path to the top of the mountain. Chairlift open June M-Sa 9:30am-1:15pm and 2:30-7pm, Su 9am-7:30pm; July-Aug. M-Sa 8:30am-7:30pm, Su 8:30am-8pm;*

Sept. M-Sa 9:30am-1:15pm and 2:30-7pm, Su 9:30am-1:15pm and 2:30-7:30pm; Mar. M-Sa 10am-1:15pm and 2:30-5:30pm, Su 9:30am-1:15pm and 2:30-6pm; Apr.-May M-Sa 10am-1:15pm and 2:30-6:30pm, Su 9:30am-1:15pm and 2:30-7pm. Oct. daily 10am-1:15pm and 2:30-6pm; Nov.-Feb. 10am-1:15pm and 2:30-5pm. €4, round-trip €5.)

ENTERTAINMENT

The 900-year-old tradition of the **Corsa dei Ceri** takes place every May 15. Intended to represent candles, the three *ceri* are huge wooden blocks carved like hourglasses and topped with little saints. Each one represents a distinct faction of the populace: the masons, the farmers, and the artisans. After 12 hours of furious preparation and frenetic flag-twirling, squads of runners *(ceraioli)* clad in Renaissance-style tights heave the heavy objects onto their shoulders and run a wild relay race up Monte Ingino. This orgiastic festival turns the quiet medieval streets of Gubbio into stomping grounds for frenzied locals and entranced visitors.

During the **Palio della Balestra,** held on the last Sunday in May in P. Grande, archers from Gubbio and nearby Sansepolcro gather for the latest rematch of a fierce crossbow contest that dates to 1461. If Gubbio wins, an animated parade ensues. A recent industry in Gubbio is the production of *balestre* (toy crossbows).

SPOLETO   ☎ 0743

A mere 43 years ago, Spoleto had little but its magnificent gorge, spanned by the medieval Ponte delle Torri. In 1958, composer Giancarlo Menotti selected Spoleto as the trial site for a summer performing arts festival, and it never left. The *Festivali Due Mondi* (Festival of Two Worlds) proved that art could be the bread and butter of an entire city. In 1962, modern artists traveled to Spoleto to place sculptures throughout the town, even in the Roman amphitheater. One of Alexander Calder's first sculptures will greet you as you exit the train station.

TRANSPORTATION

Trains: (☎0743 48 516), in P. Polvani. Ticket window open 6am-8pm. **Luggage storage** available (see below). To: **Ancona** (2hr., 9 per day, from €7.90); **Assisi** (40min., 5 per day, €2.40); **Perugia** (1½hr., 8 per day, €3.50); and **Rome** (1½hr., every 1-2hr., from €6.82). Additional trains to Assisi and Perugia via Foligno.

Buses: SSIT (☎0743 21 22 05; www.spoletina.com) departs from P. della Vittoria by P. Garibaldi. To **Foligno** (45min., M-F 4 per day, €2.60) and **Perugia** (1 per day, 6:23am, €5.40).

Taxis: (☎0743 44 548) in P. della Libertà, (☎0743 49 990) in P. Garibaldi, and (☎0743 22 04 89) at the train station.

ORIENTATION AND PRACTICAL INFORMATION

Have patience with Spoleto's narrow, cobblestoned streets; they are navigable with the assistance of a map, available from the tourist office in **Piazza della Libertà.** To get there from the train station, walk straight up **Viale Trento e Trieste,** and bear right into **Piazza della Vittoria.** Pass through the double gate in the old city wall and through **Piazza Garibaldi** straight onto **Corso Garibaldi.** Follow the Corso as it winds uphill and into **Piazza Torre dell'Olio.** Continue uphill on the narrow street, crossing over a wider, paved one. To the left of the church is **Corso Mazzini,** the main street of the *centro storico*, which leads to P. della Liberta; the tourist office is ahead on the left of the piazza (30min., most of which is up a fairly steep hill). You can also take an ATAF bus from the station (dir.: Centro, €0.80)—buy tickets at the newsstand in the station. From C. Mazzini, turn left up **Via del Mercato** to **Piazza del Mercato**, the bustling center of the city. Many streets radiate from P. del Mercato. **Via del Municipio** runs to **Piazza del Municipio** and **Piazza Campello**, while **Via Saffi** leads to **Piazza del Duomo**. These three squares contain most of the city's sights.

Tourist Office: P. della Libertà, 7 (☎0743 23 89 20). Offers detailed info and a map of the city. Arranges tours, but no hotel or event reservations. Some English spoken. Open Apr.-Oct. M-F 9am-1pm and 4-7pm, Sa-Su 10am-1pm and 4-7pm. Nov.-Mar. M-F 9am-1pm and 3:30-6:30pm, Sa 10am-1pm and 3:30-6:30pm, Su 10am-1pm.

Bank: Cassa di Risparmio di Spoleto, P. Mentana, 3, just off C. Mazzini. 24hr. **ATM.** Open M-F 8:20am-1:20pm and 2:50-3:50pm, Sa 8:20-11:50am.

Luggage Storage: In train station €2.58 per 12hr. Go to cashier at the bar. Open daily 5am-11pm.

Theater Box Office: Buy advance tickets for events during the Spoleto festival at **Teatro Nuovo** (☎0743 44 097). Open Tu-Su 10:30am-1pm and 4-7pm.

Emergency: ☎113. **Medical Emergency:** ☎118.

Police: V. dei Filosofi, 57 (☎0743 22 38 87).

Late-Night Pharmacy: Farmacia Scoccianti (0743 22 32 42), on V. L. Marconi. From train station, head straight and then take 1st right. Posts after-hours pharmacy.

Hospital: V. Loreto, 3 (☎0743 21 01), outside Porta Loreto.

Post Office: V. L.G. Matteotti, 2 (☎0743 40 373). Walk down V. Matteotti from P. della Libertà; the entrance is on your right. Open M-F 8:10am-6:30pm and Sa 8:10am-12:30pm.

Postal Code: 06049.

ACCOMMODATIONS

Finding accommodations is almost impossible during the summer music festival (the last week of June and the first week of July). If you arrive during the festival, contact **Conspoleto**, P. della Libertà, 7. (☎0743 22 07 73; www.conspoleto.com. Open M-Sa 9am-1pm and 3-7pm.) The tourist office keeps a list of camping and *agriturismo* options. Prices are higher during the festival.

Hotel Panciolle, V. del Duomo, 3 (☎/fax 0743 45 677), in the *centro storico* near the duomo. Bright, airy rooms with modern furnishings and bath. Breakfast €5. Singles €37; doubles €52; triples €62. ❹

Albergo Due Porte, P. della Vittoria, 5 (☎0743 22 36 66), a 10min. walk from train station; follow Viale Trento e Trieste and bear right into P. della Vittoria. Hotel just outside the walls to the left of passage through city gates. Or take short bus trip (every 10min., €0.80). Spotless bathrooms. TV and phone. Cribs available. Wheelchair-accessible. Breakfast included. Singles €35; doubles €62; triples €75; quads €83. MC/V. ❹

Hotel Charleston, P. Collicola, 10 (☎0743 22 00 52; fax 22 12 44; www.hotelcharleston.it), adjacent to the Museum of Modern Art. Quirky decor in rooms draws inspiration from nearby art museum. Walls are covered with posters from past Spoleto Festivals. All rooms with bath, TV, VCR, minibar, telephone, and hair dryer. Breakfast included. Singles €52-68; doubles €80-109. Additional bed €10. AmEx/MC/V. ❺

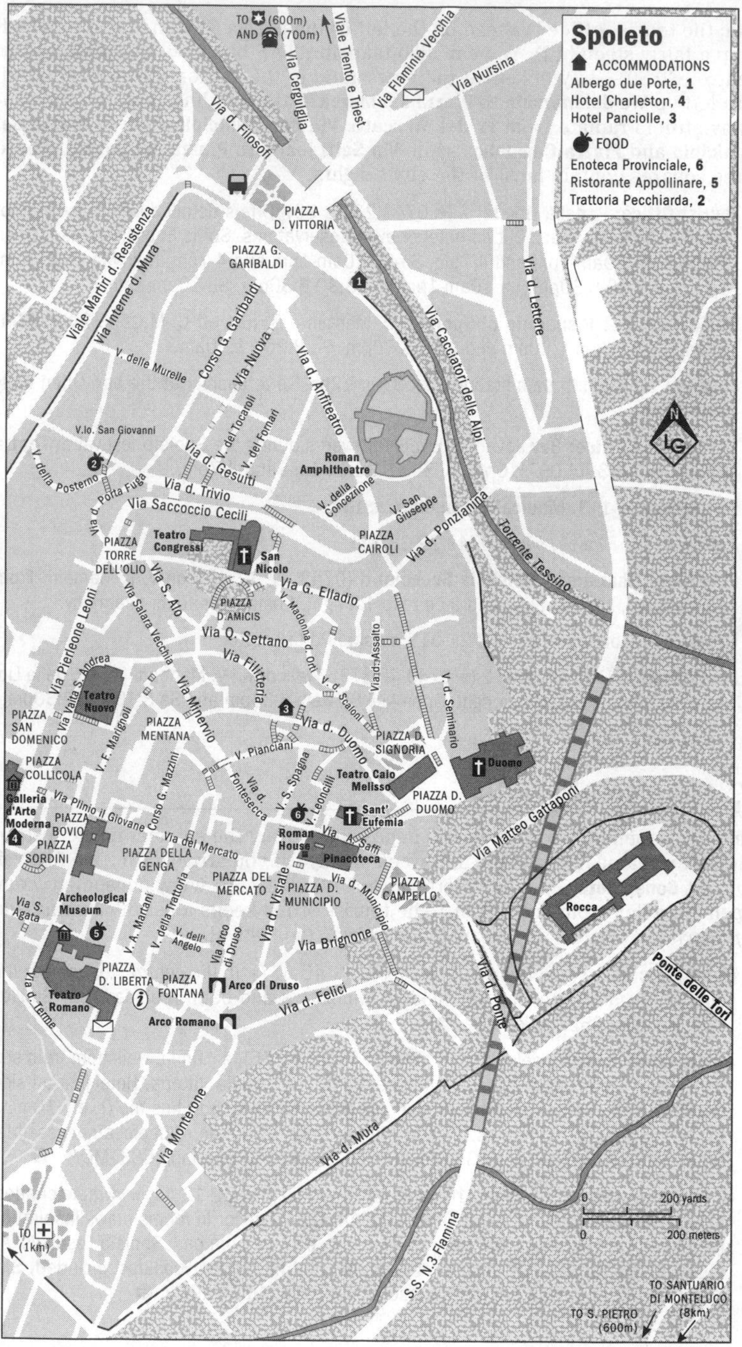
Spoleto
ACCOMMODATIONS
Albergo due Porte, 1
Hotel Charleston, 4
Hotel Panciolle, 3
FOOD
Enoteca Provinciale, 6
Ristorante Appollinare, 5
Trattoria Pecchiarda, 2
TO (600m) AND (700m)
Viale Trento e Triest
Via Flaminia Vecchia
Via Nursina
Via Cerguglia
Via d. Filosofi
PIAZZA D. VITTORIA
PIAZZA G. GARIBALDI
Viale Martiri d. Resistenza
Via Interne d. Mura
Corso G. Garibaldi
Via Nuova
Via d. Anfiteatro
Via Cacciatori delle Alpi
Via d. Lettere
V. delle Murelle
V. del Tocacoli
V. del Fornari
V.lo. San Giovanni
V. della Posterno
Via d. Gesuiti
Via d. Trivio
Via d. Porta Fuga
Via Saccoccio Cecili
Roman Amphitheatre
V. della Concezione
V. San Giuseppe
Via d. Ponzianina
Torrente Tessino
PIAZZA CAIROLI
Teatro Congressi
San Nicolo
PIAZZA TORRE DELL'OLIO
Via S. Alo
Via Salara Vecchia
PIAZZA D.AMICIS
Via G. Elladio
V. Madonna d. Orti
Via Q. Settano
Via Filitteria
Via d. Assalto
V. d. Scaloni
V. d. Seminario
Via Pierleone Leoni
Via Vaita S. Andrea
Teatro Nuovo
Via Minervio
PIAZZA SAN DOMENICO
PIAZZA MENTANA
V. F. Marignoli
Via d. Duomo
PIAZZA D. SIGNORIA
Duomo
V. Pianciani
PIAZZA COLLICOLA
Corso G. Mazzini
Via d. Fontesecca
V. S. Spagna
V. Leoncilli
Teatro Caio Melisso
Galleria d'Arte Moderna
Via Plinio il Giovane
PIAZZA BOVIO
PIAZZA SORDINI
Sant' Eufemia
PIAZZA D. DUOMO
Via Matteo Gattaponi
Roman House
Via A. Saffi
Pinacoteca
Via del Mercato
PIAZZA DELLA GENGA
PIAZZA DEL MERCATO
PIAZZA D. MUNICIPIO
Via d. Municipio
PIAZZA CAMPELLO
Rocca
Via S. Agata
Archeological Museum
V. A. Martani
V. della Trattoria
V. dell' Angelo
Via Arco di Druso
Via d. Visiale
Via Brignone
Ponte delle Tori
Via d. Terme
Teatro Romano
PIAZZA D. LIBERTA
PIAZZA FONTANA
Arco di Druso
Via d. Felici
Arco Romano
Via d. Ponte
Via Monterone
Via d. Mura
S.S. N.3 Flamina
TO (1km)
0 200 yards
0 200 meters
TO SANTUARIO DI MONTELUCO (8km)
TO S. PIETRO (600m)

◘ FOOD

An **open-air market** enlivens P. del Mercato. (Open M-Sa 8:30am-1pm.) The **STANDA supermarket,** in P. Garibaldi, stocks basics. (Open M-Sa 9am-1pm and 4-8pm.)

▨ **Trattoria Pecchiarda,** Vicolo San Giovanni, 1 (☎ 0743 22 10 09). Walk up C. Garibaldi and turn right on V. della Posterna, then left up some stairs. Fresh pasta (€6.20-9.30) and *secondi* grilled over wood fire (€6.71-8.26). Filling *gnocchi* with tomato basil sauce €7.23. Open daily 1-3:30pm and 8pm-midnight. ❸

    Enoteca Provinciale, V. Saffi, 7 (☎ 0743 22 04 84), near *La Pinacoteca.* Cozy place to sample local wines. Try the *frittata al tartufo* (truffle omelette; €6.19) or *strangozzi alla spolentina* (€5.16). Open W-M 11am-3pm and 7-11pm. MC/V. ❸

    Ristorante Appollinare, V. S. Agata, 14 (☎ 0743 22 32 56), just off P. della Libertà. Tuxedo-clad waiters serve imaginative variations of traditional Umbrian dishes. Menu changes seasonally. In summer start with the *caramella* (a *caciotta* cheese-filled puff pastry with black truffle sauce; €9). *Primi* €9-15, *secondi* €10-18. Open Easter-Oct. daily 12:30-2:30pm and 7:30-10:30pm. Nov.-Easter closed Tu. AmEx/MC/V. ❺

◗ SIGHTS

ROCCA AND PONTE DELLE TORRI. The **papal fortress,** named **Rocca,** up V. Saffi from P. del Duomo, sits on the hillside above Spoleto. This fortress, a prison until 1982, was used during the war to confine Slavic and Italian prisoners. In 1943, the prisoners staged a dramatic escape to join the partisans in the Umbrian hills. The impressive Rocca is under perpetual renovation, although the courtyard and larger rooms are used for music and film events. On the far side of the Rocca, you'll come to the massive ▨**Ponte delle Torri,** a stunning achievement of 14th-century engineering. The 80m bridge and aqueduct span the channel of the river Tessino. On the far bank, the craggy medieval towers for which the bridge was named rise up beyond a small waterfall. *(Rocca open June 11-Sept. 15 daily 10am-8pm; Mar. 15-June 10 and Sept. 16-Oct. M-F 10am-noon and 3-7pm, Sa-Su 10am-7pm; Nov.-Mar. 14 M-F 2:30-5pm, Sa-Su 10am-5pm. Guided tours every hr. Entrance €4.65.)*

DUOMO. Spoleto's glowing Romanesque cathedral was built in the 12th century and later augmented by a portico (1491) and 17th-century interior redecoration. The soaring bell tower is an amalgam of styles and materials, cobbled together from fragments of Roman structures. Eight rose windows animate the facade, the largest one bearing the symbols of the four evangelists. Brilliantly colored scenes by Fra Filippo Lippi fill the domed apse. *The Annunciation,* in the lower left of the fresco cycle, is particularly impressive. Lorenzo the Magnificent commissioned Lippi's tomb, which was decorated by the artist's son, Filippino, and is now located in the right transept. *(Down shallow flight of steps from Pinacoteca. Open Mar.-Oct. daily 7:30am-12:30pm and 3-6:30pm; Nov.-Feb. 8am-12:30pm and 3-6pm.)*

ART MUSEUMS. Spoleto's **La Pinacoteca,** on the first floor of the city hall, houses the work of medieval and modern Umbrian artists. The all-star roster includes Perugino and his student, Lo Spagna. *(Up a flight of stairs from P. del Duomo. ☎ 0743 21 82 70. Open daily 10am-1pm and 3-6pm. Ticket includes the Roman House and Museum of Modern Art. €4.13.)* The **Museum of Modern Art** hosts a variety of changing exhibits. *(From C. Mazzini, turn left on V. Sant'Agata and then right on V. delle Terme. The museum lies ahead on your right. Open Mar. 16-Oct. 15 daily 10:30am-1pm and 3-6:30pm, Oct. 16-Mar. 15 W-M 10:30am-1pm and 3-5pm. Museum only €3.10.)*

CHIESA DI SANT'EUFEMIA. Situated on the grounds of the bishop's residence, this Romanesque church was constructed in the beginning of the 12th century. It houses sweeping arches, rhythmic windows, and concentric decorations on the heavy portals. *(Left from P. del Duomo, in P. Archi Vescovile. Enter off V. Saffi. Open M, W-Sa 10am-1pm and 4-7pm, Su 10:30am-6pm. €2.50.)*

ROMAN RUINS. Spoleto's many classical ruins testify to the city's prominence in Roman times. The well-preserved **theater** stands just beyond the Roman walls, visible from P. della Libertà. Take V. S. Agata from the piazza to reach the entrance of the adjacent **Museo Archeologico**, which houses ceramic and statuary artifacts from the area. *(☎0743 22 32 77. Open daily 8:30am-7:30pm. €2, includes interior of the theater. EU citizens 18-26 €1, EU citizens under 18 or over 65 free.)* The **Arco Romano**, at the top of V. Monterone, once marked the entrance into town. Farther along, the **Arco di Druso** led to the forum (now P. del Mercato). Duck into the restored **Casa Romana,** ancient home to Emperor Vespasian's mother. *(Beneath city hall, entrance at V. di Visiale, 9. From P. del Duomo, take right on V. del Duomo, then 1st left. Open daily 10am-8pm. Entrance included in the Galleria Civico d'Arte ticket, house only €2.07.)*

MONTELUCO. Spoleto's "mountain of the sacred grove" lies an invigorating hour-long climb away, through the forest, past tiny mountain shrines and elegant villa retreats. At the crest of the mountain you'll find a park, several bars, hotels, a skeet-shooting range, and the tiny Franciscan **Santuario di Monteluco,** once the refuge of St. Francis and San Bernadino of Siena. At the base of Monteluco, a 5min. stroll down the right fork of the road brings you to the Romanesque **Chiesa di San Pietro.** Note the wolf to the right of the door wearing a monk's cowl and holding a book. *(Buses leave P. della Libertà for Monteluco about every 1½hr. when the sanctuary is open. Cross the Ponte delle Torri and follow the stony stairway up to trail #1, which leads to the sanctuary. Sanctuary open daily 9am-5:30pm. Free.)*

▌♫ ENTERTAINMENT

The ▨**Spoleto Festival** (formerly known as the **Festival dei Due Mondi** or Festival of Two Worlds) is held from the end of June to mid-July and has become one of the world's most prestigious international arts events. The festival features concerts, operas, ballets, and also brings film screenings, modern art shows, and local craft displays to Spoleto. Tickets may be purchased in late April from the ticket office at P. Duomo, 8, and in late May from another ticket office in P. della Libertà. (☎0743 44 700; fax 22 03 21.) During the festival, the box offices at **Teatro Nuovo** and **Rocca Albornoziana** are open one hour before the start of most performances. (Open Tu-Su 10am-12:30pm and 3:30-7pm.) Advance bookings are recommended. Contact the Associazione Festival dei Due Mondi, Biglietteria Festival dei Due Mondi, 06049 Spoleto (PG), Italia. The renowned **Stagione del Teatro Lirico Sperimentale di Spoleto** (Experimental Opera Season) runs from late August to September. The **Istituzione Teatro Lirico Sperimentale di Spoleto "A. Belli,"** P. G. Bovio, 1, 06049 Spoleto, provides information. (☎0743 22 16 45; www.caribusiness.it/lirico.)

▌♫ DAYTRIP FROM SPOLETO: TREVI

Take an SSIT bus from Foligno, a major station that is the branching point for the Rome-Florence line (30min.; M-Sa 8 per day; last bus to Trevi 7pm, last bus to Foligno 6:30pm). The Foligno train schedule is posted outside the Trevi tourist office and at the tabacchi next to P. Garibaldi in Trevi. The energetic can take a train to Trevi and hike up the steep bluff to the town center (30min.).

Trevi's ancient pastel buildings, perched jaggedly along near vertical slopes, form a small island amidst vast silvery-green olive groves. Contact the **Pro Loco Tourist Office,** P. del Comune, 5 (☎ 0742 78 11 50; www.protrevi.com), in the shadows of an impressive bell tower, to find out about the town's attractions. **Pinacoteca Rascolta d'Arte di San Francesco** houses a collection of religious Renaissance art. (Follow V. S. Francesco from P. Mazzini to reach the museum. Open June-July Tu-Su 10:30am-1pm and 3:30-7pm; Aug. daily 10am-1pm and 3-6:30pm; Oct.-Mar. F-Su 10am-1pm and 2:30-5pm; Apr.-May and Sept. Tu-Su 10:30am-1pm and 2:30-6pm. €2.58, students €1.80.) The **Flash Art Museum,** V. P. Riccardi, 4, is associated with the trendy contemporary Italian art magazine *Flash* and hosts changing exhibits of modern and contemporary art. (☎ 0742 38 18 18; www.flashartonline.com. Open Tu-Su 3-7pm.) The **Illumination Procession,** one of the oldest festivals in Umbria, takes place every January 28th. Hotels in Trevi are costly, but try **Il Terziere ❹,** V. Salerno, 1, just off P. Garibaldi. It's a modern hotel with immaculate rooms and a great **restaurant ❸.** Try the *strangozzi al tartufo* (stringy pasta with truffles) for €8.26. (☎ 0742 78 359. Singles €47; doubles €62; triples €72.30. AmEx/MC/V.)

ORVIETO ☎ 0763

Orvieto sits, as it has for the past 3000 years, above an incredible volcanic plateau rising from the rolling farmlands of southern Umbria. In the 7th century BC, Etruscans began to burrow under the city for *tufo* (a volcanic stone out of which most of the medieval quarter is built), creating the subterranean companion city beneath Orvieto's surface. Five centuries later, the Romans sacked and reoccupied the plateau, calling their "new" city, strangely enough, *"urbus ventus"* (old city), from which the name Orvieto is derived. In medieval times the city became a center of worship. Thomas Aquinas lectured in local academies, fervent Christians planned their crusades, and countless churches sprang up along the winding city streets. In the 14th and 15th centuries, the Masters of Orvieto, alongside those of Siena, Assisi, and Perugia, formed a highly influential school of painters. Today, Orvieto is a popular tourist destination; visitors are drawn to the stunning 13th-century duomo, the city's steeples, streets, and underground chambers, and the renowned *Orvieto Classico* wine.

⌐ TRANSPORTATION

Trains: Luggage storage available (p. 444). To: **Arezzo** (1hr., every hr., €5.70); **Florence** (2½hr., every hr. 7:29am-8:32pm, €9.70) via **Cortona** (45min.); and **Rome** (1½hr., every 1-2hr., 4:25am-11:28pm, €6.82).

Buses: Leave from P. Cahen or the train station. **COTRAL** (☎ 0763 73 48 14). Buy tickets at *tabacchi* in train station. To **Viterbo** (8 per day, 6:20am-5:45pm, €2.80). **ATC** (☎ 0763 30 12 24) runs buses to **Perugia** (1½hr., 5:55am, €6) and **Todi** (1hr., 1:40pm, €4.80). Buy tickets at funicular ticket office, at *tabacchi* on C. Cavour, or on the bus.

✈ ⚡ ORIENTATION AND PRACTICAL INFORMATION

Orvieto lies midway along the Rome-Florence train line. From the train station, cross the street and take the funicular (every 15min.; €0.80, with shuttle €0.90) up the hill to **Piazza Cahen,** where ATC buses stop. A shuttle leads from P. Cahen to **Piazza del Duomo.** If you choose to walk, you can follow **Corso Cavour** to its intersection with **Via Duomo.** The left branch leads to the duomo and surrounding museums; the right, to **Piazza del Popolo.** Sprinkled between V. Duomo and the **Piazza della Repubblica** along Corso Cavour are most of the city's restaurants, hotels, and shops. Past P. della Repubblica is the medieval and oldest section of town.

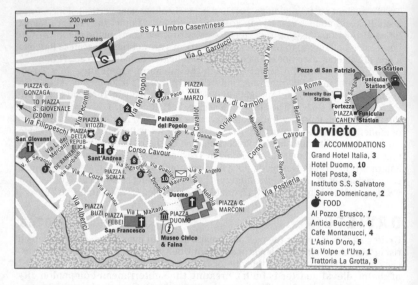

Orvieto

🏠 ACCOMMODATIONS
Grand Hotel Italia, **3**
Hotel Duomo, **10**
Hotel Posta, **8**
Instituto S.S. Salvatore
  Suore Domenicane, **2**
🍴 FOOD
Al Pozzo Etrusco, **7**
Antica Bucchero, **6**
Cafe Montanucci, **4**
L'Asino D'oro, **5**
La Volpe e l'Uva, **1**
Trattoria La Grotta, **9**

Tourist Office: P. del Duomo, 24 (☎0763 34 17 72; fax 34 44 33). English spoken. Offers info on hotels, restaurants, and sights. Has special deals on underground tours of Orvieto, as well as sells the **Orvieto Unica card** (€12.50, students €10.50), which includes underground tour, round-trip ticket for funicular-minibus, and entrance to Museo Faina, the Torre del Moro, and the Cappella della Madonna di San Brizio. Open M-F 8:15am-1:50pm and 4-7pm, Sa 10am-1pm and 4-7pm, Su 10am-noon and 4-6pm. The **Tourist Information Point,** Borgo Largo Barzini, 7 (☎0763 34 22 97), just off V. Duomo, helps find accommodations free. **Traveler's check** and **currency exchange** for 5% commission. Open M-Sa 9am-1pm and 4-7pm.

Luggage storage: At the train station ticket office. €2.58 for 12hr. Open daily 6:30am-8pm.

Emergency: ☎113. **Medical Emergency:** ☎118.

Police: (☎0763 34 00 88), in P. della Repubblica.

Hospital: (☎0763 30 91), across tracks from train station.

Post Office: (☎0763 34 12 43), on V. Cesare Nebbia. Stamps are available at *tabacchi,* and mailboxes dot the town. Open M-Sa 8am-4:45pm.

Postal Code: 05018.

🏠 ACCOMMODATIONS & CAMPING

▨ **Hotel Duomo,** V. Maurizio, 7 (☎0763 34 18 87; fax 39 49 73; www.argoweb.it/hotel_duomo), off V. Duomo, 1st right as you leave P. del Duomo. Steps away from the cathedral. Completely refurbished rooms feature classy new furniture, sparkling bathrooms, and modern sculpture. A/C, satellite TV, modem jacks, and minibar. Breakfast included. Singles €63; doubles €93. AmEx/MC/V. ❺

▨ **Hotel Posta,** V. Luca Signorelli, 18 (☎076 33 41 909). Halcyon setting with high-ceilinged rooms full of antique furniture. Lobby and hallway renovations in progress; call ahead. Breakfast €6. Reserve 20 days in advance July-Aug. Singles €26-31, with bath €37; doubles €40-43/€51-56. ❸

Istituto S.S. Salvatore Suore Domenicane, V. del Popolo, 1 (☎/fax 0763 34 29 10). Nuns to the rescue. Clean rooms at a decent value. Breakfast €3. 2-night min. Curfew 11pm; in winter 9:30pm. Closed July. Singles €41.32; doubles with bath €51.65. ❹

Grand Hotel Italia, V. del Popolo, 13 (☎0763 34 20 65; fax 34 29 02; www.bellaumbria.net/Grand-Hotel-Italia). Lounge in the spacious, comfortable lobby, or on the 3rd-floor panoramic terrace. Bright, modern rooms with bath, satellite TV, minibar, and telephone. Breakfast included. Singles €60; doubles €94. AmEx/MC/V. ❹

Camping: Scacco Matto (☎0744 95 01 63; fax 95 03 73), on Lake Corbara, 14km from center of town. From station, take local Orvieto-Baschi bus; get dropped off at site. Bus service between campsite and Orvieto's station infrequent. Beach and hot showers. €5.50 per person, €5.50 per tent, €3 per car. ❶

◘ FOOD

Reasonable options exist among Orvieto's crowd of pricey *ristoranti*. Track down an Umbrian gem that serves baked *lumachelle* (snail-shaped buns with ham and cheese), *tortucce* (fried bread dough), anise seed or almond cookies, pizza topped with pork cracklings, chickpea and chestnut soup, *rigatoni* with nuts and chocolate, and *mazzafegate* (sweet or salty sausages). Tellingly, Orvieto was known in ancient times as *Oinarea* (city where wine flows). Today the stream is still steady, with bottles starting as low as €2.50. Don't leave town without sampling its world-renowned wine, *Orvieto Classico.* **Alimentari** with local treats dot the city; stop by the charming, family-run **Panini Imbottiti,** V. del Duomo, 36. Bottles of *Orvieto Classico* start at €2.50. (Open M-Tu and Th-Sa 7:30am-noon and 5-8:30pm, W 7:45am-2pm.)

▨ **Trattoria La Grotta,** V. L. Signorelli, 5 (☎/fax 0763 34 13 48), near the duomo. Feast on *pappardelle al cinghiale* (pasta with boar sauce; €7.80). Finish with *tiramisù* (€4). *Primi* and *secondi* €4-13. Open W-M 12:30-3pm and 7:30-11pm. AmEx/MC/V. ❹

▨ **La Volpe e L'Uva,** V. Ripa Corsica, 2/A (☎/fax 0763 21 72 99). On corner of V. della Pace behind the Palazzo del Popolo. Vegetarian heaven with intimate setting and orgasmic dishes. Gorge on the *ombrigelli con la carbonara ai fiori di zucca* (€5.68) or *salsicce e uva* (sausages with grapes; €7.75). Open daily W-Su 7-11pm. ❸

Al Pozzo Etrusco Ristorante, P. de' Ranieri, 1/A (☎0763 34 44 56). Follow V. Garibaldi from P. della Repubblica and walk diagonally left across P. de' Ranieri. *Al Pozzo Etrusco* means "the Etruscan well," and they've actually got one. *Primi* €4.50-7.50, *secondi* €5.50-11.50. Open W-M noon-3pm and 7-10pm. AmEx/MC/V. ❸

Ristorante Antica Bucchero, V. de' Cartari, 4 (☎0763 34 17 25), off C. Cavour. Traditional Orvieto fare served outside in quiet piazza or in the sunken dining room. Try the *tagliatelle al ragu di coniglio* (pasta with rabbit; €6.20). *Primi* and *secondi* €6.20-10.50. Open noon-3pm and 7-10pm. AmEx/MC/V. ❹

L'Asino D'oro, V. lo del Popolo I, 9 (☎0763 34 33 02), in the piazza between C. Cavour and P. del Popolo. At intersection of V. Duomo and C. Cavour, head toward P. della Repubblica and take 1st alley to right. Exquisite and reasonably priced food. Wheelchair-accessible. *Primi* and *secondi* €4-7. Open Tu-Su 12:30pm-midnight. MC/V. ❸

Cafe Montenucci, C. Cavour, 25 (☎0763 34 12 61). Enjoy delectable regional specialty pastries while you check email. Pastries €0.70-1.55. Internet €3.10 per 30min. Open Oct.-Mar. daily 7am-midnight; Nov.-Apr. Th-Tu 7am-midnight. ❶

CENTRAL ITALY

⊙ SIGHTS

■ **DUOMO.** The facade of Orvieto's pride and joy was designed around 1290 by Lorenzo Maitani and dazzles the admirer with spires, mosaics, and sculptures. Initially envisioned as a smaller Romanesque chapel, the duomo was later enlarged with a transept and nave. The bottom level features carved bas-reliefs of the Creation and Old Testament prophecies as well as the final panel of Maitani's *Last Judgment.* Set in niches surrounding the rose window by Andrea Orcagna (1325-1364), bronze and marble sculptures emphasize the Christian canon. Thirty-three architects, 90 mosaic artisans, 152 sculptors, and 68 painters worked for over 600 years to bring the duomo to this point, and the work continues—the bronze doors were only installed in 1970. Newly restored frescoes by Ugolino dé Prete Ilario are found behind the altar.

The ■**Cappella della Madonna di San Brizio** (sometimes called the **Cappella Nuova**), off the right transept, includes Luca Signorelli's dramatic Apocalypse frescoes, considered to be his finest works. His vigorous craftsmanship, mastery of human anatomy, ability to skewer residents of the town with grace and ease, and dramatic compositions inspired Michelangelo. Skeletons and muscular humans pull themselves out of the earth while apparitions of the damned swarm about in the unsettling *Resurrection of the Dead.* Beside it hangs the *Inferno*, depicting Signorelli as a blue devil, embracing his mistress. Signorelli modeled the "Whore of Babylon," carried above the masses on his back, after an Orvieto woman who rejected his advances. The Cappella also holds the gold-encrusted **Reliquario del Corporale** (chalice-cloth), said to have been soaked with the blood of Christ. *(Duomo open M-Sa 7:30am-12:45pm and 2:30-7pm, though afternoon hours vary, Su and holidays 2:30-6:45pm. Tickets at tourist office across street. Free. No shorts or short skirts permitted. Capella Nuova open Apr.-Sept. M-Sa 10am-12:45pm and 2:30-7:15pm, Su 2:30-6pm; Mar., Oct. M-Sa 10am-12:45pm and 2:30-6:15pm, Su 2:30-5:45pm; Nov. 1-Feb. 28 M-Sa 10am-12:45pm and 2:30-5:15pm, Su 2:30-5:15pm. €3, before 10am free.)*

PALAZZO DEI PAPI. From this austere, 13th-century "Palace of the Popes," Pope Clement VII rejected King Henry VIII's petition to annul his marriage with Catherine of Aragon, condemning both Catherine and English Catholicism to a bleak fate (not to mention the other five women Henry married before his death in 1547). Set back in the *palazzo* is the **Museo Archeologico Nazionale,** where you can examine Etruscan artifacts from the area and walk into a full-sized tomb. *(Right of the duomo. Open daily 8:30am-7:30pm. €2, under 18 or over 60 free.)*

UNDERGROUND CITY. For the most complete tour of Etruscan Orvieto, consider the **Underground City Excursions,** which will lead you through the dark and twisted bowels of the city. The ancient Etruscan town of Velzna was burrowed into the soft *tufa* of the cliff below modern Orvierto. Although Velzna was sacked by Romans, its cisterns, mills, pottery workshops, quarries, wine cellars, and burial sites lie preserved beneath the earth. *(☎0763 34 48 91. 1hr. tours leave from the tourist office daily 11:30am, 12:45pm, 4:30pm and 5:45pm. €5.50, students €3.50.)*

MUSEO CIVICO AND MUSEO FAINA. These *musei* hold an extensive collection of Etruscan artifacts found in excavations of local necropoli. Exhibits include coins, bronze urns, red and black figure vases from the 6th century BC, and Roman ornaments. *(Directly opposite duomo. Open Apr.-Sept. daily 9:30am-6pm; Oct.-Mar. Tu-Su 10am-5pm. €4.20, students and seniors €2.50.)*

CHIESA DI SANT'ANDREA. This church marks the beginning of Orvieto's medieval quarter. Built upon the ruins of an Etruscan temple, it served as a meeting place, or *comune*, in medieval Orvieto. Inside, the **crypt** (at the beginning of the right aisle) contains recently excavated remains from an underground Etruscan temple. *(In P. della Repubblica, 500m down Corso Cavour from P. Cahen.)*

CHIESA DI SAN GIOVENALE. The city's oldest church was dedicated to the city's first bishop; a fresco of him is found on the left wall as you enter. Directly next to the doors on the left is a 14th-century "Tree of Life"—a family tree of the church's founders. Just inside the old city walls, the church offers stunning views of the countryside below. The soils of the verdant slope below P. San Giovanni are filled with the graves of those who died in the Black Death of 1348. *(From P. della Repubblica, follow V. Filippeschi, which turns into V. Malabranca, to San Giovenale.)*

🎵 🎭 ENTERTAINMENT AND NIGHTLIFE

Orvieto likes to party. In the spring there is the **Palio dell'Oca**, a medieval game testing dexterity on horseback. On Pentecost (50 days after Easter), Orvieto celebrates the **Festa della Palombella.** Small wooden boxes filled with fireworks are set up in the Campo della Fiera. At the stroke of noon, the fireworks are set off when a white dove descends across the wire to ignite the explosives. In June, the historical **Procession of Corpus Domini** celebrates the Miracle of Bolsena. A week of medieval banquets precede the procession at which ladies and flag wavers dance in the streets to period music. From December 29 to January 5, **Umbria Jazz Winter** swings in Orvieto's theaters, churches, and *palazzi* (with the grand finale in the duomo). For festival specifics, contact **Servizio Turistico Territoriale IAT dell'Orvietano,** P. Duomo, 24 (☎0763 34 19 11 or 34 36 58) or **Informazioni Turistiche** (☎0763 34 17 72; fax 34 44 33) at the same address. For less formal fun, try club **Zeppelin,** V. Garibaldi, 28. (☎0763 34 14 47. Open daily 12:30-3pm and 7:30pm-1am. MC/V.) Otherwise follow signs from P. Duomo for **Engel Keller's Tavern,** on V. Beato Angelico, just off P. I. Scalza. (Open Th-Tu 7pm-3am.)

THE MARCHES (LE MARCHE)

Green foothills separate the umbrella-laden beaches along the Adriatic Sea from the craggy Apennines. The agricultural towns dotting these hills are filled with the architectural and archaeological remains of the Gauls, Picenes, and Romans. The Renaissance geniuses Raphael and Donato Bramante left their legacy in Urbino, arguably the highlight of unassuming Le Marche.

HIGHLIGHTS OF LE MARCHE

FROLIC with the natives of Ascoli Piceno at the annual **Quintana Festival** (p. 369).

WHILE AWAY the afternoon on the tranquil **beaches of Fano** (p. 451).

STROLL among **Urbino's** cobblestoned streets and dream-like buildings. (p. 452).

TRAVERSE the waters of the **Adriatic** on a ferry from Ancona to Slovenia (p. 455).

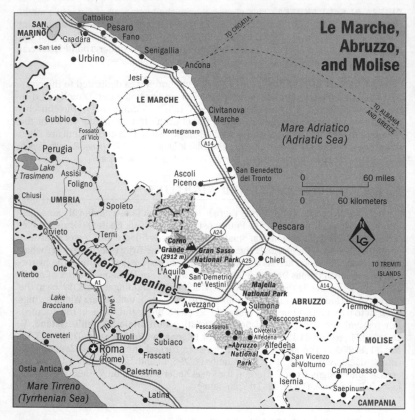

PESARO

☎ 0741

Pesaro strikes a balance between the boisterous hipness of Rimini and the relaxation of Fano. Its historic center is appealing, and its beaches relatively uncrowded. While surf shops and fast food eateries occupy much of the space along the beach, a number of museums and churches decorate the old quarter.

⌷ TRANSPORTATION

Trains: At the end of V. Risorgimento and V. della Liberazione. Ticket counter open daily 7am-8:30pm. **Luggage storage** available (see p. 449). To: **Ancona** (1hr., 2 per hr., 5am-11pm, €2.90); **Bologna** (1 per hr., 4:43am-9:20pm, €7.35); **Fano** (15min., every hr., 5:44am-11:19pm, €1.30); and **Rimini** (30min., 2 per hr., 6:42am-11pm, €2.32).

Buses: In Piazzale Matteotti, down V. S. Francesco from P. del Popolo. Buses #1, 2, 4, 5, 6, 7, 9, and 11 stop at Piazzale Matteotti. Buses leave from Piazzale Matteotti and the train station, and run to **Fano** (15min., every 30min., €1) and **Gradara** (20min., every hr., 7am-7pm, €1.25). **SOBET** runs buses to **Urbino** (1hr.; M-Sa 10 per day, 7am-8:05pm; Su 4 per day, 8:30am-8:05pm; €1.91). Buy tickets on the bus. **Bucci** runs an express bus to Tiburtina station in **Rome** from Piazzale Matteotti (4½hr., 6am, €20). Buy tickets on the bus.

Bicycle Rental: (☎0721 90 13 77) in Piazzale d'Annunzio, at the intersection of Viale Trieste and V. Verdi. €2 per hr. Also has mountain bikes and the *ciclocarrozzella*. Open May-Sept. daily 8:30am-midnight.

Scooter Rental: (☎0721 30 980) in Piazzale d'Annunzio. Right next to the bike rental. €14 per hr., €51 per day.

✦ ⁈ ORIENTATION AND PRACTICAL INFORMATION

As you exit the train station, take **Via Risorgimento**, facing you at 2 o'clock. Walk straight into **Piazza del Popolo**, the center of the old city. **Corso XI Settembre** runs west toward Chiesa di Sant Agostino, while **Via San Francesco** runs east to **Piazzale Matteotti** and the bus station. **Via Rossini** leads straight out of the piazza towards Largo Aldo Moro which leads to **Viale Repubblica, Piazzale Liberta,** and the sea. **Viale Trieste** runs along the beach.

Tourist Office: IAT (☎0721 69 341; fax 30 462), at P. della Libertà, to the right of the giant bronze globe, called the *Sfera Grande*. Open M-Sa 8:30am-1pm and 3-7:30pm. For guided tours of the town center call ☎0721 38 77 14.

Regional Tourist Office, V. Rossini, 41 (☎0721 35 95 01; www.provincia.ps.it/turismo). Past P. del Popolo, heading toward the sea, on your left, just off Largo Aldo Moro. Info on the region, including tours and recommended sights. Internet access available for research. Open M-Sa 9:30am-1pm and 4-7pm, Su 9:30am-12:30pm.

Luggage Storage: Near the sign that says **Taxis,** just outside the train station. €2.58 for 12hr. Open daily 6am-11pm.

Emergency: ☎113. **Ambulance:** ☎118.

Medical Services: ☎0721 21 344. For late-night and holiday medical care, V. Trento, 300 (☎0721 22 405).

Police: Questura (☎0721 61 803), P. del Popolo.

Post Office: P. del Popolo, 28 (☎0721 43 22 23). *Fermo Posta* at *sportello* #1. Open M-Sa 10am-7:15pm.

Postal Code: 61100.

▐ ACCOMMODATIONS & CAMPING

Pesaro, with its many reasonably priced accommodations, is a real bargain in the off season. High season runs from mid-June through August.

Hotel Athena, V. Pola, 18 (☎0721 30 114; fax 33 878). From the train station, catch the C/B bus, and get off at V. Fiume. Turn right on V. Trento and left on V. Pola. Walking from Largo Aldo Moro, take Viale della Vittoria and turn left on V. Pola. Large, sunny, and clean rooms in an old hotel right off the beach. All with bath, phone, and TV, some with balcony. Singles €32; doubles €42; triples €52. MC/V. ❸

San Marco, Viale XI Febbraio, 32 (☎/fax 0721 31 396). From the train station, follow V. Risorgimento and bear right into Piazzale Garibaldi. The Viale is to the right. Heavily trafficked street. 40 spacious rooms, all with bath, phones, and TV. 2 are wheelchair-accessible. Breakfast included. Singles €38.73-44.93; doubles €61.97-69.72; triples €77.47-85.47. AmEx/MC/V. ❹

Camping Panorama (☎/fax 0721 20 81 45), 7km north of Pesaro on *strada panoramica* to Gabicce Mare. Bus #13 from Piazzale Matteotti drops you at site, but be sure to ask the driver if the bus goes to the campgrounds. Open May-Sept. Hot showers and swimming pool free. €5-7 per person. €8-10.49 per tent. Bungalows from €46. ❶

◘ FOOD

▓ **Harnold's,** P. Lazzarini, 34 (☎0721 65 155), 2 doors from Teatro Rossini. From P. del Popolo, follow V. Branca away from the sea. Locals recommend this fresh and cheap option, with its wide range of *panini*, pasta, and salad options. Takeout and outdoor seating available. *Panini* €2-4. Open daily 8am-3am. MC/V. ❶

Casetta Vaccai, V. Mazzolari, 22 (☎0721 69 201). Off V. Rossini, right next door to the Museo Civico. Delicious pasta dishes served in a wine bar set in Pesaro's oldest house (1st floor from the 1200s). Open M-Sa 8:30am-9:30pm. MC/V. ❸

◉ SIGHTS

PIAZZA DEL POPOLO. Pesaro's main square holds the **Ducal Palace**, with its splendid facade and sprawling courtyard, commissioned in the 14th century by Alessandro Sforza. *(Open to visitors as part of a guided tour. Ask the tourist office.)*

MUSEO CIVICO. This museum houses a superb collection of Italian ceramics and primitive artifacts, showcasing the talents of Pesarese potters. There is also an impressive gallery of paintings, including the remarkable *Padre Eterno* by Bellini, the elaborate *Fall of the Giants* by Guido Reni, and four still-life paintings by Benedetto Sartori. *(Toschi Mosca, 29. From P. del Popolo, head down Corso XI Settembre and turn right on V. Toschi Mosca. ☎0721 387 5541. Open July-Aug. M-Su 9:30am-12:30pm and 5-8pm; Sept.-June W, F-Su 9:30am-12:30pm and 4-7pm, Tu and Th 9:30am-12:30pm and 4-11pm. €2.58 cumulative ticket with Casa Rossini.)*

CASA ROSSINI. The 1792 birthplace of Rossini is now a museum containing an extensive collection of photographs, portraits, theatrical memorabilia, letters, and opera scores. *(V. Rossini, 34. ☎0721 38 73 57. Open July-Aug. M-Su 9:30am-12:30pm and 5-8pm; Sept.-June W, F-Su 9:30am-12:30pm and 4-7pm, Tu and Th 9:30am-12:30pm and 4-11pm. €2.58 included with Museo Civico, under 25 or over 65 free.)*

VILLA IMPERIALE. Girolamo Genga commenced work on this villa in 1530. It features frescoes by the Dossi brothers and Raffaellino del Colle. The villa and lavish surrounding gardens are accessible by tours led by the IAT tourist office. *(☎0721 69 341. Tours leave Piazzale della Libertà. June 14-Aug. 23 W. Call for times and prices.)*

ORTI GIULI. Classic example of 19th-century gardens built along a 15th century wall and lined with avenues of trees and Neoclassical statues. *(Free entrance. Open daily 8am-4pm. Call ☎0721 31 990 to arrange a tour.)*

♫ ENTERTAINMENT

Pesaro hosts the **Mostra Internazionale del Nuovo Cinema,** the International Festival of New Films (☎0644 56 643), during the second and third weeks of June. Movies are shown in the buildings along V. Rossini and at the **Teatro Comunale Sperimentale** (☎0721 38 75 48), on V. Rossini, just off P. del Popolo. Native opera composer Rossini founded the **Conservatorio di Musica G. Rossini,** which sponsors events throughout the year. Contact the **Teatro Rossini** (☎0721 387 5548), in P. Lazzarini, off V. Branca, for show times and prices. The annual **Rossini Opera Festival** begins in early August, but opera performances and orchestral concerts continue through September. Reserve tickets through the second floor office at V. Rossini, 37. (☎0721 30 161. Open M-F 9am-12:30pm and 3:30-6pm.)

▶ DAYTRIPS FROM PESARO

FANO

Fano is accessible from Pesaro by train (€1.30) and by bus (€1). Buy bus tickets on the bus or in any tabacchi. *For the beach, exit the train station on V. Cavallotti, and take a right on V. C. Battisti. To reach P. XX Settembre, the town center, turn left onto V. Garibaldi from V. Cavallotti and then right onto Corso Giacomo Matteotti.*

Fano is a sleepy town along a 12km beach that stretches from Pesaro to some of the quietest retreats on this side of the Adriatic. Even in summer, vacationers are scarce on the beaches north of Fano. Inland, the picturesque historic center is lined with busy cafes. The **tourist office**, V. Battisti, 10, provides a map of the city and a list of local events. (☎0721 80 35 34; fax 82 42 92; www.turismofano.com. Open M-Sa 9am-1pm and 3:30-6:30pm.)

Although Fano makes a good daytrip from Pesaro, those planning to stay overnight should contact **Associazione Albergatori**, V. Adriatico, 132, an organization that helps travelers find lodging free of charge. (☎0721 82 73 76 or 82 57 10. Open M-Sa 9am-1pm and 4-7:30pm, Su 9:30am-12:30pm). **Trattoria Quinta ❸**, V. d'Adriatico, 42, at the north edge of town, provides inexpensive home-cooked meals. (☎0721 80 80 43. *Primi* €5.20, *secondi* €9. Open M-Sa noon-3pm and 7-11pm. MC/V.) Inland, **La Vecchia Fano ❸**, V. Vecchia, 8, makes tasty meals in a quaint, romantic setting. (Take a right off V. Cavour heading away from P. XX Settembre. *Primi* €6.50-8, *secondi* €9-10. Open Tu-Su noon-2:45pm and 7:45-10:45pm. MC/V.)

GRADARA

Buses leave Pesaro from Piazzale Matteotti daily (20min., 7am-7pm, every hour, €1.25). Buy tickets at any tabacchi *or on the bus. Be forewarned that the last bus back to Pesaro is at 7pm and there are no overnight accommodations within 3km of Gradara. Check bus schedules to see what time the last one leaves Gradara. Buses stop in Gradara at P. Paolo e Francesca. Walk up V. Borgo Mercato into P. Mancini. Take V. XVII Novembre into the historic center, heading for the castle.*

Gradara's main attraction is its romantic fairy-tale **Rocca di Gradara** (1150), one of the Marche's most visited castles. Beautifully preserved and decorated with period furnishings, it offers picturesque views of the countryside from its high interior windows. (☎0541 96 46 97. €4. Open M 8:30am-1:15pm and Tu-Su 8:30am-6:30pm.) The **tourist office**, to the left as you enter the main gate, offers guided tours of the city and castle. (☎0541 96 41 15; comune.gradara@provincia.ps.it. Open Mar.-Sept. daily 9am-1pm; Sept.-Feb. Tu, Th and Sa 9am-1pm. Tours in Italian, French, or German Tu 10am and Th 5pm, in English or Italian F 9:30pm. Tours leave from the office, no reservations necessary. €3.) To the right as you enter the main gate is the **Girodi Ronda**, the once-fortified castle walls. Walk around the top for a great view. (Open daily 9:30am-12:30pm and 4:30-7:30pm. €1. Nighttime tours 8:30-11:30pm, €1.50.) The **Chiesa S. Giovanni Battista** has an intriguing wooden crucifix and the **Museo Storico Strumeti di Tortura** has a tiny, dark basement room with some chains and a rack. (Chiesa open daily 8am-6:30pm. Free. Museo open daily 8am-1pm. €3.) For lunch or dinner, try **L'Osteria "La Botte" ❷**, P. V Novembre, 11 (☎0541 96 44 04; www.gradara.com/botte). An array of tasty sandwiches (€3-4) and *secondi* (€6-7) are served by the friendly owner. (Open Th-Tu noon-2:30pm and 7-11pm. AmEx/MC/V.)

URBINO ☎ 0722

With its picturesque, humble stone dwellings scattered along steep city streets and an immense, turreted palace, Urbino seems to have changed little over the past 500 years. The fairy-tale city is home to many art treasures and Renaissance monuments, including Piero della Francesca's *Ideal City* and Raphael's ornately decorated house. The cultural beauty within the city walls is rivaled only by the magnificence of the region's surrounding countryside. Urbino's youthful vitality is kept up by its university population and a stream of international visitors.

⌐ TRANSPORTATION

Buses: Borgo Mercatale. Urbino's bus and Pesaro's train timetables are posted at the beginning of C. Garibaldi, at P. della Repubblica, under the portico at the corner bar. Blue **SOBET** (☎ 0722 22 333) buses run to P. Matteotti and the train station in Pesaro (1hr.; M-Sa 10 per day, 6:30am-6:45pm; Su 4 per day, 7:10am-5:20pm; €2.10). Buy tickets on bus. **Bucci** (☎ 0721 32 401) runs a bus to **Rome** (5hr., 4pm, €18.50). **Luggage storage** available (see p. 452).

Taxis: In **P. della Repubblica** (☎ 0722 25 50) and near **bus stop** (☎ 0722 37 79 49).

▆✚ ▐ ORIENTATION AND PRACTICAL INFORMATION

After winding up steep hills, the bus stops at **Borgo Mercatale** below the city center. A short walk up **Via Mazzini** leads to **Piazza della Repubblica,** the city's hub, from which **Via Raffaello, Via Cesare Battisti, Via Vittorio Veneto,** and **Corso Garibaldi** branch out. Another short walk uphill on V. V. Veneto leads to **Piazza Rinascimento.**

Tourist Office: P. Rinascimento, 1 (☎ 0722 32 85 68; fax 30 94 57; iat.urbino@regione.marche.it), across from Palazzo Ducale. Open mid-June to mid-Sept. M-Sa 9am-1:30pm and 3-7pm, Su 9am-1pm; in winter M-Sa 9am-1pm and 3-6pm. **Tourist info booth** at bus stop in Borgo Mercatale. Open M-Sa 9am-1pm and 3-7pm.

Budget Travel: CTS, V. Mazzini, 60 (☎ 0722 20 31; fax 32 78 80). Train or plane tickets and student tour info. Open M-F 9am-1pm and 3:30-7:30pm, Sa 9am-1pm.

Luggage Storage: At the car parking office in Borgo Mercatale. €1.50 for 24hr. Open daily 8am-midnight.

Laundromat: Powders, V. Battisti, 35. €3.75 per load. Open M-Sa 9am-10pm.

Emergency: ☎ 113. **Ambulance:** ☎ 118.

Police: (☎ 0722 30 93 00).

Hospital: (☎ 0722 30 11), on V. B. da Montefeltro, off V. Comandino. Bus #1 and 3 from Borgo Mercatale stop in front.

Internet Access: Tourist office allows free computer use for up to 10min. **The Netgate,** V. Mazzini, 17 (☎ 0722 24 62), has over 20 computers. €4.99 per hr., students €3.99. 50% discount M-F mornings. Open M-F 10am-2am, Sa-Su noon-midnight.

Post Office: V. Bramante, 22 (☎ 0722 27 78 15), just off V. Raffaello. Traveler's checks and **currency exchange** available. Open M-F 8am-6:30pm, Sa 8am-12:30pm.

Postal Code: 61029.

ACCOMMODATIONS & CAMPING

Cheap lodgings are relatively rare in Urbino, and reservations are a good idea. You may want to consider staying in Pesaro and taking a daytrip to Urbino.

Pensione Fosca, V. Raffaello, 67 (☎0722 32 96 22 or 25 42), top fl. Signora Rosina treats her guests well. 9 large, charming rooms. Communal bath. Singles €21; doubles €40; triples €43. ❷

Hotel San Giovanni, V. Barocci, 13 (☎0722 28 27; fax 32 90 55). From P. della Repubblica, head towards V. Mazzini and take a right, following the sign. Modern hotel in medieval building, with simple rooms and small bathrooms. Restaurant downstairs. Open Aug.-June. Singles €21-27; doubles €37-48; triples €56. AmEx/MC/V. ❸

Piero della Francesca, V. Comandino, 53 (☎0722 32 84 28; fax 32 84 27), in front of hospital. Bus #1 from Borgo Mercatale. 15min. by foot: from P. della Repubblica, take V. Raffaello and turn right onto V. Bramante. Follow to end and turn left, then right onto V. Gramsci, which becomes V. Comandino, following signs for hospital. Rooms with bath, TV, and phone. Singles €38; doubles €53; triples €69. AmEx/D/MC/V. ❹

Camping: Camping Pineta (☎0722 47 10; fax 47 34), Loc. Monti delle Cesane. 2km from city walls. Take bus #4 or 7 from Borgo Mercatale; ask to be let off at camping. Mostly level, secluded sites. Open from Apr. to mid-Sept. Office open daily 9-11am and 3-10pm. €6 per person, €12.50 per tent. AmEx/D/MC/V. ❶

FOOD

Urbino's cuisine is simple but delicious. Hearty soups are typically eaten around Christmas. *Caciotta* is a delicate cheese that should be enjoyed with a glass of sparkling *Bianchello del Metauro.* **Supermarket Margherita,** V. Raffaello, 37, is open M-Sa 7:30am-2pm and 3-8pm. The **University MENSA,** on V. Budassi, offers a huge dinner for around €4 with any student ID. (Closed June-Aug.)

Pizzeria Le Tre Piante, V. Voltaccia della Vecchia, 1 (☎0722 48 63). From P. della Repubblica, head up V. Veneto, turn left on V. Nazario Sauro, right on V. Budassi, and left on V. Foro Posterula (5min.). Packed with locals and students, this restaurant serves sizeable pizzas. Pizza €4-7, *primi* €5.20-6.20, *secondi* €7-8.30. Open Tu-Su 12:30-3pm and 7:15-11:30pm. ❸

Ristorante La Vecchia Fornarina, V. G. Mazzini, 14 (☎0722 32 00 07). Small, cozy, and quiet, it serves traditional Urbino cuisine. *Primi* €7-10, *secondi* €10-12. Open daily noon-2:30pm and 7pm-10:30pm. AmEx/MC/V. ❹

Un Punto Macrobiotico, V. Pozzo Nuovo, 4 (☎0722 32 97 90), walk down C. Battisti from P. della Repubblica and take 1st right. Friendly waitstaff and long wooden benches promote communal feel at this student-filled eatery. Daily menu of fresh, wholesome dishes (€2.10-9.30). Open M-Sa noon-2pm and 7:30-9pm. ❷

Caffè del Sole, V. Mazzini (☎0722 26 19), across from the Netgate. For local personality, this is the best place in town. *Panini* and drinks. Sept.- May W-Th nights, students and locals gather for jazz concerts. Open Tu-Su 7pm-2am. ❶

Bar del Teatro, C. Garibaldi, 88 (☎0722 29 11), at base of Palazzo Ducale. Best view in town, with Palazzo Ducale on one side and valley on other. *Espresso* €1.10, *cappuccino* or tea €1.50-2.25. Open daily 7:30am-midnight. Off-season open M-Sa only. ❶

CENTRAL ITALY

👁 SIGHTS

🖼 **PALAZZO DUCALE.** The Renaissance Palazzo Ducale has a facade by Ambrogio Barocchi, comprised of two slender towers enclosing three stacked balconies. Inside the *palazzo*, a staircase to the left leads to the **National Gallery of the Marches,** housed in a duke's one-time private apartments. The gallery contains the most important collection of art in Urbino: Piero della Francesca's fascinating *Flagellation of Christ* shows Christ being whipped in the background, and Francesca's *Ideal City* exhibits the artist's renowned talent for manipulating perspective. Berruguete's famous *Portrait of Duke Federico,* Raphael's *Portrait of a Lady,* and Paolo Uccello's narrative panel, *The Profanation of the Host,* are here as well. The *palazzo* also contains the **Museo Archeologico,** an interesting and varied collection of Roman art and artifacts. *(P. Rinascimento. ☎0722 27 60. Open M 8:30am-2pm, Tu-Sa 8:30am-7:15pm, Su 8:30am-7:15pm. €4, students €2.)*

ORATORIO DI SAN GIOVANNI BATTISTA. The 14th-century Oratorio di San Giovanni Battista is decorated with Gothic frescoes by L.J. Salimbeni (1416), representing events from the life of St. John. The fresco painters are said to have drawn their sketches with lamb's blood instead of ink. *(At the end of V. Barocci. From P. della Repubblica, head down V. Mazzini and turn right up the small path on the right, following the sign. ☎0722 26 13. Open M-Sa 10am-12:30pm and 3-5:30pm, Su 10am-12:30pm. €1.55.)*

CASA DI RAFAELE. The site of Raphael's birth in 1483 is now a vast and delightful museum with period furnishings and paintings. The only decoration in the museum attributed to Raphael is a fresco of the Virgin and child. Raphael's father, Giovanni Santi, painted the beautiful *Annunciation.* *(V. Raffaello, 57. ☎0722 32 01 05. Open M-Sa 9am-1pm and 3-6pm, Su 10am-1pm. €3.)*

🎵 ENTERTAINMENT

Urbino's nightlife picks up in August, but the main piazzas are always bustling at night with locals and young travelers enjoying *cappuccini* and pastries, and the steep streets are crowded with those taking nighttime *passeggiate*. By midnight during the school year, **The Bosom Pub,** V. Budassi 14, is packed with dancers. Watch for their occasional festival parties, such as the costume party *Festa di Bacco* (Festival of Bacchus) in mid-July. (☎0722 47 83. Beer €2-3, wine from €5-8. No cover. Open Aug.-May daily 4:30pm-3am; June-July 10:30pm-3am.)

In July, the **Antique Music Festival** brings concerts to churches and theaters around town. Saturday nights are amateur nights—if you have a 3rd-century harp, feel free to join. Every second Sunday in August brings the ceremony of the **Revocation of the Duke's Court**. The **Festa dell'Aquilone,** held on the first Sunday in September, is a kite-flying competition between different cities.

ANCONA   ☎071

Ancona is Italy's major transportation hub for those bound to Croatia, Slovenia and Greece. Loud, pungent, and industrial Ancona is hardly an ideal vacation destination. However, the *centro* is comprised of several attractive piazzas, and from the hilltop duomo, the port-side cranes shimmer like sculptures in the water.

▣ TRANSPORTATION

Trains: (☎071 42 474), in P. Rosselli. Ticket office open daily 6am-7:30pm. To: **Bologna** (2½hr., 1-2 per hr., about €12); **Milan** (5hr., 24 per day, 12:36am-7:20pm, €21); **Paris-Lyon** (12-15hr., 7:18pm, €140); **Pesaro** (1hr., 1-2 per hr., €3.30); **Rimini** (1½hr., 1-2 per hr., €4.80); **Rome** (3-4hr., 9 per day, 2:50am-7:10pm, €15); and **Venice** (5hr., 4 per day, €15).

Ferries: Ancona offers ferry service to **Croatia, Greece,** and **Northern Italy.** Schedules available at **Stazione Marittima** (☎071 20 11 83) on waterfront, off P. Kennedy. Call ticket offices the day before to check hours of operation, as most companies close if no ship is preparing to depart. Reserve July-Aug. **Luggage storage** available (see below).

Adriatica: (☎071 20 49 15, 20 49 16, or 20 49 17; fax 20 22 96; www.adriatica.it). To: **Durazzo, Albania** (15hr.; €70, July-Aug. €90); **Spalato, Croatia** (8hr.; €45, July-Aug. €49); and **Bar, Yugoslavia** (16hr.; €48.50, July-Aug. €53).

ANEK: (☎071 207 2346; fax 207 7904; www.anek.gr). Offers a 20% discount for students and 10% discount for seniors. To **Greece** (€50; July-Aug. €65). Return trips roughly half-price.

Jadrolinija: (☎071 20 43 05; fax 20 02 11; www.jadrolinija.tel.hr/jadrolinija) runs to **Split, Croatia** (€47 one way).

SEM Maritime Co (SMC): (☎071 20 40 90; fax 20 26 18; www.sem.hr). To: **Split, Croatia** (€40; round-trip €70; July-Aug. €44, €76 round-trip); and **Hvar Island.**

Blue Star Ferries (Strintzis): (☎071 207 1068; fax 207 0874; www.strintzis.gr) to **Greece** (€53, July to early Sept. €70).

▣▣ ORIENTATION AND PRACTICAL INFORMATION

The train station is a 35min. walk to **Stazione Marittima.** From the island directly in front of the entrance to the train station, buses #1, 1/3 and 1/4 head along the port toward **Stazione Marittima** and up **Corso Stamira** to **Piazza Cavour,** the city center. Buy tickets (€0.80, full day €1.40) at the *tabacchi* in the train station. For the Stazione Marittima, disembark at P. Repubblica (the first stop after turning inland), walk back toward the ocean, and take a right on the waterfront. To get to the **tourist office** from the train station, take bus #1/4 from platform 2 under the canopy outside the train station and stay on until **P. IV Novembre.** The office is at the beginning of **Via Thaon,** across the street from the parking lot on the right.

Tourist Office: V. Thaon de Revel, 4 (☎071 35 89 91; fax 358 9929; iat.ancona@regione.marche.it). Open Su-M 3-7pm, Tu-F 10:30am-1:25pm and 3-7pm, Sa 9:40am-2pm and 3-7pm. **Branch** office (☎071 21 11 83) in Stazione Marittima has ferry info. Open June-Sept. Tu-Sa 8am-8pm, Su-M 8am-2pm.

Luggage storage: In the Stazione Marittima. Free for 1st 2 days, then €2 per bag per day.

Emergency: ☎ 112 or 113. **Ambulance:** ☎118.

Hospital: Umberto Primo, in P. Cappelli, near P. Cavour and C. Matteotti.

Police: ☎071 22 881.

Post Office: P. XXIV Maggio, (☎071 50 121), right off P. Cavour. Open M-Sa 8am-6:30pm.

Postal Code: 60100.

▣ ACCOMMODATIONS

Pensione Euro, C. Mazzini, 142, 2nd fl. (☎071 53 183) right off of P. Cavour. 9 large, airy rooms with communal baths. Singles €21; doubles €30; triples €50. V/MC. ❷

Ostello della Gioventù (HI), V. Lamaticci, 7 (☎/fax 071 42 257). Upon exiting train station, cross piazza and turn left. Take 1st right, and immediately make sharp right up steps behind newsstand; hostel is on the right. Clean rooms, each with 4-6 beds. Immaculate bathrooms and a common area. Breakfast €1.50. Lockout 11am-4:30pm. Curfew midnight. Reception 6:30-11am and 4:30pm-midnight. Dorms €13. ❶

Pensione Milano, V. Montebello 1/A (☎071 20 11 47; fax 207 3931). With back to the port, walk to far end of P. Cavour and take a right onto V. Vecchini. Walk straight and go up staircase. 14 clean, simple rooms. Communal baths. Singles €21; doubles €32; triples €46.15. ❷

Hotel City, V. Matteotti, 112/114 (☎071 207 0949; fax 207 0372). From P. Cavour, facing away from the port, turn left down the street just before Largo 24 Maggio, and turn left at the end onto V. Matteotti. 3-star hotel with modern conveniences. All rooms with bath, A/C, TV and minibar. Breakfast buffet included. Singles €53.50; doubles €96; triples €103. AmEx/MC/V. ❹

◪ FOOD

The best grocery deals are at **Supermarket CONAD,** V. Matteotti, 115. (Open M-F 8:15am-1:30pm and 5-7:35pm, Sa 8:15am-12:45pm and 5-7:40pm.)

Mercato Pubblico, P. della Erbe, 130. From P. Roma, head toward the horse fountain and turn right on V. Mazzini. Turn left into P. dell Erbe. Pack a meal for your ferry ride at this old-fashioned market. Open Mar.-Sept. M-Sa 7:30am-12:45pm and 5-8pm, Nov.-Feb. M-Sa 7:30am-12:45pm and 4:30-7:30pm. ❶

Bonta' delle Marche, C. Mazzini, 96 (☎071 53 985; www.bontadellemarche.it). From P. Roma, head toward the horse fountain and turn left. An extensive selection of gourmet meats and cheeses at this specialty food shop. Fresh, inexpensive pre-cooked meals. Takeout only. Open M-Sa 8am-1:15pm and 4:45pm-8:15pm. MC/V. ❸

La Dolce Vita, P. Cavour, 31-32 (☎071 20 33 75). Friendly, family-run restaurant, offering delectable pastries and a rotating menu of pasta favorites. Ideal for a quick bite. Pastries from €5, pasta €5-6. Open M-Sa 6am-8pm. ❶

Osteria Brillo, C. Mazzini, 109 (☎071 207 2629). From P. Roma, head toward the horse fountain and turn right onto C. Mazzini. Small, pub-style eatery for a casual meal. Hearty Italian fare at outstanding prices. Pizza €2.60-7, *secondi* €5.50-8.50. Open M-Sa 12:30-3pm and 7:30-11pm. AmEx/MC/V. ❷

◪ SIGHTS

THE OLD CITY. The **Piazzale del Duomo,** atop **Monte Guasco,** offers a view of the industrial town below, with the Anconan sea and sky as backdrop. In the Piazzale stands the **Cattedrale di San Ciriaco,** a Romanesque church in the shape of a Greek cross. It was erected in the 11th century on the site of an early Christian basilica, which was in turn built on the ruins of a Roman temple dedicated to Venus. *(To reach the duomo from P. Cavour, follow C. Mazzini to the port and turn right onto V. Gramsci at P. Repubblica. Follow it to P. Del Senato, and climb the 244 steps up to the duomo. ☎071 222 5045. Open M-Sa 8am-noon and 3-7pm, Su viewing hours vary depending on mass schedule.)*

PINACOTECA COMUNALE FRANCESCO PODESTI. Ancona's painting gallery, the Galleria Comunale Francesco Podesti, housed in the 16th-century **Palazzo Bosdari,** has amassed a collection of work by the Camerte school. Carlo Crivelli's *Madonna col Bambino* competes with Titian's *Apparition of the Virgin.*

Titian's dark, brooding depiction of the crucifixion is the collection's highlight. *(V. Pizzecolli, 17. From P. Roma, head down C. Garibaldi towards the port. Turn right at P. Repubblica onto V. Gramsci and go straight. ☎071 222 5045. Open M 9am-1pm, Tu-F 9am-7pm, Sa 8:30am-6:30pm, Su 3-7pm. €4.)*

MUSEO ARCHEOLOGICO NAZIONALE DELLE MARCHE. Housed in the 16th-century **Palazzo Ferretti** is the Marches's foremost archaeological museum. The impressive collection includes the Ionian *Dinos of Amandola*, Greek vases, and two life-size equestrian bronzes of Roman emperors. *(V. Ferretti, 6. From Palazzo Bosdari, continue towards the duomo. ☎071 207 5390. Open Tu-Su 8:30am-7:30pm. €4.)*

RIVIERA DEL CONERO. Smooth pebble **beaches** lie a few kilometers outside of Ancona. Surrounded by towering cliffs, the nearby coastal villages, collectively known as the Riviera del Conero, attract many Italian tourists. *(Autolinee RENI runs buses from Ancona's P. Cavour and train station to Sirolo, Numana, and Marcelli. Buy tickets at P. Cavour from the Pink Ladies bar, at the intersection of P. Cavour and V. Camerini, or from the bar in the train station.)*

ASCOLI PICENO ☎0736

According to one legend, Ascoli was founded by a small group of Sabines guided westward by a *picchio* (woodpecker). The bird gave the city its name and the Marches a feathered mascot. By another account, Ascoli was the metropolis of the Piceno, a quiet Latin tribe that controlled much of the coastal Marches and had the woodpecker as its clan totem. Whatever the origins of its name, Ascoli Piceno is one of Le Marche's most interesting cities. Tucked away in the mountains, this travertine paved city's charm remains untouched by tourism.

⌐ TRANSPORTATION

Trains: Piazzale della Stazione (☎0736 34 10 14), at the end of V. Marconi. To **San Benedetto** (30min., M-Sa 13 per day, 5:30am-8:30pm, €2.22). Ticket counter open M 6:20-11:30am and 4-5:30pm, Tu-Sa 8am-noon and 3-5pm.

Buses: Buses to San Benedetto are more crowded than trains and take twice as long. **Start** (☎0736 25 23 91), V. Dino Angelini, 129, just off P. Roma, runs buses to **San Benedetto** (1hr., 1-2 per hr., 5:10am-11pm, €3.45) and **Acquasanta Terme** (1¼hr., 13 per day, 6:45am-7:10pm, €3.45). Buses leave from the V. le Gasperi stop behind the duomo. Buy tickets at the newspaper shop near the bus stop. Buses to **Rome** (3hr.; M-Sa 3:20, 4:30, 9:30pm; Su 5:30pm; €12) depart from P. Orlini. Office open M-Sa 8am-1pm and 3-7pm, Su 30min. before departure.

◪ ⓐ ORIENTATION AND PRACTICAL INFORMATION

From the **train station**, walk straight for one block to **Viale Indipendenza**, turn right, and walk straight to **Piazza Matteotti**. Turn right onto **Corso Mazzini** and follow it into **Piazza del Popolo** (10min.). Or take bus #1 2, 3, 4a, or 9 (€0.70) from V. le Indipendenza to the main bus stop on **Via le Gasperi**, behind the duomo. Walk around the duomo to **Piazza Arringo**, and then on to **Via XX Settembre** and **Piazza Roma**. From there, **Via del Trivio** leads to C. Mazzini and P. del Popolo.

Tourist Offices: Centro Visitatori (☎0736 29 82 12; fax 298 2322), in P. Arringo. Open Apr.-Oct. daily 9am-7pm; Nov.-Mar. 9am-5:30pm (summer hours during Carnevale). **Ufficio Informazioni,** P. del Popolo, 17 (☎0736 25 30 45; fax 25 23 91; iat.ascolipiceno@regione.marche.it). Open M-F 8am-1:30pm and 3-7pm, Sa 9am-1pm and 3-7pm, Su and holidays 9am-1pm.

Ascoli Piceno

🔺 ACCOMMODATIONS
Cantina dell'Arte, 3
Ostello dei Longobardi, 1

🍴 FOOD
Cantina dell'Arte, 2
Ristorante dal Vagabondo, 4
Trattoria Laliva, 5

Currency Exchange: Banca Nazionale del Lavoro, C. Trento e Trieste, 10c (☎0736 29 61). Open M-F 8:20am-1:20pm and 3-4:30pm, Sa 8:20am-11:50pm.

Emergency: ☎ 113. **Police:** (☎ 112) on V. Indipendenza. **Ambulance:** ☎ 118.

Pharmacy: Farmacia Sebastiani, P. Roma, 1 (☎0736 25 91 83). Open daily 9am-1pm and 4:30-8pm. Green sign outside indicates pharmacy open on weekends.

Internet: Edinternet, C. Mazzini, 97 (☎0736 24 72 95), near P. S. Agostino. 5 computers. €3 per hr. Open daily 8:30am-1pm and 4-9pm. Closed M mornings.

Post Office: (☎0736 24 22 11), on V. Crispi. Open M-F 8:15am-6pm, Sa 8:15am-1pm. *Fermo Posta* M-F 8:30am-1pm and 4-7:15pm. **Currency exchange.**

Postal Code: 63100.

🏠 ACCOMMODATIONS

🏨 **Ostello dei Longobardi,** R. dei Longobardi, 12 (☎0736 26 18 62). From P. del Popolo, take C. Mazzini to P. S. Agostino and turn right onto V. delle Torri. Go straight, and turn left on V. Solderini. 11th-century building with 20th-century plumbing. Walk up the stairs for a view of the beach. Reception closes at 11pm. 16 beds. €11 per person. ❶

Cantina dell'Arte, V. della Lupa, 8 (☎0736 25 57 44 or 25 56 20; fax 25 51 91), in the heart of town. Follow C. Trento e Trieste to P. S. Maria Intervias and turn right on V. delle Canterine. Take a right on V. della Lupa. Quaint little *albergo* decorated with family photos. Marble floors and patios. Rooms have bath, TV, and phone. Singles €26-30; doubles €40; triples €60. 5-person apartments with huge kitchens and tubs in recently remodeled bathrooms €90. AmEx/MC/V. ❸

🍴 FOOD

Ascoli's cuisine relies heavily upon local produce—including wild mushrooms (especially truffles), onions, capers, garlic, fennel, and anise. Olives cultivated in this province have been enjoyed since Roman times. Ascolian chefs specialize in the complicated *olive all'ascolana*, soft green olives stuffed with minced meat and fried. During holidays, they typically fry sweet cream ravioli and savory anise-flavored cakes topped with powdered sugar. The region's specialty wines include *Rosso Piceno* and *Falerio dei Colli Ascolani;* the local liquor of choice is *Anisetta Meletti*. The **open-air market** is in P. S. Francesco behind P. del Popolo. (Open M-Sa 8am-1pm.) **Tigre Supermarket** is in P. S. Maria Inter Vineas, at the end of C. Trento e Trieste. (Open M-Sa 8:30am-1pm and 5-8pm.)

▧ **Ristorante dal Vagabondo,** V. D'Argillano, 29 (☎0736 26 21 68). Take C. Mazzini from P. del Popolo and turn left down the street, following signs. Tasteful modern art graces the walls of this newly opened restaurant. Gennaro cooks up a feast of authentic Ascoli-Picenian cuisine in mere minutes. Try his special *menù* of *bruschetta, olive all'ascolana,* fried veal cutlet, and dessert (€10); or choose from one of his many pasta and risotto dishes (€5-7). Open daily noon-3pm and 7-10pm. AmEx/MC/V. ❷

Cantina dell'Arte, V. della Lupa, 5 (☎0736 25 56 90), across from the hotel of same name. Spacious restaurant has a generously portioned set menù (€8.75). *Primi* €4-5, *secondi* €5-6. Open M-Sa noon-2:30pm and 6:30-10pm, Su noon-5pm. MC/V. ❷

Trattoria Laliva, P. della Viola, 13 (☎0736 25 93 58). Take V. Giudea from P. del Popolo. Small, casual, and perfect for a quick bite. *Primi* €4-4.70, *secondi* €5-6. Open Su-T, Th-Sa 11:30am-4:30pm and 6:30-10pm; W 11:30am-4:30pm. ❷

ⓖ SIGHTS

Almost all of the buildings and roads in Ascoli are made of travertine, a light-colored, porous version of marble.

PIAZZA DEL POPOLO. Beneath the piazza, polished by centuries of footsteps, are Roman ruins. 16th-century *portici* line two sides of the square, and the 3rd side houses the 13th-century **Palazzo dei Capitani del Popolo.** The *palazzo* boasts a massive portal and a statue of Pope Paul III dating from 1548. The building was burned on Christmas Day 1535 in a familial squabble. A decade later the palace was refurbished and dedicated to the Pope, and stood without controversy until 1938, when it served as a seat of the Fascist party. Works from Roman antiquity are visible along the wooden pathway that weaves beneath the *palazzo*. Every month, the upstairs rooms show modern art. (☎0736 24 47 75. *Open daily 10am-1pm and 5-7pm.)*

The eastern end of the Romanesque-Gothic **Chiesa di San Francesco** borders the 4th side of P. del Popolo. It contains a 14th-century wooden crucifix, the only art saved from the 1535 fire. The "singing columns," two sets of five low columns flanking the outer door on the V. del Trivio side of the church, sound if you draw your hand quickly across them. *(Open daily 8am-1:30pm and 4-7pm. Call ☎0736 25 28 83 for all of Ascoli's church viewing times. Hours change frequently.)* The **Loggia dei Mercanti** (Merchants's Gallery, 1509-1513), abutting the church on the side facing V. del Trivio, has Renaissance wood carvings. A left on C. Mazzini from the piazza leads to the austere 14th-century **Chiesa di Sant'Agostino,** visible only from the outside.

PIAZZA ARRINGO. On the other side of town is **Piazza Arringo** (Oration Square), which derives its name from its role as a local podium. The massive travertine **duomo** is a blend of artistic eras. A Roman basilica forms the transept, topped by an 8th-century octagonal dome. The two towers were built in the 11th and 12th centuries, while the lateral naves and central apse were constructed in the 1400s. Inside, freshly restored frescoes decorate the walls and ceiling. Next to the cathedral stands the compact 12th-century **baptistery,** decorated with a *loggia* of arches. *(Open daily 7am-12:30pm and 3:30-7:45pm.)*

> **GETTING AHEAD.** Legend has it that St. Emidio, patron saint of Ascoli, was so pious that when he was martyred by decapitation in AD 301, he picked up his detached head and hurried to the Christian cemetery to avoid burial on pagan soil. He was credited with protecting the city from the rash of earthquakes that razed other central Italian cities in the 1700s, inspiring many surrounding towns to claim him as their patron saint as well.

MUSEO ARCHEOLOGICO STATALE. Inside the Palazzo Panichi is a three-floor museum with a diverse collection of Greek and Roman artifacts, some excavated from San Benedetto. The most impressive piece is a large, round mosaic floor which depicts the face of a boy in the center; when viewed from the opposite side, it displays the face of an old man. (*Open daily 11:30am-5:30pm. €2, students €1.*)

PINACOTECA CIVICA. In the **Arengo Palace**, medieval and Renaissance works line the walls of the elaborately decorated Palazzo. Most noteworthy are those by Crivelli, Titian, van Dyck, and Ribera. Upstairs is a collection of handsome stringed instruments and Impressionist art. (*To the left as you exit the duomo in P. Arringo. ☎0736 29 82 13. Open Tu-Su 9am-1pm and 4-7pm. €5, reduced €3.*)

WALKING NORTH OF PIAZZA DEL POPOLO. From the piazza, turn left onto C. Mazzini and right on V. del Trivio. Bear left on V. Cairoli, which turns into V. delle Donne, pass the church on your left, and follow tiny **Via di Solestà** as it curves to the right past the old stone house. V. di Solestà leads to the single-arched **Ponte di Solestà,** one of Europe's tallest Roman bridges. Cross this bridge and follow **V. Berardo Tucci** straight ahead for about two blocks to the **Chiesa di Sant'Emidio alle Grotte,** whose Baroque facade is grafted onto the natural rock wall. Inside are catacombs where the first Ascoli Christians were buried.

◑ FESTIVALS

On the first Sunday in August, Ascoli holds the **Tournament of Quintana,** a colorful medieval pageant in honor of the city's patron St. Emidio. The tournament features armed jousting (man-on-dummy) and a torch-lit procession to P. del Popolo. Ascoli's **Carnevale** is one of Italy's liveliest. Insanity reigns on the Tuesday, Thursday, and Sunday preceding Ash Wednesday. On the 3rd Sunday of each month (except in July and August), there is an **Antique Market** in the center of town.

SAN BENEDETTO DEL TRONTO ☎0735

With over 7000 palm trees and nearly as many children playing under their waving fronds, San Benedetto draws summering Italian families and a smattering of foreign tourists. Do not come to San Benedetto expecting to temper your beach time with a little culture—local art appreciation entails checking out art-deco sand castles on the miles of beach. Rest and relaxation are this town's priorities.

▣ TRANSPORTATION

Trains: Viale Gramsci, 20/A (☎848 88 80 88). Ticket counter open daily 6:40am-1:30pm and 1:50-8:30pm. To: **Ancona** (1½hr., 1-2 per hr., 6am-9:22pm, €4.13-7.02); **Bologna** (2½-3½hr., every hr., €20.77); and **Milan** (5hr., 8 per day, 7am-11:30pm, €34.29).

Buses: Start buses to Ascoli Piceno leave from the train station (1hr., 25 per day, 6am-12:02am, €1.70). Buy tickets in bar at train station or Caffè Blue Express, across from station. Local lines stop in front of train station. Bus #2 leaves across street from station and travels along waterfront (every 10min., 6am-midnight, €0.75).

■ 🛈 ORIENTATION AND PRACTICAL INFORMATION

From the train station, cross the street and take bus #2 to the seaside, or turn left onto **Via Gramsci** and left again onto **Via Monfalcone** towards the beach. **Viale Trieste**, the *lungomare*, intersects V. Monfalcone and runs along the shore, changing from **Viale Marconi** to **Viale Europa/Scipioni,** and then to **Viale Rinascimento. Via Trento,** which becomes **Via Volta,** runs parallel to the *lungomare.*

Tourist Office: I.A.T., Viale dell Tamerici, 5 (☎0735 59 22 37; fax 58 28 93; iat.sanbenedetto@regione.marche.it). From the train station, turn left onto V. Gramsci and take a left onto V. Fiscaletti; follow it down to the sea and turn right on V. le dei Tigli. Open June-Sept. M-Sa 9am-1pm and 4-7pm, Su 9am-1pm.

Emergency: ☎113. **Police:** V. Crispi, 51 (☎112). **Ambulance:** ☎118.

Hospital: Ospedale Civile, V. Silvio Pellico, (☎0735 79 31). Turn left on V. Gramsci as you exit the train station, head right onto V. Montello and then left onto V. Silvio Pellico.

Post Office: At the train station. Open M-F 8am-1:30pm and Sa 8am-12:30pm. **Currency exchange.**

Postal Code: 63039.

🏠 ACCOMMODATIONS & CAMPING

V. Volta has a number of budget accommodations. Most hotels own a private beach with access included in the price. A public beach sprawls in front of the tourist office. Countless chalets along the waterfront rent storage cabins from €5.20 and umbrellas from €6.20.

Albergo Patrizia, V. A. Volta, 170 (☎0735 81 762; fax 78 63 18). Bus #2, stop 35. Excellent location. Private beach. 36 rooms, all with private bath. Breakfast included. Full-pension available. €32.50-56.50 per person. €5 less without breakfast. ❹

La Playa, V. Cola di Rienzo, 25/A (☎/fax 0735 65 99 57), at end of beach. Take bus #2 or head straight on V. San Giacomo from Viale Rinascimento, take a right onto V. F. Ferrucci, continue 3 blocks, and then turn left onto V. Cola di Rienzo. *The* budget locale in this pricey area. Rooms with bath and balcony. Singles €23-52; doubles €39. ❸

Hotel Dino, Viale Europa/Scipioni, 106 (☎0735 82 147; fax 82 175). Take bus #2 to stop 11. From bus stop, turn right on V. Montessori. 34 clean, bright rooms with A/C, TV, phone, and patio. Private beach, parking, and bicycles free. Breakfast included. Full-pension available. Singles and doubles €44-72. ❹

Camping: Seaside, V. dei Mille, 125 (☎0735 65 95 05; seaside@libero.it). Take bus #2 to stop 11, or from Viale Rinascimento, turn onto V. A. Negri and bear left onto V. dei Mille. Pool, supermarket, and restaurant. Open June-Sept. €5-8 per person, €11.50-18.50 per tent. ❶

🍴 FOOD

San Benedetto's specialty is *brodetto alla sambenedettese,* a stewed medley of fish, green tomatoes, peppers, and vinegar. On Tuesday and Friday mornings, head to the **open-air market** on V. Montebello. The **Tigre supermarket,** V. Ugo Bassi, 10, is open M-Sa 8:30am-1pm and 4:30-8:30pm, Su 9am-1pm.

CENTRAL ITALY

▨ **Bagni Andrea,** V. le Trieste (☎0735 83 834; www.digiworld.net/daAndrea), on the left heading away from the train station. Dine by candlelight at this elegant restaurant right on the beach. Specializes in fish; menu changes daily (€10-15). Make reservations F-Sa dinner. F-Sa piano bar at 10pm. Latin/swing *discoteca* closes at 3am (free entrance). Open daily 12:30-3:30pm and 8:30pm-midnight. MC/V. ❸

Molo Sud, Porto Molo Sud (☎0735 58 73 25). From V. le Trieste, heading towards the station, turn right on V. le delle Tamerici. Located on the water, right before the bend in the road. This local favorite specializes in tasty fish dishes. Casual atmosphere. *Primi* from €8, *secondi* €10-11. Always packed. Reservations recommended. ❹

Marina Al Centro Ristorante, V. lo Colombo, 7. From the train station, turn left on V. Gramsci, and left on V. Francesco Fiscaletti; it's on the right. Stylish new restaurant with outdoor seating on the patio. *Primi* €5.50, *secondi* €7-12. MC/V. ❸

Bar San Michele, V. Piemonte, 111 (☎0735 82 429). From train station, turn left onto Viale Gramsci, which becomes Ugo Bassi and V. Piemonte. Pizza €3.10-5.20, *panini* €4.20. Open daily 12:15-3pm and 7:15pm-2am. AmEx/MC/V. ❷

ABRUZZO AND MOLISE

Clusters of orange thatched roofs, green wooden doors, and the occasional medieval castle lie scattered through the foothills of the Apennine mountains. Abruzzo and Molise's artisans, agriculture, and regional dialects are remnants of a pristine ancient world. About two hours from Rome, and a far cry from the frenzy of tourism, these highlands offer tranquil retreat. Women tote copper pots of well water and shirtless men lead donkeys, while youngsters listen to their Discmans.

Abruzzo and Molise, a single region until 1963, lie at the junction of northern and southern Italy. The wealthier of the two, Abruzzo offers beach and ski resorts, as well as mountain lakes, lush pines, and wild boars in the Abruzzo National Park. Dubbed a religious center by the Samnites, the smaller Molise is home to phenomenal ruins, medieval festivals, and fresh food.

Having a car in Abruzzo and Molise is advisable, since bus service is often inconsistent and runs short of many rural destinations. In both regions, however, the **ARPA bus** service can be useful, and FS trains run between major cities with some frequency. For information, call their office in L'Aquila (☎0862 41 28 08) or Avezzano (☎0863 26 561). Service is always sharply reduced on Sundays.

HIGHLIGHTS OF ABRUZZO AND MOLISE

LEARN that L'Aquila is brought to you by the **number 99** (p. 462).

WATCH out for wild boars, wolves, and eagles in the **Abruzzo National Park** (p. 467).

GO back to medieval times at the huge **jousting** tournament in Sulmona (p. 467).

SEE both of Italy's coasts—at once!—from Gran Sasso's **Corno Grande** (p. 464).

HAGGLE in L'Aquila's lively daily **market** (p. 463).

L'AQUILA   ☎0862

In 1254, 99 lords from 99 nearby castles established the majestic capital of Abruzzo. The lords honored the founding of L'Aquila (The Eagle) by building a 99-spout fountain. Local legend claims that the town has 99 medieval streets, 99 piazzas, and 99 churches—one of which tolls 99 times at 9:09 each evening.

TRANSPORTATION. L'Aquila has two bus systems: municipal buses and ARPA regional buses. The **yellow municipal buses** (€0.80) stop at **ASM** markers and serve surrounding towns and sights. Tickets are available at *tabacchi*, newsstands, or bars. On Mondays through Saturdays, **blue ARPA buses** connect L'Aquila to: **Avezzano** (50min., 32 per day, 5:50am-8:30pm, €4.50); **Pescara** (1½hr., 9 per day, 6am-8:30pm, €7.23); **Rome** (1¾hr., 18 per day, 4:40am-8pm, €8.73); and **Sulmona** (1hr., 7 per day, 6:20am-7:20pm, €5.06). Buses depart from the **Fontana Luminosa**, near the *castello*. The **ticket office** (☎0862 41 28 08) is open M-Sa 5:30am-8:30pm, Su 7:30am-1:15pm and 2:30-8pm. The **train station** (☎0862 41 92 90) is on the outskirts of town. Take bus #M11, 30, or 79C to the center, or follow signs to the Fontana delle 99 Cannelle, and hike 2km uphill. Trains head to **Sulmona** (50min.-1hr., 10 per day, 6:30am-8pm, €3.50) and **Terni** (2hr., 9 per day, 6:30am-8:20pm, €5.73).

■ ORIENTATION AND PRACTICAL INFORMATION. The main street, **Corso Vittorio Emanuele II**, stretches between the **Castello Cinquecentesco** and the ARPA bus terminal to the north and **Piazza del Duomo**, the heart of the city's historic district, to the south. Beyond P. del Duomo, the street continues as **Corso Federico II** until it reaches the lush gardens of the **Villa Comunale** and **Via XX Settembre**, which separate the southern half of the city. Pick up a map at the tourist office to aid in navigating the small streets.

The **EPT Information Office**, is at V. XX Settembre, 8. The office provides everything from maps and taxi services to info on helicopter rentals. (☎0862 22 306. Open M-Sa 9am-1pm and 4-7pm, Su 9am-1pm.) Closer to the *castello* is a second office, in **P. Maria Paganica**. Turn off C. Vittorio Emanuele onto V. Leosini. The office is uphill on the right. (☎0862 41 08 08 or 41 03 40. Open M-F 8am-2pm and 3:30-6pm, Sa 8am-2pm.) **Club Alpino Italiano**, V. Sassa, 34, provides **hiking information**. (☎0862 24 342. Open M-Sa 7-8:15pm.) The **Centro Turistico Aquilano**, C. Vittorio Emanuele, 49, has local bus and train schedules and info on the Gran Sasso park. (☎0862 22 146. Open M-F 9am-1pm and 3:30-7pm, Sa 9am-1pm.) The **police** (☎112 or 113) are at V. del Beato Cesidio. Surf the web and sip a cold one at **Gli Internauti**, V. Cimino, 51, opposite the duomo. (☎0862 40 48 38. €4 per hr. Open Sept.-June daily 6pm-1am.) The Baroque **post office** is in P. del Duomo, along with **currency exchanges**. (Open M-F 8:15am-7:40pm.) **Postal Code:** 67100.

■ ACCOMMODATIONS AND FOOD. There are no convenient budget accommodations in L'Aquila, so try to avoid spending the night. The tourist office on V. XX Settembre has a list of religious institutions in town that will rent cheap rooms for a night (mostly dorms of the Catholic schools), and will call to arrange a stay. The cheapest hotel is **Albergo Orazi ❷**, V. Roma, 175. Walking from P. Duomo on C. V. Emanuele, take a left onto C. Umberto, which turns into V. Roma. (☎0862 41 28 89. All rooms with shared bath. Singles €20.68; doubles €30.98.)

Torrone, a honey and almond nougat, is a specialty of L'Aquila. The most popular kind, *Sorelle Nurzia*, is available at **Caffè Europa ❶**, C. Emanuele, 38. (Open daily 7am-7:50pm.) **Trattoria Da Lincosta ❸**, P. S. Pietro a Coppito, 19, off V. Roma, offers substantial regional fare from a verbal menu. (☎0862 28 662. Open Sa-Th noon-4pm and 7-10:30pm.) Find everything from fresh fruit and cured meats to clothes at the **market** in P. Duomo. (Open M-Sa 8am-noon.) The **STANDA supermarket**, C. Federico II, is two blocks up from V. XX Settembre. (Open M-Sa 8am-8pm.)

◙ SIGHTS. Dating from 1292, the **Fontana delle 99 Cannelle** (Fountain of 99 Spouts) is the oldest monument in L'Aquila. Take V. Sallustio from C. Vittorio Emanuele and bear left onto V. XX Settembre. Follow the small roads down the hill, staying to the left at the bottom. The fountain is a symbol of the city's historic foundation by 99 local lords who built a fortress to protect the surrounding hill towns. Each spout represents a different town. The source of the water remains unknown. Its quality is similarly murky; don't drink from the fountain.

L'Aquila's **Castello Cinquecentesco** dominates the park at the end of C. V. Emanuele. The Spanish viceroy Don Pedro da Toledo built this fort in the 16th century to defend himself against the rebelling Aquilans, who were forced to pay for its construction. Within the walls of the fort, the **Museo Nazionale di Abruzzo** showcases art and artifacts of Abruzzo's history: sacred paintings, Roman sarcophagi, Renaissance tapestries, a million-year-old elephant skeleton, and local modern art. (☎0862 63 32 39. Open Tu-Su 9am-8pm. €4.13, students €2.)

For the **Basilica di Santa Maria di Collemaggio,** take C. Federico I past V. XX Settembre and turn left on V. di Collemaggio, after the Villa Comunale. Construction of this church began in 1287 at the urging of local hermit Pietro da Marrone (later Pope Celestine V). The pink-and-white-checked facade conceals an austere interior—the Baroque embellishments were stripped away in 1972 to bring back the plain, dark medieval design. (Open in summer daily 8:30am-1pm and 3-7pm.)

Chiesa di San Bernardino looks out over the mountains south of L'Aquila. To reach the splendid view, walk down V. S. Bernardino from C. V. Emanuele. Built in the 15th century and restored after an earthquake in 1703, the interior boasts the sculpted tomb of San Bernardino. (Open daily 7:30am-1pm and 4-7:30pm.)

NEAR L'AQUILA

The forested terrain around L'Aquila conceals isolated medieval towns, abandoned fortresses, ancient churches, and monasteries. Many of the sights remain difficult to access without a car, as buses are generally unreliable and inconvenient. East of L'Aquila lies the 15th-century **Rocca Calascio,** a sophisticated example of military architecture. It is surrounded by the medieval towns of **Santo Stefano di Sessanio** and **Castel del Monte,** as well as the 9th-century **Oratorio di San Pellegrino** in the town of **Bominaco.** To the west of L'Aquila lie the Roman ruins at **Amiternum** and the enormous **Lago di Campotosto,** the largest man-made lake in Italy. **ARPA buses** service these sights from both L'Aquila and Sulmona (1-2hr., 2-3 per day, €2.58-4.13). North of L'Aquila, the town of **Assergi** houses a beautiful 12th-century abbey, **Santa Maria Assunta.** To get there, take municipal bus #6, 6D, or 6S (20min., 2 per hr., €0.80) from the piazza near the castle.

The **Grottoes of Stiffe** at **San Demetrio ne' Vestini,** 21km southeast of L'Aquila, are a series of subterranean caves beneath Abruzzo. A prehistoric underground river carved striking caves and rock formations that now form waterfalls and small lakes. A recent cavern collapse has restricted access, but what remains open is stunning. (☎0862 86 142; www.grottestiffe.it. Open all year. Tours depart at 10am, 1, 3, and 6pm.) To get there, take the **Paoli bus** from **Porta Paganica** (25min., 5 per day, €2.58). For more information, contact the **EPT** of L'Aquila. For reservations, call or write the **Gruppo Speleologico Aquilano** at Svolte della Misericordia, 2, 67100 L'Aquila (☎/fax 0862 41 42 73).

GRAN SASSO D'ITALIA (BIG ROCK OF ITALY)

From L'Aquila, take yellow bus #6 or 6D (30min., 5 per day, €0.80) from the fontana luminosa. Buy tickets at newsstands and tabacchi. The funivia is closed during parts of June and October. Trails start at the upper funivia station. Call Club Alpino Italiano (☎0862 24

342) for the most current Apennine advice. For information on guides ask at the tourist office, Club Alpino Italiano, or write to Collegio Regionale Guide Alpine, V. Serafino, 2, 66100 Chieti (☎ 0871 69 338).

Just 12km north of L'Aquila rises the snow capped **Gran Sasso d'Italia,** the highest ridge contained entirely within Italy's borders. Midway up the Sasso (and above the tree line) is a flat plain called Campo Imperatore, home to herds of wild horses, shepherds, and amazing views of the peaks and landscape below. On a clear day, one can see forever, or at least to both of Italy's coasts, from the range's highest peak, the 2912m **Corno Grande.** Before starting a hike, pick up the Club Alpino Italiano **trail map** in town at the **Club Alpino Italiano** near P. Duomo or at the base of the mountain (€7.75). The *sentieri* (paths) are marked by difficulty—only the more taxing routes reach the top. The peaks are snowed-in from September to July, and only experienced mountaineers should hike near the summit during this period. A **funivia** ascends the 1008m to Campo Imperatore (every 30min., 9am-5pm, round-trip €10), making the Sasso an easy afternoon excursion from L'Aquila.

In winter, Gran Sasso teems with skiers. The trails around the funicular are among the most difficult, offering several 1000m drops and one of 4000m. Ten trails descend from the funicular and the two lifts. Weekly passes can be purchased at the *biglietteria* at the base of the funicular. **Campo Felice,** at nearby Monte Rotondo, has 16 lifts, numerous trails of varying difficulty, and a ski school.

Both the map and information booklet from L'Aquila's EPT or IAT list overnight *rifugi* (hiker's huts), which cost €6-12 per night. Another option is the youth hostel, **Campo Imperatore ❶.** Call from the lower rope way station and ask to be picked up. (☎ 0862 40 00 11. €15.50 per bed.) There is also **Camping Funivia del Gran Sasso ❶,** an immaculate patch of grass downhill from the lower cable way. (☎ 0862 60 61 63. €4-5 per person, €6-7.50 per large tent.) Always call these lodgings before setting out, and bring food and warm clothing; it's windy and cool at Campo Imperatore year round. Prices rise and temperatures drop with altitude.

SULMONA
☎ 0864

Sulmona is hidden deep within the Abruzzo highlands in the Gizio River Valley, surrounded on all sides by extensive national parks. Small and overlooked by many tourists, it boasts pleasant public gardens and piazzas, *fabbriche* churning out its famous *confetti* candy (sold in bouquets, bags, and handfuls), and great pride in their most famous son, Latin poet Ovid, known for his epic *Metamorphoses* and erotic *Amores.* The "SMPE" frequently seen throughout Sulmona stands for its famous proclamation *"Sulmo mihi patria est"* ("Sulmona is my homeland"). The mountains around Sulmona offer wonderful low-impact hiking, but even a day spent meandering the streets of the city is enjoyable.

🚍 TRANSPORTATION. Two kilometers outside of the city center, Sulmona's train station (☎ 0864 34 293) joins the Rome-Pescara and Carpione-L'Aquila-Terni lines. **Trains** run to: **Avezzano** (1½hr., 4 per day, 6:38am-2:04pm, €3.50); **L'Aquila** (50-60min., 8 per day, 6:57am-8:30pm, €3.50); **Naples** (4hr., 4 per day, 6:30am-3:30pm, €12); **Pescara** (1-1¼hr., 19 per day, 6:14am-9:18pm, €3.50-6); and **Rome** (1½-2½hr., 7 per day, 5:47am-8:09pm, €7-12). **Bus A** runs from the train station to the town center (5:30am-8pm, €0.60); ask to stop at P. XX Settembre.

🛈 PRACTICAL INFORMATION. Corso Ovidio runs from the train station west of Sulmona, past P. XX Settembre and P. Garibaldi, and through Porta Napoli and the eastern wall, changing its name often. There's an English-speaking staff at the **IAT Tourist Information Office,** C. Ovidio, 208. (☎/fax 0864 53 276. Open M-Sa 9am-1pm and 4-7pm, Su 9am-noon.) A cheery crew mans the **Ufficio Servizi Turistici** office across the street in P. dell'Annunziata, in the same building as the museum. (☎0864 21 02 16; fax 20 73 48. Open in summer daily 9am-1:30pm and 4-8pm, in winter 9am-1:30pm and 3:30-7:30pm.) For **police** call ☎113 or 0864 35 661. Access the web at **Internet Etman Technology,** V. Barbato, 9. (☎0864 21 27 75. €2.58 per hr. Open daily 9am-1pm and 4-8pm.) The **post office** is on P. Brigata Maiella, behind P. del Carmine. (Open M-F 8am-6:30pm, Sa 8:15am-1pm.) **Postal Code:** 67039.

⌐Ⓒ ACCOMMODATIONS AND FOOD. Reservations are a good idea in summer. **Albergo Stella ❸,** V. Panfilo Mazara, 18/20, off C. Ovidio, near the aqueduct, has nine well-maintained rooms with bath, phone, and TV. (☎/fax 0864 52 653; www.albergostellaristorante.com. Breakfast included. Singles €31-35; doubles €50-55. MC/V.) **Hotel Italia ❷,** P. S. Tommasi, 3, to the right off P. XX Settembre, has 27 rooms, several with views of the dome of S. Annunziata and the mountains. Formerly occupied by the University of Colorado's Italian program in the summer, the hotel put up a sign when they were dismissed promising "Tranquility for all." (☎ 0864 52 308. Singles €18.23, with bath €31; doubles €41/€51.50.) The **UST tourist office** also rents three **private apartments ❶** with bath and kitchen in the center of town. Two of these hold four people (€39); the other holds up to seven (€52-€72). Call the office for information and booking (☎0864 21 02 16).

▨Cesidio ❸, V. Sulmona, 25, has been offering reasonably priced local fare, such as the full-course tourist menù (€13) and their specialty, spicy *spaghetti al Cesidio* (€4.13), for 50 years. (☎0864 34 940. Open Tu-Su noon-3:30pm and 7-10:30pm. AmEx/MC/V.) At the popular **Ristorante Clemente ❸,** V. del Vecchio, 7, off C. Ovidio, Clemente and his father serve regional favorites under their creed: *"Si mangia bene, si spende giusto"* ("Eat well, spend fairly"). Brush up on your Italian, as the menu is verbal. (☎0864 52 284. *Primi* €4.65, *secondi* €5.16-9.30. Cover €1.55. Open daily 1-3pm and 7pm-midnight.)

⑥🅙 SIGHTS AND ENTERTAINMENT. The Romanesque-Gothic **Cattedrale di San Panfilo** is at one end of C. Ovidio. Its center was built 1000 years ago on the ruins of a temple for Apollo and Vesta. From the gardens near P. XX Settembre, follow C. Ovidio to the **Chiesa and Palazzo di Santissima Annunziata.** The 15th-century Gothic *palazzo* adjacent to the Baroque church has a small **museum.** If fond of Renaissance *sulmonese* gold work, you may have found your version of *paradiso;* there's also a collection of wood statues collected from local churches. (☎0864 21 02 16. Open Tu-Su 10am-1pm. €0.55.) Behind, one block off C. Ovidio, the **Museo in Situ** features the intact ruins of a Roman house. (Open Tu-Su 9:30am-1pm. Free.) The colossal **Piazza Garibaldi** surrounds the Renaissance **Fontana del Vecchio,** which flows with mountain water from the nearby medieval aqueduct.

Sulmona's prized *confetti* candy is made at, among other places, the Pelino family's **factory,** V. Stazione Introdaqua, 55. Turn right after the arch at the end of C. Ovidio onto V. Trieste, continue 1km up the hill as it becomes V. Stazione Introdaqua, and enter the Pelino building. The Pelinos have been making *confetti* since 1783 with the same types of machines, the older of which are on display in the free **confetti museum.** Check out the slightly sacrilegious (even for Italy) pictures of past popes and Padre Pio munching on candied religious instruments. Delight in *confetti* flowers and fish, and behold the ancient cauldrons, ovens, bottles, and pipes with which the Pelinos blazed the trail for Willy Wonka. (☎ 0864 21 00 47. Open M-Sa 8am-12:30pm and 3-6:30pm.)

The last weekend of July brings the **Giostra Cavalleresca di Sulmona,** a festival in which mounted, beacon-bearing knights run figure eights around P. Garibaldi in celebration of the seven *borghi* (neighborhoods) of medieval Sulmona. Buy seated tickets (€15-18), or find a place from which to watch for free. In preparation, the *borghi* host public *feste* on June weekends. The first weekend of July brings another joust, the **Giostra Cavalleresca di Europa,** this time with international knights. In October, Sulmona hosts international film and opera festivals.

🖪 **HIKING.** The mountains towering over Sulmona are part of the **Majella National Park,** and several trails are easily accessible by foot or bus from the town center. High up on the cliffs perches the mountain retreat of the saintly hermit who became Pope Celestine V; you can see the small cave where he lived. It's a fairly easy 45min. each way from the town of **Badia,** which is a 20min. bus ride from Sulmona (€0.77; bus leaves from Sulmona's public gardens on C. Ovidio). The helpful **Club Italiano Alpino** map from the tourist office (€6.20) lists each hike and the color of the blazes that mark the trails. The difficulty level refers to mountaineering experience, not hiking experience, so hikes of moderate difficulty may be challenging for those not used to mountain climbing. The early sections of almost all trails are manageable. **Hike 7a** from the village of Fonte D'Amore is a 45min. trek that will bring you to **ruins** of a sanctuary dedicated to Hercules (or, according to old Sulmonan belief, a villa belonging to Ovid). Take the first section of **Hike 7 or 8** from the village of Fonte D'Amore for a 5km hike through the forested hills to Marane. These trailheads, 4km from Sulmona, are served by local bus. Pick up a schedule from the tourist office, and watch out for mid-afternoon gaps in service.

ABRUZZO NATIONAL PARK

The Parco Nazionale d'Abruzzo is the region's 4th-largest park, protecting 44,000 hectares of mountainous wilderness from the resort hotels so loved by Italians. The mountains provide spectacular views of lush woodlands and crystal-clear lakes. Lynx have recently been reintroduced near Civitella Alfedena, joining Marsican brown bears, Apennine wolves, and Abruzzo chamois antelopes. Despite reported glimpses of the exciting wildlife, incidents of confrontation with visitors are rare. Leave the animals alone, and they will leave you alone. Pescasseroli, the park's administrative center, provides the best base for its exploration.

▐ TRANSPORTATION

Take the **ARPA bus** (☎ 0863 26 561 or 22 921), which runs from Avezzano through the park to **Castel di Sangro** (2¾hr., M-Sa 6 per day, Su reduced service, 6:40am-6:35pm, €3.62), making five stops: **Barrea** (2¼hr., €3.51); **Civitella Alfadena** (2hr., €3.41); **Opi** (1¾hr., €3.20); **Pescasseroli** (1½hr., €3.10); and **Villetta Barrea** (2hr., €3.36). Buses run to Pescasseroli from Rome's Tiburtina station (3hr., daily 7:45am, one-way €11.93). **Trains** run from Avezzano to: **Pescara** (1¾-2hr, 8 per day, 6:30am-8pm, €8.50); **Rome** (1½-2hr., 8 per day, 5am-9pm, €8); and **Sulmona** (1-1¼hr., 10 per day, 6:30am-8pm, €5).

🔁 PRACTICAL INFORMATION

In Pescasseroli, check in at the **Ufficio di Zona,** Vico Consultore, 1, by the P. Antonio bus stop, for hiking information, local animal t-shirts, and an essential park map. (☎0863 91 955. Map €5.60. Open daily 9am-noon and 3-7pm.) For information on accommodations and restaurants, drop by the **IAT Information Office,** V. Piave, 2, off P. Antonio. (☎/fax 0863 91 04 61. Open daily 9am-1pm and 4-7pm.)

🛏️🍴 ACCOMMODATIONS AND FOOD

PESCASSEROLI. In the middle of the park, alpine Pescasseroli is a popular place to stay, though solo travelers may have a hard time finding a single room. **Pensione Claudia ❷,** V. Tagliamento, 35, 200m across the gravel lot on the main street that leads out of town, has 10 quiet rooms with bath. (☎0863 91 837; m.finamore@ermes.it. Sept.-July singles €18; doubles €25.82-30.99. July-Aug. required half-pension €36.15 per person.) **Pensione al Castello ❹,** V. Gabriele d'Annunzio, 1, opposite the park office, has seven clean and pleasant rooms, all with bath, phone, and TV. (☎0863 91 07 57. Breakfast €2.58. Doubles €42; triples €53; quads €64. Aug. and Christmas required half-pension €36-52. MC/V.) A bit more expensive is **Monte Marsicano ❷,** on V. della Piazza in the center of town, with 24 large rooms, all with bath, phone, and TV. (☎0863 91 10 55. Singles €20.65-41.31; doubles €41.32-82.63. Half-pension €38.73-67.14 per person. MC/V.) Five campgrounds are within 21km of town. The best is **Campeggio dell'Orso ❶,** 1km from Pescasseroli on the main road to Opi. Call to reserve; there's often no staff at the site. (☎0863 91 955. €3.10 per person, €3.10 per tent.)

For picnic supplies head to **Delfino A&O** supermarket on V. S. Lucia, the main highway, past the zoo and park office. (Open daily 8:30am-1pm and 4-8pm. AmEx/MC/V.) **Pasticceria Alpina ❶,** Traversa Sangro, 6, serves an array of award-winning sweets. (☎0863 91 05 61. Open Tu-Su 7am-10pm.)

OPI. ARPA buses follow the winding road through the park to the village of Opi, named for the pagan goddess of abundance, whose temple was here in ancient times. Two kilometers past the village, on the bus route, lies the campground **Vecchio Mulino ❶.** (☎0863 91 22 32; ilvecchiomulino@tiscalinet.it. €5 per person, €5.50 per small tent. AmEx/MC/V.) The campground has a restaurant and bar, and the friendly owners also own a bed & breakfast in Opi. In late August, Opi hosts the **Sagra degli Gnocchi** (Gnocchifest), a nationally renowned eat-along where thousands converge to consume large quantities of *gnocchi,* sausages, and cheese.

CIVITELLA ALFEDENA. Ten kilometers past Opi, the bus reaches the village of **Villetta Barrea.** The turn-off to Civitella Alfedena, 200m farther down the road, leads to **Camping Le Quite ❶.** The site is bordered by the River Sangro. (☎0864 89 141. €2.58-3.10 per person, €3.10-3.62 per large tent.) In Civitella Alfedena, **Alberghetto La Torre** and **Albergo Autico Borgo ❹,** V. Castello, 3, both under the same management, offer great rooms with bath, TV, and phone. (☎0864 89 01 21. Doubles €39-52; triples €49-70; quads €59-80.) The **Museo del Lupo,** on the left as you enter town, records the Apennine wolf and lynx. (☎0864 89 01 41. Open daily 10am-1pm and 3-7pm. €2.58.) Ice-cold **Barrea Lake** cuts majestically into the mountains, stretching 7km between Villetta Barrea and the neighboring village of **Barrea.**

AVEZZANO. You can say one thing about Avezzano: it was beautiful before the earthquake in 1915. But now it is known primarily for its *telespazio,* a satellite transmission system. It is also one of the main gateways to the park. Buses into the

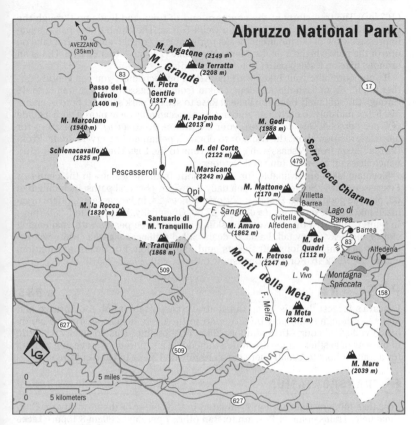

Abruzzo National Park

TO AVEZZANO (35km)

M. Argatone (2149 m)

la Terratta (2208 m)

M. Grande

83

Passo del Diávolo (1400 m)

M. Pietra Gentile (1917 m)

17

M. Marcolano (1940 m)

M. Palombo (2013 m)

M. Godi (1988 m)

Schienacavallo (1825 m)

M. del Corte (2122 m)

Serra Bocca Chiarano

Pescasseroli

M. Marsicano (2242 m)

479

Opi

M. Mattone (2170 m)

Villetta Barrea

M. la Rocca (1830 m)

F. Sangro

Lago di Barrea

Santuario di M. Tranquillo

Civitella Alfedena

Barrea

M. Amaro (1862 m)

Via S. Lucia

83

Alfedena

M. Tranquillo (1868 m)

M. dei Quadri (1112 m)

M. Petroso (2247 m)

Monti della Meta

509

L. Vivo

L. Montagna Spaccata

158

627

F. Melfa

la Meta (2241 m)

N

LG

509

M. Mare (2039 m)

0   5 miles

0   5 kilometers

627

park leave from the side of the tracks opposite the station—take the *sottopassagio*. **Hotel Creati ❷,** on V. XX Settembre near the bus station, offers pleasant, inexpensive rooms. (☎ 0863 41 33 47. Singles €20; doubles €30.)

🗺 OUTDOORS

The scenic ascent on the road from Avezzano to Pescasseroli, past fields of poppies, dazzling valleys, and rocky outcrops, marks the beginning of the park. If the wildlife in the park eludes you, there's always Pescasseroli's **Centro di Visita,** Viale Colle dell'Orso, 2, off V. S. Lucia as you head toward Opi. The center has a museum and small zoo. (Open daily 10am-1pm and 3-7pm. €5.16.)

Purchase the indispensable trail map (€5.60) from the **Pescasseroli Ufficio di Zona,** which indicates prime wildlife-viewing spots (and the locations of other *uffizi di zona* throughout the park). You might see brown bears, chamois, deer, wolves, and eagles. The trails are arranged so that all paths that begin with the same letter start from the same point. For a short hike, take **trail B1** to the castle ruins at Monte Ceraso (50min. round-trip). To really stretch those legs, brave the beautiful 5hr. round-trip hike on **trail C3** to **Vicolo (Pass) di Monte Tranquillo**

CENTRAL ITALY

(1673m). The trail starts at the southern end of town and leads up through the green Valle Mancina, past the Rifugio Della Difesa. The climb to the pass has an impressive view of the mountain peaks to the north. True adventurers can take on one of the park's highest peaks, **Monte Marsicano** (2245m)—**trail E6** from Opi is an arduous hike on a steep path (7-8hr. round-trip).

If you coordinate your hikes with the ARPA bus schedule, you can venture farther afield. From Civitella Alfedena (15km from Pescasseroli), take **trail I1 to K6** through the sublimely beautiful **Valle di Rose** to see the park's largest herd of chamois. From mid-July to early September, this area can only be explored with a guide (€7 per person). One day before your excursion, go to an *ufficio di zona* for more information about the trails or to obtain a permit and reserve a guide. From Barrea (20km from Pescasseroli), **trail K5** runs to the **Lago Vivo** (3½hr. round-trip), which dries up between June and October.

Mountain bikes are available for €2 per hour from the agency in the center of Pescasseroli at V. Sorgenti, 1. (Open daily 9am-7pm.) Several paths, including **trail C3,** provide good biking. **Ecotur,** P. Vittorio Veneto, 24, in Pescasseroli, offers organized hikes and excursions. (☎0863 91 27 60. Open daily 9am-1pm and 3:30-7pm.) In winter, this area offers excellent skiing across three peaks, with challenging slopes and heavy snowfall. Package deals called **settimane bianche** (white weeks) provide accommodations, lift tickets, and half-pension. For ticket information, call ☎0863 91 22 16. For a regional snow bulletin, call ☎0862 66 510.

PESCARA   ☎085

Pescara's biggest draw is being the central transportation hub for Abruzzo and Molise, although some may be attracted to the lively beach resorts and sandy beach volleyball courts that compose 20km of shoreline. This noisy city has little in the way of aesthetic appeal, but those spending an afternoon or evening waiting for a train or boat to Croatia here can certainly find some fun and culture.

▐▀ TRANSPORTATION

Pescara's modern train station is situated in the center of the new city on C. V. Emanuele. Trains connect Pescara to: **Bari** (4hr., 7 per day, 2:30am-8:15pm); **Lecce** (6hr., 11 per day, 1:50am-4:15pm); **Milan** (6½hr., 15 per day, noon-11:15pm); **Naples** (5hr., 2 per day, 5:15am and 7am); **Rome** (4hr., 6 per day, 4:50am-7pm); **Sulmona** (1hr., 15 per day, 6:25am-9:45pm); and **Termoli** (1½hrs., 11 per day, 6:30am-8:45pm). **ARPA** buses run from in front of the train station to **l'Aquila, Sulmona, Avezzano,** and **Rome** on varying schedules; consult booth in front of train station for times. **SNAV** (☎085 451 0873; www.snavoli.com) runs ferries in season to the Croatian Isles of **Hvar, Brac, Korcula,** and **Spalato.** Contact SNAV for times. One-way prices €98.50-114. **Jetline** (☎085 451 6241) runs ferries to the **Tremiti Islands** (2½hr., 1 per day, 8am, €20.50). Ferries leave from beyond the tourist harbor in the old city across the river from the main beach. Pescara's **airport** connects to major Italian cities and cities in Germany and Ireland. Take bus #38 from the station to the airport.

◢◣ ⁊ ORIENTATION AND PRACTICAL INFORMATION

Buses and trains drop off at Central Station in the center of the new city, on the main street, **Corso V. Emanuele.** To the right, C. V. Emanuele extends toward the **River Pescara.** Across the bridge to the right is the **old city,** and a short walk to the left leads to the **tourist harbor.** If you keep walking straight across the bridge, you will come to Pescara's extensive **park.** In front of the train station exit lies the main stretch of beach, running parallel to C. V. Emanuele. To reach the **IAT tourist office,** V. Paolucci, 3, turn right onto C. V. Emanuele, exiting the station, and make a left when you hit the river. (☎ 085 4290 0212; iat.pescara@abruzzoturismo.it. Open M-Sa 9am-1pm and 4pm-7pm, Su 9am-1pm.) The **post office** is on C. V. Emanuele between the station and the river. (☎ 085 27 541. Open M-Sa 8am-12pm, 2-5pm.) For **police,** dial ☎ 113; the station is at P. Duca D'Aosta. **Sport Net Centre,** V. Venezia, 14, off C. V. Emanuele, offers Internet access. (☎ 085 421 9368. Open M-Sa 9:30am-1pm and 4:30-8pm. €3 per hr.)

ACCOMMODATIONS AND FOOD

The best budget accommodations are in the area off C. V. Emanuele, opposite the train station. Beachfront hotels aren't worth the prices—the only views are of the colorful groupings of closely-spaced beach umbrellas. From the train station, walk down C. V. Emanuele away from the river and turn right onto V. Piave to get to **Albergo Planet ❷,** V. Piave, 142, the cheapest option in town. Low, low rates mean wearing flip-flops in the shower. (☎/fax 085 421 1657. Singles without bath €15.49-18.08; doubles €30.99-36.15, with bath €41.32.) **Hotel Adria ❸,** V. Firenze, 141, is a pleasant and clean three-star on a street running parallel to C. V. Emanuele, one block toward the waterfront. All 30 rooms are equipped with private bath and TV. (☎ 085 422 4246; fax 422 2427. Singles €25.83-36.16; doubles €41.32-61.98. MC/V.)

Food in Pescara falls into two categories: seafood and traditional Abruzzo cuisine. The best seafood options are along the waterfront. **Berardo da Eriberto ❸,** V. le Rivera, 40, is a slightly upscale restaurant with a classy patio dining room. The *gnocchi agli scampi* (€7.80) will have seafood fans rejoicing. (☎ 085 421 5444. Open daily 12:30-4:30pm and 8:30pm-12:30am. AmEx/MC/V.) Also along the beach is **Alcione da Umberto ❸,** V. le Rivera, 24, where a lively crew serves up local seafood and pizzas. The house specialty is *tagliatelle alla Umberto* (pasta, fish, and eggs; €10). (☎ 085 34 150. Pizzas €3.50-10.50. Cover €1.50. Open Tu-Su 9am-1am. MC/V.) The popular **La Cantina di Jozz ❷,** V. delle Caserme, 61, offers atmospheric outdoor seating across from the museum in the old city. (☎ 085 451 8800. Open Tu-Sa noon-3pm and 8pm-midnight, Su noon-3pm. AmEx/MC/V.)

SIGHTS AND ENTERTAINMENT

Pescara's **beach** is vibrant and crowded with all the attractions of a seaside resort: courts for basketball, soccer, and volleyball, music, windsurfing, bars, and, of course, miles of sunbathing. Those looking for active beachside recreation can do no wrong here, but it's certainly not the place for quiet relaxation.

On the other side of the river is Pescara's more cultural area, with a couple decent museums and a pleasant harbor. Cross the bridge and make first right to reach the **Museo delle Genti d'Abruzzo,** V. delle Caserme, 22, which celebrates 4000 years of Abruzzo's history in a chronological series of galleries. The time-line extends from paleolithic Abruzzo to the present, emphasizing the development of local products and crafts. (☎ 085 451 0026. Open M-F 9:30am-1pm and 3:30-6pm, Su 10am-1pm. €4, EU students 18-24 €1.50, EU citizens under 18 and over 65 free.) Straight ahead across the bridge, the **Museo Civico,** V. Marconi, 45, celebrates the remarkable 20th-century artwork of six members of the Cascella family, who were behind the modern fountain at the beach. (☎ 085 428 3515. Open M-F 9am-1pm and 4:30-6:30pm. €3, EU students 18-24 €1.50, EU citizens under 18 or over 65 free.)

Pescara hosts a large **annual jazz festival** in mid-July, attracting renowned Italian and international acts for performances in P. della Rinascità. (☎ 085 29 22 04; www.pescarajazz.com. Tickets €10-18.)

CENTRAL ITALY

TERMOLI
☎0875

With a pretty expanse of untainted coastline and an enjoyable old city, Termoli is surprisingly small and untouristed. Its central draw is that it offers ferry connections to the Tremiti islands. The **FS train** station lies at the west end of town. **Corso M. Milano** extends to **Lungomare Colombo**, the waterfront strip lined with hotels on one side and beaches on the other. **Corso Umberto**, running from the station to the small old town, is lined with restaurants and shops. To get to the port, walk down Corso Milano and turn right at the intersection with Lungomare Colombo. The ferry docks and ticket offices are past the fishing boats on the long breakwater. The **tourist office** is on Lungomare Colombo, a block to the right of the intersection with C. Milano. (☎0875 70 83 42. Open M-Sa 9am-1pm and 5-7:30pm.)

Those waiting for a boat have a few options for accommodations and food. **Hotel Rosary ❹**, Lungomare Colombo, 42, at the intersection with C. Milano, is a short walk from the station and a stone's throw from the beach. All rooms have bath and TV. (☎0875 84 944. Open Apr.-Oct. Doubles €47-57. AmEx/MC/V.) Coming from the train station, turn right from C. Nazionale onto V. Alfano and then right on V. Ruffino for **La Sacrestia ❶**, V. Ruffini, 48. Divine pizzas (€2.58-5.16) are in tune with the Holy Land pilgrimage theme. (☎0875 70 56 03. Open daily noon-2pm and 7-11pm. MC/V.) For fresh bread or other baked goods for the ride, stop by **Lineapane ❶**, V. Milano, 18. (Open daily 7am-1:15pm and 4:30-9pm.)

TREMITI ISLANDS
☎0882

▐ TRANSPORTATION. Ferry service from **Termoli** only operates June-Sept. Hydrofoils make the trip in 1hr., ferries in 1½hr. Several companies serve the islands: **Navigargano** (☎0875 70 59 90; daily 9:15am, return 5:15pm; round-trip €14.46-16.53); **Navigazione Libera** (☎0875 70 48 59; hydrofoils daily 8:40am, 10:55am, and 5:20pm; return 9:45am, 4:10pm, and 6:40pm; one-way €13; also a daily ferry at 9:15am from Termoli, €7.50); **Adriatica ferries** (daily 9am, return 5pm; €7.23-8.31); and **hydrofoils** (daily 8:35am, return 9:35am; varying afternoon service; €12.65-14.56).

▐ ORIENTATION AND PRACTICAL INFORMATION. There are four Tremiti islands—**San Domino, San Nicola, Capraia,** and **Pinosa**. San Domino is the largest, with the archipelago's only hotels, while San Nicola is home to an 11th-century abbey. The latter two are small and desolate and only of interest to seagulls. **Motorboats** run throughout the day between San Nicola and San Domino (€1). The **carabinieri** can be reached at ☎0882 46 30 10. A **first aid station** is at the port in San Domino. (☎0882 46 32 34. Open 24hr.) A **pharmacy** is in the village on San Nicola. (☎0882 46 33 27. Open June-Sept. daily 9am-1pm and 5-9:30pm; Oct.-May 9:30am-12:30pm and 5-7:30pm.)

▐ ACCOMMODATIONS. Hotels are on San Domino, and most offer doubles and require half- or full-pension. Make reservations during the summer; there are few rooms and they get filled quickly. **Hotel La Vela ❺**, on V. San Domino, offers half-pension rooms a short walk up from the boat harbor on San Domino—call to be picked up. (☎0882 46 32 54; www.hotel-lavela.it. Aug. €60-67 per person; Sept.-July €41-52.) **Villagio International ❹**, at Punta del Diamente, is an economical choice in a quiet area near the shore, with two kinds of housing—prefabricated hut/tent hybrids or bungalows. (☎0882 46 34 05. Prefab units €23.24 per person, required half-pension in Aug. €50; bungalows €34-39 per person, required half-pension in Aug. €60; surcharge for singles €15.)

🔍📷 HIKING, SPEAR-FISHING, AND SIGHTS. The **pine forests** that cover much of the island are the highlight of San Domino. Paths snake through the protected forest, alive with the sound of cicadas and the smell of dried pine needles. Many paths extend down to small rocky coves along the coast, where vacationers swim in the sapphire waters—in secluded spots, sans suits. Many Italians take to the seas with **spear guns** for fishing adventures. If you'd rather explore moderately interesting religious buildings, ride to the island of San Nicola, where a **fortified abbey** crowns the cliffs. Accessible by a short path from the harbor, the monastery was founded in the 11th century. Portions of the original mosaic floor have survived numerous renovations. A tradition of exile in the abbey began when Emperor Augustus' adulterous granddaughter Julia was banished here, and continued with the Fascist regime's purges.

ROME

Italy will return to the splendors of Rome, said the major. I don't like Rome, I said.
It is hot and full of fleas. You don't like Rome? Yes, I love Rome. Rome is the
mother of nations. I will never forget Romulus suckling the Tiber. What? Nothing.
Let's all go to Rome. Let's go to Rome tonight and never come back. Rome is a
beautiful city, said the major.
    —Ernest Hemingway, *A Farewell to Arms*

Italy's massive capital city is an eruption of marble domes, noseless statues, and
motorcycle dust. Rome is sensory overload, rushing down the hills of Lazio to
knock you flat on your back, leaving you gasping for air and dying for more. The
city and those it controlled were responsible for the development of over 2000
years of world history, art, architecture, politics, and literature. Rome has been the
capital of kingdoms and republics; from this city, the Roman Empire defined the
Western world and the Catholic Church spread its influence worldwide. For the
traveler, there is so much to see, hear, eat, smell, and absorb that the city is both
exhilarating and overwhelming, as if it's impossible to experience everything, or
even anything. Never fear, however, because in *bella Roma*, everything is beautiful and everything tastes good. Liberate your senses from the smog eroding the
monuments and from the maniacal rush of motorcyclists, and enjoy the dizzying
paradox that is the *Caput Mundi*, the Eternal City, Rome.

✈ INTERCITY TRANSPORTATION

FLIGHTS

Most international flights arrive at **da Vinci International Airport** (☎06 65 951),
known as **Fiumicino**. When you exit customs, follow the signs to your left for **Stazione FS/Railway Station.** Take the elevator or escalators up two floors to the pedestrian bridge to the airport train station. The **Termini line** runs nonstop to Rome's
main train station, **Termini Station** (30min.; 2 per hr., 12 and 37min. past the hr.
7:37am-10:37pm, extra trains 7:37am, 6:37, 8:37pm; €20 on board). Buy a ticket at
the FS ticket counter, the *tabacchi* on the right, or from one of the machines in the
station. A train leaves Termini for Fiumicino from track #22 or 23, which is at the
end of #22 (40min.; every hr. at 20min. past the hour, 7:20am-9:20pm; extra trains
6:50am, 3:50, 5:50, 7:50pm; €8.26). Buy tickets at the Alitalia office at track #22 at
the window marked *Biglietti Per Fiumicino* or from other designated areas and
machines in the station. Validate your ticket before boarding.

EARLY AND LATE FLIGHTS. For flights that arrive after 10pm or leave before
8am, the most reliable option is to take a **cab.** (Request one at the kiosk in the airport or call ☎06 35 70, 06 49 94, or 06 66 45. €35-45. Decide upon a price with the
driver before you get into the cab. Drivers have been known to charge upwards of
€150 for the fare between the airport and the city.) The cheapest option is to take
the blue **COTRAL bus** to Tiburtina from the ground floor outside the main exit doors
after customs (1:15, 2:15, 3:30, 5am; €4.50 on board). From Tiburtina, take bus
#40N to Termini. To get to Fiumicino from Rome late at night or early in the morn-
ing, take bus #40N from Termini to Tiburtina (every 20-30min.), then catch the
blue COTRAL bus to Fiumicino from the plaza (12:30, 1:15, 2:30, 3:45am; €4.20).

DOMESTIC FLIGHTS. Most charter and a few domestic flights arrive at Ciampino airport (☎06 79 49 41). To get to Ciampino from Rome, take the COTRAL bus (every 30min., 6:10am-11pm, €1.03) to Anagnina station on Metro Linea A. After 10pm and before 8am, take a cab. There will be a supplemental charge of €2.50.

TRAINS

Stazione Termini is the focal point of most train and subway lines. Trains arriving in Rome between midnight and 5am usually arrive at Stazione Tiburtina or Stazione Ostiense, which are connected to Termini at night by the #40N and 20N-21N buses, respectively. Station services include: **hotel reservations** (across from track #20); **ATMs; luggage storage** (track #1); and **police** (track #13, ☎112). Not to be missed are ▧**Termini's bathrooms,** a black-lit wonderland off track #1 (€0.50). Trains leave Termini to: **Naples** (2-2½hr., €9.70); **Florence** (2-3hr., €24.50); **Bologna** (2¾-4¼hr., €19.10); **Milan** (4½-8hr., €27); and **Venice** (5hr., €35).

⚔ ORIENTATION

From the **Termini** train station, **Via Nazionale** is the central artery connecting **Piazza della Repubblica** with **Piazza Venezia,** home to the immense wedding-cake-like **Vittorio Emanuele II monument.** West of P. Venezia, **Largo Argentina** marks the start of **Corso Vittorio Emanuele,** which leads to Centro Storico, the medieval and Renaissance tangle of sights around the **Pantheon, Piazza Navona, Campo dei Fiori,** and **Piazza Farnese.** From P. Venezia, V. dei Fori Imperiale leads southeast to the **Forum** and **Colosseum,** south of which are the ruins of the **Baths of Caracalla** and the **Appian Way,** and the neighborhoods of southern Rome, the Aventine, Testaccio, Ostiense, and EUR. **Via del Corso** stretches from P. Venezia north to **Piazza del Popolo.** East of the Corso, fashionable streets border the **Piazza di Spagna** and, to the northeast, the **Villa Borghese.** South and east are the **Fontana di Trevi, Piazza Barberini,** and the **Quirinal Hill.** Across the Tiber to the north are **Vatican City,** and, to the south, **Trastevere,** the best neighborhood for wandering. It's impossible to navigate Rome without a map. Pick up a free map from a tourist office or a ▧*Let's Go* **map guide.** The invaluable **Roma Metro-Bus map** (€4.20) is available at newsstands.

▐ LOCAL TRANSPORTATION

Bus and subway tickets (€0.77) are one and the same, and can be bought at *tabacchi,* newsstands, some bars, and vending machines. Vending machines are in stations, on occasional street corners, and at major bus stops. Look for the ATAC label. Each ticket is valid for either one ride on the Metro or for unlimited bus travel within 75min. of validation. A BIG daily ticket costs €4.13 and allows for unlimited bus or train travel everywhere in the *Comune di Roma,* including Ostia but not Fiumicino; a CIS weekly ticket costs €16.32.

SUBWAY (METROPOLITANA)

The two lines (A and B) of the *Metropolitana* intersect at Termini and can be reached by several entrances, including the stairway between the station and P. del Cinquecento. Entrances to Metro stations elsewhere are marked by poles with a white "M" on a red square. **The subway runs daily from 5:30am to 11:30pm.**

BUSES

Although the network of routes may seem daunting, Rome's buses are an efficient means of getting around the city. The **ATAC** intracity bus company has a myriad of booths, including one in Termini. (☎800 55 56 66. Open daily 8am-8pm.) Each bus

ROME

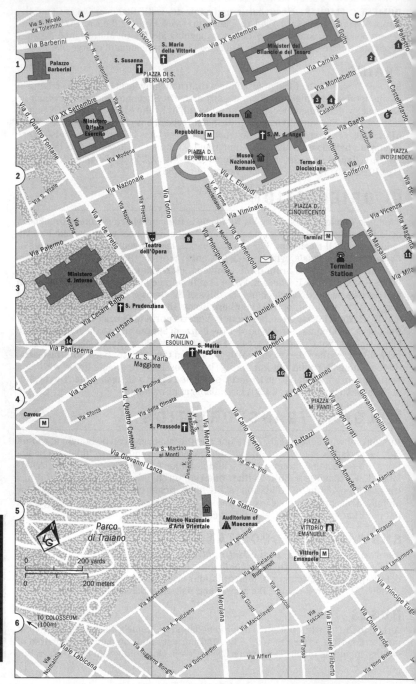

ROME

TO COLOSSEUM
(100m)

0   200 yards
0   200 meters

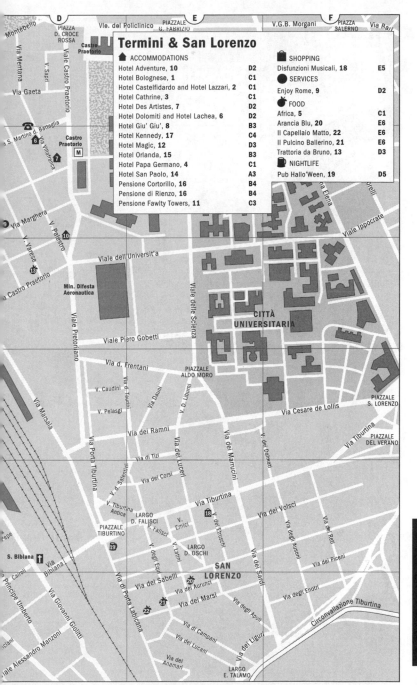

Termini & San Lorenzo

🏠 ACCOMMODATIONS

Hotel Adventure, **10**	D2
Hotel Bolognese, **1**	C1
Hotel Castelfidardo and Hotel Lazzari, **2**	C1
Hotel Cathrine, **3**	C1
Hotel Des Artistes, **7**	D2
Hotel Dolomiti and Hotel Lachea, **6**	D2
Hotel Giu' Giu', **8**	B3
Hotel Kennedy, **17**	C4
Hotel Magic, **12**	D3
Hotel Orlanda, **15**	B3
Hotel Papa Germano, **4**	C1
Hotel San Paolo, **14**	A3
Pensione Cortorillo, **16**	B4
Pensione di Rienzo, **16**	B4
Pensione Fawlty Towers, **11**	C3

🛍 SHOPPING

Disfunzioni Musicali, **18**	E5

● SERVICES

Enjoy Rome, **9**	D2

🍎 FOOD

Africa, **5**	C1
Arancia Blu, **20**	E6
Il Capellaio Matto, **22**	E6
Il Pulcino Ballerino, **21**	E6
Trattoria da Bruno, **13**	D3

🍷 NIGHTLIFE

Pub Hallo'Ween, **19**	D5

ROME

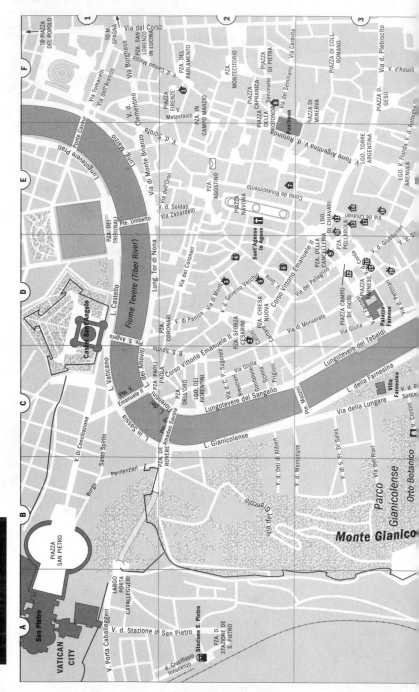

ROME

VATICAN CITY

PIAZZA SAN PIETRO

Monte Gianico

Parco Gianicolense

Orto Botanico

Centro Storico & Trastevere

⛰ ACCOMMODATIONS

Albergo Abruzzi, 8	F2
Albergo della Lunetta, 13	E3
Albergo Pomezia, 14	C5
Hotel Carmel, 29	E2
Hotel Navona, 7	E3
Hotel Piccolo, 17	E3
Hotel Trastevere, 27	C5

🍴 FOOD

Al 16, 21	E4
Augusto, 23	D4
Giardino del Melograno, 18	E3
Hostaria Grappolo d'Oro, 9	D3
L'Insalata Ricca, 11	E3
L'Oasi della Pizza, 15	D3
Ouszeri, 31	E5
Pizzeria Baffetto, 5	D2
Pizzeria Corallo, 3	D2
Pizzeria Ivo, 28	C5
Pizzeria San Calisto, 26	D4
La Pollarola, 10	E3
Ristorante a Casa di Alfredo, 30	C5
Trattoria a Giggetto, 22	E4
Trattoria da Luigi, 2	D2
Trattoria da Sergio, 19	D3
Trattoria dal Cav. Gino, 1	F2

🍷 NIGHTLIFE

Artu Cafe, 25	C4
The Drunken Ship, 12	D3
Groove, 6	D2
Jonathan's Angels, 4	D2
Rock Castle Café, 20	E4
Sloppy Sam's, 16	D3

🛍 SHOPPING

Porta Portese Market, 32	D6

★ ENTERTAINMENT

Il Pasquino, 24	C4

ROME

stop *(fermata)* is marked by yellow signs listing all routes that stop there and key streets/stops on those routes. Some buses run only on weekdays *(feriali)* or weekends *(festivi)* while others have different routes on different days of the week. Most buses start running around 5 or 6am and stop at midnight, when some routes are replaced by the less reliable **night routes** *(notturni)*.

Board through the front or back doors, not through the middle, then immediately stamp the ticket in the orange machine at the back; the ticket is then valid for any number of transfers over the next 75min. Consider buying several tickets at once; they can be hard to find at night and on weekends. Useful bus routes are: **46:** Vatican area, C. V. Emanuele, Largo Argentina, P. Venezia; **81:** P. Malatesta, S. Giovanni, Colosseo, Bocca della Verità, P. Venezia, Vatican; **170:** Termini, V. Nazionale, P. Venezia, Largo Argentina, V. Marmorata, S. Paolo Basilica; and **492:** Tiburtina, Termini, P. Barberini, P. Venezia, C. Rinascimento, P. Risorgimento.

TAXIS

Taxis in Rome are convenient but expensive. You can flag one down, but they are easily found at stands near Termini and in major piazzas. Ride only in yellow or white taxis, and make sure your taxi has a meter (if not, settle on a price before you get in the car). The meter starts at €2.50. Surcharges are levied at night (€2.55), on Sunday (€1.03), and when heading to or from Fiumicino (€7.23) and Ciampino (€5.16), with a charge per suitcase of €1.05. Standard tip is 15%. Taxis between the city center and Fiumicino should cost around €37. **Radio taxis** will pick you up at a given location within a few minutes of your call. Beware: radio taxis start the meter the moment your call is answered!

BIKES AND MOPEDS

Before you decide on your gladiatorial chariot, keep in mind that Rome is hilly and largely cobblestoned, making navigation difficult without a motor. In summer, try the stands on V. d. Corso at P. d. San Lorenzo and V. di Pontifici. (Open daily 10am-7pm.) You need to be 16 years old to rent. Helmets are required by a strictly enforced law, and will be included with your rental. Prices do not include 20% tax. For an adventurous afternoon on a bike, **Enjoy Rome** offers an informative, albeit harrowing, tour of the city's best sights. See **Tourist and Financial Services,** below.

▨ PRACTICAL INFORMATION

TOURIST AND FINANCIAL SERVICES

▨ **Enjoy Rome,** V. Marghera, 8/a (☎06 445 1843 or 445 6890; fax 445 0734; www.enjoyrome.com). From middle concourse of Termini (between trains and ticket booths), exit right, with trains behind you. Cross V. Marsala. It's on 3rd block down V. Marghera. Owners Fulvia and Pierluigi answer questions and offer useful tidbits about the city in English. Arranges hotel accommodations, walking and bicycle tours, and bus service to Pompeii. Full-service travel agency, booking transportation worldwide and lodgings throughout Italy. Branch office at V. Varese, 39; walk 1 block down V. Marghera and go right. Open M-F 8:30am-7pm, Sa 8:30am-2pm.

Currency Exchange: Banca di Roma and **Banca Nazionale del Lavoro** have good rates, but **ATMs,** scattered all over town and especially near Termini, are the best. Banking hours are usually M-F 8:30am-1:30pm. Expect long lines and cranky tellers.

American Express: P. di Spagna, 38 (☎06 67 641, lost or stolen cards and checks 06 72 282; fax 6764 2499). Sept.-July M-F 9am-7:30pm, Sa 9am-3pm; Aug. M-F 9am-6pm, Sa 9am-12:30pm. Mailing address: P. di Spagna, 38; 00187 Roma.

LOCAL SERVICES

Luggage Storage: In train station Termini, by track #1.

Lost Property: Oggetti Smarriti, V. Nicolo Bettoni, 1 (☎06 581 6040; items lost on trains 06 4730 6682). Open Tu and F 8:30am-1pm, M and W 8:30am-1pm and 2:30-6pm, Th 8:30am-6pm. In **Termini** at glass booth in main passageway. Open daily 7am-11pm.

▨ **Libreria Feltrinelli International,** V. V.E. Orlando, 84-86 (☎06 482 7878), near P. della Repubblica. Open M-Sa 10am-7:30pm, Su 10am-1:30pm and 4-8pm. AmEx/MC/V. **Anglo-American Bookshop,** V. di Vite, 102 (☎06 679 5222; www.aab.it). To the right of the Spanish Steps. In summer open M-F 9am-1pm and 3:30-7:30pm, Sa 9am-1pm; in winter. Closed M morning.

Bisexual, Gay, and Lesbian Resources: The Roman branches of **ARCI-GAY** and **ARCI-Lesbica** share offices at V. Orvinio, 2 (☎06 8638 5112) and V. Lariana, 8 (☎06 855 5522). Both hold discussions, dances, and special events. ARCI-GAY membership card (€10.33 per yr.) gains admission to all Italian gay clubs. **Circolo Mario Mieli di Cultura Omosessuale,** V. Corinto, 5 (☎06 541 3985; fax 541 3971; www.mariomieli.it). M: B-San Paolo. Walk 1 block to Largo Beato Placido Riccardi, turn left, and walk 1½ blocks to V. Corinto. Open Sept.-July M-F 9am-1pm and 2-6pm. **Libreria Babele** (☎06 687 6628), V. d. Banchi Vecchi, across from Castel Sant'Angelo. Open M-Sa 10am-2pm and 3-7:30pm.

Laundromat: OndaBlu, V. La Mora, 7 (info ☎800 86 13 46). Many locations. Wash €3.20 per 6.5kg load; dry €3.20 per 6.5kg load; soap €0.75. Open daily 8am-10pm.

EMERGENCY AND COMMUNICATIONS

Police: ☎113. **Carabinieri:** ☎112. **Medical Emergency:** ☎118. **Fire:** ☎115.

Crisis Line: Centro Anti-Violenza, V. d. Torrespaccata, 157 (☎06 2326 9049 or 2326 9053). For victims of sexual violence. Branches throughout city. Available 24hr. **Samaritans,** V. San Giovanni in Laterano, 250 (☎06 7045 4444). Native English speakers. Counseling available. Open for calls and visits daily 1-10pm. Call ahead.

Medical Services: Policlinico Umberto I, Viale di Policlinico, 155 (emergency ☎06 49 971). M: B-Policlinico or #9 bus. First aid *(pronto soccorso).* Open 24hr.

24-Hour Pharmacies: Farmacia Internazionale, P. Barberini, 49 (☎06 487 1195). MC/ V. **Farmacia Piram,** V. Nazionale, 228 (☎06 488 0754). MC/V.

Hospitals: International Medical Center, V. G. Amendola, 7 (☎06 488 2371; nights and Su 488 4051). Call 1st. Prescriptions filled, paramedic crew on call, referral service to English-speaking doctors. General visit €68. Open M-Sa 8:30am-8pm. On-call 24hr. **Rome-American Hospital,** V. E. Longoni, 69 (☎06 22 551 for 24hr. service, 225 5290 for appointments; fax 228 5062; www.rah.it). Private emergency and laboratory services, HIV tests, and pregnancy tests. No emergency room. On-call 24hr.

Internet Service: ▨ **Marco's Bar,** V. Varese, 54 (☎06 4470 3591). €2.50 per hr. with *Let's Go* or student ID, otherwise €4 per hour. Open daily 5:30am-2am. **Trevi Tourist Service: Trevi Internet,** V. d. Lucchesi, 31-32 (☎/fax 06 6920 0799). €2.50 per hour, €4 for 2hrs. Open daily 9:30am-10pm.

Post Office: Main Post Office (Posta Centrale), P. San Silvestro, 19 (☎06 679 5044 or 06 678 0788; fax 06 678 6618). Open M-F 9am-6:30pm, Sa 9am-2pm. Another **branch** V. d. Terme di Diocleziano, 30 (☎06 481 8298; fax 474 3536), near Termini. Same hours as San Silvestro branch. **Vatican Post Office** (☎06 6988 3406), 2 locations in P. San Pietro. No *Fermo Posta,* but supposedly faster than its counterparts over the wall. Open M-F 8:30am-7pm, Sa 8:30am-6pm. **Branch office** on 2nd fl. of Vatican Museum. Open during museum hours.

Postal Code: Rome's postal codes fall between 00100 and 00200.

ROME

⌐ ACCOMMODATIONS

HOTELS AND PENSIONI

Rome swells with tourists around Easter, from May through July, and in September. Prices vary widely with the time of year, and a proprietor's willingness to negotiate increases with length of stay, number of vacancies, and group size. Termini is swarming with hotel scouts. Many are legitimate and have IDs issued by tourist offices; however, some imposters have fake badges and direct travelers to rundown locations with exorbitant rates, especially at night.

CENTRO STORICO

If being a bit closer to the sights is worth it to you, then choosing Rome's medieval center over the area near Termini may be worth the higher prices.

Albergo Pomezia, V. d. Chiavari, 13 (☎/fax 06 686 1371; hotelpomezia@libero.it). Off C. V. Emanuele II, behind Sant'Andrea della Valle. 3 floors of recently renovated, clean, and quiet rooms with fans and heat in the winter. Breakfast included (8-10:30am). Handicapped-accessible room on the 1st floor. Singles €50, with bath €60; doubles €77.50/ €110; triples €120/€127.50; extra bed 35% additional. AmEx/MC/V. ❹

Albergo della Lunetta, P. d. Paradiso, 68 (☎06 686 1080; fax 689 2028). The 1st right off V. Chiavari from C. V. Emanuele II behind Sant'Andrea della Valle. Clean, well-lit rooms; some face a small, fern-filled courtyard. Great location between Campo dei Fiori and P. Navona. Reservations recommended (with credit card or check). Singles €52, with bath €62; doubles €83/€109; triples €112/€147. MC/V. ❹

Albergo Abruzzi, P. d. Rotonda, 69 (☎06 679 2021). A mere 200 ft. from the Pantheon. Some rooms have a terrific view. Old but clean facilities. Communal bath; rooms have sink. A/C €10. Singles €43-65; doubles €73-95; triples €125. ❹

Hotel Piccolo, V. d. Chiavari, 32 (☎06 689 2330), off C. Vittorio Emanuele II behind Sant'Andrea della Valle. Recently renovated, family-run establishment. English spoken. Curfew 1am. Check-out noon. Singles €51.60, with bath €62; doubles €62/€82; triples with bath €87.60; quads with bath €90. AmEx/MC/V. ❹

Hotel Navona, V. d. Sediari, 8, 1st fl. (☎06 686 4203; fax 6880 3802, call before faxing; www.hotelnavona.com). Take V. d. Canestrari from P. Navona, cross C. del Rinascimento, and go straight. This recently refurbished 16th-century building has been used as a *pensione* for over 150 years, counting Keats and Shelley among its guestsy. Brand-new bathrooms with heated towel racks. Check-out 10am. Breakfast included. Singles €84; doubles €110; triples €150. A/C €15. Reservations with credit card and 1st night pre-payment. Otherwise pay in euros or US dollars. ❺

NEAR PIAZZA DI SPAGNA

These accommodations might run you a few more euros, but can you really put a price tag on living but a few steps from Prada? John Keats couldn't.

▩ **Pensione Panda,** V. d. Croce, 35 (☎06 678 0179; fax 6994 2151; www.webeco.it/ hotelpanda), between P. di Spagna and V. d. Corso. Lovely, immaculate rooms and arched ceilings (some with frescoes). Centrally located. English spoken. Check-out 11am. Reservations recommended. All rooms except some singles have bath. Mar-Dec. singles €42, with bath €62; doubles €83; triples €124; quads €168. Jan.-Feb. singles €37, with bath €57; doubles €83; triples €109; quads €145. Jan.-Feb. *Let's Go* discount 5%. AmEx/MC/V. ❹

▩ **Hotel Pensione Suisse S.A.S.,** V. Gregoriana, 54 (☎06 678 3649; fax 678 1258; info@HotelSuisseRome.com). Turn right at the top of the Spanish Steps. Close to the wisteria-hung heights of the Steps, but away from the hubbub. Sleek, old-fashioned furniture, comfortable beds, phone and fan in every room. Internet access, TV available. Continental breakfast included. All rooms with bath (bathtubs available). Singles €88; doubles €134; triples €184; quads €208. MC/V. ❺

Hotel Boccaccio, V. d. Boccaccio, 25 (☎/fax 06 488 5962; www.hotelboccaccio.com). M: A-Barberini. Off V. d. Tritone. This quiet, well-situated hotel offers 8 elegantly furnished rooms near many sights. Reception 9am-11pm, late-night access via key. Singles €42; doubles €62, with bath €84; triples €84/€112. AmEx/D/MC/V. ❹

BORGO AND PRATI (NEAR VATICAN CITY)

While not the cheapest in Rome, the *pensioni* near the Vatican have all of the sobriety and quiet that one would expect from a neighborhood where the nun-to-tourist ratio is 5:1.

▩ **Colors,** V. Boezio, 31 (☎06 687 4030; fax 686 7947; www.colorshotel.com). M: A-Ottaviano, or take a bus to P. Risorgimento. V. Cola di Rienzo to V. Terenzio. Wonderful English-speaking staff and guests. 18 beds in rooms painted with a bravado that would put Caravaggio to shame. Internet €3 per hr. Laundry service €2.10 per load (the best deal in town). Beautiful flower-filled terrace and kitchen open 7:30am-11pm. Dorm beds €20; doubles €67.50-83; triples €77.50-98.50. Credit card for private room reservations; for dorm beds, call 9pm the night before. ❷

▩ **Pensione Ottaviano,** V. Ottaviano, 6 (☎06 3973 7253 or 06 3973 8138; www.pensioneottaviano.com), just north of P. del Risorgimento. A few blocks from the Metro stop of the same name and steps from St. Peter's. 6-8 beds per dorm room. Amenities include satellite TV, individual lockers, fridges, a microwave, hot showers, free linens, and free email access for guests (10min. per day). Smoking allowed in common room. No curfew. Lock-out 11:30am-2:30pm. Dorm rooms Oct.-June €15; July-Sept. and winter holidays €18. Doubles €62/€50; one triple €70/€62. Credit card for reservations. ❶

Hotel Lady, V. Germanico, 198, 4th fl. (☎06 324 2112; fax 06 324 3446; venneri@libero.it), between V. Fabbio Massimo and V. Paolo Emilio. The 8 rooms, some with beautiful loft-style open wood-work ceilings and tile floors, lack A/C but are cool in the summer. Spacious common room. All rooms with sinks and desks. Singles without bath €65; doubles €82, with bath €100; triples €106/€130. Prices quoted include a *Let's Go* discount, so mention it when you reserve. AmEx/MC/V. ❺

Hotel Florida, V. Cola di Rienzo, 243 (☎06 324 1872 or 324 1608; fax 324 1857; www.hotelfloridaroma.it), on the 1st-3rd floors, reception on 2nd. Floral carpets, bedspreads, wall decorations. Comfortable, with English-speaking staff. A/C (€10 per night), TV, phone, and hair dryers in each of the 18 rooms. 1 single with sink €31, with bath €72; doubles €68/€103; triples with bath €134; quads with bath €155. Call ahead to reserve; ask about discounts. 5% discount if you pay in cash. AmEx/MC/V. ❸

TRASTEVERE

Trastevere is a beautiful old Roman neighborhood famous for its separatism, medieval streets, and pretty-far-from-the-tourist-crowd charm. Hotels here are scattered, most of them too pricey for budget travelers, but the area does offer great nightlife and a location near the Vatican.

Hotel Carmel, V. G. Mameli, 11 (☎06 580 9921; fax 581 8853; hotelcarmel@hotmail.com). Take a right onto V. E. Morosini (V. G. Mameli) off V. d. Trastevere. A short walk from central Trastevere. Simple hotel with 9 small rooms with bath. A comfortable atrium-like sitting room leads to a lovely garden terrace with breakfast seating. Breakfast included. Singles €75; doubles €85; triples €110; quads €130. AmEx/MC/V. ❺

Hotel Trastevere, V. Luciano Manara, 25 (☎06 581 4713, fax 588 1016). Take a right off V. d. Trastevere onto V. d. Fratte di Trastevere, which becomes V. Luciano Manara. This homey establishment overlooks P. S. Cosimato. Neighborhood murals give way to 9 simple and airy rooms with bath, TV, and phone. English spoken. Breakfast included. Singles €77; doubles €98-103; triples €129; quads €154. Short-term apartments for 2-6 persons with little kitchens and loft beds available. AmEx/D/MC/V. ●

TERMINI AND SAN LORENZO

Welcome to budget traveler and backpacker central. While Termini is chock-full of traveler's services, the area south of Termini is a little sketchy at night.

▨ **Pensione Fawlty Towers,** V. Magenta, 39 (☎/fax 06 445 0374; www.fawltytowers.org or www.fawltytowersrome.com). Exit Termini to the right from the middle concourse, cross V. Marsala onto V. Marghera, and turn right onto V. Magenta. The flower-filled terrace provides a peaceful respite from Termini. Common room with satellite TV, library, refrigerator, microwave, and free Internet access. Frequently full, but the reception will help you find a room elsewhere. Check-out 9am for dorms and 10am for private rooms. Reservations possible a week in advance; confirm all reservations 48hr. before arrival. English speaking staff. Dorms €23; dorm-style quads €18 per person (no children); singles €44, with shower €51; doubles €62, with shower €67, with bath €77. ●

▨ **Hotel Des Artistes,** V. Villafranca, 20 (☎06 445 4365; fax 446 2368; www.hoteldesartistes.com). From the middle concourse of Termini, exit right, turn left onto V. Marsala, right onto V. Vicenza, and then left onto the 5th cross-street. 3-star, 40-room hotel with clean, elegant rooms, some with safes, refrigerators, and TVs. Amenities include a rooftop terrace (open until 1am) and lounge with satellite TV. Free Internet access. Breakfast included with rooms with a bathroom, otherwise €4.50. 24hr. reception. Check-out 11am. Singles €39-57, with bath €98-140; doubles €46-85/€103-150; triples €57-114/€103-150; quads €72-130/€146-195. Winter 20-30% less. €15 discount with cash payment. AmEx/MC/V. ●

▨ **Hotel Papa Germano,** V. Calatafimi, 14/a (☎06 48 69 19 or 4788 1281; fax 4782 5202; www.hotelpapagermano.com). From the middle concourse of Termini, exit right; turn left onto V. Marsala, which becomes V. Volturno. V. Calatafimi is the 4th cross-street on the right. Clean rooms with TV, and outstanding service. English, French, and Spanish spoken. Internet access €2.60 per hr. Check-out 11am. Dorms €18-25; singles €23-40; doubles €42-70, with bath €52-93; triples €54-78/€72-105. Prices vary depending on season and demand. Nov.-Mar. 10% discount. AmEx/MC/V. ●

Hotel Dolomiti and **Hotel Lachea,** V. S. Martino della Battaglia, 11 (☎06 495 7256 or 49 10 58; fax 445 4665; www.hotel-dolomiti.it). From the middle concourse of Termini, exit right, turn left onto V. Marsala and right onto V. Solferino (V. d. Battaglia). Aging 19th-century *palazzo* houses sparkling new 3-star hotels, with the same reception (on 2nd floor) and management. Bar, breakfast room, and Internet access (€2.60 per 30min.). Rooms have satellite TV, minibars, safes, hair-dryers, and A/C. Some with balcony. Breakfast €6. A/C €13 per night. Check-out 11am. Check-in 1pm. Singles €52-67; doubles €73-93; triples €83-108; quads €114-135; quints €145-155. ●

Hotel Cathrine, V. Volturno, 27 (☎06 48 36 34). From the middle concourse of Termini, exit right, and turn left onto V. Marsala (V. Volturno). 2 common bathrooms serve the 8 spacious singles and doubles with sinks. More rooms at the modern **Affittacamere Aries** at V. XX Settembre, 58/a. Breakfast €2. *Let's Go* discount available, depends on season. Singles €35-45; doubles €47-62, with bath €52-72. €15 per extra bed. ●

Hotel Adventure, V. Palestro, 88 (☎06 446 9026; fax 446 0084; www.hoteladventure.com). From Termini's middle concourse, exit right, cross V. Marsala onto V. Marghera, and take the 4th right onto V. Palestro. Newly renovated rooms with bath, satellite TV, telephone, and fridge. Breakfast included. Check-out 11am. A/C €12.91. Singles €100, including A/C; doubles €120; triples €140. AmEx/MC/V. ●

Hotel Bolognese, V. Palestro, 15 (☎/fax 06 49 00 45). From the middle concourse of Termini, exit right. Walk down V. Marghera and take your 4th left on V. Palestro. In a land of run-of-the-mill *pensioni*, this place is spruced up by the artist-owner's impressive paintings. Some rooms have balconies. Probably the only hotel near Termini to have won an award from the Knights of Malta for hospitality. Check-out 11am. Singles €31, with bath €43; doubles €47-60/€72; triples €62-77.50. ❸

Hotel Magic, V. Milazzo, 20 (☎06 495 9880 or 4938 6679; fax 444 1408). From the middle concourse of Termini, exit right. Take a right onto V. Marsala and your 1st left onto V. Milazzo. Clean, modern rooms and a bar will appear right before your very eyes. All rooms have bath, TV, hair-dryers and in-room safes. A/C €10. Singles €52; doubles €77; triples €103; quads €118. Student discounts possible. MC/V. ❹

VIA XX SETTEMBRE AND ENVIRONS

Dominated by government ministries and private apartments, this area is less noisy and touristy than the nearby Termini.

▨ **Pensione Tizi,** V. Collina, 48 (☎06 482 0128; fax 474 3266). A 10min. walk from the station. Take V. Goito from P. dell'Indipendenza, cross V. XX Settembre onto V. Piave, then go left onto V. Flavia and right onto V. Collina; or take bus #319 or 270 from Termini. Serving student travelers for years. Marble floors and inlaid ceilings adorn spacious and recently renovated rooms. Check-out 11am. Singles €42; doubles €52, with bath €62; triples €80/€90; quads €100/€110. AmEx/MC/V. ❹

Hotel Castelfidardo and **Hotel Lazzari,** V. Castelfidardo, 31 (☎06 446 4638; fax 494 1378; www.castelfidardo.com). Two blocks off V. XX Settembre. Both run by the same friendly family. Renovated rooms with spanking clean floors and soothing pastel walls. 3 floors of modern, shiny comfort and plenty of bathroom space. Communal bath. Check-out 10:30am. English spoken. Singles €42, with bath €52; doubles €60/€70; triples €77/€93; quads with bath €108. AmEx/MC/V. ❹

SOUTH AND WEST OF TERMINI

Esquilino (south of Termini) is home to many cheap hotels close to the major sights. The neighborhood west of Termini is slightly more inviting, with busy streets and lots of shopping.

▨ **Pensione di Rienzo,** V. Principe Amedeo, 79/a (☎06 446 7131; fax 446 6980). A tranquil, family-run retreat with spacious, newly renovated rooms. Large windows overlook a courtyard. Extremely helpful, English-speaking staff. 20 rooms, with balconies, TV, and bath. Breakfast €7. Check-out 10am. Singles without bath €19.11-46.48; doubles €22.72-56.81, with bath €25.31-67.14. Prices depend on season. MC/V. ❷

▨ **Pensione Cortorillo,** V. Principe Amedeo, 79/a, 5th fl. (☎06 446 6934; fax 445 4769). This small *pensione* has TV and A/C in all 14 rooms. English, French and Spanish spoken. Breakfast included. Check-out 10am. Singles €30-70; doubles €40-100. Extra bed €10. Prices depend on season. AmEx/D/MC/V. ❸

Hotel San Paolo, V. Panisperna, 95 (☎06 474 5213; fax 474 5218; www.hotelsanpaoloroma.com). Exiting from the front of the train station, turn left onto V. Cavour. After you pass Santa Maria Maggiore (on the left), bear right onto V. d. Santa Maria Maggiore (V. Panisperna). 10min. from Termini, San Paolo's 23 rooms are housed in a bright little *palazzo* with tranquil, whimsically decorated rooms. Hall baths are clean and private. English spoken. Breakfast €5.16. Check-out 11am. Singles €39; doubles €57, with bath €78; triples €78. Lovely, large 6-10 person suite €26 per person. AmEx/MC/V. ❹

Hotel Kennedy, V. Filippo Turati, 62-64 (☎06 446 5373; fax 446 5417; www.hotelkennedy.net). Leather couches and a large color TV in the lounge. Private bath, satellite TV, phone, and A/C. Hearty breakfast included. English, French, Spanish, and Portuguese spoken. Check-out 11am. Reservations by fax/email. Singles €45-88; doubles €70-139; triples €80-159; quads €90-258. 10% *Let's Go* discount. AmEx/D/MC/V. ❹

Hotel Il Castello, V. Vittorio Amedeo II, 9 (☎06 7720 4036; fax 7049 0068; www.ilcastello.com). M: A-Manzoni. Far beyond Termini, but well within the backpacker's budget. Walk down V. S. Quintino and take the 1st left. Housed in a castle with smallish white rooms. Spot damsels in distress from the quaint balcony outside four of the rooms. Continental breakfast €3. Check-out 10:30am. Dorms €17; singles €42; doubles €57, with bath €68; triples €65/€75-95. MC/V. ❷

Hotel Giù Giù, V. d. Viminale, 8 (☎/fax 06 482 7734; hotelgiugiu@libero.it). 2 blocks south of Termini, in an elegant but fading *palazzo*. Pleasant breakfast area, 12 quiet rooms. English spoken. Breakfast €7. Check-out 10am. Singles €36-45; doubles €57-70, with bath €67-70; triples with bath €90-105; quads with bath €120-140. ❹

Hotel Orlando, V. Principe Amedeo, 76, 3rd fl. (☎06 488 0124; fax 488 0183; hotelorlanda@traveleurope.it). At V. Gioberti. Frequented by Italian businesspeople. All 23 rooms have sink and TV; some have hair dryers. English spoken. A/C €15.50. Breakfast included. Reception 24hr. Check-in noon. Check-out by 10am. Singles €39, with bath €79; doubles €57/€83; triples €83/€111; quads €104/€124. AmEx/D/MC/V. ❹

ALTERNATIVE ACCOMMODATIONS

BED & BREAKFASTS

"Bed & Breakfast" services in Rome differ from the typical American concept. In some, guest rooms are arranged in private homes throughout the city, with the owners generally obliged to provide breakfast. In others, apartments have kitchens where clients can make their own breakfast. The rooms and apartments can vary greatly in quality and size. Be sure to pinpoint just how "centrally located" your apartment is, as some are flung toward the city outskirts. The **Bed and Breakfast Association of Rome,** P. del Teatro Pompeo, 2, can advise. (☎06 5530 2248; fax 5530 2259; www.b-b.rm.it. Call ahead M-F 9am-1pm for an appointment.)

Daphne B&B ❺, V. d. Avignonesi, 20, just off P. Barberini, receives rave reviews from guests. Friendly English-speaking owners and proximity to P. di Spagna and Trevi Fountain. (☎/fax 06 4782 3529; www.daphne-rome.com. A/C, daily maid service. Check-in 2pm. Check-out 10am. Reservations strongly recommended. Mar.-July 18 and Aug. 28-Nov. singles €100; doubles €110; triples €165; quads €220. July 19-Aug. 27 singles €85; doubles €90; triples €135; quads €180. Jan. 3-Feb. 28 and Nov. 3-Dec. 26 singles €55; doubles €60; triples €90; quads €120. MC/V.)

RELIGIOUS HOUSING

Certain convents and monasteries host guests for a fee of about who come with letters of introduction from their local diocese for €25 or more per night. Contact your home parish for details. Most accommodations are single-sex with early curfews, services, and light chores.

▨ Domus Nova Bethlehem, V. Cavour, 85/a (☎06 478 2441; fax 4782 2033; www.suorebambinogesu.it/DNB). Walk down V. Cavour from Termini, past P. d. Esquilino on the left. A modern and centrally located hotel 1am curfew. Room have A/C, bath with shower, and TV. Singles €67.14; doubles €46.48 per person; triples €41.32 per person; quads €36.15 per person. AmEx/MC/V. ❹

Santa Maria Alle Fornaci, P. S. Maria alle Fornaci, 27 (☎06 3936 7632; fax 3936 6795; ciffornaci@tin.it). Facing St. Peter's Basilica, take a left (through the basilica walls) onto V. d. Fornace. Take your 3rd right onto V. d. Gasperi, which leads to P. S. Maria alle Fornaci. Just south of the Vatican, this hotel offers 54 rooms, each with private bath. Simple, small, and clean. No curfew. Breakfast included. Singles €47; doubles €78; triples €104. AmEx/MC/V. ❹

WOMEN'S HOUSING

Associazione Cattolica Internazionale al Servizio della Giovane, V. Urbana, 158 (☎06 4890 4523; fax 482 7989; www.acisjf.it). From P. Esquilino (in front of Santa Maria Maggiore), walk down V. d. Pretis and turn left. Church-run establishment makes living arrangements for 18-25-year-old women of any religion. The garden will make you weep, but so may the 10pm curfew. Open M-Sa 6:30am-10pm, Su 7am-10pm. 5- or 8-bed dorms €15; doubles and triples €18 per person. ❶

◨ FOOD

Ancient Roman dinners were once lavish ten-hour affairs. Food orgies went on *ad nauseam*—after gorging themselves for hours, guests would commonly retreat to a special room called the *vomitorium*, throw it all up, and return to the party. Meals in Rome are still lengthy affairs, though they generally involve less vomiting, depending on the restaurant. Restaurants tend to close between 3 and 7pm.

ANCIENT CITY

The area around the Forum and the Colosseum is home to some of Italy's finest tourist traps. If you forgot to pack a lunch and the stroll to the Centro Storico seems too long and hot, there are a few places that offer tasty meals at fair prices.

▨ **Buoni Amici,** V. Aleardo Aleardi, 4 (☎06 7049 1993). From the Colosseum, take V. Labicana to V. Merulana. Turn right, then left onto V. A. Aleardi. A long walk, but cheap and excellent food. Try the *linguine all'astice* (linguini with lobster sauce; €6.50). Cover €1.29. Open M-Sa noon-3pm and 7-11:30pm. AmEx/D/MC/V. ❷

Taverna dei Quaranta, V. Claudia, 24 (☎06 700 0550), off P. del Colosseo. Shaded by the trees of Celian Park, outdoor dining at this corner *taverna* is a must. The menu changes weekly, and in summer often features the sinfully good *oliva ascolane* (olives stuffed with meat and fried; €3.87). Cover €1.29. Reservations suggested, especially for a table outside. Open daily 12:30-3:30pm and 7:45-11:30pm. AmEx/D/MC/V. ❷

PIAZZA NAVONA

There are plenty of delicious, inexpensive *trattorie* and *pizzerie* near P. Navona. A walk down V. del Governo Vecchio reveals some of the best restaurants in the city. Where ever you eat, you can expect to witness street performances.

▨ **Pizzeria Baffetto,** V. d. Governo Vecchio, 114 (☎06 686 1617), at the intersection of V. d. Governo Vecchio and V. Sora. Once a meeting place for 60s radicals, Baffetto now overflows with hungry Romans. Be prepared to wait for a table outdoors (and for your delicious pizza). Pizzas €4.50-7.50. Open daily 8-10am and 6:30pm-1am. ❶

▨ **L'Oasi della Pizza,** V. d. Corda, 3-5 (☎06 687 2876; www.info.pizzeriaoasi.tiscalinet.it), near C. dei Fiori. To say that L'Oasi serves pizza worthy of paradise is no hyperbole. The *capricciosa* (tomato, mozzarella, ham, eggs, and mushrooms; €8) is great. Open Th-Tu noon-3pm and 7-11:30pm. ❷

Pizzeria Corallo, V. d. Corallo, 10-11 (☎06 6830 7703), off V. d. Governo Vecchio near P. del Fico. Great place to grab a cheap, late dinner before hitting nearby bars. Pizzas €3.62-7.75. Excellent *primi* €5.16-8.26. Open Tu-Su 6:30pm-1am. MC/V. ❷

Trattoria dal Cav. Gino, V. Rosini, 4 (☎06 687 3434), off V. d. Campo Marzio across from P. del Parlamente. Sign proclaims owner Gino's mantra: *In Vino Veritas*. Agreed. *Primi* €5.15-6.20, *secondi* €7.20-9.30. Open M-Sa 1-3:45pm and 8-10:30pm. ❶

CAMPO DEI FIORI AND THE JEWISH GHETTO

While you might get yourself horribly lost in the labyrinth of crooked streets and alleyways that surround the Campo, you will certainly find several exceptional *ristoranti* that can provide sustenance until the search party arrives. Across V. Arenula from the Campo, the proud community of the former Jewish Ghetto serves up traditional Roman-Jewish cuisine as it has for hundreds of years.

▨ **Trattoria da Sergio,** V. d. Grotte, 27 (☎06 654 6669). Take V. d. Giubbonari and take your 1st right. Just far enough away from the Campo to keep away the tourists, Sergio offers an authentic Roman ambiance (the waiters don't bother with menus) and hearty portions. Try *spaghetti Matriciana* (with bacon and spicy tomato sauce; €6), a front-runner for the city's best plate of pasta and the *Straccetti* (shredded beef; €8). Fresh fish Tu and F. Reservations suggested. Open M-Sa 12:30-3pm and 6pm-midnight. MC/V. ❶

▨ **Hostaria Grappolo d'Oro,** P. della Cancelleria, 80-81 (☎06 689 7080), between C. V. Emanuele II and the Campo. This increasingly upscale *hostaria*'s front window is filled with awards they've won over the years. The small menu, which changes daily, offers both home-style dishes and original creations. *Primi* €7-8, *secondi* €12-13. Cover €1.03. Open M-Sa noon-2:30pm and 7:30-11pm. Closed M lunch. AmEx/MC/V. ❸

▨ **Trattoria da Luigi,** P. S. Cesarini, 24 (☎06 686 5946), near Chiesa Nuova, 4 blocks down C. V. Emanuele II from Campo dei Fiori. Enjoy inventive cuisine such as the delicate *carpaccio di salmone fresco con rughetta* (€8), as well as simple dishes like *vitello con funghi* (veal with mushrooms; €9.50). Great *antipasti* buffet. Bread €1.03. Open Tu-Su noon-3pm and 7pm-midnight. AmEx/MC/V. ❷

La Pollarola, P. Pollarola, 24-25 (☎06 6880 1654), off V. d. Biscione on the right as you approach Campo dei Fiori. Typical dishes like *spaghetti alla carbonara* (with egg and *pancetta*; €7) are well-done. Open M-Sa noon-3:30pm and 7:30pm-midnight. Service charge included in prices. AmEx/MC/V. ❷

L'Insalata Ricca, Largo di Chiavari, 85-6 (☎06 6880 3656), off C. V. Emanuele II near P. S. Andrea della Valle. Huge variety of salads (€5.20-8.30). 11 other locations around town, including: P. Pasquino, 72; V. d. Gazometro, 62-66; P. Albania, 3-5; V. Polesine, 16-18; P. Risorgimento, 5; and V. F. Grinaldi, 52-54. Reservations suggested for dinner. Open daily 12:30-3:30pm and 6:45-11:45pm. AmEx/D/MC/V. ❷

Giardino del Melograno, V. d. Chiodaroli, 16-18 (☎06 6880 3423). From Campo dei Fiori, take V. Giubbonari, a left on V. Chiavari, and then your 1st right. Some of the best Chinese food in Rome. Try the *gamberi con zenzero* (shrimp with ginger; €12). Lunch *menù* €1, dinner €15. Open Th-Tu noon-3pm and 7-11:30pm. AmEx/MC/V. ❸

Trattoria da Giggetto, V. d. Portico d'Ottavio, 21-22 (☎06 686 1105). Rightfully famous, Giggetto serves up some of the finest Roman cooking known to man in outdoor tables overlooking the ruins of the Teatro Marcello. Their *carciofi alla Giudia* (€4.50) are legendary, but be daring and go for the *fritto di cervello d'abbacchino, funghi, zucchine* (fried brains with mushrooms and zucchini; €11.50). Cover €1.55. Reservations needed for dinner. Open Tu-Su 12:30-3pm and 7:30-11pm. AmEx/MC/V. ❸

Al 16, V. d. Portico d'Ottavio, 16 (☎06 687 4722), around the corner from the Teatro di Marcello. A neighborhood favorite run by very friendly neighborhood guys, Al 16 offers traditional dishes alongside delicious house specialties like *Pennette al 16* (with eggplant, sausage, and tomato; €7.50), all at reasonable prices. Be fearless and try the *Coda alla Vaccinara* (ox-tail Roman style stew; €9.50). Cover €1.29. Reservations recommended for dinner. Open W-M 12:30-3pm and 7:30-11pm. AmEx/MC/V. ❸

OF BREAD AND CIRCUSES
An insider's guide to traditional cuisine

The poet Juvenal once said disparagingly of the Roman populace that all it needed was *panem et circenses* (bread and circuses) to remain free of rebellious thought. Luckily for even a temporary resident of the Eternal City today, Romans no longer live by bread (or circuses) alone, and Roman bread, in fact, is generally nowhere near as praise-worthy as its Gallic counterpart to the north. The two notable exceptions to this are *pizza bianca* and *pizza rossa*, both light, crispy, olive-oil-drizzled flatbreads, the latter of which is slathered with a mouth-tantalizing tomato-herb mixture.

Roman cuisine has not yet enjoyed the same sort of notoriety that surrounds that of Tuscany, with its game dishes, wonderful *pecorino di Pienza*, and hearty soups. The invention of pizza itself is a Neapolitan, not Roman, accomplishment. But Roman cuisine remains a distinct (if generally underappreciated) entity, with a history of its own. Traditionally, much of Roman cuisine was based on the *quinto quarto*, the "fifth fourth"–that is to say, what was left of a cow, sheep or pig after it was butchered: the innards and organ meats. Happily, although you can still find dishes based on these in some Roman restaurants, such as *coda alla vaccinara* (oxtail stew) and *rigatoni con pajata* (pasta with the intestines of a milk-fed calf), Roman cuisine today is predominantly created out of the freshest ingredients of the markets in the city, and enjoying it does not necessitate familiarity with a butcher's anatomical chart.

At the open markets, be prepared to find a colorful abundance of fresh produce, including greens the likes of which you've never seen before. Romans love cooked, wilted greens such as *spinaci* and *broccoletti* (spinach and broccoli rabe) dressed in garlic and olive oil and spritzed with a douse of lemon juice, but one of the more unusual is *agretti*, which looks like grass, and when boiled for 5 minutes takes on the consistency of green spaghetti. Another, which, like *agretti*, is in season in winter, is *puntarelle*, stiff green shoots which are cut and then plunged into cold water, causing them to curl up in a spiral shape. Served cold with an anchovy and oil dressing the dish makes a wonderful companion to grilled fish. *Rughetta* is a wild version of *rucola* (arugula) which is grown only around Rome. It is a small, pleasantly bitter-tasting treat as a base for the sweetest tomatoes you'll ever taste (*pomodorini*) and a hunk of *mozzarella di bufala* (buffalo-milk mozzarella). *Fiori di zucca*, zucchini flowers which have been stuffed with mozzarella and perhaps an anchovy, and *carciofi alla giudea* are both deep-fried Roman delicacies; the latter is a whole artichoke plunged in oil, providing crispy, chip-like leaves as an antipasto. *Carciofi alla romana* are equally delectable artichokes, braised with garlic and *mentuccia*, roman mint. If you're in the mood for a walk through Rome's largest park, the Villa Doria-Pamphilj, you can still find Roman matrons gathering *mentuccia* and pine nuts from the park's plentiful pine trees.

Each region in Italy has its preferred pastas, but in Rome the main idea is to keep things simple. *Spaghetti all'amatriciana* and *alla carbonara* are both flavored with *guanciale* (pork jowl); the former has tomatoes and a dash of *peperoncini* (chili pepper), the latter beaten egg and cheese. But the most simple Roman pasta is *cacio e pepe*, in which the spaghetti is mixed with ground black pepper and grated *pecorino romano* cheese; purists add no oil whatsoever, using just a bit of the pasta's cooking liquid for moisture. Another excellent way to start off a meal is *pasta e ceci*, a thick soup made of pasta and chick-peas, a Roman staple. Other simple pasta dishes include those with sauces of *porcini* mushrooms over *pappardelle*, a wide pasta, or fresh pasta in a *tartufo* (truffle) sauce, whose smoky, earthy flavor will leave you wanting more. For a tasty delicacy, try spaghetti topped with grated *bottarga*, an orange-hued fish roe that comes in solid form and lends a salty fish taste to a simple pasta dish. *Gnocchi*, small potato dumplings which originated in the south of Italy, are traditionally served in Rome on Thursday; for a new twist, however, you might want to try Rome's own version, *gnocchi alla romana*, which aren't made with potato at all, but with semolina, and are flat and circular.

Andria Derstine was a Researcher-Writer for Let's Go: Italy 1990 and 1992 and Let's Go: Greece 1991. After living in Rome for 3 years, she recently returned to the U.S. to complete her Ph.D. at the Institute of Fine Arts, New York University.

PIAZZA DI SPAGNA

Though the Spanish Steps area may seem very different from the less affluent environs of Termini, there is one big similarity—lots of lousy food. A mediocre meal here will cost twice as much. Some exceptions:

■ **Trattoria da Settimio all'Arancio,** V. d. Arancio, 50-52 (☎06 687 6119). Take V. d. Condotti from P. di Spagna; take the 1st right after V. d. Corso, then the 1st left. Join Romans as they clamor to escape the tourists. They'll order the fried artichokes (€4.50) and the squid's ink risotto (€7.50). Follow their example, and don't forget the perfectly grilled calamari (€11.50). No meal is complete without *panna cotta*, the Italian cream custard with fresh fruit. Extensive wine list. Bread €1. Reservations suggested at night. Open M-Sa 12:30-3pm and 7:30-11:30pm. AmEx/D/MC/V. ❸

■ **Vini e Buffet,** P. Torretta, 60. (☎06 687 1445). From V. d. Corso, turn into P. S. Lorenzo in Lucina. Take a left onto V. Campo Marzio, a quick right onto V. Toretta. Vini e Buffet is a favorite spot for chic Romans with a penchant for regional wines. Its popular salads are creative and fresh—the *insalata con salmone* (€8.50; *gigante* €10) is delightful. Also available are pates, *crostini,* and *scarmorze* (€6.50-8.50). Don't leave without getting one of their signature yogurt, almond, and cassis combination bowls (€4). Reservations are recommended. M-Sa 12:30-3pm and 7-11pm. ❸

Il Brillo Parlante, V. Fontanella, 12 (☎06 324 3334 or 323 5017; www.ilbrilloparlante.com), near P. del Popolo. The wood-burning pizza oven, fresh ingredients, and excellent wine attract many lunching Italians. Sophisticated food and shady outdoor tables. Pizza €5.16-7.75. Restaurant open Tu-Su noon-3pm and 7:30pm-1am; *enoteca* (wine bar) open Tu-Su 11am-2am. MC/V. ❷

UKIYO Japanese Restaurant, V. d. Propaganda, 22 (☎06 678 6093). Sushi Chef Yoichi Takumi brings Japanese cuisine along with attentive service to Italy for the delight of both tourist and Roman Japanophiles. The fish (1 piece nigiri sushi; €2.50-5.50) is fresh and prepared to exacting standards. Their specialty is a subtle mackarel, ginger, and sesame roll (€5). Full sushi meal (€28.50) and tasting menù available (€42). Open daily noon-2:45pm and 7-10:45pm. Closed W. Wheelchair-accessible. AmEx/MC/V. ❺

BORGO AND PRATI (NEAR VATICAN CITY)

The streets near the Vatican are paved with bars and *pizzerie* that serve mediocre sandwiches at hiked-up prices. For far better and much cheaper food, head to the residential district a few blocks north and east of the Vatican Museums.

■ **Franchi,** V. Cola di Rienzo, 204 (☎06 687 4651; www.franchi.it). Benedetto Franchi ("Frankie") has been serving the happy citizens of Prati superb *tavola calda,* prepared sandwiches, and picnic supplies, for 50 years. Delicacies include various croquettes (€1.29), marinated munchies (anchovies, peppers, and olives; sold by the kg), and pastas (vegetarian lasagna or *cannellini* stuffed with ricotta and beef; €5). More expensive than bread and cheese, but worth it. Open M-Sa 8:15am-9pm. AmEx/MC/V. ❷

Guido, V. Borgo Pio, 13 (☎06 687 5491), near Castle Sant'Angelo. There's no sign, but you can recognize this authentically Roman spot at the foot of Borgo Pio by the men playing cards in the sun. Guido himself holds court behind a counter filled with the makings of a beautiful *tavola calda*. Prices vary, but a full meal (*primi, secondi,* and wine) will run you less than €8. Usually open M-Sa 9am-8pm. ❷

San Marco, V. Tacito, 27-29 (☎06 323 5596), off P. Cavour. Front runner in the competition for best pizza in Rome and certainly the best north of Trastevere, this spacious institution has been dousing hungry Romans with mozzarella for 50 years. Good pastas (€7), great plates of the day (prices vary). Perfect Roman crust and fresh toppings (€6-9). Heavenly *tiramisù* (€4.10). Open daily 7:30pm-midnight. M-F also noon-3:30pm. ❸

TRASTEVERE

By day, Trastevere's cobblestone streets rumble only with the sounds of children and Vespas, but when night falls, P. di Santa Maria di Trastevere is packed with expatriates and Italian out for a night on the town.

🖾 **Pizzeria San Calisto,** P. S. Calisto, 9a (☎06 581 8256). Right off P. S. Maria in Trastevere. Best damn pizza in Rome. Gorgeous thin crust pizzas so large they hang off the plates (€4.15-7.75). The *bruschetta* (€2.07) is worth a postcard home. Management shoos the rose-sellers away for a peaceful meal. Open Tu-Su 7pm-midnight. MC/V. ❶

Ristorante a Casa di Alfredo, V. Roma Libera, 5-7 (☎06 588 2968). Off P. Cosimato. Whether you opt for the "sea" menù or the "land" menù, you are destined to find something to your liking. Try the *gnocchi tartufo e gamberi* (€9.30) or tonarelli with tomatoes, sausage, porcini mushrooms, and rocket (€10.33) to start and the *filetto a pepe verde* (€12.40) as a main dish. Open daily noon-3pm and 7:30-11:30pm. ❸

Ouszeri, V. d. Salumi, 2 (☎06 581 8256). Either go left off V. d. Trastevere or take V. Vascellari from Lungotevere Ripa and then go right onto V. d. Salumi. Greek restaurant/ cultural association. Ring doorbell to get in. Live music in cool weather. Great food— share the *piatto misto* with a friend (€7-15). €1.50 membership required. ❷

Augusto, P. de' Rienzi, 15 (☎06 580 3798). North of P. S. Maria in Trastevere. Enjoy the daily pasta specials at lunch (around €4.90), and the *pollo arrosto con patate* (€6). Dinner is chaotic; lunch tends to feature laid-back discussions between waiters and clientele. Amazing homemade desserts. Either way, you have to be pushy to get service. No reservations. Open Sept.-July M-F 12:30-3pm and 8-11pm, Sa 12:30-3pm. ❶

Pizzeria Ivo, V. d. S. Francesco a Ripa, 158 (☎06 581 7082). Take a right on V. d. Fratte di Trastevere off V. Trastevere and another right onto V. S. Francesco a Ripa. A long-standing favorite in Trastevere, Ivo rests on its laurels a bit, but still makes a good pizza. Long waits. Pizzas €4-8. Open Sept.-July W-M 5pm-2am. MC/V. ❷

TERMINI AND SAN LORENZO

You're by the train station, hungry, and in a rush. This is no reason to subject yourself to the nightmare of a shady tourist trap offering a €5 quick lunch. Instead, try:

🖾 **Africa,** V. Gaeta, 26-28 (☎06 494 1077), near P. Indipendenza. Decked out in yellow and black, Africa continues its 20-year tradition of serving excellent Eritrean/Ethiopian food. The meat-filled *sambusas* (€2.50) are a flavorful starter; both the *zighini beghi* (roasted lamb in a spicy sauce; €7) and the *misto vegetariano* (mixed veggie dishes; €6) are fantastic entrees. Try your hands at the spongy Ethiopian flatbread, *injera.* Cover €1. Open M-Sa 8pm-midnight. AmEx/MC/V. ❷

Trattoria da Bruno, V. Varese, 29 (☎06 49 04 03). From V. Marsala, next to the train station, walk three blocks down V. Milazzo and turn right onto V. Varese. A neighborhood and tourists' favorite. Start with the tasty homemade *gnocchi* (€6) and continue with the delicious *ossobuco* (€7.80). Bruno, the owner, makes *crèches;* note the picture of him shaking hands with the Pope in front of one of his little masterworks. Open Sept.-July daily noon-3:30pm and 7-10:15pm. AmEx/MC/V. ❷

SAN LORENZO

San Lorenzo is Rome's university district, and poor students with discriminating palates means good and cheap eateries with loads of local character. From Termini, walk south on V. Pretoriano to P. Tiburtino, or take bus #492 to P. Verano. Don't walk alone at night.

🖾 **Il Pulcino Ballerino,** V. d. Equi, 66-68 (☎06 494 1255). Take a right off V. Tiburtina. An artsy atmosphere with cuisine to match. The cook stirs up dishes like *conchiglione al "Moby Dick"* (shells with tuna, cream, and greens) and *risotto* (€5.16-6.20). Excellent vegetarian dishes like potato casserole (€6.20). You can also skip the chef altogether and prepare your own meal on a warm stone at the table. Cover €1. Open M-Sa 1-3:30pm and 8pm-midnight. Closed 2nd and 3rd weeks of Aug. AmEx/MC/V. ❷

Arancia Blu, V. d. Latini, 65 (☎06 445 4105), off V. Tiburtina. This elegant and popular little vegetarian restaurant serves up an inventive and excellent food. Enjoy elaborate dishes like *tonnarelli con pecorino romano e tartufo* (pasta with sheep cheese and truffles; €6.20) or fried ravioli stuffed with eggplant and smoked *caciocavallo* with pesto sauce (€8.50). Extensive wine list. Open daily 8:30pm-midnight. ❷

Il Capellaio Matto, V. d. Marsi, 25. From V. Tiburtina, take the 4th right off V. d. Equi. Vegetarians, rejoice! This offbeat place (named for the Mad Hatter) offers pasta and rice dishes like *risotto al pepe verde* (with green peppercorn; €5), imaginative salads (arugula and pears with parmesan; €3.75), and a variety of crepes (€3.62-4.65). Plenty of meat dishes, too. Cover €1. Open W-M 8pm-midnight. ❶

TESTACCIO

Once home to a giant slaughterhouse, this working-class southern neighborhood is the seat of many excellent restaurants serving traditional Roman, meat-heavy fare, as well as the center of Roman nightlife.

La Cestia, V. di Piramide Cestia, 69. M: B-Piramide. Walk across P. di Porta San Paolo to V. di Piramide Cestia; restaurant is on the right. La Cestia's offerings, particularly their fish, are so beloved that employees of the Food and Agriculture Organization make the trek from their headquarters near the Circus Maximus to grab lunch. The pizza and pasta are excellent for light meals. Pasta €4.20-7.20, pizza €4.20-7.80, fish €6.20-15, *secondi* €6.20-11. Open Tu-Su 12:30-3pm and 7:30-11pm. D/MC/V. ❷

Trattoria da Bucatino, V. Luca della Robbia, 84-86 (☎06 574 6886). Take V. Luigi Vanvitelli off V. Marmorata, then the 1st left. A friendly neighborhood *trattoria* bringing you delicious animal entrails, such as heaping mounds of *tripe alla romana* (€7), and gutless dishes such as *cosse alla marinara* (mussels; €5). Pizza €4-7. Cover €1.50. Open Sept.-July Tu-Su 12:30-3:30pm and 6:30-11:30pm. D/MC/V. ❸

Volpetti Piu, V. Alessandro Volta (☎06 574 4306). Take a left onto V. A. Volta off V. Marmorata. Join the locals at this authentic *gastronomica* for a quick lunch. Fresh salads, pizza, and daily specials from €4. Open M-Sa 10am-10pm. ❶

DESSERT

Cheap *gelato* is as plentiful on Roman streets as pairs of leather pants. Unfortunately, often you get what you pay for. Look for *gelato* with very muted (hence natural) colors, or try some of our favorite *gelaterie* and other sweetshops.

▨ The Old Bridge, V. le. dei Bastioni di Michelangelo (☎06 3972 3026), off P. del Risorgimento, perpendicular to Vatican museum walls. Huge cups and cones (€1.50-3) filled with your choice of 20 homemade *gelato* flavors, some of the best in the city. Open M-Sa 9am-2am, Su 3pm-2am.

San Crispino, V. d. Panetteria, 42 (☎06 679 3924). Very near the Trevi Fountain. Facing the fountain, turn right onto V. Lavatore and take your 2nd left; it is inset on the right. Almost universally acknowledged as the best *gelato* in Rome. Fastidious attention to purity (no cones or garnish other than cream) from stainless steel *gelato* canisters. Cups €1.70-6.30. Also at V. Acaia, 56 (☎06 704 50412), south of the center in Appio. Both locations open M, W-Th, Su noon-12:30am, F-Sa noon-1:30am.

Da Quinto, V. d. Tor Millina, 15 (☎06 686 5657). West of P. Navona. Eccentric interior decoration, huge lines, and icy, lighter *gelato*. The fruit flavors are especially good, as are the house specialty banana splits (€4.13). Enormous *macedonia* of fruit (with yogurt, *gelato,* or whipped cream topping; €6.50). Open daily 11am-2am.

COFFEE

Italian coffee is the solution to all travel hassles: early hostel lock-outs, hangovers, and belligerent tourists.

■ **Bar Giulia (a.k.a. Caffè Peru),** V. Giulia, 84 (☎06 686 1310), near P. V. Emanuele II. No other bar is crazy enough to open near this tiny, 50-year-old institution, serving what may be the cheapest (and most delicious) coffee in Rome (€0.57 at bar, €0.72 sitting). Your favorite liquor added at no extra charge. You may have to crowd-surf over the hordes of locals to get your cup of *caffè.* Open M-Sa 4am-9:30pm.

■ **Tazza d'Oro,** V. d. Orfani, 84-86 (☎06 679 2768). Stand with your back to the Pantheon's portico; the yellow-lettered sign is on your right. No seating, but the best coffee in Rome (their own "regina" blend of arabica coffees from around the world) at great prices (*caffè* €0.65; *cappuccino* €0.80). Jamaican Blue Mountain available (€1.50). Superlative *granità di caffè* with fresh whipped cream (€1.30). Open M-Sa 7am-8pm.

ENOTECHE (WINE BARS)

Wine bars, often tucked away in the corners of small piazzas, range from laid-back and local to chic and international. Have a bite to eat and a delicious glass of wine without the unrefined drinkers of the pub scene.

■ **Bar Da Benito,** V. d. Falegnami, 14 (☎06 686 1508), off P. Cairoli in the Jewish Ghetto. For 40 years and counting, a *tavola calda* lined with bottles and hordes of hungry workmen. Glasses of wine from €1; bottles from €5.50. One hot pasta prepared daily (€4.13), along with fresh *secondi* like *prosciutto* with vegetables (€4.65). Spacious and highly functional seating area next to takeout bar. Packed, noisy, and incredibly hectic, with excellent staff. Open Sept.-July M-Sa 6:30am-7pm; lunch noon-3:30pm.

Cul de Sac, P. Pasquino, 73 (☎06 6880 1094). Off P. Navona. One of Rome's 1st wine bars, Cul de Sac has kept the customers coming with a huge selection of great wines, outdoor tables, and tasty dishes. House specialty pate (pheasant and mushroom; €5.10) is exquisite, as are the scrumptious *escargot alla bourguigonne* (€4.50). Open M 7pm-12:30am, Tu-Sa noon-4pm and 6pm-12:30am. MC/V.

◉ SIGHTS

Rome wasn't built in a day, and it's nearly impossible to see even a portion of it in 24 hours. Ancient temples, medieval churches, Renaissance basilicas, Baroque fountains, and 19th- and 20th-century museums all cluster together in a city bursting with masterpieces from every era of Western civilization. Rome's 981 churches and 280 fountains boast everything from Etruscan busts to modern canvases.

THE ANCIENT CITY

THE ROMAN FORUM

Main entrance: V. d. Fori Imperiali (at Largo C. Ricci, between P. Venezia and the Colosseum). Other entrances are opposite the Colosseum at the start of V. Sacra (from here, you can reach the Palatine Hill, too) and at the Clivus Capitolinus, near P. del Campidoglio. M: B-Colosseo, or bus to P. Venezia. Open in summer M-Su 9am-6:30pm; in winter M-Su 9am-3:30pm; sometimes closes M-F 3pm, Su and holidays noon. Free. Guided tour with archaeologist €3.50; audioguide tour for Forum in English, French, German, Italian, Japanese, or Spanish €4; both available at main entrance. Access to the Forum is unpredictable–areas are fenced off at irregular intervals.

The Forum was originally a low marshland prone to flooding from the Tiber. Rome's Iron Age inhabitants (1000-900 BC) eschewed its low, unhealthy swampiness in favor of the Palatine Hill, descending only to bury the dead. In the 7th

BEST OF ROME: THE COLOSSEUM TO THE VATICAN

1 COLOSSEUM. The bad news: millions of Christians, contrary to a number of Hollywood movies, did not meet their unfortunate ends within these deteriorated walls. The good news: at least 5000 wild animals did during the stadium's inaugural festivities in AD 80. Titus's grand addition to the principle of bread and circuses may look like a heap of sun-bleached rock today (thanks to Julius II's not-so-clandestine pillaging during the Renaissance), but in its youth, it was an engineering

TIME: 3-4hr. walk; longer if you visit the museums along the way.

DISTANCE: 5 mi.

SEASON: A sunny day is preferable; bring lots of water.

A highlights tour of ancient and Renaissance Rome

marvel, containing, among other things, a system of awnings that protected the bloodthirsty populace from the inconveniences of sun and rain. Allow an extra 20 minutes if you plan to make the worthwhile climb to the upper tiers of the structure, or stride confidently across the new wooden walkway–just don't look down (p. 498).

2 SANTA MARIA IN ARACOELI. The archetypal Roman Church. In the 1st century AD, the Romans worshipped the spirit of money in the guise of Jupiter Moneta. Later, piety replaced productivity, and the mint originally located here became a meeting place for the Franciscans, who were generally uninterested in making money. In the meantime, the Sibyl once quartered within the walls of the old temple informed Augustus that although he did enjoy divine status, one greater than even he would come to rule Rome. In response, the emperor erected the Ara Coeli, or the altar to heaven (p. 500).

3 IL GESU. The Jesuits were an order known throughout Europe for their commitment to evangelism and their love of extravagant luxury items. The Gesu is the living incarnation of both strains, built in 1584 but left undecorated for more than 100 years (the prescient founders of the Order apparently realized that only Baroque could provide the gilded opulence that such a project required). The Chapel of St. Ignatius and its crowning piece of artistic achievement, the altar topped with an enormous globe of lapis lazuli are rendered almost unholy by their grandeur. However, the real triumph of the church is Baciccia's Triumph of the Holy Name of Jesus, in which sinners, cast from the communion of souls, appear to be hurtling from heaven towards the observers on the ground.

4 TEATRO DI MARCELLO. Arranging a walk past the Marcello on a summer evening is a rewarding enterprise: some of Rome's best classical musicians often use the crumbling structure as a venue for concerts. At noon on a February day, this is the required homage to the Forum that must be paid by all tourists upon entering the city. Without venturing too far into the stark, dusty collection of ruins, one can visit the oldest building in Rome permanently designated as a theater (p. 500).

5 ISOLA TIBERINA. A stroll around this island, enclosed by the Romans with travertine marble so that it would resemble a ship, is a good way to cross the Tiber on the way to the Vatican. The first structure on the island was a temple to Aesculapius, son of Apollo and god of medicine. During the plague of 293 BC, a statue of him was brought from Greece to the island, which has been dedicated to healing ever since. The **Fatebenefratelli** (literally "do good brothers") Hospital and San Bartolomeo, Holy Roman Emperor Otto III's church of choice, are both located on the grounds (p. 504).

6 CASTEL SANT'ANGELO. The popes frequently used this former site of Hadrian's mausoleum as an escape from the pressures, problems, and riots that often plagued St. Peter's. The

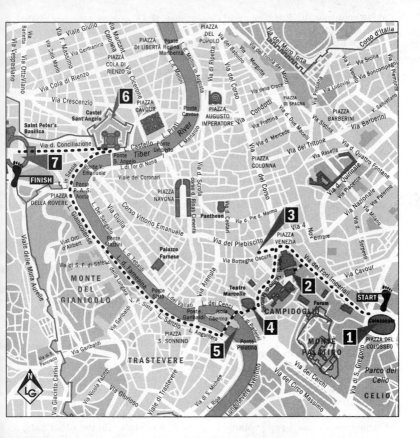

wealth of the Vatican was kept here when the Holy Roman Emperors decided that a little trip to the south was the perfect way to fill their coffers. The lower building served as quarters for some of Rome's more rowdy residents, including the boastful autobiographer and sometime artist Benvenuto Cellini, heretical monk Giordano Bruno, and Beatrice Cenci, accused of incest and patricide and memorialized by Shelley's *The Cenci*. The papal apartments are worth a look, especially the Camera d'Amore e Psiche (p. 504).

7 PIAZZA SAN PIETRO. Far too often, tourists eager to rub flesh with millions of other pensive pilgrims in the Sistine Chapel rush past Bernini's masterpiece without a second look. The artist is undoubtedly taking the proverbial route of disgruntled dead people and turning over in his grave; his work was meant to awe the Protestant heretics who came to Rome in order to talk politics with the pope. A set of four colonnades crowned by 140 distinct saints was part of the visual effect planned by Bernini, in addition to the sensation of leaving the narrow streets of the medieval quarter for the comparative openness of the square. Mussolini ruined the characteristic Baroque metaphor (darkness into light) by constructing the Via di Conciliazione, but the square, and the obelisk placed in the middle by Sixtus V, are nonetheless impressive to even the worst heretic in the crowd today (p. 503).

and 8th centuries BC, Etruscans and Greeks used the Forum as a weekly market. The Romans founded a thatched-hut shantytown on the site of the Forum in 753 BC, when Romulus and Sabine leader Titus Tatius joined forces to end the war triggered by the famous rape of Sabine women. Now the Forum bears witness to centuries of civic building. The entrance ramp to the Forum leads to the Via Sacra, the oldest street in Rome, near the area once known as the Civic Forum. The other sections of the Roman Forum are the Market Square, the Lower Forum, the Upper Forum, and the Velia.

CIVIC FORUM. The **Basilica Aemilia**, built in 179 BC, housed the guild of the *argentarii* (money changers). It was rebuilt several times after fires, particularly one started by Alaric and his merry band of Goths in AD 410; in the pavement you can still see marks from the melted coins that the *argentarii* lost in these blazes. Next to the Basilica Aemilia stands the **Curia**, or Senate House, one of the oldest buildings in the Forum. It was converted to a church in AD 630 and restored by Mussolini. The Curia also houses the **Plutei of Trajan,** two parapets that depict the burning of the tax registers and the distribution of food to poor children. The broad space in front of the Curia was the **Comitium,** or assembly place, where citizens came to vote and representatives gathered for public discussion. This space was home to the Twelve Tables, bronze tablets upon which the first laws of the Republic were inscribed. Bordering the Comitium is the large brick **Rostrum,** or speaker's platform, erected by Julius Caesar just before his death. Augustus's rebellious daughter Julia is said to have voiced dissent here by engaging in amorous activities with some of her father's enemies. The hefty **Arch of Septimius Severus,** to the right of the Rostrum, was dedicated in AD 203 to celebrate Septimus's victories in the Middle East.

MARKET SQUARE. A number of shrines and sacred precincts, including the **Lapis Niger** (Black Stone), once graced the square in front of the Curia. It was in this square that a group of senators murdered Julius Caesar. Below the Lapis Niger rest the underground ruins of a 6th-century BC altar, along with a pyramidal pillar with the oldest known Latin inscription in Rome warning against defiling the shrine. In the square the **Three Sacred Trees** of Rome—olive, fig, and grape—have been replanted by the Italian state. On the other side, a circular tufa basin recalls the **Lacus Curtius,** the chasm into which the legendary Roman warrior Marcus Curtius threw himself in 362 BC to seal the occult fissure and save the city. The newest part of the Forum (aside from the Neoclassical info booth) is the **Column of Phocas,** erected in 608 BC for the visiting Byzantine emperor, Phocas.

LOWER FORUM. Though built in the early-5th century BC, the **Temple of Saturn** has its mythological origins in the Golden Age of Rome. The temple became the site of Saturnalia, a raucous Roman winter bash where class and social distinctions were forgotten, masters served slaves, and all was permitted. Around the corner, rows of deserted column bases are all that remain of the **Basilica Julia,** a courthouse, built by Julius Caesar in 54 BC. At the far end of the Basilica Julia, three white marble columns and a shred of architrave mark the massive podium of the recently restored **Temple of Castor and Pollux.** According to legend, the twin gods Castor and Pollux helped the Romans defeat the rival Etruscans at the Battle of Lake Regillus (496 BC). Legend says that immediately after the battle, the twins appeared in the Forum to water their horses at nearby **Basin of Juturna** *(Lacus Juturnae)*. Down the road from the Temple of Castor and Pollux is the rectangular base of the **Temple of the Deified Julius,** which Augustus built in 29 BC to honor his murdered adoptive father and proclaim himself the nephew of a god. Augustus built the **Arch of Augustus,** which frames the V. Sacra. The circular building behind the Temple of the Deified Julius is the restored **Temple of Vesta,** dating back to the time of the Etruscans. Here the Vestal Virgins tended the city's eternal, sacred fire, keeping it continuously lit for over a thousand years. In a secret room of the temple, accessible only to the Virgins, stood the **Palladium,** the small statue of Minerva that Aeneas was said to have taken from Troy to Italy. Across the square from the Temple of Vesta lies the triangular **Regia,** office of the Pontifex Maximus, Rome's high priest and titular ancestor of the Pope.

UPPER FORUM. The **House of the Vestal Virgins,** shaded by the Palatine Hill, occupied the sprawling complex of rooms and courtyards behind the Temple of Vesta. For 30 years, the six virgins who officiated over Vesta's rites, each ordained at the age of seven, lived in spacious seclusion here above the din of the Forum. The Vestal Virgins were among the most respected people in Ancient Rome. They were the only women allowed to walk unaccompanied in the Forum and also possessed the right to pardon prisoners. This esteem had its price; a virgin who strayed from celibacy was buried alive with a loaf of bread and a candle—to allow her to survive long enough to contemplate her sins. Back on V. Sacra is the **Temple of Antoninus and Faustina** (to the immediate right as you face the entrance ramp), whose strong foundation, columns, and rigid lattice ceiling kept it well-preserved. In the 7th and 8th centuries, after numerous unsuccessful attempts to pull the abandoned temple down, the **Church of San Lorenzo in Miranda** was built in its interior. To the right of the temple as you face it lies the **necropolis.** Excavations uncovered Iron Age graves from the 8th century BC, lending credence to the city's legendary founding date of 753 BC. Here V. Sacra runs over the **Cloaca Maxima,** the ancient sewer that drains water from the valley. The street passes the **Temple of Romulus** (the round building behind scaffolding), named for the son of Maxentius (not the legendary founder of Rome). The original bronze doors have a 4th century AD working lock.

VELIA. V. Sacra leads out of the Forum proper to the gargantuan **Basilica of Maxentius** (also known as the Basilica of Constantine). Emperor Maxentius began construction in AD 306, until Constantine deposed him and completed the project. The uncovered remains of a statue of Constantine, including a 6½ft. long foot, are at the **Palazzo dei Conservatori** on Capitoline Hill. The Baroque facade of the **Church of Santa Francesca Romana** is built over Hadrian's Temple to Venus and Rome—the palindromic *Roma* and *Amor*—and hides the entrance to the **Antiquarium Forense,** a museum that displays necropolis funerary urns and skeletons. (Open daily 9am-1pm. Free.) On the summit of the Velia, the road down from the Palatine, is the **Arch of Titus,** built in AD 81 by Domitian to celebrate his brother Titus, who had destroyed Jerusalem 11 years earlier. V. Sacra leads to an exit on the other side of the hill, and to the Colosseum. The path crossing in front of the arch climbs up to the Palatine Hill.

CIRCUS MAXIMUS AND BATHS OF CARACALLA. Today's Circus Maximus is only a grassy shadow of its former glory. After its construction in 600 BC, the circus drew more than 300,000 Romans, who gathered here to watch chariots careen around the quarter-mile track. The Baths of Caracalla are the largest and best-preserved in Rome, with beautiful mosaics covering the floors. *(Walk down V. d. San Gregorio from the Colosseum. Open 24hr.)*

▨ THE COLOSSEUM

M: B-Colosseo. Open daily May-Oct. 9am-6:30pm; Nov.-Apr. 9am- 3:30pm. €8 for a combined ticket to the Colosseum and the Palatine Hill. EU citizens under 18 or over 65 free. EU citizens 18-24 €4. To avoid long lines at the Colosseum, buy tickets at entrance to the Palatine Hill in the Roman Forum. Archaeologia Card (7-day ticket book) good for entrance to the four Musei Nazionali Romani, the Colosseum, the Palatine Hill, the Terme di Diocleziano, and the Crypti Balbi €20, EU citizens 18-24 €10, EU citizens under 18 or over 65 free. Tours with archaeologist €3.50; multilingual audioguides €4.

The Colosseum stands as the enduring symbol of the Eternal City—a hollowed-out ghost of travertine marble that dwarfs every other ruin in Rome, once holding as many as 50,000 crazed spectators. Within 100 days of its AD 80 opening, some 5000 wild beasts perished in the bloody arena, and the slaughter went on for three more centuries. The floor (now partially restored and open for concerts) covers a labyrinth of brick cells, ramps, and elevators used to transport animals from cages to arena level. Between the Colosseum and the Palatine Hill lies the **Arco di Costantino,** one of the best-preserved imperial monuments in the area. The arch commemorates Constantine's victory at the Battle of the Milvian Bridge in AD 312, using fragments from monuments to Trajan, Hadrian, and Marcus Aurelius.

THE PALATINE HILL

The Palatine rises south of the Forum. Open daily 9am-6:30pm; in winter M-Sa 9:30am-1hr. before sunset, Su 9am-3:30pm; sometimes closes M-F 3pm, Su and holidays noon. Last entrance 45min. before closing. Combined ticket to the Palatine Hill and the Colosseum €8, EU citizens 18-24 €4, EU citizens under 18 or over 65 free. Archaeologia Card (7-day ticket book) good for entrance to the four Musei Nazionali Romani (p. 512), the Colosseum, the Palatine Hill, the Terme di Diocleziano, and the Crypti Balbi €20, EU citizens 18-24 €10, EU citizens under 18 or over 65 free. Sections of the Farnese Gardens, the hills best for viewing, were closed for renovation in summer 2002, but most of the botanical gardens are open.

The best way to attack the **Palatine** is from the access stairs steps away from the Arch of Titus in the Forum, which ascend to the **Farnese Gardens.** The hill, actually a plateau between the Tiber and the Forum, was home to the she-wolf that suckled Romulus and Remus. It was here that Romulus built the first walls of the city. During the Republic, the Palatine was the city's most fashionable residential quarter, where aristocrats and statesmen, including Cicero and Marc Antony, built their homes. Augustus lived here in a modest house, but later emperors capitalized on the hill's prestige, building themselves gargantuan quarters. By the end of the first century, the imperial residence swallowed up the entire hill, whose Latin name, Palatium, became synonymous with the palace that dominated it. After the fall of Rome, the hill suffered the same fate as the Forum.

Lower down, excavations continue on a 9th-century BC village, optimistically labeled the **Casa di Romulo.** To the right of the village is the podium of the **Temple of Cybele,** built in 191 BC during the Second Punic War. The stairs slightly to the left lead to the **House of Livia.** Augustus's wife Livia, the first Roman empress, had the house, with its vestibule, courtyard, and three vaulted living rooms, connected to the **House of Augustus** next door.

Around the corner, the **Cryptoporticus** connected Tiberius's palace with the buildings nearby. Used by slaves and couriers as a secret passage, it may have been built by Nero in one of his more paranoid moments. The solemn **Domus Augustana** was the private space for the emperors. Adjacent to the Domus Augustana lies the other wing of the palace and the sprawling **Domus Flavia,** site of a gigantic octagonal fountain that occupied almost the entire courtyard.

Between the Domus Augustana and the Domus Flavia stands the **Palatine Antiquarium,** the museum that houses artifacts found during excavations. *(30 people admitted every 20min. 9:10am-6:20pm. Free.)* Outside on the right, the palace's east wing contains the curious **Stadium Palatinum,** or Hippodrome, a sunken oval space once surrounded by a colonnade but now decorated with fragments of porticoes, statues, and fountains.

THE DOMUS AUREA

On the Oppian Hill, below Trajan's baths. From the Colosseum, walk through the gates up V. d. Domus Aurea and make 1st left. ☎ 06 3996 7700 for reservations. Open daily 9am-6:45pm, closed Tu. Groups of 30 admitted every 20min. €5, EU citizens 18-24 €2.50, EU citizens under 18 or over 65 free. Reservations recommended for €1. Guided tour €1.55.

This park houses a portion of Nero's "Golden House," which once covered a substantial chunk of Rome. An enclosed lake was positioned where the Colosseum now stands, and the Caelian Hill became private gardens. The Forum was reduced to a vestibule of the palace; Nero crowned it with a colossal statue of himself as the sun. Nero pillaged all of Greece to find works of art worthy of the quarters of an emperor, including the famous *Laocoön.* The party didn't last long; Nero committed suicide only five years after building his hedonistic pad. Out of civic-mindedness or jealousy, the later Flavian emperors tore down his house and replaced all the palace with monuments built for the public good. The Flavian Baths were built on the Caelian Hill, the lake was drained, and the Colosseum was erected.

FORI IMPERIALI

The sprawling Fori Imperiali lie on either side of V. d. Fori Imperiali, stretching from the Forum to P. Venezia. Excavations will proceed through summer 2003; **the area is closed off,** but you can still get free views peering over the railing from V. d. Fori Imperiali. The large conglomeration of temples, basilicas, and public squares was constructed by emperors from the first century BC to the 2nd century AD, in response to increasing congestion in the old Forum.

FORUM OF TRAJAN. Built between AD 107 and 113, the entire forum celebrated Trajan's victorious Dacian campaign. The complex included a colossal equestrian statue of Trajan and triumphal arch. At one end stands the ▧**Trajan's Column,** an extraordinary and intact specimen of Roman relief-sculpture, carved in 113 with 2500 climbing legionnaires. In 1588, a statue of St. Peter replaced Trajan's.

MARKETS OF TRAJAN. This three-floor semicircular complex is a glimpse of Rome's first shopping mall, featuring an impressive, albeit crumbling, display of sculpture from the imperial forums. *(Enter at V. IV Novembre, 94, up the steps in V. Magnanapoli, to the right of the 2 churches behind Trajan's column. ☎ 06 679 0048. Open Tu-Su 9am-6:30pm. Free.)*

FORUMS. Across V. dei Fori Imperiali, in the shade of the Vittorio Emanuele II monument, lie the paltry remains of the **Forum of Caesar,** including the ruins of Julius Caesar's **Temple to Venus Genetrix** (Mother Venus, from whom he claimed descent). Nearby, the gray tufa wall of the **Forum of Augustus** commemorates Augustus's victory over Caesar's murderers at the Battle of Philippi in 42 BC. The aptly named **Forum Transitorium** (also called the **Forum of Nerva**) was a narrow, rectangular space connecting the Forum of Augustus with the Republican Forum. Emperor Nerva dedicated the temple in 97 BC to the goddess Minerva. **Vespatian's Forum,** the mosaic-filled **Church of Santi Cosma e Damiano** is across V. Cavour, near the Roman Forum. *(Open daily 9am-1pm and 3-7pm.)*

THE CAPITOLINE HILL

Santa Maria in Aracoeli open daily 7:30am-noon and 3:30-5:30pm. Mamertime Prison ☎ 06 679 2902. Open daily 9am-12:30pm and 2:30-6:30pm. Donation requested. To get to the Campidoglio, take bus to P. Venezia. From P. Venezia, face the Vittorio Emanuele II monument, walk around to the right to P. d'Aracoeli, and take the stairs up the hill.

Home to the original capital, the Monte Capitolino still serves as the seat of the city's government. Michelangelo designed the spacious **Piazza di Campidoglio.** Surrounding the piazza are the twin Palazzo dei Conservatori and Palazzo Nuovo, now the home of the **Capitoline Museums.** From the Palazzo Nuovo, stairs lead up to the rear entrance of the 7th-century **Chiesa di Santa Maria in Aracoeli.** Its stunning **Cappella Bufalini** is home to the *Santo Bambino,* a cherubic statue that receives letters from sick children. The gloomy **Mamertine Prison,** consecrated as the **Chiesa di San Pietro in Carcere,** lies down the hill from the back stairs of the Aracoeli. St. Peter baptized his captors with the waters that flooded his cell here.

At the far end of the piazza, the turreted **Palazzo dei Senatori** houses the offices of Rome's mayor. Paul III had Michelangelo fashion the imposing statues of the twin warriors Castor and Pollux, and also had the famous equestrian **statue of Marcus Aurelius** brought here from the Lateran Palace. The original now resides in the courtyard of the Palazzo dei Conservatori—a sturdier copy crowns the piazza.

THE VELABRUM. The Velabrum lies in a flat flood plain of the Tiber, south of the Jewish Ghetto. At the bend of V. del Portico d'Ottavia, a shattered pediment and a few columns are all that remain of the once magnificent **Portico d'Ottavia.** The **Teatro di Marcello** next door bears the name of Augustus's unfortunate nephew. The Colosseum was modeled upon its facade (11 BC). Down V. di Teatro toward the Tiber, the **Chiesa di San Nicola in Carcere** incorporates the Roman temples to the gods Juno, Janus, and Spes. One block south along V. Luigi Petroselli are the **Piazza della Bocca della Verità,** the site of the ancient **Foro Boario,** or cattle market. Across the street, the **Chiesa di Santa Maria in Cosmedin** harbors lovely medieval decoration. The portico's ▨**Bocca della Verità,** a drain cover with a river god's face, was made famous in Audrey Hepburn's *Roman Holiday.* Medieval legend had it that the mouth would bite a liar's hand. (*Chiesa di San Nicola ☎ 06 686 9972. Open Sept.-July M-Sa 7:30am-noon and 2-5pm, Su 9:30am-1pm and 4-8pm. Portico open daily 10am-7pm.*)

CENTRO STORICO

PIAZZA VENEZIA AND VIA DEL CORSO. Following the line of the ancient V. Lata, **Via del Corso** takes its name from its days as Rome's premier racecourse. It runs nearly a mile between P. del Popolo and the rumbling P. Venezia. The crumbling **Palazzo Venezia,** on the right of the piazza, was one of the first Renaissance *palazzi* in the city. Mussolini used it as office space and delivered some of his most famous speeches from its balcony. The *palazzo* is home to the **Museo Nazionale del Palazzo Venezia.** The *loggia* of the interior courtyard dates from the Renaissance. Off V. del Corso, **Piazza Colonna** was named for the colossal **Colonna di Marco Aurelio,** designed in imitation of the emperor Trajan's triumphal column. Sixtus V had the statue of St. Paul added to the top of the column in the 16th century. On the opposite side of the piazza, **Palazzo Wedekind,** home to the newspaper *Il Tempo,* was built in 1838 with columns from the Etruscan city of Veio. The northwest corner of the piazza flows into **Piazza di Montecitorio,** overseen by Bernini's **Palazzo Montecitorio,** now the seat of the Chamber of Deputies.

PIAZZA DELLA ROTONDA. With granite columns and pediment, bronze doors, and a soaring domed interior, ▨**The Pantheon** has changed little since it was built nearly 2000 years ago. Architects still puzzle over how it was erected—its dome, a perfect half-sphere constructed from poured concrete without the support of vaults, arches, or ribs, is the largest of its kind. The light entering the roof served as a sundial. In AD 606, the Pantheon was consecrated as the **Church of Santa Maria ad Martyres.** *(Open M-Sa 8:30am-7:30pm, Su 9am-6pm; holidays 9am-1pm. Free.)*

The piazza centers on Giacomo della Porta's late Renaissance fountain, which supports an Egyptian **obelisk** added in the 18th century. Around the left side of the Pantheon, another obelisk, supported by Bernini's curious elephant statue, marks the center of tiny **Piazza Minerva.** Behind the obelisk, the **Chiesa di Santa Maria Sopra Minerva** hides some Renaissance masterpieces, including Michelangelo's *Christ Bearing the Cross,* Antoniazzo Romano's *Annunciation,* and a statue of St. Sebastian recently attributed to Michelangelo. The south transept houses **Cappella Carafa,** with a brilliant Lippi fresco cycle. From the upper left-hand corner of P. della Rotonda, V. Giustiniani goes north to V. della Scrofa and V. della Dogana Vecchia. Here stands **Chiesa di San Luigi dei Francesi,** the French National Church, home to three of Caravaggio's most famous paintings: *The Calling of St. Matthew, St. Matthew and the Angel,* and *The Crucifixion. (1 block down V. d. Salvatore from C. Rinascimento as it passes P. Navona. Open F-W 7:30am-12:30pm and 3:30-7pm, Th 7:30am-12:30pm.)*

PIAZZA NAVONA. Opened in AD 86, P. Navona housed wrestling matches, chariot races, and mock naval battles, with the stadium flooded and fleets skippered by convicts. Bernini's **Fontana dei Quattro Fiumi** (Fountain of the Four Rivers) commands the center of the piazza. Each of the river gods represents a continent: the Ganges for Asia, the Danube for Europe, the Nile for Africa (veiled, since the source of the river was unknown), and the Rio de la Plata for the Americas. At the ends of the piazza are the **Fontana del Moro** and the **Fontana di Nettuno,** designed by Giacomo della Porta in the 16th century. With a Borromini-designed exterior, the **Church of Sant'Agnese** holds the skull of its namesake saint, martyred after refusing an arranged marriage. *(Western side of P. Navona, opposite Fontana di Quattro Fiumi. Open daily 9am-noon and 4-7pm.)* West of P. Navona, where V. di Tor Millina intersects V. della Pace, the semicircular porch of the **Chiesa di Santa Maria della Pace** houses Raphael's gentle *Sibyls* in its **Chigi Chapel.** On nearby C. del Rinascimento, the **Chiesa di Sant'Ivo's** corkscrew cupola hovers over the **Palazzo della Sapienza,** the original home of the University of Rome. Continue down, turn left onto C. V. Emanuele, and walk to P. del Gesù to see **Il Gesù,** mother church of the Jesuit Order. *(Open daily 6am-12:30pm and 4-7:15pm.)*

CAMPO DEI FIORI. Campo dei Fiori lies across C. V. Emanuele from P. Navona. During papal rule, the area was the site of countless executions. The stately Renaissance **Palazzo Farnese,** built by Alessandro Farnese, the first Counter-Reformation pope (1534-1549), dominates P. Farnese, south of the Campo. Since 1635, the French Embassy has used it in exchange for the Italian Embassy's use of space in Paris's Hotel Galiffet. To the east of the *palazzo* is the **Palazzo Spada** and the collection of the **Galleria Spada** (p. 512).

THE JEWISH GHETTO

The Jewish community in Rome is the oldest in Europe—Israelites came in 161 BC as ambassadors from Judas Maccabei, asking for Imperial help against invaders. The Ghetto, the tiny area to which Pope Paul IV confined the Jews in 1555, was closed in 1870, but it is still the center of Rome's vibrant Jewish population of 16,000. Take bus #64; the Ghetto is across V. Arenula from Campo dei Fiori.

PIAZZA MATTEI. This square, centered on Taddeo Landini's 16th-century **Fontana delle Tartarughe,** marks the center of the Ghetto. Nearby is the **Church of Sant'Angelo in Pescheria,** installed inside the Portico d'Ottavia in 755 and named after the fish market that flourished here. Jews were forced to attend mass here every Sunday—an act of forced evangelism that they quietly resisted by stuffing their ears with wax. *(Open for prayer meetings W 5:30pm, Sa 5pm.)*

IN RECENT NEWS

GONE FISHING

Roberto Cercelletta was no stranger to the Roman *carabinieri,* who shook their heads but turned their policing eyes away as the otherwise unemployed and mentally unstable man drove his scooter to the Trevi Fountain, pulled on his galoshes and splashed his way among the statues, with a pole hung with a magnet in hand.

Six mornings a week, Cercelletta would arrive to fish out the coins tossed into the fountain by tourists eager to make a return to the Eternal City. When civic officials representing Roman charities, unofficially entitled to the donations, made their weekly trip to collect tourists' donations, they found far fewer coins than anticipated, given the huge volumes of wishes regularly flung at the Trevi's Neptune and Tritons.

Cercelletta's 34-year coin pinching spree never broke any well-defined laws. The coins didn't officially belong to Rome's charities or municipal government. A 1999 ordinance passed to protect city monuments, however, forbade wading in the fountain and led to Cercelletta's repeated detainment and fining.

Police were unsuccessful in their efforts to collect the fines from Cercelletta; this despite the fact that his dangling magnet was reportedly bringing in a staggering 1000 euros a day.

SINAGOGA ASHKENAZITA. Built between 1874 and 1904 at the corner of Lungotevere dei Cenci and V. Catalan, this temple incorporates Persian and Babylonian architectural techniques. Terrorists bombed the building in 1982; guards now search all visitors. The synagogue houses the **Jewish Museum,** a collection of ancient torahs and Holocaust artifacts. (☎ 06 687 5051. Open for services only.)

PIAZZA DI SPAGNA AND ENVIRONS

▧ THE SPANISH STEPS. Designed by an Italian, paid for by the French, named for the Spaniards, occupied by the British, and currently under the sway of American ambassador-at-large Ronald McDonald, the **Scalinata di Spagna** are, well, international. The pink house to the right of the Steps was the site of John Keats's 1821 death; it's now the **Keats-Shelley Memorial Museum.**

▧ FONTANA DI TREVI. Nicolo Salvi's (1697-1751) sparklingly clean **Fontana di Trevi** emerges from the back wall of **Palazzo Poli,** fascinating crowds with the rumble of its cascading waters. Anita Ekberg took a dip in the fountain in Fellini's movie *La Dolce Vita.* Legend has it that a traveler who throws a coin into the fountain is ensured a speedy return to Rome, and one who tosses two will fall in love in Rome. Opposite the fountain is the Baroque **Chiesa dei Santi Vincenzo e Anastasio,** rebuilt in 1630. The **crypt** preserves the hearts and lungs of popes from 1590-1903. *(Open daily 8am-7:30pm.)*

PIAZZA BARBERINI. Over the busy traffic circle at the end of V. d. Tritone, Bernini's **Triton Fountain** spouts a stream of water high into the air. A modern feel pervades, despite the **Fontana delle Api,** constructed in the 17th century for the Barberini pope Urban VIII. Maderno, Bernini, and his rival Borromini are responsible for the 1624 **Palazzo Barberini,** which houses the Galleria Nazionale d'Arte Antica (see **Museums**). The severe Church of the Immaculate Conception is the home of Cardinal Antonio Barberini's tomb, and a frightening **Capuchin Crypt.** *(V. V. Veneto, 27a. Walk up V. V. Veneto away from P. Barberini. Open F-W 9am-noon and 3-6pm. Donation requested.)*

PIAZZA DEL POPOLO. P. del Popolo, once a favorite venue for the execution of heretics, is now the "people's square." In the center is the 3200-year-old **Obelisk of Pharaoh Ramses II,** which Augustus brought back as a souvenir from Egypt. The early Renaissance **Church of Santa Maria del Popolo** holds Renaissance and Baroque masterpieces. *(☎ 06 361 0487. Open M-Sa 7am-noon and 4-7pm, holidays and Su 8am-*

1:30pm and 4:30-7:30pm.) The **Della Rovere Chapel** holds Pinturicchio's *Adoration*. Two exquisite Caravaggios, *The Conversion of St. Paul* and *Crucifixion of St. Peter*, are in the **Cappella Cerasi.** The **Cappella Chigi** was designed by Raphael for the Sienese banker Agostino Chigi, reputedly once the world's richest man. At the southern end of the piazza are the 17th-century **twin churches** of Santa Maria di Montesano and Santa Maria dei Miracoli.

VILLA BORGHESE

M: A-Spagna and follow the signs. Alternatively, from the Flaminio (A) stop, take V. Washington under the archway into the Pincio. From P. del Popolo, climb the stairs to the right of Santa Maria del Popolo, cross the street, and climb the small path. BioParco, V. d. Giardino Zoologico, 3. ☎06 321 6564. Open M-F 9:30am-5pm, Sa-Su 9:30am-6pm. €8; ages 3-12 €6, under 3 or over 60 free. Santa Priscilla catacombs, V. Salaria, 430, and the gardens of Villa Ada, are best reached by bus #310 from Termini, or the #630 from Venezia or P. Barberini. Get off at P. Vescovio and walk down V. d. Tor Fiorenza to P. d. Priscilla to the entrance to the park and the catacombs. ☎06 8620 6272. Open Tu-Su 8am-noon and 2:30-5pm. €6.

A recently ordained Scipione Borghese celebrated his new status as cardinal by building the **Villa Borghese** north of P. di Spagna and V. V. Veneto. Its park is now home to three art museums, including the world-renowned **Galleria Borghese** (see p. 510), and the intriguing **Museo Nazionale Etrusco di Villa Giulia** (see p. 510). The Borghese is also home to a second-rate zoo, the **Bio-Parco.** North of Villa Borghese are the **Santa Priscilla catacombs** and the **Villa Ada** gardens.

VATICAN CITY

M: A-Ottaviano, A-Cipro/Musei Vaticani, bus #64 (beware of pickpockets), 492 from Termini or Largo Argentina, 62 from P. Barberini, or 23 from Testaccio. Central Vatican ☎06 69 82.

Occupying 108½ independent acres entirely within the boundaries of Rome, Vatican City, the foothold of the Catholic Church, once wheeled and dealed as the mightiest power in Europe. The Lateran Treaty of 1929 which allowed the Pope to maintain all legislative, judicial, and executive powers over this tiny theocracy also requires the Church to remain neutral in Italian national politics and Roman municipal affairs. The nation has historically preserved its independence by minting coins (in Italian *lire* but with the Pope's face), running a separate postal system, maintaining an army of Swiss Guards, and hoarding fine art in the **Vatican Museums** (see p. 509).

BASILICA DI SAN PIETRO (ST. PETER'S)

Dress appropriately when visiting or you'll be refused entrance—nothing exposing the knee or shoulder, though jeans and a t-shirt are fine. Men requested to remove hats upon entering. Multilingual confession available. The Pilgrim Tourist Information Center is located on the left between the rounded colonnade and the basilica, and offers a multilingual staff, free brochures, and currency exchange. Next to the Information Center is a 1st aid station and free bathrooms. Open daily 7am-7pm; Oct.-Mar. 7am-6pm. Mass M-Sa 9, 10, 11am, noon, 5pm; Su 9, 10:30, 11:30am, 12:10, 1, 4, 5:30pm. Plan on spending at least 2hr. in St. Peter's.

PIAZZA AND FACADE. As you enter **Piazza San Pietro,** Bernini's colonnade draws you toward the church. Mussolini's broad V. della Conciliazione, built in the 1930s to connect the Vatican to the rest of the city, opened a wider view of St. Peter's than Bernini had ever intended. The obelisk in the center is framed by two fountains. Round disks mark spots where you should stand so that the quadruple rows of Bernini's colonnades visually resolve into one perfectly aligned row. One hundred and forty statues perch above on the colonnade. Those on the basilica represent Christ (at center), John the Baptist, and the Apostles (except for Peter).

ROME

ENTRANCE AND PIETÀ. The pope opens the **Porta Sancta** (Holy Door), the last door on the right side of the entrance porch, every 25 years by knocking in the bricks with a hammer. The basilica rests on the reputed site of St. Peter's tomb. The interior of St. Peter's measures 186m by 137m along the transepts. Metal lines on the marble floor mark the lengths of other major world churches. To the right, Michelangelo's *Pietà* has been protected by bullet-proof glass since 1972, when an axe-wielding fiend attacked it, smashing Christ's nose and breaking Mary's hand.

INTERIOR. The crossing under the dome is anchored by four niches with statues of saints. In the center of the crossing, Bernini's bronze **baldacchino** rises on spiral columns over the marble altar. The bronze bees on the canopy are the symbol of the Barberini family, of which Bernini's patron Urban VIII was a member.

CUPOLA. The entrance to the cupola is near the exit from the grottoes. You can take an elevator to the walkway around the interior of the dome or ascend 350 steps to the cupola's top ledge, which offers an excellent view of the piazza and the Vatican Gardens. *(Open daily Apr.-Sept. 7am-5:45pm; Oct.-Mar. 7am-4:45pm.)*

VATICAN GROTTOES. The Vatican Grottoes, well-lit and anything but creepy, are lined with the ancient and modern tombs of Catholic VIPs, from emperors to Queen Christina of Sweden. *(Open Apr.-Sept. daily 7am-6pm; Oct.-Mar. 7am-5pm.)*

TREASURY OF SAINT PETER'S. The Treasury contains gifts bestowed upon St. Peter's tomb. Highlights include the Solomonic column from the Basilica of Constantine; the "dalmatic of Charlemagne" (the illiterate Holy Roman Emperor's intricately designed robe); a statue of one of Bernini's angels; and the magnificent bronze tomb of Sixtus IV. *(Open Apr.-Sept. daily 9am-6:30pm; Oct.-Mar. 9am-5:15pm. Closed when the Pope is celebrating in the basilica and on Christmas and Easter. €5, children 12 and under €3. Photographs not allowed. Wheelchair-accessible. Plan to spend 30min.)*

CASTEL SANT'ANGELO

Down V. d. Conciliazione from St. Peter's. To enter the castle, walk along the river with St. Peter's behind you and the towering castle to your left. Alternately, cross the Tiber on Bernini's Ponte S. Angelo, which leads directly to the entrance of the Castel. ☎06 687 5036 or 06 697 9111. Open Tu-Su 9am-7pm; in winter daily 9am-7pm. €5, EU students 18-25 €2.50, EU citizens under 18 or over 65 free. Guided tour with archaeologist summer Tu-F 10:30am and 4:30pm, Sa-Su 4:30pm. €4.13. Free tour with admission price Sa-Su 3pm. Multilingual audio guides. €3.62. No photos in rooms with frescoes.

Built by Hadrian (AD 117-138) as a mausoleum for himself and his family, this mass of brick and stone has served as a fortress, prison, and palace. When the city was wracked with plague in 590, Pope Gregory the Great saw an angel sheathing his sword at the top of the complex; the plague abated soon after, and the edifice was rededicated to the angel. The fortress offers an incomparable view of Rome and the Vatican. Outside, the marble **Ponte Sant'Angelo,** lined with statues of angels designed by Bernini, is the starting point for the traditional pilgrimage route from St. Peter's to the **Church of San Giovanni in Laterano.**

TRASTEVERE

To get to Trastevere, take bus #75 or 170 from Termini to V. Trastevere, or tram #13 from Largo Argentina.

ISOLA TIBERINA. According to Roman legend, the Tiber Island emerged with the Roman Republic; after the Etruscan tyrant Tarquin raped the virtuous Lucretia, her outraged family killed him and threw his corpse in the river, where muck and silt collected around it. Home to the Fatebenefratelli Hospital since AD 154, the island has long been associated with healing. The Greek god Aesclepius appeared to the Romans as a snake and slithered out of the river; his symbol, the caduceus, is visible all over the island. The eclectically composed 10th-century **Church of San**

Bartolomeo has a Baroque facade, a Romanesque tower, and 14 antique columns. *(Open M-Sa 9am-12:30pm and 4-6:30pm.)* The **Ponte Fabricio** (62 BC), commonly known as the **Ponte dei Quattro Capi** (Bridge of Four Heads), is the oldest in the city.

CENTRAL TRASTEVERE. Off the Ponte Garibaldi stands the statue of the dialect poet, G. G. Belli, in the middle of his own piazza, which borders P. Sonnino and marks the beginning of V. di Trastevere. On the left is the **Casa di Dante,** where readings of *The Divine Comedy* occur every Sunday from November to March. On V. di Santa Cecilia, beyond the courtyard full of roses, is the **Basilica di Santa Cecilia in Trastevere.** *(Open M-Sa 8am-12:30pm and 4:15-6:30pm, Su 9:30-10am, 11:15am-noon, and 4:15-6:30pm. Cloister open Tu and Th 10-11:30am, Su 11:30am-noon. Donation requested. Crypt €2.)* From P. Sonnino, V. della Lungaretta leads west to P. di S. Maria in Trastevere, home to the **Chiesa di Santa Maria in Trastevere,** built in the 4th century by Pope Julius II. Although the church is being restored, the 12th-century mosaics in the apse and the chancel arch glimmer in full splendor, depicting Jesus, Mary, and a bevy of saints and popes. *(Open M-Sa 9am-5:30pm, Su 8:30-10:30am and noon-5:30pm.)* North of the piazza are the Rococo **Galleria Corsini,** V. della Lungara, 10 (see **Museo Nazionale dell'Arte Antica,** p. 511), and, across the street, the **Villa Farnesina,** the jewel of Trastevere. Peruzzi built the suburban villa for banker Agostino Chigi ("il Magnifico") between 1508-1511. The museum's frescoed walls are the main attraction (see p. 511).

GIANICOLO. At the top of the hill, the **Chiesa di San Pietro in Montorio** stands on what is believed to be the site of St. Peter's upside-down crucifixion. The church contains del Piombo's *Flagellation,* from designs by Michelangelo. Next door in a small courtyard is Bramante's tiny ⬛**Tempietto.** A combination of Renaissance and ancient architecture, it was constructed to commemorate the site of Peter's martyrdom and provided the inspiration for the larger dome of St. Peter's. Rome's **botanical gardens** contain a **garden for the blind** as well as a rose garden that holds the bush from which all the world's roses are supposedly descended. *(Reach the summit via bus #41 from the Vatican or the medieval V. Garibaldi from V. della Scala in Trastevere (about a 10min. walk). Church and Tempietto open May-Oct. daily 9:30am-12:30pm and 4-6pm; Nov.-Apr. 9:30am-12:30pm and 2-4pm. Gardens: Largo Cristina di Svezia, 24, at the end of V. Corsini, off V. della Lungara. Open Apr.-Sept. Tu-Sa 9:30am-6:30pm; Oct.-Mar. M-Sa 9:30am-5:30pm.)*

NORTH OF TERMINI

BATHS OF DIOCLETIAN. From AD 298 to 306, 40,000 Christian slaves were kept busy building these 3000-person capacity public baths. They contained a heated marble public toilet with seats for 30 people, several pools, gymnasiums, art galleries, gardens, libraries, and concert halls. In 1561, Michelangelo undertook his last architectural work and converted the ruins into a church, the **Chiesa di Santa Maria degli Angeli.** In the 4th-century rotonda, to the right as you exit the church, statues from the baths are displayed. Viewing windows look down into the excavations. *(Open Tu-F 9am-2pm, Sa-Su 9am-1pm. Church open M-Sa 7am-6:30pm, Su 8am-7:30pm. Free.)*

PIAZZA DEL QUIRINALE. At the southeast end of V. del Quirinale, this piazza occupies the summit of the tallest of Rome's seven hills. The President of the Republic resides in the imposing **Palazzo del Quirinale,** a Baroque architectural collaboration by Bernini, Maderno, and Fontana. Down V. del Quirinale, V. Ferrara on the right leads down the steps to V. Milano. Farther along the street lies the marvelous facade of Borromini's **Chiesa di San Carlo alle Quattro Fontane.**

VIA XX SETTEMBRE. V. del Quirinale becomes V. XX Settembre at the intersection with V. delle Quattro, where the four corner buildings feature fountains with reclining figures. A few blocks down, Domenico Fontana's colossal 1587 **Fontana dell'Acqua Felice** graces the Baroque P. San Bernardo. The beefy statue of Moses was carved by Antichi. The facing **Church of Santa Maria della Vittoria** was built in honor of an icon of Mary that accompanied the Catholics to victory in a 1620 battle near Prague. Inside, Bernini's fantastic *Ecstasy of St. Theresa of Ávila* (1652) resides in the Cornaro Chapel. *(Open daily 7am-noon and 3:30-7pm.)*

VIA NOMENTANA. This road runs northeast from Michelangelo's **Porta Pia** out of the city. Hop on bus #36 in front of Termini, or head back to V. XX Settembre and catch bus #60. A 2km walk from Porta Pia past villas, embassies, and parks brings you to **Chiesa di Sant'Agnese Fuori le Mura,** V. Nomentana, 349. Its apse displays Byzantine-style mosaic of St. Agnes. Underneath the church wind some of Rome's most impressive ■**catacombs.** *(☎ 06 8620 5456 or 328 565 2414 to reach Danilo, the tour guide. Open Tu-Su 9am-noon and 4-6pm; M 9am-noon. Catacombs €5.)*

SOUTH OF TERMINI

BASILICA DI SANTA MARIA MAGGIORE. As one of the five churches in Rome granted extraterritoriality, this basilica, crowning the Esquiline Hill, is officially part of Vatican City. In 352, Pope Sixtus III commissioned the basilica when he noticed that Roman women were still visiting a temple to the pagan mother-goddess Juno Lucina. Sixtus tore down the temple to build his new basilica, substituting a Christian cult for a pagan one and celebrating the Council of Ephesus's recent ruling of Mary as the Mother of God. To the right of the altar, a marble slab marks **Bernini's tomb.** The 14th-century mosaics in the church's **loggia** recount the story of the miraculous August snowfall that showed the pope where to build the church. *(From Termini, exit south onto V. Giolitti, and walk down V. Cavour. Walk around to southeastern side to enter. Open daily 7am-7pm. Loggia open daily 9:30am-noon and 2-5:30pm. Tickets in souvenir shop; €2.70. Museum entrance through souvenir shop. Dress appropriately.)*

PIAZZA VITTORIO EMANUELE II AND ENVIRONS. The shabby P.V. Emanuele is home to one of Rome's largest outdoor **markets.** *(At the end of V. C Alberto, from S. Maria Maggiore.)* Scores of pilgrims come to the Rococo **Church of Santa Croce in Gerusalemme** to see the Fascist-era **Chapel of the Relics,** which contains fragments of the "true cross." Perhaps the eeriest of the chapel's relics is St. Thomas's dismembered finger, with which he probed Christ's wounds. *(P. S. Croce in Gerusalemme. M: A-San Giovanni. From P. S. Giovanni north of the Metro stop, go east on V. C. Felice; the church is on the right. From P. V. Emanuele II, take V. Conte Verde (V. S. Croce in Gerusalemme). Open M-Su 7am-7pm.)*

CHURCH OF SAN PIETRO IN VINCOLI. Dating from the 4th century, San Pietro in Vincoli is named for the sacred chains *(vincoli)* which bound St. Peter after his imprisonment on the Capitoline. The two chains were separated for more than a century in Rome and Constantinople, brought back together in the 5th century, and now lie beneath the altar. Michelangelo's ■**statue of Moses** presides over the church. *(M: B-Cavour. Walk southwest on V. Cavour, down toward the Forum. Take stairs on left up to P. S. Pietro in Vincoli. Open daily 7am-12:30pm and 3:30-7pm. Dress appropriately.)*

SOUTHERN ROME

CAELIAN HILL: CHURCH OF SAN CLEMENTE. The Caelian and the Esquiline are the biggest of Rome's seven original hills. In ancient times, Nero built his decadent Domus Aurea between them (see p. 499). **San Clemente** consists of a 12th-century church on top of a 4th-century church, with an ancient **mithraeum** and sewers at the bottom. The upper church holds medieval mosaics of the

Crucifixion, saints, and apostles, and a 1420s Masolino fresco cycle graces the **Chapel of Santa Caterina.** The 4th-century level contains the tomb of St. Cyril and a series of frescoes depicting Roman generals swearing in Italian, the first written use of the language. Farther underground is a creepy 2nd-century **mithraeum,** below which is the insulae, a series of brick and stone rooms where Nero is said to have played his lyre in AD 64 while the rest of Rome burned. A functional complex of Republican sewers lies 30m down. *(M: B-Colosseo. Turn left and walk east on V. Fori Imperiali (V. Labicana) away from the Forum; turn right into P. S. Clemente. From Manzoni (A) stop, walk west on V. A. Manzoni (V. Labicana); turn left into P. S. Clemente.* ☎ *06 7045 1018. Open M-Sa 9am-12:30pm and 3-6pm, Su and holidays 10am-12:30pm and 3-6pm. Lower basilica and mithraeum €3.)*

SAN GIOVANNI. The immense **Church of San Giovanni in Latero,** the cathedral of the diocese of Rome, was home to the pope until the 14th century. Founded by Constantine in 314, it is the city's oldest Christian basilica. The Gothic *baldacchino* houses two golden reliquaries containing the heads of **St. Peter** and **St. Paul. Scala Santa** houses the *acheropite* (a depiction of Christ not created by human hand) and what are believed to be the 28 marble steps used by Jesus outside Pontius Pilate's home in Jerusalem. Pilgrims win indulgence for their sins if they ascend the steps on their knees, reciting prayers on each step. Martin Luther experienced an early break with Catholicism while on pilgrimage here—in the middle of his way up the cathedral's steps, he realized the false piety of his climb and left. *(M: A-San Giovanni or bus #16 from Termini. Open daily 7am-7:30pm. Cloister open daily 9am-6pm. €2. Museum €1. Dress code enforced. The baptistery, just west of the church on the south end of P. di S. Giovanni in Laterano, is open only for masses and baptisms, usually on Su.)*

THE AVENTINE HILL. The easiest approach to the Aventine is from the western end of the Circus Maximus (the end farthest from the Circo Massimo Metro stop) at P. Ugo la Malfa. From here, V. di Valle Murcia climbs past some of Rome's swankiest homes and a beautiful public rose garden to a park with orange trees and a sweeping view of southern Rome. Across the park, another gate opens onto the courtyard of the **Chiesa di Santa Sabina,** with a porch of ancient columns and a towering *campanile.* V. S. Sabina continues along the crest of the hill to **Piazza dei Cavalieri di Malta,** home of the crusading order of the Knights of Malta. Through the ▓**keyhole** in the pale yellow gate, the dome of St. Peter's is perfectly framed by hedges. *(The rose garden is open daily 8am-7:30pm.)*

THE APPIAN WAY

CHURCH OF SANTA MARIA IN PALMIS. In this church, known as Domine Quo Vadis, a fleeing St. Peter had a vision of Christ. Asked "Domine Quo Vadis?" ("Lord, where are you going?"), Christ replied that he was going to Rome to be crucified again because Peter had abandoned him. Peter returned to Rome and suffered his own martyrdom. In the middle of the aisle, Christ's alleged footprints are set in stone. *(At the intersection of V. Appia Antica and V. Ardeatina. Bus #218 from P. S. Giovanni. Open M-Sa 7am-12:30pm and 2:30-7:30pm, Su 8:30am-1pm and 3-7:45pm.)*

CATACOMBS

M: A-San Giovanni. Take bus #218 from P. S. Giovanni to intersection of V. Ardeatina and V. d. Sette Chiese. €5, 15 and under €3. Free guided tour in the language of choice every 20min. San Sebastiano: V. Appia Antica, 136. From the #218 bus stop near S. Calisto and S. Domitilla, walk down V. Sette Chiese to V. Appia Antica and turn right. ☎ *06 785 0350. Open*

Dec.-Oct. M-Sa 8:30am-noon and 2:30-5:30pm; closed Nov. Adjacent church open daily 8am-6pm. San Calisto: V. Appia Antica, 110. Take the private road that runs northeast to the catacombs's entrance. ☎06 513 015 80. Open Th-Tu 8:30am-noon and 2:30-5pm; closed Feb. Santa Domitila: V. d. Sette Chiese, 282. Facing V. Ardeatina from San Calisto exit, cross street and walk right up V. Sette Chiese. ☎06 511 0342. Open Feb.-Dec. W-M 8:30am-noon and 2:30-5pm; closed Jan.

Since burial inside the city walls was forbidden during ancient times, fashionable Romans made their final resting places along the Appian Way, while early Christians secretly dug maze-like **catacombs** under their persecutors. **San Calisto** is the largest catacomb in Rome, with nearly 22km of subterranean paths. Its four levels once held 16 popes, seven bishops, St. Cecilia, and 500,000 other Christians. **Santa Domitilla** enjoys acclaim for an intact 3rd-century portrait of Christ and the Apostles. **San Sebastiano** was the temporary home for the bodies of Peter and Paul and contains three recently unearthed pagan tombs in remarkable shape.

TESTACCIO AND OSTIENSE

South of the Aventine Hill, the working-class district of Testaccio is known for its cheap and delicious *trattorie* and raucous nightclubs. Take Metro (B) to the Piramide stop or bus #27 from Termini. The neighborhood centers on the castle-like **Porta San Paolo** (an original remnant of the Aurelian walls) and the colossal **Piramide di Gaius Cestius,** which was built in about 330 days by the slaves of Gaius.

CIMITERO ACATOLICO PER GLI STRANIERI. This peaceful Protestant cemetery, or the "Non-Catholic Cemetery for Foreigners," is one of the only burial grounds in Rome for those who don't belong to the Catholic Church. Keats, Shelley, and Antonio Gramsci were interred here. *(From the Piramide station, follow V. R. Persichetti onto V. Marmorata, immediately turning left onto V. Caio Cestio. Ring bell for admission. Donation requested. Open Apr.-Sept. Tu-Su 9am-5:30pm; Oct.-Mar. 9am-4:30pm.)*

MONTE TESTACCIO. Monte Testaccio began as a Roman dumping ground for terracotta pots. The pile grew and grew, and today the ancient garbage heap, with a name derived from *testae*, or pot shards, rises in lush, dark green splendor over the drab surrounding streets. *(Follow V. Caio Cestio from V. Marmorata until it ends at V. Nicola Zabaglia. Continue straight onto V. Monte Testaccio. The hill is ahead and to the right.)*

BASILICA DI SAN PAOLO FUORI LE MURE. The Basilica di San Paolo Fuori le Mure, another of the churches in Rome with extraterritorial status, is the largest church in the city after St. Peter's. St. Paul is believed to be buried beneath the altar. Be sure to buy a bottle of monk-made **benedictine** (€5-15) in the gift shop. *(M: B-Basilica San Paolo, or take bus #23 or 769 from Testaccio at the corner of V. Ostiense and P. Ostiense. Open in summer daily 7am-6:30pm; in winter 7am-6pm. Cloister open in summer daily 9am-1pm and 3-6:30pm; in winter 9am-1pm and 3-6pm. Dress code enforced.)*

EUR. South of the city stands a monument to a Roman empire that never was. **EUR** (AY-oor) is an Italian acronym for Universal Exposition of Rome, the 1942 World's Fair that Mussolini intended to be a showcase of Fascist achievements. Apparently, the new, modern Rome was to shock and impress the rest of the world with its futuristic ability to build lots of identical square buildings. **Via Cristoforo Colombo,** EUR's main street, is the first of many internationally ingratiating addresses like "Viale Asia" and "Piazza Kennedy." It runs north from the Metro station to **Piazza Guglielmo Marconi** and its 1959 **obelisk.** *(Take bus #714 or the Metro B.)*

ABBAZIA DELLE TRE FONTANE (ABBEY OF THE THREE FOUNTAINS). According to legend, when St. Paul was beheaded here, his head bounced on the ground three times, creating a fountain at each bounce. The Trappist monks who live here today sell their own potent eucalyptus liquor for €7-12 and enormous bars of divine chocolate for €2-4. *(M: B-Laurentina. Exit the metro station and walk straight ahead to V. Laurentina; take a right and proceed about ¾ mi. north on V. Laurentina and turn right onto V. d. Acque Salve. The abbey is at the bottom of the hill. Open daily 8am-1pm and 3-7pm.)*

🏛 MUSEUMS

Etruscans, emperors, and popes have been busily stuffing Rome's belly full with artwork for several millennia, leaving behind a city teeming with galleries. Museums are generally closed and holidays, Sunday afternoons, and all day Monday.

VATICAN MUSEUMS

Walk north from the right-hand side of P. S. Pietro along the wall of the Vatican City about 10 blocks. From M: Ottaviano, take a left onto V. Ottaviano and continue walking until you reach the Vatican City Wall; turn right and follow the wall to the museum's entrance. ☎06 6988 4947 or 6988 4341. Information and gift shop (with the useful official guidebook, €7.50) on the ground level past the entrance of the building. Valuable CD-ROM audio guide €5.50. Guides are available in major languages, and most of the museums' staff speak some English. All major galleries open M-F 8:45am-3:30pm, Sa 8:45am-1:30pm. Last entrance 1hr. before closing. Closed on major religious holidays. €10, with ISIC card €7, children under 1m tall free. Free last Su of the month 8:45am-1:45pm. Most of the museum is wheelchair-accessible, though less visited parts, such as the upper level of the Etruscan Museum, are not. Snack bar between the collection of modern religious art and the Sistine Chapel; full cafeteria near main entrance. Plan to spend at least 4-5hr.

The Vatican Museums constitute one of the world's greatest collections of art, a vast storehouse of ancient, Renaissance, and modern statuary, painting, and sundry papal odds and ends. The museum entrance at V. Vaticano leads to the famous bronze double-helix ramp that climbs to the ticket office. A good place to start your tour is the stellar **Museo Pio-Clementino,** the world's greatest collection of antique sculpture. Two slobbering Molossian hounds guard the entrance to the **Stanza degli Animali,** a marble menagerie that highlights Roman brutality. Among other gems are the ▇**Apollo Belvedere** and the unhappy **Laocoön** family. The last room of the gallery contains the enormous red sarcophagus of Sant'Elena, Constantine's mother.

From here, the Simonetti Stairway climbs to the **Museo Etrusco,** filled with artifacts from Tuscany and northern Lazio. Back on the landing of the Simonetti Staircase is the Stanza della Biga (room of an ancient marble chariot) and the Galleria della Candelabra. The long trudge to the Sistine Chapel begins here, passing through the Galleria degli Arazzi (tapestries), the Galleria delle Mappe (maps), the Apartamento di Pio V (where there is a shortcut to *la Sistina,* for all the cheaters out there), the Stanza Sobieski, and the Stanza della Immaculata Concezione.

From the Room of the Immaculate Conception, a door leads into the first of the four ▇**Stanze di Rafaele,** apartments built for Pope Julius II in the 1510s. One *stanza* features Raphael's **School of Athens,** painted as a trial piece for Julius, who was so impressed that he fired his other painters, had their frescoes destroyed, and commissioned Raphael to decorate the entire suite. From here, there are two paths: a staircase leading to the brilliantly frescoed Borgia Apartments, the **Museum of Modern Religious Art,** and another route leading to the Sistine Chapel.

SISTINE CHAPEL. Since its completion in the 16th century, the Sistine Chapel (named for its founder, Pope Sixtus IV), has been the site of the College of Cardinals' election of new popes. Michelangelo's unquestioned masterpiece of a ceiling, gleaming from its recent restoration, is flat but appears vaulted. The simple compositions and vibrant colors hover above, each section depicting a story from Genesis.

The scenes are framed by the famous *ignudi*, young nude males. Michelangelo painted not flat on his back, but standing up and craning backward, and he never recovered from the strain to his neck and eyes. Michelangelo's *The Last Judgement* fills the altar wall. The figure of Christ as judge hovers in the upper center, surrounded by his saintly entourage and the supplicant Mary. The frescoes on the side walls predate Michelangelo's ceiling. On the right, scenes from the life of Moses complement parallel scenes of Christ's life on the left. The cycle was completed between 1481 and 1483 by a team of artists under Perugino including Botticelli, Ghirlandaio, Roselli, Pinturicchio, Signorelli, and della Gatta.

PINACOTECA. This is one of the best painting collections in Rome, including Filippo Lippi's *Coronation of the Virgin*, Perugino's *Madonna and Child*, Titian's *Madonna of San Nicoletta dei Frari*, and Raphael's *Transfiguration*. On your way out of the Sistine Chapel, take a look at the **Room of the Aldobrandini Marriage**, which contains a series of rare ancient Roman frescoes.

PRINCIPAL COLLECTIONS

GALLERIA BORGHESE

M: A-Spagna; take the exit labeled "Villa Borghese," walk to your right past the metro stop to V. Muro Torto and then to P. Porta Pinciana; Viale del Museo Borghese will be in front of you, and leads directly to the museum. Piazzale Scipione Borghese, 5. ☎ 06 841 6542, reservations 06 32 810. Open daily 9am-7pm. Entrance every hr., visits limited to 2hr.; last entrance 30min. before closing. Tickets may be reserved in advance by phone or in person for €1. Guided tours by reservation €5; audioguide rental €5. Tickets include ground floor galleries and Pinacoteca. €7, EU nationals under 18 or over 65 or students €4.25. Only 360 people are allowed in the museum at once; reservations are a must. The basement of the palace contains the ticket office and a bookshop selling an guidebook (€13). Expect to spend 2hr.

The exquisite Galleria's **Room I**, on the right, houses Canova's sexy statue of **Paolina Borghese** portrayed as Venus triumphant. The next rooms display the most famous sculptures by Bernini: a magnificent **David,** crouching with his slingshot; **Apollo and Daphne;** the weightless body in **Rape of Proserpina;** and weary-looking Aeneas in **Eneo e Anchise.** Don't miss six **Caravaggio** paintings, including his *Self Portrait as Bacchus and St. Jerome*, which grace the side walls. The collection continues in the *pinacoteca* upstairs, accessible from the gardens around the back by a winding staircase. **Room IX** holds Raphael's **Deposition** while Sodoma's *Pietà* graces **Room XII.** Look for self portraits by Bernini, del Conte's Cleopatra and Lucrezia, Rubens's **Pianto sul Cristo Morto,** and Titian's **Amor Sacro e Amor Profano.**

MUSEO NAZIONALE ETRUSCO DI VILLA GIULIA

In Villa Borghese at P. Villa Giulia, 9. M: A-Flaminio or bus #19 from Piazza Risorgimento or #52 from P. S. Silvestro. From Galleria Borghese, follow V. dell'Uccelliera to the Zoo, and then take V. d. Giardino to V. d. Belli Arte. The museum is to the left, after the Galleria Arte Moderna. ☎ 06 320 1951. €4, EU citizens and Canadians under 18 or over 65 free. Audioguide €4, guidebook €15, available at bookstore. Open Tu-Su 8:30am-7:30pm. Extended hours June-Sept. Sa 9am-11pm. Plan to spend 1½-2hr.

The villa was built under Pope Julius III, who reigned from 1550 to 1555. Highlights include a graceful sarcophagus of a married couple in **Room 9** and an Etruscan chariot, or *biga*, and the petrified skeletons of two horses found beside it in **Room 18.** Upstairs, archaeologists have put together the fragments of the entire facade of an Etruscan temple, complete with terracotta gargoyles, chips of the original paint, and a relief of the Greek warrior Tydaeus biting into the brain of a wounded adversary. Don't miss the famous Euphronios vase in a special exhibit near the giftshop.

CAPITOLINE MUSEUMS

On Capitoline Hill, behind the Vittorio Emanuele II monument. ☎06 3996 7800. Open Tu-Su 9:30am-7pm. Ticket office closes 1hr. before closing. €7.75, with ISIC €5.68, EU citizens under 18 or over 65 free. Guidebook €7.75-15.50, audioguide €3.61, daily tours in English €3.10. Reservations €1. Plan to spend 2-3hr.

The collections of ancient sculpture in the Capitoline Museums are among the largest in the world. The Palazzo Nuovo contains the original statue of **Marcus Aurelius** that once stood in the center of the piazza. The sculpture rooms have notables like *Dying Gaul, Satyr Resting,* and *Venus Prudens.* The sculpture collections continue across the piazza in the Palazzo dei Conservatori. See the fragments of the **Colossus of Constantine** and the famous **Capitoline Wolf,** an Etruscan statue that has symbolized the city of Rome since ancient times. At the top of the stairs, the pinacoteca houses an assortment of 16th- and 17th-century Italian paintings. Among the masterpieces are Bellini's Portrait of a Young Man, Titan's Baptism of Christ, and Rubens's Romulus and Remus Fed by the Wolf. Caravaggio's St. John the Baptist and Gypsy Fortune-Teller are worth seeing.

MUSEO NAZIONALE D'ARTE ANTICA

M: A-Barberini. Bus #492 or 62. Palazzo Barberini: V. delle Quattro Fontane, 13. ☎06 4200 3669. Open Tu-Su 8:30am-7:30pm. €6.03, EU citizens 18-25 €3.53, EU citizens under 18 or over 65 or EU university students €1.03. Plan to spend 1-1½hr. Palazzo Corsini: V. della Lungara, 10. Opposite Villa Farnesina in Trastevere. Take the #23 bus and get off between Ponte Mazinni and Ponte Sisto. ☎06 6880 2323. Open Tu-Su 8:30am-7:30pm. €4, EU students €2, EU citizens over 65 free. Wheelchair-accessible. Plan to spend 1hr.

This collection of 12th- through 18th-century art is split between Palazzo Barberini and Palazzo Corsini. The former houses more masterpieces, but both deserve a visit. **Palazzo Barberini** contains paintings from the medieval through Baroque periods, including works by Lippi, Raphael, El Greco, Carracci, Caravaggio, and Poussin. **Galleria Corsini** holds a collection of 17th- and 18th-century paintings, from Dutch masters Van Dyck and Rubens to Italians Caravaggio and Carracci.

VILLA FARNESINA

Just across from Palazzo Corsini on Lungotevere Farnesina. Bus #23; get off between Ponte Mazinni and Ponte Sisto. At V. della Lungara, 230. ☎06 6802 7268. Open M-Sa 9am-1pm. €4, under 18 €3, EU citizens over 65 free. Plan to spend 1hr.

The Villa was the sumptuous home to Europe's one-time wealthiest man, Agostino "il Magnifico" Chigi. For show, Chigi had his banquet guests toss his gold and silver dishes into the Tiber River after every course. However, he would secretly hide nets under the water to recover his treasures. To the right of the entrance lies the breathtaking **Sala of Galatea,** mostly painted by the villa's architect, Baldassare Peruzzi, in 1511. The vault displays symbols of astrological signs that add up to a symbolic plan of the stars at 9:30pm on November 29, 1466, the moment of Agostino's birth. The masterpiece of the room is Raphael's **Triumph of Galatea.** The stucco-ceilinged stairway, with its gorgeous perspective detail, ascends to the **Loggia di Psiche,** for which Raphael received the commission. The **Stanza delle Prospettive,** a fantasy room decorated by Peruzzi, offers views of Rome between trompe l'oeil columns. The adjacent bedroom, known as the Stanza delle Nozze (Marriage Room), is the real reason for coming here. Il Sodoma, who had previously been busy painting the pope's rooms in the Vatican, frescoed the room until Raphael showed up and stole the job. Il Sodoma bounced back, making this extremely masterful fresco of Alexander the Great's marriage to the beautiful Roxanne.

GALLERIA SPADA

From Campo dei Fiori, take any of the small streets leading to P. Farnese. With your back to Campo dei Fiori, take a left onto Capo di Ferro. Bus #64. P. Capo di Ferro, 13, in the Palazzo Spada. ☎06 32 81 01. Open Tu-Sa 8:30am-7:30pm, Su 9am-7:30pm. Last tickets sold 30min. before closing. €5, EU students €2.50, EU citizens under 18 or over 65 free. Reservations €1.03 extra. Guidebooks €10.33. Guided tour Su 10:45am from museum bookshop. Pamphlet guides in English available for each room of the exhibit. Plan to spend 1hr.

Seventeenth-century Cardinal Bernardino Spada bought a grandiose assortment of paintings and sculpture and commissioned an even more opulent set of great rooms to house them. Time and good luck have left the palatial apartments nearly intact—a visit to the gallery offers a glimpse of the luxury surrounding Baroque courtly life. In the first of the gallery's four rooms, the cardinal hung three portraits of himself by Guercino, Guido Reni, and Cerini. In the portrait-studded **Room 2,** look for paintings by the Venetians Tintoretto and Titan and a frieze by Vaga, originally intended to be placed in the Sistine Chapel. In **Room 4** are three canvases by the father-daughter team of Orazio and Artemisia Gentileschi.

MUSEI NAZIONALI ROMANI

Museo Nazionale Romano Palazzo Massimo: Largo di Via Peretti, 1. In the left-hand corner of P. dei Cinquecento. ☎06 481 5576; group reservations 06 3996 7700. Open Tu-Su 9am-7:45pm; ticket office closes 7pm. €6, EU citizens ages 18-24 €3, EU citizens under 18 or over 65 free. Audio guide in Italian and English €4. Museo Nazionale Romano Terme di Diocleziano: P. dei Cinquecento, 78. Opposite Termini. ☎06 3996 7700 for reservations. Open Tu-Su 9am-7pm. €5, EU citizens 18-24 €2.50, EU citizens under 18 or over 65 free. Audioguide €4; guided tour with archaeologist €3.50. Aula Ottogonale: V. Romita, 8. ☎06 3996 7700. Open Tu-Sa 9am-2pm, Su 9am-1pm. Free. Museo Nazionale Romano Palazzo Altemps: P. Sant'Apollinare, 44. Just north of P. Navona. Museum ☎06 783 3566 or ticket office ☎06 683 3566. Open Tu-Su, 9am-7pm. €5, EU citizens 18-24 €2.50, EU citizens under 18 or over 65 free. Audioguide €4.

The fascinating **Museo Nazionale Romano Palazzo Massimo** is devoted to the history of Roman art during the Empire, including the Lancellotti Discus Thrower, a rare mosaic of Nero's, and ancient coins and jewelry. Nearby, the **Museo Nazionale Romano Terme di Diocleziano,** a beautifully renovated complex partly housed in the huge **Baths of Diocletian** (p. 505) has exhibits devoted to ancient epigraphy (writing) and Latin history through the 6th century BC. The Aula Ottogonale, another wing, holds 19 classical sculptures in a gorgeous octagonal space. Across town is the Renaissance man of the trio, **Museo Nazionale Romano Palazzo Altemps,** P. S. Apollinaire, 44, just north of P. Navona. On display is ancient Roman sculpture, including the famous 5th-century *Ludovisi Throne.*

EUR MUSEUMS

P. G. Agnelli, 10. M: B-EUR-Palasport or B-EUR-Fermi. ☎06 592 6041. Open Tu-Sa 9am-6:45pm, Su and holidays 9am-1:30pm. €4.13, under 18 or over 65 free. V. Lincoln, 3. ☎06 5422 8199. Open Tu-Su 9am-8pm. €2, under 18 or over 65 free. Wheelchair-accessible. Museo Nazionale delle Arti e Tradizioni Popolari P. G. Marconi, 8. ☎06 591 0709. Open Tu-Su 9am-8pm.€4, under 18 or over 65 free. P. G. Marconi, 14. ☎06 54 95 21. Reservations ☎06 841 2312; guided tours in Italian, ☎06 841 2312. Open daily 9am-8pm. €4, EU citizens ages 18-25 €2, under 18 or over 65 free.

If anything good came of Mussolini's regime, it just might be the extensive collections in that bastion of fascist organization and architecture, EUR. The expansive **Museo della Civiltà Romana** contains excellent and comprehensive exhibits on ancient Rome, including incredibly intricate scale models of Trajan's Column (p. 499) and Republican and Imperial Rome. The smallest of the museums, the **Museo**

dell'Alto Medievo, exhibits weapons and other artifacts from the Dark Ages. The **Museo Nazionale delle Arti e Tradizioni Popolari** preserves Italian folk art and incredible replicas of traditional attire and farming equipment. Finally, the **Museo Preistorico ed Etnografico Luigi Pigorini** contains a collection of ethnographic artifacts, including the skull of the Neanderthal Guattari Man, found in Circeo.

OTHER COLLECTIONS

■ **MUSEO CENTRALE MONTEMARTINI.** The building, a turn-of-the-century electrical plant, contains a striking display of Classical sculpture. Highlights include *Hercules' Presentation at Mount Olympus,* a huge well-preserved floor mosaic of a hunting scene. *(V. Ostiense, 106. M: B-Piramide. From P. Ostiense, walk right of the train station to V. Ostiense. Then, walk or take bus #23 or 702 three stops. ☎ 06 574 8030. Open Tu-Su 9:30am-7pm. €4.13, EU citizens ages 18-24 €2.58, EU citizens under 18 or over 65 free.)*

GALLERIA COLONNA. Despite its disorganization and inhospitable opening hours, the Galleria Colonna remains an impressive collection of art. The *palazzo* was designed in the 18th century to show off the Colonna family's collection of art work, including Tintoretto's *Narcissus.* *(V. della Pilotta, 17. Just north of P. Venezia in the Centro Storico. ☎ 06 6678 4330. Open Sept.-July Sa 9am-1pm. €7, students €5.50, under 10 or over 65 free. Guide included in ticket at 11am in Italian and 11:45am in English.)*

GALLERIA DORIA PAMPHILJ. The Doria Pamphilj family, whose illustrious kin included Pope Innocent X, remain in custody of this stunning private collection, which they display in their palatial home. The villa's Classical art is arranged by size and theme. Caravaggio's *Rest During the Flight in Egypt,* Raphael's *Double Portrait,* and the preserved corpse in the small chapel are worth seeking out. *(From P. Venezia, walk up V. del Corso and take your 2nd left. P. del Collegio Romano, 2. ☎ 06 679 7323. Open F-W 10am-5pm, last tickets 4:15pm. €7.30, students and seniors €5.70. Audioguide included. Useful catalogue with €5.16 deposit. Private apartments 10:30am-12:30pm €3.10.)*

MUSEO MARIO PRAZ. This eccentric, smallish museum is housed in seven ornate rooms, the last home of Mario Praz (1896-1982), an equally eccentric and smallish professor of English literature and 18th- and 19th-century art collector. Superstitious neighbors spat or flipped coins when they saw him. *(At the east end of Ponte Umberto, right next to Museo Napoleonico. V. Zanardelli, 1, top fl. ☎ 06 686 1089. Must visit museum with small tour groups (35-45min.) that leave every hr. in the morning and every half-hr. in the afternoon. Open M 2:30-6:30pm, Tu-Su 9am-1pm and 2:30-6:30pm.)*

MUSEO NAZIONALE D'ARTE ORIENTALE. A wide array of artifacts from prehistory to the 1800s are divided into six sections: evolution of art in the Near East, Islamic art, Nepalese and Tibetan art, Indian Buddhist art, Southeast Asian art, and Chinese history. Also here are Stone Age fertility dolls and paintings of the Buddha. *(In Palazzo Brancaccio on the Esquiline Hill. V. Merulana, 248. ☎ 06 487 4415. Open M, W, F 9am-2pm; Tu and Th 9am-7pm; Su 9am-1pm. Closed 1st and 3rd M of each month. €4.13.)*

MUSEO CRIMINOLOGICO. After overdosing on "artwork" and "culture," get your aesthetic stomach pumped at this museum dedicated to crime and punishment. Torture devices cover the first floor, as well as some old English etchings, among them *A Smith Has His Brains Beaten Out With a Hammer.* On the second floor, learn the secrets of criminal phrenology and the language of tattoos. The third floor contains terrorist, spy, and drug paraphernalia. *(On Ponte Mazzini. V. del Gonfalone, 27. ☎ 06 6830 0234. Open Tu-W 9am-1pm and 2:30-6:30pm, Th 2:30-6:30pm, F-Sa 9am-1pm. May be closed Aug. €2, under 18 or over 65 €1.)*

🎵 ENTERTAINMENT

Check out the weekly *Roma C'è* (with an English-language section) or *Time Out*, both available at newsstands, for comprehensive and up-to-date club, movie, and event listings.

LIVE MUSIC

Rome hosts a variety of worthwhile musical performances, most of them during the summer. *Telecom Italia* hosts a classical music series at the Teatro dell'Opera. At 9am on concert days, unsold tickets are given out for free at the box office. Be prepared to get in line early; tickets go on a first come, first served basis. Local churches often host free choral concerts—check newspapers tourist offices and church bulletin boards for details. Finally, and perhaps most interestingly, the *carabinieri* frequently give rousing concerts of various Italian composers in P. di San Ignazio and other outdoor forums free of charge.

■ **Alexanderplatz Jazz Club**, V. Ostia, 9 (☎ 06 3974 2171). M: A-Ottaviano. Near Vatican City. From the station, head west on V. G. Cesare, take 2nd right onto V. Leone IV and 1st left onto V. Ostia. Night buses to P. Venezia and Termini leave from P. Clodio. Known as one of Europe's best jazz clubs, the stuffy, smoky atmosphere conveys the mythical feeling of a 40s jazz joint, while sparkling walls and a funky bar suggest a modern side. Cocktails €6.20. Required *tessera* (€6.20), good for 2 months. Open Sept.-June daily 9pm-2am. 10pm showings. Moves outside in summer to Villa Celimontana.

Accademia Nazionale di Santa Cecilia (☎ 06 361 1064; www.santacecilia.it). Bus #64. This conservatory, named for the martyred patron saint of music, was founded by Palestrina in the 16th century and is home to Rome's official symphony orchestra. Concerts are held at the **Auditorio Pio,** V. di Conciliazione, 4 (☎ 06 6880 1044), near the Vatican, while the Academy's grand new concert hall is being built. Regular season runs Oct.-June, covering the classics. From late June to late July, the company moves outdoors to the *nymphaeum* in Villa Giulia or to the Baths of Caracalla; see **Summer Events**, below. Auditorio Pio box office open Th-Tu 11am-7pm, on concert days to until show time. Tickets €10.33-39. Bad acoustics make expensive seats worth the splurge.

Teatro Ghione, V. d. Fornaci, 37 (☎ 06 637 2294; www.ghione.it), near the Vatican. This red velvet theater hosts Euromusica's classical concerts. Season Oct.-Apr. Box office open daily 10am-1pm and 4-8pm. English-speaking staff. Tickets from €8.26. Call for info on discounted morning concerts.

Cornetto Free Music Festival Roma Live (☎ 06 592 2100; www.bbcom.it), at a number of different locations around the city, including Stadio Olimpico and Valle Giulia. Concerts by the likes of Pink Floyd, the Cure, the Backstreet Boys, Ziggy Marley, Lou Reed, and Joan Baez, among others. Shows at 9:30pm.

Amici di Castel Sant'Angelo, Lungotevere Castello (☎ 329 414 0166; www.santangeloestate.it). Livens up Hadrian's Mausoleum in the summer with free concerts, part of **Sant'Angelo Estate**, daily 11pm-1am. Casual concerts are aimed at those simply strolling by the Castel. Look for occasional concerts by the Accademia Filarmonica Romana.

THEATER

Roman theaters, though not on par with those in other major European cities, still generate a number of quality productions, ranging from mainstream musicals to black-box experimental theater. For information on English theater, check the tourist office, *Roma C'è*, or online at www.musical.it or www.comune.rome.it.

Teatro Argentina, Largo di Torre Argentina, 52 (☎ 06 6880 4601 or 687 5445). Bus #64 from Termini or Tram #8. The most important theater in Rome, Argentina hosts plays (in Italian), concerts, and ballets. Sponsors many drama/music festivals around Rome. Call for shows and schedules. Box office open M-F 10am-2pm and 3-7pm, Sa 10am-2pm. Tickets around €20.60; students €15.50. AmEx/D/MC/V.

Teatro Colosseo, V. Capo d'Africa, 5a (☎06 700 4932 or 7720 4958). M: B-Colosseo. Walk away from the station with the Colosseum to your right for 1 block. Turn right and walk 2 blocks through P. Colosseo, then turn left onto V. Capo d'Africa. Offers a selection of alternative plays (Italian or translated into Italian), but also has an English theater night, featuring contemporary American and British works. Box office open Tu-Sa 6-9:30pm. Tickets €5-15.50, students €7.75. Closed in summer.

CINEMA

Unfortunately, most theaters in Rome show dubbed movies. Look for a "v.o." or "l.o." in any listing; it means *versione originale* or *lingua originale* (undubbed). In the summer, huge screens come up in piazzas around the city for **outdoor film festivals.** One of the most popular is the **San Lorenzo sotto le Stelle** film festival at Villa Mercede, V. Tiburtina, 113, with shows at 9 and 11pm (€5.16-7.75). Films are also usually shown outdoors on the southern tip of Tiber Island. Visit the **I Love Rome** web site (www.alfanet.it/welcomeItaly/roma/default.html) for an excellent searchable database of films, theaters, and show times, or check *Roma C'è.*

▨ **Il Pasquino,** P. Sant'Egidio, 10 (☎06 5833 3310 or 5833 3214), off P. S. Maria in Trastevere. Take Tram #8 from Largo Argentina to the 1st stop across the river. Go right on V. della Lungaretta to P. S. Maria in Trastevere. Rome's biggest English-language movie theater. Program changes daily; call ahead. €6.20. Theaters 2 and 3 are a film club, pay €1.03 for a 2-month membership and €5.16 for the ticket. Check in *Roma C'e* or *EstateRomana* for information on the summer Roma International Film Festival.

Nuovo Sacher, Largo Ascianghi, 1 (☎06 581 8116). Take V. Induno from V. d. Trastevere. Owned by famed Italian director Nanni Moretti; shows a host of indie films. M and Tu films €6.70; matinee and W €4.13.

SPECTATOR SPORTS

Though May brings tennis and equestrian events, sports revolve around *calcio,* or soccer. Rome has two teams in Serie A, Italy's prestigious league: the 2000 European champion **A.S. Roma** and **S.S. Lazio.** The wild games at the **Stadio Olimpico,** in Foro Italico, are held almost every Sunday (sometimes Saturdays) from September to June, with European cup matches often played mid-week. The can't-miss matches of the season are the two Roma-Lazio games, which often prove decisive in the race for the championship. Single-game tickets, typically starting at €15.50, can be bought at the stadium before games (although lines are long and tickets often run out), or at team stores: **A.S. Roma Store,** P. Colonna, 360 (☎06 678 6514; www.asroma.it; open daily 10am-10pm, tickets sold 10am-6:30pm; AmEx/MC/V); another store is at V. Appia Nuova, 130 (☎06 7759 0656); and **Lazio Point,** V. Farini, 34/36, near Termini. (☎06 482 6688; www.laziopoint.superstore.it. AmEx/D/MC/V.)

☐ SHOPPING

Everything you need to know about Italian fashion is summed up in one simple phrase: *la bella figura.* It describes a beautiful, well-dressed, put-together woman, and it is essential in Rome. Think whole picture: tinted sunglasses, Armani suit, Feragamo stilettos, and, stuffed in your Dolce & Gabbana bag, a *telefonino* with a signature ring. For men, a single gorgeous black suit will do the trick. If you're not a telecom heir or heiress, there are still ways to purchase grace and aplomb. Sales happen twice a year, in mid-January and mid-July, and a number of boutiques, while not as fashionable as their counterparts on the Via Condotti, won't require the sale of a major organ.

ROME

BOUTIQUES

Most of Rome's designer shops cluster around the Spanish steps, particularly on and about V. d. Condotti. If your shopping indulgences bring you to spend over €155 at one store, remember that you are eligible for a tax refund.

▨ **Dolce & Gabbana,** V. d. Condotti, 52 (☎06 6992 4999). Open M-Sa 10am-7:30pm.

▨ **Prada,** V. d. Condotti, 88-95 (☎06 679 0897). Open M-Sa 10am-7pm, Su 2-8pm.

▨ **Salvatore Ferragamo,** Men: V. d. Condotti, 64-66 (☎06 678 1130). Women: V. d. Condotti, 72-74 (☎06 679 1565). Open Sept.-May M 3-7pm, Tu-Sa 10am-7pm; June-July M-F 10am-7pm, Sa 9am-1pm.

Bruno Magli, V. d. Gambero, 1 (☎06 679 3802). Open M-Sa 10am-7:30pm.

Emporio Armani, V. d. Babuino, 140 (☎06 3600 2197). Houses the less expensive Armani line. Same hours as Armani.

Fendi, V. Borgogna, 36-40 (☎06 679 4824). Open M-Sa 10am-7:30pm, Su 11am-7pm.

Gianni Versace, Men: V. Borgognona, 24-25 (☎06 679 5037). Women: V. Bocca di Leone, 26 (☎06 678 0521). Open M-Sa 10am-7pm.

Giorgio Armani, V. d. Condotti, 75 (☎06 699 1460). Open M-Sa 10am-7pm.

Gucci, V. d. Condotti, 8 (☎06 678 9340). Open M 3-6pm, Tu-F 10am-7pm, Sa 9:30am-1:30pm.

CHEAP AND CHIC

Designer emporiums like **David Cenci,** V. Campo Marzio, 1-7 (☎06 699 0681; open M 4-8pm, Tu-F 9:30am-1:30pm and 4-8pm, Sa 10am-8pm); **Antonelo & Fabrizio,** C. V. Emanuele, 242-243 (☎06 6880 2749; open daily 9:30am-1:30pm and 4-8pm, in winter 3:30-7:30pm); and **Discount dell'Alta Moda,** V. Agostino Depretis, 87 (☎06 4782 5672; open M 2:30-7:30pm, Tu-Sa 9:30am-7:30pm) stock designer clothes and shoes at great discounts. Unless otherwise noted, all accept AmEx/MC/V.

▨ **Diesel,** V. d. Corso, 186 (☎06 678 3933). Off V. d. Condotti. Also at V. d. Babuino, 95. Italian-made Diesel is *the* label in European fashion. Stock up on jeans and t-shirts at prices far lower than elsewhere in the world. Open M-Sa 10:30am-8pm, Su 3:30-8pm.

Mariotti Boutique, V. d. Frezza 20 (☎06 322 7126). This elegant boutique sells modern, sophisticated clothes in gorgeous materials. Prices are steep; watch for sale discounts. Open M-Sa 10am-1:30pm and 3:30-8pm; in winter closed M morning.

Ethic, V. d. Corso, 85 (☎06 3600 2191), V. d. Pantheon, 46 (☎06 6830 1063), and V. d. Carozze, 20. The hip yet less adventurous can find a balance between the avant garde and tasteful. Prices won't break the bank. Open daily 10am-7:30pm.

SHOES

It's said that a building's only as good as its foundation; in high-fashion, an outfit's only as good as its shoes.

▨ **Trancanelli,** P. Cola di Rienzo, 84 (☎06 323 4503), V. d. Croce 68-9 (06 679 1503). A must for anyone looking to return home well-shod, but with their bank account intact. Open M 4-7:45pm, Tu-Sa 10am-7:45pm.

▨ **Bata,** V. Nazionale, 88a (☎06 679 1570), V. d. Due Macelli, 45 (06 482 4529). Bata has 250 shops in Italy and 6000 shops worldwide stocked floor to ceiling with affordable designer-esque shoes. Open M-Sa 9:30am-8pm, Su 4pm-8pm.

MISCELLANEOUS

▨ **Alcozer,** V. d. Carozze, 48 (☎06 679 1388). Near P. d. Spagna. Gorgeous old-world jewelry at decent prices. Earrings €22; a jeweled crucifix that would have suited Lucrezia Borgia for €65. Open M 2-7:30pm, Tu-Sa 10am-7:30pm. AmEx/MC/V.

■ **Materozzoli,** P. S. Lorenzo in Lucina, 5, off V. d. Corso (☎06 6889 2686). Old-world *profumeria* carries exclusive soap and perfume lines and shaving brushes. Open Sept.-July M 3:30-7:30pm, Tu-Sa 10am-1:30pm and 3:30-7:30pm. 10-28. AmEx/MC/V.

Campo Marzio Penne, V. Campo Marzio, 41 (☎06 6880 7877). Gorgeous fountain pens (€26+), leather goods, and brightly colored journals and photo albums (€25+). Open M-Su 10am-1pm and 2-7pm. AmEx/MC/V.

Disfunzioni Musicali, V. degli Etruschi, 4 (☎06 446 1984; fax 445 1704), in San Lorenzo. CDs, cassettes, and LPs available in a variety of languages and genres. Helpful staff. Board posted with ads for musicians and apartments. Open M-Sa 10:30am-8pm. Closed holidays and Ferragosto. MC/V.

▣ NIGHTLIFE

The following lists the best places in Rome to drink, grind, and go bump in the night. Romans find nighttime diversion at the pubs of San Lorenzo, the clubs of Testaccio, and everywhere in between. Check *Roma C'è* for the latest news on clubs openings and closings. *Time Out* covers Rome's sparse but solid collection of gay nightlife listings, many of which require an **ARCI-GAY pass** (€10.33 yearly). Also try checking with the **Circolo di Cultura Omosessuale Mario Mieli** (☎06 541 3985).

PUBS

If you long for organized, indoor drunkenness, try one of Rome's countless pubs. Diverse crowds and lively music draw huge crowds.

■ **Jonathan's Angels,** V. d. Fossa, 14-16 (☎06 689 3426), west of P. Navona. Take V. Pasquino (V. Governo Vecchio) from the southwest end of P. Navonna, a right on V. Parione, and a left on V. d. Fossa and head for the lights. Even Michelangelo's accomplishments pale before the loo, the **finest ▣ bathroom** in Rome, nay, Italy. Jonathan himself holds court in the right bar, his son, Jonathan II, spins underground techno on the left. Medium beer on tap €5; delicious cocktails/long drinks €8. Mercifully free of pub-crawlers. Open daily 9:30am-2am.

■ **Trinity College,** V. d. Collegio Romano, 6 (☎06 678 6472), off V. d. Corso near P. Venezia. Offers degrees in such diverse curricula as Guinness and Harp. Tuition €3.20-4.50. Happy hour noon-8pm. Classes daily noon-3am. AmEx/MC/V.

■ **Nuvolari,** V. degli Ombrellari, 10 (☎06 6880 3018), off V. Vittorio. This cocktail bar (serving beer and tropical drinks) also functions as an *enoteca* with wine by the glass (€3.50), a diverse wine list, salads (choose from 30 at €6 each), and meat and cheese platters (€7.50). Homemade deserts €3.50. Sporadically hosts live music. Open M-Sa 8pm-2am. Kitchen closes M-Th 12:45am, F-Sa 1:30am.

Rock Castle Café, V. B. Cenci, 8 (☎06 6880 7999; claudiorockcastle@libero.it). In the Jewish Ghetto. Discopub atmosphere. Resist the urge to drink Budweiser; the Beamish (€3.60) is much better for you. Popular in winter with study-abroad students. DJs and specials every night; W 9-10pm all you can drink beer €5. M 70s and 80s revival night. Open daily 9pm-2am.

Artu Cafe, Largo Fumasoni Biondi, 5 (☎06 588 0398). In P. San Egidio, directly behind Santa Maria in Trastevere. A small dark wood bar bathed in colored light located in a beautiful nook. Drinkers on their way to dinner or fresh from partying in Trastevere. Beer €4.50, wine €3-5.50 per glass, cocktails €6.20-7.20. Enjoy fresh-juice cocktails. Free *aperitivi* buffet 6:45-9pm. Open Tu-Su 6pm-2am. MC/V.

Il Simposio, V. d. Latini, 11 (☎0328 9077 8551). In San Lorenzo, off V. Tiburtina. Ah, the sweet smell of turpentine. The symposium's walls are cluttered with the Jackson Pollock-esque works of local artists, and chances are good that on any given night a splattered painter will be hard at work beautifying a discarded refrigerator. With cocktails from €3.50 and a glass of *fragolino* for €2.75, even starving artists can afford the place. Open Sept. to mid-July daily 9pm-2am.

ROME

Pub Hallo'Ween, P. Tiburtino, 31 (☎06 444 0705). In San Lorenzo, at the corner of V. Tiburtina and V. Marsala. Abandon all hope of not having fun, ye who enter here. The plastic skulls and spiderwebs confirm your suspicions that this is a gateway to the pits of Hell. Draft beer €3.50-5.50. Cocktails €5. Open Sept.-July daily 8:30pm-2:30am.

The Proud Lion Pub, Borgo Pio, 36 (☎06 683 2841). The outside of the pub says "Rome, Borgo Pio," but the beer and scotch says "hey, I don't forget my Highland roots." Affiliated with the Italian Dart Club; call and ask about upcoming tournaments. Beer and cocktails €4; single malts €4.50-5. Open M-Sa 8:30pm-everyone leaves.

The Drunken Ship, Campo dei Fiori, 20-21 (☎06 6830 0535; www.drunkenship.com). Because you're tired of meeting Italians. Because you feel the need to have an emotion-free fling with a kindred spirit. Because you're proud to be an American, dammit. Beer €5. Nightly themes 8-10pm; ask about drink specials. Happy hour daily 5-8pm. W 9-10pm power hour with all you can drink for €6. Open daily 11am-2am. AmEx/MC/V.

Sloppy Sam's, Campo dei Fiori, 9-10 (☎06 6880 2637). The poor cousin of the Drunken Ship. Happy hour 4-9pm. Beer €4; shots €3. Open Su-Th 4pm-12:30am, F-Sa 4pm-1:30am. AmEx/MC/V.

Zazerkalje, V. d. Equi, 57 (☎06 590 2237). In San Lorenzo, off V. d. Sabelli. Live music, every night is this place's big draw. Shows start after 11pm; €2.50 *tessera* required. In the morning, music and painting lessons are given to the disabled, in the afternoon a music school hosts jam sessions. Weekends offer the most credible music sessions, although the school's performances during the week attract decent crowds of music lovers. Beer €3, cocktails €4.50. Bar open 9pm-5am. Closed late July to Aug.

CLUBS

Italian discos are flashy and fun, but keep in mind that they often have dress codes and are generally not frequented by the backpacker set. Although many clubs close for the summer, the Testaccio clubs are dependable for most of the summer (through early August). Check *Roma C'è* or *Time Out* for the latest.

Chic and Kitsch, V. S. Saba, 11a (☎06 574 7417). Uniting the elegant with the eclectic. House is the music of choice. Cover: men €13, women €10.33 (include a drink). Open Sept.-July Th-Sa 11:30pm-4am.

Groove, V. Savelli, 10 (☎06 687 2427). Head down V. d. Governo Vecchio from P. Pasquino and take the 2nd left. Look for the black door. Lose it to acid jazz, funk, soul, and disco. F and Sa 1 drink min. (€5.16). Open W-Su 10pm-2am. Closed most of Aug.

Alien, V. Velletri, 13-19 (☎06 841 2212; www.aliendisco.it). One of the biggest discos in Rome attracts a well-dressed crowd and plays the house you know and love. As of this writing, the comfy chill-out room had not yet reached 1987. Cover about €15, including 1 drink. Open Tu-Su 11pm-5:30am. In summer, moves to Fregene.

Charro Cafe, V. di Monte Testaccio, 73 (☎06 578 3064). So you wanted to go to Tijuana, but got stuck in Rome. Weep no more, *mis amigos:* make a run for Charro, home of the €2.60 tequila *bum bum.* Italians guzzle a good selection of beer (€5) and strong Mexican mixed drinks (€5.50), while dancing to pop and house. Summer no cover; winter €5, with 1 drink. Restaurant M-Sa 8:30pm-midnight; club midnight-3am.

Aquarela, V. di Monte Testaccio, 64 (☎06 575 9058). A plethora of pottery shards—a fine example of Roman-style urban renewal. Built out of trash, then used for years as a vegetable market, the club consists in part of 2 underground tunnels that remain cool even when the party's heating up. Entrance €10, includes 1 drink. Arrive early to lounge in swank booths while you eat expensive Brazilian food. Open Tu-Su 8:30pm-3am.

Piper, V. Tagliamento, 9 (☎06 841 44 59; www.piperclub.it). North of Termini. From V. XX Settembre, take V. Piave (V. Salaria). Take a right onto V. Po (V. Tagliamento). Alternatively, take bus #319 from Termini to Tagliamento. A popular club that occasionally hosts gay nights. 70s, rock, disco, as well as the standard house and underground. Very gay friendly all the time. Teenaged crowd on some afternoons. Cover €10-18 (includes a drink). Open F-Sa 11pm-4:30am; in summer Sa and Su 11pm-4:30am.

Classico Village, V. Libetta, 3 (☎06 3751 8551). M: B-Garbatella. Exit onto V. Argonauti and take a left on V. Libetta. Women probably don't want to travel alone in this area at night. One of the best-known *centri sociali* in Rome—your one-stop shop for all things countercultural. Hosts live music, films, art exhibits, poetry readings, and African cuisine tastings. Summer theme nights. Hours and cover vary (€8-10).

ketumbar, V. Galvani, 24 (☎06 5730 5338). In Testacccio. Miss SoHo? Willing to pay €10 for a cocktail and €5 for a Coke in the original glass bottle? A taste of New York decadence in the middle of Italy. It even doubles as a Japanese restaurant (sushi €18-36). Wear black; everyone else will. Open M-Sa 8pm-3am. Closed Aug. AmEx/MC/V.

Jungle, V. di Monte Testaccio, 95. A small, smoky disco bar full of black leather-wearing Italian Goths (on Sa) variously dancing to the Cure and Italian pop. Extravagant, if somewhat disorienting, light effects. Cover €5-8. Admission free before 11pm. Beer €5; cocktails €7.75. Open F-Sa 11pm-5am.

NEAR ROME

Rural Lazio was originally called *Latium*, Latin for "wide land." Lazio stretches from the low Tyrrhenian coastline through volcanic mountains to the foothills of the *Abruzzese* Apennines. Romans, Etruscans, Latins, and Sabines all settled here, and their contests for supremacy make up some of the first pages of Italy's recorded history. When Rome's mayhem overwhelms you, head for the hills.

TIVOLI

Water is the chief attraction of the city of Tivoli, a hilltop town perched 120m above the Aniene River, only an hour from Termini. Poets Horace, Catullus, and Propertius once vacationed in villas lining the rocks overhanging the river. Modern Tivoli stretches beyond the original narrow strip, providing dynamic views of Rome from its hilly streets and gardens. Three distinct, extravagant villas are its principal sites.

📧⁊ TRANSPORTATION AND PRACTICAL INFORMATION. Take the **Metro (B)** to Rebibbia from Termini (15min.). Exit the station; follow the signs for Tivoli through an underpass to reach the other side of V. Tiburtina. Find the marker for the blue **ACOTRAL bus** to Tivoli. Tickets (€1.60) are sold in the bar next door or in the subway station. Once the bus climbs up to Tivoli (25min.), get off past P. Garibaldi at P. delle Nazioni Unite. The bus back to Rome leaves from P. Garibaldi. The **tourist office,** a round shack with a big "I" in front, is on the street leading from P. Garibaldi. It has information on the villas, maps, and bus schedules. (☎0774 31 12 49. Open M and W 9am-1pm, Tu and Th-Sa 9am-3pm and 4-7pm.) **Villa d'Este** is through the souvenir stands in P. Trento and to the left. For **Villa Gregoriana,** follow V. di Sibilla across town. For **Villa Adriana,** 5km from Tivoli proper, take the orange #4x bus from P. Garibaldi's newsstand, which also sells tickets (€0.77).

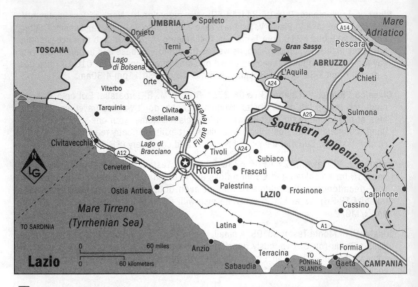

◉ SIGHTS. ▓Villa d'Este, a castle-garden, was laid out by Cardinal Ercole d'Este (the son of Lucrezia Borgia) and his architect Piero Ligorio in 1550 with the idea of recreating an ancient Roman nymphaea and pleasure palace. Spectacular terraces and fountains abound. (☎0774 31 20 70. Open May-Aug. Tu-Su 8:30am-6:30pm; Sept.-Apr. 9am-1hr. before sunset. €6.50, EU citizens 18-24 €3.25, EU citizens under 18 or over 65 free.) **Villa Gregoriana** is a park with paths that descend past temples and scattered grottoes carved out by rushing water. The star of the show is the **Great Cascade,** where the river plunges 160m from the opening of Gregory XVI's tunnel. (Open daily 9am-1hr. before sunset. €1.88, under 12 €0.52. The Villa has been closed indefinitely for restorations. Call the Tivoli tourist office at ☎0774 31 12 49 for more information.) Make time to visit the vast remains of **Villa Adriana,** the largest and most expensive ever built during the Roman Empire. Emperor Hadrian, inspired by his travels, designed its 2nd century buildings with an international flair. Look for the Pecile, built to recall the famous Stoa Poikile (Painted Porch) of Athens, and the Canopus, a statue-lined expanse of water built to replicate a canal in Alexandria, Egypt. (☎0774 53 02 03. Open daily 9am-1½hr. before sunset. €6.50, EU citizens 18-24 €3.25, EU citizens under 18 or over 65 free.)

ETRURIA

Welcome to Etruscanland, former home of a mythologized tribe that dominated North and Central Italy during the first millennium BC. Since the Etruscans' buildings were wood, only their carved-out tufa tombs survive. Tomb paintings (at Tarquinia) celebrate life, love, eating, drinking, and sport in the hilly countryside.

TARQUINIA

Trains (sometimes with a bus connection at Civitavecchia) leave Termini (1hr., 11 per day, last train leaves Tarquinia at 10:28pm, €5.60). Buses run from the train station to the beach (€0.60) and to the city center (€0.80) every 30min. Last bus to the station at 9:25pm.

When Rome was but a village of mud huts on the Palatine hill, Tarquin kings commanded this fledgling metropolis. Although little remains of the city, a subterranean necropolis lined with vibrant frescoes illustrates Tarquinia's history. In P. Cavour stands the majestic **Museo Nazionale,** one of the most comprehensive collections of Etruscan art outside Rome. It houses a superb patrimony of Etruscan sarcophagi with paintings still visible on the sides, votive statues, and an enormous range of Etruscan and Greek vases. Look for the famous **Winged Horses** upstairs. (☎ 0766 85 60 36. Open Mar.-Nov. Tu-Su 8:30am-7:30pm; Dec.-Feb. Tu-Su 2-7:30pm.) The ticket from the museum will admit you to the **necropolis.** Take the bus (dir.: Cimitero) from Barriera S. Giusto or walk 15min. from the museum. Head up C. V. Emanuele from P. Cavour and turn right onto V. Porta Tarquinia. Follow this road as it becomes V. delle Tombe Etruschi and runs to the necropolis. (☎ 0766 85 63 08. Open Mar.-Nov. 8:30am-7:30pm; Dec.-Feb. 8:30am-2pm.)

CERVETERI

First take the Metro (A) or bus #70 to Lepanto, and then take the blue COTRAL bus to Cerveteri from Lepanto (every 30min.-1hr., €2.50). To the necropolis, it's 1.5km from the village along a country road; follow the signs downhill and then to the right. Whenever you see a fork in the road without a sign to guide you, choose the fork on the right, but don't follow the "Da Paolo Vino" sign at the final fork. From Cerveteri, the last bus leaves for Rome at 8:05pm, with less frequent service on Su. The tourist office, V. d. Necropoli, 2, will answer queries. ☎ 06 995 2304. Open Tu-Su 9:30am-1pm. In winter, additional hours 2-7:30pm. Tombs: ☎ 06 944 0001. Open daily 9am-7:30pm; Oct.-Apr. Tu-Sa 9am-4pm. €4.13.

The Etruscans, believing they could take it with them, built **Cerveteri's Banditaccia Necropolis** and the ▨**Etruscan tombs,** stone houses for their dead. The houses for the living have decayed into oblivion, but the multi-room tombs are accessible.

LAKE BRACCIANO

Take Metro (A) to Lepanto, then take the COTRAL bus from Lepanto to Lake Bracciano (every hr., 6:40am-10:15pm, €2). Anguillara and Bracciano are also accessible by train on the Rome-Viterbo line (every hr.; from Rome's San Pietro station 5:35am-9:45pm, last return to Rome 10:14pm; €2.50).

About an hour away by bus, Lake Bracciano's volcanic sands and huge body of water provides Rome with its nearest freshwater beach. Fresh air, cool water, and a lush and hilly surrounding landscape compensate for its minor flaws. The impressive 15th-century **Orsini-Odescalchi Castle** dominates the town and offers some stunning frescoes and stuffed wild boars. (☎ 06 9980 4348; www.odescalchi.it. Open via tour Tu-F 11am-noon, 3pm-6pm; Sa-Su 9am-12:30pm, 3-6:30pm Tours in English available by booking in advance.) See *Roma C'è* for listings of classical concerts often held here in the summer. Bracciano's many *trattorie* cook up mounds of fresh lake fish and eel (the local specialty), though hours of operation are inconsistent. A ferry ride from the beach to nearby **Anguillara** or **Trevignano** across the lake offers more spectacular scenery.

PONTINE ISLANDS

The ▨Pontine Islands, a stunning archipelago of volcanic mountains 40km off the coast of Anzio, were once a haven for the notorious Saracen and Corsican pirates. The cliff-sheltered beaches, turquoise waters, assorted coves, tunnels, and grottoes provided the pirates a place to unwind after pillaging and plundering.

Take *aliscafi* (hydrofoils) or slower, cheaper *traghetti* (larger car ferries) to the islands. From **Rome,** take the **train** from Termini to Anzio (1hr., every hr., 6am-11pm, €2.90) and then the **CAREMAR ferry** from Anzio to Ponza (1hr.; June 16-Sept. 15 M-F 9:25am, Sa 8:30am, Su and holidays 8:30am and 3pm; return M-F 5pm, Sa 5:15pm, Su and holidays 11am and 5:15pm; €18.07). The **CAREMAR ticket office** in is in the white booth on the quay in Anzio (☎ 06 9860 0083; www.caremar.it) and in

ROME

Ponza (☎ 0771 80 565). The **Linee Vetor** hydrofoils (1hr.; 3-5 per day, 8:10am-5:15pm, return 9:50am-7pm; M-F €20, Sa-Su and Aug. €23) are faster. **Linee Vetor ticket offices** are on the quay in Anzio (☎ 06 984 5083; www.vetor.it) and in Ponza (☎ 0771 80 549). From **Formia**, CAREMAR runs 2 boats a day (3hr.; 9am and 5:30pm, return 5:30am and 2:30pm; €10.70), as does **Vetor** (M 2:30pm, Tu and Th-Su 8:30am and 2:30pm; return M 6:30pm, Tu and Th-Su 10am and 5:30pm; €20).

PONZA

In Ponza, Autolinee Isola di Ponza buses leave from V. Dante (every 15-20min. until 1am; buy tickets from driver; €1). Follow C. Pisacane as it becomes V. Dante (past the tunnel); the stop is on the left. Buses stop by request; flag them down at stops. Water taxis leave near the docks for beaches and harbors around the island (from €3 round-trip; arrange pick-up time with driver). Pro Loco tourist office is in the red building on V. Molo Musco, at the port's far right next to the lighthouse. (☎ 0771 80 672; prolocoponza@libero.it. Open in summer M-Sa 9am-1pm and 4-8:30pm, Su 9am-1pm and 5-8:10pm.)

Excellent beaches are everywhere on Ponza, including **Cala dello Schiavone** and **Cala Cecata** (on the bus line). **Chiaia di Luna** and ■**Piscine Naturali** are musts for any beach lover. A 10min. walk from the port will take you to Chiaia, set at the foot of a spectacular 200m cliffside. A lovely ride through Ponza's hillside will take you to the even lovelier Piscine Naturali. (Take the bus to Le Foma and ask to be let off at the Piscine. Cross the street and go down the long, steep path.) Cliffs crumbling into the ocean create a series of deep, crystal-clear natural pools separated by smooth rocky outcroppings perfect for sunbathing. Although there are spots for cliff-diving in the area, *Let's Go* does not recommend jumping off 15m cliffs.

Hotel rooms on Ponza hover in the €100 zone. *Let's Go* recommends foregoing hotels entirely and checking out one of many *immobiliare vacanze* (vacation property) offices instead. The tourist office has a list of over ten helpful agencies that can assist you in finding a room or apartment. The folks at ■**Isotur ❹**, Corso Piscacane, 18, are friendly and, more importantly, can set you up with a cheap double room in nearby Santa Maria, which is really an extension of Ponza. (☎ 0771 80 339; www.isotur.it. Open May M-F 9:30am-12:30pm and 4:30-8pm, Sa 9:15am-1pm and 4-8:30pm; June-August daily 9:15am-8:30pm. €45 in June; €60 in August; apartments for six for a week €400-1300.) Restaurants are on the expensive side, with plates of pasta generally around €10. The seafood and view at **Ristorante da Antonio ❹**, on the water at V. Dante, make it worth the splurge. (☎ 0771 80 98 32.)

PALMAROLA

Palmarola is an uninhabited islet perched off the northeast coast of the island. The irregular volcanic rock formations and steep white cliffs of the island are incredible. As you approach Palmarola, you will see **Dala Brigantina**, a natural lime amphitheater. Most excursions visit the **Pilatus Caves** at Ponza, a breeding ground for fish. To get to Palmarola, you have to rent a **boat** (from €35 per day), or sign up for a **boat tour** advertised at the port as *"una gita a Palmarola."*

ZANNONE

Zannone is only accessible by boat. Try Cooperativa Barcaioli Ponzesi, C. Piscacane at the S. Antonio tunnel. (☎ 0771 80 99 29. 10:30am, return 6pm; €20.)

Zannone is a nature and wildlife preserve, offering nature-lovers a refreshing break from the beach. Tours will take visitors around the coast, with time for walks on the *mufloni*-strewn island, through the *leccese* forests, and to the medieval monastery S. Spirito.

VENTOTENE

Aliscafi Alilauro hydrofoils travel from Ponza to Ventotene July-Aug. (45min.; 9:25am and 3:10pm, return 4:30pm; €9, Sa-Su €13). The tourist office, Tourist Quality Point, is at the port. ☎ 0771 85 341. Open daily 9am-1pm and 4:30-7pm; in winter 4-7pm.

On Ventotene, cars and *motorini* are verboten and the calm of island life is disturbed only by the hum of outboard motors. The tourist office offers tours of various archaeological sites, and splendid beaches flank the port.

SABAUDIA

CO.TRA.L buses leave EUR-Fermi for Sabaudia, on the Termini-Rebibbia side of the metro station (2hr.; one bus approximately every 2hr.; 6:45am-7:30pm, return 5:35am-6:20pm, or catch the 8:20pm bus to Latina where a connecting bus to Rome awaits; €3.60). CO.TRA.L buses arrive in P. Oberdan. A right onto C. Vittoria Emmanuele II leads to P. del Comune, where the tourist office is located. Pro Loco tourist office, P. del Comune, 18-19 (☎ 0773 51 50 46; fax 51 80 43; www.proloco.sabaudia.net) offers hotel and restaurant listings, as well as maps and info on the National Park and how to hike it. The office also sells train and bus tickets, as do tabaccherie. Open daily 9am-noon and 5-8pm. Near P. del Comune is V. Principe di Piemonte, which runs to the Giovanni XXIII bridge, V. Lungomare, and the beach. Orange city buses to the beach leave from P. Oberdan during the week, every 10min. from P. Savoia on weekends (€1).

Constructed as a part of Mussolini's grandiose vision to re-build the Ancient Roman Empire and extend Rome's boundaries to the coastline during the 30s, Sabaudia is an odd mix of astounding natural beauty and stupefyingly unappealing fascist architecture. Located in the Pontine region, Sabaudia is surrounded by Roman ruins, quiet farmland, and the **Circeo National Park** (with its four coastal lakes), all of which more than compensate for the town's rather dour gridded streets and industrial piazzas. Sabaudia retains its vitality by its proximity to Monte Circeo and serving as a stopover point for caravans of sun-lovers heading over kayak-filled **Lake Paola** to 23km of dazzling dunes and stretches of beautiful **free beaches**.

SOUTHERN ITALY

CAMPANIA

To the casual observer, life in Campania might appear to gravitate around natural disasters. The submerged city at Baia, lava-smothered Pompeii, and the ruins of Benevento attest to a land at the mercy of the ancient mythical elements of water, fire, wind, and earth. The human element asserts itself in the bustle of Naples's nightlife, stolid churches and museums, and ancient cities frozen in time. But when the city streets get too hot and the water calls, the islands off the Amalfi coast are sprinkled with windswept beaches and hidden coves. Invigorating hikes over jutting cliffs and extraordinary volcanoes dotting the coast and countryside provide unrivaled panoramas.

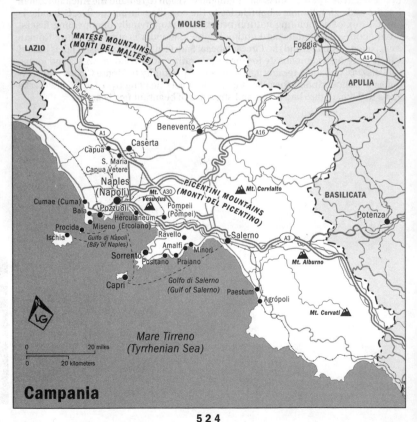

Campania

HIGHLIGHTS OF CAMPANIA

DELIGHT in the *Farnese Bull,* the largest ancient sculpture, and marvel at the Alexander mosaic in Naples's **Museo Archeologico Nazionale** (p. 602).

CATCH Pompeii (p. 546) in the act as you play volcanic voyeur.

DIVE into Capri's glowing **Grotta Azzurra** (p. 558).

RELISH the glorious beaches and stunning seascapes of the **Amalfi Coast** (p. 564).

REVERBERATE in the **Temple of Mercury** in Baia (p. 543).

GO templing in **Paestum** (p. 578), home to remarkably preserved Greek monuments.

TEMPT your hunger with chili-laced chocolate (p. 537), then satisfy it with one of Naples's legendary pizzas (p. 534).

BURN your toes in Ischia's boiling hot springs (p. 562).

PRETEND to be a toga-clad Roman noble at the intact villas in **Herculaneum** (p. 550).

NAPLES (NAPOLI) ☎ 081

Italy's third-largest city is trying desperately to emerge from the shadow of its *brutta reputazione* (bad reputation). Rampant poverty, unemployment rates closing in on 25%, and a northern Italian political party itching to cut the country in half at Rome assure that problems abound. Naples is nonetheless making progress, and many old stereotypes are becoming obsolete. More police officers on the streets and the advent of the *Napoli 99*, a group of citizens determined to maintain the city's art and restore public monuments, have made Naples a *luoga bella* (lovely locale) with some surmountable vices. UNESCO recently declared Naples's historic center the most architecturally varied in the world. The narrow streets are a constant flurry of people and cars, and the historic center is a treasure trove of piazzas, palaces, exquisite churches and public art, artisan's workshops, and colorful *trattorie.* Naples is also a cheap and convenient place to stay near Capri, Pompeii, Mt. Vesuvius, and the surrounding beaches.

◼ INTERCITY TRANSPORTATION

Flights: Aeroporto Capodichino (☎081 789 6742) V. Umberto Maddalena, northwest of city. Convenient **CLP bus** (☎081 531 1706 or 531 1707) leaves from P. Municipio (20min., 6am-10:30pm, €1.55). The #15 and 3S city buses run from P. Garibaldi to airport (€0.77). A **taxi** from the center costs €15. **Alitalia,** V. Medina, 41/42 (☎848 86 56 43), off P. Municipio. Open M-F 9am-4:30pm. **British Airways** (☎848 81 22 66). Open M-F 8am-8pm, Sa 9am-5pm. **Lufthansa** (☎066 568 4004).

Trains: Naples is served by 3 train companies that each leave from **Stazione Centrale.**

FS: Frequent connections to: **Brindisi** (5hr., 5 per day, 11am-8pm, €8.85); **Milan** (8hr., 13 per day, 7:30am-10:30pm, €49.58); **Rome** (2hr., 34 per day, 4:30am-10:06pm, €9.61); **Salerno** (45min., 8 per day, 8am-9pm, €2.74); and **Syracuse** (10hr., 6 per day, 10am-9:30pm, €28.41).

Circumvesuviana: (☎081 772 2444). From Stazione Centrale (1 floor underground) to: **Herculaneum** (€1.55); **Pompeii** (€1.90); and **Sorrento** (€2.84). Trains depart every 30min. 5:09am-10:42pm.

Ferrovia Cumana and **Ferrovia Circumflegrea:** (☎800 00 16 16). Luggage storage available (p. 531). Both run Metro lines from Montesanto station to **Pozzuoli** and **Cumae.** Trains depart every 20min. Info booth in Stazione Centrale open daily 7am-9pm.

Ferries: Ferry schedules and prices change constantly; check ahead. *Qui Napoli* (free at the tourist office) and the newspaper *Il Mattino* (€0.77) both carry current ferry schedules. Prices listed here are for May-Oct. Weekend prices are often higher. Nov.-Apr. ferries run slightly less frequently. Ask about port taxes. Hydrofoils depart from **Molo Beverello** and **Mergellina,** and ferries from **Molo Beverello, Stazione Marittima,** and **Pozzuoli.** Stazione Marittima is for longer trips to Palermo and the Isole Eolie. Molo Beverello is at the base of P. Municipio. Take the R2 bus from P. Garibaldi to P. Municipio.

Caremar: (☎081 551 3882). Ticket office on Molo Beverello. Open daily 6am-10pm. Ferries and hydrofoils depart for: **Capri** (ferry: 1½hr., 6 per day, 5:45am-6:30pm, €5; hydrofoil: 1hr., 4 per day, 7:55am-8:30pm, €10); **Ischia** (ferry: 1½hr., 8 per day, 6:25am-9:55pm, €5; hydrofoil: 1hr., 6 per day, 7:50am-8:10pm, €10); and **Procida** (ferry: 1hr., 7 per day, 6:25am-9:55pm, €5; hydrofoil: 40min., 6 per day, 7:40am-7:45pm).

Siremar Lines: (☎081 580 0340; fax 580 0341). Ticket office at Molo Angioino. Depart from Stazione Marittima. Open daily 9am-7pm. Ferries 2 per wk.; in winter 3 per wk. To: **Lipari** (12hr.), **Stromboli** (8hr.), **Vulcano** (13hr.), and points along the routes. Prices vary.

Tirrenia Lines: (☎081 199 123 199). Ticket office at Molo Angioino. Depart from Stazione Marittima. Open daily 8:30am-1:15pm and 2:30-5:30pm. Ferries to **Cagliari** (15hr., 2 per wk., in winter 1 per wk.) and **Palermo** (11hr.). Required supplemental port tax. Schedules and prices vary.

SNAV: (☎081 761 2348; www.snavali.com). Open daily 9am-7pm. Runs hydrofoils Apr.-Oct. to: **Capri** (1 hr., 6 per day, 7:10am-6:10pm); **Ischia-Cassamicciola Terme** (1hr., 4 per day, 8:30am-6:25pm, €10); **Palermo** (5hr., varying schedule and prices); and **Procida** (40min., 4 per day, 8:30am-6:25pm, €10). AmEx/MC/V.

Linee Lauro: (☎081 551 3352 or 552 2838). Ticket office at Molo Angioino. Depart from Molo Beverello. Open daily 9am-7pm. Ferries to **Ischia** (3 per day, 8:40am, 1:55pm and 7pm, €10-20) and **Tunis** (19hr., varying schedules and prices, call Linee Lauro for details).

■ ORIENTATION

Think of Naples as divided into five areas: **train station, waterfront, hilltop, downtown,** and **historic center.** The **train station** is dominated by **Piazza Garibaldi,** a jumbled mess of buses and vendors selling their wares (don't buy them). There are several budget accommodations around here, but the area is fairly seedy, so use caution when selecting a hotel. P. Garibaldi is also the central hub for the Naples bus lines. The main road leading out of P. Garibaldi is Corso Umberto I, which splits at Piazza Bovio (just after the University) into V. G. Sanfelice on the right leading to downtown, and V. De Pretis on the left leading to the waterfront. The waterfront is accessible from several key piazzas: **P. Municipio,** the destination of the R2 bus line; **P. Trieste e Trento/P. Plebiscito,** adjoining piazzas on the other side of Castel Nuovo and Palazzo Reale; **P. dei Martiri,** arrived at by following V. Chiaia out of P. Trieste e Trento; and **P. Amadeo,** where there is a Metro stop, and which can be reached by following V. Filangieri out of P. dei Martiri. **Mergellina,** the last part of the waterfront, is accessible by Metro. Linking the waterfront, downtown, and historical district is the chic pedestrian shopping street of V. Toledo. Piazzas Dante and Carita, both along V. Toledo, are on the western extreme of the historical district. Taking a right (walking from the waterfront) at either of these will lead to the winding and church-filled roads of the historical district, home also to good budget accommodations, beautiful sights, and lively nightlife. A right off V. Toledo onto V. Maddaloni (between P. Carita and Dante, coming from the waterfront) will lead you through the central piazzas of the historical district, P. Gesu Nuovo, and P. San Domenico Maggiore, and will then intersect V. Duomo before almost reaching P. Garibladi and the train station, accessible by taking a right and then a left. The Vomero hilltop can be reached by using the various funiculars around town, at P. Amadeo, V. Toledo, and P. Montesanto. The hilltop has lovely museums and great views of the city sprawling below. Reach the Capodimonte hilltop by the #160 bus from the Museo Nazionale. If you plan to be in town for a few days, the tourist office, hostels, museums, and the like eagerly hand out detailed maps. Pick up a free *Napoli by Bus* brochure for bus system assistance.

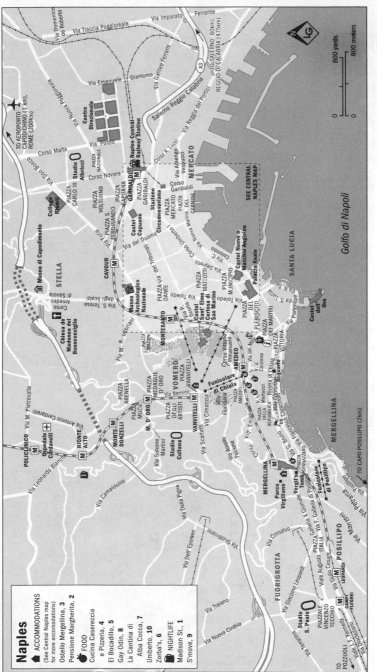

Naples

▲ ACCOMMODATIONS
(See Central Naples map
for more accomodations)
Ostello Mergellina, **3**
Pensione Margherita, **2**

🍴 FOOD
Cucina Casereccia
e Pizzeria, **4**
El Bocadillo, **5**
Gay Odin, **8**
La Cantina di
Alba Cocca, **7**
Umberto, **10**
Zorba's, **6**

🎵 NIGHTLIFE
Madison St., **1**
S'move, **9**

Golfo di Napoli

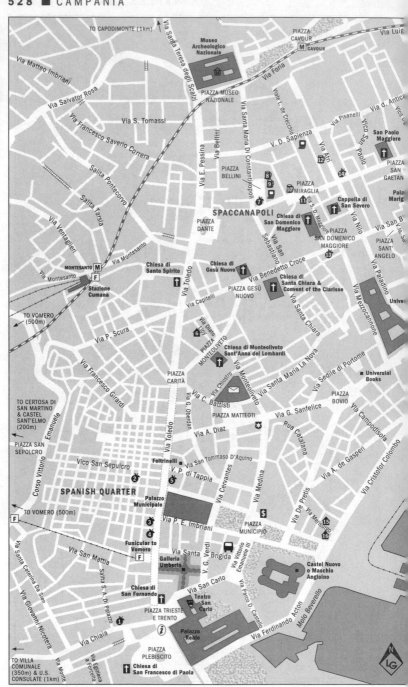

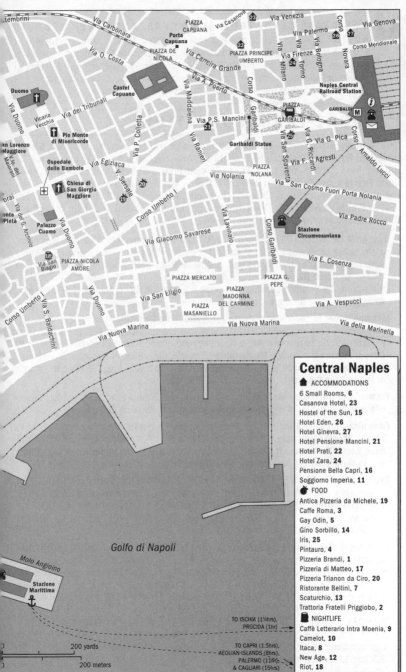

Central Naples

🏠 **ACCOMMODATIONS**
6 Small Rooms, **6**
Casanova Hotel, **23**
Hostel of the Sun, **15**
Hotel Eden, **26**
Hotel Ginevra, **27**
Hotel Pensione Mancini, **21**
Hotel Prati, **22**
Hotel Zara, **24**
Pensione Bella Capri, **16**
Soggiorno Imperia, **11**

🍽 **FOOD**
Antica Pizzeria da Michele, **19**
Caffe Roma, **3**
Gay Odin, **5**
Gino Sorbillo, **14**
Iris, **25**
Pintauro, **4**
Pizzeria Brandi, **1**
Pizzeria di Matteo, **17**
Pizzeria Trianon da Ciro, **20**
Ristorante Bellini, **7**
Scaturchio, **13**
Trattoria Fratelli Priggiobbo, **2**

🎵 **NIGHTLIFE**
Caffè Letterario Intra Moenia, **9**
Camelot, **10**
Itaca, **8**
New Age, **12**
Riot, **18**

Golfo di Napoli

TO ISCHIA (1½hrs),
PROCIDA (1hr)

200 yards

200 meters

TO CAPRI (1.5hrs),
AEOLIAN ISLANDS (8hrs),
PALERMO (11hr)
& CAGLIARI (15hrs)

❗ DON'T TAKE CANDY FROM STRANGERS, AND OTHER GOOD ADVICE. Though violent crime is rare in Naples, theft is common (unless you're in the *Camorra*, the Neapolitan mafia, in which case the opposite is true). Be smart. Don't carry your money in wallets or purses. Do not wear eye-catching jewelry or flaunt expensive cameras. Young women should avoid eye contact with strangers and should travel in mixed company whenever possible.

⊑ LOCAL TRANSPORTATION

One "Giranapoli" ticket is valid for all modes of transport in Naples: **bus, Metro, tram,** and **funicular.** Tickets are available at *tabacchi* in 3 types: 1½hr. for €0.77, full-day for €2.32, month for €23.24. To visit Pozzuoli, Vesuvius, or Cumae, take **Unico Fascia 1** and **Fascia 2** on the cost-effective ANM, CTP, Sepsa, FS, and Circumvesuviana transport lines. Unico Tickets cost between €1.29 and €3.36 and are also available at *tabacchi*. Everything stops running around midnight, except for the unreliable *notturno* (nighttime) buses.

Bus: ANM (☎ 081 763 2177). Open Su-F 8:30am-6pm. Remember to validate your ticket at the yellow boxes and pick up a copy of the essential *Naples by Bus* brochure. All stops have signs indicating their routes and destinations. **R1** travels from P. Bovio to Vomero (P. Me. Oro) and **R2** runs from P. Garibaldi to P. Municipio. **3S** connects "3 Stations": the airport, the Stazione Centrale in P. Garibaldi, and the Bay of Naples Molo Beverello, where boats leave for Capri, Sorrento, and Ichia.

Metropolitana: To cover long distances (e.g., from the train station to P. Cavour, Montesanto, P. Amedeo, or Mergellina), use the efficient Metro that runs west to Pozzuoli from P. Garibaldi. Go to platform #4, 1 floor underground at Stazione Centrale. Stops at **P. Cavour** (Museo Nazionale), **Montesanto** (Cumana, Circumflegrea, funicular to Vomero), **P. Amedeo** (funicular to Vomero), **Mergellina,** and **Pozzuoli.** If you're going to Procida or Ischia, take the Metro to Pozzuoli and depart from there.

Trams: From the station to Mergellina along the coast. Tram #1 stops at the Molo Beverello port. Catch it in front of the Garibaldi statue near Stazione Centrale.

Funiculars: 3 connect lower city to Vomero: **Centrale,** most frequently used, runs from V. Toledo; **Montesanto** from P. Montesanto; **Chiaia** from P. Amedeo. Centrale and Chiaia have intermittent stops at Corso Vittorio Emanuele. A 4th, **Mergellina,** connects Posillipo to Mergellina. (M-Sa 4 per hr., 7am-10pm; Su reduced service, 8am-7pm.)

Taxis: Cotana (☎ 081 570 7070), **Napoli** (☎ 081 556 4444), or **Partenope** (☎ 081 556 0202). Only take taxis with meters. No English spoken. **Consortaxi** (☎ 081 552 5252). **Radiotaxi** (☎ 081 551 5151). Radiotaxi's **Taxi Rosa** provides a safe taxi service for women who call 10pm-6am. €2.10 surcharge 10pm-7am. An additional €2.60 from the airport and a €4.15 minimum.

Car Rental: Avis (☎ 081 128 4041; fax 554 3020), C. A. Lucci, 203, just off of P. Garibaldi near the train station. Cars from €165.20 for 2 days; €355.82 per wk.. Open M-F 8am-7:30pm, Sa 8:30am-1pm and 4-6pm, Su 9am-1pm. Another office in the airport (☎ 081 780 5790). Additional 12% tax on cars rented at the airport. Open M-Su 7am-midnight. AmEx/MC/V. **Hertz,** P. Garibaldi, 91 (☎ 081 20 62 28, fax 554 8657). From €57.80 per day, €300-350 per wk. Another office near the airport at V. Scarfoglio, 1 (☎ 081 570 8701; fax 570 7862). Additional 12% tax applies. Open M-F 8am-1pm and 2-7pm, Sa 8:30am-1:30pm. AmEx/MC/V. **Maggiore Budget** (☎ 081 28 78 58), in Stazione Centrale. From €78 per day; €312 per wk. Open M-F 8am-1pm and 3-7pm, Sa 8:30am-1:30pm. AmEx/MC/V.

🗹 PRACTICAL INFORMATION

TOURIST, FINANCIAL, AND LOCAL SERVICES

Tourist Offices: EPT (☎081 26 87 79; fax 20 66 66), at Stazione Centrale. Calls hotels and ferry companies. Grab a map and the indispensable ▨ *Qui Napoli*, a monthly updated tourist publication full of schedules, events, and listings. English spoken. Open M-Sa 8:30am-8pm, Su 8am-2pm. **Main office**, P. dei Martiri, 58 (☎081 40 53 11). Open M-Sa 9am-8pm. Branch at **Stazione Mergellina** (☎081 761 2102). Open M-Sa 8:30am-8pm, Su 8am-2pm. **OTC** (☎081 580 8216; fax 41 03 59; osservatorio@comune.napoli.it), at Palazzo Reale in P. Plebiscito, is eager to assist you. Open M-F 9am-6:30pm.

Budget Travel: CTS, V. Mezzocannone, 25 (☎081 552 7960), off C. Umberto on the R2 line. Student travel info, ISIC and FIYTO cards, and booking services. Open M-F 9:30am-1:30pm and 2:30-6:30pm, Sa 9:30am-12:30pm. **Other CTS branches at:** V. Cinthia, 36 (☎081 767 7877; open M-F 9:30am-1:30pm and 2:30-7pm, Sa 9:30am-2pm) and V. Scarlatti, 198 (☎081 558 6597; open M-F 9:30am-7:30pm, Sa 9:30am-2pm). **CIT,** P. Municipio, 69 (☎081 552 5426), is a comprehensive travel agency. Open M-F 9am-1pm and 3-6pm. **Italian Youth Hostel Organization** (☎081 761 2346), at the Mergellina hostel (see p. 533). HI info. HI cards €15. Open M-F 9am-1pm and 3-6pm.

Consulates: US (☎081 583 8111; 24hr. emergency ☎033 794 5083), P. della Repubblica at the west end of Villa Comunale. Open M-F 8am-5pm. **South Africa,** C. Umberto, 1 (☎081 551 7519). **UK,** V. dei Mille, 40 (☎081 423 8911). **Canada,** V. Carducci, 29 (☎081 40 13 38).

Currency Exchange: Several banks operate in P. Municipio and P. Garibaldi. **Thomas Cook** at airport has decent rates. Open M-F 9:30am-1pm and 3-6:30pm. Additional branches at P. Municipio, 70 (☎081 551 8399) and **Minichini** at V. Depretis 141 (☎081 552 4213). **Stazione Centrale** has expensive 24hr. currency exchange.

American Express: Every Tour, P. Municipio, 5 (☎081 551 8564). Open 9am-1:30pm and 3:30-7pm.

Luggage Storage: In Stazione Centrale train station. Near Ferrovia Circumflegrea and Stazione Centrale info desk. €2.58 for 12hr. Open 8am-8pm.

English-Language Bookstores: Feltrinelli, V. S.T. d'Aquino, 70/76 (☎081 552 1436), north of Palazzo Municipale. Turn right off V. Toledo and onto V. Ponte di Tappia. It's 20m ahead on the left. Extensive English selection. Open M-F 9am-8pm, Sa 9am-2pm and 4-8:30pm. MC/V. **Libreria Universal Books,** C. Umberto, 22 (☎081 252 0069; fax 542 4488; unibooks@tin.it). In a *palazzo* off C. Umberto by P. Bovio. Open daily 9am-3:30pm and 4-7pm. MC/V.

Laundromats: Bolle Blu, C. Novara, 62 (☎033 8894 2714 or 5664 3057), 3 blocks from train station. Fast machines (wash and dry in under 1hr.). One of the only self-service laundromats in Naples. Wash €4-6; dry €3-5. Prices depend on load size. Open M-Sa 8:30am-8pm. **Lavanderia a gettone,** V. Montesanto, 2 (☎081 542 2162). From the metro or funicular, walk down V. Montesanto toward Commissariato Dante and Teatro Bracco; it's on the right on the corner of V. Michele Sciuti. With Internet, free soap and disinfectant, and a waiting room with TV, music, and magazines. €2 per wash and dry. Ironing €0.50 per article. Internet €2.50 per 30min. Open daily 9am-8:30pm.

EMERGENCY AND COMMUNICATIONS

Emergency: ☎113. **Police:** ☎113 or 081 794 1111. **Carabinieri:** ☎112.

Tourist Police: Ufficio Stranieri, at the **Questura,** V. Medina, 75 (☎081 794 1111), near P. Municipio on the R2 bus line. Assists with passport problems and helps travelers who have been victims of crime.

THE LOCAL STORY

BUYERS BEWARE

LG has an ice-cold Peroni at a small café in Calabria with a trio of American backpackers who have just left Naples. The most vociferous of the bunch passes on his story and a lesson for travelers everywhere.

Stepping off the train at Naples's bus station, the backpackers were immediately affronted by a street salesman. Hawking electronics, he pitched the boys a deal: if they bought a DVD player for a hundred euros, he would throw in a free portable CD player. The boys jubilantly accepted what seemed to be the bargain of the summer.

As the three excitedly rummaged through their wallets for crisp euro notes, they became conscious of an undue amount of attention being paid them from the passing crowds of Italians. Afraid they wouldn't be able to hold onto their new gadgets for long, they anxiously fled the scene.

Once safely seated at a cafe, and relieved to have escaped imminent robbery, the boys ripped open the packages to examine their purchases. The plastic wrappings came off, the boxes were thrown open, but nothing more than rocks tumbled onto the table.

Ambulance: ☎ 081 752 0696.

Late-Night Pharmacy: (☎ 081 26 88 81), at Stazione Centrale by FS ticket windows. Open in summer M-F 4pm-9am. *Il Mattino* lists the schedule.

Hospital: Cardarelli (☎ 081 747 2859 or ☎ 747 2848), north of town on R4 bus line.

Internet Access: Internetbar, P. Bellini, 74 (☎ 081 29 52 37). Chic, with A/C. Expensive drinks available to wash down your emails. €2.50 for 1hr. (required minimum). Open M-Sa 9am-2am, Su 8am-2am. **Internet Multimedia,** V. Sapienza, 43 (☎ 081 29 84 12). From Museo Archeologico Nazionale, head down V. S. Maria di Constaninopoli and turn left on V. Sapienza. Behind gate and up a flight of stairs to your right lie the lowest prices in town, at €1.55 per hr. 1hr. minimum. Buzz in to get in. Scanning and printing also available. Open daily 9:30am-9:30pm.

Post Office: (☎ 081 552 4233), in P. Matteotti, at V. Diaz. Take the R2 line. Also in Galleria Umberto (☎ 081 552 3467) and outside Stazione Centrale. Notoriously unreliable *Fermo Posta* €0.77. All offices open M-F 8:15am-6pm, Sa 8:15am-noon.

Postal Code: 80100.

◪ ACCOMMODATIONS

The hectic and seedy-by-night area around **P. Garibaldi** is packed with hotels, many of which solicit customers at the station. Don't trust anyone who approaches you in the station—people working on commission are more than happy to lead naive foreigners with heavy backpacks to unlicensed, overcharging hotels or to spread false information about reputable establishments. P. Garibaldi has options that are close to the station, comfortable, and inexpensive (though none are really quiet). Be aware that some inexpensive hotels rent rooms by the hour during the day for purposes best left undescribed. In the historic district between P. Dante and the duomo, lodgings are harder to come by, but if you can find space, this area is most conveniently located. The waterfront and downtown are home to more expensive options, and the hilltop provides great views and quiet rooms, but a guaranteed 15min. commute to the sights.

Although Naples has some fantastic bargain lodgings, be cautious. Don't surrender your passport before seeing your room, bargain for lower prices, and always agree on the price *before* you unpack your bags. Be alert for shower charges, obligatory breakfasts, and other unexpected costs. When selecting a place to stay, check for double-locked doors and night attendants. The **ACISJF/Centro D'Ascolto**, at Stazione Centrale near the EPT, helps women find safe, inexpensive rooms. (☎081 28 19 93. Open M, Tu, Th 3:30-6:30pm.) For **camping**, check out **Pozzuoli** (see p. 543), **Pompeii** (see p. 546), and other small towns on the Bay of Naples.

WATERFRONT

Ostello Mergellina (HI), V. Salita della Grotta, 23 (☎081 761 2346; fax 761 2391). M: Mergellina. From Metro station, make 2 sharp rights onto V. Piedigrotta and then a right onto V. Salita della Grotta. Turn right on long driveway after overpass. Outstanding views of Vesuvius and Capri from terrace area. 200 beds in 2-, 4-, and 6-person rooms vary in quality but are well-maintained. Computer, cafeteria, free storage downstairs, and a pleasant lounge. Breakfast, shower, and sheets included, but no towels. Laundry €5.16. Breakfast 7-9am, dinner 7-9:30 pm. Lockout 9am-3pm. Curfew 12:30am. Reservations advised July-Aug. Dorms €13.50; doubles €53.34; family rooms €16 per person, although if more than 2 beds are squeezed into the room, rates drops to €13. ❷

TRAIN STATION

▨**Casanova Hotel**, C. Garibaldi, 333 (☎081 26 82 87; fax 26 97 92; www.hotel-casanova.3000.it). From P. Garibaldi, continue down C. Garibaldi and turn right before V. Casanova. Clean, 2-star hotel with airy rooms and a rooftop terrace with bar in summer. 18 rooms with A/C, some with TV, fridge, and phone. Breakfast €4. Luggage deposit. Check-out 12pm. Reserve ahead. Singles €20, with bath €26; doubles €36/€46; triples €49-57; quads €69. 10% discount with *Let's Go*. AmEx/MC/V. ❷

Hotel Eden, C. Novara, 9 (☎081 28 53 44). From station, turn right on C. Novara; it's on the left. A quick, well-lit walk from the station leads to 40 rooms that are a convenient option for backpackers arriving late at night without reservations, although some have a slightly unpleasant odor. English, Spanish, and some French are spoken by the brothers in charge, and all rooms come with private bath. Free luggage storage. With *Let's Go* reservation: singles €30; doubles €40; triples €60. ❸

Hostel Pensione Mancini, V. Mancini, 33 (☎081 553 6731; fax 554 6675; www.hostel-pensionemancini.com), off far end of P. Garibaldi from station. Multilingual, tourist-friendly owners. Simple, spacious, newly renovated, and right in Naples's transportation hub. 6 rooms with TV and Internet. Breakfast included. Check-in and check-out noon. Reservations suggested 1 wk. in advance. Dorms €16; singles €30; doubles €40, with bath €50; triples €70; quads €80. 10% discount on rooms with *Let's Go*. ❷

Hotel Ginevra, V. Genova, 116 (☎081 28 32 10; fax 554 1757; www.hotelginevra.it). Exit P. Garibaldi on C. Novara, then turn right on V. Genova. Clean, family-run establishment. Bathrooms have showers with doors. English and French spoken. 14 rooms. Singles €25, with bath €45; doubles €45/€50; triples €60/€75; quads €70/€80. 10% *Let's Go* discount when paying cash. AmEx/MC/V. ❸

Hotel Zara, V. Firenze, 81 (☎081 28 71 25; fax 26 82 87, www.hotelzara.it). Quiet, spacious rooms. Charge for Internet access and washing machines. Reservations recommended. Singles €23; doubles €37, with bath €47; triples €57/€62. ❷

Hotel Prati, V. Cesare Rosaroll, 4 (☎081 26 88 98; fax 554 1802; www.hotelprati.it) on the side of P. Garibaldi opposite the train station. Spacious 3-star with 43 rooms, all with full bath, TV, minibar, and phone, and some with terraces and AC. Restaurant and beautiful garden on the 5th floor offer an escape from the frenzied piazza below. Singles €70; doubles €100. 10% discount with *Let's Go*. AmEx/MC/V. ❺

HISTORIC CENTER

Hostel and Pensione Soggiorno Imperia, P. Miraglia, 386 (☎/fax 081 45 93 47). Take R2 from train station, get off at the University, walk up V. Mezzocannone through P. S. Domenico Maggiore, and buzz at the 1st set of green doors to left on P. Miraglia. Climb 6 flights of stairs to get to this refurbished 16th-century *palazzo*. Bright and clean, inexpensive, and conveniently located, with kitchen, Internet, and no curfew or lockout. English, Spanish, and Polish spoken. 11 rooms. Reservations recommended. Dorm €16; singles €30; doubles €42, with bath €62; triples €60/€72; quad €75/€80. ❷

6 Small Rooms, V. Diodato Lioy, 18 (☎081 790 1378; www.at6smallrooms.com). From P. Monteoliveto, turn right on V. Diodato Lioy, and go up about half a block. There is no sign; look for the name on the call button. A bit out of the way, but worth the trek. Chill with hip Australian owners and their 2 friendly cats. English video collection. Key (€5 deposit) available for after midnight curfew. Big rooms and *cornetti* and coffee every morning. Singles €20.66; dorms €16, €15 for longer stays. ❷

Pensione Bella Capri, V. Melisurgo, 4, door B, 6th fl. (☎081 552 9494; fax 552 9265; www.bellacapri.it), at corner of V. Cristofor Colombo, across street from the port. Take the R2 bus to the end of V. de Pretis, cross the street, and turn onto V. Melisurgo. From courtyard enter door B and go to the 6th floor. Inexpensive alternative to high-priced hotels on waterfront, with view. Coin-operated elevator, and 9 rooms with bath, TV, and phone; some with A/C (€10 surcharge) and balcony. Reserve 1 wk. ahead. Singles €62; doubles €72; triples €90; quads €100. 10% *Let's Go* discount. AmEx/MC/V. ❺

Hostel of the Sun, V. Melisurgo, 15 (☎/fax 081 420 6393; www.hostelnapoli.com), across the street from Bella Capri. Buzz #51 to get in. Young owners make this a lively, happening spot. Large dorms and excellent private rooms. Browse the Internet €2.60 per hr. Wash and dry your laundry €3. Full breakfast included. Kitchen open to guests. No curfew or lockout. Dorms €16; doubles €45, with bath €61. Triple room with communal bath, but a fantastic terrace €60. ❷

HILLTOP

Pensione Margherita, V. Cimarosa, 29, 5th fl. (☎081 578 2852; fax 556 7044), in the same building as the Centrale funicular station (go outside and around the corner to the right and buzz to enter). 19 big rooms, some with terraces. Endearing management, excellent views of Vesuvius and Capri, and the lowest prices available in this posh, peaceful residential area. €0.05 for the elevator or take the stairs. Check-out 11am. Curfew 1am. Closed Aug. 1-15. Singles €32; doubles €58; triples €82. MC/V. ❸

◘ FOOD

PIZZERIE

If you ever doubted that Neapolitans invented pizza, Naples's *pizzerie* will take that doubt, beat it into a ball, throw it in the air, spin it on their collective finger, punch it down, cover it with sauce and mozzarella, and serve it to you *alla margherita*. And then you'll beg for more.

Gino Sorbillo, V. Tribunali, 32 (☎081 44 66 43; www.accademiadellapizza.it), in the historic center near Vco. S. Paolo. The only *pizzeria* with 21 pizza-making children in this generation. Their grandfather invented the *ripieno al forno* (calzone). 40 types of pizza. The *gusta pizza* (€6.19) is the only wine made to compliment pizza. *Marinara* €2.06, *margherita* €2.58, beer €0.77-3.35. Open daily noon-3:30pm and 7-11:30pm. ❷

Pizzeria Di Matteo, V. Tribunali, 94 (☎081 45 52 62), near V. Duomo. Former President Clinton ate here during the G-7 Conference in 1994. The *marinara* is your best cheap bite (€2). Open M-Sa 9am-midnight. ❶

Antica Pizzeria da Michele, V. Cesare Sersale, 1/3 (☎081 553 9204). From P. Garibaldi, walk up C. Umberto 1 and take the 1st right. The huge line outside the door says "Quality!" more loudly than a legion of reviewers. It serves only 2 traditional pizzas: *marinara* (tomato, garlic, oregano, oil) and *margherita* (tomato, mozzarella cheese, basil). Pizza €3.10-4.15, drinks €1.05. Open M-Sa 10am-11pm. ❶

Pizzeria Brandi, Salita S. Anna di Palazzo, 1 (☎081 41 69 28; fax 400 2914), off V. Chiaia. In 1889, Mr. Esposito invented the *margherita* in Brandi's ancient oven to symbolize Italy's flag with the green of basil, red of tomato sauce, and white of *mozzarella di bufala*. While Bill Clinton munched at Di Matteo in 1994, daughter Chelsea ate here. Other famous customers include Pavarotti, Isabella Rossellini, and Gerard Depardieu. Reservations advised. *Margherita* €4.14. Cover €1.55. Tip 12%. Open daily 12:30-3pm and 7:30pm-late. AmEx/MC/V. ❷

Pizzeria Trianon da Ciro, V. Pietro Colletta, 42/44/46 (☎081 553 9426; www.napolibox.it/trianon), 1 block off C. Umberto I. Big place with A/C. The house speciality is the pizza *"Gran Trianon"* (€6.50), with 8 different sections of different toppings. Pizza €3-7, beer €1.10-3. Service 15%. Open daily 10am-3:30pm and 6:30-11pm. ❷

Iris, P. Garibaldi, 121/125 (☎081 26 99 88). The sign of the Napoli DOC is on display here, indicating that Iris' pizzas uphold the Neapolitan standard. The specialty is the pizza *gamerone brace* (€7.75), covered in small, white open-eyed fish. Toast to trying new things. Cover €0.50, tourist *menù* €9.29. Open Su-F 6am-midnight. MC/V. ❷

RESTAURANTS AND TRATTORIE

Neapolitans love **seafood,** and they prepare it well. Enjoy *cozze* (mussels) with lemon or as soup. Savor *vongole* (clams) in all their glory, and don't miss their more expensive cousin, the *ostrica* (oyster). Try not to gawk as true Neapolitans suck the most elusive juices from the heads of *aragosta* (crayfish) or devour *polipo* (octopus), one of the cheapest sources of protein around. Meanwhile, when asking for *spaghetti*, don't mention any nonsense about Marco Polo and China if you want to stay on the Neapolitans' good side: this Italian trademark was reputedly first boiled in their kitchens. Today, the city's most famous pasta dishes are *spaghetti alle vongole* (with clams) and *alle cozze* (with mussels). For fresh fruits and seafood, explore Neapolitan **markets,** such as the one on V. Soprammuro, off P. Garibaldi. (Open M-Sa 8am-1:30pm.) Fruit stands, groceries, and pastry shops line V. Tribuali in Spaccanapoli.

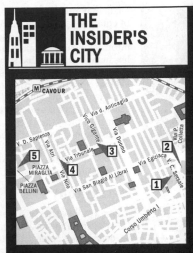

THE INSIDER'S CITY

PIZZA PARADISO

A tour of the pizza capital of the world is best for two—it would take prodigious gastronomic capabilities to single-handedly devour an entire pizza at each of the four best Neapolitan *pizzerie*. Consider fasting for a couple days, or just take a friend.

1 Start with the basics at **Antica Pizzeria da Michele**—only *margherita* and *marinara* pizzas grace their purist menu. (☎081 553 9204).

2 Cross the street to **Pizzeria Trianon da Ciro,** and try a sizzling pie by da Michele's rival. (☎081 553 9426).

3 Re-ignite your appetite with a short walk to the ever-packed **Pizzeria di Matteo,** where Bill Clinton once ate. (☎081 45 52 62).

4 Polish off another version of the pie from the inventors of the *calzone* at **Gino Sorbillo.** (☎081 44 66 43.)

5 Retreat to the open-air bars of **Piazza Bellini,** to bask in the sun and brag about your monstrous feat over a cold drink.

The **waterfront** offers a combination of traditional Neapolitan fare and a change of culinary pace. Take the Metro or the C25 bus to P. Amedeo for Greek or Spanish. Take the Metro to Mergellina, southwest of P. Amedeo on the waterfront, for informal, hearty Neapolitan seafood. P. Sannazzaro, in the center of Mergellina, has many *trattorie* that serve the beloved local *zuppa di cozze* (mussels in broth with octopus). Among the shops of **downtown,** small options can be found on the side streets, hiding from the louder, more expensive *trattorie* that one would expect to find around a galleria. The narrow, winding streets around the **historic center** and P. Dante shelter the city's most delightful *trattorie* and *pizzerie.* Some of the cheapest, most authentic options lie along V. dei Tribunali in the heart of Spaccanapoli. Tourist-ridden and expensive restaurants dominate P. Garibaldi in the **train station** area, but a few high-quality, low-cost meals hide on the side streets just off the piazza. Like most areas around train stations, P. Garibaldi becomes seedy at night, so eat early before it gets too dark.

WATERFRONT

Zorba's, V. Martucci, 5 Mergellina (☎081 66 75 72). M: Mergellina. 2 blocks off P. Amedeo, to the right as you exit the station; at the sign turn left, and Zorba's will be 3 doors down. *Satanas* (devilishly spicy mini sausages) €6.50. Greek salad €4.20. Baklava €3. Open Su-F 8pm-1am, Sa 8pm-3am. ❷

El Bocadillo, V. Martucci, 50 (☎081 66 90 30; www.elbocadillo.it). M: Mergellina. Dine on Spanish and South American dishes, in view of a mini jungle lit by neon-green lights. Entrees €5-10. *Paella* €8.26. 1L pitcher of *sangría* €5.68. Open daily 7pm-3am. ❷

La Cantina di Albi Cocca, V. Ascensione, 6 (☎081 41 16 58). Take V. Vittoria Colonna from P. Amedeo, take the 1st right down a flight of stairs, turn right, and then left onto V. Ascensione. This hard-to-find restaurant maintains its Italian authenticity with traditional Neapolitan fare in a small, romantic setting. *Primi* €6-8, *secondi* €8-10. Cover €1. Open M-Sa 1-3pm and 8pm-midnight. MC/V. ❸

Ristorante Bellini, V. Santa Maria di Constantinopoli, 79-80 (☎/fax 081 45 97 74), just off P. Bellini, escape the *pizzerie* for a slightly upscale dinner. Try the *linguine al cartoccio* (€11), or a dish from the *pesce* menu. Fish in troughs displayed in front. Open daily 9am-4pm and 7pm-1:30am, closed Su in the summer. MC/V. ❸

Umberto, V. Alabardieri, 30/31 (☎081 41 85 55; www.umberto.it). V. Alabardieri leads out of P. dei Martiri; the restaurant will be on your left. This classy waterfront locale serves well-made local dishes. Try the house specialty *menù:* the *primi tubettoni d' 'o treddata* (tube pasta stuffed with seafood; €9.30), followed by the *secondi polpettine di nonna Ermelinda* (meatballs with tomato sauce; €4.65). Open Tu-Su noon-3pm and 7:30pm-midnight. Closed 2 wk. in Aug. Reservations advised. AmEx/MC/V. ❸

Cucina Casereccia e Pizzeria, P. Sanazzaro, 69 (☎081 66 65 64), in Mergellina. Gentlemen greet you in front, shucking mussels. Fine, authentic Neapolitan food. Specializes in *cozze* (mussels), found in their popular *zuppa di cozze* for €6.71, and its upgrade for the hungry, the *zuppa di cozze super* (€9.30). Open daily noon-late. ❸

DOWNTOWN

Trattoria Fratelli Prigiobbo, V. Portacarrese, 96 (☎081 40 76 92). From V. Toledo, turn left (walking from the waterfront) onto V. Portacarrese. Simple little restaurant with friendly atmosphere. Pizza €2.50. *Primi* €3, including *gnocchi alla mozzarella.* Seafood *secondi* (roasted calamari, €4), though servings are small. Wine €2.50 per bottle. Open M-Sa 8am-midnight. ❷

GELATERIE AND PASTICCERIE

Naples's most beloved pastry is *sfogliatella*, filled with sweetened ricotta cheese, orange rind, and candied fruit. It comes in two forms: the popular *riccia*, a flaky-crust variety, and *frolla*, a softer, crumblier counterpart.

■ **Gay Odin,** V. V. Colonna, 15b (☎081 41 82 82; www.gay-odin.it), off P. Amedeo; V. Toledo, 214 (☎081 40 00 63); and V. Luca Giordano, 21 (☎081 57 83 80). No Norse gods, just delicious chocolate treats that have poured from their *fabbriche* (factories) on V. Vetriera since 1824. Try the *foresta* (a sweet and crumbly chocolate stalk; €3.62 per kg) or *chocolate con peperoncino* (chocolate bars with chili peppers; €4.13). Open M-Sa 9:30am-1:30pm and 4:30-8pm, Su 10am-2pm. AmEx/MC/V.

Pintauro, V. Toledo, 275 (☎081 41 73 39), near the central funicular station. This tiny bakery invented *sfogliatella* in 1785. Try it piping hot for €1.30. Open M-Sa 9:15am-8:15pm.

Scaturchio, P. S. Dominico Maggiore, 19 (☎081 551 6944; fax 55 29 86). One of the best pastry shops and *gelaterie* in the historic district, ideal for a break from church-viewing. Cones €1.29. The *ministeriale*, a chocolate and rum pastry, is their specialty. Though the fancy sign and counter suggest this place is a tourist trap, the taste says, "Kiss me, I'm Italian!" Open M-Sa 7:20am-8:40pm.

Caffe Roma, V. Toledo, 325 (☎081 40 68 32), on V. Toledo near the Centrale funicular station. Try the *pofiteral* (€1.50) and enormous variety of pastries and *gelato*. Open M-Sa 9am-9pm. MC/V.

◎ SIGHTS

Naples's streets are packed with people, *motorini*, churches and museums. The architecture that lines the streets is a narrative of the successive Greek, Roman, Spaniard and Italian conquerers of this land. Excavations *in sito* can be found at the Museo Archeologico Nazionale or Museo and Gallerie di Capidomonte. The Palazzo Reale's apartments and the city's castles give a taste of 18th-century royal Neapolitan life. If you plan to spend a few days touring Naples's museums and sights, the **Napoli artecard** (☎800 60 060; www.napoliartecard.com; €10, ages 18-25 €8) is a worthwhile investment. The card grants admission to two of the six museums featured, and half-price admission to the other four, in addition to free public transportation and discounts on audioguides and in museum stores.

HISTORIC CENTER

SPACCANAPOLI

Naples's most renowned neighborhood is replete with brilliant architecture and merits at least a 30min. stroll. The main sights get lost among ornate banks, *pensioni*, and *pasticcerie*, so watch for the shoebox-sized signs on buildings. But don't lose track of yourself while gaping at picturesque churches, *palazzi*, and alleyways or you'll soon find yourself staring at an oncoming *motorino*. To get to the Historic Center from P. Dante, walk through **Porta Alba** and past **P. Bellini** before turning down **V. dei Tribunali,** the former route of an old Roman road that now contains some of the city's best **pizzerie** (see **Food,** p. 534).

■ **MUSEO ARCHEOLOGICO NAZIONALE.** Situated within a 16th-century *palazzo* and former barracks, one of the world's most important archeological museums houses exquisite treasures from Pompeii and Herculaneum. Unreliable labeling makes the color guidebooks a helpful investment. The ground floor's Farnese Collection displays sculptures snatched from Pompeii and Herculaneum, as well as imperial portraits and colossal statues from Rome's Baths of Caracalla. Highlights include the massive **Farnese Hercules,** showing the exhausted hero after his last labor. Which labor this is remains uncertain: diverging myth traditions introduce the possibility that he is worn out not from the 12th labor, but from his 13th—bedding 100 women in one night. Check out the **Farnese Bull,** the largest extant ancient sculpture. The bull was carved out of a single piece of marble, then touched up by Michelangelo. The mezzanine contains a room filled with exquisite mosaics taken from Pompeii, ranging from pictures of food to the **Alexander Mosaic,** which shows a young and fearless Alexander the Great routing a Persian army. The **Secret Collection** contains erotic paintings and objects from Pompeii, ranging from images of godly love to phallic good luck charms. Call ahead to gain entrance to this room. Also of note are the **Jewels,** a collection of ancient trinkets and ornaments which includes the sparkling **Farnese Cup.** On the top floor, the **Pompeii in Minatura** puts Capri's (p. 559) to shame. In the basement is a sporadically open Egyptian collection. *(M: "P. Cavour." Turn right as you exit the station, and walk 2 blocks. It's a short walk from anywhere in the historical center. ☎ 081 44 01 66. Open W-M 9am-7:30pm. Entrance €6.50, EU students €3.25, under 18 or over 65 free. Included under Napoli artecard.)*

DUOMO. Like every good Italian town, Naples has its duomo. It lies quietly on a small piazza, and its modest facade hides its size. Twice a year throngs of people crowd around it to celebrate the **Festa di San Gennaro** (see **Entertainment**). Subject to countless additions and renovations since its inauguration in 1315 by Robert of Anjou, the duomo's most recent feature is a 19th-century neo-Gothic facade. On the right, the main attraction is the **Capella del Tesoro di San Gennaro,** decorated with Baroque paintings. A beautiful 17th-century bronze grille protects the high altar, which possesses a reliquary containing the saint's head and two vials of his coagulated blood. According to legend, disaster will strike the city if the blood does not liquefy on the celebration of his *festa;* however, it miraculously transforms while Neapolitans crowd the church and streets. Beneath the main altar of the church lies the saint's crypt, decorated with Renaissance carvings in white marble. Halfway up the right side of the church, the **Chiesa di Santa Restituta** marks the entrance to the excavations of the **Greek and Roman roads** that run beneath the city. *(Walk 3 blocks up V. Duomo from C. Umberto I or take the #42 bus from P. Garibaldi. ☎ 081 44 90 97. Open M-F 8am-12:30pm and 4:30-7pm, Sa-Su 8am-3:30pm and 5-7:30pm.)*

PIO MONTE D. MISERICORDIE. This small chapel was built by a group of nobles dedicated to helping the needy and sick, ransoming Christian slaves held prisoner by infidels, and housing pilgrims, activities which continue (at least in part) to this day. The church houses seven arches, each with its own altar and painting, and the main archway boasts Caravaggio's *Our Lady of Mercy,* the central attraction of the chapel. In the piazza outside resides a spire dedicated to S. Gennaro for having saved the city from the 1656 plague. *(1 block down V. Tribunali after V. Duomo, on a small piazza. ☎ 081 44 69 44. Call in the morning to book a tour.)*

OSPEDALE DELLE BAMBOLE. Old Naples's most endearing shop (or most creepy, depending on how many Hitchcock movies one has seen), this tiny doll hospital is one-of-a-kind. The mirthful proprietor reassembles dolls with a collection of appendages in his one-room shop. It's hard to believe there are that many dolls in Naples in need of repair, but the shop's been getting by since 1800. *(V. S. Biagio dei Librai, 81. Head 2 blocks up V. Duomo from P. N. Amore and take a left. ☎ 081 20 30 87; www.ospedaledellebambole.it. Open daily 10:30am-2pm and 6-8pm. MC/V.)*

CHIESA DI SANTA CHIARA. One of the most important Angevin monuments in Naples, Santa Chiara was originally built in the 1300s by the rulers of the house of Anjou and has been renovated several times, most recently after a WWII bombing in 1943. The church is littered with sarcophagi and tombs from the Middle Ages, and the 14th-century tomb of Robert of Anjou can be seen behind the main altar.

Spend some time in the adjoining garden and monastery, adorned with Gothic frescoes and brightly colored majolica tiles, before exiting into the utmost in beatnik piazzas. *(From P. Dante, head down V. Toledo and turn left on V. B. Croce. The church sits in P. Gesù Nuovo. ☎ 081 552 6209. Open M-F 9:30am-1pm and 3:30-5:30pm, weekends and holidays 9:30am-1pm. €4, students €2.50.)*

GESÙ NUOVO. The church's 15th-century Jesuit facade consists entirely of raised stone diamonds. The interior is awash in Baroque inlaid marbles, with colorful frescoes adorning the ceiling and chapels everywhere. Outside the church is a spectacular Baroque spire, or *guglia*, glorifying the lives of Jesuit saints, surrounded by a bunch of bongo-playing bohemians. *(Across from the Chiesa di Santa Chiara, in P. Gesù Nuovo. ☎ 081 551 8613. Open daily 7:15am-12:15pm and 4:15-7:15pm.)*

SAN LORENZO MAGGIORE. This large church retains a striking Gothic beauty. It was here that medieval writer Boccaccio first met his true love Fiammetta in 1334. Inside lie the tombs of Catherine of Austria and Robert of Arlois. Recent excavations beneath the church and monastery have uncovered Greek and Roman remains that will soon be on public display. *(P. San Gaetano, 316. 2 blocks down V. dei Tribunali from V. Duomo walking towards the historical center. ☎ 081 29 05 80.)*

TRAIN STATION

🖼 **PALAZZO REALE.** The exterior facing P. Plebiscito is decorated with huge statues of the various rulers of Naples. Inside the 17th-century *palazzo* is the **Museo di Palazzo Reale,** composed of opulent royal apartments decorated with the original Bourbon furnishings, paintings, statues, and porcelains. A wander through the immense chambers reveals lavish royal life, including the king's ornate throne and walls lined with mirrors and paintings. The *palazzo* is an intellectual mecca, housing the 1,500,000-volume **Biblioteca Nazionale.** The library contains the carbonized scrolls from the **Villa dei Papiri** in Herculaneum. *(Take the R2 bus from P. Garibaldi to P. Trieste e Trento and walk around the palazzo to the entrance on P. Plebiscito, or make the short walk from anywhere in the historical center. ☎ 081 794 4021. Open M and W-Su 9am-8pm. Included under Napoli artecard. Library ☎ 081 40 12 73; public access varies so call for details.)*

Also in the *palazzo* is the famous **Teatro San Carlo,** reputed to have better acoustics than the revered La Scala in Milan (see p. 102). For more information on performances, see **Entertainment,** p. 541. *(The theater's entrance is on P. Trieste e Trento. ☎ 081 797 2111. Tours July Sa-Tu and Th 10am; Sept.-June Sa-Su 2pm. €3.)*

🖼 **NAPOLI E LA CITTA SOTTERANEA/NAPOLI SOTTERRANEA.** These tours of the subterranean alleys beneath the city are fascinating, but not for the claustrophobic: they will have you crawling through narrow underground passageways, grottoes, and catacombs, spotting Mussolini-era graffiti, and exploring Roman aqueducts. *Napoli e la Città* explores the area underneath Castel Nuovo and downtown, and *Napoli Sotterranea* drags you through the area under the historic center. *(**Napoli e La Città' Sotterranea,** office at Vco. S. Anna di Palazzo. ☎ 081 40 02 56. Tours Th 9pm; Sa 10am and 6pm; Su 10am, 11am, and 6pm. €5. Tours leave from Bar Gambiunes in P. Trieste e Trento, but call first. **Napoli Sotterranea,** P. S. Gaetano, 68. Go down V. Tribunali and turn left right before San Paolo Maggiore. ☎ 081 29 69 44 or 0368 354 0585; www.napolisotterranea.com. Tours every 2hr. M-F 12pm-4pm, Sa, Su, and holidays 10am-6pm. €5.)*

CASTEL NUOVO. It's impossible to miss this huge, five-turreted landmark looking out over the Bay of Naples. Known also as the **Maschio Angioino,** the fortress was built in 1286 by Charles II of Anjou to be his royal residence in Naples. Perhaps its most interesting feature is the triumphal entrance with reliefs commemorating the arrival of Alphonse I of Aragon in 1443. Inside is the magnificent cubical **Hall of the Barons,** where King Ferdinand once trapped rebellious barons and where Naples's city council holds spirited meetings today, as well as the splendid **Capella Palatina,** also called the Chapel of St. Barbara. The **Museo Civico** has a collection of 14th- and 15th-century frescoes, as well as a set of bronze doors depicting Charles of Aragon defeating rebels. *(P. Municipio. Take the R2 bus from P. Garibaldi or walk from anywhere in the historical center. Museum ☎081 795 2003. Open M-Sa 9am-7pm. Admission €5.16.)*

CAPELLA SANSEVERO. The chapel, founded in 1590 and now a private museum, has several remarkable statues, including the **Veiled Christ** by Giuseppe Sanmartino. While admiring the marble marvel, don't forget to look up at the breathtaking fresco on the ceiling. Legend claims that the chapel's builder, alchemist prince Raimondo of the S. Severi, murdered his wife and her lover by injecting them with a poison that preserved their veins, arteries, and vital organs. Sadly, these aren't on display. *(V. De Sanctis, 19. Near P. S. Domenico Maggiore. ☎081 551 8470; www.icnapoli.com/sansevero. Open M and W-F 10am-5pm; in summer, Christmas, and Easter M and W-F 10am-7pm; on other holidays 10am-1:30pm. €5, students €2.50, group discounts available.)*

CHIESA DI SAN DOMENICO MAGGIORE. This 13th-century church has been restructured several times over the years and now has settled on a 19th-century, spiked Gothic interior. To the right of the altar in the Chapel of the Crucifix hangs the 13th-century painting that allegedly spoke to St. Thomas Aquinas, who lived in the adjoining monastery when Naples was a center of learning in Europe. Fine Renaissance sculptures decorate the side chapels. *(P. S. Domenico Maggiore. ☎081 45 91 88. Open M-F 8:30am-noon and 5-8pm, Sa-Su 9:30am-1pm and 5-7pm.)*

HILLTOP

CAPODIMONTE

■ **MUSEO AND GALLERIE DI CAPODIMONTE.** Housed in a royal *palazzo*, this museum is surrounded by a pastoral park where youngsters play soccer and lovers, well, play. In addition to its plush royal apartments and their furnishings, the palace houses the National Picture Gallery. The **Farnese Collection** on the first floor is full of artistic masterpieces, many of them removed from Neapolitan churches for safety's sake, including Bellini's *Transfiguration*, Masaccio's *Crucifixion*, and Titian's *Danae*. The 2nd floor traces the development of the Neapolitan realistic style and its dramatic use of light, from Caravaggio's visit to Naples (his *Flagellation* is on display) to Ribera and Luca Giordano's adaptations. *(Take the #16 bus from the Archaeological Museum, and get off when you see the gate to the park on your right. The park has 2 entrances, the Porta Piccola and the Porta Grande. ☎081 749 9111. Open Tu-F 8:30am-7:30pm, Su 8:30am-7:30pm. €7.50, after 2pm €6.50.)*

CHIESA DI MADRE DEL BUON CONSIGLIO. Dubbed "Little St. Peter's" when architect Vincenzo Vecchia was inspired by St. Peter's in Rome, it features copies of Michelangelo's *Pietà* and *Moses*. Outside, the 2nd-century **Catacombe di San Gennaro** are decorated with early frescoes. *(Down V. Capodimonte from the museum. ☎081 741 1071. Guided tours of catacombs daily 9:30am, 10:15am, 11am, and 11:45am.)*

VOMERO

MUSEO NAZIONALE DI SAN MARTINO. Once a monastery, the massive Certosa di S. Martino is now home to an excellent museum of Neapolitan history and culture. In addition to extensive galleries, the monastery includes a chapel lavishly decorated in Baroque marbles and statuary, featuring one of Ribera's finest works, *The Deposition of Christ,* and an excellent *Nativity* by Guido Reni. Numerous balconies and a multilevel garden provide superb views. *(From V. Toledo, take the funicular to Vomero, make a right on V. Cimarosa. A left on V. Morghen and a right onto V. P. L.*

Architetto lands you in Piazzale S. Martino. ☎ 081 578 1769. Open Tu-F 8:30am-7:30pm, Sa 9am-7:30pm. €6, EU students €3, EU citizens under 18 and over 65 free. Included under Napoli artecard.) The massive **Castel Sant'Elmo** next door was built to deter rebellion and hold political prisoners. Ignore the oppressive past; there are great panoramic views from the battlements. *(☎ 081 578 4030. Open Tu-Su 9am-2pm. €1.)*

MUSEO DUCA DI MARLINA. Ceramics fans should visit this crafts gallery inside the lush gardens of the **Villa Floridiana** for 18th-century Italian and Asian porcelain. *(V. Cimarosa, 77. To get to the entrance, take the funicular to Vomero from V. Toledo, turn right out of the station, and then turn left onto V. Cimarosa. Enter the gardens and keep walking downhill. ☎ 081 229 2110. Visitors admitted 9:30am, 11am, 12:30pm, 2pm. €2.50, EU students €1.50, EU citizens under 18 or over 65 free.)*

WATERFRONT

■**VIRGIL'S TOMB.** *Mirabile dictu!* Anyone who studied Latin in high school may have at least a passing interest in seeing the poet's resting place at Salita della Frotta. Below the tomb is the entrance to the closed *Crypta Neapolitana*, a tunnel built during the reign of Augustus, connecting ancient Neapolis to Pozzuoli and Baia. Nearby lies the Tomb of Leopardi, moved from the church of S. Vitale in Fuorigrotta in 1939. Call ahead and arrange a translator, or just come for the amazing view. Either way, you will feel like this is your own personal monument. *(From M: "Mergellina," take 2 quick rights. Entrance between overpass and tunnel. ☎ 081 66 93 90. Open Tu-Su 9am-1pm. Free. Guided tours upon request.)*

CASTEL DELL'UOVO (EGG CASTLE). This massive Norman castle of yellow brick and odd angles sits on a rock that was later connected to the mainland, dividing the bay in half. Legend has it that Virgil hid an egg within the castle walls and that with the collapse of the egg would come the collapse of the castle. It offers beautiful views of the water and Naples. *(Take bus #1 from P. Garibaldi or P. Municipio to S. Lucia and walk across the jetty. ☎ 081 764 5343. Only open for special events; call ahead.)*

AQUARIUM. If you're tired of seeing marine life on your dinner plate, try the aquarium in the Villa Comunale. Founded in the late 19th century, it's Europe's oldest, displaying 30 tanks with 200 local species. *(Easily accessible by the #1 tram from P. Garibaldi or P. Municipio. ☎ 081 583 3263. Open Tu-Sa 9am-6pm, Su 10am-6pm; in winter M-Sa 9am-5pm, Su 9am-2pm. €1.55, children and groups €0.77.)*

🎭 ENTERTAINMENT

Once famous occasions for revelry, Naples's religious festivals have since become excuses for sales and shopping sprees. On September 19, December 16, and the first Saturday in May, the city celebrates its patron saint with the **Festa di San Gennaro.** Join the crowd to watch the procession by the duomo (in May) and see S. Gennaro's blood miraculously liquefy in a vial (see **Duomo,** p. 538). The festival of **Madonna del Carmine** (July 16) features a mock burning of Fra' Nuvolo's *campanile* and culminates in a fireworks show. In July, concerts are held in P. S. Domenico Maggiore, while summers are full of neighborhood celebrations, *Rioni Festivali*, fireworks, sporting events, processions, music, and shows.

The **Cinema Teatro Amedeo,** V. Marcucci, 69 (☎ 081 68 02 66), four blocks off P. Amedeo, shows films in English during the summer. **Teatro S. Carlo,** at Palazzo Reale (☎ 081 797 2111), hosts performances by the Opera (Oct.-June) and the Symphony Orchestra (Oct.-May). Gallery tickets cost €12.91 and should be purchased in advance. Consult the ticket office and *Il Mattino* for both schedules.

For a portrait of Neapolitan life, catch a soccer game at **Stadio S. Paolo** (☎081 239 5623), in Fourigrotta. Take the Metro to "Campi Flegrei." **S. S. Napoli** is in Serie B, the lower division, but still is a soccer powerhouse, with packed games on Saturdays and Sundays August through June. Tickets start at €20.

Two weekends of every month (one weekend a month in June and July) **Fiera Antiquaria Napoletana** hosts flea markets filled with ancient and expensive artifacts. While buying such items will likely exceed most budgets, hundreds browse the stands along V. F. Caracciolo on the waterfront, looking at ancient and modern stamps, books, coins, and artwork. (☎081 62 19 51. Open 8am-2pm.)

☐ SHOPPING

A thriving black market and low prices make Naples a wonderful, if risky, place to shop. If you choose to buy from street vendors, understand that they are craftier than you. If a transaction seems too good to be true, it is. Clothing is usually a good deal, though your new shirt (with the Lacoste croc looking a bit too large) may come apart in the washing machine or turn your other clothes a ghastly shade of purple. *Never* buy electronic products from street vendors—even brand-name boxes have been known to be filled with newspaper, bottled water, or rocks. **V. S. Maria di Constatopoli,** south of the Archaeological Museum, has old books and antique shops, Spaccanapoli and its side streets near the Conservatorio house music shops, V. Toledo provides high-class shopping for a lower budget, and the streets south of San Lorenzo Maggiore house craftsmen of Neapolitan *creches*.

P. Martiri houses a roll call of Italian designers, including Gucci, Valentino, Versace, Ferragamo, Armani, and Prada. The most modern and expensive shopping district is in the hills of Vomero along the perpendicular **V. Scarlatti** and **V. Luca Giordano.** If you're looking for jeans, head to the market off Porta Capuana. (Most markets are open M-Sa 9am-5pm, but many close at 2pm.)

☒ NIGHTLIFE

Neapolitan nightlife is seasonal. Content to groove at the small clubs and discos during the winter, Neapolitans instinctively return to the streets and piazzas in warmer weather. In the winter, clubs and pubs usually open at around 11pm and remain open until everyone goes home, which is normally around 4 or 5am. In the summer, the Sunday evening *passeggiata* fills the Villa Comunale along the bay (#1 tram), and amorous young couples flood picturesque V. Petrarca and V. Posillipo. For obvious reasons, most take their cars. According to eager Italian men, a kiss here means seven years of good luck.

For less exclusive gatherings, head to the piazzas to relax and socialize. **P. Vanvitelli** in Vomero (take the funicular from V. Toledo or the C28 bus from P. Vittoria) is where kids hit on each other. In **P. Gesù Nuovo,** near the University of Naples (close to P. Dante) and the Communist headquarters, it ain't cigarette smoke you're smelling. Here the sound of bongos resonates as students, tired out from spray-painting high-brow *contro lo stato* (anti-establishment) graffiti, recuperate and socialize with tourists and drifters. Outdoor bars and cafes are popular in **P. Bellini** (a short walk from P. Dante) and **P. San Domenico Maggiore** (a quick walk up V. Mezzocannone from C. Umberto I), where hundreds of people socialize at sidewalk tables. *Il Mattino* and *Qui Napoli* print decent club listings. **ARCI-GAY/Lesbica** (☎081 551 8293) has information on gay and lesbian nights at different clubs.

CAFES, BARS, AND PUBS

Caffè Letterario Intra Moenia, P. Bellini, 70 (☎081 29 07 20; www.intramoenia.it). *Caffè Letterario* appeals to the intellectuals by keeping books amidst the wicker furniture. Enjoy a salad (€7-8), cocktail (€6-7), beer (€3.50-5.50), or the sumptuous dessert *Delizia Caprese* (€8). Open daily 10am-2am. AmEx/MC/V.

Itaca, P. Bellini, 71 (☎081 8226 6132). Formerly "1799," Itaca's black decor and dim lighting appeal to your dark side. Eerie trance music keeps you from noticing the exorbitant cocktail prices. Beer €3-4, cocktails €6-7. Open daily 10am-3am. AmEx/MC/V.

S'Move Light Bar, Vico dei Sospiri, 10/A (☎081 764 5813; www.smove-lab.com). Head out of P. dei Martiri on V. Chiaia toward Poerio, take 1st right, then 1st left. Futuristic watering hole provides good company and cocktails (€5). Open daily 8am-6am.

NIGHTCLUBS AND DISCOTHECHE

Camelot, V. S. Pietro a Majella, 8 (☎0380 713 6017; camelot118@hotmail.com). Just off P. Bellini in the Historic Center, Camelot provides 2 stories of dim lighting and popular music. Except for the 3 or 4 live performances each month, Camelot specializes in beer and dancing. Beer €2.58. Open Sept.-June T-Su 10:30pm-5am.

Madison Street, V. Sgambati, 47 (☎081 546 6566), in Vomero. Features a large dance floor for weekend revelry. Cover €10. Open Sept.-May F-Su 10pm-4am.

Riot, V. S. Biagio, 39 (☎081 767 5054), off C. Umberto I. Gives you a chance to hear local artists play jazz and sing the blues. While not exactly Robert Johnson and the Mississippi Delta, these folks try hard. Open Th-Su 10:30pm-3am.

New Age, V. Atri, 36 (☎081 29 58 08). Gay and lesbian *discoteca* with an active dance floor, right in the heart of the Historical Center. No cover. Tu-Su 10pm-late.

◪ DAYTRIPS FROM NAPLES

CAMPI FLEGREI

To Baia, take the SEPSA bus from M: Pozzuoli (30min.). Don't be confused by the yet-to-be-updated signs on the Ferrovia Cumana; this rail line no longer goes through Baia. In Baia itself, buy an Unico Fascia 1 ticket (€1.70) and ride all modes of transportation all day. To Cumae, take the SEPSA bus marked Miseno-Cuma from the train station at Baia to the last stop in Cumae (15min.), and walk to the end of the V. Cumae. The "Cuma" stop on the Ferrovia Circumflegrea is in the modern town, several km away from the archaeological sites. Reach Miseno using the Miseno-Cuma SPESA bus from either Baia or Cumae, and Pozzuoli using either the Ferrovia Cumana, Ferrovia Circumflegria, or Naples Metro.

The **Campi Flegrei,** or **Phlegraean Fields,** are a group of tiny coastal towns west of Naples nestled among a chain of lakes and inactive volcanoes. Ancient Greeks colonized this area and associated the thermal nature of the land with Hades, god of the Underworld. The Greek legacy lives on in the ruins at **Cumae,** also immortalized in Virgil's *Aeneid* as Aeneas's landing point in Italy. Later, the Roman elite used the region's hot springs for their intricate bath houses that still stand on the hill over **Baia,** and built an impressive ampitheater near their believed gate to hell in **Pozzuoli.** Modern Italians dot the scorching coast of **Miseno** with their own culture, fishing boats, relaxing beachline, *pizzerie* and restaurants. With the sights spread out as much as they are, using the ubiquitous orange SEPSA buses is essential to an enjoyable day. Frequent bus stops are on the side of the road, the front of the bus will list the towns its route stretches between.

SOUTHERN ITALY

Perched on a hill overlooking the bustling port center of **Baia,** where SESPA buses drop you off, is Baia's central attraction: the luxurious **Roman Baths.** Climb up the stairs and stroll through the well-preserved ruins, remarkable for their multiple stories, beautiful mosaics and detailed ceilings. At the base of the hill sits the gem of the bath houses known misleadingly as the ◙**Temple of Mercury** or the Temple of Echoes. Light shines through the oldest dome ceiling in the world, bounces off the water and reflects onto the wall. Faint of heart be warned: lizards and snakes abound in the ancient stone walls. (☎ 081 868 7592; http://www.ulixes.it. Open daily 9am-7pm. The ticket is a 2-day pass that will get you into the Baths, the Archaeological Museum in Baia, the Scavi in Cumae, and the Ampitheater in Pozzuoli. €4; with student pass €2.) A short bus ride from the center of Baia will bring you to the **Castello Aragonese,** the **Museo Archeologico dei Campi Flegrei** with a small collection of ancient artifacts from the area, and a beautiful view of Baia's harbor. (☎ 081 868 7592. Open Tu-Su 10am-6pm. Entrance with archaeological pass.) For a less conventional view of ruins, try the glass-bottomed boat *Cymba* out of Baia's port to see the **Submerged Roman City.** The boat runs from March 18th to November 3rd and can hold 48 people. (☎ 081 526 5780. Launches Sa 12pm, 4pm; Su 10:30am, 12pm, and 4pm. €7.75, children 6-12 €6.20, under 5 free.)

Cumae (Cuma), founded in the 8th century BC, was the earliest Greek colony on the Italian mainland. Mythologically, it was the place where Aeneas, father of Rome, first washed up after being shipwrecked in Virgil's *Aeneid.* The highlight of Cumae's **scavi** (excavations) is the ◙**Antro della Sibilla,** a man-made cave gallery that had been used as a pizza oven until archaeologists realized what it was in 1932. Stroll through the cave and see where Sibyl, the most famous oracle this side of Delphi, gave her prophecies in myth. Then gape at the **Augustan Tunnel,** a deep and intricate shaft used for transportation inland from the Cumaean coast. Remnants of the Cumaen Greek past are found in the **Temple of Apollo,** located one flight of stairs above Sibyl's cave, and the **Temple of Jupiter,** a short hike up the hill from the Temple of Apollo. Though little remains of the original temples, the spectacular view of Ischia and the coastline make the hike worthwhile.

Pozzuoli, the Campi Flegri town most accessible from Naples, is a busy port to Ischia and Procida. Be sure not to miss the famous volcanic crater **Solfatara,** accessed either by hiking from the center of Pozzuoli (follow the frequent signs) or by riding bus #152. Solfatara was believed by the ancients to be a portal to Hades—not an unwarranted superstition, considering its eerie glowing yellow rocks, jets of sulfuric gas, rank odor, and unnatural warmth. (☎ 081 1526 2341; http://www.solfatara.it. Open daily 8:30am-1hr. before sunset; Apr.-Sept. 8:30am-7pm. €4.60, children 5-10 €3, groups greater than 15 €4.) Beneath the Solfatura crater, a short walk from both the waterfront and the train station, is the ◙**Flavian Ampitheater,** built in the first century AD. Wander around the beautiful remains and pretend you're Russell Crowe. (☎ 081 526 6007. Open daily 9am-8pm in summer; 9am-7pm in winter. With Campi Flegri archaeological pass €4, students €2.)

Although Baia and Cumae are ideal daytrips from Naples, take advantage of the pleasant beachfront hotels in **Miseno.** Take the **SEPSA** bus from Baia or Cumae to Miseno. The **Villa Palma Hotel ❹,** V. Misena, 30, is at the last Miseno bus stop. This modern and comfortable choice is steps from the beach. (☎ 081 523 3944. 15 rooms all with bath. Breakfast included. Doubles €36-62. AmEx/MC/V.) On the high promontory at the tip of the Campi Flegrei is the **Cala Moresca ❺,** V. Faro, 44, with an amazing view that extends from Miseno's beach all the way to Naples. (☎ 081 523 5595. 28 rooms fully equipped. Breakfast included. Singles €62-67; Doubles €93-108. Make reservations. AmEx/MC/V.) On the other side of the Miseno Port, there is the **Hotel Miseno ❹,** V. Miseno, 30, with breezy, small rooms overlooking fishing boats. (☎ 081 523 5000. 17 rooms with bath. Breakfast included. Singles €36-46; doubles €41-52. AmEx/MC/V.)

CASERTA
☎ 0823

Caserta is easily accessible by train. Trains to and from Naples (30-50min., 35 per day, 4:50am-9:20pm, €2.48) and Rome (2½-3½hr., €9.30). The Caserta station, in the center of town across from the Reggia, is a major stop for local buses (€0.77-0.88). The Reggia is directly opposite the train station, across P. Carlo III. ☎ 0823 32 14 00. Palazzo and gardens open Tu-Su 9am-7:30pm. €6 for entrance to both. EPT tourist offices are at C. Trieste, 43, at the corner of P. Dante. ☎ 0823 32 11 37. Open M-F 9am-7:30pm. The post office is on V. Ellittico, off P. Carlo III, in front of the train station to the left. Postal Code: 81100. To Capua, take the train to "Santa Maria Capua Vètere" (€1.19) from Caserta, walk straight 1 block, and make the 1st left. Take the next left onto V. Achille, walk 150m, and turn right onto V. E. Ricciardi, which becomes V. Amfiteatro. Or, the blue bus from the Caserta train station (€0.88) will take you straight to P. Adriano near the ruins. To Naples, buses leave from the intersection 1 block north of the Capua train station.

Tourists flock to Caserta, "the Versailles of Naples," to see the magnificent ■**Reggia.** When Bourbon King Charles III commissioned the palace in 1751, he intended it to rival that of Louis XIV. The complex was finished in 1775, including the gigantic Royal Palace and the 120-hectare **parco** (palace garden). Lush lawns, fountains, sculptures, and carefully pruned trees culminate in a 75m man-made waterfall, setting for the final scene of the 1977 *Star Wars*. Sculptural groups at the bottom show Diana transforming the hunter Actaeon into a deer as his hounds pounce on him. To the right are the "English Gardens," complete with fake ruins inspired by Pompeii and Paestum. If you'd rather not make the 3km walk, you can take a romantic horse-and-buggy ride from the entrance to the gardens. The **palazzo** itself boasts 1200 rooms, 1742 windows, and 34 staircases. The main entrance stairway is a highlight of the palace's architecture. Frescoes and intricate marble floors adorn the gaudy royal apartments.

One train stop from Caserta lies **Capua,** and an impressive **Roman amphitheater,** as intact as (though smaller than) the Colosseum in Rome. The tunnels beneath brought gladiators and beasts into the arena. (Open daily 9am-7:30. €2.50).

Most of the hotels in Caserta are in the dilapidated area around the train station. If you're too tired to trek elsewhere after touring the Reggia, **Hotel Baby ❹,** V. G. Verdi, 41, to the right as you exit the station, has ten well-furnished rooms. (☎ 0823 32 83 11. Singles €40; doubles €52; triples €67; quads €82). Caserta's cuisine is simple—the town has numerous **pizzerie** (takeout available). One of the most popular is **Pizzeria La Ciociara ❶,** V. Roma, 13, serving up large slices for €0.62-1.29. From the train station, walk two blocks toward the Reggia and take a right on V. Roma. (☎ 0823 32 26 14. Open daily 9am-midnight.) If you're spending a night in Caserta, try **Grande Caffè Margherita** in P. Dante for some nocturnal action (☎ 0823 32 11 07; open daily 7am-2am) or any of the bars around lush P. Vanvitelli, a short walk down V. Mazzini from P. Dante.

BENEVENTO
☎ 0824

Benevento is accessible by train from Caserta (1hr., €3.05), Naples (1½hr., €3.87), and Rome (3hr., €11.36). Local buses (☎ 0824 21 015) leave from the train station, including bus #1 (€0.52) to C. Garibaldi, the center of town. Buses to Naples and local towns leave from the Terminal Autobus Extraurbani, several blocks north of the Castel on C. Garibaldi. For taxis call ☎ 0824 20 000. The EPT tourist office in P. Roma (off C. Garibaldi) is a storehouse of knowledge. ☎ 0824 31 99 38. Open M-F 8am-1:45pm and 3-5:45pm. Postal Code: 82100.

According to legend, this town's original name was *malaventum* (bad wind) until 275 BC, when the Romans defeated Pyrrhus here and decided it was a *benevento* (good wind) after all. Even after being bombed during WWII, this peaceful mountain enclave retained its ancient monuments and old-town charm.

From the 6th to the 4th century BC, Benevento was the center of the Samnite kingdom. The bell tower in P. Matteotti, off C. Garibaldi, proudly commemorates Benevento's ancient heritage. The **Church of S. Sofia** (AD 762), also in P. Matteotti, has an attached monastery that is now the **Museo del Sannio.** The museum exhibits Samnite artifacts, headless Roman statues, and contemporary works by local artists. (☎ 0824 21 818. Open Tu-Su 9am-1pm. €2.58. €1.03 students.) South of the museum, down Vico Noce, is a sculpture garden with works by Mino Palladino. North of P. Roma is the **☒Arch of Beneventum** (114-117 BC), which elaborately depicts the ruling tactics of the Emperor **Trajan.** At the other end of town (walking from the arch, a left off of C. Garibaldi past the duomo) is a well-preserved 2nd-century **Roman theater** that today hosts concerts (€2, students €1). Every September the town hosts a theater festival; contact the tourist office for details.

Albergo della Corte ❸ is in an alley at P. Piano di Corte, 11. Follow the narrow V. Bartolomeo Camerario off C. Garibaldi. Although no English is spoken at this historic *palazzo* hotel, 11 renovated rooms have bath, phone, and TV. (☎ 0824 54 819. Singles €33.60; doubles €46.50. AmEx/MC/V.) Near Trajan's Arch, **Ristorante e Pizzeria Traiano ❷,** V. Manciotti, 48, serves simple but delectable meals. (☎ 0824 25 013. *Primi* €4.13; *secondi* €4.13. Open W-M noon-4pm and 7pm-midnight.) The area is known for its rich *mozzarella di buffala;* the only thing more sumptuous is Benevento's bewitching **☒*Strega*** liqueur, named after the town's legendary spell-casters. If swigging it straight will have you falling off your broom, at least try the bright yellow *Strega*-flavored *gelato.*

The long way back to Naples takes you through the rugged backcountry. Buses stop at the small village of Montesarchio, easily explored in two hours. Covering a steep hill, its winding streets lead to an **☒Aragonese tower** and fabulous views. The Benevento tourist office can provide a bus schedule.

BAY OF NAPLES

POMPEII (POMPEI)   ☎ 081

On August 24, AD 79, the prosperous Roman city of Pompeii was buried in a fit of towering flames, suffocating black clouds, and lava from Mt. Vesuvius. Except for the prudent few who dropped everything and ran at the first tremors, Pompeiians suffered a live burial. You may well feel apprehensive at the thought of viewing the ghastly and evocative relics of the town's demise: the ash casts of the victims' bodies and their preserved contortions and expressions, the enduring walls and frescoes. Mount Vesuvius broods nearby, still active and terrifying. Since the first unearthings in 1748, discoveries are made every decade, providing a vivid picture of daily life in the Roman era.

▐ TRANSPORTATION

The quickest route to Pompeii (25km south of Naples) is the **Circumvesuviana** train (☎ 081 772 2444), which can be boarded at Naples's Stazione Centrale (dir.: "Sorrento," 2 per hr., 5:39am-10:42pm, €1.90), or from Sorrento's station. Get off at the "Pompeii Scavi/Villa dei Misteri" stop, ignoring "Pompeii Santuario." Eurail passes are not valid. The entrance to the ruins is downhill to the left. An alternative is the less frequent **FS** train that leaves from the Naples station and stops at modern Pompeii on route to Salerno (30min., every hr., €1.90). The FS train station is a 10min. walk from the east entrance to the excavations. To get there, continue straight on V. Sacra to the end and then turn left onto V. Roma.

MODERN POMPEII

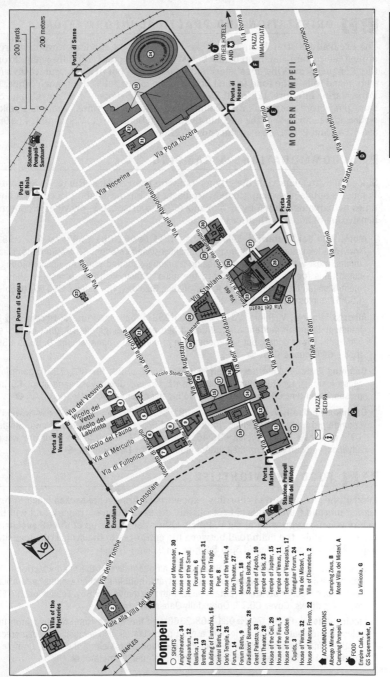

Pompeii

○ SIGHTS

Amphitheater, **34**
Antiquarium, **12**
Basilica, **13**
Brothel, **19**
Building of Eumachia, **16**
Central Baths, **21**
Doric Temple, **25**
Forum, **14**
Forum Baths, **9**
Gladiators Barracks, **28**
Great Palestra, **33**
Great Theater, **26**
House of the Ceii, **29**
House of the Faun, **5**
House of the Golden
  Cupids, **3**
House of Venus, **32**
House of Marcus Fronto, **22**

House of Menander, **30**
House of Pansa, **7**
House of the Small
  Fountain, **6**
House of Tiburtinus, **31**
House of the Tragic
  Poet, **8**
House of the Vettii, **4**
Little Theater, **27**
Macellum, **18**
Stabian Baths, **20**
Temple of Apollo, **10**
Temple of Isis, **23**
Temple of Jupiter, **15**
Temple of Venus, **11**
Temple of Vespasian, **17**
Triangular Forum, **24**
Villa dei Misteri, **1**
Villa of Diomedes, **2**

▲ ACCOMMODATIONS

Albergo Minerva, **F**
Camping Pompeii, **C**

Camping Zeus, **B**
Motel Villa dei Misteri, **A**

● FOOD

Empire Cafe, **E**
GS Supermarket, **D**

La Vinicola, **G**

✚ 🛈 ORIENTATION AND PRACTICAL INFORMATION

The excavations stretch on an east-west axis, with the modern town clustered around the eastern end. Stop by the **tourist office**, V. Sacra, 1, for a free map. From the "Pompeii Scavi/Villa dei Misteri" stop, take a right out of the Circumvesuviana station and follow the road to the bottom of the hill to get to the branch office, P. Porta Marina Inferiore, 12. (☎081 850 7255. Both offices open M-F 8am-3:30pm, Sa 8am-2pm.) Store your pack for free at the entrance to the ruins. There is a **police station** at the entrance to the site, but the main stations are at P. Schettini, 1 (☎081 850 6164), and P. B. Longo, at the end of V. Roma.

⌂ ACCOMMODATIONS & CAMPING

Since most travelers visit the city as a daytrip from Naples, Rome, or Sorrento, Pompeii's hotels and campgrounds are eager for business, and prices can sometimes be bargained down by 15% or more. The tourist office provides a comprehensive list of hotels with prices.

Motel Villa dei Misteri, V. Villa dei Misteri, 11 (☎081 861 3593; fax 862 2983; www.villadeimisteri.it), uphill from the Circumvesuviana station. 33 comfortable, clean rooms, most with balconies overlooking a uniquely shaped pool. An upscale lounge, sumptuous rooms, and proximity to the ruins attracts visitors, so reserve about 3 months ahead for summer stays. A/C available. Breakfast €5. Singles €50-57; doubles €50-57; triples €66-75. AmEx/MC/V. ❹

Albergo Minerva, V. Plinio, 23 (☎081 863 2587), between Porta di Nocera and P. Immacolata in the modern town. Wedged between buildings are 10 quiet rooms, all with bath. Lower prices, but some complain of unfriendly management. Doubles €39; triples €47; quads €57. ❹

Camping Zeus, V. Villa dei Misteri, 1 (☎081 861 5320; fax 861 7536; camping-zeus@libero.it), located outside the "Villa dei Misteri" Circumvesuviana stop. €5 per person, small tent €4, large tent €6. 2- to 5-person bungalows €40-70. MC/V. ❶

Camping Pompeii, V. Plinio, 121-8 (☎081 862 2882; fax 850 2772; www.wei.it/cpompei), downhill on V. Plinio, the main road from the ruins. 45 bungalows. Singles €25; doubles €31-41; triples €36-46; quads €51-61. If you fail to reserve 1 wk. in advance, you can sleep on their indoor lobby floor for €6 per night. ❷

🍴 🍷 FOOD AND NIGHTLIFE

Food at the site cafeteria is horribly expensive, so bring a **pre-packed lunch.** A few restaurants and fruit stands cluster outside the excavation entrances, and will try to lure you in as you walk along V. Pilino. Otherwise, stock up at the **GS supermarket,** on V. Statale, the main road between the entrances to the archaeological site. (Open M-Sa 9:30am-1pm and 5pm-8:30pm, Su 9:30am-1pm.)

La Vinicola, V. Roma, 29 (☎081 863 1244), an alternative to the nearby McDonald's. Tempts visitors with a pleasant outdoor courtyard, bubbling Italian waiters, and abundant *gnocchi con mozzarella* (potato pasta with mozzarella, €3.65). Tourist lunch €13, excluding drinks. Cover €0.77. Open daily 9am-midnight. ❸

Empire Cafe, V. Plinio, 71 (☎081 863 2366), on the way to Hotel Minerva from the ruins. The ultimate Italian all-in-one: a pizza place that is also a music hall/*discoteca*. Youthful, friendly atmosphere perfect for relaxation after visiting the ruins. Complete meals €6-11. Open daily 9am-2am. Discotheque open 9pm-2am. ❷

◙ SIGHTS

Pompeii entrances are open 8:30am to 7:30pm. A comprehensive exploration will probably take all day. (Tickets €10, EU students €5, and EU citizens under 18 or over 65 free). **Guided tours,** which allow you to savor the details of life and death in the first century AD, are quite expensive and usually only take groups. Call **GATA Tours** (☎ 081 861 5661) or **Assotouring** (☎ 081 862 2560) for information. Some of the tour guides are wise to freeloaders and will actually yell at offenders; others remain oblivious. Those with neither the cash nor the savvy to join a tour can use the helpful *Brief Guide to Pompeii,* given out at the entrance along with a map to get around, or buy one of the various guidebooks available outside site entrances (from €5). Endure a hefty admission price and a poor labeling system to get a peek under 2000-year-old molten lava.

NEAR FORUM. The **basilica** (Roman law court) walls, on the right entering the ruins, are decorated with stucco made to look like marble. Walk farther down V. D. Marina to reach the ◙**Forum,** which is surrounded by a colonnade. Once dotted with statues of emperors and gods, this site was the commercial, civic, and religious center of the city. Cases along the side display some of the gruesome bodycasts of Vesuvius's victims. At the upper end rises the **Temple of Jupiter,** mostly destroyed by an earthquake that struck 17 years before the city's bad luck got worse. To the left, the **Temple of Apollo** contains statues of Apollo and Diana (originals in Naples's **Museo Archeologico Nazionale,** p. 602) and a column topped by a sundial. On the opposite long side of the forum, the **Temple of Vespasian** houses a delicate frieze depicting preparation for a sacrifice. To the right, the **Building of Eumachia** has a door frame carved with animals and insects in acanthus scrolls.

NEAR HOUSE OF THE FAUN. At the **Forum Baths,** archaeologists have chipped away parts of the bodycasts to reveal teeth and bones beneath. The ◙**House of the Faun** was where a bronze dancing faun and the spectacular Alexander Mosaic were found (originals in the **Museo Archeologico Nazionale,** p. 537). The sheer opulence of this building leads archaeologists to believe that it was the dwelling of one of the richest men in town. The ◙**House of the Vettii,** decorated with vivid frescoes, was the home of two brothers, whose rivalry seems to have left its mark on every wall. The famous painting featured on all the postcards of Priapus, god of fertility, showing off his endowment, is in the vestibule. And while in ancient times, phalli were believed to scare off evil spirits, these days they only seem to make tourists titter. *(Exit the Forum through the upper end, by the cafeteria, and the Forum Baths are on the left. A right on V. della Fortuna leads to the House of the Faun. Continuing on V. della Fortuna and turning left on V. dei Vettii will bring you to the House of the Vettii on the left.)*

NEAR BROTHEL. The Romans who were repaving this worn path when the volcano struck were forced to leave their work unfinished. A quick right leads to the small **brothel** (the Lupenar) containing several bedstalls. Above each stall, a pornographic painting depicts with unabashed precision the specialty of its occupant. After 2000 years, this remains the most popular place in town; you may have to wait in line. The street continues down to the main avenue, V. dell' Abbondanza. To the left lie the **Stabian Baths,** which were privately owned and therefore fancier than the Forum Baths. The separate men's and women's sides each include a dressing room, cold baths *(frigidarie),* warm baths *(tepidarie),* and hot steam baths *(caldarie),* with the remnants of an intricate system that led hot steam underneath the floor still visible. *(Back down V. dei Vetti, cross V. della Fortuna over to V. Storto, and then turn left on V. degli Augustali.)*

NEAR GREAT THEATER. The **Great Theater** was built in the first half of the 2nd century BC, and the **Little Theater,** built later for music and dance concerts. North of the theaters stands the **Temple of Isis,** Pompeii's monument to the Egyptian fertility goddess. Through the exit on the right, the road passes two fine houses, the **House of the Ceii** and the **House of Menander.** At the end of the street, a left turn will return you to the main road. The Romans believed that crossroads were vulnerable to evil spirits, so they built altars like one here to ward them off. *(Across the street, V. dei Teatri leads to a huge complex consisting of the Great Theater and the Little Theater.)*

NEAR AMPHITHEATER. On V. dell'Abbondanza, red writing glares from the walls, expressing everything from political slogans to love declarations. Popular favorites include "Albanus is a bugger," "Restitutus has deceived many girls many times," and the lyrical "Lovers, like bees, lead a honey-sweet life"—apparently, graffiti hasn't changed much in 2000 years. At the end of the street rest the **House of Tiburtinus** and the **House of Venus,** huge complexes with gardens replanted according to modern knowledge of ancient horticulture. The nearby **amphitheater** (80 BC), the oldest standing in the world, once held 12,000 spectators. When battles occurred, crowds decided whether a defeated gladiator would live or die with a casual thumbs up or thumbs down.

The ◪**Villa of the Mysteries** is the most intact Pompeiian villa. The *Dionysiac Frieze* is one of the largest paintings from Roman antiquity, depicting a bride's initiation into the cult of Dionysus. Head through the Porta for a great view of the entire city. *(For the Villa of the Mysteries go to the far west end of V. della Fortuna, turn right on V. Consolare (near the "Cave Canem" mosaic), and walk all the way up Porta Ercolano.)*

◨ DAYTRIPS FROM POMPEII

HERCULANEUM (ERCOLANO)

To reach Ercolano, take a Circumvesuviana train from Naples's central train station to the "Ercolano" stop (dir.: Sorrento, 20min.). Walk 500m downhill to the ticket office. The Municipal Tourist Office, V. IV Novembre, 84 (☎081 788 1243) is on the way (open M-Sa 9am-3pm). The archaeological site is open daily 8:30am to 7:30pm. €10, EU students €5, EU citizens under 18 or over 65 free. Tours offered from the tourist office, but are only worthwhile for a large group. Illustrated guidebooks are available at any of the shops flanking the entrance, or get the free Brief Guide to Herculaneum and map at the entrance.

Neatly excavated and impressively intact, the remains of the prosperous Roman town of Herculaneum (modern Ercolano) hardly deserve the term "ruins." Indeed, exploring the 2000-year-old houses, complete with frescoes, furniture, mosaics, small sculptures, and even wooden doors, feels like an invasion of privacy.

Herculaneum does not evoke the tragedy of Pompeii—most of its inhabitants escaped the ravages of Vesuvius. Only a small part of the southeastern quarter of the city has been excavated, and between 15 and 20 houses are open to the public. One of the more alluring is the **House of Deer** (named for the statues of deer found in the courtyard), where archaeologists found the statue, *Satyr with a Wineskin,* and one of Hercules in a drunken stupor trying to relieve himself. The **baths,** with largely intact warm and hot rooms and a vaulted swimming pool, conjure up images of ancient opulence. The **House of the Mosaic of Neptune and Anfitrite,** which belonged to a rich shop owner, is famous for its breathtaking namesake mosaic, and the front of the house has a remarkably well-preserved wine shop. A mock colonnade of stucco distinguishes the **Samnise House.** Down the street, the **House of the Wooden Partition** still has a door in its elegant courtyard, and an ancient clothes press is around the corner. Cardo IV shows you what a Roman street must have looked like. Outside the site, 250m to the left on the main road, lies the **theater,** perfectly preserved underground. (☎ 081 739 0963. Occasionally open for visits; call to check.) The **Villa dei Papiri,** 500m west of the site, recently caused a stir when a trove of ancient scrolls in the library appeared to include works by Cicero, Virgil, and Horace. The villa is not open to the public.

MT. VESUVIUS

Trasporti Vesuviani buses run from Ercolano up to the crater of Vesuvius (round-trip €3.50, buy tickets on the bus; schedule at the tourist office or on the bus). They leave from outside the Ercolano Circumvesuviana station. Bus stop is part way up the crater; it's a 20-30min. walk to the top. Admission to the area around the crater €6.

Peer into the only active volcano on mainland Europe. Scientists say that, on average, volcanoes should erupt every 30 years—Vesuvius hasn't since March 31, 1944. Nevertheless, experts say the trip is safe.

SORRENTO ☎ 081

Sorrento is popularly visited both on its own and as a base for exploring the Bay of Naples and Amalfi Coast. With 20,000 residents, it is the largest town in the area, and with 13,000 hotel beds, the most touristed. So popular is the town with British tourists that it is easier to find a cup of tea than a *cappuccino*, and prices are often listed in pounds. Still, Sorrento has its charms— the streets of the old city and the **Marina Grande.** Frequent ferry connections provide links to the rest of the bay.

▛ TRANSPORTATION

The Sorrento **tourist office** has full ferry, bus, and train schedules.

Trains: Circumvesuviana (☎ 081 772 2444), just off P. Lauro. 39 trains per day, from 5am-11:30pm to: **Herculaneum** (45min., €1.65); **Naples** (1hr., €2.84); **Pompeii** (30min., €1.65).

Ferries and **Hydrofoils:** All boats dock at the port, accessible from P. Tassi by bus (€0.93). **Linee Marittime Partenopee** (☎ 081 807 1812) runs ferries (40min., 5 per day, 8:30am-4:50pm, €6.50) and hydrofoils (20min., 17 per day, 7:20am-5:40pm, €8.50) to **Capri.** It also runs hydrofoils to **Ischia** (45min., 9:30am, €12.50) and **Naples** (35min., 7 per day, 7:20am-6:35pm, €7). Ticket offices open daily 7:30am-7pm. **Caremar** (☎ 081 807 3077) runs fast ferries to **Capri** (20min., €5.70). Ticket offices open daily 7am-5pm.

Buses: SITA buses leave from Circumvesuviana station for the Amalfi coast. 18 buses per day 6:35am-8:05pm to: **Amalfi** (1¼hr., €2.12) and **Positano** (40min., €1.19). Buy your tickets at a bar, *tabacchi,* or hotel in P. Lauro.

◢✦ 🛈 ORIENTATION AND PRACTICAL INFORMATION

Most of Sorrento is on a flat shelf with cliffs rapidly descending to the Bay of Naples. **Piazza Tasso,** at the center of town, is connected by a stairway (and roads) to the **Marina Piccola** port, but those coming with luggage from a ferry are better advised to catch one of the buses. **Corso Italia** runs through Piazza Tasso—facing the sea, the train and bus station at Piazza Lauro are to the right, while the old city is to the left. **Corso S. Caesaro** runs parallel to Corso Italia on the old city side of Piazza Tasso and has a lively outdoor market.

Tourist Office: L. de Maio, 35 (☎ 081 807 4033). From P. Tasso, take L. de Maio through P. S. Antonio and continue toward the port. The office is to the right in the Circolo dei Forestieri compound. English spoken. Grab a free copy of *Surrentum,* the monthly tourist magazine. Open Apr.-Sept. M-Sa 8:45am-7:45pm; Oct.-Mar. M-Sa 8:30am-2pm and 4-6:15pm.

Currency Exchange: No-commission currency exchange is everywhere and easy to find.

Car and Scooter Rental: Sorrento Car Service, C. Italia, 210a (☎081 878 1386). Scooters from €38.73 per day. Helmet and insurance included. Driver's license required. Cars and chauffeurs available. Open daily 8am-1pm and 4-8pm. AmEx/V/MC.

English-language Bookstore: Libreria Tasso, V. S. Cesareo, 96 (☎081 807 1639; libreriatasso@tin.it). Stocks thrillers, including the shocking *Let's Go.* Open M-Sa 9:30am-1:30pm and 5-10:45pm, Su 11am-1:30pm and 7-10:45pm.

Laundromat: Terlizzi, C. Italia, 30 (☎081 878 1185), in the old quarter. €8 per load. Detergent €0.50. Dry cleaning. Open M-Sa 7:55am-1:30pm and 5-8pm.

Emergency: ☎113.

Police: (☎081 807 3088) on Vco. 3° Rota. From the station, go right on C. Italia and left after V. Nizza.

Medical Assistance: Pronto Soccorso (☎081 533 1111) at **Ospedale Civile di Sorrento,** C. Italia, 129 (☎081 533 1111).

Internet Access: Blublu.it, V. Fuorimura, 20d (☎/fax 081 807 4854; www.blublu.it). Take V. Fuorimura from P. Tasso. English-speaking staff and fast connections. €3 per 30min. Open M-F 10am-1pm and 4:30-12pm, Sa 4:30pm-12:30am.

Post Office: C. Italia, 210u (☎081 807 2828), near P. Lauro. Open M-F 8am-6:30pm, Sat 8am-12:30pm.

Postal Code: 80067.

▗ ACCOMMODATIONS AND CAMPING

Sorrento's reasonably priced accommodations, convenient transportation, and Internet access make it a great place to stay while touring along the Amalfi Coast. Many visitors choose to head off to the beaches and small towns during the day and return to crowd Sorrento's hotels at night. Make reservations in the peak summer months. Some hotels charge more than their established prices—ask to see the official price list and you can write a letter to the EPT if you're being overcharged. Prices listed below are for high season.

Hotel Elios, V. Capo, 33 (☎081 878 1812), halfway to the Punta del Capo. Take bus A from P. Tasso. Though the 14 rooms are not particularly dazzling, the hotel's hilltop location gives a great view from 2 large terraces. Singles €25-30; doubles €40-50. ❸

Hotel City, C. Italia, 221 (☎081 877 2210; hotelcity@libero.it), left on C. Italia from the station. Currency exchange, bus tickets, maps, English newspapers, and bar. Convenient location in the heart of Sorrento. Internet €5.20 per hr. In summer, reserve 1 month ahead. Singles €37-46; doubles €40-50. AmEx/MC/V. ❹

Hotel Savoia, V. Fuorimura, 46 (☎/fax 081 878 2511; www.hotel-savoia.com), 4 blocks from P. Tasso. This tranquil hotel has 15 spacious rooms, all with TV, ceiling fan, and clean bath. Breakfast included. Singles €65; doubles €80. AmEx/MC/V. ❺

Ostello Le Sirene, V. Degli Aranci, 160 (☎081 807 2925; info@hostel.it). From C. Italia, turn right onto V. S. Renato, and take 1st right. Prepare to wake up to the 1st train or to guests stumbling in just before the 4am curfew. Co-ed dorms with bath outside €14, with bath inside room €16. ❷

▓ **Nube d'Argento,** V. del Capo, 21 (☎081 878 1344; fax 807 3450; www.nubedargento.com). Bus A from P. Tasso €0.93. Campground near the ocean, with a pool, hot showers, market, and restaurant. Laundry €7. Reservations only for bungalows, in Aug. reserve 2 months ahead. €7-9 per person, €4-8.50 per tent. 2-person bungalows €45-78. 10% discount with Magic Europe camping brochure (available at any campsite) or International Camping Card. AmEx/MC/V. ❶

◨ FOOD

Local specialties at reasonable prices await in Sorrento's restaurants and *trattorie*. Forgo the crowded central restaurants, and you'll find the Italian fare rather than the British. Sorrento is famous for its *gnocchi alla Sorrentina* (potato pasta smothered in tomato sauce, mozzarella, and basil), its *cannelloni* (pasta tubes stuffed with cheese and herbs), and its *nocillo* (a dark walnut liqueur). **Fabbrica Liquori,** V. S. Cesareo, 51, provides free samples of this, as well as of the ubiquitous *limoncello*, a heavy lemon liqueur. For **market** stands, follow V. S. Cesareo from P. Tasso, where ripe, sweet, juicy fruit awaits.

▨ **Ristorante e Pizzeria Giardiniello,** V. Accademia, 7 (☎081 878 4616). Take the 2nd left off V. Giuliani, which runs off C. Italia at the cathedral. Mamma Luisa does all the cooking in this family-run establishment. Try her delightful *gnocchi* €4.65, and *linguini al cartoccio* (with mixed seafood) €6.70. Cover €1.05. Open June-Sept. daily 11am-2am; Oct.-May F-W 11am-2am. AmEx/MC/V. ❷

▨ **Davide,** V. Giuliani, 39 (☎081 878 1337). Right off C. Italia, 2 blocks from P. Tasso, you'll find Sorrento's best *gelato*. 60 spectacular flavors await, making a decision close to impossible: should I go for the watermelon, peach delicate, fig heavenly, or butterscotch savory? €1.90 for 2 scoops. Open daily 10am-midnight. ❶

La Pasteria Di Corso, V. Pietà, 3/5 (☎081 877 3432), in the alley behind the Tasso statue in P. Tasso, serves up old-style Sorrento cuisine in a beautiful candlelit setting. *Antipasti* €7.50-13, *secondi* €8-12. End a satisfying meal with their delectable fruit brandy. Cover €2. Open W-Su 7pm-midnight. ❸

Taverna Azzura, V. Marina Grande, 166 (☎081 877 2510). From C. Italia towards the old city, go right on V. Giuliani to the end; Marina Grande is a pleasant 10min. walk to the left on the small road past P. della Vittoria. Fresh seafood and pasta cooked to perfection; the owner recommends the *linguine frutti di mare*. *Primi* €5.50, *secondi* €7.50. Cover €2. Open daily 12-3pm and 7pm-12am, in winter. closed M. MC/V. ❸

Ristorante La Laterna Pizzeria, V. S. Caesaro, 23/25 (☎081 878 1355). Flip through the extensive wine listings and indulge in the large *antipasti* buffet at this classy spot. Outdoor dining, often accompanied by live music, is incomparable in the setting of the beautiful old city. *Pasta* €6.50-21.50, *pesce* €6.50-17. AmEx/MC/V. ❹

Pizza a Metro, V. Nicotera, 15 (☎081 879 8309), in Vico Equense, a 10min. train ride. Take the Circumvesuviana to V. Equense, go straight as you exit the station, and follow the winding road uphill to P. Umberto. Take a left on V. Roma and another left on V. Nicotera. Unofficially the world's largest pizzeria, this 2-story, 3000-seat facility has wood-burning ovens that cook 1m-long pizzas (€18-30). Smaller pizzas €5.16-7.75. Cover €1.03. Service 13%. Open daily 12pm-1am. AmEx/MC/V. ❷

The Red Lion, V. Marziale, 25 (☎081 807 3089; www.theredlion.it), a right off of C. Italia going to the train station from P. Tasso. Popular among the younger Sorrento set for its convivial atmosphere, great food, and low prices, this spot is packed every night. Full meal €10. AmEx/MC/V. ❷

◉ ♫ SIGHTS AND ENTERTAINMENT

Sorrento's popularity among tourists (and tourist vendors) is remarkable when one considers the dearth of traditional Italian attractions, the duomo-*torre-palazzo* combination. The **Marina Grande** provides a beautiful setting for a later afternoon stroll, far from the crowds around Piazza Tasso, and the walk goes through the equally charming streets of the **old city.**

The walk to Punta del Capo is picturesque as well, with the ruins of the **Villa di Pollio** around a beautiful cove fit for exploring at the tip of the cape. Take bus A (€0.93) from P. Tasso to the end of the route and take the footpath from the right of the stop. Bring your suit and a towel for a memorable swim among the ruins.

The old city and the area around P. Tasso heat up after dark, as locals and tourists stroll the streets, gaze over the bay, and cavort about town on mopeds. Hands down the most stylish bar in Sorrento, **Gatto Nero,** V. Correale, 21, has a garden and creative interior—each wall is painted in the style of a Modernist painter, among them Picasso and Matisse. Jazz and blues animate the crowd that gathers by 11pm in the summer. (☎081 877 3686. Open Tu-Su noon-3pm, 7pm-midnight.) The **Merry Monk Guinness Pub,** at V. Capo, 4, is as dark as any Guinness Pub should be. What's more, there's a room with eight computers. (☎081 877 2409. Internet €5 per hr. Open daily from 11am until everyone leaves.) In the summer months, a fun-loving crowd collects after 10:30pm in the rooftop lemon grove above **The English Inn,** at C. Italia, 56, where 80s music gets dancers moving. (☎081 807 4357. Open daily 9am-1am, much later on weekends.) **Chaplin's Pub,** C. Italia, 18, across the street, is packed with a boisterous crowd in the evening, and the best place to celebrate Irish pride in Italy. (☎081 807 2551. Open daily 11am-3am.)

BAY OF NAPLES ISLANDS

The pleasure islands **Capri, Ischia,** and **Procida** beckon the weary traveler with promises of breathtaking natural sights, comfortable accommodations, and gorgeous beaches. The islands can be reached by ferries *(traghetti)* or faster, more expensive hydrofoils *(aliscafi)*. But the tranquility of sun-baked landscapes has its price, and you might end up spending more than you want for accommodations. For jaunts to Ischia and Procida, the route through Pozzuoli (easily reached on the Naples Metro) is shortest and cheapest; for Capri, Sorrento is an efficient starting point. The most frequented route to Capri and Ischia is through Naples's Mergellina and Molo Beverello ports. To reach Molo Beverello from Stazione Centrale, take tram #1 from P. Garibaldi to P. Municipio on the waterfront. Ferries and hydrofoils also run between the islands, but with much less frequency than between the major ports.

CAPRI AND ANACAPRI   ☎081

Augustus fell in love with this island's fantastic beauty in 29 BC, but traded it in for the fertility of Ischia. His successor Tiberius passed his last decade on Capri, leaving a dozen scattered villas. Visitors today pay exorbitant rates to tour the renowned **Blue Grotto,** a cave where the water shimmers bright blue, and to gawk at the rich and famous. Away from the throngs flitting between Capri's expensive boutiques, Anacapri is home to budget hotels, spectacular vistas, and empty mountain paths. Crowds and prices soar with summer, so the best times to visit are in the late spring or early fall, though it is well worth the trip any time of year.

▐ TRANSPORTATION

Ferries and Hydrofoils: Ticket office, arrivals and departures at **Marina Grande.** For more info about how to get to Capri, check out ferries from Naples and Sorrento. Caremar usually is the best deal. Ferries and hydrofoils are also available to Ischia and Amalfi. Check ticket offices at Marina Grande for details.

Caremar (☎081 837 0700) runs ferries and hydrofoils. Ferries to **Naples** (1¼hr., 6 per day 5:45am-7:50pm) and **Sorrento** (50 min., 4 per day, 7am-6:15pm, €5.68). Hydrofoils to **Naples** (40min., 4 per day, 6:50am-5:40pm, €11). Ticket office open daily 7am-8pm.

SNAV (☎081 837 7577) runs hydrofoils to **Naples's** Mergellina port (40min., 13 per day, 7:15am-8:10pm, €11). Ticket office open daily 8am-8pm.

Linea Jet (☎081 837 0819) runs hydrofoils to **Naples** (40min., 10 per day, 8:30am-6:25pm, €11) and **Sorrento** (20min., €7.23). Ticket office open daily 9am-6pm.

Local Transportation: SIPPIC buses (☎081 837 0420) depart from V. Roma in Capri for Anacapri (every 15min., 6am-1:40am), Marina Piccola, and points in between. In Anacapri, buses depart from P. Barile, off V. Orlandi, for the *Grotta Azzura* (Blue Grotto), the *faro* (lighthouse), and other points. Direct line between Marina Grande and P. Vittoria in Anacapri which runs (every hr. on the hr.; €1.30, day pass €6.70).

Taxis: Convertible taxis are at the bus stop in Capri (☎081 837 0543), and at P. Vittoria in Anacapri (☎081 837 1175.)

⊁ 🔃 ORIENTATION AND PRACTICAL INFORMATION

There are two towns on the island of Capri—**Capri proper** near the ports and **Anacapri,** higher up the mountain. Ferries dock at **Marina Grande,** where a **funicular** runs to **Piazza Umberto** in Capri (every 10min., 6:30-12:30am in summer, €1.30). The alternative is an arduous 1hr. hike up a narrow stairway. Expensive boutiques and bakeries line the narrow streets radiating off Piazza Umberto. **Via Roma,** to the right upon exiting the funicular, leads to Anacapri. The bus to Anacapri stops in **Piazza Vittoria.** Villa S. Michele and the Monte Solaro chairlift are nearby. **Via Giuseppe Orlandi,** running from Piazza Vittoria, leads to the best budget establishments. Except for the port road, Capri is comprised of narrow pedestrian paths.

Tourist Office: The **AAST information Office** (☎081 837 0634) lies at the end of the dock at Marina Grande in Capri. Another branch is at P. Umberto in Capri, under the clock (☎081 837 0686). In Anacapri, there's one at V. Orlandi, 59 (☎081 837 1524), off the main piazza, to the right when you get off the bus. Pick up the annual handbook *Capri è...* and a detailed map (€0.80). Open Jun.-Sept. M-Sa 8:30am-8:30pm; Oct.-May M-Sa 9am-1:30pm and 3:30-6:45pm.

Currency Exchange: There are official exchange agencies at V. Roma, 31 (☎081 837 4768), across from the main bus stop, and in P. Umberto. Another agency in P. Vittoria, 2 (☎081 837 3146), in the center of Anacapri. No commission. Open daily 9am-8pm, reduced hours in winter.

Luggage Storage: Just outside Capri's funicular. Open daily 8am-8pm; in winter 8am-6pm. €2.60 per bag.

Public Toilets: On Marina Grande, at the funicular in Capri, and at P. Vittoria, 5, in Anacapri. Not for the faint of heart. Open daily 8am-9pm. All €0.30.

Emergency: ☎113 or 081 838 1205.

Medical Emergency: Pronto Soccorso (☎081 838 1205) at **Ospedale Capilupi,** V. Provinciale Anacapri, 5 (☎081 838 1111), a few blocks down V. Roma from P. Umberto.

Police: V. Roma, 70 (☎081 837 4211).

Tourist Medical Emergency Service: V. Caprile, 30, Anacapri (☎081 838 1240).

Internet Access: The Newsstand (☎081 837 3283) in P. Vittoria, Anacapri. Open daily 9am-2pm and 4-9pm. €5.16 per hr. **Capri Graphic,** V. Listrieri, 17 (☎081 837 5212). Head out of P. Umberto on V. Longano and take a right on V. Listrieri. Open M-Sa 9:30am-1pm and 4-9pm. €2.50 per 15min.

Post Office: Central office in Capri at V. Roma, 50 (☎081 837 7240), downhill from P. Umberto. Open M-F 8:30am-7:20pm, Sa 8:30am-1pm. **Anacapri office** at V. de Tommaso, 8 (☎081 837 1015). Open M-F 8:30am-1:30pm, Sa 8:15am-noon.
Postal Code: Capri 80073; Anacapri 80021.

ACCOMMODATIONS

Lodging in Capri proper, expensive year-round, becomes prohibitively exorbitant in mid-summer. You will not be able to find a deal in July or August. The lower price ranges listed here usually apply from October to May. Call in advance to reconfirm reservations and prices. It's possible to find vacancies in June but difficult in July and August. Makeshift camping is illegal and heavily fined.

ANACAPRI

■ **Alla Bussola di Hermes,** V. Traversa La Vigna, 14 (☎081 838 2010; bus.hermes@libero.it). This clean, welcoming spot is run by the enthusiastic and super-friendly Rita, who knows everything about Capri and loves hosting young American travelers. Reserve in the summer for this home away from home. Call from P. Vittoria in Anacapri to be picked up. Dormitory €20-24 per person; doubles €50-65 with breakfast and bath. AmEx/MC/V. ❷

Villa Eva, V. La Fabbrica, 8 (☎081 837 1549 or 081 837 2040; www.villaeva.com) Before trying to navigate the 15min. walk through Anacapri's side streets, call from Marina Grande and wait to be picked up. 28 bungalows, and beautiful indoor rooms, but some guests complain of insects in the bungalows. Pool and bar. Most rooms with bath. Internet €5 per hr. Reserve early. Singles €25-30; doubles €70; triples €75; quads €100 and up. AmEx/MC/V. ❸

Il Girasole, V. Linciano, 47 (☎081 837 2351; fax 837 3880; www.ilgirasole.com). Call from Marina Grande to be met, or walk from the last bus stop and follow the signs up the stairway. 24 well-furnished rooms with shuttered doorways around a gorgeous terrace. Bath, fridge, and TV in every room. With *Let's Go*, singles from €20 (without private bath) to €32; doubles €70-95; triples €100-120. If you can get a group of eight, it's €15 per person with *Let's Go*. AmEx/MC/V. ❷

Hotel Loreley, V. G. Orlandi, 16 (☎081 837 1440; fax 837 1399), 20m toward Capri from P. Vittoria on your left. Avoid a confusing walk through Anacapri side streets by staying at this comfortable hotel on the edge of P. Vittoria. 15 large rooms and baths. With *Let's Go*, doubles €90; triples €110; quads €130. Open Apr.-Oct. AmEx/MC/V. ❺

CAPRI

Bed and Breakfast Tirrenia Roberts, V. Mulo, 27 (☎081 837 6119; bbtirreniaroberts@iol.it). Walk away from P. Umberto on V. Roma and take the stairs on your right a little bit before the fork in V. Roma to find this B&B with a gorgeous view of the Marina Piccola over the pool and sauna. Quick access to the beach and center of Capri. Reserve 2 wk. to a month ahead. 3 double rooms €80-105. ❺

Pensione Stella Maris, V. Roma, 27 (☎081 837 0452; fax 837 8662), across from the bus stop. Capri's cheapest option, near the center of town, with consequent noise. 10 rooms with shared bath and TV. Doubles €80-100. AmEx/MC/V. ❺

Pensione 4 Stagioni, V. Marina Piccola, 1 (☎081 837 0041; www.hotel4stagionicapri.com). From P. Umberto, walk 5min. down V. Roma. Turn left at the 3-pronged fork in the road, and look for the green gate on the left. Cheaper rooms do not have the great view of Marina Piccola that the others have, but many open onto a lush garden. Breakfast included. Doubles €110; in winter €90. AmEx/MC/V. ❺

◘ FOOD

Capri's food is as glorious as its panoramic vistas. Savor the local mozzarella with tomatoes, oil, and basil in an *insalata caprese*—many consider it the quintessential summer meal. The *ravioli alla caprese* are hand-stuffed with blend of tasty local cheeses. Conclude your meal with the indulgent *torta di mandorle* (chocolate almond cake). Local red and white wines bear *Tiberio* or *Caprense* labels. A step up (especially price-wise) is the *Capri Blù*. Restaurants often serve *Capri DOC*, a light white. There is a **Dimeglio supermarket** on the right fork at the end of V. Roma. (Open M-Sa 8am-1:30pm and 5-9pm.) In Anacapri, try the **supermarket** at V. G. Orlandi, 253. (Open M-Sa 8am-1:30pm and 4:30-9pm, Su 8am-1pm.)

ANACAPRI

⊠ Ristorante Il Cucciolo, V. Fabbrica, 52 (☎081 837 1917). Follow signs for Villa Damecuta from bus stop or call for a free ride from P. Vittoria. Fresh at low prices on a lavish terrace over the ocean. Considerably less expensive menu with *Let's Go: primi* and *secondi* €6-9, *ravioli Caprese* €5. Cover €1.50. Service 6%. F-Su reservations recommended. Open daily Mar.-Oct. noon-2:30pm and 7:30-11pm; July-Aug. 7:30-11pm. AmEx/MC/V. ❸

La Rondinello, V. G. Orlandi, 295 (☎081 837 1223). Follow V. G. Orlandi out of P. Vittoria, the restaurant will be on your left. Conveniently located, enjoy the wide seafood menu, *antipasti,* and dessert buffets in the classy candlelit atmosphere. *Primi* €7-12. Cover €2. AmEx/MC/V. ❹

Ristorante Materita Bar-Pizzeria, P. Diaz (☎081 837 3375; fax 837 3881). Friendly staff and outdoor dining facing the Church of Santa Sofia. Reasonable *primi* and *secondi* (€6-8.50) and great pizza from €4.50. Cover €1.50. Open noon-3:30pm and 7pm-midnight, or until everyone leaves. AmEx/MC/V. ❷

Trattoria-Pizzeria da Mamma Giovanna, V. Boffe, 3 (☎081 837 2057), next to the church in P. Diaz. Tasty large Caprese meals in a sophisticated atmosphere. *Primi* from €5.50, pizza €5-8. Cover €1.50. Reservations recommended on summer weekends. Open daily 11:30am-3pm and 7pm-midnight. ❸

Il Grottino Ristorante, V. G. Orlandi, 95 (☎081 837 1066), a few blocks from P. Vittoria. Munch excellent food in style at the 45-year-old Il Grottino's cheery, outdoor tables. Enjoy some of the best *ravioli alla Caprese* €7.75. Lunch *menù* €8.50. Cover €1.20. Open daily 11:30am-3:30pm and 7:30-11pm. ❸

Trattoria Il Solitario, V. Orlandi, 96 (☎081 837 1382), 5min. from P. Vittoria to your right. The food is tasty and the Spanish-speaking staff friendly. *Pizza Rosse* €3.10-5.20; *Pizza Bianche* €5.20-7.80. Cover €1.30. 5% discount with *Let's Go.* Open W-M 12-3:30pm and 7:30pm-12am. AmEx/MC/V. ❷

CAPRI

⊠ Villa Verde, V. sella Orta, 6a (☎081 837 7024). Follow clear signs from V. V. Emanuele, off P. Umberto. Reserve ahead to eat as you have never eaten before. Large portions of fresh lobster, fish, vegetables, and ornate desserts call to those with a discerning palate. Prices are a bit VIP, but size and quality is worth the extra €5. Try the house specialty, *linguine "fra diavolo"* (pasta with lobster, €22). Chef's daily specialties €10-15. Open daily noon-4pm and 7pm-1am. AmEx/MC/V. ❹

⊠ Longano da Tarantino, V. Longano, 9 (☎081 837 0187), just off P. Umberto. Possibly the best deal in town, featuring an ocean view and a €15 *menù,* complete with *primi, secondi,* coffee, dessert, and a shot of the local *limoncello* to finish it off. Pizza from €3.10. Open Mar.-Nov. Th-Tu noon-3:30pm and 7pm-midnight. AmEx/MC/V. ❸

Buca di Bacco, V. Longano, 35 (☎081 837 0723), off P. Umberto I. Specialty *sfilatio*, a calzone jam-packed with a hodge-podge of meats and cheeses (€8). Pizza (€4-8) at night only. Open Sept.-July Th-Tu noon-3pm and 7:30pm-midnight; in Aug. open daily noon-2:30pm and 7pm-midnight. AmEx/MC/V. ❷

🔍📷 SIGHTS AND OUTDOOR ACTIVITIES

CAPRI'S COAST. Every day, **boat tours** reveal Capri's coast from Marina Grande for €10.50, and leave at 9:30, 10:30, and 11:30am. Many rock and pebble **beaches** surround the island. Take a boat from the port (€5) or descend between vineyards from P. Umberto to **Bagni di Tiberio,** a bathing area amid the ruins of an imperial villa. *(A bus or a 10min. walk down the path on left fork where V. Roma splits in three leads to the gorgeous southern stretch of Marina Piccola. Buy tickets and get info for all boat tours at the Grotta Azzurra Travel Office, V. Roma, 53, across the street from the bus stop. ☎081 837 0702; g.azzurra@capri.it. Open M-Sa 9am-1pm and 3-8pm, Su 9am-12:30pm.)* Cavort in the clear water among immense lava rocks or rent a **motor boat** (€80 for two hours) from **Banana Sport.** *(Main office on dock at Marina Grande. ☎081 837 5188. Open daily 9am-6pm.)*

CAPRI'S CLIFFS. For those who prefer land to sea, Capri's hiking trails lead to some stunning panoramas; less known than Capri's legendary shopping, the island's natural beauty can be a needed break from the crowded piazzas. Take a short but very uphill hike to check out the Roman Emperor Tiberius's ruined but magnificent **Villa Jovis,** the largest of his 12 Capri villas. Always the gracious host, Tiberius tossed those who displeased him over the precipice. The view from the **Cappella di Santa Maria del Soccorso,** built onto the villa, is unrivaled. *(Head out of P. Umberto on V. Longano. Don't miss the left onto V. Tiberio. Open daily 9am-6pm.)*

A path winds along the cliffs, connecting the **Arco Naturale,** a majestic stone arch on the eastern cliffs, and the **Faraglioni,** three massive rocks seen on countless postcards. The walk between the two takes about 1hr. A vista is at every bend. *(V. Tragara goes from Capri Centro to the Faraglioni, while the path to the Arco Naturale connects to the route to Villa Jovis through V. Matermania.)* The scenic overlook from **Punta Cannone** serves as a foreground for the dramatic cliffs of the southern coast. The tourist office map details several walking tours of the less-populated parts of the island.

THE BLUE GROTTO. *La Grotta Azzurra* is water-filled cave where light shining through the water creates the illusion of brilliantly blue walls. Some who visit are amazed by the bright blue color of the water; others think it's pretty, but certainly nowhere near pretty enough to justify the €8.10 fee for a six minute boat ride.

THRILL-SEEKERS, LOOK NO FURTHER than

the orange buses that bomb around Capri. Wedging two to roads lined with sheer cliffs that no American SUV would dare approach, the SIPPIC bus drivers show more driving skill and gusto than you'll see even on Ischia and Procida, where buses attempt similar feats. It's not uncommon for the Capri buses to have to stop and position themselves so that another bus can pass, brushing within inches of each other but never colliding or even scraping. Perhaps this is the reason for enforced ticket validation on Capri. Elsewhere, bus drivers don't seem to mind if you ride for free, creating what one *Let's Go*-carrying backpacker calls "the ultimate moral challenge of traveling in Italy." Try this on Capri and they'll slam you with a €30 penalty. These skilled drivers risk their lives so that you can go see a grotto, and don't take kindly to sneaky free-loaders.

Despite the narrowness of the cave opening and the sign warning that it is "strictly forbidden," many choose to go for a swim in the Grotto after the boats stop at 5pm. *(Take the bus marked Grotta Azzurra from the intersection of V. De Tomaso and V. Catena.)*

VILLA SAN MICHELE. Henry James once declared this Anacapri villa a clustering of "the most fantastic beauty, poetry, and inutility." Built in the early 20th century by Swedish author-physician Axel Munthe on the site of a Tiberian villa, it houses 17th-century furniture and Roman sculpture. The gardens boast a remarkable view and host Friday night concerts June through August. *(Upstairs from P. Vittoria and to the left, past Capri's Beauty Farm. Open daily 9:30am-6pm. €5.)*

OTHER SIGHTS. From the top of **Monte Solaro** on a clear day, you can see the Apennines to the east and the mountains of Calabria to the south. *(From P. Vittoria in Anacapri, a 12min. climb in a chairlift takes you to the summit. Open daily Mar.-Oct. 9:30am-4:45pm. Round-trip €5.50.)* You can also take a difficult hike up the mountain, starting from the base near the Villa San Michelle. A bus from P. Vittoria leads to the **Faro,** Italy's second-tallest lighthouse. Countless Italians tan, snorkel, and dive off its rocks. The yellow-brick V. G. Orlandi, off P. Vittoria in Anacapri, leads to the most inexpensive (but still rather pricey) tourist **shopping** on Capri.

▐ ENTERTAINMENT

Nighttime action carries a hefty pricetag, though Anacapri's prices are slightly lower. In typical Italian fashion, no one really goes out until around midnight. **Underground,** V. Orlandi, 259, is the town's most popular nightspot except for Saturdays when everyone heads to Club Zeus. There is no cover charge for access to €5 cocktails and squealing study abroad students. **Zeus,** V. Orlandi, 103, a few blocks from P. Vittoria, is a cinema most of the week, but morphs into a packed *discoteca* on Saturdays (and Thursdays in July and August), complete with over-the-top Greek theme, smoke machines, and international DJs. (☎ 081 83 79 16. Cover €12. Open weekends midnight-4am.) During the day, the back of Zeus boasts **Capri in Miniatura,** a tiny scale replica of the island, for the lazy tourist who wants to circle the island in only 10min. (☎ 081 837 1169 or 837 1082; fax 837 4921; www.capri.it/it/caprimini. Open all day. €3.) The Capri scene is classier and much more expensive. Covers are high and gatherings exclusive at the lounges and clubs near P. Umberto. **Number Two** V. Camerelle, 1 (☎ 081 837 7078) is a popular spot for celebs; it's an older, richer crowd than you'll find at Zeus. Also in Capri is **Bara Onda,** V. Roma, 8 (☎ 081 837 7147), which hosts many themed weekend nights. Both open all night. If you want to try your luck hanging out with crowds of dressed-to-kill Italians, remember that the **buses** stop running at 1:40am, but people don't start arriving until around 2am. A **taxi** will cost about €15.50.

ISCHIA ☎ 081

Upon first setting foot on Ischia (EES-kee-yah), you may think you have left Italy entirely, not just because the island is an Edenic vision, with luscious beaches, natural hot springs, ruins, vineyards, lemon groves, and a once-active volcano, but also because the signs, newspapers, and conversations are all in German. The island is immensely popular with German tourists, who take over for much of the summer. In August, however, Italians on holiday swarm to Ischia and reclaim it, leading to sky-high prices and boisterous crowds. Bargains and breathing room become hard to find, but with good reason: Ischia's beaches possess the perfection of Hollywood's digitally-enhanced notion of a beach. Its hot springs have drawn tourists since ancient times, meriting mention in the *Iliad* and the *Aeneid*.

SOUTHERN ITALY

⊑ TRANSPORTATION

Ferries: Ischia is best reached by **ferry** or **hydrofoil** from Pozzuoli, though ferries run from Naples as well. Most ferries arrive and leave from **Ischia Porto,** where the main ticket offices are. Schedules and prices subject to change. Call ferry line for details.

Caremar (☎ 081 580 5111) runs ferries to: **Naples** (1½hr., 14 per day, 6:45am-8:10pm, €5.06); **Pozzuoli** (45min., 3 per day, 8:25am-5:35pm, €3.87) via Procida; **Procida** (17min., 11 per day 7am-7pm, €3.62). Hydrofoils to **Naples** (1hr., 14 per day, 7am-8pm, €5.15) and **Procida** (25min., 11 per day, 6:45am-7:30pm, €2). Ticket offices open daily 7am-9pm.

Traghetti Pozzuoli (☎ 081 526 7736; www.traghettipozzuoli.it). To **Pozzuoli** from Casamicciola Terme (50min., 17 per day, 7am-7pm, €4.13). Ticket offices in Casamicciola Terme. Open daily 7am-7pm.

Alilauro (☎ 081 99 18 88; www.alilauro.it) runs hydrofoils to: **Mergellina** in Naples (40min., 15 per day, 8am-10pm from Ischia Porto; 6 per day, 9am-8:30pm from Forio); **Molo Beverello** in Naples (45 min.; 6 per day, 6:35am-6:50pm from Ischia Porto, 6 per day, 7am-6:30pm from Forio); **Capri** from Ischia Porto (1 per day, 10:40am); **Sorrento** from Ischia Porto (6 per day, 8:35am-5:20pm).

Linee Lauro (☎ 081 551 3352; www.lineelauro.it) runs ferries to **Molo Beverello** in Naples (1½hr., 6 per day, 6:40am-6:50pm) and **Pozzuoli** (18 per day, 2:30am-8:30pm).

Buses: SEPSA buses depart from just to the right of where the ferries drop off; look for the gathered orange buses. The main lines are **CS, CD,** and **#1.** CS circles the island counter-clockwise, hitting Ischia Porto, Casamicciola Terme, Lacco Ameno, Forio, Panza, Sant'Angelo, Serrara Fontana, and Barano. The CD line follows the same route in a clockwise direction (both every 20min., 5:45am-1am; late at night every 30min.). The #1 bus follows the CS route as far as Sant'Angelo and then comes back (every 20min., 6am-11:30pm). Other routes are shorter, run less frequently, and stop running earlier, and are helpful only in reaching specific locations (€0.93, half-day pass €1.65, full-day pass €2.74).

Taxis: Microtaxi (☎ 081 99 25 50).

⬛ ◪ ORIENTATION AND PRACTICAL INFORMATION

Ischia's towns and points of interest are almost all on the coast, connected by the main road, which the major bus routes follow. On the east coast is **Ischia Porto,** Ischia's largest town and the entrance point for most travelers. The road continues to **Casamicciola Terme,** on the north coast, with its overcrowded beach and legendary thermal waters, and **Lacco Ameno.** The road then reaches **Forio,** Ischia's most touristed area, full of restaurants and hotels. In the south, **Fontana,** reached by the CS and CD lines, is a good departure point for Mt. Epomeo, and **Sant'Angelo** has a great beach and boat taxis to the beach at **Sorgeto.**

Tourist Office: AAST Tourist Office (☎ 081 507 4231; fax 507 4230), on Banchina Porto Salvo, next to ticket offices on main port. Provides local tour listings and accommodations info. Open in summer daily 8am-2pm and 3-8pm; winter M-Sa 9am-1pm.

Vehicle Rental: Del Franco, V. de Luca, 133 (☎ 081 98 48 18). Rents cars, bikes, *motorini,* boats. *Motorini* €15.50-25.82 per day. Open daily 8am-10pm.

Police: Polizio della Stato, V. delle Terme, 80 (☎ 081 507 4711), 2 blocks up from V. de Luca in Ischia Porto. Help with passport problems. Open M, W, F 9am-12pm.

Medical Emergency: Pronto Soccorso, V. Fundera, 1 (☎ 081 507 9267), at the **Ospedale Anna Rizzoli,** in Lacco Ameno. Accessible by the CS, CD, or #1 bus.

⚑ ACCOMMODATIONS & CAMPING

Despite the island's popularity, Ischia has several budget options. Options in Ischia Porto, Casamicciola Terme, and Lacco Ameno tend to be very expensive because many hotels have pools (allegedly) fed by hot springs. The heavy tourist population on Ischia demands the presence of hotels everywhere, and among these, some are truly appealing to the budget-minded traveler.

⬛ Ostello "Il Gabbiano" (HI), Strada Statale Forio-Panza, 162 (☎ 081 90 94 22), on the main road between Forio and Panza. CS, CD, and #1 bus stop right outside. Bar, pool, sea view, and easy beach access. Guests love the very friendly English-speaking staff. 100 beds. Breakfast, shower and sheets included. Lockout 10am-1pm. Curfew 12:30am. Open Apr.-Sept. All beds €16 per person. ❷

Hotel Villa Franca and **Baia Verde,** Strada Statale, 270, #183 (☎ 081 98 74 20; fax 98 70 81). Take the CS, CD, or #1 bus and get off at "S. Francesco" stop between Forio and Lacco Ameno. 2 hotels near the beach with same prices and management. Patio and 3 pools (2 cold mineral baths and 1 thermal bath). Breakfast included. 35 rooms. Open Mar.-Oct. Singles €30; doubles €60. AmEx/MC/V. ❸

Pensione di Lustro, V. Filippo di Lustro, 9 (☎ 081 99 71 63). Take a slight left at the end of the long beach at Forio. Truman Capote slept here in 1968; will you in 2003? 10 rooms with TV, bath, A/C, and breakfast. Singles €31 in the summer, €22.50 in the winter; doubles €45-62. Discount with *Let's Go* in the winter. AmEx/MC/V. ❸

Albergo Macri, V. Lasolino, 96 (☎ 081 99 26 03), along the docks, just off where the buses board. A tranquil family-run hotel. All 22 rooms have baths. With *Let's Go*: singles €22-27; doubles €51-64; triples €70-83. AmEx/MC/V. ❷

Pensione Crostolo, V. Cossa, 48 (☎ 081 99 10 94). From Porto Ischia bus station, ascend the main street and turn right. Perched well above the port, this 3-star hotel has terraces and 15 rooms with bath, TV, fridge, and safe. €25-50 per person. ❸

Pensione Quisisana, P. Bagni, 34 (☎ /fax 081 99 45 20). Take bus #3 from Ischia Porto to the piazza. Near the beach. Homey establishment with a roof garden. Open May-Oct. Doubles with bath €41. Full-pension in Aug. €44. Extra bed €13. ❹

Camping Internazionale, V. Foschini, 22 (☎ 081 99 14 49; fax 99 14 72), a 20min. walk from the port. Take V. Alfredo de Luca from V. del Porto and bear right onto V. Michele Mazzella (*not* V. Leonardo Mazzella) at P. degli Eroi. Open May 1-Sept. 30. €6-9 per person, €3-10 per tent. Clean 2-person bungalows with bath €30-50. ❶

Eurocamping dei Pini, V. delle Ginestre, 28 (☎ 081 98 20 69), a 20min. walk from the port. Take V. del Porto to V. de Luca, walk uphill and take a right on V. delle Terme, where you'll see arrow indicating camping. Friendly management and a mini-soccer field. €5.20-8 per person, €4.20-6.20 per tent. 2-person bungalows €26-52. ❶

🍴 FOOD

While Ischian food, especially the seafood and fruit, is a treat, it is almost impossible to find a local eatery that is not tourist-oriented. Explore side streets in order to escape the €5.50 *pizza margherita* offered by the prominently-advertised restaurants targeting tourists and find authentic Ischian cuisine.

Emiddio, V. Porto, 30, at the docks. Enjoy locally caught fish on the water. *Primi* €3-7. Cover €1. Open daily noon-3pm and 7pm-midnight. AmEx/MC/V. ❷

Ristorante Zelluso, V. Parodi, 41 (☎ 081 99 46 27), to the left as you enter Casamicciola from Ischia Porto. Look for the sign and walk down the alley. Scrumptious pizza. Cover €1. Open daily noon-3pm and 7pm-midnight. ❷

Mastu Peppe, V. Iasolino, 10 (☎ 081 98 19 12), on the water near the ferry docks. Specializing in fish soup, this restaurant offers a friendly staff and pleasant atmosphere along the fishing wharf of Ischia Porto, and a meal for under €10. ❷

👁 🔼 SIGHTS AND OUTDOOR ACTIVITIES

CASTELLO ARAGONESE. Providing some brooding time away from fun and surf, this castle resides on a small island of its own, Ischia Ponte, connected to the rest of civilization by a 15th-century footbridge. The stronghold, built in 1441, contains both the holy and the macabre. The **cathedral** in the castle, mostly destroyed by WWII bombing, displays a mix of Roman and Baroque styles. Below, the **crypt** houses colorful 14th-century frescoes crafted by those in the school of Giotto. The **nuns' cemetery** has a ghastly history; when a nun died, the order would prop the decomposing body on a stone as a (fragrant) reminder to the other nuns of their mortality. For more family fun, visit the castle's **Museum of Arms and Instruments of Torture**, 200m past the main ticket booth, which contains things guaranteed to make the strongest stomachs groan. *(Bus #7 runs to Ischia Ponte from Porto Ischia. Castle ☎ 081 99 28 34. Open daily 9am-7:30pm. €8 entrance.)*

BEACHES, HOT SPRINGS, AND HIKING. Ischia's best and most popular beach is at **Maronti**, on the island's south coast. *(Take the #5 bus from Ischia Porto to the Maronti stop.)* Another popular choice is the beach at **Citara**, 1km down the coast from Forio. *(The #1 and #3 buses head there directly from Ischia Porto.)* For steamier adventures, the hot springs at **Sorgeto** (on the far side of the island) range from tepid to boiling. The beach is the perfect spot to lounge and soak aching feet. Locals say that the cleansing lather formed by rubbing the light-green porous rocks together is fantastic for the skin. *(Reach the beach from Panza by a 20 min. hike or from Sant'Angelo by boat taxi at €5 per person, with possible group discounts and arranged pick-ups.)* **Lacco Ameno** and **Casamicciola Terme** are densely packed with the thermal baths that originally attracted visitors to Ischia. Hikers should take the CS or CD bus to **Fontana**, which rests above most towns, making it a good departure point. Head for **Mt. Epomeo** (788m); on a clear day, the summit has a view of Capri to Terracina.

🎵 ENTERTAINMENT

Ischia's liveliest nocturnal scene is in Ischia Porto, along V. Porto and C. V. Colonna. The best of the bunch is the *discotheca* **New Valentino**, C. V. Colonna, 97, adjoining **Ecstacy** piano bar. C. V. Colonna runs parallel to V. de Luca from the port, one block farther away from Ischia Porto. (☎ 081 99 26 53. Open F-Su 11pm-6am.) **Blue Jane**, on V. Iasolino, at Pagoda Beach near the port, advertises on the sides of nearly every bus on the island. The club features a *discoteca* and a smooth hangout. (☎ 081 99 32 96. Open July-Aug. daily 11:30pm-4am; June and Sept. F-Su 11:30pm-4am. Cover €10-20.)

PROCIDA
☎ 081

Sun-baked pastel buildings with ample gardens overlook ports of netted fishing boats to create a scene so perfectly unreal that Procida has been used as the setting for such films as *Il Postino* and *The Talented Mr. Ripley*. The florid tones of the southern dialect still can be heard drifting from narrow streets and family-owned stores that still shelve only essentials. No boutiques. No souvenir stores. You've discovered authentic, untouristed Southern Italy; cross your fingers that other travelers don't do the same.

SOUTHERN ITALY

▣ ⃗ TRANSPORTATION AND PRACTICAL INFORMATION

Ferries and **hydrofoils** run to Procida from Naples, Pozzuoli, and Ischia. All boats dock at Marina Grande, near ticket offices. Caremar (☎081 896 7280; open daily 6:30am-8pm) runs hydrofoils to **Naples** (40min., 5 per day, €8.78). It also runs **ferries** to **Ischia** (30min., 10 per day, €3.62) and **Naples** (1hr., 5 per day, €4.65). Procida Lines (☎081 526 4611; open daily 6am-8pm) runs ferries to **Pozzuoli** (30min., €2.50).

While a walk across the island only takes an hour, four SESPA **bus** lines (tickets €0.77 in *tabacchi*) leave from the port, with varying frequencies according to route and season. **L1** covers the middle region running past the hotels and campgrounds before stopping at the port of **Chiaiolella**, site of the liveliest restaurants and beaches (every 20min., 8am-7pm, but check schedule). **C1** follows much the same route, but also hits the southwestern part of the island (varying times, see schedule). **C2** runs to the southeastern part of the island (every 40-50min., 6:55am-8:30pm). **L2** serves the quiet northwestern part of the island (about every hr., 7am-9pm). Another means of transportation from the port is the cramped **Microtaxi** (☎081 896 8785). The **AAST tourist office,** V. Roma, 92, near the ferry ticket offices to the far right of the main port, has free maps. (☎081 810 1968. Open daily 9am-1pm and 3:30-6:30pm.) For **medical emergencies,** the **Pronto Soccorso,** V. V. Emanuele, 191 (☎081 896 9058), accessible by L1 or C1 buses, is open 24hr.

▣ ⃗ ACCOMMODATIONS AND FOOD

Spending an inexpensive night on Procida is difficult—budget travelers may want to access the island only as a day trip from Naples. But for those willing to pay, Procida offers some gorgeous lodging with beautiful panoramic views.

La Casa sul Mare, V. Salita Castello, 13 (☎081 896 8799; www.lacasasulmare.it). Take the C2 bus. Just outside the walls of the Terra Murata, in a building dating to 1700. Complete with balconies looking out onto the fishing village of Marina Corricella, La Casa gives guests a refined bed and breakfast experience. Reservations advised. 10 rooms, all doubles €88-155. AmEx/MC/V. ❺

La Rosa dei Venti (☎081 523 1496), perched on a hill with ocean views and a manageable cliff pathway down to a private beach area. The hotel is difficult to reach on foot. Take the 3-wheeled microtaxi from the port. 22 spacious *cassete* (houses with kitchenettes and dining areas). Internet and breakfast €1.55. *Cassete* can hold between 2 and 6 people for a rental price of €50 a night. AmEx/MC/V. ❹

Hotel Riviera, V. Giovanni da Procida, 36 (☎/fax 081 896 7197; hotelrivieraprocida@libero.it). Take the L1 or C1 bus. Provides comfortable accommodations overlooking a garden. 25 rooms, all with their own bath and phone. Reserve 1-2 wk. in advance. Breakfast included. Open Apr.-Sept. Singles €36-39; doubles €68-72. 10% discount with *Let's Go,* excluding July and August. AmEx/MC/V. ❹

Albergo Savoia, V. Lavadera, 32 (☎081 896 76 16), is accessible by the L2 bus. Snug rooms, a roof terrace, and a narrow back patio with potted flowers and lemon trees. Singles €26; doubles €44. Extra bed €13. ❸

Vivara, on V. IV Novembre (☎ summer 081 896 9242, winter 556 0529). This campground is accessible by the L1 or C1 bus. €5.16 per person, €4.13-7.32 per tent, €51.65 for 4-person bungalow with private bath. Open June 15-Sept. 15. 10-tent capacity, so make reservations in June for Aug. trips. ❶

Graziella, V. Salette, 18 (☎081 896 7747). Campground on the beach. Take the L1, L2, or C1 bus to P. Olmo and from there walk on V. F. Gioia until you make a left onto V. Salette. It's the last campsite on the left. 4-person bungalows €40. ❶

Da Michele, V. Marina Chiaiolella, 22/23 (☎081 896 7422). Authentic fare in a spot looking onto the fishing harbor. *Primi* (€4-9), rabbit €7, pizza (€2.50-6.50). After your meal, ask at any bar for the potent *limoncello,* made from Procidan lemons. ❸

🔘 SIGHTS

You can walk or take the **C2** to the **Abbazia San Michele Archangelo** (St. Michael's Abbey) on Procida's easternmost and highest hilltop. Take V. V. Emanuele from the left side of the port and turn left on V. Principe Umberto. The plain yellow facade hides the interior's ornate 15th-century gold frescoes and bleeding Christ figures. Enjoy the outlook from the summit and view the deeds of St. Michael emblazoned on the domes. (☎081 896 7612. Open daily 9am-1pm and 3-6:30pm. Free.) The route passes the medieval walls of **Terra Murata** (☎081 896 7612), the old city below the monastery on V. S. Michele. Procida has several decent **beaches** that are usually uncrowded. The one at **Ciraccio** stretches across the western shore. Its western end, near Chiaiolella, is at the end of the **L1** line. Another popular beach is **Chiaia,** on the southeastern cove, accessible by **L1** and **C1.**

Take a sea excursion with **Procida Diving Center.** (☎081 896 8385; www.vacanzeprocida.it. Offices at Marina di Chaiolella offer 2hr. tours from the entrance. M-Sa, starting between 9 and 9:30am. €12.91.) Lemons are ubiquitous in Procida, and are honored for their place in Procidan culture in the May **Festa del Limone.** The festival features food tastings, a fashion show, and a debate on the, er, lemon.

AMALFI COAST

The beauty of the Amalfi coast is one of contrasts and extremes. Immense rugged cliffs plunge downward to crashing waves, and the sides of narrow ravines are dotted with tightly nestled coastal towns. The natural splendor and unique character of these towns attracts many tourists. Although some coastal areas are expensive, budget gems do exist. The coast is easily accessible from Naples, Sorrento, Salerno, and the islands by ferry or SITA buses. The harrowing bus ride along the Amalfi coast is unforgettable—just remember to sit on the right side of the bus heading south (from Sorrento to Amalfi) and on the left heading back. Those with weaker stomachs should opt for sea service.

POSITANO ☎089

When American author John Steinbeck visited Positano in the 1950s, he estimated that its vertical cliffs were already piled so high with homes that no more than 500 visitors could possibly fit, negating the possibility of tourism. He underestimated local ingenuity. After running through a series of industries (including fashion—the bikini was invented here in 1959) with variable success, Positano embraced its role as an intellectual and cultural resort. Soon its classy reputation began to draw ordinary millionaires in addition to the writers, painters, actors, and filmmakers, and the *Positanese* squeezed not 500, but over 2000 hotel beds into their town. Today, Positano's most frequent visitors are the wealthy few who can appreciate the beachfront ballet and afford the French chefs in the four-star hotels. There is no denying, however, that Positano has its charms, and most who come here linger. As Steinbeck observed, "Positano bites deep."

▐ TRANSPORTATION

Buses: 18 blue **SITA** buses, from 7am-9pm, run to **Amalfi** (€1.19) and **Sorrento** (€1.19). There are 2 main stops in Positano, at the 2 points where the road that runs through town at the base of the hill meets the main coastal road. Tickets can be bought at bars or *tabacchi* near the stops.

Ferries and **Hydrofoils: Linee Marittime Salernitane** (☎089 81 11 64) runs ferries (50min., 9:20am, €10) and hydrofoils (30min., 10am, €13) to **Capri. Travelmar** (☎089 87 29 50) runs ferries to **Amalfi** (25 min., 6 per day, 10am-6:15pm, €4); **Minori** (40 min., 3 per day, 12:15-6:15pm, €4.50); **Salerno** (80min., 6 per day, 10am-6:15pm, €5); **Sorrento** (50 min., 2 per day, 9:45am and 3:40pm, €6.50).

▄ ▌ ORIENTATION AND PRACTICAL INFORMATION

Positano clings to the zeniths of two cliffs over the Tyrrhenian Sea. The main center of town lies around **Spiaggia Grande**. To get there, take **Viale Pasitea** down from the main road between Sorrento and Amalfi at **Chiesa Nuova**. Viale Pasitea turns into **Corso Colombo** when it starts going uphill, and eventually makes its way up to the main road again at the other end of town. To get over to **Fornillo** beach, take the footpath from Spiaggia Grande. Make use of the orange local bus (every 20min., 7am-midnight, €0.77) marked "Positano Interno" that circles through the town, terminating at **Piazza dei Mulini** at the center of town.

Tourist Office: V. del Saraceno, 4 (☎089 87 50 67), near duomo. Provides maps. Open M-Sa 8am-2pm and 3:30-8pm; in winter M-F 8:30am-2pm, Sa 8:30am-noon.

Emergency: ☎113. **Carabinieri:** (☎089 87 50 11) near the top of the cliffs, down the steps opposite Chiesa Nuova. Nearest **hospital** in Sorrento.

Late-Night Pharmacy: V. Pasitea, 22 (☎089 87 52 26). Open in summer daily 9am-1pm and 5-9pm.

Internet Access: D.S. Informatica, V. G. Marconi, 188 (☎089 81 19 93; www.positanonline.it), on the main coastal road, accessible by the local bus. €5 per hr. Open M-Sa 9:30am-1pm and 3-7:30pm.

▐ ACCOMMODATIONS

Positano has over 70 hotels and residences, and spare rooms are available for rent. Since many hotels are rather expensive, contact the tourist office for help in arranging inexpensive rooms for longer stays.

Ostello Brikette, V. G. Marconi, 358 (☎089 87 58 57; fax 812 2814; brikette@syrene.it), 100m up the main coastal road to Sorrento from Viale Pasitea. Squeaky clean and incredible views from 2 large terraces. 45 beds. Shower and sheets included. Lockout 1am-5pm. Curfew varies from 12-2am with Positano's nightlife, but curfew means all in bed, lights out. Reservations available. Dorms €20; doubles €65. ❷

Il Gabbiano Hotel, V. Pasitea, 310 (☎089 87 53 06; fax 81 17 13; www.wel.it/Hilgabbiano), offers 19 gorgeous, open rooms all with view of the harbor, private bath, phone, and TV. Breakfast included. Doubles €98; triples €130; quads €162. ❺

Pensione Maria Luisa, V. Fornillo, 42 (☎/fax 089 87 50 23). Take the local bus down V. Pasitea to V. Fornillo. A jolly owner keeps 12 bright rooms, most with views from their private seaside terraces. All rooms with bath. Small breakfast included. Singles €35-40; doubles €110-120. Extra bed €20. ❹

THE BIG SPLURGE

IL SAN PIETRO DI POSITANO

Positano's Il San Pietro is carved into the monolithic cliffs of the Sorrentine Peninsula. Guests enter by way of an elevator that descends through rock into an airy, terracotta-tiled hall and lounge. Far from cave-like, the expansive interior is filled with stone statues, murals, carved wooden and plush white furniture, and bouquets of fresh flowers.

One of the flower-filled slopes beneath the hotel has a large, semi-circular pool; another has a tennis court surrounded by rose gardens. The rock beach, sunbathing platform, and hotel bar are on a promontory at the foot of the cliffs, set at the gaping mouth of a seaside cave.

Hotel San Pietro's 61 rooms and suites are hewn into a myriad of natural ledges. Each has a luxurious bathroom (with a jacuzzi and tropical plants), A/C, TV, radio, phone, mini-bar, and a private terrace.

Dine high above the bay in the enchanting open-air restaurant, on a terrace shaded by arbors spilling grape vines and bougainvillea. Watch the frenzied movements of chefs as they prepare typical regional cuisine in front of gaping brick ovens, then enjoy the piano bar's mellow background music at a romantic meal lit by the Tyrrhenian sunset.

V. Laurito, 2, Positano (SA) 84017. ☎089 87 54 55; fax 81 14 49; www.ilsanpietro.it. Children over 12 welcome. Standard or deluxe doubles €385-833.

Casa Guadagno, V. Fornillo, 22 (☎089 87 50 42; fax 81 14 07), next door to Pensione Maria Luisa. Pampers its patrons with 15 spotless rooms, tiled floors, sublime views, and winter heating. Breakfast and bath included. Reserve in advance. With *Let's Go:* doubles €85; triples €95; quads €105. ❺

◘ FOOD

Prices in the town's restaurants reflect the high quality of the food. For a sit-down dinner, thrifty travelers head toward the beach at Fornillo.

▩ **Da Costantino,** V. Corvo, 95 (☎089 87 57 38). Serves tasty cuisine, though the ocean view overshadows even the most succulent meal. Try the specialty *crespolini al formaggio* (crepes filled with cheese, €5.50). Pizza €4.50, *primi* €5.50-8.50, *secondi* €8-13. Open in summer daily noon-3:30pm and 7pm-midnight; in winter Tu-Th noon-3:30pm and 7pm-midnight. AmEx/MC/V. ❷

▩ **Mediterraneo Ristorante,** V. Pasitea, 236-238 (☎089 812 2828). This family-run restaurant offers a wide array of meals and manages to break away a little from the seafood dishes served up by every restaurant on the coast. Try the fried zucchini flowers and the popular *calamarato con polipetti e pomodorini* (squid-shaped pasta with octopus and tomato). *Primi* €6-17.50. Open daily 9:30am-12:30pm. MC/V. ❸

Vini e Panini, V. del Saracino, 29-31 (☎ 089 87 51 75), near the church. For the frugal, this shop sells reasonable sandwiches to go and interesting cheeses to try. Mozzarella and *pomodori panino* €2.60. Bottle of *limoncello* €10. Open M-Sa 8am-2pm and 4:30-10pm; closed Dec.-Mar. ❶

Trattoria Grottino Azzurro, Chiesa Nuova (☎089 87 54 66), next to Bar International near the hostel. Frequented by local celebrities, it serves up local specialties at reasonable prices. Homemade pasta and fresh seafood from €5.50. Cover €1.50. Open Th-Tu 1-3pm and 8-11pm. Closed Dec. to mid-Feb. ❷

Il Saraceno D'Oro, V. Pasitea, 254 (☎089 81 20 50). Delicious pizza to go (evenings only) from €4. Try the incredible *gnocchi alla Sorrentina* (€6.50). Cover €1. Open in summer daily 1-3pm and 7-11pm; in winter Th-Tu 1-3pm and 7-11pm. ❷

Bar-Pasticceria La Zagara, V. dei Mulini, 6 (☎089 87 59 64). Exquisite pastries, tarts, and *limoncello*. The *torta afrodisia* (chocolate cake with fruit, €2.50) promises to raise your libido. Prices are slightly higher if you choose to eat on the shaded patio, which becomes a piano bar in the evenings. Open daily 8am-midnight. ❶

La Taverna del Leone, V. Laurito, 43 (☎089 87 54 74), on the left side of the main road to Praiano; serviced by infrequent SITA buses. Escape the crowds of central Positano to enjoy a meal in this spacious, open tavern. Open May-Sept. daily 1-3pm and 7:30pm-midnight; Oct.-Dec. and Mar.-Apr. W-M 1-3pm and 7pm-midnight. AmEx/MC/V. ❷

◎ SIGHTS

For some, Positano's gray beaches are its main attractions. Each has public (free) and private sections. The biggest, busiest, and priciest is **Spiaggia Grande,** in the main part of town. At the private **Lido L'Incanto** (☎089 81 11 77), spend the day with the other people who shelled out €10 for a beach chair *(lettino)*, umbrella, shower, and changing room. Outside the entrance, **Noleggio Barche Lucibello** (☎089 87 50 32 or 87 53 26), rents motorboats from €30 per hour and rowboats from €10.50 per hour. To reach the quieter, smaller **Spiaggia del Fornillo,** take V. Positanese d'America, a footpath that starts above the port and winds past **Torre Trasita.** While parts of the Fornillo are public, you can get your own spot at one of three private beaches. **Marinella** beach (€5) features a little sand underneath a time-worn boardwalk; **Fratelli Grassi** beach (€12) offers boat excursions; and **Puppetto** beach (€5-7) gives guests from Hostel Briskette a 10-15% discount. The three **Isole dei Galli,** poking through the water off Positano's coast, were home to Homer's mythical sirens, who lured unsuspecting victims with their spellbinding songs. In 1925, perhaps to honor this tradition, the quartet of Stravinsky, Picasso, Hindemith, and Massine bought one of the *isole*. While swimming around these beautiful islands is permitted, setting foot on land is not.

Positano offers tremendous hikes for those with quads of steel. **Montepertuso,** a high mountain pierced by a large *pertusione* (hole), is one of three perforated mountains in the world (the other two are in India). To get there, hike the 45min. trail up the hillside, or take the bus from P. dei Mulini, near the port or from any other bus stop. For those who want to lighten their pocketbooks by several pounds, Positano offers endless possibilities. The tragically chic spend afternoons in the exorbitantly priced city boutiques. Others take boat excursions to tour the coast and neighboring islands. The adventurous (or really hungry) take squid-fishing expeditions at night. Frequent cruises embark to the **Emerald** and **Blue Grottoes,** beautiful water-filled caves in the area. As numerous boating companies compete for these excursions, the prices can sometimes be reasonable for shorter trips; check the tourist office and booths lining the port area.

◪ ENTERTAINMENT

The swank piano bar and disco, **Music on the Rocks,** on the far left side of the beach as you face the water, packs in the well-dressed thirtysomethings like sardines. Handfuls of celebrities, from Sharon Stone to Luciano Pavarotti, have been known to stop by. The cover charge can only get you in if you're wearing fancy threads. (☎089 87 58 74. Cover €20.) **Easy Pub** on Spiaggia Grande, at D. del Brigantino, is a happening spot from mid-Mar to Nov. (☎089 81 14 61. Open all day and night, live music and other events on occasions.)

PRAIANO

A winding 6km bus ride down the coast from Positano (15min., €1.19), Praiano (pop. 800) is less of a town than a loose conglomeration of hotels and restaurants along 10km of coastline. Without the tourism and commotion of the bigger towns, Praiano gives relaxation and quietness against the Tyrrhenian's blue, and the most popular nightlife on the Amalfi Coast.

ACCOMMODATIONS. Enjoy the expansive panorama from the campground **Villaggio La Tranquillità** and the **Hotel Continental ❶,** V. Roma, 10, which are part of the same complex, on the road to Amalfi (ask the bus driver to stop at the Ristorante Continental). A long stairway descends to a stone dock. The restaurant-hotel-campground complex is staffed by a friendly family (everyone knows your name), and all rooms include bath and bread-and-butter breakfast. (☎089 87 40 84; fax 87 47 79; www.continental.praiano.it. Parking available. Camping €15 per person (tent not included); doubles and 2-person bungalows €60-88. MC/V.) **La Perla ❹,** V. Miglina, 2, 100m toward Amalfi from La Tranquillità on the main road, offers rooms with bath and a terrace overlooking the sea. (☎089 87 40 52. Breakfast included. With *Let's Go:* singles €40-62; doubles €93-100. AmEx/MC/V.) **Tramonto D'oro Praiano ❺,** near the duomo, offers a touch of elegance that is fitting for the magnificent coastline sprawling behind the hotel. The Isole dei Galli and Capri are both visible from the immaculate rooms' terraces. Rooftop pool and bar, gym and Turkish baths in the basement. (☎089 87 49 55; www.starnet.it/tramontodoro. Breakfast included. Doubles in the summer €125-180, in the winter €105-150; triples €142-203/€170-245; quads €160-230/€189-270. AmEx/MC/V.)

FOOD. Ristorante Continental ❹, downstairs from Villagio La Tranquillità, specializes in local seafood *primi* (€8-11) and *secondi* (€11-15), and local wine (from €5). (☎089 87 42 93. Cover €1.70. Open Easter-Nov. daily noon-3pm and 8pm-midnight. MC/V.) On the road from Positano, next to the San Gennaro Church (with blue and gold domes), **Trattoria San Gennaro ❸,** V. S. Gennaro, 99, lets you choose between their terrace and the garden as the setting for your meal. Enjoy the view and a big serving of the *sciaiatielli San Gennaro* (mushrooms and clams, €6.50), or pizza (€4.50). They also offer rooms and scooters for rent; ask at the restaurant for details. (Cover €1.50. Open daily noon-5pm and 7pm-midnight.)

SIGHTS AND ENTERTAINMENT. Praiano's openness and natural beauty make it the best place on the coast to take a scenic drive on a **scooter.** Praia Costa (☎/fax 089 81 30 82; www.praiacosta.com) offers rentals starting at €30 for three hours. Around the bend from Praiano toward Amalfi, V. Terramare, a ramp which starts at **Torre a Mare** (a well-preserved tower which now serves as an art gallery for lauded sculptor and painter Paolo Sandulli) leads down to **Marina di Praia.** This 400-year-old fishing village, tucked in a tiny ravine, hides restaurants, bars, and the Amalfi Coast's most popular club since the early 1960s, **▓Africana,** on V. Terramare. Fish swim through the grotto under the glass dance floor crowded with twenty and thirty somethings. Music echoes off the dimly lit cave roof above and boats dock at the stairwell right outside. Met a cute Italian? Drop a flower in the well and make a wish; if the flower floats out of the grotto below, your wish will come true. If it doesn't, drown your sorrows in a *cocktail africana* €5. (☎089 87 40 42. Cover charge €15, Tu women free. Open mid-June to Sept. daily 10pm-3am.)

A bit farther between Praiano and Amalfi lies the **Grotta Smeralda** (Emerald Grotto). The SITA bus stops at the elevator leading down to the cave. If you didn't make it to the Blue Grotto, haven't had your fill of water-filled caves, or enjoy dropping €5 and then being hassled to tip the boatman, the 22m high cavern has green water with a slight glow and walls dripping with stalactites. Multilingual guides reveal an underwater nativity scene and a rock formation profile of Garibaldi, Churchill, or G. Dubya Bush (depending on your nationality). Sorry, no swimming in this grotto. (Tour €5. Open daily 10am-4pm.)

AMALFI ☎089

Between the jagged rocks of the Sorrentine peninsula and the azure waters of the Adriatic, the narrow streets and historic monuments of Amalfi are at home in incomparable natural beauty. As the first sea republic of Italy and the preeminent maritime powerhouse of the southern Mediterranean, Amalfi ruled the neighboring coast, no doubt thanks to the compass, invented here by Flavia Gioia. Pisan attacks and Norman conquests hastened Amalfi's decline in influence, but the vigor remains in spirit, and the city's past survives in its arsenal, duomo, medieval paper mills, and other monuments. Visitors crowd the waterfront and the shops, restaurants, and cafes around the duomo. During festivals, music and fireworks echo off the steep mountains around the town.

TRANSPORTATION

Buses: Buses arrive at and depart from P.F. Gioia, on the waterfront. Buy tickets at bars and *tabacchi* on the piazza. Blue **SITA buses** (☎089 87 10 16) connect Amalfi to: **Positano** (35min., €1.19); **Salerno** (1¼hr., 24 per day, 5:15am-10pm, €1.65); **Sorrento** (1¼hr., 19 per day, 6:30am-8pm, €1.86).

Ferries and **hydrofoils:** Ticket booths and departures from the dock off P.F. Gioia.

Travelmar (☎089 87 29 50) runs hydrofoils to: **Minori** (5min., 3 per day, 12:45-7pm, €1.50); **Positano** (25min., 7 per day, 8:40am-4:20pm, €4); **Salerno** (35min., 6 per day, 10:35am-7pm, €3.50); **Sorrento** (80min., 2 per day, 9:15am and 3pm, €7). All times and prices subject to change; check with tourist office or ferry line.

Taxis: ☎089 87 22 39.

ORIENTATION AND PRACTICAL INFORMATION

The easiest way to navigate Amalfi is to think of it as a T, with the main coastal road (heading towards Atrani on the left, Praiano on the right facing the water) perpendicular to Amalfi's main street, **Via Lorenzo d'Amalfi,** which leads from the port to the hills above. Ferries and buses stop in **Piazza Flavio Gioia,** the point of intersection of the two roads, on the waterfront. **Piazza del Duomo** lies up Via d'Amalfi through the white arch. **Piazza Municipio** is 100m up Corso delle Repubbliche Marinare, the coastal road, toward **Atrani** from Piazza Gioia. Go through the tunnel on **Corso delle Repubbliche Marinare** to reach **Atrani,** 750m down the coast, or follow the public path through the restaurant next to the tunnel.

Tourist Office: AAST, C. delle Repubbliche Marinare, 27 (☎089 87 11 07), through a gate on the left as you head up the road towards Atrani. Don't count on finding a free map though. Open May-Oct. daily 8am-2pm and 3-8pm; Nov.-Apr. M-Sa 8am-2pm.

Police: Carabinieri, V. Casamare, 19 (☎089 87 10 22), on the left up V. d'Amalfi.

Medical Assistance: American Diagnostics Pharmaceutics (☎033 545 5874). On-call 24hr. Clean and modern. Blood tests, lab procedures, and English-speaking doctors.

Post Office: C. delle Repubbliche Marinare, 35 (☎089 87 13 30), next to the tourist office. Offers currency exchange with good rates. Commission €0.52, €2.58 on checks over €51.65. Open M-F 8:15am-7:20pm.

Postal Code: 84011.

SOUTHERN ITALY

ACCOMMODATIONS

Staying in Amalfi can be expensive, but you get what you pay for. Accommodations fill up in August, so reserve at least one month in advance.

Beata Solitudo Campeggio Ostello (HI), P. Generale Avitabile 6, Agerola (☎/fax 081 802 5048; www.beatasolitudo.it). 30min. bus ride from Amalfi; get off at the piazza in Agerola. 3 rooms and 16 beds, a kitchen, laundry facilities, Internet €4 per hr., and TV. Gorgeous views make up for the long ride from Amalfi. Dorms €9.30; 4-person bungalows with bath and kitchen €50; campsites €4 per person. MC/V. ❶

Hotel Lidomare, V. Piccolomini, 9 (☎089 87 13 32; fax 87 13 94; www.amalficoast.it/hotel/lidomare), through the alley across from the duomo, left up the stairs, then across the *piazzetta*. Very spacious rooms with terraces. Halls and common areas decked with local antiques. 15 rooms with bath, TV, phone, fridge, and A/C. Breakfast included. Singles €34-43; doubles €70-95. AmEx/MC/V. ❹

A'Scalinatella, P. Umberto, 6 (☎089 87 19 30 or 87 14 92; www.hostelscalinatella.com), up V. dei Dogi in Atrani. Look for arrows painted on wall to the right. Genial brothers have rooms in Atrani, plus campsites and scenic rooms above Amalfi. Laundry €5.50. Seasonal variations in prices, highest in Aug. Dorms €10-25; doubles €26-45, with bath €40-80; camping €7.75 per person. Call to check prices at any given time. ❷

Hotel Amalfi, V. dei Pastai, 3 (☎089 87 24 40; fax 87 22 50; www.starnet.it/hamalfi), left off V. Lorenzo onto Salita Truglio, uphill. A 3-star establishment with 42 immaculate rooms, attentive management, terraces, and citrus gardens with restaurant. Bar, telephone, safe, and TV in all rooms; A/C in some. English spoken. Continental breakfast included. Singles €70-90; doubles €93-120. AmEx/MC/V. ❺

Vettica House, V. Maestra dei Villaggi, 92 (☎089 87 18 14). Call Gabriele from SITA bus stop in Amalfi for directions. A paradise for those seeking rest and quiet among natural beauty. Ten rooms sit high above lemon grove 270 steps from the road, with quick access to great hiking trails. Kitchens available, *alimentari* nearby. All rooms with bath. With *Let's Go:* doubles €52; quads €60; €15 per person for a bed with other people. ❹

Hotel Fontana, P. Duomo (☎089 87 15 30). A bit noisy with a friendly staff, Hotel Fontana provides 16 comfortable, clean rooms in the center of Amalfi. Breakfast included. Singles €50; doubles €78; triples €105; quads €132. ❹

Hotel La Bussola, Lungoar dei Cavalieri, 16 (☎089 87 15 33; fax 87 13 69; www.labussolahotel.it), on the right side of the beach facing the water, gives 3-star treatment with great views of the sea. All rooms with bath. Singles €57-72; doubles €94-124. AmEx/MC/V. ❺

Hotel Residence, V. delle Repubbliche Marinare, 9 (☎089 87 11 83; fax 87 30 70), right near P. Flavio Gioia, where the buses terminate, offers a touch of splendor with its winding marble staircases, lavish rooms, and large balconies. All rooms with bath, shower, TV, phone, and balcony. Singles €78-93; doubles €114-124; triples €144-155; quads €155-180. AmEx/MC/V. ❺

FOOD

Food in Amalfi is good, but expensive. Indulge in seafood, *scialatelli* (a coarsely cut local pasta), and the omnipresent pungent lemon liqueur *limoncello*. The town's many **paninoteche** (sandwich shops) are perfect for a tight budget.

Da Maria, P. Duomo (☎089 87 18 80). In the quest for quality Neapolitan cuisine, Da Maria should be your one and only stop. In this family-run restaurant owners instruct the adventurous on the daily specials and the house favorites like the Amalfitan Pasta, a dish of *scialatelli* and seafood for €4.50. *Primi* from €10.33, pizza from €2.58. Reservations recommended. Open Tu-Su 11am-3pm and 7pm-midnight. AmEx/MC/V. ❹

EAT YOUR WORDS. For Italians, the desecration of pasta is a mortal sin, akin to murder or buying French wine. Pasta must be chosen correctly and cooked *al dente* (firm, literally "to the tooth"). To avoid embarrassment, get to know the basics. The spaghetti family includes all variations that require twirling, from hollow cousins *bucatini* and *maccheroni* to the more delicate *capellini*. Flat spaghetti include *fettuccini*, *taglierini*, and *tagliatelle*. Short pasta tubes can be *penne* (cut diagonally), and *rigate* (ribbed), *sedani* (curved), *rigatoni* (wider), or *cannelloni* (usually stuffed). *Fusilli* (corkscrews), *farfalle* (butterflies or bow-ties), and *ruote* (wheels) demand shoveling rather than twirling. Don't be alarmed if you see pastry displays labeled "pasta"; the Italian word refers to anything made of dough.

Trattoria La Perla, Via dei Pastai, 5 (☎089 87 14 40), around corner from the Hotel Amalfi. Moderately priced. Try the bountiful *scialatielli ai frutti di mare* served in a giant conch shell (with seafood, €8), or the *bigné al limone* (pastry with lemon cream, €4). *Menù turistico* (including dessert) €16. Cover €2. Open Mar.-Nov. daily noon-3pm and 7pm-midnight; Apr.-Oct. W-M noon-3pm and 7-11:30pm. AmEx/MC/V. ❹

Lo Sputino, Lgo. Scavio, 5 (☎333 247 6628), on the left as you walk up C. delle Repubbliche Marinare. Hearty and imaginative *panini* €2.60-6.80. Beer from €1.80. Open Mar.-Oct. daily 10am-3am. ❸

Al Teatro, V. E. Marini, 19 (☎089 87 24 73). From V. d'Amalfi, turn left up the staircase (Salita degli Orafi) with a sign immediately after a shoe store, then follow the signs. Providing great atmosphere in a lively little locale, Al Teatro simply produces good, inexpensive food. Try the *scialatelli al Teatro* (with tomato and eggplant, €6.71). *Primi* and *secondi* from €4. *Menù* €15. Open mid-Feb to early Jan. Th-Tu 11:30am-3:15pm and 7:30-11:30pm. AmEx/MC/V. ❸

Barracca, P. Dogi, 16 (☎089 87 12 85), in the piazza abutting P. Duomo, offers fresh seafood set apart from the noise and chaos of the center of Amalfi. Special *spaghetti alla pescatore* (pasta with fish, €8.30). *Primi* €6.20-8.30. Tourist *menù* in the afternoon €15.50. Open W-M 12-3pm and 6-10:30pm, open daily in Aug. AmEx/MC/V. ❸

Ristorante Pizzeria S. Andrea, P. Duomo, 26 (☎089 871 023), just to the left of the duomo. Grab a table in the pleasant outdoor seating and take your pick from the huge menu with 40+ types of pizza and calzone. Pizza €4.40-8.30. Cover €2.10. MC/V. ❷

Caffe Royal, V. Lorenzo d'Amalfi, 10 (☎089 87 19 82), near the duomo. Follow the smell to Amalfi's best ice cream and Neapolitan pastries. Cones €2-3. Delectable *gelato* made from the local wine with a wide range of flavors. Lip-smacking crepes with nutella €5. Open 7am-3am daily; closed F Jan.-Feb. AmEx/MC/V. ❶

Andrea Pansa, P. Duomo, 40 (☎089 87 10 65). This pastry shop opened in 1830, and their experience is evident with the 1st bite of their tasty confections. In winter ask for *sprocollati* (fig with ground almond); year-round, the *Baba au limon* (€2) and *Baba con crema* (€1.50) are delicious. Open 7am-midnight daily. AmEx/MC/V. ❶

🔄 SIGHTS

The 9th-century Duomo di Sant'Andrea imparts grace, elegance, and dignity to the P. del Duomo. The piazza may need it; the nearby **Fontana di Sant'Andrea** features a marble female nude squeezing her breasts as water spews from her nipples. Those who can put their Freudian complexes aside drink from the fountain, which was rebuilt in the 19th century according to the original medieval plan. The cathedral features a facade of varied geometric designs typical of the Arab-Norman style. The handsomely-wrought **bronze doors,** crafted in Constantinople in 1066, started a bronze door craze throughout Italy. (Open daily 9am-6:45pm. Appropriate dress required.)

To its left, the **Chiostro del Paradiso** (Cloister of Paradise), a 13th-century cemetery, has become a graveyard for miscellaneous columns, statues, and sarcophagus fragments. The elegant interlaced arches, like the *campanile* in the square, show the Middle Eastern influence. Its museum houses mosaics, sculptures, and the church's treasury. Underneath is the crypt containing the body of the church's namesake, Saint Andrew the Apostle. (Open June-Sept. daily 9am-6:45pm. Free multilingual guides available. €1.50 for cloister, museum, and crypt.)

The 9th-century **Arsenal** on the waterfront, by the entrance to the city center, contains relics of Amalfi's former maritime glory. As you walk up V. D'Amalfi, the road changes its name to **Valle dei Mulini** (Valley of the Mills). Find here the **Paper Museum** with collections of, surprisingly enough, sundry paper items and the water-powered medieval machines that made Amalfi a paper-producing powerhouse. (☎089 830 4561; www.museodellacarta.it. Open Tu-Su 10am-6pm. €1.50.)

🏖️🥾 BEACHES AND HIKING

While there is a small beach in Amalfi, a 5-10min. trip will bring you to a much better (and free) beach in **Atrani**. A beachside village of 1200 inhabitants just around the bend from Amalfi, Atrani used to be home to the Republic's leaders; today it's a quiet place to escape from Amalfi's crowds by day, and lively with bars and music in the evening. Try **Casbah'r**, P. Umberto, 1 (☎089 87 10 87), with super-friendly bartenders and a fun-filled atmosphere. After the tunnel, descend a small winding staircase to the beach and P. Umberto. Atrani's one cobbled road, V. dei Dogi, leads from the beach up past P. Umberto, at which point a white stairway leads to **Chiesa di San Salvatore de Bireto**, with its 11th-century bronze doors from Constantinople. The name refers to the ceremonial hat placed on the Republic's doge when he was inaugurated.

Hikers often tackle paths from Amalfi into the imposing **Monti Lattari**, winding through lemon groves, mountain streams, and past beautiful vistas. From Amalfi, you can head up the **Antiche Scale** toward Pogerola. Trek through the **Valley of the Dragons**, named for the torrent of water and mist (like smoke from a dragon) exploding out to sea every winter. Another favorite is the four-hour **Path of the Gods**, leading from Bomerano to Positano, with great views along the way. Many enjoy the beautiful hike from Atrani to Ravello, or the hike past the old paper mills in **Valle delle Ferriere** that begins at the paper museum. Naturally, the hikes can get steep, and a good map, available anywhere in Amalfi, is essential for orientation.

If you prefer a short walk, a path leads through the streets along the cliffs to the cave where the famous rebel Masaneillo hid from Spanish police. Although the cave is sporadically closed, the view of Atrani alone is worth the one hour ascent.

📍 DAYTRIPS FROM AMALFI

MINORI

SITA buses from Amalfi stop on V. G. Capone, which changes its name to V. G. Amendola as it heads north to Minori, 1km away. Roman villa. (☎089 85 28 43. Open daily 9am-7pm. Free.)

Minori's main attraction is its beaches, less frequented by tourists than those at Amalfi and Positano. Hotels are more expensive than in Maiori, so it's best to stay there and dodge the tourist buses on the 1km walk along the coastal road. Unlike Maiori, where only a tiny section of the beach is public, a large swath of Minori's waterfront is free to all. Minori also has the remains of a Roman villa, with monochrome mosaics of a hunt, well-preserved arcades, and a small museum. The site is several blocks up from the beach on V. S. Lucia.

MAIORI

The pedestrian-only Corso Regina intersects V. G. Capone by the SITA bus stop. Several blocks up C. Regina, inside a garden on the left, is the tourist office, C. Regina, 73. (☎089 87 74 52; fax 85 36 72. Open M-Sa 8:30am-1:30pm, 3-6pm.) The nearest medical facilities are in Amalfi; however, there are carabinieri *(☎089 87 72 07).*

Only a few kilometers from well-known and touristed Amalfi, this beachfront town has few foreign visitors among the many Italians drawn to its shores. Though it lacks neither the style of Positano nor the history of Amalfi, Maiori has low priced hotels, excellent beaches, and several historical sights. Much of Maiori was damaged during WWII, and what was left was destroyed in a flood several decades ago. Thus, the architecture is noticeably more modern than in the other towns along the coast.

Most visitors come to Maiori to lounge on the beaches. Although much of the beach is privately owned (€5-10 fee for access with chair and umbrella) there is a small public section near the SITA bus stop. If you'd rather see sights than sun, the town's main attraction is **Chiesa di S. Maria a Mare,** up a flight of stairs on the left side of a mini piazza three blocks up C. Regina from the beach. It has a beautiful 15th-century alabaster altar kept in front of the crypt.

Maiori has several inexpensive hotels near the beach. **Albergo De Rosa ❸,** V. Orti, 24, a left two blocks up C. Regina from the beach, has English-speaking management and rooms with bath and breakfast included. (☎/fax 089 87 70 31. Singles €26-37; doubles €42-57; triples €54-71.) An inexpensive local restaurant is **Dedalo ❸,** on V. Cerasuoli just off C. Regina one block up from the beach. They serve up a €14 *menù* and €3-6 pizzas in a stylish air-conditioned interior. (☎089 87 70 84. Open daily noon-3pm and 6pm-2am.) For a bit more expensive fare at a beautiful spot along Maiori's beach, try **Ristorante La Vela ❹,** Lungomare G. Amendola to pick from their huge selection of local fish, including the house specialty *scialatelli* with seafood and vegetables for €10. *Primi* €7-10, *secondi* €11-22. (☎089 85 28 74. Open all year noon-3:30pm, 6pm-midnight. AmEx/MC/V.)

RAVELLO   ☎089

Ravello perches atop cliffs 330m high, above a patchwork of villages and ravines extending to the sea. Settled in AD 500 by Romans fleeing barbarian invasions, it grew into an opulent town of 70,000 during the heyday of the Amalfi Republic, and then later under Norman rule in the medieval era. But epidemics and raiding Saracens ended the town's prosperity and left only 2700 people. Though plague and civil war sapped its strength, the town's natural beauty and romantic decay drew artists and intellectuals alike. The exquisite gardens of Villa Rufolo inspired Giorgio Boccaccio's literary masterpiece, *The Decameron*, as well as Richard Wagner's opera, *Parsifal*. In fact, Ravello is still known as "*La Città della Musica*," thanks to the many concert series and performances it hosts throughout the year. For those needing creative inspiration, and even just those wanting to gaze at peaceful natural beauty, Ravello is well worth the trip up the mountain.

⌂✈ TRANSPORTATION AND PRACTICAL INFORMATION. Take the blue SITA bus from Amalfi (20min., 18 per day, 6:45am-10pm, €0.93) marked Ravello-Scala. If you'd rather take the gorgeous walk on foot, hike the footpaths along the hills and lemon groves from Minori (1hr.), Atrani (2hr. via Scala), or Amalfi (2½hr. via Pontone). Check the maps available in Amalfi for details. The **AAST Information office,** P. Duomo, 10 (☎089 85 70 98), is to the left of the **Piazza Duomo** as you face it. The English-speaking staff provides brochures, event and hotel listings, and a map. More maps are available at magazine and book shops; the best one is published by the *Club Alpino Italiano*. For a **taxi,** call ☎089 85 79 17. The **carabinieri**

(☎089 85 71 50) are convenient to the piazza, close by on V. Roma. There's a **pharmacy** at P. Duomo, 14, on the left side of the piazza as you face the duomo. (☎089 85 71 89. Open in summer daily 9am-1pm and 5-8:30pm.) The **post office** is at P. Duomo, 15. (Open M-F 8am-1:30pm, Sa 8am-12:30pm.) **Postal Code:** 84010.

⌂⌂ ACCOMMODATIONS AND FOOD. Ravello offers several affordable options. **Hotel Villa Amore ❹,** V. dei Fusco, 5, on the road to Villa Cimbrone, has 12 cute, tidy rooms and a garden overlooking cliffs and the sea. As their welcome sign says, "A stay at Villa Amore gives peace to the soul and joy to the heart." All rooms have terraces and views; some have bath. (☎/fax 089 85 71 35. Breakfast included. Reserve 1 month in advance. Singles €47-53; doubles €70-76. MC/V.) **Albergo Garden ❹,** V. G. Boccaccio, 4, before the tunnel into Ravello, by the SITA bus stop, offers a great view of the cliffs. All ten rooms have bath and balcony. English is spoken. (☎089 85 72 26; fax 85 81 10; www.starnet.it/hgarden. Breakfast included. Reserve 1 month in advance for Aug. Doubles €77-88. Closed Nov. 15-Feb. 15.) On the other side of the piazza, **Hotel Parsifal ❺,** V. G. d'Anna, 5, hosts guests in a former Augustinian convent with lush gardens overlooking the cliffs. (☎/fax 089 85 79 72; www.hotelparsifal.com. Breakfast included. Singles €55-95; doubles €85-180 for full-pension.)

Although many wines savored around the globe appear under a Ravello label, actual wine from the area is neither common nor commercially available—make friends in the town if you hope to try some. **Cumpà Cosimo ❸,** at V. Roma, 44/46, caters to the indecisive, with a huge menu of local specialties that are a welcome change from the seafood along the coast. Try the house specialty *mista di pasta fatta in casa*, a mix of five homemade pastas for €14. (☎089 85 71 56. Open noon-4pm and 6:30pm-midnight. €2 cover. AmEx/MC/V.)

◪⌂ SIGHTS AND ENTERTAINMENT. The beautiful churches, ivy-covered walls, and meandering paths of **Villa Rufolo** inspired Wagner's magic garden in the second act of *Parsifal*. In the summer, Villa Rufolo is home to a concert series on stages erected in some of the most picturesque spots of the villa. A medieval **tower** with Norman-Saracen vaulting and statues representing the four seasons serves as the entry to the famous Moorish cloister. Enter through the arch off P. Duomo near the tunnel. (☎089 85 76 57. Open daily 9am-8pm. €4, €2 under 12 or over 65, €3 per person in groups of more than 10.)

In the portal of Ravello's **duomo** you can see the Amalfi Coast's third set of famous bronze doors, cast by Barisano of Trani in 1179. Inside, a group of antique columns sets off two pulpits with elaborate mosaics. To the left of the altar stands the Cappella di S. Pantaleone, the town's patron saint. Behind the painting, you can see his blood, preserved in a cracked vessel. Saint Pantaleone was beheaded on July 27, AD 290, at Nicomedia. Every year on this day the city holds a religious **festival,** during which the saint's blood is mysteriously liquefied. The **museum** within depicts the duomo's history during pagan and Christian eras with beautiful ancient mosaics and sculpture. (Duomo open Mar.-Nov. daily 9:30am-1pm and 3-7pm; Dec.-Feb. Sa-Su 9am-1pm and 2-5pm. Museum €1.50. Proper dress required.)

Follow Viale dei Rufo out of P. Duomo to **Villa Cimbrone.** Renovated by Lord Grimmelthorpe in the 19th century in a probable attempt to draw attention away from his name, the villa sports floral walkways and majestic gardens. Greek temples and statued grottoes hide among Cimbrone's twisty paths, which harbor some of the most magnificent views on the Amalfi coast. A procession of notables made it a retreat, including Greta Garbo and Leopold Stokowski, who had romantic interludes here, and Jacqueline Kennedy, resident in 1962. (Open daily 9:30am-7:30pm. €4.50, €3 children under 12. Group rates available.)

Ravello deserves its "Città della Musica" moniker. During the year, internationally renowned musicians come to perform at the **classical music festivals** held around New Year's Day, Easter, and often throughout the summer. Concerts are performed in the gardens of the Villa Rufolo (in winter, concerts move indoors, into the Villa or the duomo). Tickets are usually around €10-20, and can be purchased at the AAST Information Office. Call the *Società di Concerti di Ravello* for more information (☎089 85 81 49).

SALERNO   ☎089

The capital of the Norman Empire from 1077 to 1127 and home to Europe's first medical school, Salerno is more recently famous as the site of an Allied landing during WWII. After being blasted to bits, it was remodeled and the consequently postwar urban landscape may shock those accustomed to the Amalfi Coast's peaceful coastal villages. Though lacking notable sights, Salerno is a cheap base from which to visit the Amalfi coast and Paestum.

⌐ TRANSPORTATION

Trains: Station in P. Veneto. To: **Naples** (45min., 29 per day, €5-10); **Paestum** (40min., 9 per day, 6am-9:30pm, €3); **Reggio Calabria** (3½-5hr., 22 per day, €17-35); **Rome** (2½-3hr., 19 per day, €20-30); and **Venice** (9hr., 1am, €35).

Buses: Blue **SITA** buses leave from the train station for **Amalfi** (1¼hr., 23 per day, 6am-10:30pm, €2.74) and **Naples** (1hr., 47 per day, 6am-9pm, €2.74). Purchase tickets from a bar or *tabacchi*, and ask where the bus leaves—many departures are not central.

Ferries and **Hydrofoils:** 1 dock is in P. della Concordia, 2 blocks from the train station. Another is in M. Marittimo Manfredi, a 15min. walk up the waterfront. **Linee Marittime Salernitane** (☎089 23 48 92) runs ferries to **Capri** (2hr., 2 per day, 7:50am and 8:10pm, €11). **Travelmar** (☎089 87 29 50) runs ferries to **Amalfi** (35min., 6 per day, 8:20am-3:30pm, €3.50); **Minori** (30min., 3 per day, 8:20am-2:10pm, €3.50); **Positano** (80min., 6 per day, 8:20am-3:30pm, €5); and **Sorrento** (2hr., 2 per day, 8:20am and 2:10pm).

Local Transportation: The orange **city buses** connect the train station neighborhood to the rest of the city. For routes and schedules, check the ticket booth in P. Veneto. Tickets €0.67 for 1hr., €1.29 for an all-day pass.

Taxis: ☎089 22 99 63 or 22 99 47.

◢* ⁊ ORIENTATION AND PRACTICAL INFORMATION

From the train station on **Piazza Vittorio Veneto**, the expansive-pedestrian **Corso Vittorio Emanuele** veers to the right. C. V. Emanuele becomes **Via dei Mercanti** in the **old quarter**, the most historically interesting and lively part of Salerno, approaching the **duomo**. **Via Roma** runs parallel to C. V. Emanuele one block toward the waterfront and is home to many of Salerno's best restaurants. Along the waterfront from the train station is **Piazza della Concordia,** where many intercity buses depart, and the **Lungomare Trieste,** which runs to the **Molo Marittimo Manfredi,** Salerno's port.

Tourist Office: EPT (☎089 22 47 44 or 22 49 16), in P. Veneto to the right as you leave the train station. The *Agenda del Turista* has practical info for Salerno and the Amalfi coast, while the bi-weekly *MEMO* lists hotel, restaurant, club, and special events. English spoken. Open M-Sa 9am-2pm and 3:30-7pm.

Car Rental: Travelcar, P. Veneto, 33 (☎089 22 77 22). Cars from €36 per day. Open daily 7:30am-1:30pm and 2:30-8:30pm. AmEx/MC/V.

English-Language Bookstore: Libreria Leona, V. Settimnio Mobilio, 38 (☎089 40 51 59). Take a left out of the train station and another left under the railroad tracks. Classics and new fiction. Open M-Sa 9am-1:15pm and 3:30-9pm. MC/V.

Laundromat: Onda Blu, V. Mauri, 128 (☎089 33 32 26), in Salerno's Mercatello neighborhood. City's only self-service laundry. Take bus #6 or #25 from C. Garibaldi, opposite the train station, to P. Grasso. Walk 1 block down V. Mauri. €3.50 wash, €3.50 dry for up to 7kg. Soap €0.50. Open daily 8am-10pm.

Work Opportunity: Italian-speaking travelers could try asking at the P. Veneto tourist office and at any of the many rental car services nearby about short-term work.

Emergency: ☎113. **Carabinieri:** ☎112.

First Aid: ☎089 24 12 33.

Hospital: S. Leonardo (☎089 67 11 11).

Internet Access: Mailboxes, Etc., V. Diaz, 19 (☎089 23 12 95), off C. V. Emanuele, 500m from the station. With *Let's Go* €1.55 for 30min. Also offers FedEx, UPS, Western Union, and fax service. Open M-F 8:30am-2pm and 4-8:30pm, Sa 8:30am-1pm and 5:30-8:30pm.

Post Office: C. Garibaldi, 203 (☎089 22 99 70). Open M-Sa 8:15am-6:15pm. **Branch office** (☎089 22 99 98) at P. Veneto. Open M-Sa 8:15am-1:30pm. **Currency exchange** only at the main office.

Postal Code: 84100.

ACCOMMODATIONS

Ostello della Gioventù "Irno," V. Luigi Guercio, 112 (☎089 79 02 51). Exit train station and turn left onto V. Torrione and left under the bridge onto V. Mobilio. It's 700m ahead, across from gas station. No longer with HI, this spot has since become a social center for recent immigrants, so prepare to be woken up as early as 4am by roommates getting up for work. Hot showers, restaurant, TV, spacious rooms, and Internet for €5 per hr. Breakfast and sheets included. Curfew 1:30am. Dorms €10. ❶

Albergo Santa Rosa, C. V. Emanuele, 14 (☎/fax 089 22 53 46), 1 block from the train station, on the right. 12 clean, comfortable rooms. Helpful proprietors full of crafty tips to save money and heartache. Singles €25, with bath €35; doubles €35/€55. ❷

Hotel Salerno, V. Vicinanza, 42 (☎089 22 42 11; fax 22 44 32), the 1st left off C. V. Emanuele. Close to the train station, up a few flights of stairs. Some of the 27 rooms have phone and TV. Singles €27-34, with bath €42-47; doubles €39-42/€49-57; triples €52-57/€67-77. AmEx/MC/V. ❸

Hotel Plaza, P. Veneto, 42 (☎089 22 44 77; fax 23 73 11; www.plazasalerno.it), right across from the tourist information office. High-ceilinged rooms with amenities in a convenient location. Singles €54-60; doubles €80-92; triples €92-110. AmEx/MC/V. ❹

FOOD

Salerno serves typical Campanian cuisine, including *pasta e fagioli* (pasta and bean soup), as well as unusual specialties of its own, such as *milza* (spleen).

❖ **Hosteria Il Brigante,** V. F. Linguiti, 4 (☎089 22 65 92). From P. Duomo, head up the ramp and look for the sign on the left. You know you've found an authentic spot when you have to wait for the 1 copy of the menu, hand-written on brown laminated paper, and the waiter/manager/only visible employee fills your wine glass with the bottle of the guy sitting across from you. Try the *pasta alla Sangiovannara,* a hodge-podge of pasta, tomato, cheese, and sausage (€3). Open daily 1:15-3pm and 8:45pm-2am. ❸

Taverna del Pozzo, V. Roma, 216-7 (☎089 25 36 36), serves some of the street's best pizza on a pleasant patio. Pizzas €2.60-7.20. Cover €1.10. Open M-Sa 1-3:30pm and 8pm-2am. AmEx/MC/V. ❷

Cueva del Sol, V. Roma, 218-220, serves delicious Mexican food and exotic drinks. Small portion of tacos €3.70. House cocktail *agave spinosa* (tequila, papaya juice, and lime; €3.70). Open daily 9pm-2am. MC/V. ❷

Mimmo e Lucio, V. Roma, 264/266 (☎089 22 59 70), is a pleasant family-run spot with outdoor seating on V. Roma. Serves traditional Salerno cuisine. *Pasta e fagioli* €3.10, pizza €3.10-4.10. Cover €1.10. AmEx/MC/V. ❷

🔍 🎵 SIGHTS AND ENTERTAINMENT

Though most of Salerno is dominated by aesthetically uninteresting modern buildings, the old city teems with pleasant narrow roads with wonderful little shops. Especially nice is the walk starting along C. V. Emanuele that winds through back alleys leading to the **duomo.**

First constructed in 845, the **Duomo San Matteo** was destroyed and then rebuilt 200 years later by Norman leader Robert Guiscard— explaining its design in the cosmopolitan style of the Norman regime. The arches of the portico, floor of the apse, and two pulpits in the nave are decorated with beautiful geometric mosaics and patterns influenced by those of the Islamic world. The ubiquitous design of rings around a star of David is symbolic of the belief of evil things (the rings) eventually leading to good (the star). The duomo is also home to many relics usually not shown to the public, such as a tooth of the Evangelist Matthew, a hair of the Virgin Mary, and a splinter believed to be from Jesus's cross. (Turn right off V. Mercanti or V. Roma onto V. Duomo and walk uphill. Open daily 10am-noon and 4-6:30pm.) One block down V. Duomo from the duomo, the **Museo della Ceramica** exhibits local ceramic art. (☎089 22 77 82. Open M-W and F-Sa 9am-1pm, Th 9am-1pm and 4-7pm. Free.) Exotic plants grow in the **Parco del Mercatello** east of the city. CTSP bus #6 (€0.67) runs to the gardens. If you want to soak up some rays, there is a sandy beach after the sailboat harbor. (Take the bus along Lungomare Trieste until you see the beach.)

During the month of July, the **Salerno Summerfestival,** at the Arena del Mare, near the Molo Marittimo Manfredi, includes a concert series with jazz and blues. (☎089 66 51 76. Concerts usually start at 10pm. Prices vary.)

At night, the youngest crowd gathers near the fountain at **Bar/Gelateria Nettuno,** V. Lungomare Trieste, 136-138 (☎089 22 83 75). Discos rock the coastal towns around Salerno, but prices are steep unless you can get your hands on one of the free passes often dispensed at random, often at the bars along V. Roma. Women can usually enter for free, but let that be its own warning. In summer, locals flock to gigantic open-air discos on the western and southern coasts. **Movida, Villaggio del Sole, Morgana,** and **Mermaid's Tavern** along the southern coast are difficult to reach without a car. The nighttime hotspot **Fuenti,** in Cetara (4km west of Salerno), has three floors of open-air dancing on the coastal cliffs. (☎089 26 18 00. Cover €10-15. Open June-Sept. F-Sa 10:30pm-5am.) ▨**Africana,** the most spectacular club around but far away in Praiano, sometimes charters boats to Salerno and back in the summer (see **Praiano,** p. 567). Check the magazine *MEMO* (at the tourist office or the hostel) for special events and club listings, including those outside Salerno.

Nearby **Vietri sul Mare** is home to hundreds of artisans and a pleasant beach. Bus #4 and 9 run from the station (10min., €0.67). Check out the neon-lit **Café degli Artisti,** V. C. Colombo, 35. Dance to Latin music and choose the *sangria* over the local red. (☎089 76 18 42. Open nightly 7:30pm-3am. Cover €10.)

DAYTRIP FROM SALERNO: CERTOSA DI SAN LORENZO

Without a car, the Certosa is best reached from Salerno, and can be seen in an easy daytrip. A bus leaves from Piazza Concodia at 6:25am, 10:30am, noon, and 2:30pm. The last bus returning to Salerno leaves Padula at 5:45pm (2½hr., €5.42). Buses do not stop at Padula itself, but at the crossroads about 2km away which seem to be in the middle of nowhere, so make sure you tell the driver that you want to stop in Padula. From the crossroads, follow the signs for "Certosa di Padula" 1km to the monastery.

Beneath the small town of **Padula** in the beautiful hilly farmland of southern Campania, sits the magnificent Certosa di San Lorenzo, one of the largest monasteries in Europe and a magnificent example of Baroque architecture. Angevin kings founded the monastery for Carthusian monks in the early 14th century to maintain control over routes into Calabria, but in the 17th century it was redecorated in lavish Baroque style. Charles V stopped here, and he and his court were served an omelette made from 1000 eggs. Though you won't be able to eat the embryos of 1000 chickens today, the splendid architecture and beautiful setting of the Certosa make it well worth a visit.

The *certosa* is divided into two sections, "Upper" and "Lower." Lay people could visit the lower section, which is the 1st courtyard through the main gate, but only the monks could pass through the ornate facade into the main body of the monestary. (Open daily 9am-7:30pm. Free for those under 18 and over 65, €2 18-25, €4 25-65.) The path through the monastery leads through two halves of the chapel, with choir stalls covered in inlaid wood depicting landscapes and Biblical scenes, along with a marble altar adorned with ornate friezes. The path leads through the dining hall and kitchen, decorated in colorful majolica tiles, to the staircase to the library, which winds precariously up, without railings or pillars for support. Pass the staircase into the huge and serenely beautiful **Great Cloister,** a massive courtyard decorated with carved miniatures of religious symbols in the entablature. At the far end of the cloister, the **Grand Staircase,** an architectually masterful double staircase, curves up to the upper level.

Although you can easily see the *certosa* as a daytrip from Salerno, if you want to relax (or if you missed the last bus), **Albergo La Rosa ❶**, attached to a farm, offers six clean rooms with a kitchen for €15-per person. (Call ☎ 0975 55 81 04 to be picked up from anywhere in Padua.)

PAESTUM ☎ 082

Not far from the Roman ruins of Pompeii and Herculaneum, the three Greek temples of Paestum are among the best-preserved in the world, even rivaling those of Sicily and Athens. Paestum's perfectly constructed temples remained standing even after the great earthquake of AD 69 reduced Pompeii's Temple of Jupiter to a pile of rubble. The city began as a prosperous Greek colony dedicated to the sea god Poseidon, then changed hands between the Greeks, the native Lucanians and eventually the Romans, until it faded out, not to be discovered again until the 18th century. Because Paestum is not urbanized, you may think that you missed your stop as you step off the train or bus. Fear not the dearth of modern urban squalor; the ruins alone are a must-see, especially when the *Sovrintendenza Archeologica* lets visitors walk around on the temples (sometimes they are fenced off).

TRANSPORTATION AND PRACTICAL INFORMATION. CTSP buses from Salerno (1hr., every hr., 7am-7pm, €2.53) stop at **Via Magna Graecia,** the main modern road. Buy a ticket from the *tabacchi* in the station. The tourist office in Salerno provides a helpful list of all return buses and trains from Paestum.

Trains run from **Naples** (1¼hr., 7 per day, 5:15am-8:54pm, €5.73) via **Salerno** (35min., €3.10). The **AAST Information Office**, V. Magna Graecia, 887, is next to the muscum. (☎082 81 10 16. Open June-Sept. 15 M-Sa 9am-1pm and 2-7pm, Sept. 16-June 9am-1pm, 2-5pm.)

ACCOMMODATIONS. There is really no reason to stay in Paestum when local hotels and restaurants are overpriced, and the site can easily be visited as a daytrip. The beachside **Ostello "La Lanterna" (HI) ❶**, V. Lanterna, 8, in Agropoli, is the nearest budget option. (☎/fax 0974 83 83 64. lanterna@cilento.peoples.it Sheets and shower included. 56 beds. Dorms €10; quads €42.) To get to Agropoli take the **CTSP buses** from Paestum (10min., 1 per hr., 7:30am-9:15pm, €1.10) or from Salerno (1hr., 23 per day, 6:30am-8:15pm, €2.53). Agropoli is also connected by train to Paestum (10min., 9 per day, 6:10am-10:22pm, €1.154); Salerno (45min., 21 per day, 5:30am-9:49pm, €3.10); and Naples (1½hr., 16 per day, 5:15am-8:54pm, €5.73).

SIGHTS. Paestum's three Doric temples rank among the best-preserved in the world. Amazingly, these massive structures were built without any mortar or cement. When excavators first uncovered the three temples, they misidentified (and thus misnamed) them. Although recent scholarship has provided new information about the temples's dedications, the old names have stuck. Restoration work on the temples occasionally leaves them fenced off or obscured by scaffolding. (Temples open daily 9am-4pm in winter, 9am-7:30pm in summer. Closed 1st and 3rd Monday of each month for maintenance. €6.50 for the ruins and museum, half-price for students from the EU, free for EU citizens over 60 and under 18.)

There are three entrances to the ruins. The northernmost entrance leads to the **Temple of Ceres.** Built around 500 BC, this temple became a church in the early Middle Ages but was abandoned in the 9th century. The ancient Greeks built Paestum on a north-south axis, marked by the paved V. Sacra. Farther south on V. Sacra is the Roman **forum,** which is even larger than the one at Pompeii, although less preserved. The Romans leveled most of the older structures in the city's center to build this proto-piazza, the commercial and political arena of Paestum. To the left, a shallow pit marks the pool of an ancient **gymnasium.** East of the gymnasium lies the Roman **amphitheater.**

South of the forum lies the 5th-century BC **Temple of Poseidon** (actually dedicated to Hera), which incorporates many of the optical refinements that characterize the Parthenon in Athens. Small lions' heads serve as gargoyles on the temple roof. The southernmost temple, known as the **basilica,** is the oldest, dating to the 6th century BC. Its unusual plan, with a main interior section split by a row of columns down the middle, has inspired the theory that the temple was dedicated to two gods, Zeus and Hera, rather than one. A **museum** on the other side of V. Magna Graecia houses extraordinary pottery, paintings, and artifacts taken primarily from Paestum's tombs, narrated by outstanding bilingual descriptions and essays. It also includes samples of 2500-year-old honey and paintings from the famous **Tomb of the Diver,** dating to 475 BC. (Museum open daily 9am-6:30pm. Ticket office open daily 9am-5:30pm. Closed 1st and 3rd Monday of each month. €4, half-price for EU students, free for EU citizens over 60 and under 18.)

If visiting the temples puts you in the mood for worship, bow down on golden sand toward the sun at the beach, 2km to the west. Unfortunately, much of it is owned by resorts that charge for beach access and chair rental. For a free dip in the Mediterranean, head to a *spiaggia pubblica*—ask for directions.

APULIA (PUGLIA)

Welcome to absolute Italy, where scorching sun rays and volatile tempers continually threaten to bring things to a boil. Conversations, complete with elaborate hand gestures, quickly progress from pleasant joking to frenzied yelling and then back again. Some travelers interpret southern mercurial passions as rudeness, but you'll have a better understanding (and a better time) if you try to see it as part of an uninhibited zest for life. Women may find the persisting legacy of *machismo* a little too much for them, especially in large cities.

The heel of Italy's boot, Apulia has been prized throughout the centuries for its fertile plains and natural ports (still used today in the modern Brindisi, Bari, and Otranto). The Greeks, and later the Romans, controlled the region as a vital stop on the trade route to the East. With the Middle Ages came an onslaught of invaders who shaped the area's culture and built its gorgeous cathedrals and castles. Modern Apulia, long considered the unsophisticated country cousin of northern Italy, is regaining stature as a wealthy and educated region. Within its borders, remote medieval villages and cone-roofed *trulli* houses dot a cave-ridden plain, and ports have a distinctly Middle Eastern flair.

Direct train lines run from Naples to Bari and from Bologna to Lecce, and rail service is supplemented within the region by several private train and bus companies. Eurail passes and *cartaverdi* are not valid on these private carriers.

HIGHLIGHTS OF APULIA

MARVEL at Alberobello's mortarless houses, *trulli* (p. 588).

SPELUNK in the stalactite-filled caverns of **Castellana Grotte** (p. 587).

GET LOST in the winding streets of Trani's **old city** as you search for the stunning **cathedral** (p. 589).

TAKE A BREATHER in **Bari**. It's free (p. 580).

BARI
☎ 080

Se Parigi ci avesse lo mare, sarebbe una piccola Bari.
(If Paris had the sea, it would be a little Bari.)
—— An Italian proverb

Vibrant, modern, and indisputably Italian, Apulia's capital is a chaotic melange of seemingly incompatible ingredients. Begin with a tiny old city, whose monuments date from its days as a Byzantine stronghold. Add a well-organized, modern city grid, a port with ferries to Greece, hip nightlife fueled by a large university population, and vast quantities of delectable Puglian cuisine. Sprinkle in Rome's drivers and Naples's pick-pockets, and broil the whole mishmash in some scorching southern Italian weather. While the city has been called dirty, violent, and nightmarishly inefficient, and most tourists stay only long enough to buy a ferry ticket to Greece, the reputation's bark is far worse than Bari's bite. The old city has several excellent monuments, and the new city is an easily-navigated grid of tree-lined shopping streets and piazzas with fountains. Proud of their effort to alter their city's image, the *Baresi* strive to make tourists feel welcome.

Apulia, Basilicata & Calabria

TRANSPORTATION

Airport: Bari Palese Airport (☎080 921 2172), 8km west of the city. Alitalia, Air France, British Airways, and Lufthansa fly to major European cities. A **shuttle bus** leaves from P. Aldo Moro (12 per day, 5:15am-6:30pm, €4.13).

Trains: Bari is connected to 4 different railways, all of which leave from P. Aldo Moro. The higher prices listed below are for InterCity (IC) or EuroStar (ES) trains.

FS to: **Brindisi** (1-1¾hr., 26 per day, 4:50am-11pm, €6.20-10.33); **Foggia** (1-1¾hr., 41 per day, 12:40am-11:55pm, €6.70-13.94); **Lecce** (1¾-2¼hr., 21 per day, 4:50am-11pm, €7.50-12.19); **Milan** (9hr., 9 per day, 7am-midnight, €37.70-58.31); **Naples** (4½hr., noon, €14.31); **Reggio Calabria** (7½hr., 3 per day, noon-10pm, €23.50-35.48); **Rome** (5-7hr., 6 per day, 12:40am-6:42pm, €26.12-36); and **Termoli** (2-3hr., 6 per day, 1am-9:39pm, €9.80-21.28).

FSE (☎080 546 2444) from the main station to **Alberobello** (1½hr., 14 per day, 5:30am-7:15pm, €3.05), sometimes via **Castellana Grotte** (1hr., 4 per day, 8:25am-7:15pm, €2.43).

Ferrotramviaria Bari Nord (☎080 521 3577), next to the main station. Trains run to: **Barletta** (1¼hr., 19 per day, 6am-10pm, €3.05) via **Bitonto** (30min., €1.55); **Ruvo** (45min., €2.01); and **Andria** (1¼hr., €2.63). On Su the route is served by a bus leaving from P. Aldo Moro.

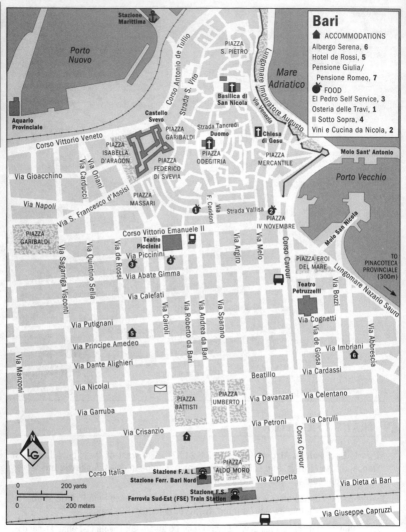

FAL (☎ 080 524 4881) runs to **Matera** (1½hr., 8 per day, 6:30am-9pm, €3.62) via **Altamura** (1¼hr., €2.58). Next door to the Bari-Nord station in P. Aldo Moro.

Buses: SITA (☎ 080 556 2446) usually leaves from V. Capruzzi on the other side of the tracks. Call ahead for fares and schedules.

Public Transportation: Local buses leave from P. Aldo Moro, in front of the train station. Tickets €0.77.

Taxis: ☎ 080 55 43 33.

◪ FERRIES

Although there are no discounts for Interrail or Eurail pass holders (as there are in Brindisi), Bari is an important port for ferries to Greece, Turkey, Albania, and Israel. Because Bari's *Stazione Marittima* and the surrounding area can be intimidating, you should take one of the many buses to the port rather than walking the 2km through the old city. **Check in at least 2hr. before departure.** Many lines offer special student rates and discounts on round-trip tickets (Poseidon discounts 30% on return-trips). The list of companies below gives the lowest prices (deck class) for each destination on weekdays. The higher figure denotes high-season (July-Aug.) prices, while the lower figure represents low-season prices. Call ahead, as schedules and prices vary, especially on weekends. Obtain tickets and information at the *Stazione Marittima* or at the offices listed below.

Ventouris Ferries, V. Piccinni, 133, c/o P. Lorusso & Co. (☎080 521 7699; fax 521 7734; www.ventouris.gr). Windows #18-20. To: **Corfu** (11hr., Sept. 17-June 16 M and W only, June 17-Sept. 16 daily with some exceptions) and **Igoumenitsa** (13hr.; Sept. 17-June 16; daily, June 17-Sept. 16, 4 per wk.).

Marlines (☎080 523 1824; fax 523 0287). To **Kotor, Montenegro** (8hr.; June 29-Sept. 7, 5 per wk.; Sept. 8-Dec. 31, 4 per wk.; €22-39).

Superfast Ferries (☎080 528 2828; fax 528 2444), to **Igoumenitsa** (9½hr.; June 28-July 24, 3 per wk.; July 25-Aug. 11, daily; €42-52) and **Patras** (15½hr.; June 28-July 24, 3 per wk.; June 25-Aug. 11, daily; €42-52).

Adriatic Shipping Company (☎080 527 5452; fax 575 1089) to **Dubrovnik** (9hr.; July 5-June 24 and Aug. 29-Sept. 13, 2 per wk.; June 25-Aug. 28, 3 per wk.; €43).

◪ ◪ ORIENTATION AND PRACTICAL INFORMATION

Via Sparano runs straight from the train station to **Piazza Umberto I,** Bari's main square. Farther along V. Sparano, fancy boutiques line the street and provide some of the city's best window-shopping. The end of V. Sparano intersects **Corso Vittorio Emanuele II** and the edge of the **old city** *(Bari Vecchia)*. Those attempting the long walk to the **port** should skirt the old city's winding streets by turning left on C. V. Emanuele II and right at P. della Libertà onto **Via Giuseppe Massari.** Walk around the castle, head right, and follow the coast. Otherwise, take the bus from the station (one per hr.). For a more leisurely stroll, turn right off V. Sparano onto C. V. Emanuele II; this path takes you past **Corso Cavour** to **Piazza Eroi del Mare.**

Tourist Office: APT, P. Aldo Moro, 33a, 2nd fl. (☎080 524 2361; fax 524 2329), to the right, from the station. Maps of Apulia and Bari. English spoken. Open M-F 9am-12pm.

American Express: Morfimare, C. de Tullio, 36/40 (☎080 521 0022), near the port. Open M-F 9am-1pm and 3:30-7:30pm, Sa 9am-noon.

English-Language Bookstores: Feltrinelli, V. Dante 91/95 (☎080 521 9677). Open M-Sa 9am-8:30pm.

Laundromat: V. Toma, 35 (☎080 556 7056). Take the overpass over the train tracks onto C. Cavour, and continue a long way until a left onto V. Toma. €3 wash, €2 dry. Open M-Sa 9am-1:15pm and 4-6:15pm.

Short-term Work: Short-term work is readily available in Bari. The **Lavoro Temporaneo Office,** P. Aldo Moro, near the FAL station, can help you find jobs lasting a couple of months. The daily business page in the Bari newspaper also lists temporary jobs.

Emergency: ☎ 113. **Police:** ☎ 113. **Carabinieri:** ☎ 112.

Late-Night Pharmacy: Lojacono di Berrino, V. Cavour, 47 (☎080 521 2615), across from Teatro Petruzzelli. Open M-F 4:30-11pm, Sa-Su 4:30-8pm. **De Cristo,** V. Kennedy, 75 (☎080 51 31 38).

Internet Access: Netcafe, V. Andrea da Bari, 11 (☎/fax 080 524 1756; www.netcafebari.it). €4 per hr. Open M-F 8:30am-midnight, Sa 8:30am-2:30pm, 4:30pm-midnight, Su 4:30pm-midnight.

Post Office: (☎080 575 7187; fax 575 7007), in P. Battisti, behind the university. From P. Umberto, turn left on V. Crisanzio, then take the 1st right on V. Cairoli. Recently discovered, to everyone's shock, to be Italy's most efficient. Open M-F 8:20am-8pm, Sa 8:20am-1pm.

Postal Code: 70100.

ACCOMMODATIONS

Most travelers don't stay long in Bari, but cheap accommodations are plentiful.

Pensione Romeo, V. Crisanzio, 12 (☎080 521 6352; fax 523 7253; hotelpensioneromeo@tim.it). Below his star-crossed love, Pensione Giulia. 25 rooms. Singles without bath €25.80, with bath €36; doubles with bath €54. AmEx/MC/V. ❸

Albergo Serena, V. Imbriani, 69 (☎080 554 0980; fax 558 6613). The most spacious option, all 14 rooms with shower. Many past guests have been cigarette smokers. Singles €25.82; doubles €51.65. ❷

Pensione Giulia, V. Crisanzio, 12 (☎080 521 6630; fax 521 8271; www.pagineitaliahotelgiulia.it). 13 spacious rooms with balconies. Breakfast included. Singles €40, with bath €50; doubles €50/€65. 3-5 person rooms also available. AmEx/MC/V. ❸

Hotel de Rossi, V. de Rossi, 186 (☎080 524 5355). In the heart of downtown, these good-sized rooms have bath, TV, and A/C. Singles €31; doubles €52. AmEx/MC/V. ❸

FOOD

Bari offers delicious Apulian food at outrageously low prices. Restaurants in the old town give a taste of old-world style, often providing neither menus nor itemized checks. Purchase food for the ferry ride at **Super CRAI,** V. de Giosa, 97, three streets to the right of P. Umberto I if you are facing away from the station. (☎080 524 7485. Open M-Sa 8am-2pm and 5-8:30pm.) There is a daily **vegetable market** in P. del Ferrarese, closer to the port.

Osteria delle Travi, Largo Chiurlia, 12 (☎339 157 8848), at the end of V. Sparano. Turn left through the arches at the entrance to the old city. True *mezzogiorno* cuisine including pasta with arugula, and the local delicacy *orecchiette con cavallo* (ear-shaped pasta with horse). Full meal with drink, €16-19. Open Tu-Su 1-3:30pm and 8-11pm. ❹

Vini e Cucina Da Nicola, Strada Vallisa, 23 (☎0330 43 30 18), in the old city. From the left of P. IV November, enter the old city; the restaurant is on the left. Inexpensive dining at its best. No-frills service. Dishes change daily; the fried calamari is exquisite. *Menù* with drink, €9.81. Open M-Sa 8am-3pm and 7pm-1am. ❷

AGRITURISMO. Somewhat comically translated as "farm holiday houses," Southern Italy's *agriturismo* is growing in popularity. Tourists flock to tranquil retreats in Apulia's countryside to relax, bike, or hike in the open terrain. Agritouring options are wide, and almost universally inexpensive. From renovated barns to well-equipped apartments, accommodations vary along with rental policies. Some agritouring spots require a minimum stay or half-pension. If you've got a craving for southern Italy's colorful countryside, start by contacting the tourist bureau in the nearest city.

El Pedro Self-Service, V. Piccini, 152 (☎/fax 080 521 1294), off V. Sparano. Turn left (when heading away from the station) a block before C. V. Emanuele. Not a Mexican restaurant, but a busy cafeteria serving authentic Apulian specialties. Expect to wait in line, but the food's certainly worth it. Complete meal with drink €7.32. Open M-Sa 11am-3:30pm and 6-10pm. MC/V. ❷

Il Sotto Sopra, V. Piccini, 110/112/114 (☎080 521 4995), offers Apulian pastas in a big arched dining room. Tasty takeout pizzas for under €5. *Primi* €5, *secondi* €6-10. Cover €1. Open daily 12:30-3:30pm and 7:30pm-midnight. AmEx/MC/V. ❷

◎ SIGHTS

As a strategic port on the Italian coast, Bari has always been a favorite target for invading armies. To help defend against approaching troops, Bari's citizens built the old city as a labyrinth; residents could hide in the twisting streets or use them to ambush those less familiar with the city. Thieves have learned to use this maze of streets to their advantage, and careless tourists are their favorite victims. **Do not venture alone into the old city at night.** Avoid flashy watches and jewelry, keep valuables inside front pockets, and hold on tightly to purses, bags, and cameras. If you use a map, use it discreetly. At the same time, petty criminals should not scare you off entirely. The old city is of great historic interest and well-worth visiting.

▓ BASILICA DI SAN NICOLA. In 1087, 60 *Baresi* sailors stole the remains of St. Nicholas from Demre, Turkey—they don't call Bari *scippolandia* (land of the petty thieves) for nothing. Although the victorious sailors initially refused to hand over the saint to the local clergy, the Catholic Church built the Chiesa di San Nicola as Santa's final resting place. The church's spartan appearance would be better suited to a fortress—in fact, the tower on the right survives from a Byzantine castle that originally occupied the site. Inside, an 11th-century Episcopal throne hides behind the high altar, and 17th-century paintings with gaudy trim adorn the ceiling. The crypt, with its windows of translucent marble, holds the remains of jolly old Saint Nick himself. To the left of the entrance, a Greek Orthodox shrine welcomes pilgrims visiting from the east. On the back wall, several 17th-century paintings commemorate the saint's life, including a scene of the resurrection of three children sliced to bits and plunged into a barrel of brine by a nasty butcher. On a 3rd wall, stockings are hung by the chimney with care. *(Open daily 7am-noon and 4-7:30pm, except during Mass.)*

CASTELLO SVEVO. Fortifying the old maze of streets near the port is the colossal Swabian Castle, built in the 13th century by Frederick II on Norman and Byzantine foundations. Isabel of Aragon and Sona Sforza added bulwarks in the 16th century. Although you can't climb the ramparts, you can check out the frequently changing art exhibits inside the medieval keep, as well as artifacts from the cathedrals and castles of the region. *(Just outside the old city, off C. V. Veneto near the water. ☎080 528 6111. Open Tu-Su 8:30am-7:30pm. Mid-June to mid-Sept. open until 11pm on Sa.)*

DUOMO. Bari's most important monument, this Apulian-Romanesque cathedral was built in the late 12th century, during years of peaceful Norman rule. The duomo displays a typically austere tripartite Romanesque facade, augmented by rose windows on the transepts and Baroque decorations around the doors. *(In the old city at P. Odegitria. Open daily 8am-12:30pm and 3-7:30pm.)*

OTHER SIGHTS. The **Pinacoteca Provinciale** displays in 17 rooms paintings by Veronese, Tintoretto, Bellini, and the Impressionist Francesco Netti, Bari's most acclaimed artist. It also houses a collection of 18th- and 19th-century Apulian landscapes. *(Down Lungomare N. Sauro, past P. A. Diaz, 4th fl. ☎ 080 541 2422. Open Tu-Sa 9am-1pm and 4-7pm, Su 9am-1pm. €2.58, students €1.03.)* The **Acquario Provinciale** has a large collection of marine life. *(On Molo Pizzoli across P. Garibaldi. ☎ 080 521 2229. Open M-F 9am-1pm and 3-5pm, Sa-Su 10am-1pm.)*

🎵🎤 ENTERTAINMENT AND NIGHTLIFE

Pubs and **clubs** pepper this university town. Most are open daily from around 8pm until 1 or 2am (3am on Saturdays); they are generally closed during the August holidays. On weekends, students cram into Largo Adua and the other piazzas along the coast east of the old city. Here, **Deco**, P. Eroi del Mare, 18 (☎ 080 524 6070), serves American food and has live music. V. Sparano and P. Umberto are packed in the evenings as well, with young *Baresi* in their flashy finest, revving their Vespas to impress the girls.

Bari is the cultural nucleus of Apulia. **Teatro Piccinni** offers a spring concert season and opera year-round (purchase tickets at the theater). Consult the *Bari Sera* section of *La Gazzetta del Mezzogiorno* (the local newspaper) for the latest information or the ticket office at the theater.

Bari's **soccer** team was successful enough in 1997 to move up to Serie A, but since has been booted back down to Serie B. For true Italian culture, catch a game any Sunday (and often other days of the week) from September through June. Tickets, starting at €15, are available at the stadium or in bars. The great commercial event of the year, the **Levante Fair,** runs for 10 days in mid-September, and similar smaller commercial fairs occur on weekends throughout the year. The largest fair in southern Italy, it displays goods from all over the world in the huge fairgrounds by the municipal stadium. May 7, 8, and 9 bring the **Festival of San Nicola.** Every Sunday *Baresi* carry an image of the saint from church to church.

🏛 DAYTRIPS FROM BARI

The numerous train lines that radiate from Bari make daytripping easy and affordable. Nearby towns are arranged in groups along five routes: Barletta, Trani, and Bisceglie to the northwest along the coast; Bitonto, Ruvo di Puglia, and Castel del Monte to the west; Altamura and Gravina in Puglia in the southwest; Castellana Grotte, Alberobello, and Martina Franca to the south; and Polignano a Mare, Monopoli, Egnazia, Fasano, and Ostuni to the southeast.

CASTEL DEL MONTE

In summer, take Ferrotramviaria Bari Nord train (☎ 0883 59 26 84) to Andria (1¼hr., 19 per day, 5:30am-10:20pm, €2.63) and then take bus from station to the castle, 17km away (30min.; 8:30am, 1:30pm, and 5pm; returns 10:15am, 2:15pm, and 7pm; €1.03). Call ☎ 0883 29 03 29 or contact Pro Loco tourist office (☎ 0883 59 22 83) to confirm the schedule. Castel del Monte (☎ 0883 56 98 48) is open daily 10am-1:30pm and 2:30-7pm. €3, EU students 18-25 €1.50, EU citizens under 18 and over 65 free.

Halfway between the High Murge and the sea, Castel del Monte sits majestically atop a hill, surrounded by rolling farmlands. It is easily the most impressive of the castles of Frederick II, the Swabian king who ruled southern Italy in the 13th century. According to legend, the castle housed the Holy Grail; in reality, it served as a hunting lodge and, later, a prison. Now the castle hosts various exhibits covering a broad range of local art. Check out the majestic gateway, inspired by a Roman triumphal arch—Frederick tried to revive classical principles of art and good government—and many neoclassical details can be seen throughout the castle. The striking octagonal layout is aligned astronomically, leading scholars to hypothesize that the castle was designed as an observatory rather than a military structure. Atop one of the spiral staircases sits a small room used as a roost for hunting hawks, one of the emperor's hobbies.

CASTELLANA GROTTE

The FSE train from Bari toward Alberobello stops at "Grotte di Castellana Grotte" (1hr., 8 per day, 8:30am-7:15pm, €2.43). Do not disembark at "Castellana Grotte." This stop is for the city, 2km away from the grotte down V. Grotte. The next (unmarked) stop is for the grotte. Check schedules carefully; not all trains stop here. Walk across the parking lot and turn left to get to the caves. Short tours (50min.; every hr., 8:30am-7pm; in winter, every hr., 8:30am-1pm; €8), longer tours (2hr., every hr., 9am-6pm except 1 and 2pm; in winter, every hr., 9am-noon; €13), and English tours available (long tour 11am and 4pm, short tour 1pm and 6:30pm).

The breathtaking, natural caverns of ▓**Castellana Grotte,** discovered in 1938, are famed for their size, age, and beauty. Stalactites and stalagmites have developed over time into all sorts of whimsical shapes, including a Madonna, a camel, a wolf, an owl, and an ice-cream cone. Even if you don't see the resemblances, the various formations invite the imagination to run wild. Those with time to kill can even watch them grow—at the rate of 3cm per century. Visiting the caverns is expensive but worthwhile. To enter, you must join one of two **guided tours** (☎ 0167 21 39 76 or 0804 98 55 11). A short 1km jaunt and a longer 3km trek both start at La Grave, an enormous pit that superstitious locals feared was an entrance to hell. The longer tours culminate in the stunning Grotta Bianca (White Cave), a giant cavern filled with white stalactites.

THE GARGANO MASSIF

For Siponto, take the train to Foggia from Bari (1-1¾hr., 41 per day, 12:40am-11:55pm, €6.70-13.94) or Termoli (1-1¼hr., 13 per day, 7:45am-10:15pm, €3.82-6.40). From there, another train will take you to Siponto (20min., 27 per day, 5am-10:30pm, €1.80). To get to the church, take the path that starts across the tracks next to the small amusement park. For Monte Sant'Angelo, take the SITA bus from the train station in Foggia (40min., 10 per day, 5:45am-6:45pm, €3.62). Ferrovie del Gargano buses also run to Vieste (2hr., 5 per day, 6:45am-5:45pm, €4.65), via Pugnochiuso (1¾hr., €4.65). SITA buses also run to San Giovanni Rotondo, home of the famous Padre Pio—his tomb and the church built in his honor draw droves of Italian pilgrims. (10 per day, noon-10:15pm, €2.58. Crypt open daily 9:30am-1:30pm and 4-7pm.)

The Gargano Massif once ranked among the most popular pilgrimage destinations in Europe. The Archangel Michael was said to have appeared in a cave in **Monte Sant'Angelo** in the 5th century, and in ancient times, a respected oracle supposedly occupied the same cavern. Now the peninsula is renowned for its stretches of sand (65km) on the north and east coasts. Popular beach destinations include **Vieste, San Menaio,** and **Pugnochiuso.** Unfortunately, the Gargano is gradually succumbing to the twin blights of the southern coastal areas—smokestacks and beach umbrellas—so visit soon. Inland from the shore is the **Foresta Umbra,** which abruptly gives way to classic Mediterranean terrain in the south.

Residents of **Siponto,** 3km southwest of Manfredonia, abandoned the ancient city after a 12th-century earthquake and plague. The sole remains of Siponto surround the remarkable **Chiesa di Santa Maria di Siponto,** built during the 11th century in the Apulian-Romanesque style. The blind arcade shows strong Pisan influence and the square plan and cupola reveal Byzantine roots. Ask the caretaker to allow you to visit the 7th-century **crypt.**

RUVO

For Ruvo, take the Ferriovie Bari Nord train line from Bari's main FS station in P. Aldo Moro. (40 min., 19 per day, 6am-10pm, €1.65). Ruvo is served by bus on Su. Bitonto is on the same train line, between Ruvo and Bari (30min., €1.14).

An easy half-day trip from Bari, Ruvo is home to one of the most beautiful Romanesque cathedrals of medieval Puglia. Exit the station, take a right on V. Scarlatti, then a left down the road onto V. Fornaci, which turns into C. Cavour; the ■**cathedral** is to the left when you reach the public gardens, also on the left. Built in the 13th century, its doorway is ornamented with a wild assortment of motifs derived from the Saracen, German, and French conquerors who ruled Puglia, in high contrast with the cathedral's simple facade.

The town of **Bitonto** also boasts an impressive Romanesque cathedral, modeled after the church of San Nicola in Bari (p. 585). From the train station, head up V. Matteotti until you reach a squat tower—turn right and continue through the winding streets a short way until you reach the large piazza with the church. At the central portal, carved scenes from the life of Christ contrast with abstract patterns. Inside, be sure to check out the beautifully carved pulpit and its reliefs of Frederick II. (Open daily 8am-noon and 4-7pm.)

ALBEROBELLO AND THE TRULLI DISTRICT   ☎0804

The **Valley of Itria,** stretching between Bari and Taronto, is crowded with hundreds of *trulli*—peculiar huts that have been around since ancient times. The current, mortarless form of the *trulli* did not appear until 1654, when a local court required that the squalid peasant inhabitations be built without mortar, so that they could be dismantled for royal visits. While many *trulli* are still inhabited by farmers, the conglomeration of over 1000 in Alberobello, a UNESCO World Heritage site, is primarily a tourist attraction. The Tolkien-esque image of the town's *trulli*-covered hills is well worth the trek out to Alberobello. A night spent in a *trullo* will be the most memorable slumber you'll have in southern Italy.

◪◪ TRANSPORTATION AND PRACTICAL INFORMATION. Alberobello is just south of Bari. Take the **FSE train** from **Bari** (1½hr., 14 per day, 5:30am-7:15pm, €3.62). To reach the *trulli* from the train station, bear left and take V. Mazzini (which becomes V. Garibaldi) to P. del Popolo. The staff at the **tourist information office,** in P. Fernando IV, off P. del Popolo, provides helpful maps marked with all the sights, hotels, and restaurants. (☎080 432 5171. Open M-F 8am-2pm and 2:30-5:30pm.) There's also a **Pro Loco Information Office** at V. Montenero, 1, in the *trulli* district, where English is spoken. (☎080 432 2822; www.prolocoalberobello.it. Open M-Sa 9am-1pm, 3:30-7:30pm.) **Postal Code:** 70011.

◪◨ ACCOMMODATIONS AND FOOD. Eating and sleeping in Alberobello can be expensive; it's less costly to visit the *trulli* as a daytrip. ■**Trullidea ❹,** V. Montenero, 18, rents *trulli* by the night. As you face the *trulli* district, V. Montenero leads uphill from your left. The spacious *trulli* include kitchen and bathroom; breakfast in a nearby restaurant is included in the price. (☎/fax 080 432 3860; www.trullidea.com. Singles €34-46; doubles €68-92; triples €77-114. Prices vary with season. AmEx/MC/V.) **Albergo da Miniello ❸,** V. Balenzano, 14, a block down V. Bissolati from P. del Popolo, is one of the only hotels in town without the word *trullo* in its name, and it's also the least expensive. The *albergo* has 15 rooms, all with bath, TV, phone, and fridge, many with great views of the you-know-whats. (☎/fax 080 432 1188. Singles €34; doubles €47;

triples €64. AmEx/MC/V.) The local restaurant, **L'Olmo Bello ❷**, V. Indipendenza, 33, to the left before entering the *trulli* district, serves local specialties in a century-old *trullo*. Try the *orechiette alla buongustaio*, ear-shaped pasta. (☎ 080 432 3607. Dishes from €5. Cover €1.60. Open W-M noon-2:30pm and 8-11pm.)

■ **SIGHTS.** V. Monte S. Michele leads up the hill to the *trullo* **Church of St. Anthony.** To reach the **Trullo Sovrano** (Sovereign *Trullo*), take C. V. Emanuele from P. del Popolo and continue past the church at the end. This two-story structure, the largest *trullo* in Alberobello, was built as a seminary in the 16th century. It's decorated to show how *trulli* were originally used, with signs explaining the rooms and displayed farming tools. (Open daily 10am-7:30pm. €1.50.) To get to the **Museo del Territorio** from P. del Popolo, turn left by the Eritrea store to P. XXVII Maggio. Composed of 23 *trulli* linked together, the museum has various temporary exhibits and a permanent display explaining the history and structure of the *trulli*. (Open daily 10am-8pm. €3.10.)

TRANI   ☎ 0883

One of the many stops on the coastal train ride to Bari, Trani is a lovely, clean space to relax. The town is easily navigable and refreshingly free from visitors despite the major touristic draw that is its brilliant Norman cathedral.

▆▆ TRANSPORTATION AND ORIENTATION. Trani is on the FS line between **Foggia** and **Bari.** Trains run frequently to both destinations (4:30am-11:30pm; €1.58 to Bari, €7.30 to Foggia). Trains also run to **Barletta** (12 per day, 6:24am-8:18pm, €1.58). The train station lies in an unappealing area in Piazza XX Settembre. From here walk straight onto **Via Cavour,** the main street of town, which leads through **Piazza della Republica** and **Piazza Plebiscito.** The **AAST office,** V. Cavour, 140, is on the left just before P. della Republica. (☎ 0883 58 88 23. Open M-F 8:30am-12:30pm and 3:30-5pm, Sa 8:30am-12:30pm.) The disorienting but beautiful **old city** can be reached by taking a left at P. della Republica. The **harbor** is to the left at P. Plebiscito, while the **public gardens** are straight ahead.

▐ ▐ ACCOMMODATIONS AND FOOD. Trani doesn't draw as many tourists as its neighbors along the coast, and lodging options are limited. The two best accommodations are on opposite sides of the harbor and opposite ends of the price range. **Hotel Regia ❺,** right next to the cathedral, is an 18th-century *palazzo* with spectacular views of the sparkling harbor, but it's going to cost you. Ten rooms with full bath, A/C, and TV. (☎ 0883 58 45 27. Breakfast included. Doubles €110-130. AmEx/MC/V.) On the other side of the harbor, **Padri Barnabiti ❷,** P. Tiepolo, 1, just to the left of P. Plebiscito, can give you sizeable rooms at a decent price. (☎ 0883 48 11 80. Curfew 11pm. Reception closed 1-5pm. Singles €13.43-16.53, with bath €16.53-20.66; doubles €26.86/ €26.86-34.09; triples and quads also available.)

The virtually unnavigable streets of the old city hold many small **pizzerias** with atmospheric outdoor seating. The area around the public gardens on the other side of the harbor has good local seafood. **Il Melograno ❸,** V. G. Bovio, 189, near P. della Republica, has shellfish favorites like *spaghetti alle vongole* (€8-11). The hefty whole fried fish *secondo* is delicious, despite the scales and bones. (☎ 0883 48 69 66. Open Th-Tu 12-3pm and 8pm-midnight. Cover €2. AmEx/MC/V.)

■ **SIGHTS.** Trani's **old city** is charming, but navigation around the 18th-century *palazzi* is close to impossible. Allow for extra time to meander. Either wind through the tiny streets or follow the coast from the harbor to the town's stunning **cathedral.** The wind-swept structure unites three individual churches, and many levels of history: Roman columns on the ground level, 6th-century Christian architecture in the crypt, and plain Norman style in the main church. Remains of 12th-century mosaics decorate the altar, including a cartoonish Adam and Eve. Within sight of the cathedral is the town's **castle,** open to the public after years of use as a prison. *(Cathedral open M-Sa 8:15am-12:15pm and 3:15-6:30pm, Su 9am-12:45pm and 4-5pm. Castle open daily 8:30am-7:30pm. Mid-June to mid-Sept. open Sa until 10:30pm. €2.)*

BRINDISI   ☎0831

Everyone comes to Brindisi to leave Italy. Pompey made his escape from Julius Caesar's army here in the first century BC, and Crusaders used this port to sail for the Holy Land. Nowadays, Brindisi is the main departure point for travelers heading to Greece, who crowd the town and stay only long enough to pick up their ferry ticket. Brindisi is more than just a convenient port town, however, and nearby Lecce and Ostuni amply repay travelers who stop to explore.

◪ FERRIES

Brindisi is Italy's central port for passenger boats to Greece; it is also the only port with boats to Corfu and the only Adriatic-side port to accept Eurail and Interrail passes. Ferries leave for **Corfu** (8hr.), **Igoumenitsa** (10hr.), **Paxi** (13hr.), **Kephalonia** (16½hr.), and **Patras** (17hr.). Ferries usually follow the Corfu-Igoumenitsa-Patras route, occasionally stopping in Paxi and Kephalonia. From **Patras,** buses (2½hr.), buy tickets at the *stazione marittima*) and trains service **Athens.** Ferries run to **Çesme,** in Turkey (30hr.) and **Durres,** in Albania (9hr.), but there are no Interrail or Eurail discounts to those destinations.

The area between the train station and port in Brindisi is littered with travel agencies that sell tickets for all of the ferry companies that service Brindisi. Prices for each ferry line are fixed, and all agencies charge the same amount for tickets. The only ferry lines to officially accept Eurail and Interrail passes are **Hellenic Mediterranean Lines** and **Italian Ferries;** however, almost all companies will provide unofficial discounts. There is a surcharge for traveling with Eurail in high season (usually around €20), but not with Interrail. If you are traveling with Eurail, check the prices carefully—the price of deck passage (the cheapest option) may be less expensive than the Eurail surcharge.

Use appropriate caution when buying tickets: sometimes tickets are for nonexistent or overbooked ferries. Use a reputable agency, and always ask for other options. Well-known and established ferry lines include **Strintzis Lines** (Corso Garibaldi, 65; ☎0831 56 22 00); **Med Link Lines** (Corso Garibaldi, 49; ☎0831 52 76 67); and **Fragline** (V. Spalato, 31; ☎0831 54 85 34). The catamarans operated by **Italian Ferries** (Corso Garibaldi, 96/98; ☎0831 59 08 40), sail to Corfu in only 4hr. and are only slightly pricier than ferries.

Not included in the ticket price are the port tax (€6), the reservation fee (€3), and a supplement (if you want to move up from deck passage). Most lines provide a free shuttle bus that runs 1km from the **stazione Marittima,** at the end of Corso Garibaldi, to **Costa Morena,** where the boats depart. It is a 1km walk otherwise, so plan accordingly. **Check in 2hr. before departure.** Bring your own food to avoid the overpriced snack bars on board.

◪ TRANSPORTATION

Trains: (☎0831 166 105 050) in P. Crispi. Open daily 8am-8pm. Luggage storage available (p. 592). Prices higher for Intercity trains. **FS** to: **Bari** (1¼-1¾hr., 31 per day, 4am-11:30pm, €6-10); **Lecce** (20-30min., 33 per day, 5:45am-12:30am, €2.32); **Milan**

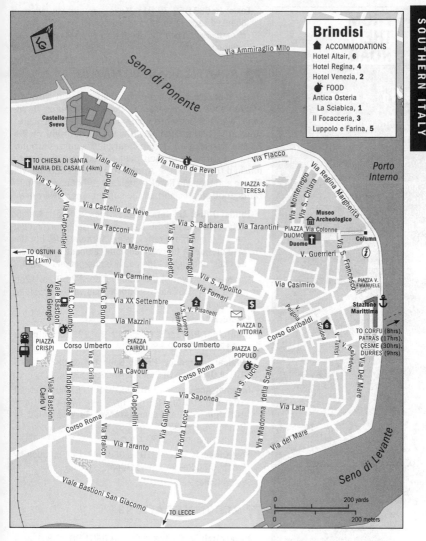

(10hr., 6 per day, 7:45am-9:30pm, €41-65); **Rome** (6-9hr., 6 per day, 6:30am-10:45pm, €27-45); and **Taranto** (1¼hr., 20 per day, 4:45am-10:30pm, €3.62).

Buses: FSE, at the train station, handles buses throughout Apulia. Buy tickets for both companies at **Grecian Travel,** C. Garibaldi, 79 (☎0831 56 83 33; fax 56 39 67). Open M-F 9am-1pm and 4-8pm, Sa 9am-1pm. **Marozzi buses** travel to **Rome** (7½-8½hr., 3 per day, 11am-10pm, €32.55-35.65). **Miccolis** runs to **Naples** (5hr., 3 per day, 6:35am-6:35pm, €21.17).

Public Transportation: City buses (☎0831 54 92 45) run between train station and port and to destinations around city. Buy tickets (€0.62) from bars and *tabacchi.*

FROM THE ROAD

IT'S NOT A HOTEL...

Southern Italian cities are hot in the summer. This was my only thought as I wiped my brow, waiting for the *pensione* to answer their buzzer. Finally, *"Pronto?"* shot out of the intercom, and I asked to enter in my broken Italian. A portly man planted behind a large oak desk awaited me on the third floor office.

Sweating under the weight of my pack, I quickly asked about singles prices. When I asked to see a room, he seemed caught off-guard by my request (did he think I wasn't going to ask?), but proceeded to fumble for his keys anyway. Leading me down a narrow hallway, lined with doors from which strange noises emanated, the owner leaned his ear toward one door and quickly shrank back. It appeared that every room was occupied, despite the fact that it was midday.

At the *pensione* one floor down, the owner pounced on me, dragging me by the arm into her office. Visibly distressed, the little woman could do no more than gesture madly upstairs. Shaking her head at my blank face, she finally made an all-too explicit gesture with her left hand and right pointer finger. Her unspoken meaning became clear—the *pensione* above worked days as a brothel.

—Chris Kukstis

Taxis: (☎0831 59 79 01). Make sure that you are in a licensed taxi, as unofficial taxi services tend to overcharge. Taxis from the station to the ferry departure point cost €15.

🛈 PRACTICAL INFORMATION

Corso Umberto runs from the train station through **Piazza Cairoli** and to **Piazza D. Populo** and **Piazza D. Vittorio,** where it becomes Corso Garibaldi and heads to the port. The **Stazione Marittima** is to the right on **Via Regina Margherita.** V. Regina Margherita curves around the waterfront to the left past the column that once marked the end of the Appian Way, and becomes **Via Flacco** and then **Via Revel,** which are full of bars, restaurants, food stands, and, in the summer, carnival rides.

Tourist Office: APT Information Office, V. Regina Margherita, 5 (☎0831 52 30 72). From C. Garibaldi, turn left on V. Margherita. Pretty useless for ferry info, but the staff provides a free map and advice about hotels, local services, and sights. Open daily 8am-2pm and 3-8pm.

Luggage Storage: At the train station. €2.50 per 12hr. Open daily 6:30am-10:30pm. Also at the *stazione marittima.*

Emergency: ☎113.

Municipal Police: ☎0831 22 95 22. **Carabinieri:** ☎112 or 0831 52 88 48.

Medical Emergency: Pronto Soccorso (☎0831 53 75 10) at **Ospedale Di Summa** (☎0831 53 71 11).

Internet Access: Sala Giochi, V. B.S. Giorgio, 1st left after the station. €5 per hr. Open M-Sa 8:30am-10:30pm, Su 9am-1pm. **Internet Service Point,** C. Roma, 54, (☎0831 52 64 28), near P. del Popolo. €4 per hr. Open daily 3:30-10pm.

Post Office: P. Vittoria, 10 (☎0831 47 11 11). Open M-F 8am-6:30pm, Sa 8am-1:30pm.

Postal Code: 72100.

🛏 ACCOMMODATIONS

Hotel Altair, V. Giudea, 4 (☎/fax 0831 56 22 89), near port and center. From *stazione marittima,* walk up C. Garibaldi and take the 2nd left. 15 big rooms with high ceilings, TV, and fridge. Singles €12-23, with bath €20-33; doubles €30-35/€35-49. MC/V. ❷

Hotel Venezia, V. Pisanelli, 4 (☎0831 52 75 11). After the fountain, take the 2nd left off C. Umberto onto V. S. Lorenzo da Brindisi, then right onto V. Pisanelli. 12 cheap rooms with a shared bath. Reserve 4 days in advance. Singles €12.91; doubles €24.79. ❷

Hotel Regina, V. Cavour, 5, off P. Cairoli (☎ 0831 56 20 01; fax 56 38 83; www.hotel-reginaweb.com). This 3-star option is a strikingly modern alternative to the smaller hotels in town. All 43 spotless rooms have A/C, fridge, and TV. Buffet breakfast included. Laundry service available. Singles €44-70; doubles €55-90. AmEx/MC/V. ●

☐ FOOD

An open-air **market,** on V. Fornari off P. Vittoria, sells fresh fruit. (Open M-Sa 7am-1pm.) Pick up supplies for your ferry ride at the **Gulliper supermarket,** C. Garibaldi, 106, a block from the port. (Open M-Sa 8am-1:30pm and 4:30-8:30pm, Su 9am-1pm.) Avoid the restaurants and cafes on the main strip, where the ubiquitous "tourist *menù*" provides smaller portions and steep drink prices. Better options lie on nearby side streets.

Il Focacceria, V. Cristoforo Colombo, 5 (☎ 0831 56 09 30), offers much more than what its name implies. Favorite of US military personnel in Brindisi. Takeout pizza and lasagna on the quick. Lasagna €3, pizzas €3-4. Open daily 8am-11pm. ●

Antica Osteria la Sciabica, V. Thaon de Revel, 29/33 (☎ 0831 56 28 70) is in a quiet spot on the harbor with seating on a lovely, candlelit patio. Seafood is the specialty of the house, especially the *maltagliata alle cozze nere* (local pasta with mussels, €6.71). *Primi* and *secondi* €7-10. Open daily noon-3pm and 8:30pm-midnight. AmEx/MC/V. ●

Luppolo e Farina, V. Pozzo Traiano (☎ 0831 59 04 96), just off C. Garibaldi near P. del Popolo. A great alternative to the tourist-targeting *pizzerie* along the main strip, serving pies cooked in a wood oven (€2.80-7.80). Try the house pizza, with mozzarella cheese and fresh and sun-dried tomatoes (€5.30)! Open daily 7pm-midnight. AmEx/MC/V. ●

☑ ☐ SIGHTS AND ENTERTAINMENT

From the port, V. Regina Margherita leads three blocks to stairs facing the water. The huge **column** here marked the end of the Appian Way. The marble capital is graced by the figures of Jove, Neptune, Mars, and eight tritons. The column's twin, which once stood on the adjacent base, now resides in Lecce. V. Colonne runs from behind the column to P. Duomo. In the 11th-century **duomo** (rebuilt in the 18th century), Emperor Frederick II married Jerusalem's Yolande. (Open daily 7am-noon and 4-7pm.) The **Museo Archeologico** next door traces Brindisi's rich history though pottery, tablets, and other artifacts. (☎ 0831 22 14 01. Open M-F 9:30am-1:30pm, Tu 9:30am-1:30pm and 3:30-6:30pm, Sa-Su 9:30am-1:30pm. Free.)

Follow the signs out of town from the station to the pride of Brindisi, the **Chiesa di Santa Maria del Casale.** The interior is decorated with 13th-century frescoes, including one of Mary blessing the Crusaders. (Open daily 7am-noon and 4-7pm.)

☑ DAYTRIP FROM BRINDISI: OSTUNI

Ostuni is on the train line between Brindisi (30min., 20 per day, 7am-10:30pm, €2.01) and Bari (1hr., 26 per day, 5am-11pm, €4.10). From train station (☎ 0831 30 12 68), take city bus to P. della Libertà, the center of town (5min.; M-Sa every 30min., Su every hr.; 7am-9:30pm; €0.85). Buy tickets at train station bar.

Rising out of a landscape of sea, dark-red earth, and olive trees, Ostuni's *città bianca* (white city) appears ethereal. The *centro storico*'s white walls protect the city from the elements and lend a fairy-tale touch to the serpentine streets. The terrace at the top of C. V. Emanuele boasts a beautiful view of the old city. Just off the piazza, the little church of **Santo Spirito** has a doorway with impressive late-medieval reliefs. From the piazza, V. Cattedrale runs up through the old town center. The **Convento delle Monacelle** (Convent of Little Nuns), V. Cattedrale, 15, has a Baroque facade and a colorful, white-tiled dome of Moorish inspiration, as well as a museum inside with a 24,500-year-old human skeleton. (☎0831 33 63 83. Museum open daily 9:30am-12:30pm and 3:30-7:30pm. €1.50.) Crowning Ostuni's hill, the **duomo,** built in 1437, was the last Byzantine building erected in southern Italy. The remarkable facade, in the Spanish Gothic style, contrasts sharply with the austere Norman styles common in Apulia. (Open daily 7:30am-12:30pm and 4-7pm.) On August 26 and 27, Ostuni celebrates St. Oronzo with the **Cavalcata,** a parade of costumed horses and riders. Many praise Ostuni's nearby beach, accessible from P. della Libertà (15min., every 30min., 8am-7:30pm, €0.85). Buses are not numbered; ask the driver if you're on the right one.

Ostuni's **AAST Information Office,** C. Mazzini, 6, just off P. della Libertà, provides both assistance and a booklet catchily named *Ostuni.* (☎0831 30 12 68. Open June-Aug. M-F 9:30am-1:30pm and 3-8pm; Sept.-May M-F 9:30am-noon and 4-7pm.) If you choose to stay the night, try the 26 rooms at **Hotel Orchidea Nera ❸,** C. Mazzini, 118, 0.5km from P. della Libertà. (☎0831 30 13 66. Singles €30, with bath €36; doubles €38/€49-61.) Another option is **Lo Sperone ❷,** on V. per Cisternino, 2km outside the town in beautiful farmland. Three- to five-person apartments available with kitchen, bathroom, and TV. Call ahead to reserve and get directions. (☎0831 33 91 24. €23.50 per person.)

Rustic taverns and *osterie* abound in the old city. The streets can be tricky to navigate, but there are signs everywhere directing you to the restaurants. Restaurants only serve pizza in the evening. **Porta Nova ❹,** V. Gaspare Petrolo, 38, is a little expensive, but offers fresh seafood and a panoramic view of the countryside from the elegant dining room. (☎0831 33 89 83. *Primi* €7-15, *secondi* from €15. €2 cover. Open daily 11am-4pm and 7:30-midnight. Closed W in low season.) **Locanda dei Sette Peccati ❷,** on V. F. Campana off V. Cattedrale, has pizza from €2.58, and similarly priced *panini.* (☎0831 33 95 95. *Primi* €3.62. Open Sept.-May Tu-Su 11am-4pm and 6:30pm-1am; July-Aug. also open M.) Nearby on Largo Lanza, **Ristorante Vecchia Ostuni ❸** has outdoor seating and a menu specializing in all types of *carne* and *pesce* (meat and fish; from €8). Call ahead to have fish prepared for you. (☎0831 30 33 08. Open W-M noon-3pm and 7pm-midnight. AmEx/MC/V.)

LECCE ☎0832

The hidden pearl of Italy, Lecce is where Italians go when foreign tourists invade their country. Once here, they can hardly help but to marvel at the city's architecture, a spectacularly ornate style known as Leccese Baroque. Made from *tufigna,* a soft local stone that hardens when exposed to air, most of Lecce's perfectly preserved *palazzi* and elaborate churches are covered with intricate floral carvings, lavishly embellished balconies, and finely decorated portals. At night, the lighted buildings are extraordinary, making for an outstanding *passegiata.* Although a succession of conquerors—Cretans, Romans, Saracens, Swabians, and more—passed through here, the Spanish Hapsburgs solidified the old city's current form in the 16th and 17th centuries. Lecce, the "Florence of the Mezzogiorno," is a great starting point for a tour of the Salento Peninsula, the heel of Italy's boot. The university lends the city a vibrant nightlife, made up almost exclusively of Irish pubs.

▐ TRANSPORTATION

Trains: P. Stazione, 1km from the town center. Buses #24 and 28 run from the train station to the center of town. Lecce is the southeastern terminus of the state railway. **FS** trains (☎0832 30 10 16) to: **Bari** (1½-2hr., 18 per day, 5am-11pm, €6-13); **Brindisi**

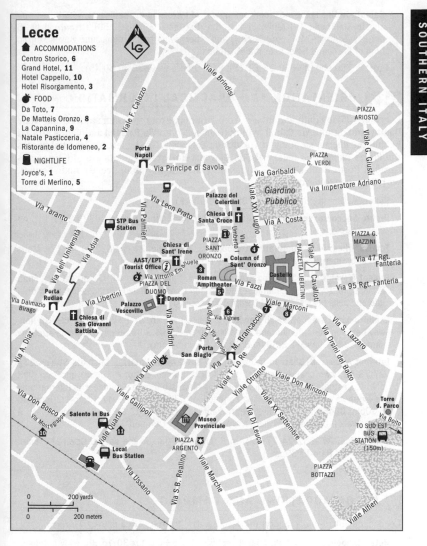

Lecce

🏠 ACCOMMODATIONS
Centro Storico, **6**
Grand Hotel, **11**
Hotel Cappello, **10**
Hotel Risorgamento, **3**

🍴 FOOD
Da Toto, **7**
De Matteis Oronzo, **8**
La Capannina, **9**
Natale Pasticceria, **4**
Ristorante de Idomeneo, **2**

🛏 NIGHTLIFE
Joyce's, **1**
Torre di Merlino, **5**

(20-40min., 18 per day, 5am-11pm, €2.01-8.26); **Reggio di Calabria** (9hr., 3 per day, 7:30am-9:15pm, €30); **Rome** (6-9½hr., 8 per day, 6am-11pm, €30-44); and **Taranto** (2½hr., 7 per day, 7am-9:15pm, €6-12). **FSE** trains (☎0832 66 81 11) criss-cross the Salento. To **Gallipoli** (1hr., 11 per day, 6:25am-8:40pm, €3.10) and **Otranto** (1¼hr., 9 per day 6:45am-7:30pm, €2.58), **via Maglie.**

Buses: FSE, V. Boito (☎0832 34 76 34), easily accessible by bus #4 (€0.62) from the train station. To **Gallipoli** (1hr., 5 per day, €2.84) and **Taranto** (2hr., 5 per day, 7am-4pm, €4.58). **STP** (☎0832 30 28 73), V. Adua, heads to the smaller towns of the Salento Peninsula. Pick up a schedule at the tourist office. In the summer months,

Salento in Bus is the most convenient way of traversing the peninsula, with buses running to: **Gallipoli** (70-100min., 10 per day, 8:10am-9:30pm, €2.50); **Otranto** (1 hr., 6 per day, 9:45am-11:40pm, €2.50); and other towns on the peninsula. Buses stop in front of the Grand Hotel near the FS station.

Taxis: P. Stazione (☎0832 24 79 78); P. S. Oronzo (☎0832 30 60 45).

◆ 🔁 ORIENTATION AND PRACTICAL INFORMATION

Lecce lies 35km south and inland from Brindisi. From the train station, take **Viale Quarta** straight into **Via Cairoli,** which turns left onto **Via Paladini** and winds around behind the **duomo,** stopping at **Via Vittorio Emanuele.** To the left, **Via Libertini** passes the **Piazza Duomo** and **Chiesa di San Giovanni Battista** and exits the old city walls through Porta Rudiae. To the right lies **Piazza Sant'Oronzo,** Lecce's main square, with the *castello* beyond.

Police: V. Otranto, 5 (☎113 or ☎0832 30 90 19).

Pronto Soccorso: (☎0832 66 14 03), at **Ospedale Vito Fazzi** (☎0832 66 11 11), on V. S. Cesario.

Tourist Office: AAST Information Office, V. V. Emanuele, 24 (☎0832 31 41 17). Maps and info. Open M-F 9am-1:45pm and 4-7:30pm.

Budget Travel: Centro Turistico Studentesco, V. Palmieri, 91 (☎0832 30 18 62). From P. Sant'Oronzo, take V. Emanuele and turn right on V. Palmieri. Provides flight and train info and sells tickets. Open M-F 9am-1pm and 4-7:30pm.

Laundromat: Lavanderia Self-Service, V. dell'Università, 47 (☎0339 683 6396), halfway between Porta Rudiae and Porta Napoli. Wash €1.30-6.50 depending on size. Dry same prices. Open M-F 8:30am-8:30pm, Sa 9am-1pm.

Internet Access: ▧**Chatwin Internet Cafe & Traveller Point,** V. Castriota 8b (☎0832 27 78 59; www.chatwin-netcafe.it). Follow V. Rubichi out of P. Oronzo and turn right onto V. Castriota. Friendly English-speaking staff, a bar, and a lounge with international newspapers and guidebooks. Fast connection; €3 per hr. Open M-F 10am-1:30pm and 5-10pm. **Cliocom,** V. 95° Regimento Fanteria, 89 (☎0832 34 40 41; www.clio.it). A 5min. walk from castle. €4 per hr. Open daily 9am-1pm and 4-8pm.

Post Office: (☎0832 24 27 12), in P. Libertini, behind the castle. Open M-F 8am-6:30pm, Sa 8am-12:30pm.

Postal Code: 73100.

🏠 ACCOMMODATIONS AND CAMPING

Lecce lacks ultra-cheap accommodations. The tourist office lists *affittacamere.*

Hotel Cappello, V. Montegrappa, 4 (☎0832 30 88 81; fax 30 15 35; www.hotelcappello.it). From the station, take the 1st left off V. Quarta onto V. Don Bosco and follow the signs. Modern, comfortable, and convenient. All 35 rooms with bath, A/C, TV, and fridge. Singles €28; doubles €44; triples €57. AmEx/MC/V. ❸

Centro Storico, V. Andrea Vignes, 2b (☎0832 24 28 28; fax 24 27 27; www.bedandbreakfast.lecce.it). Go to the *tabacchi* at V. Fazzi, 12, just off P. Oronzo for information. Fantastic, small B&B close to the center of the old town. Reservations advised 1-2 wk. in advance. All 5 huge rooms with A/C, cooking facilities, TV, and balconies. Singles €26-31; doubles €47-52; quad €120. MC/V. ❸

Grand Hotel, V. Quarta, 28 (☎ 0832 30 94 05; fax 30 98 91), half a block from the train station. A little faded, but still as elegant as the name suggests. Large rooms, gorgeous building. Singles €32-34, with bath €41-48; doubles €49-54/€76-84. AmEx/MC/V. ❸

Hotel Risorgimento, V. Imperatore Augusto, 19 (☎ 0832 24 21 25; fax 24 55 71), in a wonderful location just outside P. S. Oronzo. Rooms with A/C, phone, TV, and fridge. Singles €44-47, with bath €60; doubles with bath €105. AmEx/MC/V. ❹

Torre Rinalda (☎ 0832 38 21 61; fax 38 21 65). Campground on the beach, 15km from town. Bus #32 (€0.62) from P. S. Oronzo. Virtually every amenity. €7 per person; €4 per tent. AmEx/MC/V. ❶

◖ FOOD

Regional specialties range from the hearty *cicerietria* (chickpeas and pasta) and *pucce* (sandwiches made with olive-bread rolls) to *confettoni* (traditional and locally made chocolate candies). Picnic supplies have been bought for a century at at **Salumeria Loiacono,** V. Fazzi, 11, in P. Sant'Oronzo, a long-established meat and cheese establishment. (Open daily 7am-2pm and 4:30-8:30pm.) The indoor **market,** behind the post office, provides a chance to haggle over meat and fruit. (Open M-F 4am-2:30pm, Sa 4am-2:30pm and 3:30-9pm.)

Ristorante de Idomeneo, V. Libertini, 44 (☎ 0832 24 49 73), just a few blocks from the duomo. Reasonably priced, with endearing staff and plates fit for a king. In the winter, enjoy traditional *cicerietria* (€5.16). Pizza €2.84-6.20, *primi* €5.16-6.71, *secondi* €5.58-7.32. Open W-M noon-3pm and 7:30pm-1am. AmEx/MC/V. ❸

La Capannina, V. Cairoli, 13 (☎ 0832 30 41 59), between the train station and P. Duomo. Excellent outdoor dining in the tranquil piazza opposite the restaurant. Pizza €2.60-5.20, *primi* €3.65-5.20, *secondi* €4.10-7.35. Cover €1.30. Open Tu-Su 9am-2:30pm and 6:30pm-midnight. ❶

Da Toto, Viale F. Lo Re, 9 (☎ 0832 30 10 00), near the cinema on Viale Marconi. A good bet for local cuisine, this restaurant and pizza is quite popular among *Leccesi* looking for a quieter setting. Try the hearty *orecchiette al pomodoro* for €4.50. Pizzas €2.50-5, *primi* €4.50-6.50. Cover €1.50. Open M-Sa noon-3:30pm, 7:30pm-midnight. ❷

De Matteis Oronzo, Viale Marconi, 51 (☎ 0832 30 28 00), near the castle. This fantastic candy store sells *confettoni* (€0.40) and *cotognata leccese* (dried fig candies so delicious, they're special-ordered by the Pope; €0.40). Open daily 7am-9:30pm. ❶

Natale Pasticceria, V. Trinchese, 7 (☎ 0832 25 60 60), near the McDonald's. Pastry shop is full of *Leccese* pastries, *gelati,* and candies. Cones €1.50-4. Local cream-filled delights €0.70. Open daily 8am-midnight. MC/V. ❶

◖ SIGHTS

Lecce's downtown is filled with Baroque **churches,** and the best are all within a 15min. walk of each other.

BASILICA DI SANTA CROCE. The most outstanding of Lecce's churches, this *chiesa* (1549-1695) is the supreme expression of *Leccese* Baroque. Most of the area's accomplished architects contributed their efforts to this church at some time or another; if you look closely, you can see the profile of Gabriele Riccardi, the original designer, hidden between the upper window and the column to its left. Inside you'll find two rows of massive Corinthian columns. F. A. Zantimbalo's altar (1614) adorns the chapel to the left of the apse. *(From P. S. Oronzo, head down V. Templari toward the basilica's extravagant facade. Open daily 8am-1pm and 4:30-8:30pm.)*

PALAZZO CELESTINI. Giuseppe Zimbalo, nicknamed "Lo Zingarello" (the gypsy) due to his tendency to wander from one church project to another, designed the lower half of the *palazzo*'s facade. His pupil, Giuseppe Cino, finished the upper part. Visitors can view the inner courtyard of the building now used for offices. In the summer, rock and classical music concerts are held here; keep an eye out for posters or ask at the AAST office for more information. *(Next to Chiesa d. S. Croce. Concerts vary in price but are generally under €10.)*

PIAZZA DEL DUOMO. Constructed in 1114, the duomo was "Zingarelloed" between 1659 and 1670. With the exception of two *Leccese* altars, the interior dates from the 18th century. The **campanile** (bell tower; 1682) rises from the left side of the cathedral. Opposite, the **Palazzo Vescovile** (Bishop's Palace) has been remodeled several times since construction in 1632. On the right, with a Baroque well in its center, stands the **seminary** (1709), designed by Cino. Be sure to come at night, when the lighting on the building facades is spectacular. *(From P. S. Oronzo, take V. Emanuele. Duomo open daily 6:30-noon and 5-7:30pm.)*

ANCIENT RUINS. The **Column of Sant'Oronzo,** one of two that marked the termination of the Appian Way in Brindisi (see p. 593), towers over P. Sant'Oronzo. A statue of the saint now tops the column. Also in P. S. Oronzo lie the ruins of a second-century amphitheater, thought to have held 20,000 spectators (at least that many young people gather here on summer nights to flirt), which blends remarkably well into the modern piazza. Half of the structure was filled in to build the nearby church. Near the station, the **Museo Provinciale** is home to Apulian ceramics from the 5th century BC. *(V. Gallipoli, 30. ☎0832 24 70 25. Open M-F 9am-1:30pm and 2:30-7:30pm, Sa-Su 9am-1:30pm. Wheelchair-accessible. Free.)*

OTHER SIGHTS. The complex **Chiesa di San Giovanni Battista** (Church of the Rosary) was Lo Zingarello's last work. Here, the artist surrendered to the Baroque with reckless abandon. The decorated columns of the facade were novel at the time, as were the 13 altars around the Roman cross design inside. *(Take V. Libertini from P. del Duomo.)* The ornate **Porta Napoli** once stood on the road from Naples. This arch was erected in 1548 in honor of Holy Roman Emperor Charles V, whose coat of arms adorns the front. *(From P. del Duomo, take V. Palmieri.)*

🎭 ENTERTAINMENT

Lecce's soccer team has bounced between Serie A and Serie B in recent years, and is currently (to the shame of most citizens) stuck in Serie B. (Stadium ☎0832 45 38 86. Games held Sept.-June. Tickets from €15. Buy at *tabacchi* and lottery agencies.) The AAST office distributes *Calendario Manifestazioni*, which describes seasonal events in the province and Lecce's annual summer festivals. Every night, crowds gather outside the many bars, Irish pubs, and *pizzerie* along V. V. Emanuele and P. Oronzo. **Torre di Merlino,** V. G. Battista del Tufoi, 10 (☎0832 24 18 74), near the Roman Theater, is a favorite among the university crowd. (Open Th-Tu 8pm-3am. Draft beer €3. MC/V.) **Joyce's,** V. Matteo da Lecce, 4, is another hot spot, with walls covered in U2 album covers and glass cases containing texts of *Ulysses*. (Walk out of P. Oronzo towards the basilica and turn left onto V. Matteo da Lecce. ☎0832 27 94 43. Open daily 8pm-2am.) **Road 66,** at V. Dei Perroni, 8 (☎0832 24 65 68), near Porta San Biagio, and **Douglas Hyde Irish Pub,** on V. B. Ravenna, are also good bets for nocturnal action. Most nightclubs, especially during the summer, are on the coast and only accessible by car. For current information on nighttime hot spots, ask for the monthly *Salento in Tasca* at local bars.

SALENTO PENINSULA

Foreign tourists often overlook Italy's sun-baked heel, home to beautiful sandy beaches on two seas, hidden grottoes, medieval fortresses, and some of Italy's oldest and best-preserved art and architecture. With cultural roots stretching back to the Greeks, the peninsula is worthy of exploration. Visitors can roam an enchantingly varied coastline, or venture to inland villages to sample wine and olives.

OTRANTO ☎ 0836

Although Otranto is swamped with tourists in July and August, its winding streets, crystal-clear waters, and medieval sights make it tranquil and picturesque during the rest of the year. The town's history teems with legend—the story is that when conquered by Ottoman Turks, the town's Christian survivors opted to be executed rather than convert to Islam—an act of faith that managed to convert their executioners to Christianity, which brought about their death as well as that of the Otranto citizens. The bones of the *Martiri d'Otranto* (Martyrs of Otranto), in glass cases in the duomo, attract some, while the majority are content to wade in the warm waters of Otranto's gorgeous beaches.

🖪🖬 TRANSPORTATION AND PRACTICAL INFORMATION. Otranto is 40km southeast of Lecce on the Adriatic coast and is downright hard to get to by public transportation during the year. Rustic **FSE trains** run from Lecce (1¼hr., 9 per day, 6:45am-7:30pm, €2.58) to Maglie. Get off and take the waiting bus to Otranto. The FSE ticket to Lecce covers both. In July and August, **Salento in Bus** will take you straight to the castle. Pick it up in Lecce in front of the Grand Hotel, near the train station. (30min., €2.50.) The town's main strip of beach is along the **Lungomare d'Otranto,** ending at the **public gardens.** From the gardens, V. V. Emanuele leads to **Piazza de Donno** and the entrance to the *centro storico.* Enter through the city gate and turn right on **Via Basilica** to reach the **duomo.** Past the duomo, in the piazza in front of the castle, the **APT tourist office** provides advice on lodgings and transportation to towns on the peninsula. (☎ 0836 80 14 36. Open daily 9am-1pm and 3-9pm.) The **carabinieri** can be reached at ☎ 0836 80 10 10. **Pronto Soccorso,** V. Pantaleone, 4, is downhill from the information office. (☎ 0836 80 16 76.) **Pharmacy Ricciardi** is at V. Lungomare, 101. (☎ 0836 80 136. Open daily 8:30am-1pm and 4:30-9pm.) The **post office** is at the stoplight on V. Pantaleone. (☎ 0836 80 10 02. Open M-Sa 8:15am-6pm.) **Postal Code:** 73028.

🖪🖸 ACCOMMODATIONS AND FOOD. Lodging in Otranto is very expensive from mid-July to August, when most hotels require half-pension and all require reservations. The tourist office can help find rented rooms in local homes. The monolithic, recently renovated **Hotel Miramare ❹,** Lungomare, 55, has 55 well-furnished rooms, some with balcony and TV, right on the beach. Call in March for a room in July or August. (☎ 0836 80 10 23; fax 80 10 24; www.cliotranto.clio.it/hotelmiramare. Singles €45; doubles €70. AmEx/MC/V.) **Bellavista Hotel ❺,** V. Vittorio Emanuele, 19, is right across from the public gardens and beach and has 22 rooms with bath, TV, and A/C. (☎ 0836 80 10 58. Singles €47-55, required full-pension from July 27-Aug. 30 €78; doubles €65-78/€103.)

The **market** by P. de Donno sells fruit, meat, and fish. (Open daily 8am-1pm.) Across from the public gardens, **Boomerang Self-Service ❷,** V. V. Emanuele, 14, offers tasty Italian dishes served cafeteria-style. (☎/fax 0836 80 26 19; www.otrantovacanze.it. Pizza €3.10-5.50, *primi* €4.50, *secondi* €4.50-7. Open

Mar.-Sept. daily 12pm-12:30am.) **Acmet Pasia ❸**, at the end of V. Emanuele provides covered, outdoor dining with a gorgeous view. (☎0836 80 12 82. *Primi* €5-8, fish *secondi* €7-16. Open Tu-Su 10am-3:30pm and 7pm-1:30am. AmEx/MC/V.)

◙♫ SIGHTS AND ENTERTAINMENT. Otranto's picturesque old city is surrounded by fortifications. Dante visited here while he wrote *The Divine Comedy*. Lending a majestic air to this enclosed city is the famous **duomo,** paved with a phenomenal 11th-century ▧**floor mosaic** of the Tree of Life. The mosaic extends the entire length of the nave and depicts religious, mythological, and historical figures from Adam to Alexander the Great to King Arthur—and that's just the A's. Another section shows the 12 zodiac signs and the farm work done each month. Among the dead bodies and columns pilfered from Greek, Roman, and Arab sites, the crypt also houses the **Capella dei Martiri,** a small chapel with large glass display cases housing the skulls and bones of all 800 who died for their faith. (Duomo open daily 8am-noon and 3-6:30pm, excluding mass times. Modest dress required.)

Red, pink, and blue frescoes of the Garden of Eden brighten the intimate interior of 8th-century Byzantine **Chiesa di San Pietro.** Take C. Garibaldi to P. del Popolo and follow the signs up the stairs on the left. (Open on request 9:30am-1pm and 3:30-7:30pm.) The 16th-century **Aragonese castle,** with its imposing walls and newly excavated moat, casts a shadow over the town. You can't see much of the castle besides the courtyard, but a gate in the ramparts on a side street leads down to a pier that runs along the small boat harbor, offering views of the old town and anchored sailboats. (Open daily 10:30am-12:30pm and 6-11:30pm.)

In August, Otranto's **beaches** are packed; the fine sand and light-blue waters are even more enjoyable during the first part of the summer. The public strips along the *lungomare* and farther along on V. degli Haethey are the most popular and accessible. The beach closest to V. Pantaleone will neatly extract €4.50 from your wallet for entry alone, plus more for an umbrella and chair, but the beach one block down the road is free. Both of these beaches are just as nice as the more crowded ones along the *lungomare*, although some may not enjoy swimming in sight of rusty old freighters belching out smoke as they dock at the port. In the evenings, vendors arrive in droves to feed the crowds—try the delicious *noccioline zuccherate* (candy coated peanuts; €1).

After dark, Otranto's *lungomare* fills with people walking the waterfront and patronizing the pubs; those with cars head to the *discoteche* 5-6km away. On August 13, 14, and 15, Otranto welcomes tourists to the **Festa dei Martiri d'Otranto,** a festival in honor of the martyrs. On the first Sunday in September, the town celebrates the **Festa della Madonna dell'Altomare** (Festival of the Virgin of the High Seas). Every Wednesday the castle is surrounded by a **market.** (Open 9am-1pm.)

TARANTO ☎0994

In ancient times, Taranto was a proud Greek city-state with a navy ruling the seas and 300,000 seafaring citizens prospering on numerous merchant routes. Today Taranto still houses 300,000 citizens, a busy, dirty port, and Italy's fine naval fleet. The downward spiral of high unemployment, government corruption, welfare dependency, and Mafia control has taken its toll. However, Taranto is beginning to experience an urban renewal, and well-to-do young professionals pack trendy downtown cafes and restaurants. Reasonably-priced accommodations aren't hard to find, and a world-famous archaeological museum, delicious and inexpensive seafood, and sailboat-packed beaches give Taranto some hearty Italian charm.

☞ TRANSPORTATION

Trains: (☎ 1478 88 088), in P. Libertà, across the old city from the center of town. **FS** to: **Bari** (1¾hr., 25 per day, 4:40am-10:22pm, €6.20); **Brindisi** (1¼hr., 25 per day, 5am-10pm, €3.62); **Naples** (4hr., 6 per day, 6:15am-midnight, €22.41-40.31); and **Rome** (6-7hr., 7 per day, 6:15am-midnight, €23.50-36).

Buses: Buses stop at P. Castello (near the swinging bridge); buy tickets at the **Marozzi Ticket Office,** C. Umberto, 67 (☎ 0994 59 40 89), 1 block up from P. Garibaldi. **SITA buses** run to **Matera** (1¾hr., 4 per day, 6am-7:20pm, €4.62). Several companies serve **Bari** (1¾ hr.) and **Lecce** (1¾ hr.) every day; consult the Marozzi office about timetables for the various lines.

Public Transportation: Tickets on local AMAT buses cost €0.67; 90min. €0.93; 1 day €1.65.

◼◼ ORIENTATION AND PRACTICAL INFORMATION

Taranto's old city is on a small island between two promontories. Bridges join the old city to the new port area and the train station. Be wary of pickpockets during the day, and avoid the old city at night. From the station, buses to the new city take you near **P. Garibaldi,** the main square. On foot, take **V. Duca d'Aosta** over Ponte Porta Napoli into **P. Fontana,** in the old city. Walk for 10min. along the shore to P. Castello and across the swinging bridge to reach the new city; P. Garibaldi is one block ahead.

Tourist Office: APT Information Office, C. Umberto, 113 (☎ 0994 53 23 92; fax 52 04 17; apttaranto@pugliaturismo.com), 4 blocks from P. Garibaldi away from the old city. Good maps available. Open M-F 9am-1pm and 4:30-6:30pm, Sa 9am-noon. The **Info Booth** in the station stocks city maps.

Emergency: ☎ 113.

Police: ☎ 112.

Internet Access: Chiocciolin@it, C. Umberto I, 85 (☎/fax 0994 53 80 51). Next to P. Garibaldi. Sony Playstation and Dreamcast available. Open Tu-Su 9am-1pm and 4:30-9pm, M 4:30-9pm.

Post Office: (☎ 0994 35 951), on Lungomare V. Emanuele. Open M-Sa 8:15am-6pm.

Postal Code: 74100.

◪◪ ACCOMMODATIONS AND FOOD

Albergo Pisani ❷, V. Cavour, 43, off P. Garibaldi, is conveniently located, reasonably priced, and provides comfortable accommodations. (☎ 0994 53 40 87; fax 70 75 93. Breakfast included. Singles with bath €25; doubles €44, with bath €46.) Nearby, **Hotel Plaza ❺,** V. d'Aquino, 46, has luxurious rooms with bath, A/C, and TV. (☎ 0994 59 07 75; fax 59 06 75. Breakfast included. Singles €65; doubles €68. AmEx/MC/V.) **Albergo Sorrentino ❷,** P. Fontana, 7, has 13 well-priced rooms overlooking the sea. Some solo travelers might feel uncomfortable in the untouristed fishing harbor, but the 11pm curfew will prevent late-night sojourns through the neighborhood. (☎ 0994 70 74 56. Singles €19; doubles €34, with bath €37.)

Taranto's prosperous fishing industry translates into delicious, plentiful, and inexpensive seafood. Try *cozze* (mussels) in basil and olive oil or spaghetti with *vongole* (clams). Grab your bread, sandwiches, and pizza at **Panificio due Mari ❶,** between P. Garibaldi and the swinging bridge at V. Matteoti, 16. (Open daily 7am-1:30am.) Fruit is available at the **market** in P. Castello. (Open daily 7am-1:30pm.) **☒Queen ❷,** V. di Cesare, 20-22, offers delectable seafood, local specialties, impeccable service, and affordable prices. The €12 meal is offered the entire next day and includes wine. The *menù* changes daily, but the ace is the Queen pizza with everything on it for €5. (☎ 099 459 1011. Beer from €1. *Primi* €3.50, *secondi* €3.10-6.70. Evening cover €1.30. Open M-Sa 7:30am-midnight.)

🔴 SIGHTS

The ▨**Museo Nazionale Archeologico,** C. Umberto, 41, in P. Garibaldi, houses the world's largest terracotta figurine collection, as well as ancient pots, marble and bronze sculptures, mosaics, jewelry, and coins. (☎ 099 453 2112. Open M-F 8:30am-1:30pm and 2:30-7:30pm, Sa 9am-midnight. Free.) From P. Garibaldi, a **swinging bridge** built in 1887 hangs over the shipping canal to the *città vecchia*. The first of its kind, it opened sideways to let ships through. The bridge still swings, and is fun to watch—check the daily schedule of opening times posted on either side.

🎵 ENTERTAINMENT

V. d'Aquino pulses with crowds every night between 6 and 11pm. On P. Garibaldi, the navy band accompanies the lowering of the flag at sundown. Taranto's **Holy Week Festival** draws hordes from around the country. In a ceremony rooted in medieval Spanish ritual, sheet-covered men carrying papier-maché statues parade to all the churches. Festivities begin the Sunday before Easter.

BASILICATA

Depicted in Carlo Levi's *Christ Stopped at Eboli* as a land of poverty and pagan mysticism, small, sparsely populated Basilicata is seldom visited. The region begins in the rugged Lucan Apennines and stretches across the Murge to the Ionian and Tyrrhenian coastlines. Mountainous, almost landlocked, and lacking natural resources, it never attained the strategic importance or prominence of neighboring coastal regions. Fortunately for the travelers who do make the trip, its fascinating prehistoric caves, breathtaking vistas, colorful local culture, and smooth beaches remain unspoiled.

HIGHLIGHTS OF BASILICATA

DESTROY a papier-maché cart in Matera's frenzied **Assalto al Carro** (p. 606).

WANDER through 7000-year-old cave houses in the *sassi* **district** (p. 602).

PLUNGE into the sparkling Ionian in **Metaponto** (p. 606).

MATERA   ☎ 0835

Matera's claim to fame are the *sassi*, ancient homes carved directly in the rocks of the Materan terrain. The settlements remained livable until 1952, when the government deemed the 7000-year-old homes unsafe and unsanitary, displacing the residents. Yuppies and several high-tech firms recently went slumming and restored and occupied several *sassi*. Strikingly beautiful and oddly captivating, the city that calls itself "The Heritage of Humanity" has expanded to become the second-largest in Basilicata, earning it the nickname "Capital of Nowhere." The city is still relatively isolated, and remains the only provincial capital in Italy not connected by FS trains. Nonetheless, its extraordinary sights, inexpensive accommodations, and engaging local culture, including the exhilarating **Festa di Santa Maria della Bruna** (see **Entertainment,** p. 606), make getting to Matera worth the trouble.

⌐ TRANSPORTATION

Trains: Station at P. Matteotti. **FAL** trains run to **Altamura** (30min., 13 per day, 6:30am-9pm, €3.46) and **Bari** (1½hr., 13 per day, 6:30am-9pm, €3.62).

Buses: FAL buses leave from P. Matteotti for **Bari** on Sunday, when train service is suspended (1¾hr., 6 per day 6am-2pm, €3.62). Buy tickets at train station. **SITA buses** leave from the same piazza; buy tickets at P. Matteotti, 3 (☎0835 38 50 70). Buses run to: **Altamura** (30min., 4 per day, 12:30-6:30pm, €1.60); **Gravina** (50min., 3 per day, 1-6:30pm, €2.43); **Metaponto** (1hr., 5 per day, 8:15am-5:30pm, €2.63); and **Taranto** (1½hr., 6 per day 6am-5pm, €5.16). All bus lines have reduced service on Su.

◥ ◢ ORIENTATION AND PRACTICAL INFORMATION

Matera's grottoes split into two small valleys overlooking a deep canyon in the **Parco della Murgia Materana.** From the train and bus stations at **Piazza Matteotti,** head down **Via Roma** or **Via Minzoni** to **Piazza V. Veneto,** the heart of the city. The first valley, **Sasso Barisano,** the more modern area, is straight ahead; descend through the stairway across from the Banco di Napoli. To reach **Sasso Caveoso,** the cavernous *sasso,* continue to the right down **Via del Corso,** which bears right to **Via Ridola,** and descend to the left at **Piazza Pascoli.** Some of the more important *chiese rupestri* (rock churches) are on the other side of the ridge opposite the Sasso Caveoso. A detailed map of the *sassi* can be found at the tourist office and hotels.

Tourist Office: APT, V. di Viti de Marco, 9 (☎0835 33 19 83; fax 33 34 52). From the station, walk down V. Roma and take the 2nd left. Some English spoken. Open M and Th 9am-1pm and 4-6:30pm, Tu-W and F-Sa 9am-1pm. The city has an **information office** on V. Madonna della Virtù, the road along the ridge in the *sassi* district. Open Apr.-Sept. 9:30am-12:30pm and 3:30-6:30pm.

Emergency: ☎113.

Police: ☎0835 33 42 22.

Ambulance: ☎0835 24 32 70.

Hospital: (☎0835 24 31), on V. Lanera.

Internet Access: Qui PC Net, V. Margherita (☎0835 34 61 12), to the left of the Banco di Napoli. €4.40 per hr. Open daily 8am-1pm and 5-8:30pm.

Post Office: (☎0835 33 25 91), on V. del Corso off P. Veneto. Open M-Sa 8:30am-6pm.

Postal Code: 75100.

⌐ ACCOMMODATIONS

Matera has a great hostel, making it an inexpensive base for regional exploration.

▨ **Sassi Hostel (HI),** V. S. Giovanni Vecchio, 89 (☎0835 33 10 09; fax 33 37 33; hotelsassi@virgilio.it). From the station, take V. Minzoni to P. Veneto and take V. S. Biagio to the church, where signs leading to the hostel appear on the right. This hostel and hotel amid the prehistoric caves will fulfill your troglodyte fantasies. The rooms are renovated *sassi,* each with private bath. Sheets and towels included. Curfew midnight. Dorms €15.50. AmEx/MC/V. ❶

Albergo Roma, V. Roma, 62 (☎0835 33 39 12), by tourist office. 10 unremarkable rooms at low prices. Singles €21; doubles €31, with bath €36. ❷

Il Piccolo Albergo, V. De Sariis, 11 (☎/fax 0835 33 02 01). V. De Sariis is off V. Lucana and close to the tourist office. 11 rooms close to the center of town with full amenities, including bath, TV, fridge, and A/C. Singles €55; doubles €75. AmEx/MC/V. ❹

Hotel De Nicola, V. Nazionale, 158 (☎/fax 0835 38 51 11). Follow V. A. Moro from P. Matteotti to V. Anunziatella on the left, which becomes V. Nazionale, or take orange city bus #7 or 10 from the station (every 10min., €0.67). A 15min. walk from the station, and even farther from the sights. 99 modern rooms, all with bath, TV, and phone. Pay supplement for a room with fridge and A/C. Singles €43; doubles €66. AmEx/MC/V. ❶

🖪 FOOD

Try some of Matera's specialties: *favetta con cicore* (soup of beans, celery, chicory, and croutons, mixed in olive oil) or *frittata di spaghetti* (pasta with anchovies, eggs, bread crumbs, garlic, and oil). Experience true Materan grit with *pane di grano duro*, made of extra-hard wheat, from **Divella supermarket,** V. Spine Bianche, 6. (Open M-W and F-Sa 8:30am-1:30pm and 5-8:30pm, Th 8:30am-1:30pm.)

Ristorante Pizzeria La Terrazzina, V. S. Giuseppe, 7 (☎0835 33 25 03), off P. Veneto near Banco di Napoli. Savor immense portions of local delicacies in a cave dug into the cliffs. The cave doubles as wine cellar. Try handmade pasta in *cavatelli alla boscaiola* (pasta with tomatoes, mushrooms, and *prosciutto* for €5.16). Pizza €2.50-6. Cover €1.55. *Primi* under €6. Open W-M noon-3:30pm and 7pm-midnight. AmEx/MC/V. ❷

Trattoria Lucana, V. Lucana, 48 (☎0835 33 61 17), off V. Roma. Begin with the *orecchiette alla materana* (ear-shaped pasta with tomatoes and fresh veggies; €5.16) and continue with their specialty, the *bocconcini alla lucana* (thinly sliced veal with mushrooms; €6.70). Cover €1. Service 10%. Open M-Sa 12:30-3pm and 8-10:30pm. Closed early Sept. AmEx/MC/V. ❷

Ristorante Il Castello Tramontano, V. Castello, 1 (☎/fax 0835 33 37 52.) Take V. del Corso out of P. Veneto, turn right onto V. Scotellaro, left onto V. Lucana, and right again onto V. Castello. Excellent location looking out from the hill onto the *sassi*-filled valley, and great cheap eats under the castle. *Menù* €15, €18 with *antipasti*. Open daily 8pm-midnight. AmEx/MC/V. ❸

Ristorante Il Casino del Diavolo, V. La Martella (☎0835 26 19 86). Take the #10 bus. With great food at moderate prices, this huge restaurant is always packed with locals, despite its distance from P. Veneto. Main courses €5.60-12. Open Tu-Su 12:30-3:30pm and 8pm-1am. AmEx/MC/V. ❸

Carpe Diem, V. Minzoni, 32/4 (☎0835 24 03 59), between the station and P. Veneto. *Tavola calda,* a stylish, mirrored interior, and great *focaccia* served quickly and cheaply. Open daily 7am-9:30pm. ❷

Gran Caffè, P. Veneto, 6. No seating. Grab a sandwich, soda, and *cannoli* for less than €5 and eat on the pleasant benches in the piazza. Open daily 6am-11pm. ❶

🖪 SIGHTS

ALONG THE WAY TO THE SASSI. The 7000-year-old homes lie amid a maze of stone pathways, so you will need a **detailed map** to negotiate them properly. Enter the heart of *sassi* zone from P. Veneto by taking V. del Corso past the Chiesa di S. Francesco d'Assisi to P. Sedile, on your left. From there, V. Duomo leads to the Apulian-Romanesque **duomo** in P. del Duomo—check out the beautiful carving on the outside portals. Inside, the 15th-century carved choir stalls compete with the 16th-century **Cappella dell'Annunziata.** *(Open daily 9am-1pm and 3:30-6pm.)* From P. S.

YOU WANT A PIECE OF ME? The frenzied excitement of the *Festa di Santa Maria della Bruna* reaches its apex during the thrilling *"Assalto al Carro,"* when a beautiful papier-maché cart is led through town by people in medieval garb. When it reaches P. V. Veneto, melee sets in, as reveling natives destroy it in seconds. Dating to the Middle Ages, what seems like a simple exercise in mob violence actually has specific rules of etiquette: the cart can't be touched until it is entirely within P. V. Veneto (a SWAT team of terrified *carabinieri* tries to ensure this), and once the bullies who pushed to the center of the piazza have grabbed a piece of the cart, they flee as quickly as possible, holding the best fragments high over their heads, to the applause of the crowd. Occasionally, though, the first rule is broken, and the cart is attacked before it has quite entered the piazza. The first person gets the best piece (actually, the second person usually gets the best piece, while the first gets trampled), and the *carabinieri* melt away at the first inkling of resistance. Those who manage to seize chunks of the cart sprint off, triumphantly displaying their prizes.

Francesco, V. Ridola leads past the creepy **Chiesa del Purgatorio,** with its skeleton and skull-covered facade, to the **Museo Ridola** on your right, which displays the area's archaeological treasures. The museum houses excellent prehistoric and early Classical art in a 17th-century monastery and a room on early 20th-century excavation techniques. *(V. Ridola, 24. ☎0835 31 12 39. Open T-Su 9am-8pm, M 2-8pm. €2.50, €1.25 for students 18-24, under 18 or over 65 free.)*

THE SASSI. Of obscure origin, the *sassi* are carved from a soft limestone (calcarenite) in several styles. The oldest, inhabited around 7000 years ago, are crumbling structures that line Sasso Barisano along V. Addozio. The 2nd type, dating from 2000 BC, includes the carved nooks around Sasso Caveoso in the valley to the east of the duomo. The more elaborately carved *sassi*, about 1000 years old, are clustered near V. Buozzi (which stems from V. Madonna delle Virtù near the duomo). Most of the 6th-century *chiese rupestri* (rock churches) remain unmodified, still displaying remnants of 12th-century frescoes. As you roam the Sasso Caveoso, you may be approached by children offering "tours;" the organized ones are more enlightening. Try **Tour Service Matera,** P. Veneto, 42 (☎0835 33 46 33). For a comprehensive, self-guided tour, buy a book at any magazine stand.

CHURCHES... WITH *SASSI.* Churches carved into the rock and decorated with centuries-old frescoes dot the *sassi.* From the piazza past the museum, head down the narrow street to the right of the *palazzo,* continue down V. Buozzi, and follow the signs to reach the Convicino di S. Antonio, a large complex of painted rock churches with a great view of the *sassi.* From here follow the path along the cliffs to reach the churches of **San Pietro Caveoso, Santa Maria d'Idris,** and **Santa Lucia alle Malve,** which preserve beautiful 11th-century Byzantine frescoes in their caves. *(All the rock churches in the sassi district are open daily 9:30am-1:30pm and 2:30-7pm. 1 church €2.10, 4 churches €4.20, all 7 churches €5.20.)* A nearby **sasso** is furnished as it was when ten people and two horses shared its two small rooms. *(☎/fax 0835 31 01 18. Open daily 9am-9:30pm. €1.20. Tours in English.)* Farther along is the multilevel complex of Madonna delle Virtù and S. Nicola dei Greci, which contains both ancient frescoes and rough-hewn houses and the frantic modern sculpture of famed artist Leoncillo. *(Open daily 9am-9pm. €2.50, students €1.25. Tours in English.)*

PARCO DELLA MURGIA METERANA. For the best **hiking** in the area, this park inhabits the ridge across the canyon from the *sassi.* The entrance to the park is off Strada Statale, down V. Annunziatella and then V. Marconi.

🎵 ENTERTAINMENT

Matera celebrates the ▓**Festa di Santa Maria della Bruna** during the last week of June and the first week of July. The festival includes numerous musical and cultural events, nightly fireworks displays, and open-air markets where you can buy power tools or have a parakeet predict your future. The culmination of the festival with the **Assalto al Carro** on July 2.

🌄 DAYTRIPS FROM MATERA

ALTAMURA

The city is on the FAL line between Bari (1hr., 8 per day, 6:30am-9pm, €2.58) and Matera (40min., 8 per day 6:30am-9pm, €1.81).

The urban center for the farm country of inland Puglia, Altamura boasts an impressive Romanesque **cathedral.** The beautiful rose window sits above one of the best decorated church portals in Puglia. Scenes from the life of Christ surround the main carving showing the last supper. (Cathedral in P. Duomo, on V. Frederico in the old city.) Altamura also has an interesting archaeological museum displaying the finds of lots of academic grave-digging in the region of both Greek and prehistoric tombs. At the entrance into the old city, take a left and continue on the road until you see signs for the museum. (Open daily 8:30am-7:30pm. €2.)

V. L. Regina Margerita runs from the station to the old city, where it becomes V. Frederico di Svevia. Just after the old city, V. Federico di Svevia splits into V. Pietro Colletta and V. Matera. A **hospital** is on V. Regina Margherita (☎ 0803 10 811), and **Guardia Medica** can be reached at ☎ 080 310 8201. The **carabinieri** (☎ 0803 10 29 92) are in P. S. Teresa, down V. N. Melodia from P. Duomo.

GRAVINA

Gravina is most accessible from Altamura by FAL train (15min., 13 per day, 7:15am-9pm, €1.03), while FS trains run to rural spots in the area. Museum ☎ 080 325 1021. Open Tu-Su 9am-1pm.

Gravina is perched along a steep gorge that gives the town its name. The town's highlight is the beautiful view of the city and Apulian countryside from the ravine.

Both train stations are at the end of **Corso Aldo Moro** (on the other side of the tracks from the FAL station), which runs to the old city, becoming **Via V. Veneto** midway down, and dissolving into a tangled mass of streets in the old city. Keep heading downhill to reach P. Notar Domenico and the **Chiesa del Purgatorio,** decorated with statues of reclining skeletons. The bears supporting the columns represent the Roman Orsini family, feudal lords of Gravina. Next to the church in a large *palazzo* is the small **Archaeological Museum.** Free admission includes tours of the collection of Lucanian grave relics, including some huge Greek *amphora*. Next to the stations, the facade of **Chiesa di Madonna di Grazie** has a massive relief of an eagle spreading its wings. On C. A. Moro, heading away from the stations, turn left down V. Fontana La Stella to the stone bridge leading across the ravine to the cliffs on the other side and a lovely pastoral view of town. Prehistoric caves dug into the cliffs were used by locals in the 5th century to hide from attacking barbarians.

METAPONTO   ☎ 0835/0831

Metaponto consists of a few packed campsites and restaurants along the beach, some lonely Greek ruins, a museum, and a train station 3km inland. Although the sand along the sparkling Ionian is a delight, it is better enjoyed in early July or September. Metaponto feels like a ghost town for most of the year, but from mid-July through August the campsites burst with flocks of Italians scrambling to the sea.

TRANSPORTATION. Metaponto is best reached by train, although both the beach and the ruins are a short bus ride away from the station. **Trains** to: **Bari** (2-2½hr., 7 per day, 5:30am-3pm, €6.78); **Reggio di Calabria** (4½-5½hr., 2 per day, 10am-2:15pm, €18.60); **Rome** (5½-6hr., 3 per day, 6:30am-12:30am, €22.70); **Salerno** (3-3½hr., 5 per day, 6:30am-10pm, €11.60); and **Taranto** (30-45min., 29 per day, 5am-11pm, €3.60). Blue **SITA buses** run from the train station to **Matera** (1hr., 5 per day, 7:05am-4:30pm, €2.63). Local **Chiruzzi buses** serve the area. **Bus #1** runs between the train station, the museum, and *lido* (14 per day, 7:30am-9:30pm, €0.62), while the less frequent **#2** runs between the train station and the ruins, first the *zona archeologica* and then the Tavole Palatine, 5 km away (7 per day, 8am-7pm, €0.62 tickets on the bus). The *lido* district is a small area around P. Nord, where the bus stops and bicycles can be rented, a five minute walk from the beach.

ORIENTATION AND PRACTICAL INFORMATION. The town can be divided into four areas: *scalo* (the train station), *borgo* (the museum), *lido* (beach and hotels), and the **ruins** of an archaeological park. While Scalo, Borgo, and the ruins are all 1-2km apart, the *lido* is farther away. Metaponto's best reserved ruin, the **Tavole Palatine**, is 5km from Borgo. In case of **medical emergency**, contact the **Pronto Soccorso** (☎0835 74 19 97), off the beach. The **post office** is near the Museo Archeologico, a 10 minute walk straight ahead out of the station. (Open M-Sa 8am-1:15pm.) **Postal Code:** 75010.

ACCOMMODATIONS AND FOOD. Metaponto's many cheap campgrounds host most of its beach-goers. **Camping Magna Grecia ❶**, V. Lido, 1, is on the right of the highway V. L. Jonio when leaving the *lido* (connecting the *lido* to the station). The campground's noisy *discoteca* is next door to a quiet national forest. There are also tennis courts, game rooms, bars, a swimming pool, and a shuttle to the beach. (☎0831 74 18 55. Open July 21-Aug. 25. €8.50 per person, €8.50 per tent, €3.50 per parking space. Electricity €3.50. AmEx/MC/V.) Finding a cheap hotel on the *lido* isn't likely; the best value option is **Hotel Kennedy ❹**, Viale Jonio, 1, just off of P. Nord. Good-sized rooms have bath, A/C, TV, and fridge; some have kitchen facilities. (☎/fax 0835 74 18 32; www.hrkennedy.it. Breakfast included. Singles €47-57; doubles €62-72. AmEx/MC/V.) **l'Oasi Ristorante Pizzeria ❸**, V. Lido, 47, is a good bet for a beachside lunch break, with tasty cheap seafood and pizzas just off the sand. (☎0835 74 18 83. 4-course tourist menù €16. Open daily noon-3pm and 7pm-midnight. MC/V.) **Maria's ❶** is a mini-market off P. Nord that makes good sandwiches for under €5. (Open daily 7am-6pm.)

SIGHTS. Most people go to Metaponto for the beach, and with good reason: the sand is powdery-fine, the water bright turquoise and clean, and large stretches are public. The drawback, of course, is the massive congestion that overtakes the beach in the summer months. If the sun starts to get to you, catch the #1 bus from the *lido* or the train station to the **Museo Archeologico.** The museum displays ancient jewelry, vases, and figurines, most of which come from the nearby ruins. (☎0831 74 53 27. Open daily 9am-7pm. €2.50, ages 18-26 €1.25, under 18 or over 60 free.) From the museum you can head through the park, past the post office down a lonely country road to the **ruins** of the Doric **Temple of Apollo Licius** and a **Greek Theater** (6th century BC), although be warned before taking the long walk: there's not that much to see. It's another 5km to the **Tavole Palatine,** the ruins of a Greek temple of Hera and the best-preserved temple in Metaponto. The Greek mathematician **Pythagoras**, inventor of the Pythagorean theorem, taught here until his death in 479 BC. (The #2 bus connects the train station with all the ruins.)

TYRRHENIAN COAST

MARATEA ☎097

A collection of small, tranquil towns on the Tyrrhenian Sea, Maratea is the only portion of Basilicata that touches the water. The natural landscape, running 30km along the coastline, boasts beaches of rock and sand, creeks and caves, and pines, oaks, and olive trees. Wild rosemary, myrtle and other blooms dot the greenery of the surrounding mountains. Summer, particularly August, brings tourists who flock to admire the coast's natural splendor, raising hotel prices; during this high season, advance reservations are recommended. **Maratea Centro** is closest to the train station and has many secrets worth discovering, but if you came to Maratea to see the sea, **Fiumicello (Santavenere)** and **Maratea Porto** are closer to the water. Fiumicello melts down to the hillside in the form of small shops and *ristoranti* along Via Santavenere until joining the sea on a gorgeous beach. Maratea Porto's cove houses both modern boats and old fishing vessels, as well as an array of restaurants and shops. Watching over the coast from atop Mount Biagio, a 22m statue of *il Redentore* (Christ the Redeemer) stands cloaked in white marble. It has stood with arms outstretched in benediction of the beauty below since 1963.

⊑ TRANSPORTATION. Trains run from **Maratea Station** to **Cosenza** (13 per day), **Naples** (13 per day), and **Reggio di Calabria** (9 per day). (☎097 387 6906. Open 7:15am-noon, 3:40-6pm, and 9-11pm. AmEx/MC/V.) Fiumicello, Maratea Centro, and Maratea Anziana are accessible by **bus** from Cosenza during the summer (June-Aug., 9am-1am, every hr.; Sept.-May service more erratic). Local buses are far less frequent, follow no particular schedule, and only run between the station, Fiumicello, and Porto. Though the main bus stop is down the road from the train station, don't hesitate to flag down a bus—they'll usually stop anywhere. If you prefer to walk, **Maratea Porto** (4km) and **Fiumicello** (2km) may be reached on foot from the train station. Exit the station, turn right, and continue down V. Profiti under the bridge. Turn left down the hill to Fiumicello. Porto is down the same road. Signs appear frequently along the way. **Cabmar taxis** are recommended if arriving at Maratea Station in the evening. (☎097 387 0084 or 033 790 1579.)

⊠ PRACTICAL INFORMATION. The **AAST tourist office,** V. Santa Venere, 40, is on P. Gesù as you curve down the hill on V. Santa Venere. (☎097 387 6908. Open June-Sept. M-Su 8am-8pm; Oct.-May M, W, and F-Sa 9am-2pm, Tu and Th 9am-2pm and 3-6pm.) There is a Banco di Napoli with an **ATM** at V. S. Venere, 61. The closest **post office** is in Maratea Porto, V. Porto, 27 (☎ 097 387 6711. Open M-Sa 8am-1:15pm.) From mid-May to October, **Porto Turistico di Maratea** (☎097 387 7307) in Maratea Porto, rents out **motorboats** for €77.50.

⊓ ⊡ ACCOMMODATIONS, CAMPING, AND FOOD. With hotels, the closer you get to the water, the closer you get to the bottom of your wallet. Closest to the train station, and about a 10min. walk from the beach, **Hotel Fiorella ❸,** V. Santa Venere, 21, is on the hill on the right as you enter Fiumicello. The bus from the train station drives by the hotel; ask the driver to drop you off. Alternatively, to walk from the train station, continue down the curving V. Profiti until you reach a set of stairs heading down on your left. Follow the steps until you reach the bottom; the hotel will be right in front of you. The Fiorella provides spacious, if simple, rooms at a decent price. (☎097 387 6921; fax 387 7343. Sept.-June: singles with bath €26; doubles with bath €45. July-Aug.: singles €35; doubles €64.

Half-board €54 per person, full-board €63 per person. AmEx/MC/V.) **Hotel Sette-bello ❺**, V. Fiumicello, 52 (☎097 387 6277, fax 387 7204; www.costadima-ratea.com/settebello), sits right on the beach, with a beautiful view of the coast. Rooms have private bathroom and shower, direct-dial phones, and satellite TVs; most also have large balconies overlooking the seaside. (Breakfast included. Open Easter-Oct. High season singles €78, doubles €104; low season singles €52, doubles €69. Half-board €54-€80, full-board €65-€96.) Located in **Maratea Castrocucco**, 8km down the coastal road from Maratea's port, **Camping Maratea ❶**, Località Castrocucco, 72 (☎ 097 387 7580 or 387 1680, fax 387 1699), is close to the sea and popular. Make reservations early in the summer.

CALABRIA

Calabria is the most under-developed of Italy's provinces, as well as the most under-appreciated. Shunned by tourists in favor of the flashier and more expensive North, Calabria has developed an isolated culture of its own. Two and a half millennia ago, when the northern cities that sniff at her today were small backwaters, Calabria was the center of the world, home to leading philosophers, artists, and athletes. Fortunately for Calabrese pride, traces of this illustrious past remain in abundance, from the Greek ruins at Locri to the Norman Castle at Cosenza.

HIGHLIGHTS OF CALABRIA

ENCOUNTER wildlife in the parks of the **Sila Massif** (p. 613).

GLIMPSE at the remarkable Riace Bronzes in Reggio's **National Museum** (p. 602).

LOLL on the beautiful **beaches** of Scilla (p. 617).

COSENZA   ☎0984

Cosenza has a slight case of split personality, with the Busento River separating its modern, traffic-plagued half from the cultured *Centro Storico*. The latter, highlighting the city's ties to its ancient history, is the real pride of Cosenzians. It is said that the Busento River is the burial place of Alaric I, king of the Visigoths, who died of malaria in Cosenza in AD 410. Many frantic and unsuccessful searches have been carried out to find the bones of this notorious king, along with the treasure he and his troops plundered from Rome. This legend, captured in August von Platen's famous poem, *La tomba sul Busento*, caused an "Alaric fever," as Alexandre Dumas put it, that boosted tourism in Cosenza for ages. Today, the *Centro Storico* is the major draw, with each ruin a tangible link to Cosenza's past.

▣ TRANSPORTATION

Public transportation shuts down on Sundays, so be sure to plan ahead.

> **Trains: Stazione Cosenza** (☎0984 39 47 46), V. Popilia, at the *superstrada*. Ticket office open daily 6:30am-8:25pm. **FS** (☎1478 88 088; 7am-9pm) trains run to: **Naples** (3½-4hr., 7 per day); **Paola** (30min., 15 per day); **Reggio** (3hr., 4 per day); **Rome** (6½hr., 2 per day); **Sibari** (1hr., 9 per day). Station serviced by **Ferrovie della Calabria** trains to **Camigliatello** (1½hr, 2 per day, €1.70) and buses (most blue buses stop at the blue "fermata" sign in front of the train station).

Buses: Autostazione (☎ 0984 41 31 24), on V. Autostazione. Where C. Mazzini ends in P. Fera, turn right and walk down the marked sloping street to the station. **Ferrovie della Calabria** regional buses for inland destinations leave from here and the train station, where you can buy bus tickets at windows opposite those for train tickets. To **Camigliatello** and **San Giovanni** (10 per day, €1.76) and **Villagio Palumbo** (€3.)

Public Transportation: All orange **buses** stop at P. Matteotti; buy tickets (€0.67) at any one of the magazine stands (main stand where V. Trieste crosses C. Mazzini near P. dei Bruzi) and at most *tabacchi*. Buses #22 and 23 serve the old city, stopping in P. Prefettura (every 30min., 5:30am-11pm). Buses #27 and 28 go between P. Matteotti and the train station (every 7min., 5am-midnight.) For more detailed bus routes look for yellow hanging street signs in P. Matteotti and at all bus stops. A word of caution: posted schedules are your only clue as to which bus stop you're at. Ask the driver or a fellow passenger to tell you when your stop comes up.

■✚ 🛈 ORIENTATION AND PRACTICAL INFORMATION

The **Busento River** divides the city into two distinct regions: the traffic-heavy "new city," north of the Busento, and the "old city," with its ancient buildings, south of the river. **Corso Mazzini,** the main thoroughfare and shopping center, begins in **Piazza dei Bruzi,** continues through the small **Piazza Kennedy,** and ends in **Piazza Fera.** To get to C. Mazzini, hop on any bus to **Piazza Matteotti** and with your back to the bus stop walk a block up C. Umberto into **P. dei Bruzi.** The central bus station is on **Via Autostazione,** just to the right off P. Fera at the end of C. Mazzini, where the *corso* splits seven ways.

Cosenza's *centro storico* rests across the Ponte Mario Martiri, three blocks to the right from P. Matteoti when facing away from P. dei Bruzi. A labyrinth of medieval multi-level stone buildings, the old city features winding "roads," some of which are just elaborate, cobblestone staircases. Its only identifiable street, narrow **Corso Telesio,** begins in the petite **Piazza Valdesi,** near the Busento, and climbs through the recently revived section of the old city to the statue of the philosopher Telesio himself in the well-lit and immaculate **Piazza Prefettura** (Piazza XV Marzo).

Emergency: ☎ 113. **Carabinieri:** ☎ 112.

Police: Municipale (☎ 0984 25 422), in P. dei Bruzi, behind the town hall. Open 24hr.

Red Cross: V. Popilia, 35 (☎ 0984 41 11 55).

Late-Night Pharmacy: P. Kennedy, 7 (☎ 0984 24 155), open M-Sa 2:30pm-1am, Su 10pm-8am. **Farmacia Berardelli,** C. Mazzini, 40, open 8:30am-1pm and 4:30-8pm.

Hospital: Ospedale Civile dell'Annunziata, (☎ 0984 28 409), on V. Felice Migliori.

Ambulance: Croce Bianca, V. Beato Angelo d'Acri, 29 (☎ 0984 39 35 28).

Internet Access: Casa delle Culture, C. Telesio, 98. With your back to the duomo, follow C. Telesio until you reach an area on your right set back from the road. Only 7 terminals. Reservation 1hr. ahead of time recommended.

Post Office: V. Veneto, 41 (☎ 0984 252 84; fax 732 37), at the end of V. Piave, off C. Mazzini. Open M-F 8:10am-4pm, Sa 8:10am-1:30pm.

Postal Code: 87100.

🛏 ACCOMMODATIONS

Hotel Grisaro, Viale Trieste, 38 (☎ 0984 27 952, fax 27 838). Walk 1 block up C. Mazzini from P. dei Bruzzi, then make a left onto V. Trieste. V. Monte Santo is 1 block up on the right, marked by a large, bright sign. Spacious rooms with TV and comfy beds are easily accessed by elevator. Friendly common room downstairs with TV and armchairs. Wheelchair-accessible. Reservations suggested. Singles €28.40, with bath €36.15; doubles, €51.65; triples, €67.15; quads, €77.50. ❸

Hotel Excelsior, Piazza Matteotti, 14 (☎0984 74 383; fax 74 384). The 1st hotel you hit after stepping off any of the buses at Piazza Matteotti. Rooms come with color TV, nice bathroom, and telephone. Singles €34; doubles €52; triples €68; quads €78. ❸

🍴 FOOD

Cosenza is a well-fed city, and the city's bounty of restaurants draw on the rich mushrooms and fresh *prosciutto* of the Sila forests, plentiful fish from the sparkling Tyrrhenian, and the fruit of the region's orchards. For sumptuously fresh fruits and vegetables, stop at **Cooper Frutta,** Viale Trieste, 25/29, a block from C. Mazzini, and acquire everything else from **Cooperatore Alimentare** next door at Viale Trieste 35; have yourself a picnic in nearby P. Vittoria—just you, a peach, a loaf, and the old men playing *gioca tresete*, a local card game.

Gran Caffè Renzelli, C. Telesio, 46 (☎0984 26 814), in the piazza behind the duomo. With pictures and newspaper clippings on the wall, this cafe loves to boast of its 200-year history. The Bandiera brothers, famous patriots of the Risorgimento, stopped by for a cup of Renzelli's excellent coffee; an hour later Bourbon troops caught and executed them beneath the Valle di Rovina aqueduct. Find out if the *cappuccino* is really to die for. Mini *pizza rustica* €1. Table service an additional €0.52. Open W-Su, from early afternoon to late night, depending on the crowd and the owner's fancy. ❶

Taverna L'Arco Vecchio, P. Archi di Ciaccio, 21 (☎0984 72 564). Take 4T bus to hillside village, or follow signs along V. Petrarca. An elegant cove within a rustic, crumbling stone village locale, the restaurant is located right beside the city's old arch. Large wine selection and a menù with dishes that change daily. Cover €1.55. Lunch served starting at 1pm, dinner 8:30-11pm. MC/V. ❸

Da Giocondo, V. Piave, 53 (☎0984 29 810). Left off of C. Mazzini onto V. Piave, then 2 blocks up on left. From the friendly atmosphere to the *centro storico* artwork on the walls, this 3-room restaurant has a local character that can't be topped. Bow-tied waiters serve local fish, regional specialties, and tasty fruit desserts to go with the long wine list. Dishes from €4. Cover €2. Open M-Sa noon-3pm, 7-10pm. AmEx/MC/V. ❷

Yankee, V. Piave, 17-19 (☎0984 27 032). Left off C. Mazzini, then 1 block up on V. Piave, on the left. Ever wonder what Italians really think of America? The decor of this establishment throws randomly combines Coca-Cola signs, Popeye cartoons, a mural of the wild west, Pokemon, and outdated radio hits. But don't worry; you're still in Italy. The pizza is delicious and cheap (€0.77). Good ol' American food comes in the form of a hot dog (€1.81), or hamburger (€2.58). Open daily noon-3pm and 5pm-midnight. ❶

👁 SIGHTS

DUOMO. The Duomo was erected in the middle of the 12th century, according to Romanesque design, only to be almost completely rebuilt in 1184, after an earthquake struck. Its original design struggles through Baroque and other stylistic influences. Inside is Cosenza's second most-prized artwork after the famed cross: *La Madonna del Pilerio*, a 12th-century painting in the Byzantine style with influences from Sicily and Campania. The work is framed by an ornate baroque chapel, the first on the left side of the church as you enter. The next chapel belongs to the *Arciconfraternità della Morte* (Archbrotherhood of Death). Not to be confused with a heavy metal band, the brothers actually belonged to a religious order charged by ancient privilege to aid those condemned to death. Many Cosentini executed for their part in the Risorgimento are buried in the chapel, as well as Isabella of Aragon, whose tomb is the left side of the chapel. *(Cross the M. Martini bridge into the old city, and head left up C. Telesio. Or take bus #22 or 23 up to P. Prefettura, and with your back to P. del Governo, turn right down C. Telesio. Open mornings and late afternoons.)*

CHIESA DI SAN FRANCESCO D'ASSISI. This small church's plain exterior, rebuilt after an earthquake in 1854, hides a lavish but tired white Baroque cruciform interior. In the far right aisle is a portal leading to the chapel of Santa Caterina, the main attraction of the church, which is graced by the paintings of the Flemish artist William Borremons. Behind the altar, a wooden tomb contains the angelic but shriveled body of a 500-year-old Franciscan monk, on full display. The chambers above (reached by a stairway from the adjoining sacristy) contain astounding views of the city, but are not normally accessible to the public—so ask nicely. The greatest treasure to be found here, however, lies just below the church. When the duomo was reconsecrated in 1222 following an earthquake, Frederick II gave the city a gilt **Byzantine crucifix** containing a splinter said to have come from the True Cross. A skilled work in fine gold, the cross is truly exquisite. Once on public display in the duomo, then moved to the Archbishopric, it is now safe and sound in the basement of the Convento di San Francesco d'Assisi. Call ahead to see it. *(☎ 0984 75 522. Cross the Mario Martiri bridge, turn left up narrow C. Telesio to the Duomo. Continue on C. Telesio just past the cathedral's facade, then turn right onto V. del Seggio (don't be fooled by its staircase-like appearance; it is a street). Take a right at the top; church is around the corner. For the cross, follow the church's left flank down to the last door and press the buzzer for "Laboratorio di Restauro." Free.)*

CASTELLO NORMANNO-SVEVO (NORMAN CASTLE). This fairytale structure on the hill high above the city predates most of the *centro storico* and, in its ruined state, provides a silent and meditative testament to the city's tumultuous past. Originally built by the Saracens but refurbished by Frederick II after the Cosentini tried to overthrow him, the castle offers impressive views of the surprisingly compact city. Now overrun with grass and a few trees, the castle has been a barracks for the armies of three different monarchs, a prison, and a seminary. Though three earthquakes have destroyed most of its ornaments, the castle's flowered columns and roofless chambers remain. *(Take bus #22 or 23 to P. Prefettura, and with your back to Rendano Theater (with the Telesio statue to your left), walk up the curved road. Or take bus 4T to the elevated village and follow signs 10-15min. uphill. Word of caution: the climb is steep, unshaded, and the light colored roads reflect the harsh sunlight. Be extra cautious on hot days and bring water. Open daily 9am-1:30pm. Free.)*

RENDANO THEATER. Calabria's most prestigious venue, the Rendano Theater was originally constructed in 1895 but was destroyed by WWII bombing. It has since been rebuilt to its former glory. Crimson, white, and gold, its plush interior has showcased the likes of José Carreras. Reservations for non-Calabresi are extremely difficult to get during the opera season (Oct.-Dec.); you might have more luck stopping in during the theater season (Jan.-May). If it's performance itself you want, the Rendano hosts regional performance groups during the summer, with readily available tickets. *(☎ 0984 81 32 20. Behind the statue of Telesio in P. Prefettura. For plays, tickets may be available 10am-1pm and 5-8pm on day of performance, but you cannot check by phone. €18. Student discounts.)*

PIAZZA TOSCANO. The piazza contains the ancient ruins of the Cosenza. Original stone work is covered by plexiglass, allowing visitors to walk over the remains of ancient buildings. Remnants of the artwork that once covered the stone walls are also on display. Excavators continue to uncover the old city lying beneath the new. *(Directly behind the Duomo, off to the left of C. Telesio.)*

VILLA VECCHIA. Also known as the public gardens, are located off P. Prefettura, from the road beside the palace. The gardens engulf old stone fountains and benches. Projects are at work to restore the rest of it to its original splendor.

⬛ NIGHTLIFE

Cosenza is the center of action for smaller neighboring towns. **Planet Alex,** C. Mazzini, 12 (☎0984 79 53 37), is a disco-pub in the new city that plays loud music into the wee hours of the morning. In the *Centro Storico*, settle down at the **J. Joyce Irish Pub,** V. Cafarone, 19 (☎0984 22 799), a bar packed with locals on the weekends. €5 cover includes one drink.

CAMIGLIATELLO AND SILA MASSIF   ☎098

A billboard near the train station depicting an untainted green landscape says of Sila, "Its nature will amaze you." Sila's glorious woods, lakes, mountains, and valleys are ready and waiting to be explored by intrepid independent travelers. Calabria's hikers, campers, and skiers flock here to take advantage of the countless cross country and few downhill trails. Often neglected by foreign tourists, Sila is as worthwhile a destination as the coast.

⬛ TRANSPORTATION AND PRACTICAL INFORMATION. Camigliatello is the best base to visit elsewhere in the Sila. **FS** trains run from **Cosenza** (1½hr., 12 per day, €1.70), and buses leave from the Cosenza **Autostazione** (40min., €1.91) Maps and information on Sila's attractions, events and trails can be found at the **Pro Loco tourist office,** V. Roma, 5, uphill to the right from the train station and bus stop. The **bank,** Banca Carime, is at V. del Turismo, 73. (☎098 457 8027. Open M-F 8:30am-1:20pm and 2:35-3:35pm.) For **medical emergencies,** call ☎098 457 8328. Camigliatello's **post office,** V. Tasso, is at the intersection of V. del Turismo and V. Roma, next to Hotel Tasso. (☎098 457 8076. Open M-Sa 9am-1pm.)

⬛ ACCOMMODATIONS AND FOOD. La Baita ❸, V. Roma, 99, 100m from the train station, and just up the road on the right from the bus stop, is a comfortable family-run hotel. All rooms with bath. (☎098 457 8197. Singles €20; doubles €40. During August and ski season, singles €26; doubles €47.) Slightly more expensive lodgings can be found at **Hotel Meranda ❺,** V. del Turismo, 29, has 90 rooms with bath and color TV, as well as an elegant restaurant/bar, *discoteca*, and video game room. (☎098 457 8022; fax 457 9293. Doubles with full board om June from €37 per person, €62 in Aug.) Buses run from Camigliatello to the **La Fattoria ❶** campsite (☎0984 57 82 41), near a vineyard. (€5.16 per person, tent provided.) **Le Tre Lanterne ❸,** V. Roma, 142, is a popular and friendly spot that specializes in *funghi porcini*, or Sila-style mushrooms. Dinner prices generally run €20-€30. (☎098 457 8203. Cover €1.55. Open Tu-Su noon-3:30pm and 7pm-12am.) **La Stragola ❺,** V. Roma, 160 (☎0984 57 83 16), offers fresh mushroom pasta and other local favorites. Expect to pay between €30 and €50, plus €1 cover. For a change of pace, try the *salumerie* (deli-like eateries) that overflow with smoked cheeses, cured meats, and marinated mushrooms. Picnic grounds lie 10min. from the *centro*, up V. Tasso and past the post office.

S **L** **SIGHTS AND ENTERTAINMENT.** If it's snow you want, you'll get plenty of it at the **Tosso Ski Trail,** on Monte Curcio, about 2km from town up V. Roma and left at Hotel Tosso. In winter, minibuses leave for the trailhead from Camigliatello's bus stop (buy tickets at Bar Pedaggio, next door to the stop). Though Tosso offers 35km of beautiful cross-country skiing, it has only two downhill trails (2km each). (☎ 098 457 8136 or 457 9400. Lifts open daily when snow is on the ground, 8am-5pm. Round-trip lift ticket €2.58; full-day pass €15.50. Getting to the **Parco Nazionale di Calabria** (☎ 098 457 9757), 10km northwest is not quite as easy. The state bus service sends just two buses into the park per day, in the morning and afternoon at varying times. **Altrosud,** V. Corado, 20 (☎ 098 457 8154), offers guided tours of the park in Italian for large groups. Arrange times and prices through reservation.

If you seek traditional Calabrian culture, ignore the stores filled with knick-knacks and instead hop on the bus for **San Giovanni in Fiore** (33km from Camigliatello), where you can view a 12th-century abbey, exhibitions of handicrafts at the museum, and traditional festivals (including the world-renowned **Potato Festival**).

Camigliatello is geared more towards the summer nature-lover or winter skiier than towards the party animal. Local youth often escape to nearby Cosenza for kicks at night; others remain for the blaring Eurotechno music, video games, foosball, and pool at **Le Bistro,** at V. C. Alvaro, 68. (Internet access €5 per hr.)

REGGIO DI CALABRIA   ☎0965

Though often regarded as merely a jumping off point for reaching Sicily, Reggio and its environs encompass some of the finest landscapes in Italy. With the Tyrrhenian Coast to the north and the Ionian to the east, amazing beaches are easily accessible in all directions. (Be sure to check out the nearby towns of **Scilla** (see p. 617) and **Gerace** (see p. 616). The former has a beach paramount to any in Italy, and the latter is one of the best-preserved medieval towns in the country.) More than two thousand years ago, Reggio was one of the greatest cities of Magna Graecia, the western end of the ancient Greek world. Those days of glory are now only to be found in the city's prized **Museo Nazionale,** Reggio having since fallen on hard times. Hundreds of year of raids and sacks left the region in disarray, with a devastating earthquake in 1908 providing the city with a chance to renew and rebuild. From the rubble arose a new town, lacking in old-world charm but brimming with designer stores and ornate turn-of-the-century *palazzi*.

▉ TRANSPORTATION

Flights: Aeroporto dello Stretto (☎0965 64 05 17), 5km south of town. Orange bus #113, 114, 115, 125, or 131 from P. Garibaldi outside Stazione Centrale (€0.52). Service to **Bologna, Florence, Milano, Rome,** and **Torino.**

Trains: Reggio has 2 train stations. All trains stop at **Stazione Centrale** (☎0965 27 427), on P. Garibaldi at southern end of town. To: **Cosenza** (2½hr., 3 per day, €11.36); **Naples** (5hr., 10 per day; €30.47, *rapido* €36.15); **Rome** (9hr., 10 per day, €40.28, *rapido* €45.45); **Scilla** (30min., 20 per day, €2.27); **Tropea** (2hr., 5 per day, €4.65). The less-frequented **Stazione Lido** (☎0965 86 36 64) sits at the northern end of town off V. Zerbi, close to the museum, port, and beaches.

Ferries: From Reggio's port, at the northernmost end of the city, boats and hydrofoils service Messina as well as the Aeolian Islands (Lipari, Salina, Vulcano). **FS** (☎0965 81 76 75), all the way to left, against the water as you enter the port, shares Reggio's hydrofoil service with **SNAV** (☎090 66 25 06 or 36 40 44), just to right of FS. FS open daily 6:30am-8:15pm; SNAV's hours vary. **NGI** (☎0335 842 7784), across from the "Onda Marina" bar to the right of the port's entrance, runs a ferry service. (M-F 12:20am-10:20pm, Sa 12:20am-8:20pm.) **Meridiano** (☎0965 81 04 14) is on the corner of the water nearest the port entrance. (Ferries run daily 2:10am-11:50pm, fewer on Su.)

🔶 🛈 ORIENTATION AND PRACTICAL INFORMATION

Reggio's main artery is **Corso Garibaldi**, which runs 1km parallel to the sea and to all the major sights. With your back to **Stazione Centrale**, walk straight through **Piazza Garibaldi** to C. Garibaldi; a left turn leads to the heart of the town. At the end of C. Garibaldi and down V. L.G. Zerbi is Reggio's **port**, from which hydrofoils and boats zip off to Messina and the Aeolian Islands. One block to the left of the station, the twin roads **Corso Vittorio Emanuele III** and **Viale Matteotti** trace the **Lungomare** on the sea. City buses run continuously up and down C. Garibaldi and along the two roads toward the **Stazione Lido**, 1½km to the north.

Tourist Office: APT booth (☎ 0965 27 120), at the central train station. Free maps as well as transportation and hotel information. Open M-Sa 8am-2pm and 2:30-8pm. Other branches with similar hours at the **airport** (☎ 0965 64 32 91) and the **main office** at V. Roma, 3 (☎ 0965 21 171 or 0965 89 25 12), which includes a wider variety of information and some English-speaking staff. Another **APT office** lies at C. Garibaldi, 327 (☎ 0965 89 20 12), next to the theater.

Currency Exchange: Banca Nazionale del Lavoro, C. Garibaldi, 431 (☎ 0965 85 11). Open M-F 8:20am-1:20pm and 2:35-4:05pm. C. Garibaldi has many **ATMs.**

Emergency: ☎ 113. **Carabinieri:** ☎ 112.

Police: (☎ 0965 41 11), on C. Garibaldi near central station.

24-Hour Pharmacy: Farmacia Caridi, C. Garibaldi (☎ 0965 24 013); **Farmacia Curla,** C. Garibaldi, 327 (☎ 0965 33 23 32).

Hospital: Ospedale Riuniti (☎ 0965 39 111), on V. Melacrino.

Internet Access: Agen Service (☎ 0965 581 8762.) At port, next to FS ticket office. €1.03 per 15min. Open 8am-12:40pm and 5:30-7:30pm. **PuntoNet,** C. Garibaldi, 70 (☎/fax 0965 33 16 68). €4.13 per hr. Open daily 3:30-8:30pm.

Post Office: V. Miraglia, 14 (☎ 0965 31 52 68), bear left from P. Italia on C. Garibaldi.

Postal Code: 89100.

🔶 ACCOMMODATIONS

Hotel Diana, V. Diego Vitrioli, 12 (☎ 0965 89 15 22), left off C. Garibaldi 4 blocks past and across from the duomo. Simple rooms with TV, bath, and phone. 1-month advance reservation required in Aug. Singles €25.82; doubles €51.65; triples €69.72; quads €87.80. A/C 20% more. ❷

Albergo Noel, V. Genoese Zerbi, 13 (☎ 0965 33 00 44 or 89 09 65), near port at opposite end of C. Garibaldi from Stazione Centrale. With the sea behind you, turn left from station. Dusty rooms and plastic furniture. Great location. The port, beach and museum are within a few blocks. Reduced baths and color TV. Wheelchair-accessible. Reservations recommended July-Sept. Singles €27; doubles €57. ❸

🔶 FOOD

In Reggio, chefs serve *spaghetti alla calabrese* (with pepper sauce), *capocollo* ham (spiced with local hot peppers), and *pesce spada* (local harpoon-hunted swordfish). Stock up for the beach at **Di per Di supermarket,** opposite the train station on C. Garibaldi. (Open M, W-Sa 8am-1:30pm and 5-8:30pm, Tu 8am-2pm.) Bars along C. Garibaldi often offer baked goods. Pick up a few of the region's favorite *biscotti* to make your outings a little sweeter.

✦Pizzeria Rusty, V. Romeo, next to the museum, by the Antica Gelateria. Nothing rusty about this fine eatery. Double-folded Neapolitan slices the size of Fiats, priced by weight. Another branch at V. Crocefisso, 14, to the right of the duomo. Both restaurants open daily 3:30-11pm. ❶

La Pignata, V. Demetrio Tripepi, 122 (☎0965 27 841), up V. Giutecca from C. Garibaldi. A sparkling interior and sociable waiters create the perfect atmosphere to sample specialties. La Pignata is the place to go when you want a little luxury at a little price. *Primi* from €5.16; *secondi* from €8.26. MC/V. ❷

Glenduff House, V. Ravagnese Inf., 83 (☎0965 63 67 40), near the airport. This nice bar and restaurant is filled to the brim with locals come nighttime; there may be a wait for a table. Wide variety of drinks available, with cocktails starting at €3.10. ❸

👁 SIGHTS

▩MUSEO NAZIONALE. Reggio's famed **Museo** celebrates the city's past as a great ancient Greek *polis*. The preeminence the city enjoyed in antiquity may have passed, but the Nazionale preserves the Reggio's historical claim to fame with one of the world's finest collections of art and artifacts from Magna Graecia (Greater Greece). In the first-floor galleries, a wealth of *amphorae* and *pinakes*, wine jars and votive tablets, show scenes from mythology and daily life. The floor above the gallery contains a large coin collection and a 2300-year-old novelty sarcophagus shaped like a huge sandaled foot.

The centerpiece of the collection is in the **Sezione Subacquea,** downstairs. Treasures formerly submerged in the Ionian Sea, such as pottery, anchors, and broken statues, are showcased here. More monumental finds include the **Bronze di Riace,** arguably the most valuable and important of known Greek sculptures. The Riace Bronzes stand casually in all their muscular glory in a gallery shared with the **Head of the Philosopher,** thought to be the Greek tradition's first life-like portrait. The Bronzes, two male nude warriors of stunning anatomical detail, date from the 5th century BC and are believed to be Greek originals, rather than Roman copies. Discovered by chance in 1972 near Riace, they have since stood guard in Reggio. A comprehensive display before you enter the gallery documents the bronzes's 9 year restoration process. (*P. de Nave, on C. Garibaldi toward the Stazione Lido.* ☎0965 81 22 55; www.museodellacalabria.com. Open daily 9am-7pm. Closed 1st and 3rd M of the month. €4.13; ages 18-25 €2.07; under 18 and over 65 free.)

🏖 🎭 BEACHES AND ENTERTAINMENT

As the day cools, Reggesi mingle on the **lungomare,** a long, narrow botanical garden stretching along the seaside that Italian author d'Annunzio immortalized as the "most beautiful kilometer in all of Italy." When they want to take a dip, pale travelers sprawl on the beach near **Lido Communale.** Playgrounds, an elevated boardwalk, and monuments to the city's more famous citizens dot the *lungomare,* and a sunset behind the misty blue mountains of nearby Sicily is a sight not to be missed. Calabrians finish the summer with the **Festival of the Madonna della Consolazione.** The four-day festival, celebrated in mid-September, concludes with an elaborate fireworks display.

🔄 DAYTRIPS FROM REGGIO DI CALABRIA

LOCRI AND GERACE
From Reggio, trains (2hr.; 23 per day; €5) run to and from Locri on the coast. From the station, the Audino bus (€1) runs 7:20am-5:30pm up to Gerace and back; to avoid getting stuck find out from the driver when he'll stop by again.

An easy and relaxing vacation from the urban energy of Reggio, **Locri** features the very best qualities of Ionian Coast: expansive beaches and ancient ruins. Between Bianco and Siderno, Locri is at the center of the coast's most pleasant and explorable beaches. The long, under-populated stretches of sand and stone allow for low-key and private afternoons lolling in the sun. Despite its location, Locri is not a "beach town," containing all regional government offices. The grand **Communale** (now being refurbished) presides over a square that is more park than piazza. With flowers, trees, grass, and benches, **Piazza Re Umberto** is a pleasant spot to watch the locals play cards and just relax.

On the outskirts of town, **Locri Epizephyri** offers those up to the 2km stroll a remarkable expanse of ancient Greek ruins. Various remaining foundations and supports give a sense of the Locri of old. Visitors can explore the Sanctuary of Persephone, the Necropolis, and the Ionic Temple of Marasa. The highlight of the site is the theatre, built into the hillside. Much of the seats and the stage remain, moving some visitors to give impromptu performances. The nearby museum (☎ 0964 39 04 33) displays objects and maps of the site. There is a **Pro Loco** office on V. M. di Savoia, 1 block to the left as you exit the piazza in front of the station, with helpful maps of the town. (Open 8am-2pm, 4-8pm.) A 24hr. Banco di Napoli **ATM** is on V. Mileto. After a right out of the station's piazza, take the first left.

Gerace is among the best-preserved medieval towns in Italy. Since losing the government seat to Locri, Gerace has become something of a "ghost town," but this has only served to maintain its medieval beauties in pristine, untouched splendor. The bus from Locri drops passengers off uphill from the duomo beside **Largo delle Tre Chiese,** a piazza enclosed by three churches. **The Chiesa di San Francesco** (to your left if you stand facing the Largo from the street) has a beautiful portal decorated in the Arabic-Norman style; inside is an elegant wooden altar fully decorated with exquisite black and white marble. Take a short walk up Gerace's pinnacle for the astounding view from **Castello di Roberto Il Guiscardo.** Down V. Caduti sul Lavoro from the bus stop, Gerace's immense **cathedral**—the largest in Calabria—occupies most of P. Duomo. Twenty-six Greek columns pilfered from Locri support the grand Romanesque interior. Highlights of the church are ancient Greek graffiti and Bishop Calceopulo's 16th-century tombstone.

There is a **Banca Carical** with an **ATM** and currency exchange in Largo Barlaam, downhill from the duomo on toward P. del Tocco. (Open M-F 8:20am-1:20pm and 2:35-3:35pm, Sa 8:20-11:50am.) The **post office** is in P. del Tocco. In **medical emergencies,** call the **Guardia Medica** (☎ 0964 39 91 11).

SCILLA

You can access Scilla from Reggio by train (30min, 20 per day, €2.27) or by bus (20min., 12 per day, €1.29).

Homer immortalized the town's great cliffs in *The Odyssey* as the home of the terrible monster Scylla (Italian: Scilla), whose six heads, 12 feet, and foul temper destroyed many a ship that steered away from Charybdis, a whirlpool in the straits where the oceans meet. Tourists today need not fear being devoured by a scaly monster, but beware of being seduced by Scilla the town. This fishing village-cumbeach resort is just 23km from Reggio, but its slow pace, white sands, and turquoise waters feel a world away. About ten times a year, however, the world can seem a lot closer as the *Fata Morgana*—a meteorological oddity wherein the light on the ocean air creates a natural magnifying glass—make the Aeolian Islands seem to be within walking distance. The town is built directly into the cliffs enclosing the beach, creating level after level of incredible vistas. In quiet moments, listen for the soft music of the merfolk. Scilla may be gone, but local legend contends that beautiful mermaids still grace the waters.

If Scilla proves too enticing to leave, consider spending the night at the seaside **Pensione Le Sirene,** V. Nazionale, 57,(☎0965 75 40 19 or 75 41 21; www.svagocalabria.com/pensionelesirene) across from the train station. A clean, cozy haven with nine rooms, Le Sirene is sandwiched between the station and the beach. (Breakfast included in summer. Reservations recommended during the summer. Singles €24; doubles €43.) Being eaten by Scylla is not fun, but eating in Scilla can be most enjoyable. The cheapest meals are served at the air-conditioned **Pizzeria San Francesco,** V. Cristoforo Colombo, 29, (☎0349 32 60 670) along the beach. This family-run establishment prides itself on its specialty, the Pizza Stefania. (Pizza €2.58-5.16.) To dine with a Homerian epic view, climb the stairs to **Vertigine,** P. San Rocco, 14 (☎0965 75 40 15) at the top of the town. Devour some speciality seafood. (*Primi* from €3.62; *secondi* from €5.16. Drinks from €1.29. Cover €1.29. Open daily noon-3pm and 7:30pm-midnight. MC/V.)

Scilla's most famous cliff now supports the 17th-century **Castello Ruffo,** evidence of Scilla's important historical role as a control base for the Straits of Messina. For over 2000 years, the cliffs have been valuable real estate when it comes to controlling the region, and everyone from the Italiots to Garibaldi himself has fought to take possession. Just down hill from the castle, **Chiesa di Maria S. S. Immacolata** is the largest and most impressive of Scilla's many churches. An enormous altarpiece and 14 bronze sculptures of Christ cannot contend with the beauty of the landscape, but are well worth the trip uphill. In August, Scilla celebrates the Festival of S. Rocco, the town's patron saint, with a grand fireworks display.

TROPEA ☎0963

Tropea's sandy beaches are among the most beautiful in all of Italy. Cold water slips between rock cliffs, upon which ancient buildings perch over the town below. Its winding streets create a maze of hidden piazzas and dignified churches. By day, the town is abandoned as everyone heads to the beach. By night, the piazzas become a brimming ocean of bronzed bodies. Tropea was once known for its nobility and its red onions. The nobility has long since replaced by international tourists that flood it beyond capacity in the summer, but the onions remain.

🖬🖪 TRANSPORTATION AND PRACTICAL INFORMATION. Trains (2hrs., 10 per day; open M-Sa 9am-1:50pm and 4:30-6pm; AmEx/MC/V) run from the Reggio train station and return to Reggio directly 3 times a day, all other trains must change at Rosarno. **Autoservizi** (☎0963 61 129) operates convenient *pullmini* (blue buses), which pick up passengers on V. Stazione every 30min. For €0.52 per person, the vans travel 27 different routes, going as far as 24km out, and are often the easiest or only way to access some of the more remote attractions and Accomodations around Tropea. For exact stops, ask the English-speaking staff at the **Pro Loco tourist office,** down V. Stazione at P. Ercole. (☎0963 61 475. Open daily 9:30am-1pm; Aug. 4:30-10pm.) **Banca Carime,** V. Stazione, has an **ATM** and an automatic currency-exchange machine (Open M-F 8:20am-1:20pm and 2:35-3:35pm.) In an **emergency,** call the **police** (☎113 or 0963 60 42 11) or the **Carabinieri** (☎112 or 0963 61 018). For medical emergencies, call **Pronto Soccorso** (☎0963 61 366). The **post office** is on C. Rigna. (☎0963 61 290. Open M-Sa 8:15am-7pm.) **Postal Code:** 89861.

🖬🖪 ACCOMMODATIONS AND FOOD. As long as you make reservations, staying in Tropea need not be expensive. The best deal in town is 🖼**Da Litto** (or **Hotel Hibiscus**) ❷, V. Carmine, 25. The road to the hotel is uphill along trafficked s-curves, but is also serviced by the blue buses. If you'd rather make the hike, exit the train station and walk down V. Stazione past the gas station at left. Turn right onto the angular V. degli Orti, then right onto V. Carmine. After the full s-curve of the road, follow the first driveway on the right; then follow the bright yellow signs. Each bungalow in the hotel's garden has a patio, kitchenette and TV. (☎ 0963 60 33 42 or 0339 332 15 35; www.tropea.it/deluca. Sept.-June €13; Summer €24.20-€33.) For camping right by the sea, try the tree-shaded **Campeggio Marina dell'Isola ❶**, on V. Marina dell'Isola at the bottom of the stairs that lead down to the beach. (Summer ☎ 0963 61 970; winter ☎ 0963 60 31 28; www.italiaabc.it/a/marinaisola. €4.50 per person in winter; €8.50 per person in summer. €2.50 extra per light and per car. Tents provided. Hot showers included. MC/V).

Tropea's sweet red onions spice up local dishes. **Ristorante Porta Vaticana ❸**, through the gate on V. Regina Margherita, serves up local specialties in an elegant indoor dining room. (☎ 0963 60 33 87; fax 66 96 80. Open Mar.-Oct., 9:30am-2:30pm, 6pm-12am.) With tables that flow into the small piazza of the three-headed fountain, the restaurant **Le Tre Fontane ❹** claims to have perfected the local dish *fileya alla tropeana*. Expect to pay between €18-20. Open Mar.-Oct. 12:30-3pm, 7pm-midnight. To dine on local fish with an ocean view, try **Pimm's Restaurant ❹**, Largo Migliarese (☎ 0963 66 61 05), next to the lookout at the end of C. Emanuele. The *alimentare* on V. Stazione in the center of town across from V. V. Veneto is great for grabbing snacks on the way to the beach.

⑥ SIGHTS. The gleaming **Santuaria di Santa Maria** presides over the white cliffs at the edge of town. In its isolated beauty, the church mirrors Tropea's character. Townsmen take the church's pink-clad *Madonna and Child* out to sea every August 15. Up the cliff is Tropea's graceful **Norman cathedral**. Besides some nice polychrome marble work and several dead sword-bearing Tropeans, the elegant interior houses two bombs that miraculously failed to destroy Tropea when an American warplane dropped them in 1943. To reach the **beach**, take a winding set of stairs down the cliffs at the end of V. Umberto (turn off V. Stazione to the left).

THE IONIAN COAST

From Reggio to Riace, the Ionian Coast offers miles of beaches. Ranging in type from white sand to rocks to dunes, the beaches cater to every taste and contrast the mountains visible in the distance. Though the ancient Greeks once made these shores as crowded as modern Tropea, the beaches are now frequented primarily by locals. Even the more established sites at **Bovalino Marina, Bianco**, and **Soverato** are largely unknown and waiting to be enjoyed. A train ride along the coast is a pleasant trip in itself. Since trains along the Ionian coast often have erratic schedules and multiple connections, allow ample time to reach your destination.

SICILY (SICILIA)

> Without Sicily, Italy cannot be fully understood. It is here one finds the key to all things.
> ——J.W. von Goethe

Sicily is a land of sensuous sunshine and sinister shadows. Ancient Greek influences lauded the golden island as the second home of the Gods; now eager tourists seek it as the home of *The Godfather*. While the *Cosa Nostra* does remain a presence in Sicilian life, it makes up only the smallest part of the vivacious and varied island's culture. The boiling sun has melted together the traditions, dialects, and architecture of the countless peoples who have coveted the island's beauty, creating a diverse society. Evidence of prehistoric, Carthaginian, Greek, Roman, Arab, Norman, Bourbon, and Aragonese eras are to be found in exquisite temples, local foods, hilltop castles, and dialects. On the whole, Sicily has very little to do with Italy; its physical separation from the mainland makes Sicilians' determined independence literal. The many volcanoes that cover Sicily and its lesser isles seem to echo the Sicilian character: timeless and beautiful, but prone to passionate volatility. The volcanoes are just one element of this exciting landscape. A 1000km coastline encompasses rocky shores, intriguing grottoes, impossible cliffs, and beaches whose sand ranges from pure white to dirty black. Inland, the view changes from a sea of turquoise waters to one of golden grain and craggy jutting cliffs to gentle whitecapped waves. Orchards of olive, citrus, and almond trees alternate with vineyards to produce some of Italy's sweetest culinary delights. The locals working the rich soil do so with love and skill, create a postcard image of a Sicily untouched by time. As Palermo and other cities illustrate, however, Sicily is hardly behind the times. Vespas, cell phones, chic boutiques, and high rises are as much a part of Sicilian life as the farms that lie just outside—and sometimes inside—the city limits. Sadly, modernization has had negative effects as well. As unemployment rises, petty crime and poverty mar the island's progress. Nevertheless, Sicily remains an extraordinary island, full of myth and mystery, traditions and history.

NORTHERN SICILY

PALERMO   ☎ 091

The largest city in Sicily, Palermo is like a concentrated version of the region's most potent wine. It retains the overall flavor, but is stronger and works faster on your poor, befuddled mind. A gritty urban environment with over a million inhabitants, the pace of life here dimspels any myth of a sleepy Sicily. Cars, buses, scooters, and horse-drawn carriages infest the streets day and night—except for Sundays, when the city is all but abandoned to baby strollers and roller skaters. Despite Sicilians' best attempts to make Palermo seem like a slightly run-down version of Berlin or Madrid, the city is still very much grounded in both its medieval and its more recent *Cosa Nostra* identities. The knotted tiny streets in the old sections wind past ancient ruins, Norman structures, and bombed-out buildings. The 1993 election of a publicly anti-Mafia mayor, however, brought an end to the mob's knee-bashing control. Much of Palermo backs the mayor's efforts, and with political clean-up underway, the city is now restoring its architectural treasures.

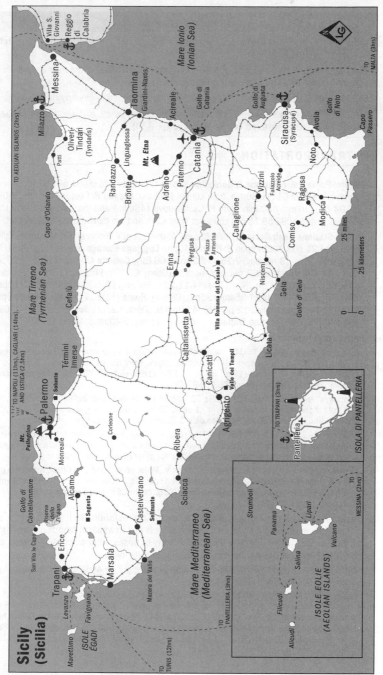

Sicily (Sicilia)

SICILY

TO NAPOLI (11hrs), CAGLIARI (14hrs), AND USTICA (2.5hrs)

TO AEOLIAN ISLANDS (2hrs)

NALIA (3hrs)

Mare Tirreno (Tyrrhenian Sea)

Mare Ionio (Ionian Sea)

Mare Mediterraneo (Mediterranean Sea)

Villa S. Giovanni
Reggio di Calabria
Messina
Milazzo
Oliveri Tindari (Tyndaris)
Patti
Capo d'Orlando
Randazzo
Bronte
Linguaglossa
Mt. Etna
Adrano
Paternò
Catania
Taormina
Giardini-Naxos
Acireale
Golfo di Catania
Golfo di Augusta
Golfo di Noto
Siracusa (Syracuse)
Avola
Capo Passero
Noto
Vizzini
Falazzolo Acreide
Ragusa
Modica
Comiso
Caltagirone
Piazza Armerina
Villa Romana del Casale
Niscemi
Gela
Golfo di Gela
Enna
Pergusa
Cefalù
Caltanissetta
Canicatti
Licata
Valle dei Templi
Agrigento
Termini Imerse
Solunto
Mt. Pellegrino
Palermo
Monreale
Corleone
Ribera
Sciacca
Castelvetrano
Selinunte
Mazara del Vallo
Marsala
Alcamo
Segesta
Erice
Trapani
San Vita lo Capo
Golfo di Castellammare
Riserva dello Zingaro
Levanzo
Favignana
Marettimo
ISOLE ÉGADI

TO TRAPANI (3hrs)
Pantelleria
ISOLA DI PANTELLERIA

Stromboli
Panarea
Filicudi
Alicudi
Salina
Lipari
Vulcano
ISOLE EOLIE (AEOLIAN ISLANDS)
TO MESSINA (2hrs)

TO PANTELLERIA (3hrs)
TO TUNIS (12hrs)

25 miles
25 kilometers

HIGHLIGHTS OF SICILY

VISIT Grecian glories at **Segesta, Selinunte, Syracuse,** and the world famous **Valle dei Tempii** (p. 679) in Agrigento.

VENTURE onto Sicily's many volcanoes: Stromboli and Vulcano of the Aeolian Islands, and the volatile **Mt. Etna,** Europe's tallest (p. 665).

ENJOY Enna (p. 666), the best all-around little medieval hilltop city anywhere.

APPLAUD Palermo's traditional puppet shows in local theaters and world-class performances in the newly-restored **Teatro Massimo** (p. 630).

▛ TRANSPORTATION

Flights: Punta Raisi/Falcone & Borsellino airport (domestic info ☎091 601 9250; international info ☎702 0111). 30min. from central Palermo. **Prestia & Comande** buses (☎091 58 04 57) run every 30 min. from P. Castelnuovo (45min.) and the central station (1hr., €4.65). Taxis (☎091 59 16 62) charge at least €30, and are parked outside the airport.

Trains: Stazione Centrale, in P. Giulio Cesare. At the foot of V. Roma and V. Maqueda. Ticket office (☎091 603 3088) open 6:45am-8:40pm. **Luggage storage** available (p. 625). To: **Agrigento** (2hr., 13 per day, 7:25am-8:25pm, €6.82); **Catania** (3½hr., 8:15am-2:20pm, €11.21); **Cefalù** (1hr., 23 per day, 4am-9:10pm, €3.62); **Firenze** (16hr., 3 per day, €46.66); **Messina** (3hr., 4am-9pm, €11.21); **Milan** (19½hr., 11am and 2:10pm, €49.63); **Milazzo** (2½hr., 7:55am-8:35pm, €8.99); **Rome** (11hr., 7 per day, 7:55am-9pm, €52.63); **Termini** (30min., 12 per day, 4:50am-9:10pm, €2.32); **Torino** (21hr., 11:20am and 1:35pm, €49.63); and **Trapani** (2½hr., 11 per day, 6:40am-8:40pm, €6.82).

Ferries and Hydrofoils:

Grimaldi Group (☎091 58 74 04). 100m before Tirrenia with the sea to your left. Luxury ships have gyms and discos. Office open M-F 8:30am-5:30pm. Ferry leaves at 2:15pm; Sa 9am-noon, 4:30pm. Ferries to **Livorno** (17hr.; Tu, Th, and Sa 11pm; *poltrona* €53.20-31.50) and **Genoa** (20hr., 6 per wk. M-Sa, *poltrona* €63.52-93.48).

Siremar, V. Francesco Crispi, 118 (☎091 58 24 03). On the last street before the waterfront, just in front of port. Ferries to **Ustica** (2½hr., 1 daily, €9.81). From July-Aug. Siremar also runs hydrofoils (1¼hr., 2 per day, €16.01). Open daily 8:30am-1pm and 4-6:30pm.

SNAV (☎091 33 33 33 or 611 8525). Off V. Francesco Crispi, inside the port gates; the office is at the far end of Stazione Marittima. Runs hydrofoils twice a day to the Aeolian Islands. All hydrofoils stop in **Lipari** and **Vulcano**; check schedule for other islands. More erratic in winter.

Tirrenia (☎091 602 1111), on the waterfront on V. Molo, off V. Francesco Crispi, within the port gates. Open M-F 8:30am-12:30pm and 3:30-8:45pm, Sa 3:30-8:45pm, Su 5-8:45pm. Ferries to **Naples** (10hr.; 8:45pm; armchair *poltrona* €38, cabin €55) and **Sardinia** (14hr.; Sa 7pm; *poltrona* €42, cabin €60).

Buses: All 4 lines run along V. Balsamo, by the train station. With your back to the tracks, turn right; exit with McDonald's on your left and newspaper stands on your right; V. Balsamo is straight ahead, hidden by an army of buses. After purchasing tickets, ask exactly where your bus will be arriving and find out its logo.

Cuffaro, V. Balsamo, 13 (☎091 616 1510). Opposite Segesta. To **Agrigento** (2½hr.; M-Sa 7 per day, Su 3 per day; €6.71).

Segesta, V. Balsamo, 14 (☎091 616 9039). Sometimes uses buses confusingly marked "Sicilbus," "EtnaTransport," or "Interbus." To: **Alcamo** (1hr.; M-F, 10 per day, 6:30am-8pm; Sa 8 per day, 6:30am-8pm; Su 2 per day, 11:30am-8pm; €4.65, €7.20 roundtrip); **Rome** (12hr.; from Politeama 6:30pm; from the station 6:45pm; €35, roundtrip €60.50); **Terrasini** (1hr.; M-Sa 6 per day, 6:30am-8pm; €2.50, €4.10 roundtrip); and **Trapani** (2hr.; M-F 26 per day, 6:30am-9pm; Sa every hr., Su 13 per day; €6.20).

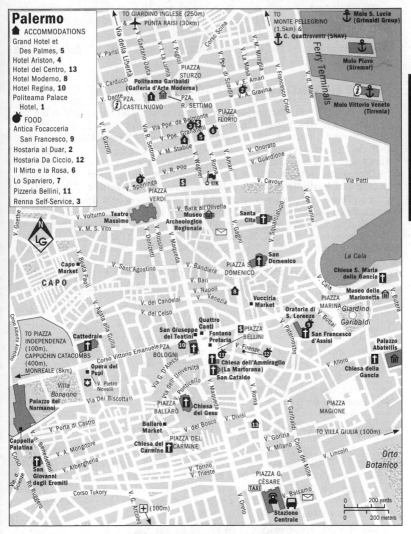

Palermo

ACCOMMODATIONS
Grand Hotel et
  Des Palmes, **5**
Hotel Ariston, **4**
Hotel del Centro, **13**
Hotel Moderno, **8**
Hotel Regina, **10**
Politeama Palace
  Hotel, **1**

FOOD
Antica Focacceria
  San Francesco, **9**
Hostaria al Duar, **2**
Hostaria Da Ciccio, **12**
Il Mirto e la Rosa, **6**
Lo Sparviero, **7**
Pizzeria Bellini, **11**
Renna Self-Service, **3**

SICILY

SAIS Transporti, V. Balsamo, 16 (☎091 617 1141). To **Corleone** (1¼hr.; 5 per day, 6am-6pm; €3.87).

SAIS, V. Balsamo, 16 (☎091 616 6028). On the right from the train station and just next door to SAIS Transporti. To: **Catania Airport** (3¼hr., 8 per day, €11.82); **Catania** (2½hr., every hr. M-Sa., 5am-8:30pm, €11.82); **Messina** (3¼hr.; M-Sa, every hr., 5am-8pm; Su every hr. 9am-7pm; €12.39); and **Piazza Armerina** (1½hr., 8 per day, 6:15am-8pm, €9.55).

Public Transportation: Orange **city buses (AMAT).** Main terminal in front of train station, under a dark green overhang. €0.77 for 1½hr., €2.58 per day. Buy tickets from any *tabacchi* or on-site mini offices. 17 **metropolitana** stations around the city are useful for getting to spots north or south of the **centro storico. Metro trains** to suburbs use normal train tracks. Catch trains at the central station. Ticket prices are the same as bus fares. Ask at one of the mini offices or info booths for a combined metro and bus map. Most bus stops are labeled and have route maps posted.

Taxis: Station office (☎ 091 616 2001); **Autoradio** (☎ 091 51 27 27); **Radio Taxi** (091 22 54 55); in front of the central station next to the bus stop.

✴ 🛈 ORIENTATION AND PRACTICAL INFORMATION

Palermo, Italy's 4th largest city, is Sicily's most urban. The newer half of the city follows a regular grid pattern, but the older sections to the south, near the train station, form a tangled knot. The **station** dominates **Piazza Giulio Cesare,** from which the city's two primary streets define Palermo's central axis. **Via Roma** begins directly across from the station and passes the **post office. Via Maqueda** is parallel to V. Roma and to the left from the front of the station. It runs to the Teatro Massimo and **Piazza Verdi,** where it becomes **Via Ruggero Settimo.** After 300m, it runs into **Piazza Castelnuovo (Politeama),** home to the tourist office and **Politeama Theater.** When Via Ruggero Settimo becomes the stylish **Via della Libertà,** it signals the beginning of the new city and leads to the **Giardino Inglese.** At **Quattro Canti, Via Vittorio Emanuele** intersects V. Maqueda, connecting **Piazza Independenza** to the sea. **Via Cavour** travels in the same direction from **Piazza Verdi** toward the port.

> ❗ **A CRASH COURSE IN SICILIAN STREET SMARTS.** Palermo shuts down at night and its streets are poorly lit. Knowing where to go and how to get there is essential, especially after dark. When possible, stay on the main streets of V. Roma, V. Maqueda, V. R. Settimo, V. della Libertá, or C. V. Emanuele—you may feel like the only pedestrian, but the stream of cars and scooters, which continues into the night, is reassuring. The areas behind the train station and around the port are particularly sketchy after shops close in the evening. Daylight hours are safer, but still be cautious—don't carry cameras around your neck or wear backpacks, flashy jewelry, or watches. Women should not carry purses slung sideways across the body. **Walk with a purposeful stride at all times and avoid openly consulting maps.**

TOURIST, LOCAL, AND FINANCIAL SERVICES

Tourist Office: P. Castelnuovo, 35 (☎ 091 605 8111; fax 58 27 88; wwww.palermotourism.com). Detailed maps and brochures. Ask for the monthly *Agenda.* Open M-F 8:30am-2pm and 2:30-6pm. 2 other **branches,** at the train station (☎ 091 616 5914) and airport (☎ 091 59 16 98; fax 652 5053). Airport office open daily 8:30am-midnight. Smaller info kiosks in small dark blue tents with maps scattered throughout the city, at most parks, and at the port.

Consulates: UK, V. C. Cavour, 117 (☎ 091 32 64 12). **US,** V. G.B. Vaccarini, 1 (☎ 091 30 58 57). Emergencies only. Open M-F 8am-12:30pm and 3-5pm.

Currency Exchange: *Cambio* at the central post office and train station. **Banca Nazionale del Lavoro,** V. Roma, 201, and **Banco di Sicilia,** on V. R. Settimo, both open M-F 8:20am-1:20pm. **ATMs** on V. Roma and V. Maqueda often reject international cards; **Bankomat 3-plus** ATMs are newer and more reliable.

American Express: G. Ruggieri and Figli Travel, V. E. Amari, 40 (☎ 091 58 71 44). From P. Castelnuovo (Politeama), follow V. E. Amari toward the water. Cashes traveler's cheques for cardholders only. Ask for the red city map "Palermo in your pocket." Open M-F 9am-1pm and 4-7pm, Sa 9am-1pm.

Luggage Storage: In the train station at the end of track #8. €2.58 per bag for 12hr. Open daily 6am-10pm.

English-Language Bookstore: Feltrinelli, V. Maqueda, 395 (☎091 58 77 85), a few blocks before Teatro Massimo from the train station. A selection of classics and mysteries on the 2nd fl. Open M-Sa 9am-8pm. **Mondadori,** on the corner of V. Roma and P. S. Domenico, adjacent to UPIM Department Store, on P. S. Domenico. 7 shelves of mystery, romance, classics, and sci-fi.

Gay and Lesbian Resource Center: ARCI-GAY and **ARCI-Lesbica,** V. Genova, 7 (☎091 33 56 88), off V. Roma. Info on events and clubs. Open M-F 5-7pm.

EMERGENCY AND COMMUNICATIONS

Carabinieri: ☎112. **State Police:** ☎113. **Fire Brigade:** ☎115. **Municipal Police:** ☎091 22 29 66.

First Aid: (☎118 or 091 666 2207), in Ospedale Civico.

Late-Night Pharmacy: Lo Cascio, V. Roma, 1 (☎091 616 2117). Look for a green cross near the train station. Open daily 4:30pm-8:30am. **Di Naro,** V. Roma, 207 (☎091 58 58 69), on the right after C. V. Emanuele. Open M-F 8:30am-1pm, 4-8pm. Frequent pharmacies throughout the city are marked by bright green lit crosses above the door. **Hospital: Policlinico Universitario,** V. del Vespro (☎091 655 1111), or **Ospedale Civico** (☎666 1111), on V. Lazzaro, near the train station.

Internet Access:

Mondadori Bookstore, V. Roma, on P. S. Domenico. 2 computers at €2.58 per 30min.

Nick Carter/Cr@zy Village, V. Roma, 182/188 (☎091 33 12 72), is a burger joint/Internet cafe with 2 computers. €5.16 per 30min., €5 per hr. Open after 3pm.

Navigando Internet Point, V. della Libertà, 73 (☎091 34 53 32), down V. della Libertà from the Politeama, on the right after Giardino Inglese and before V. Notarbartolo. 8 computers with medium connection. €3.10 per hr. Open M-Sa 10am-1am and Su afternoon.

Candelai (see **Insider's City,** p. 631) €4.13 per hr. Open F-Sa 7pm-late.

Post Office: V. Roma, 322 (☎091 160 or 695 9111). Massive white-columned building 5 blocks up V. Roma past V. E. Emanuele. Open M-Sa 8am-6:30pm. **Branch office** also at Central Station (☎091 617 5357), to the right of the station, beside the tracks. Open M-F 8am-6:30pm, Sa 8am-12:30pm.

Postal Code: 90100.

▐ ACCOMMODATIONS AND CAMPING

Palermo is packed with places to stay at all levels of price and luxury, though the two seldom have any discernible relationship; always ask to see the room before accepting. V. Roma and V. Maqueda have high concentrations of budget accommodations, but the neighborhoods near the train station are dangerous at night. Women should be especially cautious when staying in this area.

▨ **Hotel Regina,** C. V. Emanuele, 316 (☎091 611 4216; fax 612 2169), at the intersection of V. Maqueda and C. V. Emanuele, across from the larger Hotel Centrale. Central location beside the old city of Palermo easily accessible. Carved bureaus, ornate tables, light pine, and glass light fixtures adorn lengthy corridors at the top of worn marble staircases. All rooms with TV, fan, and free car-parking. Beach passes available. Singles €18, with bath €30; doubles €34/€44. ❷

▨ **Hotel del Centro,** V. Roma, 72 (☎091 617 0376; fax 617 3654; hoteldelcentro@libero.it; www.hoteldelcentro.it), 5 blocks up V. Roma from the station, on 2nd fl. Old-world-style rooms have stratospheric ceilings, classy curtains, and cream-colored details. Bath, A/C, and TV. Breakfast included. Singles €62; doubles €80. MC/V. ❺

Hotel Moderno, V. Roma, 276 (☎091 58 86 83 or 58 85 26; fax 58 86 83), at V. Napoli. Colorful rooms with bath, A/C, and TV. Bar and communal TV room. Singles €47; doubles €62; triples €83; quads €90. AmEx/MC/V. ❹

Hotel Ariston, V. M. Stabile, 139 (☎091 33 24 34). Take V. Roma 4 blocks past V. Cavour, or take bus #122 and get off before V. Amari. Hotel is in the middle of town between Teatro Massimo and the Politeama, 6 floors above small courtyard. Bright, modern rooms in impeccable minimalist style. All 7 rooms with bath, A/C, and TV. Singles €36-40; doubles €54-60. AmEx/DC/MC/V. ❹

Grand Hotel et Des Palmes, V. Roma, 398 (☎091 602 8111; fax 33 15 45; www.thi.it), on V. Roma between V. Pipe Granatelli and V. Stabile, in the heart of Palermo's *centro.* As its name implies, this hotel is pure elegance. Dining halls lit by chandeliers and large rooms complete with bath, A/C, and TV. Breakfast included. Singles €119; doubles €181. July and Aug. singles €111; doubles €168. AmEx/MC/V. ❺

Politeama Palace Hotel, P. R. Settimo, 15 (☎091 32 27 77; fax 611 1689; www.hotel-politeama.it), right beside the Politeama. In an enviable location on P. R. Settimo and P. Castelnuovo, this hotel offers every possible comfort in rooms with bath, A/C, TV, and Internet access. Breakfast included. Singles €124; doubles €181; triples €207. Half-pension: singles €145; doubles €222; triples €270. Full-pension: singles €163; doubles €258; triples €324. AmEx/MC/V. ❺

Camping: Campeggio dell'Ulivi, V. Pegaso, 25 (☎/fax 091 53 30 21), 35min. outside Palermo. Take bus #101 from Palermo's central station to P. de Gasperi; then take bus #628 to V. Sferracavallo. Walk downhill a block and turn right on V. dei Manderini just after the post office. Campground is on the right. Neurotically clean facilities with free hot showers. Bungalows available. €6.50 per person, tent included. ❶

🖸 FOOD

Palermo is famous for its *spaghetti ai broccoli affogati alla palermitana* (with spicy fried cauliflower), *pasta con le sarde* (with sardines and fennel), *pesce spada* (swordfish), and *rigatoni alla palermitana* (with meat and peas). *Arancini* (fried balls filled with rice, spinach, or meat) and *panini con panelle* (fried balls of chickpea flour) are also rich Sicilian delicacies. *Sfincione,* a thicker Sicilian version of pizza, is a hallmark of the Palermo New Year. Palermitans claim to have invented their own *cassata* (a sweet ricotta pastry), discovered *paste con gelo di melone* (pastries with watermelon-paste filling), and perfected *gelato.* The best restaurants in town are positioned between Teatro Massimo and Politeama. Palermo's bustling markets provide better budget opportunities than most supermarkets, and more interesting selections. **Ballarò** sprawls through the intricate streets behind V. Maqueda and C. V. Emanuele, while **Capo** covers the streets behind Teatro Massimo. **Vucciria** completes the trio in the area between C. V. Emanuele and P. S. Domenico. All three are open Monday through Saturday during daylight. Saturday mornings are the most chaotic.

🍽 **Lo Sparviero,** V. Sperlinga, 23 (☎/fax 091 33 11 63), 1 block toward P. Politeama from Teatro Massimo, off a small, private piazza. A local secret shrouded in antique interior, with cloudy brown glass walls and dark wood tables. Pizza from €3, *primi* from €6.50, *secondi* from €7. Cover €1; service fee 15%. Open Su-M 12:30-4pm and 7:15pm-midnight, Sa 12:30-4pm and 7:15pm-1am. AmEx/MC/V. ❸

🍽 **Antica Focacceria San Francesco,** V. A. Paternostro, 58 (☎091 32 02 64; fax 612 8855), in P. S. Francesco, across from the church. This *focacceria* and bar has been serving popular Palermo fare since 1834. On the counter sits an infamous bowl of *milza* (spleen); the brave can try it alone in a *panino,* or with maritata cheese (€1.55). Medum lunch about €12.50. Cover €1.03. Open daily 9am-midnight. AmEx/MC/V. ❸

■ **Pizzeria Bellini,** P. Bellini, 6 (☎091 616 5691), to the left of P. Pretoria in the shadow of the Teatro Bellini and the churches La Martorana and San Cataldo. With its location among the ancient beauties of Palermo and its comfortable outside tables, this restaurant is an ideal spot for a romantic meal. Pizza from €3.10, *primi* from €5.50, *secondi* from €8.50. Cover €1.50. Open W-M 6am-1am. AmEx/MC/V. ❸

Hostaria al Duar, V. Ammiraglio Gravina, 31 (☎0347 473 5744 or 347 701 7848). Off V. Roma, 3 blocks north toward the port. Terrific mingling of Sicilian and Arabic flavors. Complete meals €10.33. *Primi* from €4.13, *secondi* from €6.20. Cover €1.55. Open Tu-Su noon-3:30pm and 7pm-midnight. AmEx/MC/V. ❸

Il Mirto e la Rosa, V. Principe di Granatelli, 31/33 (☎091 32 43 53). Upscale vegetarian fare amid cathedral-like arches and 30-something *Palermitani*. Try *fettuccine al profumo d'estate* (in an aromatic sauce of tomatoes, pine nuts, peppers, garlic, and basil). *Primi* from €6, *secondi* from €5. Modest-sized fish and meat *secondi* €8-9. A tea room adds chamomile-tinged flavor. Open daily 12:30-3pm and 8-11pm. ❷

Hostaria Da Ciccio, V. Firenze, 6 (☎091 32 91 43; fax 602 3259), at V. Roma, 178. This small restaurant has been serving fresh Sicilian fare since 1938. Outdoor dining on the street. *Primi* from €5, *secondi* from €7. Cover €1.50. AmEx/MC/V. ❷

Renna Self-Service, V. Principe di Granatelli, 29 a/b/c (☎091 58 06 61; fax 611 6756; rennass@tin.it). Fast-food joint as crowded as a high school cafeteria. The only difference is the food—Renna doesn't skimp on taste or portions. *Primi* from €1.81, *secondi* from €3.10. Open daily noon-3:30pm and 7-10pm. AmEx/MC/V. ❶

⊙ SIGHTS

Ancient glory, seven centuries of neglect, and heavy World War II bombing have made Palermo a city of both splendor and deterioration—the beauty of the past hides behind the face of urban blight. The bizarre sight of Palermo's half-crumbled, soot-blackened 16th-century *palazzi* startles visitors accustomed to the cleaner historic districts of northern Italy. For much of the 20th century, corrupt politicians and Mafia activity diverted funds and attention from the dilapidated landmarks. In the past several years, however, cleaning and rebuilding efforts have slowly begun to reopen sights such as the magnificent Teatro Massimo.

■ **MONREALE.** Palermo's greatest treasure actually rests 8km outside of the city. The exterior of the extraordinary **Monreale Cathedral** is an example of the Sicilian take on Norman architecture, mixing Arabic and local styles on the northern template. The interior, however, is a complete original. The cathedral's walls glisten with 6340 square meters of golden mosaics, the largest display of Byzantine religious art outside the Hagia Sofia. The series of 130 panels depict the massive **Christ Pantocrator** (Ruler of All) over the main altar, the mystical flavor of the locale emphasized by the minimal light from the cathedral's small windows. Every few minutes, someone pays the €1 necessary to activate electric lighting in a portion of the church; the sudden illumination never fails to startle.

I'VE HAD IT UP TO HERE. With one arm outstretched, Carlo V presides over Piazza Bologni. This statue of the 5th Emperor of the Holy Roman Empire and King of Spain and Sicily was erected in the mid-16th century to commemorate his visit to Palermo. The official story is that the statue captures him in the act of pledging allegiance over Sicily's constitution—hence the extended arm. *Palermitani*, however, have their own ideas. One local interpretation has the king exclaiming, "To survive in Palermo, one needs a mountain of money this high!" Another expresses the citizens' discontent with the city council: "The garbage of Palermo comes up to here!"

SICILY

LA FAMIGLIA

Powerful because people owed them favors, strong because they supported one another, and feared because they did not hesitate to kill offenders, the Sicilian Mafia founded a brutal tradition that has dominated life since the late 19th century. The Mafia system has its roots in the *latifondi* (agricultural estates) of rural Sicily, where land managers and salaried militiamen protected their turf and people. Today, Sicilians shy away from the topic, referring to the Mafia as *Cosa Nostra* (Our Thing).

At a grass-roots level, the Mafia is said to have long controlled public works infrastructure, and farmers for years have lived in fear of land seizure and extortion. The Mafia was reported to have capitalized upon a drought in the summer of 2002 by stealing water from private wells and public water systems. Recent local resistance includes a farmers' group, Libera, that sells what it calls "anti-Mafia pasta," made from wheat grown on land seized from the Mafia by the government. Another jailed Mafia don's estate has been converted to a cooperative olive oil production site.

Since the mid-80s, Italian government efforts to curtail Mafia influence have met with some success. Dozens of members of Mafia strongholds like the Corleone, mythologized by *The Godfather* films, have been arrested, and in August 2002, Palermo police confiscated an estimated 500 million euros in Mafia property.

From the side entrance, visitors face the beginning of Genesis at the upper left of the central aisle. The two-tiered Old Testament narrative continues clockwise with images of Adam and Eve. *(Bus #389 leaves from Palermo's P. Independenza for Monreale's P. V. Emanuele (40min., 3 per hr., €0.77). To get to P. Independenza, take bus #109 or 318 from Palermo's Stazione Centrale. Tourist info (☎ 091 640 4413) to left of church. Cathedral open daily 8am-6pm. Treasury open daily 9:30am-noon, 3:30-5:30pm. €2.07. Modest dress required.)*

Beside the cathedral, the quiet, light-flooded **cloisters** offer a contrast to the solemn shadows of the cathedral. Though seemingly empty, this courtyard contains one of the best and most unusual collections of Sicilian sculpture. Alternately plain and inlaid with Arabic tiles, 228 paired columns ring the interior. Each capital is unique, constructed alternately in Greco-Roman, Islamic, Norman, Romanesque, and Gothic styles. In the corner near the lesser colonnade and its fountain, a capital shows William II offering the Cathedral of Monreale to the Virgin. A balcony along the cathedral's apse looks over the cloisters and beyond to all of Palermo. Two doors down from the cloister is the entrance to a series of quiet **gardens** that survey Palermo. *(Cloister open M-Sa 9am-7pm, Su 9am-1pm. €4.13, students €2.07. Roof access €1.55.)*

■ **CAPPELLA PALATINA.** This chapel, in the monstrous conglomerate **Palazzo dei Normanni,** houses a smaller and more local version of the mosaics at Monreale. Norman kings imported artists from Constantinople to cover every inch of the interior with continuing colors of gold, glass, wood carvings, and sculpture. Many Palermitans and their city pride claim to prefer this local treasure to that of Monreale, citing this Christ Pantocrator as being softer and more compassionate. Local Arab craftsmen created the artful wooden ceilings and the geometric designs on the walls. Upstairs, guards lead tours through the **Sala di Ruggero** (King Roger's Hall). *(Follow C. V. Emanuele all the way up to Palazzo dei Normanni; entrance on the far right from P. Independenza. ☎ 091 705 4879. Chapel open M-F 9-11:45am and 3-4:45pm, Sa 9-11:45am, Su 9-9:45am and noon-12:45pm. Closed Easter M. Tours run M, F, and Sa 9am-noon; other days by arrangement only. Call ahead.)*

■ **CAPPUCHIN CATACOMBS.** The set of a horror movie or the backstage of the most macabre puppet show in history? These murky subterranean chambers plunge skull-first into the grotesque and theatrical. Over the course of 350 years, the friars of the Cappuchin order preserved the remains of over 8000 bodies. Attached to wall niches by wires and nails;

grimacing, sneering skeletons in varying degrees of decomposition scream silently at visitors. The bodies are dressed in their finest clothes and sorted by sex and profession. The highlight of this grim collection is the remains of a young girl, Rosalia, in a glass box. Alarmingy well-preserved, the child appears to be merely sleeping, as if she could awake at any moment. Several bishops and the painter Velázquez also inhabit these corridors. *(Take bus #109 or #318 from Stazione Centrale to P. Indipendenza. From there hop on #327 to catacombs. P. Cappuccini. ☎091 21 21 17. Open daily 9am-noon and 3-5:30pm. €1.50.)*

TEATRO MASSIMO. Constructed between 1875 and 1897 in a robust Neoclassical style, the **Teatro Massimo** is the largest indoor stage in Europe after the Paris Opera House. After undergoing a 30 year renovation, the theater reopened in grand Sicilian style (with trumpets and confetti) for its 100th birthday in 1997. Word on the street is that the long restoration was not a question of artistry but of Mafia feuding. Cleaned, polished, and shined, the exterior has now regained its light sandcastle-colored appearance, and the interior its former gleam. It was here that Francis Ford Coppola shot the climactic opera scene in *The Godfather Part III*. Operas, plays, and ballets are performed throughout the year. The **Festival della Verdura** (late June to mid-Aug.) brings famous international performers for one or two night shows. During this period, however, shows are transferred from the Massimo to nearby Villa Castelnuova. *(Across V. Maqueda from the Museo Archeologico, 500m up V. Maqueda from the Quattro Canti intersection with C. V. Emanuele. Toll free ☎800 65 58 58; box office ☎091 605 3515. Open Tu-Su 10am–5:30pm for 20min. tours in English, French, and German. Under 18 or over 65 €1.55. Admittance prohibited during rehearsals.)*

PALERMO'S CATHEDRAL. Legend has it that the kings of Palermo and Monreale had a contest to see who could construct the most beautiful church. While Palermo's cathedral is breathtaking from the outside, the Monreale's interior caused Palermo's king to bow down in worship and defeat. Continually renovated from the 13th through the 18th century, the cathedral's enormous exterior shows the resultant stylistic clash. Arabic columns, Norman turrets, and an 18th-century dome crowd the facade and walls. Note the inscription from the Qu'ran on the first left column before the entrance; in 1185 the Palermitan archbishop chose to plunk his cathedral down on top of a mosque, and this column was part of its stonework. The *cattedrale* is connected by flying buttresses to the former **archbishop's palace** (1460), larger and more opulent than the church itself. *(On C. V. Emanuele. ☎091 33 43 76. Open daily 9:30am-5:30pm. Closed Su mornings and during liturgy. Treasury and crypt open M-Sa 9:30am-6:30pm. €1.55.)*

QUATTRO CANTI AND LA FONTANA PRETORIA (THE FOUNTAIN OF SHAME). The intersection of V. Maqueda and C. V. Emanuele forms the Quattro Canti (the four corners). Each sculpted angle of this little 17th-century piazza contains the statue of a season on the lower level, of a king of Spain (and thus, of the region) on the middle level, and of one of the city's patron saints on the top level. Covered in soot and smog for decades, the sculptural works are now benefitting from Palermo's city-wide restoration. Large posted drawings give a picture of what lies beneath the scaffolding. Piazza Pretoria, down V. Maqueda, houses the oversized Fontana della Vergogna (Fountain of Shame) under Teatro Bellini. The statue-bedecked fountain was given its name by irate churchgoers who didn't like staring at mythological monsters and nude figures as they left Chiesa di San Giuseppe dei Teatini (1612), across the street. An even more shameful story explains its inappropriate size—the Fountain of Shame was not intended for the small piazza. In the early 16th century, a rich Florentine commissioned the fountain for his villa, sending a son to the Carrara marble quarries to ensure its safe delivery. The son, in need of quick cash, sold the fountain to the Palermo senate and shipped it to Sicily. Due to restoration and previous acts of vandalism the fountain is disappointingly surrounded by a wooden blockade—visitors must gaze at the nude figures through clear windows. *(630m down V. Maqueda from the train station.)*

MUSEO ARCHEOLOGICO REGIONALE. Housed at a quiet *palazzo* in the center of town, this museum features an impressive collection of Sicilian archeological treasures. The collection has several fine Greek and Roman works (including a large section of the Punic Temple of Himera) whose grinning lion heads stick out their tongues in celebration of a victory over Greece, and the Greek *Ram of Syracuse* (3rd century BC), notable for its realistic sneer. The top floor features prehistoric cave carvings, and large Roman mosaic floors. *(Head away from the train station on V. Roma, and turn left onto V. Bara all'Olivella across from Teatro Massimo. P. Olivella, 24. ☎ 091 611 6805 or 611 0740. Open M-Sa 9am-1:45pm and 9am-1pm; T, W, and F also 3-6:30pm. €4.13, students €2, under 18 or over 65 free.)*

PALAZZO ABATELLIS. Signs in P. Marina point toward this 15th-century *palazzo* (1495), which houses one of Sicily's best art museums, the **Galleria Regionale della Sicilia.** Dozens of religious panel paintings and sculptures from the Middle Ages through to the Baroque period culminate with Antonello da Messina's unusual *Annunciation.* The massive and morbid fresco *The Triumph of Death* merits a room of its own on the lower level. *(V. Alloro, 4. From P. G. Cesare in front of train station, take V. Abramo Lincoln, then go left for 2 blocks on V. N. Cervello. ☎ 091 623 0011. Open W, F, and M 9am-1pm, T and Th 9am-1pm and 3-7:30pm. Ticket counter closes 30min. before museum. €4, under 18 or over 65 free. Student discount available.)*

CHIESA DEL GESÙ (CASA PROFESSA). V. Ponticello winds through a crowded neighborhood to this stucco church (1363-1564), crowned by a green mosaic dome. Nicknamed Il Gesù, the church has a dazzling multicolored marble interior and surrealist depiction of the Last Judgment. World War II bombing scarred its courtyard and the neighboring **Quartiere dell'Albergheria,** which droops with ruined buildings and bomb-blackened facades. *(In P. Casa Professa, on V. Ponticello, across V. Maqueda. Open M-Sa 7:30-11:30am and 5-6:30pm, Su 7am-12:30pm. No visits during mass.)*

OTHER CHURCHES. The famous **Santa Maria dell'Ammiraglio** ("La Martorana") was built for an admiral of Norman King Roger II. The Byzantine mosaics inside are the 12th-century equivalent of celebrity photos: Roger I stands with Jesus, and Admiral George admires the Mother of God. *(P. Bellini, a few steps from P. Pretoria. ☎ 091 616 1692. Open M-Sa 8am-1pm and 3:30-5:30pm, Su 8:30am-1pm.)* Next door lies the smaller **Chiesa di San Cataldo** (1154), whose red domes and arches liken it to a mosque. *(Open M-F 9am-3:30pm, Sa 9am-12:30pm, Su 9am-1pm.)* Perhaps the most romantic spot in Palermo, the garden and cloister of the **Chiesa di San Giovanni degli Eremiti** (St. John of the Hermits) comes complete with fanciful bulbous pink domes designed by Arab architects. Gazebos and little fountains dot this vine-wreathed paradise. *(V. dei Benedettini, 3. Walk west from the train station on C. Tukory to Porta Montalto and take a right. Open M-Sa 9am-7pm, Su 9am-1pm. €4.)*

PUPPETS. There are no small parts, only small actors. For 300 years, Sicilian-made puppets have taken the main stage at the **Museo Internazionale delle Marionette,** offering a playful glimpse at Sicilian stage culture. Viewing galleries also display puppets from India, Africa, Burma, China, Thailand, France, and Britain. *(V. Butera, 1. Follow signs from P. Marina. ☎ 091 32 80 60; fax 32 82 76. Open M-F 9am-1pm and 4-7pm. Closed in Aug. €2.58, under 14 or over 65 €1.55. Demonstrations on request.)* Catch an authentic Palermo puppet show at Vincenzo Argenti's **Opera dei Pupi.** Three-foot tall armored puppets whale away at each other, fight dragons, behead Saracens, and reenact scenes from the chivalric romance of *Orlando Furioso*. (V. P. Novelli, 1. ☎ 091 611 3680. Shows daily 6pm. Min. audience of 15 required. €7.75.)

GARDENS. Relief from Palermo's dense urban environment is found in the fresh air of the city's gardens and parks. The large and refined **Giardino Inglese** off V. della Libertà harbors many a picnicker under its shady palms and marble busts. During the summer, the park hosts free concerts. Down C. V. Emanuele toward the port, **Giardino Garibaldi** features several enormous and strange banyan trees, whose limbs and roots seem to drip down from leaf to land. The large **Villa Giulia,** at the end of V. Lincoln from the station, is a Parisian-style park with white sand pathways, meticulous flower beds, and large fountains. (All open daily 8am-8pm.)

🎨 🎷 BEACHES AND ENTERTAINMENT

As part of Palermo's recent attempts to better its tourism, the city has established **Mondello Lido** as a free, tourist-only beach. All registered hotels have tickets for guests, which are good for the day and must be shown at the beach entrance. Otherwise, beach-goers must pay €8 to set up camp in the area near the Charleston (or sit for free directly on the shoreline). Palermo packs buses every weekend to seaside **Mondello,** a beach by day and playground of clubs and bars by night. Take bus #101 or #102 from the station to reach the Politeama and V. della Libertà, and then bus #806 in the same direction to reach Mondello (after going through the tree-filled area known as "La Favorita," you will reach the beach). On the beach, watch for the frequent vendors that walk up and down the sand with all types of goodies. *Ciambelle* (donuts caked in sugar; €1) are not to be missed. Palermo's nightlife centers around bars that are hard to find and even harder to stagger home from. For information on cultural events and nightlife, pick up a copy of *Un Mese a Palermo,* a monthly brochure available at any APT office, or the far-from-redundant *News-News.* **Fuso Orario** (☎ 091 32 03 56), in P. Olivella, 2, and **Champagneria,** a block from the Teatro Massimo, are home to the mob of young *Palermitani* that floods the street opposite Teatro Massimo every weekend night. **I Candelai,** V. Candelai, 65, tends to pick up around midnight. It has one of central Palermo's few dance floors, with live, mainstream rock. The place is usually packed, so arrive early for time on Candelai's three net-connected computers. (☎ 091 32 71 51; www.candelai.it. Open F-Su 7pm-late.) For more on nightlife, see **The Insider's City.**

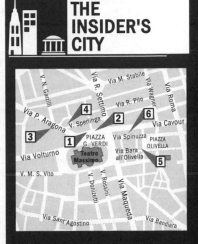

NIGHTLIFE OF THE TEATRO MASSIMO

As night falls, the majestic Teatro Massimo illuminates the surrounding area and sidestreets, bringing to life a host of restaurants and bars open until 1 or 2 am. As always, when venturing out of the well-lit and populated Massimo area, make sure to stay on main streets, especially when nearing the train station neighborhood.

1. Dine in the shadow of the Massimo at **Ristorante al 59** (☎ 091 58 31 39).

2. Indulge your sweet tooth at **Caffé Opera** (☎ 091 33 28 36).

3. Scarf down crêpes at **Torquemada** (☎ 091 32 88 29).

4. Ogle expert pizza chefs at **La Taverna di John** (☎ 091 33 46 78).

5. Munch kebab sandwiches (€3.10) on the heavily frequented Piazza Olivella at **Onifur.** Continue down for small, popular pubs.

6. Down shots of neon alcohol in test tubes (€1) at **Aboriginal Internet C@fe** (☎ 091 662 2229). Check your email—if you can remember how to type.

Finish the night crooning Italian vocals in the quiet piazza at **Havana's** outdoor tables (☎ 091 32 06 08), in P. S. Onofrio. Follow tiny Vicolo dei Fiovenchi off V. Maqueda, just opposite the intersection of V. Maqueda and V. Bari. The crowd is older and more sedate than those in many of Palermo's other bars.

🔰 DAYTRIPS FROM PALERMO: M. PELLEGRINO AND USTICA

🔳**Monte Pellegrino,** an isolated mass of limestone rising from the sea, is Palermo's principal natural landmark, separating the city from the beach at Mondello. Near its peak, the **Santuario di Santa Rosalia** marks the site where Rosalia, a young girl, sought escape from a planned marriage and wandered into ascetic seclusion. After dying there, she appeared in an apparition to a woodsman many years later, and told him to carry her bones throughout the city in a procession. The procession is believed to have brought an end to the raging plague that was destroying the city. The real bones of Rosalia, the patron saint of Palermo, can be found in Palermo's cathedral, and are paraded around the city every year on July 15. (*Monte Pellegrino.* ☎ *091 54 03 26. Open daily 7am-7pm. Take bus #812 from P. Castelnuovo*). The volcanic island of **Ustica** lies 36 miles off the coast. Settled first by the Phoenicians, then by pirates and exiled convicts, it offers prime snorkeling and grotto exploration. **Siremar** runs ferries and hydrofoils to Ustica (see **Ferries,** p. 622).

CEFALÙ   ☎ 0921

Dominated by its grand duomo, Cefalù is a labyrinth of cobblestone streets curling around the base of Rocca, an enormous stone promontory. The city's love for the sea draws its aging terra-cotta and stone buildings right up to the water's edge and its people to the social *lungomare* (beaches). The Sicilian proverb "good wine comes in small bottles" captures the timeless nature of little Cefalù, whose paradisal qualities were featured in the Academy Award-winning film *Cinema Paradiso.* Be warned: Cefalù's charms do not come cheaply. The city's reputation as a beach resort and its close proximity to Palermo allow *pensioni* to charge what they please.

▐ TRANSPORTATION

Trains: At P. Stazione, 1 (☎ 0921 42 11 69). From the intersection of V. Roma, V. Mazzini, and V. Matteotti, take V. A. Moro. Station is 3 blocks up on the left. Station open daily 4:30am-11:30pm. Ticket counter open daily 7:05am-8:50pm. AmEx/DC/MC/V. To: **Messina** (3hr., 11 per day, 4:45am-9:50pm, €7.80); **Milazzo** (2hr., 7 per day, €6.15); **Palermo** (1hr., 30 per day, 5:13am-10:20pm, €3.60); and **S. Agata di Militello** (50 min., 13 per day, 7:03am-9:50pm, €3.20).

Buses: Spisa buses run from the train station and the waterfront P. Colombo to 26 local towns (€1). Schedules posted in station bar's window and tourist office.

Taxis: Kefautoservizi, in P. Stazione (☎ 0921 42 25 54), near P. Colombo, or in P. del Duomo (☎ 0921 42 11 78).

▰ 🔃 ORIENTATION AND PRACTICAL INFORMATION

From the station, **Via Aldo Moro** curves downhill to the city's biggest intersection. To the left, **Via Roma** cuts through the center of the new city. Straight and to the left, **Via Matteotti** leads into the **old city,** changing at **Piazza Garibaldi** into **Corso Ruggero. Via Cavour,** across the intersection from V. A. Moro, turns to the *lungomare.*

Tourist Office: C. Ruggero, 77 (☎ 0921 42 10 50; fax 42 23 86), in the old city. English-speaking staff has a vast supply of brochures, maps, hotel listings, and schedules. In summer, open M-Sa 8am-2:30pm and 3:30-8pm, Su 9am-1:30pm.

Currency Exchange: Banca S. Angelo (☎ 0921 42 39 22), near the station at the corner of V. Giglio and V. Roma. Open M-F 8:30am-1:30pm and 2:45-3:45pm. The **ATM** at the **Banca di Sicilia** (☎ 0921 42 11 03 or 42 28 90), in P. Garibaldi, has 24hr. access.

Carabinieri: ☎ 112. **Municipal Police:** ☎ 0921 42 01 04.

First Aid: ☎ 0921 42 45 44. **Guardia Medica:** V. Roma, 15 (☎ 0921 42 36 23), in a modern yellow building in the new city, behind an iron fence. Open daily 8am-8pm.

Late-Night Pharmacies: Dr. V. Battaglia, V. Roma, 13 (☎ 0921 42 17 89), in the new city. Open M-Sa 9am-1pm and 4-8pm. MC/V. **Cirincione,** C. Ruggero, 144 (☎ 0921 42 12 09). Open M-F 9am-1pm and 4-8pm. Call ahead in Aug.

Hospital: V. A. Moro (☎ 0921 92 01 11), at the intersection with V. Matteotti.

Internet Access: Kefaonline, P. S. Francesco, 1 (☎ 0921 92 30 91), where V. Umberto meets V. Mazzini. €5 per hr. Open M-Sa 9:30am-1:30pm and 3:30-7:30pm. **Bacco On-Line,** C. Ruggero, 38 (☎ 0921 42 17 53), across from the tourist office. Wine store has 2 IBM computers in back. Would you like red, white, or rosé with your email? Slow connection gives time to decide. €2.58 per 30min. Open daily 9am-midnight.

Post Office: V. Vazzana, 2 (☎ 0921 42 15 28). In a modern concrete building on the right off the *lungomare*, 2 long blocks down from P. Colombo. Open M-F 8am-6:30pm, Sa 8am-12:30pm.

Postal Code: 90015.

ACCOMMODATIONS AND CAMPING

Cangelosi Rosaria, V. Umberto I, 26 (☎ 0921 42 15 91), off P. Garibaldi. The best deal in the city. Private residence has 4 large, simply furnished rooms just off a dining room with shared fridge and TV. Separate sex communal baths. Reserve ahead. Single €20; doubles €36.15. ❷

Hotel Mediterraneo, V. A. Gramsci, 2 (☎/fax 0921 92 26 06 or 92 25 73), 1 block left when exiting the station. 13 well-furnished rooms boast heavenly beds, A/C, TV, and sparkling baths with hairdryers. Breakfast buffet included. Singles €44-73; doubles €62-104; triples €75-135; quads €86-156. ❹

Hotel Riva del Sole, V. Lungomare, 25 (☎ 0921 42 12 30; fax 42 19 84). This classy waterfront hotel provides easy beach access and a gorgeous view. *Discoteca,* bar and garden. 28 rooms with A/C. Half-pension €85.50; full-pension €96. 10% less in winter. AmEx/MC/V. ❺

Camping: Costa Ponente (☎ 0921 42 00 85; fax 42 44 92), 3½km west of Cefalù at Contrada Ogliastrillo. 45min. walk or short ride on Cefalù-Lascari bus (€1) from P. Colombo. Swimming pool and tennis court. Hot showers free. Sept.-June €5.50 per person, €4.50 per tent, €3.50 per car; July-Aug. €6 per person, €5 per tent, €4 per car. ❶

FOOD

Several affordable *trattorie* in the old city beckon the hungry with sizzling Sicilian scents. Prices increase in the new city, however, and some appealing restaurants on the *lungomare* feature prices that are clearly a result of the view. Just off the *lungomare*, next door to the post office on V. Vazzana, a **MaxiSidis** supermarket sells all the basics. (☎ 0921 42 45 00. Open M-Sa 8am-6:30pm.)

Osteria la Botte, V. Veterani, 6 (☎0921 42 43 15), off C. Ruggero, 2 blocks past P. Duomo. Intimate interior and candlelit exterior whisper of romance and history. Leather-bound menus overflow with *primi* and *secondi* (from €6), but try the delicious house special *Casarecce alla Botte* (traditional Sicilian pasta with meat sauce; €5.16). Cover €1. Open Tu-Su 12:30-3pm and 7-11:30pm. AmEx/DC/MC/V. ❷

L'Arca di Noé, V. Vazzana, 7/8 (☎0921 92 18 73), across from the post office. Crowded wooden booths docked among nautical maps, anchors, and ropes fill half of this popular nightspot, while a fully stocked bar and *gelateria* serve those on the run. Pizza from €3.50. Also offers Internet access. Open M-Sa 6am-5am. AmEx/MC/V. ❶

Pasticceria-Gelateria Serio Pietro, V. G. Giglio, 29 (☎0921 42 22 93), a well-advertised 1st left from the train station when heading into town. 30 flavors of *gelato*, a dozen cakes, and piles of cookies make this sleek bar a palace of delights equal to the magnificent marzipan duomo on display. Marzipan €18 per kg. Open Sept.-July daily 7am-1pm and 3-9:30pm, Aug. 7am-10pm. ❸

Al Porticciolo, V. di Bordonaro, 66 (☎0921 92 19 81), off C. Ruggero, near the duomo. 2 locations on V. Bordonaro serve up unique seafood dishes. Pizza from €3.50, *primi* from €4, *secondi* from €7. Open Th-Tu noon-3pm and 7pm-midnight. AmEx/MC/V. ❷

Ristorante-Pizzeria Trappitu, V. di Bordonaro, 96 (☎0921 92 19 72), near the water. Paintings and artifacts line the walls of this museum-like restaurant. An impressive wine list enhances the typical Sicilian menu. Excellent sea view on terrace. *Primi* from €6, *secondi* from €10. Open daily 7:30pm-midnight. AmEx/MC/V. ❷

Al Gabbiano, V. Lungomare G. Giardina, 17 (☎0921 42 14 95), along the lungomare. This breezy restaurant-*pizzeria* sits right on the water. Outdoor patio. *Primi* from €5, *secondi* from €8. Open Th-Tu noon-3pm. AmEx/MC/V. ❷

👁 🏖 SIGHTS AND BEACHES

DUOMO. The grand duomo appears suddenly to those traveling the city's narrow streets. This dramatic off-white structure combines Arabic, Norman, and Byzantine architectural styles, a result of the diverse craftsmen King Roger II hired for its construction in AD 1131. Legend has it that the king promised to build a great monument to the Savior if he lived through a terrible shipwreck. Once a potential fortress, with crenellated towers and firing outposts, it now only protects the king's body. The duomo's more famous contents, are the enormous Byzantine mosaics covering the apse. The great **Christ Pantocrator** surveys with glistening calm all who enter. *(Open daily 8am-noon and 3:30-7:30pm. Modest dress required.)*

MUSEO MANDRALISCA. Stuffed alligator cases and ancient vases are presented with equal flourish in this museum, the chaotic collection of local Baron Mandralisca, who once lived here and who bequeathed his collection to the city. The 19th-century connoisseur amassed an impressive array of medieval and early Renaissance Sicilian paintings by anonymous artists, many of which are undergoing restoration. For every good painting, however, there are a few hundred seashells, a shelf of old books, and a half-dozen lamps of questionable taste. A 4th-century BC Greek *krater* showing a cartoon-like tuna vendor merits attention, but the collection's centerpiece is the **Ritratto di Ignoto** (Portrait of an Unknown) by Sicilian master Antonello da Messina. The image is inescapable in Cefalù, smirking at tourists from every postcard rack and hotel wall, but the real thing is surprisingly fresh and lively. *(V. Mandralisca, 13, opposite the duomo. ☎0921 42 15 47. Open Sept.-June 9am-7pm; July-Aug. 9am-9pm. €4.15, €2.50 per person for groups of 10 or more.)*

STICKS AND STONES MAY BREAK MY BONES, BUT WHIPS AND CHAINS EXCITE ME.

As the home of the mythical giant Gargantua, Cefalù has a history of monstrous associations. Perhaps this is why the notorious English occultist and sadist Aleister Crowley (rhymes with "holy") chose to found his new "abbey" (nicknamed Thelema) here in 1920. "Do what thou wilt shall be the whole of the law" was the motto of Crowley and his followers. It was in Cefalù that the "magician," or the "Purple Sacerdote," as he liked to be called, practiced his particular flavor of sexual occultism. "All [sexual] acts are allowed, if they injure not others; approved, if they injure not self," he proclaimed from Cefalù. When one of Crowley's students died in the 1920s, his widow claimed that her husband's death was caused by drinking cat's blood during a Black Mass in Thelema. Crowley and his followers were expelled from Italy in 1923. Thelema is known among students of the occult for the grotesque, demonic frescoes that cover its walls. Though the site was closed in summer 2002, the regional department of Cultural Resources promises to restore and reopen the abbey soon.

ROCCA. The massive cliffs above Cefalù have always stood at the center of the city's history. They now offer extraordinary vistas and serene ruins. Medieval walls from long-abandoned fortifications lace the edges, while crumbling cisterns and ovens line forgotten avenues. Ancient foundations cluster under trees and lead to the monolithic **Tempio di Diana** (Temple of Diana). The nimble huntress's temple, surrounded by pines and overlooking the city and the sea, was used first as a place of sea worship and later as a defensive outpost. Morning is the best time for pictures, when the sun's direction does not dull the vivid colors of the city below. *(Accessible by the Salità Saraceni, a 30min. hike up the side. From P. Garibaldi, follow the signs for "Pedonale Rocca" from between the fountain and the Banco di Sicilia. Use caution, as the volcanic rock path is quite slippery when wet. Gates close 1hr. before sunset.)*

BEACHES. Cefalù's most attractive beaches, **Spiaggia Mazzaforno** and **Spiaggia Settefrati**, lie west of town on Spisa's Cefalù-Lascari bus line. Popular **Spiaggia Attrezzata** lies just off the *lungomare*. Crowded for good reason, the beach has white sand, turquoise shallows, and free showers. At the beach in Cefalù, seven stones jut out from the waves said to have been placed in memory of seven brothers who died here while trying to save their sister from pirates.

▶ DAYTRIP FROM CEFALÙ: THE RUINS OF TYNDARIS

Tyndaris is a popular destination, but difficult to reach without private transportation. You must arrive through Patti or Oliveri. Buses to Tyndaris leave from P. Marconi in Patti (20min., M-Sa 6 per day, 6:30am-1:30pm.) To reach Patti, take the train from Cefalù (13 per day; 4:50am-9:38pm; €4.65, express €6.20). Buses also leave from Oliveri (1 daily M-Sa, 9:55am) and return to Oliveri at 12:05pm. Reach Oliveri from Cefalù by train (1¾hr.; 5 per day; 4:50-4:46pm; €5.73, express €7.28). Tourist office in Patti, P. G. Marconi, 11, ☎ 0941 24 62 18. Office is also at the site, V. Teatro Greco, 15. ☎ 0941 36 91 84. Both have maps, brochures about Tyndaris and performance information. Ruins open daily 9am-1hr. before sunset. €2, students €1. Santuario (☎ 0941 36 90 03) open M-F 6:45am-12:30pm and 2:30-7pm, Sa-Su 6:45am-12:30pm and 2:30-8pm. Proper attire required.

The ancient ruins of Tyndaris sit in majesty atop an enormous rock promontory. A view that stretches from Patti to Milazzo over the Aeolian Islands has made this site a valuable strategic position since the 4th century BC and a popular tourist destination. The ancient Greeks first adopted Tyndaris as a refuge from the onslaughts of the Peloponnesian War. Excavated at the beginning of the 20th century, the site is in surprisingly good condition. A large **theater** is cut into the hill at one end of the town. Over the years the original stone seats have witnessed theatrical performances and gladiator fights, as well as the original Greek plays that are still performed in front of the buildings during the summer. From behind the stage the **decumanus,** the main thoroughfare, passes through the center of town to the **Agora,** the old marketplace and town center. At right are the foundations of the **Villa Romana,** of which just a few columns and walls remain. Stylish mosaic floors whisper of the life once lived among its crumbling walls. The **Gymnasium (Basilica),** currently under restoration, retains many harmonious arches and columns.

The ruins of Tyndaris share their rocky perch with a more modern marvel, the **Santuario di Tindari,** erected in the 1970s in honor of **Madonna Nera** (Black Madonna). Local lore has it that a statue of this Byzantine Madonna washed up on the shores of Tindari hundreds of years ago. The current sanctuary stands on the site of the first church built in her name. The designers did not miss an inch when covering the interior with marble, gilt, pastels, sculpture, painting, and stained glass. Solemn statues command visitors to turn off their cell phones.

AEOLIAN ISLANDS (ISOLE EOLIE)

Residents refer to this archipelago as *Le Perle del Mare* (the pearls of the sea), and each summer boatloads of visitors second the motion. Homer thought the **Aeolian Islands** were the second home of the gods, and indeed these unspoiled shores border on the divine. Sparkling seas, incomparable beaches, and fiery volcanoes all contribute to the area's stunning beauty. **Lipari,** the central and largest island, has ancient ruins, a bustling port, and one of the finest museums in Italy. Visit nearby **Vulcano** for bubbling mud baths and a sulfurous crater, **Stromboli** for spectacular colors and a restless volcano, **Panarea** for inlets and an elite clientele, and **Salina** for cliffs and luxurious vegetation. The more remote sister islands of **Filicudi** and **Alicudi** feature untouched wilderness and intriguing rock formations. Although pleasantly affordable in the off-season, the islands suffer an exponential rise in prices at the end of July and August. Those planning a summer excursion should make reservations no later than May.

▶ TRANSPORTATION

The archipelago lies off Sicily, north of **Milazzo,** the principal and least expensive embarkation point. **Trains** run to Milazzo from **Messina** (45min., 18 per day, €2.45) and **Palermo** (3hr., €8.01). **Giuntabus** (☎090 67 37 82 or 67 57 49) brings you directly to Milazzo's port from **Messina** (45min.; M-Sa 14 per day, Su 1 per day; €2.58) and from the **Catania airport** (Apr.-Sept. daily, 4pm, €9.30). From the Milazzo train station, you can buy a ticket for an orange **AST bus** to the seaport (10min., every hr., €0.75). **Ferries** leave less frequently from Molo Bevellero in **Naples. Hydrofoils** *(aliscafi)* and **ferries** *(traghetti)* run regularly in late July and August from **Messina, Naples, Cefalù, Palermo,** and **Reggio Calabria.** Rates vary from each destination; check with local offices.

Three hydrofoil and ferry companies serve the islands, and all have ticket offices in Milazzo on V. dei Mille, directly across from the docks in the port. Hydrofoils run twice as often as ferries for twice the price (and half the time). Off-season runs from Sept. 1 to June 30. High-season is July 1 to August 31. Some travelers enlist the aid of Aeolian residents, who are charged far less than tourists when buying hydrofoil tickets.

Siremar: (☎090 928 3242; fax 928 3243), V. dei Mille in **Milazzo**, sends both ferries and hydrofoils to the islands. Offices also in Lipari (☎090 981 2200) and in Naples (☎081 551 2112). See **Naples, p. 525**.

SNAV: (☎090 928 4509), V. dei Mille in **Milazzo**, sends hydrofoils to the islands. Also has office in Lipari (☎090 981 2448)

Navigazione Generale Italiana (NGI): V. dei Mille, 26 (☎090 928 4091; fax 928 3415) in **Milazzo**; V. Ten. Mariano Amendola, 14, Porto Sottomonastero (☎090 981 1955) in **Lipari**; Porto Levante (☎090 985 2401) in **Vulcano**; and P. Santa Marina (☎090 984 3003), in **Salina**.

The following schedules list hydrofoil and ferry information from Milazzo on **Siremar**. The numbers are guidelines and change often; contact the company directly before planning your journey.

FERRY DESTINATION	TIME	HIGH-SEASON
Vulcano	40min.	8 per day, 7:05am-6:10pm, €10.33
Lipari	55min.	9 per day, 7:05am-6:10pm, €11.10
Salina: S. Marina	1hr. 25min.	8 per day, 7:05am-6:10pm, €12.65
Panarea	2hrs.	4 per day, 7:05am-2:50pm, €13.17
Alicudi	3hrs.	2 per day, 7:05am-2:50pm, €21.17
Filicudi	4½hr.	2 per day, 7:05am-2:50 pm, €17.30
Stromboli	2½hr.	4 per day; 6:05am-3:30pm, €16.01

HYDROFOIL DESTINATION	TIME	HIGH-SEASON
Vulcano	1½hr.	7 per day, 7am-6:30pm, €5.97
Lipari	2hr.	7 per day, 7am-6:30pm, €6.39
Salina	3hr.	4 per day, 7am-2:30pm, €8.10
Panarea	4hr.	4 per day, 7am-2:30pm, €7.67
Alicudi	6hr.	2 per day, 7am-2:30pm, €12.32
Filicudi	5hr.	4 per day, 7am-2:30pm, €11.08
Stromboli	6hr.	4 per day, 7am-2:30pm, €10.22

LIPARI ☎090

...a floating island, a wall of bronze and splendid smooth sheer cliffs.
—Homer

Centuries ago, wild-eyed pirates ravaged Lipari's shores. Today, boats and hydrofoils let loose swarms of equally ravenous visitors. Lipari is, and has always been, the most developed of the islands off the coast of Sicily. Because it is the largest of the Aeolians, however, it has always been the first to get burned, razed, and sacked during 2000 years of invasions. You can hear the influence of the raiding civilizations in the local dialect, which is interspersed with French adjectives, Arabic nouns, and Spanish verbs. In the town, pastel houses and bright shops surround the base of a medieval *castello*, the site of an ancient Greek acropolis. From the busy port, crowds move to **Spiaggia Bianca** and **Spiaggia Porticello,** the most popular beaches, to splash idly in the waves and bask in luxurious sunshine. For those who prefer the colors of the surrounding sea and mountains to neon umbrellas and swimsuits, short hikes often lead to private beaches. Inexpensive hotels, luscious beaches, and one of Italy's best museums have made Lipari the ideal launching point for daytrips to the six neighboring islands.

⌐ TRANSPORTATION

Public Transportation: Autobus Urso Guglielmo, V. Cappuccini, 9 (☎090 981 1262 or 981 1026; fax 981 1835). Ticket office open daily 9am-1pm; tickets also available on the bus. Hits most spots on the island. The company also runs tours of Lipari, leaving at 2pm daily; reservations required.

Bike/Moped Rental: ▨**De. Sco.,** V. Stradale Pianoconte, 5 (☎090 981 3288 or 368 753 5590), at the end of C. V. Emanuele closest to the hydrofoil docks. Shiny scooters lined up showroom-style. Helmets provided. 24hr. rental includes gas. €18; Aug. €30. Open 8:30am-8pm. MC/V. **Ditta Carbonaro Paola** (☎090 981 1994), on C. V. Emanuele just a few steps away from De. Sco. 12hr. rental. €15; July €20; Aug. €29.

Taxis: (☎338 563 29 21, 339 577 6437, or 090 988 0616) wait at either port.

◪ ▨ ORIENTATION AND PRACTICAL INFORMATION

Two ports are on either side of the large rock promontory supporting the *castello* and **museum.** Restaurants, hotels, and shops are along or between the roughly parallel **Corso Vittorio Emanuele II** and **Via Garibaldi.** V. Garibaldi runs from the hydrofoil port around the base of the *castello*, and is accessible by large stone stairs up the street. C. V. Emanuele, Lipari's main thoroughfare, ends at the ferry docks.

Tourist Office: AAST delle Isole Eolie, C. V. Emanuele, 202 (☎090 988 0095; fax 981 1190; www.netnet.it/aasteolie). From the hydrofoil docks, take a right up V. Garibaldi for 200m, then turn left on V. XXIV Maggio. Turn right onto C. V. Emanuele—the office is 100m down on the right; a white sign with the black letter "i" will be out front. This office is the information hub for all 7 islands. Offices elsewhere are either nonexistent or hard to find. *Ospitalità in blu*, which contains helpful visitor information for all of the islands. Find maps at *tabacchi*. Open July-Aug. M-Sa 8am-2pm and 4-10pm, Su 8am-2pm; Sept.-June M-F 8am-2pm and 4:30-7:30pm, Sa 8am-2pm.

Currency Exchange: C. V. Emanuele is lined with banks and **ATMs.** Exchange money at **Banco Antonveneta** (☎090 981 2117 or 988 0576; open M-F 8:20am-1:20pm and 2:35-3:35pm), **Banco di Roma** (☎090 9813 275; open M-F 8:25am-1:35pm and 2:10-4:10pm, Sa 8:25am-1:35pm), or at the **post office** (cash only). ATMs are not common on the other islands, so be sure to stock up here.

Books: La Stampa (☎090 981 1282), on C. V. Emanuele near the port. 4 shelves of various romance novels in English. Open M-Sa 9am-2pm and 4:30-10pm. MC/V.

Laundry: Lavanderia Caprara Andrea (☎090 981 3177), off of C. V. Emanuele. Wash and dry €3 per kg.

Emergency: ☎113.

Carabinieri: (☎112 or 090 981 1333 in emergencies). Carabinieri can also be reached at ☎090 981 2757 or 988 0030.

Ambulance: (☎090 989 5267). **First Aid (Pronto Soccorso)** (☎090 988 5267 or 981 1010.) **Medical Officer: Guardia Medica** (☎090 988 5226), office 50m up V. Garibaldi from the waterfront, on the left under the Italian flag. Open M, W, and F 8:30am-1pm; Tu and Th 3:30-5:30pm.

Pharmacies: Farmacia Internazionale, C. V. Emanuele, 128 (☎090 981 1583). Open M-F 9am-1pm and 5-9pm. MC/V. **Farmacia Cincotta,** V. Garibaldi, 60 (☎090 981 1472). Open M-F 9am-1pm and 5-9pm. AmEx/MC/V. Mini screen on storefront window of every pharmacy lists the pharmacist and phone number on call 24hr.

Hospital: Ospedale Civile di Lipari Centralino (☎090 98 851), on V. Santana, off the southern end of C. V. Emanuele. At end of C. V. Emanuele, descend the side street between scooter rental places and take a right up V. Roma. V. Santana is the 2nd left. Open daily 8am-8pm.

Internet Access: Internet Point, C. V. Emanuele, by the post office. Open 9am-8pm. €3 for 30min., €5 per hr. **Net C@fe,** V. Garibaldi, 61 (☎090 981 3527), offers 2 computers and a cool atmosphere. €7.75 per hr.

Post Office: Main branch on C. V. Emanuele is undergoing restorations. Temporary office 1 block away towards *porto* (off of C. V. Emanuele). Open M-F 8:15am-6:30pm, Sa 8:15am-1:20pm.

Postal Code: Lipari 98055; **Canneto-Lipari** 98052; all **other islands** 98050.

⚐ ACCOMMODATIONS & CAMPING

Three steps down the swaying hydrofoil exit ramp, you will be swamped with offers for *affittacamere* (private rooms for rent). Although many such rooms are not registered, they may become a viable option come July and August, when hotels and pensions overflow. Ask to see the room before accepting, and don't be afraid to show a bit of hesitation, as prices tend to drop when you do so. Because many private rooms are not registered (and thus are technically illegal), it is always a good idea to politely **ask for your price quote in writing.** As the summer progresses, Lipari is increasingly invaded by tourists, and the island reaches its saturation point in August. Hotels fill almost instantaneously and owners raise their prices by as much as 25%. Reserve far in advance, even for early July.

Casa Vittorio di Cassara, Vico Sparviero, 15, off of V. Garibaldi, 78 at the end of the short stairway. (☎/fax 090 981 1523, 988 0729, or 338 392 3867). Take V. Garibaldi from the hydrofoil dock and make a U-turn around the first possible left. From the small alley, turn right at first chance onto Vico Sparviero. It is the yellow building with blue window frames. If door is locked, continue to the end of the street and turn right. At the red iron gate, ring the top white button on the left for the owner. Ideal location near the port and centro. Rooms with bath vary in size and style from intimate singles to 5-person penthouses. Top-floor communal kitchen and open terrace with an ocean view. €16-€37 per person, depending on season. ❷

Pensione Enso Il Negro, V. Garibaldi, 29 (☎090 981 3163, 981 2473, or 368 370 9548), 20m up V. Garibaldi, to the left, under a small doorway and up 3 flights of stairs. Painted tiles lead the way into 8 rooms with patio, fridge, A/C, and roomy baths. Elegant archways, blond wood furniture, and a location 3min. from the hydrofoil dock means class and comfort. Singles €30-€47; doubles €50-€80. AmEx/MC/V. ❸

Hotel Europeo, C. V. Emanuele, 98 (☎090 981 1589), has a convenient location in the center of C. V. Emanuele and near both ports. Small bright rooms have few furnishings, but comfortable beds. Top floor has external doors and terrific view of the city. Open Apr.-June and Sept. €25; July €30; August €37. ❸

Hotel Rocce Azzurre, Porto delle Genti, V. Maddalena, 69 (☎090 981 3248; fax 090 981 3247; rocceazzurre@interfree.it). On the beach and built into a quiet bay, this hotel offers 33 rooms with bath and private balcony. Daily island and sailing excursions offered as well. Rates per person: with breakfast, €37-57. July-Aug. *pensione* required: half-pension €47-93; full-pension €57-112. AmEx/MC/V. ❺

Camping: Baia Unci, V. Marina Garibaldi, 2 (☎090 981 1909 or 981 2527 in low season; fax 981 1715; www.campeggitalia.it/sicilia/baiaunci). 2km from Lipari at the entrance to the beachfront town Canneto. 10 min. from the beach. Amiable management and cheap self-service **restaurant** open daily noon-3pm and 7pm-11am. Grounds open Mar. 15-Oct. 15. Reserve for Aug. €6.20-€11 per person with tent. ❶

⚫ FOOD

Legions of lovers have sprinkled sauces, garnished salads, and spiced meats with the island's *capperi* (capers), renowned for their aphrodisiac powers. The sweet local Malvasia dessert wine perfectly complements dinner. The *alimentari* (grocery stores) lining C. V. Emanuele are open daily and sell cheap fruit. Lipari's lip-licking restaurant cuisine can get a little expensive, however, and the budget-minded may want to self-cater at the **UPIM supermarket,** C. V. Emanuele, 212. (☎090 981 1587. Open M-Sa 8:30am-1:30pm and 4-9:30pm. AmEx/D/MC/V.)

■ **Da Gilberto,** V. Garibaldi, 22-24 (☎090 981 2756), has become famous nationwide for what may well be Italy's best sandwiches. Invent your own hot *panini* with any of the ingredients on Gilberto's shelves: prosciutto, capers, fresh and dried tomatoes, olives, garlic, mint, etc. Gilberto also stocks everything needed for a complete picnic. *Panini* €3.50. Open daily 7am-midnight or closing, 7pm-2am in low season. MC/V. ❷

La Cambusa, V. Garibaldi, 72 (☎349 476 6061). This intimate *trattoria* is a family affair, service courtesy of the owner and his wife. Regulars rave about the exceptionally tasty pasta from €4.32. Cover €1.03. Open daily 7-11pm. ❷

La Piazzetta, off of C. V. Emanuele (☎090 981 2522; fax 981 2511), directly beside Pasticceria Subba. Has an elegant patio that extends into a small piazza. Walls and menus contain the signatures of many famous satisfied customers, including Audrey Hepburn. Pizza from €4, *primi* from €7, *secondi* from €9.50. Open for lunch July-Aug. noon-2pm; dinner year-round 7:30pm-midnight. MC/V. ❸

Ristorante Sottomonastero, C. V. Emanuele, 232 (☎090 988 0720; fax 981 1084), is a versatile bar-ristorante-*pizzeria* that also specializes in Aeolian sweets. The restaurant's action spills from the indoor bar to an outdoor patio. Pizza from €3.50. Open 7am-midnight. AmEx/MC/V. ❷

Pasticceria Subba, C. V. Emanuele, 92 (☎090 981 1352). The archipelago's oldest *pasticceria* is one of Italy's best. Heavenly *pasta paradiso*, (almond paste dumpling). Pastries from €1.03. Open daily May-Oct. 7am-3am; Nov.-Apr. 7am-midnight. ❶

⚫ 🎵 SIGHTS AND ENTERTAINMENT

Lipari's best sights, aside from its beaches, are all to be found in the *castello* on the hill between the ports. The gigantic fortress with ancient Greek foundations dwarfs the surrounding town. Prehistoric ruins encircle it, running along the outside of the **museum,** which shares the hill with the **San Bartolo church.**

■ **MUSEO ARCHEOLOGICO EOLIANO.** Highlights of the collection include several gigantic *Liparite* burial urns, galleries full of Greek and Sicilian red figure-ware pottery from the 4th and 5th centuries BC, and the treasures of underwater exploration around the Aeolians. An entire building, the **Serione Geologico-Vulcano-logica,** is devoted to the island's natural history. *(Up the stone steps to the right off V. Garibaldi. Turn left at the church. ☎090 988 0174. Open May-Oct. M-Su 9am-1:30pm and 4-7pm; Nov.-Apr. M-Su 9am-1:30pm and 3-6pm. €4.32, under 18 or over 65 free.)*

CHURCH AND ARCHEOLOGICAL PARK. All around the church and museum, ancient ruins await exploration. Comprehensive charts show the process of excavation and the age of structures. The centerpiece of the park—and the best preserved site—is the theater, which still functions as a performance space. *(Both sites are across from the museum. Open daily 9am-1pm. Church €0.52.)*

ENTERTAINMENT

Lipari's summer excitement reaches its height (and surpasses the island's capacity) on August 24 during the **Feast of St. Bartholomew**. Processions, parties, and pyrotechnics take over the city in celebration. The quieter **Wine and Bread Festival** in mid-November features more delectable activities in the Pianoconte district.

BEACHES, BATHING, AND BUMMING AROUND

Lipari is known for its beaches and views of Salina, Panarea, and Stromboli. Take the Lipari-Cavedi bus to Canneto, a couple of kilometers north, for the popular beaches at **Spiaggia Bianca** (White Beach) and **Porticello**. Protect your flesh—the pebbles are sharp and the sun is hot. From Canneto's center, the secluded, sandy coves flanking Spiaggia Bianca can be explored by renting one of the rafts, kayaks, or canoes that line the beach at V. M. Garibaldi. (€3-5 per hr., €13-20 per day.) Just a few kilometers north of Canneto lies **Pomiciazzo**, where white pumice mines line the road. Farther north at Porticello, you can bathe at the foot of the mines while small flecks of stone float on the sea's surface.

For the island's finest view, take the Lipari-Quattropani bus to the Pianoconte stop, and head over to **Monte S. Angelo**. The path to Monte S. Angelo is tiny and hidden; ask or you'll never find it. A beach closer to the port can be found at **Porto delle Gente**. From the docks, take a left along the lungomare and up the slight incline. Turn right up the stairs and take the first left away from the hotel. Take a right when you reach the next road, and follow it to the beach. From July to September, bus tours of Lipari (€2.58) run at 2pm from Autobus Urso Guglielmo on V. Cappuccini (☎ 090 981 1262 or 981 1026). The best way to see the island's many beaches is a leisurely day aboard a rented boat from the hydrofoil port in Lipari.

VULCANO ☎ 090

Stretch out and immerse yourself; the hand of the god Vulcan will hold you gently, transforming thoughts into bubbles of music and culture.
—A signpost in Vulcano

From miles away you'll be able to smell the sulfuric winds off Vulcano. Thought at various points to be the home of the Greek wind gods Aeolus and Hephaestus (Vulcan), god of the smiths, as well as the gate to Hell, the islands are now known for their four volcanoes, 470 *vulcanarí* (those diehard folks living near the volcanoes), and wild landscapes. Black beaches, bubbling seas, and natural mud spas attract tourists from all over the world during the summer months. The largest volcano is the heavily touristed Fossa di Vulcano. For now, the great furnace lies dormant at the island's center, but beware that some geologists predict an eruption from the gurgling volcano within the next 20 years.

TRANSPORTATION

Hydrofoils: Siremar (☎ 090 985 2149), atop an elevated stone walkway at the Porto Levante intersection. To: **Lipari** (10min., 20 per day, €2.32) and **Milazzo** (40min., 18 per day, 7am-8pm, €10.33). **SNAV** (☎ 090 985 2230), in a tiny cranny directly off the port, next to Cantine Stevenson. To: **Lipari** (10min., 20 per day, €2.32); **Milazzo** (40min., 18 per day, €10.33); and **Palermo** (4hr., 2 per day, 7:40am-4pm).

Ferries: N.G.I. Biglietteria (☎ 090 985 2401), under a blue awning on V. Provinciale, just off P. Levante. Open daily 8:15am-12:15pm.

Buses: Scaffidi Tindaro (☎ 090 985 3047), in front of the Ritrovo Remigio bar, just off the port on V. Provinciale. Infrequent buses run to Vulcano Piano (€1.81).

Taxis: (☎ 339 600 5750, 347 813 0631, or 339 579 1576), or at the stand in the port. Call **Centro Nautico Baia di Levante** (☎ 090 982 2197 or 339 337 2795). For 24hr. watertaxi service see **boat rental,** below.

■✴ 🛈 ORIENTATION AND PRACTICAL INFORMATION

Vulcano's casual atmosphere is emphasized the lack of posted street names and numbers. Frequent directional signs and arrows, however, make this pedestrian island easy to navigate. All ferries and hydrofoils dock at **Porto di Levante** on the eastern side of **Vulcanello,** one of four volcanoes on the island. With your back to the hydrofoil dock at the far left of the port, **Via Provinciale** heads left toward the largest volcano and the **Gran Cratere.** Straight ahead is **Via Porto Levante,** a semicircular road that loops through the center of town and reconnects to the part of the ferry side. From the hydrofoil docks, V. Porto Levante stretches straight until splitting in three directions at the small statue of Aeolus at rest. The pharmacy is straight ahead, while the famed *acquacalda* and **Laghetto di Fanghi** are on the right. Continuing along and to left of the pharmacy, after green pastures on the left, is the black shoreline of **Sabbie Nere.**

Tourist Office: Stagionale summer counter at V. Provinciale, 41 (☎ 090 985 2028 or 090 985 2142). Open late June-Aug. daily 8am-1:30pm and 3-5pm. Provides information on **rented rooms** *(affittacamere).* All other information is at the AAST office in Lipari.

Bank: Banco Sicilia (☎ 090 985 2335), 100m down from the port on V. Provinciale, has an **ATM.** Open M-F 8:30am-1:30pm and 2:45-3:45pm.

Currency Exchange: SNAV Office (☎ 090 985 2230), at Porto di Levante.

Boat Rental: Centro Nautico Baia di Levante (☎ 090 982 2197 or 339 337 2795), in a shed on the beach behind the Ritrovio Remigio bar, near the hydrofoil dock. 4-person motorboats. €77.47-103.29 depending on boat style, plus gas. Open daily 8am-9pm.

Scooter and Bicycle Rentals: *Noleggio* nemeses **da Paolo** (☎ 090 985 2112 or 338 139 2809) and **Sprint** (☎ 090 985 2208 or 0347 760 0275), just a block apart at the intersection of V. Provinciale and V. Porto Levante, wage a constant rate war. Scooters per hr. May €12.91-15.50; June €15.50-18.08; July-Aug. €18.08-25.62; Sept. €15.50. Bikes €5.16 per hr. Sprint has a novelty tandem surrey bike for €7.75 per hr.

Carabinieri: ☎ 090 985 2110.

City Police: ☎ 090 985 2577

First Aid (Medical Officer): ☎ 090 985 2220.

Late-Night Pharmacy: Farmacia Bonarrigo, V. Favaloro, 1 (☎ 090 985 2244; emergencies 985 3113), straight ahead of the port, at the far end of the small piazza where V. Provinciale breaks off. Open M-F 9am-1pm and 5-8pm, Sa 9am-1pm. MC/V.

Post Office: down V. Provinciale, at Vulcano Piano. Open M-F 8am-1:30pm, Sa 8:30am-12:30pm.

Postal Code: 98050.

🏠 ACCOMMODATIONS & CAMPING

Along with the temperature, hotel prices rise significantly in the months of July and August, when tourists saturate the island. While finding a room is easy in the colder winter months, summer reservations far in advance are recommended.

■ **Hotel Torre,** V. Favaloro, 1 (☎/fax 090 985 2342), straight down V. Porto Levante from the hydrofoil docks, near the pharmacy. This centrally located hotel is a perfect retreat after a day at the nearby *acquacalda*. All 8 enormous rooms come with terrace, kitchen, TV, A/C, and grand, airy bathrooms. Many of the rooms offer extraordinary views. Cribs available. Doubles Oct.-Apr. €38; May €40; June-Sept. €47; Aug. €75. Extra person 35% more. Solo travelers may receive discounts. ❹

Residence Lanterna Bleu di Francesco Corrieri, V. Lentia, 58 (☎/fax 090 985 2178; lanternableu@virgilio.it), along V. Lentia, which breaks from V. Provinciale before the pharmacy. 1-or 2-room apartments 400m from thermal and mudbaths come with bathroom, A/C, kitchenette, and terrace. Breakfast €4 per person. Oct.-Apr. 1 room €31, 2 rooms €52; May-Sept. 1 room €42-68, 2 rooms €83-135. Extra bed €13-19. ❹

Hotel Residence Mari del Sud, V. Porto Ponente (☎090 985 3250; fax 985 3328; dipanesrl@tin.it), continuing down the road to the left of the pharmacy to reach the black sand beach, the hotel will be on the left along the shore. This resort-style establishment, with an enviable location over the black sand beach, hosts activities ranging from diving lessons and excursions to Caribbean dance parties. Doubles with breakfast €39-88; half-pension €52-103; full-pension €65-118. AmEx/MC/V. ❺

Camping: Campeggio Togo Togo (☎090 985 2303), at Porto Ponente on the opposite side of Vulcanello's isthmus neck, 1½km from the hydrofoil dock and adjacent to *Sabbie Nere* (the Black Beach). Showers and hot water included. In summer, the *pizzeria* is open and internet access is available. Open Apr.-Sept. Reservations suggested for August. €10.50 per person includes tent and light. Larger bungalows with TV, fridge and kitchenette also available. July-Aug. €83 per night for up to 4 people; Apr.-June and Sept. 1-7 €21 per person per night. ❶

◖ FOOD

The **Tridial Market** in the little white piazza off the Aeolus center, has all the basics, including toiletries and an inexpensive sandwich counter. (Open daily 8am-1pm and 5-8pm.) For fruit and vegetables, there is an *alimentari* on V. Provinciale, toward the crater from the port. (☎090 985 2222. Open daily 8am-1pm and 5-8pm. MC/V.) *Granite* and *gelato* are in abundance at the port, but take a plunge off the main roads for a good full meal.

■ **Ritrovo Remigio/Il Sestante,** V. Porto Levante (☎090 985 2085), right at end of hydrofoil dock. Popular with tourists and locals alike, this large bar offers hot and cold made-to-order sandwiches €2, and a beguiling terrace on the port to eat them in. The *gelato* is delicious, but skip it in favor of any of the delicious desserts from the largest selection on the islands. *Tiramisù* €1.55, *cassata* €2. Open daily 6am-2am. ❶

Cafe Piazzetta, Piazzetta Faraglione (☎090 985 3267), down V. Provinciale from the hydrofoil docks. You can slurp up tasty *gelato* cups or cocktails (€5.20) or order a more serious pizza meal from €5. In June-Sept. enjoy live music in the evenings on the outdoor patio. AmEx/MC/V. ❷

Ristorante-Bar Vincenzino, V. Porto Levante, 25 (☎090 985 2016; fax 985 3370), down from the hydrofoil docks, up V. Provinciale. This little restaurant and bar, separated from the main road, serves up typical Aeolian specialties, with *primi* from €6 and *secondi* from €7. Open 7am-midnight. AmEx/MC/V. ❸

Cantine Stevenson, V. Porto Levante (☎090 985 3247), to the right as you exit the hydrofoil docks. Lounge with locals until wee hours of the morning at this popular nightlife location over-looking the water. Try local *Malvasia* wines, as well as cocktails and long drinks (€5.50), *panini* (€3.50), and pizza (€6.50). After your meal, enjoy cups of *gelato* (€5) and crepes (€4). Open daily noon-3am. AmEx/MC/V. ❷

SICILY

👁 SIGHTS

Vulcano's natural wonders are perfect for casual thrill-seeking. The aura of danger at the hands of the volcano coupled with ancient tradition makes for unusual and relaxing experiences. If you can stand the sulfuric aroma, lounging on the beach at Sabbie Nere or taking a dip in the mudbaths is truly an unforgettable experience.

■ **GRAN CRATERE.** Anyone visiting Vulcano for more than a day should tackle the one-hour hike on a snaking footpath to the inactive crater. The summit rewards trekkers with unsurpassed views of the island, sea, and volcanic landscape. The hike winds through bright yellow *fumaroli*, emissions of noxious smoke, and bizarre orange rock formations powdered with white dust. Between 11am and 3pm, the sun transforms the volcano into a furnace, so head out in the early morning or late afternoon. Bring a hat, sunscreen, plenty of water, and sturdy climbing shoes. Portions of the trail are quite strenuous and should be approached with caution by the inexperienced. Obey the signs, and don't sit or lie down, as poisonous gases tend to accumulate close to the ground. Some travelers risk taking an unpleasant spill by sprinting straight down the side of the volcano, but they do shave a good 30min. off the time required for descent (and is quite a rush). *(With your back to the water at the port, turn left onto V. Provinciale, and follow it until you reach a path with "Cratere" signs. The notices point to a dirt turn off 300m on the left.)*

LAGHETTO DI FANGHI. The water's murky gray-brown color blends right in with the volcanic rock formations that surround it, but the putrid smell makes this natural spa impossible to miss. Hundreds of visitors flock to the pit to spread gray goo all over their bodies for its therapeutic effects. Therapeutic or not, the mud is radioactive and high in sulfuric acid. Remove all silver and leather accessories, and keep the actual mud away from your eyes. If contact occurs, *immediately* rinse eyes with running water and a few drops of lemon juice from a nearby restaurant. *(Up V. Porto Levante and to the right from the port. €0.77.)*

ACQUACALDA. Directly behind the mud pits, Vulcano's shoreline bubbles like a jacuzzi, courtesy of volcanic *fumarole* beneath the surface. The sulfuric nature of the water is known to have quite an effect on the human blood circulation, creating a heavenly sensation upon emerging—that is, until you see the new sulfuric holes in your bathing suit. If you love your designer suit, don't wear it here. Ugly bathing suits are available nearby for €10.

BEACHES. If sulfur burns and radioactive mud aren't appealing, join carefree sunbathers on Vulcano's best beach, **Sabbie Nere.** Black sands, blue water, white crests, and colorful swimsuits make for a rainbow of relaxation. *(Follow V. Provinciale from the port and then take the road that veers off to the left of the pharmacy. Continue along the pastures and past the Hotel Eolie until you reach the sandy black shore.)*

OTHER ISLANDS

STROMBOLI   ☎ 090

Stromboli has the Aeolians' only active volcano, a fact that keeps residents few (pop. 370) and visitors many. Though the great Stromboli is always active, the island itself is quiet until the summer. For those intimidated by the volcano's dangers, renting a boat is a great way to visit. The tourist deluge lasts from mid-June to September, making cheap accommodations almost impossible to find. In the off-season, many *pensioni* are closed and owners are reluctant to rent rooms for fewer than three nights at a time. Ferries are rare, so it is worthwhile to call ahead.

TRANSPORTATION. Along the shorefront lungomare, **Siremar** (☎ 090 98 60 11), **SNAV** (☎ 090 98 60 03), and **N.G.I.** (☎ 090 98 30 03) run infrequent ferries and hydrofoils to the islands. Boat rentals are available at the port from the **Società Navigazione Pippo.** (☎ 090 98 61 35 or 338 985 7883. Open daily 9am-noon and 2-10pm. Boats from €60 per day; larger boats run up to €200, gas not included.)

ORIENTATION AND PRACTICAL INFORMATION. On the calmer slopes of smoking Stromboli, the three villages of Scari, Ficogrande, and Piscita have melded into one continuation of whitewash known as the town of Stromboli. From the ferry docks, the wide *lungomare* is on the right, continuing to the beach and two large hotels, while the narrow **Via Roma** heads from the ticket offices up to the town center, and ultimately to the restaurant L'Osservatorio, the last establishment before the volcano takes over. Twisting uphill to the left, V. Roma passes the **carabinieri** station (☎ 090 98 60 21) on the left, the island's **only ATM** on the right, and the **pharmacy** just before the piazza (☎ 090 98 67 13; open June-Aug. 8:30am-1pm and 4-8:30pm; Sept.-May 8:30am-1pm and 4-7:30pm; AmEx/MC/V), before finally reaching **Piazza San Vincenzo.** V. Roma then dips downhill becoming **Via Vittorio Emanuele,** which runs past the **Guarda Medica** (☎ 090 98 60 97).

ACCOMMODATIONS. Stromboli's hotels are solidly booked in August, and your best bet may be one of the *affittacamere.* You should expect to pay between €15 and €30 for your room. Ask to see the room before paying, and don't be afraid to check for hot water and good beds. **Casa del Sole ❷** is down the alleyway from Pensione Brasile. Large, hostel-style communal rooms face a shaded terrace and communal kitchen. Private doubles painted in sea colors are upstairs. Four separate bathrooms are downstairs. (☎/fax 090 98 60 17. June €18 per person; July-Aug. €20 per person.) **Pensione Brasile ❹,** V. D. Cincotta, offers simple rooms and great home-cooked meals. Off of V. Regina, follow the small sidestreet across from St. Bartholomew's church at the end of town. (☎ 090 98 60 08. Half-pension €39-57; full-pension €49-67. MC/V.) If a room on the beach is your calling, head to the **Hotel Miramare ❺,** along the *lungomare* to the right from the ferry docks, right on the water. Each room has bath and sea view. (☎ 090 98 60 47; fax 98 63 18; http:// www.netnet.it/miramare. Singles €39-65; doubles €68-114, triples, €90-153; quads €110-174. Half-pension offered July-Aug. €73-81. AmEx/MC/V.) **Pensione Villa Petrusa ❹,** off V. V. Emanuele, 10min. from the sea, offers colorful gardens, a communal TV room and bar, and 26 rooms with private baths. (☎ 090 98 60 45; fax 98 61 26. With breakfast €30-60 per person.)

FOOD. Stuff your pack at the **Duval Market,** on V. Roma just before the church. (☎ 090 98 60 52. Open daily 8am-1pm and 4-9pm. AmEx/MC/V.) For those who cannot, for any reason, make the trek up to the *vulcano,* fear not. Some of the explosive activity can be seen from the restaurant and bar **L'Osservatorio ❹,** Punta Labronzo (☎ 090 98 60 13 or 337 29 39 42), is the last establishment along V. V. Emanuele. The restaurant is a long walk away, and for those heading over at nighttime, a flashlight and sneakers are highly recommended. Taxis also part for the restaurant from S. Bartolo every hour from 5-11pm. Locals say the best pizza on the island is **La Lampara ❸,** V. V. Emanuele, 27, just after Piazza San Vincenzo, on the left. (☎ 090 98 64 09; fax 98 67 21. Pizza from €7, *primi* from €8, *secondi* €7.50. Open daily 6pm-midnight. AmEx/MC/V.) At the rosticceria **La Trattola ❷,** V. Roma, 34, delve into the *pizza Stromboli,* a cone-shaped creation bursting with mozzarella, tomatoes, and olives. (☎ 090 98 60 46. Pizza from €3.62. Open daily 8am-2pm and 4pm-midnight. MC/V.)

SICILY

■ ENTERTAINMENT. The plateau of Piazza San Vincenzo is Stromboli's geographic center, and its most happening 500 square feet (besides the crater itself). Each night around 10pm, islanders flock to **Bar Ingrid** for drinks, *gelato* €1.55, and conversation. (☎ 090 98 63 85. Open daily 8am-1am, and until 3am in July-Aug.) Its neighbor, **Ristorante-Pizzeria Il Conte Ugolino** (☎ 090 986 5765), serves typical Aeolian and Sicilian favorites. The piazza is abuzz with voices, occasional singing, and half the town's population. The moon rising directly over the piazza is quite a sight, and from behind the church there's a great view of the *vulcano*.

◙ SIGHTS. At the volcano each evening, orange cascades of lava and molten rock spill over the slope, lighting the **Sciara del Fuoco** (trail of fire) at 10min. intervals. The **Società Navigazione Pippo** (☎ 090 98 61 35), at the port, runs a boat trip for the very adventurous (1hr., 10pm, €12.91).

> **▮ STOP IN THE NAME OF LAVA.** *Let's Go* does not recommend, advocate, or take responsibility for anyone hiking Stromboli's volcano, with or without a guide. A red triangle with a black, vertical bar means "danger."

An ordinance passed in 1990 made hiking the volcano without a guide officially illegal, and with good reason: not long ago a photographer was burnt to death after getting too close to the volcanic opening; in 1998, a Czech diplomat, lost in the fog, walked off the cliff's edge. So if such criminality is not your style, look into a trip with **Magmatrek,** located on V. Vittorio Emanuele (☎/fax 090 986 5768). The group runs a 6-7hr. afternoon trek to the craters (Mar. 1-June 30 3:30pm, July 1-Aug. 31 6pm, Sept. 1-Oct. 31 3:30pm; €21) as well as a 7-8 hr. night excursion (July 1-Sept. 15, departure at 12:30am; €34). Helmets are required and provided. Mario Zaia, known as Zaza, is a highly regarded guide. Equipment and supplies for the trek can be rented at **Totem Trekking** (☎ 090 986 5752), on P. S. Vincenzo.

Those who choose to ignore the law (feigning ignorance of the four languages on the warning signs) and head up alone, can and should arrange to do the more dangerous descent with a returning group. Hikers should take sturdy shoes, a flashlight, extra batteries, snacks, lots of water, and warm clothes for the exposed summit. Don't wear contact lenses, as the wind sweeps ash and dust everywhere. During the day only smoke is visible, so plan to reach the summit around dusk to snuggle into a rock dugout and watch the brilliant lava bursts. Climbing shoes, daypacks, flashlights, and walking sticks can be rented at the GAA office. Helmets are also available; every couple years, someone gets hit by a piece of flying rock.

To reach the volcano, follow C. V. Emanuele from P. Vincenzo for a kilometer until you reach a large warning sign; bear right at the fork in the road. The path turns upward when a secluded stretch of beach comes into view and (after 400m) cuts between two white houses. Smart hikers take only the well-trodden shortcuts—anything else will lead to a maze of thick brambles and reeds. Halfway up the slope, the trail degenerates into a scramble of volcanic rock and ash; follow the striped red, orange, and white rock markings. Follow markings very carefully or you'll end up stranded in a landslide of loose volcanic ash, sand, and soil. The warning signs at the top ridge are sincere. The risk of walking off the edge is greater during the spring and fall fogs. The most important rule of all: **when hiking down the volcano at night, use the same path you took up.** The professional guides' shortcuts are tempting but infinitely easier to get lost on.

Strombolicchio, a gigantic rock with a small lighthouse, rises 2km in the distance from the black beach at **Ficogrande.** The ravages of the sea have eroded the rock from 56m to a mere 42m in the past 100 years. Beachgoers should check out the small cove at the end of V. Giuseppe Cincotta, off V. V. Emanuele near Casa del Sole. Large rocks encircle the stretch of black sand.

PANAREA ☎ 090

Panarea, the smallest of the Aeolian islands, has a reputation as an elite playground for celebrities. Until July and August, Panarea attracts an older crowd that wants a quiet place to relax and enjoy the view. In the high season, however, the island explodes with younger generations that fill the various *discoteche*, persuading once-tame waterside bars to pump up the volume on the *lungomare*.

▚ ⁊ ORIENTATION AND PRACTICAL INFORMATION. Panarea is accessible by ferry and hydrofoil (See **Ferry Schedules**, p. 636). A purely pedestrian island, Panarea's only wheeled objects are scooters and golf-carts, owned by hotels or serve as taxis. All directional signs list distances by foot rather than kilometers. Street signs and numbers are nonexistent. The main road is **Via San Pietro**, running past Chiesa San Pietro along an undulating stone path to **Punta Milazzese**. **Banca Antonveneta**, on V. S. Pietro, on the left from the port, has an **ATM**. Another ATM through **Banca di Sicilia** can be found on the patio of the Hotel Cincotta. The **post office**, on V. S. Pietro, past the bank on the right, changes cash and AmEx traveler's checks. (☎ 090 98 32 83 or 98 30 28. Open daily 8:30am-1:30pm.) In an **emergency** call the **carabinieri** (July-Aug. ☎ 090 98 31 81; Sept.-June in Lipari 090 981 1333) or the **Guardia Medica** (☎ 090 98 30 40). A 24 hr. **Taxi** service (in the form of golf carts) is run by **Paola+Angelo** on V. S. Pietro (☎ 333 313 8610).

⌐⊡ ACCOMMODATIONS AND FOOD. Larger hotels can be pricey, especially in July and August. The **Da Bruno minimarket** is on V. S. Pietro by the post office. (☎ 090 98 30 02. Open July-Aug. daily 8am-9pm; Sept.-June 8am-1pm and 4:30-9pm.) At the *panificio* next door to Da Bruno, locals line up for baked goods, including *biscotti, foccacia,* and pizza slices. (Open Sept.-July daily 7am-1:30pm and 5-8pm; Aug. 7am-8pm.)

▨ **Hotel Raya** (☎ 090 98 30 13; fax 090 98 31 03; info@hotelraya.it.), on V. S. Pietro, is known over the island for its *discoteca,* open late July-Aug., emitting action until the first rays of the morning. Its manta ray symbol can be seen as you exit the docks, off to the left along the *lungomare.* Charming rooms with beguiling architecture. Different parts of the hotel overlook different vistas, and prices vary accordingly. Low season €77-154 (depending on view); high season €129-253. AmEx/MC/V. ❺

Pensione Pasqualino (☎ 090 98 30 23), half a block from the port. Turn right from the port and follow signs up the stairs. Sharing space and management with Trattoria da Francesco, it has spacious rooms and friendly staff. Breakfast included. Apr.-June €20.66-36.15; July-Aug. €51.65. ❹

Da Francesco/Pasqualina (☎ 090 98 30 23), on the *lungomare* along the water. Turn right coming off the docks and continue up the stairs to the white and blue houses. All rooms have bath and view of the sea. The patio *trattoria* (under the same management and name) extends from the deck. B&B €21-52 per person; half-pension €47-83. ❹

Hotel Tesoriero, V. S. Pietro (☎ 090 98 30 98 or 98 31 44; fax 98 30 07; info@hoteltesoriero.it). It has grand rooms with bath, AC, TV, and access on to a bamboo-shaded terrace with an ocean view. Breakfast included. Double rooms €37-73 per person; €11-52 charged if used as a single. AmEx/MC/V. ❹

Hotel Cincotta, V. S. Pietro (☎ 090 98 30 14; fax 98 32 11). Coming off the docks, turn left and follow the road past the ATM, to steps leading up to the right. Look for the signs. Rooms contain bathroom, color TV, minibar and a terrace overlooking the sea. Among the more posh hotels of Panarea, the Cincotta also offers a pool and outdoor dining. With breakfast €55-110; half-pension €81-140. ❺

Ritrovo da Tindero, V. Comunale Iditella (☎ 090 98 30 27). Find a filling *panino* (€1.81-2.58), feast on huge salads (€4.50), and sample *cannoli* (€2.07) oozing with fresh *ricotta. Primi* from €6, *secondi* €7.75-9.30. Open Apr.-Oct. daily 8am-1am. ❸

SICILY

Ristorante Da Pina, V. S. Pietro (☎090 98 30 32 or 98 33 24; fax 98 31 47), near the port. A formal restaurant that serves specials like *gnocchi di melanzane* and *cous cous di pesce*. Lobster €75 per kg, *primi* from €9, *secondi* from €14. AmEx/MC/V. ❹

Ritrovo Naif, V. S. Pietro (☎090 98 31 88), near the port. Feast on *gelato* and sandwiches, or choose from a large selection of typical Sicilian sweets. ❷

◙ ⬛ SIGHTS AND ENTERTAINMENT. From Punta Milazzese, Panarea's three famous beaches extend along the coastline. Gradually changing from rocks to sand, this trio gives a wide spectrum of Aeolian shores. Taking two rights from the center of town to **Calcara** (also known as **"Spiaggia Fumarole"**), you'll reach a beach near the thermal springs at **Acquacalda.** Another beach can be reached by following V. S. Pietro and the signs for "Spiagietta Zimmari" (the small beach of Zimmari). In a 25min. stroll along a scenic road alive with tiny lizards and colorful flowering cacti, rock gives way to sand in this perfect marriage between shore and sea. Panarea comes alive in the summer with disco-fevered youngsters and their older counterparts. Bars and cafes spill out onto the beachfront. Arrive early if you'd like a corner on which to spread your beach towel. For scuba diving try **Amphibia** (☎335 613 8529), with offices located on the *lungomare*, up the stairs next to the accommodation **Da Francesco.**

SALINA ☎090

Though close to Lipari in both size and distance, Salina is far removed from its more developed neighbor. Untouched landscapes, quiet villages, and the most dramatic beaches in the Aeolian Islands make Salina a lush paradise. With its vast variety of plants and flowers, Salina's natural wonders equal those of the more boisterous volcanic isles. The island's most astounding rock formations are found at **Semaforo di Pollara,** the enchanting setting of Massimo Troisi's *Il Postino.* The lack of steady tourism has its downside, however, for there are few budget accommodations to be found, making Salina more suitable for daytrips.

▮ TRANSPORTATION. From Lipari, Salina (Porto S. Marina, its main port) is accessible by **hydrofoil** (30min., 8-9 per day, €5.08) and **ferry** (4 per day, €2.84). The smaller port of **Rinella** on the opposite side of the island also receives hydrofoils (at an additional 15min. and €0.73) and ferries (additional 30min., €0.52). **SNAV** (☎090 984 3003) and **Siremar** (☎090 984 3004) have offices on either side of the church of S. Marina, in front of the port. The island's blue **buses** (C.I.T.I.S. Autobus, V. Nazionale, 10 (Malfa; ☎090 984 4150) stop in front of the church (monthly schedules posted at SNAV office). Buses to **Pollara** (40min., 7 per day, 6:05am-5:15pm) and **Leni, Valdichiesa, Malfa, Pollara, Gramignazzi, Rinella,** and **Lingua** (12 per day each, 6:05am-8pm).

▮ ⬛ ORIENTATION AND PRACTICAL INFORMATION. The main road in Salina is **Via Risorgimento,** which runs parallel to the lungomare in front of the port which contains the hydrofoil ticket centers. Rent **scooters** from **Buongiorno Antonio,** V. Risorgimento, 240, S. Marina (☎090 984 3409 or 984 3264). Facing away from the hydrofoil docks, turn left up the curving road uphill. Turn left up the first side street past a row of parked scooters to reach the office. **Caution:** Salina's roads are extremely narrow, high, and riddled with blind curves and fast-moving cars and buses. Only those with experience should attempt to drive. (Scooters €8-8.50 per hr., €26-31 per day; mountain bikes €2.50-3.50/€8-10.50. Helmet and technical assistance included. Gas not included. Open daily 8:30am-8pm.)

In case of emergency, call the **Carabinieri** (☎ 090 984 3019 or 984 3042) or the **City Police** (☎ 090 984 3021). **First Aid** can be reached at ☎ 090 984 3064 or 984 4005. The **Farmacia Comunale**, V. Risorgimento, 111, is at the bottom of the street. (☎ 090 984 30 98. Open M 5:30-8:30pm, Tu-F 9am-1pm and 5:30-8:30pm, Sa 9am-1pm.) **Banco di Sicilia**, V. Risorgimento, cashes **traveler's checks, exchanges money,** and has an **ATM.** (☎ 090 984 3365. Open M-F 8:30am-1:30pm and 2:45-3:45pm.) There is a **post office,** at V. Risorgimento, 13, which changes AmEx traveler's checks. (☎ 090 984 3028. Open daily 8am-1:20pm.) **Postal Code:** 98050.

⌂⌂ ACCOMMODATIONS AND FOOD. Restaurants are crowded into Santa Marina, the town by the docks, but most accommodations are farther afield in neighboring towns. To stay in Santa Marina, consider the **Pensione Mamma Santina ❹**, V. Sanità, 40, which offers first-rate rooms painted in traditional Aeolian colors. Guests mingle on the melon-colored terrace and the enthusiastic owner makes everyone feel at home. The owner/chef has been featured in *Cucina Italiana.* (☎ 090 984 3054; fax 984 3051; www.mammasantina.it. Half-pension Jan. €47, Aug. €83; full pension Jan. from €62, Aug. €99. AmEx/D/MC/V.) Take the bus or aliscafo to Rinella for Salina's only true budget accommodations, **Campeggio Tre Pini**, V. Rotabize, 1, which has a market, bar, and restaurant. Terraced sites drop down to the sea. (☎ 090 980 9155 or 980 9041. Reserve July-Aug. €4.13-6.20 per person, €10.33-12.91 per tent.)

Ristorante da Franco ❹, V. Belvedere, 8 (☎ 090 984 3287), up the hill from Mamma Santina until you get to the main road, then right down to the small and winding V. Belvedere, promises "courtesy, hospitality, and quality" from "the best of nature." The 15min. walk uphill works up a healthy appetite and rewards the intrepid with the best views in Salina. The chef and owner, who has been featured in a number of international cuisine magazines, mixes up specialties with a smile. *Primi* (from €9.30) overflow with home-grown vegetables, and *secondi* (from €10.33) are made with fresh fish from around the island. Homemade wine goes for €7.75. (Open June-Sept. daily noon-2:30pm and 8pm-midnight; closed Jan.-May. AmEx/MC/V.) At night, **Ni Lausta ❸**, V. Risorgimento, 188 (☎ 090 984 3486) crowds locals and tourists into the bar downstairs for quick drinks and the latest gossip. Evening diners come upstairs to enjoy *pasta modo mio*, an ever-changing original pasta dish, in the more relaxed garden terrace. (Open Apr.-Oct. Bar open 5pm-3am, and earlier for coffee; restaurant open for dinner 7pm-midnight. MC/V.) As always, the cheapest way to eat is the cold lunch; assemble a beach picnic at any *alimentari* on V. Risorgimento.

◙ SIGHTS. Seeing Salina's finest sight involves a harrowing hour-long bus ride from Santa Marina to the dramatic ☒**beach** at Pollara, which lies 100m straight down from the town's cliffs, in the middle of a half-submerged volcanic crater. The trip is worth every twist and turn. Black sand, crumbling boulders, and raked sandstone walls create the rough crescent of land that embraces impossibly blue water. To the far right, a natural rock archway bursts out of the water, sunning itself against the cliff. On the other side of the island, **Valdichiesa** rests at the base of **Monte Fossa delle Felci,** the highest point in the Aeolians. Trails lead from the town 962m up the mountain to superb vistas. Those not willing to climb relax at Malfa's luxurious beach, offering views of the *sconcassi* and huge sulfur bubbles. The first Sunday in June, the population of Salina heads to Pollara for the festivities of the **Sacra del Cappero.** Each restaurant and volunteering family brings their own special dish, where the *cappero* is key, and all present feast. Visitors to the town during this time should try to blend in and bring their own goodies to contribute. Partying with the locals is always a treat.

FILICUDI AND ALICUDI ☎ 090

Filicudi and its distant neighbor Alicudi are the best-kept secrets of the Aeolians. Outside the summer rush, Filicudi is left entirely to its 250 inhabitants, though even in July and August the island is seldom found on the standard Sicilian itinerary. The lack of developed towns and related activity makes Filicudi ideal for outdoor exploration and hiking. A thick tangle of cacti, fruit trees, and flowers, climb up lush slopes and rocky terraces. The rewarding climb up Fossa delle Felci (774m) takes visitors to the rewarding view of La Canna, the impressive rock spike that bursts 71m out of the sea. Enchanting beaches and grottoes encircle the mountainous terrain. Some sandy stretches, including the Grotta del Bue Marino, lie in front of interesting caves. Exploration by water is also a great way to see Filicudi's charms from a distance. Contact **I Delfini,** V. Pecorini (☎/fax 090 988 9077) in Pecorini Mare, a village near the port, for boat, moped, and scuba diving rentals. In case of emergency call the **carabinieri** (☎ 090 988 9942) or **Guardia Medica** (☎ 090 988 9961). The **post office** (☎ 090 98 80 53) is uphill to the right of the port. Filicudi does not have an ATM or a hospital.

Even reaching accommodations in Filicudi is an adventure. Its two most affordable hotels are perched atop the cliff directly over the port. The island's one paved road reaches it eventually, but the most direct route (though not necessarily the easiest) is a steep 15min. climb up staggered rock steps. The steps begin at your right as you step off the dock, before you reach Hotel Phenicusa. When you finally make it up to the top, you will first hit **Hotel La Canna ❹,** V. Rosa, 43, a traditional house with a fantastic view of Filicudi's natural landscape. All rooms have bath, A/C, and TV. The hotel features a communal terra-cotta terrace, Internet access, and a restaurant that serves typical Sicilian cooking and seafood specialties. (☎ 090 98 89 56 or 336 92 65 60; fax 988 9966; vianast@tin.it. With breakfast: €33.57-€64.56; half-pension €49.06-€87.80; full board €18. AmEx/MC/V.) Hotel-restaurant **Villa La Rosa ❹,** V. Rosa, 24, is the social center of the island for locals and tourists. The hotel contains anything you could possibly need, including a restaurant, bar, mini-supermarket, video arcade and *discoteca.* (☎ 090 988 9965 or 331 83 16 55; fax 988 9291; www.wel.it/VillaLaRosa. Half-pension Sept-May €38.73, June €41.32, July 1-19 €51.65, July 20-Aug. €61.97; full-pension year-round €15.49. AmEx/MC/V.) If the thought of the steep climb gives you butterflies, consider staying at the **Hotel Club Phenicusa ❹,** at the Porto. Each room contains a bath and a balcony with a view of the ocean or the mountainside. (☎ 090 988 9946; fax 988 9955; www.capocalava.com. With breakfast and ocean view €34-40, mountain view €30-37; half board €50-85/€46-80; full-pension €67-100/€63-95. Bed and breakfast option not available July-Aug. MC/V.) If you get hungry while seaside, stop by Restaurant-Bar **Da Nino ❸,** V. Porto (☎ 090 988 9984), with tables by the water. Da Nino also rents out motorbikes (Aug. €30 per day) and boats (Aug. €90-230 per day).

EASTERN SICILY

MESSINA ☎ 090

Messina is a transportation hub; better air-conditioning and a duty-free shop would turn this fast-paced town into an airport. While its role as a major port and the main commercial connection between Sicily and the mainland has brought prosperity, it has been threatened throughout the years by invaders (Carthaginians took over in the 4th century BC, followed by the Mamertines, the Normans and Richard the Lionheart), plagues (1743 and cholera in 1854) and major earthquakes in both 1783 and 1908, with other lesser earthquakes and disasters in between. Despite all obstacles, the town maintains its dignity in points of historical interest such as the duomo, the tall and allegorical clock tower next door, and the church of Santa Maria Annunziàta dei Catalani, must-sees on any Messina itinerary.

TRANSPORTATION

Trains: Central station (☎ 090 67 97 95 or info 147 88 80 88), on P. della Repubblica. Call ahead; schedules change frequently. To: **Naples** (4½hr., 7 per day, €21.59); **Palermo** (3½hr., 15 per day, €10.07); **Rome** (9hr.; 7 per day; €29.44, less-frequent rapido trains €40.28); **Syracuse** (3hr., 14 per day, €6.71); and **Taormina** (1hr., 26 per day, €2.84). Trains to the west stop in **Milazzo**, the main port of the Aeolian Islands (45min., €2.32). **Luggage storage** available (p. 652).

Buses: Messina has 4 bus carriers, many of which serve the same routes.

AST (☎ 090 66 22 44, ask for "*informazioni*"). The province's largest carrier; their *biglietteria* is in an orange minibus across P. Duomo from the cathedral. They service all destinations including smaller and less-touristed areas all over Southern Italy and Sicily.

SAIS, P. della Repubblica, 6 (☎ 090 77 19 14). The ticket office is behind the trees, across from the far left tip of the train station. To: **Airport** (1-2hr., 6 per day, €6.71); **Catania** (1½hr., 9 per day, €6.20); **Florence** (19hr., 1 on Su, €28.92); **Naples** (22hr., 3 per wk., €25.31); and **Palermo** (1½hr., 8 per day, €12.39).

Interbus P. della Repubblica, 6 (☎ 090 66 17 54), has blue offices left of train station, beyond the line of buses. To **Giardini Naxos** (1½hr., 9 per day, €2.58); **Naples** (1 on Su, €20.40); **Rome** (2 per day, €12.91); and **Taormina** (1½hr., 12 per day, €2.58).

Giuntabus, V. Terranova, 8 (☎ 090 67 37 82 or 67 57 49), 3 blocks up V. 1 Settembre, left onto V. Bruno, right onto V. Terranova. To: **Catania Airport** (Apr.-Sept. daily 4pm, €10.33) and **Milazzo** from the Terranova station (45min., M-Sa 14 per day, 6am-6pm, 1 on Su, €3.10).

Ferries: NGI (☎ 0335 842 7785) and **Meridiano** (☎ 347 910 0119 or 090 641 3234), under the 1st pair of yellow cranes on the waterfront, 300m from the FS station. To **Reggio** on NGI: 40min., M-F 12 per day, Sa 10 per day, Su 1 per day, €0.52) and on **Meridiano** (40min., M-F 15 per day, Sa 11 per day, Su 3 per day, €1.55).

Hydrofoils: From the waterfront wing of the central rail station, Messina Marittima, **FS** sends hydrofoils to **Reggio** (25 min., 12 per day, €2.58) and **Villa S. Giovanni** (30min., 3 per hr., €0.93). **SNAV** (ticket office ☎ 0903 64 044; fax 28 76 42), has offices in a blue building on the waterfront side of C. V. Emanuele, 2km north of the train station off C. Garibaldi. Hydrofoils to: **Aeolian Islands** (2hr., 3-6 per day for each destination from June-Sept.); **Lipari** (40min., 6 per day, €16.53); **Salina** (1¼hr., 4 per day, €19.11); and **Panarea** (1¾hr., 3 per day, €19.11).

Public Transportation: Orange **ATM** buses leave either from P. della Repubblica or from the bus station, 2 blocks up V. 1 Settembre from the station, on the right. Purchase tickets (€0.52) at any *tabacchi* or newsstand. Detailed bus info on yellow-bordered signs outside the *autostazione*. Note that bus #79, stopping at the duomo, museum, and aquarium, can only be taken from P. della Repubblica.

Taxis: Radio Taxi Jolly (☎ 090 65 05), to the right of duomo.

ORIENTATION AND PRACTICAL INFORMATION

Messina's transportation center is **Piazza della Repubblica,** in front of the train station, home to the tourist office and headquarters for several bus lines. **Via G. la Farina** runs directly in front of the train station. Beyond the highrises to the left, **Via Tommaso Cannizzaro** leads to the center of town, meeting palm tree-lined **Viale S. Martino** at **Piazza Cairoli.** Enter P. della Repubblica from the train station. At the far right end begins **Via Primo Settembre,** which intersects **Corso Garibaldi.** C. Garibaldi runs along the harbor to both the hydrofoil dock and **Corso Cavour.**

SAFETY FIRST. Women should **not** walk alone in Messina at night, and no one should roam the streets near the train station or the harbor after 10pm. Stay near the more populated streets around the duomo and the university. Be wary of pick-pockets and purse-snatchers, and keep money in a secure place.

Tourist Office: Azienda Autonoma Per L'Incremento Turistico (AAPIT), V. Calabria, 301 (☎090 64 02 21or information office 67 42 36). The office is on the right corner facing P. della Repubblica from the train station. Well-staffed, with a deluge of maps and helpful info on Messina, the Aeolian Islands, and even Reggio Calabria. Open M-Th 9am-1:30pm and 3-5pm, F 9am-1:30pm.

Currency Exchange: Cambio/Ufficio Informazioni (☎147 88 80 88), just inside the train station. Good rates and info on trains and buses. Open daily 7am-8pm. Another exchange is available at **F. III. Grosso,** V. Garibaldi 58 (☎090 77 40 83). Open M-F 8:30am-1pm, Sa 8:30am-12:30pm. There are **ATMs** just outside the train station, to the right and at V. Cannizzaro, 24, and **Banco di Napoli** on V. Emanuele facing the port.

English-Language Bookstore: Libreria Nunnari e Sfameri, V. Cannizzaro, 116 (☎090 71 04 69), is a university bookstore that contains 4 shelves of familiar English and American classics—stock up on Shakespeare and Hemingway here. Open M-F 8:30am-1pm and 4-8pm, Sa 8:30am-1pm.

Luggage Storage: Central station (☎090 678 6433), €3.87 per day. Open daily 6am-10pm (see p. 651).

Emergency: ☎113. **Police:** ☎113. **Carabinieri:** ☎112.

First Aid: ☎118. **Accidents:** ☎090 77 10 00.

Guardia Medica: (☎090 34 54 22), V. Garibaldi, 242.

Late-Night Pharmacy: Farmacia Abati, Viale S. Martino, 39 (☎090 71 75 89 for info on all pharmacies in town). Up V. del Vespro 4 blocks, then left, from the station. All pharmacies open M-F 8:30am-1pm and 4:30-8pm. Posted schedules show weekly late-night rotation among local pharmacies.

Hospital: Ospedale Piemonte, Viale Europa, (☎090 222 4347).

Internet: Internet Point, V. dei Mille, 200. (☎090 678 3289). About €4 per hour. Open M-Sa 9am-1pm and 4pm-8pm. Military and student discounts. **Stamperia,** V.T. Cannizzaro, 170 (☎090 640 9428; stamperi@tin.it). €5.16 per hr. Open M-F 8:30am-1:30pm and 3:30-8pm.

Post Office: (☎0906 68 64 15), on P. Antonello, off C. Cavour and across from Galleria. Open M-Sa 8:30am-6:30pm.

Postal Code: 98100.

ACCOMMODATIONS

Messina continues to be a fly-by, not a stop-over, on the travel itinerary. The handful of hotels the city does possess cater not to cost-conscious travelers, but to businessmen with deep pockets. Messina's cheaper hostels tend to be in a shadier neighborhood near the train station; be extremely careful during the evening.

Hotel Cairoli, (☎090 67 37 55). From the station, 4 blocks up V. del Vespro and left 1 block. A white and blue vertical sign is prominent over the doorway. The small rooms are plain and minimally furnished, but come with TV, A/C, and phone. Ask at the front desk for a coupon that will get you a free breakfast at the cafè around the corner. Singles €38, with bath €46; doubles €62.50/€77; triples €77/€103. AmEx/MC/V. ❸

Hotel Mirage, V. N. Scotto, 3 (☎090 293 8844). Turn left from the train station, pass the buses, and continue under the *autostrada* bridge onto V. Scotto. Mission-style simplicity in airy rooms with tall windows. Curfew midnight. Singles €21; doubles €37, with bath and TV €45-51. MC/V. ❷

Hotel Touring, V. N. Scotto, 17 (☎090 293 8851), a few steps from Hotel Mirage. Mirrors and faux marble-lined halls lead to simple rooms with dark wood furniture and armoirs. Midnight curfew. Singles €20, with bath and TV €35; doubles €35/€45. ❷

The Royal Palace Hotel, V. T. Cannizzaro, 224 (☎090 65 03; fax 292 1075, ricevimento.royal@framon-hotels.it), offers spacious, elegant rooms and a fancy restaurant to match. Breakfast included. Singles €105; doubles €158. AmEx/MC/V. ❺

❏ FOOD

Ristorante and *trattorie* cluster in the area around V. Risorgimento, reached by following V. Cannizzaro two blocks past P. Cairoli. Messina is hooked on swordfish, whether baked, fried, or stewed *(pesce stocco)*. Eggplants are stuffed or mixed into *caponata* (fried eggplant, onion, capers, and olives in a red sauce). The *cannoli* and sugary *pignolata* are sinfully rich. The **STANDA supermarket,** P. Cairoli, 222, in the center of town, is a great place to stock up on the basics. (☎090 292 7738. Open M-Sa 9am-8pm.) Fresh fruit and vegetables are cheaper and readily available on nearly every street.

▨ **Osteria del Campanile,** V. Loggia dei Mercanti, 9-13 (☎/fax 090 71 14 18), behind the duomo. Locals flock to the elegant dining room or the sidewalk tables for *linguini all'inferno marina* and other tasty traditional treats. *Primi* €5.20, *secondi* €6.20. Open Tu-Su 12:30-2:30pm and 7:30pm-midnight. AmEx/MC/V. ❸

Osteria Etnea, V. Tommaso Cannizzaro, 155-57 (☎090 71 80 40), near the university. Art-deco rooms with fancy tablecloths bearing delicious signature pasta and fish dishes from €4.13. Cover and bread €1.55. Open daily noon-4pm and 8:30pm-midnight. ❷

Trattoria Del Popolo, P. Francesco Lo Sardo, 30 (☎090 67 11 48). Offers a quiet meal off a busy piazza. Open Su-F for lunch and dinner. ❸

Pizza e Coca, V. C. Battisti, N47 (☎090 67 36 79). Take V. Primo Settembre one block down from the duomo and turn right. The pizza (from €3.62) and *bruschette* (€1.03), in this local hangout are delicious and inexpensive. Open daily 7:30pm-midnight. ❷

❻ SIGHTS

Though Messina has lost many of its monuments to earthquakes, invasions, and bombings, the town features a number of great sights, many of which have been recently restored. Messina's churches, ranging from Romanesque to Baroque design, dot the city. Some of the churches on the outskirts of town, such as **Montalto,** offer sweeping views of the city and port.

PIAZZA DEL DUOMO. Bright flagstones and shady trees provide a relaxing respite from the bustling city that surrounds this central piazza. The great duomo, originally built in Norman times and dedicated in 1197 to the Virgin Mary, dominates the square with an enormous sandstone face that can be blinding in the afternoon sun. The surprisingly long nave rolls past fourteen niche sculptures of saints to arrive at a massive altar dedicated to *Madonna della Lettera*, the city's patroness. **Il Tesoro** (the Treasury), a modern two-story museum, houses the church's most valuable possessions, including gold reliquaries, chalices, and candlesticks. The highlight of the collection is the ornate *Manta d'Oro* (Golden Mantle), a special cover, decorated with precious stones and jewels, for the picture of the Madonna and Child in the church's altar, now on display for the first time in three centuries. Plans for the ▓bell tower began in the early 16th century, and at 90m, the structure was to be the highest bell-tower in Sicily. After being struck by lightning in 1588, restorations continued throughout the ages until in 1933, when the tower acquired the large clock it hosts today. The structure displays man's arduous ascension from a base being to a noble creature, as well as an astrological wheel. At noon, a creaky recording of Schubert's *Ave Maria* booms and the gigantic lion lets out a mechanical roar. Below the clock tower, mythology and local lore meet in stone at the **Fontana di Orione** (1547), designed by a pupil of Michelangelo, Angelo Montorsoli. The intricate fountain glorifies Orion, the mythical founder of Messina. *(Duomo open daily 8am-6:30pm. Guided tours of Il Tesoro in English, French, and German available. €2.58, under 18 or over 65 €1.55.)*

MUSEO REGIONALE. This museum was created in a converted spinning mill to house whatever could be salvaged from the monastery of St. Gregory and churches throughout the city after the devastating earthquakes of 1894 and 1908. A series of galleries around a quiet courtyard display the chronological development of the surprisingly rich Messinese artistic tradition. The most notable pieces are *The Polyptych of the Rosary* (1473) by local master Antonello da Messina, Andrea della Robbia's terra-cotta of the *Virgin and Child*, and Caravaggio's life-size *Adoration of the Shepherds* (1608) and *Resurrection of Lazarus* (1609). Inside the entrance, bronze door panels tell the story of the Madonna della Lettera. *(Down from the hydrofoil port. Take bus #8 or #79 from the station or P. Duomo to P. Museo. ☎ 090 36 12 92. Open Oct.-May M, W, F 9am-1:30pm; Tu, Th, and Sa 9am-1:30pm and 3-5:30pm, Su 9am-12:30pm; June-Sept. M, W, F 9am-1:30pm; Tu, Th, Sa 9am-1:30pm and 4-6:30pm, Su 9am-12:30pm. €4.13.)*

PORT. Messina's history and character largely centers on its naval prowess. The modern port is more than a place to catch a hydrofoil; it is a destination in itself. The impossibly blue waters are protected by the city's most important icons: the enormous **La Madonnina,** a 6m golden statue, watches over the comings and goings of the city from a 60m column across the water in the port's center; while on the city side, the pristine **Fontana di Nettuno** by Montorsoli graces the intersection of V. Garibaldi and V. della Libertà. The muscular marble god extends one arm to calm the seas and stands above the monsters Scylla and Charybdis. Locals crowd the sides of the docks for leisurely afternoons fishing and sunning, or lounge at the outdoor cafes. The port becomes dangerous during the evening and night, however, so be sure to make this a daytime visit.

CHURCH OF THE SANTISSIMA ANNUNZIATA DEI CATALANI. On V. Garibaldi, this church was built between 1150 and 1200 on the remains of a pagan temple, and then again after its front section collapsed in a flood in the Middle Ages. The church still shows Islamic and Byzantine influence in its archways and layout. Known by the name "Catalani" since it was given to the guild of Catalan merchants in the 16th century, it was turned into their headquarters.

🎵 ENTERTAINMENT

The *Festa di Madonna della Lettera* on June 3rd celebrates the city's protector. Parades throughout the town end at the duomo, where the *Manta d'Oro* is restored to the altar for one day every year. Messina overflows with sightseers and approximately 150,000 white-robed pilgrims during the nationally celebrated **Ferragosto Messinese** festival from August 13-15. During the first two days of Ferragosto, two huge human effigies called Mata and Grifone are motored around the city in the *Processione dei Gianti* (Procession of the Giants).

MILAZZO ☎ 090

In times past, one or two boats at most would leave Milazzo's calm port each day. Today, however, ferries and hydrofoils leave the docks every hour, heading towards the Aeolians or towards the Italian mainland. Though this has created a fast-paced, hectic transportation center, Milazzo is nonetheless a worthwhile tourist destination in itself. Older parts of the city boast beautiful ancient churches, a grand castle, and breathtaking views over the water.

⊟🔁 TRANSPORTATION AND PRACTICAL INFORMATION. Trains run to **Messina** (30min., every hr., €2.45) and **Palermo** (2½hr., €8.78). Milazzo's center is a 10min. orange bus ride from the train station (€0.75). **Giuntabus** (☎ 090 67 37 82 or 067 57 49) runs **buses** to **Messina** (45min., every hr., 14 per day, €3.10). Both Giuntabuses and city buses arrive in **Piazza della Repubblica** at the center of the port. **Lungomare Garibaldi** runs the length of the port. Take a left down **Via Crispi** and right into **Piazza Caio Duilio** and follow the yellow signs to the **tourist office**, P. C. Duillo, 20. (☎ 090 922 2865. Open July-Aug. M-F 8am-2:30pm and 3-6:30pm.) Milazzo's *castello* in the old center is well-regarded. Hourly guided tours in summer.

🔋🔲 ACCOMMODATIONS AND FOOD. Milazzo has a good number of reasonably priced accommodations. The **Hotel Central ❷**, V. del Sole, 8, is a family-run establishment with 12 clean rooms and a cheery ambience. (☎ 090 928 1043. Communal baths and TVs in rooms. €18 per person, doubles in August €36. AmEx/MC/V for longer stays only.) Across the street is **Hotel California ❷**, V. del Sole, 9, such a lovely place. (☎ 090 922 1389. Singles with shared bathroom €18-21; doubles with bath €31-42.) **The Petit Hotel ❺**, directly across from the port, is a new establishment with high quality facilities. Paintings line spacious rooms equipped with organic linen bedding, private bathroom, TV, telephone, and A/C. Their **restaurant** serves all organic food on a top-floor terrace overlooking the coast. (☎ 090 928 6784; www.petithotel.it. Singles €70-120; doubles €100-200.) **Campground: Riva Smerelda ❶**, Strada Panoramica (☎ 090 928 7791), is 6km out of town on Capo Milazzo and can be reached by bus from P. della Repubblica.

Milazzo is designed for eating on the go. Bars line the *lungomare* and fruit vendors set up along V. Regis in P. Natasi and at the intersection with V. del Sole. There is a large **supermarket** at V. del Sole, 34, a block away from the Hotels Central and California. Head to **Pizzeria da Tonino ❷**, V. Cavour, 27 (☎ 090 928 3839) for 30 varieties of pizza €3.62, served in air-conditioned turquoise Tex-Mex splendor. For an elegant sit-down meal try **Ristorante Al Gambero ❷**, V. Luigi Rizzo, 5/7, at the end of the port under a large sign. (Pizza from €3.50, *primi* €5, *secondi* €8. Open 11am-4pm and 7pm-2am. AmEx/MC/V.)

TAORMINA ☎ 0942

Legend has it that Neptune wrecked a Greek boat off the eastern coast of Sicily in the 8th century BC, and that the sole survivor, so inspired by the spectacular scenery onshore, founded Taormina. Historians tell a different tale: the Carthaginians founded Tauromenium at the turn of the 4th century BC, only to have it wrested away by the Greek tyrant Dionysius. Disputed origins aside, Taormina is a city of unsurpassed beauty, where mansions and pines crown a cliff above the sea. Disoriented, fanny-packed foreigners, hearty backpackers, and elite VIPs come for a glimpse of what millions of photographic flashes and hyperbolic statements can't seem to dull: the vista dizzily sweeping from boiling Etna to the straits of Messina.

▐ TRANSPORTATION

Taormina is accessible by bus from **Messina** or **Catania**. Although **trains** from Catania and Messina are more frequent, the train station lies far from Taormina in Giardini Naxos. **Buses** run from the train station to **Taormina** (every 30min., 6:50am-midnight) and **Giardini-Naxos** (M-Sa 6:50am-midnight, Su 9am-midnight).

Trains: (☎0942 51 026 or 51 511). Station at the bottom of Giardini-Naxos's hill. To: **Catania** (45min., 36 per day, 1:20am-8:16pm, €2.84); **Messina** (50min., 31 per day, 4:02am-11:25pm, €2.84); and **Syracuse** (2hr., 16 per day, 4:10am-8:02pm, €6.46).

Buses: Interbus (☎0942 62 53 01). Ticket office open daily 6am-8:15pm. Located at the end of V. Pirandello, off C. Umberto. **CST** (☎0942 62 60 88) offers *Etna Tramonto*, a sunset trip up the volcano (July-Aug. M and W 3:45pm; Sept. M and W 3:15pm; Oct. M and W 2:15pm; €55). To: **Catania** (M-Sa 15 per day, 6:30am-9pm; Su 12 per day, 6:30am-6pm; €3.80, €6.20 round-trip) and **Messina** (M-Sa 10 per day, 6:30am-7:20pm; Su 8:50am, 12:30pm, 6pm; €2.50, €4.10 round-trip). Same bus runs to **Giardini-Naxos** and train station (dir.: Recanti or Catania; M-F every 30min., 6:50am-midnight; €1.20, €2 round-trip). Also to **Gole Alcantara** (M-Sa 4 per day, 9:30am-6:30pm, Su 9:30am; €4.30 round-trip) and **Isola Bella, Mazzaro,** and **Spisone** (M-Sa 14 per day, 6:30am-7:40pm; Su 4 per day, 8:40am-5:40pm; €1.50, €2 round-trip).

Moped and Car Rental: Autonolo "City," P. Sant' Antonio, 5 (☎0942 23 161), around corner from post office at the end of C. Umberto. **Scooters:** €24 per day, €145 per wk. **Vespas:** €37 per day, €235 per wk. 2 seats. Must be 18+ and have a Vespa license. **Cars:** €59-130 per day, €272-491 per wk. 21+ only, must have had license for at least 1 year. Gas not included in price. Open daily 8am-noon and 4-8pm.

▐ ▐ ORIENTATION AND PRACTICAL INFORMATION

To reach the city from the train station, hop on the blue Interbus that makes the trip uphill (10min., every 30min., 7:45am-11:45pm, €1.30). Taormina's steep and narrow streets are closed to cars; all automobiles are directed into a small lot at the base of **Via Pirandello.** From the bus depot, the center is a brief walk left up V. Pirandello to **Corso Umberto I,** which runs the length of town. Beginning under a stone archway, the road runs left through four principal piazzas. Small stairways and sidestreets wind downhill to countless restaurants, shops, and bars. **Via Naumachia** leads downhill to **Via Bagnoli Croci,** which continues to the public gardens.

Tourist Office: AAST, P. Corvaja (☎0942 23 243; fax 24 941), off C. Umberto across from P. V. Emanuele. English-speaking staff provides several pamphlets and a generic, rather non-specific map; the turquoise fold-out "SAT Sicilian Airbus Travel" map is more helpful. Open M-Sa 8:30am-2pm and 4-7pm.

Luggage Storage: In train station, €3.87 per bag. Open 6am-9pm.

Currency Exchange: Dozens of banks line C. Umberto and V. Pirandello. **ATMs** are in great supply, as are **currency exchange** offices, including **Cambio Valute,** C. Umberto, 224, right before P. Sant'Antonio. Open M-Sa 9am-1pm and 4-7pm.

American Express: La Duca Viaggi, V. Don Bosco, 39 (☎0942 62 52 55), on P. IX Aprile. Mail held. Open Apr.-Oct. M-F 9am-1pm and 4-7:30pm; Nov-Mar. M-F 9am-1pm and 2-6pm.

Emergency: ☎113 or 0942 61 111.

Police: ☎112 or 0942 23 232.

Medical Assistance: Guardia Medica (☎0942 62 54 19 or 57 92 97).

Late-Night Pharmacy: Farmacia Ragusa, P. Duomo, 9 (☎0942 23 231), posts the weekly rotation. Open Th-Tu 8:30am-1pm and 5-8:30pm.

Hospital: Ospedale San Vincenzo (☎0942 57 92 97), in P. S. Vincenzo.

Internet: Internet Cafe, C. Umberto, 214 (☎0942 62 88 39), has a large number of fast computers at €2 for 20min., €5 per hr. Open daily 9am-11pm.

Post Office: (☎0942 21 108), on P. Sant' Antonio at the very top of C. Umberto near the hospital. Temporary building is directly next to old office, which is undergoing restoration. **Cashes traveler's checks.** Open M-Sa 8am-4:30pm.

Postal Code: 98039.

▐ ACCOMMODATIONS

Taormina's popularity as a resort town makes cheap accommodations difficult to find. If your budget is tight, consider staying in nearby Mazzarò, Spisone, or Giardini-Naxos (see p. 659). Hike down steep trails to Mazzarò and Spisone or take the bus; service stops around 9pm.

Pensione Svizzera, V. L. Pirandello, 26 (☎0942 23 790; fax 62 59 06; svizzera@tao.it; www.tao.it/svizzera), 100m from the bus station. Pricey, but worth every euro. Magnificent sea views. Clean rooms with bath and TV. Breakfast buffet included on a garden terrace by the sea. Reservations advised in Aug. Open Feb.-Nov. and Christmas. Singles €52; doubles €80, with ocean view €88; triples €108; quads €120. AmEx/MC/V. ❹

La Campanella, V. Circonvallazione, 3 (☎0942 23 381; fax 62 52 48), around the bend of the middle road at the end of V. Pirandello. Hallways and lobby cluttered with Sicilian memorabilia, but rooms as tidy as can be. Singles €45; doubles €75. ❹

Inn Piero, V. Pirandello, 20 (☎0942 23 139), near base of C. Umberto after gas station, in 2 buildings overlooking the sea. Small, pristine rooms, all with bath. Breakfast included. Reserve in summer. Singles €49.42-56.81; doubles €64.20-82.37. Extra bed 30%. Discount of 10-15% for students. AmEx/MC/V. ❹

▐ FOOD

Taormina's restaurants are of consistently high quality, but have consistently high prices. Try **STANDA supermarket,** V. Apollo Arcageta, 49, at the end of C. Umberto, one block from the post office. (☎0942 23 781. Open M-Sa 8:30am-1pm and 5-9pm.)

▨ **Trattoria da Nino,** V. Pirandello, 37 (☎0942 21 265), between the buses and town center. Trust Nino to guide you through the delicious dishes on an extensive menu. The fish and pasta are the best in town. *Primi* €3-8, *secondi* €5-10. Cover and service included in price. Discount for students and with *Let's Go.* AmEx/MC/V. ❷

▨ **Bella Blu,** V. Pirandello, 28 (☎0942 24 239). A terrace dining room with seaside view. Waiters burst into song regularly and perform Sicilian classics on guitar. *Primi* from €4.50, *secondi* from €6.50. Cover €1. Open 10am-3:30pm and 6pm until the last person leaves. MC/V. ❷

San Pancrazio, P. San Pancrazio, 3 (☎0942 23 184), at the end of V. Pirandello. Breezy outdoor tables. Pizza from €5, fresh fish plates from €8, and *primi* and *secondi* from €6. Cover €1. Open W-M noon-2:30pm and 7-11pm. AmEx/MC/V. ❸

Gastronomia la Fontana, V. Constantino Patricio, 28 (☎0942 23 478), up the hill (at the end of V. Pirandello) on the middle street, to the right of the arch. Follow the smell of rotisserie chicken to a popular takeout spot. A variety of pizza, *panini,* and savory snacks including *cipolline* and *arancine* (€1-1.50). Open Tu-Su 11:30am-11pm. ❶

◉ SIGHTS

▓ GREEK THEATER. This almost-perfectly preserved theater is Taormina's greatest treasure. It offers an unsurpassed view of Etna, whose sultry smoke and occasional eruptions beat out the plays of Sophocles and Euripedes when it comes to drama. In ancient days, the 3rd-century cliffside arena seated 5000 spectators; today, that same number packs in for the annual summer-long festival **Taormina Arte** (see **Entertainment**). *(Walk up V. Teatro Greco, off C. Umberto at P. V. Emanuele. Open daily 9am-1hr. before sunset. €4.15, EU residents under 18 or over 65 €2.)*

DUOMO. This 13th-century cathedral, rebuilt during the Renaissance, takes center stage. The Gothic interior shelters paintings by Messinese artists and an alabaster statue of the Virgin Mary. A two-legged female centaur, Taormina's mascot, crowns the nearby fountain. *(Up C. Umberto, at P. del Duomo. Under construction in summer 2002; reopening date uncertain.)*

OTHER SIGHTS. Behind the tourist office, the **Church of Santa Caterina** protects a small theater, the **Roman Odeon.** Slip into the **Church of St. Augustine** in Piazza IX Aprile, now the town library. The short walk down V. di Giovanni leads to one of Taormina's most enjoyable and least-visited sights, the **Villa Comunale.** These lush gardens look out over Giardini-Naxos below and Etna in the distance. A trek to the **piccolo castello** offers an escape from boisterous crowds. V. Circonvallazione, which runs parallel to and above C. Umberto, leads to a small stairway that snakes up the mountainside to the castle.

♪ ◉ ENTERTAINMENT AND BEACHES

While the wildest nights are spent below in action-packed Giardini-Naxos, Taormina also stays up well past its bedtime. Chic bars line C. Umberto and its tributary side streets. The **Re Di Bastoni,** C. Umberto, 120, in the center of town, serves sandwiches and large salads (from €7.20) all day, and cocktails with fresh fruit (from €5.70) late into the night. Live jazz on Friday evenings. (☎ 0942 23 037. Open daily 11:30am-3am. AmEx/MC/V.) **Mediterraneo,** V. di Giovanni, 6, packs in a lively crowd that devours crepes and cocktails. Head to the area around P. Garibaldi, off C. Umberto, for a number of small and unique bars and clubs. The lively **Casanova Pub,** V. Paladini, 2, off C. Umberto before P. Garibaldi, serves pizza (from €6.50) and cocktails (from €6), on colorful tables. (☎ 0942 23 945. Open daily 10am-7am. AmEx/MC/V.) **Cafe Marrakech,** P. Garibaldi, 2, seduces party-goers under Arabic tents, with cocktails from €5.50. (☎ 0942 62 56 92. Open daily 6pm-3 or 4am.) Next door, **Shateulle,** mixes things up late into the night. (☎ 0942 62 61 75. Open daily 6pm-3:30am.) A 30min. jaunt down the hill leads to **Tout Va,** V. Pirandello, 70 (☎ 0942 23 824), an open-air club with good food and great views.

Every summer from late July to September, the city pleases crowds with **Taormina Arte,** an international festival of theater, ballet, music, and film. Past performances have attracted the likes of Jose Carreras, Bob Dylan, and Ray Charles. (☎ 0942 62 87 49. Ticket office at C. Umberto, 19.)

Tourists and locals lounge on beach **Lido Mazzarò,** just below town, where shallow sparkling waters flow around the tiny **Isola Bella,** a national nature preserve, 100m off-shore. **Cable cars** zip from V. Pirandello to Lido. (☎ 0942 23 605. In summer every 15min., 8:30am-1:30am; €1.60, €2.70 round-trip.) The island beach is just a 200m walk uphill to the right. The strong-stomached can travel the narrow, winding route by bus to **Castelmola,** the highest point of Taormina, complete with medieval castle and fantastic panorama. **Gole Alcantura** is a nearby haven of waterfalls, gorges, and rapids. The Gole Alcantara office has a monopoly on tours. (☎ 0942 98 50 10. €4.15; wetsuit €7.75.) Bring sunscreen, a towel, a change of clothes, and sturdy shoes for hiking. Restaurants and a bar are on the premises.

GIARDINI-NAXOS   ☎ 0942

Giardini-Naxos was the site of the first Greek colony in Sicily (734 BC). Naxos enjoyed moderate success, at its height reaching a population of 10,000. An alliance with Syracuse in its 5th-century BC war for independence against Athens resulted in the devastation of Naxos. The modern town now has fewer splintered ancient Greek remains and more *Giardini* (gardens), with fertile slopes, shady palms, and wild flowers clinging to volcanic cliffs. The eastern coast's ultimate beach town, with a long *lungomare* and an impressive collection of clubs, Giardini-Naxos swims all day and swings all night.

⌐⚡ TRANSPORTATION AND PRACTICAL INFORMATION. Only 5km away from Taormina, Giardini-Naxos shares a train station with its neighbor. **Interbus** (☎ 0942 62 53 01) runs frequently from Giardini to the train station and Taormina's central bus station (40 per day, 7:35am-11:35pm, €1.55). Signs throughout town point the way to the **AAST tourist office,** V. Tysandros, 54 (☎ 0942 51 010; fax 52 848), along the *lungomare.* English spoken. Open M-F 8:30am-2pm and 4-7pm, Sa 8:30am-2pm. In an **emergency,** call the **carabinieri** (☎ 112) or **first aid** (☎ 0942 53 932). There is a **post office** at V. Erice, 1 (☎ 0942 51 090).

⌐⚡ ACCOMMODATIONS AND FOOD. As in Taormina, hotels in Giardini are often filled in August, but prices are better. Make reservations in advance. The beachfront V. Tysandros is packed with hotels, varying considerably in quality and price. The ▨**Hotel Villa Mora ❹,** V. Naxos, 47, is set back from the *lungomare* promenade, with direct access to the beach. Ask for a room with a view. (☎/fax 0942 51 839; hotelvillamora@tin.it. All rooms with bath, TV with CNN, and fan; some with A/C. Breakfast included. Singles €35-45; doubles €60-84. MC/V.) **Pensione Otello ❷,** V. Tysandros, 62, along the *lungomare,* has simple rooms overlooking a beach. (☎ 0942 51 009. Oct.-July €25 per person. Aug.-Sept. €35 per person.)

Buy necessities at **Sigma supermarket,** V. Dalmazia, 31, down from the central bus stop. (Open M-Sa 8:30am-1pm and 5-10pm.) **Angelina ❷,** V. Calcide Eubea, 2, specializes in seafood. At the tip of Giardini-Naxos's curved port, the dining room has ocean views on two sides, an airy interior and an impressive wine shelf. (☎/fax 0942 51 477. (☎ 0942 62 56 92. *Primi* from €5.16, *secondi* from €7.23. Open daily noon-4pm and 6:30pm-1am. AmEx/MC/V.) **Trattoria Pizzeria Nettuno ❸,** V. Tysandros, 68, along the *lungomare,* offers seafood specialties in a light dining area with a summer atmosphere. Pizza emerges from a wooden stove, starting at €3.50. (☎/fax 0942 57 12 76. *Primi* from €5, *secondi* from €8. Cover €1. Open F-W 12:30-3pm and 6:30pm-midnight. AmEx/MC/V.) For a sea view, head over to **Ristorante-Pizzeria Lido da Angelo ❸,** V. Umberto, 523, which has a patio over a private beach. (☎ 0942 51 902. Pizza from €3.50, *primi* from €5, *secondi* from €7.50. Cover €1. Open daily noon-4pm and 6pm-1am. AmEx/MC/V.)

◙ ☷ SIGHTS AND ENTERTAINMENT. Excavations in the 1960s unearthed traces of a **Greek city,** with walls built of solidified lava blocks. The two-room **Museo Archeologico** records that city's earliest days, and includes an inscribed ceramic cup, the colony's earliest surviving writing. (☎ 0942 51 001. Open 9am-1hr. before sunset. Entrance €2.07; ages 18-25 half-price; under 18, over 65 free).

Beach by day, fluorescent-lit pub promenade by night, Giardini-Naxos seems to casually lose the hours in between. Things light up around 11pm, as busloads of glitzed-up revelers head to pubs, restaurants, and flashy *discoteche*. The party starts 20m from the bus stop at *pizzeria*/karaoke bar **Mister Roll**, V. Jannuzzo, 31. (☎0942 65 30 87. Open daily 8:30pm-5am; in winter closed Tu.) The disco-happy should hang a left to **Marabù**, on V. Jannuzzo. Follow back-lit palm trees and the neon blue cursive sign to this red-carpeted complex, complete with rotating techno, oldies, Latin, and international pop music. (☎0942 65 30 29. Live piano before 1am. Cover €13. Open in summer 11:30pm until morning.) Let your dancing shoes and inner child fly at **Discoteca Peter Pan**, V. Stracina, 4. (Must enter in couples. Cover €10. Open 11pm-4am.) Farther to the left, a poorly lit but well-trafficked road leads down to the all-night *lungomare* party at V. S. Naxos/V. Tysandros, an extra-sensory experience with live music, popcorn and cotton candy vendors, whizzing pre-teen in-line skaters, and people, people, people.

CATANIA
☎095

With the smoking Etna looming above and a reputation as Sicily's crime capital, Catania is a city seemingly fraught with danger. From beneath the squalid veneer of sooty *palazzi*, however, Catania exudes elegance. Leveled repeatedly, most often by the nearby volcano, it has been rebuilt several times since its founding as a Greek colony in 729 BC. After the monstrous 1693 earthquake, G. B. Vaccarini recreated the city with his Baroque piazzas and duomo. The virtuoso composer Vincenzo Bellini brought another type of harmony to Catania: the opera.

▐ TRANSPORTATION

Flights: Fontanarossa (☎095 34 05 05). Take the *alibus* from train station or pay about €20 for the 15min. cab ride. 2 daily flights to Malta with **Air Malta**, V. Libertà, 188 (☎095 31 33 08; fax 31 65 58). Open daily 8:30am-1pm and 2:30-7pm.

Trains: in P. Papa Giovanni XXIII (☎095 730 6255). To: **Agrigento** (4hr., 5 per day, 5:55am-1:35pm, €9.05); **Enna** (1½hr., 4 per day, 5:55am-1:35pm, €4.50); **Florence** (12hr., 4 per day, 4:48-8:15pm, €43.02); **Messina** (2hr., 27 per day, 3:15am-10:40pm, €4.90); **Palermo** (3½hr.; 2:15, 4, and 7:20pm; €11); **Rome** (10hr., 5 per day, 9:10am-10:40pm, €33.47); **Syracuse** (1½hr., 19 per day, 5am-8:50pm, €4.50); and **Taormina/Giardini-Naxos** (1hr., 20 per day, 3:15am-9:40pm, €1.85).

Buses: All companies are on V. D'Amico, across the city bus-filled piazza in front of train station, behind the construction. Reduced service Su. **SAIS Trasporti** (☎095 53 62 01) to **Agrigento** (3hr., 13 per day, 6:45am-9pm, €9.81) and **Rome** (14hr.; 7:50pm and 9pm; €38.73, under 26 or over 60 €33.57). **SAIS Autoline** (☎095 53 61 68) to: **Enna** (1½hr.; M-Sa 7 per day, 6:40am-8pm; Su 3 per day, 9am-8pm; €5.94); **Messina** (1½hr.; M-Sa 28 per day, 5am-9pm; Su 8 per day, 5am-9pm; €6.20); **Palermo** (3hr., 17 per day, €11.62). **Interbus** and **Etna** (☎095 53 27 16), both to: **Brindisi** (8hr.; 1pm and 10pm; €33.57); **Giardini-Naxos** (1hr., 14 per day, 7am-6:45pm, €2.58); **Noto** (2½hr., 8 per day, 8:30am-7pm, €5.68); **Piazza Armerina** (2hr., 7 per day, 8:15am-7:30pm, €4.91); **Ragusa** (2hr., 12 per day, 6am-8pm, €6.20); **Rome** (10hr.; M, Th, F, and Su 8pm; Tu, Th, and Sa 9:30am; €33); and **Taormina** (1¼hr.).

Ferries: La Duca Viaggi, P. Europa, 1 (☎095 722 2295). Walk up V. Africa from train station. Ferry tickets to **Malta** (high season €85.22).

Public Transportation: AMT buses leave from train station in P. Papa Giovanni XXIII. *Alibus* goes to airport and bus #27 to beach. Tickets (€0.77) valid for 1½hr. are sold at *tabacchi* and newsstands.

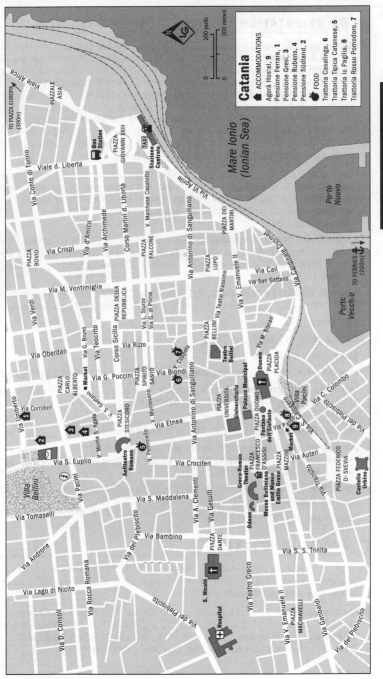

SICILY

Catania

▲ ACCOMMODATIONS
Agorà Hostel, 9
Pensione Ferrara, 1
Pensione Gresi, 3
Pensione Rubens, 4
Pensione Sidiland, 2

● FOOD
Trattoria Casalinga, 6
Trattoria Tipica Catanese, 5
Trattoria le Paglia, 8
Trattoria Rosso Pomodoro, 7

Mare Ionio
(Ionian Sea)

Porto
Nuovo

Porto
Vecchio

TO FERRIES
(200m)

0   200 yards
0   200 meters

✈❓ ORIENTATION AND PRACTICAL INFORMATION

Via Etnea, running from the **duomo** to the **Giardini Bellini,** is Catania's chic main street. From the **train** and **bus stations** in the waterfront **Piazza Giovanni XXIII, Corso Martiri della Libertà** heads west into the city center, changing into **Corso Sicilia** in Piazza della Repubblica. Corso Sicilia bisects V. Etnea in Piazza Stesicoro, under the watchful eye of a pigeon-covered Bellini monument. A right on V. Etnea leads to budget accommodations, fashionable boutiques, the post office, and the gardens; the **Teatro Bellini** and city **University** cluster around the duomo to the left. Although notorious for petty thievery, Catania can be conquered by the cautious traveler. At night, stick to the populated and well-lit areas along V. Etnea; be wary of staged distractions.

Tourist Office: AAPIT, V. Cimarosa, 10 (☎095 730 6233 or 730 6222), near the Bellini gardens. From V. Etnea, turn on V. Pacini before post office and follow signs. English-speaking staff offers brochures on city, region, and Etna. Open daily 8am-8pm. **Branches** at station (☎095 730 6255) and airport (☎095 730 6266 or 730 6277). Open M-Sa 8am-8pm.

Budget Travel: CTS, V. Ventimiglia, 151-153 (☎095 53 02 23; fax 53 62 46; ctscatania@tiscalinet.it), off the piazza where C. Sicilia becomes C. Martiri della Libertà. Useful info on travel in Sicily, Italy, and beyond. Open M-F 9:30am-1pm and 4:30-7:30pm, Sa 9:30am-12:30pm.

American Express: La Duca Viaggi, P. Europa, 1 (☎095 722 2295), up V. Africa from train station. Mail held for 1 month. Open M-F 9am-1pm and 3-6:30pm, Sa 9am-noon.

Emergency: ☎113.

Carabinieri: ☎112 or 095 53 78 22.

State Police: ☎095 736 7111.

First Aid: ☎095 49 77 77. **Guardia Medica:** C. Italia, 234 (☎095 37 71 22 or 38 21 13).

Late-Night Pharmacy: Crocerossa, V. Etnea, 274 (☎095 31 70 53). Open M-Su 4pm-1am. **Croceverde,** V. G. D'Annunzio, 45 (☎095 44 16 62), at the intersection of C. Italia and C. della Provincia.

Hospital: Garibaldi (☎095 759 4371), on P. Santa Maria del Gesù.

Internet: Internet Caffetteria, V. Penninello, 44 (☎095 31 01 39), has a number of speedy computers. €1 for up to 30min., €2 per hr. Open Sept.-June M-Sa 8:30am-9pm, July-Aug. M-Sa noon-10pm.

Post Office: V. Etnea, 215 (☎095 715 5111), in the big building next to the Villa Bellini gardens. Open M-Sa 8am-6:30pm.

Postal Code: 95125.

🏠 ACCOMMODATIONS

Though the plethora of posh stores lining the streets suggests high *pensione* prices, many hotels along V. Etnea can be surprisingly affordable. Make reservations early for late July through September.

▨ **Pensione Rubens,** V. Etnea, 196 (☎095 31 70 73; fax 715 1713). Amicable owner and well-kept, spacious rooms, all with A/C, TV, and phone. Beautiful interior and cozy, clean rooms are an escape from the busier, darker outside streets. Singles €32, with bath €40; doubles €48/€60. Extra bed €15. AmEx/MC/V. ❸

Pensione Gresi, V. Pacini, 28 (☎095 32 27 09; fax 715 3045), off V. Etnea before Villa Bellini and the post office. Decorated hallways lead to social bar, breakfast room, and reading room. Clean rooms with gorgeously painted ceilings have bath, A/C, TV, phone, and minibar. Breakfast €5. Singles €40; doubles €60; triples €75. AmEx/MC/V. ❹

Pensione Ferrara, V. Umberto, 66 (☎095 31 60 00; fax 31 30 60), off V. Etnea across from the gardens. Clean, rosy rooms vary in noise and light levels, but are comfortable and appealing. Singles €26, with bath €40; doubles €41/€51; triples €60/€70; quads €72/€85. ❸

Pensione Südland, V. Etnea, 270 (☎095 31 24 94 or 31 13 43), opposite the post office. Rooms with bath and TV. Reserve 1wk. in advance in summer. Singles €21, with bath €26; doubles €31/€39; triples €40/€51; quads €52/€62. ❷

Agora Youth Hostel, P. Curro, 6 (☎095 723 3010; agorahost@hotmail.com; http://agorahostel.hypermart.net), beside the duomo and the marketplace. Color-coded rooms are well kept, and the nighttime live music and bar keep visitors entertained. Internet available. Includes small breakfast. €15.50 per person. ❶

🍴 FOOD

When Catanians ring the dinner bell, they enjoy eggplant- and ricotta-topped *spaghetti alla Norma*, named for Bellini's famous opera. Other local favorites are fresh anchovies known as *masculini*. The marketplace off P. del Duomo and V. Garibaldi features excited vendors advertising fruits, vegetables, fresh fish, meats, and traditional sweets. The action runs M-Sa in the morning and early afternoon. A **SMA supermarket** is at C. Sicilia, 50. (Open M-Sa 8:30am-10:30pm.) **Bar Savia,** V. Etnea, 304, across from Bellini Gardens, displays *pizzete* and *arancini* and serves the city's best *granite di Gelsi*. (Open Th-Tu 8am-9pm.) **Gelateria del Duomo,** across from the elephant fountain, serves 24 flavors from €1.30. The *latte di mandorla* (almond milk) makes a cool treat. (☎095 715 0556. Open Su-F 5am-midnight, Sa 5am-3am.)

🔲 **Trattoria la Paglia,** V. Pardo, 23 (☎095 34 68 38). Lunch in the heart of the bustling marketplace near P. del Duomo. Tired of tomatoes? Trade red sauce for black with *spaghetti al nero di seppia* (pasta with squid ink, €4.65). Cozy indoor tables. *Primi* from €4, *secondi* from €5.50. Open M-Sa noon-midnight. MC/V. ❷

Trattoria Tipica Catanese, V. Monte S. Agata, 11-13 (☎095 31 54 53), off V. Etnea just after the Stefanel store on P. Stesicoro. Authentic Catanese charm accompanies the food. Wooden-covered menus in many different languages list *primi* and *secondi* from €7. Cover €1.55. Open daily noon-3pm and 7-11pm. AmEx/MC/V. ❸

Trattoria Tipica Catanese Da Mario, V. Penninello, 34 (☎095 32 24 61), off V. Etnea near the amphitheater. This family-run restaurant serves a great variety of *Catanese* cuisine between walls decorated with Sicilian souvenirs. Coperto €2.07. *Primi* from €4, *secondi* from €5.16. Open M-Sa 11am-4pm and 7pm-midnight. AmEx/MC/V. ❷

Trattoria Rosso Pomodoro, V. Coppola, 28 (☎095 250 0010), off V. Biondi near Teatro Bellini. Checkered country-style tablecloths display a mouth-watering *antipasto* buffet. Specialty mixed seafood dish €8. *Primi* from €4, *secondi* from €4.50. Cover €1. Open Tu-Su noon-3:30pm and 7pm-midnight. AmEx/MC/V. ❷

Trattoria Casalinga, V. Biondi, 19 (☎095 31 13 19). Popular with the locals, this little restaurant offers *primi* for €5 and *secondi* for €7. Planned full *menùs* are perfect for larger groups. Cover €1. Open M-Sa noon-4pm and 8pm-midnight. MC/V. ❸

BEWARE THE ANIMAL SPIRITS! According to Catanian legend, each of the city's many animal fountains is inhabited by an animal spirit. Anyone who falls asleep by one of these fountains will lose his soul to the resident animal spirit and never wake up. *Let's Go* does not recommend losing your soul to a resident animal spirit, so nap elsewhere.

SIGHTS

PIAZZA DEL DUOMO. In P. del Duomo, Giovan Battista Vaccarini's little lava **Fontana dell'Elefante** (Elephant Fountain; 1736) commands the city's attention. Vaccarini carved his elephant (the symbol of the city) without visible testicles. When the statue was unveiled, horrified Catanian men, who concluded that this omission was an attack on their virility, demanded corrective measures. Vaccarini's acquiescence was, um, monumental. Residents claim that visitors may attain citizenship by smooching the elephant's tush, but the height of the pachyderm's backside precludes the fulfillment of such aspirations. The other buildings on the piazza, the 18th-century **Palazzo del Municipio** on the left and the former **Seminario dei Chierici** on the right, are striped black and white to mirror the duomo's side.

DUOMO. Restoration in 1950 revealed glimpses of the duomo's interior before its Baroque makeover. Teams discovered stumps of old columns and tall, pointed arches of the original three apses. In the Norman **Cappella della Madonna,** on the right, the sparkling walls surround a beautiful Roman sarcophagus and a 15th-century statue of the Virgin Mary. Nine meters from the chapel, the body of Catania's beloved priest, the Beato Cardinal Dusmet, lies with his bronze head and bony fingers protruding from his vestments. To the right as you enter through the main door is **Bellini's tomb,** guarded by a life-size marble angel. The words and music from his *Sonnambula* are inscribed above the tomb and translate as "Ah, I didn't think I'd see you wilt so soon, flower." *(Modest dress required.)*

OTHER SIGHTS. Uphill from P. del Duomo lies the entrance to the **Greco-Roman Theater,** built in 415 BC. Behind the theater is the similar but smaller **Odeon,** with an entrance around the back. Mt. Etna's 1669 eruption coated the marble of both theaters in lava. *(V. V. Emanuele, 266. Open daily 9am-1hr. before sunset. Free.)* The centerpiece of Catania's restoration efforts rests just up V. Etnea. The **Bellini Gardens** sprawl over several small hills, around tiny ponds, and through miniature forests. Below an elegant Victorian bandstand, a small plot displays the day's date in perfect grass figures, replanted daily. Sunday afternoons find half the city strolling here with *gelato* in hand. A few blocks away in P. Stesicoro, modern streets surround the ruins of a second-century **Roman amphitheater.** The tunnels and entrances that gladiators and monsters used to enter the arena are still visible.

ENTERTAINMENT

The **Teatro Massimo (Bellini)** mesmerizes audiences with opera and concerts. Sink into plush red seats during symphony season (Sept.), or wait for the thrill of the opera (Oct.-June). Student discounts are available for all tickets; contact the tourist office. (☎095 730 6111 or 715 0921. Box office open M 9:30am-12:30pm, Tu-F 5-7pm.) The AAPIT's free monthly bulletin *Lapis*, available at bars and the tourist office, details Catania's hot nightlife, movies, concerts, and festivals.

Participants in the nightly *passeggiata* (the Italian slow stroll) circulate the P. del Duomo and swarm near Teatro Bellini. Cafes liven up on weekends, drawing a sometimes raucous crowd. Local university students, urban thirty-somethings, and eager travelers all enjoy the bounty of drinking holes that fill this area. **Mythical Pub,** V. Michele Rapisardi, 8, in the shadow of Teatro Bellini, is where Catania's beautiful people watch one another on weekend nights. (Imaginative cocktails €3.62. Open 9pm.) From the *centro*, locals drive to the dance floor of **Banacher,** V. XXI Aprile S.S., 114, a 15min. taxi ride from Catania. Lights capture dancing crowds until 5am at what is reputed to be Europe's largest outdoor *discoteca*. (☎095 27 12 57. Cover €10. Open Tu-Su 10pm-3am.) Weekend summer crowds also scooter 20min. away to the nightly destination of *passagiate*, seaside bars, and general mayhem known as **Aci Castello.** This side of Catania's coast is far from the city chaos, but it isn't out of reach of Etna's fury; huge black boulders thrown from a boiling Etna line the jagged shore. Catania's biggest feast day is that of **Saint Agata,** the city's patron saint. The first five days of February are saved from winter gloom by a non-stop fireworks display and partying. The pleasant but crowded beach **La Plaja** has a view of a nearby power plant (bus #427, June-Sept. "D"). Farther from the port, an alternative lies at **La Scogliera,** with fiery cliffs and a bathing area (30min., bus #334 from P. del Duomo).

DAYTRIP FROM CATANIA: MOUNT ETNA

An AST bus leaves from Catania's central train station at 8:30am for Rifugio Sapienza. The bus returns to Catania at 4:45pm (times subject to change; round-trip €3.56).

At 3350m, Mt. Etna is one of the world's largest active volcanoes and the tallest in Europe. Etna's history of volcanic activity is the longest documented of any volcano—the first recorded eruption was in 1500 BC. The Greek poet Hesiod envisioned Etna as the home of Typhon, the last monster conceived by Earth to fight the gods before the dawn of the human race. Apparently Typhon's aggressions aren't over yet; a 1985 eruption destroyed much of the summit tourist station, and an eruption in late July of 2001 sent lava rolling down the hillside at 100m per hour. The volcano continues to emit ash.

From Sapienza (1900m), where the AST bus stops, a 2½hr. hike to **Torre del Filosofo** (Philosopher's Tower; 2920m) gives full view of the looming peaks of Etna's steaming craters. Anyone wearing sturdy shoes can safely maneuver around the crater in front of the parking area for a 30min. taste of the peaks.

From the Philosopher's Tower, a 2hr. hike leads to the **craters** themselves. While the view of the hardened lava, huge boulders, and unearthly craters is incredible, the trail is so difficult and the volcanic activity so unpredictable that all guided tours have been suspended. Eleven tourists died several years ago when one of the craters erupted unexpectedly. Those who brave the trip should take precautions; notify someone when you leave, don't go alone, carry water, and bring warm clothing, as winds are ferocious and pockets of snow remain even in mid-July. Returning from the tower, you will pass **Valle de Bove,** Etna's first volcanic crater.

For tour information, call **CST,** C. Umberto, 99-101 (☎0942 62 60 88; fax 23 304; csttao@tiscalinet.it), which runs tours to 3000m (June-Aug. M and W 3:45pm; Sept. 3:15pm; Oct. 2:15pm; €55) and to 2000m (T and Th 8am, €25) or **Gruppo Guide Alpine,** V. Etna, 49 (☎095 53 98 82). **SAT,** C. Umberto, 73, operates day-long tours from Taormina. (☎0942 24 653; www.sat-group.it. Bus tours for Etna leave M 6:40am, €25; tours of the crater area in bus and jeep Tu and Th 3pm, €55). In an **emergency,** call ☎0942 53 17 77.

After a hard day's hike, campers can curl up in a tent at **Camping La Timpa ❶,** V. Nazionale, 31, in the nearby countryside of Acireale. With elevators that descend to sea level, late-night scuba excursions, and unique pizza concoctions at **Pizzeria "A Cumarca" ❸,** it's the perfect place to relax in nature. (☎095 764 8155; fax 764 0049; www.campinglatimpa.it. €4-6 per person, €3-7 per tent, €1.50-2.80 per car. Bungalows: doubles €32-65; triples €38-70; quads €46-75.)

CENTRAL SICILY

ENNA ☎ 0935

Enna, *l'ombelico della Sicilia* (the navel of Sicily), is an isolated city of ancient charms, with worn stone streets, shockingly beautiful vistas, and simple churches. At night, the intimate piazzas are abuzz with youthful faces and winding *passegiate*. Strolls inevitably lead to railings overlooking the mountainside and fields of golden grain that extend as far as the eye can see. For the best view in town, walk the short distance to the towers of the **Castello di Lombardia** (p. 668). On good days, the eye is treated to a panorama that runs all the way to Etna.

▐▌ TRANSPORTATION

Enna is serviced by both buses and trains, but arriving by bus saves you the 8km uphill hike from the train station.

Trains: (☎ 0935 50 09 10). Buses connect station to town center (M-Sa 11 per day, 6:50am-8:55pm, €1.29). Schedule posted in station. To: **Agrigento** (5 per day, 7:17am-2:59pm, €5.06); **Catania** (1hr., 7 per day, 6:13am-7:53pm, €3.72); and **Palermo** (2hr.; 3:42, 5:21, and 8:31pm; €6.56).

Buses: All buses depart from the *autostazione* on V. Diaz, a short walk uphill from P. Matteotti. **Interbus** (☎ 0935 50 23 90) and **SAIS** (☎ 0935 50 09 02) are under 1 roof, with an additional Interbus office on V. Roma by the tourist office (☎ 0935 50 08 99). Buses also pass various stops throughout the city—check with information to find one near you. To: **Catania** (2hr.; M-Sa 6-7 per day, 6:30am-7:15pm; Su 7:30am, 5:30pm, and 6:30pm; €7) continuing to **Noto, Ragusa,** and **Syracuse; Palermo** (2hr., 9 per day, 5:45am-6:30pm, €7.75) and **Piazza Armerina** (35min., 8 per day, 7:10am-6pm, €2.58).

Taxis: (☎ 0935 68 950 or 50 09 05) in P. Scelfo.

✴❷ ORIENTATION AND PRACTICAL INFORMATION

The bus station lies outside Enna's central historic district. **Via Vittorio Emanuele** runs from the station to **Piazza Matteotti,** where **Via Roma** branches in two directions. Straight ahead, V. Roma passes **Piazza Vittorio Emanuele** and the duomo, ending at the **Castello di Lombardia.** To the right, V. Roma cuts an arc through residential areas to the **Torre di Federico II.**

Tourist Offices: AAPIT, V. Roma, 411-413 (☎ 0935 52 82 28). Information on the province of Enna. Open M-Sa 9am-1pm and 3-7pm. For information on the city, schedules and lodgings, head to the AAST office at P. Cloajanni, 6 (☎ 0935 50 08 75; fax 26 119), beside the Hotel Sicilia. English spoken.

Currency Exchange: Banks line V. Roma between P. V. Emanuele and P. Umberto I. Currency exchange also available at the post office.

ATM: There is a Bankomat 3 in P. Umberto on V. Roma.

Emergency: ☎ 113.

Police: ☎ 0935 50 12 89.

Carabinieri: (☎ 112 or 0935 50 13 21), in P. Europa.

Ambulance: ☎ 0935 21 933.

First Aid/Emergency Room: ☎0935 50 08 96.

Guardia Medica: (☎0935 52 04 89 or 50 08 96). Open daily 8pm-8am.

Late-Night Pharmacy: Farmacia del Centro, V. Roma, 315 (☎0935 50 06 50), posts the rotation schedule of the city's late-night pharmacies, as does **Farmacia Librizzi,** P. V. Emanuele, 21 (☎0935 50 09 08). Open 9am-1-m and 4-8pm.

Hospital: Ospedale Umberto I (☎0935 45 245 or 50 08 99), on V. Trieste.

Internet Access: Bar Panorama, V. Belvedere, 16 (☎0935 24 803) has 1 speedy net-connected computer. €5 per hr. Open daily 9-11am and 4pm-midnight.

Post Office: V. Volta, 1 (☎0935 56 23 27 or 56 21 11). Take a left off V. Roma just before the AAPIT and walk to the right, behind the "Provincia" building. Open M-F 8am-6:30pm, Sa 8am-12:30pm.

Postal Code: 94100.

ACCOMMODATIONS

Enna's only accommodation is Hotel Sicilia, with another option out in nearby Pergusa, reached from Enna by **bus #5.** Buses depart from Enna's bus station and in front of Agenzia Coppola on V. Roma; ask to be let out at the Miralago in Pergusa (€0.77).

Hotel Sicilia, P. Colajanni, 7 (☎0935 50 08 50), just up V. Roma from AAPIT in Enna. Posh rooms with bath, TV, hairdryer, and antique furniture. Breakfast buffet included. Singles €57; doubles €91; triples €110. Rooms for 4-5 €155. AmEx/D/MC/V. ❹

Hotel Miralago (☎0935 54 12 72), 3km outside Pergusa's center on V. Nazionale. Area's only budget accommodation. Next to a noisy *discoteca* and somewhat far from any *centro*, the hotel still offers decent prices. Breakfast included. Singles €30; doubles €43; triples €60. ❸

FOOD

Enna's relaxed pace makes eating an enjoyable and lengthy affair. Good restaurants cluster along the aptly titled Viale Belvedere (beautiful view) behind V. Roma and P. Crispi. **Salumeria F. lli Caruso,** V. Roma, 406 (☎0935 51 146), sells the essentials and picnic materials. (Open M-Sa 8:30am-2pm and 5:30-9pm.) A sweeter option is the **Bar del Duomo,** in P. Mazzini next to the duomo, whose glass shelves boast rows of perfect cookies; **Caffe Roma,** V. Roma, 312, sells sweets and *gelato* (€1.30). Picnickers may also want to wander along **Via Mercato Sant'Antonio,** which is filled with *alimentari,* fruit stands, and bakeries.

▨ Ristorante La Fontana, V. Volturo, 6 (☎0935 25 465), in P. Crispi. The indoor dining area, lovely as it is, should be passed over for the flower-covered terrace on popular P. Crispi, overlooking the valley. *Primi* from €4.65, *secondi* from €7.30. Cover €1.04. Open daily noon-3:30pm and 7:30pm-close. AmEx/MC/V. ❷

San Gennaro da Gino, Viale Belvedere Marconi, 6 (☎0935 24 067; fax 50 61 94). Serves fabulous food with a view to match. Start with extensive *antipasti* buffet and finish with delicious *pannacotta* (€2.50), their specialty. Piano bar Tu and F. Pizza from €3.10, *primi* from €5.16, *secondi* from €6.20. Cover €0.77. Service 15%. Open daily 12:30-3pm and 8pm-12:30am. MC/V. ❷

Ristorante Pizzeria Ariston, V. Roma, 353 (☎0935 26 038), with another entrance on V. Volturo. Head here for an elegant indoor meal. Mirror-lined walls, peach flowers and tablecloths. Pizza from €3.10, *primi* from €6.20, *secondi* from €11.36. Cover €1.30. Open M-Sa 1-2:30pm and 8-10:30pm. AmEx/MC/V. ❷

SICILY

◉ SIGHTS

CASTELLO DI LOMBARDIA AND ENVIRONS. Enna's history as a defensive city is most apparent at the **Castello di Lombardia.** The enclosed courtyards are now covered with grass and vines, but most of the thick walls and towers remain. A view of the entire province and Mt. Etna, on clear days, merits fending off roosting pigeons at **La Pisana,** the tallest of the towers. Named for a Lombardian siege, the castle was constructed by the Swabians in the Norman period and later used by Federico II. Fred really liked to feel secure; one of the city's other architectural marvels is the **Torre di Federico II,** visible from the Castello. Next to the castle, a natural fortress also offers excellent views of the city. The **Rocca di Cerere,** on the path below the *castello,* is supposedly where the weeping Demeter mourned the loss of her daughter Persephone to Hades. *(From the duomo, V. Roma curves uphill and becomes V. Lombardia before ending at the Castello. Castello ☎ 0935 50 09 62. Open daily 8am-8pm, though gates often stay open later. Rocca di Cerere on path leading up to left of castle. Turn left onto V. IV Novembre for public gardens. Open daily 9am-8pm. Free.)*

DUOMO. The more than dozen religious fraternities throughout the city have their own churches, but they all ultimately share the curious duomo, which combines as many architectural styles as there are brotherhoods. Construction began in the early 14th century, but the cathedral was remodeled throughout the 15th and 16th. The result is a walking tour through three centuries of Italian architectural movements. The interior sports Gothic doors, medieval walls, Renaissance paintings, and gilded Baroque flourishes. The sacrilegious stretch out on wooden pews to appreciate the marvelous wood-paneled ceiling.

The **Museo Alessi** is housed in the rectory immediately behind the cathedral on V. Roma, and the eclectic collection mirrors the duomo in its veneration of variety. Oil paintings and ancient coins and pottery share space with the duomo's treasures, including a fine silver model cathedral. At the first left on the ground floor, look for Paolo Vetri's watercolor plans for cathedral frescoes and the *Portrait of an Elder Man.* *(☎ 0935 50 31 65. Open daily 8am-8pm. €2.60, students or over 60 €1.50.)*

♫ ENTERTAINMENT

For the **Festa della Madonna** (July 2), the entire town turns out to watch the procession of three enormous votive statues throughout the streets of the city. *Ennesi* celebrate with fireworks, music, and *mastazzoli* (apple cookies). The party continues through the summer, with similar festivities for the feasts of **Sant'Anna** and **San Valverde,** the last Sundays of July and August, respectively. Ever Easter, each fraternity dons hoods and capes to parade through the streets.

Processions of a faster sort take place down the hill at the **Autodromo di Pergusa** (☎ 0935 25 660; fax 25 825), where the city hosts **Grand Prix auto races** from March through October. The most important are the Formula 3 in July. In other months, the Autodromo hosts everything from motorcycle races to dog shows.

PIAZZA ARMERINA ☎ 0935

Like the neighboring Ennesi, the founders of Piazza Armerina headed for the hills. The medieval city is perched in the Erei Mountains, and dominated by its green-domed duomo and King Martino's *Castello Aragonese.* Time has changed little here, and many streets are no more than twisting stone staircases. The city's greatest attraction lies in the foothills below; the famed Villa Romana at Casale has the largest and finest collection of ancient mosaics in the world.

🖪🖬 TRANSPORTATION AND PRACTICAL INFORMATION. Piazza Armerina is a bus ride from **Enna** (35min., 8 per day, 7:10am-6pm, €2.58). **Buses** arrive at P. Senatore Marescalchi at the city's northern end. From the piazza, V. D'Annunzio becomes V. Chiaranda and then V. Mazzini before arriving at **Piazza Garibaldi,** the historic center. The **tourist office,** V. Cavour, 15, is in the courtyard of a *palazzo* just off P. Garibaldi. (☎ 0935 68 02 01. Open M-Sa 10am-1:30pm and 2:30-6pm.) In P. Garibaldi, **Farmacia Quattrino** posts the night-shift rotations. (☎ 0935 68 00 44. Open daily 9am-1pm and 4-8pm.) In **emergencies,** call the **carabinieri** (☎ 0935 68 20 14) or **first aid** (☎ 0935 68 15 00).

🖪🖸 ACCOMMODATIONS AND FOOD. For the best budget accommodation, follow the yellow signs to **🖪Ostello del Borgo ❷**, Largo S. Giovanni, 6, a recently renovated 14th-century monastery in the heart of historic Piazza Armerina. 20 rooms have dignified dark wood furniture and excellent beds. (☎ 0935 68 70 19; fax 68 69 43; www.ostellodelborgo.it. Breakfast included. Dorms €18.50; singles €39, with bath €33.50; doubles with bath €52; triples with bath €67.50; quads with bath €83. AmEx/MC/V.) **Hotel Villa Romana ❹**, V. De Gasperi, 18 offers rooms with bath, TV and A/C, and has three restaurants, two of which also contain a bar. (☎ 0935 68 29 11; fax 68 29 12; hotelvillaromana@piazza-armerina.it. Singles €51.65; doubles €77.47; triples €92.96; quads €103.29. AmEx/MC/V.)

Only a handful of restaurants sprinkle Piazza Armerina's old streets. A *panino* from **Spaccio Alimentari ❷**, P. Garibaldi, 15 (☎ 0935 68 10 84), can be enjoyed in the small garden nearby, down V. Roma. If only a restaurant will do, try the centrally located **Ristorante Pizzeria Pepito ❸**, V. Roma, 140, off P. Garibaldi and across from the garden, serves quality local dishes, such as house specialty *agnello al forno* (baked lamb; €10). (☎ 0935 68 57 37. *Primi* from €5.20, *secondi* from €7. Cover €1.10. Open W-M noon-3:30pm and 7-11pm. AmEx/MC/V.)

🖸 SIGHTS. 🖪 **Villa Romana "Del Casale"** lies 5km southwest of town in a fertile green valley. This remarkable site, known locally as *"I Mosaici,"* is thought to have been constructed at the turn of the 4th century AD, but a landslide in the 12th century kept it mostly hidden for 800 years. In 1916, famed archaeologists Paolo Orsi and Giuseppe Culterra unearthed 40 rooms of extraordinary stone mosaics. Glass walls and shaded ceilings now cover the mosaics, but still allow for a sense of what the villa would have looked like at the height of its glory. Guidebooks at nearby vendors explain the finer points of the villa's construction and history. The entrance passes first through the **baths,** for which water was warmed by visible hot air vents running under the entire structure. A large **ovoid hall** on the left, just past the baths, depicts a chariot race; flying legs, at left, are all that remain of the poor driver, believed to have been Maximenius Herculeus, co-ruler of the western half of the Roman Empire with Diocletian. Max's great wealth, fondness for the hunt, and side business as an importer of exotic animals, are all apparent in the tiles. One of the largest rooms shows the dramatic capture of lions, tigers, and bulls. The enormous **Triclinium** depicts the Battle of the Giants and the Feats of Hercules. The famed **Salle delle Dieci Raggazze** (Room of Ten Girls) shows buff bikini-clad beauties engaged in various aerobic activities. While the **Cubicolo Scena Erotica** is not quite as racy as the title suggests, the bare tush and intimate kiss have kept people talking for centuries. A room off the great hall showcases the battle between Odysseus and Polyphemus. The artist blurred the finer details of the story; the Cyclops has three eyes instead of one. *(☎ 0935 68 00 36. Buses run to the villa from P. Marescalch (6 per day; 10:30am-4pm, last return 4:30pm). Call ☎ 0935 85 605 for bus info at V. Umberto, 6. If you'd prefer to walk the 5km, the way is well-marked with signs toward the Mosaici. Bring lots of water—the P. Armerina sun can be brutal. Villa and ticket office open daily 8am-6:30pm. €4.50, under 18 or over 65 €2.)*

SOUTHERN SICILY

SYRACUSE (SIRACUSA) ☎ 0931

The most beautiful and noble of the Greek cities.
—Titus Livius (Livy), on Syracuse

At its height, Syracuse rivaled Athens as one of the greatest cities in the west, cultivating such luminaries as Theocritus, Archimedes, and the great Greek lyric poet Pindar. Hard times followed in 211 BC, however, when the Romans conquered the city, and again in AD 668, when the bathing emperor Constans was bludgeoned to death with a soap dish. The city's prominence was perhaps most seriously undermined in AD 879, when Arabs conquered Sicily and established Palermo as the capital of the island. Though no longer the titan of its youth, modern Syracuse is hardly crestfallen, but rather is content to rest upon laurels long since won. Pride has always been one of the city's most noticeable qualities, a characteristic over a millennium of decline has yet to tarnish. Ask a citizen to point to the pride of Syracuse and a tanned arm may gesture wordlessly toward the stunning archaeological park, with its extraordinary theater, or toward Ortigia and its elegant churches.

▐ TRANSPORTATION

Trains: (☎ 0931 67 964), V. Francesco Crispi, halfway between Ortigia and archaeological park. To: **Catania** (1½hr., 18 per day, 4:50am-9:10pm, €4.39); **Florence** (14hr., 4 per day, 3:25pm-6:35pm, €43.90); **Messina** (3hr., 16 per day, 4:50am-9:10pm, €8.26); **Milan** (19hr., 4 per day, 3:25-6:35pm, €49.78); **Noto** (30min., 10 per day, 5:20am-8:30pm, €4.91); **Ragusa** (2hr., 5 per day, 5:20am-3:10pm, €5.68); **Rome** (12hr., 5 per day, 8am-9:10pm, €37.70); **Taormina** (2hr., 12 per day, 4:50am-9:10pm, €6.46); and **Turin** (20hr., 1:30 and 2:30pm, €49.63). **Luggage storage.**

Buses: AST office (☎ 0931 46 48 20 or 46 27 11), next to the post office on Ortigia, to left after stone bridge. While construction continues, blue buses leave from P. Marconi on the mainland side of the stone bridge. To: **Gela** (4hr., 2 per day, 7am and 1:30pm, €7.23); **Piazza Armerina** (3hr., 1 daily, 7am, €7.23); and **Ragusa** (3hr., 6 per day, 5:30am-5:30pm, €5.42). **Interbus,** V. Trieste, 28 (☎ 0931 66 710), 1 or 2 blocks from P. delle Poste toward center of Ortigia, 2nd street to left after stone bridge. To: **Catania** (M-F 17 per day, 5:45am-6:30pm; Sa-Su 8 per day, 6:30am-6:30pm; €4.10); **Giardini-Naxos** (2hr.; 1 per day, 7:15pm; €7.20, €13.40 round-trip); **Noto** (1hr., 9 per day, 7:10am-8:30pm, €2.50); **Palermo** (3hr., 5 per day, 6am-5pm, €13.40, €18.50 round-trip); **Rome** (12hr.; 1 per day; 7:15pm; €36, €60 round-trip); and **Taormina** (2hr.; 1 per day; 7:15pm; €7.20, €13.40 round-trip).

Local Transportation: Orange **AST** buses depart from P. delle Poste. Bus #21, 22, and 24 run past Fontane Bianche. #23 to Aranella. Tickets €0.77 in *tabacchi*.

Taxis: (☎ 0931 69 722 or 60 980). From train station to Ortigia about €7.75.

■※▐ ORIENTATION AND PRACTICAL INFORMATION

The **Ponte Umbertino** connects the island of **Ortigia** to mainland Syracuse. **Corso Umberto I** links the bridge to the **train station** and passes through **Piazza Marconi,** from which **Corso Gelone** courses through town up to the **archaeological park.** Corso Umberto continues past Foro Siracusano to the train station.

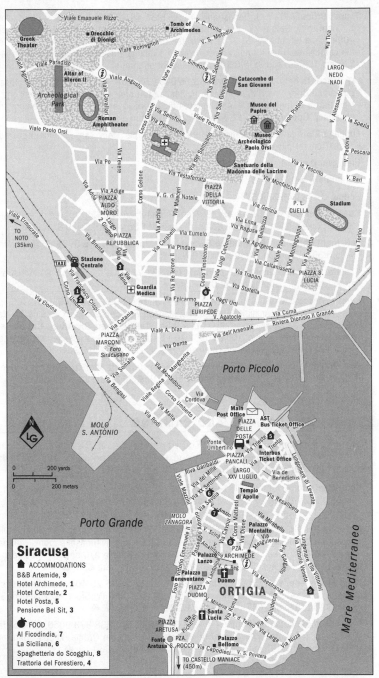

Greek Theater

Tomb of Archimedes

V. C. Bruno

■ Orecchio di Dionigi

Viale Romagnoli

V. S. Metodio

Via Tica

Viale Emanuele Rizzo

Via Teracati

V. Simeone

V. San Sebastiano

Catacombe di San Giovanni

LARGO NEDO NADI

Viale Paradiso

Altar of Hieron II

Viale Augusto

Via San Giovanni

Archeological Park

Viale Cavallari

Corso Gelone

Via Senofonte

Via Demostene

Viale Teocrito

Museo del Papiro

Via A. von Platen

V. Alessandria

V. la Spezia

Roman Amphitheater

Museo Archeologico Paolo Orsi

V. Padova

Pescara

Via le Teocrito

V. Bari

Viale Paolo Orsi

Via Po

Santuario della Madonna delle Lacrime

Via Monfalcone

Via Tevere

Via Testaferrata

PIAZZA DELLA VITTORIA

Via Gorizia

P. L. CUELLA

Stadium

Viale Ermocrate

Via Adige

Via Adda

PIAZZA ALDO MORO

V. G. di Natale

Via Manceri

Via Enna

Via Ragusa

Via Torino

TO NOTO (35km)

Corso Gelone

Largo 2 Giugno

PIAZZA REPUBBLICA

Via Archia

Via Carabelli

Via Eumelo

Via Agrigento

Via Caltanissetta

Viale Piave

Via Montegrappa

Via Fulgetta

PIAZZA S. LUCIA

Via Brenta

Via Oglio

Via Re Ierone II

Via Pindaro

Corso Timoleonte

Via Luigi Cadorna

Via Trapani

TAXI

Stazione Centrale

Via Reno

Guardia Medica

Via Statella

Via Francesco Crispi

Via Epicarmo

V. degli Orti

PIAZZA EURIPEDE

Via Cuma

Via Umberto I

Via Elorina

Via Catania

Viale A. Diaz

Via Agatocle

Riviera Dionisio II Grande

PIAZZA MARCONI
Foro Siracusano

Via Dante

Via dell'Arsenale

Via Somalia

Via Margherita

Via Montedoro

Porto Piccolo

Via Bengasi

Viale Regina

Corso Umberto I

Via Cordova

Via Malta

Via Rodi

Main Post Office

AST Bus Ticket Office

PIAZZA DELLE POSTA

MOLO S. ANTONIO

Ponte Umbertino

PIAZZA PANCALI

Interbus Ticket Office

Via de Benedictus

Lungomare di Levante

0   200 yards
0   200 meters

Riva Garibaldi

LARGO XXV LUGLIO

Tempio di Apollo

Via Resalibera

Porto Grande

Viale Mazzini

Via del Mille

Via XX Settimbre

Via Savoia

Via Trento

MOLO ZANAGORA

Via Arezzo

Via Scinà

Via Capuli

Via Dione

Palazzo Montalto

Via Mirabella

Via Meligulensi

Corso Matteoti

Via de' Gaboli

Siracusa

🏠 ACCOMMODATIONS

B&B Artemide, 9
Hotel Archimede, 1
Hotel Centrale, 2
Hotel Posta, 5
Pensione Bel Sit, 3

Via Amalfitania

Foro Vittorio Emanuele II

Palazzo Lanzo

PZA. ARCHIMEDE

Palazzo Beneventano

V. C. Reg

Duomo

Via Roma

Via Maestranza

Via Vittorio Veneto

🍴 FOOD

Al Ficodindia, 7
La Siciliana, 6
Spaghetteria do Scogghiu, 8
Trattoria del Forestiero, 4

PIAZZA DUOMO

Via Minerva

Via Pichirelli

ORTIGIA

Santa Lucia

Via d. Teatro

Via Larga

PIAZZA ARETUSA

Fonte Aretusa

PZA. S. ROCCO

Palazzo Bellomo

Via Capodieci

V. S. Privitera

Via Nizza

Via Giudecca

Mare Mediterraneo

▼ TO CASTELLO MANIACE (450m)

SICILY

Tourist Office: APT, V. S. Sebastiano, 43 (☎0931 48 12 32). From the station, take V. F. Crispi to C. Gelone (V. V. Catania on the left). Turn right onto Viale Teocrite after 400m, then left onto V. S. Sebastiano; the office is 150m up on the left, across from the catacombs. Useful tourist map includes a mini-guide. English spoken. Open M-Sa 8:30am-1:30pm and 3:30-6:30pm. Closed Su afternoon.

AAT Office: Ortigia, V. Maestranza, 33 (☎0931 65 201 or 46 42 55). After crossing Umbertino Bridge, turn right through P. Pancali to uphill C. Matteotti. Turn left onto V. Maestranza at fountain in P. Archimede; office in courtyard of the *palazzo* across from pharmacy. Open M-F 8am-1:50pm and 2:45-5:30pm, Sa 8am-1:50pm.

Luggage Storage: In train station. €3.90 for 24hr. Open daily 7am-7pm for deposit and 7am-10pm for pickup.

Emergency: ☎113.

Carabinieri: ☎0931 44 13 44.

Police: ☎0931 46 35 66.

Guardia Medica: ☎0931 48 46 39. From P. Archimede on Ortigia, turn down V. Maestranza; take 1st left onto V. S. Coronati. Open M-F 8pm-8am, Sa-Su 8am-8pm.

Late-Night Pharmacy: Mangiafico Farmacia, C. Matteotti, 33 (☎0931 65 643). Open M-Sa 8:30am-1pm and 4:30-8pm. MC/V.

Hospital: Ospedale Generale Provinciale (☎0931 72 41 11), a beige brick monstrosity on V. Testaferrata, off the end of C. Gelone.

Internet Access: W@W: Web and Work, V. Roma, 16/18 (☎0931 46 59 60), in Ortigia. Take V. Roma from P. Archimede at end of C. Matteoti. Fast connections, €4.65 per hr. Many other multimedia services available. Open M-Sa 11am-9:30pm. **Ricevitoria-Cartoleria S. Bongiovanni,** Viale Teocrito, 103 (☎0931 46 11 70), in upper Siracusa, has a speedy computer. €0.50 per min., €6 per hr. Open daily 8:30am-1:30pm and 3:30-8:30pm.

Post Office: P. delle Poste, 15 (☎0931 68 416). Turn left after crossing the bridge to Ortigia. BancoPosta offers **currency exchange.** Open M-Sa 8:15am-7:40pm.

Postal Code: 96100.

■ ACCOMMODATIONS AND CAMPING

Many budget accommodations have staked out the area between the station and the bridge to Ortigia. While prices are good, the quality is not. This area **can be dangerous at night.** Ortigia's few options are more expensive, but of higher quality.

Hotel Centrale, C. Umberto I, 141 (☎0931 60 528; fax 61 175), near train station. Small entryway leads to clean, affordable rooms with astounding sea views and A/C. Singles €17, with view €18; doubles €26, with bath €35; triples with bath €37. ❷

Pensione Bel Sit, V. Oglio, 5 (☎0931 60 245; fax 46 28 82), on the 5th floor. Follow signs from C. Gelone, close to the train station. Large, simply furnished rooms with bath are cooled by a fan and windows. Upstairs rooms also have A/C and TV. Reserve 1wk. in advance for July-Aug. Singles €20; doubles €26, with bath €35. ❷

Hotel Archimede, V. F. Crispi (☎/fax 0931 46 24 58 or 46 20 40), near the train station, has comfortable and clean rooms with bath, A/C, and TV. Breakfast included. Singles €31-41; doubles €47-62; triples €62-78. AmEx/MC/V. ❸

B&B Artemide, V. Vittorio Veneto (☎/fax 0931 69 005 or 338 373 9050; info@bedandbreakfastsicily.com; www.bedandbreakfastsicily.com), on Ortigia, keeps bright and clean rooms with A/C and color TV. Singles €40; doubles €60-70. ❹

Hotel Posta, V. Trieste, 33 (☎0931 21 819; fax 61 862; bookinghotelposta@hotmail.com; www.hotelpostasiracusa.com), on Ortigia. Large, classy rooms on the port are at the height of comfort. All have bath, A/C, and TV. Singles €70; doubles €98; triples €132. AmEx/MC/V. ❺

Camping: Fontane Bianche, V. dei Lidi, 476 (☎0931 79 03 33), 20km from Syracuse, near the beach of the same name. Take bus #21 or 22 (€0.77) from P. delle Poste on Ortigia. Open May-Sept. €6 per person. Showers included. No tents. ❶

🄵 FOOD

While hotel prices can run fairly high, restaurants are affordable. On the mainland, the area around the station and the archaeological park offers some of the best deals. Ortigia has an **open air market** on V. Trento, off P. Pancali, as well as several budget options on V. Savoia and V. Cavour.

Spaghetteria do Scugghiu, V. D. Scinà, 11, a tiny street off P. Archimede, on Ortigia. A large spaghetti selection of over 20 varieties accompanies *primi* and *secondi* from €5.50. Cover €1.50. Open Tu-Su noon-3pm and 7-11pm. ❷

Al Ficodindia, V. Arezzo, 7/9 (☎0931 46 28 38), off V. Cavour in Ortigia. An antipasto buffet (€4.15) and daily "chef recommends" section display typical Sicilian kitchen specialties. Pizza from €2.58, *primi* from €5.16, *secondi* from €4.13. Open Th-Tu 12:30-3:30pm and 7:30pm-close. ❶

La Siciliana, V. Savoia, 17 (☎0931 68 944 or 74 91 04), in Ortigia, next door to Hotel Gran Bretagna. In the evening, 54 different varieties of pizza (from €3.10) are served between picture-filled walls or at breezy outdoor tables. Try the seafood appetizer for €5. Service €1.20. Open Tu-Su noon-3pm and 7pm-midnight. AmEx/MC/V. ❶

Trattoria Del Forestiero, C. Timoleonte, 2 (☎0931 46 12 45 or 335 843 0736), on mainland. From the start of C. Gelone, take V. Agatocle to P. Euripede; restaurant is on the far side at start of C. Timoleonte. High-quality food served in big portions with small prices. *Primi* from €3.10, *secondi* from €4.20, pizza to eat-in or takeout from €2.20. Cover €1.10. Open W-M noon-2:30pm and 7pm-midnight. ❶

🄶 SIGHTS

▨ARCHAEOLOGICAL PARK. Syracuse's three centuries as the most important city on the Mediterranean left behind a collection of immense monuments. The Greek ruins are the most impressive, but Roman remains also attest to a rich heritage. Two theaters, an ancient quarry, and the world's largest altar share a fenced compound, visited with a single ticket. Take a deep breath before plowing through the paper fan- and bead-hawkers. *(Follow C. Gelone to V. Teocrito; park entrance down V. Augusto to the left, following frequent signs. Ticket office open daily 9am-6pm, closing 1hr. before the park. €4.50, ages 18-25 €2, under 18 or over 65 free.)*

GREEK THEATER. While sitting in one of the theater's rows, carved into the hillside in 475 BC, it's easy to understand why Syracuse became such a successful Greek colony. If the 15,000 spectators watching Aeschylus's original production of *The Persians* got bored, they could lift their eyes over the now-ruined scenic building to look out over green fields, colorful flowers, the sparkling sea in the distance and oncoming attackers—Syracuse's location was spectacularly strategic. Original Greek inscriptions line the walls along the mid-level aisles, and the track for the *deus ex machina*, a large crane that made the gods "fly," is still visible around the orchestra.

THE LOCAL STORY

NO STRINGS ATTACHED

Alfredo Mauceri is a third-generation puppeteer at Il Piccolo Dei Pupi, Fratelli Mauceri, Syracuse's only traditional Sicilian puppet show. (☎/fax 0931 46 55 40; www.pupari.com.)

Q: Is the Syracuse version of puppetry different from the Catania or Palermo versions?
A: Sure. Every city has its own puppets. For example, in Syracuse, the puppets' faces are made of papiermaché, and the knees can be bendable instead of rigid.
Q: How many different stories are run by the company?
A: Originally, there was only one called *Il Paladini di Francia* (The Paladins of France) that lasted for three years, running every evening for two hours.
Q: What if a fan missed a night?
A: It was like a soap opera. If someone missed a night, they would miss a new piece of the story, and would have to catch up. With television, there's not the same kind of audience. We have every month with a different story, or even a different story every night.
Q: Is there a show this evening?
A: Yes, we are putting on *Rinaldo and the Dragon*, where Rinaldo encounters a kidnapping thief as well as, obviously, a dragon. I'm not telling how it ends.
Q: Is there a character that you especially like impersonating?
A: Not really. I find that every character has a part of my own personality, so every one brings out a different side of me.

PARADISE QUARRY. The floral valley next to the theater derives its name from the fertile gardens that line the base of large, chalky cliffs. It is from these quarries that most of the characteristic gray stone that built old Syracuse was taken. Two large artificial caves now cut into the walls, the **Orecchio di Dionigi** (Ear of Dionysius) and the **Grotta dei Cordari** (Ropemakers's Cave). The latter is closed to the public for safety reasons, but visitors can still see the former, which is famous for the echoes that ricochet off its walls. Legend claims the tyrant Dionysius put his prisoners here in order to eavesdrop on their rebellious conversations. Dionysius wouldn't dare to spend long hours listening now: the cave rings with the delighted high-pitched shrieks of visiting children.

OTHER SIGHTS IN THE PARK. Outside this area lies Ara di Ierone II, the altar of Heiron II (241-215 BC), once used for public sacrifices. At 198m by 23m, this is the world's largest altar. Walk up the hill and through the other gate to reach the well-preserved, 2nd-century AD Roman amphitheater. Visitors can also see the tunnels through which wild gladiators and brave animals entered.

MUSEO ARCHEOLOGICO PAOLO ORSI. Named for the most famous archaeologist in Sicily, this museum has an overwhelming collection of objects from prehistory through Ancient Greece. From the circular introductory room at the museum's core, hallways branch out into chronologically arranged galleries that wind through time and place. Exquisite *kouroi* torsos, grimacing Gorgons, elegant vases, and a couple of Pygmy elephant skeletons rest in dimly-lit galleries. *(V. Teocrito. ☎0931 46 40 22. Open 9am-2pm and 3:30-7:30pm. Ticket office closes 1hr. earlier. €4.50, ages 18-25 €2, under 18 or over 65 free.)*

CATACOMBE DI SAN GIOVANNI. Dating from AD 415-460, this subterranean maze has over 20,000 tombs carved into the walls. There are no corpses to be seen here; only ghostly frescoes, an occasional sarcophagus, and a few wall-carvings remain. The 4th-century **Cripta di San Marziano** (the first bishop of Syracuse) lies below the ruins. *(Across from tourist office on V. S. Giovanni, off Viale Teocrito from C. Gelone. Mandatory guided tours run every 15-20min., 9:10am-12:30pm and 2:40-5:30pm. €3.50, under 15 or over 65 €2.50, school groups €1.50 per person.)*

SANTUARIO DELLA MADONNA DELLE LACRIME. For three days in 1953, a small mass-produced statuette of the Madonna began to weep in the home of the Iannuso family, on V. degli Orti. As word spread, the number of pilgrims grew too large for their little place, and a larger sanctuary was built in 1966 on the competition-winning plans of Frenchmen Michel Arnault and Pierre Parat. Later chemical tests proved the liquid coming from the Madonna's eyes to be of similar makeup to human tears. Timetables placed outside of the sanctuary now tell the statue's tale. (☎ 0931 21 446. Both open daily 6:30am-12:30pm and 4-6pm. Sanctuary free. Museum of the Tears €1.55, Museum of Liturgy €1, both museums €2.)

MUSEO DEL PAPIRO. This collection of papyrus texts and woven objects displays four or five pages from the ancient Egyptian Book of the Dead, with invocations (translated into Italian) to the Eater of Souls and the Snake-that-Rises. (Up the street from the Orsi museum. ☎ 0931 61 616. Open Tu-Su 9am-1:30pm. Free.)

ORTIGIA. The Greeks first landed in Ortigia, using the island as an embarkation point for their attack on the mainland. At the end of the Ponte Umbertino, the fenced-in ruins of the **Tempio di Apollo** catch the golden evening sun and many a tourist's eye. The temple, dating from 575 BC, is the oldest peripteral (columns on all sides) Doric temple in Sicily. The island flourished in the Baroque period, leaving a smattering of elegant churches and the **Palazzo Impellizzeri,** V. Maestranza, 22. The island is best enjoyed during the evening *passegiata*, when citizens from all over the city and their rambunctious children take to strolling in the streets.

DUOMO. The 18th-century exterior of Syracuse's cathedral may look like the standard Baroque compilation of architectural fancies, but the interior is anything but. The duomo was built upon the site of the 5th-century BC Temple of Athena, but rather than demolishing the pagan structure, the architects incorporated it directly into their own construction. Fluted columns line both sides of the interior, in an unusual but aesthetically effective design. According to legend, the temple became a church with the arrival of St. Paul. Large, shiny letters proclaim this the first Christian church in the west. The first chapel on the right as you enter the church is dedicated to St. Lucia, the light-bearer and Syracuse's patron saint. The elaborate reliquary in the glass case holds a piece of her left arm. Hidden from view above the reliquary is a masterpiece of Sicilian silver work, a life-sized statue of Lucia that is paraded through the street on her feast day (see **Entertainment,** below). Lest you forget how she died, the silversmiths kindly included a dagger sticking out of her throat, the punishment dealt the saint by the Inquisition. (Down V. Minerva from P. Archimede. Open daily 8am-noon and 4-7pm. Modest dress required.)

FONTE ARETUSA. This small, ancient pond fed by a "miraculous" fresh-water spring near the sea overlooks Porta Grande. *Siracusani* believe that the nymph Arethusa escaped the enamored river god Alpheus by diving into the ocean and that the goddess Diana rescued her by transforming her into this fountain. Alpheus, pining for his love, transformed himself into a subterranean river so their waters could mingle eternally. The river surfaces here at the Fonte Aretusa. (P. Aretusa. From P. Duomo, walk down V. Picherale.)

🎵 ENTERTAINMENT

Siracusani, like all Italians, fall prey in summer to powerful ancestral instincts that force them from the cities to the beach. **Fontane Bianche** is a fleshy beach with many discos by night. Staying at the *campeggio* (campgrounds) there ensures you a place to sleep when the buses stop. Take bus #21 or 22 (30min., €0.77).

On Ortigia, nightlife consists of a grand tour of the island, stopping at any of several bars along the way. In winter, check out **Troubador,** off P. S. Rocco. In summer, the Ortigia hotspot is **Nonsolobar Bar,** behind the Fonte Aretusa. Patrons drink in a mossy natural grotto below street level. (Open W-M 7am-2am, cave open after

6pm.) In May and June, the city stages **classical Greek drama.** The APT office has all the details. Tickets for **Istituto Nazionale del Dramma Antico** are available at the theater box office. (☎ 0931 48 35 31. Open M-F 3:30-6:30pm.) Syracuse's biggest festival is the **Festa di Santa Lucia,** December 13. Local men carry the silver statue of the city's patron saint in a 6hr. procession from the duomo to S. Lucia al Sepolcro on the mainland. The statue stays on the mainland for a week and is carried back to the duomo on December 20.

▓ DAYTRIP FROM SYRACUSE: NOTO

Interbuş and AST buses head from Syracuse in a steady stream (1hr., 9 per day, 7:10am-8:30pm, €2.50). Ticket office opposite bus stop in the Bar Efirmmedio. You can also reach Noto by train (30min., 10 per day, 5:20am-8:30pm, €1.65). The station is a 20min. uphill walk from town.

A haven of Baroque unity, Noto is a pleasure to the eyes. After the 1693 earthquake shook Sicily's shore, the noble Landolina and Nicolaci families made Noto their favorite renovation project, restoring its architectural elegance with monumental staircases, chubby cupid moldings, and pot-bellied balconies. Things have slowed to a more relaxed pace since the earthquake, making Noto a calm and educational retreat from frenzied tourist destinations.

To reach the **APT tourist office** from the bus stop at the **Giardini Pubblici** (Public Gardens), cross the paved way with the fountain on the right. Turn left through the tunnel of low hanging trees and pass under the **Porta Nazionale** (built in 1838) onto **Corso Vittorio Emanuele.** The tourist office is in the garden **Villetto Ercole,** behind the Fontana d'Ercole. Off C. V. Emanuele, enter the garden through the gate and head to the back behind the fountain. English is spoken; pick up your free map. (☎ 0931 57 37 79. Open 8am-2pm and 3:30-6:30pm.) To reach the town center from the train station, follow the road leading uphill and to the right; at the second traffic light, turn right, and then right again.

Toward the city center from C. V. Emanuele stands the immense **Chiesa di San Francesco all'Immacolata,** built in 1704, which houses one of the bloodiest crucifixes you'll find in Sicily. (Open daily 9am-12:30pm and 3:30-7pm.) While on C. V. Emanuele, stop at the **Teatro Comunale "Vittorio Emanuele"** to gaze up at its bright red seats and hanging drapes. (Open M-Sa 8:30am-1:30pm and 3-8pm. €1, show tickets €5.) From C. V. Emanuele, turn right on V. Niccolaci, and for a view of the balconies of the **Palazzo Niccolaci,** supported by cherubs, griffins, and sirens. The noteworthy duomo contains captivating frescoes, currently under renovation. Decent **beaches** are 7km away at **Noto Marina.** Buses depart from the **Giardini Pubblici** (July-Aug. M-Sa 8:30am and 12:45pm, €1.20).

Ostello per la Gioventù "Il Castello" (HI) ❶ awaits at V. F.lli Bandiera, 1 (☎/fax 0931 57 15 34; ostellodinoto@tin.it), off V. Cavour, to the right up a flight of stairs; follow the signs. Large, clean rooms create a friendly atmosphere. (HI members only. Breakfast included. €14.50 per person.) **Trattoria al Buco ❸,** V. G. Zanardelli, 1, provides *affittacamere* of varying quality, mostly within the historic district. All have kitchen, bath, and eccentric furnishings. (☎ 0931 83 81 42. Expect to pay around €30 per person.) Within the **trattoria ❷** itself, feast on homemade pasta (from €4) and fish *secondi* from €5.50. (Cover €0.70. Open Su-F noon-3:30pm and 7pm-midnight, Sa 7pm-midnight. AmEx/MC/V.) Call to reserve one of two well-furnished rooms with A/C at **Centro Storico ❸,** C. V. Emanuele, 64, run by a welcoming family. (☎ 0931 57 39 67 or 338 763 6994; chrislibra@jumpy.it. €28.50 per person for at least 2 people.) **Pasticceria La Vecchia Fontana ❶,** C. V. Emanuele, 150, scoops sinfully good *gelato* (€1.10-1.80). (☎ 0931 83 94 12. Open W-M 6am-1am.)

RAGUSA ☎ 0932

Hot Ragusa's lethargic pace contrasts with the frantic modernity of other Sicilian cities. The city, settled comfortably in the interior, is distant from even its nearest neighbors. The language cascading off the Baroque buildings has little to do with Italian, and it is rare that a tourist tongue is heard. The craggy valley that divides Ragusa Ibla from the modern Ragusa Superiore is the city's most unusual feature, with its verdant cliffs and winding paths. Antique buildings and wide vistas make Ragusa the retreat that time could not be troubled to visit.

▐▀ TRANSPORTATION

Trains: New town end of V. Roma, off P. della Libertà, behind the bus stop. To: **Caltanissetta** (3hr., 3 per day, 2:58-5:16pm, €8.26); **Gela** (1½hr., 8 per day, 4:08am-8:20pm, €4.05); **Palermo** (5hr., 2:58 and 4:17pm, €12.91); and **Syracuse** (2hr., 13 per day, 5:20am-6:30pm, €6.71).

Buses: Beside train station, just above P. della Libertà, at new town end of V. Roma. Schedules posted on wall facing stop. To: **Catania** (2hr.; M-F 5 per day, 5:30am-6pm; Sa 2 per day, 5:30am and 2pm; €6.46); **Gela** (1½hr.; M-Sa 9:45am and 4pm; €3.87, €6.20 round-trip); **Noto** (1½hr.; M-Sa 7 per day, 6:50am-7:15pm; €3.87, €6.20 round-trip); **Palermo** (4hr.; M-F 4 per day, 5:30am-5:30pm; Sa-Su 2:30 and 5:30pm; €11.62); and **Syracuse** (2hr.; M-Sa 7 per day, 6:50am-7:15pm; €5.42, €8.78 round-trip). Connections to **Agrigento** and **Enna** via **Gela.** Tickets at **Bar Puglisi,** across the street. Open daily 5am-10pm.

▟▙ ▟ ORIENTATION AND PRACTICAL INFORMATION

The **train** and **bus stations** are in **Piazza del Popolo** and neighboring **Piazza Gramsci.** To reach the center from either of these adjacent piazzas, turn left on **Viale Tenente Lena,** walk through **Piazza Libertà** on V. Roma and then across **Ponte Senatore F. Pennavaria,** the northernmost of three bridges crossing the **Vallata Santa. Corso Italia,** off V. Roma, leads downhill for several blocks, passing the **post office** in Piazza Matteotti, and becomes **Via XXIV Maggio.** It ends at the **Chiesa di Santa Maria della Scala.** Here, stairs and roads wind down to **Ragusa Ibla.**

Tourist Office: AAPIT, V. Capitano Bocchieri, 33 (☎ 0932 22 15 11; fax 22 15 09), in Ragusa Ibla beyond the duomo, behind a small entryway with flags above the door. Brochures, maps, and information are given with a smile. English spoken. Open M-F 9am-2pm, Tu 4-6pm.

Emergency: ☎ 113. **Police:** ☎ 112 or 0932 62 10 10.

Medical Emergency: ☎ 118.

First Aid: ☎ 0932 62 11 11. **Guardia Medica:** (☎ 0932 23 90 85), in P. Igea.

Hospital: Ospedale Civile (☎ 0932 60 01 11), in a peach building on V. da Vinci.

Post Office: (☎ 0932 23 21 11; fax 22 86 23), in P. Matteotti, 2 blocks down C. Italia from V. Roma. Open daily 8am-6:30pm, closed last day of the month.

Postal Code: 97100.

▐▘ ACCOMMODATIONS

Hotel San Giovanni, V. Transpontino, 3 (☎ 0932 62 10 13 or 62 12 96; fax 62 10 13). From P. del Popolo, take Viale L. da Vinci to V. Transpontino; the hotel is to the left before the bridge at the end of a long series of signs pointing the way to this central location. Ceiling fans, TVs, and views of Ragusa Ibla. Breakfast included for rooms with bath. Singles €21, with bath €31; doubles €36/€51. AmEx/MC/V. ❷

SICILY

Hotel Jonio, V. Risorgimento, 49 (☎0932 62 43 22; fax 22 91 44). Facing away from the train station entrance, walk across the piazza to V. Sicilia. Turn right, and walk past the gas station. Fine rooms near the train station and several restaurants. Breakfast included. Other meals €11 person. Singles €20, with bath €33; doubles with bath €50; triples with bath €70. AmEx/MC/V. ❷

Baia del Sole, in Marina (☎0932 23 98 44), near the beach. Tumino buses run from P. Gramsci in Ragusa to P. Duca degli Abruzzi in Marina (30min., every hr., €2.07). 1km down from the main piazza (with the water to your right) on Lungomare Andrea Doria. Hot showers until 6pm (€2.50). €6 per person, €4-10.50 per tent. ❶

🔆 FOOD

While in Ragusa, try some *panatigghie* (thin pastries filled with the unholy trio of cocoa, cinnamon, and ground meat).

Iblantica, C. XXV Aprile, 36 (☎0932 68 32 23), in the heart of Ragusa Ibla, serves the best of the old city amdist ancient buildings and piazzas. *Primi* from €4.20, *secondi* from €6.20. The fish of the day is a steal at €4.15. Cover €1.30. AmEx/MC/V. ❷

La Valle, V. Risorgimento, 70 (☎0932 22 93 41). Waiters sport retro 30s-style uniforms as they whisk tasty pizzas to tables in the curious mint-green dining room. A colorful pizza menu presents pies from €3.36. *Primi* from €4.13, *secondi* from €4.65. Cover €1.29. Open W-M noon-3pm and 7pm-midnight. AmEx/MC/V. ❷

Ristorante Orfeo, V. S. Anna, 117 (☎0932 62 10 35), off V. Roma in the *centro*, serves quality food. Fresh fish from €8, *primi* from €7.20, *secondi* from €7. Cover €1.50. Service 10%. Open M-Sa noon-3pm and 7-10pm. AmEx/MC/V. ❸

Pizzeria La Grotta, on V. G. Cartia (☎0932 22 73 70), the 2nd right off V. Roma with your back to the bridge, serves standard *tavola calda* favorites, plus a few originals like pizza topped with french fries. Pizza by the slice €1.30. Open Th-Tu 5:30pm-1am. ❶

👁 🎵 SIGHTS AND ENTERTAINMENT

The dual hilltop locations of Ragusa Superiore and Ragusa Ibla offer great views of the countryside. The latter is accessible by a steep but lovely 10min. hike down from the church at the very bottom of C. Italia (V. XXIV Maggio) and by the #1 or #3 city bus (€0.77) from the duomo or P. del Popolo. The stairs at S. Maria offer a stellar view of Ragusa Ibla, crowned by a monastery and the 18th-century dome of **San Giorgio,** which glows an unearthly turquoise at night. (Modest dress required.) Walk 200m down tricky steps to P. Repubblica. The road to the left circumvents the town, passing abandoned monasteries and lush farmland. P. del Duomo di San Giorgio sits at the top of the city. C. XXV Aprile runs downhill from the piazza, passes two churches, and ends at the **Giardino Ibleo** with views of the surrounding countryside. Ragusa Superiore's **Museo Archeologico,** below the Ponte S. Pennavaria, has a collection of pottery from the nearby Syracusan colony of Camarina. (☎0932 62 29 63. Open daily 9am-1:30pm and 4-7:30pm. €2, ages 18-25 €1.03; under 18 or over 65 free.) The **Chiesa di San Giovanni** is the religious center of the new city.

In summer, any citizen with a swimsuit spends the weekend at ▓**Marina di Ragusa**—a bikini-packing, Vespa-roaring, booty-shaking stretch of sand. **Autolinee Tumino** (☎0932 62 31 84 or 65 19 67) runs buses to Marina from P. Gramsci (40min.; 14 per day; €1.81, round-trip €3.36). A schedule is posted in Polleria Giarrosto in Marina's P. Duca degli Abruzzi. In the same piazza, savor Marina's best *gelato* at **Delle Rose** (€1.30 per scoop).

Every year since 1990, Ragusa has hosted the **Ibla Grand Prize,** an international piano/voice/composition competition that runs from late June to early July. Performances are held in the theater of Palazzo Comunale.

> **A TALE OF (ONE OR) TWO CITIES.** The tremendous earthquake of 1693 left much of Eastern Sicily in ruins. Fearing another natural disaster, the people of Ragusa rebuilt on two levels. Pioneering *Ragusani* made their way across the hills and divides to create a new center in what is now Ragusa Superiore. Their more traditional counterparts opted to stay in the Ibla area, where their ancestors had laid their stones. Baron Mario Leggio, who had studied architecture in Spain, designed new Ragusa's streets in the modern style of Barcelona, with straight intersecting roadways instead of the winding and intertwining streets that defined defensive Ibla's town. Departures from the old-style duomos followed. The contrast between old and new, between modernization and tradition, became too much—despite their proximity, the two areas lived as separate factions until 1927. It was only upon Ragusa's transition into provincehood in that year that the two were reunited.

AGRIGENTO ☎ 0922

The fantastic juxtaposition of a valley filled with ancient temples and a complex of standard city high rises makes for a surreal scene straight out of one of local celebrity Luigi Pirandello's plays. Originally founded in the 6th century BC by Greek colonists, Agrigento now prides itself on its impeccable modernity. Traces of the past linger in the form of winding cobblestone streets, excellent museums, stunning ruins, and plenty of character. Agrigento belongs on a list of Italy's most under-appreciated locations.

TRANSPORTATION

Trains: In P. Marconi, below P. Moro. Ticket office open M-Sa 6:30am-8pm, Su 7am-8pm. To **Catania** (3¼hr.; 12:20, 3:50, and 5:55pm) via **Enna** (2hr., €5.73) and **Palermo** (2hr., 11 per day, 4:50am-8:05pm, €6.60).

Buses: From P. V. Emanuele, buses are to left in P. Roselli. **Cuffaro** runs buses to **Palermo** (M-Sa 7 per day, 7am-6:30pm; Su 3 per day, 8:15am-6:30pm, €6.50) and back to **Agrigento** (M-Sa 7 per day, 5:45am-8pm; Su 3 per day, 7am-3:30pm); schedules and information available at the bar down from the SAIS offices in P. Roselli. **SAIS Trasporti,** V. Ragazzi, 99 (☎ 0922 59 59 33), behind the ticket office. To: **Caltanissetta** (1hr.; M-Sa 13 per day, 4:45am-7pm; Su 8 per day, 6:45am-7pm; €4.13); **Catania** (2¾hr., 11 per day, €9.81); and **airport.** Indirect transport to **Rome** and **Messina.**

Public Transportation: Orange **TUA city buses** depart from the train station. Ticket (€0.77) valid 1½hr. Buses #2 and 2/ run to the beach at San Leone; #1, 2, and 2/ run to the Valley of Temples; #1/ runs to Pirandello's house. Alternatively, take the bus to **Porto Empedocle** (€1.03) and get off at "La Casa di Pirandello." Tickets available at the cream-colored bar cart in the parking lot. Ask for schedules on board.

Taxis: (☎ 0922 26 670), at stand in front of train station in P. Marconi; or (☎ 0922 21 899), in P. Aldo Moro.

ORIENTATION AND PRACTICAL INFORMATION

The middle of Agrigento is a string of large piazzas. The **train station** is in **Piazza Marconi,** which spills into **Piazza Moro** at the far left corner when facing away from the station. From P. Moro, **Via Atenea** leads straight through the **centro storico.** At the far side of P. Moro is **Piazza Vittorio Emanuele,** home of the post office and the **bus station.** The temples are a bus ride (#1 or 2) or a long walk below the town.

SICILY

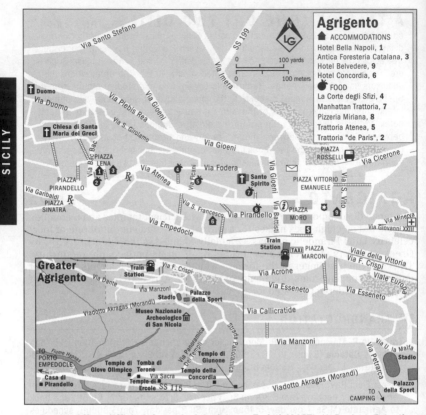

Agrigento

🏠 ACCOMMODATIONS
Hotel Bella Napoli, **1**
Antica Foresteria Catalana, **3**
Hotel Belvedere, **9**
Hotel Concordia, **6**
🍴 FOOD
La Corte degli Sfizi, **4**
Manhattan Trattoria, **7**
Pizzeria Miriana, **8**
Trattoria Atenea, **5**
Trattoria "de Paris", **2**

Tourist Office: Ufficio Informazioni Assistenza Turisti (AAST), V. Battista, 5 (☎/fax 0922 20 454), the 1st left off V. Atenea. Staff will outfit you with maps and brochures. Open in summer M-F 8:30am-1:30pm. Another summer office in **Valle dei Tempii,** adjacent to car park and bar. English spoken. Open daily 8am-7:30pm. Information stand also in train station.

Luggage Storage: At bus station, €3.87 per bag per 24hr. Open daily 8am-9:30pm.

Emergency: ☎113.

Carabinieri: (☎0922 59 63 22), at P. Moro, 2, opposite V. Atenea.

First Aid: ☎0922 40 13 44.

Late-Night Pharmacy: Farmacia Averna Antonio, V. Atenea, 325 (☎0922.26 093). Open M-F 9am-1:30pm and 5-8:30pm. **Farmacia Minacori,** P. Sinatra, 3 (☎0922 24 235), open same hours. Both post late-night and weekend rotations outside.

Hospital: Ospedale Civile (☎0922 49 21 11), on S. Giovanni XXII.

Internet Access: Libreria Multimediale, V. Celauro, 7 (☎0922 40 85 62), off V. Atenea, 2 blocks down from P. Moro. €1 for 15min., €3.10 per hr. Open M-Sa 9:30am-1:15pm and 4:45-8:15pm.

Post Office: P. V. Emanuele (☎0922 59 51 50; fax 22 926). Open M-Sa 8am-6:30pm, with break at 1:30pm when shifts change.

Postal Code: 92100.

▐ ACCOMMODATIONS & CAMPING

■ **Hotel Concordia,** V. S. Francesco d'Assisi, 11 (☎ 0922 59 62 66). At end of V. Pirandello in historic district, just after the church. Small, simply-furnished rooms in a great location. Bells from the nearby church serve as a built-in alarm clock. Singles €17, with bath and TV €21; doubles €34-42. AmEx/MC/V. ❷

■ **Hotel Belvedere,** V. S. Vito, 20 (☎/fax 0922 20 051). Follow the hotel signs in front of the train station, left to P. Moro; follow stone steps and signs leading up to your right from the piazza. Colorfully painted rooms with decorated bedcovers overlook P. Moro and the valley. Ask for a room with a view. Breakfast €3. Singles €34, with bath €47; doubles €42/60; triples with bath €85. ❸

Hotel Bella Napoli, P. Lena, 6 (☎/fax 0922 20 435), off V. Bac Bac. Take V. Atenea 1km uphill and turn right after you pass the Justice Building. Institutional hallways lead to clean white rooms with large, bare bathrooms. Rooftop terrace overlooks the valley. Renovations are providing rooms with bath, A/C, and TV. Breakfast €3. Singles €35; doubles €65; triples €95. V. ❸

Antica Foresteria Catalana, P. Lena, 5 (☎/fax 0922 20 435), beside the Hotel Bella Napoli and under the same management, offers larger, but similarly furnished rooms. with bath, AC, and TV. Singles €45; doubles €75; triples €120. V. ❹

Camping: Camping Nettuno (☎ 0922 41 62 68) lies on the beach at V. L'Acquameno at the bus stop. Take bus #2 or 2/ from the train station. Reasonable market, restaurant, bar, and *pizzeria*. €5 per person, €5 per tent, €2.50 per car. Showers €0.50. ❶

▐ FOOD

Plenty of small *alimentari* line V. Pirandello and V. Atenea. Indulge a sweet tooth at the candy stalls along V. della Vittoria. The local specialty is *torrone*, a nut-filled cream-colored nougat. Authentic, inexpensive *trattorie* lie off V. Atenea, in small stairway areas tucked off the main street.

■ **Trattoria Atenea,** V. Ficani, 21 (☎ 0922 20 247), 4th right off V. Atenea from P. Moro, just beyond the Stefanel store. Like grandma's kitchen: huge portions with no fuss. Extensive seafood offerings, such as *calamari* (squid) and *gamberi* (shrimp), starting from €5.16. Chase house specialty *grigliata mista di pesce* (mixed grilled fish; €4.65) with smooth local wine. Cover €1.29. Open M-Sa noon-3pm and 6:30-10pm. ❷

Manhattan Trattoria/Pizzeria, Salita M. degli Angeli, 9 (☎ 0922 20 911), up steps to the right off V. Atenea near P. Moro. Seating indoors and outside. Pizza from €3.10, fresh local fish from €7.75., and typical Sicilian *primi* and *secondi* from €4.15. Cover €1.03. Open noon-3pm and 7:30-10:30pm. AmEx/MC/V. ❷

Trattoria "de Paris," P. Lena, 7 (☎ 0922 25 413), beside Hotel Bella Napoli. White-and-blue tablecloths and small rooms crowded with odd figurines. Tasty *rigatoni alla Pirandello* (with tomatoes, *prosciutto*, mushrooms, and cream, €4.13) is so-called because Pirandello is said to have brought *panna* (cream), to the Italian kitchen. Open M-Sa noon-3pm and 7:30-10:30pm. AmEx/D/MC/V. ❷

La Corte degli Sfizi (☎ 0922 20 052), on Cortile Contarini, off V. Atenea. Classic Sicilian dishes like grilled fish in a peaceful open-air garden. *Primi* €4.13, *secondi* €5.16. Cover €1.55. Open daily 11am-3:30pm and 7pm-midnight. AmEx/MC/V. ❷

Pizzeria Miriana, V. Pirandello, 6 (☎ 0922 22 828), at the start of V. Pirandello off P. Moro. Quality budget food to go. Friendly chefs serve pizza by the slice (€1) and *panini* (from €1.55). Open daily 8am-10pm. ❶

SICILY

◉ SIGHTS

◼VALLE DEI TEMPII. Planted in a lesser ridge below Agrigento's hilltop perch, the five elevated temples are a picture-perfect tribute to the indomitability of paganism. Time, earthquakes, vicious Punic Wars, and the rise of Christianity have taken their toll, and the temples have been named official World Heritage Landmarks. Weathered to glowing golden hues, the temples are best viewed at sunset, as crowds thin and temperatures cool. The transition from sunset to moonlight is not to be missed. Make sure to bring a lot of water, sunscreen, light clothes, and good walking shoes, as there is no break in the valley from the hot Agrigento sun.

From the entrance, a wide avenue heads uphill along the ridge, first passing the **Tempio di Ercole** (Hercules). One row of solid, squat columns are all that remain standing from this earliest of the temples. Farther along, the **Tempio della Concordia** stands as the proud victor in the battle against fate. With 34 columns, walls intact, and evident metopes and stylobates, this temple is one of the best-preserved of the Greek world. Erected in the mid-5th century BC from limestone, it owes its preserved state to an early conversion to Christianity by the archbishop of Agrigento. Though the temple is fenced off from the public, the niches carved into the interior walls are still visible. The road ends at the contemporary 5th-century BC **Tempio di Giunone** (Juno). Elegant columns and part of the pediment remain to create one of the more interesting sunset silhouettes. To the left during the ascent, holes in the ground mark an early Christian burial site.

Across the street lies the entrance to the unfinished **Tempio di Giove Olimpico** (Jupiter). Had its construction not been interrupted by Carthaginian troops in 406-405 BC, it would have been one of the largest Greek temples ever built. The toppled jigsaw puzzle of partitioned columns and walls has challenged archaeologists for years. The temple's most interesting features are the gigantic *telamones*, 8m sculpted male figures, one of which has been reconstructed at the site. These massive figures would have encircled the temple, holding up the roof and entablature. At the far end of the ride, past the Tempio di Giove, four columns of the long-gone **Tempio di Catore e Polluce** (Castor and Pollux) stand eternal guard in case the Carthaginians should choose to come back.

The excellent **Museo Nazionale Archeologico di San Nicola**, 1km uphill from the parking lot, has a fabulous collection of red and black figureware vases, terracotta votive figures, and funerary vessels from the area's necropolis. The newly renovated interior boasts an upright *telamon*, as well as model projections of how a completed Tempio di Giove may have looked. *(Valle dei Tempii is several km from city. Starting on V. F. Crispi, it's a sunny 30min. walk from the train station to the entrance, following signs downhill and left at the lower intersection. Or take bus #1, 2, or 27 from train station; it stops in a dirt lot carpark with a snack bar and many tour buses. Tempii di Giove open 8:30am-11pm. €2; all other temples free. Museum open daily 9am-1:30pm. €4.)*

CHIESA DI SANTA MARIA DEI GRECI. Built atop a 5th-century BC Greek temple, this church is the most interesting building in medieval Agrigento. The interior contains a Norman wooden ceiling, original Doric columns, and 14th-century frescoes of a strangely wizened Christ child. *(Follow the signs up the hill from V. Bac Bac off V. Atenea. In the summer of 2002, the church was undergoing restoration.)*

CHIESA DEL PURGATORIO (S. SPIRITO). The legendary Serpotta employed all of his wizardry in making this church's stucco ornamentation look like marble. The statues of the "Virtues" are meant to help you stay out of purgatory, but most of the imagery reminds you how imminent purgatory actually is—note the unusual skull and crossbones on the confessional and the countless depictions of roasted sinners. To the left of the church, below a sleeping lion, lies a 5th-century BC Greek entrance to a network of underground channels. *(In P. Purgatorio off V. Atenea in the* centro storico.*)*

SIX TOURISTS IN SEARCH OF AN AUTHOR. Those with their eyes open need not search long—Agrigentan playwright **Luigi Pirandello** has achieved all but mythical status in his hometown. Literature aficionados will want to visit his birthplace, now a small museum of books, notes, and family photographs. Pirandello's ashes are buried below a large boulder under his favorite pine tree, a few hundred meters from the house. *(Take the Lumia bus #1 to P. Kaos. ☎0922 51 11 02. Open daily 8am-1:30pm. €2. In the summer of 2002, the church was undergoing restoration, but was expected to reopen soon.)*

ENTERTAINMENT

The first Sunday in February brings the **Almond Blossom Festival,** an international folk-dancing fest, to the Valle dei Tempii. The **Settimana Pirandelliana,** a week-long outdoor festival of plays, operas, and ballets in P. Kaos, occurs in late July and early August. *(Info ☎0922 23 561.)* During summer months, Agrigentans move to the beach and nightlife strip at **San Leone,** 4km from Agrigento by bus #2.

MARSALA   ☎0923

When Garibaldi and his red-shirted devotees landed at Marsala, the city provided them with men and means, making itself the Risorgimento's proud launchpad. Today, the streets course with hot and dusty *scirocco* wind from Africa, rather than with revolutionary fever. The city is best known for its exquisite Marsala wine, which gained fame thanks to Brit John Woodhouse. Despite its small size, the city has several worthwhile sights, including the ruins of Lilybaeum and a famed Carthaginian warship.

TRANSPORTATION AND PRACTICAL INFORMATION. Trains service the town from **Trapani** (20min., 17 per day, €2.45), as do **AST buses** (☎0923 23 222). (30min.; 4 per day; 6:50am-2:10pm; €2.58, round-trip €4.13. Return to Trapani, 4 per day, 7:10am-2:15pm.) **Salemi** buses (☎0923 98 11 20) run from **Palermo** to **Marsala** (M-Sa 17 per day, 6:15am-8:30pm; Su 5 per day, 10:30am-8:30pm) and back to **Palermo** (M-Sa 17 per day, 5:15am-5:30pm; Su 5 per day, 7:30am-6pm). **Taxis** are at ☎0923 71 29 92.

With your back to the train station, the first right facing V. A. Fazio and another slight right through the intersection onto **Via Roma** leads to Marsala's historic center. V. Roma turns into **Via XI Maggio** and then **Via Veneto.** The **Pro Loco tourist office** is at V. XI Maggio, 100, in the old city, just before Palazzo Comunale and the duomo. The staff checks bus schedules and suggests housing. (☎0923 71 40 97 or 71 44 77; www.prolocomarsala.org. Open M-Sa 8am-2pm and 3-8pm, Su 9am-noon.) In an **emergency,** call the **carabinieri** (☎112 or ☎0923 95 10 10), **state police** (☎0923 71 88 11), **first aid** (☎0923 95 14 10), or **Guardia Medica** (☎0923 78 23 43). A **pharmacy,** one block from the Pro Loco office at V. XI Maggio, 114, posts the nighttime rotation. (☎0923 95 32 54. Open Su-F 9am-1:30pm and 4:20-8pm.)

ACCOMMODATIONS AND FOOD. Marsala has few hotels of any kind, and very few budget accommodations. Those planning to spend a few days wine tasting might check out **Andrea's affittacamere ❷.** Call ahead for free pickup at the bus or train station. Though quite a distance from the center, rooms for rent located among the old salt mills and the lagoon can be great values. (☎0923 74 57 47, 328

SICILY

484 9399, or 388 941 4016; andreasbb@tiscali.it Singles €21-31; doubles €36-55.) Within the *centro*, the best bet is **Hotel Garden ❷**, V. Gambini, 36. The gritty station neighborhood and drab exterior hides a sparkling interior with marble, mirrors, and communal bathrooms. Tidy rooms have TV, fans, and woven rugs. (☎0923 98 23 20. Singles €30, with bath €35; doubles with bath €51. AmEx/D/MC/V.) Stumbling home from wine tastings at Cantine Florio, you can find comfortable beds at the nearby **New Palace Hotel ❺**, V. Lungomare Mediterraneo, 57. Refined rooms with bath, A/C, and TV await beyond the impressive courtyard. (☎0923 71 94 92; fax 71 94 96. Singles €80-98; doubles €130-181. AmEx/MC/V.)

Self-caterers should head to the **STANDA supermarket,** V. Cammareti Scurtil, 10. (☎0923 71 54 76. Open M 4-7:30pm, Tu-Sa 9am-1pm and 4-7:30pm.) The aromatic **Trattoria Garibaldi ❷**, V. Rubino, 35, on P. Addolorata across from the sanctuary of Maria S. S. Addolorata, has typical Italian fare and vegetarian options such as omelettes. (☎0923 95 30 06. *Primi* from €5, *secondi* from €6. Cover €2. Open M-F 12:30-2:30pm and 8-10:30pm, Sa 8-10:30pm, and Su 12:30-2:30pm. AmEx/MC/V.) Facing the cathedral's main door, head left through the Porta Garibaldi arch into P. Garibaldi; then take your first right and look for a sign several blocks down, on the corner with V. Sabilla, for **Nuova Trattoria da Pino ❷**, V. San Lorenzo, 27. An excellent *antipasto* buffet and seafood specialties are served on checkered tablecloths alongside impressive shelves of wine. (☎0923 71 56 52. *Primi* from €4.50, *secondi* from €5. Open M-Sa noon-3:30pm and 7-11pm, Su 7-11pm. AmEx/MC/V.) **E & N Cafe ❶**, V. XI Maggio, 130, serves delicacies such as *cannoli* (from €1.50) to crowds from dawn until drop. A case full of marzipan fruit begs to be taken home. (☎0923 95 19 69. Open Su-F 7:30am-10pm, Sa 7:30am-midnight.)

◨ ▣ SIGHTS AND ENTERTAINMENT. The **Museo Archaeologico Regional "Baglio Anselmi"** guards the famed **Carthaginian warship.** To reach the museum, follow V. XI Maggio through its portal end to P. della Libertà. Facing the bright pink cinema, take the flower-filled road slightly to the left, continuing right at its end. The museum is on the Lungomare Boeo. The now-skeletal vessel sank in the devastating final battle (241 BC) of the First Punic War, in which Rome defeated Carthage and established its permanent naval supremacy. The few wooden planks, preserved for over 2000 years in underwater sand off Marsala, are the largest existing portion of this type of ship. Across the hall, other galleries in the museum display objects from Lilybaeum and the isle of Motya, including pottery and two life-size male sculptures. (☎0923 95 25 35. Open 9am-2pm and 4-8pm. Closed M, W, and Th afternoons. €2., under 18 half-price, over 65 free.)

Visitors can walk through the wine-scented halls of the **Cantine Florio,** the oldest and most famous of the Marsala wine production areas, built in 1833. The *enoteca* at the far end of the facilities sell the strong wine products from 9am to 12:45pm and 3-5:45pm. Take V. Francesco Crispi toward the water from the main intersection of V. Roma next to the train station. At the end, follow Lungomare Mediterraneo until the painted Florio sign. (☎0923 78 11 11. Free tours July-Sept. 11am and 3:30pm. Oct.-June, call for tour arrangements.) On the way back, stop by the **Fontana del Vino** (Fountain of Wine), where a wine-loving lady drinks gustily with a barrel-bearing donkey. The piazza surrounding the fountain, with a brick pattern that mimics the Union Jack, is a subtle poke at the British presence in Marsala.

Also down V. XI Maggio and left down V. Sauro, the **Chiesa di San Giovanni** conceals the **Groita della Sibilla** (reached via a trapdoor), where an ancient oracle spent 28 years preaching to believers through a hole in the ceiling. Early Christians staked out the cave in the 4th century AD, hence the frescoes of fish and doves; St. Paul is said to have baptized converts in the pool here, and a statue of St. John covers the reclusive sibyl's grave. (Church closed to visitors. Open only on the Day of San Giovanni, June 24th). Just behind the duomo at V. Garraffa, 57, the **Museo degli Arazzi (Flemish Tapestry Museum)** contains eight violent 16th-century Flemish tapestries illustrating Titus's war against the Jews in AD 66-67, and provides information on Marsala's various churches. (☎ 0923 71 29 03. Open Tu-Su 9am-1pm and 4-6pm. €1.50, students €0.50.) A few steps down from P. Reppubblica and the duomo, the **Museo Civico** houses several of the thousand red shirts, as well as Garibaldi's own rather snazzy uniform. (Open Tu-Su 9am-1pm and 4-8pm.)

The 🅜**Marsala DOC Jazz Festival** jams it up with music and wine in the last two weeks of July, attracting the greats of the international jazz scene. The festival emblem colorfully depicts a mellowed-out bass player strumming his six-foot wooden, stained bottle of Marsala.

TRAPANI ☎ 0923

Between two perfect blue stretches of *lungomare*, ancient rooftops peek over Trapani's old city. Just below the horizon, colorful fishing boats and massive ferries barrel through waves and pull into the dock. Reliable transportation and extensive lodgings make Trapani a good base for adventures to Segesta's temple, Erice's medieval streets, San Vito's beaches, the natural splendor of the Lo Zingaro reservation, and the Egadi Islands.

📁 TRANSPORTATION

Flights: Vincenzo Florio Airport (☎ 0923 84 25 02 or 84 12 22), in Birgi en route to Marsala, 16km outside the city. Buses from P. Malta are timed to coincide with flights. Daily flights to Rome and Pantelleria. Not a heavily used airport.

Trains: P. Stazione (☎ 0923 28 071 or 28 081). **Luggage storage** available (p. 686). Ticket office open daily 5:45am-7:50pm. AmEx/MC/V. To: **Castelvetrano** (1hr., 17 per day, 4:35am-8:40pm, €4.15); **Marsala** (30min., 15 per day, 4:35am-8:40pm, €2.45); and **Palermo** (2hr., 9 per day, 5am-7:30pm, €6.45).

Buses: AST (☎ 0923 21 021). Main bus station at P. Malta. Buses to **Erice** (45min.; M-Sa 11 per day, 6:40am-7:30pm; Su 4 per day, 9am-6pm; €1.80); **Marsala** (M-Sa 4 per day, 6:40am-2:10pm, €2.58); and **San Vito Lo Capo** (1½hr.; M-Sa 9 per day, 7am-8:20pm; Su 5 per day, 8:15am-6:40pm; €3.10). Service to all destinations reduced Su. **Segesta** (☎ 0923 21 754) runs buses to local towns and to **Rome** (15hr., 1 per day, 5:30pm, €38.22).

Ferries: Ferries and *aliscafi* (hydrofoils) leave Trapani for the **Egadi Islands** (Levanzo, Favignana, and Marettimo), **Ustica, Pantelleria** (an Italian island off the Tunisian coast), and Tunisia. All boats leave from the docks across from P. Garibaldi and along V. A. Staiti. You can also purchase tickets for these lines from the travel agents and offices along V. A. Staiti. The schedule below shows high-season (June-Aug.) times and rates; low-season frequency and prices will be lower. Sea transport schedules may also suffer at the hands of bad weather. Schedules are available at all ticket offices.

Ustica (☎ 0923 22 200; fax 0923 23 289; www.usticalines.it), in a yellow booth on the waterfront.

Siremar (☎ 0923 54 54 55; www.siremar.it), with ticket offices both at a blue and white striped waterfront booth and in Stazione Marettima. Open M-F 6:15am-noon, 3-7pm and 9pm-midnight; Su 6:15-10am, 11:30am-noon, 3-3:30pm, 5:15-6:45pm, and 9pm-midnight. AmEx/D/MC/V.

Tirrenia (☎ 0923 52 18 96; www.tirrenia.it), in Stazione Marettima. Open M 6:30am-1pm and 3-6pm, Tu 9am-1pm and 4-9pm, W-F 9am-1pm and 3-6pm, Sa 9am-noon. AmEx/D/MC/V.

Lauro (☎ 092 392 4073), on the waterfront near Ustica. Open W-M 9am-1pm and 4-7pm, Tu from 7am,

DESTINATION	COMPANY	DURATION	FREQUENCY	PRICE
Favignana (Egadi Islands)	Siremar (ferry)	1hr.	2 per day	€3.10
Favignana (E.I.)	Ustica (hydrofoil)	20min.	11 per day	€5.08
Favignana (E.I.)	Siremar (hydrofoil)	25min.	10 per day	€5.16
Levanzo (E.I)	Siremar (ferry)	1hr.	7 per day	€3.10
Levanzo (E.I.)	Siremar (hydrofoil)	20min.	10 per day	€5.16
Levanzo (E.I.)	Ustica (hydrofoil)	20min.	10 per day	€5.08
Marettimo (E.I.)	Siremar (ferry)	3hr.	2 per day	€6.97
Marettimo (E.I.)	Siremar (hydrofoil)	1hr.	3 per day	€11.62
Marettimo (E.I.)	Ustica (hydrofoil)	1hr.	2 per day	€10.45
Pantelleria	Siremar (ferry)	6hr.	Midnight	€22.47
Pantelleria	Ustica (hydrofoil)	2½hr.	1:35pm	€34
Ustica via Favignana	Ustica (hydrofoil)	2½hr.	3 per wk.	€19
Cagliari (Sardinia)	Tirrenia (ferry)	11½hr.	Tu 9pm	€38.21
Tunis	Tirrenia (ferry)	8½hr.	M 10am	€51.38
Tunis	Linee Lauro (ferry)	12hr.	2 per wk.	€46.48

Public Transportation: SAU, the orange city bus, has its main terminal at P. V. Veneto, down V. Osorio from the station right on V. XXX Gennaio, and straight ahead all the way to the water. Office at left when facing water. Has posted schedules of all bus routes. Tickets sold at most *tabacchi* (€0.57).

Taxis: (☎ 0923 23 233 or 22 808), often in P. Umberto, outside the train station.

✈ 🛈 ORIENTATION AND PRACTICAL INFORMATION

Trapani sits on a peninsula 2hr. west of Palermo by bus or train. The old city began at the outer tip of the hook, growing in cautious backward steps until it tripped and spilled new wide streets and cement high-rises into the mainland. The **train station** is in **Piazza Umberto,** with the **bus station** just to the left in **Piazza Malta.** From the train station, **Via Osorio** passes the **Villa Margherita Gardens** to end at the perpendicular **Via XXX Gennaio.** A right onto this road leads to **Piazza V. Veneto** and the local city bus station. A left goes down to **Via A. Staiti,** which runs along the port. The **tourist office** is at the end of **Corso Italia,** off V. XXX Gennaio. From P. V. Veneto, **Via Garibaldi** becomes **Via Libertà** and moves into the old city.

Tourist Office: AAPIT (☎ 0923 29 000; fax 24 004; www.apt.trapani.it), at P. Saturno, up V. Torrearsa from the port. English-speaking staff can provide maps and information on activities and cultural events in Trapani and surrounding towns. Open M-Sa 8am-8pm, Su 9am-noon.

Currency Exchange: Banks on C. Italia have better rates than the train station. Open daily 8:10am-1pm. **Post office** also exchanges money and cashes traveler's checks. **ATMs** are at Stazione Marettima in the old city and along V. M.V. Scontrino in front of the train station.

Luggage Storage: In train station. €3.87 per bag per 24hr. Open daily 8am-9:30pm.

Police: (☎ 113 or 0923 59 02 98), in P. V. Veneto. **Carabinieri:** V. Orlandini, 19 (☎ 0923 27 122).

Guardia Medica: P. Generale Scio, 1 (☎ 0923 29 629). **Pronto Scorso:** (☎ 0923 80 94 50), on V. Cosenza.

Pharmacy: V. Garibaldi, 9, next to P. V. Veneto. All pharmacies open Su-F 9am-1:30pm and 4:30-8pm, with on-call night information schedule posted on the door. Look for bright green cross outside the door.

Hospital: Ospedale Sant'Antonio Abate (☎ 0924 80 91 11), on V. Cosenza, far northeast of the city center.

Internet Access: World Sport Line, V. Regina Elena, 26/28 (☎ 0923 28 866; fax 54 41 68), across from Stazione Marettima. 4 speedy computers at €2.50 per 30min. or €5 per hr. Open M-F 9am-1pm and 4-8:30pm, Sa 9am-1pm and 4-11pm.

Post Office: P. V. Veneto, 3 (☎ 0923 21 996 or 43 44 04). With your back to the train station, turn right down V. M.V. Scontrino and take a left through the small fountain park. Continue left down V. Fardella, with iron-fenced public gardens on the left. Post office on left after Palazzo del Governo. **Currency exchange,** booth #18. Open M-Sa 8:20am-6:30pm.

Postal Code: 91100.

■ ACCOMMODATIONS & CAMPING

▧ Pensione Messina, C. V. Emanuele, 71 (☎ 0923 21 198), through a Renaissance courtyard and up 4 flights of steps. Welcome to Grandma's house, complete with ticking grandfather clock, eclectic bric-a-brac, garden statues, and familial feel. Bright rooms each contain a balcony and a sink. Communal bathrooms are down the hall. Breakfast €3.50 per person. Singles €16; doubles €26-31. Extra bed 35%. ❷

Albergo Moderno, V. Genovese, 20 (☎ 0923 21 247; fax 23 348). From P. S. Agostino on C. V. Emanuele, go left on V. Roma, then right on V. Genovese after Café Moderno. Clean, white rooms with TV are brought to life by frames lining walls. All rooms except for 2 singles are with bath. Singles €16, with bath €23.50; doubles €39; triples €52.50. MC/V. ❷

Ostello per la Gioventù (HI) (☎ 0923 55 29 64), Strada Proviniciale, Trapani-Erice. The hostel is a good 6km from the station. Take city bus #23 from the train station (2 per hr., €0.77) and ask the driver to let you off at the hostel. Follow signs from the stop to the hostel, about 900m. The hostel's distance from Trapani is both its greatest selling point and its worst feature. A peaceful, wooded setting with cheery red bunks and the scent of evergreen and *cappuccino*. Many English-speaking travelers. HI members only. Breakfast (€2) served in summer. Showers and sheets included. Lockout 10am-4pm. Curfew 11:30pm (ask for a key). 6-bed dorms €11. ❶

Nuova Albergo Russo, V. Tintori, 4 (☎ 0923 22 166; fax 26 623), off V. Torre Arsa. Newly-renovated hotel with large and comfortable rooms, each with bath, A/C, and TV. Breakfast €3 per person. Sept.-June singles €39; doubles €68; triples €92; quads €116. July-Aug. and Easter wk. singles €41; doubles €78; triples €105; quads €133. AmEx/MC/V. ❹

Hotel Vittoria, V. F. Crispi, 4 (☎ 0923 873 044; fax 29 870), off P. V. Emanuele. Near train and bus stations. Large rooms offer view of rocky coast and public gardens. Communal area with bar and TV. Breakfast €5 per person. Singles €47; doubles €73; triples €98.55. AmEx/MC/V. ❺

Camping: Campeggio Lido Valderice (☎ 0923 57 30 86), on V. del Detince, in seaside town of the same name. Take bus for Bonegia or San Vito La Capo (€2.58) and tell driver your destination. Follow flower-lined road opposite bus stop and perpendicular to the highway, and turn right at its end. Well-shaded campground near a couple of beaches. €3.90 per person, €3.50 for small tent, €1.70 extra for light. €8.30 for campers (light included), €2 per car. Hot showers €0.60. ❶

◖ FOOD

In Trapani, couscous is actually touted as a Sicilian dish, with local fish added to the North African favorite. Bakeries carry *biscotti con fichi*, the Italian Fig Newton, for about €0.20 each. The old city has lots of small *alimentari*, and a daily fish and fruit market springs up each morning along the northern *lungomare*, at the intersection of V. Maggio and V. Garibaldi in the old city. Almost everything in Trapani closes on Sunday.

DRIVING US CRAZY. As one Trapani native puts it, "The street signs here are just suggestions." Trapani's streets are filled to the brim with cars: double-parked, triple-parked, and packed into the sidewalks of every street, with angry closed-in drivers honking their horns in frustration. Stop signs might as well be invisible, turn signals are unused toys, and seat belts are foreign objects of an unknown purpose. As such, visitors should take extra care, both when traversing the busy streets—cars here rarely stop for pedestrians—and especially when venturing behind the wheel of a Trapani vehicle. To cross a street, look both ways (five times each), stick out a hand in either direction, and prepare to sprint. To get out of your parking space when blocked by double parking, get behind the wheel and sound your horn like there's no tomorrow. Eventually, the owner of the offending vehicle will make his way out. If stuck in a traffic jam or waiting in line at an intersection for too long, open your window and take a lesson in colorful Sicilian phrases from your fellow drivers.

▨ **Trattoria da Salvatore,** V. N. Nasi, 19 (☎ 0923 54 65 30), 1 street toward the port from C. V. Emanuele. Small and authentic, this family-run restaurant serves perfect pasta to a regular local crowd. Debates over soccer games on the overheard TV are as hot as the house couscous. Menu changes daily. *Primi* from €3.60, *secondi* €6.20-8.26. Cover €1. Open Sept.-June M-Sa noon-3:30pm and 7-11pm; July-Aug. daily noon-3:30pm and 7-11pm. AmEx. ❷

▨ **Pizzeria Calvino,** V. N. Nasi, 71 (☎ 0923 21 464), behind C. V. Emanuele, 100m from the duomo. Customers line up at the door nightly for one of 30 varieties of the best pizza in town. Order a pie to go, or eat in small back rooms. Delivery service available. Pizzas from €3.50. Open W-M 7pm-midnight. MC/V. ❶

Trattoria Miramare (☎ 0923 20 011), on the port side *lungomare,* at the end of V. Torrearsa. Features a small dining room and a huge wine list. A non-smoking Italian anomaly. Couscous is the specialty, in a fish sauce so spicy that they won't serve it to foreigners unless prodded. *Tortellini con panna* (with cream, €6). *Primi* from €4, *secondi* €4-12. Cover €1. Open daily noon-5pm and 7pm-midnight. ❷

Taverna Paradiso, Lungomare Dante Alighieri, 22 (☎ 0923 87 37 51). This classy, bluesy tavern serves up seafood and drinks late into the night. *Primi* from €9, *secondi* €9-13. Cover €3. Kitchen closes at 11pm. Open Feb.-Dec. M-Sa noon-3pm and 8pm-1am. AmEx/MC/V. ❸

👁 SIGHTS

CHIESA DEL PURGATORIO. Delicate stone statues blend into the gray exterior of this 17th-century Baroque church, in the heart of Trapani's old city. Inside, 16 nearly life-size wooden sculptures, known as *I Misteri*, form a semi-circle around the pews, telling the story of the passions and the crucifixion. Each year on Good Friday at 2pm, these sculptures are paraded around the city, and given to the workers' guild to which they were dedicated. *(1 block up V. D.G. Giglio from P. Garibaldi, across from Stazione Marettima; follow signs from the port. Open daily 9am-noon and 4-7pm.)*

SANTUARIO DELL'ANNUNZIATA/MUSEO NAZIONALE PEPOLI. The only attraction in the modern part of town, the enormous *santuario* is a lavishly decorated church housing a 14th-century statue of the Madonna of Trapani. Legend has it that a boat carrying this statue got caught in a storm at sea. The captain promised God that if he survived, he would leave the statue as a gift to the first port at which he arrived. In the same complex is the *museo*, which features a collection of local sculptures and paintings, coral carvings, and folk-art figurines, including a frighteningly violent portrayal of the biblical story of Herod's baby hunt. *(Take SAU buses #24, 25, or 30 from P. V. Emanuele (€0.80), 2 blocks to the right of the train station. ☎ 0923 55 32 69. Open M-Sa 9am-1:30pm, Su 9am-12:30pm. Call to make sure it's open. €4.15.)*

TORRE DI LIGNY. A mini-peninsula, the Torre is at the end of a wide jetty off the tip of Trapani. Wild coastal winds stream past the tower, which is visible from both sides of Trapani's ports. The tower itself houses the **Museo di Preistoria/ Museo del Mare,** with its collection of shells, prehistoric artifacts, and underwater excavation pieces. *(☎0923 22 300. Open daily 9:30am-12:30pm. €1.55.)*

VILLA MARGHERITA. At the cusp of the old and new cities, the Villa (or Public Gardens) offers a delightful change of pace from cobblestone and cement. Palms, banyan trees, and fountains rest behind flower-lined avenues. Playgrounds and statues complete the picture of the perfect city park. Each July, the villa is the center of the **Luglio Musicale Trapanese,** an annual festival of opera, ballet, and cabaret that draws national and international stars to the temporary stage among the trees. *(☎ 0923 21 454; fax 22 934. Shows 9pm. Info booth inside park gates.)*

◗ DAYTRIPS FROM TRAPANI

SAN VITO LO CAPO

Buses to San Vito Lo Capo, the closest town to the reserve, leave from P. Malta in Trapani (1½hr.; M-Sa 9 per day, 7am-8:20pm; Su 5 per day, 8:15am-6:40pm; last return to Trapani daily 8pm; €3.10).

San Vito is defined by its popular and breathtaking *spiaggia*, with all roads in town leading to the smooth sands. Tanned bodies meander idly around the wide streets, stopping for a *gelato* on the *lungomare*. The main road is V. Savoia, where you'll find the **tourist office** at #57. (☎ 0923 97 43 00 or 97 24 64. Open daily 9am-1pm and 5-9pm.) **Albergo Costa Gaia ❸,** V. Savoia, 123-125, on the main street four blocks from the beach, has rooms with bath and A/C. (☎0923 97 22 68 or 97 23 75; www.albergocostagaia.com. Breakfast included. Sept. to early July singles €32.50; doubles €57. July 15-Aug. 1 half-pension €52 per person; full-pension €60 per person.) For a little luxury right on the beach, head to **Hotel Egitarso ❹,** V. Lungomare, 54. Services include a 24hr. bar, a restaurant with typical Sicilian fare, and a minibus excursion program. (☎0923 97 21 11; fax 97 20 62; www.hotelegitarso.it. Half-pension €45-75 per person; full-pension €60-80 per person. AmEx/MC/V.)

San Vito has several excellent nearby camping options. **International Camping Soleado ❶,** V. della Secca, 40, is straight across from the beach. It has a restaurant, bar, mini-club, and sports area. (☎ 0923 97 21 66; fax 97 40 51; soldeado@virgolio.it. Sept.-June €5 per person, €6 per tent, €6 per car; July-Aug. €6/€8/€6. Light €3, hot shower €0.50.) **Camping La Fata ❶,** V. B. Napoli, 68, two blocks from the beach, is right in town. Complete with bar and disco, the site has a secluded, bamboo-shaded rectangle for tenting. (☎0923 97 21 33; lafata@trapaniweb.it; www.trapaniweb.it/lafata. Open June-Sept. Reservations recommended. June and Sept. €4 per person, July-Aug. €6 per person; €3.50-€5.50 per tent, €3-4 per car. Light €3, hot shower €0.50. AmEx/MC/V.) **Campeggio La Pineta ❶,** V. del Secco, 88, is on the town's edge. (☎0923 97 28 18; lapineta@camping.it, www.campinglapineta.it. Reserve in Aug. €4.20-6.30 per person, €3.50-5.50 per tent, €2.50-4 per car. Hot shower €0.40. Bungalow rates with breakfast: June and Sept. doubles €54. July-Aug. half-pension €42-61 per person, full-pension €54-74 per person.)

Trattoria Galante ❸, V. Margherita, 95, off V. Savoia, serves *risotto alla pescatora* (seafood risotto) and various couscous dishes. (☎0923 97 20 07. *Primi* from €6, *secondi* from €7.50. Cover €2. Open daily 8am-3pm and 7-11pm. MC/V.) At **Le Sorelle ❸,** V. Arimondi, 15, a wooden stove yields hot pizza (from €5.20) to enjoy on the outside patio. (☎0923 97 21 19. *Primi* from €5.20, *secondi* from €7.70. Open daily noon-3pm and 8pm-midnight. D/MC/V.) In case of an emergency, call the **beach police** (☎0923 97 43 71), **Guardia Medica** (☎0923 97 20 91), **carabinieri** (☎ 0923 97 23 47), or **municipal police** (☎ 0923 97 21 60).

FROM THE ROAD

LABOR OF LOVE

Walking along Erice's medieval streets, I found peaceful, chosen isolation. I let my mind wander, imagining what the fairy-tale town must have been like one century back, five centuries back, and before. I turned a corner and suddenly came upon a man relieving himself on a wall. This wasn't exactly the "once upon a time" I was looking for. A few moments later, I stumbled upon a vicious dogfight. The two combatants looked up, snarling and turning their bared teeth toward me.

The streets had lost their initial appeal. I fled to Erice's public gardens and settled onto a shady bench. A sizeable serving of *gelato* in hand, I thought about the job at hand: the many buses and trains that would be boarded tomorrow, and the pages upon pages that would have to be written by sunrise.

The *gelato* eased my appetite and calmed my nerves. Dread gave way to anticipation as I scanned the horizon, turning a warm, glowing shade of pink. I love this job. I love the feeling of lightness that comes over me each morning as a train takes me to a new location. I embrace smelly clothing, dirty clothing, and have stopped worrying about making a fool of myself in public. Sometimes I worry about how I'll make it back into society.

—Julia Bozer

RISERVA DELLO ZINGARO

Bus tickets to the reserve available in San Vito at Mare Monti, V. Amadeo, 15 (☎ 0923 97 22 31 or ☎ 338 756 94 41; info@sanvitomaremonti.com). Buses depart from P. Marinella (M, W, F at 8am; return M, W, F at 7pm; €8, reservations required). Bluvacanze, V. Savoia, 13 (☎ 0923 62 10 85; bluvacanze@bluvacanze.net; www.bluvacanze.interfree.it) runs excursions as well (M, W, F at 9am, returning at 4pm; €15).

For shade and seclusion, drive 10km outside of San Vito to the green mountains of Riserva dello Zingaro. One unfinished half-mile of a four-lane highway hangs perilously close to the pristine reserve. A 1981 environmentalist rally march halted the highway in its tracks, sending jackhammering workers on a permanent lunch break and leaving the province of Trapani in possession of holding Sicily's (and Italy's) first nature reserve, complete with Bonelli's eagles, mountain trails, and prehistoric caves. Follow the yellow brick road (or umber dirt road for grown-ups lacking imagination) to a succession of secluded pebble beaches. With entrances on both sides of the coast, the middle two are most private. Camping is officially illegal, and motor vehicles are prohibited, but hiking is superb.

SEGESTA

Tarantola buses (☎ 0924 31 020) leave from Piazza Malta in Trapani for Segesta (4 per day, 8am-5pm; return 4 per day, 7:10am-6:35pm; one-way €2.58, round-trip €4.13). Temple site open 9am-6pm; ticket office closes 1hr. earlier. €4.13 per person, under 18 or over 65 free.

Isolated and untouched, the extraordinary ▩**Doric temple** at Segesta is one of the best-preserved examples of ancient Greek architecture. The golden stones dominate a surprisingly green landscape, sculpted by sudden valleys, tall trees, and lush vineyards. The 5th-century BC structure lacks a roof and cellar, and the gigantic columns are un-fluted. Visitors are now free to roam among the great columns and contemplate the classical lifestyle. Segesta's 2nd great treasure is a large **theater** carved into the top of Mount Barbaro. The €1 ticket for the bus ride (2 per hr.) is well worth avoiding the trek up the steep mountain. The theater has a 4000-person capacity and is used for performances of modern-day classical plays from mid-July to early August every other year. (Ask at the ticket office or tourist offices in Trapani for details.) Both the temple and theater are best in the morning and late afternoon, when the temperatures are low and the light brings out the stone's golden and silver hues.

ERICE ☎ 0923

With a magical castle, ancient stone, and mysterious fogs, you can almost see the fire-breathing dragons and damsels in distress in medieval Erice. Once upon a time, the town comprised one of the region's most powerful and wealthy forces. Myths hold that the mountain was once the home of several fertility goddesses, and cults to the Phoenician Tanit-Astarte, the Greek Aphrodite, and the Roman Venus all sought sanctuary on the cliffs. Reverence and piety are now reserved primarily for the spectacular views.

⎘⚡ TRANSPORTATION AND PRACTICAL INFORMATION. The bus from Trapani departs from P. Malta to **Erice/Montalto** (40min.; M-Sa 11 per day, 6:40am-7:30pm; M-Sa last return to Trapani 8:25pm; Su 4 per day, 9am-6pm; Su last return to Trapani 7:30pm; €1.81). Buses leave visitors on **Via Conte Pepoli**, which leads up to the **Balio Gardens**. From there, **Via Nasi** runs to **Piazza San Cataldo** and **Piazza San Domenico**. The **AAST** tourist office, at V. C.A. Pepoli, 11, is a tiny stone cottage that is uphill from the first bus stop. (☎ 0923 86 93 88. Open M-Sa 8am-2pm.)

📁📞 ACCOMMODATIONS AND FOOD. Lofty hotel prices make Erice more affordable as a daytrip, but if you're enamored with the town, try **La Pineta ❹,** Viale N. Nasì. In its own natural wonderland, this village has cottages, with bath, TV, minibar, and terrace overlooking the landscape. (☎ 0923 86 97 83; fax 86 97 86; www.lapinetaerice.it. Breakfast included. Singles €50-70; doubles €80-115; triples €114-155; quads €145-185. Half-pension €60-85 per person, full-pension €77-100 per person. AmEx/MC/V.) Alternatively, try the small and white, clean and bright accommodations at **Albergo Edelweiss ❺,** Cortile P. Vincenzo, 9, off P. S. Domenico. (☎ 0923 86 94 20; a.edelweiss@libero.it. All rooms with bath. Breakfast included. Singles €61.97; doubles €82.63; triples €100; quads €110. MC/V.)

Erice's few restaurants are charming but can have prices as steep as the town's cliffs. **Ristorante Ulisse ❸,** V. Chiaramonte, 45, serves excellent pizza in air-conditioned splendor. Getting there need not be an Odyssey—signs show the way from the city entrance nearest the bus stop. (☎ 0923 86 933 or 53 12 15; fax 86 96 29; ristoranteulisse@libero.it. Cover €2.07. Pizza from €4.15, *primi* and *secondi* from €6.20. Open daily noon-3pm and 8-11pm. AmEx/D/MC/V.) At **La Vetta ❸,** V. G. Fontana, 5, off P. Umberto I, indoor and outdoor seating await. (☎ 0923 86 94 04. Pizzas from €4.50, *primi* from €6.50, *secondi* from €7. Cover €2. Open daily noon-3:30pm and 7:30pm-midnight. AmEx/MC/V.)

The **Balio Gardens,** up Viale Conte Pepoli from the bus stop, have stone benches carved directly into the hillside, which look out over the whole valley and make an ideal location for an enchanting picnic. Before heading out, stock up on local products at the **Salumeria Bazar del Miele ❶,** V. Cordici, 16 (☎ 0923 86 91 81). Open daily 9:30am-9:30pm. AmEx/MC/V. For dessert, grab some sweets at the **Antica Pasticceria del Convento ❷,** V. Vittoria Emanuele, 14 (☎ 0923 86 93 90), in P. S. Domenico. All different shapes, styles, and colors of cookies are here (€11 per kg). Try the famous *belli e brutti* (pretty and ugly) sweets, made with almond paste. Open daily 9am-1:30pm and 3:30pm-1am.

▣ SIGHTS. Erice fits a surprising number of sights inside the 8th-century BC **Elymian walls** that encircle the city. At the hilltop's highest point, the **Norman Castle (Castello di Venere)** towers over the city. The vine-covered castle was built upon the site of several ancient temples to fertility goddesses; a large altar and several walls from the original ruins were incorporated into the fortification's foundations. At the castle's base, the flowering **Giardini del Balio** spreads its boughs over stone benches. The views from the gardens and the castle are incomparable, with most of the western countryside, the Egadi Islands, Pantelleria, and occasionally Tunisia visible. On the other side of town, the 14th-century Gothic **duomo** features original delicate stonework in its large windows. The nearby **bell tower** offers still more exquisite Erice-exclusive views for a small price. (Duomo and bell tower open M-F 9:45am-12:30pm and 3:30-5:30pm, Sa-Su 9:45am-1pm and 3:30-5:30pm. €1.) Throughout the city, 60 other quiet churches await exploration. In P. Museo, the **Museo Comunale di Erice** houses a small collection of treasures and trinkets, many of them relating to the city's sacred fertility goddesses. (Open M-Sa 8:30am-7:30pm, Su 9am-1pm. Free.)

EGADI ISLANDS (ISOLE EGADI)

Inhabited since prehistoric times, the Egadi Islands have long been treasured for their natural wonders and exquisite seas. Lying just off the coast of Trapani, the islands of Favignana, Levanzo, and Marettimo are easily accessible by frequent ferries and hydrofoils (see **Trapani Ferries**, p. 685). Favignana is the largest and the most modern of the three, with many beaches and many more tourists. Levanzo and Marettimo are tiny port towns surrounded by unspoiled natural beauty. Mules and sheep share plains with cacti, while rugged mountainous cliffs burst upward in all directions. Lush and green, these islands offer some of the best outdoor adventures in Sicily. The best way to see the islands is to choose one and spend an entire day, as the finest beaches and most intriguing discoveries lie far from the ports. Stop by the ATM in Trapani or Favignana before leaving; Levanzo and Marretimo don't have any.

FAVIGNANA ☎ 0923

Favignana is visited for one reason and one reason only: its beautiful beaches. Sicilians build summer homes on the shoreline, and vacationers arrive expecting the modern conveniences its sister islands lack. This relaxed but crowded island is ideal for those whose idea of roughing is staying in a resort beach cottage.

▐ TRANSPORTATION

Island buses are necessary to reach the more remote and beautiful beach areas of the island—they're quite a hike away.

Hydrofoils: Siremar (☎ 0923 92 13 68) and **Ustica** (☎ 0923 92 12 77) run to the island from Trapani (25min., 10 per day, 7am-7:15pm, €5.08).

Ferries: Siremar runs from Trapani to Favignana (1hr., 3 per day, 7am-5:15pm, €3.10).

Island Buses: Useful for access to more remote beach areas of the island. **Tarantola** buses (☎ 0923 92 19 44 or 31 020) run 3 different lines, all leaving from Porto Florio: **Line 1** (8per day, 8am-4:50pm) to **Calamone** (5min.), **Lido Burrone** (8min.), and **Cala Azzurra** (15min.); **Line 2** (8 per day, 7:45am-7pm) to **Calamone** and **Cala Rotonda** (13min.); **Line 3** (6 per day, 8:30am-5:40pm) to **Cala Rossa** (7min.), **Lido Burrone**, and **Calamone.** Bus tickets (€0.62) can be bought at any *tabacchi.*

24hr. Taxi Service: Francesca e Rocco, Trav. Calamoni, 7 (☎ 348 586 0676 or 586 0677; www.isoleegadi.it/rocco). Transport to Trapani and Palermo airports. Also runs minibus excursions around the island (€8 per person, min. 5 people).

Scooter and Bicycle Rental: Services all over the island. **Noleggio Isidoro,** V. Mazzini, 40 (☎ 0923 92 16 67), rents bikes (€3 per day, August €6 per day) and scooters (€20 per day, August €25 per day). Open daily 7:30am-7:30pm.

⚓ ☑ ORIENTATION AND PRACTICAL INFORMATION

Hydrofoils and ferries drop passengers off at **Florio Porto**, from which **Via V. Emanuele** leads to **Piazza Europa** and then to **Piazza Madrice**, which contains the tourist office and many of the island's useful businesses. **Via Garibaldi** breaks off of V. V. Emanuele, becoming **Via Libertà** as it leads to the island's countryside. Favignana's most beautiful beaches are each about 1km away.

Tourist Office: Pro Loco, P. Madrice, 8 (☎ 0923 92 16 47). Brochures, schedules and maps of Favignana and other islands. Open daily 9am-12:30pm and 4:30-8pm, closed Su afternoon.

Currency Exchange: Banco di Sicilia, P. Madrice, 12 (☎ 0923 92 13 47), beside the Pro Loco, also has an **ATM**. Open M-F 8:20am-1:20pm and 3:50-4:50pm.

Carabinieri: (☎ 0923 92 12 02), on V. S. Corleo, near P. Castello.

First Aid: Pronto Soccorso (☎ 0923 92 12 83), off V. Calamoni.

Late-Night Pharmacy: Farmacia Rizza Leonarda, P. Madrice, 62. Open daily 8:30am-12:30pm and 5-8pm. Another **pharmacy** at P. Europa, 41 (☎ 0923 92 16 66) is open 8:30am-12:30pm and 4:30-8:30pm. Schedules with the pharmacy on call are posted outside each.

Post Office: V. G. Marconi, 3 (☎ 0923 92 12 09), off P. Madrice. Open M-F 8am-1:30pm, Sa 8am-12:30pm.

Postal Code: 91023.

▌ ACCOMMODATIONS AND CAMPING

Casa Vacanze Mio Sogno, V. Calamoni, 2 (☎ 0923 92 16 76), off V. Libertà, past the first-aid center and down a small dirt path. This family-run *affittacamere* offers independent rooms, each with bathroom, kitchenette, TV, and patio, all structured around a small garden. €21-40 per person. ❷

Camping Village Miramare, Prov. Punta Sottile (☎ 0923 92 22 00 or 92 13 30; www.egadi.com/miramare), is far from the *centro*, but its activities and sports centers create a lively scene in Favignana's otherwise quiet countryside. The camping site is serviced by bus line 2 and by the establishment's white van shuttle from the city center (call ahead). Open April-Oct. €8.50-12 per person. Hot showers included. Bungalow with breakfast: doubles €41.50-91.50; triples €62-137; quads €72.50-160. Half-pension doubles €92.70-126.70; triples €139-190; quads €172-230. Full-pension add €12.50 per person. MC/V. ❶

Camping Villaggio Egàd (☎ 0923 92 15 55 or 92 15 67; in winter ☎/fax 0923 53 93 70; camping.egan@tiscalinet.it; www egadi.com/egad), in Favignana's countryside. A campsite bus awaits visitors at the port—call reception if it's not there. Alternatively, take bus #3 from the port. Shaded site offers numerous activities and services, including a restaurant with typical Sicilian cooking. Open Apr.-Sept. Camping €4.40-5.60 per person, €4.20-5.20 per tent (rented tents €8-10.50), €2.10-2.40 per car. Hot showers €0.30. Bungalows with A/C, bath, and kitchenette: doubles €27-42; triples €38-55; quads €48-98. ❶

◖ FOOD

Stock up for that unforgettable beach or countryside picnic at **San Paolo Alimentari**, V. Mazzini, 24. (Open M-Sa 8am-1pm and 5-8pm; closed W afternoon.) Favignana's traditional tuna products can be found at the **Antica Tonnara di Favignana**, V. Nicotera, 6 (☎/fax 0923 92 16 10) or at **La Casa del Tonno**, V. Roma, 12 (☎ 0923 92 22 27). For a change of pace, an open-air fruit and vegetable market sits at the intersection of V. Libertà and V. Di Vita until sunset.

La Bettola, V. Nicotera, 47 (☎/fax 0923 92 19 88; www.isoleegadi.it/labettola), at P. Castello. This comfortable *trattoria*, with cool indoor tables as well as an outdoor patio, serves seafood specialties. *Primi* from €6.50, *secondi* from €9. Cover €1.55. Open daily 1-3pm and 7pm-midnight. AmEx/MC/V. ❸

Trattoria-Pizzeria da Franco, V. V. Emanuele, 30 (☎347 119 4390), serves up great island pizza late into the night. Pizza from €3.10, *primi* from €7.80, *secondi* from €7.30. Cover €1.55. Open daily noon-4pm and 7pm-3am. AmEx/MC/V. ❸

Ristorante Aegusa, V. Garibaldi, 17 (0923 92 24 40), down the road from hotel of the same name. Three meals of Sicilian specialties are served a day inside an air-conditioned sea of blue and yellow tables. Local fish from €4.50. *Primi* from €6.50, *secondi* from €10.50. Cover €3. Open 8-10am, 1-2pm, and 8-10:30pm. AmEx/MC/V. ❸

🔊👁 BEACHES AND SIGHTS

About 1km each from Favignana's center, the island's best beaches are the popular **Lido Burrone,** and **Calamone, Cala Rossa,** and **Cala Azzurra.** All beach areas can be reached by the public **Tarantola** buses (€0.62; see **Transportation,** p. 692). The **Castello di Santa Caterina,** a deserted castle perched high upon a hill, watches over Favignana.

LEVANZO   ☎0923

Levanzo's town is little more than a row of whitewashed buildings hugging the cliffs on the port. The bar directly above the docks is the social center of the island (and the setting of the **Ustica hydrofoil** office). Up to the left, **Albergo Paradiso ❹,** has the island's best accommodations, including a cozy restaurant with traditional cooking, newly renovated rooms with baths and ocean views. (☎/fax 0923 92 40 80. Reserve for Aug. by mid-Mar. July-Aug. half-pension €50-67 per person, full-pension €70-80 per person. AmEx/MC/V.) Head down the *lungomare* past the **Siremar** office to catch bus #27 to the island's primary attraction, the **Grotta del Genovese,** a cave containing Paleolithic incisions and ochre-grease paintings depicting ancient tuna-fishing rituals. For information on the site, head to **Natale Castiglione,** in a ceramics shop beside the Siremar office. (☎ 0923 92 40 32; nacasti@tin.it. Organized excursions by boat €13 per person. If you take the public bus, admission €5, ages 5-11 €3. Open for visit by reservation—at least one day in advance—10am-1pm and 3-6pm.) A few kilometers along the coastal road to the left of the town, secluded grottoes and beaches await. The crystal-clear water between the rounded rock beach and the neighboring island has a ripping current when the winds pick up; snorkel carefully.

MARETTIMO   ☎0923

The most physically remote of the Egadi Islands, Marettimo is equally distant in spirit. Pristine white cubic buildings with bright blue shutters line the curve of the port, introducing visitors to Marettimo's relaxed way of life. The town itself is actually larger than Levanzo and has a few piazzas that connect the maze-like town streets. The **cultural center** on V. Scalo Vecchio, along the fishing boat docks, has information on the islands. (Open 8am-noon and 3-8pm.) Ask at **Il Pirate ❷** about renting a room (☎0923 92 30 27 or 92 31 59. €18-20 per person, Aug. €25 per person.) Their **trattoria ❹** serves fresh seafood; a full meal comes to about €20. (Open noon-2pm and 7pm-midnight.) Another option for lodging is **Marettimo Residence ❺,** the last establishment along the town, visible from the hydrofoil docks. Individual bungalows have bathroom, kitchenette, and pretty patio. A computer room with Internet access is available at customers' request. (☎0923 92 32 02 or 92 35 00; fax 92 33 86; www.marettimoresidence.it. Prices per wk.: 1-bedroom unit €450-1150; 2-bedroom unit €600-1400. AmEx/MC/V.)

Because there are few roads, you'll need a boat to see the island's most intriguing caves. The port is filled with boats to rent. Beyond the port and village, the only intrusion into Marettimo's rugged environment is an outstanding new set of stone hiking trails crossing the island. The 2½hr. hike to ▨**Pizzo Falcone** (686m), the highest point on the Egadi islands, is worth every minute. The trailhead is on the sea road, past the Siremar office and Il Pirate. Prime time to arrive at the peak is around 6pm; a view of the sun setting over the wild and uninhabited far side of the island is unforgettable. Along the way, snuggled between dramatic cliffs and lush greenery, stand the **Case Romane,** ruins dating back to Roman domination.

To the right of the little village and past an arc of beach sand at **Punta Troia,** a 17th-century Spanish castle tops the cliff. According to local legend, when a prince chose to marry one of two princess sisters over the other, the rejected princess threw her sister off the edge of the cliff. The heartbroken prince then tossed the offending sister down the same route, following her fall with his own. Locals say that at sunset, the ghosts of the two lovers find each other again at the castle.

PANTELLERIA ☎0923

Seven thousand years ago, this island of thickly wooded mountains, terraced hillsides, and jagged rock was inhabited by Neolithic people in search of **obsidian,** black, petrified lava that was once as valuable as gold. Today, the volcanic island is still home to dazzling natural phenomena, including a natural sauna, a myriad of hot springs, and the best capers in the Mediterranean (they grow wild along the island's roads). Attracted by its isolation and natural beauty, several celebrities, including Giorgio Armani and Sting, have set up camp on the island. Although Pantelleria lies six hours off the coast from Trapani, it's just five hours from Kelibia, Tunisia. If you come to Pantelleria, expect to linger; many of the best accommodations require a minimum stay of several days, and the many sights will keep you occupied for quite some time.

▐ TRANSPORTATION

The midnight ferry from Trapani may save money, but it costs one day. Opt for the hydrofoil and relax on the noon return ferry. (See Trapani ferry schedule, p. 685).

Hydrofoils: Ustica Lines (☎0923 91 15 02) has a mini ticket office at #66 on the *lungomare.* Open M-Sa 9am-noon and 6:30-10:45pm. Hydrofoil tickets available 3-4:20pm. Tickets also available at **La Cossira travel agency** (☎0923 91 10 78), left of Khamma Hotel, where V. Catania meets the *lungomare.* Open daily 9am-1pm and 5:30-7:30pm. To **Trapani** (2hr., 4:40pm, €35).

Ferries: Siremar (☎0923 91 11 20), on the waterfront at V. Borgo Italia, 22, runs to **Trapani** (5hr., noon, €23).

Island Buses: Infrequent buses run weekdays from P. Cavour to the airport and the 5 island towns of **Kamma-Tracino, Scauri-Rekale, Bukkuram, Siba,** and **Buegeber** (€1). Schedules at tourist office.

Scooter and Car Rental: Autonoleggio Policardo, V. Messina, 31 (☎0923 91 28 44 or 91 17 41; noleggiopolicar@tiscalinet.it), just off the port, up the small street to the right after giant fenced-in scooter lot. Scooters €14 per day, €77 per wk. Cars €26 per day, €126 per wk. Prices nearly double in August. Open daily 6am-9pm.

SICILY

SICILY

⚞☚ ORIENTATION AND PRACTICAL INFORMATION

Ferries and hydrofoils deposit visitors at the northwestern tip of the teardrop shaped island. The curved port is bordered by the town of Pantelleria. A long *lungomare*, first **Via Borgo Italia** then **Lungomare Paolo Borsellino**, suns itself from the docks to the private sailboat moorings. At the end of Lungomare P. Borsellino, **Piazza Almanza**, beneath the **Castello**, becomes **Piazza Cavour**, where most services are located, including the **tourist office**. Roads at either end of the *lungomare* head backward along the coast to other towns. Facing away from the water, the coastal road to the left leads to **Bue Marino, Gadir, Lago Specchio di Venere,** and **Arco dell'Elefante.** The right leads toward the **airport**, the **Sesi, Scauri town,** and **Rekhale.** An inland road (above and to the right of the southwest sea highway, past the dockside Agip station) leads to the **airport, Sibà,** and **Montagna Grande.** Be sure to get a road map from the Pro Loco office before excursions.

Tourist Office: Pro Loco (☎ 0923 91 18 38), in P. Cavour in the corner of the municipal building closest to Banco di Sicilia. Look for the language flags. Lots of brochures, maps, and bus schedules. Open daily 8am-2pm and 5:30-7pm. Closed Sept.-June Su.

Currency Exchange: Banca del Popolo (☎ 0923 91 27 32), up V. Catania from the *lungomare*. Open M-F 8:30am-2pm. **ATM** here, and across the street at **Monte dei Paschi di Siena** and **Banco di Sicilia,** in P. Cavour across from the municipal building.

Carabinieri: (☎ 0923 91 11 09), on V. Trieste, 13.

Guardia Medica: Piazza Cavour, 21 (☎ 0923 91 02 55), on the far right side of the Municipal building (opposite Banco di Sicilia). Open M-F 8pm-8am, Sa 10am-8pm, Su 8am-8pm.

Late-Night Pharmacy: Farmacia Greco, P. Cavour, 26 (☎ 0923 91 13 10). Open M-Sa 8:30am-1pm and 5-8:30pm. Night shifts on rotation with the schedule posted outside.

Hospital: (0923 91 11 10), in P. le Alamanza.

Post Office: (☎ 0923 91 13 34), on V. Verdi, 2, adjacent to the municipal building and across from Banco di Sicilia (off P. Cavour). **Changes cash** and **traveler's checks.** Open M-Sa 8:15am-1:30pm.

Postal Code: 91017.

⛏ ACCOMMODATIONS

Dammusi ❷, the square-shaped, domed dwellings of Arab descent unique to this island, are one of the most interesting sleeping options available. Their one-meter-thick black lava stone walls keep the interior cool, and water is drawn from a cistern filled by tubes running from the rain-trapping roof. The classic *dammuso* is whitewashed inside and simply furnished, with a sleeping alcove or two and several niches for storage. There are over 3000 *dammusi* on Pantelleria, and nearly every resident rents one out or knows someone who does. There are also very reasonable *affitacamere* options available in Pantelleria town (many compare to furnished apartments). Room quality varies considerably, and landing a pad often requires patient perseverance. For both *dammusi* and *affitacamere* options, the best places to start are the bars lining the beach or the tourist office, which has information on such accommodations. Flyers fill the windows advertising available rooms. *Dammusi* usually go for about €25 per person per night, and many require a minimum stay of at least 4 days. Be ready to haggle.

■ **La Vela** (☎ 0923 91 18 00 or 91 65 66), on Scauri Scalo. Follow the sea road 10km west from Pantelleria town to Scauri's port, where these 14 luxurious *dammusi*, with kitchen, bath, and terrace, await. Black volcanic stone, white domed roofs, brilliant purple bougainvillea, and bamboo-shaded porches. Small beach and restaurant with a sea view. Reserve 3 months in advance for July and Aug. €20-28 per person. ❷

Hotel Cossyra Mursia (☎ 0923 91 12 17 or 91 11 54; fax 91 10 26; cossyrahotel@pantelleria.it or mursiahotel@pantelleria.it; www.mursia.pantelleria.it), along the road from Pantelleria town to Scauri, before the *sesi*. This resort-style hotel overlooking the sea has a large deck with 3 swimming pools, plus TV lounges, a piano bar, tennis courts, archery ranges, scuba diving excursions, and a restaurant where renowned chefs mix up local specialties. Half-pension double €57-83 per person; single room add €8. Beverages excluded. ❺

Hotel Khamma, Lungomare Borgo Italia, 24 (☎ 0923 91 25 70), at end of docks. Central location and some rooms with sea views. Polished rooms with bath, TV, A/C, phone, and minibar. Breakfast included. 7-night min. stay in Aug. Reserve far ahead. Singles €39-57; doubles €67-103; triples €88-134. AmEx/D/MC. ❸

✪ FOOD

Arab domination in the 8th century AD turned Pantelleria away from fishing to the cultivation of its rich volcanic soil. A local specialty, *pesto pantesco*, is a sauce of tomato, capers, basil, and garlic, eaten with pasta or on *bruschetta*. The local variety of *zibbibi* grape yields the island's yellowish grape jelly and the sweet amber *passito* or *muscato* dessert wine (delicious Pantelleria gold). The **SISA supermarket** in Pantelleria town sits above the *lungomare*. Hike up two flights of stairs at the 90 degree bend of the *lungomare*, passing Banco de Popolo on the right. (Open M-Tu and Th-F 8am-1pm and 5:30-8:30pm, W 8am-1pm. MC/V.)

La Risacca, V. Milano, 65 (☎ 0923 91 29 75). The open-air dining room is shaded by reed mats and decorated with small lanterns. Local *Pantesche* dishes, such as the *cappero*, with tuna, capers, and oregano, are served alongside pizza (dinner only, from €3.50). *Primi* from €4.50, *secondi* from €9.50. Cover €1.55. Open June-Sept. daily 12:20-2:30pm and 8-11:30pm. ❷

Ristorante-Pizzeria Castiglione, V. Borgo Italia, 24 (☎ 0923 91 14 48), along the *lungomare*, serves up fresh pizza from a wooden stove (starting at €4.50) in an air-conditioned dining room. *Primi* from €8, *secondi* from €8. Open daily 9am-3pm and 7pm-midnight. Oct.-May closed Tu. AmEx/MC/V. ❷

La Pergola (☎ 0923 91 84 20), Loc. Suvaki, between Pantelleria town and Scauri, after the *sesi*. Bright yellow tablecloths among a large garden create a summery atmosphere. *Trattoria* serves couscous and local specialties year-round. Open noon-2:30pm and 4:30pm-1am. ❸

◉ SIGHTS

Most of Pantelleria's sights are of the spend-an-afternoon-here-with-a-book kind, rather than the peek-in-and-move-on variety, so don't plan to hit more than two of them in a single day. The island is deceptively large, and if you crave liberation from the tyranny of Pantelleria's bus system (which may leave you waiting in the sun for up to five hours), a colorful portside line of free-flying mopeds await your motor-revving inner speed demon. Motorized transportation is an absolute necessity for most destinations inland and to the south; even some coastal spots are a good hour's walk from the scattered bus stops.

⧆ BAGNO ASCIUTTO AND MONTAGNA GRANDE. Far away from the port near the inland town of Sibà, a natural rock sauna and the summit of Pantelleria's highest mountain await. Signs guide you through and beyond Sibà to the sauna; the last 10min. or so must be traveled on foot. Inside, Panteschi lie face down in a deep, low cave. Bring water and a towel and be prepared to leave and reenter several times—the oven-like heat is hard to stand. Farther along the sauna path, at the foot of Monte Gibole, the **Favara Grande** is a *fumarole* (crater) that still emits clouds of hot smoke. Many trails, most pretty but short, lead off the asphalt road, and a shady picnic area in a pine grove near the summit is the perfect place to relax after a *bagno asciutto* (sauna). If the midday heat is already steamy enough, head to Montagna Grande just for the view. The mountain road past Sibà leads almost to the top, with fantastic views of the 2nd half of the lush Piano di Ghirlanda (plain). *(To get to Sibà, take the marked bus from P. Cavour at 6:40am, 12:40, 2, and 7:40pm. Both the Bagno and the mountain are clearly marked. By car, follow signs from Pantelleria Town for Sibà.)*

THE SESI AND PUNTO DI SATARIA. The Bronze Age people who inhabited Pantelleria 5000 years ago left behind the **sesi,** dome-shaped funerary monuments built without mortar from about 1800 BC. Tunnels in the *sesi* gave access to the womb-shaped chambers where kneeling corpses were placed. The largest remaining congregation of *sesi* (many have been torn down for building material) forms a 70-tomb cemetery. Chambers can be seen in the small tunnels that lead into the domes. *(On the road from Pantelleria town to Sauri, look for a sign indicating the "zona archeologica" off to your right, past the Hotel Mursia.)* Further down the sea road from the *sesi* is the **Punto Sataria.** Stairs lead down to a cave once thought to be the home of the goddess Calypso, and of Ulysses on the island of Ogygia. The 40° water in the thermal pools, only a jump away from the much cooler sea, is believed to cure joint aches. *(Buses to Scauri-Rekale pass both sites, tell the driver where you want to get off, and leave Pantelleria at 6:40, 8, 8:40, 9:15am, 12:40, 2, and 5:20pm. Portions of this site may be blocked off due to falling rocks.)*

LO SPECCHIO DI VENERE (THE MIRROR OF VENUS). Legend has it that Venus used this lake as a mirror before her dates with Bacchus, a frequenter of Pantelleria for its superb, strong *zabbibo* wine. Mere mortals will likewise be unable to resist a long look down into this startlingly aquamarine pool, fringed with firm white mud and surrounded by its bowl of green hillsides. Sulfur springs warm the water and enrich the mud. Local practice recommends letting the sun dry the therapeutic mud to a white cake on your skin. *(Take the bus to Bugeber from P. Cavour; ask the driver to drop you off. Be sure to ask about return times. Buses depart Pantelleria Town M-F at 7:50am, noon, and 2pm. By car or scooter, head toward Bugeber and follow signs for the turnoff.)*

THE NORTHEAST COAST AND THE ARCO DELL'ELEFANTE. The best swimming off Pantelleria is along the northeastern coast in three small inlets. The first of the three, Gadir, is one of the more popular *acquacalda* spots on the island. Cement encloses the bubbly natural pool next to the sea. Superior swimming spots are just down the coast at **Cala di Tramontana** and **Cala di Levante,** unscathed by the omnipresent concrete that rings the island. Perfect for sunbathing, these twin coves are actually one, split by a rocky outcropping. Cala di Levante offers a view of the **⧆Arco dell'Elefante** off to the right. The unofficial symbol of the island, this unusual rock formation looks like a large elephant guzzling up the surf. *(All 3 inlets are on the Khamma/Tracino bus line. Buses leave P. Cavour daily at 6:40, 8, 9:15am, 12:40, 2, and 6:40pm. Be sure to check return times. Drivers should follow signs for Khamma and Tracino, then follow signs for the coastal roads.)*

IL PIANO DI GHIRLANDA. Surrounded by its own crumbled lip, this fertile crater makes a perfect 2hr. hike from Tracino. The area is one of Pantelleria's prettiest, and a reminder that the island makes its living by farming (as well as tourism). Here, terraced hills and caper fields are tended by peasants working out of small, utilitarian *dammusi*. *(By car, take the road leading out of Tracino's P. Perugio. Alternatively, take Tracino bus to the Byzantine tombs, then follow signs to the trails. Ask locals for help.)*

◪ BEACHES AND BOAT TOURS

Though surrounded with luscious turquoise water and covered with dramatic rock formations and unusual bathing opportunities, standard definition "beaches" are a rarity on Pantelleria. What sandy stretches there may have been were inexplicably replaced by concrete blocks. Swimming areas around the coast are rated on a three point scale on maps by difficulty of access. Rocky coves and swimming grottoes abound, but require some seeking out. The closest swimming to Pantelleria can be found at **Grotta del Bue Marino,** just 2km to the east (to the right when facing the water) along the *lungomare*. Snorkelers prowl the coast, sunbathers perch on volcanic rock, and maniacal young boys hurl themselves off cliffs into the deep waters below. Use **extreme caution:** the water is shallow in places and the bottom is lined with jagged rocks.

■**Boat tours** are one of the best, fastest, and most relaxing ways to see Pantelleria. Sailing over liquid glass waters provides an excellent look at hidden grottoes, caves, colorful marine life, and various volcanic remains. Passengers slip demurely in with mask and flippers or dive recklessly off top decks for an unrivaled *bagno dolce* (sweet swim). Boats also offer a view of some of Pantelleria's greatest (and otherwise inaccessible) delights, including Cinderella's Slippers, *L'Arco dell'Elefante*, and *I Cinque Centi* (The Five Teeth). The colorful portside line of boats offer various advantages; while smaller boats make it into a few grottoes, their larger cousins provide bamboo shade, napping cushions, and room for young ones to play. **Minardi Adriano,** V. Borgo Italia, 5 (☎/fax 0923 91 15 02 or 339 717 3678), runs excursions around the island. Expect to pay about €25 per person with any of the services for a day at sea.

▣ NIGHTLIFE

Pantelleria's most obvious nightlife is at the port, where *Panteschi* take 24hr. *passagiate* near two popular and interchangeable bars: **Tikirriki** (☎0923 91 10 79) and **Il Goloso** (☎0923 91 18 14). Both are open until 3am and have canopied tables outside by the water. 12km away in the small town of Scauri is the sleek, clubbish **Bar-Panineria 'U Friscu,'** C. da Scauri, 54 (☎0923 91 60 52), on the western seaside road from Pantelleria, where music blasts late into the night. The one *discoteca* open on Pantelleria during the summer is **Oxidana,** on the western seaside road near Hotel Mursìa-Cossira; look for a huge electronic scrolling banner that reads "Tutte le Sere." Come mid-summer, tourists pack the pod seats and multi-level outdoor dance floor. (☎0923 91 23 19. Open July-Sept. 15. Cover €10.33, includes 1 drink.)

SARDINIA (SARDEGNA)

When the vanity of highly cultivated mainland Italy starts to wear thin, when one more church interior will send you into the path of the nearest speeding Fiat, Sardinia's savage coastline and rugged people will reinvigorate your spirits. An old Sardinian legend says that when God finished making the world, he had a handful of dirt left over, which he threw into the Mediterranean and stepped on, creating Sardinia. The contours of that divine foot formed some of the world's most spectacular landscapes. The haphazard, rough-hewn coastlines, tiny rivers, rolling hills, and mighty mountain ranges today support about a million Sardinians, a people some describe as too sturdy to be Italians. D. H. Lawrence sought respite from the "deadly net of European civilization" that plagued him even in the outermost reaches of Sicily, and found his escape among the wild horses, wind-carved rock formations, and pink flamingos of this untamed island.

The ancient feudal civilizations of warring shepherd-kings that settled in Sardinia some 3500 years ago left about 8000 scattered *nuraghi* ruins, gutted cone-shaped tower-houses built of stone blocks and assembled without mortar. Tossed from the Phoenicians to the Carthaginians, Sardinia was temporarily grounded when the Romans pacified the island and made it an agricultural colony. In the 13th century, Sardinia was a stomping ground for the Pisans, the Aragonese, the newly united Spanish, and the *Piemontese*. It was from this exploited island that Vittorio Emanuele, Italy's first king, began his campaign to unify Italy in 1861. Only decades ago, *padroni* (landlords) still held Sardinia's land, and farmers toiled under a system akin to serfdom. Today, Sardinia's argiculturally-driven economy still relies heavily upon the farmland of the interior. Tourism is the real cash crop along the coastline, where vacationers lounge on beaches and relax in resorts.

> Like its terrain, Sardinia's cuisine is rustic and rugged. Hearty dishes like *sa fregula* (pasta in broth with saffron), *malloreddus* (shell-shaped pasta), *culurgiones* (ravioli stuffed with cheese, beets, tomato sauce, lamb, and sausage), and *pane frattau* (thin bread covered with eggs, cheese, and tomato sauce) frequent the island's menus. Celebrated dishes include *cardo* (lamb entrails), pork cooked in lamb's stomach, and grilled pig, horse, donkey, and goat. The infamous product of Sardinian shepherds, *casu fatizzu* (cheese with worms) and savory *pecorino* (sheep's milk cheese) are considered delicacies. Local wines are often sweet and strong. Try *vernaccia d'uva* (for its almond aftertaste) with fish or the robust *cannonau di Sardegna* with red meat.

✈ TRANSPORTATION

FLIGHTS
Flights link Alghero, Cagliari, and Olbia to major Italian cities. Flights are faster than water travel, but exorbitant fares discourage most travelers.

FERRIES
The cheapest way to Sardinia is by ferry to Olbia from Civitavecchia, Genoa, or Livorno; expect to pay €20-75, depending on the company, season, speed of the

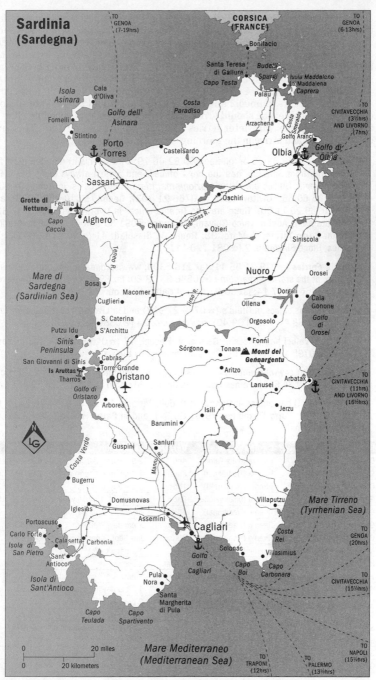

Sardinia (Sardegna)

CORSICA (FRANCE)

TO GENOA (7-19hrs)

TO GENOA (6-13hrs)

Bonifacio

Santa Teresa di Gallura
Capo Testa
Budelli
Spargi
Isola Maddalena
La Maddalena
Caprera
Palau

TO CIVITAVECCHIA (3½hrs) AND LIVORNO (7hrs)

Isola Asinara

Cala d'Oliva

Costa Paradiso

Arzachena

Costa Smeralda

Fornelli

Golfo dell' Asinara

Stintino

Porto Torres

Golfo Aranci

Olbia

Golfo di Olbia

Castelsardo

Sassari

Oschiri

Grotte di Nettuno
Fertilia

Siniscola

Capo Caccia
Alghero

Chilivani

Coghinas R.

Ozieri

Mare di Sardegna (Sardinian Sea)

Bosa

Macomer

Nuoro

Orosei

Dorgali

Cala Gonone

Golfo di Orosei

Cuglieri

Tirso R.

Ollena

S. Caterina

Orgosolo

Putzu Idu

S'Archittu

Sinis Peninsula

San Giovanni di Sinis

Cabras

Sórgono

Tonara

Fonni

Monti del Gennargentu

Is Aruttas
Tharros

Torre Grande

Oristano

Aritzo

Golfo di Oristano

Arborea

Isili

Lanusei

Arbatax

TO CIVITAVECCHIA (11hrs) AND LIVORNO (16½hrs)

Jerzu

Barumini

Sanluri

Manni R.

Guspini

Costa Verde

Bugerru

Villaputzu

Mare Tirreno (Tyrrhenian Sea)

Domusnovas

Iglesias

Assemini

Cagliari

Costa Rei

TO GENGA (20hrs)

Portoscuso

Carlo Forte

Calasetta

Carbonia

Solonas

Villasimius

Isola di San Pietro

Sant' Antioco

Golfo di Cagliari

Capo Boi

Capo Carbonara

TO CIVITAVECCHIA (15½hrs)

Isola di Sant'Antioco

Pula

Nora

Santa Margherita di Pula

Capo Teulada

Capo Spartivento

Mare Mediterraneo (Mediterranean Sea)

TO NAPOLI (15½hrs)

TO TRAPONI (12hrs)

TO PALERMO (13½hrs)

0 ——— 20 miles
0 ——— 20 kilometers

boat, and departure time (night trips cost more). The cheapest tickets are for daytime *posta ponte* (deck class) slots on the slow-moving boats, but most ferry companies require that the *poltrone* (reserved armchairs) be sold to capacity before they open *posta ponte* for sale. In the price ranges in the table below, the low number is the low-season *poste ponte* fare, and the high number is the high-season *poltrone* fare. Expect to pay an additional €10-20 if you want a *cabina* with a bed, and an extra €5-15 depending on the season, duration, and taxes. Travelers with cars, mopeds, animals, or children should arrive 1½hr. before departure; everyone else should arrive 45 minutes early. Ferry schedule chart is for summer service. All winter ferries sell at second-class *poltrona* fares, and depart at night and arrive in the morning.

Tirrenia (☎199 12 31 99 or toll-free 800 82 40 79; www.tirrenia.it) runs the most ferries to and from Sardinia, has the most offices, and almost always costs the least. *Bravo*, Tirrenia. Offices are in the *stazione marittima* in most cities, including **Cagliari** (☎070 66 60 65), **Civitavecchia** (☎0766 21 703), **Genoa** (☎010 269 8228), and **Olbia** (0789 20 71 00). There are also Tirrenia offices in **Livorno** (☎0586 42 47 30), on Calata Addis Abeba–Varco Galvani; **Palermo** (☎091 33 33 00), on Calata Marinai d'Italia; **Porto Torres,** V. Mare, 38; **Rome,** V. Bissolati, 41 (☎06 474 2041), and **Naples**, Rione Sirignano, 2 (☎081 720 1111).

Sardinia Ferries (☎019 21 55 11; fax 215 5300; www.sardiniaferries.com). Offices in **Livorno,** at the *stazione marittima* (☎0586 88 13 80; fax 89 61 03), and in **Civitavecchia** (☎0766 50 07 14; fax 50 07 18), at Calata Laurenti.

Moby Lines has offices in **Olbia's** (☎0789 27 927) and in **Livorno's** *stazione marittima* (☎0586 82 68 47; fax 44 39 40), or V. Veneto, 24 (☎0586 82 68 23).

Grand Navi Veloci has offices in **Genoa,** V. Fieschi, 17 (☎010 55 091), and in **Porto Torres** (☎0795 16 034), in the Porto Industriale, by the water.

Linea dei Golfi (www.lineadeigolfi.it) has offices in **Piombino** (☎0565 22 23 00) and Olbia (☎0789 24 656). Ferries from Piombino and Livorno to **Olbia** (€16.50-35).

Tris (www.tris.it) has offices in **Genoa,** at P. della Vittoria, 12/24 (☎010 576 2411; fax 576 2402), in **Porto Torres** (☎079 51 26 34), and in **Palau** (☎0789 70 86 31), at the port terminal.

Route	Company	Duration	Frequency	Price
Civitavecchia-Olbia	Tirrenia (unità veloce)	4hr.	2-3 per day, 8:30am	€29.70-46.99
Civitavecchia-Olbia	Tirrenia (Traditional)	8hr.	1-2 per day, 11pm	€16.78-24.53
Civitavecchia-Cagliari	Tirrenia (Traditional)	15hr.	1 per day, 6:30pm	€25.56-40.28
Genoa-Olbia	Tirrenia (unità veloce)	6hr.	June-Sept. 1 per day, 9am	€47.31-77.98
Genoa-Olbia	Tirrenia (Traditional)	13½hr.	July-Sept. 1 per day, 6pm	€27.63-45.19
Genoa Porto Torres	Tirrenia (Traditional)	11hr.	1 per day, 7:30pm	€27.63-45.19
Genoa-Cagliari	Tirrenia (Traditional)	20hr.	July-Sept. 3 per wk.	€45.19-60.17
Naples-Cagliari	Tirrenia (Traditional)	16hr.	1-2 per wk., 7:15pm	€25.26-40.80
Palermo-Cagliari	Tirrenia (Traditional)	13½hr.	1 per wk.	€25.56-38.21
Trapani-Cagliari	Tirrenia (Traditional)	11hr.	1 per wk.	€25.56-38.21
Civitavecchia-Golfo Aranci	Sardinia Ferries	3½-6hr.	1-3 per day in summer	€17-52
Livorno-Golfo Aranci	Sardinia Ferries	6-9hr.	2 per day in summer	€21-47
Olbia-Livorno	Moby Lines	10hr.	2-3 per day	€20-46
S. Teresa-Bonifacio	Moby Lines	1hr.	10 per day in summer	€8-12
Genoa-Palau	Tris	6-12hr.	2-3 per day	€29-57
Genoa-Olbia	Grand Navi Veloci	10hr.	1 per day	€36-73
Genoa-Port Torres	Grand Navi Veloci	10hr.	1-2 per day	€30-67

CAGLIARI PROVINCE

CAGLIARI ☎070

Cagliari combines the bustle and energy of a modern Italian city with the endearing rural character of the rest of Sardinia. Downtown, regal, tree-lined streets run past rows of tiny boutiques and stately piazzas. By the port, porticos shelter cafes, cinemas, and chic stores from the midday sun. Above the port, the 13th-century Castello district graces the hillside with twisting cobblestoned streets that snake around the vast Roman amphitheater. Just minutes away stretch the sparking green water and bright sands of Il Poetto.

⌐ TRANSPORTATION

Flights: (☎070 21 051), in the village of **Elmas**. ARST buses run from airport to the city terminal at P. Matteotti (30min., 24 per day, 6:25am-12:10am, €0.67).

Trains: FS (☎070 89 20 21), in P. Matteotti. Open daily 6am-8:30pm. 24hr. ticket machines. To: **Olbia** (4hr., 6:20pm, €12.95), V. Oristano or Macomer; **Oristano** (1½hr., 18 per day, 5:40am-9:55pm, €4.55); **Porto Torres** (4hr., 2:30pm and 4:28pm, €12.95); and **Sassari** (4hr., 6:49am and 4:28pm, €12.10). **Ferrovie della Sardegna** (☎070 58 00 75), in P. della Repubblica. Info office open daily 7:30am-8:45pm. Private railroad with supplementary services to **Arbatax** (6:45am and 1:45pm, €17).

Buses: Station open M-Sa 8-8:30am, 9am-2:15pm, and 5:30-7pm, Su 1:30-2:15pm and 5:30-7pm. When office is closed, buy tickets on bus. **PANI,** ticket booth in Stazione Marittima. To: **Nuoro** (3½hr., 4 per day, 5:30am-6:15pm, €11.31); **Oristano** (1½hr., 8 per day, 5:30am-6:15pm, €5.84); and **Sassari** (3hr., 7 per day, 5:30am-7pm, €12.39-13.43). **ARST,** P. Matteotti, 6 (☎070 409 8324), serves local towns, including: **airport** (10min.; 24 per day; 6:25am-10:10am, return 6:15am-midnight, €0.67) and **Arbatax** (10:25am-3pm, €7.64). **FMS** (☎800 04 45 53) runs to: **Calasetta** and **Sant'Antioco** (both 2hr., 2 per day, 10am-4pm). Buy tickets at newsstand across from Farmacia Spanno on V. Roma. Buy tickets a day in advance if traveling on Su.

Ferries: Tirrenia (☎070 66 60 65 or 800 82 40 79), in Stazione Marittima. Luggage storage available (see below). Open M-F 9:30am-noon and 3-7pm, Sa 9am-noon and 4-7pm, Su 9:30am-noon and 4-7pm.

Car Rental: Ruvioli, V. dei Mille, 11 (☎070 65 89 55; fax 65 79 69; info@ruvioli.it). All cars with A/C. Insurance included. English-speaking staff. Major credit card required. Web reservations preferred. €47 per day; €290 per wk. 21+. Open daily 9:30am-1pm and 4:30-7pm. You can make reservations here, but pick up the car at the **airport branch** (☎070 24 03 23), open daily 8:30am-9pm. AmEx/D/MC/V.

Local Buses: Orange **CTM** buses run from P. Matteotti. Tickets sold at ARST station's newsstand. €0.80 per 1½hr., €1.30 per 2hr., €2.10 per 24hr.; €7.75 for 12 tickets. **Buses P, PQ,** and **PF** go to beach from **Il Poetto**.

Taxis: ☎070 40 01 01.

✱⁊ ORIENTATION AND PRACTICAL INFORMATION

Sandwiched between the harbor, Stazione Marittima, and the PANI bus stop on one side and outdoor cafes on the other, **Via Roma** stretches before those arriving by train, boat, or bus. At one end of V. Roma, **Piazza Matteotti** houses the train station, the ARST station, and the tourist office. Across from P. Matteotti, **Largo Carlo Felice** climbs the steep hill leading to **Piazza Yenne,** and then to the *castello* and the historic center of town.

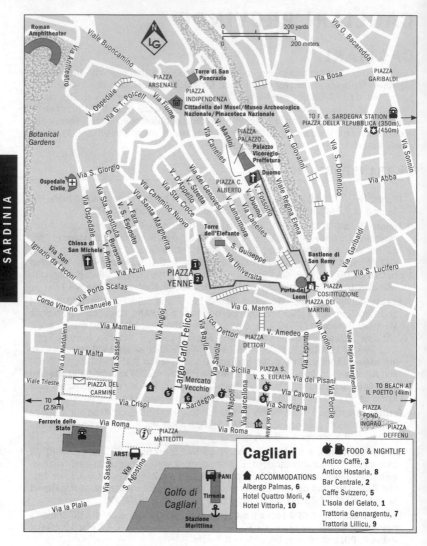

Tourist Office: (☎070 66 92 55 or 66 49 22), in P. Matteotti, in park across from train and bus stations. Multilingual staff has substantial info on local sights. Open M-Sa 8:30am-1:30pm and 2:30-7:30pm. Hours subject to change in winter. The **Stazione Marittima branch** is open daily 8am-7pm.

Budget Travel: CTS, V. Cesare Balbo, 12 (☎070 48 82 60). Info on student discounts and packages. Open M-F 9am-1pm and 4-7:30pm, Sa 9am-1pm. **Memo Travel,** V. Pitzolo, 1A (☎070 40 09 07). Open M-F 9am-1pm and 4-7:30pm, Sa 9am-1pm.

Luggage Storage: At the Stazione Marittima. Free. Open daily 7am-7pm.

Laundry: Lavanderia Self-Service, V. Sicilia, 20 (☎070 56 55 21), off V. Bayle. 6kg wash €3.50; 20min. dry €3.50. Prices decrease by €0.50 between 8-10am and 2-4pm. Open daily 8am-10pm (last wash at 9pm).

Bookstore: Libreria della Costa, V. Roma, 65 (☎070 65 02 56). English-language classics and current bestsellers. They also have **Internet Access** €3 for 30min., €5 per hr. Open M-Sa 9am-9pm. MC/V.

Emergency: ☎113. **First Aid/Ambulance:** ☎118.

Pharmacy: Farmacia Dr. Spano, V. Roma, 99 (☎070 65 56 83). Open M-F 9am-1pm and 4:50-8:10pm; in winter M-F 9am-1pm and 4:30-7:50pm.

Hospital: V. Ospedale, 46 (☎070 66 32 37 or 60 91), by Chiesa di S. Michele.

Internet Access: Mail Boxes Etc., V. Trieste, 65B (☎070 67 37 04), near the post office. €7.50 per hr. Open M-F 9am-1pm and 4-7:30pm. MC/V.

Post Office: (☎070 65 82 57), in P. del Carmine. Take V. Sassari from P. Matteotti. *Fermo Posta,* phone cards, and **currency exchange.** Open M-F 8am-6:40pm, Sa 8:10am-1:20pm.

Postal Code: 09100.

ACCOMMODATIONS

■ **Hotel Aer Bundes Jack Vittoria,** V. Roma, 75 (☎/fax 070 66 79 70). Cross V. Roma from train station or ARST station and turn right. Check in on 3rd fl. Formerly known as Pensione Vittoria, this lovely spot is still one of the best places to stay in Cagliari. 20 majestic rooms, Venetian chandeliers, bathrooms, and A/C. Breakfast €4.65. Wheelchair-accessible. Reserve ahead. Singles €36, with bath €43; doubles €60-65. ❹

Hotel Quattro Morii, V. G.M. Angioj, 27 (☎070 66 85 35; fax 66 60 87; www.hotel4mori.it). Set back a little from the noisy port and close to P. Yenne, this hotel is modern and attractively decorated. The staff is helpful and polite. All rooms with bath, A/C, and TV. Simple breakfast included. Reservations recommended. Singles €52; doubles €83. AmEx/D/MC/V. ❹

Albergo Palmas, V. Sardegna, 14 (☎070 65 16 79). Cross V. Roma and turn right. Take 1st left on Largo Carlo Felice, and 1st right on V. Sardegna. Excellent location and accommodating management—the best budget option in town. 14 rooms. Communal bath. Reservations recommended. Singles €21; doubles €31, with shower €37. ❷

FOOD

Along V. Sardegna, many small shops sell fruit, cheese, and bread. Try **Mini Market La Marina,** V. Sardegna, 43 (☎070 65 99 22), a small market with a heavenly bakery. (Open M-Sa 7:30am-2pm and 4:30-8:30pm. MC/V.) The colossal **Iper Pan La Plaia,** V. la Plaia, 15, is the mother of all grocery stores. (Open daily 9am-9pm.) On Sundays, explore the **market** on the far side of the stadium in Borgo S. Elia for fresh fruit and seafood. A down-to-earth **self-service restaurant** at V. Sassari, 16, has a €6.70 *menù.*

■ **Trattoria Lillicu,** V. Sardegna, 78 (☎070 65 29 70). Established 80 years ago and still run by the same family. Simple *trattoria* serves traditional Sardi dishes like *lacetti di agnelle* (lamb; €5.16) and expertly prepared seafood (€7.75-10.33) at clamorous communal tables. Full meal €18-20. Cover €1.55. Open M-Sa 1-3pm and 8:30-11pm. Reservations recommended. AmEx/D/MC/V. ❹

SARDINIA

AIO? EIA! If you've just sat down with a hearty plate of horse and tentacles and suddenly realize that your four years of college Italian aren't helping you eavesdrop effectively on the people at the table next to you, chances are that you've just had your first encounter with *Sardo*. The German linguist Weher divided it into four main dialects: *Logudorese* (from Logudo, near the center of the island), *Campidanese* (from the plains of Campidano around Cagliari in the south), *Sasserese* (from Sassari, in the northwest), and *Gallurese* (from Gallura, in the north). *Sardo* is influenced by Italian, but also by the tongues of its ancient conquerors: Arabs, Germans, Spanish, and the Romans. On the street of Sardinian towns, you're likely to hear locals greeting each other with *"Eia"* (pronounced eh-yah), which means "yes" but is used more like *"ciao,"* and *"Aio"* (*"ay-yoh"*) meaning—you guessed it—"let's go."

🍴 **Antica Hostaria,** V. Cavour, 60 (☎070 66 58 70; fax 66 58 78). Reputedly one of Cagliari's best restaurants. This beautiful restaurant maintains an art nouveau decor, clothes its waitstaff in tuxes, and starts your meal with a basket of bread and drink of white wine, pear juice, and a shot of gin. Try the tasty *malloreddus alla campidanese* (€7.75) or veal in *vernaccia* sauce €8. Cover €2. Open M-Sa 12:45-3pm and 8-11pm; closed Aug. AmEx/D/MC/V. ❸

Trattoria Gennargentu, V. Sardegna, 60 (☎070 65 82 47). Join the locals in this *salumeria*-restaurant for a feast of *spaghetti alle arselle e bottarga* (with baby clams and seasoned with ground fish eggs; €6.47) and zesty *salsiccia arrosto* (roasted sausage; €4). Cover €1.55. Open M-Sa 12:30-3pm and 8-11pm. AmEx/MC/V. ❸

Caffe Svizzero, Largo Carlo Felice, 6/8 (☎070 65 37 84). The best bar/cafe in town. Enjoy coffee (€0.70) and pastries (€0.65) in classy ambiance. Come for breakfast or an early evening drink. Open daily 7am-10pm. AmEx/MC/V. ❶

Antico Caffè, P. Costituzione, 10/11 (☎070 65 82 06). The haunt of Nobel Prize winners, Italian presidents, and flashy Italian TV stars; this elegant, snobbish cafe has over 150 years of history. Come for dessert, and reserve a table outside. Delicious crepes (€3.40-5.60) and decadent ice-cream sundaes (€4.13-5.16). Breakfast €4.20-8.20. 20% service charge. Open daily 8am-3am. AmEx/MC/V. ❸

👁 SIGHTS

ROMAN AMPHITHEATER. This second-century theater was constructed after the Carthaginians succumbed to the Roman juggernaut in 238 BC. Built into a rocky hillside, the amphitheater conforms beautifully to the natural slope. Underground cages once hosted ferocious animals, and the arena itself was used for gladiatorial combat. Today summer performances in the theater are a little more civilized. From July to September, an **arts festival** features ballets and concerts. *(V. Fra Ignazio. ☎070 56 25 96. Free guided tours Apr.1–Oct. 1 Tu-Su 10am-1pm and 3-6pm.)*

BASTIONE DI SAN REMY. When you get to **Piazza Costituzinoe,** you'll be dwarfed by an enormous arch and a staircase that seems to be carved into the hillside. Climb up the graceful (though graffiti-covered) double stairway, through the archway, to the terraces of the 19th-century Bastione for a spectacular view of Cagliari spread out below. Take particular notice of the Golfo degli Angeli, the pink flamingos, and the **Sella del Diavolo** (Devil's Saddle), a massive rock formation. The Bastione divides the modern city and the medieval *castello* district. For a stroll through medieval Cagliari, start at the top of the Bastione, follow narrow streets as they wind past Aragonese churches and Piedmontese palaces, and stop at the Pisan wall that runs about the hill.

DUOMO. This cathedral, dedicated to St. Mary, was modeled after the one in Pisa (p. 403). Gold mosaics sit atop each entryway. The pulpits on either side of the main entrance and the four wrestling lions at the base of the 12th-century altar are by Pisano. The ornate wooden balcony to the left and in front of the altar was for the Piedmontese king—he refused to sit among the people for fear of regicide. The **sanctuary** below the duomo was carved into the rock in 1618. Colorful marble inlays cover the 292 niches that contain the relics of early Christian martyrs. *(P. Palazzo, 4.* ☎ *070 66 38 37. Open M-F 8am-12:30pm and 4-7pm, Su 8am-1pm and 4-8pm. Free.)*

MUSEUMS. Although the menacing spear above the entrance recalls the building's original purpose, today the Arsenale houses a modern complex of research museums that includes the vaguely inspiring **Museo Archeologico Nazionale.** Among the Phoenician statuettes and Roman glass works are impressive armies of tiny, 1000-year-old bronze figurines. *(Take V. Buoncammino to P. Arsenale and pass under the Torre di S. Pancrazio to the Arsenale.* ☎ *070 65 59 11. Open Tu-Su 9am-8pm. Wheelchair-accessible. €4.13, ages 18-25 €2.07, over 65 or under 18 free.)* The **Pinacoteca Nazionale,** in the same complex as the archaeological museum, displays medieval and Baroque religious paintings. The labyrinthine museum is built around the remains of a 16th-century city fortification, visible on the ground floor. Works include portraits by the most influential Sardinian painter of the 19th century, Giovanni Marghinotti. *(*☎ *070 66 24 96 or 67 40 54. Open Tu-Su 9am-8pm. Wheelchair-accessible. €2.07, ages 18-25 €1.03, over 60 or under 18 free.)*

BOTANICAL GARDENS. A perfect spot for a picnic, the university gardens protect over 500 species of plants, many of them unique to Sardinia. *(Take V. S. Ignazio da Laconi to university. V. Fra Ignazio, 11.* ☎ *070 675 3501. Open May 2-Aug. 31 daily 8am-1:30pm and 3-8pm; Sept. 1-Oct. 15 8am-1:30pm and 3-6:30pm; Oct. 16-Mar. 31 9am-1:30pm; Apr. 8am-1:30pm and 3-6:30pm. Closed Easter, May 1, and Aug. 15. €0.50, under 6 or over 60 free.)*

BEACHES. Il Poetto, Cagliari's most popular stretch of pure white sand and emerald-sapphire water spans 10km from the Devil's Saddle to the Margine Rosso (Red Bluff). Locals claim it's ugly, but only because the nearby treasures of **Villasimus** and **Chia** put most beaches in Sardinia to shame. Behind Il Poetto, the salt-water **Stagno di Molentargius** (Pond of Molentargius) provides a habitat for flamingos. City buses P, PQ, and PF run to the beaches (20min., €0.77). To avoid more crowded areas, hold off for a few stops once you see the beach. For more private sunning and swimming, head to the less crowded **Cala Mosca,** a smaller beach surrounded by dirt paths leading to isolated coves. Take city bus #5 to Stadio Amsicora and then bus #11 to the beach.

🎵 ENTERTAINMENT

Most bars and clubs in the city are open from 9pm to 5am, but they shut down in August when dancing moves outdoors. Some bars are members-only digs—you'll have to shell out a one-time €5.16-12.91 for a nifty AICS card; look for a sticker on the window to see if that's necessary. **De Candia,** V. De Candia, 1, on top of the Bastione de San Remy, serves expensive drinks to an older crowd. (☎ 070 65 58 84. Cocktails €5. Open in summer M-Sa 8am-2am, Su 7am-1:30pm and 4pm-2am.) On summer evenings, Piazza Yenne is packed full of locals chatting at **Bar Centrale** and **L'Isola del Gelato**—a *gelateria* with an impressive selection and a waterfall in the wall that feeds a river running beneath the transparent floor.

To dance the night away, either find a ride or rent one—most *discotheche* are 15-20km outside of Cagliari, on the beaches. The best night to go out is Friday, when the clubs are packed with revelers. Check out **Buddha Beach** (☎ 070 82 44 70), at Stella di Mare, 20km east of the city.

Outdoor movies are shown (without subtitles) in July and August (around 9pm) at the Marina Piccola off Spiaggia del Poetto. Buy tickets (€2.58-5.16) at the Marina. Merchants converge on the terraces of the Bastione di S. Remy for a **flea market** on Sunday mornings and a smaller daily flea market in P. del Carmine.

On the first of May, Sardinians flock to Cagliari for the **Festival of Sant'Efisio**, honoring a deserter from Diocletian's army who saved the island from the plague but couldn't save himself from a beheading. A costumed procession escorts his effigy from the capital down the coast to the small church that bears his name.

ORISTANO PROVINCE

ORISTANO   ☎ 0783

In the 7th century, the stoic inhabitants of Tharros repelled invasion after invasion until a band of merciless Moorish pirates finally forced them to abandon their homes. With nowhere else to go, they set up camp around nearby Oristano. Today, Oristano has developed into a modest-sized city, complete with the island's largest duomo. Still, as in the 7th century, it would take nothing less than an angry mob of Moorish pirates to convince you to stay in Oristano much longer than a day. It's most notable as a base for exploring the natural and historical splendor of the nearby Sinis Peninsula, where the enticing Phoenician and Roman ruins at Tharros, the awe-inspiring arch at S'Archittu, and the beaches of Is Aruttas all beckon.

▐▀ TRANSPORTATION

Trains: (☎ 0783 72 270), on P. Ungheria, 1km from town center. **Luggage storage** available (p. 709). To: **Cagliari** (1-2hr., 18 per day, €4.45); **Macomer** (9 per day, 6:45am-9:21pm, €2.85); and **Olbia** (2½hr., 1:20pm, €8.60) V. Ozieri Chilivani or Macomer. To get to **Sassari,** go to Macomer or Chivilani for connection.

Buses: PANI, V. Lombardia, 30 (☎ 0783 21 22 68), inside Bar Blu. Open daily 7am-10pm. To: **Cagliari** (1½hr., 4 per day, 8:55am-9:34pm, €5.85); **Nuoro** (2hr., 4 per day, 7:05am-7:50pm, €5.85); and **Sassari** (2¼hr., 4 per day, 7:05am-7:50pm, €7.20). **ARST,** on V. Cagliari, runs local routes (☎ 0783 71 185 or 71 776). Ticket office open daily 7:30am-2pm and 4:30-6pm. To: **Putzu Idu** (dir.: Su Pallosu; 50min., 3 per day, 8:40am-1:53pm, €1.75); **San Giovanni di Sinis** (July-Oct.; dir.: Is Aruttas; 40min.; 5 per day; 8:25am-6:30pm, last return 7:45pm; €1.45); and **Santa Caterina** (dir.: Scano Montiferro; 40 min., 2 per day, 8:02am-7:05pm, €1.76); **ARST** runs to **Cagliari** (2hr., 2 per day, 6:15am-2:10pm, €6.04).

Taxis: At P. Roma (☎ 0783 70 280). Available 7am-1pm and 3-8:30pm; for 24hr. service, call ☎ 336 81 35 85. At the train station (☎ 0783 74 328) and from PANI (☎ 330 43 04 98).

Car Rental: Avis, V. Liguria, 17 (☎ 0783 31 06 38). Cars from €69 per day. 25+. Open M-F 9am-noon and 4-7pm, Sa 9am-1pm. AmEx/MC/V.

Scooter Rental: Marco Moto, V. Cagliari, 99/101. Scooters and tandems €26-39 per day. 18+. Open M-F 8:30am-1pm and 3:30-8pm. AmEx/MC/V.

▗▖ ORIENTATION

To get to the city center from the ARST bus station, take the back exit and turn left. Continue past the duomo and head straight onto **Via De Castro,** which spills into **Piazza Roma,** the heart of the city. From the train station, follow **Via Vittorio**

Veneto, the street farthest to the right, to **Piazza Mariano.** Then take **Via Mazzini** to P. Roma. From the PANI station on Via Lombardia on the other side of town, face the Blu Bar and turn right. At the end of the street, turn right onto **Via Tirso,** left onto **Via Cagliari,** and left on **Via Tharros,** which leads directly into P. Roma.

🛂 PRACTICAL INFORMATION

Tourist Office: Pro Loco, V. V. Emanuele, 8 (☎/fax 0783 30 32 12; proloco.oris@tiscalinet.it). Maps and info on local festivals. Open M-F 9am-12:30pm and 4:30-8pm, Sa 9am-12:30pm. Mobile tourist info booth in **P. Roma.** Open July-Sept. 9am-1pm and 4:30pm-9pm, 10pm on weekends.

Currency Exchange: Banca Nazionale del Lavoro, Banca di Napoli, and **Credito Italiano** are in P. Roma. All open M-F 8:30am-1:20pm and 3-4:30pm.

Luggage Storage: In the train station. €1.55 per day. Open daily 6am-7:30pm.

Emergency: ☎ 113. **Red Cross:** ☎ 0783 74 318. **First Aid:** ☎ 0783 31 72 13.

Pharmacy: V. Umberto 49/51 (☎ 0783 60 338). Open M-F 9am-1pm and 5-8:20pm.

Hospital: (☎ 0783 31 71), on V. Fondazione Rockefeller.

Internet Access: Center for Cultural Services at the **Community Library,** V. Carpaccio, 9 (☎ 0783 21 16 56). Free access. Open M-F 9am-1pm and 4-7pm. **Internet Point,** V. Cagliari, 288, outside of ARST bus station, across the street to the left. Slow connection €4.20 per hr. Open M-F 9:30am-1pm and 5-8:30pm, Sa 10:30am-1:30pm and 5-8:30pm.

Post Office: V. Liguria, 60 (☎ 0783 21 17 78). Open M-Sa 8:15am-6:40pm.

Postal Code: 09170.

🏠 ACCOMMODATIONS & CAMPING

Oristano caters primarily to travelers on their way to the beaches, and low competition maintains high prices. For attractive *agriturismo* options in the surrounding countryside, ask at the tourist office or **Consorzio Agriturismo di Sardegna,** P. Cattedrale, 17. (☎ 0783 73 954; fax 73 924; cas.agriturismo@tiscali.net. Open Apr.-Oct. M-F 9am-1pm and 4-7pm, Sa 9am-noon; Nov.-Mar. M-F 9am-1pm.)

ISA, P. Mariano, 50 (☎/fax 0783 36 01 01; isarose@tiscalinet.it). Exit from back of ARST station, turn left, and turn right onto V. V. Emanuele. Walk through edge of P. D'Arborea and through the adjoining P. Martini, and then follow V. Lamarmora to the end. Turn right, then immediately left. Take 1st right down V. Mazzini to P. Mariano. Immaculate rooms with bath, A/C, and TV. Breakfast included in high season. Reservations recommended July-Aug. Singles €50; doubles €83. Extra bed €12. Half-pension €68 per person. AmEx/MC/V. ❹

Piccolo Hotel, V. Martignano, 19 (☎ 0783 71 500). From the ARST station, take the back exit, turn right, and continue across P. Mannu. Head down the street to the left (it runs east to west) and take the 1st left. Turn right at the end of this street. From the PANI station, call a cab. Town's best budget option. Clean rooms and firm beds. Mosquitoes are everywhere—close your windows and lather on plenty of repellent. All 10 rooms with bath, many with balconies. Singles €31; doubles €52. ❸

Camping: Marina di Torregrande (☎/fax 0783 22 228), on V. Stella Maris, near the beach and 100m out of Torre Grande toward Oristano (7km). Orange local buses leave from V. Cagliari in front of the ARST station (10min., 2 per hr., 7:30am-12:30am, €0.80). Clean bathrooms, hot showers, a restaurant/*pizzeria*, bar, and small market with fresh produce. Unpleasant fumes may waft over from the nearby tar plant. Packed during the summer. 400 lots. Check-in 8am-2pm and 4-9pm. Open May-Sept. €5.20 per person, €3.50 for children, €5.20-6.50 per tent. 4-person tent rental €28.41. Bungalows available, prices vary. Camper €32. Electricity €1.60 per day. ❶

⬚ FOOD

The **Euro-Drink market,** P. Roma, 22, sells inexpensive basics and *Sardi* products. (Open M-Sa 8am-1:30pm and 5-9pm. MC/V.) **STANDA supermarket,** V. Diaz, 53, is at the corner of V. XX Settembre. (Open M-Sa 8:30am-9pm, Su 9am-1:30pm and 5-9pm. AmEx/MC/V.) **SISA supermarket** is at V. Amiscora, 26. (Open M-Sa 8am-8pm.)

> **Ristorante Craf da Banana,** V. De Castro, 34 (☎0783 70 669). Slightly more expensive than other restaurants near the town center, but far more elegant. Low arched brick ceilings, earthy lighting, and fine cuisine. *Primi* €6-7, *secondi* €8-13. Reservations recommended. Open M-Sa 1-4:30pm and 8-11:30pm. AmEx/MC/V. ❸

> **La Torre,** P. Roma, 52 (☎0783 70 784). Local favorite serves Sardinian fare. Pizzas €3.70-6.80, *primi* €4.20-6, *secondi* €6.20-10.80. Cover €1.10. Open Tu-Su noon-3pm and 8pm-midnight. *Pizzeria* open daily 6:30-11pm. AmEx/D/MC/V. ❷

> **Pizzeria La Grotta,** V. Diego Contini, 3 (☎0783 30 02 06), off P. Roma. Despite its name, this place is far from cave-like. *Antipasti* €2.32-€5.68, pizzas €2.58-€7.23. Cover €1.03. Open 7:30pm-1am. D/MC/V. ❷

👁 SIGHTS

CHIESA DI SAN FRANCESCO. This pastel church, the largest in Sardinia, was heavily remade in Neoclassical fashion during the 19th century, leaving little of the original interior intact. A notable remnant is the gruesome wooden crucifix draped with the emaciated and tortured body of Christ. In fact constructed by a 16th-century Catalán teacher, the cross was once attributed to Nicodemus; it was believed that such a vivid depiction could only have been captured by an eyewitness. The sacristy houses a 16th-century polyptych of *St. Francis Receiving the Stigmata* and Nino Pisano's 14th-century marble statue of San Basilio. *(In P. E. d'Arborea at the end of V. de Castro. Open M-Sa 8am-1pm, Su 7am-noon and 4-7:15pm. Free.)*

TOWER OF SAN MARIANO II. Once a fortified entrance to the medieval city, this 13th-century tower dominates P. Roma. On summer evenings, young *oristanesi* gather in this piazza and the adjoining C. Umberto to flirt, drink Ichnusa (Sardinian beer), and chatter away on their *telefonini.*

THE LORD IS MY SHEPHERDESS. Unlike most Italian cities, Oristano is heir to a matriarchal tradition, begun with the 14th-century reign of Eleonora d'Arborea. Not only did Eleonora develop the progressive *Carta de Logu* legal code (which was in use from 1392 to 1897), but she also helped her people fight off the Aragonese for five years before signing a truce, paving the way for future female leaders. In contrast to other cities, dotted with marble Vittorio Emanueles and Gramscis, Oristano's piazzas are guarded by statues of powerful *donne*. The town's estrogen appreciation is accentuated on the second Saturday of September, when crowds of women don yellow flowers and march on Oristano's streets in celebration of d'Arborea.

ANTIQUARIUM ARBORENSE. This museum shelters a small collection of Nuraghic, Punic, Phoenician, and Roman artifacts unearthed at Tharros. On display are urns, cups, containers, and earthenware of all shapes and sizes, as well as a tabletop model of ancient Tharros. *(In P. Corrias, near P. E. d'Aborea. ☎0783 79 12 62. Open daily 9am-2pm and 5-8pm. Wheelchair-accessible. €3, students and groups €1.)*

BASILICA OF SANTA GIUSTA. In its synthesis of Lombard and Pisan influences, this 12th-century basilica is typically Sardinian. Far from inspiring pious tranquility, the sculpted facade depicts two tiny lions dismembering and devouring a deer. *(V. Manzoni, 2, on the road to Cagliari, 3km out of town. Take the ARST pullman (dir.: Arborea) and get off at 1st stop (5min., every hr., 6:15am-8:05pm, €0.67). Basilica ☎0783 35 92 05. Open daily 7:30am-12:30pm and 4-7:30pm.)*

OUTDOOR ACTIVITIES. Maneggio Ippocamo in Rimedio leads day-long horseback tours. *(☎333 479 4955. Open M-Sa 9am-6pm. Tours including lunch €95. Lessons €15 per hr. Discounts for groups of 5 or more.)*

🎭 ENTERTAINMENT

Oristano comes alive for the annual **Sartiglia,** on the last Sunday of *Carnevale* and the following Tuesday (usually in March). The citizens of Oristano don traditional finery (horse-riding gear, expressionless masks, and small top-hats) and ride on horseback through the streets. One of the festive days is sponsored by the *falegnami* (woodworkers) and the other by the *contadini* (farmers). At the Sartiglia's climax, they charge down the street on horseback, trying to pierce six-inch metal stars with their spears. The more stars pierced, the better the upcoming harvest.

🚌 DAYTRIP FROM ORISTANO: SINIS PENINSULA

From July-Aug., reach Tharros by taking the ARST bus to San Giovanni di Sinis (dir.: Is Aruttas; 40min.; 5 per day; 8:25am-6:30pm, last return 7:45pm; €1.45). Ruins open daily 9am-7:30pm. €4.20. S'archittu (30min.; 8:05am and 5:25pm, last return 7:10pm; €1.45). Is Aruttas (July-Aug. 50min., 5 per day, 8:25am-6:30pm, €1.85). Putzu Idu (dir.: Su Pallosu; 1hr.; 4 per day; 6:10-5:15pm, last return 2:47pm; €1.66). Take local orange bus and follow locals to Torregrande's coarser sands (Sept.-June 15-20min., 1-2 per hr., 6am-7:10pm, €0.88).

Visiting Oristano and missing the Sinis Peninsula is like visiting Italy without trying the pasta. Tranquil beaches, stark-white cliffs, rolling country hills and ancient ruins, all within an easy day's drive, make the trip unforgettable. Public transportation is poor and infrequent; those with some cash to spare should consider renting a moped or a car.

The peninsula's southernmost tip, a narrow finger of land rising into a hill 17km west of Oristano, holds the ruins of the ancient Phoenician and Roman port of 🏛**Tharros.** Much of the city remains submerged, but excavations have revealed Punic fortifications, a Roman temple dedicated to Demeter, a Christian baptistery, and a Phoenician shrine. Two white columns rise above the rest of the ruins, framed by the blue sea in the background. A medieval Spanish watchtower crowns the hill and offers comprehensive views.

Gracing the coast slightly to the north of the peninsula proper (off the road to Caglieri) is 🏖**S'Archittu,** a sleepy town with a beautiful seaside where young locals lounge on and leap 15m from a massive, naturally-formed limestone arch into the waters of a beautiful rocky inlet.

Also well-worth the trip is the secluded beach of 🏖**Is Aruttas,** on the coast north of San Giovanni di Sinis. With no town (or refreshment stand) for miles around, white quartz sand the texture of fine caviar, and an endless stretch of Sardinia's famous blue water, this is the place to go for a relaxing day away from civilization. The shallow, sloping waters of **Putzu Idu** are dotted with bobbing fishing boats, seaweed, and sun-worshippers. The beach is on the northern tip of the peninsula, accessible by car or bus.

NUORO PROVINCE

Nuoro is by far the least-touristed Sardinian province. Few realize that the heart of Sardinia contains some of the most spectacular terrain in the country. Nuoro spans from Bosa on the west coast to the Golfo di Orosei on the east. Between these two towns lie smooth plateaus, rolling hills, and the island's highest mountain range, Gennargentu.

NUORO ☎ 0784

Although it is set against a dramatic backdrop of Sardinian mountains, the unimaginative architecture of this provincial capital betrays its agricultural heritage. A few parts of the town—notably, C. Garibaldi—are lively during the day, but Nuoro is still relatively small and underdeveloped, and offers little more than a couple of decent museums. The most attractive quality of the town is its proximity to more interesting destinations in the surrounding countryside.

⌐ TRANSPORTATION

Trains: On V. Lamarmora at V. Stazione (☎0784 30 115). Buy tickets M-Sa 7:30am-7pm. To **Cagliari** (3½-5hr., 6 per day, 6:27am-6:51pm, €10.80).

Buses: The following bus companies serve the island:

ARST (☎0784 32 201). Buses stop along V. Sardegna between the intersection with V. Toscana and the intersection with V. Lamarmora. Tickets available at bar next door or at corner of V. Lamarmora and V. Stazione. Open M-F 6:30am-8pm, Sa-Su 6:30am-2pm. To: **Cagliari** (daily, 2:05pm, €10.38); **Dorgali** (1hr., 6 per day, 6:53am-7pm, €2.01); **Olbia** (7 per day, 5:30am-8:50pm, €6.30-7.64); **Oliena** (30min., 13 per day, 6:53am-7:45pm, €0.89); and **Orgosolo** (30min., 8 per day, 5:50am-6:30pm, €1.45).

F. Deplanu (☎0784 20 15 18) runs buses from the ARST station to the **Olbia airport** (1½hr., 5 per day, 5:45am-5pm, €9.30). **Redentours** runs buses from the ARST station to the **Alghero airport** (2¾hr., 2 per day, €12.39).

PANI, V. B. Sassari, 15 (☎0784 36 856). Walk up V. Stazione and follow it to the right. Ticket office open 9am-noon, 5-7:30pm, and 30min. before each departure. Buses to: **Cagliari** (3½hr., 4 per day, 6:52am-7:31pm, €11.31); **Oristano** (2hr., 4 per day, 6:52am-7:31pm, €5.84); and **Sassari** (2½hr., 6 per day, 5:52am-7:31pm, €6.77).

Local Transportation: Buy tickets (€0.57) for the local buses at a *tabaccheria*. **Bus #4** runs from P. V. Emanuele to train station (3 per hr.) and **bus #3** runs to V. Sardegna.

Car Rental: Autonoleggio Maggiore, V. Convento, 32 (☎/fax 0784 30 461). Affiliated with National Car Rental. 23+. €69.72 per day. Open M-F 8:30am-1pm and 3:30-7pm, Sa 8am-1pm. AmEx/MC/V.

■ ⑦ ORIENTATION AND PRACTICAL INFORMATION

Facing the PANI bus stop, turn left and take **Via B. Sassari** directly into **Piazza Italia,** where you'll find the friendly tourist office and a pleasant park. As you exit the ARST bus stop, take a left down **Via Sardegna** (continuing in the direction of the bus), and then take the first right onto **Via Lamarmora** and follow it to **Piazza delle Grazie**. Turn left and follow **Via IV Novembre** uphill to **Piazza Italia**. **Via Roma** leads from P. Italia to **Piazza San Giovanni** and the town's social hub, **Piazza Vittorio Emanuele**, known to the locals simply as *giardini*.

Tourist Office: EPT, P. Italia, 7 (☎0784 30 083), on street level in summer and on the 4th floor in winter. Stocked with brochures. Enthusiastic staff is eager to offer hiking info. Open Th-Su 9am-1pm and 4-7pm; winter Tu-W 9am-1pm. **Punto Informa,** C. Garibaldi, 155 (☎/fax 0784 38 777; www.viazzos.it), is a private tourist office with lots of brochures and published guides. Staff will help sort through Sardinia's transportation system, and will set you on the right track for hikes, bike tours, and other countryside diversions. Open June-Sept. M-Sa 10am-1pm and 4-7pm.

Emergency: ☎113. **Medical Emergency:** ☎118.

Red Cross: ☎0784 31 250.

Internet Access: Informatica 2000, C. Garibaldi, 156 (☎0784 37 289). €6 per hr. Open M-F 9am-1pm and 4-8pm, Sa 9am-1pm.

Post Office: P. Crispi, 8 (☎0784 24 52 96), off V. Dante. Open M-F 8:15am-6:30pm, Sa 8:15am-12:45pm. **Currency exchange** €2.58.

Postal Code: 08100.

ACCOMMODATIONS

Inexpensive hotels are rare in Nuoro, and campgrounds are in distant towns; take the hint and head for smaller hamlets in the hills. Nearby *agriturismo* options include **Testone,** V. Verdi, 8100 (☎0784 23 05 39), to the northeast of the city.

Hotel Sandalia, V. Einaudi, 14 (☎/fax 0784 38 353), on the outskirts of town on the road to Cagliari and Sassari. As you near the hospital, you'll see Sandalia sitting atop a hill with a big sign. From the ARST station, go as far as V. Lamarmora (see directions above) and take a left, following road signs as above. The quality of rooms varies in this modern 3-star hotel. All have TV and A/C. Singles €39; doubles €55. MC/V. ❹

Il Portico, V. M. Bua, 13 (☎0784 37 535; fax 25 50 62), off the north end of P. V. Emanuele, near P. Mazzini. Reception has the same hours as the restaurant. Singles €26; doubles €30. AmEx/MC/V. ❸

Tonara, V. Muggianeddu, 2 (☎0784 61 00 05). Buses to Tonara are infrequent, so plan ahead or rent a car to get to this hostel. Dorms €10.33; doubles with bath €30. ❶

FOOD

For provisions, head to the **Comprabene supermarket** in P. Mameli. (Open M-Sa 8:30am-1:30pm and 4:30-8pm. MC/V.) **Mercato Civico,** P. Mameli, 20, off V. Manzoni and across from Comprabene, is the place to look for fresh fruit, cheese, and meat. (Open M-Sa 7am-1:30pm and 4:30-8pm. Closed Sa afternoon July-Aug.) An old-fashioned, wood-oven bakery, **Antico Panifico,** V. Ferraciu, 71, off P. delle Grazie, sells hot, fresh rolls, the Sardinian bread *pane carasau*, and scrumptious *panzerotti*, filled with cheese, tomato, and your choice of eggplant, mushroom, or ham for €1.56. (Open M-Sa 8am-8pm.)

Il Portico, V. M. Bua, 15. Excellent rustic cuisine in a new smoke-free restaurant. The house specialty, *ravioli di ricotta alla crema di carciofi* (ricotta-stuffed pasta in a cream of artichoke sauce; €5.50) is delicious. Excellent fresh fish €3 per *etto* (100g). *Secondi* €7.50-11.50. Open M-Sa 12:30-2:30pm and 8-10:30pm. AmEx/MC/V. ❸

Canne Al Vento, V. Repubblica, 66 (☎0784 20 17 62), a 15min. walk down V. Lamarmora from P. delle Grazie. Handsome decor, livened by bright flowers. Generous servings of classic Sardinian *pane frattau* (cheese, egg, and tomato sauce on a bed of thin, crisp bread; €5.16). The house specialty is *porcetto* (roast pig; €5.16). Open M-Sa 12:30-3pm and 8-10:30pm. AmEx/MC/V. ❷

Da Giovanni, V. IV Novembre, 9 (☎0784 30 562). Unremarkable ambiance, but try a delicious plate of *fettucini cinghiali* (wild boar fettucini; €7.74). *Primi* €7.74, *secondi* €7.74-10.33. Open daily noon-3pm and 8-10pm. AmEx/MC/V. ❸

👁 🎵 SIGHTS AND ENTERTAINMENT

The cement P. V. Emanuele—*giardini* for short—is the hangout spot of choice for younger locals who come to sit, talk, and smoke in the evenings. A more mature crowd converges upon C. Garibaldi to do much the same thing.

MUSEUM OF THE ART OF THE PROVINCE OF NUORO. The striking white building stands out among its dimmer surroundings, as does the local contemporary art found inside. Special exhibits change regularly. *(V. S. Satta, 15. ☎ 0784 25 21 10. Open Tu-Su 10am-1pm and 4:30-8:30pm. €2.58, students €1.55, under 18 or over 60 free.)*

MONTE ORTOBENE. A mind-blowing view, a bronze statue of Christ the Redeemer, and a shady park overlooking the neighboring hamlets await at the peak of this hill. From the bus stop on Monte Ortobene, walk 20m down the road for a view of Monte Corrasi, which dwarfs neighboring Oliena. *(To reach the summit, take the orange ATP bus #8 from P. V. Emanuele (15 per day; 8:15am-8pm, last return 8:15pm; €0.55). Or hike about 6km up the hillside. Beware: Cinghiali, or wild boar, haunt the hills.)*

SAGRA DEL REDENTORE. Nuoro celebrates The Feast of the Redeemer in the last week of August. This spartan religious procession, during which the townfolk contemplate the Resurrection, takes place on August 29. A colorful parade of revelers dressed in traditional Sardinian garb and lively productions of traditional folk dances and choral performances precede it.

🔂 DAYTRIP FROM NUORO: ORGOSOLO

Entrust your life to an ARST driver (40min., 8 per day 5:50am-6:30pm, last return 7:05pm; €1.45).

The bus ride alone merits a trip to sleepy ▨Orgosolo. With its comparatively Spartan architecture and its shaded piazza, Orgosolo is the quintessential Sardinian mountain town. The beauty of Orgosolo's mountain vistas are offset by the Picasso-esque murals that dot the buildings. **Francesco del Casino,** a local teacher, initiated this ongoing outdoor art project in 1975, after studying in Latin America. His work focuses on a broad range of topics including imperialism, fascism, commercialism, and terrorism (a World Trade Center mural has been added.) Del Casino drew his initial inspiration from the 1963 film *The Bandits of Orgosolo*, which immortalized the blood *"banditismo"* in the south of Oliena.

Exit the bus at the third stop and follow the signs to the **Hotel Sa'e Janna ❹**, V. E. Lussu, 17, a family-run establishment offering enormous rooms with bath. The **restaurant ❷** downstairs serves inventive *Sardo* dishes. (☎0784 40 12 47; fax 40 24 37. Singles €37; doubles €46. Half-pension €44-49 per person; full-pension €54. 5% discount for students. *Primi* €4-5.50, *secondi* €5.20-6.80.) More del Casino paintings decorate the cozy **Petit Hotel ❷**, V. Mannu, 9, off C. Repubblica. Backtrack from the bus stop at the small park (keeping the police station to your right), then head up the incline on the left and follow the signs. (☎/fax 0784 40 20 09. Breakfast €2.50. Singles €20.66-23.24; doubles €38.80. AmEx/MC/V.)

SASSARI PROVINCE

SASSARI   ☎ 079

Founded as the first free commune of Sardinia in 1294, Sassari held onto its medieval walled-town layout until the late 1800s. In the last 100 years, it has become an important petrochemical center and Sardinia's second-largest city. Thanks to its university, the city has a strong student presence. Congregating along the wide boulevards and the beautiful refurbished 18th-century P. d'Italia, pink-haired rebels roll their eyes at religious processions. When the preaching ends, the kids switch their phones back on and city-dwellers say "Pronto" to the highest standard of living on the island.

▐▀ TRANSPORTATION

Flights: (☎079 93 50 39), near **Fertilia**, 35km south of Sassari. Allow about 1hr. to get there from the bus station (see **ARST**, below). Domestic flights year-round; charter flights to European destinations only in summer.

Trains: (☎079 26 03 62), in P. Stazione, 1 block from P. Sant'Antonio. Take the #8 bus from P. d'Italia. Tickets (€0.57) available at newsstands. Luggage storage available (p. 716). To: **Alghero** (40min., 11 per day, 6:09am-8:55pm, €1.81); **Cagliari** (3½hr., 7 per day, 7:06am-6:51pm, €12.10); **Olbia** (2hr., 3 per day, 8:09am-5:12pm, €5.60); and **Porto Torres** (20min., 10 per day, 5:58am-7:47pm, €1.25).

Buses:

ARST (info ☎079 263 9220). Tickets at Tonni's Bar, C. M. Savoia, 11. Buses depart from V. Italia in public gardens to **Nuoro** (2hr., 2 per day, 9:35am and 2:50pm, €6.30-7.64) and **Porto Torres** (35min., 1-2 per hr., 5:20am-9:15pm, €1.19). Buses to **Castelsardo** (1hr., 11 per day, 7:20am-7:45pm, €2.01) and **Fertilia Airport** (40min., 7 per day 5:36am-6:40pm, last return 10:55pm; €1.76) leave from in front of Tonni's bar.

FDS (☎079 24 13 01), with buses leaving from V. XXV Aprile, serves the local area. Tickets are sold at Corso Vico, where the bus stops. Destinations include **Alghero** (1½hr., 13 per day, 5:35am-7pm, €1.50).

PANI, V. XXV Aprile (☎079 23 69 83; fax 26 00 66; www.comune.sassari.it/vivere_sassari/trasporti/autolinee_pani.htm). Office open daily 5:30-6:35am, 8:30am-2:15pm, and 5-7:15pm, Sa-Su 5:30-6:35am, 9-9:30am, noon-2:15pm, and 5-7:15pm. Buses go to: **Cagliari** (3-4hr., 7 per day, 6am-7:15pm, €13.43); **Oristano** (2¼hr., 4 per day, 6:36am-7:15pm, €7.18); **Nuoro** (2½hr., 6 per day, 6:36am-7:15pm, €6.77); and **Torralba** (40min.-1hr., 6 per day, 6:36am-7:15pm, €2.32).

Taxis: Radiotaxi (☎079 26 00 60). Open 24hr.

Car Rental: Avis, V. Mazzini, 2 (☎ 079 23 55 47). €72 per day. Under 25 pay more. Open M-Sa 8:30am-12:30pm and 4-7pm. AmEx/D/MC/V. **Eurorent,** V. Roma, 56 (☎079 23 23 35). Fiats or other small, "Class B" vehicles €60 per day. 21+. Credit card required. Open M-Sa 8:30am-1pm and 3:30-7pm.

◢▌ ▐ ORIENTATION AND PRACTICAL INFORMATION

All buses stop in the *giardini publici* before heading to the bus station. Since these gardens are much closer to Sassari's attractions, get off at **Via Italia** in the park. **Emiciclo Garibaldi** lies ahead, past **Via Margherita di Savoia.** To reach the town center, head straight through Emiciclo Garibaldi onto **Via Carlo Alberto,** which spills into **Piazza Italia.** To the right, **Via Roma** runs to the tourist office and the Museo Sana. To the left lies **Piazza Castello,** packed with people and restaurants, 200m from **Corso Vittorio Emanuele,** a major thoroughfare.

Tourist Office: V. Roma, 62 (☎079 23 17 77), a few blocks to the right of and behind P. d'Italia when facing the provincial administration building. Go through the gate and then the doorway on your right; the door is on the right-hand side of the hallway. The English-speaking staff provides a map and bus and train schedules. Open M-Th 9am-1pm and 4-6pm, F 9am-1pm.

Budget Travel: CTS, V. Manno, 35 (☎079 20 04 00). Also assists students in finding accommodations. Open M-F 9:30am-1pm and 4:30-7pm, Sa 9:30am-1pm. MC.

Ferry Tickets: Ajo Viaggi, P. Fiume, 1 (☎079 20 02 22; fax 23 83 11). **Agitour,** P. Italia, 13 (☎079 23 17 67; fax 23 69 52).

Currency Exchange: Banca Commerciale D'Italia, in P. D'Italia, has an **ATM** outside. Open M-F 8:20am-1:50pm and 3-4:45pm.

Luggage Storage: (☎079 26 03 62), in the train station. €3 per 12hr. Open daily 6:50am-8:50pm.

English-Language Bookstores: Demetra di Sassari, V. Cavour, 16 (☎079 201 3118). Best sellers and classics; relatively big selection. Open daily 9am-8pm. MC/V. **Gulliver Librerie,** V. Portici Crispo, 4 (☎079 23 44 75). Mostly classics. Open M-Sa 9am-9pm, Su 9am-1pm and 5-9pm. AmEx/MC/V.

Emergency: ☎113.

Police: V. Coppino, 1 (☎079 283 0500).

Ambulance: Red Cross, C. Vico, 4 (☎079 23 45 22). **First Aid: Ospedale Civile** (☎079 206 1000), V. Montegrappa 82/83.

Late-Night Pharmacy: Simon, V. Brigata Sassari, 2 (☎079 23 32 38). Open May-Oct. M-Sa 5pm-1pm, Su 8:30pm-9am; Nov.-Apr. M-Sa 4:30pm-1pm, Su 8pm-1:10am. Posts list of 24hr. pharmacies. There's another pharmacy right down the street.

Internet Access: Buffetti (☎079 215 1055), at V. Italia, 21. €5.16 per 30min. Open daily 9am-1pm and 4:30-8pm. **PC Mainia,** V. Cavour, 71A (☎079 23 49 71). €6 per hr. Open Su-F 9am-1pm and 4:30-8pm.

Post Office: V. Brigata Sassari, 13 (☎079 282 1267), off P. Castello. Open M-F 8:15am-6:15pm, Sa 8:15am-1pm. **Currency exchange,** phone cards, *Fermo Posta*.

Postal Code: 07100.

▐ ACCOMMODATIONS

Finding quality accommodations in Sassari requires a brief, but worthwhile trip outside the city.

▨ Il Gatto e la Volpe, Caniga Località Monti di Tesgia, 23 (☎079 318 0012; English-speaking cell 328 692 3248; www.ilgattoelavolpebandb.com). Call Marcello or Luigi for free pickup from the bus station. Located in the peaceful countryside just outside Sassari, this place is a gem. Some rooms have terraces, and each has its own color scheme (try to reserve the orange room). Dynamic owners will do their best to accommodate with escorted beach and archeological excursions, sailing trips, or mountain bike rental. Internet access available. 5 rooms, 2 with private kitchenettes and bathrooms. Extra beds available. Breakfast included. Reserve ahead. €20.66 per person. ❷

Frank Hotel, V. Armando Diaz, 20 (☎/fax 079 27 64 56). Lovely rooms and nice management. All rooms with bath, A/C, and TV. Breakfast €5.60. Singles €49.06; doubles €67.14. Half-pension €54.23; full-pension €67.14. AmEx/D/MC/V. ❹

Hotel Leonardo da Vinci, V. Roma, 79 (☎079 28 07 44; fax 28 07 44). All rooms have bath, A/C, phone, minibar, TV, and hairdryers. Parking available. Singles €52-72; doubles €72-92. AmEx/D/MC/V. ❹

⬛ FOOD

A wide selection of *pizzerias* line **Corso Emanuele.** Any college ID and a €2.70 ticket affords you a meal at the **University Mensa,** V. dei Mille. Meals include *primo, secondo, contorno,* and fruit. (☎079 21 64 83 or 25 82 11. Open M-Sa 12:30-2:30pm and 7:30-9pm. Closed the last week of July-Aug.) Another university *cantina* is on V. dei Manzella, 2, but is only open for lunch in the summer. A large, enclosed **market** occupies P. Mercato, down V. Rosello from V. V. Emanuele. (Open M-F 8am-noon, Sa 8am-1pm.) **Multimarkets supermarket** is on the corner of V. Cavour and V. Manno. (☎079 23 72 78. Open M-Sa 8am-8:30pm.)

⬛ **Trattoria Da Antonio,** V. Arborea, 2B (☎079 23 42 97), behind the post office. Wood-paneled interior and subdued ambiance. Expect the waitstaff to recommend horse, donkey, and tentacled creatures. Dinner *menù* €12.91 (including €1 cover). Open daily 1-3pm and 8:30-11pm. MC/V. ❸

Trattoria Da Peppina, V. Pigozzi, 1 (☎079 23 61 46), off C. Emanuele. The *menù* (with everything from horse to tripe) is delicious but unfriendly to vegetarians. The waitstaff conducts lively lunchtime banter with the patrons in rapid-fire Italian. *Primi* €3-3.50, *secondi* €4-7. You must order something else with a *primo.* Open M-Sa 12:30-2:30pm; dinner starts at 7:30pm. ❸

Ristorante/Trattoria L'assassino, V. Ospizio Cappucini, 1 (☎079 23 50 41). With your back to the statue of Tola, walk straight ahead. At the end of the street, veer right. This nook of a restaurant doesn't look like much, but the food and the friendly management are a pleasure. *Primi* €4.20-5.70, fish *secondi* €3.60-7.75. Open daily 12:30-3pm and 7:30-11pm or midnight. AmEx/MC/V. ❷

◎ ⬛ SIGHTS AND ENTERTAINMENT

Museo Giovanni Antonio Sanna, V. Roma, 64, has a lovely rose garden in front and houses *nuraghi* models, Sardinian paintings, skulls with holes drilled into them, and petrified tree stumps. (☎079 27 22 03. Open daily 9am-8pm. €2, ages 18-25 €1. EU citizens under 18 or over 60 free.) From the center of town, walk down C. Emanuele from P. Castello and turn left on V. al Duomo to P. Duomo to reach Sassari's duomo, **Cattedrale di San Nicolò.** This 15th-century Gothic Catalan-style structure has a Baroque facade. Renovations have uncovered early frescoes.

The lavish **Sardinian Cavalcade,** held on the third weekend in May, is Sardinia's most notable folk festival. Festivities include a parade of costumed emissaries from Sardinian villages, a horse exhibition, singing, and dancing. On August 14th, I **Candelieri** brings worker's guilds carrying enormous wooden candles through the streets. The festival, dating back to the Middle Ages, is one of the oldest and most colorful in Sardinia—each guild has its own costume, and the candles are bedecked with flowers and streamers.

If it weren't for the ⬛**University Pub,** V. Amendola, 49/A, Sassari would be devoid of a hip youth scene. A favorite among locals, the subdued pub offers dirt-cheap drinks (beer from €1.60) and overflows with students when school's in session. Request (but don't inhale) the cannabis beer (€4) or the mysterious Sardinia Island mixed drink (€5.16), whose contents are strong but secret. (☎079 20 04 23. Open Sept.-July W-M 8:30pm-1am.)

SARDINIA

DAYTRIP FROM SASSARI: CASTELSARDO

To reach Castelsardo, take ARST bus from Sassari. From P. Pianedda, face uphill and walk up stairs. Open M-Sa 9:30am-1pm and 2:30-9pm. Castle and museum €1.55.

Castelsardo's striking location atop a lofty crest and proximity to sandy beaches make it a popular stop along the Costa Paradiso. Renowned across the island for its beauty, the town was once described by a Sardinian poet as a "flower of light that smiles from the top of a sharp promontory upon the glimmering sea." (He wasn't known for mincing compliments.) This large, well-preserved, and well-situated castle (containing a dull wicker-work museum) crowns the village.

PORTO TORRES   ☎079

Founded in 27 BC, the village of Turris Libissonis, on the mouth of the river Mannu, was the first Sardinian outcropping of the Roman Empire and served as one of Rome's principal ports along the corn-trading routes between Sicily and Africa. Today, the town's ancient twist can be savored in its Roman ruins and Romanesque 12th-century church—but good luck getting rid of the bitter taste of the outlying industrial zones. This modern port town is best sampled as a stopover and as a point of access to luscious Stintino.

▐▆ TRANSPORTATION. Trains are synchronized with ferries, leave from the port to **Sassari** (20min., 9 per day, 5:48am-7:50pm, €1.25) and continuing on to **Olbia,** while **ARST** buses (☎079 263 9200 or 800 86 50 42) run from the ferry port. Schedule restricted on Sundays. Tickets available in the cafe at C. V. Emanuele, 38. To: **Alghero Fertilia Airport** (40min., 6 per day, 6:01am-10:01pm, €1.55); **Sassari** (35min., 1-2 per hr., 5:47am-9:55pm, €1.25); and **Stintino** (40min.; 6 per day; 5:43am-8:10pm, last return 8:20pm; €1.79).

▆▐ ORIENTATION AND PRACTICAL INFORMATION. Porto Torres has one major thoroughfare, **Corso Vittorio Emanuele,** which runs perpendicular to the ocean from the port. The first stop you should make in Porto Torres is the **Pro Loco Tourist Office,** Locali Ex Pesa Varco Alti-Fondali, in the port. The multilingual staff will provide bus schedules and information on local sights, beaches, and mountain biking. (☎/fax 079 51 50 00. Open July-Sept. M-Sa 8am-1pm and 4-8pm; Oct.-Apr. M-Sa 9am-1pm.) Farther up the street, the bank **BNL,** C. V. Emanuele, 18/20, has an **ATM** outside. (Open M-F 8:30am-1:30pm and 2:45-4:15pm, Sa 8:30am-noon.) In case of **emergency,** call the **police** (☎112, 079 50 24 32, or 070 51 01 19), **Guardia Medica** (☎079 51 03 92), or an **ambulance** (☎079 51 60 68). The town's **pharmacy,** Farmacia Rubatiu, C. V. Emanuele, 73, is down the block. (☎079 51 40 88. Open M-Sa 9am-1pm and 5-11pm.) The **post office** is at V. Sachi, 113. (☎079 50 491. Open M-F 8:15am-6:15pm, Sa 8:15am-1pm.) **Postal Code:** 07046.

▐▊ ACCOMMODATIONS AND FOOD. At **Albergo Torres ❹,** V. Sassari, 75, the decor is pink and delightful. All rooms have bath, A/C, and TV. The gorgeous *matrimonale* fits two to four people. (☎079 50 16 04; fax 50 16 05; www.hoteltorres.it. Breakfast €6.71. Singles €49.06-62.49; doubles €69.72-72; triples €77.47-87.80. In winter €40/€62/€70. Half-pension €61.97; full-pension €69.72. AmEx/D/MC/V. **Albergo Royal ❹,** V. S. Satta, 8, has comfortable decor, TV, and private baths. From the port or bus stop, walk up C. V. Emanuele away from the water until you reach a yellow "Albergo Royal" sign hanging overhead. Turn left and walk about 300m along V. Petronia and then follow the signs; it'll be another 200m or so. (☎079 50 22 78. Singles €30-36; doubles €62.) The lodging closest to the ferry port is the three-star **Hotel Elisa ❹**, V. Mare, 2, with bath, TV, phone, and a small refrigerator in each of its 27 rooms. Ask the amicable Alessandro about local beaches. (☎079 51 32 60; fax 51 37 68. Breakfast included. Singles €44-46.50; doubles €68-73. MC/V.)

In the mornings, an **outdoor market** is at the intersection of V. Delle Vigne and V. Sacchi. **Bar Trattoria Pedoni Teresa ❷**, V. G. Bruno, 5, off P. XX Settembre, has standard Sardinian cuisine specialties like donkey, horse, and octopus. Meal around €9. (Lunch at noon and dinner at 7pm. Closed Su evenings.) **La Rosa dei Venti ❸**, on V. G. Galilei, also offers local favorites. (☎079 50 25 90. *Primi* €4-7.40, *secondi* €7.80-10.80. AmEx/MC/V.) For sandwiches and pizza from €3.61, go to **Poldiavolo ❶**, in P. Settembre XX. (*Primi* €5.16-10.32, *secondi* €4.65-10.32. Open daily 11:30am-midnight.) The **SISA supermarket** is on V. Mare, 24. (☎079 50 10 24. Open daily 8am-8:30pm. MC/V.)

🅰🅰 **SIGHTS AND BEACHES.** The 11th-century **Basilica di San Gavino,** up the stairs in P. Marconi at the end of C. V. Emanuele, houses the crypts of local Saints Gavino, Proto, and Gianuario. Proto and Gianuario were Christians persecuted by the Romans around AD 300. Gavino was a Roman soldier who, while holding the Christians captive, was converted, and then set them free. All three were eventually captured and beheaded. (Open 8:30am-1pm and 3-7pm.) The ruins of the **Roman Thermal Baths,** along V. Ponte Romane, 5min. from the center of town, were ravaged in the 19th century by railway planners and dynamite-wielding quasi-archaeologists searching for the site of the martyrs' decapitation. (☎079 51 44 33. Open Tu-Su 9am-8pm. €2, under 18 or over 65 free.)

Soak up some rays at the two beaches along Porto Torres's shore. **Scoglio Lungho Spiaggia,** a sandy beach 250m from the port, is family-friendly, complete with a metal dolphin diving over a rock that juts out of the water. **Acquedolci,** right down the road, is notable for its flat stone outcroppings and blue-green water.

🅳 **DAYTRIP FROM PORTO TORRES: STINTINO.** Northwest of Porto Torres on the Capo del Falcone, Stintino was once a legitimate fishing village; then came the tourist deluge. The winter population of fewer than 1000 swells to almost 20,000 in summer. The obvious draw is the captivating ▨**Spiaggia di Pelosa,** a beach 4km outside town. Here, children fondle captured baby octopi along the rocky shore, and sparkling blue waters glisten against the bone-dry Isola Piana. On the other side of Piana lies **Isola Asinara,** which was used as a penal colony until very recently. Considering the gorgeous surroundings, maybe crime does pay. To reach a more accessible island (graced with an 18th-century Aragonese tower), walk all the way along the beach, and either tackle the 500m swim from the beach or strap on sandals and make a wet scramble 50m over the rocks. Watch out for sea urchins lurking within small crevices along the way.

Stintino has a **tourist office,** V. Sassari, 77, with maps and tips on activities and accommodations. (☎/fax 079 52 37 88; stintinoturismo@tin.it. Open daily 9:30am-1pm and 8-11pm.) Orange **line A buses** run from the beach back to Stintino (every hr., 8-12:30am, €0.67). **Buses** run from Pelosa to **Sassari** (1¼hr., 6 per day, 6:40am-8pm, €2.91) via **Porto Torres** (40min., €1.95). In Stintino you can catch the bus in P. Municipio (6:50am-8:20pm). If you get stuck waiting for a bus, head to **Lu Funali,** Lungomare C. Colombo, 89, along the water, for a drink to the tunes of Bob Marley.

ALGHERO ☎079

Vineyards, ruins, and horseback rides are all a short trip away from Alghero's palm-lined parks and cobbled streets. If you prefer to stay in town, however, you'll have plenty to see. Alghero's history spans centuries of occupation by everyone from native Sardinians to the Aragonese and the Genovese. In addition to Italian, you're likely to hear a dialect of Catalán, left in Alghero's streets by Pere I of Aragon after his 14th-century conquest; Alghero is also known as *Barcelonetta*. The Aragonese influence is also reflected in the architecture (check out S. Francesco) and the cuisine (lots of restaurants offer *paella* as well as pasta).

▛ TRANSPORTATION

Flights: (☎079 93 50 39), near **Fertilia,** 6km north of Alghero. Domestic flights year-round, charter flights to European destinations only in summer.

Trains: (☎079 95 07 85), on V. Don Minzoni, in northern part of city. Take **AP** or **AF** bus from in front of the Casa del Caffè in the park (3 per hr.), or walk 1km along port. Open daily 5:45am-9pm. Buy ticket at **FS** stand in the park and you can ride the city bus to the station for free. **Luggage storage** available (p. 721). To **Sassari** (40min.; 11 per day (fewer on Su); 6:01am-8:47pm; €1.81, €3.10 round-trip).

Buses:

ARST: (☎079 95 01 79 or 800 86 50 42). Blue buses depart from V. Catalogna next to park. Buy tickets at the stand in park. To: **Bosa** (1½hr., 4 per day, 6:35am-7:30pm, €1.76); **Porto Torres** (1hr., 8 per day, 4:50am-8:50pm, €2.58); **Sassari** (1hr., 18 per day, 5:35am-7pm, €2.58).

FS: Orange city buses (info ☎079 95 04 58). Buy tickets (€0.57) at *tabacchi*. Book of 12 tickets €5.68. Buses run from V. Cagliari in front of Casa del Caffè to the **airport** (20min., 6 per day, 5:45am-8:30pm, last return from airport 11:45pm). **Line AF** travels between **Fertilia** and V. Cagliari (Alghero's *giardini*), with a stop at the port (every 40min., 7:10am-9:30pm, return from Fertilia 7:50am-9:50pm). **AP** (from Viale della Resistenza) runs to the train station (every 40min., 6:20am-9pm). **AO** (from V. Cagliari) heads to the *lido* (beach) and the hospital (2 per hr., 7:15am-8:45pm). **AC** (from V. Liguria) runs to Carmine (2 per hr., 7:15am-8:45pm).

Taxis: (☎079 97 53 96), in Alghero, can be caught on V. V. Emanuele across from the BNL bank. At the airport, ask where to catch a taxi.

Car Rental: Avis, Piazza Sulis, 9 (☎079 97 95 77), or Fertilia airport (☎079 93 50 64). Cars from €60 per day for unlimited mileage. 25+. Credit card required. AmEx/D/MC/V. **Europcar** (☎079 93 50 32), at the airport. From €70 per day, including insurance. 150km per day limit. Open daily 8am-11pm.

Bike/Moped Rental: Cycloexpress di Tomaso Tilocca (☎/fax 079 98 69 50), at the harbor near the intersection of V. Garibaldi and V. Spano. Bikes €7.75, mountain bikes €10.33-12.91, tandem bikes €12.91, and scooters €25.82 (€154.90 credit card security deposit required to rent scooters). Open M-Sa 9am-1pm and 4-8:30pm, Su by appointment. AmEx/D/MC/V.

▛ ▟ ORIENTATION AND PRACTICAL INFORMATION

ARST buses stop at the corner of **Via Catalogna** and **Via Cagliari,** on the waterfront one block from the port. The tourist office, in **Piazza Porta Terra,** lies diagonally across the small park, on the right beyond the easily visible towers of the *centro storico*. The train station is a hike from the town center, but is accessible by local orange buses (lines AF and AP). If you'd rather walk from the station, follow **Via Don Minzoni** until it turns into **Via Garibaldi** along the waterfront.

Tourist Office: P. Porta Terra, 9 (☎079 97 90 54; fax 97 48 81; www.infoalghero.it), on the right from the bus stop, toward the old city. Cheerful, multilingual staff offers an indexed street map, tours of the city, and daytrips to local villages. Open Apr.-Oct. M-Sa 8am-8pm, Su 9am-1pm; Nov.-Mar. M-Sa 9am-1pm.

Horseback Riding: Club Ippico Capuano (☎079 97 81 98), 3km from Alghero on Strada Villanova. Daily guided excursions. They will pick you up in Alghero; €5 per carload. Reserve 2-3 days in advance. €15 per hr.

Vineyard Tours: Sella and Mosca (☎079 99 77 00), 11km up the road to Porto Torres. Has a shop (open June-Aug. daily 8:30am-8pm) and offers tours of their wine-making facilities (June 15-Sept. 30 M-Sa 5:30pm; in winter by request). **Santa Maria/La Palma Wine Growers' Cooperative** (☎079 99 90 44) has a shop and offers tours on request. (Open M-Sa 8am-1pm and 4-8pm.)

Currency Exchange: Banca Nazionale del Lavoro, V. Emanuele, 5 (☎079 98 01 22), across from the tourist office, has a 24hr. **ATM.** Open M-F 8:20am-1:20pm and 3-4:30pm. Exchange also at the **post office.**

Luggage Storage: In train station. €0.77 per day.

English-Language Bookstore: Mondolibro, V. Roma, 50 (☎079 98 15 55) has classics and bestsellers. Open daily 9:30am-1pm and 4:30pm-midnight.

Emergency: ☎113. **Carabinieri:** ☎112.

Police: P. della Mercede, 4 (☎113 or 97 20 00).

Ambulance: ☎118, 079 97 66 34, or 98 05 87. **First Aid:** ☎079 99 62 33.

Pharmacy: All pharmacies, including **Farmacia Puliga di Mugoni,** V. Sassari, 8 (☎079 97 90 26). Open May-Oct. M-Sa 9am-1pm and 5-9pm; Feb.-Apr. M-Sa 9am-1pm and 4:30-8:30pm; Nov.-Jan. 9am-1pm and 4-8pm. AmEx/MC/V.

Hospital: Ospedale Civile (☎079 99 62 00), Regione la Pietraia, V. Don Minzoni.

Internet Access: Soft, V. Tarragona, 22 (☎079 97 00 57). €7.75 per hr. Open M-Sa 9am-1pm. Also see listings for **Caffe Teatro** and **Libreria Labadinto.**

Post Office: V. XX Settembre, 112 (☎079 97 93 09; fax 98 10 29). *Fermo Posta* (next door to main office). Open M-F 9:30am-1:30pm and 2:30-6:15pm. **Currency exchange** open M-F 8:15am-5pm, Sa 8:15am-1pm. Open M-F 8:15am-6:15pm, Sa 8:15am-1pm.

Postal Code: 07041.

ACCOMMODATIONS & CAMPING

In July and August, prices escalate and rooms vanish. Unless you have a reservation or are willing to pay for half-pension, consider the youth hostel in Fertilia.

▧ **Hostal d l'Alguer (HI),** on V. Parenzo, in Fertilia (☎/fax 079 93 20 39; hostalalguer@tiscali.net). From the bus stop in Fertilia, turn right and walk down the street. Proceed until you see houses on your left; the hostel will be on your right. 100 beds. Internet access and phone in reception area. Terrific meals (lunch or dinner €8). Breakfast included. HI card required. 4-bed dorms €13 per night; family rooms with 2 beds €16. ❶

▧ **Hotel San Francesco,** V. Machin, 2 (☎/fax 079 98 03 30; hotsfran@tin.it). Walk straight from the tourist office and take the 3rd right. 20 rooms in the church cloister, all with bath, phone, and beautiful stone walls. Breakfast included. Reservations necessary June-Aug. Singles €36-43; doubles €62-77; triples €84-104. MC/V. ❹

Hotel La Margherita, V. Sassari, 70 (☎079 97 90 06), near the intersection of P. Mercedes. Easy-to-find, central location. All rooms have bath, A/C, and TV; some have a view of the ocean. Terrace on top of the hotel for socializing and sunbathing. Breakfast included. Singles €42-62; doubles €73-99. AmEx/D/MC/V. ❹

Hotel San Guian, V. G.M. Angioy, 2 (☎079 95 12 22; fax 95 10 73), 1 block east from the beach. Firm beds and immaculate bathrooms. All 22 rooms with bath. Rooftop terrace with a view. Breakfast included. Reserve for June-Aug. Singles €31-41.50; doubles €52-72.50; triples €67-93. MC/V. ❹

Camping: La Mariposa (☎079 95 03 60; fax 98 44 89; www.lamariposa.it), on V. Lido, near the beach and 1½km away from town on the Alghero-Fertilia road. Open Mar.-Oct. Reservations suggested in summer. €8.50-10.50 per person, ages 3-13 €5-8.30. €3.10-5.10 per tent, €1.76 per car; Apr.-June tents and cars free. Discount about 10% for very large groups. 4-person bungalows €72. ❶

🍴 FOOD

On V. Sassari, two blocks from the tourist office, a **market** offers fresh produce every morning. On Wednesdays, the **open-air market** on V. de Gasperi floods with crowds. Take the *linea mercato* bus from V. Cagliari. Be sure to stop by the **Antiche Cantine del Vino Sfuso,** C. V. Emanuele, 80, a *cantina sociale* that shoots inexpensive (but decent) table wine from giant, space-age machines for a mere €1 per liter. (Open M-Sa 8:30am-1pm and 4:30-8pm. MC/V.) The **SISA supermarket** is at V. Sassari, 49. (Open M-Sa 8am-9pm, Su 8am-1:30pm and 5-8:30pm.)

🏠 **Ristorante da Ninetto,** V. Gioberti, 4 (☎079 97 80 62). From P. Porta Terra, go down V. Simon and turn right onto V. Gioberti. The restaurant is housed in an 8th-century *frantoio* (olive press). Admire the arched stone ceilings while you enjoy delicious, reasonably priced fare. Try the scrumptious *maloreddus alla salsiccia* (€7) or *paella.* *Primi* €7-15.50, *secondi* €9.50-15. Open daily 12:30-3pm and 7:30pm-midnight; closed Tu in winter. AmEx/D/MC/V. ❹

Taverna Paradiso, V. Principe Umberto, 27 (☎079 97 80 01). Stone-vaulted ceilings and delicious food make for a charming dinner in the *centro storico*. *Primi* €5.20-8.30, *secondi* €5.20-12.95. Cover €1.05. Open daily noon-3pm and 7pm-1am. MC/V. ❸

Ristorante La Muraglia, Bastioni Marco Polo, 7 (☎079 97 55 77), offers a sweeping view of the sea from its upstairs room. Rather touristy, but the food is excellent. Make sure to get a seat with a view. Finish off the meal with *seadas,* a Sardinian cheese pastry doused in honey (€3). *Primi* €6.50-12, *secondi* €7-11. Cover €1.55. Open daily June-Sept. noon-3:30pm and 7pm-2am. AmEx/D/MC/V. ❸

👁 SIGHTS

A leisurely walk through the *centro storico* reveals tiny alleyways, half-hidden churches, and the ancient town walls. Unlike many of its counterparts elsewhere in Italy, it's also very clean and safe. The old city is hard to navigate without a map, so stop by the tourist office before heading inside. Don't leave without seeing Alghero's **Chiesa di San Francesco.** From P. Sulis, take V. Carlo Alberto to the intersection with V. Machin. The heavy, 14th-century Neoclassical facade of this church conceals a graceful Gothic presbytery. (Open 7:30am-noon and 5-8pm. Free.) Alghero's **duomo,** on V. Roma, was begun in 1552 and took 178 years to construct, resulting in a motley Gothic-Catalán-Renaissance facade. Rebuilt in the 19th century, the cathedral has Gothic choirs and a mosaic of John the Baptist.

🎵 ENTERTAINMENT

Alghero truly comes alive at night—with revelers streaming through the cramped streets of the *centro storico* and pouring onto the promenade until the early hours of the morning. (Be wary of indulging in the late-night scene if you're staying at the hostel; the last bus to Fertilia is at 11:30pm.) Lungomare Dante is lined with open-air bars that attract locals in search of warm evening breezes and decent bands. Closer to the water, **Bar El Trò,** Lungomare Valencia, 3, offers live music or DJs spinning after 11:30pm. (Open daily May-Oct. 9pm-6am; Nov.-Apr. 7:30pm-3am; everyone arrives after 1am.) To escape from the nighttime stampede in P. del Teatro, duck into the cool confines of **Caffe Teatro,** V. Principe Umberto, 23, where buying a drink is your ticket to free Internet access. (☎ 079 973 2119. Open daily 8pm-3am.) **Jamaica Inn,** V. P. Umberto 57, is jammin' daily 7pm-3am. (☎079 973 3050. Beer €2.50-4, mixed drinks €5.50.) For dancing, head to **La Siesta** or **Ruscello**—both are 6-7km outside the city and require a cab. Don't go until after midnight, or you'll be dancing by yourself. In July and August, the town has **outdoor movies** in Forte della Maddalena. (Info ☎ 079 97 63 44.)

⚡ DAYTRIP FROM ALGHERO: GROTTE DI NETTUNO

FDS buses (☎079 95 01 79) run to Capo Caccia and Porto Conte (50min.; 3 per day; 9:15am-5:15pm, last return 6:05pm; €1.76). Or take the frequent and pleasant Navisarda Grotte di Nettuno boat tour. Boats (☎079 97 62 02, 95 06 03, or 97 89 61) leave Alghero's Bastione della Maddalena (1hr.; 8 per day (fewer in winter); 9am-5pm; €10, under 13 €5).

The Duke of Buckingham dubbed the 🖼**Grotte di Nettuno** "the miracle of the gods." The majestic caves have been around for 60 to 70 million years and today are one of Sardinia's most coveted tourist attractions. Respect your elders and watch where you bump your head—one cubic centimeter of stalactite took 100 years of dripping rain water to form. Well-run tours are conducted in Italian, French, English, and German. The caves are in **Capo Caccia,** a steep promontory that juts out from **Porto Conte.** Once there, descend the 632 steps that plunge to the sea between massive white cliffs. (☎ 079 94 65 40. Open daily Apr.-Sept. 8am-7pm; Oct. 10am-5pm; Nov.-Mar. 9am-2pm. Groups admitted every hr. €8, under 12 €4.)

ARST buses to Capo Caccia stop along the way at the **Nuraghi di Palmavera** (☎079 95 32 00), where a central tower surrounded by several huts forms a limestone complex dating from 1500 BC. (Open daily Apr.-Oct. 9am-7pm; Nov.-Mar. 9:30am-4pm. €2.10, with guided tour €3.60. Call ☎079 95 32 00 for information on the tours offered by the S.I.L.T. cooperative; tours available in English, French, German, and Spanish if you reserve in advance.)

BOSA   ☎0785

Odd that a town with a 12th-century castle perched atop a hill overlooking the sea could remain largely untouristed—but sleepy Bosa pulls it off. Bosa proper is home to the castle and photogenically dilapidated buildings. Bosa Marina, a ten-minute bus ride away, boasts a lengthy *lungomare*, relatively unpopulated beaches, an assortment of seaside bars, and a hostel.

■📠 ORIENTATION AND TRANSPORTATION. **Bosa,** the larger of the two cities, and the one with the *centro storico*, lies on either side of the **River Temo,** about 3km inland from the ocean. **Bosa Marina** is across the river from the *centro* on the beach. Buses stop in Bosa's **Piazza Angelico Zanetti.** Buses run from Bosa to **Piazza Palmiro Togliatti** in Bosa Marina (5min., 22 per day, €0.67). Additionally, Pullman buses from **Alghero** or **Oristano** often continue to Bosa Marina. **ARST** buses run from Bosa to **Oristano** (1½hr., 4 per day, 7:30am-4:50pm, €4.44) and **Sassari** (2hr., 4 per day, 8:30am-5:25pm, €5.37-9.61). Buy tickets from the *tabacherria* at V. Alghero, 7A. **FDS buses** run to **Alghero** (*linea mare* 55min., 11

per day, €2.89; *linae montagna* 1½hr., 11 per day, €3.72) and **Nuoro** (1¾hr., 3 per day, 10:05am-7:31pm, €4.91). Tickets can be bought at the FDS office in P. Zanetti. (Open 5:30-8:30am, 9:30am-1pm, and 1:05-3:20pm; in winter 5:30-8:30am and 9:30am-7:35pm.)

◪ PRACTICAL INFORMATION. The **Pro Loco tourist office,** V. Zuni, 5, at the intersection of V. Francesco Romagna and V. Azuni, has a good, free map of the city. (☎0785 37 61 07. Open daily 9:30am-1pm and 6-8pm.) For **currency exchange,** head to **Credito Italiano,** at the corner of V. Lamarmora and V. Giovanni XXIII. (Open M-F 8:20am-1:20pm and 2:35-4:05pm.) In case of **emergency,** dial ☎113 or call the **Red Cross** (☎0785 37 38 18) or **carabinieri** (☎0785 37 31 16). Find **Internet access** at the cyber-*pizzeria* **Al Gambero Rosso,** V. Nazionale, 22, in Bosa on the Bosa Marina side of the river. (☎0785 37 41 50. €5 per hr. Open M-Sa 12:30-3pm and 7:30pm-midnight.) **Internet Web Copy,** in P. IV Novembre, offers Internet (€6 per hr.) and fax services. (Open M-Sa 9am-1pm and 6-10pm.) The **post office,** P. Pischedda, 1, has fax service and **currency exchange.** (☎0785 37 31 39. Open M-F 8:20am-6:30pm, Sa 8:20am-12:45pm.) **Postal Code:** 08013.

◪◪ ACCOMMODATIONS AND FOOD. Bosa Marina is home to a well-run **▨Youth Hostel ❶** at V. Sardegna, 1. Ask the bus driver to let you off near the hostel. From P. Palmiero Togliatti, take V. Sassari to V. Grazia Deledda and turn right. After two blocks, turn left and look for the hostel at the end of the street. Fifty meters from the beach, this hostel has a restaurant, a bar that's open until midnight, and an amicable staff. (☎0785 37 50 09. Meals €9.30, breakfast €2.07. Lockout Sept.-June noon-6pm. 50 beds. 6- to 8-bed dorms €10.33; doubles available if reserved.) For something more classy, try **Albergo Perry Clan ❷**, V. Alghero, 3, in Bosa. From the bus stop, walk along V. D. Manin and turn right—the hotel is on the left after P. Dante Alighieri. All rooms have bath and A/C; some have TV. (☎0785 37 30 74. 28 beds. Singles €20; doubles €40.) **Tattore ❸**, in P. Monumento, sates the appetite with savory, fresh seafood. (Open daily noon-3pm and 8:15pm-midnight. Closed W in winter.) **Sa Pischedda ❸**, V. Roma, 8, serves fantastic, garlic-saturated *razza alla bosana*, a sautéed flat fish. (☎0785 37 30 65. *Primi* €7-10, *secondi* 7.50-14. Open daily 12:30-3pm and 7:30pm-midnight. AmEx/MC/V.)

◪◪ SIGHTS AND OUTDOORS. Walk around the town's historic area, **Quartiere Sa Costa,** and inhale the history. A large, free **beach** awaits in Bosa Marina, with a *lungomare* lined with bars and its very own **Aragonese Tower.** (Open occasionally; check with tourist office.) The **Bosa Diving Center** (☎0785 37 56 49), V. Colombo, 2 , in Bosa Marina, offers snorkeling (€24 per person) and scuba trips (€35-52 per dive plus accessory costs), 4km river boat rides with exceptional views of the city (€5-6), and ocean trips to nearby grottoes and beaches (2hr., €13).

OLBIA ☎0789

Most visitors only stop in Olbia en route to other Sardinian destinations. Although there are archaeological sites in the area, the town itself has but a single, unremarkable medieval church, and nary a beach in sight. Unless you're willing to rent a moped or bike to explore some of the surrounding countryside, Olbia offers little more than convenient ferry connections to Corsica and the rest of Italy.

▛ TRANSPORTATION

Trains: (☎0789 84 88 or 88 088), on V. Pala. Turn off C. Umberto, pass through the bus station to the tracks, and turn right. Trains run to the port. Ticket office open M-Sa 6am-12:40pm and 1:45-7pm. **Luggage storage** available (see below). To: **Cagliari** (4hr., 6 per day, 6:46am-6:20pm, €13.25); **Golfo Aranci** (20min., 7 per day, 7am-8:10pm, €1.75); and **Sassari** (2hr., 6 per day, 6:46am-8:17pm, €5.80).

Buses: ARST, C. Umberto, 168 (☎0789 55 30 00). Waiting room open daily 7am-8pm. Tickets and schedule at train station ticket window or *tabacchi*. Fewer buses on Su. To: **Arzachena** (1hr., 11 per day, 6:30am-11:15pm, €1.76); **Nuoro** (3hr., 6per day, 8:10am-7:25pm, €6.30); **Palau** (1¼hr., 12 per day, 4:20am-11:15pm, €2.32); and **Santa Teresa di Gallura** (1½hr., 6 per day, 6:40am-8:15pm, €3.72).

Ferries: All of the ferry companies have offices in the Stazione Marittima. **Port office** open when ferries are running. Check-in 1½hr. before departure. **Tirrenia** (☎0789 20 71 00). Open M-Sa 7am-1pm and 5:30pm-midnight. To: **Civitavecchia** (4-8hr., €14.72-33.31) and **Genoa** (6-13½hr., €27.11-53.19). **Moby Lines** (☎0789 27 927). Open daily 8am-12:30pm and 3-10pm. To: **Civitavecchia** (4-8hr., €25-52); **Genoa** (6-13½hr., €30-53); and **Livorno** (10hr., €29-46). **Grand Nave Veloci** (☎0789 20 01 26). Open daily 8:30am-12:30pm and 4-8pm. To **Genoa** (6-13½hr.; runs only June 1-Sept. 30; €36-73). **Lloyd Sardegna** (☎0789 21 411). To **Livorno** (11hr., €28.40-36.50).

Car Rental: Avis (☎0789 69 540), in the airport. MC/V.

✴ ▛ ORIENTATION AND PRACTICAL INFORMATION

Blue intercity **ARST buses** and a train timed to meet incoming passengers greet **ferries** arriving at the port. To reach Olbia's *centro*, take the waiting train to the first stop. To find the tourist office, walk directly from the train station up **Via Pala** until it intersects **Corso Umberto.** The ARST bus station is 200m to the right. Turn left and continue past **Piazza Margherita** until you reach **Via Catello Piro.**

Tourist Office: V. Catello Piro, 1 (☎0789 21 453; fax 22 221), off C. Umberto. Look for the modern white building. Ask for *Annuario Hotels and Camping.* Open in summer M-Sa 8am-1pm and 3:30-7:30pm, Su 8:30am-12:30pm and 4-7pm.

Currency Exchange: Credito Italiano, C. Umberto, 167. Open M-F 8:20am-1:20pm and 2:50-4:20pm, Sa and holidays 8:20-11:50am. **Banco di Sardegna,** C. Umberto, 142, off P. Margherita. **Banca Popolare di Sassari,** C. Umberto, 3. All have **ATMs** outside.

American Express: Avitur, C. Umberto, 142B (☎0789 24 327). Holds mail for AmEx cardholders. Also books ferry and plane tickets. Friendly, English-speaking staff. Open M-F 9am-1pm and 4-7pm.

Luggage Storage: In train station. €2.58 per 12hr.

English-Language Bookstore: La Libreria dell'Isola, C. Umberto, 154 (☎0789 21 386). Good selection of English best sellers and classics. Open May.-Oct. daily 9am-1pm and 4:30-8:30pm; Nov.-Apr. 9am-1pm and 4-8pm. AmEx/D/MC/V.

Emergency: ☎113.

First Aid: Guarda Medica (☎0789 55 24 31), on V. Roma, near the hospital.

Pharmacy: Farmacia Lupacciolu, C. Umberto, 134 (☎0789 21 310), at the corner of V. Porto Romano. Open M-Sa 9am-1pm and 5-8:20pm. Local papers, *La Nuova Sardegna* and *L'Unione Sarda,* list pharmacies open on Su.

SARDINIA

Hospital: Ospedale Civile (☎0789 55 22 00), on V. Aldo Moro.

Internet Access: Mailboxes, Etc., V. R. Elena, 24A (☎0789 26 000). €6.20 per hr. Also offers Western Union, UPS, and FedEx services. Open M-F 9:30am-1pm and 4:30-8pm, Sa 9:30am-1pm.

Post Office: V. Cherubini (☎0789 23 151). Open M-F 8:30am-6pm, Sa 8:30am-1pm.

Postal Code: 07026.

ACCOMMODATIONS

▨ **Hotel Minerva,** V. Mazzini, 6 (☎/fax 0789 21 190). From P. Margherita, walk down C. Umberto toward water and take 1st right. Friendly management and bright rooms, with old-fashioned furniture and light fixtures. Some rooms have bathrooms. Breakfast €2. Singles €26, with bath €34; doubles €36.50/€51.65. ❸

Albergo Terranova, V. Garibaldi, 3 (☎0789 22 395; fax 27 255; www.paginegialle.it/terranova-07), off P. Margherita. This labor of love has been run by the same family since 1964. Recently renovated rooms have bath, TV, and A/C; some have balconies. Breakfast included. Singles €50; doubles €68; triples €90; quads €115. Half-pension €50 per person. AmEx/MC/V. ❹

Hotel Centrale, C. Umberto, 85 (☎0789 23 017; fax 26 464). Blessedly central location. Clean rooms with bath, A/C, and TV. Breakfast included. Singles €45; doubles €78; triples €105. AmEx/MC/V. ❹

FOOD

For bargains, shop at **Mercato Civico,** on V. Acquedotto (open M-Sa 8am-1:30pm and 5-8:30pm), **Superpan,** P. Crispi, 2, off V. R. Elena at the waterfront (open M-Sa 8:30am-9pm and Su 8am-1:30pm; MC/V), or **Supermercato Sisa,** V. Dettori, 10 (open daily 8am-1pm and 5-8pm; MC/V).

▨ **Antica Trattoria,** V. Pala, off C. Umberto, near the bus and train stations. Good cooking at reasonable prices. Bustling ambiance and friendly waitstaff. *Primi* €4.20-7.30, *secondi* €4.70-13. *Menùs* from €13. Open Tu-Su 12:30-3pm and 7:30-11:30pm. ❶

Ristorante da Paolo, V. Garibaldi, 18 (☎0789 21 67.5). A contrast of rugged brown stone, soft pastel tablecloths, and pleasant wall murals. Try the house specialty *porcetta* (€6.71). *Primi* €5.16-7.75, *secondi* €6.20-10.33, fish €7.75-12.91. Cover €1.55. Open daily noon-2:30pm and 7-10:30pm. MC/V. ❷

Ristorante/Pizzeria Trocadero, V. Achenza, 14 (☎0789 22 047). Located at the end of V. Temio off Corso Umberto. Peach-colored table cloths, great food. Pizza €4-7, *primi* €7-8.50, *secondi* €7-8.50. Cover €2.10. Open daily noon-3pm and 6:30-11:30pm. AmEx/DC/MC/V. ❸

◎ ♫ SIGHTS AND ENTERTAINMENT

A walk along the water in Olbia takes you through an industrial area, sadly obscuring Sardinia's peaks and blue coasts. Nearly all traces of Olbia's Greek, Roman, and medieval past have disappeared. The sole exception is the fairly uninteresting 12th-century **Chiesa di San Simplicio,** behind the train station. Built in the Pisan-Romanesque style, the imposing facade is etched in off-white granite. **Eddy's Pub,** V. Cavour, 3 (☎333 938 7490), serves drinks daily from 9pm to 3am.

If you have a car or feel up to a bike ride, consider an excursion from Olbia to **S'Abe,** an archaeological site 6km away, or to the **Giants' Tombs of Su Monte** (prehistoric burial grounds with megaliths emerging from the ground). The bus to Nuoro passes **Isola Tavolara,** a prism of rock protruding 450m out of the sea.

ARST buses run to **San Teodoro** (1hr.), where a long, luxurious beach eases into aquamarine water. **Hotel La Palma,** on V. del Tirreno, offers 18 budget rooms. (☎0784 86 59 62. Doubles €80; half-pension €57 per person. AmEx/MC/V.) One kilometer from San Teodoro, the **Cala d'Ambra campground** has satisfactory facilities and 100 lots just 250m from the beach. (☎0784 86 56 50. Open Apr.-Oct. €6.20-10.85 per person, €1.55-5.16 per tent.)

PALAU ☎0789

Palau's most famous inhabitant is the *roccia dell'orsù*, an enormous rock that the tireless mistral winds have carved into the shape of a bear. It was an object of intrigue even in Homer's day, when he immortalized it in his *Odyssey* by warning of the ferocious *Lestrigoni* people that once lived around it. The locals have mellowed a bit since then, and Palau is now a sleepy, harmless coastal town composed of modern buildings painted in typically Sardinian pastel shades of yellow and pink. The real attraction these days is the coast. Convenient ferry shuttles transport passengers across the bay to the islands of La Maddalena and Caprera.

◨ TRANSPORTATION AND ORIENTATION. The port end of **Via Nazionale**—Palau's single thoroughfare—contains a white building that houses a bar, several ferry ticket offices, and a newsstand that also sells ARST bus tickets (the buses stop outside). **ARST buses** head to **Olbia** (18 per day; €2.32 to the *centro*, €2.58 to the port) and **Santa Teresa di Gallura** (8 per day, 7:55am-9:25pm, €1.72). The **Trenino Verde** (little green train) provides a slow, indirect, and expensive means of transportation to Sassari—the train goes to Tempio from June to August (2 hr., 9:50am, €13) and on Thursdays a train runs from Tempio to Sassari (2hr., 4:50pm, €15). **TRIS** (☎0789 70 86 31) and **Saremar Ferries** (☎0789 70 92 70) serve the island of **La Maddalena** (15min.; 2 per hr.; 7:15am-11:50pm, round-trip €3.40, under 12 €2.07, cars €4.13-8.52, bicycles free). For **car rental** head to **Centro Servizio Autonoleggio,** V. Nazionale, 2. (☎0789 70 85 65. 20+. From €75 per day, with insurance and unlimited mileage. Open daily 9am-1pm and 4-7:30pm. AmEx/MC/V.)

◨ PRACTICAL INFORMATION. Palau's **tourist office,** V. Nazionale, 96, slightly uphill from the center of town, offers information on nearby beaches, outdoor activities, and tours of neighboring islands. (☎/fax 0789 70 95 70. Open M-Sa 8am-1pm and 4-8pm, Su 8:30am-12:30pm and 5-8 pm.) **Banca di Sassari,** V. Roma, 9, has **currency exchange** and **ATMs** in front. (Open M-F 8:20am-1:20pm and 2:30-3:30pm, Sa 8:20-11:50am.) In an **emergency,** dial ☎113, contact the **carabinieri** (☎112), call the **Guarda Medica** (☎0789 70 93 96), or ring the **hospital** in Olbia (☎0789 22 279). **Farmacia Nicolai** is at V. Delle Ginestre, 19. (☎0789 70 95 16; for **medical emergencies** call ☎329 953 4693. Open M-Sa 9am-1pm and 5-8pm. AmEx/MC/V.) The **post office** is at the intersection of V. Garibaldi and V. La Maddalena. (☎0789 70 85 27. Open M-F 8:15am-1:15pm, Sa 8:15am-12:45pm.)

◨ ACCOMMODATIONS & CAMPING. Accommodations in Palau are often prohibitively expensive. **Hotel La Roccia ❹,** V. dei Mille, 15, is modern and has a lobby built around an enormous boulder. All 20 rooms have bathrooms, A/C, and TV. (☎0789 70 95 28; fax 70 71 55. Breakfast included. Private parking available. Call ahead. Singles €45-67; doubles €70-105. AmEx/MC/V.) **Hotel del Molo ❹,** on V. dei

Ciclopi, is a quiet hotel with pleasant staff and 14 clean, air-conditioned rooms, all with bath, TV, and fridge. (☎0789 70 80 42. Breakfast €4. Ask about half-price meals at nearby restaurants. Singles €45-66; doubles €62-96. MC/V.) **Hotel Serra ❸**, V. Nazionale, 17, close to the port, provides 20 simple, clean rooms, all with bath. (☎0789 70 95 19; fax 70 97 13. Reserve in summer. Singles €31; doubles €45. AmEx/MC/V.) For **camping**, try ▧**Acapulco ❶**, Loc. Punta Palau. The facility has a private beach, a bar with nightly piano music (live singer July-Aug.), and a restaurant. (☎0789 70 94 97; fax 70 63 80. Open Easter-Oct. 15. Reserve in summer. Bring your own tent. €7.75-14.50 per adult, €5.30-10.30 per child ages 4-12. Bungalows €20.65-25.80; July and Aug. half-pension required €46.50-51.65. 4-person caravans €51.65-87.70. AmEx/MC/V.)

◘ **FOOD.** Numerous **bakeries** and **alimentari** line V. Nazionale. The friendly, attentive waitstaff of ▧**L'Uva Fragola ❶**, P. V. Emanuele, 2, serve a variety of crisp, refreshing salads (€5.50-10.50), pizzas (€3.50-8), and desserts in a relaxed, shaded outdoor setting. (☎0789 70 87 65. Cover €1. Open daily noon-3pm and 7-11:30pm. D/MC/V.) **Ristorante Robertino ❸**, V. Nazionale, 20, dishes out flavorful spaghetti with scallops for around €10. (☎0789 70 96 10. *Primi* €5.50, *secondi* €10-13. Cover €1.55. Open Tu-Su 1-2:30pm and 8-11:30pm. MC/V.) **Ristorante Il Covo ❸**, V. Sportiva, 12, has reasonably priced seafood. (☎0789 70 96 08. *Primi* €5-9.30, *secondi* €8.26-14. Cover €1.80. AmEx/D/MC/V. Sailors drink at **Guido's**, by the Stazione Marittima, where ferry tickets are sold. (☎0789 70 94 65. US currency accepted. Open daily 5:30am-2am.)

◖ **SIGHTS.** Tiny **Spiaggia Palau Vecchia** is the beach to the left of the port when facing the water. Palau's main curiosity is the **Roccia dell'Orsù. Caramelli buses** (15min.; 5 per day; 7:30am-6pm, last return 6:20pm; €0.62) run to the rock at **Capo d'Orso** from the port. Caramelli also runs to **Porto Pollo**, a beautiful beach (30min., 5 per day, 8:15am-7:20pm, last return 7:55pm, €1.19). An **antique steam-engine tour** departs in July and August for Tempio (9:50am, return 5pm; round-trip €12). Several private boat companies run all-day tours of the archipelago, including the islands of **Budelli** and **Spargi** (see La Maddalena's **Sights**, p. 729).

LA MADDALENA ARCHIPELAGO ☎0789

Corsica and Sardinia were once joined by a massive land bridge; La Maddalena, Caprera, and the 50-plus smaller islands that surround them are its fragmented remains. La Maddalena is clean, safe, and draws mostly upscale tourists and soldiers. The beautiful coastline is a strategically important one, and one-fifth of La Maddalena's inhabitants are members of the Italian or US Navy. Although US tourists are still a rarity, American sailors jog through the streets, kayak in the waters, and enjoy drinks at the bars of La Maddalena. You'll run into more shopkeepers and waiters who speak English here than anywhere else in Sardinia. Italian patriots mob La Maddalena for their own reasons: their national hero, Giuseppe Garibaldi, made the nearby island of Caprera his home while he was in exile.

◪◨ **TRANSPORTATION AND PRACTICAL INFORMATION. Tris** (☎0789 73 54 65) runs ferries between Palau and La Maddalena (15min., 2-3 per hr., 7:15am-11:20pm, €4.34), as does **Saremar** (☎0789 73 76 60; every 30min., 4:30am-11:45pm, €4.34). For a **taxi**, call ☎0789 73 65 00. A rented **scooter** will run you €20-50 per day at **Nicol Sport**, V. Amendola, 18. (☎0789 73 54 00. Half-day rates available. Open daily 8am-8pm.) A **tourist office** is in P. Barone de Geneys. (☎0789 73 63 21. Open May-Oct. M-Sa 8:30am-1pm and 4:30-7:30pm, Su 9:30am-12:30pm and 5-8pm.) A **Banco di Sardegna**, on V. Amendola off P. XXIV Febbraio, has **currency** exchange and a 24hr. **ATM**. (Open M-F 8:45am-1:30pm and 2:45-6pm.) In an emergency, call the **carabinieri** (☎0789 73 69 43), a **Pronto Soccorso** (☎0789 79 12 18), or the **hospital** (☎0789 79 12 00). A **Farmacia Russino** is at V. Garibaldi, 5. (☎0789 73 73 90. Open Su-F 9am-1pm and 5-8:30pm.) Use the **Internet** at **Sotta Sopra Internet Cafe,** V. Garibaldi, 48. (☎0789 73 50 07. €6.20 per hr. Open F-W 11am-3:30pm and 5:30pm-late.) A **post office** is in P. Umberto. (☎0789 73 75 95. Open M-F 8:15am-6:15pm, Sa 8:15am-noon.)

🏠🍴 ACCOMMODATIONS AND FOOD. Hotel Archipelago ❹, V. Indipedenza, 2, is the best deal, though it's a 20min. walk from the town itself. From P. Umberto, follow V. Mirabello along the water until you reach the intersection with the stoplight. Take a left here and then a right at the Ristorante Sottovento. Continue uphill to the sign directing you to your left; take the left indicated by the sign, and then take a left and a right after the grocery store. The brown stucco hotel will be on your right (15min.) Alternatively, catch the bus to Caprera from the Garibaldi column, ask to be let off at the *semaforo* (stoplight), and proceed as above. All 12 rooms have bath and TV; some have balconies. (☎0789 72 73 28. Breakfast included. Reservations necessary July-Aug. Singles €49; doubles €76.)

Pick up the basics at the **Dimeglio Supermarket,** V. Amendola, 6. (☎0789 73 90 05. Open M-Sa 8am-9pm, Su 8:30am-1pm. MC/V.) **Mangana ❷,** V. Mazzini, 2, is decent and not too expensive. (☎0789 73 84 77. Pizzas €2.50-6, *primi* €7-9, *secondi* €6.50-12. AmEx/DC/MC/V.) La Maddalena's seafaring citizens support a substantial selection of bars. For Guinness on tap (small €2.50), head to **The Penny Drops,** an Irish pub on V. Nazionale. (☎0333 349 9372. Open daily 11am-3am.)

📷 SIGHTS. The islands of **🏝Spargi, 🏝Budelli, Razzoli,** and **Santa Maria** are paradises of uninhabited natural beauty. National Park status was conferred upon the islands to protect them from development and to curb the throngs of tourists. Some spots, including the infamous **Spiaggia Rosa,** have been closed off altogether. However, boatloads of swimsuit-wearing sightseers still pack large tour ships to take all-day cruises around the archipelago, stopping at beaches along the way (Spargi's **Cala Connari** and Budelli's **Spiaggia Cavaliere**). To avoid the crowds, you have to hike along the thorny, glittering granite cliffsides that cascade down to the beaches. Even then, you're bound to share the crystalline waters with swimmers diving off anchored yachts and tiny power boats. Ticket sellers clamor along the docks of both La Maddalena and Palau every morning until the boats begin to depart (8-10:30am). Purchase tickets the day before, especially in summer, as they do sell out. The tour should include a meal and two or three 2hr. stops at beaches along the way. Most boats return around 5-6:30pm. Though fairly expensive (€27-33), the tour is the cheapest way to reach the islands.

Pine groves shade picnic tables on the quiet island nature reserve of **Caprera.** With few inhabitants, the calm is interrupted only by carloads of tourists coming for a stay at Caprera's **Club Med ❸** (☎0789 72 70 78; meals included; doubles €250-665 per wk.) or for a visit to the much-adored **House of Garibaldi.** Catch a **bus** from the Garibaldi column in P. XXIV Febbraio in La Maddalena to Caprera (13 per day; 8:45am-6:45pm, last return 7:15pm; €0.67). During the Risorgimento, Garibaldi was forced into exile in the US, where he lived in New York City for five years. He returned to Italy and settled at Caprera in 1854. Two years later, he built a home here, spending the rest of his life commuting back and forth between his Caprera home and the mainland in pursuit of his patriotic endeavors. The house contains much of Garibaldi's original furniture and possessions, as well as family portraits. (☎0789 72 71 62. Open Tu-Su 9am-6:30pm. €1.)

SARDINIA

SANTA TERESA DI GALLURA   ☎0789

Although the crowds of beach-goers here might make you forget you ever left the mainland, Santa Teresa's beautiful view and surrounding countryside will soon convince you that you could be nowhere but Sardinia. The little town is a lovely launching point for exploring coves, inlets, and the Capo Testa, a plain of wind-sculpted granite with magnificent beaches. Santa Teresa boasts its own small beach, Rena Bianca, from which the hazy shores of Corsica are visible.

▐ TRANSPORTATION

Buses: ARST (☎0789 21 197) buses depart from V. Eleonora d'Arborea, next to post office off V. Nazionale. Buy tickets at **Baby Bar** on V. Nazionale, 100m to left from bus stop. To: **Olbia** (2hr., 13 per day, 6:10am-8:50pm, €3.72); **Palau** (40min., 9 per day, 6:10am-8:50pm, €1.76); and **Sassari** (3hr., 5 per day, 5:15am-7:15pm, €5.83).

Ferries: Saremar (☎0789 75 40 05). Tickets can be purchased at the office on V. del Porto. Open daily 9am-12:30pm and 2-10:30pm. For ferry details, see p. 702. To **Bonifacio, Corsica** (1hr., 2-4 per day, 8am-5pm, €6.71-8.52 plus €3.10 port tax for entrance into Corsica).

Taxis: (☎0789 75 42 86), on V. Cavour. Open 6am-midnight.

✦⁊ ORIENTATION AND PRACTICAL INFORMATION

The ARST bus stops in front of the post office. Facing the post office, turn right, head to the intersection, and turn right onto **Via Nazionale.** Head for the church at the end of the street (in **Piazza San Vittorio**) and turn right again to reach **Piazza Vittorio Emanuele.** The tourist office is on the opposite side of the piazza.

Tourist Office: The Consorzio Operatori Turistici, P. V. Emanuele, 24 (☎0789 75 61 11). List of rooms for rent. Ask about horse, moped, and boat rentals. Open June-Sept. daily 8:30am-1pm and 3:30-8pm; Oct.-May M-Sa 8am-1pm and 3:30-6:30pm.

Boat Tours: Consorzio delle Bocche, P. V. Emanuele, 16 (☎0789 75 51 12), tours the islands of the archipelago. Daily tours last 9:30am-5:30pm, with lunch. €34 per person, ages 4-12 €18. Office open daily 9:30am-1pm and 5:30pm-midnight.

Horseback Riding: Scuola di Turismo Equestre/Caddhos Club (☎0789 75 16 40), in nearby Marazzino (4km away). Guided excursions €18 per hr.

Scuba Diving: No Limits Diving Center, V. del Porto, 16 (☎/fax 0789 75 90 26), offers a 7-day course for PADI and SSI certification (€330), guided excursions (€35-50), and help in finding accommodations. AmEx/D/MC/V.

Car Rental: Avis, V. Maria Teresa, 41 (☎0789 75 49 06). 23+. From €68 per day. Open daily 9am-12:30pm and 4:30-7pm. AmEx/D/MC/V. **GULP,** V. Nazionale, 58 (☎0789 75 56 98; info@gulpimmobiliare.it). 25+. From €58 per day. AmEx/MC/V.

Scooter and Bike Rental: Top Service Noleggio, V. Nazionale, 15/17 (☎0789 75 45 33 or 328 488 8757; topservice@tiscalinet.it). 18+. Bikes from €8 per day; scooters from €18 per day; 4-wheeler €77 per day. Discounts available for rentals longer than 2 days. Open daily 9am-1pm and 4-8pm. AmEx/MC/V.

Emergency: ☎113. **Medical Emergency:** ☎118.

Police: Carabinieri (☎112), on V. Nazionale.

First Aid: Guarda Medica (☎0789 75 40 79), V. Carlo Felice. Open 24hr.

Pharmacy: P. S. Vittorio, 2 (☎0789 75 53 38). Open June-Aug. daily 9am-1pm and 5-8:30pm; off season has reduced hours.

Internet Access: Infocell (☎/fax 0789 75 54 48), on V. Nazionale, off V. D'Arborea. €5 per hr. Open M-Sa 9am-1pm and 4:30-8pm.

Post Office: (☎0789 73 53 24), on V. Eleonora D'Arborea, across from the bus stop. Open M-F 8:05am-12:45pm, Sa 8am-12:30pm.

Postal Code: 07028.

ACCOMMODATIONS

Hotel Bellavista, V. Sonnino, 8 (☎/fax 0789 75 41 62), 2 blocks past P. V. Emanuele. Incredible views of the sea. 16 bright, airy rooms with balconies and baths. Breakfast €4. Singles €30.99-33.57; doubles €46.48-49.06. Half-pension €51.65-63; full-pension €54-67. 30% more for an extra bed. MC/V. ❸

Hotel Marinaro, V. G.M. Angioy, 48 (0789 75 41 12; www.hotelmarinaro.it). Turquoise and yellow stripes on the lobby walls; rooms have bath, A/C, and TV. Some have terraces. Spacious **restaurant** offers breakfast for €8. Singles €42-70; doubles €55-100; triples €72-120. Half-pension required in Aug. AmEx/D/MC/V. ❹

Hotel Moderno, V. Umberto, 39 (☎0789 75 42 33), off V. Nazionale. Central location. 16 white rooms with big, bright bathrooms. Breakfast included. Reservations required. Singles with bath €34-46; doubles €57-87. AmEx/MC/V. ❹

Hotel del Porto, V. del Porto, 20 (☎/fax 0789 75 41 54). From ARST stop on V. Nazionale, face post office and go left. At the intersection, take another left and then a right. Follow V. del Porto down the hill. Likely to have vacancies. 20 large rooms, some with bath and views of the nearby rocks, all close to the ferry horns. Breakfast €6. Singles €26-31; doubles €37-42. Prices increase by €6 in Aug. AmEx/MC/V. ❸

FOOD

Alimentari scattered along V. Aniscara, off P. V. Emanuele, sell inexpensive basics. A fruit and clothing **market** by the bus station opens on Thursday mornings. If you're on a really tight budget, make a picnic with food from the **SISA supermarket,** on V. Nazionale next to the Banco di Sardegna. (Open M-Sa 8am-1pm and 4:30-8pm, Su 9am-noon.)

Papè Satan, V. Lamarmora, 22 (☎0789 75 50 48). Look for the sign off V. Nazionale. Who would have thought the Prince of Darkness would be such a good cook? Try the devilishly rich *pizza alla Papè Satan* (€8), or, if you don't mind anchovies, the *quattro stagione* (€8). Cover €2. Open daily noon-2:30pm and 7-11pm. ❷

Da Thomas, V. Val d'Aosta, 22 (☎0789 75 51 33). Eat outdoors, away from the maddening crowds. *Primi* €6-12, *secondi* €8.50-13. Open daily for lunch from 12:30pm, dinner 7:30pm. AmEx/DC/MC/V. ❸

Poldo's Pub, V. Garibaldi, 4 (☎0789 75 58 60). Poldo's has blossomed from a pub to a *pizzeria, spaghetteria, birreria,* and wine bar. Pizza €3.10-7, *primi* €5.20-8.80, *secondi* €7.75-13. Open daily noon-3pm and 7pm-midnight. AmEx/MC/V. ❶

BEACHES AND HIKING

V. XX Settembre leads toward the sea. As the road forks, veer left and continue past Hotel Miramar to reach **Piazza Libertà.** The perfect **Aragonese Tower** is framed by the deep blue of the wide ocean, with the shores of Corsica just barely visible through the mist across the sea. Take a walk down the stairs in the piazza to reach **Spiaggia Rena Bianca.** Those seeking a more off-the-beaten-path sunbathing experience must sacrifice sand. Above the beach, an unkempt trail winds up and around the rocks along the coast, giving the more adventurous traveler access to the coves and lagoons. The trek is thorny and overgrown, so proper footwear is a must. Farther up, the path offers glimpses of the impressive beaches of ▧Capo Testa. If you prefer flip-flops to hiking boots but still want to get to the beach, either take the **Sardabus** from the post office to Capo Testa (10min.; 5 per day; €0.67, round-trip €1.24) or brave the traffic and walk the 3km along **V. Capo Testa** from V. Nazionale.

🎵 ENTERTAINMENT

Groove's Cafe, V. XX Settembre, 2, offers cushioned booths and outdoor balcony seating where you can nod your head to acid jazz and deep house after 11pm. (Open daily 6:30am-5:30am.) **Conti** (☎0789 75 42 71), on the other side of the piazza, has an upstairs dance floor and loft beds where you can nod your bod to the sounds of a live DJ. (☎0789 75 42 71. Open 7pm-late.) Shoot pool or surf the net with a Corona (€1.55) in hand at **Poldo's Pub.** (☎0789 75 58 60. Open all night.)

APPENDIX

TEMPERATURE AND CLIMATE

°CELSIUS	-5	0	5	10	15	20	25	30	35	40
°FAHRENHEIT	23	32	41	50	59	68	77	86	95	104

To convert from °C to °F, multiply by 1.8 and add 32. For a rough approximation, double the Celsius and add 25. To convert from °F to °C, subtract 32 and multiply by 0.55. For a rough approximation, subtract 25 from Fahrenheit and cut it in half.

AVERAGE TEMPERATURE AND PRECIPITATION											
	JANUARY			APRIL			JULY			OCTOBER		
	°C	°F	cm/in	°C	°F	cm/in	°C	°F	cm/in	°C	°F	cm/in
Florence	2/10	35/50	6.4/2.5	8/19	46/66	7.1/2.8	17/31	62/87	3.4/1.3	10/21	50/69	10.3/4
Milan	-4/6	25/42	5.2/2.0	5/17	40/63	12.5/5	15/28	59/82	6.4/2.5	6/18	43/63	8.4/3.3
Rome	3/14	38/56	8.1/3.2	7/19	45/66	5.6/2.2	17/30	62/86	1.8/0.7	11/22	52/73	12/4.6
Venice	-1/6	31/42	5.6/2.2	8/16	46/61	7.3/2.9	18/27	63/81	6.8/2.7	9/18	48/64	7.7/3.0

ABBREVIATIONS

Throughout the book, address titles have been abbreviated:

ABBREVIATIONS	
C.	Corso
D.	Di
Loc.	Locanda
P.	Piazza
Pta.	Porta
V.	Via
Vco.	Vicolo

INTERNATIONAL CALLING CODES

To call internationally without a calling card, dial the international access number ("00") + country code (for the country you are calling) + number. For operator-assisted and calling card calls, dial the international operator: 170. For directory assistance, dial 12.

TELEPHONE CODES			TELEPHONE CODES	
Australia	61		Monaco	377
Austria	43		New Zealand	64
Canada	1		Slovenia	386
France	33		South Africa	27
Germany	49		Spain	34
Greece	30		Switzerland	41
Ireland	353		UK	44
Italy	39		US	1

TIME ZONES

Italy is one hour later than Greenwich Mean Time (GMT), seven hours later than US Eastern Standard Time (EST), 10 hours ahead of Vancouver and San Francisco time, the same as Johannesburg time, 12 hours behind Sydney time, and 14 hours behind Auckland time. From the last Sunday in March to the last Sunday in September, Italy and Malta both switch to Daylight Savings Time and are two hours later than GMT but still seven hours later than US EST.

MEASUREMENTS

Italy uses the metric system. Below are metric units and English system equivalents.

MEASUREMENT CONVERSIONS

1 inch (in.) = 25.4mm	1 millimeter (mm) = 0.039 in.
1 foot (ft.) = 0.30m	1 meter (m) = 3.28 ft.
1 yard (yd.) = 0.914m	1 meter (m) = 1.09 yd.
1 mile (mi.) = 1.61km	1 kilometer (km) = 0.62 mi.
1 ounce (oz.) = 28.35g	1 gram (g) = 0.035 oz.
1 pound (lb.) = 0.454kg	1 kilogram (kg) = 2.202 lb.
1 fluid ounce (fl. oz.) = 29.57ml	1 milliliter (ml) = 0.034 fl. oz.
1 gallon (gal.) = 3.785L	1 liter (L) = 0.264 gal.
1 acre (ac.) = 0.405ha	1 hectare (ha) = 2.47 ac.
1 square mile (sq. mi.) = 2.59km^2	1 square kilometer (km^2) = 0.386 sq. mi.

ITALIAN

PRONUNCIATION

VOWELS

There are seven vowel sounds in standard Italian. **A, i,** and **u** each have one pronunciation. **E** and **o** each have two pronunciations, one tense and one lax, depending on the vowel's placement in the word, the stress, and the regional accent (some don't incorporate this distinction). It is difficult for non-native speakers to predict the quality of vowels—don't worry so much about **e** and **o**. You may hear a difference, especially with **e.** Below is the *approximate* pronunciation of vowels.

THE BASICS	
a:	a as in father *(casa)*
e: tense e: lax	ay as in bay *(sete)* eh as in set *(bella)*
i:	ee as in cheese *(vino)*
o: tense o: lax	o as in bone *(sono)* between *o* of bone and *au* of caught *(zona)*
u:	oo as in droop *(gusto)*

CONSONANTS

Save a few quirks, Italian consonants are easy. **H** is always silent, **r** is always rolled.

> **C and G:** Before **a, o,** or **u, c** and **g** are hard, as in *cat* and *goose* or as in the Italian word *colore* (koh-LOHR-eh), "color," or *gatto* (GAHT-toh), "cat." They soften into **ch** and **j** sounds, respectively, when followed by **i** or **e,** as in English *cheese* and *jeep* or Italian *ciao* (chow), "goodbye," and *gelato* (jeh-LAH-toh), "ice cream."

CH and GH: H returns **c** and **g** to their "hard" sounds in front of **i** or **e** (see above): *chianti* (ky-AHN-tee), the Tuscan wine, and *spaghetti* (spah-GEHT-tee), the pasta.

GN and GLI: Pronounce **gn** like the **ni** in on*ion*, thus *bagno* ("bath") is "BAHN-yoh." **Gli** is like the **lli** in m*illion*, so *sbagliato* ("wrong") is said "zbal-YAH-toh."

SC and SCH: When followed by **a, o,** or **u, sc** is pronounced as **sk**. *Scusi* ("excuse me") yields "SKOO-zee." When followed by an **e** or **i, sc** is pronounced **sh** as in *sciopero* (SHOH-pair-oh), "strike." **H** returns **c** to its hard sound **(sk)** before **i** or **e**, as in *pesche* (PEHS-keh), "peaches," not to be confused with *pesce* (PEH-sheh), "fish."

Double consonants: The difference between double and single consonants in Italian is likely to cause problems for English speakers. When you see a double consonant, pronounce it twice or hold it for a long time. English phrases like "dumb man" or "bad dog" approximate the double consonant sound. Failing to make the distinction can lead to confusion; for example, *penne all'arrabbiata* is "short pasta in a spicy red sauce," whereas *pene all'arrabbiata* means "penis in a spicy red sauce."

STRESS

In many Italian words, stress falls on the next-to-last syllable. When stress falls on the last syllable, accents indicate where stress falls: *città* (cheet-TAH) or *perchè* (pair-KAY). Stress can fall on the first syllable, but this occurs less often.

PLURALS

Italians words form the plural by changing the last vowel. Words ending in an **a** in the singular (usually feminine) end with an **e** in the plural; *mela* (MAY-lah), "apple," becomes *mele* (MAY-lay). Words ending with **o** or **e** take an **i** in the plural: *conto* (KOHN-toh), "bill," is *conti* (KOHN-tee), and *cane* (KAH-neh), "dog," becomes *cani* (KAH-nee). Words with a final accent, like *città* and *caffè*, and words that end in consonants, like *bar* and *sport*, do not change in the plural.

PHRASEBOOK

ENGLISH	ITALIAN	ENGLISH	ITALIAN
NUMBERS			
one	uno	twenty-one	ventuno
two	due	twenty-three	ventitre
three	tre	twenty-eight	ventotto
four	quattro	thirty	trenta
five	cinque	forty	quaranta
six	sei	fifty	cinquanta
seven	sette	sixty	sessanta
eight	otto	seventy	settanta
nine	nove	eighty	ottanta
ten	dieci	ninety	novanta
eleven	undici	one hundred	cento
twelve	dodici	one hundred five	cento cinque
thirteen	tredici	two hundred	duecento
fourteen	quattordici	eight hundred	ottocento
fifteen	quindici	one thousand	mille
sixteen	seidici	two thousand	due mila
seventeen	diciasette	eight thousand	otto mila

APPENDIX

eighteen	diciotto	hundred thousand	cento mila
nineteen	dicianove	million	un millione
twenty	venti	billion	un milliardo

DAYS			
Monday	lunedì	Friday	venerdì
Tuesday	martedì	Saturday	sabato
Wednesday	mercoledì	Sunday	domenica
Thursday	giovedì		

MONTHS			
January	gennaio	July	luglio
February	febbraio	August	agosto
March	marzo	September	settembre
April	aprile	October	ottobre
May	maggio	November	novembre
June	giugno	December	dicembre

ENGLISH	ITALIAN	PRONUNCIATION
GENERAL		
Hello/So long (informal)	Ciao	chow
Good day/Hello	Buongiorno	bwohn JOHR-noh
Good evening	Buona sera	BWOH-nah SEH-rah
Good night	Buona notte	BWOH-nah NOHT-teh
Goodbye	Arrivederci/ArrivederLa (formal)	ah-ree-veh-DAIR-chee/ah-ree-veh-DAIR-lah
Please	Per favore/Per piacere	pehr fah-VOH-reh/pehr pyah-CHEH-reh
Thank you	Grazie	GRAHT-see-yeh
How are you?	Come stai/Come sta (formal)?	COH-meh st-EYE/stah
I am well	Sto bene	stoh BEH-neh
You're welcome	Prego	PREY-goh
May I help you?	Prego?	PREY-goh
Go right ahead!	Prego!	PREY-goh
Excuse me	Scusi	SKOO-zee
I'm sorry	Mi dispiace	mee dees-PYAH-cheh
My name is...	Mi chiamo...	mee key-YAH-moh
What's your name?	Come ti chiami?	COH-meh tee key-YAH-mee
Yes/No/Maybe	Sì/No/Forse	see/no/FOHR-seh
I don't know	Non lo so	nohn loh soh
I have no idea	Boh	boh
Could you repeat that?	Potrebbe ripetere?	poh-TREHB-beh ree-PEH-teh-reh
What does this mean?	Cosa vuol dire questo?	COH-za vwohl DEE-reh KWEH-stoh
I understand	Ho capito	Oh kah-PEE-toh
I don't understand	Non capisco	nohn kah-PEES-koh
I don't speak Italian	Non parlo italiano	nohn PAR-loh ee-tahl-YAH-noh
Is there someone who speaks English?	C'è qualcuno che parla inglese?	cheh kwahl-KOO-noh keh PAR-lah een-GLAY-zeh
Could you help me?	Potrebbe aiutarmi?	poh-TREHB-beh ah-yoo-TAHR-mee
How do you say...?	Come si dice...?	KOH-may see DEE-chay
What do you call this in Italian?	Come si chiama questo in italiano?	KOH-may see key-YAH-mah KWEH-stoh een ee-tahl-YAH-no

this/that	questo/quello	KWEH-sto/KWEHL-loh
who	chi	kee
where	dove	DOH-vay
which	quale	KWAH-lay
when	quando	KWAN-doh
what	che/cosa/che cosa	kay/KOH-za/kay KOH-za
how	come	KOH-meh
why/because	perchè	pair-KEH
more/less	più/meno	pyoo/MEH-noh
good luck (literally, in the mouth of the wolf)	in bocca al lupo	in BOHKA al lOO-po

TIME

At what time...?	A che ora...?	ah keh OHR-ah
What time is it?	Che ore sono?	keh OHR-ay SOH-noh
It's 3:30 (Remember, Italians often use the 24-hour clock, so add twelve to afternoon and evening arrival times.)	Sono le tre e mezzo.	SOH-noh leh tray eh MEHD-zoh
It's noon.	È mezzogiorno.	eh MEHD-zoh-JOHR-noh
midnight	mezzanotte	MEHD-zah-NOT-eh
now	adesso/ora	ah-DEHS-so/OH-rah
tomorrow	domani	doh-MAH-nee
today	oggi	OHJ-jee
yesterday	ieri	YAYR-ee
right away	subito	SU-bee-toh
soon	fra poco/presto	frah POH-koh/ PREH-stoh
already	già	jah
after(wards)	dopo	DOH-poh
before	prima	PREE-mah
late/later	tardi/più tardi	TAHR-dee/pyoo TAHR-dee
early (before scheduled arrival time)	presto	PREHS-toh
late (after scheduled arrival time)	in ritardo	een ree-TAHR-doh
daily	quotidiano	kwoh-tee-dee-AH-no
weekly	settimanale	seht-tee-mah-NAH-leh
monthly	mensile	mehn-SEE-leh
vacation	le ferie	leh FEH-ree-eh
weekdays	i giorni feriali	ee JOHR-nee feh-ree-AH-lee
Sundays and holidays	i giorni festivi	ee JOHR-nee fehs-TEE-vee
day off (at store, restaurant, etc.)	riposo	ree-POH-zo

DIRECTIONS AND TRANSPORTATION

Where is...?	Dov'è...?	doh-VEH
How do you get to...?	Come si arriva a...	KOH-meh see ahr-REE-vah ah
Do you stop at...?	Ferma a...?	FEHR-mah ah
...the beach	la spiaggia	lah spee-AH-jah
...the building	il palazzo/l'edificio	eel pah-LAHT-zo/leh-dee-FEE-choh
...the bus stop	la fermata d'autobus	lah fehr-MAH-tah DAOW-toh-boos

APPENDIX

...the center of town	in centro	een CHEN-troh
...the church	la chiesa	lah kee-AY-zah
...the consulate	il consolato	eel kohn-so-LAH-toh
...the grocery store	l'alimentari/il supermercato	lah-lee-men-TAH-ree/eel SOO-pehr mer-CAT-oh
...the hospital	l'ospedale	los-peh-DAH-leh
...the market	il mercato	eel mehr-KAH-toh
...the office	l'ufficio	loo-FEE-choh
...the post office	l'ufficio postale	loo-FEE-choh poh-STAH-leh
...the station	la stazione	lah staht-see-YOH-neh
near/far	vicino/lontano	vee-CHEE-noh/lohn-TAH-noh
turn left/right	gira a sinistra/destra	JEE-rah ah see-NEE-strah/DEH-strah
straight ahead	sempre diritto	SEHM-pray DREET-toh
here	qui/qua	kwee/kwah
there	lì/là	lee/lah
the street address	l'indirizzo	leen-dee-REET-soh
the telephone	il telefono	eel teh-LAY-foh-noh
street	strada, via, viale, vico, vicolo, corso	STRAH-dah, VEE-ah, vee-AH-leh, VEE-koh, VEE-koh-loh, KOHR-soh
Take the bus from/to...	Prenda l'autobus da/a...	PREN-dah LAOW-toh-boos dah/ah...
What time does the... leave?	A che ora parte...?	ah kay OHR-ah PAHR-tay
...the (city) bus	l'autobus	LAOW-toh-boos
...the (intercity) bus	il pullman	eel POOL-mahn
...the ferry	il traghetto	eel tra-GHEHT-toh
...the plane	l'aereo	lah-EHR-reh-oh
...the train	il treno	eel TRAY-no
How much does it cost?	Quanto costa?	KWAN-toh CO-stah
How much does...cost?	Quanto costa...?	KWAN-toh CO-stah
I would like...	Vorrei...	VOH-ray
...a ticket	un biglietto	oon beel-YEHT-toh
...a pass (bus, etc.)	una tessera	OO-nah TEHS-seh-rah
one-way	solo andata	SO-lo ahn-DAH-tah
round-trip	andata e ritorno	ahn-DAH-tah ey ree-TOHR-noh
reduced price	ridotto	ree-DOHT-toh
student discount	uno sconto studentesco	oon-oh SKOHN-toh stoo-dehn-TEHS-koh
What time does the train for...leave?	A che ora parte il treno per...?	ah kay OH-rah PAHR-tay eel TRAY-noh pair
What platform for...?	Quale binario per...?	qwal-eh bee-NAH-ree-oh pair
From where does the bus leave...?	Da dove parte l'autobus per...?	dah DOH-vay PAHR-tay LAOW-toh-boos pair
Is the train late?	È in ritardo il treno?	eh een ree-TAHR-doh eel TRAY-no
the arrival	l'arrivo	la-REE-voh
the departure	la partenza	la par-TENT-sah
the track	il binario	eel bee-NAH-ree-oh
the terminus (of a bus)	il capolinea	eel kah-poh-LEE-neh-ah
the flight	il volo	eel VOH-loh
the reservation	la prenotazione	la pray-no-taht-see-YOH-neh
the entrance/the exit	l'ingresso/l'uscita	leen-GREH-so/loo-SHEE-tah
I need to get off here	Devo scendere qui	DEH-vo SHEN-der-ay qwee

EMERGENCY		
I lost my passport/wallet	Ho perso il passaporto/portafoglio	oh PEHR-soh eel pahs-sah-POHR-toh/por-ta-FOH-lee-oh
I've been robbed	Sono stato derubato	SOH-noh STAH-toh deh-roo-BAH-toh
Wait!	Aspetta!	ahs-PEHT-tah
Stop!	Ferma!	FAIR-mah
Help!	Aiuto!	ah-YOO-toh
Leave me alone!	Lasciami stare!	LAH-shah-mee STAH-reh
Don't touch me!	Non mi toccare!	NOHN mee tohk-KAH-reh
I'm calling the police!	Telefono alla polizia!	tehl-LEH-foh-noh ah-lah poh-leet-SEE-ah
Go away, idiot!	Vattene, cretino!	VAH-teh-neh creh-TEE-noh

MEDICAL		
I have...	Ho...	OH
...allergies	delle allergie	DEHL-leh ahl-lair-JEE-eh
...a blister	una bolla	lah BOH-lah
...a cold	un raffreddore	oon rahf-freh-DOH-reh
...a cough	una tosse	OO-nah TOHS-seh
...the flu	l'influenza	lenn-floo-ENT-sah
...a fever	una febbre	OO-nah FEHB-breh
...a headache	mal di testa	mahl dee TEHS-tah
...an itch	un prurito	eel pru-REE-toh
...a lump (on the head)	un bernoccolo	eel bear-NOH-koh-loh
...menstrual pains	delle mestruazioni dolorose	DEH-leh meh-stroo-aht-see-OH-nee doh-lor-OH-zay
...a rash	un'esantema/un sfogo/un'eruzione	oo-NEH-zahn-TAY-mah/eel SFOH-goh/loo-NEH-root-see-OHN-eh
...a stomach ache	mal di stomaco	mahl dee STOH-mah-koh
...a swelling/growth	un gonfiore	oon gohn-fee-OR-ay
...a venereal disease	una malattia venerea	OO-nah mah-lah-TEE-ah veh-NAIR-ee-ah
...a vaginal infection	un'infezione vaginale	oon-een-feht-see-OH-neh vah-jee-NAH-leh
...a wart	una verruca	OO-nah veh-ROOK-kah
My foot hurts	Mi fa male il piede	mee fah MAH-le eel PYEHD-deh
I'm on the pill	Prendo la pillola	PREHN-doh lah PEE-loh-lah
I haven't had my period for (2) months	Non ho le mestruazioni da (due) mesi	nohn oh leh meh-stroo-aht-see-OH-nee dah (DOO-eh) may-zee
I'm (3 months) pregnant	Sono incinta (da tre mesi)	SOH-noh een-CHEEN-tah (dah treh MAY-zee)
You're (a month) pregnant	Lei è incinta (da un mese)	lay eh een-CHEEN-tah (dah oon MAY-zeh)
the bladder	la vescica	lah veh-SHEE-cah
the gall bladder	la cistifellea	lah sees-tee-fehl-LAY-ah
the blood	il sangue	eel SAHN-gweh
the appendix	il appendice	eel ap-pen-DEE-chay
a gynecologist	un ginecologo	oon jee-neh-KOH-loh-goh
the skin	la pelle	lah PEHL-leh

HOTEL AND HOSTEL RESERVATIONS		
Hello? (used when answering the phone)	Pronto?	PROHN-toh
Do you speak English?	Parla inglese?	PAHR-lah een-GLAY-zeh

APPENDIX

Could I reserve a single room/double room for (the second of August)?	Potrei prenotare una camera singola/doppia per (il due agosto)?	POH-tray pray-noh-TAH-reh OO-nah CAH-meh-rah SEEN-goh-lah/DOH-pee-yah pair (eel DOO-ay ah-GOH-stoh)
Is there a free bed for tonight?	C'è un posto libero stasera?	chay oon POHS-toe LEE-ber-oh sta-SER-ah
with bath/shower	con bagno/doccia	kohn BAHN-yo/DOH-cha
with bathroom	con un gabinetto/un bagno	kohn ooh gah-bee-NEHT-toh/oon BAHN-yoh
Is there a cheaper room without a bath/shower?	C'è una stanza più economica senza bagno/doccia?	chay oo-nah STAN-zah pyoo eko-NOM-ika sen-zah BAHN-yo/DOH-cha
open/closed	aperto/chiuso	ah-PAIR-toh/KYOO-zoh
a towel	un asciugamano	oon ah-shoo-gah-MAH-noh
sheets	i lenzuoli	ee lehn-SUO-lee
a blanket	una coperta	OO-nah koh-PEHR-tah
heating	il riscaldamento	eel ree-skahl-dah-MEHN-toh
How much is the room?	Quanto costa la camera?	KWAHN-toh KOHS-ta lah KAM-eh-rah
I will arrive (at 2:30pm)	Arriverò alle (quattordici e mezzo)	ah-ree-vehr-OH ah-lay (kwah-TOHR-dee-chee eh MED-zoh)
Certainly	Certo!	CHAIR-toh
We're closed during August	Chiudiamo ad agosto	kyu-dee-AH-moh ahd ah-GOH-stoh
No, we're full	No, siamo al completo	no, see-YAH-moh ahl cohm-PLAY-toh
We don't take telephone reservations	Non si fanno le prenotazioni per telefono	nohn see FAHN-noh leh pray-noh-tat-see-YOH-nee pair teh-LAY-foh-noh
You'll have to send a deposit/check	Bisogna mandare un anticipo/un assegno	bee-ZOHN-yah mahn-DAH-reh oon ahn-TEE-chee-poh/oon ahs-SAY-nyoh
You must arrive before 2pm	Deve arrivare primo delle quattordici	DAY-veh ah-ree-VAH-reh PREE-moh day-leh kwah-TOHR-dee-chee
Okay, I'll take it	Va bene, la prendo	vah BEHN-eh, lah PREHN-doh
What is that funny smell?	Che cos'è il odore curioso?	kay kohz-EH eel oh-DOOR-eh kyoor-ee-OH-so

RESTAURANTS

breakfast	la colazione	lah coh-laht-see-YO-neh
lunch	il pranzo	eel PRAHND-zoh
dinner	la cena	lah CHEH-nah
appetizer	l'antipasto	lahn-tee-PAH-stoh
first course	il primo	eel PREE-moh
second course	il secondo	eel seh-COHN-doh
side dish	il contorno	eel cohn-TOHR-noh
dessert	il dolce	eel DOHL-cheh
fork	la forchetta	lah fohr-KEH-tah
knife	il coltello	eel cohl-TEHL-loh
spoon	il cucchiaio	eel koo-kee-EYE-yoh
teaspoon	il cucchiaino	eel koo-kee-EYE-ee-noh
bottle	la bottiglia	lah boh-TEEL-yah
glass	il bicchiere	eel bee-kee-YAIR-eh
napkin	il tovagliolo	eel toh-vahl-YOH-loh
plate	il piatto	eel pee-YAH-toh
waiter/waitress	il/la cameriere/a	eel/lah kah-meh-ree-AIR-reh/rah
the bill	il conto	eel COHN-toh
cover charge	il coperto	eel koh-PAIR-toh
service charge/tip	il servizio	eel sehr-VEET-see-oh
included	compreso/a	KOHM-preh-zoh/ah

LOVE		
I have a boyfriend/a girl-friend.	Ho un ragazzo/una ragazza.	oh oon rah-GAHT-soh/oo-nah rah-GAHT-sah
Let's get a room.	Prendiamo una camera.	prehn-DYAH-moh oo-nah CAH-meh-rah
Oh, I'm leaving tomorrow.	Oh, vado via domani.	Oh VAH-doh vee-ah doh-MAH-nee
Voluptuous!	Volutuoso!	Vol-OOP-to-oh-soh
Enamoured.	Essere innamorato di.	Eh-seh-reh en-am-mo-rah-to dee.
Just kiss me.	Giusto baciami.	gee-oo-STO BAH-cha-mee
Are you single?	Siete singoli?	see-EH-teh SIN-goh-li
You're cute.	Sei carino/a (bello/a).	SAY cah-RIN-oh/ah (BEHL-loh/lah)
I love you, I swear.	Ti amo, te lo giuro.	tee AH-moh, teh loh JOO-roh
I'm married.	Sono sposato/a	soh-noh spo-ZA-to/ta
Save a dance for me.	Lasciami un ballo.	LAH-shah-mee oon BAH-loh
Your friend is cute.	Tuo amico/tua amica è bello.	TOO-oh/ah ah-MEE-coh/cah ay BEHL-loh
She dances poorly, why don't you dance with me?	Lei balla male, perchè non balli con me?	lay BAH-lah mal-eh, pair-KEH nohn BAH-lee con meh
I only have safe sex.	Pratico solo sesso sicuro.	PRAH-tee-coh sohl-oh SEHS-so see-COO-roh
Would you touch me here?	Puoi toccarme qui?	poy toc-CAR-meh qwee
Leave her alone, she's mine.	Lasciala stare, è mia.	LAH-shah-lah STAH-reh eh mee-ah
Leave right now.	Vai via subito.	vai VEE-ah SOO-bit-oh
I'll never forget you.	Non ti dimenticherò mai.	nohn tee dee-men-tee-ker-OH my
heterosexual/straight	etero (sessuale)	EH-teh-roh (ses-SOOAH-leh)
bisexual	bisessuale	bee-ses-SOOAH-leh
gay	gay	GAH-ee
lesbian	lesbica	LEH-sbee-cah
celibate	celibe	CHEH-lee-beh
a transvestite	uno/a travestito/a	OO-noh/nah trah-veh-STEE-toh/tah

AT THE BAR		
May I buy you a drink?	Posso offrirle qualcosa da bere?	POHS-soh ohf-FREER-leh kwahl-COH-zah dah BAY-reh
I'm drunk.	Sono ubriaco/a.	SOH-noh oo-BRYAH-coh/cah
Let's drink some more!	Beviamo più!	beh-vee-AH-moh pyoo
I don't drink.	Non bevo.	nohn BEH-voh
Cheers!	Cin cin!	chin chin
Do you have a light?	Mi fai accendere?	mee fah-ee ah-CHEN-deh-reh
No thank you, I don't smoke.	No grazie, non fumo.	noh GRAH-zye nohn FOO-moh
Do you have an ashtray?	Hai un portacenere?	ah-ee oon pohr-tah-CHEH-neh-reh
I was here before this lady!	C'ero io prima io di questa signora!	CHEH-roh EE-oh PREE-mah dee QHEH-stah see-nyoh-rah
Do you believe in aliens?	Credi negli extraterrestrl?	CREH-dee neh-lyee ehx-trah-teh-REH-stree
I feel like throwing up.	Mi viene di vomitare.	mee VYE-neh dee voh-mee-TAH-reh
beer	una birra	OO-nah BEER-rah
a glass of wine	un bicchiere di vino	oon bee-KYE-reh dee VEE-noh
a liter of wine	un litro di vino	oon LEE-troh di VEE-noh

MENU READER

PRIMI	
pasta aglio e olio	garlic and olive oil
pasta all'amatriciana	in a tangy tomato sauce with onions and bacon
pasta all'arabbiata	in a spicy tomato sauce
pasta alla bolognese	in a meat sauce
pasta alla boscaiola	egg pasta, served in a mushroom sauce with peas and cream
pasta alla carbonara	in a creamy sauce with egg, cured bacon, and cheese
pasta alle cozze	in a tomato sauce with mussels
pasta al forno	oven-baked pasta, like lasagna
pasta alla pizzaiola	tomato-based sauce with olive oil and red peppers
pasta al pomodoro	in tomato sauce
pasta alla puttanesca	in a tomato sauce with olives, capers, and anchovies
pasta alla romana	cooked in milk, butter, cheese, and then baked
pasta alle vongole	in a clam sauce; *bianco* for white, *rosso* for red
polenta	deep fried cornmeal
risotto	rice dish, comes in nearly as many flavors as pasta sauce

PIZZA	
ai carciofi	with artichokes
ai fiori di zucca	with zucchini blossoms
ai funghi	with mushrooms
alla capriciosa	with ham, egg, artichoke, and more
con acciughe	with anchovies
con bresaola	with cured beef
con melanzana	with eggplant
con prosciutto	with ham
con prosciutto crudo	with cured ham (also called simply *crudo*)
con rucola (rughetta)	with arugula (rocket for Brits)
margherita	plain ol' tomato, mozzarella, and basil
peperoncini	chillies
polpette	meatballs
quattro formaggi	with four cheeses
quattro stagioni	four seasons; a different topping for each quarter of the pizza, usually mushrooms, *crudo*, artichoke, and tomato

SECONDI	
agnello	lamb
anatra	duck
animelle alla griglia	grilled sweetbreads
anguila	eel
arrosto misto di pesce	mixed grilled seafood
asino	donkey (served in Sicily and Sardinia)
bistecca	steak
cavallo (sfilacci)	horse (a delicacy throughout the South and Sardinia)
carciofi alla giudia	fried artichokes
carne alla valdostana	cutlets fried in lemon butter, baked with cheese and ham
coda alla vaccinara	stewed oxtail with herbs and tomatoes
coniglio/pollo cacciatore	rabbit/chicken served in a tomato sauce; varies widely by region

SECONDI	
coppa	cured pork shoulder
cotoletta	breaded veal cutlet with cheese
cozze	mussels
fegato alla veneziana	chicken liver cooked with onions
filetto di baccalà/merluzzo	fried cod
fiori di zucca	zucchini flowers filled with cheese, battered, and lightly fried
gamberi	prawns
granchi	crabs
involtini al sugo	veal cutlets filled with ham, celery, and cheese, with tomato sauce
manzo	beef
oca	goose
osso buco	braised veal shank
pasta e ceci	pasta with chick peas
polpo	octopus
salsiccia	sausage
saltimbocca alla romana	slices of veal and ham cooked together and topped with cheese
seppia	cuttlefish, usually served grilled in its own ink
sogliola	sole
speck	smoked raw ham, lean but surrounded by a layer of fat
suppli	fried rice ball filled with tomato, meat, and cheese
tonno	tuna
trippa	tripe (chopped, sautéed cow intestines, usually in a tomato sauce)
vitello	veal
vongole	clams
CONTORNI	
broccoletti	broccoli florets
cavolo	cabbage
cipolle	onion
fagioli	beans (usually white)
fagiolini	green beans
funghi	mushrooms
insalata caprese	tomatoes with mozzarella cheese and basil, drizzled with olive oil
insalata mista	mixed green salad
lattuga	lettuce
melanzana	eggplant
piselli	peas
radicchio	radish
sottaceti	pickled vegetables
tartufi	truffles
ANTIPASTI	
antipasto rustico	assortment of cold appetizers
bresaola	sliced cold cuts of meat, served with olive oil, lemon, salt, pepper, and *parmigiano*
bruschetta	large, crisp slices of garlic-rubbed, baked bread, often with raw tomatoes
carpaccio	extremely thin slices of lean, raw beef
crostini	small pieces of toasted bread usually served with chicken liver or mozzarella and anchovies, though other toppings abound
prosciutto e melone	cured ham and honeydew melon

FRUTTA	
anguria/cocomero	watermelon
arancia	orange
ciliegie	cherries
fragole	strawberries
lamponi	raspberries
pesca	peach
prugna	plum
uva	grape

DOLCE	
cannoli	sicilian tube pastries filled with sweet ricotta
cassata siciliana	sponge cake, sweet cream, cheese, chocolate, and candied fruit
confetti	candied almonds
fragole con panna	strawberries with cream
gelato	Italian-style ice cream
panforte	round, flat, honey-coated, candied fruit cakes originally from Siena
panna cotta	flan
sfogliatelle	sugar-coated layers of crunchy pastry with ricotta
tiramisù	marscapone, eggs, and lady fingers dipped in *espresso*
zuppa inglese	alternating layers of chocolate, egg cream, and biscuits soaked in liqueur and coffee.

PREPARATION	
al dente	firm to the bite (pasta)
al diavolo	very spicy, made with *fra diavolo* chili peppers
al forno	baked
al sangue	rare
al vino	in wine sauce
alla griglia	grilled
aromatica/o	spicy
ben cotta/o	well done
condita/o	seasoned
cruda/o	raw
fresca/o	fresh
fritta/o	fried
marinata/o	marinated
non troppo cotta/o	medium rare
piccante	spicy
poco cotta/o	undercooked
raffermo	stale
resentin	coffee in a grappa-rinsed mug
ripieno	stuffed
scottata	scorched
secca	dry
stracotta	overcooked

GLOSSARY

abbazia	also badia, an abbey
agriturismo	tourist accommodations on farms
affittacamere	rooms for rent (usually privately owned and cheaper than a hotel)
albergo	hotel
alimentari	grocery store, often the cheapest place in town to get food
aliscafi	hydrofoils
anfiteatro	amphitheater
APT	Azienda Promozione Turistica (tourist office)
architrave	the lowermost part of an entablature, resting directly on top of a column
arco	arch
apse	a semicircular, domed niche projecting from the altar end of a church
baldacchino	stone or bronze canopy supported by columns over the altar of a church
basilica	a rectangular building with aisle and apse; no transepts. Used by ancient Romans for public administration, later used by Christians for their churches.
battistero	a baptistry, usually a separate building near the town's duomo, where the town's baptisms were performed
Berber	non-Arab native inhabitants of North Africa
borgo	ancient town or village
campanile	a bell tower, usually freestanding
cappella	chapel
carabinieri	military police
cartoon	full-sized drawing used to transfer a preparatory design to the final work, especially to a wall for a fresco
castrum	the ancient Roman military camp. Many Italian cities were originally built on a rectilinear plan with straight streets, the chief of which was called the decumanus maximus.
Cenacolo	"Last Supper"; a depiction of Christ at dinner on the evening before his crucifixion, often found in the refectory of an abbey or convent
chancel	the space around the altar reserved for clergy and choir
chiaroscuro	the balance between light and dark in a painting, and the painter's ability to show the contrast between them
chiesa	church
cloister/chiostro	a courtyard; generally a quadrangle with covered walkways along its edges, often with a central garden, forming part of a church or monastery
comune	the government of a free city of the Middle Ages
condottiere	a leader of mercenary soldiers in Italy in the 14th and 15th centuries, when wars were almost incessant
corso	a principal street or avenue
cosmati work	mosaic on marble, found in early Christian churches
cupola	a dome
diptych	a painting in two parts or panels
duomo	cathedral; the official seat of a diocesan bishop, and usually the central church of an Italian town
etto	100 grams
facade	the front of a building, or any wall given special architectural treatment
fiume	a river
forum	in an ancient Roman town, a square containing municipal buildings and/or market space. Smaller towns have one forum, larger cities can have several.
fresco	a painting made on wet plaster. When it dries, the painting becomes part of the wall.

frieze	a band of decoration. Architecturally, this can also refer to the middle part of an entablature (everything above the columns of a building) between the architrave and the cornice.
FS	Ferrovie dello Stato (Italian State Railways)
fumarole	a hole in the ground from which volcanic vapor is released
giardino	garden
gabinetto	toilet, WC
Greek Cross	a cross with arms of equal length
grotesque	painted, carved, or stucco decorations of fantastic, distorted human or animal figures, named for the grotto work from Nero's buried Golden House
in restauro	under restoration; a key concept in Italy
intarsia	inlay work, usually of marble, metal, or wood
Latin Cross	a cross with the vertical arm longer than the horizontal arm
loggia	a covered gallery or balcony
lungo	"long"; a lungomare is a boardwalk or promenade alongside the *mare* (ocean)
lunette	a semicircular frame in a ceiling or vault, holding a painting or sculpture
mausoleum	a large tomb or building with places to entomb the dead above ground
mithraeum	a temple to the Roman god Mithras
nave	the central body of a church
nuraghe	cone-shaped tower-houses built of stone and assembled without mortar
palazzo	an important building of any type, not just a palace
passeggiata	a ritual evening stroll (see p. 28)
piazza	a city square
piazzale	(large) open square
Pietà	a scene of the Virgin mourning the dead Christ
pietra serena	gray to bluish stone commonly used in Renaissance constructions
pilaster	a rectangular column set into a wall as an ornamental motif
polyptych	altarpiece with more than three panels
ponte	bridge
presepio	nativity scene
putto	(pl. *putti*) the little nude babies that flit around Renaissance art occasionally and Baroque art incessantly
reliquary	holding place for a saint's relics, usually the bones, but often much stranger
sinopia drawing	a red pigment sketch made on a wall as a preliminary study for a fresco
scalinata	stairway
settimana bianca	"white week," a winter package that combines lodging, food, and skiing
sottoportico	street or sidewalk continuing under a building (like an extended archway)
spiaggia	beach
stigmata	miraculous body pains or bleeding resembling Christ's crucifix wounds
thermae	(*terme* in Italian) ancient Roman baths and, consequently, social centers
telamoni	large, often sensual, statues of men used as columns in temples
tessera	one of the small colored pieces of stone or glass used in making mosaics
transept	in a cruciform church, the arm of the church that intersects the nave or central aisle (i.e. the cross-bar of the T)
travertine	a light-colored marble or limestone
triptych	a painting in three panels or parts
trompe l'oeil	literally, "to fool the eye," a painting or other piece or art whose purpose is to trick the viewer, as in a flat ceiling painted so as to appear domed
tufa	a soft stone composed of volcanic ash (*tufo* in Italian)
via	a street or road

INDEX

INDEX

N

O

WHO WE ARE

A NEW LET'S GO FOR 2003

With a sleeker look and innovative new content, we have revamped the entire series to reflect more than ever the needs and interests of the independent traveler. Here are just some of the improvements you will notice when traveling with the new *Let's Go*.

MORE PRICE OPTIONS

Still the best resource for budget travelers, *Let's Go* recognizes that everyone needs the occasional indulgence. Our "Big Splurges" indicate establishments that are actually worth those extra pennies (pulas, pesos, or pounds), and price-level symbols (❶ ❷ ❸ ❹ ❺) allow you to quickly determine whether an accommodation or restaurant will break the bank. We may have diversified, but we'll never lose our budget focus—"Hidden Deals" reveal the best-kept travel secrets.

BEYOND THE TOURIST EXPERIENCE

Our Alternatives to Tourism chapter offers ideas on immersing yourself in a new community through study, work, or volunteering.

AN INSIDER'S PERSPECTIVE

As always, every item is written and researched by our on-site writers. This year we have highlighted more viewpoints to help you gain an even more thorough understanding of the places you are visiting.

IN RECENT NEWS. *Let's Go* correspondents around the globe report back on current regional issues that may affect you as a traveler.

CONTRIBUTING WRITERS. Respected scholars and former *Let's Go* writers discuss topics on society and culture, going into greater depth than the usual guidebook summary.

THE LOCAL STORY. From the Parisian monk toting a cell phone to the Russian *babushka* confronting capitalism, *Let's Go* shares its revealing conversations with local personalities—a unique glimpse of what matters to real people.

FROM THE ROAD. Always helpful and sometimes downright hilarious, our researchers share useful insights on the typical (and atypical) travel experience.

SLIMMER SIZE

Don't be fooled by our new, smaller size. *Let's Go* is still packed with invaluable travel advice, but now it's easier to carry with a more compact design.

FORTY-THREE YEARS OF WISDOM

For over four decades *Let's Go* has provided the most up-to-date information on the hippest cafes, the most pristine beaches, and the best routes from border to border. It all started in 1960 when a few well-traveled students at Harvard University handed out a 20-page mimeographed pamphlet of their tips on budget travel to passengers on student charter flights to Europe. From humble beginnings, *Let's Go* has grown to cover six continents and *Let's Go: Europe* still reigns as the world's best-selling travel guide. This year we've beefed up our coverage of Latin America with *Let's Go: Costa Rica* and *Let's Go: Chile;* on the other side of the globe, we've added *Let's Go: Thailand* and *Let's Go: Hawaii.* Our new guides bring the total number of titles to 61, each infused with the spirit of adventure that travelers around the world have come to count on.

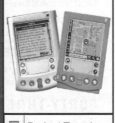

MAP INDEX

MAP LEGEND

✚ Hospital	✈ Airport	🏛 Museum	⌂ Gate
🚓 Police	🚌 Bus Station	⌂ Hotel/Hostel	✝ Trailhead
✉ Post Office	🚂 Train Station	▲ Camping	≫ Mountain Pass
ⓘ Tourist Office	Ⓜ METRO STATION	🍎 Food & Drink	⚔ Border Crossing
$ Bank	⚓ Ferry Landing	🛍 Shopping	A1 Motorway Number
⚑ Embassy/Consulate	✝ Church	★ Entertainment	🗼 Lighthouse
▪ Site or Point of Interest	✡ Synagogue	🍷 Nightlife	TAXI Taxi Stand
☎ Telephone Office	☪ Mosque	☕ Cafe	
🎭 Theater	🏰 Castle	💻 Internet Café	N LG The Let's Go compass always points NORTH.
📖 Library	⛰ Mountain	⋯ Pedestrian Zone	